D0743195

For Reference

Not to be taken from this room

Current Biography Yearbook 2016

H. W. Wilson

A Division of EBSCO Information Services, Inc.

Ipswich, Massachusetts

GREY HOUSE PUBLISHING

SEVENTY-SEVENTH ANNUAL CUMULATION—2016

International Standard Serial No. 0084-9499

International Standard Book No. 978-1-61925-731-3

Library of Congress Catalog Card No. 40-27432

Current Biography Yearbook, 2016, published by Grey House Publishing, Inc., Amenia, NY, under exclusive license from EBSCO Information Services, Inc.

PRINTED IN CANADA

CONTENTS

LIST OF BIOGRAPHICAL SKETCHES

List of Biographical Sketches

List of Biographical Sketches

List of Biographical Sketches

LIST OF OBITUARIES

List of Obituaries

List of Obituaries

Current Biography Yearbook 2016

Lenny Abrahamson

Born: November 30, 1966
Occupation: Director

The Irish filmmaker Lenny Abrahamson has an engaging visual style, deep sense of storytelling, and an ability to explore with subtlety the sad, funny, absurd, and disturbing aspects of life—all in a single film. He directed the films *Adam & Paul* (2004) and *Garage* (2007), both about odd friendships among outcasts, and *What Richard Did* (2012), about the heavy ethical consequences of violence and privilege. He then gained even more international acclaim for *Frank* (2014), about a troubled eccentric genius musician and his group, and *Room* (2015), based on a book of the same name, about a mother and her young son held prisoner in a tiny room.

EARLY LIFE AND EDUCATION

Lenny Abrahamson was born on November 30, 1966, in Dublin, Ireland. Both sides of his family were Eastern European Jews who had immigrated to Ireland in the early twentieth century. Being Jewish in Ireland made Abrahamson and his family members of a small ethnic minority. The family had a membership at a local synagogue, Abrahamson attended a *cheder* (a Jewish school where students are taught Hebrew and religious texts), and at the age of thirteen he had a bar mitzvah, a traditional Jewish ceremony in which a boy is proclaimed to be a man. Asked by Curt Schleier for *Forward* (14 Aug. 2014) if he had ever encountered anti-Semitism while growing up, Abrahamson replied, "No, I can pretty much say I didn't. I remember one kid in school, he might have called me a name sometimes, but nothing above that level. I never felt it institutionally. People were fascinated by me because there were so few Jews around."

Academic success and intellectual pursuits were highly valued in the Abrahamson household. Abrahamson's childhood was full of books and films, which in later interviews he attributed to the Jewish intellectual tradition. In an interview with Jonathan Romney for the *Guardian* (10 Jan. 2016), he recalled his "first properly aesthetic experience of film" was seeing *Way Out West* (1937), a film by the comedy duo Stan Laurel and Oliver Hardy. He also

Jeffrey Mayer/WireImage/Getty Images

recalled watching, in his teens, the early films of independent American film director Jim Jarmusch, who is known for having a unique visual aesthetic and an odd sense of humor. Abrahamson, speaking to Romney, recalled the Jarmusch film *Stranger Than Paradise* (1984), which has three main characters, and fairly spare, realistic dialogue. But what Abrahamson noticed was also the times when there was no dialogue, the long moments of silence, which he found to be "compelling." The lesson was clear: a lot could be communicated to the viewer even when the characters are not communicating. Other directors made a strong impression as well, notably the Swedish director Ingmar Bergman and the Italian directors Michelangelo Antonioni and Federico Fellini. "It was the first time," Abrahamson told Romney, "I detected in cinema the same kind of intellectual range and power and textural richness that I had in literature."

GOING BACK HOME

Abrahamson attended Trinity College Dublin, where he studied theoretical physics, then switched his major to philosophy. After making a few short films, most notably *Three Joes* (1991), he moved to the United States to pursue his doctorate degree in philosophy at Stanford University, in California. But that would not last. According to the profile of Abrahamson by Danny Leigh of the *Financial Times* (8 Jan. 2016), Abrahamson left Stanford for two reasons: first, his short film *Three Joes* began winning awards, such as the best European short award at the Cork Film Festival in Ireland, and gaining some recognition throughout Europe; and second, as he told Leigh, "I was lonely at Stanford." In part he enjoyed solitude and time for his own thoughts and studies, but that also made the graduate school experience in a completely new environment "miserable." He decided he would go back to Dublin and pursue a career as a filmmaker.

However, after returning to Dublin, Abrahamson spent several years struggling financially, unable to get any of his films made. He decided to do something he had previously been against: directing TV commercials. This venture was very successful, which gave him both a sense of purpose and at least somewhat of a creative outlet, as well as a solid income that would eventually allow him to direct the films he had originally wanted to make.

EARLY FILMS

Abrahamson's first feature film, *Adam & Paul*, came out in 2004 and got a positive critical reception. It is about two drug addicts walking around Dublin, drifting, in need of cash or drugs or both. The two lead actors in the film, Tom Murphy and Mark O'Halloran, also received good reviews, and the duo was compared to two other very different duos: Laurel and Hardy, who had made a big impression on the young Abrahamson, and Vladimir and Estragon from the existential playwright Samuel Beckett's play *Waiting for Godot*. The former duo had fast and snappy dialogue and physical comedy, and the latter a sense of existential dread and absurdist humor. As Adam and Paul wander around Dublin, they meet various other characters, such as drug dealers and other people who are down on their luck. In a review for the *Guardian* (2 June 2004), Peter Bradshaw called the film an "uncompromising bleak comedy" and pointed out, as did other reviewers, that the director "never glamorizes drugs or tries to make its comedy on the subject dishonestly flippant."

The director's next film, *Garage* (2007), continued the theme of odd friendships and exploring the lives of the down and out. Of his choice of subject matter, he told Leigh, "I don't think of myself as doing good works. It's not, 'Oh, I must give these poor people a voice.' That person on the street corner with nowhere to go, putting yourself in their shoes opens up dramatic questions." *Garage* was screened at the Cannes Festival in 2007, and won the International Confederation of Art Cinemas (CICAE) Prize. It also won

best film at the Toronto Film Festival. The film's protagonist is Josie, a middle-aged man who is not exceptionally bright and is employed at a gas station. He develops an odd friendship with David, his teenage assistant, and that brings him out of his shell somewhat. Josie then develops the confidence to pursue Carmel, a shop worker on whom he has a crush. The story is not a happy one. The themes of the film are isolation and loneliness, and Abrahamson manages to balance these heavy themes—and how they manifest themselves in human relations with people who are not who you think they are—with extraordinarily beautiful, cinematic shots. Bradshaw, writing for the *Guardian* (6 Mar. 2008), called the film a "very impressive follow-up" to Abrahamson's first film, and noted that it is a "gem of a film." Similarly, for the *Independent* (6 Mar. 2008), Anthony Quinn observed that *Garage* was "even more laconic and touching in its portrayal of narrow lives" than the director's first film. The sort of existential state of stasis seen in *Adam & Paul* is also present in *Garage*. "Indeed," wrote Quinn at the end of his review, "hardly anything at all seems to happen, yet in its patient detailing of a certain way of life—isolated, inarticulate, yet curiously hopeful—everything happens."

WHAT RICHARD DID AND FRANK

Abrahamson's third feature film, *What Richard Did* (2012), was a notable departure from the theme of loneliness and misfits, though like his previous films it received near-unanimous acclaim. Richard, the film's central character, is a handsome rugby player who has recently graduated high school. It is summertime, and he and his friends are partying and drinking and hanging out. Richard falls for Lara, who was recently going out with his friend Conor. At one point during a house party, Richard spots Lara talking to Conor, becomes jealous, and gets into a fight, beating Conor severely—but the true consequences of the fight are not evident to Richard until the next day, when he hears on the radio what had actually happened to Conor. Richard must now live with what he has done. Many people at the party witnessed what happened, but very few step forward, because Richard is bright, good-looking, and a promising athlete who is well liked in the town. Unlike Abrahamson's first two films, this one addresses privilege, but he still, through that context, manages to explore existential dread and raw emotion. Tom Robey for the *Telegraph* (10 Jan. 2013) observed that the film's scenario "isn't just skin-crawlingly plausible but morally fascinating."

The director's fourth film, *Frank* (2014), about an odd, beloved, and demanding band leader, was his most ambitious yet—and not just because the star of the film, Michael Fassbender, spends nearly the entire film wearing a giant watermelon-sized papier-mâché head with painted-on big eyes, open mouth, and triangular nose. Fassbender plays Frank, the eccentric leader of an eccentric band, which includes a moody theremin player named Clara (Maggie Gyllenhaal) and a drummer and a bassist (Carla Azar and François Civil) who rarely speak. By chance, Jon (Domhnall Gleeson), a so-called average guy who until recently had an office job, joins the band as a keyboard player. Most of the film takes place in a cabin where the band is recording an odd album that they assume very few people will listen to—which is how they like it. Jon, however, has the idea that the band should be heard by a wider audience. Through a social media campaign, he gets them a spot at the South by Southwest festival in Austin, Texas. Things do not go as planned.

Frank received mainly positive reviews, many noting Abrahamson's successful attempt to create a tone that is both funny and touching within a premise that in some other director's hands would have been a gimmick. Michael Phillips of the *Chicago Tribune* (28 Aug. 2014) called the film a "functioning, funny, weirdly touching fable of artistic angst and aspiration, a meditation on fame and its terrors and the metaphoric usefulness of masks and huge fake heads." A. O. Scott, for the *New York Times* (14 Aug. 2014), wrote that "Mr. Abrahamson's main achievement, enabled by the sensitive and resourceful cast, is to find a tone that is funny without flippancy, sincere without turning to mush."

ROOM

Abrahamson's next film was also a unique challenge, and the story behind it started with a letter. After reading the novelist Emma Donoghue's book *Room* (2010), the story of a young woman who has been kidnapped and held in a small room for years and now has a son, fathered by her kidnapper, who has never seen the world outside, Abrahamson was inspired. He wrote Donoghue a five-page single-spaced letter about why he should be the one to direct the film version of her book. In the letter, Abrahamson analyzed the book, and then went on to say how he would direct the film. The book has a narrator, the young boy Jack, but the movie should not have a narrator, wrote Abrahamson in his letter, which is available on the website IndieWire (9 Feb. 2016). "Thinking about this," he wrote, "the main challenge, which arises for me in imagining a film adaptation, is how to achieve something similar without a first person narrator. . . . At the most basic, physical level, we should always be with Jack, never seeing or hearing anything he wouldn't be able to see or hear." Donoghue was evidently moved enough by the letter to allow Abrahamson not only to direct, but also to take part in the writing of the script.

The film, starring Brie Larson as the mother and Jacob Tremblay as Jack, received nearly unanimous praise. For the *Guardian* (17 Jan. 2016), Mark Kermode pointed out that despite its very specific setting, the story has a "universal edge." He went on to conclude: "Where other film-makers might have resorted to the kind of elaborate visualizations that characterized Peter Jackson's *The Lovely Bones*, Abrahamson has the intelligence to trust his cast to show us the world through their eyes. And oh, what a world it is." The film also earned Abrahamson nominations for the Satellite and Academy Awards for best director.

PERSONAL LIFE

Abrahamson is married to the film scholar Monika Pamula, with whom he has two children.

SUGGESTED READING

Abrahamson, Lenny. "Lenny Abrahamson: 'It's a Way of Talking about Childhood and Parenting.'" Interview by Jonathan Romney. *Guardian*. Guardian News and Media, 10 Jan. 2016. Web. 12 July 2016.

Kermode, Mark. "To See the World within Four Walls." Rev. of *Room*, dir. Lenny Abrahamson. *Guardian*. Guardian News and Media, 17 Jan. 2016. Web. 12 July 2016.

Leigh, Danny. "Interview: Lenny Abrahamson." *Financial Times*. Financial Times, 8 Jan. 2016. Web. 12 July 2016.

Scott, A. O. "Music for Its Own Sake, until a Dreamer Intrudes." Rev. of *Frank*, dir. Lenny Abrahamson. *New York Times*. New York Times, 14 Aug. 2014. Web. 12 July 2016.

SELECTED WORKS

Adam & Paul, 2004; *Garage*, 2007; *What Richard Did*, 2012; *Frank*, 2014; *Room*, 2015

—*Dmitry Kiper*

Lila Abu-Lughod

Born: October 21, 1952
Occupation: Professor

Lila Abu-Lughod is a tenured professor of anthropology and women's and gender studies at Columbia University, where she also has the distinction of being the Joseph L. Buttenwieser Professor of Social Science. Her work, as she writes on the university's website, "has focused on three broad issues: the relationship between cultural forms and power; the politics of knowledge and representation; and the dynamics of gender and the question of women's rights in the Middle East."

Abu-Lughod's opinions are a frequent source of contention, especially among political conservatives and supporters of Israel, who view her as a left-leaning Islamic apologist. In an article for the *Maccabean* (Nov. 2010), feminist psychologist Phyllis Chesler described her as a "cultural relativist . . . who does not believe in universal standards of human rights." However, Abu-Lughod herself, in an interview with Nermeen Shaikh for the Asia Society website (n.d.), argued, "I don't think we need simply be cultural relativists, advocating respect for whatever goes on elsewhere and explaining it as 'just their culture.' . . . What I think we need to do is to work hard to respect and recognize difference—as products of different histories, as expressions of different circumstances, as manifestations of differently structured desires." She added, "We might still argue for justice for women, but consider that there might be different ideas about justice and that different women might want, or choose, different futures from what we envision as best."

FAMILY HISTORY AND EARLY LIFE

Lila Abu-Lughod was born on October 21, 1952. She has two sisters, Mariam and Deena, and a brother, Jawad. Her father, Ibrahim Abu-Lughod, was a respected Palestinian-born academic; her mother, Janet Lippman, was an American-born sociologist whose teaching career included stints at the University of Illinois, the American University in Cairo, Smith College, Northwestern University, and the New School for Social Research (later New School University, now simply the New School). A prolific writer, Janet was widely recognized in academic circles for her contributions to urban sociology.

Although Janet was Jewish, she and Ibrahim raised their four children as Muslims. Ibrahim grew up in the ancient port city of Jaffa, then part of British-controlled Palestine. As a youth, he volunteered with the National Committee in Jaffa, seeking to discourage residents from leaving while the state of Israel was being established and reportedly defending against attacks by Zionist groups in the region. He remained there until May 1948, when he left for Beirut to join his family, who had departed the previous month. Abu-Lughod recalled to an interviewer for *Spiegel Online* (16 May 2008) an essay she had once written about her father, in which she described "how excited he was to hear that he and his best friend had passed their national high school exams, which they took in March 1948 while the fighting was going on. But then it dawned on him that since Jaffa had fallen to the Zionists, it no longer meant anything. They were refugees with no future."

Yet Ibrahim's future soon took a positive turn after he arrived in the United States as a refugee. He earned his bachelor's degree from the University of Illinois, met and married Janet Lippman, and completed a doctoral degree in Middle Eastern studies at Princeton University in 1957. He became a well-respected professor at Smith and Northwestern, among other institutions, and served for several years as a field expert in Egypt for the United Nations Educational, Scientific and Cultural Organization (UNESCO).

Throughout his life, he was a vocal proponent for Palestinian rights, a legacy that Lila Abu-Lughod inherited. In a 2002 speech, quoted in her biography for the Institute for Middle East Understanding (IMEU) (10 Oct. 2015), she opened by saying, "I've lived with Palestine all my life." In her interview for *Spiegel Online*, she elaborated, "Only my father was Palestinian, but for both my parents the political injustice of the situation was clear. Every child of a Palestinian refugee feels the burden of the events of 1948, not just through what a parent or grandparent might tell her or through sensing their hollow feeling of exile, but because the results are with us today in the continuing violence."

EDUCATION AND EARLY CAREER

As an undergraduate, Abu-Lughod attended Carleton College, a small liberal arts school in Northfield, Minnesota. She earned her bachelor's degree in anthropology in 1974 and later entered Harvard University, where she earned her PhD in 1984. While conducting her doctoral studies, Abu-Lughod spent long periods in Egypt, living with members of the Awlad 'Ali tribe of Bedouin. "I first chose to work with them out of some romantic fascination with the desert life," Abu-Lughod explained, as quoted in her IMEU biography. "But when I got there, everything changed. I got involved in trying to understand and convey how they understood their world, especially through their poetry and storytelling. I've kept in contact with them for almost 30 years, with the amazing feeling of growing up and old together."

After receiving her doctorate, Abu-Lughod began teaching at Williams College; she would later hold positions at Princeton University and New York University before moving on to Columbia. While at Williams, she won the 1984 Stirling Award for Contributions to Psychological Anthropology for her article "Honor and the Sentiments of Loss in a Bedouin Society," which was published in the May 1985 issue of *American Ethnologist*. The article later became a chapter in her first book, *Veiled Sentiments: Honor and Poetry in a Bedouin Society* (1986), which drew on her time in Egypt, studying gender relations among the Awlad 'Ali and the oral lyric poetry through which the women of the tribe expressed themselves. Her 1993 work, *Writing Women's Worlds: Bedouin Stories*, also drew from this experience, and it garnered the prestigious Victor Turner Prize for Ethnographic Writing. Abu-Lughod subsequently edited *Remaking Women: Feminism and Modernity in the Middle East* (1998), which contained essays questioning the accepted wisdom that domesticity and tradition equate with oppression.

POLITICAL CONTROVERSY

In 2000 Abu-Lughod joined the faculty of Columbia University, where she now holds an endowed chair. She has been active in a number of progressive institutions on campus, including the Institute for Research on Women, Gender, and Sexuality, which promotes interdisciplinary feminist scholarship, and the Center for the Study of Social Difference (CSSD), which promotes interdisciplinary scholarship on gender, sexuality, ethnicity, and race.

Columbia is often viewed as a bastion of far-left extremism by right-wing critics, and Abu-Lughod's name is sometimes evoked as proof of that assertion. She has also repeatedly drawn fire from all political sides for supporting calls for boycotts, divestment, and sanctions (tactics known collectively as BDS) against Israel in response to the Israeli government's treatment of Palestinians, resulting in frequent accusations of anti-Semitism. Discussing such accusations in her interview with *Spiegel Online*, Abu-Lughod noted, "False accusations of anti-Semitism . . . trivialize an important issue because they are now routinely used to silence any discussion of Palestinian suffering and any open debate about what the Israeli government is doing." When challenged with the fact that Arab states in the region have similarly poor records regarding the treatment of Palestinian refugees, she replied, "Palestinian scholars and activists have been at the forefront of those documenting the way some of the Arab states have denied Palestinian refugees rights and opportunities, just as they deny them, incidentally, to many of their own populations. What I object to is how these facts are used to avoid talking about why these people were made refugees in the first place."

DO MUSLIM WOMEN NEED SAVING?

It was with her 2013 book, *Do Muslim Women Need Saving?*, that Abu-Lughod cemented her reputation as a contrarian. That work, an expansion of a much-discussed scholarly article from 2002, "seeks answers to the questions that presented themselves . . . with such force after September 11, 2001, when popular concern about Muslim women's rights took off," as she wrote in the introduction. In an article for the *Daily Beast* (22 Oct. 2013), she elaborated, "I was uncomfortable with disjunction between the lives and experiences of Muslim women I had known and the popular media representations I encountered in the Western public sphere, the politically motivated justifications for military intervention on behalf of Muslim women that became common sense, and even the well-meaning humanitarian and rights work intended to relieve global women's suffering." Rather than asking how the West might "save" Muslim women, she wrote, a better question might be, "How might we take responsibility for distant women's circumstances and possibilities in what is clearly an interconnected global world, instead of viewing them as victims of alien cultures?"

Of all the sections in the book, the chapter on honor crimes drew a particularly vitriolic response from her detractors, many of whom claimed that she was arguing that honor killings should be viewed within the context of the culture rather than condemned outright. In fact, rather than upholding honor killings as a cultural practice, Abu-Lughod was decrying the widespread Western view of them as such—that is, "as a culturally specific form of violence, distinct from other widespread forms of domestic or intimate partner violence, including the more familiar passion crime." She objected not to condemnation of the crimes themselves, but rather to the way that such crimes "are explained as the behavior of a specific ethnic or cultural community. The culture itself, or 'tradition,' is taken to be the cause of the criminal violence. So the category stigmatizes not particular acts of violence but entire cultures or communities." In addition, she wrote, the Western insistence on characterizing honor killings as a cultural institution, rather than another form of domestic violence, obscures the complicity and systematic failures of governments and various institutions that by turns dismiss, sensationalize, and perpetuate violence against women in all forms.

PERSONAL LIFE

A 2007 Carnegie Scholar, Abu-Lughod has also won fellowships from the National Endowment for the Humanities and the John Simon Guggenheim Foundation, among other groups. She is married to Timothy Mitchell, a British-born political scientist who also holds an endowed chair at Columbia, as the William B. Ransford Professor of Middle Eastern, South Asian and African Studies.

SUGGESTED READING

Abu-Lughod, Lila. "Do Muslim Women Need Saving?" *Time*. Time, 1 Nov. 2013. Web. 18 Mar. 2016.

Abu-Lughod, Lila. "Do Muslim Women Need Saving?" Interview by Nourhan Tewfik. *Al-Ahram Weekly*. Al-Ahram Weekly, 10 Dec. 2015. Web. 18 Mar. 2016.

Abu-Lughod, Lila. "Lila Abu-Lughod on Attitudes toward Muslim Women in the West." Interview by Nermeen Shaikh. *Asia Society*. Asia Soc., n.d. Web. 18 Mar. 2016.

Abu-Lughod, Lila. "*Spiegel* Interview with Lila Abu-Lughod: 'Any Solution Will Have to Involve More Creative Thinking.'" *Spiegel*

Online. Spiegel, 16 May 2008. Web. 18 Mar. 2016.

Abu-Lughod, Lila. "Transnational Politics and Feminist Inquiries in the Middle East: An Interview with Lila Abu-Lughod." Interview by Basuli Deb. *Postcolonial Text* 7.1 (2012): n. pag. Web. 18 Mar. 2016.

"Lila Abu-Lughod: Professor and Author." *Institute for Middle East Understanding*. Inst. for Middle East Understanding, 10 Oct. 2015. Web. 18 Mar. 2016.

SELECTED WORKS

Veiled Sentiments: Honor and Poetry in a Bedouin Society, 1986; *Writing Women's Worlds: Bedouin Stories*, 1993; *Remaking Women: Feminism and Modernity in the Middle East*, 1998; *Dramas of Nationhood: The Politics of Television in Egypt*, 2005; *Nakba: Palestine, 1948, and the Claims of Memory* (with Ahmad H. Sa'di), 2009; *Do Muslim Women Need Saving?*, 2013

—*Mari Rich*

Huntington Theatre Company/CC BY 2.0/Wikimedia Commons

Uzo Aduba

Born: February 10, 1981
Occupation: Actor

Uzo Aduba first came to widespread attention in 2013 after the premiere of the hit Netflix series *Orange Is the New Black*. On the show—a comedy-drama series based on a 2010 memoir about Piper Kerman's incarceration at a minimum-security federal prison on money-laundering charges—Aduba plays inmate Suzanne "Crazy Eyes" Warren. "If prison was a playground, Crazy Eyes would be the last one picked at recess," Celine Wright explained for the *Los Angeles Times* (12 Aug. 2013). "With her bulging eyes, wild hair, and bizarre mannerisms, she's both mocked and feared by the other prisoners."

The show has been widely praised for widening the roles available to women on television and for depicting characters of varying ethnicities, sizes, ages, and sexual orientations. Even within a large and exceptionally strong ensemble cast, Aduba and her character stand out. "In a lesser drama, Suzanne would have remained a wild card—a comic-relief character who'd occasionally appear in [the main character] Piper's orbit to display menacing or slightly clueless behavior," Maureen Ryan wrote for the *Huffington Post* (23 Aug. 2013).

Since the series premiered, Aduba has won a Screen Actors Guild Award for outstanding performance by a female actor in a comedy series, as well as a 2014 Emmy Award for outstanding

guest actress in a comedy. In 2015 she won a second Emmy, this time for outstanding supporting actress in a drama series, as the show's designation had been officially changed for the competition. (That administrative quirk made her one of only two people ever to win an Emmy in both the comedy and drama categories for the same role.)

EARLY LIFE AND EDUCATION

The actor was born Uzoamaka Aduba on February 10, 1981, in Boston and was raised in Medfield, Massachusetts, along with her four siblings. Her mother, a social worker, and her father, a banker, had immigrated to the United States after the Nigerian Civil War, and theirs was one of the few black families in their adopted suburban community. (Aduba's mother had survived not only that brutal war in the late 1960s but an earlier bout with polio; although doctors had warned her that she might never walk again after her illness, she went on to become a champion college tennis player.)

Aduba's first name means "the road is good" in the Igbo language, and although she has never considered Americanizing it as an adult, she told June Thomas for *Marie Claire* (12 May 2015), "When I was really little, teachers in my small, traditional New England town would really struggle with it. One day I came home from school and said, 'Mommy, can you call me Zoe? No one can say Uzoamaka.' Without skipping a beat, my mom was like, 'If they can learn to say Tchaikovsky and Dostoyevsky and Michelangelo, they can learn to say Uzoamaka.' That was the end of it." Her mother was equally adamant when Aduba asked for braces to fix the wide gap between her front teeth. "My mother sat me down [and said], 'Uzo, I will not close your gap and here's why. You have an Anyaoku gap, my family's gap,'" the actor wrote in an essay for *Cosmopolitan* (15 June 2014). "It's a signature in the village she grew up in. People know the Anyaokus, in large part, by that gap. They also revered them for it. In Nigeria, my mom explained, a gap is a sign of beauty and intelligence."

Aduba's parents were determined that their children take advantage of all America had to offer. All five children played instruments, and at age five, Aduba began figure-skating lessons. She competed in the sport for the next decade, often practicing six days a week. (Her younger brother joined her on the ice, eventually playing for the Missouri Mavericks, a minor-league hockey team.) After a coach began pressuring her to quit school in order to train more seriously, her parents, aghast at the possibility that she might discontinue her formal education, stopped the lessons. Aduba, however, found plenty of other pursuits to occupy her time. She took up track-and-field, developing into a state-champion sprinter at Medfield High School, and became a valuable member of the local youth choir.

Aduba's athletic abilities earned her a track-and-field scholarship to Boston University (BU), where she excelled in the 55-meter, 100-meter, and 200-meter races and won a sports leadership award during her senior year. She majored in classical vocal performance and cultivated a new love of acting. (Many fans who know Aduba only from *Orange Is the New Black* are greatly surprised to discover that she can sing.) In 2003 she appeared in *Translations of Xhosa*, a student's thesis play that was being produced at the Olney Theatre Center as part of its Potomac Theatre Festival. That role earned her a Helen Hayes Award nomination for best supporting actress in a resident play.

START OF PROFESSIONAL ACTING CAREER

Aduba earned her bachelor of fine arts degree in 2005 and set out for New York to pursue a stage career. Although her family originally expected her to become a lawyer or other white-collar professional, they were supportive.

Aduba settled in the then-relatively-affordable neighborhood of Astoria, Queens, earning her living by waiting tables. She accepted unpaid roles in several Off-Off-Broadway productions. "I didn't care because it was work," she wrote in an essay for the *Daily Beast* (8 Apr. 2014). "My uncle once told me, 'Your parents didn't leave Nigeria for you to just be standing still, Uzo.' These words resonated with me long after I had first heard them, and I took them to heart."

It was, however, difficult at times for her to remain upbeat. Aduba made her Broadway debut in 2007, in *Coram Boy*, but that little-seen show ran for only one month. Other shows closed unexpectedly or even failed to open. "Frequently, I called my mom to seek guidance (and to shed some tears)," Aduba wrote for the *Daily Beast*. "Through all of my disappointments and heartbreak, she never played 'the practical parent' or pleaded with me to pursue something more stable. Instead, she encouraged me and supported me. 'Just keep pushing,' 'Keep going,' she would say." Given that perseverance, things did occasionally appear to improve. In 2011, for example, Aduba received the prestigious Elliot Norton Award for outstanding musical performance for her role in *Prometheus Bound* at Boston's American Repertory Theater, and that year she also appeared in a hit Broadway revival of the musical *Godspell*.

There followed, however, a seemingly inevitable dry season. At her agent's suggestion, she had begun auditioning for television and film roles, but had little luck. "I heard the word 'no' so often that it started to feel like a second name," Aduba wrote for the *Daily Beast*. "I watched my savings dwindle. One day, after getting lost and arriving twenty minutes late to my audition, I hit my breaking point. I tried with all my might to salvage the audition, but in true dramatic actor fashion, I convinced myself that this was a sign that I wasn't meant for this industry."

To her surprise, that tryout had not been the disaster she had envisioned, and Aduba was cast in a guest role on an episode of the CBS police series *Blue Bloods*. But first, she got an even bigger surprise during her tearful subway ride home from that audition.

ORANGE IS THE NEW BLACK

About a month before trying to win a part on *Blue Bloods*, Aduba had auditioned for a new series titled *Orange Is the New Black*. She had hoped to win the part of an inmate named Janae, which seemed like a perfect fit for her because the character was a talented track star. On the way home from her *Blue Bloods* tryout, still clutching a handful of soggy tissues, she took a call from her agent, who informed her that although the show's creators had not chosen her to play Janae, they wanted her for a different character, who would be nicknamed Crazy Eyes. "I was like, 'What in my audition would make someone think I'd be right for a part called Crazy Eyes?'" Aduba quipped to Maureen Ryan. "But to be honest, when I got the script for it, it felt like the right fit. I was excited by the challenge of Suzanne and what she had to accomplish and by her story throughout the progression of the show." Aduba often relates the tale of that phone call to journalists, specifying that she will always remember it as among the most significant events of her life.

From the very first episode in which she appeared, critics and fans alike acknowledged Suzanne as one of the most compelling and unforgettable characters on the show. "The writer of that episode, Marco Ramirez, wrote a stage direction, describing her as, in part, someone who was innocent like a child . . . except that children aren't scary, and I remember thinking that was just loaded with so much information," Aduba told Christine Champagne for Co.Create (8 June 2014). "I thought she was like an adult carrying a sledgehammer and a pacifier, showing how an innocent child could be scary, meaning her intentions would be always good and rooted in some sort of purity but her execution might be somehow mismanaged or poorly orchestrated."

Suzanne—whose backstory reveals that she had been adopted as a child by a white couple who never fully addressed her evident mental-health issues—is romantically obsessed with the main character, Piper. Piper continually rebuffs her advances, and in one much-talked-about scene, Suzanne retaliates by urinating outside of her crush's bunk. Although the writers had initially meant the character to appear only sporadically in the first season, she was quickly bumped up to series regular, thanks in large part to Aduba's sensitive portrayal. In reviews consistently echoed during *Orange Is the New Black*'s run, Tom Meltzer wrote for the *Guardian* (17 Dec. 2013) that the "lyrical, Shakespeare-quoting loner 'Crazy Eyes' invites pity, shock, reproach, and belly-laughs in equal measure." The eagerly anticipated fourth season of the show began streaming on Netflix in June 2016.

OTHER ROLES
Despite the demands of filming an acclaimed television series, Aduba, who rarely speaks of her private life to interviewers, has concurrently taken on other roles. In December 2015, for example, she portrayed Glinda the Good Witch on the NBC remake of *The Wiz!*—a role played in the original 1978 film by the iconic Lena Horne. (An urban retelling of *The Wonderful Wizard of Oz*, the movie featured an entirely black cast and had been adapted from a 1974 Broadway musical of the same name.) "To say that *Orange Is the New Black* breakout Uzo Aduba did Lena Horne proud would be an understatement," Jaleesa M. Jones wrote for *USA Today* (4 Dec. 2015). "It would also fail to capture what her turn as Glinda the Good Witch meant for others." She explained, "Uzo's appearance . . . served as a landmark moment in which women and little girls of color felt seen and valued," and that theory was confirmed by an outpouring of enthusiastic Tweets and Facebook messages from viewers.

In early 2016 Aduba returned to the stage, appearing on London's West End in a well-received version of Jean Genet's *The Maids*. She also starred in the 2016 television film *Showing Roots*, about a pair of friends seeking to integrate their small Southern town.

SUGGESTED READING
Aduba, Uzo. "My Road to *Orange Is the New Black*." *Daily Beast*. IAC, 8 Apr. 2014. Web. 20 Apr. 2016.
Champagne, Christine. "Behind the Breakout Role: *Orange Is the New Black*'s Uzo Aduba on Creating Crazy Eyes." *Co.Create*. Fast, 8 June 2014. Web. 20 Apr. 2016.
Ryan, Maureen. "'Crazy Eyes' from *Orange Is the New Black* Talks Flirting, Jodie Foster and That Infamous Scene." *Huffington Post*. TheHuffingtonPost.com, 23 Aug. 2013. Web. 20 Apr. 2016.
Thomas, June. "*Orange Is the New Black* Star Uzo Aduba Reveals What's in Store for Season 3." *Marie Claire*. Hearst, 12 May 2015. Web. 20 Apr. 2016.
Widdicombe, Lizzie. "On Ice." *New Yorker*. Condé Nast, 7 Dec. 2015. Web. 20 Apr. 2016.
Wright, Celine. "Orange Is the New Black's Uzo Aduba on a Good Road as Crazy Eyes." *Los Angeles Times*. Tribune, 12 Aug. 2013. Web. 20 Apr. 2016.

SELECTED WORKS
Blue Bloods, 2012; *Orange Is the New Black*, 2013– ; *The Wiz! Live*, 2015; *Showing Roots*, 2016

—Mari Rich

José Eduardo Agualusa

Born: December 13, 1960
Occupation: Author

Over the course of a literary career that has spanned nearly three decades, the Angolan writer and journalist José Eduardo Agualusa has helped bring to the Western world a new perspective of Portuguese-speaking African countries, commonly referred to as Lusophone Africa. He has done so with a collection of works that has been characterized by outlandish story lines and bravura reimaginings of real-life figures and events.

Agualusa has written more than a dozen novels that have been translated into twenty-five languages. He was relatively unknown to English-speaking readers until 2007, when *The Book of Chameleons*, the English translation of his 2004 novel *O vendedor de passados*, won the United Kingdom's prestigious Independent Foreign Fiction Prize, which honored foreign-language novels that had been published

Christian Ries/CC BY-SA 3.0/GFDL/Wikimedia Commons

in English in the United Kingdom. The novel, which is told from the perspective of a gecko, was translated by British writer and editor Daniel Hahn, who has collaborated with Agualusa on all of the English translations of his works to date.

Agualusa and Hahn's fifth collaboration was *A General Theory of Oblivion* (2015), a translation of Agualusa's 2013 novel *Teoria geral do esquecimento*, set against the backdrop of the Angolan Civil War. In a review of the novel for the *Financial Times* (17 July 2015), Ángel Gurría-Quintana called Agualusa "one of Angola's most inventive novelists."

EARLY LIFE

José Eduardo Agualusa was born on December 13, 1960, in Huambo, Angola, then known as Nova Lisboa in the Province of Angola. While growing up in Angola, a country known for its abject poverty and a devastating civil war that lasted from 1975 to 2002, Agualusa, whose mother taught Portuguese, fell in love with books and the written word. "I grew up among books. I grew up among great storytellers and in a rough area in turmoil, full of extraordinary tales," Agualusa told Eric M. B. Becker for the online literature magazine *Words without Borders* (12 Apr. 2016). "Writing was a way to understand the world around me and to assert my place in it."

During his youth Agualusa was greatly influenced by Portuguese and Latin American literature. He immersed himself in works by such authors as Eça de Queirós, Jorge Luis Borges, Jorge Amado, Gabriel García Márquez, Mario Vargas Llosa, and Rubem Fonseca. Many of those

authors helped popularize the literary genre known as magical realism, which is characterized by a melding of the fantastical and absurd with the everyday. Such elements would later come to define Agualusa's fictional works.

EARLY CAREER

Agualusa studied agronomy and forestry before embarking on a literary career, first as a poet and then as a novelist. His first novel, *A conjura (The Conspiracy)*, was published in 1989. It is set in the Angolan capital of Luanda between 1880 and 1911 and offers insight into the mélange of cultures and traditions that helped shape modern-day Angola.

In 1992 Agualusa published his second novel, *A feira dos assombrados (The Market of the Damned)*, which chronicles the emergence of the Creole elite and the rise of Angolan protonationalism. The following year he published *African Lisbon*, a collaborative project with Fernando Semedo and the photographer Elza Rocha about African influence on Portuguese society.

For *Estação das chuvas* (1996; *Rainy Season*, 2009), Agualusa drew partially from his own life to tell the fictional story of Lídia do Carmo Ferreira, an Angolan poet and freedom fighter. Through the idealistic eyes of Ferreira, readers are vividly transported back to the war-torn Angola of the 1970s. In a review of Hahn's English translation for the *Independent* (30 July 2009), Boyd Tonkin noted Agualusa's "lissom, glancing style" and commented that he "has a touch and tone of such lyrical and rhythmic grace that it can make the worst horrors almost bearable."

RISE TO INTERNATIONAL PROMINENCE

In 1997 Agualusa received a literary grant from the Lisbon, Portugal–based Centro Nacional de Cultura to write *Nação crioula* (1997; *Creole*, 2002), a novel that revisits the character of Carlos Fradique Mendes, a fictional Portuguese adventurer created by Eça de Queirós in the late nineteenth century. It follows Mendes as he traverses the world and falls in love with Ana Olímpia Vaz de Caminha, a former slave who becomes one of Angola's richest women. *Nação crioula* became a best seller in Brazil and Portugal and was awarded the Grande Prémio de Literatura (Grand Prize for Literature) by Rádio e Televisão de Portugal (Radio and Television of Portugal). The novel was Agualusa's first to be translated into English and marked the author's first collaboration with Hahn; its English-language translation was published in the United Kingdom in 2002.

Agualusa's next novel, *O vendedor de passados (The Book of Chameleons)*, was first published in Portugal in 2004. It takes place in Angola and unfolds from the point of view of a gecko named Eulálio, whose recollections correspond to fragments of the life of Argentine writer Jorge Luis Borges. Throughout the novel, Eulálio eavesdrops on his housemate, a secondhand-book dealer named Félix Ventura, who specializes in recreating memories from people's pasts. "It's a novel about the construction of memory and memory's traps," Agualusa explained to Carlos J. Queirós in an interview for the AARP's bilingual Spanish- and English-language magazine *Segunda Juventud* (*Second Youth Summer* 2008). *O vendedor de passados* received widespread praise from critics, and Hahn's translation was published in the UK in 2006. The novel won the 2007 Independent Foreign Fiction Prize, making Agualusa the first African writer to win the prestigious award since its inception in 1990. In 2008 *The Book of Chameleons* became the first of Agualusa's novels to be released in the United States.

Agualusa followed *The Book of Chameleons* with *As mulheres do meu pai* (2007; *My Father's Wives*, 2008), which focuses on the country-hopping efforts of a young filmmaker named Laurentina to gather information about her mysterious father, the late Angolan composer Faustino Manso. In a review for the *Guardian* (19 Dec. 2008), Jennie Erdal called *My Father's Wives* "an artful mix of fact, reportage, politics, poetry, and personal confession, not to mention mountainous dollops of sheer unadulterated invention—all dispatched in short episodic chapters and musical, rhythmic prose." She added that Agualusa is a "master of multiple perspectives" who "remains impressively in control" of the eclectic material, resulting in "a giant melting pot, exuding intoxicating fumes of love and death that permeate the exotic, chaotic sweep of southern Africa."

MAN BOOKER INTERNATIONAL PRIZE NOMINEE

Agualusa's fifth collaboration with Hahn, *A General Theory of Oblivion*, was published in both the United Kingdom and the United States in 2015. Set in 1975 on the eve of Angola's declaration of independence from Portugal, the thirty-seven-chapter novel is based on the true story of Ludovica "Ludo" Fernandes Mano, a Portuguese woman who barricaded herself inside her Luanda apartment for the entirety of the Angolan Civil War. Agualusa originally wrote Ludo's story as a screenplay for Angolan filmmaker Jorge António, but when the film fell through, he turned the screenplay into a novel. Drawing inspiration from Ludo's personal diary entries, he colors her story with cast of fictional characters, all of whom help shed light on the culture of chaos that existed in Angola during its civil war. In a review for the *Independent* (2 July 2015), Jethro Soutar cited Agualusa's "sometimes willfully flamboyant" storytelling style, while calling the novel "a timely homage to the prize of Angolan independence."

In 2016 *A General Theory of Oblivion* was nominated for the Man Booker International Prize, which is awarded annually to a full-length novel published in English, whether originally or in translation. Agualusa was the first Angolan writer to be nominated for the prize.

OTHER WORKS

Agualusa divides his time between Angola, Portugal, and Brazil. In addition to his novels, he has written four plays, two of them in collaboration with Mozambican writer Mia Couto. He has also published a collection of poetry and several collections of short fiction, and he has written columns for Angolan and Portuguese newspapers. In 2006 he helped found a Brazilian publishing house, Língua Geral (General Language), which exclusively publishes works written in Portuguese.

SUGGESTED READING

Agualusa, José Eduardo. Interview by Paulo Polzonoff Jr. and Anderson Tepper. *Words without Borders*. Words without Borders, Sept. 2007. Web. 19 Sept. 2016.

Agualusa, José Eduardo. Interview by Carlos J. Queirós. *AARP*. AARP, Summer 2008. Web. 19 Sept. 2016.

Agualusa, José Eduardo. "2016 Man Booker International Q&A: José Eduardo Agualusa." Interview by Eric M. B. Becker. *Words without Borders*. Words without Borders, 12 Apr. 2016. Web. 19 Sept. 2016.

Erdal, Jennie. "Across the Continent." Rev. of *My Father's Wives*, by José Eduardo Agualusa, trans. Daniel Hahn. *Guardian*. Guardian News and Media, 19 Dec. 2008. Web. 19 Sept. 2016.

Gurría-Quintana, Ángel. Rev. of *A General Theory of Oblivion*, by José Eduardo Agualusa, trans. Daniel Hahn. *FT.com*. Financial Times, 17 July 2015. Web. 19 Sept. 2016.

Soutar, Jethro. Rev. of *A General Theory of Oblivion*, by José Eduardo Agualusa, trans. Daniel Hahn. *Independent*. Independent.co.uk, 2 July 2015. Web. 19 Sept. 2016.

Tonkin, Boyd. Rev. of *Rainy Season*, by José Eduardo Agualusa, trans. Daniel Hahn. *Independent*. Independent.co.uk, 30 July 2009. Web. 19 Sept. 2016.

SELECTED WORKS

A conjura (*The Conspiracy*), 1989; *A feira dos assombrados* (*The Market of the Damned*), 1992; *Estação das chuvas* (*Rainy Season*), 1996; *Nação crioula* (*Creole*), 1997; *O vendedor de passados* (*The Book of Chameleons*), 2004; *As mulheres do meu pai* (*My Father's Wives*), 2007; *Teoria geral do esquecimento* (*A General Theory of Oblivion*), 2013

—*Chris Cullen*

Michelle Alexander

Born: October 7, 1967
Occupation: Civil rights activist

Miller Center/CC BY 2.0

The civil rights lawyer and legal scholar Michelle Alexander shook up the national conversation about race, the drug war, and the prison system with the release of her book *The New Jim Crow: Mass Incarceration in the Age of Colorblindness* in 2010. In the book she makes the case that even though the drug laws in this country are written to be colorblind, the enforcement of those laws is anything but. Although white Americans are more likely to consume and sell illegal drugs than black Americans, African Americans are much more likely to get stopped and searched, arrested, convicted, and imprisoned for drug-related offenses. For example, in 2006, one out of every one hundred six white men was in prison, whereas for black men the statistic was one out of every fourteen. This racial disparity, Alexander suggests, has greatly contributed to high rates of imprisonment for drug offenses, a trend that has created many social problems among communities of color. Furthermore, four out of five drug arrests in 2005 were only for possession—with no violence involved—and about eight out of ten of those arrests were for marijuana.

Although poor whites are also burdened by this system of mass incarceration, Alexander argues it disproportionately affects communities of color and asserts that it has been used as a way to maintain racial inequality. Because individuals who have been convicted of a felony lose various essential rights, such as the right to vote; forfeit benefits such as public housing and food stamps; and can also face legal discrimination when searching for work, incarceration reduces the agency of the minority groups that are disproportionately convicted. Alexander's book helped provoke a national conversation—from both sides of the political spectrum—on the effects the criminal justice system has on millions of Americans and their families.

EARLY LIFE

Michelle Lorén Alexander was born on October 7, 1967, and initially raised in Stelle, Illinois, a small planned community where her parents' interracial marriage was not looked down upon. Her mother, Sandra, was white, and her father, John Alexander, was black. Alexander witnessed their struggles with discrimination, even from other family members. "My grandfather was extremely hostile to my mother marrying my father," she told Arnie Cooper for *Sun Magazine* (Feb. 2011), noting that her mother was disowned and her family's church excommunicated her.

Racial discrimination continued to shape Alexander's childhood. When she was eight years old, her father was transferred to San Francisco, California, so the family moved to the West Coast. Alexander's father was a successful salesperson for IBM but was continually overlooked for promotions, so he eventually left the company. Alexander attended a mix of private and public schools, where she encountered a variety of people from different ethnic and economic backgrounds. She ended up attending three different high schools because her parents' financial troubles caused the family to move around a lot.

Despite the challenges of being evicted and frequently moving, Alexander performed well in school. During her senior year of high school, in Ashland, Oregon, she was told by a family friend that she should apply to Vanderbilt University, in Nashville, Tennessee. She not only got in, she received a Gertrude Vanderbilt Minority Scholarship, which was a necessity as her family was still financially insecure. Her parents encouraged her to take advantage of the opportunity, and she left for school without even visiting the campus.

EDUCATION AND INITIAL ACTIVISM

At Vanderbilt, Alexander studied political science and became involved in various groups as a volunteer. During her junior year she joined Alternative Spring Break, a student-run organization that promotes community involvement and social action by engaging college students in service projects. Alexander worked to register voters in a black community in Lexington, Mississippi, where local politicians had historically drawn district lines and passed laws to make voting for African Americans either hard or simply impossible. "Black people would be told their names weren't on the rolls or that some technicality prevented them from registering," Alexander recalled in an interview with Cooper for *Vanderbilt Magazine* (2 Dec. 2013). "Residents were often too confused or intimidated to challenge these tactics." During her senior year, Alexander worked as a volunteer visitor at the Spencer Youth Correctional Center in Nashville. That was her first real experience with the prison system, and it made a deep impression.

Alexander earned her Bachelor of Arts degree in 1989. She then attended the Stanford University Law School, one of the nation's top law schools. At the law school Alexander was mentored by Gerald López, a professor and the cofounder of the Lawyering for Social Change program. "I think I had a little bit of a fairytale idea of civil-rights lawyers riding in on their white horses to save a community," Alexander told Cooper for *Vanderbilt Magazine*. "[López] disabused me of those notions and challenged my thinking in very important ways that have influenced how I've thought about my work as a lawyer and advocate ever since." During her time in law school, she became the director of the Civil Rights Clinic, an organization through which law school students assist professional attorneys to provide free legal services to poor people in the San Francisco Bay Area. Alexander received her law degree in 1992.

AFTER LAW SCHOOL

After graduating, Alexander clerked for Justice Harry A. Blackmun on the United States Supreme Court and for Chief Judge Abner Mikva on the United States Court of Appeals for the DC Circuit. She became an associate at the law firm of Saperstein, Goldstein, Demchak & Baller in Oakland, California, where she represented plaintiffs in class-action lawsuits who alleged discrimination based on gender or race.

In 1998 Alexander became the director of the Racial Justice Project for the Northern California chapter of the American Civil Liberties Union (ACLU), where she was in charge of grassroots organization, media advocacy, litigation, and coalition building. The Racial Justice Project focused primarily on reforming the education and criminal justice systems. Under her leadership, that ACLU branch launched a campaign against law enforcement racial profiling,

called the Driving While Black or Brown Campaign. Alexander worked with victims of racial profiling and police brutality, saw how drug laws were selectively being used against people of color, and witnessed the social and legal challenges that people who were recently released from prison faced upon reentering society.

In an interview with Dave Davies for the National Public Radio (NPR) program *Fresh Air* (17 Jan. 2012), Alexander said that during her time with the Racial Justice Project she experienced what she called an "awakening" to the problems of the criminal justice system. When she was asked to describe a case that was especially significant, she provided the example of a young black man who came to her office and said that he had been a victim of continued police harassment and had the evidence to prove it. Over the course of nine months he had taken detailed notes on his many encounters with law enforcement. Initially Alexander thought he was the perfect plaintiff to represent the ACLU's goals. But during the conversation she discovered that the young man had a drug felony on his record, and, despite his claims that the conviction was framed by the police, she told him the ACLU could not represent him due to his potential lack of credibility.

Frustrated, the young man described how the conviction prevented him from improving his life, as he could not get a job, find housing, or even collect food stamps. He accused Alexander of being as useless as the police. A few months later Alexander read in the local newspaper that drug-taskforce police officers in Oakland had indeed been planting drugs on people in the very neighborhood where the young man lived. She realized that the burden of criminal convictions, especially on nonviolent drug charges, was a significant obstacle to civil rights. As she told Davies, "That was really the beginning of my journey, of asking myself, how am I, the civil rights lawyer, actually helping to replicate the very forms of discrimination and exclusion I'm supposedly fighting against?"

THE NEW JIM CROW

In 2005 Alexander was jointly appointed to faculty positions at the Kirwan Institute for the Study of Race and Ethnicity and the Moritz College of Law at the Ohio State University (OSU). She also received an Open Society Institute Soros Justice Fellowship, which allowed her to dedicate her time and energy to completing her first book, about the criminal justice system problems she was studying. The result was *The New Jim Crow: Mass Incarceration in the Age of Colorblindness*, released in 2010. Immediately recognized as an important and timely book, it tackled the issue of how the war on drugs and the prison system were allegedly being used to maintain racial inequality.

The Jim Crow laws to which the title refers were originally state and local laws implemented after the end of the American Civil War, especially in the South. These laws created segregation in virtually all aspects of society, including public spaces such as schools, restrooms, and public transportation. As a result black people were treated as second-class citizens. The laws were finally ruled unconstitutional thanks to the civil rights movement of the 1960s, and subsequent legislation was careful to call for racial equality and a colorblind system of justice. Yet although the language of modern laws is well intentioned, Alexander argues, their implementation is highly discriminatory. As she told Davies, "many of the old forms of discrimination that we supposedly left behind during the Jim Crow era are suddenly legal again, once you've been branded a felon."

Alexander's central argument in *The New Jim Crow* is that US government policies, such as the war on drugs (begun by the US government in the early 1970s in the name of public safety), have caused disproportionate mass incarceration of minorities, which in turn prevents such groups from realizing true social equality. She suggests that this outcome may have even been an intention of the politicians who developed the modern US criminal justice system, as a way of limiting minorities' advancement just like the original Jim Crow laws did. Alexander presents statistics to support her claims, such as the fact that in 2004 three-fourths of all US prisoners on drug charges were Latino or black, despite the fact that most drug dealers and users in the country were white.

Alexander argues that law enforcement officers spend too much time and effort harassing and arresting low-level offenders, namely nonviolent offenders in possession of small amounts of illegal drugs, rather than targeting violent criminals and drug kingpins. She notes that felony convictions ruin lives and make it difficult for individuals to improve themselves and their communities. People who have been convicted of a felony can be banned from public housing, discriminated against when searching for a job, and denied food stamps and other benefits. These serious limitations, argues Alexander, make it too difficult for many Americans to live and work in the legal economy. Furthermore, in a number of states, Americans who are on parole or have felony convictions lose their right to vote, so even after they have served their sentence they are effectively disenfranchised.

BEST-SELLING AUTHOR

The New Jim Crow became a best seller and occupied a real place in the national conversation on race and the criminal justice system after its release in paperback form in 2012. The reception of the book was primarily positive and enthusiastic, often from various ideological corners. Bill Frezza praised the book in a review for *Forbes* (28 Feb. 2012), writing, "Alexander makes a compelling case that one of the key pillars of the fruitless war on drugs is selective enforcement coupled with plea bargain-driven judicial railroading," while noting that Alexander's political views could not be further from his own. In the *New York Review of Books* (10 Mar. 2011) Darryl Pinckney wrote, "*The New Jim Crow* is striking in the intelligence of her ideas, her powers of summary, and the force of her writing. Her tone is disarming throughout; she speaks as a concerned citizen, not as an expert, though she is one."

The New Jim Crow was highlighted by many national publications and spent more than a year on the *New York Times* Best Seller list. In 2011 it won the Image Award for best nonfiction book from the National Association for the Advancement of Colored People (NAACP), among other accolades. After her book's success, Alexander took advantage of her heightened profile to tour extensively, give talks on the subject of mass incarceration around the country, and work with advocacy groups. She also continues to write, including pieces in publications such as *Time* and the *Nation*.

PERSONAL LIFE

Michelle Alexander married Carter Stewart, an attorney, in 2002. They have three children, a son and two daughters.

SUGGESTED READING
Cooper, Arnie. "Strong Convictions." *Vanderbilt Magazine*. Vanderbilt Magazine, 2 Dec. 2013. Web. 9 Dec. 2015.
Cooper, Arnie. "Throwing Away the Key: Michelle Alexander on How Prisons Have Become The New Jim Crow." *The Sun*. Sun Magazine, Feb. 2011. Web. 9 Dec. 2015.
Davies, Dave. "Legal Scholar: Jim Crow Still Exists in America." *Fresh Air*. NPR, 17 Jan. 2012. Web. 9 Dec. 2015.
Pinckney, Darryl. "Invisible Black America." Rev. of *The Presumption of Guilt*, by Charles J. Ogletree Jr., and *The New Jim Crow*, by Michelle Alexander. *New York Review of Books*. NYREV, 10 Mar. 2011. Web. 9 Dec. 2015.

—*Dmitry Kiper*

Jozy Altidore

Born: November 6, 1989
Occupation: Soccer player

The American soccer star Jozy Altidore is a striker for Major League Soccer (MLS)'s Toronto Football Club (FC) and the US men's national team (USMNT). Known for playing a graceful yet physical brand of soccer, Altidore has enjoyed a "sometimes brilliant, sometimes brutal" soccer career, as Kevin Baxter wrote for the *Los Angeles Times* (14 June 2014), that has been marked by extreme highs and lows.

Altidore turned professional at age sixteen after he was selected by the New York Red Bulls in the 2006 MLS SuperDraft. After two breakout seasons with the Red Bulls, Altidore launched a professional career in Europe, where he struggled to find the same success. He had stints with five different European teams before regaining his form with the Dutch club AZ Alkmaar during the 2011–12 season.

Following a record-breaking 2012–13 campaign with AZ Alkmaar, Altidore signed a contract with Sunderland in the English Premier League. However, he remained with that team for only eighteen months, and in 2015 he returned to MLS to sign with Toronto FC.

A mainstay on the USMNT for much of the last decade, Altidore played for the United States at both the 2010 and 2014 FIFA (Fédération Internationale de Football Association) World Cups and has set a number of team records. He is currently the team's third all-time leading scorer.

EARLY LIFE

Josmer "Jozy" Volmy Altidore was born on November 6, 1989, in Livingston, New Jersey. His parents, Joseph and Giselle, are both natives of Haiti and had come to the United States in the 1970s to escape the corrupt regime of President François Duvalier, better known as "Papa Doc." They met while riding a bus together in Orange, New Jersey, and married soon after. Altidore's father is an engineer and his mother is a nurse.

When Altidore was a baby, his family, which included an older brother, Janah, and two older sisters, Lindsey and Sadia, moved to Boca Raton, Florida. Joseph, an avid soccer enthusiast, taught all his children, including Altidore, how to kick a soccer ball not long after they learned to walk.

Unlike his siblings, however, Altidore displayed a preternatural talent for handling a soccer ball. By age five, he was kicking the ball so hard that he had to play in an older age division. For the rest of his youth, Altidore would compete against older children. He joined his first travel soccer team at age eight, after Josef Schulz, a former soccer player and coach in the Austrian first division, spotted him playing in a park.

Schulz, who was then in the midst of launching an eponymous youth soccer academy, approached Altidore's father and predicted that Jozy would one day play for the US men's national team. Altidore's parents valued education above everything else, however, and initially balked at letting him attend Schulz's academy, but they relented after acknowledging Altidore's great potential in the sport. As Altidore's father said to Baxter, "Sometimes, you have to let your children do what is in their heart."

SOCCER PRODIGY

Because his parents could not afford to cover the full costs of Schulz's academy, Altidore was able to train with the youth club at a discount. Schulz started out with six players and began entering them in three-on-three tournaments; he eventually increased the academy's membership to around 300 players, and by 2007, the academy was ranked among the nation's top twenty boys' soccer clubs by *Soccer America*.

Altidore quickly stood out among his peers on the soccer pitch, and in 2004, he helped the Schulz Academy win the first of three consecutive North American championships in the Super Y-League, which is made up of teams from the United States and Canada. Altidore has credited Schulz, whose teachings emphasized an offensive-minded and tactically sound brand of soccer modeled after the Dutch, with instilling in him the importance of basic fundamentals. "I learned so much there," he recalled to Doug McIntyre for *ESPN.com* (26 June 2013). "Josef used to always tell me that when you get to the highest level, you have to do the little things on your own."

Altidore also played basketball during his youth, but by the time he reached high school, he had to choose between that sport and soccer. Despite loving basketball, Altidore decided to focus on soccer full-time. He attended Boca Prep International School, in Boca Raton, Florida, on a soccer scholarship, before leaving home at age fifteen to join US Soccer's Residency Program, located three hours away in the city of Bradenton.

Upon joining the program, Altidore initially hoped he would be able to land a college scholarship. His talents, however, put him on a fast track to a professional career. In 2005, as a member of a team made up solely of players born in 1989, he scored nineteen goals in twenty-six games. Later that year Altidore was one of just three players born in 1989 to earn a spot on the Under-17 World Cup team. During the 2005 Under-17 World Cup, he appeared in games against Italy and the Netherlands.

TURNING PROFESSIONAL

Altidore's impressive play for the Under-17 squad helped bring him to the attention of MLS scouts. Though his parents wanted him to go to college and receive a degree before turning professional, he declared himself eligible for the 2006 MLS SuperDraft, held in January of that year, and was selected seventeenth overall by the New York Red Bulls (originally known as the New York/New Jersey MetroStars).

Before Altidore could play for the Red Bulls, however, he had to finish high school. As a result, he spent the majority of his 2006 rookie MLS season away from the team. He joined the Red Bulls that summer and made his official professional debut on September 9, 2006, when he appeared in the final minutes of a game against the New England Revolution.

In just his second professional game, Altidore recorded his first career goal, notching the game-winner in a 1–0 Red Bulls victory over Columbus Crew SC. At sixteen years and 314 days, he became the fourth-youngest player to score in MLS. Altidore also became the youngest player to appear in a MLS playoff match, after playing every minute of the Red Bulls' postseason series against DC United. He finished his rookie season with four goals in nine games.

Altidore went on to enjoy a breakout season with the Red Bulls in 2007, when he recorded nine goals and four assists in fifteen games. That year he also made his first international appearance with the USMNT, coming on as a substitute in the sixty-fifth minute of a 1–0 US victory over South Africa in the Nelson Mandela Challenge Cup.

In 2008 Altidore made his first start and scored his first career goal for the USMNT in a friendly match against Mexico. He became, at eighteen, the youngest player to score for the United States in the modern era. By then, Altidore had also played well enough for the Red Bulls to draw serious interest from European clubs, and in June 2008, he moved to Europe to join Villarreal CF of Spain's major soccer league, La Liga. Altidore signed a contract with the club worth approximately $10 million, which was then the largest amount ever paid for an MLS player.

WORLD CUP DEBUT

Altidore's early career success with the Red Bulls proved difficult to replicate on European soil at first, although in November 2009 he became the first US international player to score in La Liga when he netted a goal in the ninetieth minute of a match against Athletic Bilbao. Over the next year and a half, Altidore would play on loan to a succession of other European clubs, including Xerez of the Spanish Second Division and Hull City of the English Premier League.

From his signing with Villareal in 2008 to 2011, Altidore scored just three goals in thirty-nine games with five different clubs. For the young star, playing in Europe's highly competitive leagues, which feature the best assemblage of soccer talent in the world, was a humbling experience. "You go from being a big fish in a small pond to being a very tiny fish in a huge pond," Altidore explained to Pedro Heizer for the *Boca Raton Tribune* (29 June 2012). "That's when your career really starts. You're forced to get better quickly and you begin to understand that every day matters."

Altidore, nevertheless, continued to make his mark as a member of the USMNT. In March 2009 he recorded his first away goal in a World Cup qualifying match against El Salvador, and in the following month, he became, at nineteen, the youngest American to score a hat trick in an international game, doing so in a match against Trinidad and Tobago.

Altidore subsequently started all four games for the United States at the 2010 FIFA World Cup, which was held in South Africa. Though held scoreless in those games, Altidore tallied a pivotal assist in a group match against Slovenia to help keep the United States in the tournament. (The United States would ultimately be eliminated from the tournament after losing to Ghana in the round of sixteen.) He was awarded Man of the Match honors by *ussoccer.com* for his efforts.

REGAINING HIS FORM

In July 2011, after bouncing around from club to club for the previous three years, Altidore signed a four-year contract with the Dutch club AZ Alkmaar, which plays in the Eredivisie, the top soccer league in the Netherlands. The move proved a "dream" for Altidore, as Ives Galarcep put it for FOX Sports (21 June 2012). Playing under the demanding yet nurturing manager Gertjan Verbeek, Altidore scored a team-leading twenty-two goals during the 2011–12 season.

Altidore performed even better during the 2012–13 season, netting thirty-one goals across all competitions and helping lead AZ Alkmaar to a Dutch Cup title. It was the highest scoring output by a US player in Europe's history. "Early on in my career, I think [I] went a bit blindly into things, and didn't know what I should look for," Altidore explained to Galarcep. "When I went to AZ I took my time . . . and after talking to some people, I realized this was a situation I knew I could do well in."

Altidore set his sights on greener pastures in July 2013, when he signed a four-year, $13 million deal with Sunderland of the English Premier League. Meanwhile, from June 2 to August 14 of that year, he scored in five consecutive games for the USMNT, netting seven goals in total to establish a US record. Prior to the streak, Altidore had suffered through a fifteen-month-long scoring drought in international play. He was nonetheless named 2013 US Soccer Male Athlete of the Year for his record-breaking performance.

Fulfilling one of his goals for the 2012–13 season, Altidore helped the USMNT qualify for the 2014 World Cup in Brazil. His hopes of leading the United States to victory in that tournament, however, were dashed after he pulled his hamstring in the team's opening match against Ghana. The team again advanced to the round of sixteen, where they were eliminated by Belgium. It marked the first time the USMNT advanced to the knockout stage of a FIFA World Cup in two consecutive years.

MOVE TO TORONTO FC
Unlike his tenure with AZ Alkmaar, Altidore struggled mightily with Sunderland. In fifty-two appearances with the club, he managed to score just three goals, leading some soccer observers to label his signing one of the worst in Premier League history. His eighteen-month stay in England officially came to an end in January 2015, when he signed a deal with Toronto FC, marking his return to MLS.

Upon arriving in Toronto, Altidore attributed his struggles in England to a number of factors, among them a managerial change and recurring hamstring issues. "As a professional, there are going to be times when everything is not perfect," he said, as quoted by Joe Prince-Wright for NBC Sports (16 Jan. 2015). "In those times, how you react to those moments will define you."

Altidore appeared in twenty-five games for Toronto during the 2015 season, in which he scored thirteen goals. He teamed up with forward Sebastian Giovinco, the 2015 MLS Golden Boot winner, to lead Toronto to the playoffs for the first time in franchise history. However, Altidore was unable to build on his solid 2015 campaign in 2016, with a recurring hamstring injury forcing him to miss the first half of that year's MLS season.

Altidore was also sidelined for the USMNT during the 2016 Copa America Centenario due to hamstring issues. Nevertheless, in September 2016, he became the third most prolific goal scorer in USMNT history when he scored his thirty-fifth career international goal in a match against St. Vincent and the Grenadines.

PERSONAL LIFE
Altidore has been known for his many humanitarian and relief efforts in Haiti. Following the devastating 2010 Haiti earthquake, he raised over $100,000 toward scholarships and water stations in the country. He is the founder of an eponymous charity that raises money for underprivileged youth in the United States and Haiti.

SUGGESTED READING
Altidore, Jozy. "Path to the Pros." Interview by Doug McIntyre. *ESPN.com*. ESPN Internet Ventures, 26 June 2013. Web. 19 Sept. 2016.
Baxter, Kevin. "Jozy Altidore of the U.S. Looks to Strike It Big at the World Cup." *Los Angeles Times*. Los Angeles Times, 14 June 2014. Web. 19 Sept. 2016.
Galarcep, Ives. "Altidore Finding Peace in Holland." *FOX Sports*. Fox Sports Interactive Media, 21 June 2012. Web. 19 Sept. 2016.
Heizer, Pedro. "Hometown Hero: Jozy Altidore." *Boca Raton Tribune*. Boca Raton Tribune, 29 June 2012. Web. 19 Sept. 2016.
Lewis, Michael. "The Making of a Pro." *BigAppleSoccer.com*. Sports Vue Interactive, 28 Oct. 2006. Web. 19 Sept. 2016.
Prince-Wright, Joe. "Has Jozy Altidore's Premier League Legacy Damaged the Reputation of US Players?" *NBC Sports*. NBC Universal, 16 Jan. 2015. Web. 19 Sept. 2016.

—*Chris Cullen*

Eniola Aluko

Born: February 21, 1987
Occupation: Soccer player

Eniola Aluko is one of the United Kingdom's most prominent female soccer players, or footballers, and she has never shied away from a

Johnmaxmena (Own work)/[CCO 1.0]/Wikimedia Commons

challenge. In addition to playing for the Chelsea Ladies Football Club and representing Great Britain in international tournaments such as the 2012 Olympic Games, she has studied and practiced law, specializing in entertainment- and sports-related legal matters. "I've always had a natural advocacy streak in me," she told Rebecca Waller-Davies for *Lawyer 2B* (10 Jan. 2013) of her unusual career path. "I'm very disturbed by injustice and I like solving problems for people and for myself."

Maintaining a double career is a challenge that could easily have overwhelmed a lesser player and student, and indeed, Aluko in 2015 announced that she was putting her legal work on hold to focus her energies on soccer. Still, she plans one day to resume her fusion of sports and law, viewing any setback along the way as a learning opportunity. "You are going to fail in sport, you are going to win sometimes, you are going to be criticized sometimes, you are going to be applauded," she explained to Hannah Ellis-Petersen for the *Guardian* (11 June 2016). "It gives you . . . those real-life lessons that make you bulletproof."

EARLY LIFE AND EDUCATION

Eniola Aluko, known to her fans as Eni, was born on February 21, 1987, in Lagos, Nigeria. Planning to further their education in England, her parents moved the family to the United Kingdom when Aluko was less than one year old. Aluko's father, Daniel, later became a politician in Nigeria and went on to serve in a high-level position at an oil company there. Her mother, Sheila, became an entrepreneur and ran a successful business in England. Aluko has three

younger siblings, one of whom, a brother, Sone, is a professional soccer player who plays for the Fulham Football Club.

Aluko spent her childhood and adolescence in the central England city of Birmingham. She was an avid soccer fan and a dedicated supporter of the professional club Manchester United and its star forward Éric Cantona. She frequently played soccer with her brother and other neighborhood children, and as she grew older and with the support of her parents, she became more involved in the sport. "My parents always encouraged me," Aluko recalled to BBC broadcaster Tina Daheley, as quoted by Linda Kinstler for *Women in the World* (8 Oct. 2015). "Even though I was a girl who played football and it was a bit weird at the time, they always encouraged me to play and express myself."

Aluko attended Birmingham's Broadmeadow Junior School, and by secondary school she was fully devoted to soccer but found that she did not always fit in with her peers. "A lot of the girls in school thought I was a bit weird, and it was difficult," she recalled to Ellis-Petersen. "You do get to an age where you want friends who are girls, and you want girls to like you and think you're pretty or whatever. So it was hard at times."

After completing her secondary education, Aluko enrolled in Brunel University in London, where she studied law. Although she hoped to become a professional soccer player, she also had a strong interest in the law and becoming a lawyer, a plan that was particularly practical in light of the realities of women's soccer: Unlike its wildly popular male counterpart, women's soccer has a limited number of fans and relatively low revenue, and female players are paid much less compared to male players, even in the professional leagues. Opportunities for endorsement deals and sponsorships are similarly limited. Aluko's plan to pursue a dual career was both ambitious and financially prudent. She graduated with a first-class honors degree in law from Brunel in 2008.

EARLY ATHLETIC CAREER

As a preteen and teen, Aluko established herself as a key member of her school soccer teams and soon began to impress scouts with her skills on the field. Still, her path was not always clear. "I grew up feeling like it was quite cool to play football—it was always something that was accepted. But when coaches disagreed with it, I started to question myself," she told Daheley, as quoted by Kinstler. "I looked at [American professional tennis players] Serena and Venus Williams, and I thought, 'I want to be like them because they're accepted, they're celebrated.' I didn't say anything about it—it was really an internal battle, but I think your talent just proves you right."

After a stint on the Leafield Athletic Ladies team as a young teenager, Aluko joined the youth division of the Birmingham City Ladies Football Club, where she remained until 2004 when she joined the Charlton Athletic women's team. She stayed with Charlton until 2007, when she joined the Chelsea Ladies team. Aluko was given the opportunity to play for Nigeria on the international stage, but she opted instead to compete for England, representing the country in international competitions. She notably competed in the 2005 Union of European Football Associations (UEFA) Women's Championship despite the fact that some of the games were scheduled for the same days as her A Level exams, which she also attended.

Aluko moved to the United States in late 2008, joining the Saint Louis Athletica professional soccer club. She again played forward and was the team's leading scorer and a key member of the offense. The Saint Louis Athletica disbanded in 2010 after only two seasons, and Aluko then joined the short-lived Atlanta Beat team for one season before being traded in December 2010 to the New Jersey–based Sky Blue Football Club. Aluko returned to England in 2012.

FROM THE FIELD TO THE COURTROOM

At the same time that she was impressing soccer fans, Aluko was also establishing herself in the field of law. She spent a year as a paralegal for the London-based law firm SC Andrew and then enrolled in an accelerated legal training program at London's College of Law, which is now part of the University of Law. She worked as a trainee solicitor and assisted in litigation proceedings for the media and entertainment law firm Lee & Thompson and later for the sport and media law firm Onside Law.

Aluko became a fully credentialed lawyer in 2015 but announced in March of that year that she intended to put her legal career on hold to completely focus on soccer. Nevertheless, she remained intent on pursuing a career in sports law later in life. "I think it would be a shame for me to have had a career in football and met so many influential people in the game and not bring that into law in some way," she told Waller-Davies of her plans for the future.

FULL-TIME FOOTBALL

Aluko's return to England from the United States in 2012 also marked her return to English professional soccer. She played for Birmingham briefly before returning to Chelsea in late 2012, playing a key role in the team's 2015 Football Association Women's Cup victory. In a column for *BBC Sport* (3 Aug. 2015), Aluko referred to that game as the best day of her career.

Aluko likewise returned to international play and soon found that women's soccer in England was changing, largely for the better. In 2009, England's Football Association introduced

central contracts for all players on England's women's international team, which meant that the players were finally guaranteed a certain level of pay—a significant deviation from the previous low per diem payments. "I remember when I was starting out at Birmingham I was paid per game," Aluko recalled to Riath Al-Samarrai for *MailOnline* (10 Mar. 2016). "If I got injured I wouldn't be paid. . . . Players now have sustainability—you can get a mortgage because you can show you have a contract. Before as players you simply couldn't."

The world of women's soccer was also changing in a less tangible but perhaps more satisfying way. Thanks in part to a string of strong showings in international competitions, interest in women's soccer had increased significantly, as had fan turnout at games. The increased visibility of female soccer players was particularly important to Aluko, who had at times struggled to fit in as a young female athlete. "That's the part that makes me the most proud," Aluko told Daheley, as quoted by Kinstler. "When a young girl comes up to me and says, 'Eni, I really wanna be like you.'"

Aluko played with the British women's soccer team in the 2012 London Olympics and contributed to the team's strong performance leading up to the quarterfinals when they were defeated by Canada. The national team likewise performed well in the lead-up to the 2016 Olympic Games, but in March 2016, the Football Association decided not to send any football team to the Games that year. Despite missing out on her second chance to compete for an Olympic medal, Aluko remained focused on her upcoming games and future international competitions. "We have to keep pushing on, making the game stronger," she told Al-Samarrai. "We have the European Championships in 2017 and we really have to try to win that tournament. Why set a limit to what we can do?"

PERSONAL LIFE

Aluko's younger brother, Sone, has received significant attention for his career as a forward for the professional Fulham Football Club. In light of the greater popularity of men's soccer in the United Kingdom and the higher profile of its players, some members of the media have speculated that such a disparity could be a source of conflict between the siblings. However, Aluko has noted in interviews that she is nothing but supportive of her brother and that she is not envious of his greater public profile. "Even now there are a lot of parts of my brother's life—being in the public eye like that—that I just couldn't cope with," she explained to Ellis-Petersen. "We joke about it a lot actually, and I'm grateful that at least I can still walk into Tesco in my tracksuit without being bothered."

SUGGESTED READING

Al-Samarrai, Riath. "Eniola Aluko Revels in England Women's Football Growth." *MailOnline*. Daily Mail, 10 Mar. 2016. Web. 12 Aug. 2016.

Aluko, Eniola, and Alistair Magowan. "Eniola Aluko Column: Why FA Cup Win Was the Best Day of My Career." *BBC Sport*. BBC, 3 Aug. 2015. Web. 12 Aug. 2016.

Aluko, Eniola, and Alistair Magowan. "Eniola Aluko Column: Why I'm Putting My Legal Career on Hold." *BBC Sport*. BBC, 27 Mar. 2015. Web. 12 Aug. 2016.

Brookes, Christian. "Eniola Aluko Interview: The Law of the Symphony for England's Forward." *Beats & Rhymes FC*. Brookes, 13 May 2013. Web. 12 Aug. 2016.

Ellis-Petersen, Hannah. "Eniola Aluko: 'I Won't Be Paid the Same as Wayne Rooney, Because I'm Not Wayne Rooney.'" *Guardian*. Guardian News and Media, 11 June 2016. Web. 12 Aug. 2016.

Kinstler, Linda. "Not Only Is Eniola Aluko One of the World's Top Soccer Players, She's Also a Big-Time Lawyer." *Women in the World*. Women in the World Media, 8 Oct. 2015. Web. 12 Aug. 2016.

Waller-Davies, Rebecca. "End Goal: Eniola Aluko on Juggling a Legal Career and Life as an International Footballer." *Lawyer 2B*. Centaur Communications, 10 Jan. 2013. Web. 12 Aug. 2016.

—*Joy Crelin*

Jake Arrieta

Born: March 6, 1986
Occupation: Baseball player

Joe Sargent/Getty Images

In the tradition of such late-blooming pitching greats as Sandy Koufax, Randy Johnson, and Roy Halladay, Jake Arrieta overcame early-career mediocrity to become one of the most dominant pitchers in Major League Baseball (MLB). A fifth-round draft pick of the Baltimore Orioles out of Texas Christian University (TCU) in 2007, he spent three years in the Orioles' farm system before making his MLB debut in 2010. In three-and-a-half seasons with the Orioles, Arrieta struggled to a 20–25 record and a 5.46 earned-run average (ERA). After being traded to the Chicago Cubs midway through the 2013 season, however, he was able to resurrect his career. In 2015 he posted historic pitching numbers and won the National League (NL) Cy Young Award.

With a pitching repertoire that includes four-seam and two-seam fastballs, a power curveball, an occasional changeup, and a deceptive slider-cutter hybrid, Arrieta—known for his crossfire pitching motion and unflappable demeanor—was long considered to have raw talent and high potential. His career turnaround, however, was as much about hard work and fortunate circumstances as it was about natural ability. Chicago Cubs manager Joe Maddon said of Arrieta to Tom Verducci for *Sports Illustrated* (28 Mar. 2016), "I don't think I've ever seen anybody work like he does. . . . Among all the pitchers I've ever had, he is in the present tense as well and as much as anybody."

EARLY LIFE

Jacob "Jake" Joseph Arrieta was born on March 6, 1986, in Farmington, Missouri, to Lou and Lynda (Collins) Arrieta. He has two younger brothers, Sam and Lukas. When Arrieta was four months old, his family moved to Plano, Texas, a suburb of Dallas.

Arrieta began playing baseball at the age of four. He learned how to play the game from his father, who would run him through baseball drills at a nearby Little League field each day after returning home from work. Arrieta's competitive nature was apparent from the time he joined T-ball. His father recalled to Dan Connolly for the *Baltimore Sun* (5 Apr. 2012), "Whether it was riding go-karts or home-run derby in practices . . . he always wanted to be No. 1."

Blessed with a strong arm, Arrieta became a pitcher not long after he started playing, and by age ten he was already throwing with a natural crossfire motion. He grew up idolizing Hall of Fame pitcher Nolan Ryan, baseball's all-time leader in strikeouts and no-hitters. Arrieta later credited his father, who rose from modest beginnings to become vice president of a construction company, with instilling in him the importance of hard work and perseverance. Meanwhile, he inherited his composed temperament from his mother, who juggled her domestic responsibilities with shuttling him and his brothers to school, practices, and games.

HIGH SCHOOL AND COLLEGE CAREER

Arrieta's development into an elite pitcher came gradually. Upon entering Plano East High School in 2000 he was overweight and undersized. To gain an edge over his peers he became a student of nutrition and started undergoing intensive strength and conditioning training. By his senior season Arrieta had reached his full height of six feet four inches and filled out to a lean 200 pounds. He emerged as the staff ace on Plano East's varsity squad and went 5–4 with a 1.30 ERA, helping him earn honorable mention all-district honors.

Arrieta was selected by the Cincinnati Reds in the thirty-first round of the 2004 MLB Draft. Instead of signing, however, he opted to play baseball at Weatherford Junior College in Weatherford, Texas. After finishing his freshman campaign there with a 6–2 record and a 3.58 ERA, Arrieta was drafted by the Milwaukee Brewers in the twenty-sixth round of the 2005 Draft. Yet he again chose to forgo the professional ranks and spent that summer playing for the McKinney Marshals in the Texas Collegiate League.

While playing for the Marshals Arrieta caught the attention of TCU head baseball coach Jim Schlossnagle. Originally intending to scout a Marshals relief pitcher, Schlossnagle decided instead to offer Arrieta a scholarship after watching one of his starts. The offer was "the best opportunity I've been given my entire career," Arrieta told Verducci, adding, "I never looked back from that moment."

In his first season at TCU Arrieta shined, tying for the national lead with fourteen wins and recording a team-best 2.35 ERA in nineteen games. His numbers dropped during his junior season, in which he went 9–3 with a 3.01 ERA, partly due to his overzealousness in the weight room. The addition of extra muscle affected Arrieta's command to the point that he was prohibited from lifting by TCU coaches. "[He's] very, very self-motivated and very much a perfectionist," Schlossnagle told Brittany Ghiroli for MLB. com (4 Mar. 2011). "[He is] really hard on himself, and those are some good traits and also some things he had to overcome."

BALTIMORE ORIOLES

By the end of his junior year at TCU Arrieta's fastball velocity had increased from the high-eighties miles per hour range to the high-nineties. He also added a power curveball to his repertoire and began experimenting with the slider-style cutter that later became his signature pitch. Despite some concerns about his control, scouts for the Baltimore Orioles felt Arrieta possessed the kind of talent to eventually become a top-of-the-rotation starter. The Orioles selected him in the fifth round as the 159th overall pick of the 2007 Draft and signed him to a $1.1 million bonus.

In the fall of 2007, Arrieta reported to the Phoenix Desert Dogs in the Arizona Fall League (AFL). He led the league in scoreless innings (16.0) and game appearances (14) and held opponents to a .154 batting average as the Desert Dogs won that year's AFL championship. Over the next two seasons Arrieta established himself as one of the top pitching prospects in the Orioles' farm system, rising from advanced-A to triple-A ball. In 263.2 innings during that span, he struck out 268 batters and allowed just 222 hits.

After opening the 2010 season with a sterling 1.85 ERA in twelve games with the AAA Norfolk Tides, Arrieta was called up to the big leagues. "It started to click [in Norfolk]," he told Ghiroli. "For the first time, it really felt like I was becoming a pitcher." Arrieta made his major-league debut on June 10, 2010, in a game against the defending-champion New York Yankees. He pitched six innings, allowing just four hits and three runs in a 4–3 win for the Orioles. He went on to finish his rookie campaign with a 6–6 record and a 4.66 ERA in eighteen starts.

OPENING-DAY STARTER TO CASTOFF

Over the next two seasons with the Orioles Arrieta "portended greatness in bits, pieces, and tantalizing glimpses," as Jerry Crasnick noted for ESPN.com (2 Oct. 2015). During the 2011 season he earned a regular spot in the Orioles' rotation, making twenty-two starts and recording ten wins before being shut down for the year by bone spurs in his right elbow. The Orioles nonetheless signaled their faith in Arrieta by naming him the 2012 opening-day starter. However, after going 3–9 with an atrocious 6.13 ERA in his first eighteen starts that season he was relegated back to the Norfolk Tides. He spent two months in Norfolk before being recalled by the Orioles in September 2012, at which point he was moved to the bullpen.

Arrieta returned to the Orioles' rotation for the 2013 season and started the team's home-opener against the Minnesota Twins. He was demoted back to Norfolk after just four starts, however, due to command problems. Arrieta's tenure with the Orioles reached a tipping point in June 2013, when, after being recalled from Norfolk for a start against the Detroit Tigers, he gave up ten hits and five runs in less than five innings.

Arrieta was sent back to Norfolk after the start; statistically he was one of the worst Orioles starters ever. On July 2, 2013, he was traded along with reliever Pedro Strop to the Chicago Cubs in exchange for veteran pitcher Scott Feldman and backup catcher Steve Clevenger.

Much of Arrieta's disappointing performance in Baltimore has since been attributed to his discomfort with the coaching staff. Pitching coach Rick Adair repeatedly tinkered with his pitching motion and mechanics, making Arrieta abandon his natural crossfire motion in favor of a more traditional delivery to the plate, which contributed to his control issues. The Orioles prohibited their pitchers from throwing cutters because they believed the pitch hindered fastball velocity. "I feel like I was playing a constant tug-of-war," Arrieta explained to Verducci, "trying to make the adjustments I was being told to make and knowing in the back of my mind that I can do things differently and be better."

CAREER RESURRECTION WITH THE CUBS

After being acquired by the Cubs, Arrieta was designated to the Iowa Cubs in the AAA Pacific Coast League, where he went back to his crossfire motion and developed his slider-cutter hybrid. "Sometimes you have to be your own coach and try to figure it out on your own," he told Crasnick. Arrieta joined the Cubs' major-league squad in August 2013 and showed improvement in nine starts, going 4–2 with a 3.66 ERA. He built on that success in 2014 when he went 10–5 record with a 2.53 ERA in twenty-five starts. In three of those starts he took no-hit bids into the seventh inning, hinting at his ability to dominate.

Arrieta's flashes of greatness crystallized into historic dominance in 2015, when he established himself as perhaps the best pitcher in baseball. He entered the midseason break with a strong 10–5 record and 2.66 ERA before putting together "arguably the greatest second half for any pitcher who's ever picked up a baseball," as Patrick Mooney wrote for *Baseball Digest* (Jan./Feb. 2016). In fifteen starts after the All-Star break he went 12–1 and recorded a 0.75 ERA, the lowest second-half ERA in baseball history. He finished the season as the major-league leader in wins (22), complete games (4), shutouts (3), and opponent batting average (.185), while placing second in the NL in ERA (1.77) and innings (229.0) and third in the league in strikeouts (236). He became the first Cubs starter to finish with a sub-2.00 ERA since Grover Alexander in 1920 and only the third Cubs pitcher to record twenty wins and 200 strikeouts in a season.

The highlight of Arrieta's historic season came on August 30, 2015, when he threw his first career no-hitter against the Los Angeles Dodgers. He won NL pitcher of the month awards for both August and September as he anchored a Cubs team that finished with a 97–65 record. The Cubs enjoyed a twenty-four game improvement from the previous season and advanced to the playoffs for the first time since 2008 with a wild card berth.

In the NL wild card game—his postseason debut—Arrieta pitched a complete game shutout against the Pittsburgh Pirates. He floundered in his next two postseason contests, however, due to arm fatigue caused by an increased regular-season workload, and the Cubs were ultimately swept by the New York Mets in the National League Championship Series (NLCS). Arrieta received a number of honors for his excellent season, including the 2015 NL Cy Young Award. He became the fifth Cub to win the award, which recognizes the league's best pitcher, and the first since Greg Maddux in 1992. "I've had some pretty dark times in this game in my career," Arrieta told Mooney. "But I was dedicated to getting over the hump, to putting in the time, the effort, making any adjustments necessary to get to this point."

2016 SEASON

Arrieta carried his otherworldly pitching into the beginning of the 2016 season. In five April starts, he posted a perfect 5–0 record with a 1.00 ERA, helping him become the first NL pitcher to claim three consecutive pitcher of the month awards. On April 21, 2016, he threw his second career no-hitter, this time against the Cincinnati Reds. He became the twenty-eighth pitcher in baseball history to throw multiple no-hitters in a career since 1913.

The Cubs, meanwhile, finished the month of April with an MLB-best record of 17–5. Arrieta's emergence as an ace helped make the Cubs early favorites for the World Series, which they had not won since 1908. "He wakes up every day trying to figure out how to get better," the Cubs' president Theo Epstein said of Arrieta to Mooney. "That's the kind of mindset we want in this organization."

PERSONAL LIFE

Arrieta married his wife, Brittany, in 2009. They have two children, Cooper and Palmer. His family is often featured in his regular social media updates shared with fans. A self-professed fitness nut, Arrieta won attention around the league for incorporating Pilates and other unconventional cross-training exercises into his baseball workouts.

SUGGESTED READING

Connolly, Dan. "Opening Day Starter? Arrieta Is Ready for the Challenge." *Baltimore Sun*. Baltimore Sun, 5 Apr. 2012. Web. 16 May 2016.

Crasnick, Jerry. "How Jake Arrieta Finally Tapped His Potential." *ESPN*. ESPN Internet Ventures, 2 Oct. 2015. Web. 16 May 2016.

Ghiroli, Brittany. "Arrieta Continues to Push His Limits." MLB.com. MLB Advanced Media, 4 Mar. 2011. Web. 16 May 2016.

Mooney, Patrick. "Believe the Hype." *Baseball Digest* Jan./Feb. 2016: 16–19. Print.

Verducci, Tom. "The Revenant." *Sports Illustrated* 28 Mar. 2016: 48–55. Print.

— *Chris Cullen*

Annaleigh Ashford

Born: June 25, 1985
Occupation: Actor

Annaleigh Ashford has found acclaim on Broadway and television, playing characters from Glinda the Good Witch in the musical *Wicked* to a pet dog in the play *Sylvia*. With a Tony Award already under her belt, Ashford's career is on a seemingly unstoppable upward trajectory. Known for her comedic talent, she spoke of her role models with Elysa Gardner for *USA Today* (26 Oct. 2015), highlighting "Amy Schumer, Amy Poehler, and Tina Fey, who are creating their shows, being producers. They're wearing the pants in their comedies. In the comedy world, there's always been one woman to five men. I think that's changing, that we're being respected more as writers and comedians." Ashford also provided a voice for a troll in *Frozen*, a film she believes is introducing children to musical theater.

EARLY LIFE AND EDUCATION
Ashford grew up in Wheat Ridge, a suburb of Denver, Colorado. Her mother, Holli Swanson, was a physical education teacher and she enrolled Ashford in a number of sports, which her daughter tolerated but did not enjoy. As a child, Ashford loved movies such as *All That Jazz* and *Annie Hall*. She developed a talent for doing impressions and began acting at nine years of age. She also took dance lessons, which included ballet. She explained to Kathryn Lurie for *Wall Street Journal* (18 Nov. 2014), "Well, thank God I grew up dancing, going to dance class every night in which the first hour of the evening was taken up by ballet."

When she was sixteen, she graduated from Wheat Ridge High School and at seventeen moved to New York City to attend Marymount Manhattan College. She majored in theater, graduating at nineteen. Unlike students who wait tables or take a campus job, she went to

iDominick/CC BY-SA 2.0/Flickr/Wikimedia Commons

the Lower West Side to become a go-go dancer named Hollywood Starr.

Ashford went to numerous casting calls without success. In time, she was cast in the first touring company of *Wicked* as Pfanee and the understudy of Glinda the Good. Ashford made her Broadway debut in the spring of 2007 in the original cast of *Legally Blonde: The Musical*. She played Margot, a sorority sister and was also the understudy for Elle Woods. She left the show, in September 2007, to enter the world of Oz.

WICKED
The musical, based on the novel by Gregory Maguire, provides a back story of the relationship between the Wicked Witch of the West and the Good Witch from the *Wizard of Oz*.

She took over the role of Glinda on Broadway the following year, replacing Kendra Kassebaum. She became the sixth woman to take the part. At that time the show was grossing more than a million dollars in ticket sales weekly. She told John Moore for *Denver Post* (28 Oct. 2007), "I'm getting to do what I love every night, in one of my dream roles. It's amazing. You are so tired when you get home at the end of the day, but then you put your feet up, and you are like, 'Wow. All right, Lord, my dreams have come true. I am working as an actor, and making a living. Thank you.'"

Ashford also took the roles of Jeanie in *Hair* in 2010 and Maureen Johnson in the first Off-Broadway revival of *Rent* in 2011. For the latter show, she received nominations for both the Clive Barnes and the Drama League awards.

KINKY BOOTS

Next Ashford joined the original cast of the Cyndi Lauper musical *Kinky Boots*. The musical is based on a true story of a British man who takes on the failing family shoe factory and finds unexpected success. Through his unlikely friendship with a drag queen, he begins designing women's shoes for men. Ashford was cast in the role of Lauren, a factory worker who falls in love with her boss. She prepared for the role for three years before the show opened in the spring of 2013, doing readings. She told Patrick Healy for *New York Times* (24 Feb. 2013), "I love finding ways to make familiar characters into someone unique. In *Kinky Boots* I looked for moments to be bold showing Lauren's gutsiness and smarts. She's a little bit kooky now too, and I love me some kooky." She was nominated for a Tony Award for her performance.

Ashford left the show in early 2014, which continued with another actress in her role, to take on a television series. She had already been in several shows, including *Law and Order*, *Nurse Jackie*, and *The Big C*, but this character was something quite different.

MASTERS OF SEX

In 2013 Ashford was cast as Betty DiMello in the Showtime series *Masters of Sex*, about William Masters and Virginia Johnson and their research on human sexuality during the 1950s and 1960s. Showrunner Michelle Ashford, cast her in the show and explained the growth of her character to Jeff Lunden for National Public Radio's *Weekend Edition* (1 Nov. 2015), saying, "She was supposed to be a one-off. And we cast Annaleigh. And she was so delightful and such a wonderful energy and so unlike everyone else in our cast that we thought, well, we have to keep her." Her character was a prostitute before becoming office manager for the research lab. Betty DiMello is also a lesbian trying to have a child with her partner, despite the more repressive attitudes of the time. Ashford spends five months annually in Los Angeles working on the show.

YOU CAN'T TAKE IT WITH YOU

Written in 1936 by Moss Hart and George S. Kaufman, *You Can't Take It with You* is controlled mayhem on stage. From 2014 to 2015, Ashford starred in the show on Broadway with James Earl Jones and Rose Byrne. Ashford played the role of Essie Carmichael, who dances ballet with enthusiasm, if not skill, in a family of eccentrics.

For the "bad dancing" Ashford was required to do on stage, she relied on the ballet lessons of her childhood, even though she had not worn on pointe shoes since about age fourteen. Every morning for the first month of the show, she went to a Bikram yoga class to warm up her body. Nathan Peck, who worked with Ashford for her dance scenes, handled the choreography; director Scott Ellis helped them fine tune Ashford's dancing. For authenticity, the trio relied on ballet styles of the 1930s, the time in which the play is set.

The show was the first time Ashford was cast in a play rather than a musical, giving her voice a break from singing the high notes. As she told Lurie, "It is such a treat to do a play—sometimes it takes those of us who start out in musicals a little longer to be trusted to come in and do a play so I'm just so grateful that I've gotten the opportunity."

She won a Tony Award, Outer Critics Circle Award, and a Drama Desk Award for her performance. She charmed Ben Brantley, the *New York Times* drama critic who told Lunden, "She was so good at being bad. I mean, there was a real grace in the character's clumsiness. I could eat it with a spoon. It was just delightful." The show ran until February 22, 2015.

SYLVIA

A. R. Gurney's play *Sylvia* portrays a love triangle with a twist: the other woman is a poodle mix the husband, Greg, brings home from the park. In the 2015 Broadway production Ashford was cast as the poodle, Sylvia; Matthew Broderick played the role of Greg.

To prepare for her role as a dog with humanlike emotions, Ashford read *Animals in Translation* by Temple Grandin and *The Other End of the Leash* by Patricia McConnell. She also observed her own dog, particularly at obedience training. Gurney was pleased with Ashford in the role of Sylvia. As he told Anita Gates for the *New York Times* (10 Sept. 2015), "She likes to take risks. And so does Sylvia." The play's director, Daniel Sullivan, was also pleased, as he told Lunden, "We don't have that many highly physical female clowns. I mean, she is really extraordinary in her ability to keep a thing very true and honest and, at the same time, much larger than life, physically."

The role was physically demanding for Ashford. Ashford wore kneepads in performance; she also went regularly to a physical therapist and an osteopath to prevent injury. She worked with a voice coach to perfect a bark that would not leave her voiceless during the run of eight performances a week.

Sylvia concluded its run on Broadway in January 2016. Ashford was cast as Columbia in the remake of the television movie *Rocky Horror Picture Show*, scheduled to air on Fox later in 2016. She also released on iTunes a live recording of her cabaret performance *Lost in the Stars* at the club 54 Below.

PERSONAL LIFE

Describing herself, Ashford told Lois Smith Brady for *New York Times* (4 Aug. 2013), "I'm a modern girl with old-fashioned sensibilities." Ashford did not date much until she met her husband Joe Tapper. The two met through her manager when Tapper was a master of fine arts acting student at Yale School of Drama. They married in 2013 at Devil's Thumb Ranch in Colorado, with the reception in a barn from Civil War days, with an Old West theme. The couple owns a dog, Gracie, a toy Australian sheepdog named for the comedian Gracie Allen.

SUGGESTED READING

Ashford, Annaleigh. "Annaleigh Ashford on You Can't Take It with You and Masters of Sex." Interview by Kathryn Lurie. *Wall Street Journal*. Dow Jones, 18 Nov. 2014. Web. 23 May 2016.

Brady, Lois Smith. "Onstage Together at Last." *New York Times*. New York Times, 4 Aug. 2013. Web. 11 May 2016.

Gardner, Elysa. "Annaleigh Ashford Takes a Bow-Wow." *USA Today*. Gannet, 26 Oct. 2015. Web. 10 May 2016.

Gates, Anita. "This Pooch Has a Tony: Annaleigh Ashford on Playing a Poodle in Sylvia." *New York Times*. New York Times, 10 Sept. 2015. Web. 2 June 2016.

Healy, Patrick. "Looking Out for the Revelations/From Silly to 'Kinky.'" *New York Times*. New York Times, 24 Feb. 2013. Web. 11 May 2016.

Lunden, Jeff. "Annaleigh Ashford Barks Up the Right Tree on Broadway." *NPR*. NPR, 1 Nov. 2015. Web. 11 May 2016.

Moore, John. "Ashford Making a Splash in New York." *Denver Post*. Digital First Media, 28 Oct. 2007. Web. 18 May 2016.

—*Judy Johnson*

Andrew Bacevich

Born: July 5, 1947
Occupation: Historian

"Andrew J. Bacevich is one of the most provocative—as in thought-provoking—national-security writers out there today," Mark Thompson wrote for *Time* magazine (17 Apr. 2013). Bacevich is the author of a number of books dealing with military and political issues, including *The New American Militarism: How Americans Are Seduced by War* (2005), *The Limits of Power: The End of American Exceptionalism* (2008), and *Washington Rules: America's Path to Permanent War* (2010).

Minehan/ullstein bild/Getty Images

His latest book, *America's War for the Greater Middle East: A Military History*, published in 2016, has received much press attention for its timeliness and pull-no-punches nature. In it, he writes, "As an American who cares deeply about the fate of his country, I should state plainly my own assessment of this ongoing war, now well into its fourth decade. We have not won it. We are not winning it. Simply trying harder is unlikely to produce a different outcome."

Bacevich writes from the dual perspective of one who has had lengthy careers both in the military, as a West Point graduate and Vietnam veteran, and in academia, as a professor of international relations and history at Boston University, among other posts. "I think there's massive misunderstanding between the two worlds," he told Rich Barlow for *BU Today* (23 June 2014). "Professional military officers tend to see academics as pointy-headed, airy-fairy impractical. I suspect that many academics tend to not appreciate the amount of intelligence that is found in the officer corps."

EARLY LIFE AND EDUCATION

Andrew John Bacevich Sr. was born on July 5, 1947, in Normal, Illinois, and was raised in a relatively conservative, Catholic family in northern Indiana. He has told interviewers that some people, upon hearing his name, assume that he must be Serbian or Croatian. However, his mother, the former Martha Ellen Bulfer, was of Irish, German, and English descent, and his father, also named Andrew, was Lithuanian. The family name had originally been Bacevochis, but it had been changed sometime after his paternal grandparents immigrated to the United States at the turn of the twentieth century.

"My folks really struggled after the war to put three squares on the table every day," Bacevich recalled to Patrick L. Smith for *Salon* (22 May 2016). "My dad was going through medical school, and when he finished medical school we moved into the comfortable middle class. . . . It was that classic American story of the second generation being the first generation to go to college." During his youth, Bacevich held what he has described as the typical attitudes of the day. "I remember, in the '50s, as a product of that environment, wondering why anybody would want to buy a used car," he told Smith. "And I remember thinking that after you had a new car for a year or two, why aren't you getting another new one to replace it? Why would you want to drive a car that had now become a used car? In retrospect, it's so absurd. But I think that I was absorbing what the culture was powerfully communicating."

When he was in grade school, a friend lent Bacevich a series of then popular books whose protagonist, Clint Lane, had attended the U.S. Military Academy at West Point. Bacevich's parents were both World War II veterans who often extolled the virtues of patriotism, and the books sparked in him a desire to one day attend the iconic school himself. Another factor, he has admitted to interviewers, is that he very much wanted to attend a school on the East Coast, which he imagined being more sophisticated than his native Midwest.

Bacevich graduated from West Point in 1969 with a BS. His education was interrupted for a time by his military service. In 1977 he earned a master's degree in American history from Princeton University, followed by a doctorate in American diplomatic history in 1982.

MILITARY CAREER

Upon leaving West Point, Bacevich completed a short tour of duty at Fort Riley, Kansas. He was sent to Vietnam in the summer of 1970, serving first in the Second Squadron, First Cavalry Regiment, and then in the First Squadron, Tenth Cavalry. After returning to the United States the following summer, he remained in the military and was assigned to the Third Armored Cavalry Regiment at Fort Bliss, in Texas. Bacevich ultimately spent more than two decades in the Army, retiring as a colonel. Some sources posit that his retirement in the early 1990s stemmed from his sense of responsibility for a serious munitions explosion that occurred under his command at Camp Doha, near Kuwait City.

Leaving the military in his forties presented him with a form of culture shock. "From my upbringing, and I think notably from attendance at the Military Academy, I was shaped by some powerful forces to accept a very particular worldview," he explained to Smith. "I've come to believe that the Military Academy doesn't educate, it socializes. It forms people. And maybe it should. Because it exists to prepare people to be servants of the state, as military officers . . . It took me a long time to recognize the extent to which I'd been socialized and to come to appreciate that there were alternative perspectives. It really took getting out of the Army and distancing myself from an institution that had been my life."

Gaining that distance allowed Bacevich to think critically about the role America was playing in the world and the country's evolving national psyche. While he maintains that he is sometimes abashed at his youthful naïveté and willingness to accept what he was told, he understands the reasons he was trained in that manner. "We don't want military officers to think that they are policymakers," he said to Smith. "We want military officers to be loyal servants of the state, and that's what I was for a period of time."

ACADEMIC CAREER

While still in the Army, Bacevich began a foray into academia, teaching history at West Point from 1977 to 1980. After retiring from the Army, however, he embarked upon his academic career in earnest. From 1993 to 1998 he served as the executive director of the Foreign Policy Institute (FPI) at the Paul H. Nitze School of Advanced International Studies (SAIS) at Johns Hopkins University. The FPI had been launched in 1980 with the stated mission "to unite the worlds of scholarship and policy in the search for realistic answers to international issues facing the United States and the world." While affiliated with Johns Hopkins, Bacevich also lectured in the school's department of political science.

Upon leaving that post in 1998, Bacevich joined the faculty of Boston University (BU), where he became the director of the school's Center for International Relations. During the sixteen years he ultimately spent at BU, Bacevich was a well-respected figure at the Pardee School of Global Studies, where he taught international relations, and the College of Arts & Sciences, where he taught history. He enjoyed the freedom that academia afforded him. "As scholars, our search for truth is rooted in expectations of freedom to think what we want to think and say what we want to say," he told Barlow. "In the military, that kind of freedom simply doesn't exist. There are expectations of discipline and subordination and conformity, and need to be."

When Bacevich retired from teaching in 2014, he expressed some dissatisfaction with the state of the profession. "I have come to, frankly, a recognizing of how limited our influence is as teachers on students," he admitted to Barlow. "These young people who come to us—they're all wonderful and bright and eager and ambitious, but they are influenced by so many different things, things that are far more powerful than a professor in the front of the room pontificating. I've learned to be modest in my expectations of my ability to shape the thinking of young people." While he agreed upon retirement to conduct a massive open online course (MOOC) at BU and to lecture on occasion, he also announced his intention to focus more fully on his writing career.

BOOKS AND HONORS

Bacevich has been writing steadily since 1986, when National Defense University Press published his first volume, *The Pentomic Era: The US Army between Korea and Vietnam*. (The word "pentomic" refers to the strategy of splitting a military division into five parts in response to a perceived tactical nuclear threat.) Of Bacevich's most recent book, *America's War for the Greater Middle East* (2016), David Rohde wrote for the *New York Times* (15 Apr. 2016): "[It] extends his string of brutal, bracing and essential critiques of the pernicious role of reflexive militarism in American foreign policy. As in past books, Bacevich is thought-provoking, profane and fearless. Assailing generals, journalists and foreign policy experts alike, he links together more than a dozen military interventions that span 35 years and declares them a single war. . . . Bacevich's call for Americans to rethink their nation's militarized approach to the Middle East is incisive, urgent and essential."

Bacevich's many honors have included membership on the independent, nonpartisan Council on Foreign Relations, designation as a National Security Fellow at Harvard's John F. Kennedy School of Government, and a Berlin Prize fellowship at the American Academy in Berlin, Germany.

PERSONAL LIFE

Bacevich and his wife, Nancy Bacevich, live in Walpole, Massachusetts. The couple are the parents of three daughters and a son. Their son, Andrew J. Bacevich Jr., an Army lieutenant, was killed by a bomb while on patrol in Iraq in 2007 at the age of twenty-seven. "When historians in future decades ponder America's wars in Vietnam and Iraq, the name of Andrew J. Bacevich . . . will have its own poignant chapter," Robert D. Kaplan wrote for the *Wall Street Journal* (4 Apr. 2016). "Long before his son was killed, Mr. Bacevich had carved out a niche as a fiery polemicist against not only the 2003 invasion of Iraq but the whole logic of preventive, expeditionary warfare. [Following his son's death] he became almost mythic in antiwar circles as a military man whose family had paid the ultimate price."

SUGGESTED READING

Barlow, Rich. "Good-bye, Professor Bacevich." *BU Today*. Boston University, 23 June 2014. Web. 14 June 2016.

Belluck, Pam. "Former Soldier, Now a Professor, Loses His Only Son to a War He Actively Opposed." *New York Times*. New York Times, 16 May 2016. Web. 14 June 2016.

Goodman, Amy. "Andrew Bacevich: America's War for the Greater Middle East Cannot Be Won." *Democracy Now!* Democracy Now!, 8 Apr. 2016. Web. 14 June 2016.

Kaplan, Robert D. "Freedom for Me—But Not for Thee." *Wall Street Journal*. Dow Jones, 4 Apr. 2016. Web. 14 June 2016.

Kinzer, Stephen. "Matters of Choice." *Boston Review*. Boston Review, 4 Apr. 2016. Web. 14 June 2016.

Smith, Patrick L. "'This Will Stop Only When the American People Get Fed Up': American Exceptionalism, the *New York Times*, and Our Foreign Policy after Barack Obama." *Salon*. Salon Media Group, 22 May 2016. Web. 14 June 2016.

Thompson, Mark. "The Renewed American Militarism." *Time*. Time, 17 Apr. 2013. Web. 14 June 2016.

SELECTED WORKS

Diplomat in Khaki: Major General Frank Ross McCoy and American Foreign Policy, 1898–1949, 1989; *Knives, Tanks, and Missiles: Israel's Security Revolution*, 1998; *American Empire: The Realities and Consequences of US Diplomacy*, 2002; *The New American Militarism: How Americans Are Seduced by War*, 2005; *The Limits of Power: The End of American Exceptionalism*, 2008; *Washington Rules: America's Path to Permanent War*, 2010; *Breach of Trust: How Americans Failed Their Soldiers and Their Country*, 2013; *America's War for the Greater Middle East: A Military History*, 2016

—Mari Rich

Julien Baker

Born: September 29, 1995
Occupation: Musician

Although Julien Baker has released only one album, 2015's *Sprained Ankle*, she has already caused a buzz in the music world. Writing for *Stereogum* (26 Oct. 2015), Gabriela Tully Claymore described the record as "deceptive" and opined, "On its surface it's an undeniably beautiful collection of humbly rendered folk songs; below that is a teeming pit of gut-rattling, cataclysmic feelings engulfing the songwriter."

Erika Goldring/FilmMagic/ Getty Images

Much of the excitement generated by Baker's work stems from the simplicity and raw emotion of her music. As Rebecca Haithcoat of *Noisey* (20 Apr. 2016) commented on Baker's live performance: "There are no sets, no backup singers, just a girl, her guitar, and the weight of crosses she seems too young to bear." Videos posted on sites such as YouTube helped garner attention and transformed *Sprained Ankle* from a side project released online for free to a critical indie darling. These videos feature her singing in simple settings (such as a deserted parking garage or an empty bar), accompanied by just her guitar. "All of these quotidian places become temporarily sacrosanct when Baker is performing in them; the raw purity of her vocals seems to convert the everyday into the divine," Rachel Syme wrote for the *New Yorker* (29 Apr. 2016). "Baker's voice is so exposed that listeners wonder if they are even supposed to be in the room. It's easy to feel, watching her, as if you have walked in on a private act, a girl and her guitar in secret communion. She makes you feel like an interloper, eavesdropping on someone else's prayers."

Syme is far from the only music journalist to invoke religious concepts like communion and prayer when discussing Baker, who hails from the American Bible Belt and who has made no secret of her deep faith, which she regained after a rebellious adolescence. Explaining to Syme that she tries to leave space for a supreme being to enter the room whenever she sings, she said, "Ultimately, I feel like there is just a pervasive evidence of God, though I know that is maybe a controversial thing to say."

EARLY LIFE

Baker was born on September 29, 1995, and raised in Memphis, Tennessee. Her mother was a physical therapist, and her father, who had lost a leg in a motorcycle accident, earned a living by making prosthetic limbs. The family was deeply religious, and although Baker attended church regularly, in her early teens she went through a period of rebellion and self-destruction. "You start drinking and smoking and staying out late and not answering your mom's calls," she recalled to Haithcoat. "And I'm really embarrassed of that person. There are so many people in Memphis who have real reasons to be angsty, but I was just a suburban white kid with all this misplaced rage. Like, 'Screw you, Mom and Dad, you won't let me pierce my lips and I'm twelve years old!'" Her parents, who ultimately divorced, remained supportive of their daughter. Her father often drove her to a local indoor skate park to hear the punk concerts held there. At the age of twelve she began to teach herself to play on a guitar he had originally purchased for himself. She learned largely by copying riffs from bands like Fall Out Boy and My Chemical Romance.

Baker was greatly influenced by the music scene created by Smith7, a Memphis-based independent record label that oversaw an all-ages, substance-free DIY performance space. "They were the first . . . to say, 'You don't have to be destructive to be countercultural,'" Baker told Haithcoat. "I don't know where I'd be if I didn't have this modicum of positive influences." In her early teens, Baker struggled with drug and alcohol abuse, but in 2012, she decided "not to be horrible," as she has described it, and worked to get sober. She says that her newer friends, who know her as a strict teetotaler and designated driver, are sometimes surprised to learn of this period in her life.

COMING OUT AND FINDING ACCEPTANCE

Baker's teenage years were also shadowed with worry about coming out as gay. She watched as other young gay people were ostracized or cast out of their churches, and one friend was even forcibly sent to a camp to be "cleansed" of his homosexuality through prayer and Bible study. Finally, at age seventeen, she confronted her parents with the truth about her sexuality. Her father's response was to immediately fetch his Bible from the shelf and read her passages highlighting God's acceptance and reassuring her that her family would also embrace her no matter what. Her mother reaffirmed those sentiments. "She was like, 'If I'm human and imperfect and I love you no matter what, how much do you think a perfect being loves you?'" Baker recalled to Haithcoat.

Baker has told interviewers that being accepted on her own terms, even in the seemingly repressive South, was revelatory. "I hope we can dismantle the idea that the entire south is sitting on our porches spitting tobacco and hating gay people," she told Audrey White for *Pitchfork* (18 May 2016). "Because I had access to Smith7 and the DIY punk scene, and had the option to come out in a nontraditional church, all these things happened to show me that sexuality is not one-sided, and neither is religion, and neither is the path to reconciling those things."

In the midst of her struggles with substance abuse and concerns about coming out, Baker was becoming involved in Memphis's thriving underground music scene. Along with a group of friends, she formed a band—originally called the Star Killers, though they later changed it to Forrister—and began playing in local venues. In addition to playing guitar, Baker was the lead vocalist for the band. "Every girl is a singer. I wanted to learn the solos and play lead guitar. I would meticulously teach myself solos so when dudes were like, 'Oh, you're a girl, you can't play guitar,' I could rip these insane Telecaster blues solos and tell them, 'Yeah, I can burn up a fret board,'" she mused to Haithcoat. "You're not going to tell me I'm just some girl in the punk scene. I still think the timbre of my voice is weird. I'm no Mariah." After starting at Middle Tennessee State University in Murfreesboro, she regularly hopped on a Greyhound bus back to Memphis to perform with them.

As a freshman, Baker studied audio engineering but changed her mind when a professor brought up the concept of monetizing one's passions—an idea she found mercenary and distasteful. She subsequently switched her major to literature, with minors in Spanish and secondary education, thinking that she might like to one day teach high school.

When not in class, Baker focused on her songwriting. "I was very seldom at my dorm," she recalled to Claymore, "because, you know, you just get paired with a stranger and you can't really, like, write music. They're just sitting there eating Hot Pockets and there isn't much privacy." Instead, she frequented the miniscule practice rooms in the school's music building, sometimes getting locked in because she stayed long after the building had closed for the night.

MUSIC CAREER

Many of the songs Baker was writing did not fit Forrister's post-punk sound, and she did not know what to do with them. A friend who was interning at Spacebomb Studios in Richmond, Virginia, excitedly told her that he had been given the chance to use the recording booth for two days to do a project of his choosing and invited

her to come record. Taking only her guitar and a loop pedal, Baker headed to Virginia. "We could only do what we could do with two microphones," she recalled to Syme. "And those limiting factors contributed to the way the record came out. There's a casualness to it; it's underproduced, almost. In a way, it was spontaneous creation—it feels to me like it could be played live in a living room or in a bar and it would sound the same."

Baker hand-illustrated an album cover and posted the songs on Bandcamp, a site where musicians who are not signed to a label can sell their music directly. "Whatever happened with it, I was like, oh, cool," Baker explained to Eileen Townsend of the *Memphis Flyer* (22 Oct. 2015). People began to respond to the work, particularly after Baker posted a video for "Something," shot in a Memphis parking garage by the local filmmaker Breezy Lucia, in which she sings about watching a lover drive away.

Soon after Baker posted the album, which she called *Sprained Ankle*, she was approached by 6131 Records, an independent label that wanted her to pull the recording from Bandcamp so that they could remaster, market, and release it on a wider scale. Steeped in the nonprofit, socially conscious ethos of Smith7, she was somewhat leery of the more commercial aspects of the music business. She fretted to Townsend that the industry had been known to "put best things to meanest use." Still, she ultimately agreed, explaining to Townsend, "Being able to support yourself with your art—that's the dream. . . . It sunk in for me when I was able to hand my roommate utility and rent [money]. I was like, 'Wow, that's real.'"

Sprained Ankle contains nine tracks, "and every one of them is sad," as Bob Boilen said when introducing Baker on the National Public Radio (NPR) show *Tiny Desk* (7 Mar. 2016). He continued, "But Baker's shimmering electric-guitar picking, the purity of her voice and the yearning way she sings make each of her songs lovely and memorable rather than merely somber."

Other critics concurred. Praising "how Baker operates in existential ultimatums—life or death, hope or despair, oblivion or epiphany," in a review for *Pitchfork* (5 Nov. 2015), Ian Cohen went on, "[The album's] clarity and honesty has instantly helped Baker reach across aisles. . . . If you prefer redemption songs to sound as raw as they feel, *Sprained Ankle* could bring you to your knees."

Baker told Syme that it can be gratifying to hear that fans appreciate her willingness to address difficult topics: "I have had so many kids come up to me and say a song I wrote saved them," she explained. "So now, when I sing, I know that, even if problems the songs entail are solved for me, just admitting that they happened will help solve those problems for another person. Or at least ease the struggle knowing that our pain is shared, that someone else has felt angry, spiteful, or hurt."

PERSONAL LIFE

Baker is fluent in Spanish and volunteers for a nonprofit that aids immigrant laborers. As of 2016, she was still attending college in Tennessee.

SUGGESTED READING

Baker, Julien. "An Interview with Young Phenom Julien Baker." Interview by Gabriela Tully Claymore. *Stereogum*. Spin Media, 26 Oct. 2015. Web. 15 Sept. 2016.

Gokhman, Roman. "Julien Baker: The Best of What's Next." *Paste Magazine*. Paste, 1 Dec. 2015. Web. 15 Sept. 2016.

Haithcoat, Rebecca. "He Hears Either Way: Julien Baker Is Writing a New Gospel for Broken Hearts." *Noisey*. Vice Media, 20 Apr. 2016. Web. 15 Sept. 2016.

Kaplan, Ilana. "Reeling from Substance Abuse and Questioning God, Julien Baker Sings through the Pain." *Observer*. Observer Media, 25 Jan. 2016. Web. 15 Sept. 2016.

Syme, Rachel. "Julien Baker Believes in God." *New Yorker*. Condé Nast, 29 Apr. 2016. Web. 15 Sept. 2016.

Townsend, Eileen. "Julien Baker Arrives." *Memphis Flyer*. Contemporary Media, 22 Oct. 2015. Web. 15 Sept. 2016.

White, Audrey. "Julien Baker on Being Queer, Southern, Christian, and Proud." *Pitchfork*. Pitchfork Media, 18 May 2016. Web. 15 Sept. 2016.

—*Mari Rich*

Radley Balko

Born: April 19, 1975
Occupation: Journalist

An award-winning libertarian investigative journalist, blogger, and author, Radley Balko is one of the leading experts on civil liberties and the criminal-justice system in the United States. According to Tim Mak for the *Daily Beast* (27 Aug. 2014), Balko "stands virtually peerless as a writer on the issue" of US police militarization, which has experienced an alarming upward trend since the 1970s. An alumnus of Indiana University, Balko began his professional career in the early 2000s as a policy analyst for the Cato Institute, a libertarian think tank, before becoming a writer and investigative reporter for such publications as *Reason* magazine and the *Huffington Post*.

In 2013, Balko published his first book, *Rise of the Warrior Cop: The Militarization of America's Police Forces*, which chronicles the rise of the police-industrial complex in the United States. Since 2014 he has served as an opinion blogger for the *Washington Post*.

EARLY LIFE AND EDUCATION

Radley Balko was born to Terry and Pat Balko on April 19, 1975, in Greenfield, Indiana, a suburb of the state capital of Indianapolis. Intellectually curious from a young age, Balko attended Eastern Hancock High School, in nearby Charlottesville, Indiana, where he served as editor of the school newspaper. Dave Pfaff, Balko's history teacher at Eastern Hancock and now the school principal, remembered his former pupil being "the kind of bright that kept teachers on their toes," as he told Maribeth Vaughn for the Greenfield, Indiana, *Daily Reporter* (26 Aug. 2013). "He was paying attention to the world in those days at the level that most high school juniors weren't."

After graduating from Eastern Hancock High in 1993, Balko attended Indiana University in Bloomington, Indiana, from which he graduated with degrees in journalism and political science in 1997. Afterward, Balko attended law school, but he dropped out after a year to accept a job with the Leadership Institute, a conservative recruitment organization based in Arlington, Virginia. Balko has admitted that he never had any intentions of becoming a lawyer but has said that some of his first-year law classes, in areas such as criminal and constitutional law, helped him become a well-rounded journalist.

JOURNALISM CAREER

At the Leadership Institute, which was founded in 1979 by the conservative activist Morton C. Blackwell, Balko served as a campus journalism coordinator. In that role, he helped organize and market seminars for the organization.

In 2001, Balko moved to Washington, DC, to become a policy analyst for the Cato Institute, a libertarian think tank founded by billionaire businessman Charles Koch. He held a variety of roles at the think tank over the next six years and wrote extensively about vice and civil-liberties issues. He authored a study on alcohol policy, titled "Back Door to Prohibition: The New War on Social Drinking," in 2003 and a seminal paper on paramilitary police raids, titled "Overkill: The Rise of Paramilitary Police Raids in America," in 2006.

Meanwhile, in 2002, Balko became a biweekly opinion columnist for FoxNews.com, a role he held for the next seven years. That year he also began publishing a personal blog called *The Agitator*. As a columnist and blogger during this time, Balko wrote about a wide range of topics, including police misconduct, criminal-justice reform, Social Security privatization, affirmative action, the tobacco and fast-food industries, and public-sector unions.

AWARD-WINNING INVESTIGATIVE JOURNALIST

Balko began to establish his reputation as a serious and dedicated investigative journalist in 2005, when he started reporting on the case of Cory Maye, an African American man who had been sentenced to death in Mississippi for the 2001 murder of a white police officer. Maye, who had no previous criminal record, shot and killed the officer, named Ron W. Jones, after mistaking him for a burglar during an erroneous, no-knock drug raid on his home. Nevertheless, a jury rejected Maye's plea of mistaken self-defense and sentenced him to death in 2004.

After conducting research into the case, Balko began blogging about his findings, which uncovered many flaws and failings with Maye's trial, from crucial mistakes made by Maye's defense team to the tainted testimony of longtime Mississippi medical examiner Dr. Steven Hayne, who performed Jones's autopsy. "To me, the reporting that had been done (previously) didn't dig nearly enough," Balko explained to Vaughn. "It seemed quite obvious from reading the press accounts that [Maye] just made a mistake."

Balko's blog posts gained significant Internet attention, enough to win Maye new legal representation; in 2006, a judge overturned Maye's death sentence. In October of that year, Balko chronicled his findings in a feature article for the monthly libertarian magazine *Reason*, where he became a senior editor. The article was cited in an opinion by the Mississippi Supreme Court, and Balko was widely credited with helping Maye escape the death penalty and win a new trial. Maye was released from prison in 2011.

As a senior editor for *Reason*, Balko wrote other investigative reports on the Maye case, as well as on police militarization and issues related to America's so-called war on drugs. In 2007, he wrote an exposé on Hayne, whose questionable and unethical medical practices ultimately led to him being barred from performing any more autopsies in Mississippi. That exposé earned Balko second-place honors in the investigative-reporting category at the Los Angeles Press Club awards.

Balko was honored again by the Los Angeles Press Club for a 2008 report on a Hispanic Louisiana family that was wrongly convicted of operating a crack-cocaine ring. Meanwhile, a 2009 feature on tainted forensic evidence in a Louisiana capital murder case won him the Western Publishing Association's MAGGIE Award for best news story.

RISE OF THE WARRIOR COP

In 2011, Balko left *Reason* to become a senior writer and investigative reporter for the *Huffington Post*, where he continued to write about police, civil liberties, and the criminal-justice system. Also that year, the Los Angeles Press Club named Balko journalist of the year, stating "Balko is one of those throw-back journalists that understands the power of groundbreaking reporting and how to make a significant impact through his work," as quoted by *Reason* editor in chief Matt Welch. "Time and time again, his stories cause readers to stop, think, and most significantly, take action."

Balko's growing reputation as a "one-man category creator" on police militarization in the United States, as Welch put it to Mak, led to him being approached by publishers about writing a book on the subject. Intrigued, Balko began researching the history of special weapons and tactics (SWAT) teams, which were first created in the 1960s as a response to urban race riots that were sweeping the United States at the time. Propelled by the US drug war and nationally televised raids, and further driven by both the 9/11 terrorist attacks and increased gun violence, SWAT teams, equipped with armored vehicles and other military-style equipment, grew exponentially over subsequent decades, giving rise to what Balko has called the "warrior cop mentality." "When you put on garb that was designed for a soldier to wear," Balko explained to Alex Howard for the *Nashville Scene* (3 July 2013), "it can and often does give you the mentality of a soldier or encourage you to assume that mentality."

The fruits of Balko's research resulted in the four-hundred-page book *Rise of the Warrior Cop*, which chronicles not only the unprecedented growth of SWAT teams in the United States since the 1960s but also the history of policing in the country. Peppered throughout Balko's book are brutal and tragic examples of botched police raids on innocent and unsuspecting civilians. Still, Balko affirmed to Vaughn, "This is not an anti-cop book or an attack on police officers . . . this is about policy."

Rise of the Warrior Cop received widespread acclaim from reviewers, many of whom hailed it as the definitive book on police militarization. In the online publication *The Intercept* (14 Aug. 2014), Pulitzer Prize–winning journalist Glenn Greenwald called the book the "best and most comprehensive account of the dangers of police militarization." Meanwhile, a reviewer for the *Economist* (13 July 2013) commented, "Balko manages to avoid the clichés of both right and left and provokes genuine outrage at the misuse of state power in its most brutal and unaccountable form."

MOVE TO THE *WASHINGTON POST*

In 2014, Balko joined the *Washington Post*, where he began writing an opinion blog called *The Watch*. Similar to Balko's previous work, the blog features his take on policing strategies and tactics, civil liberties, and the criminal-justice system, among other topics. In his introductory blog post, Balko wrote, "I consider myself an opinion journalist. I try to be fair and accurate in my reporting, but I do come at these issues from a perspective, which I make no attempt to hide."

The issue of police militarization in the United States came to a head in August 2014, when protests and riots swept through the city of Ferguson, Missouri, after Darren Wilson, a white police officer, fatally shot Michael Brown, an unarmed African American teenager. The local police response to the unrest in the largely black city drew heavy criticism for its violent and aggressive military-style tactics and sparked a nationwide debate about law enforcement and race relations. In response to Ferguson, Balko proposed a return to community policing, a form of policing that emphasizes citizen interaction.

PERSONAL LIFE

Balko lives in Nashville, Tennessee, in an apartment on Music Row. The apartment is known for its famous guitar-shaped swimming pool, which was designed by the late country star Webb Pierce. A passionate music fan, Balko runs a side blog, called *Nashville Byline*, dedicated to Nashville music and culture.

Among the many other publications for which Balko has written are the *Wall Street Journal*, the *Los Angeles Times*, *Forbes*, *Playboy*, *Slate*, and *Time*. He has served as a guest commentator on the BBC, CNN, Fox News, MSNBC, and NPR.

SUGGESTED READING

Balko, Radley. "An Introduction." *Washington Post*. Washington Post, 8 Jan. 2014. Web. 15 Dec. 2015.

Halperin, Alex. "Radley Balko: 'Once a Town Gets a SWAT Team You Want to Use It.'" *Salon*. Salon Media Group, 13 July 2013. Web. 15 Dec. 2015.

Howard, Alex. "Show of Force." *Nashville Scene*. CityPress Communications, 3 July 2013. Web. 15 Dec. 2015.

Mak, Tim. "Koch Brothers Take On Camo-Wearing Cops." *Daily Beast*. Daily Beast, 27 Aug. 2014. Web. 15 Dec. 2015.

Vaughn, Maribeth. "EH Grad Chronicles Trend of 'Warrior Cops' in Book." *Daily Reporter* [Greenfield, IN]. Daily Reporter, 26 Aug. 2013. Web. 1 Dec. 2015.

Welch, Mark. "Radley Balko Named 'Journalist of the Year.'" *Reason*. Reason Foundation, 28 June 2011. Web. 15 Dec. 2015.

—*Chris Cullen*

Mario Balotelli

Born: August 12, 1990
Occupation: Soccer player

After surviving a tough upbringing and a severe childhood illness, Mario Balotelli became an international sensation as a soccer player. He quickly earned a reputation for both his skill on the pitch and his at-times controversial personal life.

EARLY LIFE

Mario Barwuah Balotelli was born Mario Barwuah in Palermo, Italy, on August 12, 1990. His biological parents, Thomas and Rose Barwuah, had immigrated to Italy from Ghana. The Barwuahs had three other children: son Enoch and daughters Abigail and Angel. As an infant, Balotelli suffered from serious intestinal problems. His condition was severe enough that doctors diagnosed it as life threatening, and he underwent a series of operations. His family struggled financially during his childhood, with Balotelli's father working long hours as a metalworker and spending much of his time away from home.

As a result of his poor health and his family's financial problems, Balotelli was put in the care of social services soon after his parents relocated to the town of Brescia. He was placed with foster parents Francesco and Silvia Balotelli, who lived north of Brescia in the town of Concesio. Balotelli remained with his foster parents for the rest of his childhood. The Barwuahs claim they made attempts to regain custody of their son in court but were unable to compete with the resources and reputation of the Balotellis. In 2008, Balotelli was officially granted Italian citizenship under his foster parents' surname.

SOCCER CAREER

Balotelli began playing soccer (known as football in Europe) at a very young age, practicing for hours at a time. He began playing organized soccer at the age of five. As a member of his parish team, he was grouped with older boys because of his skill at dribbling and passing. Balotelli was recruited by the club A.C. Lumezzane of Italy's Lega Pro Prima Divisione in 2001, at the age of eleven. He made his debut with the team as a fifteen-year-old in mid-2006.

During the summer of that year, Balotelli participated in a five-day camp in Barcelona for elite young players. Although he considered signing with a Spanish team, issues related to his official citizenship prevented him from pursuing negotiations. Balotelli signed with the Italian soccer club F.C. Internazionale in August 2006. He began playing with Allievi Nazionali, one of the club's youth teams. As a teenager, Balotelli demonstrated his prolific goal-scoring abilities and earned subsequent promotions within the organization. As a member of the organization's Primavera youth team, Balotelli helped his team win the 2007 Italian soccer championship and the 2008 Viareggio Cup.

Balotelli made his debut with Internazionale's top-level Serie A squad, led by head coach Roberto Mancini, at seventeen. His performance in the Italian Cup—which included two goals against the Turin-based team Juventus—helped establish his reputation as a formidable talent. He scored his first goal as a member of the Italian under-twenty-one national team in September 2008.

In March 2009, crowds attending a match between Internazionale and Juventus greeted Balotelli with racist chants. Juventus chairman Giovanni Cobolli Gigli later admonished the spectators for their behavior, and the incident led the Juventus club to be fined and disciplined with a temporary partial stadium closure. Nevertheless, Balotelli continued to face racist taunts from fans of opposing squads throughout his career in the Italian league.

In August of the following year, Balotelli joined Manchester City of the English Premier League. At the time, the club was led by his former coach Mancini. Despite undergoing minor knee surgery in September, Balotelli proved a useful addition to the team. He was awarded the sports newspaper *Tuttosport*'s Golden Boy award, given to the year's most impressive young European player, in December 2010. Balotelli remained a valuable member of the team during the 2011–12 Premier League season, scoring thirteen goals and helping Manchester City win the Premier League championship.

Balotelli faced disciplinary action in the 2012–13 season, missing a total of eleven games as a result of suspensions (he had previously been suspended while playing for Internazionale). On the pitch, Balotelli became known for arguing with referees and other players. His off-the-pitch indiscretions included a car accident, breaking curfew, firing air pistols in a public plaza, and spending time with individuals allegedly involved in organized crime.

In January 2013, Balotelli returned to Italian professional soccer, signing a lucrative agreement with A.C. Milan. He scored twelve goals in thirteen games during the 2012–13 Serie A season and was named to the Serie A Team of the Year. During the 2013–14 Serie A season, Balotelli scored fourteen goals.

IMPACT

Throughout his career in professional soccer, Balotelli has helped call international attention to issues surrounding race relations in Italy. As one of the few black Italian soccer players to appear in major domestic and international tournaments, he was at times berated with racist taunts, including accusations that it is impossible to be both black and Italian. Nevertheless, Balotelli has persevered, stating that he is proud to be Italian and honored to represent his country on the pitch. He was included in *Time* magazine's list of the world's hundred most influential people in 2013.

PERSONAL LIFE

Balotelli has a daughter, Pia, with former girlfriend Raffaella Fico. He resides in Italy.

SUGGESTED READING

Duff, Mark. "Italian Mafia Investigators to Approach Mario Balotelli." *BBC News*. BBC, 7 Sept. 2011. Web. 16 May 2014.

Longman, Jeré. "Short-Fused and Explosive: Mario Balotelli, One of Soccer's Most Gifted and Eccentric Players." *New York Times*. New York Times, 30 June 2012. Web. 16 May 2014.

Mabry, Marcus. "Can Balotelli Make Italy Less Racist?" *New York Times*. New York Times, 29 June 2012. Web. 16 May 2014.

Mayer, Catherine, and Stephan Faris. "Why Always Mario?" *Time*. Time, 12 Nov. 2012. Web. 16 May 2014.

Williamson, Laura, and Nick Pisa. "Mario Balotelli's Double Life: The Bitter Family Feud That Haunts the £29m Manchester City Target." *Daily Mail*. Associated Newspapers, 5 Aug. 2010. Web. 16 May 2014.

—*Joshua Pritchard*

Shigeru Ban

Born: August 5, 1957
Occupation: Architect

Cutting-edge architecture is often characterized by complex experimental structures that emphasize innovation in form. For Japanese architect Shigeru Ban, however, the needs of a structure's occupants are equally important. "I'm not the architect to make a shape," he explained to Dana Goodyear for the *New Yorker* (11 Aug. 2014). "My designs are always problem solving." Known for using unusual materials such as paper tubes, cardboard, and recycled beer crates, Ban focuses on designing functional structures that meet

準建築人手札網站/Flickr/Wikimedia/CC BY 2.0

specific needs yet always retain their creator's distinctive architectural point of view.

Although Ban has designed and overseen the building of numerous structures, from homes to office buildings to exhibition pavilions, over the course of his three-decade career, he is best known for his innovative emergency shelters, designed to house populations displaced by war or natural disasters such as earthquakes. In many ways the design of his shelters and other emergency buildings, which have been used in countries such as Rwanda, Japan, and New Zealand, is heavily influenced by budgetary restrictions, environmental concerns, and limited time-frames. However, Ban is also deeply concerned with the comfort of his shelters' displaced residents, a concern he finds lacking among government relief organizations. "I've spent a lot of time in emergency shelters. I understand the argument that [a disaster] is not the place or time to think about design, but I think that's exactly what is necessary," he explained to Winifred Bird for *Dwell* (19 Jan. 2014). "The government tells people to endure their situation. They're not thinking about human rights at all. That's why I think we need to do better with emergency shelters and temporary houses."

EARLY LIFE

Shigeru Ban was born on August 5, 1957, in Tokyo, Japan. His mother was a clothing designer, while his father worked for Toyota. As a child and teenager, Ban attended schools in Tokyo, where he enjoyed taking classes in the industrial arts. He played violin as a child and later developed a passion for rugby, initially hoping

to pursue a career in the sport. However, he stopped playing rugby after his team went to the national high school championships, where he realized that the team was not truly playing on a competitive level.

Renovations made to the family home introduced Ban to the processes of architectural design and construction at an early age, and he was initially drawn to carpentry. "I liked the smell of the wood, and the wood offcuts and things that would be lying around," he told Edan Corkill for the *Japan Times* (7 Apr. 2013). "So I would collect those and make things." Those early creative efforts led Ban to develop an interest in the field of architecture, and as a teenager he studied drawing in the hope that it would help him gain entrance to a university architecture program. Ban first hoped to study architecture at Waseda University and play rugby for the school. After putting his dreams of professional sports behind him he instead planned to enroll in Tokyo University of the Arts; however, he did not pass the university's entrance exams.

ARCHITECTURAL EDUCATION

This setback, however, sent him down a different and perhaps even more productive path. During the course of his studies as a teenager Ban learned about the American architect John Hejduk, who had studied and later taught at the Cooper Union for the Advancement of Science and Art, a college in New York City with a prestigious architecture program. Inspired by Hejduk's work, Ban resolved to study at the Cooper Union, which at the time did not admit international students. In order to gain admittance, he moved to the United States, where he studied English and attended the Southern California Institute of Architecture for three years.

Ban transferred to the Cooper Union in 1980. Although he had been an upperclassman at the Southern California Institute of Technology, he entered the Cooper Union as a sophomore in accordance with the college's policy. Over the following years, Ban struggled somewhat at the institution, which proved to be a poor fit for him. "I came to realize that the education philosophy at Cooper Union didn't really suit me," he told Corkill. "I was much better than the other students but I was always fighting with the teachers and they refused to pass me. I had to redo my graduation work and so my graduation was delayed by six months." After taking a break from his studies to work for Japanese architect Arata Isozaki, Ban graduated from the Cooper Union with a bachelor's degree in architecture in 1984.

EARLY CAREER

After completing his degree Ban returned to Tokyo and started an independent architecture practice. Among his first projects was designing a new workshop for his mother, who continued to run a successful clothing business. During his early years as an architect Ban worked primarily on residential properties. He has noted that this work, which gave him extensive practical experience, was uniquely possible in Japan. "This country is very different from others in terms of practical training," he told Corkill. "I think it's because Japan is the only country where even members of the middle class are willing to employ architects. Elsewhere it is only the very rich who do that. Consequently, there are plenty of opportunities for young architects to improve their skills here."

Ban began experimenting with using paper in his buildings early in his career, and his use of the material would soon become one of the defining features of his body of work. Paper has been used in traditional Japanese architecture for centuries, typically in the form of paper partitions within homes and other buildings. Ban, however, sought to use various forms of paper as structural elements in buildings, believing that such materials could potentially stand up to natural disasters such as earthquakes, which could destroy rigid building materials such as concrete. "When people try to do something new, they always think something stronger or more acrobatic," he told Goodyear. "My development was using more humble material, or weaker material. The strength of the material has nothing to do with the strength of the building, even nothing to do with durability. I knew logically that even using a weaker material like a paper tube I could make a strong building." The tubes in question were not specially manufactured for Ban's work; rather, they were long tubes made of thick paper originally intended to be used as forms for concrete columns. As such, buildings constructed from such tubes are also more environmentally friendly than buildings made from nonrecycled materials.

Using paper tubes as key structural components, Ban designed and oversaw the building of a number of buildings to serve as case studies. The first such building, known as the Paper Arbor, was constructed in Nagoya, Japan, in 1989 and consisted of forty-eight paper tubes arranged in a circle on a concrete foundation and topped with a wood, fabric, and wire roof. The tubes were coated in paraffin and glue to make them waterproof and capable of withstanding the elements. Another of those early buildings was Ban's vacation home at Lake Yamanaka in Yamanakako, Japan, which featured more than one hundred paper tubes. Through the creation of such buildings, Ban successfully demonstrated that paper could be used for structural purposes in homes and other buildings.

EMERGENCY HOUSING

Ban's paper buildings took on a new purpose beginning in the mid-1990s, when two crises demonstrated the multitude of applications for inexpensive, environmentally friendly structures. Early in the decade a civil war in Rwanda displaced a large portion of the country's population, leading to the development of crowded refugee camps. Relief organizations struggled to provide adequate shelter to the inhabitants of the camps, facing serious logistical and environmental concerns. "They had been using local wood and four-by-six-meter tarpaulin sheets, but there was not enough wood, so people were cutting down trees and causing deforestation," Ban explained to Corkill. "The [United Nations High Commissioner for Refugees (UNHCR)] then switched to aluminum frames, but that was problematic too, because in Africa aluminum is a valuable commodity and so the refugees would sell the tubing and go back to cutting down trees. I was suggesting something completely new—that the frames could be made with paper tubes." With a budget of only fifty US dollars per shelter, Ban designed emergency shelters based on paper-tube frames, fifty of which were eventually constructed.

Paper-based shelters likewise played an important role after a severe earthquake, known as the Kobe earthquake or Great Hanshin earthquake, struck southern Japan in 1995. In response to the need for emergency housing Ban designed buildings that he called paper log houses, which consisted of numerous paper tubes arranged on a foundation made from recycled beer crates packed with sandbags and covered with a tentlike roof. In addition to demolishing many homes, the earthquake and the subsequent fires had destroyed a church in the city of Kobe. Ban set out to build a new church, partnering with more than 150 volunteers and completing the building in only five weeks. Although intended to be a temporary structure, the church remained in place until 2005, when it was disassembled. The church's materials were later sent to Taiwan, where it was reconstructed in 2008 following an earthquake there.

Committed to continuing his work with relief organizations and governments worldwide, Ban founded the Voluntary Architects' Network (VAN), a nongovernmental organization (NGO) devoted to designing and building emergency housing. He went on to create a number of emergency structures using materials such as paper, cardboard, and shipping containers over the following decades, providing shelter to refugees and survivors of natural disasters in Japan, China, India, and elsewhere. Among his most famous paper structures is Christchurch, New Zealand's Cardboard Cathedral, a triangular building designed as a temporary replacement for a church seriously damaged by the 2011 earthquake in that city.

OTHER PROJECTS

In addition to his numerous buildings incorporating paper elements, Ban created a number of other innovative structures. His furniture houses, beginning with 1995's Furniture House 1, used factory-made furniture, such as floor-to-ceiling bookcases or shelving units, as integral structural supports. Much like his paper buildings, the furniture houses were influenced by natural disasters. "In the Hanshin-Awaji earthquake, in 1995, many people were injured or killed by the furniture. On the other hand, some people were saved by sheltering under it," he told Bird. "At the time, I realized how strong cabinets could be and wondered if even without posts or [bearing] walls it would be enough just to have these furniture units as structural elements." Ban was also responsible for the design of the Nomadic Museum, a temporary building that incorporated metal shipping containers as well as paper tubes.

Ban held teaching positions at a number of Japanese universities, including Tama Art University, Keio University, and Kyoto University of Art and Design. He also served as a visiting professor at several institutions in the United States, including Columbia University and Harvard University. In recognition of his work Ban was awarded the prestigious Pritzker Architecture Prize in 2014.

PERSONAL LIFE

Ban is married to designer Masako Ban, the founder of the accessory company Acrylic. He divides his time among Tokyo, Paris, and New York.

SUGGESTED READING

Ban, Shigeru. Interview by Judith Benhamou-Huet. *Interview*. Brant, 28 Apr. 2009. Web. 12 Feb. 2016.

Ban, Shigeru. "Q&A with Japanese Architect Shigeru Ban." Interview by Winifred Bird. *Dwell*. Swell Media, 19 Jan. 2014. Web. 12 Feb. 2016.

Ban, Shigeru. "Shigeru Ban: 'People's Architect' Combines Permanence and Paper." Interview by Edan Corkill. *Japan Times*. Japan Times, 7 Apr. 2013. Web. 12 Feb. 2016.

Goodyear, Dana. "Paper Palaces." *New Yorker*. Condé Nast, 11 Aug. 2014. Web. 12 Feb. 2016.

Medina, Samuel, and Paul Makovsky. "Exclusive: Meet the 2014 Pritzker Prize Winner, Shigeru Ban." *Metropolis*. Metropolis, 24 Mar. 2014. Web. 12 Feb. 2016.

Pogrebin, Robin. "Pritzker Architecture Prize Goes to Shigeru Ban." *New York Times*. New York Times, 24 Mar. 2014. Web. 12 Feb. 2016.

—*Joy Crelin*

Courtney Barnett

Born: November 3, 1987
Occupation: Musician

Australian singer-songwriter Courtney Barnett has released only a handful of EPs (extended plays) and one full-length album (2015's *Sometimes I Sit and Think, and Sometimes I Just Sit*), but she is already being widely hailed as one of the most promising talents of recent years. "Barnett is a master of small-bore observations that smudge the line between profundity and banality, set atop swaggering garage riffs," Jonah Weiner wrote for *Rolling Stone* (1 Apr. 2015), describing her singular sound. "The geographies Barnett narrates in most songs are tiny—drinking wine with friends in a living room; regarding cracks in a plaster wall with the interpretive scrutiny of a palm reader; riding the Epping mass-transit line in Melbourne. And yet she somehow makes her world feel improbably big."

In another article for *Rolling Stone* (29 Jan. 2015), Simon Vozick-Levinson had similar praise for the young artist. "Barnett specializes in spinning seemingly mundane thoughts and events into sneakily hilarious stream-of-consciousness lyrics," he wrote. "Her best-known song to date, 2013's 'Avant Gardener,' narrates a

Aurelien Guichard/Flickr/CC BY-SA 2.0/Wikimedia Commons

lazy afternoon that suddenly turns into a spiraling allergy-slash-panic-attack. Another highlight from her new album, the bright, energetic 'Dead Fox,' finds her in the middle of the ten-hour drive from Melbourne to Sydney, wondering whether her hay fever is about to cause a fatal collision."

Barnett's willingness to draw upon the minutia of her own life have caused some to label her a music-industry Lena Dunham—a reference to the creator of the notoriously self-referential television series *Girls*. In addition to her allergies, her lyrics have touched on her relationship with her parents, her laundry schedule, and even her masturbation habits. "Most are pretty revealing of myself," she admitted to Holly Williams for the *Independent* (12 Apr. 2014).

EARLY LIFE

Barnett was born in Pittwater, a seaside town not far from Sydney, in New South Wales, Australia. She has recalled to interviewers that her family's one-story home was on the edge of the town, out in the Australian bush and surrounded by trees. She and her brother enjoyed something of an idyllic childhood, with plenty of room to ride their bikes and play at being commandos on secret missions. She also took ballet lessons (her mother was a former dancer), played tennis competitively (she briefly considered making a career of the sport), and—inspired by her brother and his friends—learned the guitar. "I wanted to hang around them, like an annoying little sister," she recalled to Amie Mulderrig for the *Enfield Independent* (4 May 2014). "Some of them taught me some guitar tunes and sent me off to learn it, so I'd keep out of their way. After that I begged mum and dad to let me have some guitar lessons." Initially, she played on a beat-up, nylon-string guitar given to her by a family friend, with the fretboard falling off the neck. She was never certain, she has quipped, if she sounded so bad because of the poor quality of the instrument or because she truly lacked talent.

Barnett's parents provided great encouragement. They were both artistically inclined and had, in fact, met when her mother was dancing professionally and her father was working as a stage manager. They were aficionados of jazz and classical music, and Barnett has told interviewers that they were thus something of an anomaly in their staid, middle-class neighborhood.

When Barnett was sixteen, her father, by then working as a graphic designer, moved the family to Hobart, the capital of the island state of Tasmania, separated from mainland Australia by the Bass Strait. "It was actually great in the end, but I thought my life was being horribly ruined by my parents," she recalled to Vozick-Levinson. "I was so miserable. I remember listening to a lot of Nirvana in my headphones and ignoring my parents on the boat to Tasmania."

EDUCATION

After graduating from high school, Barnett entered the University of Tasmania. Although she was by then regularly writing songs—most of which she describes as decidedly bad—she set her sights on becoming a fine-art photographer. After two years, however, she realized she had made a mistake and dropped out of school to pursue music instead. She subsequently moved to Melbourne, which had a thriving music scene, and supported herself by selling shoes at a high-end local store; if a customer seemed particularly nice, she tried to gently dissuade them from spending so much money on shoes that would, as she asserted, only fall apart eventually anyway.

Barnett had long suffered from anxiety and depression, but in Melbourne the conditions intensified, and she began taking prescription antidepressants. "They're never real reasons," she described her depression to Weiner. "Just, you know, general kind of esteem and stuff. I don't want to go on about it, but I basically wouldn't leave my room, and I was unemployed for quite a while, and it became a cycle of, um, one leading into the other. I just couldn't see the point in anything—that's what it always came back to." Once she felt somewhat better, however, Barnett found a job at a popular bar, Northcote Social Club, and began playing in a variety of cover bands and garage-rock groups.

EARLY MUSIC CAREER

Barnett had something of an epiphany in her mid-twenties. She had always tried writing songs that she thought other people would like and had never been satisfied with the results. Once she gave up the notion of appealing to the tastes of others, however, her songs seemed to improve. In 2012, with money she borrowed from her grandmother, she recorded an EP and released it on her own independent label, Milk! Records. Released in April 2012, *I've Got a Friend Called Emily Ferris* contained such songs as "Canned Tomatoes (Whole)," "Are You Looking After Yourself?" and "Lance Jr." (The last-named track caused a flurry of comment for its inclusion of the line "I masturbated to the songs you wrote.") Calling the EP an "honest, easy, and notable debut," Taryn Stenvei wrote for the Australian music publication *Beat* (17 Aug. 2012), "With catchy melodies and sparse production, she creates a unique brand of slacker-folk, advanced primarily by her lyrical frankness and a deadpan sense of humour. It's both real and refreshing, awash with jangly guitars, vice-heavy lyricism, and pop harmonies."

Barnett, who has drawn the cover art for all of her releases, followed that effort with another EP, *How to Carve a Carrot into a Rose*, which she put out in 2013. That collection included the songs "Avant Gardener," which the influential music magazine *Pitchfork* deemed best new track of the year. In the song, Barnett describes a pleasant morning gardening that ends in an exceptionally severe allergy attack. "Suspended within the song's shaggy-dog haze are deceptively dark themes of thwarted ambition and the paralyzing fear of wasting one's life," Weiner opined. The song was a runaway indie hit and was responsible for bringing Barnett to the attention of fans outside of Australia.

MAINSTREAM SUCCESS

Later in 2013, Barnett combined the two EPs to release *The Double EP: A Sea of Split Peas*, which gained her increased attention globally. She was invited to participate in the CMJ Music Marathon, a major industry event devoted to new music, and soon mounted a US tour of her own. In 2015 Barnett released her first full-length album, *Sometimes I Sit and Think, and Sometimes I Just Sit*, taking the title from a poster her grandmother had hanging up in her home. (The phrase has been attributed to both baseball icon Satchel Paige and Winnie the Pooh creator A. A. Milne.) The release was met with rapturous reviews. "Lyrical free-association. Stream-of-conscious rambling. An artful word salad. Call it what you will, but Barnett's spill-it-all approach to songwriting has made her first full-length record one of the most anticipated indie albums of the year," Lorraine Ali wrote for the *Los Angeles Times* (20 Mar. 2015), expressing sentiments echoed by several other critics. "An avalanche of raw internal dialogue, hook-heavy garage rock, and Barnett's own deadpan delivery are at the heart of *Sometimes I Sit and Think, and Sometimes I Just Sit*. In Barnett's hands, self-deprecation and crippling insecurity become charming attributes, and the mundane (cracks in the wall, breathing) funny if not fascinating."

Sometimes I Sit and Think, and Sometimes I Just Sit peaked at number twenty on the Billboard 200 album chart, and Barnett soon found herself being invited to perform on such television programs as *The Tonight Show with Jimmy Fallon* and *The Ellen DeGeneres Show* and making an appearance at the prestigious South by Southwest (SXSW) music festival, where *Billboard* magazine touted her as a must-see act.

At the 2015 ARIA Awards, presented by the Australian Recording Industry Association, Barnett won top honors in the categories of best female artist, breakthrough artist, and best independent release, and she took home an Artisan ARIA Award for *Sometimes I Sit and Think, and Sometimes I Just Sit*'s cover art—a simple but cheery line drawing of a chair perched on a colorful rug. Barnett also received a nod in the category of best new act at the 2016 Grammy Awards, ultimately losing to American pop star Meghan Trainor.

PERSONAL LIFE

"I don't really like talking about myself," Barnett told Dorian Lynskey for the *Guardian* (12 Mar. 2015). "I write songs because I can work on them and make myself sound clever, but in interviews I feel like a bit of a doofus." Most journalists have described the recording artist as quiet and laid-back.

Barnett—who did not quit her job at the Northcote Social Club until well after her music career seemed assured—lives in Australia with her longtime girlfriend, fellow singer-songwriter Jen Cloher, with whom she runs Milk! Records. She came out as gay to her parents the year she graduated from high school. "I was really scared," she recalled to Weiner, "And they were like, 'Yeah, we know!'"

SUGGESTED READING

Ali, Lorraine. "Singer-Songwriter Courtney Barnett Lets Her Lyrics Do the Talking." *Los Angeles Times*. Los Angeles Times, 20 Mar. 2015. Web. 7 Feb. 2016.

Greene, Jayson. "Rising: Courtney Barnett." *Pitchfork*. Condé Nast, 1 Oct. 2013. Web. 7 Feb. 2016.

Lynskey, Dorian. "Courtney Barnett: 'Every Day I Have Some Sort of Breakdown.'" *Guardian*. Guardian News and Media, 12 Mar. 2015. Web. 7 Feb. 2016.

Stenvei, Taryn. Rev. of *I've Got a Friend Called Emily Ferris*, by Courtney Barnett. *Beat*. Furst Media, 25 Mar. 2011. Web. 1 Apr. 2016.

Vozick-Levinson, Simon. "How Courtney Barnett Made One of 2015's Most Clever LPs." *Rolling Stone*. Rolling Stone, 29 Jan. 2015. Web. 7 Feb. 2016.

Weiner, Jonah. "How Courtney Barnett's Thoughts Became 2015's Sharpest Debut." *Rolling Stone*. Rolling Stone, 1 Apr. 2015. Web. 7 Feb. 2016.

Williams, Holly. "Courtney Barnett Interview: Why the Rising Star Is Happy to Sing about Panic Attacks, Parents, and Masturbating." *Independent*. Independent.co.uk, 12 Apr. 2014. Web. 7 Feb. 2016.

SELECTED WORKS

I've Got a Friend Called Emily Ferris, 2012; *How to Carve a Carrot into a Rose*, 2013; *Sea of Split Peas*, 2013; *Sometimes I Sit and Think, and Sometimes I Just Sit*, 2015

—*Mari Rich*

Mary Barra

Born: December 24, 1961
Occupation: CEO of General Motors

EARLY LIFE AND EDUCATION

Mary Barra was born Mary Teresa Makela on December 24, 1961, in Waterford, Michigan, to Ray and Eva Makela. Her father worked for Pontiac, one of several car brands owned by General Motors (GM), for nearly four decades. As the daughter of a longtime GM employee, Barra grew up immersed in the world of car manufacturing. She loved GM cars and particularly admired a vintage Chevrolet Camaro owned by a cousin. As a teenager, Barra wanted to buy a Pontiac Firebird, a sporty muscle car, but instead opted for a more affordable and practical—but slow and clunky—Chevrolet Chevette. Having to compromise between practicality and style influenced her later philosophy in designing cars for GM.

Barra graduated from Waterford Mott High School in 1980. That year she took her first job at GM, participating in the company's cooperative education program. She divided the year between working in a Pontiac manufacturing plant and studying electrical engineering at GMI Engineering and Management Institute (later known as Kettering University), a GM-affiliated university in Flint, Michigan. She graduated with a bachelor's degree in electrical engineering in 1985. She later attended the Stanford University Graduate School of Business on a GM fellowship, earning a master's of business administration in 1990.

GENERAL MOTORS

After completing her bachelor's degree, Barra began working for GM full time, taking on a variety of roles within the company over the following decades. She served for a time as an engineer in the Pontiac plant where she had worked as a student and later was named manager of manufacturing planning. In 1996 she took the position of executive assistant to GM's chief executive officer (CEO) and vice chairman.

Barra next worked in internal communications for a time before being named manager of an assembly plant that manufactured such cars as the Buick LeSabre. She became executive director of vehicle manufacturing in 2004, and was then appointed vice president of global manufacturing engineering in 2008. She served in this position until July 2009.

Like many other American car companies, GM struggled during the global recession that began in 2008. Rising gas prices and a general economic downturn decreased sales severely, and in June 2009, GM filed for bankruptcy.

The company survived the period in large part thanks to a government bailout. Shortly after the bankruptcy filing, which led to reorganization within the company and made clear the need for major changes in the immediate future, GM leadership named Barra vice president of global human resources. She remained in the position until early 2011, when she became senior vice president of global product development. Barra next served as executive vice president of global product development and global purchasing and supply chain from August 2013 to January 2014.

In late 2013 it was announced that GM CEO Dan Akerson planned to retire, and the company's leaders had assembled a short list of potential candidates to fill his position, Barra among them. By the middle of December, following much speculation, Barra was named as Akerson's successor. She officially began serving as CEO on January 15, 2014.

Barra had the difficult task of managing GM's continued financial recovery and regaining the attention and trust of car buyers in the United States and abroad. She faced significant scrutiny several months into her tenure, when a government investigation revealed that some individuals at GM had known about a dangerous defect in certain cars that had been implicated in a number of deaths but had chosen not to order a recall. In response to this controversy, which had been brewing for a decade prior to her appointment as CEO, Barra apologized on behalf of the company and noted that delays in rectifying such issues were unacceptable under her leadership.

As CEO, Barra became known for analyzing GM's products not from the viewpoint of an engineer or an executive but from that of the customer, making decisions based on factors such as comfort, design, and ease of use. She encouraged compromise and coordination among engineers and sought to improve efficiency, which in turn would decrease manufacturing costs. GM had a history of costly production delays and even cancelation of vehicles, and Barra acknowledged that if that trend continued, the company would continue to struggle.

In addition to being GM's CEO, Barra served as a member of Kettering University's board of trustees. She received the Kettering Alumni Association's management achievement award in 2010.

IMPACT

As the first female CEO of GM, Barra represented a major change in the automotive industry, a male-dominated realm that had long been considered inhospitable to women. In recognition of her work, she was ranked number seven on Forbes magazine's list of the world's hundred most powerful women for 2014.

PERSONAL LIFE

Barra is married to consultant Tony Barra. They have two children, Nicholas and Rachel.

SUGGESTED READING

"Mary T. Barra." *General Motors*. General Motors, 2014. Web. 29 June 2014.

Durbin, Dee-Ann, and Tom Krisher. "Mary Barra, a Child of GM, Prepares to Lead as First Female CEO of US Automaker." *Huffington Post*. TheHuffingtonPost.com, 24 Dec. 2013. Web. 29 June 2014.

McGregor, Jena. "The Rundown on Mary Barra, First Female CEO of General Motors." *Washington Post*. Washington Post, 10 Dec. 2013. Web. 29 June 2014.

Nisen, Max. "How Mary Barra Went from Inspecting Fender Panels to GM's First Female CEO." *Business Insider*. Business Insider, 10 Dec. 2013. Web. 29 June 2014.

Tankersley, Jim. "What Drives Mary Barra." *Stanford Alumni*. Stanford U, Sept./Oct. 2011. Web. 29 June 2014.

—*Leland Spencer*

Mary Beard

Born: January 1, 1955
Occupation: Classicist

Mary Beard, a professor of classics at the University of Cambridge, in the United Kingdom, is better known to the general public than the vast majority of academicians thanks to her many layperson-friendly books (including 2015's *SPQR: A History of Ancient Rome*), her regular appearances on the British Broadcasting Corp. (BBC), and her post as classics editor of the *Times Literary Supplement*.

While her intelligence and academic qualifications are well documented, Beard has proven to be a fiercely polarizing figure, drawing the ire of many observers for her unabashedly plain mien and strong feminist bent. A. A. Gill, the television critic for the London *Sunday Times*, has been particularly cruel, regularly mocking the state of Beard's hair and teeth—and once famously writing that she "should be kept away from cameras altogether."

Still, others applaud her for those very qualities that so anger her detractors. She has been appointed to the Order of the British Empire for services to classical scholarship, and in a poll among the readers of the political magazine *Prospect* in 2014, she was named one of the most significant thinkers in the world, just behind the Pope. In 2013 the *Oldie*, a British magazine that bills itself as "a light-hearted alternative to a

WPA Pool/Getty Images

press obsessed with youth and celebrity," named her its pinup of the year.

"Through her television appearances, she has become an avatar for middle-aged and older women, who appreciate her unwillingness to fend off the visible advancement of age," Rebecca Mead wrote for the *New Yorker* (1 Sept. 2014). "She looks comfortable both in her skin and in her shoes—much more preoccupied with what she is saying than with how she looks as she is saying it."

EARLY YEARS AND EDUCATION

An only child, Beard was born on January 1, 1955, in Much Wenlock, a picturesque village in Shropshire, England. Her father worked as an architect, and her mother was the headmistress of a school. Beard became interested in ancient history when she was about five years old, during a family trip to the British Museum in London. "I had thought people from the past weren't as good as we were, and then I saw the Elgin marbles. Suddenly, the world seemed more complicated," she recalled to Stuart Jeffries for the *Guardian* (20 Apr. 2012). "[I was allowed to touch] carbonised bread from 2,800 years ago. It gave me a thrill . . . Even today, when I hold a ring that somebody wore 2,000 years ago, I get excited."

Beard attended Shrewsbury High School, an exclusive all-girls' institution, as a scholarship student. She excelled academically, particularly in Latin and Greek, and during school breaks she took part in local archaeological digs. When asked why she loved so-called dead languages, she explained that she appreciated the fact that they were no longer spoken. "Part of the pleasure of knowing Latin is that you don't have to learn to say, 'Where is the cathedral?' or 'I would like a return ticket, second class, please,'" she quipped to Mead. "You actually get to the literature. You don't always have to be making yourself understood."

In 1972 Beard passed the entrance exam to Cambridge University. In choosing a specific school at the university, she was initially drawn to King's College, which had been founded by Henry VI and had only recently begun accepting women. She reconsidered after a mentor suggested that it would be difficult to blaze a trail at the venerable institution—and because scholarships were not yet being awarded to female students. Instead, she entered the all-women's Newnham College, where she had something of a political awakening. "Most of the people who taught us in the faculty were blokes," told Mead. "There were only twelve per cent women among the students, and you thought, actually, there is an issue here. You go into a dining hall of a men's college, and everybody's portrait was a bloke. Well, perhaps some female founder back in 1512, some lady who gave the cash—and everyone else was a bloke. For the first time I saw that, somehow, I was there as sort of a favor." Beard began attending women's consciousness-raising groups and hung a poster of American political activist Angela Davis in her room.

In the fall of 1978, while traveling by train to do student research in Rome, Beard was raped by a fellow passenger. She has since spoken openly about the incident and has even examined it in light of the classical tales of the rape of Lucretia and the rape of the Sabine women.

In 1979 Beard became a classics lecturer at Kings College London while undertaking her doctoral studies at Newnham. She earned her PhD in 1982 with a thesis entitled "The State Religion in the Late Roman Republic: A Study Based on the Works of Cicero."

ACADEMIC POSTS

After earning her doctoral degree, Beard continued to teach in London, but in 1984 she was invited back to Newnham as a lecturer and fellow. She was one of three women in the classics department—and the other two women ultimately departed. By then she had married and had children and found the absence of female camaraderie and guidance troubling. In response to that lack, she wrote *The Good Working Mother's Guide* (1989), which contained her hard-won wisdom on disposable diapers, household help, and other such topics.

In 2004 she became a full professor of classics at Newnham, where she remains, and in 2013 the Royal Academy of Arts named her a professor of ancient literature. The title is considered largely honorific, and her duties involve promoting ancient history among the members of the institution.

BOOKS

Beard's first book, *Rome in the Late Republic*, was published in 1985, and is still popular among classics students. Since then, she has published numerous others, including *Religions of Rome* (1998, with John North and S. R. F. Price), *The Parthenon* (2003), and *The Roman Triumph* (2007). *Pompeii: The Life of a Roman Town* (2008) garnered the prestigious Wolfson Prize, given to volumes that are written in a style that is scholarly but accessible to the layperson.

That accessibility is something of a Beard hallmark, as critics often note. In a review of Beard's 2013 book, *Confronting the Classics: Traditions, Adventures, and Innovations*, Joanna Scutts wrote for the *Washington Post* (18 Oct. 2013) that it "takes a particularly talented writer such as Beard—clear-eyed, witty, learned, sincere—to engage outsiders in such questions as the true meaning of Thucydides's barely penetrable Greek, the political importance of Cleopatra for Rome, the greatness of Alexander and, underneath it all, how we know what (we think) we know about ancient Greece and Rome."

Her 2015 book, *SPQR: A History of Ancient Rome*, "pitches itself firmly to the non-classicist," according to Joy Lo Dico, who interviewed Beard for the *Independent* (10 Oct. 2015). Lo Dico continued, "This . . . is a distillation of 40 years of scholarship told by someone who has managed to strip away the patina of deference that has attached itself to classical studies. The over-arching values and absolutes of Rome are gone, so too the long slog through multiple Latin names and the blood and guts of wars. SPQR—the brand standing for Senatus Populus Que Romanus, the senate and the people of Rome—is a tussle of ideas. It wakes up the once-greatest city in the world again by asking: 'Well, was it so great?'"

OTHER MEDIA

Beard has been a writer for the *London Review of Books* since the late 1980s, and in 1992 she became the classics editor of the *Times Literary Supplement* (*TLS*), a post she still holds. She writes a regular blog for the *TLS* called *A Don's Life*, which contains her musings on academic topics, stories from her life, and her other assorted interests. One post from December 2015, for example, debated naming college buildings after historical figures known to be racist, while another posted later in the month discussed her Christmas decorations.

Beard writes for both the *Guardian*, with its liberal readers, and the *Daily Mail*, which attracts a decidedly conservative audience. In addition to recording commentary for BBC Radio 4, she is a frequent presence on television and has appeared on several episodes of the public-affairs program *Question Time*, as well as on numerous BBC documentaries, including *Pompeii: Life & Death in a Roman Town* (2010), *Meet the Romans with Mary Beard* (2012), *Caligula* (2013), and *Suffragettes Forever! The Story of Women and Power* (2015).

ATTACKS

Beard maintains an active social media presence and is known for taking the time to respond to even the most offensive Internet trolls. In one widely publicized incident, university student Oliver Rawlings sent her an abusive message in which he referred to her as a "filthy old slut." She retweeted it to her tens of thousands of followers but then forgave him for what she termed his "one moment of idiocy" and wrote him job recommendations.

Despite such generosity, even Beard was taken aback after a *Question Time* appearance in which she advocated for recent immigrants to England. So abusive were users of one message board (a representative missive asserted that she was "a vile, spiteful excuse for a woman, who eats too much cabbage and has cheese straws for teeth") that the board was shut down by its administrator. "It was so ghastly it didn't feel personal, or personally critical," Beard recalled to Elizabeth Day for the *Guardian* (26 Jan. 2013). "It was such generic, violent misogyny. In a way, I didn't feel it was about me." In addition to being a strong female voice in her academic field, Beard has gained praise and become somewhat of a feminist hero for her handling of the abuse.

PERSONAL LIFE

Beard is married to art historian Robin Cormack, who focuses on the Byzantine era. They have a daughter, Zoe, an academic who specializes in the history of South Sudan, and a son, Raphael, who studies Egyptian literature. Beard and Cormack live in Cambridge, in a Victorian house filled with their antique and art collections.

Beard told Vanessa Thorpe for *Guardian* (28 Apr. 2012) that she cares little about meeting societal conventions of beauty. "I used to be scared of looking like this, but now I couldn't wish to be any different," she asserted. "Never mind the masochism of Botox. I can't even imagine dyeing my hair. It's not just the boring hours it would take. It's that every time you did it, you'd be reminded that you were hiding something. And how do you stop once you've started?"

SUGGESTED READING

Chhibber, Ashley. "Interview: Mary Beard." *Cambridge Student*. Cambridge Student, 3 May 2013. Web. 22 Dec. 2015.

Jeffries, Stuart. "The Saturday Interview: Mary Beard." *Guardian*. Guardian News and Media, 20 Apr. 2012. Web. 22 Dec. 2015.

Lo Dico, Joy. "Professor Mary Beard Talks about Her New History of Ancient Rome Book." *Independent*. Independent.co.uk, 10 Oct. 2015. Web. 22 Dec. 2015.

Mead, Rebecca. "The Troll Slayer." *New Yorker*. Condé Nast, 1 Sept. 2014. Web. 22 Dec. 2015.

Scutts, Jessica. "*Confronting the Classics: Traditions, Adventures and Innovations*, by Mary Beard." *Washington Post*. Washington Post, 18 Oct. 2013. Web. 5 Feb. 2015.

Thorpe, Vanessa. "Mary Beard: The Classicist with the Common Touch." *Guardian*. Guardian News and Media, 28 Apr. 2012. Web. 22 Dec. 2015.

SELECTED WORKS

The Parthenon, 2003; The *Roman Triumph*, 2007; *Pompeii: The Life of a Roman Town*, 2008; *Pompeii: The Life of a Roman Town*, 2008; *It's a Don's Life*, 2009; *Confronting the Classics: Traditions, Adventures, and Innovations*, 2013; *Laughter in Ancient Rome: On Joking, Tickling, and Cracking Up*, 2014; *SPQR: A History of Ancient Rome*, 2015

—*Mari Rich*

Kate Beaton

Born: September 8, 1983
Occupation: Cartoonist

When cartoonist Kate Beaton first began posting installments of her web comic *Hark! A Vagrant*, she could not have predicted that her work would bring her not only significant popularity among comics readers but also substantial critical acclaim. Dealing with a wide variety of subjects, from historical figures to literary characters to Beaton's younger self, her comic strips blend factual elements with offbeat, anachronistic humor, appealing to readers of all disciplines. "I think that I'm like a big magnet ball, running through the Internet, picking up things that I find interesting, and storing them away," she told Laura Bradley for *Slate* (10 July 2015) when asked about her comic's diverse subject matter. A native of rural Nova Scotia, Beaton started out publishing comics in her university newspaper, but she first gained extensive attention in 2007, when she began posting her work online. By the end of 2015, she was the best-selling creator of three collections of comics as well as *The Princess and the Pony*, a children's book she wrote and illustrated.

(Wikimedia/Flickr) "Kate Beaton" by 5of7 - Flickr: Kate Beaton. Licensed under CC BY-SA 2.0 via Wikimedia Commons

EARLY LIFE AND EDUCATION

Kathryn Moira Beaton was born in the Canadian province of Nova Scotia on September 8, 1983. The second of four daughters born to Marion and Neil Beaton, she grew up in Mabou, a small town on Cape Breton Island. Her mother worked at a bank when Beaton was a child, while her father was a butcher. For most of her academic career, Beaton attended Mabou Consolidated School, which taught students through twelfth grade. The school closed in 2000, and Beaton spent her final year of high school at Dalbrae Academy in Mabou, graduating in 2001.

Beaton developed a love of drawing at an early age. Mabou's schools offered little in the way of art education, but her parents encouraged her artistic pursuits and for a time arranged for her to take lessons from a local painter. Beaton has noted in interviews that although she began drawing comics early in life, she had very little exposure to the superhero comics and long-form graphic novels popular among comics readers; however, she did have the opportunity to read newspaper comics and particularly enjoyed Charles Schulz's *Peanuts* and Bill Amend's *FoxTrot*.

Although Beaton had become known in her family and school as "the one who could draw," as she told Chris Mautner for the *Comics Journal* (4 Nov. 2015), a career in art seemed far too risky for a resident of rural Nova Scotia. "[I]f I said, 'I want to be an artist,' a lot of people would have been like, 'Are you sure? Being a nurse is much safer, being a teacher,'" she explained to Mautner. She added, "People make fairly safe moves there, which is what happens when you're

in an economically disadvantaged place. Risks are for privileged people with money to fall on their face if it doesn't work out." Instead of pursuing an education in art, Beaton opted to study history and anthropology while attending Mount Allison University in Sackville, New Brunswick, from which she earned her bachelor's degree in 2005. During her time at the university, she began drawing comics for the student newspaper, the *Argosy*, and also wrote a humor column called Super Quiz. Having gained an outlet for her comics, Beaton over time began to develop the offbeat sense of humor that characterizes much of her later work, although she admitted to Mautner that many of her *Argosy* strips were "so bad."

EARLY CAREER

After graduating from college, Beaton faced the daunting prospect of paying off her student loan. Returning to Mabou was not an option. "You grow up in Cape Breton and you have to leave. If you want to make a good living you have to leave," she explained to Mautner. "There's an immense sense of loss over generations. . . . There's all kinds of songs about how much people miss home and how they had to go. But there's an emphasis on doing better for yourself." Instead, Beaton took a job in Fort McMurray, Alberta. Located in the Athabasca oil sands of northern Alberta, Fort McMurray is the site of extensive oil extraction processes and a common destination for young Canadian jobseekers, particularly those, like Beaton, from the Maritime provinces. The experience proved to be a formative one for Beaton, who told Sam Thielman for the *Guardian* (14 Sept. 2015), "I had just finished school, so you have your kind of academic-head-in-the-clouds thing that you do when you're writing a paper, and you're like: 'This is important!' And then you get to the oil sands and people are dying, and the earth is being destroyed and you're like: 'Oh, this is important.'"

Beaton remained at Fort McMurray for a year, working in a tool warehouse at a mining site. She spent the following year as an administrative assistant at the Maritime Museum of British Columbia in Victoria. A history buff, Beaton enjoyed working in a museum environment and considered enrolling in graduate school with the goal of becoming a professor.

HARK! A VAGRANT

Although Beaton no longer had a publication venue for her work after graduating from university, she continued to write and draw comics, creating many of the strips for which she would first become known while working at the Maritime Museum. Emily Horne, one of the creators of the comic *A Softer World*, was the programs manager at the museum, and upon witnessing

Beaton's talent, she encouraged her to post her drawings on the Internet. Beaton began posting her work online in 2007, initially on her Live-Journal blog and then on a personal website.

Unlike her comics for the *Argosy*, which primarily focused on campus life and current events, her *Hark! A Vagrant* strips (named after a line from one of her early comics) deal with topics such as history and literature, areas that had long been of interest to Beaton. Despite the interesting tidbits of information they present to readers, however, her comics are not solely educational in nature; rather, they blend facts with an offbeat brand of humor that is joyfully anachronistic and often employs puns and moments of sheer absurdity. "I like going back and forth between the stuff that is just silly nonsense and the stuff that is a bit more book heavy," Beaton told Mautner of her writing style. "Because if you do one or the other all the time I think you'd get tired of it and people would get tired of seeing it. I like throwing in different stuff. 'Cause we all have a broad taste like that. We like to laugh, we like to learn, we like to look at something silly, and we like to think about things a bit more sometimes."

Hark! A Vagrant frequently features historical figures such as Elizabeth I of England, inventor Nikola Tesla, and journalist Ida B. Wells as well as references to numerous literary works, including Jane Austen's 1813 novel *Pride and Prejudice* and F. Scott Fitzgerald's 1925 classic *The Great Gatsby*. In addition to its real-world and pop-cultural influences, the comic also features a number of original characters who recur from time to time. One particularly notable character is a fat Shetland pony who appears in several comics and is a favorite among Beaton's fans; the pony has made a guest appearance in an episode of the Cartoon Network program *Adventure Time* and also has a costarring role in Beaton's first children's book, *The Princess and the Pony* (2015). Other recurring characters include the Mystery Solving Teens, essentially a more realistic version of teen detectives such as the Hardy Boys, and the Strong Female Characters, who represent a satirical view of the representation of women in popular media.

SUCCESS IN COMICS
Still financially unable to commit to comics full time, Beaton ultimately returned to Fort Mc-Murray, working there for another year. She later wrote a five-part comic, "Ducks" (2014), about her experiences in Alberta during that period. Finally, in the fall of 2008, she moved to Toronto to focus on writing comics, where she lived for a time with Horne. By that point, she had also changed the name of her site to *Hark! A Vagrant*. In an interview with Raju Mudhar for the *Toronto Star* (28 Oct. 2011), Beaton explained that

as she grew into the creative process, she had learned to let her work stand on its own: "It used to be KateBeaton.com but I got rid of that because I didn't want to be the focus of the comic. I wanted the comic to *be*."

Hark! A Vagrant has amassed a dedicated readership in the years since the site's launch, and the success of the web comic has enabled Beaton to make a living from her work, in part through the sale of merchandise such as T-shirts and a stuffed animal version of the fat pony. In addition to maintaining an archive of comics on her website, Beaton has released three collections of strips, beginning with the publication of *Never Learn Anything from History* in 2009. She has drawn comics for the *New Yorker* and contributed to the Marvel Comics anthology *Strange Tales II* (2010). Not long after her second collection, *Hark! A Vagrant* (2011), became a *New York Times Best Seller*, she was the recipient of the 2012 Harvey Award for best online comics work. In December 2014, her art appeared on Google's Canadian homepage to commemorate the birthday of Canadian suffragist Henrietta Edwards.

Perhaps the most intangible yet significant of Beaton's accomplishments is her success in introducing readers to historical figures and events with which they are unfamiliar. Although Beaton does not design her comics to be educational tools, their humorous take on history has proven highly effective. "I really believe in the power of comics as an educational thing, even ones as silly as mine, because they're a gateway to the actual thing," she explained to Tasha Robinson for the *A.V. Club* (14 Oct. 2011). "They're like an easy entrance."

THE PRINCESS AND THE PONY
Following the publication of the *Hark! A Vagrant* collection in 2011, editors from the book publisher Scholastic approached Beaton about writing a children's book. Intrigued by the idea, Beaton contemplated a number of potential stories before ultimately writing what became *The Princess and the Pony*. Published in 2015, the book tells the story of Princess Pinecone, a child from a family of warriors who requests a warhorse for her birthday but instead receives a fat pony—an animal familiar to readers of *Hark! A Vagrant*. Asked about the process of writing for children rather than her usual audience of adults, Beaton told Laura Godfrey for *Publishers Weekly* (9 June 2015), "I think everyone who likes their kids knows that it's a mistake to talk down to them. You're talking to them on a level that's respecting their intelligence, because they're a very discerning audience. So are adults, but when I write for adults, I'm talking to an audience that seems invested in nostalgia, a thing that doesn't exist for kids. So the language changes." As further proof of her versatility, her third comics collection,

Step Aside, Pops (2015), also landed on the *New York Times Best Sellers* list.

PERSONAL LIFE

Beaton, who still lives in Toronto, has acknowledged that although she is grateful for the success she has experienced, she has increasingly striven to separate her work and her personal life: "My day-to-day isn't as bothered by it now. Maybe it's because I retreated, and now I'm a more private person. In the beginning, you're so excited that people are reading your work, and you're way more open and giving of yourself. . . . Then you get a little older and you want to live by the sea in a hut," she explained to Laura Hudson for *Wired* (23 Sept. 2015).

SUGGESTED READING

Beaton, Kate. "*Hark! A Vagrant's* Kate Beaton on Making History Funny and Who Should Be on the $10 Bill." Interview by Laura Bradley. *Slate*. Slate Group, 10 July 2015. Web. 16 Nov. 2015.

Beaton, Kate. "'I'm a Careful Person': An Interview with Kate Beaton." Interview by Chris Mautner. *Comics Journal*. Fantagraphics, 4 Nov. 2015. Web. 16 Nov. 2015.

Beaton, Kate. "Kate Beaton: 'We Watched Print Die from up on Our Hill of Youth.'" Interview by Sam Thielman. *Guardian*. Guardian News and Media, 14 Sept. 2015. Web. 16 Nov. 2015.

Beaton, Kate. "Q & A with Kate Beaton." Interview by Laura Godfrey. *Publishers Weekly*. PWxyz, 9 June 2015. Web. 16 Nov. 2015.

Hudson, Laura. "How Internet Magic Helped a Quirky Cartoonist Find Success." *Wired*. Condé Nast, 23 Sept. 2015. Web. 16 Nov. 2015.

Robinson, Tasha. "Kate Beaton." *A.V. Club*. Onion, 14 Oct. 2011. Web. 16 Nov. 2015.

SELECTED WORKS

Never Learn Anything from History, 2009; *Hark! A Vagrant*, 2011; *The Princess and the Pony*, 2015; *Step Aside, Pops*, 2015

—Joy Crelin

Katia Beauchamp

Born: ca. 1982
Occupation: Business executive

In 2010, while she was still a student at Harvard Business School, Katia Beauchamp cofounded the beauty subscription service Birchbox, which sends subscribers a curated box of sample-sized beauty products each month. "I think every woman needs a best friend who is a beauty editor

to curate the clutter and find the best products for them," Beauchamp explained in an interview with Jenna Wortham for the *New York Times* (20 Apr. 2011). "With four or five samples a month, you can really sink your teeth into a new product and decide if you want to buy the product in a full size." Within five years of the company's founding, Birchbox had amassed more than one million subscribers across six countries.

In 2014, Beauchamp served as the keynote speaker at the cosmetics trade organization Cosmetic Executive Women's (CEW) sixtieth anniversary celebration. As reported by Jayme Cyk for *Women's Wear Daily* (27 June 2014), Beauchamp told the crowd, "Get comfortable with uncertainty. We knew very little about the industry when we started and instead of trying to understand everything, we drove forward." At the inaugural Forbes Power Redefined Women's Summit, Beauchamp and her cofounder and co-CEO, Hayley Barna, were honored with the Award for Excellence in Leadership. When Barna left the company in 2015, Beauchamp became Birchbox's sole chief executive.

EARLY LIFE AND EDUCATION

Katia Ververis Beauchamp's mother is of Mexican descent, and her father is Greek. Her parents divorced when she was four years old, which was the beginning of a split existence for Beauchamp. She spent most of her time with her mother in El Paso, Texas. She summered in both Germany, where her father relocated, and Greece. She began traveling extensively when she was only five, accompanied by her seven-year-old brother; their travels sparked her interest in global studies.

As a high school student, Beauchamp served as the student body president and cheerleading squad captain. She also worked at Gap, spending much of her earnings on beauty products. Her prom outfit was designed to complement her Chanel nail polish. After graduating from high school in 2001, she attended Vassar College, a prestigious liberal arts college in Poughkeepsie, New York.

After her freshman year, Beauchamp landed an internship at Estée Lauder, where she became intrigued by the beauty business. Sitting in on executive meetings was transformative for her. As she told Andrew Faught for Vassar's *Alumnae/i Quarterly* (Fall 2013), "I became really obsessed with beauty on the business side. I was attracted to the fact that the business of beauty required both analytical skills and creative skills—it was right brain and left brain. Everyone I met was incredibly smart and grounded in data, while also creative, passionate, and comfortable with the unquantifiable aspects of building a brand." She graduated from Vassar in 2005 with a double major in international studies and economics, as well as a minor in Spanish.

Beauchamp's early career was in private banking. She worked for M&T Bank from 2005 until 2007, when she joined the real estate bank Eurohypo as an analyst. She remained at Eurohypo for one year before enrolling at Harvard Business School.

DEVELOPING A BUSINESS CONCEPT

Beauchamp and her Birchbox cofounder Hayley Barna met on the first day of classes at Harvard Business School in 2008. Seated near one another, they began their friendship by commenting on one another's nail polish colors. Together they wrote a business plan for an e-commerce beauty site that won second place in the Harvard Business School Business Plan competition.

The two began testing the concept for Birchbox as they were completing their final semester at Harvard. To try out their idea, Beauchamp and Barna ran a two-month beta test. They sent out e-mails to their favorite beauty companies with the subject heading "Re-imagining Beauty e-Commerce." They initially limited the trial to two hundred subscribers at an initial cost of twenty dollars a month. By the time the company was ready to launch, based on word of mouth, the number of paying customers had tripled and the subscription cost had been cut in half to ten dollars a month.

Their idea, termed "discovery retail," was a monthly subscription for a beauty box filled with four or five sample sizes of high-end beauty products. Everyone wins with this model: customers get to try new items tailored to their preferences based on the online profiles they create, cosmetics retailers get to reach more customers and are able to track the return on investment

of their sample products, and Birchbox connects the two. Birchbox initially did not pay the beauty companies for the samples, which typically give out free samples to customers who make larger purchases. "Including a gift with a purchase to an existing customer makes it very difficult to track that investment," Beauchamp explained to Wortham. "Birchbox is a way to track that return and give [companies] data about purchasing behavior."

Beauchamp explained the origin of the idea to John Patrick Pullen for *Entrepreneur* (20 Aug. 2013), "The Internet is good at what it's always been good at, which is replenishing things, but it's particularly bad at a first-time purchase. We saw that as a huge opportunity."

FOUNDING BIRCHBOX

Beauchamp and Barna launched Birchbox in September 2010 with 660 subscribers. They began with only two other employees—a friend who was a web designer and Mollie Chen, their editorial director—in a startup space in Dumbo, Brooklyn. The company name came from a desire for something simple and beautiful in all seasons, like a birch tree, but also vague enough to allow for expansion in areas other than beauty.

Investors from First Round Capital and Accel Partners, which had provided early funding for such tech companies as Groupon and Facebook, provided seed money. By October 2010, the company had raised $1.4 million in seed financing; less than a year after its founding, Birchbox had raised $10.5 million in Series A capital funding. Still, Beauchamp and Barna said that they found it difficult to win the approval of men in venture capital who controlled money but had never used makeup or understood its appeal.

The two women divided job responsibilities, with Beauchamp meeting with potential investors and beauty company stakeholders and guiding the company's press coverage. Barna focused on customer relations, operations, and technology. Power in the company is also decentralized, and Birchbox employees are encouraged to pursue their own ideas for the company. As Beauchamp explained to Colleen Leahey for *Fortune* (19 Sept. 2013), "We're building a bridge over a ravine and putting the next brick down as we step." Within the first seven months of Birchbox's existence, it had reached the five-year sales goal that Beauchamp and Barna had set.

EXPANSION

In 2012 the company launched Birchbox Man, offering a subscription for men's products at twenty dollars a month. Birchbox hired a men's editor and more male staff to oversee Birchbox Man. Beauchamp told Chris Gayomali for *Fast Company* (13 Apr. 2015), "It's very clear that it's a major opportunity for us. Men are relatively small from a subscriber perspective, but they're meaningful from a revenue perspective. Also, guys are shopping more: They shop sooner and therefore more often."

Birchbox also bought JolieBox, a competitor in Europe, in 2012, the first step toward becoming an international business. Based in Paris, JolieBox had launched only eight months after Birchbox debuted and served customers in France, Spain, and the United Kingdom, all of whom were eligible to become Birchbox members. The transition went so smoothly that neither company lost a day of business. As Beauchamp told Meghan Casserly for *Forbes* (13 Sept. 2012), "We've had the vision of global growth since day one. Because our value proposition really knows no borders."

Within two years of its launch, Birchbox had more than 400,000 subscribing members and 200 staff members and revenue of more than $40 million. The company is able to give personalized attention to subscribers as well; for example, if customers indicate particular problems with their skin or hair on a questionnaire, Birchbox will send them products to address the issue. From its website, Birchbox also offers direct sales of full-sized versions of the samples, a service half of their subscription clients use, providing some 30 percent of Birchbox's revenue.

By early 2014, Birchbox had partnered with 800 brands, employed 250 employees, and drawn more than 800,000 subscribers, generating approximately $125 million in revenue. In April 2014, Birchbox closed its Series B round of funding, having raised $60 million. Birchbox was then valued at $485 million.

RETHINKING THE BOX

By 2015 Birchbox had a brick-and-mortar presence in Lower Manhattan, after trying short-term pop-up stores in New York City and the Hamptons. More than one million people in six countries subscribed to the service in 2015. After the success of Birchbox, many other monthly subscription services began selling subscriptions for monthly deliveries of everything from coffee to razors. As Erin Griffith remarked in an article for *Fortune* (21 Apr. 2014), "All of it seemed very faddish, and indeed, many of these startups have petered out. Those that have thrived have done so with a unique value proposition that can't be matched by brick-and-mortar retailers, and more importantly, by Amazon. One such company is Birchbox." Kent Goldman, from the venture capital firm First Round Capital, explained to Olga Kharif for *Bloomberg Businessweek* (16 Feb. 2012), "It's a business model we love. You have regular subscribers; you have a direct relationship with them."

However, the white-hot market for subscription beauty products that Birchbox had pioneered began to cool as other companies competed for market share. In addition, some companies that began as brick-and-mortar stores, such as the cosmetics giant Sephora, also began to offer monthly subscription services. Concurrently, investment funds were less easily secured. Discussing the difficulty of finding venture capital in this new, increasingly competitive marketplace, Beauchamp told Khadeeja Safdar for the *Wall Street Journal* (15 June 2016), "There is a complete reversal. It is all about showing how you can operate this business profitably and it has forced us to completely change the way we operate, the way we spend money."

Two of those changes included starting to pay for samples and spending more on marketing. In addition, subscribers had been able to earn unlimited credit points by writing reviews for Birchbox's website. That was capped at five points in July 2016, upsetting some subscribers. The company had planned further international expansion to China, which has been put on hold. Likewise, plans for more brick-and-mortar stores have been halted as the company reevaluates its long-term plans.

PERSONAL LIFE

Beauchamp met her husband, Greg, on the tetherball court at school when they were both ten years old. They began dating many years later after he moved to New York City. They married on the Greek island of Crete in July 2010. Their twin sons, Guy and Alec, were born in 2014.

SUGGESTED READING

Casserly, Meghan. "Birchbox Goes Global, Acquires Paris-Based Copycat 'Joliebox.'" *Forbes*. Forbes.com, 13 Sept. 2012. Web. 13 Sept. 2016.

Cyk, Jayme. "Talent Scouting." *Women's Wear Daily* 27 June 2014: 30. Web. *EBSCO Vocational Studies Premier.* 12 Sept. 2016.

Faught, Andrew. "Boxing Beauty." *Alumnae/i Quarterly*. Vassar College, Mar. 2013. Web. 12 Sept. 2016.

Gayomali, Chris. "Opening the [Birch]box." *Fast Company*. Mansueto Ventures, 13 Apr. 2015. Web. 13 Sept. 2016.

Griffith, Erin. "Exclusive: Birchbox Banks $60 Million." *Fortune*. Time, 21 Apr. 2014. Web. 13 Sept. 2016.

Leahey, Colleen. "Thinking Outside the Box." *Fortune*. Time, 19 Sept. 2013. Web. 13 Sept. 2016.

Pullen, John Patrick. "Harvard Students Reimagine the Cosmetics Business." *Entrepreneur*. Entrepreneur Media, 20 Aug. 2013. Web. 13 Sept. 2016.

—*Judy Johnson*

Bruce A. Beutler

Born: December 29, 1957
Occupation: Geneticist

Bruce A. Beutler is one of three scientists awarded the 2011 Nobel Prize in Physiology or Medicine for his contributions to the understanding of the innate immune system.

EARLY LIFE AND EDUCATION

Bruce A. Beutler was born in 1957 in Chicago, Illinois, one of four children born to a Jewish physician father, whose family immigrated to the United States to escape Nazi Germany, and a Ukrainian American mother who worked as a technical writer. Beutler grew up in Arcadia, California, a small city outside Los Angeles, where his family relocated in 1959.

Beutler has said that his desire to become a biologist began when he was around seven years old through his fascination with the animals and plants he found in the California woods. By age fourteen, Beutler was working in his father's laboratory at City of Hope Medical Center, where he gained an introduction to laboratory work. Beutler pursued an accelerated academic program, graduating with his bachelor's in biology from the University of California, San Diego in 1976, at age eighteen. He then worked briefly in the lab of evolutionary biologist Susumu Ohno, where he was first introduced to the genetics of immune systems. Beutler opted to attend medical school at the University of Chicago in 1977, graduating in 1981. Beutler completed his medical residency at University of Texas (UT) Southwestern Medical Center, in Dallas, Texas, where he gained practical exposure to clinical and emergency medicine.

IMMUNOLOGY RESEARCH

In 1983, Beutler took a research position at New York City's Rockefeller University, where he studied the function of cachectin, a protein secreted in the immune systems of mice exposed to bacterial toxins called lipopolysaccharides (LPS). Beutler was the first to synthesize cachectin in a laboratory setting, and this helped in the realization that cachectin was involved in endotoxic shock, or septic shock, a condition that occurs when bacteria within the body release LPS, causing an immune response that can be fatal.

Beutler learned that cachectin was a mouse-specific version of a more general protein known as tumor necrosis factor alpha (TNF), found in humans and known to be active in several toxic disorders. Initially, scientists were interested in developing TNF molecules for use in medicine, but Beutler's research helped to reveal that TNF caused inflammation. Scientists then began searching for ways to block TNF activity within the body.

Beutler returned to Dallas in 1986 to head his own immunology laboratory at UT Southwestern, where he focused on researching several aspects of TNF formation and function. Beutler's team developed a neutralizing protein capable of blocking TNF activity in the body for extended periods. Beutler patented the protein for use in creating medicines, and the patent was later sold to Amgen corporation, where it is used to create the drug Enbrel, an anti-inflammatory drug used to treat the symptoms of rheumatoid arthritis and similar conditions.

Beutler's team also conducted experiments to identify the receptor mechanism in the immune system that identifies and responds to the presence of LPS resulting from gram negative bacteria. By 1993, Beutler's laboratory began using a technique called positional cloning, which allows geneticists to isolate portions of a genome and then determine the function of the isolated section.

A lack of publications and measurable results from his ongoing study led University administrators and funding agencies to question the value of Beutler's research. After numerous reviews from the Medical Advisory Board to determine the team's funding from the Howard Hughes Medical Institute (HHMI), it was decided in April 1998 that HHMI would only fund his research until August 2000. In September 1998, while reviewing a batch of results, Beutler's team located the Toll-like receptor 4 (*Tlr4*) gene, which coded for a cell surface receptor protein, and seemed a good candidate for the elusive LPS receptor mechanism.

Beutler's team found that *Tlr4* was part of a family of proteins related to the Toll gene that had been identified in *Drosophila* fruit flies and was involved in the immune system. Beutler's team published the results of their work in the article "Defective LPS signaling in C3H/HeJ and C57BL/10ScCr mice: Mutations of in *Tlr4* gene," in the journal *Science*. The paper was recognized as a major success in the field and became one of the most cited publications in immunology over the next decade.

In 2000, Beutler relocated to the Scripps Research Institute in La Jolla, California, where he worked with N-ethyl-N-nitrosourea (ENU) mutagenesis, a genetics technique that can be used to create novel versions of a gene within a test organism. Beutler began receiving worldwide recognition for his work in innate immunity in 2004 when he was awarded the Robert Koch Prize; he went on to receive the William B. Coley award from the Cancer Research Institute in 2005. In 2008, Beutler was elected to the National Academy of Science, and in 2011, he won the Shaw Prize from the Shaw Foundation in Hong Kong.

In 2011 Beutler was one of three scientists awarded the Nobel Prize in Physiology or Medicine for his contribution to the scientific understanding of immunity. Beutler shared the award with Jules A. Hoffmann from the University of Strasbourg and Ralph M. Steinman of McGill University, who died shortly before receiving the award. The 2011 prize became controversial after a group of twenty-three immunologists published a letter in the journal *Nature* criticizing the Nobel Committee for choosing Beutler and ignoring the contributions of pioneers in the field such as Ruslan Medzhitov and Charles A. Janeway.

Beutler returned to Dallas in March 2011, where he established a Center for the Genetics of Host Defense. In 2013, Beutler was elected to the American Academy of Arts and Sciences (AAAS) in recognition of his contributions to the field of immunology.

IMPACT

Beutler's lab has produced research that led to the development of drugs and therapies used to treat immune system disorders, inflammatory diseases, and various types of cancer. Ongoing research into the nature of the *Tlr4* gene and the Toll family of genes is one of the cornerstones of modern immunology research.

PERSONAL LIFE

Beutler married Barbara Lanzl, a dental student he met while attending medical school in Chicago, in 1980. The couple had three sons, Danny, Elliot, and Jonathan, before divorcing in 1988.

SUGGESTED READING

Beutler, Bruce A. "Autobiography of Bruce A. Beutler." *Shaw Prize*. Shaw Prize Foundation, 2011. Web. 24 Apr. 2014.

"Bruce A. Beutler – Biographical." *Nobelprize. org*. Nobel Media, 2013. Web. 24 Apr. 2014.

"Bruce Beutler Wins the 2011 Nobel Prize in Physiology or Medicine." *Scripps Research Institute*. Scripps Research Inst., 3 Oct. 2011. Web. 24 Apr. 2014.

"Bruce Beutler, M.D." *UT Southwestern Medical Center*. UT Southwestern Medical Center, 2014. Web. 24 Apr. 2014.

Garwood, Jeremy. "Nobel Prize Critiques: Bruce Beutler." *Lab Times Online*. Lab Times, 14 Feb. 2012. Web. Apr. 24, 2014.

Johnson, Dirk. "Life after Nobel." *Medicine on the Midway* 65.1 (2012): 7–9. Print.

—*Micah Issitt*

Mhairi Black

Born: September 12, 1994
Occupation: Politician

In 2015, Mhairi Black became the youngest member of Parliament (MP) in the United Kingdom since at least 1832. Only twenty years old at the time of the election, Black stunned political insiders when she ousted Douglas Alexander, a long-serving Labour MP who was a former national campaign strategist and cabinet minister. Jeremy Paxman noted for the *Financial Times* (31 July 2015) that Black's success was especially surprising considering she is a member of the Scottish National Party (SNP). SNP supporters were once a political minority in her constituency, the blue-collar Paisley and Renfrewshire South, located southwest of Glasgow, Scotland. "It's the sort of town that once had the reputation for being a place where the Labour Party could stick a red rosette on the studded collar of a child-eating bull terrier and see it elected to Parliament," as Paxman colorfully put it. In an article for the *New York Times* (8 May 2015), Katrin Bennhold deemed Black's victory so shocking as to be "unthinkable."

Black won her election by a whopping 27 percentage points, but her success was part of a larger sweep across the country. The SNP, which had unsuccessfully led the charge for Scottish independence from the United Kingdom in September 2014, won fifty-six of Scotland's fifty-nine parliamentary seats. The once-dominant Labour Party lost forty seats, leaving it with only one. The SNP's victory

LESLEY MARTIN / Stringer from GettyImages

suggests that, far from putting the issue to rest, the failed referendum for an independent Scotland actually energized voters to reconsider the country's relationship to the United Kingdom. Labour was once considered the party of liberal ideals, but the SNP has now assumed that title for the Scottish public. After dazzling the country with her maiden speech in Parliament in July 2015, Black seems to be a leader in this burgeoning movement for change.

EARLY LIFE AND EDUCATION

Black was born in Paisley, fifteen minutes west of Glasgow, on September 12, 1994. Her parents are math teachers. Growing up, Black played soccer with her older brother, who now works as a railway conductor. When she went to try out for her primary school team, she was told that the team was for boys only. Black persisted in her desire and the school ultimately relented. She was the first girl to play for the team. Black appears to exhibit the same amiable toughness in nearly every facet of her life. She and her family knew she was gay from a young age, though she told Janice Turner for the London *Times* (25 July 2015), she never officially came out. "Why should I have to come out when my brother didn't have to talk about how he's straight?" she said. Other gay children were bullied at her school, she added, but no one ever gave her a hard time because her classmates knew she could stand up for herself. As a child, she thought about becoming an astronaut, a farmer, or a judge, but when she went to school she was preparing to become a teacher, like her parents. She studied politics and public policy at the University of Glasgow and graduated shortly after her election in 2015.

THE SCOTTISH NATIONAL PARTY

Her parents were longtime supporters of the Labour Party, but a few years ago, her parents began to vote with the SNP. Her father worked the picket lines in a teachers' strike when Black was a child. Her mother, the daughter of a man who worked in the Glasgow shipyards, was the first in her family to go to university. Black's own politics, encouraged by her family, are motivated by a "hatred for unfairness," Turner wrote. As a teenager, Black worked with her mother's Catholic charity and joined Amnesty International. The Blacks are very much a typical, middle-class Scottish family, and in many ways, their political conversion is emblematic of the change happening across Scotland. "My dad and I used to argue for hours at the dinner table," Black told Paxman. "I just couldn't understand how anyone could continue to believe in the Union when things weren't really changing at all."

Black herself was impressed by the SNP minority government in 2007 that ended tuition fees—a postgraduation fee that students paid in lieu of yearly tuition—and stopped charging people money for prescription drugs. Black joined the SNP and was elected women's officer at her first meeting. She began passing out leaflets for the party and knocking on doors. Soon, she was speaking at public meetings, lobbying for the 2014 referendum for Scottish independence.

2015 PARLIAMENTARY ELECTION AND "THE FIFTY-SIX"

The idea to run as a candidate in the 2015 parliamentary election was first suggested to Black in February 2015. She did not think she stood a chance against Douglas Alexander, the influential Labour incumbent who had served in his post since 1997. In 2010, his last reelection, he had won 60 percent of the vote. But when Black and her father, who served as her campaign manager, began knocking on doors in their district, Paisley and Renfrewshire South, they found hardly a single Labour voter. In a Labour-stronghold council estate called Johnstone, Black recalled to Turner, a man approached her holding a beer. She expected him to drunkenly berate her, but the man clapped her on the shoulder and said, "I'm voting for you!" Vote for her, they did. Black won the May election 23,548 votes to Alexander's 17,864 votes—a margin of 27 percent. Black did not believe it until it was over. She sat by herself that election night, playing guitar while her father watched the results come in. He did not tell her she had won until it was time for her to make her victory speech. She had written two speeches but had only practiced her concession. (Black's campaign went smoothly save for one gaffe involving her Twitter account. Unlike her much older opponents, Black has had the page since she was fourteen years old, and in it, her political rivals found fodder for embarrassment. In one older tweet, she had likened the alcoholic beverage Smirnoff Ice to "the drink of the gods.")

Black was among the fifty-six SNP members who won elections in 2015. The tight-knit group calls itself "the fifty-six." Many of them, like Black, were unfamiliar with the parliamentary protocol and got in trouble for unintentionally breaking rules during their first weeks. For her part, Black seated herself directly behind Labour heavyweight Harriet Harman on her first day in the House of Commons. The press interpreted the seating choice as a bold statement, an intimidation of the old party by the new party that threatens to take its place. Black admitted later that she just did not know that she was not supposed to sit there. Other aspects of the Commons, of which she is well aware, infuriate her and she has not been shy about voicing her frustration. For instance, members of the UK Parliament must be present in the House of Commons to vote on an issue. (In the Scottish and European parliaments, members can vote electronically.) She also takes issue with the long-standing, though unwritten, rule against clapping. "So you're not allowed to clap like an ordinary person, but you're allowed to bray like a donkey?" she quipped to Turner.

EARLY POLITICAL CAREER

Black's distaste for convention was best demonstrated in her maiden speech, ten weeks after the election, in July. (A maiden speech is an MP's introductory speech to the chamber. Traditionally, these speeches are pro forma and fairly uncontroversial.) Black's speech—which went viral, racking up eleven million views on the Internet by the end of the day of its posting—was a blistering indictment of austerity, the program of severe budget cuts that Britain implemented in 2010 following the global recession. Black said that Britain currently had "one of the most uncaring, uncompromising, and out-of-touch governments that the UK has seen since [conservative Prime Minister Margaret] Thatcher." Austerity has proved a tough road for Britain, where, as of the 2015 election, real wages were lower than they were before the recession in 2008. Young people, like many of Black's friends, are among the hardest hit, working low-wage jobs with few social benefits. Black criticized Chancellor George Osborne for cutting the budgets of programs that help people, imploring, "When the chancellor spoke in his budget about fixing the roof while the sun is shining, I would have to ask, on who[m] is the sun shining?" Black also noted the growing number of food banks in her constituency and revealed that one in five children in her district go to bed hungry. She argued that lawmakers' praise of food banks was misplaced. "Food banks are not part of the welfare state, they are a symbol that the welfare state is failing," she said.

Black's speech was rife with stinging sound bites, but her ire was specifically directed at the Labour Party. To fully understand the depth of Black's frustration—a frustration she shares with an overwhelming number of Scots—one has to go back several years to the administration of former British prime minister Tony Blair and the New Labour movement. In an effort to win conservative voters after the Thatcher years, the Labour Party compromised some of its liberal ideals and adopted a more centrist platform. The hugely unpopular war in Iraq and the financial crisis further tarnished New Labour's reputation, but the party's capitulation to conservative austerity measures a few years ago was the nail in the coffin for New Labour. Many Scots felt betrayed by the party, which was once considered the champion of the working class. They felt that the party was more closely aligned with the conservative Tories than with trade unions. As Black put it, the Labour Party left the Scots, not the other way around. Still, several months

into Black's first term, she told Zoe Williams for the *Guardian* (13 Oct. 2015) that the biggest difference between her and the Labour Party was in their stances on Scottish independence. In 2014, the Scottish Labour Party was against Scottish independence because it claimed solidarity with English Labour, and did not want to see the party lose power in England. "I don't think Scotland can reach its potential or get the society it deserves until we've got independence," Black told Williams. "I don't see the Labour Party backing that any time soon, and that's a fundamental difference between us. It's a big one." The SNP hopes to raise the issue again in the near future, and Black hopes that next time, the people will vote differently. Westminster makes her "fundamentally uncomfortable," she told Williams. "I don't want to be there. I don't want to make decisions there."

PERSONAL LIFE

Black still lives in Paisley, though she keeps an apartment in East London for her work as an MP. Her city apartment—as is the case for all MPs—is subsidized by the government. In her maiden speech, she noted that the chancellor recently abolished housing benefits for any citizen under twenty-one. "We are now in the ridiculous situation whereby, because I am an MP . . . I am also the only twenty-year-old in the whole of the UK that the chancellor is prepared to help with housing," she said.

SUGGESTED READING

Bennhold, Katrin. "Scottish Nationalists Rejoice in Big British Election Win." *New York Times*. New York Times, 8 May 2015. Web. 11 Nov. 2015.

Paxman, Jeremy. "Lunch with the FT: Mhairi Black." *Financial Times*. Financial Times, 31 July 2015. Web. 14 Nov. 2015.

Turner, Janice. "Mhairi Black: The SNP Firebrand." *Times*. The Times, 25 July 2015. Web. 14 Nov. 2015.

Williams, Zoe. "Mhairi Black: 'I Was Born. I Went To School. I Left. I Fried a Fish. Now I'm an MP.'" *Guardian*. Guardian News and Media, 13 Oct. 2015. Web. 15 Nov. 2015.

—*Molly Hagan*

Bruce Bochy

Born: April 16, 1955
Occupation: Baseball manager

Baseball manager Bruce Bochy is, as he told Steve Kettmann for *San Francisco Magazine* (19 Apr. 2013), "a believer in instincts," and judging from his career trajectory, Bochy's instincts are

Dilip Vishwanat/Getty Images

particularly good ones. Starting as a player in the minor leagues, Bochy made his major-league debut as a catcher for the Houston Astros in 1978 and went on to play for the New York Mets and the San Diego Padres. He found his true calling, however, in the late 1980s when he retired from playing the game and transitioned into team management. Over the following decades, he worked his way up through the Padres' minor-league affiliates before serving as manager for the team for more than a decade. In 2007 he was hired as manager for the San Francisco Giants and led them to the World Series three times.

A highly regarded manager who has amassed more than one thousand wins and four National League pennants during his years in the position, Bochy is a firm believer in collaboration between manager, coaches, and other team leaders. At the same time, he recognizes the value of the unique viewpoint and skill-set that successful managers possess. "You have to trust yourself," he explained to Kettmann. "You can't get caught up in thinking, 'We've got to do it this way, we've got to go by the book!' Sometimes you go against that book. It doesn't mean that you're always right, but, hopefully, you're right more than you're wrong, or chances are that you won't be doing the job long."

EARLY LIFE AND EDUCATION

Bruce Douglas Bochy was born on April 16, 1955, at Landes de Bussac, a US military installation in France. He was one of four children born to Gus and Melrose Bochy. Gus was a sergeant major in the US Army, and the family moved several times during Bochy's youth, depending on where his father was stationed. In

addition to France, the Bochy family lived in Panama and several US states before settling in Melbourne, Florida.

Bochy became interested in baseball at a young age, in large part because of his parents' interest in the sport. He played on Little League teams and went on to play for Melbourne High School. After graduating from high school in 1973, he enrolled in Brevard Community College, later known as Eastern Florida State College. He spent two years at the school, where he led Brevard's baseball team to the state championship in 1975. Bochy initially planned to transfer to a four-year college and continue to play college baseball. However, he ultimately opted to pursue a career in professional baseball instead.

EARLY CAREER

In the first phase of the 1975 Major League Baseball (MLB) draft, Bochy was drafted by the Chicago White Sox but decided not to sign with them. He was then drafted by the Houston Astros in the secondary round later that year and opted to join the National League team, spending several years playing for the Astros' minor-league affiliate teams, beginning with the Virginia-based Covington Astros, part of the Appalachian League. Bochy also played for affiliate teams based in Dubuque, Iowa, and in Columbus, Ohio.

During his time in the minor leagues, Bochy established himself as catcher and as a capable batter. He also became known for a characteristic that had far less to do with his athletic performance—the size of his head. "When I signed with the Houston Astros, they realized they didn't have a helmet big enough. They had to special-order one," he recalled to Tyler Kepner for the *New York Times Magazine* (27 Mar. 2015). "My nickname was Headly. When I was traded to New York and San Diego, I made sure my helmet went, too."

MAJOR LEAGUE PLAYER

In 1978, at the age of twenty-three, Bochy was called up to the major leagues and officially joined the Houston Astros. He made his debut with the team on July 19, 1978, in a game against the New York Mets. He played in fifty-four games that first season, accumulating a batting average of .266. In the 1980 postseason, he accompanied the team to the National League Championship Series, where the Astros were eventually defeated by the Philadelphia Phillies.

Bochy remained with the Astros until February 1981 when he was traded to the Mets. He spent all of the 1981 and a portion of the 1982 seasons playing for the Mets-affiliated Tidewater Tides minor-league team before joining the main team partway through 1982. His tenure with the

Mets was brief, and he was released by the team in early 1983.

It was Bochy's third and final major-league team that would prove the most significant to his career. He joined the San Diego Padres as a free agent shortly after leaving the Mets. He had a successful career with the Padres, assisting the team in the 1984 World Series, which the Padres ultimately lost to the Detroit Tigers. Serving as a backup catcher at the time, Bochy played in one game in the series and singled his only time at bat. He remained with the team until 1987 and spent a season with the minor-league Las Vegas Stars before retiring from play. However, Bochy's baseball career was far from over.

TAKING THE LEAD

Soon after retiring from professional baseball as a player, Bochy realized that he wanted to devote his career to managing teams. He was appointed manager of the Spokane Indians, the Padres' rookie-level minor-league team in 1989, and the team's first game under Bochy's leadership further underscored his newfound devotion to management. "We were playing Boise," he recalled to Kepner. "I was nervous, doing the lineup and looking at it five or six times, making sure I didn't mess up the first one. But it was an unbelievable experience. I didn't know if I'd ever get the opportunity to manage in the major leagues, and I probably would have been fine with that. That's how much I loved it."

Bochy went on to manage several of the Padres' minor-league affiliates over the years, leading teams to various championships. In late 1992, Bochy was promoted to third-base coach for the Padres, and although the role of coach differed significantly from that of manager, the move was crucial because it brought him into the main Padres organization. He remained as third-base coach throughout the 1994 season and in October was named the Padres team manager for the 1995 season, replacing outgoing manager Jim Riggleman.

Bochy's first season as manager came at a challenging time for major-league baseball. In response to a proposed salary cap and related salary disputes, major-league players went on strike during the summer of 1994. They remained on strike well into the spring of 1995, which resulted in the cancellation of many games, including the entire scheduled 1994 postseason. In a controversial move, some major-league teams, including the Padres organization, opted to bring in replacement players to try to hold an abbreviated 1995 season. "It was a nightmare for a first-year manager," Bochy told Emily Wilson for *SF Weekly* (15 June 2016). "I had to manage replacement players—I had plumbers and fire fighters. It was like the Bad News Bears. I was worried about losing credibility with my team." Despite these initial challenges, Bochy

found success and remained the Padres manager for more than a decade. He was named the National League's manager of the year in 1996 and oversaw the Padres when they won the National League pennant in 1998 and played in the World Series, eventually losing to the New York Yankees in a four-game sweep.

SUCCESS AS A MANAGER

Bochy's managerial style is to avoid micromanaging and preferring instead to ask for and then assess input from key figures in a team's organization. It is a style that did not come naturally but evolved as he gained more experience as a manager. "When I was young, I did everything. I ran every meeting, whether it was a pitching meeting or how we were going to defend opposing teams," he explained to Kettmann. "But I've learned that you have to let your coaches coach. . . . Delegating has become an important part of my job." Bochy is no pushover, though, especially when it comes to dealing with players. "You try to be as honest as you possibly can be, and I think they respect that," he told Kepner. "Players are smart. They know when you're sugarcoating something."

After twelve seasons with the team, Bochy left the Padres in 2007 and headed north to take over as manager of the San Francisco Giants, a move that proved beneficial to both Bochy and his new team. The Giants won the National League pennant three times under his leadership (2010, 2012, and 2014) and not only advanced to the World Series each time, but also won the world championship title each year, defeating the Texas Rangers, the Detroit Tigers, and the Kansas City Royals, respectively. Prior to Bochy's arrival in San Francisco, the Giants had not won a World Series in more than fifty years. Bochy's only focus, however, has been on the rare opportunity he has been given: "I know how fortunate I am to be doing what I'm doing and to have been doing it for so long," he told Kettmann.

A BOOK OF WALKS

In addition to his work playing and managing professional baseball, Bochy is an avid walker. "What got me into walking really was, with all the years of catching, the wear and tear on the legs. With my left knee at a point now where I can't run, I still wanted to stay active and, of course, stay in decent shape. So I took up walking," he explained to Kettmann. "Every city I go to, I get away, particularly after a game that didn't go well. I can say, 'I don't wanna sit in the bus. I'm gonna walk back by myself.' It is still kind of my therapy, I guess." In 2015, Bochy published *A Book of Walks*, a short book devoted to his thoughts on walking and favorite walking routes.

PERSONAL LIFE

Bochy met his wife, Kim, while in college. They married three years later and had two sons. Their younger son, Brett, is a pitcher who made his major-league debut with the San Francisco Giants in the fall of 2014. "It's never happened before in the major leagues: a father bringing his son in from the bullpen," Bochy told Kepner. "I told Dave Righetti, our pitching coach, 'This is the most stress I've ever felt.' I put Brett in a really tough situation: bases loaded. The game wasn't close, but still."

SUGGESTED READING

Bochy, Bruce. "Bruce Bochy Won't Let Success Go to His Head." Interview with Tyler Kepner. *New York Times Magazine*. New York Times, 27 Mar. 2015. Web. 12 Aug. 2016.

Keri, Jonah. "Is Bruce Bochy One of the Best Managers in Baseball History? (Yes. Here's Why.)" *Grantland*. ESPN Internet Ventures, 9 Oct. 2014. Web. 12 Aug. 2016.

Kettmann, Steve. "The SF Interview: Bruce Almighty." *San Francisco Magazine*. Modern Luxury, 19 Apr. 2013. Web. 12 Aug. 2016.

O'Connell, Robert. "Bruce Bochy and Ned Yost, Baseball's Great and Powerful Scapegoats." *Atlantic*. Atlantic Monthly Group, 29 Oct. 2014. Web. 12 Aug. 2016.

Schulman, Henry. "Meet Bruce Bochy: New Head Man. *SFGate*. Hearst Communications, 11 Mar. 2007. Web. 12 Aug. 2016.

Wilson, Emily. "Walking, Preparing, and Letting Players Be Themselves: Inside the Mind of the Giants' Bruce Bochy." *SF Weekly*. SF Weekly, 15 June 2016. Web. 12 Aug. 2016.

—*Joy Crelin*

David Bossie

Born: November 1, 1965
Occupation: President and chairman of Citizens United

David Bossie heads Citizens United, a conservative nonprofit corporation and lobbying group. He made his name in the 1990s, investigating the private lives and financial practices of President Bill Clinton and First Lady Hillary Clinton. He became a go-to source for information regarding the Whitewater scandal, and later served as the lead investigator in a congressional probe of the subject. In 2000 Bossie assumed his current position at Citizens United, and a few years later, motivated by the success of the left-wing political documentary *Fahrenheit 9/11* (2004), began producing political films with a right-wing point of view. Miffed that one of those films, *Hillary: The Movie* (2008), was found to be in

Gage Skidmore/CC BY-SA 3.0

conflict with the campaign finance regulations set forth by the Federal Election Commission (FEC), Bossie sued the FEC.

The resulting case, *Citizens United v. Federal Election Commission*, was heard before the Supreme Court and decided in 2010 in favor of Citizens United. This victory changed the narrative of Bossie's life and was a landmark moment in US politics, as it overturned a key provision of the 2002 McCain-Feingold campaign finance reform law. After having left Washington to become the producer of agitprop films that garnered little attention, Bossie was suddenly at the center of a hugely influential Supreme Court decision. Most notably, the decision fostered the formation of entities called super PACs (political action committees), which are not directly affiliated with specific candidates or their campaigns, but may collect donations of unlimited size and engage in unlimited political spending on an independent basis. In 2014, according to Gabrielle Levy for the US *News and World Report* (21 Jan. 2015), the Brennan Center for Justice found that outside spending in Senate races had more than doubled since the case was decided in 2010. The report further stated that this additional spending was coming from a very small slice of the population. Super PACs spent around $1 billion in federal elections from 2010 to 2014, and "nearly 60 percent of the money came from just 195 individuals and their spouses," Levy wrote.

EARLY LIFE

David Norman Bossie was born in Boston, Massachusetts, on November 1, 1965. His father worked as an x-ray technician and his mother was a nurse. He is the second of four children, and grew up in Connecticut and Michigan before settling in Montgomery County, Maryland. Bossie attended both Towson University in Baltimore and the University of Maryland, though he never earned a degree. In 1984, when he was eighteen years old, Bossie volunteered on President Ronald Reagan's reelection campaign. He worked on a congressional campaign in 1986, and in 1988, he served as Senator Bob Dole's Maryland youth organizer in the presidential primary. Through the Dole campaign, he met a political activist named Floyd Brown, who was working as a Dole organizer in the Midwest. (Brown was responsible for the infamous "Willie Horton" attack ad in 1988. The ad, which used the case of escaped inmate Willie Horton to paint Democratic presidential candidate Michael Dukakis as soft on crime, was one of the first ads run by an outside group during an election, and derailed Dukakis's campaign. Brown founded Citizens United the same year.) Bossie worked briefly for conservative political activist Morton Blackwell before joining Citizens United in 1991.

"THE SECRET SPINNER"

In 1992 Bossie was living in a firehouse in Burtonsville, Maryland, where he was a volunteer firefighter, and working for President George H. W. Bush's reelection campaign against Arkansas governor Bill Clinton. He was also a top official at Citizens United. During the 1992 election, Citizens United oversaw the publication of Brown's book *"Slick Willie": Why America Cannot Trust Bill Clinton* (1992). Bossie is credited with tracking down most of the salacious stories in the book, including one for which he hounded the family of one of Clinton's former students who had committed suicide years earlier. According to a report on the *CBS Evening News* in 1992, Bossie located the woman's parents after discovering that her father was in a hospital in Georgia, recovering from a stroke. Bossie and an associate went to the hospital, where they interrogated the mother and father, asking them if their daughter committed suicide because she was pregnant with Clinton's child. Bossie's story turned out to be baseless; Bossie apologized for his error, then turned his attention to Clinton's finances.

Bossie spent 1993 and 1994 travelling to Arkansas, investigating Bill and Hillary Clintons' involvement in the failed Whitewater Development Corporation, a real estate venture in which they had invested starting in 1978. The Whitewater scandal, as it soon became known, was a convoluted tale that first came to national attention with Clinton's 1992 presidential campaign. Bossie became a go-to source on Whitewater for major news outlets including the *New York Times* and the *Washington Post*. His role led *Newsweek*

to dub him "the secret spinner" a few years later. It was through these activities that Bossie befriended Republican Congressman Dan Burton in 1994, and in 1995, Bossie became Republican Senator Lauch Faircloth's personal aide on the Senate Whitewater Committee. In that role, he quickly rose from being a tipster to an active participant in directing the investigation. In 1996, Bossie joined Congressman Burton's Government Reform and Oversight Committee, which was investigating President Clinton's 1996 campaign finance practices, as a chief investigator. He was forced to resign his position in 1998, after he released a selectively edited transcript of a conversation he had with Webster L. Hubbell, a former senior Justice Department official who was serving a jail sentence for overbilling clients at his private law firm.

By some accounts, Bossie's departure was overdue. Both Democrats and Republicans were uncomfortable with Bossie's presence on a committee whose purpose was becoming an embarrassment to the Republican Party. Within a very short period of time, Bossie had become one of the most hated men in Washington. In a short profile of Bossie for the *Washington Post* (13 Nov. 1997), Lloyd Grove wrote that "not since Roy Cohn—the bare-knuckled chief counsel for Sen. Joe McCarthy in the Red-hunting hearings of the 1950s—has a congressional staffer been so thoroughly demonized by his enemies." Some accused him of grandstanding, and one member of Burton's committee, according to Eric Schmitt of the *New York Times* (7 May 1998), said in a statement that the committee could not function because of Bossie's "unrelenting, self-promoting actions." In his resignation letter, Bossie blamed his departure on Democrats who had subjected Burton "to never-ending and unjustified attacks."

HILLARY: THE MOVIE (2008)

In June 2004, four months before President George W. Bush faced reelection, controversial filmmaker Michael Moore released a documentary called *Fahrenheit 9/11*, which was highly critical of Bush's decision to invade Iraq and Afghanistan in the wake of the terrorist attacks on September 11, 2001. The film won numerous awards and became the highest-grossing documentary of all time. Bossie had never produced a film before, but felt that Moore's film called for a rebuttal. He therefore had Citizens United fund a documentary called *Celsius 41.11* (2004)—its title a reference to temperature at which brain cells start to die—as a response to *Fahrenheit 9/11* but also as an attack on Democratic presidential nominee John Kerry. The FEC ruled that Citizens United was bound by a provision of campaign finance law that prohibited corporations from paying to broadcast or promote the film on television within sixty days of the general election, because it qualified as "electioneering communication." "I mean Michael Moore made his movie and we saw its impact," Bossie told Brian Lamb for C-SPAN (12 Feb. 2010). "We decided to try and answer that and so we were told by the Federal Election Commission, you can't."

Bossie was irked by the decision. He, like many conservatives, was not a fan of the law on which the ruling was based, the McCain-Feingold Act (or the Bipartisan Campaign Reform Act of 2002); the law sought to regulate the influence of money in political elections, but conservatives felt it infringed on the right to free speech. (For many years, outside individuals, corporations, and labor unions spent millions on "issue" television ads that promoted or attacked specific candidates but avoided language that made them subject to laws that regulated official campaign ads—such issue ads, and the money behind them, were one of McCain-Feingold's largest targets.) So, in 2008, Bossie and Citizens United made another movie, this time about Senator Hillary Clinton, who was running in the Democratic presidential primary against Senator Barack Obama. Bossie was candid about his reason for making the film. Despite his long-standing vendetta against the Clintons, he told Lamb, "[I]t had nothing to do with Hillary Clinton. Hillary Clinton was a vehicle, if you will. The movie was a vehicle. And so we knew we were going to run into road blocks and obstacles because of 2004, what happened there." Bossie and Citizens United knew that the FEC would try to block their attempts to broadcast the film as an on-demand cable movie, and they preemptively sued the FEC for violating their right to do so. "It was 100 percent calculated toward fighting the FEC," Bossie told David Weigel for *Slate* (9 Aug. 2011).

CITIZENS UNITED V. FEDERAL ELECTION COMMISSION

The FEC indeed deemed the film, *Hillary: The Movie*, "electioneering communication"—essentially a campaign ad, as opposed to journalism or entertainment—and a three-judge panel at the federal district court in Washington upheld that ruling, writing, as quoted by Jeffrey Toobin for the *New Yorker* (21 May 2012), that the movie is "susceptible of no other interpretation than to inform the electorate that Senator Clinton is unfit for office, that the United States would be a dangerous place in a President Hillary Clinton world, and that viewers should vote against her." For his appeal, Bossie hired prominent attorney Theodore Olson, who had served as US solicitor general under President George W. Bush, to represent Citizens United. (Olson's wife Barbara was a conservative commentator and outspoken Hillary Clinton critic who died in the terrorist attacks on September 11, 2001; Bossie dedicated

Hillary: The Movie to her.) Olson had successfully argued numerous cases before the Supreme Court, including *Bush v. Gore* in 2000, so Bossie was confident in the choice.

As the case proceeded, it became clear that the Supreme Court, or rather, the conservative majority on the court, was looking to overturn several major decisions regarding campaign finance law—the court upheld most of McCain-Feingold in *McConnell v. Federal Election Commission* (2003). The final ruling—which split the court 5–4—was handed down on January 21, 2010. Justice Anthony Kennedy, who wrote the majority opinion, took the view that the provision of McCain-Feingold that stipulated pre-election bans on corporate-funded political advertisements (the ones with which *Hillary: The Movie* was in conflict) was a form of government censorship and thus in violation of Citizen United's First Amendment right to free speech. His framing of the argument paved the way for the rise of entities like super PACs and confirmed that in the eyes of the Supreme Court, corporations like Citizens United were entitled to the same inalienable rights possessed by individuals under the Constitution. The ruling struck a blow to over a century of campaign finance law. "Clearly McCain-Feingold was a hindrance on every American's freedom of speech," Bossie told Weigel a year after his victory, citing the rousing success of the Republican Party in the 2010 midterm election. "The American people got to hear more information, not less, and the American people are incredibly smart. I for one am glad that our victory shed light on that and I think the new freshman class in Congress would agree."

PERSONAL LIFE

Bossie is married to Susan Bossie, with whom he has four children: Isabella, Griffin, Lily Campbell, and Margaret Reagan. They live in Montgomery County, Maryland.

SUGGESTED READING

Grove, Lloyd. "A Firefighter's Blazing Trail; David Bossie Is Throwing Sparks on the GOP Campaign Finance Probe." *Washington Post.* Washington Post, 13 Nov. 1997. Web. 9 Dec. 2015.

Lamb, Brian. "Q&A with David Bossie." *C-SPAN.* National Cable Satellite, 12 Feb. 2010. Web. 9 Dec. 2015.

Levy, Gabrielle. "How Citizens United Has Changed Politics in 5 Years." *US News and World Report.* US News and World Report, 21 Jan. 2015. Web. 10 Dec. 2015.

Miller, Mark. "The Secret Spinner." *Newsweek.* Newsweek, 18 Feb. 1996. Web. 8 Dec. 2015.

Schmitt, Eric. "Testing of a President: The Congressional Aide; Top Investigator for House Panel Leaves under Fire." *New York Times.*

New York Times, 7 May 1998. Web. 9 Dec. 2015.

Toobin, Jeffrey. "Money Unlimited: How Chief Justice John Roberts Orchestrated the Citizens United Decision." *New Yorker*. Condé Nast, 21 May 2012. Web. 9 Dec. 2015.

Weigel, David. "David Bossie, President and Chairman, Citizens United: How Citizens United Changed the American Political Campaign." *Slate*. Slate, 9 Aug. 2011. Web. 9 Dec. 2015.

—*Molly Hagan*

Nick Bostrom

Born: March 10, 1973
Occupation: Philosopher

In 2014 an unusually dense and philosophical book became a *New York Times* best seller: Nick Bostrom's *Superintelligence: Paths, Dangers, Strategies*, which carefully and cogently lays out the author's concerns about the likely impending development of artificial intelligence (AI). Bostrom believes that AI poses an existential threat to humanity—far greater than any previous threat, including the advent of nuclear weapons—because AI, with its presumed ability to improve itself exponentially, could easily outstrip the human race as the most intelligent life form on the planet. Although this idea sounds like the plot to any number of science-fiction stories, Bostrom's serious take on the issue has

Future of Humanity Institute/[CC BY-SA 4.0]/Wikimedia Commons

earned plaudits from a number of noteworthy technology giants, including Microsoft founder Bill Gates and Tesla Motors and SpaceX founder Elon Musk.

Bostrom has been studying these potential risks to the human race for more than twenty years. As the founding director of the Future of Humanity Institute at the University of Oxford, he conducts research into the field of superintelligence, as well as into related areas of philosophical study such as existential risk, the anthropic principle, and ethics of human enhancement. Although he expresses concern about AI, he supports the idea of a transhumanist future in which human beings could overcome many of their current genetic, mental, and physical limitations, possibly by transforming their consciousness into software. He also believes that AI could be a useful tool to humanity, provided its scope is limited and controlled by humans.

EARLY LIFE AND EDUCATION

Niklas Bostrom was born on March 10, 1973, in Helsingborg, Sweden. An only child who was raised on the southern coast of Sweden, he found himself growing bored by school at a very young age. In a brief description of his background written for his personal website, he recalled, "At age fifteen or sixteen I had an intellectual awakening, and [felt] that I had wasted the first one-and-a-half decades of my life." He came to this realization after stumbling across a collection of nineteenth-century German philosophy at a local library. Taking the book into a nearby forest and absorbing the works of Friedrich Nietzsche and Arthur Schopenhauer, he had something of an epiphany about the potentials available for his intellectual discovery. Bostrom continued, "I resolved to focus on what was important. Since I did not know what was important, and I did not know how to find out, I decided to start by trying to place myself in a better position to find out. So I began a project of intellectual self-development, which I pursued with great intensity for the next one-and-a-half decades." To this end, he isolated himself from old friends and took special exams so that he could complete his last year of high school from home in just ten weeks.

After graduating, Bostrom first attended Umeå University, where he immersed himself in his studies—so much so that he ended up expelled for it. "I was called in to the head of [psychology] department's office, and he told me that he'd found out I'd been studying mathematics, physics, and philosophy alongside psychology," he recalled to Jamie Condliffe for the University of Oxford's *Blueprint* magazine (July 2012). "He computed that it was psychologically impossible to cope with such a heavy course load—so I was asked to leave!" Undaunted, Bostrom enrolled in the University of Gothenburg, where he completed his bachelor of arts degree in philosophy, mathematics, mathematical logic, and artificial intelligence in 1994, setting a national record for undergraduate studies in the process. He went on to earn master's degrees in philosophy and physics from Stockholm University, where he studied the writings of W. V. Quine, an analytical philosopher who studied the relationship between language and reality.

For his additional postgraduate work, Bostrom left Sweden for England, where he earned master of science degrees in physics, philosophy, and computational neuroscience from King's College London in 1996, followed by a doctorate in philosophy from the London School of Economics in 2000. His dissertation was selected by Professor Robert Nozick to be a part of Routledge's Studies in Philosophy: Outstanding Dissertations series, for which only seven dissertations in the world are chosen each year. A revised version was published under the title *Anthropic Bias: Observation Selection Effects in Science and Philosophy* in 2002.

MAIN AREAS OF STUDY

From 2000 to 2002, Bostrom was a lecturer at Yale University in the United States. In 2003 he joined the faculty of the University of Oxford, first as a postdoctoral fellow and then as a university fellow, before becoming a professor with the Faculty of Philosophy in 2008. Since 2005 his primary work at Oxford has been to serve as the director of the Future of Humanity Institute, which he founded as part of the Faculty of Philosophy and the Oxford Martin School. In 2011 he took on the additional role of director of the Programme on the Impacts of Future Technology at the Oxford Martin School. In these roles, Bostrom has five main fields of study: existential risk; the simulation argument; anthropics, specifically observational selection effects; transhumanism, and the bioethics thereof; and the implication of consequentialism.

In the field of existential risks, Bostrom looks at the ways technology could bring about the end of the human race. Unlike many intellectuals who look at such present risks as plague or nuclear war, he focuses on the areas of future technologies that may cause the extinction of the human race, such as weaponized nanotechnology—machines that could attack human beings on the cellular level—or AI not under human control. In *Global Catastrophic Risks* (2008), a volume he coedited with Milan M. Ćirković, Bostrom outlines the differences between such existential risks and so-called global catastrophic risks, a broader category of dangers that includes nuclear war, plagues, and climate change.

The simulation argument, first postulated by Austrian roboticist and futurist Hans Moravec, raises the possibility that what human beings experience as reality could very well be a computer simulation. Bostrom has expanded on this idea, arguing that there is essentially a one-in-three chance that the entire human race is living in a virtual-reality simulation that is indistinguishable from the real world, similar to the plot behind the 1999 film *The Matrix*. This is one of three possibilities raised in Bostrom's 2003 paper "Are You Living in a Computer Simulation?"; the other two are (1) that the human race will become extinct before it develops technology capable of creating such a simulation, or (2) that any civilization that does develop such technology would not produce the number of simulations necessary to create a convincing reality, either for ethical reasons or because the computational power required would be too great. Bostrom's argument is that at least one of these three possibilities must be correct.

In the field of anthropics—the philosophical idea that the universe must be compatible with a conscious and sapient life-form able to observe it—Bostrom seeks to develop "the first mathematically explicit theory of observation selection effects," according to his website. As he explained to Ross Andersen in an interview for the *Atlantic* (6 Mar. 2012), "An observation selection effect is a selection effect introduced not by limitations in our measurement instrument, but rather by the fact that all observations require the existence of an observer." His book *Anthropic Bias*, derived from his dissertation, discusses this topic at length.

Transhumanism is a field that Bostrom has long been involved with. In 1997 he cofounded the World Transhumanist Association (now Humanity+), which seeks to enhance human abilities and the human condition through "the ethical use of technology." One major area of interest, according to Bostrom, is the possibility of slowing or even reversing the aging process. However, he is also keenly aware of the ethical concerns involved in such an undertaking. "It's one thing if we are talking about adult, competent citizens deciding what to do with their own bodies," he explained to John Sutherland for the *Guardian* (9 May 2006). "If, on the other hand, we are thinking of modifying children, or selecting embryos, then there is another set of ethical questions that arise. There is a further set of ethical questions relating to access. If some of the technologies . . . turn out to be very expensive, then what mechanisms should be in place to ensure fairness?" *Human Enhancement* (2009), which Bostrom coedited with Australian philosopher and bioethicist Julian Savulescu, explores some of these ethical questions.

Bostrom's final field of study is the implications of consequentialism, that is, the belief that the consequences of one's actions are the only way to understand the rightness or wrongness of those actions. It is also sometimes known by the shorthand phrase "the end justifies the means."

SUPERINTELLIGENCE

The work that has made Bostrom one of the more quotable philosophers today is *Superintelligence: Paths, Dangers, Strategies*, his 2014 book that explores the ways superintelligent agents such as AIs could produce profound benefits for human society if controlled properly but, if left unchecked, could create an existential risk for the human race. Although the modern concept of artificial intelligence has been around since the earliest mainframe computers, many living computer experts believe that humanity could now be on the verge of a breakthrough in AI—possibly within the next couple of decades. (Some experts theorize that human-level intelligent computers could be created as early as 2040; others believe that it could come later in the century, around 2075.) Regardless of the time frame, Bostrom believes that unchecked AIs could easily outclass human beings, regardless of biological advancements humans may have undergone by then.

Throughout his book, Bostrom postulates various ways AI could be achieved. However the means, he argues that the only ways to properly contain AI would be through either capability control methods or motivation selection methods. Capability control methods would limit the AI's capacity in some way, such as by "boxing" it, either physically or informationally; it would not be linked to the Internet and would not have access to other computers, thus preventing it from upgrading itself or interacting with the outside world. Motivation selection methods involve designing an AI in such a way that it would not "want" to act in a harmful manner—for example, establishing a set of rules to follow, such as Isaac Asimov's Three Laws of Robotics.

In addition to impressing thinkers such as Gates and Musk, *Superintelligence* wowed a number of leading book critics. In a review for the *Financial Times* (13 July 2014), Clive Cookson wrote, "Bostrom's writing, often clear and vivid, sometimes veers into opaque language that betrays his background as a philosophy professor. But there is no doubting the force of his arguments. While he does not claim that an existential catastrophe is an inevitable long-term consequence of AI research, he shows the risk is large enough for society to think now about ways to prevent it by endowing future AI with positive human values." In *Reason* (12 Sept. 2014), Ronald Bailey wrote, "Bostrom cogently argues that the prospect of superintelligent machines is 'the most important and most daunting challenge humanity has ever faced.' If we fail to meet this challenge, he concludes, malevolent or indifferent artificial intelligence (AI) will likely destroy us all." He later added, "Bostrom is most likely right that once a superintelligent AI is conjured into existence, it will be impossible for us to turn it off or change its goals. He makes a strong case that working to ensure the survival of humanity after the coming intelligence explosion is, as he writes, 'the essential task of our age.'"

AWARDS AND RECOGNITIONS

Bostrom has been interviewed more than five hundred times for various media outlets and has given addresses to a wide variety of audiences. In 2009 he received the inaugural Eugene R. Gannon Award for the Continued Pursuit of Human Advancement and in 2009 and 2015 the editors of *Foreign Policy* included him in their list of the Top 100 Global Thinkers (renamed the Leading Global Thinkers list in 2013). His works have been translated into more than twenty-four languages, and more than one hundred translations and reprints of his works have been published around the world.

PERSONAL LIFE

Nick Bostrom's wife, Susan, holds a doctorate in the sociology of medicine. Despite having been together for more than a dozen years and having a young son together, they have rarely lived on the same continent; Bostrom makes his home in Oxford, England, while Susan prefers to remain in Montreal, Canada.

SUGGESTED READING

Bailey, Ronald. "Will Superintelligent Machines Destroy Humanity?" Rev. of *Superintelligence: Paths, Dangers, Strategies*, by Nick Bostrom. *Reason.com*. Reason Foundation, 12 Sept. 2014. Web. 14 Apr. 2016.

Bostrom, Nick. *Nick Bostrom's Home Page*. Author, Apr. 2016. Web. 14 Apr. 2016.

Bostrom, Nick. "We're Underestimating the Risk of Human Extinction." Interview by Ross Andersen. *Atlantic*. Atlantic Monthly, 6 Mar. 2012. Web. 14 Apr. 2016.

Condliffe, Jamie. "Back to the Future." *Blueprint* July 2012: 11. *University of Oxford*. Web. 14 Apr. 2016.

Cookson, Clive. Rev. of *Superintelligence: Paths, Dangers, Strategies*, by Nick Bostrom. *FT.com*. Financial Times, 13 July 2014. Web. 14 Apr. 2016.

Khatchadourian, Raffi. "The Doomsday Invention." *New Yorker*. Condé Nast, 23 Nov. 2015. Web. 14 Apr. 2016.

Sutherland, John. "The Ideas Interview: Nick Bostrom." *Guardian*. Guardian News and Media, 9 May 2006. Web. 14 Apr. 2016.

SELECTED WORKS

Anthropic Bias: Observation Selection Effects in Science and Philosophy, 2002; *Global Catastrophic Risks*, 2008; *Human Enhancement*,

2009; *Superintelligence: Paths, Dangers, Strategies*, 2014

—Christopher Mari

Jamelle Bouie

Occupation: Journalist

Jamelle Bouie is the chief political correspondent for *Slate* and a political analyst for *CBS News*. He began his career with the liberal magazine *American Prospect* in 2010, joined the staff of the *Daily Beast* in 2013, and later joined *Slate* in 2014. He has also contributed to the *New Yorker*, the *Washington Post*, the *Nation* and the *Atlantic*. Bouie, who is also a regular guest on the television show *Face the Nation*, is best known for his articles about politics and race, and has spent much of the past year chronicling the rise of real estate mogul turned Republican presidential nominee Donald Trump. A number of Bouie's articles explore Trump's racist rhetoric: his proposed ban on Muslim immigrants, his characterization of Mexican immigrants as "criminals" and "rapists," and his refusal to disavow connections to white supremacist groups like the Ku Klux Klan. These views are not exclusive to Trump, Bouie argues—Bouie first wrote about a troubling strain of racism in the conservative Tea Party movement for the *American Prospect* in 2010—but Trump's candidacy has certainly given them a voice, welcoming once-ostracized fringe groups into mainstream politics.

EARLY LIFE AND EDUCATION

Bouie was born in Jacksonville, Florida. He and his younger brother Jarin, who serves in the Navy, grew up mostly in Virginia Beach, Virginia with their parents. Bouie attended school in the rural, predominantly white town of Pungo, where, as a dark-skinned African American boy, he learned to deal with racism at a young age. Bouie traces his interest in American history back to middle school, when he first participated in political debates. In high school, he joined the Model United Nations (also known as Model UN or MUN). He enrolled at the University of Virginia (UVA) in Charlottesville with a notion to pursue work in public policy, and graduated with bachelor's degrees in political and social thought and government in 2009, after completing his thesis on white evangelicals and their response to the civil rights movement.

Bouie stayed in Charlottesville to work for the university's Miller Center for Public Affairs before accepting a writing fellowship with *American Prospect* magazine in 2010. His early assignments focused on the 2010 midterm elections.

Jamelle Bouie/[CC BY 2.0]/Flickr/Wikimedia Commons

During his three years with the magazine, Bouie also chronicled the rise of the conservative Tea Party movement and the racialized acts of violence—beginning with the murder of Trayvon Martin in February 2012—that would give birth to the Black Lives Matter movement. His articles introduced readers to his preferred mode of political analysis: using historical events to contextualize contemporary ones. Describing his outlook to a reporter for the University of Wisconsin–Madison (20 Apr. 2016), Bouie said, "My hobbyist interest in American history has centered my thinking in terms of 'this can't be the first time something like this has happened so what like this happened before and what lessons can we pull from it to help us explain what is happening now.'" Bouie was named a Knobler Fellow at the Nation Institute in 2011.

HOUSING POLICY AT THE *DAILY BEAST*

Bouie joined the staff of the *Daily Beast* in 2013. In addition to his usual beat covering politics, Bouie also began writing about housing policy. In an article called "How We Built the Ghettos" (13 Mar. 2014), Bouie explored the history of housing discrimination in the United States. He touched on a practice called redlining, which began in the 1930s. Redlining deemed black neighborhoods ineligible for home loans and insurance, all while actively preventing black people from moving into white neighborhoods. "In short, redlining forced blacks into particular areas and then starved those areas of affordable capital," Bouie wrote. "Combined with widespread job discrimination—which barred blacks from public employment and forced them into low-wage labor—you had neighborhoods that were impoverished by design." These neighborhoods would later be referred to in coded terms like "inner city" or "ghetto." In the same article, Bouie also wrote about a practice called "contract buying," in which white real estate agents offered black homebuyers low down payments only to charge them nearly double (and in some cases, more than double) their home's actual purchase price. Missed payments resulted in automatic eviction, and without equity or formal processes of recourse (which would have been available to white tenants), black tenants lost both their homes and their wealth. Bouie also wrote about blockbusting, in which white real estate agents drove black tenants into white neighborhoods. As white tenants flocked to suburban areas, the real estate agents routinely broke up spaces meant for single families into multiple units, renting more and smaller spaces for sometimes quadruple the previous rent of the space as a whole. All of these practices continued through the 1960s. The Fair Housing Act of 1968 was meant to address these practices and the social woes that arose because of them, but as Bouie wrote, the law was only sporadically enforced. "After a half century (or more), it's not hard to see how we get to here from there: When you prevent a whole class of people from building wealth, accessing capital, or leaving impoverished areas, you guarantee cultural dysfunction and deep, generational poverty," he concluded. "When it comes to inner-city poverty—we built that."

"WHY DO MILLENNIALS NOT UNDERSTAND RACISM?"
Bouie joined *Slate* as a political correspondent in 2014. In May of that year, he wrote a widely read piece called "Why Do Millennials Not Understand Racism?" The article was inspired by an MTV poll that found that most young people, although ideologically more committed to equality and fairness than their parents, upheld "colorblindness," and were opposed to measures like affirmative action that specifically address race. Bouie attributes these seemingly mutually exclusive opinions to a general confusion about what racism actually is. "From these results, it's clear that—like most Americans—millennials see racism as a matter of different treatment, justified by race, that you solve by removing race from the equation," he wrote. According to Bouie, this view is woefully inadequate. Citing the nefarious creation of the "ghettos" he wrote about for the *Daily Beast*, Bouie wrote that racism "isn't just different treatment— it's unequal treatment rooted in unequal conditions." He continues: "Millennials have grown up in a world where we talk about race without racism—or don't talk about it at all—and where 'skin color' is the explanation for racial inequality, as if ghettos are

ghettos because they are black, and not because they were created" by white supremacy.

Bouie covered similar territory in an article for the *Nation*—"Race, Millennials and Reverse Discrimination" (26 Apr. 2012)—but the *Slate* article received far more attention. Bouie was asked to share his views on National Public Radio (NPR), while his article drew ire from conservative websites and publications like the *National Review,* where Bouie is a perennial target. The *Review* published a column by Kevin D. Williamson a few days later (responding to a different article about racism) called "Jamelle Bouie, Wrong as Usual." As the website for World Trust, a nonprofit social justice organization, observed, Bouie's article "touched a national nerve" (17 July 2014).

COVERING THE 2016 PRESIDENTIAL ELECTION
Bouie was named a political analyst for CBS News in November 2015. He had previously appeared on the CBS program *Face the Nation,* but the official title meant that he would also become a regular on other CBS programs like *CBS Evening News with Scott Pelley* and *CBS This Morning.* He is currently a part of the core team of commentators covering the 2016 presidential election.

Bouie has also covered this topic extensively for *Slate.* In an early 2016 article for *Slate* called "How Trump Happened" (13 Mar. 2016), Bouie theorizes that this contemporary strain of overt racism in the political right is a direct response to the presidency of Barack Obama. Although Obama's politics are quite moderate, Bouie wrote, Obama as an African American man is a radical "political symbol." For many poor and middle class white people, his ascendancy came as a shock. "When coupled with the broad decline in incomes and living standards caused by the Great Recession, it seemed to signal the end of a hierarchy that had always placed white Americans at the top, delivering status even when it couldn't give material benefits," Bouie wrote. Bouie wrote that whites have become "hyperaware" of their status, and often blame Obama for sowing racial division. In reality, Obama has given voice to minorities, particularly African Americans, who have hitherto been comfortably ignored. Trump is a perfect surrogate for these disgruntled white voters who view gains for black people, Muslims, or Mexicans as a threat to their way of life. He rose to political prominence by touting "birtherism," the conspiracy theory that Obama is actually a foreigner (and a Muslim) masquerading as an American citizen. Rather than distance himself from such erroneous views, Trump, even after clinching the Republican nomination, doubled down on them. In an article for *Slate* published in July called "Our Political Culture Doesn't Know What to Do with Trump's Explicit Prejudice"

(5 July 2016), Bouie, citing the candidate's penchant for retweeting white supremacist and neo-Nazi accounts on Twitter, wrote that Trump's rhetoric was unprecedented in modern political discourse. "Right now, Trump is showing his dedicated following of white supremacists that you can deny the humanity of other people and still thrive in mainstream politics," Bouie wrote. Trump's rhetoric does not bode well for minorities, he added; "If this all feels dangerous—like the beginning of a new, more frightening kind of politics—that's because it is."

Bouie has also written about former presidential candidate Senator Bernie Sanders and his influence on the Democratic Party platform; Democratic nominee Hillary Clinton's troubled history with voters; and even the politics—made pertinent by Clinton's candidacy—of President Bill Clinton's 1994 crime bill. In the latter, Bouie called for historical perspective as he recalled the complex stew of political forces that created the deeply flawed bill. "We can't lose sight of the fact that the crime bill did real damage to countless communities, harming people it was supposed to help. But we also can't turn this into a simple morality play of good guys and bad ones," he wrote (11 Apr. 2016). "With the crime bill, there is a real gap between good intentions and actual consequences that is worth considering, not as an excuse or a defense, but as a lesson. A reminder that politics is full of the unintended, and that as a profoundly human endeavor, it's almost never a story of perfect heroes and simple villains."

PERSONAL LIFE
Bouie is a prolific photographer and culinary enthusiast. He married Tess Krovetz, an elementary school teacher, in 2016. The two met as students at the University of Virginia and live in Washington, DC.

SUGGESTED READING
Bouie, Jamelle. "A Conversation with Jamelle Bouie." *Hairpin*. Hairpin, 14 Mar. 2014. Web. 18 Aug. 2016.
"Slate Writer in Residence Puts Today's Politics in Historical Context." *Robert M. La Follete School of Public Affairs*. U of Wisconsin–Madison, 20 Apr. 2016. Web. 1 Aug. 2016.
Williamson, Kevin D. "Jamelle Bouie, Wrong as Usual." *National Review*. National Review, 28 May 2014. Web. 4 Aug. 2016.

SELECTED WORKS
"Our Political Culture Doesn't Know What to Do with Trump's Explicit Prejudice." *Slate* 5 July 2016; "The Messy, Very Human Politics of Bill Clinton's Crime Bill." *Slate* 11 Apr. 2016; "How Trump Happened." *Slate* 13 Mar. 2016; "Why Do Millennials Not Understand Racism?" *Slate*

16 May 2014; "How We Built the Ghettos." *Daily Beast* 13 Mar. 2014

—Molly Hagan

Heather Boushey
Born: 1970
Occupation: Executive director of Washington Center for Equitable Growth

For economist Heather Boushey, income inequality is one of the most serious issues plaguing the United States in the early twenty-first century. The executive director of the Washington Center for Equitable Growth, an organization dedicated to researching and determining how to combat such inequality, Boushey has spent decades analyzing the root causes and exacerbating factors that keep many Americans in poverty, among them ineffective government assistance programs, gender disparities in the workforce, and an overall lack of work-family balance in US society.

In light of such persistent issues, Boushey has dedicated much of her career to explaining the need for major economic and social reforms to policymakers, transforming complex economic data into easy-to-understand reports. The author of numerous papers and articles on economic inequality, she has testified before congressional committees on multiple occasions and in 2015 began to advise Democratic presidential candidate Hillary Clinton on economic

Heather Boushey/CC BY 3.0/Wikimedia Commons

inequality. Although policymakers ultimately have a long way to go, Boushey has been delighted by the newfound willingness of some politicians to discuss issues such as the wage gap between male and female workers, paid family leave, and welfare reform. "It is beyond exciting to see things that you have been . . . working on spreadsheets for and thinking about for a really long time actually entering the political discourse," she told Eric Garcia for the *Atlantic* (12 June 2015).

EARLY LIFE AND EDUCATION

Heather Marie Boushey was born in 1970 to Bobbi and Michael Boushey. Her mother was a bookkeeper, while her father worked as a machinist for the aerospace company Boeing. Boushey has noted on multiple occasions that her family was a union household, indicating that this fact may have had some influence on the development of her point of view regarding workplace- and income-related reforms.

Boushey grew up in Mukilteo, a suburb of Seattle, Washington. After graduating from Mariner High School in 1988, she enrolled in Hampshire College in Amherst, Massachusetts, where she studied economics. Boushey earned her bachelor's degree from the college in 1992. She went on to attend the New School for Social Research in New York City, completing her PhD in economics in 1998. Her dissertation concerned New York City's Work Experience Program (WEP), a program in which individuals seeking government assistance were required to work in exchange for the benefits they receive, which she argued did not adequately address the causes of poverty facing the city's residents.

While still at the New School, Boushey contributed to a number of publications as a writer and editor. She coedited the books *Gender and Political Economy: Incorporating Diversity into Theory and Policy* (1997) and *Workfare, Welfare, and Jobs: An Educator's Guidebook* (1997) and contributed writing to the former as well as to publications such as *Review of Political Economy*.

EARLY CAREER

After earning her PhD, Boushey completed a postdoctoral fellowship with the New York City Housing Authority (NYCHA). During that time, she researched welfare reform and authored reports and papers on the transition from welfare to work for the housing authority.

Boushey next joined the Economic Policy Institute (EPI) in Washington, DC, as an economist. In that role, she continued to research the transition from welfare to work as well as the needs of low-income working families. In early 2002 she testified before the US Senate Committee on Health, Education, Labor, and Pensions, discussing the difficulties faced by many Americans who had stopped receiving government assistance and had entered or reentered the workforce. In many cases, such individuals remained in poverty despite their employment and were thus unable to maintain access to housing, healthcare, food, and other necessities. This result, Boushey argued, was in direct conflict with the implicit contract the federal government had made with the United States' low-income workers. "That contract held that if the jobless poor would go to work, we would strengthen work supports to ensure that they and their families would not be left in privation," she explained in her testimony (14 Feb. 2002). "We have failed to honor that contract." Although the majority of individuals who had received government assistance had joined the workforce, doing so was no guarantee of escaping poverty. "In most cases," Boushey added, "the standard of living did not improve for recipients after they moved from the welfare rolls to the payrolls. This is because of a persistent gap between earnings and needs."

In addition to testifying before Congress, Boushey cowrote the publication *The State of Working America 2002/2003* while working for the EPI. In early 2003 she left the institute to take the position of senior economist with the Center for Economic and Policy Research (CEPR). During her time in that role, she continued to research and write about many of the issues that had long been of interest to her, including the minimum wage, welfare reform, and the wage gap between male and female workers. Boushey remained with the center until late 2007 and went on to spend a year as a senior economist for the Joint Economic Committee (JEC) of the US Congress. While advising the committee, she authored and coauthored reports on such topics as paid family leave, unemployment benefits, and the effects of layoffs on female workers.

CENTER FOR AMERICAN PROGRESS

Boushey joined the Center for American Progress as a senior economist in December 2008. She remained with the center, a progressive policy institute, for just under five years, taking on the title of chief economist in early 2013. During her tenure there, she focused extensively on working families and especially the challenges and economic iniquities faced by women in the workforce.

The global economic recession that began in late 2007 and extended through 2009 provided a number of key insights to Boushey and other economists who studied the ways in which layoffs, unemployment, and other consequences of the financial downturn affected American workers—particularly women. Boushey noted during this period that women's participation in the workforce had shown some improvement, with women making up half of the nation's workforce as of late 2009; however, this was not necessarily a sign of improved work-life policies or of a more woman-friendly workplace. In a September 2009 opinion piece for the *Guardian*, she argued that the apparent increase in the percentage of women in the workforce was actually the result of the recession, which had had a particularly devastating effect on male-dominated industries such as construction, causing numerous layoffs in such fields. Three-quarters of the jobs lost between December 2007 and September 2009, Boushey noted, had been held by men. Thus, as the number of employed men decreased and the number of employed women remained little changed, the gender breakdown of the workforce shifted. In her article Boushey cautioned that substantial reforms were still needed to ensure the economic well-being of female workers, regardless of their supposed statistical equality.

Among other key issues Boushey addressed during her time with the Center for American Progress was an issue that was receiving significant media attention at the time—that women often left the workforce to care for children. Boushey noted in her writings on the subject that the narrative around this supposedly common phenomenon varied in presentation depending on the economic status of the women in question: professional women were said to be "opting out" of the workforce, whereas articles about lower income women who stayed home to care for their children often raised questions about whether those women should be eligible for government assistance. In an interview with Judi Casey for *Network News*, a publication of the Sloan Work and Family Research Network at Boston College (July 2010), Boushey argued that the media emphasis on women leaving the workforce distracted from major issues facing women with children such as paid maternity and family leave, work-life balance, and the wage gap. For most women, she asserted, the decision to work or remain home was based not on choice but necessity. "Most mothers work outside the home, especially among working-class and middle-income families where there is little choice about whether to work," she explained to Casey. "Most families need the income that women bring into the home. Continuing to frame the narrative in terms of 'choice' does a disservice to millions of families because it takes the responsibility off of policymakers to address the very real work-family conflicts that most families struggle with."

WASHINGTON CENTER FOR EQUITABLE GROWTH

In late 2013 Boushey left the Center for American Progress to take the position of executive director and chief economist of the Washington Center for Equitable Growth. A newly formed organization dedicated to researching economic inequality in the United States, the center also provides grants to researchers in the field. As executive director and chief economist, Boushey has continued to research income inequality and the ways in which public policy addresses or exacerbates it. She is especially interested in presenting economic data and complex research in forms that can be easily understood by both policymakers and the public. "Where I think you hit the sweet spot in research is when what you . . . tease out of these datasets actually resonates with people's real lived experiences," she explained to Garcia. Boushey received significant additional attention beginning in 2015 when she began to be widely identified as one of the primary economists advising Democratic presidential hopeful Hillary Clinton. "In terms of what I have been talking to her about, it has been about the big questions about what we should do for our economy and how we should think about the interventions that policymakers should make," she told Garcia of her work with Clinton.

In addition to her years of work with various Washington organizations dedicated to research and public policy, Boushey has been associated with a number of additional research institutions, including the National Poverty Center at the University of Michigan, the Institute for Public Policy Research (IPPR) in the United Kingdom, and the Berkeley, California–based Opportunity Institute. She has served on the boards of various journals, including the *Journal of Poverty*. Her book *Finding Time: The Economics of Work-Life Conflict* was published in April 2016 by *Harvard University Press*.

PERSONAL LIFE

Boushey married fellow economist Todd Tucker in Seattle in 2007. A former research director for the nonprofit consumer-rights think tank Public Citizen, Tucker is a researcher at the University of Cambridge in the United Kingdom. Boushey and Tucker live in Washington, DC.

SUGGESTED READING
Boushey, Heather. "Equal Work without Equal Pay." *Guardian*. Guardian News and Media, 7 Sept. 2009. Web. 12 Feb. 2016.

Boushey, Heather. "Strengthening the Middle Class: Ensuring Equal Pay for Women." *Senate.gov*. US Senate, 11 Mar. 2010. Web. 12 Feb. 2016.

Boushey, Heather. "Testimony of Heather Boushey." *Senate.gov*. US Senate, 14 Feb. 2002. Web. 12 Feb. 2016.

Boushey, Heather. "The Three Faces of Work-Family Conflict." Interview by Judi Casey. *Network News* 12.7 (2010). PDF file.

Garcia, Eric. "Hillary Clinton's Economic Inequality Whisperer." *Atlantic*. Atlantic Monthly Group, 12 June 2015. Web. 12 Feb. 2016.

"Heather Boushey, Ann O'Leary." *Politico Magazine*. Politico, 2015. Web. 12 Feb. 2016.

—*Joy Crelin*

Isaac Brock

Born: July 9, 1975
Occupation: Musician

Isaac Brock is the singer, guitarist, and songwriter of the indie rock band Modest Mouse. Brock founded the band in 1993 while still a teenager, and within a few years the group began to make an impact in the indie rock scene. They achieved greater recognition and critical acclaim with the album *The Moon & Antarctica* (2000). About four years later they attained mainstream success with the album *Good News for People Who Love Bad News* (2004), which featured the hit singles "Float On" and "Ocean Breathes Salty." The album and "Float On" received Grammy Award nominations, solidifying Modest Mouse's unique position between underground rock and mainstream pop.

Through all his success Brock cultivated a notoriously misanthropic personality to match his complex lyrics. As James Montgomery wrote for MTV News (18 Aug. 2009), the songwriter earned a reputation as "the surliest loner in all of indie rock, and rather proudly so." After releasing the chart-topping album *We Were Dead Before the Ship Even Sank* in 2007, Modest Mouse put out no full-length album for eight years. Brock and his band continued to tour, however, and finally returned with *Strangers to Ourselves* (2015).

EARLY LIFE

Isaac Brock was born on July 9, 1975, in Helena, Montana. When Brock was around three years old, his parents divorced and his mother, Kris, married her former husband's brother. They were briefly involved in a hippie commune and then lived as part of the Grace Gospel Christian sect, moving in with the preacher due to financial difficulties. Brock would later recall being told to speak in tongues and making up nonsense to please the church leaders, though he felt awkward and disillusioned. Brock's family eventually moved to Issaquah, Washington, a small town outside of Seattle.

Brock's unusual childhood deeply influenced his outlook, and by the time he became famous many elements of his upbringing had become a sort of mythology for fans, often misinterpreted and distorted. This is why when Jonathan Valania did a profile of Brock for *BuzzFeed* (30 Mar. 2015), Brock wanted to set the record straight—or at least did not want to contribute any more

Tim Mosenfelder/GettyImages

tall tales to the legend of his rough upbringing. "Brock is wary about talking about his childhood," wrote Valania, "because the more outlandish anecdotes he shared with journalists early on—the commune! the trailer park! the Christian death cult!—have become part and parcel of his lore and legend and are often misinterpreted as indicators of hardship and neglect." One of the most important stories, one that relates directly to Brock becoming interested in playing and recording music, is that Brock lived in a shed outside his parents' home. This piece of legend, however, is true. After a flood ruined the family's home, Brock's mother, stepfather, sister, and step siblings lived in a cramped trailer, so Brock opted to live in a shed in the backyard, where he could have time to himself. It was there that, starting around the age of fourteen, he taught himself to play bass and guitar.

MUSICAL BEGINNINGS

What Brock would continue to refer to as "The Shed" became his first recording studio of sorts. He played guitar and recorded some songs. It would also become a place where he and his new friends—bass player Eric Judy and drummer Jeremiah Green—could rehearse and jam. When Brock was sixteen years old he dropped out of high school and went on to do a series of various jobs: janitor, dishwasher, test subject in scientific research, and nude model for artists.

Eventually he left his little hometown and moved to Washington, DC, where he lived in an artistically and politically minded collective called Positive Force. There he developed the "Dial-A-Song" project, for which he would record a song on his outgoing answering machine message, to be heard only by calling that number. Brock earned his high school diploma by taking classes at a community college. In one of those classes he read the Virginia Woolf story "The Mark on the Wall," and was struck by the phrase "modest mouse-like people." He began using the name Modest Mouse for his evolving musical projects.

In 1993, when Brock was just eighteen years old, Modest Mouse officially came together as a band with the addition of Judy and Green. It would only take a few years for the band to release its first album; in the meantime Brock continued putting out cassette demos. In 1994 the group recorded its official first album as Modest Mouse, titled *Sad Sappy Sucker*, but it was not released. (The album would actually come out in 2001 on the coattails of the group's success in the indie rock scene.)

Though passed over by Sub Pop, a prestigious indie rock music label, Modest Mouse was picked up by Up Records, for which the group released its first full-length album, *This Is a Long Drive for Someone with Nothing to Think About* (1996). The record, a mix of moody and fast songs about desperation and loneliness, was well received among independent music enthusiasts. The group's next album on Up Records, *The Lonesome Crowded West* (1997), "put Modest Mouse on the indie rock map," according to Valania. The album earned critical acclaim, eventually becoming regarded as one of the defining records of 1990s indie rock, and also sold relatively well, setting the band up for a breakthrough.

SHIFT TO A MAJOR LABEL

Modest Mouse was eagerly pursued by record labels looking for the next big thing. However, in early 1999 Brock was embroiled in controversy when a woman accused him of date rape. Although no charges were filed and the accusation was later dropped, the incident threw Brock's life into turmoil and split the opinions of the Seattle indie rock scene. The band Murder City Devils, whose guitarist Dann Gallucci had become a part-time member of Brock's band, even quit their tour with Modest Mouse over the allegations.

A different kind of controversy emerged when Modest Mouse signed to the major label Epic Records, a division of Sony, leading some to claim the band was selling out. Brock justified the move by asserting, "I wouldn't mind actually getting paid [for making music]. I love the record label I'm on, but I've got people knocking at the door. Commercial rock is usually pretty s——, but it doesn't have to stay that way. I think we could go to a major label and still fly under the radar," as quoted by Cam Lindsay for Exclaim. ca. The band was budgeted $100,000 to complete an album for Epic, but during the process

Brock's personal troubles continued. In Chicago he had his jaw broken in a fight when he was attacked by a group of more than a dozen teens. The break required his jaw to be sealed shut for a period of time. Brock also admitted to heavy drug use, and live performances were often sloppy due to his frequent inebriation.

Modest Mouse's eventual major-label debut album, *The Moon & Antarctica* (2000), reached number one hundred twenty on the Billboard 200 chart. The album received mostly very positive reviews. In a review for the influential music website Pitchfork (13 June 2000), Brent DiCrescenzo called the album "monumental, groundbreaking, hypnotic, sublime" and wondered how the band would ever top it. "That they manage to go beyond any other rock band out there is staggering," DiCrescenzo added. "The sequencing weaves a dramatic ebb and flow of emotion. Every song is packed with fantastic sounds that reach out for space and salvation." Despite the album's strong reception, Brock did receive criticism from some fans after he licensed songs for use in corporate advertisements.

OTHER PROJECTS AND LEGAL TROUBLE

The Moon & Antarctica was followed a year later by *Everywhere and His Nasty Parlor Tricks* (2001), an EP of eight outtakes and demos. That record reached one hundred forty-seven on the Billboard 200 chart. Brock also formed a side project known as Ugly Casanova, allowing him to explore different musical territory from that of Modest Mouse. That project resulted in the album *Sharpen Your Teeth* in 2002 on the Sub Pop label. Brock also helped sign new bands to Sub Pop during this period.

In 2002 Brock was arrested for driving under the influence (DUI) after he crashed his van in Oregon. One of his passengers dislocated her thumb, which under Oregon law led to a charge of attempted murder against him due to the involvement of alcohol in the incident. Brock hired a lawyer to deal with the charge but apparently it remained unresolved; as a result there was an arrest warrant out for him—a fact that Brock discovered while driving back to the United States from Canada. At the border he was stopped, detained, and sent to a jail in upstate New York. After spending over a week in prison Brock was able to hire a lawyer to negotiate probation, and he served time on a road work crew. Because of the DUI he attended mandatory Alcoholics Anonymous (AA) meetings.

Brock's troubles were not limited to his own actions. In 2003 Jeremiah Green, Modest Mouse's founding drummer, had a mental breakdown and quit the band. And in 2004 Brock's adopted brother, Ansel, was killed in an avalanche on Mount Rainier.

GOOD NEWS FOR PEOPLE WHO LOVE BAD NEWS

Following this stretch of personal and professional setbacks, Brock and the band put out an album that would truly catapult them to widespread success. Recorded at Sweet Tea Studio, in Oxford, Mississippi, and produced by Dennis Herring, *Good News for People Who Love Bad News* (2004) put Modest Mouse on the map of the mainstream rock and pop world, reaching number eighteen on the Billboard 200. With the temporary departure of Green and the return of guitarist Dann Gallucci, the album had a more commercially appealing sound while retaining many of the band's signature quirks. The best example was the single "Float On," which *Rolling Stone* would eventually name as the thirty-ninth best song of the 2000s. The single and the album were both nominated for Grammys, though they did not win.

Strong reviews accompanied the album's commercial success. Barry Walters wrote for *Rolling Stone* (7 Apr. 2004) that Modest Mouse "refine their weirdness and become a pop band while grasping at dark truths that pop ordinarily denies. Although the group still builds its sound around jammy live grooves, two new members and various guests flesh out Brock and bassist Eric Judy's singular brand of psychedelic rock, art punk, and pastoral Americana. Brock now writes and sings more melodically—a little less Pixies, a bit more Talking Heads." The band appeared on television shows and Epic gave Brock his own record label, Glacial Pace, to sign other artists.

Modest Mouse continued to evolve. Green returned and Gallucci left, to be replaced first by Jim Fairchild and then by Johnny Marr, former guitarist of the Smiths. The revamped lineup released *We Were Dead Before the Ship Even Sank* (2007), which reached number one on the Billboard 200. Brock's erratic behavior did not disappear; in 2007 he slashed himself with a knife while performing on stage and he suffered a facial fracture after being hit with a bottle at another show. Although they continued to tour and release outtakes, Modest Mouse did not put out a new album for eight years.

STRANGERS TO OURSELVES

Brock continued to collaborate with other artists (including a cameo on the television series *Portlandia*) and reissue Modest Mouse's back catalog. When the band's next album, *Strangers to Ourselves* (2015), finally arrived, it was met with much excitement and anticipation. The lineup had changed again: Marr had left and Fairchild was brought back, founding bassist Eric Judy departed, and several new members joined, including Brock's girlfriend, Lisa Molinaro.

Strangers to Ourselves received many positive reviews, but there were also plenty of lukewarm ones. Kyle McGovern of *Spin* (19 Mar. 2015) opened his review by asking, "Eight years and this is it?" He later added, "This band has never made an out-and-out *bad* album, but now it has made an uninspired one." On the other hand, in a review for *New Musical Express* (*NME*) (11 Mar. 2015), Al Horner, citing the album's genre hopping, observed that it is an "impressively unpredictable record that veers down wildly different paths, in ways no previous Modest Mouse album has dared."

SUGGESTED READING

Lindsay, Cam. "Modest Mouse: Building Something Out of Nothing." *Exclaim.ca*. Exclaim!, 26 Mar. 2015. Web. 4 Nov. 2015.

Modell, Josh. "Modest Mouse" *A. V. Club*. Onion, 7 Apr. 2004. Web. 4 Nov. 2015.

Montgomery, James. "Modest Mouse: Misanthrope Music." *MTV News*. Viacom, 18 Aug. 2009. Web. 4 Nov. 2015.

Valania, Jonathan. "Modest Mouse's Isaac Brock Wants to Be More Than a Myth." *BuzzFeed Music*. BuzzFeed, 30 Mar. 2015. Web. 4 Nov. 2015.

SELECTED WORKS

This Is a Long Drive for Someone with Nothing to Think About, 1996; *The Lonesome Crowded West*, 1997; *The Moon & Antarctica*, 2000; *Good News for People Who Love Bad News*, 2004; *We Were Dead Before the Ship Even Sank*, 2007; *Strangers to Ourselves*, 2015

—*Dmitry Kiper*

Elizabeth Stoker Bruenig

Occupation: Journalist

Elizabeth Stoker Bruenig is a journalist and an assistant editor for Outlook/Post Everything at the *Washington Post*. Formerly a staff writer for the *New Republic*, as well as a contributing writer to the *Atlantic*, the *Week*, *Salon*, and *Ethika Politika*, Bruenig earned a master's degree in Christian theology at the University of Cambridge on a Marshall Scholarship. As a writer, Bruenig examines contemporary issues—poverty, politics, gender, the death penalty, inequality—through a leftist, Christian lens. "The conflation of faith with American political conservatism is absurd to me," Bruenig told the writers of *Politico* in an interview (2 Feb. 2015). She takes issue with the general lack of religious thinkers, but also with the catch-all term "religion," itself, stressing the variety of beliefs in the world and their function in structuring one's worldview.

Bruenig herself, who is deeply influenced by the early Christian philosopher Saint Augustine, applies her own Catholic views to politics and questions of social justice. For instance, Bruenig defended her views on abortion in an article for the *Week* titled "Why I'm a Pro-Life Liberal" (16 Apr. 2014), in which she took an all-encompassing view of the word "life," writing that "a genuine pro-life political position takes its commitment to human life seriously, and is, therefore, willing to commit to supporting the *lives* of mothers and children rather than simply their births." She has criticized pro-life activists who focus on punishing mothers rather than promoting social programs that would support them after the child is born. Although her specific view of laws crafted to limit abortion is unclear, Bruenig presents the issue in ethical terms, landing on a larger doctrine of social responsibility.

Bruenig's writing has won her a diverse collection of fans as well as commentary from several outspoken critics. John Zmirak, for example, writing for the conservative website the Stream (18 Mar. 2015), accused her of "cherry-picking" and distorting Catholic doctrine for her own political purposes. With converts like Bruenig—who joined the Catholic Church in 2014—"who needs apostates?" Zmirak wrote. But Bruenig is not alone in her desire to see a stronger relationship between liberal politics and Christianity. She wrote about the rise of the Christian left in an article for Salon (21 July 2014). Its emblems, she writes, are socially liberal Christian millennials who grew up during the culture wars of the 1990s and 2000s, and the popular Pope Francis, who has condemned corporate greed and income inequality from his pulpit. As young people come into positions of authority, Bruenig writes, she hopes to see an emphasis on "some of the finest features of the Christian tradition: to resist categorization, pull hard for the oppressed and downtrodden and insist upon hope while coping with the realities of power."

EARLY LIFE AND EDUCATION

Bruenig was born in Fort Worth, Texas, and grew up in nearby Arlington. She was raised in the teachings of the United Methodist church, and her parents encouraged her to engage intellectually with its teachings. She has recalled having lengthy discussions about the Bible and its meaning over dinner and on long car trips with her family. She was diagnosed with juvenile myoclonic epilepsy at the age of fourteen after having a seizure in her high school cafeteria.

In high school, she was a member of the debate team and a competitive essay writer. She won a statewide essay writing competition during her junior year. Bruenig also taught Sunday school at her church. She fretted about misleading her students with her own secondhand knowledge of the Bible—so she decided to sit down and read the whole thing. "I've heard this process turns some people into atheists," she wrote on her personal blog (8 Sept. 2013); "it turned me into a hardcore leftist."

Bruenig's parents, she wrote in the same essay, were "predictably right-wing," and growing up, Bruenig, following their lead, was too. But reading the Bible stirred in her a sense of community with others, which led her to craft her own liberal philosophy. In high school, she also read Saint Augustine's *Confessions* for the first time. Saint Augustine posited that human beings were inherently imperfect and taught his followers to be skeptical of wealth and power and to be benevolent to the poor.

After graduating from high school, she enrolled at Brandeis University in Waltham, Massachusetts. "Brandeis was the only school I interviewed or toured at, because as soon as I visited its campus, I knew it was the place for me," she said for the university's website. Bruenig continued to read Saint Augustine in college, but she also read other religious scholars such as Thomas Aquinas, Julian of Norwich, Alasdair MacIntyre, and John Milbank.

As an undergraduate, Bruenig coached high school debate teams, served on the campus newspaper, and founded a program called Brandeis: Be Our Guest, which allows students to donate unused guest meals on their school meal plans to a local homeless shelter. During her sophomore year, she completed an internship at the Epilepsy Foundation in Washington, DC. She was also heavily involved in the Waltham Group's Hunger and Homelessness program and served as a board member at the Community Day Center, a local homeless shelter.

She graduated in 2013 with a double major in English and sociology, as well as a minor in Near Eastern and Judaic studies. The same year, she won a coveted Marshall Scholarship to study theology and Christian ethics at Jesus College at the University of Cambridge in England. Bruenig had attended meetings of the Religious Society of Friends while she was in college and briefly became a Quaker, but, led by her affinity for Catholic thinkers, she joined the Catholic Church in 2014.

Bruenig earned a master's degree in Christian theology in 2014. While she was a student, Bruenig, a prolific blogger, began writing for *Salon*, the *Boston Review*, and the *Atlantic*. She was also a columnist for the *Week*. Bruenig attended Brown University, where she was a doctoral candidate studying religion, politics, and philosophy and earned a 2014–15 Presidential Fellowship, which are awarded on a competitive basis to "the most outstanding applicants to doctoral programs across the disciplines."

JOURNALISM CAREER

Bruenig joined the *New Republic* as a staff writer in 2015. Her hiring came after a serious shake-up at the one-hundred-year-old magazine in 2014, when executives announced a plan to restructure the magazine as a digital media company and two-thirds of the editors and staff writers whose names appeared on the editorial masthead resigned. The position was Bruenig's first major job as a journalist, providing her with "hands-on learning," as she told *Politico*. "One of the things I found most appealing about the opportunity was the chance to work with experienced editors who are willing to make time for young writers." In March 2016, she became an assistant editor for Outlook/PostEverything at the *Washington Post*, which features freelance contributions, news analyses, and opinions.

A substantial share of Bruenig's writing addresses poverty and the social stigma of being poor. In 2015, she chided conservative columnist David Brooks, who had written an opinion piece for the *New York Times* (10 Mar. 2015) arguing that poor and less-educated people were prone to unwanted pregnancies, violent crime, and drug use because of a lack of social norms—a basic understanding of how a person should function in society. He wrote that "sympathy is not enough. It's not only money and better policy that are missing in these circles; it's norms," arguing that people, even people born in extreme poverty, must be held responsible by society for their dysfunctional behavior. Bruenig, writing for the *New Republic* (10 Mar. 2015), took a different view. Citing a slew of books and polls, Bruenig wrote that both poor and wealthy people share roughly the same moral baseline, and that behaviors such as drug use arise from the condition of poverty itself. Social policies that seek to reduce or eradicate poverty address these behaviors by default. When people are financially secure enough to feed their families and pay rent, they are statistically less likely to violate Brooks's "social norms."

Bruenig's views about poverty are research-based but also deeply rooted in the philosophy of Saint Augustine, who believed that success and wealth were not virtues in themselves. Brooks's moral assessment—that college-educated people are more virtuous than non-college-educated people because of their privileges—is a direct contradiction to this belief. Her philosophical, ethical, and theological framework distinguishes Bruenig from other writers who share her views, like her husband, Matt Bruenig. The two wrote a thought-provoking article for the *Atlantic* (29 Oct. 2013) in which they proposed a solution to reduce the poverty rate in the United States—15 percent of the population in 2012—by half. Their plan is popularly known as universal basic income, but they called it "Social Security for all, not just the elderly." Social Security, they argued, has historically been one of the most effective tools in fighting poverty followed by other social programs such as Supplemental Security Insurance, disability insurance, unemployment benefits, and other benefits such as food stamps. But these programs are not enough. They argued that an annual cash income of about three thousand dollars to every American adult and child would be economically feasible, cut the poverty rate by half, and give the working poor a springboard from which to move up the economic ladder. Advocates of such a plan have included Martin Luther King Jr. and conservative economists F. A. Hayek and Milton Friedman.

Although poverty is perhaps the issue closest to Bruenig's heart, she has also written about the death penalty. After the 2013 Boston marathon bombing, she closely followed the case of Dzhokhar Tsarnaev. Bruenig, who was living in Boston at the time of the bombing, wrote an essay about Tsarnaev for the *New Republic* (8 Apr. 2015) after he was convicted of killing three and injuring more than two hundred people. Tsarnaev was later given the death penalty, but at the time he had yet to be sentenced. Bruenig argued against giving Tsarnaev the death penalty—a policy that dovetails with Bruenig's expanded definition of "pro-life." In prison, she wrote, Tsarnaev would no longer be in a position to cause harm. She quoted Pope Francis, who called the death penalty "an offense against the inviolability of life and the dignity of the human person." (Four Massachusetts Catholic bishops used this quote in a statement appealing to the jury in Tsarnaev's trial.) Further, she wrote, killing Tsarnaev would make him a martyr to a population of angry youth. "It would be better not to give such people an emblem for their cause, especially given that Tsarnaev's original crime was, in his thinking, an act of revenge [for killing innocent Muslims overseas]," she wrote. "At some point the cycle simply has to stop, and with Tsarnaev, the jurors in Boston have a chance to contribute to that effort."

PERSONAL LIFE

Elizabeth Stoker Bruenig married Matt Bruenig, a blogger and journalist who writes about politics and economics at MattBruenig.com and for the Demos blog *Policy Shop*, in 2014. The two occasionally write articles together, and Bruenig often cites her husband's research in her own work. The couple's first child, Jane Grace, was born in June 2016.

SUGGESTED READING

Bruenig, Elizabeth Stoker. "The Curious Case of Christian Libertarians." *Elizabeth Stoker Bruenig*. ElizabethStoker-Bruenig.com, 8 Sept. 2013. Web. 7 June 2016.

Rose, Devin. "Joy and Truth: A Conversation with Elizabeth Stoker." *St. Joseph's Vanguard*. HeroicVirtueCreations.com, 10 Feb. 2014. Web. 8 June 2016.

"The 60-Second Interview: Elizabeth Stoker Bruenig, Staff Writer, the *New Republic*." *Politico*. Politico Media, 2 Feb. 2015. Web. 6 June 2016.

SELECTED WORKS
"How to Cut the Poverty Rate in Half (It's Easy)," *Atlantic*, 29 Oct. 2013; "Why I'm a Pro-Life Liberal," *Week*, 16 Apr. 2014; "Rise of the Christian Left: Why the Religious Right's Moment May Be Ending," *Salon*, 21 July 2014; "Poor People Don't Need Better Social Norms. They Need Better Social Policies," *New Republic*, 10 Mar. 2015

—*Molly Hagan*

Aidy Bryant

Born: May 7, 1987
Occupation: Comedian

Mireya Acierto/FilmMagic/Getty Images

Aidy Bryant might be one of *Saturday Night Live*'s most valuable players. Since joining the long-running sketch comedy show in 2012, Bryant has won acclaim for her memorable original characters as well as her impressions of celebrities such as pop singer Adele. "I like to play characters that have an inner confidence about them that maybe you wouldn't expect them to have and that they aren't afraid to unleash occasionally," she told Kevin Fallon for the *Daily Beast* (31 Oct. 2014) of her performances.

Having ascended quickly from featured cast member to repertory player on *Saturday Night Live* (SNL), Bryant has fit in seamlessly with both veteran cast members and later additions, becoming a core part of countless sketches and gaining widespread notice as a comic. For Bryant, however, joining the show was both the exciting next step in her career in improvisational and sketch comedy and the realization of a childhood dream. "I was a religious *SNL* watcher all through middle school. I was obsessed with Molly Shannon, Ana Gasteyer, Cheri Oteri—they were on right when I found the show," she explained to Laia Garcia for *Yahoo! Style* (30 Jan. 2015). "Then I started watching the older episodes and it just totally blew my mind that my dream show already existed."

EARLY LIFE AND EDUCATION
Aidy Bryant was born on May 7, 1987, in Phoenix, Arizona. She is the older of two children born to Tom and Georganne Bryant. Her father is a real estate agent, and her mother was a homemaker who later opened a boutique in Phoenix, called Frances Vintage, when Bryant was in her late teens. Bryant and her younger brother, Patrick, grew up in Phoenix, where Bryant attended Xavier College Preparatory, an all-girls Catholic high school. She graduated from the school in 2005.

Bryant developed an interest in comedy at an early age, in large part due to the influence of her family. "Funny was very valued in my house," she told Katie Connor for *Cosmopolitan* (8 Apr. 2014). "My parents are both very funny, and my brother has great timing." She also became interested in the performing arts and initially pursued studies in traditional forms of theater through various workshops and summer camps. However, she soon decided to take a different route. "When I found out about improv and sketch, I was like, 'Oh, this is my jam,'" she explained to Connor.

Although Bryant's family approved of and encouraged her comedic efforts, her natural inclination toward comedy sometimes got her into trouble. In high school, Bryant earned the ire of the administration with her manner of reading the televised morning announcements. "One time, the dean stopped me in the hallway and was like, 'The flipness isn't gonna fly on the TV.' I was like, 'All right, lady,'" she recalled to Sara Benincasa for *Bust* (Oct./Nov. 2015). "But then when I got hired at *SNL*, I was like, 'Ha, ha, the flipness is about to fly on the TV, baby.'"

After graduating from high school, Bryant enrolled in Columbia College Chicago in Illinois, where she studied theater. While in college, she began to get involved in the thriving improv comedy scene in Chicago, which is home to well-regarded comedy theaters and training centers such as the Second City and the iO Theater. Bryant completed a training program in improv at the latter while an undergraduate. She earned her bachelor's degree from Columbia College in 2009.

EARLY COMEDY CAREER

Following her graduation, Bryant became more deeply involved in improvisational and sketch comedy, joining troupes such as Baby Wants Candy. She was eventually asked to join one of the Second City troupes. A comedy institution, the Second City has produced numerous well-known performers in the decades since its creation in 1959, including *SNL* alumni such as John Belushi, Mike Myers, Rachel Dratch, and Tina Fey.

Bryant enjoyed performing at the Second City e.t.c. Theater, viewing her time with the troupe as an opportunity to evolve as a comedian. "In Second City, it's all about ensemble and working together," she told Claire Lawton for the *Phoenix New Times* (2 Oct. 2014). "Everyone helps write every scene, but it's all about improv and saying yes to different people's ideas, and I think that was such a great way for me to start." During her tenure at Second City, she performed in and cowrote various sketch shows. She also worked for a time at a barbershop.

JOINING *SNL*

With the Second City's history of supplying cast members for *Saturday Night Live*, it was perhaps unsurprising that Bryant would one day have the chance to join the show. In 2012, Bryant learned that members of *SNL*'s staff, including showrunner Lorne Michaels, were visiting Chicago and planned to attend a new sketch show she had cowritten, in which she was also performing. "I think maybe the night after our opening night—or something—our Second City producers were like, 'OK, Lorne is coming tonight and some of the producers and writers from *SNL*,'" she told Fallon (2014). "I was like, 'OK. If they're ever going to see me in any capacity, this is how I want them to see me.'"

Michaels and his companions were impressed. Within about a week, Bryant received a call asking her to come out to New York City for an official audition. After several in-person auditions and meetings, *SNL*'s showrunners offered the twenty-five-year-old Bryant a featured player slot starting at the beginning of the show's thirty-eighth season. She joined *SNL* at the same time as Cecily Strong and Tim Robinson, both of whom were affiliated with Chicago-based comedy groups. Robinson left the performing cast for the *SNL* writers' room after one season, while

Strong has joined Bryant as a cornerstone of the show's new lineup.

As a new featured player, Bryant did not immediately make her mark on-screen; she has recalled in interviews that she had only one line in her first televised sketch. However, she soon reached one particularly meaningful *SNL* milestone. Several episodes into her first season, Bryant portrayed CNN political correspondent Candy Crowley in an episode's cold open. At the end of the sketch, which satirized the presidential debate Crowley had moderated, Bryant had her first opportunity to say the traditional line that ushers in the show's opening credits: "Live from New York, it's Saturday Night!"

FROM NEW KID TO VETERAN

For Bryant, being an *SNL* cast member was a daunting yet exciting experience. "It is overwhelming. And it is really scary. And you are aware of people who are some of the funniest people ever and still got fired after one year, or two years," she explained to Fallon (2014). "That is very present in your mind. So you want to work as hard as you can, but you also want to figure out where you fit in this moving machine."

Over the following years, however, it became clear to many *SNL* viewers that Bryant was a key piece of that machine, particularly as longtime cast members left the show and a new crop of featured players arrived. She was promoted from featured player to repertory player in 2013, a move that signaled she was not going anywhere. Even as Bryant grew accustomed to the show's strenuous pace and to appearing on live television each week, however, she remained acutely aware of the unique position she was in. "I still get super excited," she told Fallon (2014). "I try to really make myself, even if I'm tired or something, go and watch the musical guests rehearse just so that I enjoy it all. Sometimes you're like, 'Ugh. I want to go to see, but I'm sitting under a blanket. . . . ' But then you go, 'What am I doing?'"

In addition to being a popular cast member among *SNL* viewers, Bryant has received critical acclaim for her work on the show. Along with fellow cast member Kate McKinnon and three other members of the *SNL* staff, she was nominated for the 2014 Emmy Award for outstanding original music and lyrics for the song "Home for the Holiday (Twin Bed)," a comedic song featured in the episode that aired on December 21, 2013.

OTHER WORK

In addition to *SNL*, Bryant has made a number of guest appearances in television shows such as *Comedy Bang! Bang!*, *Broad City*, and *Documentary Now!* She has played recurring roles in several series as well, including *Girls* and *Horace and Pete*. A live performer at heart, Bryant has continued to appear on stage in comedy and sketch shows when not filming *SNL*.

In 2016, Bryant took her career in yet another direction, starring in the short film *Darby Forever*, which she also cowrote. Released online via the video-streaming service Vimeo, the short revolves around a woman named Darby, played by Bryant, who works in a fabric store and spends her time daydreaming about those around her. In making the film, Bryant worked alongside friends and acquaintances from many stages of her life, including childhood friends, roommates, and *SNL* colleagues. "It felt like a full circle Oprah moment for me," she explained to Fallon for the *Daily Beast* (24 Feb. 2016), describing a scene in which confetti falls on Darby. "We had all these people positioned to shoot off the little confetti cannons and each one of them was from a different portion of my life. I was, like, looking around and having this beautiful moment while confetti rained down on me."

PERSONAL LIFE
Bryant met her longtime boyfriend, Conner O'Malley, when they were both performing at the Annoyance Theater in Chicago in 2008. They began dating shortly afterward. O'Malley is a member of the writing staff for *Late Night with Seth Meyers*, which is hosted by the titular former *SNL* cast member. Bryant and O'Malley live in the Chelsea neighborhood of New York.

SUGGESTED READING
Benincasa, Sara. "*SNL*'s Aidy Bryant Talks Boyfriends, Best Friends, and Being Prom Queen." *Bust*. Bust, Oct./Nov. 2015. Web. 15 July 2016.

Bryant, Aidy. "Girl You Need to Know: Aidy Bryant." Interview by Laia Garcia. *Yahoo! Style*. Yahoo!, 30 Jan. 2015. Web. 15 July 2016.

Connor, Katie. "32 Things You Didn't Know about the Women of 'SNL.'" *Cosmopolitan*. Hearst Communications, 8 Apr. 2014. Web. 15 July 2016.

Fallon, Kevin. "How Aidy Bryant Stealthily Became Your Favorite 'Saturday Night Live' Star." *Daily Beast*. Daily Beast, 31 Oct. 2014. Web. 15 July 2016.

Fallon, Kevin. "The Adorable Rise of Aidy Bryant, *SNL*'s Next Big Thing." *Daily Beast*. Daily Beast, 24 Feb. 2016. Web. 15 July 2016.

Lawton, Claire. "Aidy Bryant's Made It Big on *Saturday Night Live*, But Phoenix Still Feels Like Home." *Phoenix New Times*. Phoenix New Times, 2 Oct. 2014. Web. 15 July 2016.

Metz, Nina. "Aidy Bryant, Tim Robinson, Cecily Strong Join Cast of 'SNL.'" *Chicago Tribune*. Chicago Tribune, 10 Sept. 2012. Web. 15 July 2016.

SELECTED WORKS
Saturday Night Live, 2012– ; *Girls*, 2015–16; *Darby Forever*, 2016; *Horace and Pete*, 2016

—*Joy Crelin*

Christine Jensen Burke
Born: July 2, 1968
Occupation: Mountaineer

Mountaineer Christine Jensen Burke has climbed peaks all over the world. She is the first New Zealand–born woman to successfully climb all of the Seven Summits, the highest mountains on each of the seven continents.

EARLY LIFE AND EDUCATION
Christine Jensen Burke was born in the port city of Timaru, New Zealand, on July 2, 1968. Timaru is located on New Zealand's South Island at the foot of the Southern Alps. As a child, Burke, along with her seven older siblings, accompanied her parents on long walks through the surrounding hills.

After graduating from Timaru Girls' High School, Burke attended the University of Otago in Dunedin, New Zealand, where she earned her undergraduate law degree in 1990. She then moved to Sydney, Australia, but returned to Timaru following the death of one of her brothers. Although Burke had originally intended to practice criminal law, while in Timaru she worked for a property lawyer and was inspired to change her focus. She moved back to Sydney to pursue graduate studies at Macquarie University and received her master's degree in environmental law in 1997. She specialized in property and development law, including commercial real estate and infrastructure expansion.

Burke got her start in mountain climbing during a visit to Nepal in 1998, after having suffered a series of running-related injuries. While in Nepal, she discovered that her body adapted easily to high-altitude conditions, as she is one of a small percentage of people who produce red blood cells more quickly than usual.

CLIMBING HIGH
Since her introduction to mountaineering in 1998, Burke has climbed peaks all over the world. Her training involves regular circuits of trail climbing, rock-climbing exercises, and training in the technical aspects of climbing, including the use of ropes, carabiners, tents, and oxygen masks. Despite this preparation and her native physiological advantage, however, she has twice experienced life-threatening health issues while climbing. In 2009, while scaling Cho Oyu

in the Himalayas not long after recovering from pneumonia, Burke developed a pulmonary edema and had to be evacuated. The following year, she developed a chest infection shortly before climbing Ama Dablam in Nepal. Burke started the climb but turned back before achieving the summit.

In 2011, Burke took part in an expedition to reach the summit of Mount Everest, the world's highest peak. Although she began the trip in good health, she soon experienced her first bout of the so-called Khumbu cough, a persistent dry cough caused by the low temperatures and lack of humidity at high altitudes. Nevertheless, Burke pushed on and reached the summit in May 2011. She was the fourth New Zealand woman to do so.

In addition to health risks, mountain climbing can pose other dangers as well. While attempting to summit Indonesia's highest peak, Puncak Jaya—also known as the Carstensz Pyramid—in August 2012, Burke and the other members of her climbing team were taken prisoner by a West Papuan antigovernment militia. The group was held captive for a period of sixteen hours before being released. They did not complete their expedition.

The month before, in July 2012, Burke had successfully climbed to the top of Mount Elbrus, Russia's highest peak, located in the Caucasus Mountains along the country's border with Georgia. Burke's ascent of Mount Elbrus marked her completion of the original "Seven Summits" list—the highest peaks on each of the seven continents. For the purposes of the list, Mount Elbrus is considered to be on the European side of the Eurasian divide; the other six summits are Argentina's Aconcagua (South America), Alaska's Mount McKinley (North America), Tanzania's Mount Kilimanjaro (Africa), Mount Kosciuszko (Australia), Mount Vinson (Antarctica), and Mount Everest (Asia).

A second Seven Summits list exists that replaces Mount Kosciuszko with Puncak Jaya, approximately 2,656 meters (8,714 feet) taller, as Indonesia is considered to be part of the Australian continent. In January 2013, only five months after her hostage experience, Burke returned to the Indonesian province of West Papua to make another attempt. This time she was successful, becoming both the first New Zealand woman and the fourth Australian woman to complete both lists.

Having gained a variety of insights from experiences at the top of the world, Burke retired from practicing law in 2012 and began appearing as a motivational speaker. In her presentations to corporate audiences and students, Burke addresses the tools necessary to overcome significant obstacles through hard work and perseverance. Her audiences have praised her ability to inspire and entertain.

IMPACT

Burke has put the renown she has achieved as a successful mountaineer to good use. She has worked for a variety of philanthropic organizations, including the Christchurch Earthquake Appeal, dedicated to rebuilding Christchurch and the surrounding region following two major earthquakes in September 2010 and February 2011, and the Eggtober Foundation, which raises money for research and treatment of gynecological cancers. Burke also works in support of the Australian Himalayan Foundation, which undertakes development initiatives in Nepal, India, and Bhutan.

PERSONAL LIFE

Burke holds dual Australian and New Zealand citizenship. She lives in Sydney, Australia.

SUGGESTED READING

Australian Associated Press. "West Papua Militia Frees New Zealand Mountaineer Hostages." *Australian*. News Corp Australia, 14 Aug. 2012. Web. 18 July 2014.

Burke, Christine Jensen. "Attempting Makalu and K2/Broad Peak in 2014." Interview by Raheel Adnan. *Altitude Pakistan*. Blogger, 19 Mar. 2014. Web. 18 July 2014.

"Christine Achieves Seven Summits." *Timaru Herald*. Fairfax New Zealand, 26 Jan. 2013. Web. 18 July 2013.

Cogle, Fleur. "High Achiever." *Timaru Herald*. Fairfax New Zealand, 27 June 2011. Web. 18 July 2014.

Jones, Chris. "Conquering Mt. Everest." *Edge* Dec. 2011: 22–24. Print.

Quine, Stephanie. "Mountain of Similarities between Everest and the Office." *Lawyers Weekly*. Cirrus Media, 8 Mar. 2013. Web. 18 July 2014.

—*Joshua Pritchard*

Carter Burwell

Born: November 18, 1954
Occupation: Composer

Carter Burwell has composed music for some of the most beloved and critically acclaimed American films of the late twentieth and early twenty-first centuries. He has worked most frequently on films written and directed by the Coen brothers, such as *Fargo* (1996), *Big Lebowski* (1998), *No Country for Old Men* (2007), and *Hail Caesar!* (2016). He has provided music for

the complex films of Charlie Kaufman, such as *Being John Malkovich* (1999), *Adaptation* (2002), and the animated *Anomalisa* (2015). Burwell has also created scores for relatively small films, such as *Kinsey* (2004) and *Howl* (2010), as well as popular ones, such as *Twilight* (2008) and *The Blind Side* (2009). Prior to getting into film scoring, he was a computer programmer, animator, and musician. After decades of creating film scores, he finally received his first Oscar nomination for his work on the film *Carol* (2015).

EARLY LIFE

Carter Benedict Burwell was born on November 18, 1954, to parents Natalie and Charles. He has a sister, Belinda Lee Burwell, who is a veterinarian and the founder of Blue Ridge Wildlife Center, dedicated to wildlife rescue and conservation. Burwell's father, Charles, founded Thaibok Fabrics, a fabrics company well known for its designs. Burwell spent his first two years in New York City, but in 1956, the family moved to Darien, Connecticut. Burwell's mother taught math at a Darien elementary school, which Burwell and his sister attended. His mother also sang and played guitar. One day, according to a story that appears on the Steinway piano company's official website, Natalie Burwell was walking down the street and saw a Steinway piano on the street. It was a bit burned, having survived a fire, but it sounded fine, the damage having been only superficial. She asked the owners if she could take it home for her son, and they agreed. Burwell took piano lessons, but that appears to be the only official musical training he ever had.

He never studied performance or composition, but he loved music.

WEARING MANY HATS AT HARVARD

Burwell attended Harvard University, in Cambridge, Massachusetts, where he studied animation with Mary Beams and George Griffin. He was also a cartoonist for the famous satirical campus newspaper the *Harvard Lampoon*. As graduation approached, he became interested in electronic music. After graduation, in 1977, he stayed at Harvard, in part so he could learn from the experimental composer Ivan Tcherepnin, who had a substantial impact on Burwell. "The type of music that he made was completely different than what everyone else was doing at Harvard, which was more what passed for academic concert music in the '70s," Burwell told Steve Chagollan for *Variety* (18 Feb. 2016). "Ivan would take a parabolic microphone, stick it out the window and point it at a sidewalk down below and send it into tape loops. . . . His open definition of what could be music was really important to me. Exactly the opposite of what you would have experienced if you would have taken most of the music classes at Harvard." Burwell also did some independent study at the Massachusetts Institute of Technology (MIT) Media Lab, which at the time was known as the Architecture Machine Group. In 1979, he became the chief computer scientist at Cold Spring Harbor Laboratory, and in 1981, he joined the staff of the New York Institute of Technology, where he eventually became the director of digital sound research.

NEW YORK CITY PUNK

From an early age, Burwell had multiple passions and pursuits. He was interested in animation, music, and computer science. By the time he was finishing college he had started playing in various bands. That time, the late 1970s, saw the dawn of the ubiquity of punk music, which was not about musical virtuosity but about attitude, emotion, defiance of authority, and pushing boundaries—everything that appealed to Burwell in his early twenties. He starting living in New York City in 1981, and he actively pursued music in the evenings. He even played at CBGBs, the seminal punk and alternative music club of New York City, where such groups as Television, the Ramones, and the Talking Heads got their start. By this point, Burwell had played with several bands, including the Same, Radiante, and Thick Pigeon. Thick Pigeon was a duo with Stanton Miranda, who played bass and sang, while Burwell played percussion, sang, and did the effects. They released the album *Too Crazy Cowboys* (1984) for Factory Records. That year, Burwell began his rise to one of the preeminent soundtrack composers in contemporary American film.

JOINING THE COEN BROTHERS

Sometime in the early 1980s a friend of Burwell from the punk music scene was working on an independent film as a sound editor, and he asked Burwell to write music for the film. The film in question was written and directed by Joel and Ethan Coen, best known as the Coen brothers. It was their first feature film, *Blood Simple* (1984), a neo-noir crime thriller set in Texas about a jealous husband who hires someone to murder his cheating wife and her man. Burwell had never composed a film score, but he agreed to take the job. The decision changed the lives of both Burwell and the Coen brothers, with whom he would work for decades.

Writing for the *CounterPunch* magazine website (8 Jan. 2016), David Yearsley described that soundtrack thusly: "That score begins with a fateful synthesizer ticking . . . Enter circling, predatory left-hand piano chords that cannot escape their own claustrophobic desires. These harmonies seethe coolly as if in a smoke-filled air-conditioned bar." As Yearsley and other film music critics observed, Burwell's soundtrack was essential to the mood and feel of the film. In fact, Burwell's scores became integral to the success of the Coen brothers' films. Yearsley notes that "With compelling artistic economy, Burwell's contribution was from the start crucial to evoking the shadowy, seedy world of this vision of rural Texas. Little wonder that this inspired debut would be the beginning of an illustrious career."

THE FILM SCORING PROCESS

Although Burwell was quite knowledgeable about music, he was still a novice when it came to both the technical aspects of film scoring and the purpose music is meant to serve in a particular film. Speaking to Aubrey Page for the independent film website *Indiewire.com* (30 Oct. 2015), Burwell confessed that when he first started doing film soundtracks, he was not aware of the delicate balance between the three audio elements of a film: dialogue, sound effects, and the soundtrack music. The more he learned about sound design over the years, he said, the more he has tried to fit his soundtrack music within the full context of the film's sound, particularly the dialogue, "so the notes fall in between dialogue."

Speaking to Page, Burwell revealed another element in his process: he prefers to see as much of the film as possible in order to provide the soundtrack, because the script itself reveals little about the film's pacing, colors, angles, shots, actors' facial expressions, and other such details. Furthermore, he told Page, unlike many other soundtrack composers, particularly those from the middle of the twentieth century, he aims for mystery and subtlety. "In movies from the '40s, they're telling you who everyone is and what they're like. It's on top of, if not a little ahead of the action," Burwell said. "What I prefer is very much the opposite, to leave the audience a little more uncertain about what's going on." With his music, he added, he aims to find and bring to light "something in the film that's not already there on the screen."

MORE WORK WITH THE COENS

After *Blood Simple*, Burwell composed the soundtrack for the Coens' screwball comedy *Raising Arizona* (1987), which included banjo and a sense of whimsy. That was followed by the organized-crime film *Miller's Crossing* (1990), which had orchestral elements and a certain grandiosity in the soundtrack. A year later he worked on *Barton Fink* (1991), a psychological thriller about a writer suffering from writer's block, which starred John Goodman and John Turturro. In *Barton Fink* Burwell incorporated sound effects and sounds in general into the soundtrack. The next soundtrack was for another screwball comedy, *The Hudsucker Proxy* (1994), and then two cult classics, *Fargo* and *Big Lebowski*. For the latter, Burwell used a variety of music, including an electronic pop number and big-band, swinging jazz music.

Burwell composed a rather minimal—yet highly effective—soundtrack for the Coen brothers' unsettling psychological thriller *No Country for Old Men*. The music in that film was non-invasive, hiding underneath other sounds of the film. In fact, the entire film has less than fifteen minutes of total score music. Burwell decided on this approach in order to keep the tension high throughout the film. His next film with the Coens was *A Serious Man* (2009), which takes place in 1967 in a Jewish suburb outside Minneapolis, Minnesota. In an interview with David Schwartz of *Moving Image Source*, a website of New York City's Museum of the Moving Image, Burwell discussed how he tried to fit the music in that film to the personality of the central character, Larry Gopnik. "I found it was useful to have a motif that would repeat endlessly, to suggest that no matter what goes on in the film, he's not really getting anywhere," said Burwell of the main character. "He's blocked at every point in his personal, professional, and spiritual life. And there's something about the delicacy of the harp that I think on the one hand seems sympathetic to this character's travails, but on the other hand is a little bit funny, because in fact none of these characters reveals any delicacy whatsoever."

After the Western film *True Grit* (2010), for which Burwell used hymns as part of the score, he had one of his biggest challenges. The Coen brothers' film *Hail Caesar!* (2016), a slapstick comedy about the "golden age" of Hollywood filmmaking, had within it at least five types of film, including a Roman epic, a Western, and a film featuring water ballet. The Coens wanted Burwell to do a distinct soundtrack for all of them. "A lot of film music is putting on a hat and being like an actor," Burwell said in an interview about the film on National Public Radio's *Morning Edition* (7 Feb. 2016). "In this case, I had to put on lots of different hats. But I love a challenge."

JONZE, HAYNES, AND OTHER MASTERS

Burwell has worked with many well-respected film directors in addition to the Coens, including Spike Jonze and Todd Haynes. For the latter he composed the soundtracks for *Velvet Goldmine* (1998) and *Carol* (2015), for which he received his first Academy Award nomination. For Jonze he composed the scores for such mind-bending films as *Being John Malkovich* (1999), *Adaptation* (2002), and *Where the Wild Things Are* (2009).

He also did scores for legendary director Sidney Lumet's last feature film, *Before the Devil Knows You're Dead* (2007), the renowned Charlie Kaufman's stop-motion animation film *Anomalisa*, and the critically acclaimed cinematic television series *Mildred Pierce* (2011) and *Olive Kitteridge* (2014).

PERSONAL LIFE

Burwell is married to the artist Christine Sciulli. The couple has three children.

SUGGESTED READING

Burwell, Carter. "Behind the Music." Interview by David Schwartz. *Moving Image Source*. Museum of the Moving Image, 28 Dec. 2009. Web. 3 June 2016.

Page, Aubrey. "*Carol* Composer Carter Burwell Talks the Coen Brothers." *Indiewire.com*. Penske Business Media, 30 Oct. 2015. Web. 3 June 2016.

Yearsley, David. "The Curious Case of Carter Burwell." *CounterPunch*. CounterPunch, 8 Jan. 2016. Web. 3 June 2016.

SELECTED WORKS

Blood Simple, 1984; *Miller's Crossing*, 1990; *Fargo*, 1996; *Big Lebowski*, 1998; *Being John Malkovich*, 1999; *Adaptation*, 2002; *No Country for Old Men*, 2007; *Where the Wild Things Are*, 2009; *Carol*, 2015; *Hail Caesar!*, 2016

—*Dmitry Kiper*

Robert Califf

Born: 1951
Occupation: Commissioner of Food and Drugs

On February 24, 2016, Dr. Robert Califf officially became the twenty-second commissioner of the United States Food and Drug Administration (FDA)—the government agency charged with assuring the safety and effectiveness of human drugs and medical devices; overseeing the safety of the nation's food supply, dietary supplements, and cosmetics; regulating tobacco; and ensuring the safety of animal feed and veterinary products. Although Califf was overwhelmingly confirmed by the Senate, in a vote of eighty-nine to four, his nomination had not been without controversy. "Califf, a cardiologist, is a renowned clinical researcher who has deep respect for the system in which he works, and no one who knows him thinks he wants to weaken the regulatory agency he has been chosen to lead," Sabrina Tavernise wrote for the *New York Times* (19 Sept. 2015). "But he has deeper ties to the pharmaceutical industry than any FDA commissioner in recent memory, and some public health advocates question whether his background could tilt him in the direction of an industry he would be in charge of supervising." As Tavernise pointed out, the answer was of major importance because "Califf will be steering a vast and powerful federal agency that regulates about a quarter of every dollar spent in the United States."

Califf had thoughtful answers for his critics, explaining to Massimo Calabresi for *Time* magazine (19 Feb. 2015) that partnerships between

Michael J. Ermarth/Flickr/FDA/Wikimedia Commons

academia, industry, and government were going to be vital in the future. "The greatest progress almost certainly will be made by breaking out of insular knowledge bases and collaborating across the different sectors," he said. While he admitted that there is "a tension which cannot be avoided between regulating an industry and creating the conditions where the industry can thrive," he asserted that the FDA must and would do both.

EARLY LIFE AND EDUCATION

Robert McKinnon Califf, one of four siblings, was born in 1951 in Anderson, South Carolina. His mother, Sarah, was a teacher, and his father, John, was a faculty member of Clemson University and an architect. Califf's father was particularly noted for his contributions to the restoration of the historic quadrangle at the University of South Carolina.

When Califf was in elementary school, his family moved to the town of Columbia, South Carolina. When he failed to make the local Little League baseball team at age nine, his mother petitioned the coaches until they changed their minds. Califf, whose nickname was "Grin," was deeply passionate about basketball. As captain of the basketball team at A. C. Flora High School, he led his teammates to the 1969 AAAA South Carolina State Championships.

Califf spent much of his adult life at Duke, a renowned university in Durham, North Carolina. There, he earned a bachelor's degree in psychology, summa cum laude, in 1973 and planned on pursuing a career in clinical psychology. The summer after graduation, he took a job in the work-release section of the South Carolina state prison system. One day, he took the work-release prisoners out on a bus to play basketball and some of the inmates picked his pocket, which prompted him to switch his career from psychology to medicine. He had to take an extra year of courses to prepare for medical school and then he returned to Duke to earn a medical degree, which he completed in 1978. He completed an internship and a residency in internal medicine at the University of California, San Francisco, but he returned to Duke in 1980 to undertake a fellowship in cardiology.

GOVERNMENT CAREER

In January 2015, Margaret A. Hamburg, then the head of the FDA, appointed Califf as the FDA's deputy commissioner for medical products and tobacco. In that capacity he oversaw the Center for Drug Evaluation and Research (CDER), the Center for Biologics Evaluation and Research (CBER), the Center for Devices and Radiological Health (CDRH), and the Center for Tobacco Products (CTP). (Other deputies reporting to Hamburg oversaw such areas as foods and veterinary medicine, medical and scientific affairs, and global regulatory operations and policy.)

Although his appointment as deputy commissioner incited little controversy, when President Barack Obama nominated him to replace Hamburg as commissioner in September 2015, there was an outcry. Califf's detractors pointed out that among his peer-reviewed papers were several coauthored by pharmaceutical company researchers and that a 2014 financial disclosure form listed, as Tavernise reported, "seven drug companies and a device maker that paid him for consulting and six others that partly supported his university salary, including Merck, Novartis, and Eli Lilly. A conflict-of-interest section at the end of an article he wrote in the *European Heart Journal* last year declared financial support from more than twenty companies." While those facts fueled his critics' allegations that he was too deeply beholden to pharmaceutical companies, Tavernise noted, "Califf had been donating all his consulting fees to nonprofits since the mid-2000s. . . . A résumé studded with industry funding is not unusual in academic medicine." She continued, "Doctors are paid consulting fees all the time, and universities routinely conduct clinical trials on behalf of companies. Those contracts help support university researchers' salaries, a standard practice. Many emphasize that it does not imply an inherent conflict."

Other defenders pointed out despite that Califf's professional relationships with the pharmaceutical companies, data compiled by the public-interest group ProPublica show the vast majority of payments to Califf were for travel, meals, or consulting fees amounting to less than five thousand dollars. (One exception was a 2012 consulting fee of $87,500 from industry giant Johnson & Johnson.)

For his part, Califf has continually stressed that collaboration is not only virtually unavoidable but beneficial and that only an ivory-tower academic would suggest a strict division between industry and government-funded university researchers. Describing the division as a "false dichotomy," he said in an interview for *The Bob Harrington Show* (29 July 2009), "What we need is a venue where all sides can be represented and you end up with something that represents a common ground in terms of evaluating therapeutics."

COMMISSIONER OF FOOD AND DRUGS

Although many senators on both sides of the aisle initially opposed his nomination, Califf ultimately won them over and sailed relatively easily through his confirmation hearings. "I think my record shows that I'm for medical products that work and are effective. When they're not I've been outspoken," Califf said of his confirmation hearings to Brady Dennis for the *Washington Post* (25 Feb. 2016). "I think the best testament is that I went through an amazing rigorous committee, hundreds of pages of written documentation, and then a full Senate review, and came out pretty well." On February 24, 2016, the US Senate confirmed his nomination, and he was sworn into office the following day.

Back in 2007, in a conversation with Steven E. Nissen for *TheHeart.org*, Califf had said of the FDA: "If we don't take this agency, which is regulating over 25 percent of our economy [and] has responsibility for our food supply, our agricultural products, and the drugs and devices that we use, and start putting serious money into it and demand that we have a nonpolitical scientific base for what it does, we are going to see more catastrophes along the lines of what we saw in the past with thalidomide. . . . I can tolerate easily differences of opinion about exactly how to do it, but fundamentally this is not something that can be fixed with a patch; it really is systemic, in my view."

Now in a position to make desired changes, he told Dennis, "This is an unprecedented time of evidence generation, ranging from genomic medicine to use of social media to the astonishing opportunity with electronic health records. We really want to bolster the scientific infrastructure at FDA and take advantage of the opportunity that we have to have much better evidence. My experience in the year I've been there is that we do really well at FDA when we have good evidence. And when we don't have good evidence, it's a matter of opinion and politics, and it often doesn't go as well."

PERSONAL LIFE

Califf married his high school sweetheart, the former Lydia Carpenter, in 1974. Together, they have three children, Sharon, Sam, and Tom. Their oldest child, Sharon, had congenital heart defects that required open heart surgery. (Califf drew upon that experience in front of his Senate Hearing Committee, telling its members, "My family has experienced firsthand how important it is to find a critical balance between innovative treatments and appropriate safeguards for patients.")

Califf continues to love basketball, and when the Duke team has a game, he has been known to sport school colors that day in support. He also enjoys playing golf.

Califf has served on several medical committees, including the Institute of Medicine (IOM), the American Board of Medical Specialties (ABMS), the American College of Cardiology (ACC), and the American Heart Association (AHA).

SUGGESTED READING

Bergengruen, Vera. "Tough Questions for Robert Califf, Obama's Pick to Head FDA." *McClatchyDC*. McClatchy Washington Bureau, 7 Dec. 2015. Web. 8 June 2016.

Calabresi, Massimo. "Candidate to Lead FDA Has Close Ties to Big Pharma." *Time*. Time, 19 Feb. 2015. Web. 8 June 2016.

Dennis, Brady. "New FDA Head Robert Califf Vows to Use 'Bully Pulpit,' Better Explain Agency Decisions." *Washington Post*. Washington Post, 25 Feb. 2016. Web. 8 June 2016.

Husten, Larry. "Califf to Leave Duke to Become FDA Deputy Commissioner." *Forbes*. Forbes Media, 26 Jan. 2015. Web. 8 June 2016.

Kroll, David. "Duke's Rob Califf Named FDA Deputy Commissioner." *Forbes*. Forbes Media, 26 Jan. 2015. Web. 8 June 2016.

Tavernise, Sabrina. "F.D.A. Nominee Califf's Ties to Drug Makers Worry Some." *New York Times*. New York Times, 19 Sept. 2015. Web. 8 June 2016.

—*Mari Rich*

Peter Capaldi

Born: April 14, 1958
Occupation: Actor

Peter Capaldi is an award-winning Scottish actor best known for his work on the television comedy series *The Thick of It* (2005–12) and for being cast as the twelfth incarnation of the Doctor on the popular science fiction series *Doctor Who* (2005–) in 2013.

EARLY LIFE AND EDUCATION

Peter Dougan Capaldi was born on April 14, 1958, in Glasgow, Scotland, to Irish and Italian parents who owned an ice cream delivery business. Capaldi grew up in the inner city Springburn district of Glasgow, a working-class area where his family lived in a tenement building. He attended St. Teresa's Primary School in Glasgow, then St. Matthew's Primary School in Bishopbriggs, Scotland. At St. Ninian's High School in Kirkintilloch, Scotland, he was a member of the Antonine Players, a theater group that performed at the Fort Theatre in Bishopbriggs. Capaldi continued his education at the Glasgow School of Art, where he pursued artistic endeavors such as acting and music. While at school, he sang in a punk rock band called the Dreamboys, which featured future talk show host Craig Ferguson on drums. The band released one record before breaking up. Capaldi left the Glasgow School of Art in 1980 with a degree in graphic design. Capaldi played a small part in the romantic comedy film *Living Apart Together* (1982) before getting his big break. Returning to his apartment in Glasgow one day, Capaldi found Scottish director Bill Forsyth talking with his landlady, who was a costume designer. Forsyth was taken by Capaldi's appearance and cast him in his film *Local Hero* (1983), which was praised by critics in the United Kingdom and the United States.

TELEVISION AND FILM ACTOR

After *Local Hero*, Capaldi landed roles in a variety of films and television series. He worked consistently throughout the 1980s, appearing in films such as the television movie *John and Yoko: A Love Story* (1985), in which he played Beatles member George Harrison, and the comedy *The Lair of the White Worm* (1988). On television, he had leading roles on the miniseries *The Chain* (1990) and *Selling Hitler* (1991).

In the 1990s Capaldi proved his talent was not restricted to acting. He wrote the screenplay for *Soft Top Hard Shoulder* (1993), which he partially based on his life. The film, which Capaldi also starred in, is about a man who is set to inherit his family's ice cream business. It won the Audience Award at the London Film Festival. In 1995, Capaldi wrote and directed the black-and-white short film *Franz Kafka's It's a Wonderful Life*, which won the Academy Award for best live action short film. He believed this to be his big Hollywood break, but though he was attached as a writer to several subsequent film projects, none came to fruition. Disappointed, he returned to Scotland.

Capaldi continued acting consistently in both television series and films throughout the 1990s. He starred in the television miniseries *Neverwhere* and the television movie *Giving Tongue* in 1996, and the comedy film *Bean* the following year, which was commercially successful in the United States, earning $45 million. In 2001 he went behind the camera again to direct *Strictly Sinatra*, which most critics gave negative reviews.

ACCLAIM AND NEW DIRECTIONS

Capaldi achieved mainstream success in 2005 when he starred in the comedy series *The Thick of It*, for which he received high acclaim. In the critically praised series he played Malcolm Tucker, a communications director working in politics. Capaldi appeared in all four of the show's seasons, the last of which aired in 2012. For his performance, Capaldi won an award for best performance in a comedy role at the 2010 British Academy Film Awards (BAFTA). The series produced a spin-off film, *In the Loop* (2009), which was praised by critics and introduced Capaldi to a large audience in the United States.

With his increased profile and success Capaldi remained busy. He directed several episodes of the British sitcom *Getting On* (2009–10) and was nominated for another BAFTA for his role in the first season of the television crime drama *The Field of Blood* (2011–13). He received another BAFTA nomination for his role on the drama series *The Hour* (2012).

On August 4, 2013, during a live BBC broadcast, it was announced that Capaldi would be the twelfth actor to play the Doctor on the popular British science fiction series *Doctor Who*, which started in 1963 and was revived in 2005 after being off the air since 1989. In his youth, Capaldi was a big fan of the show and a drawing of his even appeared in an issue of *Doctor Who International Fan Club Magazine* in 1976. He made his premiere as the Doctor on the television special *The Time of the Doctor* (2013).

IMPACT

Capaldi is an award-winning actor, director, and screenwriter who has had a consistently busy career in a diverse range of movies and television series. His work has made him a well-known figure in both the United Kingdom and the United States. As the twelfth incarnation of the Doctor on *Doctor Who*, Capaldi will be contributing to one of the most significant shows in British popular culture.

PERSONAL LIFE

Capaldi is married to Elaine Collins. They live in London, England, and have one daughter, Cecily.

SUGGESTED READING

"Doctor Who: Peter Capaldi Revealed as 12th Doctor." *BBC News*. BBC, 4 Aug. 2013. Web. 2 Mar. 2014.

Duerden, Nick. "Peter Capaldi: From Oscar Winner to Hollywood Reject." *Independent*. Independent Digital News and Media, 6 Oct. 2005. Web. 3 Mar. 2014.

Jefferies, Mark. "Peter Capaldi Says Doctor Who Is 'in His DNA' As He Starts Work as Time Lord." *Daily Mirror*. Trinity Mirror, 9 Jan. 2014. Web. 3 Mar. 2014.

Jeffries, Stuart. "No More Mr. Nice Guy." *Guardian*. Guardian News and Media, 30 Aug. 2006. Web. 2 Mar. 2014.

"Peter Capaldi Biography." *Biography Channel*. A+E Television Networks, n.d. Web. 3 Mar. 2014.

SELECTED WORKS

Local Hero, 1983; *The Lair of the White Worm*, 1988; *Soft Top Hard Shoulder*, 1993; *Franz Kafka's It's a Wonderful Life*, 1995; *Bean*, 1997; *Strictly Sinatra*, 2001; *In the Loop*, 2009; *Selling Hitler*, 1991; *Neverwhere*, 1996; *The Thick of It*, 2005–12; *Getting On*, 2009–10; *The Hour*, 2012; *Doctor Who*; 2013–14

—*Patrick G. Cooper*

Alessia Cara

Born: July 11, 1996
Occupation: Singer and songwriter

Alessia Cara's debut single, "Here," which encapsulates her feelings of awkwardness and alienation while attending a friend's crowded house party, instantly struck a chord with audiences when it was released in the spring of 2015. The infectious antisocial anthem also earned Cara a legion of celebrity fans, including rapper and fellow Canadian Drake and pop singer Taylor Swift, leading *H & M Magazine* (7 Aug. 2015) to dub her "the next big thing in music." Within months Cara's ode to wallflowers and introverts had charted as one of the most viral tracks on the popular music-streaming service Spotify, and the single's success carried over to her EP and full-length album debuts later in 2015. Several publications, including *Billboard*, *Entertainment Weekly*, and *Rolling Stone*, designated "Here" as one of the year's best songs.

However, it was in 2016 that Cara claimed her first number-one hit, as "Here" reached the top of the Billboard Hot R&B/Hip-Hop Songs chart in January. Later that month the song reached number one on Billboard's Pop Songs chart for radio airplay as well; it would go on to be certified double platinum. Cara followed her breakthrough success with two more singles: "Wild Things," which champions self-acceptance, and the heartfelt "Scars to Your Beautiful," a positive song aimed at getting young women to embrace themselves.

EARLY LIFE AND EDUCATION

Alessia Cara was born Alessia Caracciolo on July 11, 1996, in Brampton, Ontario, a suburb located just outside of Toronto, Ontario. Her father, a welder, was a first-generation Italian-Canadian, and her mother, a hairdresser, was an Italian immigrant who at first hardly spoke English. Despite growing up in a nonmusical household, Cara would credit her parents with introducing her to multiple genres of music, ranging from classic rock bands such as the Beatles and Queen to Michael Jackson to contemporary Italian singers Laura Pausini and Tiziano Ferro.

Cara, who grew up with a younger brother, Dario, recalled her childhood as relatively uneventful. "I didn't do things other kids did because my parents were very strict—I stayed at home, quiet in my room," she told Chris Martins

Umusic (Umusic)/CC BY-SA 4.0/Wikimedia Commons

for *Billboard* (28 Aug. 2015). From an early age, the self-described introvert spent her free time watching Sesame Street and obsessively listening to the show's soundtrack, including her favorite track, "I Love Trash" by Oscar the Grouch.

By the time Cara reached middle school, she had become more outgoing and creative, expressing herself through painting and drawing as well as by writing short stories and poetry. However, music quickly became her passion after seeing the video for Amy Winehouse's single "Rehab" on MTV. "I just fell in love with her and her music," she told Jenn Pelly for *Pitchfork* (30 June 2015). "I was nine or ten at the time and I didn't know that current music could sound like it was old. That's when I started falling in love with soul and jazzy-sounding stuff: Michael Bublé, Frank Sinatra."

During this period, Cara received her first guitar—a tenth birthday gift from her parents. After a few months of guitar lessons, she decided instead to teach herself to play, eventually adding the piano and ukulele to her repertoire. Although she formed a band called the Lilacs with her cousins and performed at some family gatherings, she lacked confidence in her voice. "There was this period of time where I would be home alone for an hour because my parents were still at work and my brother was still at school," she revealed to Lauren Nostro for *Complex* (10 July 2015). "I would close myself in a closet and just sing really loud. . . . As soon as I heard someone come home, I would stop. I'd get scared because sometimes I'd think that they heard me."

YOUTUBE STAR

Cara reached a turning point after her mother discovered her secret and demanded an impromptu performance. "I made her close her eyes because I was so shy," she told Martins. The young singer emerged from the closet to find her mother weeping and insisting that music was her daughter's calling. In 2011, at her mother's suggestion, a guitar-playing Cara posted an acoustic version of Adele's "One and Only" on the social media site Facebook in order to build up her confidence. Months later she launched her own channel on the video streaming service YouTube and uploaded her first video: a cover of Jessie J's "Price Tag."

To become a more confident performer, Cara joined her high school choir and took theater classes at Cardinal Ambrozic Catholic Secondary School in Brampton, where her drama instructor further convinced her to enter school talent shows and drama club open mic events. Over the next year, she continued to upload YouTube videos of her performing—in her closet and bedroom—with an acoustic guitar. Beyoncé, Lianne La Havas, Lana Del Rey, idol Amy Winehouse, and fellow Canadian Justin Bieber were among the artists whose songs she covered.

In February 2013, after posting videos with little fanfare, the budding singer's cover of Justin Timberlake's "Mirrors" went viral after television and radio personality Ryan Seacrest included it as part of a cover song contest on his website. However, three months later, it was surpassed in popularity by her version of the Neighbourhood's "Sweater Weather," which attracted the attention of the production company EP Entertainment. The company contacted her via Twitter, much to Cara's disbelief. "I thought it was spam," she told Pelly. "I made sure that my dad talked to them, and as they talked more and more, I realized, 'OK, it's legit.'"

After flying out with her father to the entertainment firm's New York City headquarters, Cara performed two of her covers at a showcase and was signed to a management deal by company cofounder Tony Perez. Determined to pen her own material, the then-sixteen-year-old collaborated with songwriter and fellow EP Entertainment signee Sebastian Kole. "I was not developed. I had no original songs," she told Jane Stevenson for the *Toronto Sun* (23 Nov. 2015). "All I had was my guitar and a voice."

RECORDING PROFESSIONALLY AND SIGNING WITH DEF JAM

Cara and Kole met in Toronto for a brainstorming session intended to develop the direction and sound of a potential album. During her senior year of high school Cara, who kept her music-industry ambitions a secret from classmates, would sneak off to the recording studio after school, often working until midnight on demo tracks. As part of the songwriting process, Kole would have Cara record her thoughts and feelings and send them to him via e-mail. In her journal entries, Cara embraced being an awkward teenager and loner. "I wanted not only to talk about my own experiences, but to really make an album for everyone. I wanted at least one song to resonate with every person," she recalled to Julianne Escobedo Shepherd for *Rookie* (28 May 2015). "I have a lot of talk about body image for women, self-acceptance for everyone, accepting that you might be weird or you might be a little uncool but you could still be cool if you find your own space."

Within a few months Cara had produced several songs, including "Here," a tune about feeling alienated at a house party inspired by a real event she attended while in high school. Armed with her guitar, Cara spent nearly a year visiting various labels in the United States, where she performed stripped-down, acoustic versions of her demo tracks for A&R representatives. Cara continued to attend high school and even applied to colleges, although her parents allowed her to take a year off to pursue her dream of a singing career.

Cara's dedication paid off. In July 2014 she and her EP Entertainment management met an agent who happened to be leaving his label for Def Jam Recordings—the last label Cara visited. Excited that his former label had not immediately signed Cara, the agent enthusiastically lobbied Def Jam's executives to sign her, which they did. After signing, Cara entered the studio with producers including Pop & Oak, Malay, and Fredro in order to develop her demos into finished songs. For "Here," Pop & Oak came up with the idea of including a sample from an Isaac Hayes song ("Ike's Rap II"). Cara and Kole also began writing more material to fill out a full-length album.

FROM "HERE" TO *KNOW-IT-ALL*

Despite her label's desire to release a more radio-friendly song, Cara fought to have "Here" as the lead single from her upcoming EP. "The other song that we had, I feel like it wouldn't separate me from the crowd as much," she told Jon Caramanica for the *New York Times* (19 May 2015). "As a new artist and as a teen girl, I didn't want to be compared. I wanted people to be, like, 'Who is this girl?'" Her instinct would prove to be right. Within four months of its April 2015 release, "Here" had become a viral hit, amassing more than 11 million Spotify streams; the accompanying video, which debuted in May 2015, had racked up 2.5 million views on YouTube. She also made her late-night television debut, performing the song on *The Tonight Show Starring Jimmy Fallon* in July 2015.

Cara's debut five-song EP, *Four Pink Walls,* was released in late August 2015. The album, whose title references the bedroom where Cara had recorded most of her YouTube clips, peaked at number eleven on Billboard's Canadian Albums charts and number thirty-one on the Billboard 200. "Wild Things," Cara's follow-up single, was released in October 2015—the same month that her debut track achieved gold status. "'Wild Things' is about self-acceptance no matter how old you are, what you look like or what you're choosing to do with your life," she shared with *H & M Magazine* (7 Aug. 2015). "It's about rebelling against standards and what is expected of you." The song, which has an accompanying video costarring Cara's friends filmed in Toronto quickly achieved gold status and reached the top twenty of Billboard's Mainstream Top 40 and Dance Club Songs.

Know-It-All, Cara's full-length studio album, hit the shelves in November 2015, entering the Billboard 200 at number nine. To promote the record, she embarked on a headlining tour in January 2016, the same month "Here" reached double platinum. The album, boosted by her hit singles, was a success and was certified gold in May 2016. For her twentieth birthday Cara launched a video for her third single, "Scars to Your Beautiful," in July 2016, while "Wild Things" reached platinum that August.

PERSONAL LIFE
In an August 9, 2016, essay for *Lipstick,* Cara revealed the inspiration behind "Scars to Your Beautiful": her struggle with hair loss, which has left her with visible bald spots. Cara, who feels most comfortable in jeans, a T-shirt, and Converse sneakers, does not consider herself a fashion plate. "I just don't see the point in focusing on what I'm wearing . . . or how I do my hair or what I look like or if I'm fat or skinny," she revealed to Josh O'Kane for the *Globe and Mail* (2 Oct. 2015). "I'm not a fitness model; I'm just a singer. If people focus on that, that's what I care about."

SUGGESTED READING
Cara, Alessia. "Alessia Cara: Antisocial Optimist." Interview by Jenn Pelly. *Pitchfork*. Condé Nast, 30 June 2015. Web. 14 Sept. 2016.

Cara, Alessia. "Alessia Cara Dishes on *Know-It-All* and Getting Thumbs Up from Drizzy and Swifty." Interview by Jane Stevenson. *Toronto Sun*. Postmedia, 23 Nov. 2015. Web. 14 Sept. 2016.

Cara, Alessia. "Let's Do This for Real: An Interview with Alessia Cara." Interview by Julianne Escobedo Shepherd. *Rookie*. Rookie, 28 May 2015. Web. 14 Sept. 2016.

Cara, Alessia. "Meet Alessia Cara, the Soulful Voice behind This Year's Antisocial Pop Anthem." Interview by Lauren Nostro. *Complex*. Complex Media, 10 July 2015. Web. 14 Sept. 2016.

Caramanica, Jon. "Alessia Cara Speaks Up for the Outsiders on 'Here.'" *New York Times*. New York Times, 19 May 2015. Web. 14 Sept. 2016.

O'Kane, Josh. "Rising Pop Star Alessia Cara's Mission: To Craft a Narrative that Focuses on Being Herself." *Globe and Mail*. Globe and Mail, 2 Oct. 2015. Web. 14 Sept. 2016.

—*Bertha Muteba*

Mirinda Carfrae
Born: March 26, 1981
Occupation: Triathlete

When Australian native Mirinda "Rinny" Carfrae competed in her first triathlon at age nineteen, she had no background in swimming, cycling, or running. She nonetheless displayed talent in all three disciplines and, in 2001, earned a spot on the Australian junior elite team. After representing Australia at the International Triathlon Union (ITU) World Championship from 2001 to 2005, Carfrae began competing in half-Ironman 70.3 races, so-called because the total distance covered in the race is 70.3 miles. In 2007 she won the Ironman 70.3 World Championship, helping her qualify for the full-distance Ironman World Championship in Kailua-Kona,

Sandra Mu/Getty Images

Hawaii, commonly known as the Hawaii Ironman or Kona.

Since making her Hawaii Ironman debut in 2009, Carfrae has established herself as one of the best female long-distance triathletes in the world. She has secured podium finishes in all but one of her seven appearances at Kona, winning Ironman world titles in 2010, 2013, and 2014. She has also won more than twenty half-Ironman races. Known as a marathon specialist, Carfrae has won many of her races in dramatic come-from-behind fashion after overcoming significant time deficits during the run phase. She holds both the Kona marathon record (2:50:38) and overall course record (8:52:14). Carfrae is a "fierce competitor," Bradley Stulberg wrote for *Outside* (30 Sept. 2015). "In events where it is common for competitors to slow down, stumble, and, in some cases, literally crumble from fatigue," Stulberg continued, "Carfrae is known for racing like a metronome."

EARLY LIFE AND EDUCATION

Mirinda Carfrae was born on March 26, 1981, in Brisbane, the capital of the state of Queensland in Australia. With her two brothers and three sisters, Carfrae grew up on a farm in Logan City, located just south of Brisbane. Carfrae's parents raised lettuce and, later, passion fruit, and they assigned various farm chores and responsibilities to their children. Carfrae has said that these tasks helped her develop a strong work ethic at an early age.

Growing up on a farm, Carfrae and her siblings "never wore shoes and we lived outside," as she noted to Damien Stannard for the Brisbane *Courier-Mail* (17 Mar. 2015). "We played, and ran." A self-professed tomboy, Carfrae was introduced to sports by her older brothers, and at age seven, she followed them into basketball. Her mother was actively involved in the sport, managing several teams and founding a local basketball club.

Despite often being much shorter than her peers, Carfrae had exceptional agility and athleticism. She played the point guard position and was a standout basketball player at Rochedale State High School in Queensland. She also played touch football and participated in gymnastics and kung fu during her youth.

BASKETBALL PLAYER TO TRIATHLETE

After graduating from high school, Carfrae went on to university to study business and human movement science. During this time, she continued to play basketball, earning a spot on the Southern District Spartans in the Queensland state basketball league. According to Carfrae, she was not "an amazing basketball player" but "was competitive on the regional level" and "okay at the state level," as she put it to Julia Polloreno for *Triathlete* magazine (28 June 2013).

Still, Carfrae, who stands only five feet three inches tall, realized that her height would serve as a major impediment to her basketball future. To make up for her short stature, Carfrae participated in an off-season strength and conditioning program. It was during her training sessions that she first came in contact with triathletes. The Spartans' physiotherapist, Miles Browning, also coached a group of triathletes and invited Carfrae to join the group based on her speed. "I was intrigued by what they were doing," Carfrae told Stannard.

When Carfrae began triathlon training, the only bike she had ever ridden was a BMX bike and her only swimming experience had come in the form of Marco Polo games in her family's backyard pool. Carfrae had also, admittedly, never been a fan of running, despite her natural talent. She was such a poor swimmer, in fact, that when Browning watched her swim for the first time, he dissuaded her from taking her triathlon training any further. "But something inside of me was ignited," Carfrae explained to Polloreno. "I was so excited about the possibility of this new challenge."

Carfrae quit playing basketball and began training in earnest. She received her first triathlon bicycle from her basketball coach, and in late 2000, she competed in her first triathlon. Carfrae placed third in the race, which was held in her hometown and consisted of a 300-yard swim, a 6-mile bike ride, and a 1.8-mile run. "Finishing the race," she wrote in an article for *Self* (12 Oct. 2015), "was the hardest thing I'd ever done. But as soon as the pain went away, I wanted to feel that sense of accomplishment again."

BUILT FOR IRONMAN

In 2001, after placing well in other local triathlon competitions, Carfrae made the Australian junior elite team. She also won backing from the Australian Institute of Sport (AIS), which started covering part of her training and traveling expenses. At this point, Carfrae quit her university studies to focus full time on her triathlon career.

During the beginning of Carfrae's triathlon career, she competed mostly in standard Olympic-distance, or short-course triathlons, which consists of a 0.93-mile (1.5-kilometer) swim, a 24.9-mile (40-kilometer) bike ride, and a 6.2-mile (10-kilometer) run. (Other short-distance triathlons, such as mini or sprint triathlons, vary from race to race.) From 2001 to 2005, Carfrae represented Australia at the short-course ITU World Championships, now known as the ITU World Triathlon Series. She earned silver medals at the 2002 and 2003 championships.

As Carfrae participated in more competitions, she arrived at the realization that she was better built for long-course triathlons. "I learned pretty quickly I didn't break down," she said in her interview with Stannard, "and could keep going a lot longer than the other girls, or get as tired." Carfrae began working toward competing in Ironman-distance triathlon events but did so gradually after learning that most Ironman athletes did not peak until their mid-thirties. She explained to Stannard, "My approach became calculated and long-term. . . . I became a student of the sport, looked at the best, and wondered what it took them to get there."

In 2004 Carfrae won the Nice, France, Long Course Triathlon, and in the following year, she captured the silver medal at the ITU Long Course World Championships, held in Fredericia, Denmark. In 2006 Carfrae placed third in the inaugural Ironman 70.3 World Championship, a half-marathon race consisting of 1.2-mile (1.9-kilometer) swim, a 56-mile (90-kilometer) bike ride, and a 13.1-mile (21.1-kilometer) run. Then, in 2007, she notched her first world title at the Ironman 70.3 World Championship, setting a world record with a time of 4:07:25. Later that year she was named *Triathlete* magazine's Ironman 70.3 athlete of the year.

IRONMAN WORLD CHAMPION

Carfrae's Ironman 70.3 world title victory paved the way for her entry into the Ironman World Championship in Kailua-Kona, Hawaii. Held every year in Hawaii since 1978 and organized by the World Triathlon Corporation (WTC), the Hawaiian Ironman is considered the "holy grail" of triathlon events and is "one of the toughest competitions on the planet," Cristina Goyanes wrote for *espnW* (8 Oct. 2015). The event, like all full Ironmans, consists of a 2.4-mile (3.86-kilometer) swim, a 112-mile (180.25-kilometer) bike ride, and a 26.2-mile (42.2-kilometer) run, but it is distinguished from others by its harsh and unpredictable weather conditions. More than eighty thousand athletes from around the world compete each year for slots to the championship, which is limited to roughly two thousand participants. Less than one hundred of those slots are allotted to professionals, who are granted entry based on points earned in qualifying Ironman triathlon events around the world.

When Carfrae made her Kona debut at the 2009 Ironman World Championship, she was "nervous and scared and just wanted to survive," as she wrote in her article for *Self*. Carfrae not only survived but placed second, posting a marathon course record time of 2:56:51. Her overall time of 9:13:59 was nineteen minutes behind England's Chrissie Wellington, then a two-time

defending Ironman champion and arguably the greatest female triathlete in history.

Carfrae relished the opportunity to challenge Wellington again at the 2010 Hawaii Ironman, but the British champion was forced to make a last-minute withdrawal due to illness. In Wellington's absence, Carfrae ended up taking home her first Ironman world title, bettering her time from the previous year by more than fifteen minutes. "It was unreal, kind of like an out-of-body experience," she said to Polloreno.

At the 2011 Ironman World Championship, Carfrae again finished second to Wellington but in much closer fashion, losing by just two minutes and forty-nine seconds. She nonetheless achieved a then-personal-best course time of 8:57:57. Following Wellington's retirement, Carfrae returned to Kona in 2012 expecting to reclaim her title, but she finished third. She famously collapsed at the finish line and reportedly lost ten pounds during the race as a result of insufficient hydration.

SECOND AND THIRD IRONMAN WORLD TITLES

Carfrae made history in 2013 when she won Kona in a course-record time of 8:52:14, eclipsing Wellington's 2009 record by almost two minutes. Carfrae finished the bicycle portion of the race eight minutes behind the leader but ended up winning by more than five minutes after posting a blistering and then course-record marathon time of 2:50:35. With her victory, she became the first Australian woman to win multiple Ironman world titles.

Coming out of the bike leg of the 2014 Hawaii Ironman, Carfrae's chances of defending her title were highly improbable. She trailed race leader Daniela Ryf of Switzerland by more than fourteen minutes and reasoned that she would have to run a marathon in under two hours and fifty minutes in order to regain the lead and win. Carfrae nearly accomplished that feat, breaking her own marathon course record with a time of 2:50:27 to defeat Ryf by two minutes and claim her third Ironman world title. Her come-from-behind win marked the biggest deficit overcome in Kona history, surpassing American Mark Allen's thirteen-minute deficit in 1995. "When you don't have a positive mindset, you don't achieve your best," she asserted to Goyanes. "It weighs you down and it's tough to perform."

Three days before the 2015 Ironman World Championship, Carfrae was involved in a minor cycling accident when a car hit her while out on a prerace bike ride. She was ultimately forced to withdraw from the championship halfway through the bike leg due to back soreness caused by the accident. "I keep coming back to Kona because I believe I can still do better there, and that is what drives me," Carfrae explained in the *Outside* article. "I want to see how fast I can go.

I want to see if I can have my perfect race. And while I've had some amazing days out there, I still think there's more to do."

Though Kona remains her main focus, Carfrae has continued to race in Ironman 70.3 series competitions. To date, she has won more than twenty half-Ironman races.

PERSONAL LIFE

As a three-time Ironman world champion, Carfrae can lay claim to being one of the best athletes in the world. That title has been earned, however, as much through talent as through hard work, dedication, and perseverance. During her peak training season, Carfrae trains roughly thirty to thirty-five hours per week, with three training sessions a day. She typically puts in seven runs, six swims, and five bike rides a week, totaling 50 to 60 miles of running, 12 miles of swimming, and 280 miles of cycling. At the end of each triathlon season, Carfrae takes two weeks completely off to allow her body to rest and recover.

In December 2013 Carfrae married her longtime boyfriend, the American triathlete Timothy O'Donnell, who placed third in the 2015 Ironman World Championship. The couple reside in Boulder, Colorado.

SUGGESTED READING

Carfrae, Mirinda. "Three-Time Ironman World Champion Mirinda Carfrae Shares What Makes Her a Fierce Competitor." *Self.* Condé Nast, 12 Oct. 2015. Web. 24 Feb. 2016.

Goyanes, Cristina. "Mirinda Carfrae's Seemingly Impossible Surge to Win." *espnW.com.* ESPN Internet Ventures, 8 Oct. 2015. Web. 24 Feb. 2016.

Polloreno, Julia. "Mirinda Carfrae Talks about Her Childhood, Training, Running Form and More." *Triathlete.* Competitor Group, 28 June 2013. Web. 24 Feb. 2016.

Stannard, Damien. "Mirinda Carfrae's Bumpy Road to Becoming a Triple Hawaiian Ironman Champion." *Courier-Mail.* News, 17 Mar. 2015. Web. 24 Feb. 2016.

Stulberg, Bradley. "Ironman World Champ Mirinda Carfrae Shares Her Training Wisdom." *Outside.* Mariah Media Network, 30 Sept. 2015. Web. 24 Feb. 2016.

—*Chris Cullen*

Eleanor Catton

Born: September 24, 1985
Occupation: Author

Eleanor Catton is a New Zealand novelist. Born in Canada, she was raised in New Zealand and attended the University of Canterbury in Christchurch. Her 2013 novel, *The Luminaries*, won the prestigious Man Booker Prize for Fiction.

EARLY LIFE AND EDUCATION

Eleanor Catton was born in London, Ontario, Canada, on September 24, 1985. She has one sibling. Her father is American, and her mother is from New Zealand.

Catton's family moved to the city of Christchurch on New Zealand's South Island when she was six years old, after her father accepted a position as a philosophy professor at the University of Canterbury. Catton's mother was a librarian and later worked in the New Zealand Ministry of Education.

Catton's parents were enamored with New Zealand's natural beauty and took their children on numerous tours of the country's diverse wilderness. The Cattons' devotion to both nature and the arts was reflected in their refusal to own an automobile or a television, a stoic upbringing that Catton later credited for fostering her passion for literature. She began writing at age five, starting with short stories and picture books for her parents and siblings. Catton attended high school in Burnside, New Zealand, before enrolling as an undergraduate at the University of Canterbury, where she majored in English.

THE REHEARSAL

After her undergraduate study, Catton earned a master's degree in creative writing from Victoria University in Wellington. Her thesis in the program ultimately became her debut novel, *The Rehearsal*, released by Granta Books in 2008 and first published in the United States in 2010, when Catton was just twenty-two years old. *The Rehearsal* centers on the scandal that erupts in a small community following an affair between a music teacher and his pupil. The plot also follows the school's theater department, which scandalously produces a play based on the incident.

The book was well received by both international critics and the literary community in Catton's native New Zealand. It earned her numerous awards, including the 2009 Betty Trask Award from the Society of Authors. Catton was also included in Amazon's Rising Stars list of authors in 2009. In 2011, she was awarded the Ursula Bethell Residency at the University of Canterbury, her undergraduate alma mater.

THE LUMINARIES

The success of Catton's first book led to her acceptance in the venerable Iowa Writers' Workshop at the University of Iowa. During her two years at the university, she began work on an ambitious new project that became her second novel.

The Luminaries (2013) is a Dickensian work based on a gold rush town in nineteenth-century New Zealand. The book's protagonist, Walter Moody, stumbles upon a series of complex unsolved crimes. He is pulled into the mystery by a council of twelve men, whom Catton based on the twelve signs of the Western zodiac, while Moody and other main characters are based on the sun, the moon, and five planets of the solar system.

Praised by critics across the globe, *The Luminaries* affirmed Catton's place among the top authors in contemporary literature. Critics lauded the book's breadth, intricacy, and diverse narrative patterns. Catton drew inspiration for the work from her trips around the mountains of New Zealand with her parents as a child, as well as her father's lifelong passion for astronomy.

The novel earned Catton the prestigious Man Booker Prize for Fiction in 2013, making her only the second New Zealand author in history to win the award. At twenty-eight, she was also the youngest author to win the award to date. The book earned other crucial accolades as well, including Canada's Governor's General Award for English-language fiction.

IMPACT

Catton has emerged as a unique talent, bringing global attention to an insular yet burgeoning community of authors working in New Zealand and becoming something of a national treasure. The dense, overarching narratives in *The Luminaries* have drawn critical comparison to the works of such authors as Charles Dickens and Herman Melville, evoking a time when ambitiously layered works of prose were the cultural norm.

PERSONAL LIFE

Catton lives in Auckland, New Zealand, with her partner, American poet Steven Toussaint. She teaches creative writing at the Manukau Institute of Technology.

SUGGESTED READING

Catton, Eleanor. "Eleanor Catton: The Land of the Long White Cloud." *Guardian*. Guardian News and Media, 17 Oct. 2013. Web. 12 June 2014.

Clark, Nick. "Eleanor Catton Interview: Kiwi Author Describes the Journey That Led to Her Booker Prize Win." *Independent*. Independent.co.uk, 16 Oct. 2013. Web. 12 June 2014.

Houpt, Simon. "Canadian-Born Author Eleanor Catton Wins Prestigious Man Booker Prize." *Globe and Mail*. Globe and Mail, 15 Oct. 2013. Web. 12 June 2014.

Lyall, Sarah. "A Writer Thanks Her Lucky Stars." *New York Times*. New York Times, 19 Nov. 2003. Web. 12 June 2014.

Rahim, Sameer. "Eleanor Catton Interview: Money Doesn't Transform You—Only Love Can." *Telegraph*. Telegraph Media Group, 17 Oct. 2013. Web. 12 June 2014.

Taylor, Phil. "Interview with Eleanor Catton." *New Zealand Herald*. APN New Zealand, 21 Sept. 2013. Web. 12 June 2014.

SELECTED WORKS

The Rehearsal, 2008; *The Luminaries*, 2013

—*John Pritchard*

Wyatt Cenac

Born: April 19, 1976
Occupation: Comedian and actor

Wyatt Cenac is, as the title of his 2011 stand-up special proudly proclaims, a comedy person. Best known for his four-year stint as a correspondent on *The Daily Show*, Cenac began his career performing stand-up comedy as a college student in North Carolina and later honed his craft in the comedy clubs and improv theaters of Los Angeles. Much of his most noteworthy work has occurred behind the scenes; he spent several years on the writing staff of the animated series *King of the Hill* and was the recipient of three Emmy Awards for his writing work on *The Daily Show*. After leaving *The Daily Show* in 2012, he returned to his stand-up roots, hosting a popular comedy showcase in Brooklyn, New York. Despite his off-screen success, Cenac has made it clear that any departures from the screen are merely temporary. "[T]his face can't stay off the television. Not because it's so beautiful. It's just I have a medical condition that needs the radiation that comes off the cameras," he joked to Bradford Evans for *Splitsider* (19 Sept. 2013). "Otherwise, it's like a weird *Dorian Gray* thing."

EARLY LIFE AND EDUCATION

Wyatt Cenac was born on April 19, 1976, in New York City. He spent the first several years of his life in the city, where his father worked as a taxi driver. After his father was shot and killed while on the job when he was still a young child, his mother remarried. The family moved to Texas when he was four, settling in Dallas.

Amanda Edwards/WireImage/Getty Images

Following his graduation from the Jesuit College Preparatory School of Dallas, he enrolled in the University of North Carolina at Chapel Hill (UNC-CH), where he studied communications. He earned his bachelor's degree in 1998.

While in college, Cenac began to take his first steps into the world of stand-up comedy. He had long been interested in comedy and particularly enjoyed the work of veteran comedians such as Bill Cosby, Richard Pryor, and Jerry Seinfeld. He first took the stage at an open mic in Raleigh, North Carolina, where he was given three minutes to perform. The experience was a nerve-wracking one for Cenac, but it ultimately played a crucial role in the development of his career. "I was so nervous I burned through my whole set in a minute flat," he recalled to Mychelle Vasvary for *Laughspin* (14 Oct. 2014). "I remember walking off the stage feeling scared, but then I got encouraged because after my set the headliner for the night came up to talk to me. . . . He told me I did a good job, and I should get a few minutes more. So I remember thinking, 'this is a professional comedian that thinks I've got something.'"

EARLY CAREER
Cenac began his career in television while still in college, completing an internship at *Saturday Night Live (SNL)*, the long-running late-night sketch show that has accelerated the careers of numerous up-and-coming comedians since its inception in 1975. Cenac's time at *SNL* gave him firsthand knowledge of the behind-the-scenes operations of a comedy television show. "I was an intern in the research department," he

told Tom Whitcomb for *Isthmus* (29 Oct. 2015). "If a cast member was doing an impression of a politician, I'd go down to the Today show and get some video clips for them. And for *Weekend Update*, they would do a lot of stuff with Associated Press photos. I would go to the AP and get a stack of those photos, and then the *Update* writers would look at them to come up with jokes. I got to kind of watch and absorb, and it was a very cool experience."

Although he was later offered a position as *SNL's* receptionist, Cenac decided not to take it, doubting that it would lead to work as a writer or performer on the show. Instead, he opted to move to Los Angeles following his graduation from the University of North Carolina. While in California, he focused on performing stand-up and also began to explore improvisational comedy, performing in the Los Angeles branches of the Upright Citizens Brigade and ImprovOlympic theaters.

Around 2003, Cenac joined the writing staff of *King of the Hill*, an animated television comedy set in suburban Texas. Two of the show's writers, John Altschuler and Dave Krinsky, were alumni of the University of North Carolina, and Cenac had had the opportunity to meet with them and show them samples of his writing while in college. He remained in touch with the two writers after graduating, and he credits them with helping him get the job. He enjoyed writing for *King of the Hill* and found that he was able to bring some personal experience to the table. "[I]t was great because I grew up in Texas so there was a lot about the show that I felt like I could relate to," he told Evans. "Even the way that I write today is all based on lessons that I learned from John and Dave. And [show creator] Mike [Judge] too." Cenac worked in *King of the Hill's* writers' room for several years and later lent his voice to characters in several episodes.

THE DAILY SHOW
Although he had found success as a stand-up comic and television writer, Cenac did not become widely known among the public until 2008, when he joined the cast of *The Daily Show*. He had previously auditioned for the popular satirical news program on several occasions, with no success, and was reluctant to audition again when his agent told him of the opportunity. However, for his final audition he was allowed to write his own audition piece. The opportunity to demonstrate more of his personality and particular brand of humor proved to be the key; he was called to a second audition and hired shortly thereafter. Joining *The Daily Show* as a writer and correspondent, he left Los Angeles and returned to New York, where the show was filmed.

Thanks to his time working on *King of the Hill*, Cenac was already familiar with what went into writing a television show. Still, the transition from performing stand-up and improv on stage to filling a more behind-the-scenes role was challenging at times. "It was an adjustment just from the standpoint that you're spending all day writing jokes for somebody else, and you kind of have to put your own stand-up career on hold a little bit. It kind of happens on weekends and after work, and it becomes this sort of extracurricular thing," he explained to Joel Keller for the *A.V. Club* (13 May 2011). While a member of *The Daily Show's* staff, he wrote for the show and appeared on screen, filming comedic interviews and sometimes traveling to film pieces in the field. He also wrote for and performed at the 2010 Rally to Restore Sanity and/or Fear, a televised event in Washington, DC, that was a collaboration between *The Daily Show* and the satirical news program *The Colbert Report*.

Although his commitment to *The Daily Show* rendered his stand-up career "extracurricular," as he described it to Keller, Cenac nevertheless found some opportunities to perform during his tenure with the program. His first stand-up special, *Wyatt Cenac: Comedy Person*, was released on DVD and CD in 2011. In recognition of his work on *The Daily Show*, Cenac, along with his fellow writers, received the Emmy Award for outstanding writing for a variety series in 2009, 2011, and 2012.

Cenac remained with *The Daily Show* until 2012, at which time he decided to move on. He later revealed on the podcast *WTF with Marc Maron* that his decision to leave the show was more complicated than he had initially made public. In 2011 Cenac had come into conflict with *The Daily Show* host Jon Stewart after Stewart performed an impression of Republican presidential candidate Herman Cain that Cenac considered racist. The ensuing argument contributed to his discomfort at work and played a significant role in his decision to leave the following year. Despite the less than positive terms of his departure, however, Cenac later returned to *The Daily Show* in the summer of 2015 for Stewart's final episode. In an interview with Andy Beta for the *Wall Street Journal* (20 Oct. 2014), he also emphasized that he had wanted to explore more independent opportunities that would give him greater control: "*The Daily Show* was a great job, but at some point the urge to spread my wings and steer my own ship took over."

RETURN TO STAND-UP

Following his departure from *The Daily Show*, Cenac returned to his stand-up roots, performing more extensively and filming a second special, *Wyatt Cenac: Brooklyn*. Released in 2014, the special premiered on Netflix and featured, among other guest appearances, an appearance

by a puppet version of Cenac. "When you think about it, a televised special is not the ideal way to experience stand-up," he told Whitcomb of his thought process while preparing to record the special. "The best way is to be at the show, and second best is probably just to listen to it, because you can focus in on it. If it's on television, you're listening but you can also check your phone or walk away to make a sandwich. So I felt like [I should do] something visually to add to the televised experience of it—and that was puppets."

Along with his own stand-up shows, Cenac has hosted the stand-up showcase Night Train since 2012. "[I]t's nice to sit and just watch all the comedians and see them and get to be a fan," he told Evans. "I'll always try to sit in the wings and watch through a slit in the curtain and see friends or people I've just met." Held weekly at the Littlefield performance space in the Gowanus neighborhood of Brooklyn, Night Train features performances by both new and established comedians as well as occasional live music.

OTHER WORK

In addition to his work on *The Daily Show*, Cenac has made guest appearances on television comedies such as the *Eric Andre Show, Maron*, and *Inside Amy Schumer* and has appeared in films such as 2014's *Hits* and the 2016 mockumentary *Jacqueline (Argentine)*. Also an occasional voice actor, he has lent his voice to more than twenty episodes of the cartoon *Fanboy & Chum Chum* as well as single episodes of the *Venture Bros.* and *BoJack Horseman*. In early 2016 the cable channel Turner Broadcasting Station (TBS) announced that it had ordered ten episodes of *People of Earth*, a comedy series starring Cenac.

SUGGESTED READING

Beta, Andy. "Wyatt Cenac Skewers Brooklyn's Preciousness in Netflix Comedy Special." *Wall Street Journal*. Dow Jones, 20 Oct. 2014. Web. 16 May 2016.

Cenac, Wyatt. "The People in Your Neighborhood: Wyatt Cenac." Interview by Kristin Iversen. *Brooklyn*. Brooklyn Magazine, 2 Sept. 2014. Web. 16 May 2016.

Cenac, Wyatt. "Talking to Wyatt Cenac about *The Daily Show*, Writing for *King of the Hill*, and What's Next for Him." Interview by Bradford Evans. *Splitsider*. Splitsider, 19 Sept. 2013. Web. 16 May 2016.

Cenac, Wyatt. "What's Your Story, Wyatt Cenac?" Interview by Tom Whitcomb. *Isthmus*. Red Card Media, 29 Oct. 2015. Web. 16 May 2016.

Cenac, Wyatt. "Wyatt Cenac." Interview by Joel Keller. *A.V. Club*. Onion, 13 May 2011. Web. 16 May 2016.

Cenac, Wyatt. "Wyatt Cenac on Brooklyn, Net-flix Special, and Getting Personal." Interview by Mychelle Vasvary. *Laughspin*. Laughspin, 14 Oct. 2014. Web. 16 May 2016.

SELECTED WORKS
The Daily Show, 2008–12; *Wyatt Cenac: Comedy Person,* 2011; *Wyatt Cenac: Brooklyn,* 2014

—*Joy Crelin*

Michael Cerveris

Born: November 6, 1960
Occupation: Actor

For many critics and theater fans, Michael Cerveris is one of the most versatile stage actors working today. He first received notice for his pioneering lead role in The Who's *Tommy,* a musical adapted for the stage from the classic rock opera, which premiered on Broadway in 1993. Since *Tommy,* he went on to perform in many Broadway and Off-Broadway productions, accrue numerous acting award nominations, and win two Tony Awards for his roles in the musicals *Assassins* (2004), and *Fun Home* (2015).

Cerveris has also had a successful career in film and on television. He is particularly beloved for his turn as September, an observer, on the cult sci-fi television series *Fringe* (2008–13), as well as for his scene-stealing roles in *Treme,* from 2011 to 2013, and on *The Good Wife,* from 2013

Noam Galai/WireImage/Getty Images

to 2014. Cerveris also finds time to moonlight as a singer and guitarist on various musical projects, including his country band Loose Cattle. Yet, for Cerveris, what matters most is not the accomplishments or the praise, but the opportunity to continue to do quality work. "I have an ambivalence about awards in the arts, especially competitive awards," he said to Joanne Kaufman for the *New York Times* (27 May 2016). "But I'm grateful to have them and grateful for the memory of the work they represent."

EARLY LIFE AND EDUCATION
Michael Cerveris was born in Bethesda, Maryland, on November 6, 1960, and raised in Huntington, West Virginia. He is one of three children. His mother was a dance teacher; his father a music professor at Marshall University. His parents, who met at the Juilliard School in New York City, always encouraged their children to pursue their creative interests. For young Michael, that meant playing music and acting from his early childhood. He began performing in second grade, appearing in his father's university productions whenever there was a role for a small child.

The first show Cerveris saw in a Broadway theater was *Sweeney Todd: The Demon Barber of Fleet Street,* a musical thriller with music and lyrics by Stephen Sondheim. He has since called seeing the show a formative experience. Cerveris told Kathy Henderson of *Broadway.com* (18 Apr. 2012): "*Sweeney* has always been, for me, the standard for what music theater can and should be. The original production was the first Broadway show I ever saw—and I saw it seven times! It made me think there might be a place for someone like me, who was not a typical musical theater performer."

After graduating from Phillips Exeter Academy in New Hampshire in 1979, Cerveris studied theater and voice at Yale University in New Haven, Connecticut. He graduated cum laude in 1983. He immediately headed to New York City, in the hopes of making it as a stage actor.

BECOMING THE PINBALL WIZARD
During his first three years in New York City, Cerveris lived the fabled starving artist lifestyle. He bounced from sublets to friends' couches, living in thirteen locations over those three years. He became involved in the downtown and experimental theater scenes, both through acting and by exploring the punk music scene. He had early success in a series of Off-Broadway productions, including roles in *Macbeth* (1983), *Total Eclipse* (1985), *Abingdon Square* (1987) and *Blood Sports* (1986), as well as a role as a British guitar student, Ian Ware, on the television series *Fame,* from 1986 to 1987. He stayed in Los Angeles, where *Fame* was filmed, for a number of

years, making appearances in films like *Strangers* (1990), *Rock 'n' Roll High School Forever* (1991), *Steel and Lace* (1991), and *A Woman, Her Men, and Her Futon* (1992). It wasn't long before he returned to the stage. He landed the title role in the musical adaptation of The Who's *Tommy*, which premiered at the La Jolla Playhouse in California in 1992.

Cerveris played the title role of the deaf, dumb, and blind pinball wizard for 110 performances in La Jolla before being asked, along with the rest of the cast, to audition for the same roles in the Broadway version, which was scheduled to open at the St. James Theater in 1993. He won the part and made his Broadway debut later that year to critical and commercial success. He also played the role in the European premiere in Germany. Cerveris recalled to Henderson, "Everything about *Tommy* was unexpected and new. It was the Broadway debut of almost all of us: Sherie Rene Scott, Norm Lewis, Alice Ripley. [Director] Des McAnuff was not a Broadway insider at that point. We were total underdogs, a scrappy bunch of kids bringing a rock opera by the Who to Broadway at a time when *Rent* wasn't even a thought in Jonathan Larson's mind. I think *Tommy* really changed the landscape of Broadway."

Tommy also changed the direction of Cerveris's career. Always involved with music, he was taken under the wing of Pete Townsend, the Who's lead guitarist and principal songwriter, and asked to perform on Townsend's solo record, *Psychoderelict*. He also toured with Townsend, performing a number of songs from *Tommy* at each concert.

AN ESTABLISHED ACTOR

Cerveris returned to Broadway in 1997 to appear as Thomas Andrews in *Titanic* (1997) and then received considerable acclaim Off-Broadway for his leading performance as the transsexual punk rocker Hedwig in *Hedwig and the Angry Inch* in 1998. He played Hedwig in Los Angeles and then made his West End debut in London in the same role in 2000.

While Cerveris's stage career continued to blossom in the early 2000s, he also found time to work as a character actor in films and television, including having roles in *CSI: Crime Scene Investigation* (2001), *The Mexican* (2001), and *The American Embassy* (2002).

When he returned to Broadway in 2004, he played John Wilkes Booth in the Stephen Sondheim musical *Assassins*, a role that earned him the Tony Award for Best Featured Actor in a Musical. The next year, in 2005, he played the title role in *Sweeney Todd*—the musical that began his fascination with musical theater—and again earned a Tony nomination. He followed these runs with acclaimed performances in

the Broadway versions of *Lovemusik* (2007), in which he played Kurt Weill, *Cymbeline* (2007), in which he played Posthumus Leonatus, and *Hedda Gabler* (2009), in which he played Jorgen Tesman. He was also active during this period in Off-Broadway productions, including *King Lear* (2007), in which he played the Earl of Kent.

GAINING ACCLAIM AND A WIDER AUDIENCE

By the late 2000s, Cerveris was well-known in the world of Broadway, but he became known to a larger audience with his, and most notable, television role as the otherworldly character known as September in the cult sci-fi drama *Fringe* (2008–13). September was originally intended to appear in a single episode, but was later developed into both a series regular and a character integral to the series main plot.

As one of the figures known as the Observers—so-called because they had appeared as bystanders at key moments of history—Cerveris's character became pivotal to the mythology of the show. In *Entertainment Weekly* (18 Jan. 2013), Cerveris discussed with Emily Rome the evolution of his character shortly before the *Fringe* finale: "Yeah, it's been kind of astounding. It's true that in the very beginning I understood it as just being a one-off. Almost before I started working actually, they had already started to feel differently. Both [executive producers] Jeff Pinkner and J. J. [Abrams]—they saw September as having a crucial role to play, a role that was going to continue to play out throughout the series as long as it lasted. But you never know when people say that—no matter how well-intentioned, how much they believe it themselves—you never know if that's how things are actually gonna play out."

While acting in *Fringe*, Cerveris also appeared as music manager Marvin Frey in the HBO series *Treme*, from 2011 to 2013. He later appeared in the role of James Castro, a charismatic state's attorney, on the 2014–2015 season of the long-running CBS political and legal drama *The Good Wife*.

In 2015 Cerveris received considerable praise for his leading role in the Broadway musical production of *Fun Home*, based on the graphic memoir by Alison Bechdel about her childhood. In it, Cerveris plays Alison's father, Bruce Bechdel, who dies under mysterious circumstances and is revealed to be a closeted gay man. Cerveris won his second Tony for his performance, this time in the category of best actor in a musical. Of his diverse stage roles, he remarked to Karu F. Daniels for *New York* (20 May 2015): "I'm always interested in a new challenge or trying to do something I haven't done before. Maybe I'm just impatient or schizophrenic. I'm just interested in too many different things and nobody ever told me that I couldn't."

MUSICAL CAREER

In addition to his work as a stage and screen actor (and the soundtrack recordings he has made as a cast member of musicals), Michael Cerveris has been actively involved in the music scene for decades—though he doesn't consider music his primary career. In an interview with Jeryl Brunner for *Parade* (4 Apr. 2016), Cerveris noted: "I sometimes see my acting life as my day job. Because I've never looked to music to make a living, I'm able to do it with relatively few compromises. I grew up playing music and acting in equal measure. My father is a classical pianist and music educator. So I grew up with a very specific idea of what it took to call yourself a musician and that was study and training to a degree that I didn't have. I still don't really read music. I can kind of read relatively to learn to sing. I can read guitar charts. I guess my training is more practical than theoretical."

As a young man Cerveris considered bands like Hüsker Dü, the Pixies, and the Replacements among his musical influences. In 1998 he took a sabbatical from the stage to play guitar on former Hüsker Dü guitarist and vocalist Bob Mould's 1998 tour of the United States and the United Kingdom. His first solo album, *Dog Eared*, came out in February 2004. A road trip through the southern United States in 2007 found him in Meridian, Mississippi, where he reconnected with his southern upbringing through the music of Meridian hometown music legend Jimmy Rogers. He recorded and released *North of Houston*, a southern-tinged country live album with his band, Loose Cattle, in 2013. His most recent solo album, *Piety*, was more pop/rock oriented and was released in 2016. Cerveris told Brunner, "My second solo record, *Piety* . . . It's lushly string orchestrated so it's not as strictly country as the Loose Cattle stuff. The songs are all originals and they range a bit stylistically."

PERSONAL LIFE

Fun Home closes on September 10, 2016. When not on stage, Cerveris continues to play music with Loose Cattle. He has homes in New York City and in New Orleans, Louisiana.

SUGGESTED READING

Cerveris, Michael. "Exclusive Q&A: Actor Michael Cerveris on Broadway and Making Music." Interview by Jeryl Brunner. *Parade*. AMG/Parade, 4 Apr. 2016. Web. 14 June 2016.

Cross, Lucy E, and Michael Cerveris. "Michael Cerveris." *Masterworks Broadway*. Sony Music Entertainment, n.d. Web. 9 June 2016.

Daniels, Karu F. "10 Things You May Not Know about Me: Michael Cerveris of *Fun Home*." *NewYork.com*. NewYork.com, 20 May 2015. Web. 20 July 2016.

Henderson, Kathy. "*Evita* Star Michael Cerveris on *Sweeney*, *Tommy*, and His Most Difficult Role Ever." *Broadway.com*. Broadway.com, 18 Apr. 2012. Web. 10 June 2016.

Kaufman, Joanne. "Michael Cerveris's 'Fun Home' in Chelsea." *New York Times*. New York Times, 27 May 2016. Web. 9 June 2016.

Rome, Emily. "*Fringe*: Michael Cerveris on the Return of September and the Series Finale Full of 'Surprise and Heartbreak.'" *Entertainment Weekly*. Entertainment Weekly, 18 Jan. 2013. Web. 9 June 2016.

SELECTED WORKS

The Who's *Tommy*, 1993; *Titanic*, 1997; *Hedwig and the Angry Inch*, 2000; *Assassins*, 2004; *Sweeney Todd*, 2005; *Fringe*, 2008–13; *Hedda Gabler*, 2009; *Treme*, 2011–13; *Evita*, 2012; *The Good Wife*, 2014–15; *Fun Home*, 2015

—*Christopher Mari*

Nuri Bilge Ceylan

Born: January 26, 1959
Occupation: Director

Writer and director Nuri Bilge Ceylan is Turkey's most acclaimed filmmaker and "one of the most important auteurs working today," Rachel Donadio declared for the *New York Times* (22 Dec. 2014). Ceylan is known for making highly atmospheric, slow-burning films that probe various facets of the human condition. "My films are mostly about humans, trying to understand human relations. The story, or what's happening, is not that important," he told Donadio.

A former professional photographer, Ceylan did not become a full-time filmmaker until the 1990s, when he was already in his mid-thirties. He quickly established his reputation, however, with his first film effort, *Cocoon* (*Koza*, 1995), which became the first Turkish short film to be selected for competition at the Cannes Film Festival. He subsequently went on to release seven feature-length films, all of which received international acclaim and won awards. A mainstay at Cannes for more than a decade, Ceylan won the festival's second-highest honor, the Grand Prix, for his films *Distant* (*Uzak*, 2002) and *Once Upon a Time in Anatolia* (*Bir Zamanlar Anadolu'da*, 2011). His career reached a high point in 2014, when he won Cannes's coveted top honor, the Palme d'Or, for his film *Winter Sleep* (*Kiş Uykusu*, 2014).

EARLY LIFE AND EDUCATION

Nuri Bilge Ceylan was born on January 26, 1959, in Istanbul, Turkey, to Fatma and Mehmet

Venturelli/WireImage/GettyImages

Emin Ceylan. He grew up with an older sister, Emine. When Ceylan was two, his father, an agricultural engineer, moved the family back to his hometown of Yenice, a small town in Turkey's northwestern Çanakkale province. Ceylan lived in Yenice until the age of ten, after which his family returned to Istanbul so his sister could attend high school. The family settled in the city's Bakirköy neighborhood, where Ceylan attended fifth grade, middle school, and high school.

When Ceylan was a child, "there was no art at all around me," he noted to Geoff Andrew for the *Guardian* (6 Feb. 2009), in an interview sponsored by that publication at the British Film Institute. As a high-school student, however, he developed an interest in photography after receiving a book on the subject as a present. He created a darkroom and began printing his own photographs, "and with time I began to realize that it's an art," he told Andrew.

Upon graduating from high school in 1976, Ceylan began studying chemical engineering at Istanbul Technical University. His studies there, however, were regularly interrupted by political unrest, forcing him to drop out after two years. "Every day," he recalled to Jonathan Romney for the *Independent* (17 Mar. 2012), "there was fighting, shooting and killings." In 1978 he won acceptance to Istanbul's prestigious Boğaziçi University, where he switched his focus to electrical engineering.

It was during his time at Boğaziçi that Ceylan rekindled his passion for photography. He joined the university's photography club and earned money by taking passport photographs. Still, he initially considered photography nothing more than a hobby, and in 1985, he earned his Bachelor of Science degree in electrical engineering.

LATE-BLOOMING FILMMAKER

Uninterested in working as an engineer after university, Ceylan turned his attention to traveling. He spent six months in London before traveling to Nepal and India to pursue mountaineering exploits.

After approximately a year abroad, Ceylan returned to Turkey to complete his eighteen months of compulsory military service. During that time, he started reading books on a wide array of topics, including filmmaking. One of those books included Roman Polanski's 1984 bestselling autobiography *Roman*, which chronicles the celebrated French-Polish director's dramatic journey from Nazi-occupied Poland to Hollywood. For Ceylan, the book proved to be a transforming experience and inspired him to become a filmmaker. Polanski's life "seemed very adventurous," he observed to Andrew, "starting from absolute zero in a Nazi camp up to Hollywood. And in that book, film-making seemed easy to me."

While studying film at Istanbul's Mimar Sinan Fine Arts University, Ceylan supported himself by working as a commercial photographer. He left the four-year course after two years, however, to learn the craft on his own. In addition to pouring over technical books about cinematography and other aspects of filmmaking, he also became a devoted cinephile, studying the works of international masters such as Robert Bresson, Yasujirō Ozu, Michelangelo Antonioni, Ingmar Bergman, Andrei Tarkovsky, and Abbas Kiarostami.

Ceylan's professional career began as an actor, when he landed a role in a short film directed by his friend Mehmet Eryilmaz. The experience allowed Ceylan to witness firsthand the various stages of the filmmaking process. Afterward, he purchased an Arriflex thirty-five millimeter camera, which he began using to photograph his own short film.

COCOON AND THE "PROVINCIAL TRILOGY"

Ceylan's first and only short film, *Cocoon*, was released in 1995. Shot in black and white and featuring no dialogue, the fourteen-minute short starred his parents as an estranged older couple who reunite after much time apart. It screened at the 1995 Cannes Film Festival, becoming the first Turkish short to be selected for competition at the festival.

The positive response to *Cocoon* at Cannes prompted Ceylan to focus his attention on feature-length films. His debut feature, *The Small Town* (*Kasaba*, 1997), was entirely self-financed and featured a cast comprised of family, relatives, and close friends. Partly adapted from an autobiographical story by Ceylan's sister, the eighty-five-minute, black-and-white film follows, through the gaze of a young girl and her brother, a three-generation family living in a rural area around Yenice. The film, for which Ceylan served as writer, director, producer, cinematographer, and editor, premiered at the 1998 Berlin International Film Festival, where it won the Caligari Prize. It also captured the Special Jury Prize at that year's Istanbul Film Festival.

For his next two features, *Clouds of May* (*Mayıs Sıkıntısı*, 1999) and *Distant*, Ceylan again enlisted family and friends as actors and, in addition to writing, directing, and producing, held virtually every technical role. "I think a director should know many things . . . otherwise you are a slave of the technical people," he asserted to Andrew. Similar to *The Small Town*, *Clouds of May* and *Distant* touch on themes that would become common in his work, such as rural versus city life, family dynamics, and marital conflict. Together, the three films have come to be affectionately known as Ceylan's "provincial trilogy."

Clouds of May tells the story of a film director who journeys back to his hometown of Yenice to make a film using his own family and friends. Shot in color and again featuring Ceylan's parents in principal roles, the film is largely based on his experiences making *The Small Town* and also draws on elements from *The Cherry Orchard* (1904), the final play by Russian author Anton Chekhov, to whom it is dedicated. Ceylan, who became enamored with Chekhov as a teenager, told Romney that Russian literature is "maybe the biggest influence in my films." *Clouds of May* took home best film prizes at both the 1999 Antalya and Istanbul film festivals, in Turkey, and the FIPRESCI (Fédération Internationale de la Presse Cinématographique) Award at the 2000 European Film Awards.

Distant, however, was the film that first brought Ceylan widespread international recognition. Mostly filmed in his apartment in Istanbul, the drama centers on a middle-class commercial photographer whose solitary life in the ancient Turkish city is interrupted when a distant male relative comes to live with him. Praised for its sophisticated cinematography and contemplative tone, *Distant* won a total of forty-seven awards, most notably the prestigious Grand Prix award at Cannes.

CANNES MAINSTAY

Ceylan stepped back in front of the camera for his next film, *Climates* (İklimler, 2006), in which he starred alongside his second wife, Ebru Ceylan, who also served as a cowriter. The film, shot on high-definition video, marked the beginning of his relationships with cinematographer Gökhan Tiryaki and producer Zeynep Özbatur

Atakan. In it, Ceylan plays Isa, an Istanbul university professor whose growing self-involvement leads him to break up with his much-younger wife, Bahar, during a summer holiday on Turkey's Aegean coast.

Climates won the FIPRESCI Award at the 2006 Cannes Film Festival and was well received by critics. Manohla Dargis, in her review for the *New York Times* (27 Oct. 2006), called *Climates* "a haunting portrait of existential solitude. . . . [Ceylan's] scenes play out to the natural rhythms of life, their meaning often articulated in silences, digressions and awkward laughter." Meanwhile, *Variety*'s chief film critic Scott Foundas, in a profile of Ceylan for that publication (3 Nov. 2014), later observed that the film echoed John Cassavetes "in its feverish emotional pitch" and Bernardo Bertolucci "in the reckless abandon of its sex scenes."

Ceylan's next two features, *Three Monkeys* (Üç Maymun, 2008) and *Once Upon a Time in Anatolia* (2011), marked a departure from his first four films. Moving away from the autobiographical nature of those films, *Three Monkeys* adopts the narrative style of a classic Hollywood film noir. It tells the story of an indigent Istanbul family who get caught up in a web of deceit, double-dealing, and murder after its patriarch accepts an ill-fated bribe. The film, which Ceylan cowrote with his wife and actor Ercan Kesal, premiered at the 2008 Cannes Film Festival and earned him the best directing award.

Once Upon a Time in Anatolia furthered Ceylan's reputation as one of international cinema's most prominent directors. Like *Three Monkeys*, the 157-minute film, which he again cowrote with his wife and Kesal, contains noir elements, taking on the form of a police procedural. Divided into three parts, it follows a dozen men over a single night as they search for a dead body in the desolate countryside of Anatolia in western Turkey. The film garnered universal critical acclaim for its deep probing of the human condition and won the Grand Prix at the 2011 Cannes Film Festival. Romney called the production "utterly absorbing" and declared Ceylan to be "one of today's great directors—an artist whose unapologetic seriousness, tempered by mischievous wit, makes him as close as we have now to a Bergman or a Tarkovsky."

PALME D'OR WINNER

Ceylan and his wife spent six months writing *Winter Sleep* (2014), his seventh feature film. Based on two Chekhov stories, "Excellent People" and "The Wife," and set in the Cappadocia region of central Anatolia, the film centers on Aydin (Haluk Bilginer), a former actor who runs a scenic mountaintop hotel that was bequeathed to him by his late parents, as well as other nearby properties that he rents out to local tenants.

Aydin lives at the hotel with his much-younger wife, Nihal (Melisa Sözen), and his recently divorced sister, Necla (Demet Akbağ). When the region is beset by winter, Aydin is forced to confront his wife and sister's deep-rooted animosities toward him.

Despite a running time of three hours and sixteen minutes, long and meandering dialogue sequences, and an ambiguous ending, *Winter Sleep* was widely hailed by critics. The film premiered at the 2014 Cannes Film Festival, where it won the prestigious Palme d'Or. Ceylan became only the second Turkish director to win the honor after Yilmaz Güney and Serif Gören, who won for their film *The Way* (*Yol*) in 1982. *Winter Sleep* was also Turkey's official selection for the Academy Award for best language film, but it failed to earn a nomination. Commenting on his goal in making films, Ceylan explained to Foundas, "Socrates said that the aim of philosophy is to know oneself. For me, cinema is the same thing. I try to know myself better, to relieve my pain about life."

Ceylan, who returned to photography as a hobby in 2003, held his first US photography exhibition, titled *The World of My Father*, at the Tina Kim Gallery in New York in 2014. "I feel a different kind of satisfaction when I finish a photograph," he said to Foundas. "In film, you deal with hundreds of people. . . . But with photography, you are like God. You are alone. It's a kind of meditation."

PERSONAL LIFE

Ceylan lives in Istanbul. He and his wife have two children.

SUGGESTED READING

Cardullo, Robert, ed. *Nuri Bilge Ceylan: Essays and Interviews*. Berlin: Logos, 2015. Print.

Ceylan, Nuri Bilge. "Nuri Bilge Ceylan." Interview by Geoff Andrew. *Guardian*. Guardian News and Media, 6 Feb. 2009. Web. 15 Dec. 2015.

Donadio, Rachel. "A Director Holds Up a Mirror to Turkey." *New York Times*. New York Times, 22 Dec. 2014. Web. 15 Dec. 2015.

Foundas, Scott. "Nuri Bilge Ceylan on *Winter Sleep* and Learning to Love Boring Movies." *Variety*. Variety Media, 3 Nov. 2014. Web. 15 Dec. 2015.

Romney, Jonathan. "Nuri Bilge Ceylan: 'Death Was Always with Us—And That Is a Good Thing.'" *Independent*. Independent.co.uk, 17 Mar. 2012. Web. 15 Dec. 2015.

SELECTED WORKS

Cocoon (*Koza*), 1995; *The Small Town* (*Kasaba*), 1997; *Clouds of May* (*Mayıs Sıkıntısı*), 1999; *Distant* (*Uzak*), 2002; *Climates* (*İklimler*), 2006; *Three Monkeys* (*Üç Maymun*), 2008; *Once Upon*

a Time in Anatolia (*Bir Zamanlar Anadolu'da*), 2011; *Winter Sleep* (*Kiş Uykusu*), 2014

—*Chris Cullen*

Chai Jing

Born: January 1, 1976
Occupation: Journalist, filmmaker

In 2015 a journalist named Chai Jing released a documentary film called *Under the Dome*, about air pollution in China. Chai, a former reporter for China's state television service, made the film for her infant daughter who was born with a benign tumor in her lung. The child's poor health was exacerbated by chronic air pollution. Chai explained that she let her daughter go outside only on days when the air quality in Beijing was graded excellent or good. In 2014 there were 175 days that did not meet that mark. "I'd never felt afraid of pollution before, and never wore a mask no matter where," Chai says in the documentary, as quoted by Mark Tran for the *Guardian* (2 Mar. 2015). The masks Chai refers to, surgical masks that cover nose and mouth, are ubiquitous in heavily polluted cities like Beijing. "But when you carry a life in you," Chai said, "what she breathes, eats and drinks are all your responsibility, then you feel the fear." Chai is the star of her film. She speaks to an audience from a stage in the manner of a Technology, Entertainment, and Design (TED) talk, with interviews and statistics interspersed throughout her narrative. *Under the Dome* has been compared to *Silent Spring*, Rachel Carson's 1962 book about pesticides that helped spur the creation of the Environmental Protection Agency (EPA) in the United States. It has also been compared to former Vice President Al Gore's documentary *An Inconvenient Truth* (2006), a call to arms in the face of a changing global climate. Chai's documentary has certainly had more of an impact on the Chinese public than some—including the Chinese government—ever anticipated. The movie was viewed more than 200 million times within a few days of its Internet release. In China, Chai is also the best-selling author of a 2013 memoir, *Kanjian* (translated as "Insight" or "Bearing Witness") about her experiences working for China Central Television (CCTV). In 2015 she was named one of *Time* magazine's 100 Most Influential People.

EARLY LIFE AND EDUCATION

Chai was born on January 1, 1976, in the Shanxi province in North China. She studied accounting at the Changsha Railway Institute (now Central South University) in the Hunan province.

When she was fifteen, she was given a job with a local radio program. In 1994 she began hosting her own program about literature on Hunan Arts Radio called *Gentle Moonlight*. The show ran for four years. In 1998 she moved to Beijing to study journalism at the Beijing Broadcasting Institute (now the Communication University of China), and landed a job hosting a program called *Horizon Connection* with China's national broadcaster, China Central Television (CCTV), in 2001. Chai embarked on a fruitful career as an investigative reporter, earning a Correspondent of the Year award for her coverage of the outbreak of severe acute respiratory syndrome (SARS) in 2003. (That year, SARS infected more than 5,300 people in China and killed 349.) In 2008 she reported on a magnitude 7.9 earthquake in the Sichuan province. The quake, considered one of the worst in human history in terms of loss, killed almost 70,000 people. She was praised for her fearless reporting, and, according to *Want China Times*, has said "Journalism is my profession and also way of life" (2 Mar. 2015). In 2009 Chai became a news anchor, hosting the CCTV programs *24 Hours* and *One on One*; in 2010, she began hosting the weekend edition of the program *Insight*, akin to the long-running television news magazine *60 Minutes* in the United States.

Chai became known for her candid, yet accommodating interview style. She once interviewed the parents of a girl stabbed to death by a man who hit her with his car. On camera, Chai let the girl's mother cry in silence. Chai also wrote a blog in which she discussed each of her interviews. In one post, she wrote that she pressed the tip of her pen into her palm to restrain her anger when she interviewed the aforementioned killer's father.

UNDER THE DOME (2015)

In 2013 Chai gave birth to a daughter, Chai Zhiran. Zhiran was born with a tumor in her lung and needed life-saving surgery. Chai decided to quit her job to take care of her daughter. The nature of the girl's malady made air pollution an immediate concern. "While I was taking care of her, my feelings about the smog became more and more intense; my whole life was affected by it," Chai told a reporter for *People's Daily*, as translated by Mengyu Dong for *China Digital Times* (2 Mar. 2015). "Professional training and the instinct of a mother made me think it was necessary to answer these questions: What is smog? Where did it come from? What should we do about it?" Chai's investigation began as a personal quest. She interviewed experts and found satellite photos of polluted Beijing, but, at least at first, did not consider making her findings public. Then she met with Tang Xiaoyan, the director of the Air Quality Guarantee Team for the

2008 Beijing Olympics. Tang showed her air pollution data from a month in 2004. The air quality had been so bad that authorities briefly shut down the Beijing airport. The media had reported that the airport was closed because of fog. As a former member of the media, Chai felt personally responsible for the misreporting. She began to wonder what other lies about China's environment she had unwittingly spread, and decided she had to share her findings in a documentary.

Chai funded the film herself, putting up 1 million yuan (about $160,000) to make it. She released *Under the Dome* on February 28, 2015. The video was hosted on several Chinese websites, including the video-hosting sites Youku and Tencent. By March 2, it had been viewed more than 150 million times. The public embraced the film and its message became a popular topic of discussion. The Chinese government also appeared to approve of the film, at least at first. Authorities had even allowed her to interview government regulators and factory owners. The *People's Daily*, a state-run newspaper, promoted the film and interviewed Chai. The minister of environmental protection publicly thanked Chai for her documentary. But by March 3, the government reversed itself. The *People's Daily* interview was deleted from the paper's website and the Ministry of Truth instructed media outlets to stop promoting the film. By March 7, the film was deleted from the Chinese Internet. In an opinion piece for the *Baltimore Sun* (11 Mar. 2015), Jess Fong speculates that the Chinese government initially supported the film because they did not expect it to "resonate so deeply." Pollution in China is talked about but most often described as a nuisance. Chai's framing device—the well-being of her child—made it immediate, dangerous, and heartbreaking. In one interview, quoted in a piece written by Steven Mufson for the *Washington Post* (16 Mar. 2015), a six-year-old child from Chai's own Shanxi province tells Chai that she's never seen a real star or white clouds. "'What about blue sky?' Chai asks. 'I've seen one that's a little blue,' the child replies."

CHINA'S RESPONSE TO THE FILM

Comparisons between *Under the Dome* and *Silent Spring*—the book that helped create the EPA—are inadequate, Steven Mufson wrote. For China, the problem is not a lack of regulatory bodies—the country has several environmental organizations—but a system in which those regulatory bodies fail to operate. "Chinese industry," Mufson said, "much of it state-owned, disregards regulations, sets its own standards, or manages to play off different parts of the bureaucracy against one another." According to Chai, the burning of oil and coal accounts for 60 percent of China's air pollution. Against standing regulations, that oil and coal is predominantly low quality, producing more pollutants than higher-grade materials. Chai went further, accusing Sinopec and the China National Petroleum Corporation (CNPC), two of China's largest state-owned oil companies, of strong-arming the Chinese government to keep environmental standards low. In the documentary, an anonymous official from China's National Development and Reform Commission says that when the government wanted to reform fuel standards, the companies threatened to stop supplying oil. Sinopec alone reported more than $400 billion dollars in revenue in 2014—shouldn't they "take some social responsibility?" Chai asks in the film, as quoted by Yiqin Fu for *Foreign Policy* magazine (2 Mar. 2015).

Chai also urged viewers to take action themselves—a directive that did not sit well with the Chinese government. In the wake of the film's release, the state showed an uncharacteristically divided front. The government embraced Chai, only to drop her and then embrace her again. As the *People's Daily* deleted its interview with her, the *Global Times*, another hard-line, state-owned outlet, praised her, writing, as quoted by Yiqin Fu, "Criticizing [Chai] for pointing out the problems of state-owned enterprises . . . is not a patriotic thing to do." Pollution may be bad press for China, but even the Chinese government seems to agree that the health risks are too alarming to ignore. According to Yiqin, air pollution has been linked to a spike in lung cancer rates in Beijing. In some regions, life expectancy has dropped by nearly 5.5 years. Battling the smog has become its own competitive industry as air mask and filter companies vie for dominance, and apps that measure air quality consistently rate among the most downloaded in China. Chai remains optimistic for change. "To put it simply, everyone wants to have clean air," she told *People's Daily*, as quoted by Yiqin. "What is a social consensus? There is no consensus stronger than this one."

PERSONAL LIFE
Chai and her husband, photographer Zhao Jia, were married in early 2013. The couple has one daughter.

SUGGESTED READING
Chai Jing. "Translation: Interview with Chai Jing." Trans. Mengyu Dong. *China Digital Times*. China Digital Times, 2 Mar. 2015. Web. 22 Oct. 2015.
Fong, Jess. "China's Silenced Jing." *Baltimore Sun*. Tribune Publishing, 11 Mar. 2015. Web. 21 Oct. 2015.
Mufson, Steven. "This Documentary Went Viral in China. Then It Was Censored. It Won't Be Forgotten." *Washington Post*. Washington Post, 16 Mar. 2015. Web. 21 Oct. 2015.
Staff Reporter. "Chai Jing Praised for 'Under the Dome' Film on China's Smog." *Want China Times*. WantChinaTimes.com, 2 Mar. 2015. Web. 5 Nov. 2015.
Tran, Mark. "Phenomenal Success for New Film That Criticizes China's Environmental Policy." *Guardian*. Guardian, 2 Mar. 2015. Web. 21 Oct. 2015.
Yiqin Fu. "China's National Conversation on Pollution Has Finally Begun." *Foreign Policy*. Foreign Policy, 2 Mar. 2015. Web. 29 Oct. 2015.

—*Molly Hagan*

Kartik Chandran
Born: ca. 1974
Occupation: Environmental engineer

Many people do not devote much thought to the wastewater produced by agricultural processes, manufacturing techniques, and everyday human life. Environmental engineer Kartik Chandran is not one of them, however. Over the course of a distinguished career, the Columbia University professor consistently worked to develop new means of removing harmful bacteria and contaminants from wastewater in ways that are inexpensive, efficient, and environmentally responsible. Of significant concern to Chandran and his team is the need for adequate waste processing technology throughout the world, particularly in developing countries. "Clean water and

John D. and Catherine T. MacArthur Foundation/CC BY 4.0/ Wikimedia Commons

sanitation are global issues," he told Anushree Singh for *Business Insider India* (5 Oct. 2015). "Clean water from waste form just doesn't need money. It needs energy, chemicals, technology, access to technology in whatever form. It also needs technical education and know how. These things, individual or combined, are not available around the world for some reason."

Undaunted by the challenges facing his mission, Chandran designed and tested a variety of waste-treatment processes that address issues such as pollution—for instance, by removing nitrogen-containing compounds from wastewater while minimizing the expulsion of greenhouse gases such as nitrous oxide into the air. His work with more solid forms of waste has been similarly innovative, as he collaborated with international researchers to transform fecal sludge into usable biofuel. In recognition of his work he was named one of the 2015 class of MacArthur Fellows, a highly selective group of individuals who are seen as making extraordinary achievements in the arts, sciences, and other fields. For Chandran, however, the prestigious fellowship and associated grant are less a reward for his previous work and more a motivating factor that will fuel additional forays into developing practical solutions to complex problems. "It's good to look at questions that need answers," he told Singh.

EARLY LIFE AND EDUCATION
Kartik Chandran was born in India and grew up in Delhi. As a child he enjoyed playing music and for a time took lessons from K. M. Vaidyanathan, a well-known musician who specialized in the ghatam, a southern Indian percussion instrument. Chandran also enjoyed participating in sports such as soccer and cricket. Although he would go on to a career in academia, scholastic pursuits were not forced upon him during his childhood and teen years. "I didn't sit and study at all," he told P. Rajendran for *India Abroad* (16 Oct. 2015). "I had it pretty easy, I think—go to bed at nine and get up at six, go to school and have fun. That's it! It was not about academics." Although studies in biology were essential to his later work, he avoided the subject while attending Delhi's Springdale High School, preferring subjects such as math, chemistry, and computer science.

After completing high school, Chandran enrolled in the University of Roorkee, later known as the Indian Institute of Technology at Roorkee (IITR), where, based on the results of his entrance exams, he was assigned to study chemical engineering. No longer intent on avoiding subjects related to biology, he took a class in biotechnology that proved influential. Indeed, Chandran would later credit his time at the University of Roorkee with providing him with a strong foundation for his later research. He graduated from the university with honors in 1995, having earned a bachelor's degree in chemical engineering.

EARLY CAREER
Chandran next traveled to the United States to pursue graduate studies at the University of Connecticut (UConn). There, he served as a graduate research assistant in the department of civil and environmental engineering and completed his doctoral research under adviser Barth F. Smets, a professor of environmental engineering who was particularly interested in the treatment of wastewater. While at UConn, Chandran worked on a project that concerned the removal of nitrogen from wastewater at the Hockanum River Water Pollution Control Facility in Manchester, Connecticut. "I had to go sample, analyze everything and give a recommendation to the city of Manchester," he told Rajendran. "And then I really, *really* got into it—because I was there alone, sampling, making sense of it, and making recommendations." Chandran earned his PhD in environmental engineering in 1999, completing a dissertation titled "Biokinetic Characterization of Ammonium and Nitrite Oxidation by a Mixed Nitrifying Culture Using Extant Respirometry."

After earning his doctorate from UConn Chandran remained at the university as a postdoctoral research fellow until the summer of 2001. In September of that year he took a position as a senior technical specialist at Metcalf and Eddy, an engineering firm specializing in waste management. He continued to investigate wastewater treatment in that role and also contributed to the company's annual academic design competition, which tasked teams of environmental engineering students from a number of institutions with designing a variety of systems and processes relevant to their field. Chandran remained with Metcalf and Eddy until mid-2004, when he took the position of research associate at the Virginia Polytechnic Institute and State University, or Virginia Tech. He conducted research at Virginia Tech for a year, during which time he also served as a guest lecturer in environmental engineering microbiology.

WASTEWATER TREATMENT
Chandran joined Columbia University in New York City as an assistant professor in the fall of 2005, and it was there that he would do the work that would bring him widespread acclaim. He taught numerous courses in the department of earth and environmental engineering, including classes in subjects such as environmental microbiology and environmental engineering. The author of numerous papers on subjects such as water treatment and microbial ecology,

he also presented at numerous conferences and conducted workshops and short courses at Columbia and other universities on topics such as environmental biotechnology.

Perhaps the most significant result of Chandran's time at Columbia, however, was his research into the problem of wastewater treatment. Wastewater is any water that has been degraded by human influence, whether through direct use, as in household sewage, or indirectly, as in agricultural runoff. Long a subject of concern among environmental engineers, sewage and other concentrated forms of wastewater are generally treated—that is, processed in order to remove harmful bacteria and other contaminants—to protect public and environmental health. However, most common treatment processes are costly and require substantial amounts of energy. Furthermore, such processes frequently introduce other pollutants into the environment.

Chandran sought to address these issues, focusing particularly on the removal of nitrogen from wastewater. Nitrogen, which naturally exists in the environment, is introduced into wastewater in greater levels through human waste and fertilizer runoff, among other sources. Compounds that contain nitrogen, including nitrate and ammonia, are harmful to animals and humans in large quantities and thus must be removed from wastewater to render it usable for other purposes. However, some traditional methods of wastewater treatment result in the emission of nitrous oxide, a so-called greenhouse gas, into the air, where it can contribute to climate change. "We are looking specifically at the emissions of nitrous oxide and the metabolic level mechanisms of nitrous oxide emissions in wastewater treatment," Chandran told Julia Apland Hitz for the Columbia University Earth Institute's *State of the Planet* blog (24 Mar. 2010) of his work to combat such pollution. "The idea there is to remove nitrogen from the waste stream, but not at the expense of blowing nitrous oxide into the atmosphere."

In addition to his research into more environmentally friendly forms of wastewater treatment, Chandran became particularly concerned with the accessibility of such methods of treatment in the developing world, where access to clean water is of the utmost importance and traditional treatment methods may not be feasible. He paid close attention to making the solutions he developed economically feasible. By creating, testing, and modifying sustainable treatment processes in the United States, Chandran hoped to be able to implement perfected versions of such processes globally. "One of the things we should keep in mind is we should not make all the mistakes again in the developing world that we've made in the United States, which is what

we're working towards in some of these sustainable technologies," he told Apland Hitz. "We can really leapfrog everything that's happened here, before we put them out in the developing world."

OTHER RESEARCH

Although much of his research concerned liquid waste, Chandran also conducted research into treatment of more solid forms of waste. In 2011 he and his Columbia University team, along with partner organizations, were awarded a $1.5 million grant from the Bill and Melinda Gates Foundation to fund a waste-processing facility in Ghana that would transform fecal sludge into biodiesel fuel that could then be used for a wide range of applications. A pilot facility opened in 2012.

Chandran also delved into the issue of bacterial resistance—that is, the phenomenon in which bacteria develop resistance to chemicals, such as those used in waste treatment or medicine—and the prevalence of resistant bacteria in wastewater. "I think [bacterial resistance] is already ranked in the top five in terms of impending human health threats," he told Apland Hitz for *State of the Planet* (22 Mar. 2010). As pharmaceutical companies create drugs to treat diseases, the bacteria that cause such illnesses can over time become resistant to them and pose a major risk, thus necessitating the development of new, more powerful drugs.

However, this is not the only factor contributing to the presence of drug-resistant bacteria; Chandran found that pollution also plays a significant role in bacterial resistance. "There is a very strong link between metal pollution and resistance to antibiotics," he explained to Apland Hitz. "So the more metals we discharge, the more the organisms are exposed to these metals. Some of them always find a way to cope with the metal concentrations. In many cases, metal resistance and drug resistance are coded on the same genetic element, and so it is very likely that they are coexpressed." To enable the reuse of treated wastewater and related products, such drug-resistant bacteria must be eliminated.

MACARTHUR FELLOWSHIP

As a successful researcher in his field, Chandran received ample recognition for his work from organizations and institutions both within and beyond academia. Perhaps the most significant recognition came in the fall of 2015, when he was named one of that year's MacArthur Fellows. The prestigious fellowship, known colloquially as the genius grant and administered by the John D. and Catherine T. MacArthur Foundation, recognizes exceptional work in a variety of fields and awards its recipients a grant of $625,000, which may be used for any purpose. In naming Chandran one of the 2015 fellows, the foundation cited his work in processing and treating wastewater to render it usable in a variety of applications, including fertilizers, energy sources, and usable water, as well as his research into fecal sludge and biofuels.

Chandran, who learned that he had been named a MacArthur Fellow just after returning from a trip to India, noted that he planned to use the grant to continue his groundbreaking research. "The fellowship is a great honor, which carries with it immense responsibility and provides ever more motivation to continue expanding my scientific horizons and boundaries and help solve global societal and human challenges," he said, as quoted by Holly Evarts for the website of Columbia's Fu Foundation School of Engineering and Applied Science (29 Sept. 2015).

SUGGESTED READING

Chandran, Kartik. "Microbial Drug Resistance: Interview with Kartik Chandran, Part 1." Interview by Julia Apland Hitz. *State of the Planet*. Earth Inst., Columbia U, 22 Mar. 2010. Web. 11 Mar. 2016.

Chandran, Kartik. "Nitrogen and Wastewater: Kartik Chandran Interview Part 2." Interview by Julia Apland Hitz. *State of the Planet*. Earth Inst., Columbia U, 24 Mar. 2010. Web. 11 Mar. 2016.

Evarts, Holly. "Fecal Sludge–Fed Biodiesel Pilot Plant Opens in Ghana." *Fu Foundation School of Engineering and Applied Science*. Columbia U, 19 Nov. 2012. Web. 11 Mar. 2016.

Evarts, Holly. "Professor Kartik Chandran Wins MacArthur 'Genius' Grant." *Fu Foundation School of Engineering and Applied Science*. Columbia U, 29 Sept. 2015. Web. 11 Mar. 2016.

"Kartik Chandran." *MacArthur Fellows Program*. MacArthur Foundation, 28 Sept. 2015. Web. 11 Mar. 2016.

Rajendran, P. "The Genius Lab." *India Abroad* 16 Oct. 2015: A6–A7. Print.

Singh, Anushree. "Why MacArthur 'Genius' Kartik Chandran Remembered IIT Roorkee on Receiving $625,000 Grant for His Innovation." *Business Insider India*. Times Internet, 5 Oct. 2015. Web. 11 Mar. 2016.

—Joy Crelin

Emmanuelle Charpentier

Born: December 11, 1968
Occupation: Scientist

After years as an itinerant scientist, traveling from institution to institution and scraping

Bianca Fioretti, Hallbauer & Fioretti/CC BY-SA 4.0/ Wikimedia Commons

together funding and resources for her labs, French-born researcher Emmanuelle Charpentier is at last gaining widespread recognition for her groundbreaking work. Charpentier is one of the scientists credited with discovering the CRISPR-Cas9 technique of editing genes, a method drawn from existing processes that occur naturally within certain bacteria. In recognition of her work, which has major implications in fields such as biomedicine, she has won a number of prestigious awards, including the 2015 Gruber Prize in genetics (shared with research partner Jennifer Doudna), awarded by the Yale University–based Gruber Foundation. Charpentier's focus, however, remains on her work rather than her newfound acclaim. "Jean-Paul Sartre, the French philosopher, warned that winning prizes turned you into an institution," she told Alison Abbott for *Nature* (27 Apr. 2016). "I am just trying to keep working and keep my feet on the ground."

In addition to her work on the CRISPR-Cas9 technique, Charpentier actively researches a variety of topics related to infection biology. In 2015, she became a director of the Max Planck Institute for Infection Biology in Berlin, Germany. As a researcher and public figure, Charpentier seeks to remind government and industry bodies as well as the public of the importance of funding scientific research. "This is a technology that originates from our doing pure, basic science," she told Katie L. Burke for *American Scientist* (July–Aug. 2015), referring to the CRISPR-Cas9 gene-editing technology. "Politicians and funding agencies need to support basic science, because all discoveries, whether it's in biology, chemistry, physics, or other fields, come from this kind of research."

EARLY LIFE AND EDUCATION

Emmanuelle Marie Charpentier was born on December 11, 1968, in Juvisy-sur-Orge, a town just south of Paris, France. Her father was a park manager, and her mother managed a psychiatric hospital. She has two older siblings.

During Charpentier's childhood, her parents encouraged her to explore numerous interests, including dance and music. However, her chief interests were academic and spanned multiple subjects. "I was a serious student, but I was interested in a number of things," she recalled, as quoted in a brief biography published on the Gruber Foundation website. "I liked pure science and mathematics, but I was also interested in the human sciences—psychology, sociology, and philosophy." The young Charpentier soon developed major aspirations. According to her parents, as a preteen she told them that she would one day work for the Pasteur Institute, a scientific institution in Paris dedicated to studying subjects such as biology and infectious disease.

For her undergraduate studies, Charpentier attended Pierre and Marie Curie University (Université Pierre-et-Marie-Curie, or UPMC) in Paris, where she studied biology, microbiology, biochemistry, and genetics. After earning her degree in biochemistry in 1991, she pursued graduate studies microbiology at UPMC. Her studies included research at the Pasteur Institute, just as she had predicted years before. She also worked for several years as a teaching assistant at UPMC before earning her PhD in 1995.

EARLY CAREER

After completing her doctorate, Charpentier served as a postdoctoral assistant at the Pasteur Institute until 1996, when she traveled to the United States to take the position of postdoctoral research associate at New York's Rockefeller University. There she studied *Streptococcus pneumoniae*, the pathogen that causes pneumonia and several other illnesses, under researcher Elaine Tuomanen. Charpentier remained in the United States for several years, subsequently serving as an assistant research scientist at the New York University (NYU) Langone Medical Center (1997–99) and as a research associate at the NYU School of Medicine's Skirball Institute of Biomolecular Medicine (1999–2002), before returning to Europe.

As a student, Charpentier had intended to complete some postgraduate work abroad and then return to France, where she would spend the rest of her career. Her postgraduate career in the United States, however, demonstrated to her the importance of being exposed to a variety of different perspectives and approaches. In light of this, she decided not to return to France, instead taking a position as laboratory head and guest professor at the University of Vienna's Institute of Microbiology and Genetics in 2002.

AN ITINERANT RESEARCHER

Over the following years, Charpentier held positions at several institutions and became known as an itinerant researcher with a talent for securing the necessary resources for her work, even in the face of budgetary and other challenges. "I always had to build up new labs from scratch, on my own," she told Abbott. She remained at the University of Vienna through 2009, serving in a variety of roles, including assistant professor in the Department of Microbiology and Immunobiology and lab head and associate professor in the Max F. Perutz Laboratories.

Charpentier left the University of Vienna in 2009 to take the position of lab head and associate professor in the Department of Molecular Biology at Sweden's Umeå University. In 2013 she was named department head of the Helmholtz Centre for Infection Research at Hannover Medical School in Germany. She continued to serve as a visiting professor at Umeå University and in 2015 was named a director of the Max Planck Institute for Infection Biology. Based in Berlin, Germany, the institute is dedicated to researching and developing treatments for infectious diseases. Within the institute, Charpentier heads a division focused on regulation in infection biology, an area of research that considers the ways in which certain processes within bacteria are controlled. Among the topics studied by researchers at the institute are clustered regularly interspaced short palindromic repeats, or CRISPR for short, which are segments of deoxyribonucleic acid (DNA) that have significant implications for infection biology.

CRISPR

Charpentier began her research into CRISPR in the early 2000s, while at the University of Vienna. "When my lab started to work on CRISPR, we were interested in how bacteria, such as *Streptococcus pyogenes*, cause diseases. We were trying to decipher regulatory mechanisms that explain how the bacteria are virulent and how they survive in the human host," she explained to Burke. She added, "We showed that it is a defense system that protects the bacteria from viruses, which are composed of DNA. There are different defense systems that bacteria have evolved to destroy these invading genomes. CRISPR is such a system, one that is a little bit similar to our adaptive immune system. The CRISPR system first recognizes the invading genome and once it does so, it memorizes it. Upon a second infection, it can destroy the foreign DNA."

When the CRISPR system identifies a foreign genome, it uses specific proteins to cut the invader's DNA. Through her research, Charpentier determined that one particular variety of CRISPR system—the simplest—uses only one protein, Cas9 (short for CRISPR-associated protein 9. She theorized that the CRISPR-Cas9 system, which occurs naturally in some bacteria, could be used by scientists for genetic engineering purposes. She presented some of her early research into CRISPR at a meeting in the Netherlands in 2010, sharing it with fellow scientists interested in the phenomenon.

The next major step in Charpentier's research came through her work with Jennifer Doudna, a biologist working at the University of California, Berkeley. The two researchers met in 2011 and soon began to work together to study how the protein Cas9 cuts specific DNA. They determined that the CRISPR-Cas9 system could, in fact, be used as a tool to make specific changes to DNA. Charpentier and Doudna published a paper on the topic in the journal *Science* in 2012 and attempted to patent their newly discovered gene-editing technology, which would allow scientists to make specific, targeted changes to DNA for a variety of purposes. The latter process proved more difficult than expected, as another team, based out of Massachusetts's Broad Institute, had likewise been studying CRISPR-Cas9 and argued that they had discovered the process first. The ownership of the CRISPR-Cas9 technology has remained a subject of controversy several years after the first publication of the pertinent studies.

IMPLICATIONS AND APPLICATIONS

For Charpentier, her research into CRISPR-Cas9 is important on a number of levels. First, and perhaps most basic, is the fact that it brought to light information about bacteria that was not yet known to scientists. Also important is CRISPR-Cas9's suitability for a wide range of functions. "It has major implications for biotechnology and biomedicine," she told Burke. "Companies have started to use it to form a library of knock-outs of human cells [cells with gene deletions] to screen for novel targets for new therapeutics. We can also generate animal models that are better for testing new therapeutics, because the model may mimic what is happening to humans more accurately. I think with CRISPR-Cas9, human genetic disorders could be cured."

In an attempt to both encourage the responsible use of CRISPR-Cas9 technology (and discourage its irresponsible use) and protect her intellectual property, Charpentier has cofounded two companies dealing with the technology. The first, CRISPR Therapeutics, conducts research and seeks to develop therapies for diseases based on gene-editing technology. The second, ERS Genomics, is dedicated to licensing the CRISPR-Cas9 intellectual property to other firms.

RECOGNITION

Charpentier has received numerous awards for her work, including the Göran Gustafsson Prize in molecular biology (2014), the Gruber Prize in genetics (2015), and the Breakthrough Prize in life science (2015). She has been a member of various scientific organizations, including the European Molecular Biology Organization and the American Academy of Microbiology. For Charpentier, though, such recognition is far less important than the work itself. "Sometimes I wonder whether I would have had my research funded if I had proposed exactly what I wanted to do—to decipher the CRISPR-Cas9 system," she told Burke. "It's an example that shows how important it is to provide scientists with some budget where they are allowed to do some blue-sky research. For sure one always needs to have some kind of big hypothesis or direction or interest, but sometimes you just hit something, certain components that you want to put together in a way that maybe does not make sense but you just want to do it. Scientists need to have the support to be able to do some crazy experiments to see where they go. My discovery has been a lesson for me that it's important to give scientists the freedom and the time to do such work."

PERSONAL LIFE

Charpentier lives in Germany. Frequently asked about her personal life in interviews, she often responds that her research is her life. "I chose that science would be the main focus of my life," she told Gina Kolata for the *New York Times* (30 May 2016). "It is a little bit like entering a monastery. This is really the thing that drives you. You tend to be focused and obsessional—you *need* to be a bit obsessed."

SUGGESTED READING

Abbott, Alison. "The Quiet Revolutionary: How the Co-Discovery of CRISPR Explosively Changed Emmanuelle Charpentier's Life." *Nature*. Macmillan, 27 Apr. 2016. Web. 15 July 2016.

Charpentier, Emmanuelle. "Emmanuelle Charpentier's Still-Busy Life after Crispr." Interview by Gina Kolata. *New York Times*. New York Times, 30 May 2016. Web. 15 July 2016.

Charpentier, Emmanuelle. "Interview with a Gene Editor." Interview by Katie L. Burke. *American Scientist* July–Aug. 2015: 247–49. Web. 15 July 2016.

Charpentier, Emmanuelle, and Jennifer Doudna. "A Conversation with CRISPR-Cas9

Inventors Charpentier and Doudna." Interview by Ricki Lewis. *DNA Science Blog*. PLOS, 3 Dec. 2015. Web. 15 July 2016.

Connor, Steve. "The More We Looked into the Mystery of Crispr, the More Interesting It Seemed." *Independent*. Independent.co.uk, 6 Nov. 2013. Web. 15 July 2016.

"Emmanuelle Charpentier." *Gruber Foundation*. Yale U, 2015. Web. 15 July 2016.

Kahn, Jennifer. "The Crispr Quandary." *New York Times*. New York Times, 9 Nov. 2015. Web. 15 July 2016.

—*Joy Crelin*

Steve Coll

Born: October 8, 1958
Occupation: Writer, Journalist

In addition to numerous other awards and distinctions, journalist Steve Coll has twice been awarded the Pulitzer Prize—in 1990 for Explanatory Reporting and in 2005 for General Non-Fiction. He is the author of numerous books and articles on business, national security, and American foreign policy.

EARLY LIFE AND EDUCATION

Steve Coll was born in Washington, DC, on October 8, 1958. He graduated from Thomas S. Wootton High School in Rockville, Maryland, in 1976, and he graduated with honors from Occidental College in Los Angeles in 1980, earning a degree in English and history. Coll took his first job as a journalist with *California* magazine in 1982. In 1985, he took a position as a general correspondent for the style section of the *Washington Post*. He later transitioned to the role of New York–based financial reporter for the paper. In 1989, he published his first book, *The Deal of the Century: The Breakup of AT&T*. In 1987, he published *The Taking of Getty Oil: The Full Story of the Most Spectacular and Catastrophic Takeover of All Time*.

From 1989 to 1992, Coll served as the Asian bureau chief for the *Washington Post*, where he covered events in Afghanistan and Pakistan. In 1990, he and his *Post* colleague David A. Vise were awarded the Pulitzer Prize for Explanatory Journalism in recognition of a series of articles they wrote on the relationship between Wall Street power brokers and members of the United States Securities and Exchange Commission (SEC). The series of articles was published in book form in 1991 under the title *Eagle on the Street*. Coll writes of his experiences living in Asia in his 1994 book *On the Grand Trunk Road: A Journey into South Asia*. The work is both a travelogue and an overview of the region's political and social history.

GHOST WARS

Coll served as a managing editor and foreign correspondent at the *Washington Post* from 1998 to 2004. His January 2000 article on the civil war in Sierra Leone entitled "Peace without Justice: A Journey to the Wounded Heart of Africa" earned him a Robert F. Kennedy Journalism Award and an Ed Cunningham Award from the Overseas Press Club. Coll left the *Washington Post* in 2005 to join the *New Yorker*, where he began publishing long-form reports on national security, terrorism, and American foreign relations in the Middle East and Asia. In 2004, Coll published his fourth book, *Ghost Wars: The Secret History of the CIA, Afghanistan, and Bin Laden, from the Soviet Invasion to September 10, 2001*. *Ghost Wars* brought international attention to the relationship between White House officials, the Central Intelligence Agency (CIA), and Pakistan's Inter-Services Intelligence (ISI) unit. Coll recounts how the ISI used CIA funding to set up militant groups in Pakistan to combat the Soviet Union's presence in Afghanistan. Coll's research reveals how the CIA was directly involved in the creation of both the Taliban and al-Qaeda—groups that would later constitute America's central foes in the global war on terror. *Ghost Wars* was widely lauded, receiving the 2004 Lionel Gelber Prize and the 2004 Cornelius Ryan Award. The following year, the book was awarded the Pulitzer Prize for General Nonfiction as well as an Arthur Ross Book Award.

In 2007, Coll was named director of the New America Foundation, a Washington, DC, think tank specializing in foreign policy, technology, economics, and education. He published *The Bin Ladens: An Arabian Family in the American Century* in 2008. The book details the global business and political relationships cultivated by the bin Laden family: the immediate and extended family of al-Qaeda leader Osama bin Laden. The book was a finalist for the 2008 National Book Critics Circle Award. In 2009, *The Bin Ladens: Oil, Money, Terrorism and the Secret Saudi World* was awarded the PEN/John Kenneth Galbraith Award.

Coll was named to the Pulitzer Prize Board in 2012. That same year, he published his seventh book, *Private Empire: ExxonMobil and American Power*. The book tells the story of ExxonMobil—one the largest and most profitable privately owned companies in the world. In addition to detailing the company's relationship with the United States government, Coll recounts the company's influence on global politics and the environment. The book received the *Financial Times* and Goldman Sachs Business Book of the Year Award in 2012. In July 2013, Coll was named dean of the Columbia University Graduate School of Journalism.

IMPACT

Coll has become one of the most widely respected figures in journalism. Over the course of his career, he has helped expand the scope and reach of long-form journalism, providing a detailed behind-the-scenes view into the world of global power brokers in business and government.

SUGGESTED READING

Coll, Steve. "Gusher." *New Yorker*. Condé Nast, 9 Apr. 2012. Web. 8 Apr. 2014.

"Coll, Steve." *The Pulitzer Prizes*. Columbia University, n.d. Web. 8 Apr. 2014.

Garner, Dwight. "Oil's Dark Heart Pumps Strong." *New York Times*. New York ean." New York Times. New York Times, 18 Mar. 2013. Web. 8 Apr. 2014.

Kakutani, Michiko. "The Bricklayer's Sons: The Family That Spawned 9/11." *Times*, 26 Apr. 2012. Web. 8 Apr. 2014.

Kaminer, Ariel. "Columbia Picks New Journalism D *New York Times*. New York Times, 1 Apr. 2008. Web. 8 Apr. 2014.

Ricks, Thomas E. "The Best Defense Interview: Steve Coll on White House Leaks and What Might Happen." *Foreign Policy*. Slate Group, 27 Mar. 2013. Web. 8 Apr. 2014.

Risen, James. "'Against All Enemies' and 'Ghost Wars': Connecting the Dots." *New York Times*. New York Times, 29 Mar. 2004. Web. 8 Apr. 2014.

So, Jimmy. "Steve Coll on ExxonMobil's Sinister Kingdom and 'Private Empire.'" *Daily Beast*. Daily Beast Company, 6 May 2012. Web. 8 Apr. 2014.

SELECTED WORKS

The Deal of the Century: The Breakup of AT&T, 1986; *The Taking of Getty Oil: The Full Story of the Most Spectacular and Catastrophic Takeover of All Time*, 1987; *On the Grand Trunk Road: A Journey into South Asia*, 1994; *Ghost Wars: The Secret History of the CIA, Afghanistan, and Bin Laden, from the Soviet Invasion to September 10, 2001*, 2004; *The Bin Ladens: An Arabian Family in the American Century*, 2008; *The Bin Ladens: Oil, Money, Terrorism and the Secret Saudi World*, 2008; *Private Empire: ExxonMobil and American Power*, 2012

—*Joshua Pritchard*

Ryan Coogler

Born: May 23, 1986
Occupation: Director and screenwriter

Despite being just thirty years old and with only two full-length feature films under his belt, Ryan Coogler is quickly gaining recognition as one of the best filmmakers at work in Hollywood today. He made his reputation as the screenwriter and director of his debut feature, *Fruitvale Station* (2013), which wowed critics and audiences with its complex portrayal of Oscar Grant, a young African American man who was fatally shot by a Bay Area Rapid Transit police officer on January 1, 2009, while waiting for a train in Oakland, California.

Coogler has since cemented his reputation by penning and directing *Creed* (2015), the seventh film in the long-running Rocky series, which has not only revitalized the franchise but brought to it a new generation of fans. Moreover, Coogler had done something for Rocky creator and star Sylvester Stallone that Stallone had never been able to capture for himself: a Golden Globe Award and an Oscar nomination for best supporting actor. Coogler is now poised to jump into the world of blockbuster filmmaking as he prepares to helm the film *Black Panther*, starring Chadwick Boseman in the title role as the first black superhero in mainstream American comics, created by comic book giants Stan Lee and Jack Kirby in 1966.

Desiree Navarro/Wirelmage/Getty Images

EARLY LIFE

Ryan Kyle Coogler was born on May 23, 1986, in Oakland, California, and later grew up in Richmond, California, where his family moved when he was eight years old. His parents, Ira and Joselyn Coogler, worked hard to provide for him and his two younger brothers, Noah and Keenan. Coogler's father worked as a probation officer at San Francisco's Juvenile Justice Center, where Coogler himself worked as a youth counselor for a time. His mother worked as a community organizer in Oakland.

Coogler credits much of his professional success to his parents. "I have real good parents, I have two brothers, and we got good educations. My parents didn't have a whole lot of money, but they spent the money they had on private school for us, Catholic school," he recalled in an interview with Patt Morrison for the *Los Angeles Times* (17 July 2013). "My school was pretty much all African Americans, but it was still a little tough to be in because I didn't have a lot of money. And when I came back to my neighborhood, it was tough to fit in there too because I was wearing Catholic school clothes, and I had two parents, which was rare."

Growing up, Coogler loved to read, excelled at science and math, and, having inherited his father's athleticism, played football. He also loved to watch movies with his parents, who were film buffs. He developed a love of Martin Scorsese movies from his mother and a love of sports films, especially the Rocky series, from his father. In a conversation with Kristopher Tapley for *Variety* (5 Jan. 2016), Coogler recalled, "My dad's thing was 'Rocky.' He would make me watch the 'Rocky' movies all the time. So I can't even remember not knowing who Rocky was. I was watching it probably before I could talk. He would watch the films and get really emotional at the same parts every time. And it was really the only time I ever saw my dad get choked up. It's the only time I ever saw him cry."

Coogler later discovered that the reason his father grew so emotional: his father had watched the same films with his mother as she battled breast cancer over a ten-year period, from the time his father was eight until she died when he was eighteen. "In the last year or so of her life, she was really debilitated from the disease and from the treatment. She was bedridden and my pops was her primary caretaker. And the only activity they could do together was watch movies," Coogler told Tapley.

FILM SCHOOL AND EARLY CAREER

Coogler earned a football scholarship to Saint Mary's College in Moraga, California. The college's football program was canceled after Coogler's freshman year, so he transferred to California State University, Sacramento. It was during his time at Saint Mary's, however, that he began to consider his job options, deciding that if he failed to have a football career he would attend medical school to become a doctor. At this time, he took a creative writing class with Rosemary Graham, who asked her students to write about the most emotionally intense experience of their lives. After submitting his assignment, Coogler was called to her office, expecting to be in trouble for what he wrote about in his assignment. Graham, however, praised his work. "She got my assignment and said: 'This is really visual; that's rare to be able to do that. You should think about becoming a writer instead of a doctor,'" Coogler recalled to Morrison. "She said: 'Maybe you could even go to Hollywood and write screenplays.' I thought she was crazy at the time." Nevertheless, Coogler began looking into how to go about writing screenplays, buying a DVD pack of *Pulp Fiction* that included a CD of the film's screenplay. "I put it in my computer and saw a screenplay for the first time. I opened up Microsoft Word and tried to duplicate the physical structure of it, started doing my own script, and I really liked it," he told Morrison.

While attending Sacramento State, he majored in business administration and was a wide receiver for the Sacramento State Hornets, but in his spare time he wrote screenplays and took as many film classes as he could fit into his schedule. After graduating in 2007, he studied film at the University of Southern California (USC) School of Cinematic Arts, graduating in 2011 with an MFA in film and television production. During his time at USC, Coogler made three notable short films: *Locks* (2009), about a young man who decides to cut his dreadlocks off one morning; *Fig* (2011), about Figueroa, an area in Los Angeles known as a prostitution hub; and *The Sculptor* (2011).

FRUITVALE STATION

As Coogler was about to begin filming his first feature, *Fruitvale Station* (2013), his father became seriously ill with a neuromuscular condition that doctors had difficulty diagnosing. Initially they believed it might be amyotrophic lateral sclerosis (ALS) or multiple sclerosis (MS), but his condition continued to deteriorate rapidly and the doctors did not think he had long to live. Ultimately, it was discovered that his father's body was not processing vitamin B12, among other vitamins, and the vitamin deficiency was causing his muscles to atrophy. The experience made Coogler question his understanding of manhood for the first time in his life. He remarked in an interview with Mike Fleming Jr. for *Deadline Hollywood* (19 Nov. 2015): "It really messed my head up, but it raised questions. What makes you a man? What's the definition of masculinity? Is it the strength that my father had when I was a kid and I ran to him and he would pick me up with one arm? When that strength goes away, is he still that same person? What is the relationship between a father and a son?"

While he would revisit these questions in *Creed*, he channeled his energy into completing work on *Fruitvale Station*. Coogler's debut film examines the true story of the murder of Oscar Grant III, a young African American man who was both a devoted father and an ex-con trying to straighten out his life. Grant was shot in the back while lying face down on a subway platform in Oakland, California, by a white police officer. Video of the incident, recorded on a cell phone, helped to expose some of the dynamics at work in modern America when it comes to policing, race, racism, and law and order.

Coogler, in his debut film, presented a nuanced view of the incident that impressed film critics and audiences. In his review for the *New York Times* (11 July 2013), A. O. Scott cheered: "[Coogler] examines his subject with a steady, objective eye and tells his story in the key of wise heartbreak rather than blind rage. It is not that the movie is apolitical or disengaged from the painful, public implications of Mr. Grant's fate. But everything it has to say about class, masculinity, and the tricky relations among different kinds of people in a proudly diverse and liberal metropolis is embedded in details of character and place." In a review for *All Things Considered* (11 July 2013), Bob Mondello remarked, "*Fruitvale Station* isn't really a surprising film, except insofar as it's rare to see such a warmly emotional big-screen portrait of black family life. The director, who grew up just north of Oakland and is about the age Oscar would be today, has said that for him there was a jarring that-could-have-been-me aspect to the story. He's given it an immediacy and resonance on screen that reflects that—with help from a striking performance by [Michael B.] Jordan. . . . Together, star and director get you to look at, and think about, a flawed young man you might not give a second thought if you saw him on the street." *Fruitvale Station* won the audience award and the grand jury prize at the 2013 Sundance Film Festival, and Coogler earned the New York Film Critics Circle Award and the Independent Spirit Award for best first film.

CREED

Coogler began working on a script for a seventh film in the Rocky series around the time he was completing work on *Fruitvale Station*. In it, the main character of Rocky (played by Stallone) becomes a mentor to Adonis "Donnie" Johnson (played by Michael B. Jordan), the son of Apollo Creed (played by Carl Weathers), Rocky's archrival in two films and later his good friend. Coogler's film centers on Donnie's attempt to make a name for himself in the ring outside of his father's shadow. Donnie never knew his father, who was killed in the ring during *Rocky IV* (1985), and finds in Rocky a surrogate father. Coogler channeled much of his own relationship with his father into the relationship between the characters of Adonis and Rocky. "I learned in film school that the type of movies I like to make are the ones that are extremely personal to me. Personal to a point they were almost like my own kids," Coogler explained to Fleming. "I also learned that I like to make movies with questions that keep me up at night."

When Coogler contacted Stallone about the script, Stallone was initially reluctant to return to his signature character, feeling that he had concluded the character's story in the well-received *Rocky Balboa* (2006). Stallone, however, was so impressed with Coogler's take on the story that he willingly agreed to portray Rocky again and to produce the film with Coogler directing. Prior to the film's release, many critics and fans believed that *Creed* would be a mediocre installment in the franchise and that Coogler and Jordan's careers would be sullied by it. Yet the film was met with almost universal acclaim and earned a host of awards.

In *Time* (25 Nov. 2015), Stephanie Zacharek proclaimed: "Coogler honors and builds upon the *Rocky* formula so that it feels both comfortingly old-fashioned and bracingly new. Audiences instantly adored *Rocky*, for good reason—it's a great date movie, and *Creed* is too." In a review for National Public Radio (NPR) (25 Nov. 2015), Chris Klimek echoed this assessment, writing: "While one hopes Coogler won't stay in franchiseville after *Creed*, he can feel good about having made an honorable, heart-tugging crowd-pleaser that should attract a more diverse crowd to the series while satisfying older fans with the best Rocky movie since *Rocky*." Reviewing the film for *AV Wire* (13 Nov. 2015), Herman Dhaliwal wrote that, with the success of *Creed*, "Ryan Coogler cements himself as one of the best rising filmmakers working today."

SUGGESTED READING

Fleming, Mike, Jr. "How Director Ryan Coogler's Own Father-Son Saga Fueled 'Rocky' Revival 'Creed.'" *Deadline Hollywood*. Penske Business Media, 19 Nov. 2015. Web. 15 Mar. 2016.

Klimek, Chris. "Vital and Tear-Jerking, 'Creed' Is the Best Rocky Movie since 'Rocky.'" *NPR Movie Reviews*. NPR, 25 Nov. 2015. Web. 15 Mar. 2016.

Mondello, Bob. "A New Day, a Last Day, for One Man at 'Fruitvale Station.'" *All Things Considered*. NPR, 12 July 2013. Web. 21 Feb. 2016.

Morrison, Patt. "'Fruitvale Station's' Ryan Coogler, the Message Maker." *Los Angeles*

Times. Los Angeles Times, 17 July 2013. Web. 21 Feb. 2016.

Scott, A. O. "A New Year, and a Last Day Alive." *New York Times*. New York Times, 11 July 2013. Web. 21 Feb. 2016.

Tapley, Kristopher. "Ryan Coogler on 'Creed,' Filmmaking as Journalism and the Need for Female Voices (Q&A)." *Variety*. Variety Media, 5 Jan. 2016. Web. 15 Mar. 2016.

—*Christopher Mari*

Jeremy Corbyn

Born: May 26, 1949
Occupation: Politician

Jeremy Corbyn is a long-serving member of Parliament (MP) for the London constituency of Islington North who came to prominence when, in 2015, he became the unlikely candidate—and then the even more unlikely victor—of an election that made him the leader of the United Kingdom's liberal Labour Party. At the time the party continued to suffer through an identity crisis that began during Margaret Thatcher's opposing Conservative Party (Tory) administration in the 1980s. Labour MP Tony Blair, who served as prime minister from 1997 to 2007, rose to power by finding common ground with the Tories and positioning the party as more centrist—ushering in the period of "New Labour"—but he alienated many who believed that he had eschewed some of the party's core liberal principles.

RevolutionBahrainMC/CC BY 3.0

Under the leadership of Prime Minister David Cameron the Tories won a parliamentary majority in the May 2015 elections. The defeat prompted Labour leader Ed Miliband to resign. Three centrist candidates joined the race to replace him, and several MPs, hoping to rally some fringe support, urged Corbyn—an uncompromising, bicycle-riding vegetarian who long opposed austerity, the monarchy, and the war in Iraq—to throw his hat in the ring as well. Corbyn's election drew hundreds of thousands of new voters to Labour but created a deep rift between leftists and moderates in the party.

EARLY LIFE AND EDUCATION

Jeremy Bernard Corbyn was born in Chippenham in Wiltshire, England, as the youngest of four boys on May 26, 1949. His mother, Naomi, was a scientist and a math teacher, and his father, David, was an electrical engineer. Corbyn's parents, who met at a London rally supporting Spain's Republicans in the fight against Francisco Franco's fascists during the Spanish Civil War, nurtured a passion for liberal causes in their children. Corbyn spent his early years in the village of Kington St. Michael in Wiltshire, and when he was seven years old, his family moved to a manor house in Shropshire—a conservative, upper-middle-class county that Corbyn has jokingly referred to as "Tory-shire." He attended private school called Adams' Grammar School in Newport, where he was one of only two Labour supporters in his class; he ran in a mock election and lost in a landslide. While finishing high school at a public school, he joined the Campaign for Nuclear Disarmament in 1966.

After graduation, Corbyn spent two years in Jamaica with Voluntary Service Overseas, an international development organization focused on eradicating poverty, and adopted his trademark beard. When he returned to the United Kingdom, he became an organizer for the (now defunct) National Union of Tailors and Garment Makers. He enrolled at North London Polytechnic where he began a major in trade union studies, but he left after a series of disagreements with his professors. He never completed his degree. Corbyn continued to work with trade unions, first with the Amalgamated Engineering and Electrical Union (AEEU) and then the National Union of Public Employees (NUPE), but he eyed a larger role in politics. In 1974, he was elected to Haringey District Council in North London.

PARLIAMENTARY CAREER AND POLITICAL CAUSES

As Brian Wheeler remarked in a profile of the politician for the British Broadcasting Corp. (BBC) (12 Sept. 2015), Corbyn's allure is in his zeal for hard work. Corbyn, unlike his mentor, the late Tony Benn, is not a great orator. Nor is he a "firebrand," Wheeler wrote, "like labor leader Arthur Scargill." Corbyn is an ascetic—he does not drink alcohol, eat meat, or own a car—and a tireless pamphleteer who won acolytes by putting in countless hours at the copy machine and out on the street. In the early 1980s he ran the leftist newspaper the *London Labour Briefing*, advocating for gay rights, nuclear disarmament, and Irish republicanism throughout his political career.

He was elected to Parliament, serving his hometown of Islington North in Greater London, in 1983. Despite his new title as MP, Corbyn did not forsake his activist roots. In 1984, while serving on the National Executive of the Anti-Apartheid Movement (AAM), he was arrested for protesting outside the South African diplomatic mission in London. Later, he employed Ronan Bennett, an Irish Republican dissident who went on to become a successful novelist and screenwriter, on his staff at Westminster. But the year in which Corbyn was elected was also a year of serious defeat for the national Labour Party. Having introduced its most radical platform in decades—vowing to renationalize the industries that Thatcher had privatized, pull out of the European Union (EU), and create a national investment bank—Labour suffered a resounding defeat with British voters as Thatcher's popularity soared. Licking its wounds, Labour promised to modernize and began adopting more centrist policies that constituted the New Labour movement.

Corbyn, however, refused to embrace New Labour. He maintained his radical stance on key liberal issues and came to be known, during his thirty-two years as MP, as an outlier within his own party. According to Wheeler, Corbyn voted against the party's orders over five hundred times. He chaired the Stop the War Coalition, which demanded an end to the wars in Afghanistan and Iraq, and when Prime Minister Cameron introduced harsh austerity measures in the wake of the financial collapse in 2008, Corbyn became a leading figure in the anti-austerity movement. The latter won him many young fans and comparisons to liberal outlier and US presidential hopeful Senator Bernie Sanders. But Lane, who has been critical of Corbyn, dismissed the comparison: "Nice try, but no. Corbyn makes Bernie Sanders look like Ted Cruz," referring to the ultra-conservative US senator from Texas. Despite his rising popularity, Corbyn remained a fringe figure, ideologically pure and unwilling to compromise.

2015 ELECTION

After a resounding defeat to the Tories in the 2015 parliamentary elections, Labour leader Ed Miliband resigned. British voters were unhappy with the way the party kowtowed to Tories after the 2008 recession, backing harsh austerity measures that failed to relieve the financial woes of ordinary citizens. The decision to support austerity, one Labour MP told John Cassidy for the *New Yorker* (13 Sept. 2015), was political but also quite cynical: parliamentarians just did not think voters would listen to reason. Cutting spending during a recession is counterproductive, but "we had no confidence in our own arguments," the Labour MP told Cassidy. "The Tory lie became hegemonic, despite being a lie." Unsurprisingly, Corbyn maintained his anti-austerity stance, telling Simon Hattenstone for the *Guardian* (17 June 2015), "Austerity is used as a cover to reconfigure society and increase inequality and injustice. Labour needs to offer a coherent economic alternative."

When the time came to choose a successor to Miliband, some people came knocking at Corbyn's door—but not because they were supporters. Several of his colleagues urged him to throw his hat into the ring only, as Rowena Mason for the *Guardian* (10 Sept. 2015) put it, in order to "widen the debate." The candidates already in the race included MPs Andy Burnham, Yvette Cooper, and Liz Kendall—all three were centrist in their views and had previously served as shadow ministers. (Shadow ministers are foils to the real thing while their party is out of power; they develop policies in response to those crafted by the actual cabinet ministry). Corbyn never served as a minister nor a shadow minister, but he was something different: an old-time Labour liberal with socialist leanings. His colleagues agreed he could not win but would certainly enliven debate. Corbyn collected the requisite thirty-five nominations from Labour MPs to put him on the ballot quite literally at the last moment. The last MP registered their support for him one minute before the official deadline.

None of the Labour MPs anticipated what happened next, significantly underestimating just how far left many British voters had shifted in recent years. Two major British trade unions, Unite and Unison, threw their support behind Corbyn, and hundreds of thousands of people joined the party just to vote for him. The MPs themselves used to vote on new leadership, but under new rules, any member of the Labour Party could vote if they had paid three pounds for the membership fee. Previously unregistered members flocked to the voting booth and elected Corbyn, who won in a landslide with nearly 60 percent of the vote. Burnham, Corbyn's closest competitor, trailed him by nearly 40 percentage points. Corbyn was gleeful in his victory. After the results of the election were announced, he gave a speech at a London pub in which he thanked the surge of new voters that had elected him. "It's been a campaign of hope," he said, as quoted by Cassidy. "It's been a campaign of justice. It's been a campaign of inclusion."

LEADER OF THE OPPOSITION

As the party's leader, Corbyn dictates Labour's ideological course, but his election engendered a massive split within the party. Corbyn, who had called for an end to the British monarchy, drew ire from party members after refusing to follow tradition and kneel before the queen as he was sworn in as a member of the Privy Council, and at a separate public event, he failed to sing the national anthem, "God Save the Queen." Though the incidents have little to do with public policy, they risked alienating key supporters needed in the lobby for Corbyn's comprehensive new economic program, which called for reversing some spending cuts, nationalizing energy and railway companies, getting rid of college tuition fees, and setting up a national investment bank to invest in infrastructure and housing. The bold plan sought to redistribute the country's wealth from its richest citizens—who had enjoyed low tax rates and corporate tax benefits—to its poorest.

A measure of Corbyn's success was expected in 2016 with local and regional elections in Wales, Scotland (which had previously ousted nearly all of its Labour MPs in favor of members of the new, left-wing Scottish National Party), and parts of England. But Steven Fielding, a political history professor at the University of Nottingham, told Stephen Castle for the *New York Times* (13 Oct. 2015) that the results of those elections might be less important than Corbyn's overall impact. "I don't think his priority is to win the next election," he said. "It is to change the nature of the Labour Party."

PERSONAL LIFE

In 1974, Corbyn married Jane Chapman, a fellow Labour councilor (Corbyn had just been elected to the Haringey District Council) and university lecturer. Corbyn's single-minded focus on his political causes drove the two apart, and they divorced in 1979. In 1987, Corbyn married a Chilean woman named Claudia Bracchita. Together they had three sons: Ben, Seb, and Tommy. Corbyn and Bracchita divorced in 1999. Corbyn married Laura Alvarez, a Mexican fair trade coffee importer, in 2015.

SUGGESTED READING

Cassidy, John. "Jeremy Corbyn's Victory and the Demise of New Labour." *New Yorker*. Condé Nast, 13 Sept. 2015. Web. 5 Jan. 2016.

Castle, Stephen. "New Labour Party Leadership Widens Rift Between Left and Center." *New York Times*. New York Times, 13 Oct. 2015. Web. 5 Jan. 2016.

Lane, Anthony. "The Corbyn Supremacy." *New Yorker*. Condé Nast, 13 Sept. 2015. Web. 4 Jan. 2016.

Mason, Rowena. "Labour Leadership: All Eyes on Jeremy Corbyn as Voting Ends." *Guardian*. Guardian News and Media, 10 Sept. 2015. Web. 5 Jan. 2016.

Wheeler, Brian. "The Jeremy Corbyn Story: Profile of Labour's New Leader." *BBC News*. BBC, 12 Sept. 2015. Web. 4 Jan. 2016.

—*Molly Hagan*

Carlos Correa

Born: September 22, 1994
Occupation: Baseball player

Houston Astros shortstop Carlos Correa is, as Ben Reiter wrote for *Sports Illustrated* (6 Oct. 2015), "a phenom, a prodigy who continually exceeds lofty expectations." Such expectations followed the six-feet-four, 210-pound Correa after he was selected first overall by the Astros in the 2012 Major League Baseball (MLB) Draft. The highest draft pick ever from Puerto Rico, he drew comparisons to fellow MLB stars Alex Rodriguez for his size and skill set and Derek Jeter for his poise and all-out style of play.

Correa expectedly breezed through the Astros' farm system, and had played in only fifty-three games above Class A ball when he made his major-league debut with the Astros in June 2015 at the age of twenty. Despite being the

Ronald C. Modra /Sports Imagery/Getty Images

youngest position player in the majors, Correa made an immediate impact, putting up offensive numbers that have rarely been seen from a shortstop his age. He served as a catalyst for the Astros' first postseason berth since 2005 and won the American League (AL) Rookie of the Year Award. Unusually tall for a shortstop, Correa quickly established himself among the best defenders at his position. He also entered the conversation as one of baseball's best all-around players with his ability to hit for both average and power and his speed on the basepaths.

EARLY LIFE

Carlos Javier Correa was born on September 22, 1994, in Ponce, Puerto Rico, to Carlos Correa Sr. and Sandybel Oppenheimer. He was raised in Barrio Velázquez on the outskirts of Santa Isabel, Puerto Rico, with his younger brother and sister. The family was poor, and Correa's father earned the nickname "24/7" for his nonstop schedule at up to three jobs at a time just to get by.

Correa began playing baseball at the age of five under the tutelage of his father. Carlos Correa Sr. had limited baseball experience and knowledge, but he saw the game as a way out of poverty for his son and worked hard to mold him into a ballplayer. He closely observed local baseball coaches and studied major-league players on television, passing down what he learned. Despite his busy work schedule he made time every day to play catch with his son.

Much to his father's delight Correa developed an insatiable love for baseball early on. "I was everywhere throwing the ball," he recalled to Joseph Duarte for the *Houston Chronicle* (17 June 2012), "against walls, against the houses, hitting all over the place." As a child, Correa was reportedly so devoted to the game that he would continue throwing baseballs against a wall even after having them ricochet into his face. That unflinching devotion was matched only by his preternatural abilities.

Correa pitched and played shortstop for his youth-league teams because of his natural arm strength and fielding prowess. He also had exceptional hand-eye coordination and an effortless ability to hit home runs. Throughout his youth Correa was a standout player on American Amateur Baseball Congress (AABC) teams.

DEVELOPING AS A PLAYER

One of Correa's idols growing up was the perennial All-Star shortstop Derek Jeter of the New York Yankees. He admired Jeter as much for the professional way he handled himself off the field as for his relentless play and sought to shape himself in that mold. By the time Correa reached third grade he already had the foresight to realize that learning English might be helpful in his mission to become a major-leaguer. He

worked hard in school and won a partial scholarship to Raham Baptist Academy, which had courses in English. Meanwhile, he was recruited by a more competitive AABC team, which helped him improve his skills but required a long commute to practice. The family also struggled to raise money to send Correa to tournaments in Atlanta, Georgia.

To pay for Correa's training and schooling his parents took on extra jobs and held fundraisers, with much community support. His father continued to dedicate all of his free time to his son, developing rigorous nightly fielding and batting-practice sessions at a local field. In addition to baseball workouts, Correa often helped his father on job sites and was responsible for performing household chores, which instilled in him the value of hard work and sacrifice. "My dad never treated me like a little boy," he explained to Reiter. "He wanted me to be like him: a man at a young age who could go out and work for his family."

Correa's maturity and work ethic served him well when he began attending the Puerto Rico Baseball Academy and High School (PRBAHS), an MLB-sponsored organization offering a unique curriculum combining academics with intensive baseball instruction. He had established himself as one of the best young players in Puerto Rico and won a scholarship to the school, but his family continued to struggle financially. Long drives on mountainous roads to practice ruined the family car, and Correa's father even crashed a borrowed vehicle after one exhausting nightly trip.

The PRBAHS staff recognized Correa's talent, however, and determined to help get him to school and practice. He got up early every day to carpool with a coach at six in the morning, getting home at six in the evening to eat before returning to the field for more drills. His father recalled to Gabrielle Paese for ESPN (3 June 2012) that Correa was so dedicated "we never had to tell him to practice or do more, and he never complained about the long days and the hard work." Soon crowds of locals were coming to watch his practices, increasingly joined by MLB scouts.

NUMBER ONE DRAFT PICK

Prior to his senior season Correa turned down offers to finish high school in Florida, as other recent top Puerto Rican prospects had done before him to increase their visibility and draft prospects. The decision to continue his development in Puerto Rico was a risky one: though once a breeding ground for baseball stars, the island had seen a decline in prospects over the previous two decades due to the increased popularity of other sports and a more stringent MLB draft process. As a backup plan, Correa signed a letter of intent to attend the University of Miami.

Still, Correa was widely expected to be selected in the first round of the 2012 MLB Draft. He had been on the radar of major-league scouts since his sophomore year with his rare combination of size, speed, and power, and had also impressed many with his strong mental make-up. Correa's stellar performances in MLB-sanctioned showcase events on the US mainland helped further increase his profile. Among those who closely followed his development was the scout Mike Elias, who worked for the St. Louis Cardinals organization under Jeff Luhnow and joined the Astros when the team hired Luhnow as general manager in 2012.

In May 2012 Elias recommended the Astros bring Correa in for a workout. The Astros held the top pick in that year's draft and were looking to draft a cornerstone player that they could build their franchise around for years to come. Though Correa was initially not among the Astros' top choices and was not considered a top pick in most rankings, Luhnow agreed to give him a closer look and invited him to participate in a simulated game. In that game Correa "stood out from the professionals," Luhnow noted to Brian McTaggart for MLB.com (5 June 2012), adding that he was "an impact player we need for the future. . . . He's driven to be successful."

In June 2012 the Astros selected Correa with the first overall pick in the draft, making him the highest player ever drafted out of Puerto Rico. Correa agreed to a signing bonus of $4.8 million, which was significantly less than the value of his draft slot but gave the team more resources to lock up other key draft picks. Several days after signing his contract Correa graduated from the PRBAHS as class valedictorian with a 4.0 grade point average.

RISE TO THE MAJOR LEAGUES

By the time Correa entered the Astros' system he had reached the height of six feet four inches but only weighed 185 pounds. Many scouts believed that Correa would fill out his frame and hit for both average and power. They also projected that Correa would physically outgrow the shortstop position and ultimately end up at third base, much like Alex Rodriguez. Correa was determined, however, to make it in the big leagues as a shortstop and resolved to follow a strict diet that would keep him under 220 pounds. As he told McTaggart, "I think I have the ability, and I will work hard. . . . I want to be one of the best."

Making good on his pledge, Correa established himself not only as the Astros' top prospect but also as one of the best prospects in all of baseball. He played in 282 games over parts of four minor-league seasons, in which he batted .313 with 28 home runs and 199 runs batted in

(RBIs). Correa's rapid ascension through the Astros' farm system was only briefly halted in June 2014, when he fractured his right fibula while sliding into third base during a game with the Astros' advanced-A affiliate, the Lancaster JetHawks of the California League. The injury required surgery and sidelined Correa for the remainder of the 2014 season.

When Correa returned for the 2015 season, the Astros assigned him to the Corpus Christi Hooks of the AA Eastern League. After posting a blistering .385 batting average in 29 games with the club, Correa was promoted to the AAA Fresno Grizzlies of the Pacific Coast League. He played in just 24 games with the Grizzlies, hitting .276 with 3 home runs and 12 RBIs, before the Astros decided to call him up to the majors in early June.

ROOKIE PHENOM

Correa was expected to provide an extra spark for the Astros' team that had opened the 2015 season with a surprisingly strong 34–24 record. The Astros were just one year removed from a ninety-two-loss season and had suffered through three consecutive seasons with at least one hundred losses prior to that. The team, however, was enjoying a resurgence under manager A. J. Hinch and led the AL West Division when Correa joined the big league club. At twenty years and 259 days old, Correa became the youngest player in the majors at the time and would remain the youngest position player that year.

Youth and inexperience notwithstanding, Correa quickly justified the Astros' decision to promote him by authoring a historic rookie season. He batted .287 with 9 doubles, 5 home runs, 15 RBIs, and 4 stolen bases in 21 games for the month of June and was named the AL Rookie of the Month. He proceeded to hit 14 home runs in his first 51 games, becoming the first shortstop in more than a century to accomplish such a feat. In addition to putting up rare power numbers Correa won attention around the league for his spectacular defensive plays, many of which ended up on television highlight reels.

Correa finished his rookie season with a solid .279 batting average to go along with an .857 on-base plus slugging (OPS) percentage, 22 home runs, 68 RBIs, 22 doubles, and 14 stolen bases in 99 games. He became only the fourth player in MLB history age twenty-one or younger to post an .850 OPS with at least 250 at-bats. Correa's play fueled the Astros to an 86–76 record and a second-place finish in the AL West, helping the team secure their first winning season since 2008 and first postseason berth since 2005.

In the AL one-game wild-card elimination round, the Astros defeated the New York Yankees, 3–0. The Astros then faced the Kansas

City Royals in the AL Division Series, which they lost in five games. In Game 4 of that series Correa hit two home runs, becoming the youngest player in AL postseason history with a multi-homer game. He also committed a momentum-shifting error in the eighth inning of that game, which the Astros lost, but was praised by teammates and coaches for demonstrating poise and accountability after the defeat.

In November 2015 Correa won the AL Rookie of the Year Award, receiving seventeen of thirty first-place votes from the Baseball Writers' Association of America (BBWAA). He became just the second Astro to receive the honor.

2016 SEASON

Correa entered the 2016 season hoping to solidify his status as one of the game's best all-around talents. "I don't put limitations on him, in terms of what's possible" Hinch told Ted Berg for USA Today's sports news site For the Win (29 Feb. 2016). "He has got a lot of talent. He has good makeup. He has tremendous drive. I think he can be as good as anyone expects." Correa himself explained his philosophy to Berg: "For me, it's not only about baseball. I want to be a great baseball player, but an even better human being."

One of Puerto Rico's most marketable sports figures, Correa signed a record-setting five-year endorsement contract with sportswear company Adidas in February 2016.

PERSONAL LIFE

Correa lives in a penthouse apartment in downtown Houston overlooking the Astros' Minute Maid Park.

SUGGESTED READING

Berg, Ted. "Carlos Correa Adjusts to Life on the Brink of Superstardom." For the Win. USA Today Sports, 29 Feb. 2016. Web. 10 Mar. 2016.

Duarte, Joseph. "Astros Top Pick Carlos Correa Already a Hero at Home in Puerto Rico." Houston Chronicle. Hearst Newspapers, 17 June 2012. Web. 10 Mar. 2016.

McTaggart, Brian. "Astros Make Correa Draft's Leading Man." Astros.com. MLB Advanced Media, 5 June 2012. Web. 10 Mar. 2016.

Paese, Gabrielle. "Carlos Correa Jr.: Special Bonds." ESPN. ESPN Internet Ventures, 3 June 2012. Web. 10 Mar. 2016.

Reiter, Ben. "Made Man: At 21, Astros Shortstop Carlos Correa Is Already a Star." Sports Illustrated. Time, 6 Oct. 2015. Web. 10 Mar. 2016.

—Chris Cullen

Robert Costa

Born: October 14, 1985
Occupation: Journalist

In the midst of a severe partisan deadlock and a shutdown of the federal government, Marc Tracy wrote for the New Republic (14 Oct. 2013), "The most important news in the country over the past few weeks has been driven by a cohort of Republican politicians, activists, and operatives, and that means that the most important reporter in the country over the past few weeks has been National Review's Robert Costa." He continued, "For decades, the premium in conservative journalism has been on opinion-mongering. Costa defies this trend, working sources, focusing on scoops and objective analysis, and rarely, if ever, betraying a political lean."

Other media observers concurred. Joe Coscarelli wrote for New York magazine (17 Oct. 2013), "Costa has been celebrated by his colleagues and subjects alike as a must-read this month, his reporting from behind the closed doors of Republicans in Congress held up as indispensable, a shining beacon of the form in which a man tirelessly asks questions and prints the answers without fluff or bluster." Others grudgingly admitted Costa's talent, albeit with a measure of sniping. "It's unusual to see a conservative reporter win universal praise for his reporting, if for no other reason than that there aren't that many conservatives who do straight journalism. Which brings us to Robert Costa," Paul Waldman wrote for the progressive publication American Prospect (17 Oct. 2013), in

Paul Marotta/Getty Images for SiriusXM

a piece sarcastically headlined, "Conservative Does Journalism, Gets Hailed as Demi-God." Waldman added, "Costa is without question an excellent reporter, and he got information that even other conservatives weren't getting. . . . So when the fate of the entire world seemed to hinge on what Ted Cruz told a few dingbat Tea Partiers in a clandestine meeting in the basement of a Capitol Hill restaurant, Costa was the only one in the media who could explain it to everyone else."

Costa is known to keep his political opinions to himself, but many people have assumed that he endorses the positions of the Republican politicians he has reported on. "If you worked at *Car and Driver* magazine, it doesn't mean you necessarily love cars, but you have the best car-industry sources and you know what's coming around the bend in terms of next year's models," Costa told Tracy. "That's how I look at covering conservatism. It's one of the best stories in American politics." Explaining his position to Coscarelli, Costa said, "I have my own views, but every day I try to wipe the board clean. Basically, I'm a middle-of-the-road guy who's mostly conservative, who loves to report."

EARLY LIFE

Robert Costa was born on October 14, 1985, in Richmond, Virginia. He has a twin brother named James. He grew up in Lower Makefield, Yardley, Pennsylvania. Costa attended Pennsbury High School, in Fairless Hills, Pennsylvania, a town in Bucks County, near Trenton. Well before he became known for his reporting, Costa's high school years were chronicled in the 2004 nonfiction book *Wonderland: A Year in the Life of an American High School* by Michael Bamberger, a senior writer for *Sports Illustrated*. Costa's leadership activities and compelling personality attracted Bamberger's attention, and he ended up being a major figure in the book.

Because Costa's father, a lawyer for pharmaceutical companies, always carried business cards, Costa had his own made, which read, "Bob Costa, Pennsbury High School." While still a student, he wrote concert reviews for the local paper, the *Bucks County Courier Times*, earning fifty dollars for each review. For a time, he was in charge of reading the daily announcements over the school's PA system, and he frequently appeared on the student-run television station, PHS-TV.

Active in student government, he was president of his junior class and is particularly remembered for his role in planning the Pennsbury prom. (The school's proms have traditionally been so lavish—featuring a celebratory parade through town before the event—that they have received national attention.) Costa was determined to get pop star John Mayer, already

at the height of his fame, to perform at the 2003 prom. While backstage at a Mayer concert he was covering for the local paper, Costa slipped the musician a letter asking him to perform. Although those efforts were unsuccessful, he did manage to convince Mayer's opening act—Maroon 5—to appear at his prom. The following year, impressed by Costa's doggedness, Mayer did make a surprise appearance, singing three songs at Costa's senior prom.

HIGHER EDUCATION

Costa, who was also elected senior-class president, graduated from Pennsbury in 2004. During the summer before entering college, he worked as a strategist on the special election campaign for Republican Mike Fitzpatrick, who was vying to become the representative for Pennsylvania's Eighth Congressional District. He credits Fitzpatrick with sparking his interest in conservatism. Previously, he had identified as a liberal Democrat. While in high school, Costa had traveled to Harrisburg to attend the 2003 inauguration of Pennsylvania's newly elected Democratic governor Ed Rendell, and the day after the junior prom, he journeyed to Trenton, New Jersey, where former president Bill Clinton was making an appearance. (He used his PHS-TV credentials to gain access to the event.)

After leaving Fitzpatrick's ultimately successful campaign, Costa entered the University of Notre Dame, where he majored in American studies and was active with the student-run television station and wrote for the school newspaper, just as he had been at Pennsbury. Long a fan of such political television shows as *Meet the Press* and *Face the Nation*, he was excited to learn of Notre Dame's Washington Program, which is run by the Rooney Center for the Study of American Democracy and sends students to the nation's capital to take courses and visit government policymakers and other leaders. The students are also assigned internships at the White House, congressional offices, media outlets, and nongovernmental organizations, and Costa landed at ABC (American Broadcasting Company), where he worked on *This Week with George Stephanopoulos* and assisted commentator George Will during the 2006 congressional elections. He also was a Robert L. Bartley Fellow at the *Wall Street Journal*, which allowed him to contribute to the newspaper's editorial page. He also worked as an intern for a time with Charlie Rose at PBS (Public Broadcasting System).

After earning his bachelor's degree in 2008, Costa entered the University of Cambridge, in England, where he was a member of the Cambridge Union debating society, wrote a thesis on Winston Churchill, and completed his master's degree in politics in less than one year.

NATIONAL REVIEW

Upon leaving Cambridge, Costa joined the *National Review* as the magazine's first-ever William F. Buckley Fellow. (The fellowship was named for the famed conservative commentator who had founded the magazine in 1955 following his death in 2008.) Since the outset of his career, Costa has focused on old-fashioned, shoe-leather reporting. "From Day One, I've never written a column or an editorial," Costa recalled to Coscarelli. "I was not comfortable even aspiring to be Buckley or George Will, but I felt comfortable aspiring to be a solid reporter." After his fellowship ended in 2009, Costa was hired by the *National Review* as a political reporter, working at the publication's New York headquarters. In 2012, he was named editor of the Washington bureau, where he covered the White House, Congress, and national campaigns.

Costa gained widespread attention, even among those who did not read the *National Review*, in 2013, during the shutdown of the federal government that had been precipitated by a partisan stalemate over funding for President Barack Obama's Patient Protection and Affordable Care Act. Costa was identified as the most vital source for information on what Republican leaders were thinking and doing, beating out major news organizations such as the Associated Press and the *New York Times* for scoops. "His ability to take all sides seriously may have earned him as many ins as having the *National Review* on his business card," Coscarelli wrote. In his interview with Tracy, Costa explained, "My job is connecting the dots with all these sources I have on the right. It gives me the ability to understand the language of conservatism. When I cover Tea Party activists and conservative House members, it's not like I'm a reporter going into a zoo and raising my eyebrows at the scene and filing some color piece. I'm really taking seriously the ways conservatives think, use power, and practice politics, and reporting that straight."

When Obama gathered several conservative journalists for an off-the-record meeting at the White House in the midst of the shutdown, Costa was included along with such better-known figures as Fox News contributor Charles Krauthammer and syndicated columnist Kathleen Parker.

THE WASHINGTON POST

In January 2014, Costa joined the staff of the *Washington Post* as a national political reporter. His method of reporting remained the same despite switching from a right-leaning magazine to a more mainstream publication. "I'm a reporter. Wherever I work, that's how I operate," he asserted in an interview with *Politico Media* (11

Nov. 2014). "The setting is certainly different, going from a political magazine to a national newspaper, but the process remains the same. You hustle, you write, and then you search for your next story. Sources have not treated me differently. They recognize that a reporter's integrity is what matters, not just where he or she works." Several reporters have commented on Costa's ability to gain the trust of his sources and understand the mindset of right-wing politicians. "There aren't actually that many people who take the time to understand who these guys are and what their motivations are as individuals," Dave Weigel, a political reporter for *Slate* magazine, told Coscarelli. "There are [reporters] who pop up when there's a problem. He tries to understand them at all times." In 2015, in addition to his duties at the *Post*, Costa signed on as a political analyst for NBC (National Broadcasting Company) News and MSNBC (Microsoft National Broadcasting Company).

While Costa respects the figures he covers, he does not venerate them. "My political hero is [biographer] Robert Caro, not any politician," Costa told Coscarelli. "With his [Lyndon B.] Johnson books he chronicled power. I try to get beyond the glib quote and get inside the cloak room to find out who's using power and why. That's not a partisan pursuit."

SUGGESTED READING

Calderone, Michael. "Robert Costa's Moment." *Huff Post Media*. TheHuffingtonPost.com, 10 Oct. 2013. Web. 17 Feb. 2016.

Coscarelli, Joe. "How Robert Costa Became the Golden Boy of the Government Shutdown." *New York*. New York Media, 17 Oct. 2013. Web. 17 Feb. 2016.

Costa, Robert. "The 60-Second Interview: Robert Costa, National Political Reporter, the Washington Post." Interview. *Politico Media Beta*. Politico, 11 Nov. 2014. Web. 17 Feb. 2016.

Costa, Robert. "Q&A with Robert Costa." Interview by Brian Lamb. *C-SPAN*. Natl. Cable Satellite, 11 Sept. 2015. Web. 17 Feb. 2016.

Smerconish, Michael. "Bucks Native Makes a Splash in Washington." *Philly.com*. Philadelphia Media Network, 27 Oct. 2013. Web. 17 Feb. 2016.

Tracy, Marc. "Robert Costa: I'm Not on the 'Conservative Team.'" *New Republic*. New Republic, 14 Oct. 2013. Web. 17 Feb. 2016.

Waldman, Paul. "Conservative Does Journalism, Gets Hailed as Demi-God." *American Prospect*. Prospect, 17 Oct. 2013. Web. 17 Feb. 2016.

—*Mari Rich*

Kirk Cousins

Born: August 19, 1988
Occupation: Football player

Kirk Cousins, referred to by his teammates as "Captain Kirk" for his command in the huddle and resolve under pressure, overcame long odds to become a regular starting quarterback in the National Football League (NFL). An unheralded quarterback prospect coming out of high school, Cousins spent two years as a backup at Michigan State University before becoming the school's starter. Despite setting all-time school records for wins, completions, passing yards, and passing touchdowns, he fell to the fourth round of the 2012 NFL Draft before being selected 102nd overall by the Washington Redskins, the NFL team that plays in Washington, DC. He was immediately cast as a backup on a Washington team that had selected Robert Griffin III, the 2011 Heisman Trophy winner, second overall in the draft.

As Griffin's backup, Cousins played only sparingly in his first three seasons with Washington, during which he showed glimpses of promise despite being prone to inconsistency and occasional mistakes. That promise was enough for the team to name Cousins the starter prior to the 2015 season as Griffin struggled with injuries. Cousins went on to have a breakout 2015 campaign, leading the NFL in completion percentage (69.8 percent) and guiding Washington to an unexpected National Football Conference (NFC) East Division title and playoff berth. The team then signed Cousins to a one-year franchise tag and parted ways with Griffin. Cousins, as Robert Klemko wrote for MMQB.com (1 Dec. 2015), "may not be the best QB in the NFL . . . but he's making the case that he belongs."

EARLY LIFE

The second of three children of Don and MaryAnn Cousins, Kirk Daniel Cousins was born on August 19, 1988, in Barrington, Illinois. His father was an evangelical preacher who served as the senior pastor at the Orlando, Florida–based Discovery Church; his mother was a flight attendant. He grew up with an older brother, Kyle, and a younger sister, Karalyne.

Cousins endured his first bout with adversity at just nineteen months old, when he suffered severe burns to his neck and torso after knocking over a pot of boiling water while playing in his family's kitchen. He spent two weeks in the hospital recovering and was forced to wear a compression jacket for almost a year so his skin would heal properly. Though Cousins was too young to recall the incident later in life, his family was informed that he might never be able to do things like throw a ball correctly due to the

Keith Allison/Flickr/CC BY-SA 2.0/Wikimedia Commons

extent of his injuries. Yet after healing he excelled early on in sports, particularly football. He started tossing footballs around with his father not long after he could walk. "My life," Cousins told Mark Schlabach for *ESPN.com* (21 Oct. 2011), "has been a living evidence of God's ability to do the unexplainable."

Cousins started playing organized football in the sixth grade. Thanks to his strong arm, he was immediately placed as quarterback and led his suburban Chicago youth team to a league championship. When Cousins was in seventh grade, his family moved to western Michigan, settling in the city of Holland.

HIGH SCHOOL CAREER

Cousins attended Holland Christian High School, where he starred not only in football but also in basketball and baseball. He had to earn his way onto the varsity squads for each of those sports. As a sophomore, Cousins started out as a reserve on the varsity baseball team before becoming the starting third baseman and emerging as a standout hitter. Then, as a junior, he opened the basketball season as the varsity team's third-string before winning the starting point guard spot in his first game.

On the gridiron, Cousins played quarterback for Holland Christian's freshman and junior-varsity teams before advancing to the varsity level. His chances of playing college football were put in jeopardy, however, after suffering a broken ankle during his junior year. Cousins recovered in time for his senior season when he earned all-conference honors after throwing for 2,088 yards and making twenty-eight touchdowns.

Still, "when you looked at him, you never said 'oh yeah, this is definitely a D-I prospect," as his high-school coach, Tim Lont, noted to Dan Steinberg for the *Washington Post* (14 July 2016).

Despite his intense work ethic and exceptional leadership skills, Cousins lacked the physical gifts of other high school quarterback prospects. As a result, Lont tried to steer him toward Division II and Division III colleges. Cousins nonetheless set his sights on playing at the highest level possible and eventually won a scholarship to Michigan State University (MSU), in East Lansing, a Division I school that plays in the Big Ten Conference. An academic standout, Cousins graduated as the valedictorian of his senior class with a perfect 4.0 grade-point average (GPA). "He's a goal setter. He's an achiever . . . . He just sets goals and goes after them," Don Cousins said of his son to Schlabach.

MICHIGAN STATE RECORD HOLDER

Cousins was recruited to Michigan State by coach Mark Dantonio, who decided to redshirt him for the 2007 season. Upon returning for his redshirt freshman season in 2008, he served as the primary backup quarterback behind senior Brian Hoyer. Following Hoyer's senior season, Cousins battled Keith Nichol for the Spartans' starting quarterback spot. He not only won the job but was also named a team cocaptain for his redshirt sophomore season in 2009, in which he led the Spartans to a 6–7 record.

Proving himself "a capable if not spectacular quarterback," as Albert Chen noted for *Sports Illustrated* (16 Aug. 2011), Cousins returned in 2010 to lead the Spartans to an 11–2 record and a share of the Big Ten title. That season he threw for 2,825 yards with twenty touchdowns and ten interceptions, and he displayed toughness playing through several injuries. "He embraces the big moments and doesn't shy away from anything," Dantonio told Chen. "The players look up to his toughness and feed off of it."

During his 2011 redshirt senior season, Cousins led the Spartans to an 11–3 overall record and a runner-up finish in the first ever Big Ten championship game. He finished his career at MSU as the school's all-time leader in a number of offensive categories, including passing touchdowns (66), passing yards (9,131), and completions (723). He also finished as the winningest quarterback in school history and became the first MSU quarterback to defeat instate rival Michigan Wolverines three straight times. A four-time Academic All-Big Ten Conference honoree, Cousins, who was initially a pre-med student, graduated from MSU in December 2011 with a 3.68 GPA and a degree in kinesiology. After completing his collegiate career, Cousins said, as quoted by Steinberg: "There were a lot of people who didn't believe

in me, a lot of people who didn't give me a chance. . . . I think I was able to prove those people wrong."

Cousins subsequently entered the 2012 NFL Draft thinking he would be selected in the first couple of rounds. However, he slipped to the fourth round and, as a surprise to many, was selected by the NFL team that plays in Washington, DC, which, with the second overall pick, had already taken Robert Griffin III, better known as RG3, the reigning Heisman Trophy winner. Griffin was immediately designated as the new face of the franchise, while Cousins was simply considered an insurance policy if Griffin was injured.

NFL DEBUT

Disappointed but not defeated, Cousins settled into a backup role behind Griffin, who proceeded to have a record-breaking rookie season. Griffin's highly athletic style of play, however, left him susceptible to injury, leaving the door open for Cousins, who played in three regular-season games in the 2012 season, including one start. In that game, against the Cleveland Browns, Cousins passed for 329 yards and two touchdowns in a 38–21 Washington victory. The team won the NFC East title and advanced to the postseason for the first time since 2007. In the NFC wildcard playoff round, Griffin was forced to leave in the fourth quarter after tearing two ligaments in his right knee. Cousins struggled in his place, completing just three of ten passes, and Washington was defeated by the Seattle Seahawks, 24–14.

Griffin's injury, which required surgery, ultimately proved to be the turning point in Cousins's career. Though Griffin recovered in time for the 2013 season opener, his performance declined greatly in his sophomore season, so much so that Washington coach Mike Shanahan decided to bench him for the season's final three games in favor of Cousins. Shanahan, who had rebuilt the team's entire offense around Griffin's unique skill set, was heavily criticized by the national sports media, with some pundits even accusing him of making the move in a deliberate attempt to get himself fired.

Cousins went 0–3 in his three starts, and Washington finished last in the NFC East with a disastrous 3–13 record. Shanahan, along with the bulk of his coaching staff, was indeed fired at the conclusion of the regular season. Cousins appeared in five games in total during the 2013 season, finishing with 854 passing yards, four touchdowns, and seven interceptions.

Cousins was the subject of trade rumors during that offseason, with the Browns and the New York Jets expressing interest in acquiring him. He remained with Washington, however, and entered the 2014 season again as the backup to Griffin, who was reinstated as the starter by Shanahan's replacement, Jay Gruden. In just the second week of the season Griffin dislocated his ankle and Cousins stepped in. The following week Cousins started and passed for a career-high 427 yards with three touchdowns and a 103.4 passer rating. Yet he failed to duplicate that success in his next few outings and was benched in favor of third-string quarterback Colt McCoy for the remainder of the season. Washington again finished last in the NFC East. "It was tough," Cousins said of his benching to David Whitley for the *Orlando Sentinel* (12 Sept. 2015). "At the same time, tough times don't last. Tough people do. I just had to keep going, and if I kept doing that, I'd have another chance."

RECORD-BREAKING 2015 SEASON
Cousins's chance for redemption came during the 2015 preseason, when he out-battled Griffin to win Washington's starting quarterback spot. Cousins went on to start all sixteen games in the regular season. Despite amassing eight interceptions and just six touchdown passes in the first six games, in which the team posted a 2–4 record, he overcame his inconsistent play in the second half of the season and finished with 4,166 passing yards, twenty-nine touchdowns, and eleven interceptions for a 101.6 passer rating.

Cousins led the NFL with a 69.8 completion percentage, becoming the first Washington signal-caller to accomplish the feat since 1970. He also established a new NFL mark for the highest completion percentage (74.7) in home games and set single-season team records for passing yards, attempts (543), completions (379), and 300-yard passing games (7).

Bolstered by Cousins's regular-season performance, Washington finished with a 9–7 record, which was good enough to claim the NFC East title. In his first postseason start, Cousins threw for 329 yards with one passing touchdown and one rushing touchdown. However, the team lost to the Green Bay Packers in the NFC wildcard game, 35–18. "He's a natural leader, and he's what a QB is supposed to be," Washington defensive tackle Ricky Jean Francois said of Cousins to Klemko, "He beats himself up too much. . . . But that's just a quarterback searching for perfection."

In March 2016 Washington placed the nonexclusive franchise tag on Cousins, which allowed them to match any contract offers he received from other teams. That month the team also released Griffin, who was inactive for the entire 2015 regular season. Cousins remained unfazed by the prospect of having to play under the one-year franchise tag after he and the team failed to negotiate a longer-term deal. "I'll let my play do the talking," he explained, as quoted by John Keim for *ABC News* (15 July 2016).

"Nothing in this league is promised to you. Whether it's a one-year deal or a ten-year deal, I have to prove myself every game and every year."

PERSONAL LIFE
On June 28, 2014, Cousins married his wife, Julie, in a ceremony held in Atlanta, Georgia. He is known for his strong Christian faith and for being, at times, "painfully humble, to the point that it may have impacted his play," as Steinberg wrote. In 2013 he published the book *Game Changer: Faith, Football, & Finding Your Way*, which chronicles how he integrates his faith and values into his life and career.

SUGGESTED READING
Chen, Albert. "Tough, Tested and Ready to Lead." *Sports Illustrated* 16 Aug. 2011: 72–73. Print.
Clarke, Liz. "'Captain Kirk' Cousins May Boldly Go Where Few Redskins Quarterbacks Have Gone." *Washington Post*. Washington Post, 21 Nov. 2015. Web. 28 Aug. 2016.
Klemko, Robert. "The Books of Cousins." *MMQB*. Time, 1 Dec. 2015. Web. 28 Aug. 2016.
Schlabach, Mark. "Kirk Cousins Used to Playing Long Odds." *ESPN.com* ESPN Internet Ventures, 21 Oct. 2011. Web. 28 Aug. 2016.
Steinberg, Dan. "Kirk Cousins Has Never Been Afraid of Betting on Himself." *Washington Post*. Washington Post, 14 July 2016. Web. 28 Aug. 2016.
Whitley, David. "Kirk Cousins, Father Face Different Challenges with Same Faith." *Orlando Sentinel*. Orlando Sentinel, 12 Sept. 2015. Web. 28 Aug. 2016.

—*Chris Cullen*

Stephen Curry
Born: March 14, 1988
Occupation: Basketball player

The Golden State Warriors' point guard Stephen Curry, who stands six feet three inches and weighs about 185 pounds, does not have the kind of imposing physique and athleticism of prototypical superstars in the National Basketball Association (NBA). He does, however, possess an inimitable shooting ability that strikes fear into the hearts of even the most formidable opponents. That ability has helped him establish a reputation as not only the best three-point shooter in the NBA, but also as one of the greatest shooters of all time. Curry has "mesmerizing talent," Sam Amick wrote for *USA*

Photo by Keith Allison from Hanover, MD, USA (Stephen Curry) [CC BY-SA 2.0], via Wikimedia Commons

Today (12 Feb. 2015). "On his best nights, he's a combination of Steve Nash, Pete Maravich, and Reggie Miller."

Drafted by the Warriors in 2009, Curry was hampered by ankle injuries early in his professional career, but he eventually overcame them to ascend to the ranks of the NBA's elite. He reached superstar status during the 2014–15 season, when he won the NBA's Most Valuable Player (MVP) Award and led the Warriors to their first NBA championship since 1975. That season he broke his own NBA record for the most three-pointers made in a single season (286) and set the league record for most threes made in a single postseason (98). A two-time All-Star selection, Curry is equally known for his humble, down-to-earth demeanor, which has made him one of the NBA's most popular and relatable stars.

EARLY LIFE

Wardell Stephen "Steph" Curry II was born on March 14, 1988, in Akron, Ohio. He grew up with his younger brother, Seth, and younger sister, Sydel. His father, Dell, was a professional basketball player who played shooting guard over a sixteen-year NBA career, from 1986 to 2002. His mother, Sonya, was also an accomplished athlete, playing volleyball at Virginia Tech University.

Curry was raised mostly in Charlotte, North Carolina, where his father spent the bulk of his career with the Charlotte Hornets. He grew up watching his father play and reportedly attended his first NBA game when he was just two weeks

old. As youngsters, Curry and his brother often accompanied their father on road trips, where the two would help shag balls during pregame warm-ups. During free time at home, Dell, who was known as one of the NBA's best three-point marksmen, would run his sons through drills that emphasized proper shooting mechanics and other fundamentals of the game. On a daily basis, Curry challenged his brother to shootouts and one-on-one games on the family's lighted backyard basketball court.

Though Curry was undersized and possessed only modest athletic gifts, he had excellent hand-eye coordination and a tireless work ethic, which enabled him to develop remarkable shooting skills from an early age. By age six, he was already putting on dazzling shooting displays. "He'd hit one, then another, and you'd see this smirk on his face, and you knew it was over," his first basketball coach, Malcolm Sanders, told Lee Jenkins for *Sports Illustrated* (25 May 2015). "People came to watch him. He gave shows."

Curry spent his middle school years in Toronto, Ontario, Canada, where his father played his final three NBA seasons for the Toronto Raptors. As an eighth-grader at Queensway Christian College, he routinely scored forty to fifty points per game for the school's basketball team, helping them go undefeated.

HIGH SCHOOL CAREER

After Curry's father retired from the NBA, his family moved back to Charlotte. Curry attended Charlotte Christian School, a private college prep school. As a freshman, he stood only five feet six inches tall and was "so scrawny that his jersey fit him like a hand-me-down nightgown," Cory Collins wrote for the *Sporting News* (27 Apr. 2015). Due to his size, Curry began on the school's junior-varsity basketball squad during his freshman season.

During his sophomore season, Curry became a varsity starter for Charlotte Christian. At the time, he had an unorthodox shooting form in which he would push the ball from his chest. Knowing that form would not stand up against more physically imposing competition, Dell Curry forced his son to remake his shot so that his release point was above his head. Though Curry initially struggled with the change, it eventually helped him take his game to the next level. "Every year he brought something new to his game," his high-school coach Shonn Brown noted to Collins. "And that was truly just a function of him working."

Curry led Charlotte Christian to three consecutive state tournaments from his sophomore to senior seasons, and earned all-state and team MVP honors as both a junior and senior. As a senior, Curry teamed up with his brother, then a sophomore and varsity backup shooting guard, to lead Charlotte Christian to a runner-up finish in the 2006 state tournament.

STAR AT DAVIDSON COLLEGE

Curry finished his high-school career at Charlotte Christian as the school's all-time leading scorer, with a 48 percent three-point field goal percentage. Those accomplishments notwithstanding, Curry was overlooked by every major college basketball program because of his size. As a result he chose to enroll at Davidson College, a small, academically prestigious liberal arts college near Charlotte that competes in the National Collegiate Athletic Association's (NCAA) Division I. Davidson's head basketball coach, Bob McKillop, recognized not only Curry's technical abilities but also his many intangible qualities, and promised to build the school's basketball program around him. "He doesn't overpower you with slam dunks and with muscle," McKillop explained to Stephen Kruse for *Bleacher Report* (5 Mar. 2015). "He overpowers you with an IQ that is extraordinary."

McKillop's instincts proved true as Curry emerged as a national sensation at Davidson, where he played both shooting guard and point guard. As a freshman he finished second in the nation among first-year players in scoring (21.5 points per game), and led the Wildcats to a berth in the NCAA tournament.

Curry entered the mainstream consciousness during his sophomore season, when he set the NCAA record for three-pointers in a season, with 162, and led Davidson on an improbable run to the NCAA tournament's Elite Eight. Curry's prolific scoring output in the tournament earned him appearances on a number of national talk shows and a nomination for best breakthrough athlete at the 2008 ESPY (Excellence in Sports Performance Yearly) Awards. He returned for his junior year in 2008–9 to lead the nation in scoring (28.6 points per game) and was named a consensus first-team All-American.

GOLDEN STATE WARRIOR

Curry decided to forgo his senior season to enter the 2009 NBA Draft. Unlike his experience of being overlooked in high school, he was selected by the Golden Gate Warriors in the draft's first round, as the seventh overall pick. In July 2009 he signed a four-year contract with the Warriors worth $12.7 million.

Prior to the 2009–10 season, the Warriors' then head coach, Don Nelson, named Curry, who by then had grown to his full height and added bulk to his frame, the team's starting shooting guard. That decision, however, did not sit well with the Warriors' veteran starting point guard, Monta Ellis, who publicly declared that their backcourt pairing would never work in Nelson's free-flowing offensive system. Undaunted, Curry settled into his role, and in eighty games during his first NBA season he averaged 17.5 points, which ranked second among rookies. He also led all NBA rookies in assists per game (5.9), steals per game (1.9), three-point field-goal percentage (.437), and free throw percentage (.885). He was a unanimous selection to the NBA All-Rookie First Team and finished second in the voting for the NBA Rookie of the Year Award. "It kind of made me even more focused on what I was doing," Curry later said of the Ellis controversy to Chris Ballard for *Sports Illustrated* (2 Apr. 2013).

Despite Curry's impressive rookie performance, the Warriors were beset by injuries throughout the season and finished fourth in the Pacific Division with a dismal 26–56 record. In the summer of 2010, the team was purchased by an ownership group headed by Joe Lacob and Peter Guber. One month before the start of the 2010–11 season, the new owners fired Nelson and replaced him with longtime Warriors assistant Keith Smart, who implemented a more defensive-minded team philosophy. That season Curry improved his scoring average to 18.6 points per game and led the NBA in free-throw percentage (.934), despite missing eight games due to multiple right ankle sprains. The Warriors, however, did not fare much better under Smart, who was fired after leading the team to a mediocre 36–46 record.

OVERCOMING ADVERSITY

Following the 2010–11 season, Curry underwent surgery to repair torn ligaments in his right ankle. He returned in time for the 2011–12 season, which was shortened from eighty-two to sixty-six games due to a lockout. One week into the season, Curry aggravated his right ankle injury, which would plague him the rest of the season and ultimately limit him to just twenty-six games. In those games, he averaged career-lows of 14.7 points and 5.3 assists. That off-season he underwent a second successful surgery to repair the instability in his right ankle.

Though many questions surrounded Curry's long-term health, the Warriors gave him a four-year, $44 million contract extension before the start of the 2012–13 season. Curry rewarded the Warriors' faith in him by having a breakout season. In seventy-eight games, he averaged 22.9 points, 6.9 assists, and 1.6 steals, and broke the NBA record for three-pointers made in a season, with 272. He led the Warriors to a 47–35 record and helped them reach the playoffs for the first time in six years. "When people count you out, tell you there's no chance, that's when it's easy for me to really focus," Curry told Jenkins.

Curry continued his ascension during the 2013–14 season, in which he averaged career-highs in points (24.0) and assists (8.5). He earned his first All-Star selection, as a starter for the Western Conference, and was named to the All-NBA Second Team. He helped the Warriors improve to 51–31 and earn a second straight playoff appearance. Polarizing third-year head coach Mark Jackson was fired after the team's first-round playoff exit, however, due to his poor relationship with the owners. He was replaced by Steve Kerr, a former NBA guard and television analyst who had never coached at any level.

MVP SEASON AND FIRST NBA TITLE

Although he had enjoyed significant success in Jackson's isolation-heavy offense, Curry flourished even more under Kerr, who implemented a faster-paced system that relied heavily upon motion and ball movement. Curry subsequently transformed himself into one of the NBA's best players during the 2014–15 season, in which he also became "the new face of his sport," as Kruse wrote. He began the season by winning the Western Conference Player of the Month Award after averaging nearly twenty-four points, eight assists, and two steals in the first sixteen games. He then recorded his one-thousandth career three-point field goal, becoming the fastest player ever to accomplish the feat. He was selected to his second straight All-Star team, again as a starter, after finishing as the league's top overall vote-getter, and won his first three-point contest during the 2015 NBA All-Star Weekend.

Curry continued his electrifying play during the second half of the season. He eclipsed his own NBA record for most three-pointers in a season, finishing with 286, and led the league in free throw percentage (.914) for the second time in his career. In eighty games, he averaged 23.8 points, 7.7 assists, and two steals, good for sixth, sixth, and fourth in the league, respectively. Those numbers helped him earn All-NBA First Team honors and, ultimately, the NBA MVP Award. He became only the second player in Warriors history to receive the latter honor, after Wilt Chamberlain in 1959–60.

With Curry as their anchor, the Warriors finished with an NBA-best and franchise-record sixty-seven regular-season wins, which were the third-most in league history. The Warriors cruised to the NBA Finals, where they defeated the LeBron James–led Cleveland Cavaliers in six games to win their first league title in forty years. In twenty-one postseason games, Curry averaged 28.3 points, 6.4 assists, and five rebounds, and made a league-record 98 three-pointers, which obliterated the previous mark of 59 set by Reggie Miller in 2000.

In the 2015–16 season-opener, Curry picked up where he left off, scoring 40 points in a 111–95 Warriors victory over the New Orleans Pelicans. Through the first six games of that season, he tallied 213 points, which were the most since

Michael Jordan scored 214 to begin the 1989–90 campaign.

PERSONAL LIFE

Curry, who is known for his strong Christian faith, is "one of the most humble superstars there is, by far," the Warriors' veteran backup point guard Shaun Livingston explained to Amick. "His faith, his beliefs, and his value system is unprecedented." Curry's wholesome reputation has contributed to his popularity and has helped him land endorsement deals with such brands as Under Armour, State Farm Insurance, Muscle Milk, and Express. His first signature shoe, the Curry One, was released by Under Armour in 2015.

In addition to his NBA career, Curry has represented the US men's national basketball team in a number of international competitions. He captured gold medals as a member of the team at both the 2010 and 2014 world championships.

Curry married his high-school sweetheart, Ayesha Alexander, in July 2011. The couple's daughters, Riley and Ryan, were born in 2012 and 2015, respectively.

SUGGESTED READING

Amick, Sam. "Stephen Curry: Family Man, Everyman, NBA Megastar." *USA Today*. USA Today, 12 Feb. 2015. Web. 21 Oct. 2015.

Ballard, Chris. "Warriors' Stephen Curry Perfecting the Imperfect Art of Shooting." *Sports Illustrated*. Time, 2 Apr. 2013. Web. 21 Oct. 2015.

Collins, Cory. "Stephen Curry Started Small, But He's Always Been Big-Time." *Sporting News*. Sporting News, 27 Apr. 2015. Web. 21 Oct. 2015.

Jenkins, Lee. "Curry Flurry." *Sports Illustrated* 25 May 2015: 38–45. Print.

Kruse, Stephen. "Meet Steph Curry, the NBA's Most Beloved Megastar." *Bleacher Report*. Bleacher Report, 5 Mar. 2015. Web. 21 Oct. 2015.

—*Chris Cullen*

Andra Day

Born: December 30, 1984
Occupation: Singer and songwriter

At a time when the mainstream musical landscape is being dominated by pop singers, Andra Day has distinguished herself with a unique "retro soul" sound that has evoked comparisons to other notable jazz-influenced female vocalists. "Who is Andra Day? Some might say 'the Black Amy Winehouse,' or 'the next Eartha Kitt,'"

slgckgc/CC BY 2.0/Wikimedia Commons

Matthew Allen wrote in his introduction to an interview for *Ebony* (19 Nov. 2015). "The San Diego–born singer/songwriter . . . may reach back to a foregone time when doo-wop, jazz and blues moved the musical needle. But she's her own artist with both feet planted firmly in the present."

Day's 2015 debut album, *Cheers to the Fall*, impressed critics and audiences alike, garnering two Grammy Award nominations and spawning the inspirational and empowering hit ballad "Rise Up." Equally distinctive is Day's personal style—her beehive hairdo, silk bandannas, cat-eye makeup, classic red lips, and hoop earrings—which is heavily inspired by legendary comedian Lucille Ball. Her signature look was on full display as the face of Gap's 2014 Summer Loves campaign.

EARLY LIFE AND EDUCATION
The second oldest of four children, Cassandra Monique Batie, nicknamed Andra (Day is her stage name), was born on December 30, 1984, in Spokane, Washington. Her family moved to San Diego, California, when she was three years old. She credits her mother, a facilities manager, and her father, a US Navy veteran, with introducing her to different genres of music. "My father . . . loved Motown and R & B, and my mother loved Journey and Fleetwood Mac, so they were always listening to it and playing it," Day recalled to Stacy-Ann Ellis for *Vibe* (28 Aug. 2015). She also had a passion for dance, having started taking tap, jazz, and ballet lessons at the age of five.

Day first honed her performing skills as a member of the praise band at First United Methodist Church in Chula Vista. Her formal music education began at Valencia Park Elementary School, then a performing-arts magnet school located in southeast San Diego. Day subsequently attended the San Diego School of Creative and Performing Arts (SCPA), also an arts-focused magnet school, where she was actively involved in musical theater, appearing in productions of *Once on This Island* and *Sweet Charity*.

It was at SCPA that Day seriously started to consider pursuing a singing career. As a vocal performance major, she also became acquainted with classical music, as well as the works of influential female vocalists from the 1940s through the early 1960s. "When I heard Billie Holiday's voice, Nina Simone's and Ella Fitzgerald's—there was something about their voices to me that was such a different texture than what I was used to listening to at the time," she said to Aisha I. Jefferson for Xfinity's television blog (8 Apr. 2016). "Hearing those jazz voices [was] so different and I think I just gravitated toward it."

Upon graduating from SCPA in 2003, the eighteen-year-old made the decision to pursue a singing career. She was initially steered toward contemporary pop and R & B, genres that did not strongly resonate with her. "I tried for a little while but I just realized my voice wasn't quite fitting some of the records that I was doing," she told Sarah A. McCarty for *Paste* (Jan. 2016). "So that's when I started to incorporate more jazz back into what I do and the soul music that my father had me listen to when I was young. And that's when it really clicked for me. That's exactly where I wanted to be."

DISCOVERED BY STEVIE WONDER
Day began performing under her stage name and, over the next several years, became a mainstay of the local nightclub circuit. To support herself, she worked various odd jobs, including managing a paper route, working at a taco joint, and manning the desk at a video store. "I was willing to do whatever it took, even if that meant scrubbing apartment floors by day and gigging at night," she told Arianna Davis for Oprah.com (Dec. 2015).

Day performed in relative obscurity until 2010, when a YouTube clip of her singing in front of a Malibu strip mall caught the attention of Kai Millard Morris, who shared the video with her husband at the time, R & B legend Stevie Wonder. Impressed by what he heard, Wonder personally contacted Day, who was living at her mother's small, cramped Chula Vista apartment. "He reached out to talk about music and writing songs and astrology," she confided to Allison Stewart for the *Chicago Tribune* (10 Mar. 2016). "He wanted to work with me, but it didn't end up working out." Day cites the contentious business relationship with her then-manager/producer as a contributing factor.

About a year-and-a-half later, after Day had parted ways with her manager, she was contacted again by Wonder. He invited her to Los Angeles and introduced her to musician and producer Adrian Gurvitz, cofounder of the Buskin Entertainment record label. After signing with Buskin in 2011, Day entered the studio to begin writing and recording the songs that would eventually appear on her debut album. She also enlisted Jeffrey Evans, Buskin's other cofounder, as her manager.

In addition to Gurvitz, Day was later joined in the studio with former Tony! Toni! Toné! frontman Raphael Saadiq, who served as album coproducer and cowriter. With the encouragement of Gurvitz and Saadiq, Day drew inspiration for the song lyrics from her own life, including the end of an eight-year relationship as a result of her indiscretion. "Being vulnerable and telling the whole truth while allowing yourself to be judged or criticized is one of the scariest things to do. That's something I had to do because I wasn't living right," she told Ellis. She added, "Growing from it was a scary thing, but the freedom that I experienced on the other side of that is something I'll never go back from."

BECOMING A YOUTUBE SENSATION

Among the songs Day recorded with Buskin were a number of covers of popular songs, which she decided to post online to generate public interest. She spent a day in the studio recording several videos for the covers, starting with her take on Muse's "Uprising," which she uploaded on YouTube in October 2012. Day's subsequent renditions of Jessie J's "Mamma Knows Best," which reached number 2 on the YouTube Music Charts, and of Florence and the Machine's "Cosmic Love" quickly gained popularity among YouTube viewers. They also earned her a phone call from comedian and talk-show host Ellen DeGeneres, who offered to help promote her. Day went on to record and upload a mash-up of the Notorious B. I. G.'s "Big Poppa" and Marvin Gaye's "Let's Get It On," inspired by an impromptu jam session with her sister, as well as one combining Amy Winehouse's "He Can Only Hold Her" with Lauryn Hill's "Doo-Wop."

However, it was Day's unique spin on Eminem's "Lose Yourself," which would prove to be her most viewed YouTube cover, that attracted the attention of executives at Warner Bros. Records. In December 2012, Warner Bros. signed her to their label through Buskin, partnering with the latter in order to release her debut. The following summer, "Coolin' in The Street," Day's pop/reggae duet with Ziggy Marley, was featured in the Bud Light Lime national television campaign. In October 2013, she headlined the after-party at the Global Fund for Women's twenty-fifth anniversary gala in San Francisco. She ended the year by releasing a four-track Christmas EP and posting a YouTube video for one of its singles, the Christmas classic "God Rest Ye Merry Gentlemen."

CHEERS TO THE FALL

In 2015, Day performed in a musical tribute to Nina Simone at the 2015 Sundance Film Festival, where a documentary about Simone was being screened. Her performance caught the attention of filmmaker Spike Lee, who offered to direct the video for her upcoming album's debut track, "Forever Mine." The single and Lee's accompanying music video were released in May 2015, followed by Day's second single, "Rise Up," in June. Over the summer, Day performed at both the BET (Black Entertainment Television) Awards and the Essence Festival in New Orleans.

Day's debut album, *Cheers to the Fall*, was officially released in August 2015 to critical acclaim. "This confident, stylish pop R & B record ushers in a sophisticated vocalist who faithfully reflects past influences while remaining contemporary and relevant," Ken Capobianco wrote in his review for the *Boston Globe* (27 Aug. 2015). Ellis agreed, writing in her *Vibe* interview, "*Cheers to the Fall* . . . is definitely a body of work that sticks out like a sore thumb alongside some of the major music releases of 2015, and that's a great thing. It signifies timelessness, embodying all the things to love about nostalgia when it comes to vintage-style music." Day followed up the release by serving as the opening act for eleven dates of the fall 2015 leg of Lenny Kravitz's Strut Tour.

Although "Rise Up" had been released earlier that year, it received a major publicity boost in September, when the track was featured in a commercial for Beats by Dre headphones starring tennis player Serena Williams. The commercial, which debuted during television coverage of the 2015 US Open, catapulted Day to stardom. Two months later, she and pop singer Nick Jonas performed a gospel-tinged version of the song for A+E Networks' Shining a Light concert promoting racial unity.

GRAMMY NODS AND POPULAR SUCCESS

Day's career came full circle in November 2015 when she appeared alongside mentor Stevie Wonder in Apple's annual holiday commercial, belting out his 1967 classic ballad "Someday at Christmas." Her year ended on a high note with two Grammy Award nominations, one for best R & B album and one for best R & B performance (for "Rise Up"). The following February, Day attended the 2016 Grammy Awards, where she and fellow nominee Ellie Goulding dazzled viewers with a mash-up of "Rise Up" and Golding's single "Love Me Like You Do." Although Day did not win an award, she experienced the biggest increase in album sales among all Grammy nominees following her performance.

As Day embarked on her first headlining concert tour in late February 2016, "Rise Up" continued to gain in popularity. After performing the tune on the March 24 episode of the *Ellen DeGeneres Show*, she partnered with Coca-Cola and McDonald's for a May campaign featuring the song's lyrics and Day's image on forty million Coca-Cola cups at the fast-food restaurant. Customers who received the cups were also able to view *I Rise* (2016), a short film inspired by the single that celebrates trailblazing African American women. Also in May, Day released two music videos for the ballad, one of which was directed by filmmaker M. Night Shyamalan. She subsequently returned to perform at the Essence Festival for the second year in a row, this time on the main stage.

PERSONAL LIFE

Day is a supporter of the Global Fund for Women, an organization that promotes women's human rights, and the anti–human trafficking group Unlikely Heroes.

SUGGESTED READING

Davis, Arianna. "This Jazz Artist's Voice Will Blow You Away." *Oprah.com*. Harpo, Dec. 2015. Web. 12 June 2016.

Day, Andra. "Andra Day Is Having It All Happen, All at Once." Interview by Allison Stewart. *Chicago Tribune*. Tribune, 10 Mar. 2016. Web. 12 June 2016.

Day, Andra. "Andra Day Sings Back to the Future." Interview by Matthew Allen. *Ebony*. Johnson, 19 Nov. 2015. Web. 12 June 2016.

Day, Andra. "Get Familiar: Andra Day Is a Big Voice in Bloom." Interview by Stacy-Ann Ellis. *Vibe*. SpinMedia, 28 Aug. 2015. Web. 12 June 2016.

Day, Andra. "Singer Andra Day on Her 'Rise Up,' Lessons Learned as Stevie Wonder's Protégé." Interview by Aisha I. Jefferson. *Xfinity TV Blog*. Comcast, 8 Apr. 2016. Web. 12 June 2016.

McCarty, Sarah A. "Andra Day: The Best of What's Next." *Paste Monthly*. Paste Media Group, Jan. 2016. Web. 12 June 2016.

Varga, George. "Andra Day Rises Up to Music Stardom." *San Diego Union-Tribune*. Tribune, 25 Feb. 2016. Web. 12 June 2016.

—*Bertha Muteba*

Rob Delaney

Born: January 19, 1977
Occupation: Comedian

Comedian Rob Delaney's rise to fame is in many ways a testament to the power of the Internet. A stand-up comic performing largely under the radar in the early years of his career, he found a wider audience when social media was still in its infancy, becoming one of the earliest users of the website MySpace. Upon joining the social network Twitter, Delaney gained the ability to share short, comedic snippets with hundreds of thousands of followers, earning a reputation as one of the site's funniest users. Even his highest profile on-screen role, on the television comedy *Catastrophe*, owes much to the Internet: Delaney met his costar and cowriter for the series, Sharon Horgan, on Twitter, and the series is available to US viewers through the Amazon Prime Instant Video service.

As a comedian who has worked in a range of media, from one-man live shows to 140-character tweets to television, Delaney has an appreciation for the many forms of his chosen calling. "I like comedy of all kinds," he told Lindy West for *GQ* (9 Apr. 2016). "I even enjoy formal roasts—like, I love to watch the Dean Martin ones. I enjoy a good mean joke if it's a heat-seeker, and the game is to find the most sensitive part between two plates of armor." At the same time, Delaney also attempts to meld comedy with a degree of social responsibility. "Life is really hard," he told West, "so I think it's a good idea

David Livingston/Getty Images

to acknowledge that and try to leave the world better than you found it."

EARLY LIFE AND EDUCATION

Rob Delaney was born in Boston, Massachusetts. He and his younger sister, Maggie, grew up primarily in Marblehead, a coastal town north of Boston, where the family moved when Delaney was two years old. His parents later divorced. As a child, Delaney worked a paper route in town, delivering both the local paper, the *Marblehead Reporter*, and the *Boston Globe*. Later, he taught sailing and found work piloting a launch boat. A fan of the performing arts, Delaney appeared in plays and musicals while in school. After graduating from high school, he enrolled in New York University's Tisch School of the Arts to study musical theater. He earned his bachelor's degree from the school in 1999.

In addition to his studies in theater, Delaney developed an interest in comedy, particularly stand-up comedy, while in college. "In 1998, during my senior year of college, I started going to comedy shows and realized, 'Whoa, you can do this,'" he recalled to Phoebe Reilly for *Rolling Stone* (17 June 2015). "These people were just a few years older than me, we're in the same city, and if you saw me in a lineup with them, you wouldn't be like, 'Hey, he sticks out.' So it occurred to me that this was a possibility." However, he did not pursue a career in comedy seriously at first. "I would . . . only develop a laser-like focus on it after getting sober and older, which I hope is good news for younger people who feel like scattershot idiots," he told Reilly.

EARLY CAREER

After graduating from New York University (NYU), Delaney worked various jobs in New York, supplementing stage acting roles with stints in restaurants and hotels. In 2001, he moved to Los Angeles, California, with the hope of finding work in television. The following year, after spending time in rehab for alcohol abuse, Delaney decided to finally try out stand-up for himself. The process of establishing himself as a comic was a slow one; Delaney has noted that in those early days, he sometimes performed for audiences of as few as four people. Still, he found that he enjoyed performing stand-up more than anything else he had tried. "At the end of the day, my favorite thing to do was what I did last night and what I'll do tonight, and that's stand-up," he told Rocco Castoro for *Vice* (19 Sept. 2011). "If everything else went away and there was just stand-up, that would be OK. I'd be able to live with that."

Over the next several years, Delaney began to attract a small following, and his audiences grew steadily larger. However, comedy was not yet a viable full-time career. "It's extraordinarily hard to have success as a stand-up," he explained to Castoro. "So I did some writing on TV shows, and when that slowly started to happen I could afford food, so when I spoke to audiences at night I would make sense because I had sugar in my blood." For a time, Delaney worked in Internet marketing at Intermix Media, a marketing company that owned the social networking website MySpace. One of the site's early users, Delaney has credited his early use of social media with helping him book shows that he might otherwise not have gotten.

In addition to stand-up, Delaney found intermittent work as an actor, appearing in projects such as the television movie *Sweetwater Tides* and the short film *Nature of the Beast*. In 2009, Delaney starred in the web series *Coma, Period.*, about a man who is trapped in his subconscious after falling into a coma.

TWITTER FAME

One of the most significant steps in the evolution of Delaney's career essentially happened on a whim. In 2009, Delaney learned that comedian Louis C. K., whose work he enjoyed, had joined the social networking site Twitter. Founded three years earlier but not yet widely popular, Twitter enabled users to post 140-character messages known as tweets. Delaney followed C. K.'s example and created a Twitter account, soon realizing that the short-form messages used on the site were an ideal vehicle for comedy. Posting various humorous tweets, he quickly drew a substantial following of Twitter users attracted to a particular brand of humor, which often concerns the human body as well as more absurd topics. By 2012, his account, @robdelaney, had 600,000 Twitter followers; by August 2016, that number had doubled. On several occasions, Delaney was dubbed the funniest person on Twitter.

Although online fame does not always translate into real-world success, for Delaney, Twitter presented numerous new opportunities. Most obviously, his Twitter account exposed him to new audiences and attracted fans to his stand-up shows, ensuring that he would never again perform for only four people. His tweets also garnered him a book deal, and in 2013, he published the humorous memoir *Rob Delaney: Mother. Wife. Sister. Human. Warrior. Falcon. Yardstick. Turban. Cabbage.* Perhaps most significant, however, were the connections Twitter allowed him to make with fellow performers, including Irish comedian and future collaborator Sharon Horgan. Having met on Twitter in 2010, the two soon established a close friendship that would prove to be one of Delaney's most productive yet.

CATASTROPHE

Several years after meeting on Twitter, Delaney and Horgan began to collaborate on a television show. The resulting comedy, *Catastrophe*, was filmed in the United Kingdom and released on Britain's Channel 4 as well as online retailer Amazon's video-streaming service. The series focuses on American businessman Rob, played by Delaney, and Irish teacher Sharon, portrayed by Horgan, who attempt to build a life together after a brief fling results in an unexpected pregnancy. *Catastrophe*'s first two seasons, each six episodes long, won critical acclaim following their release, and Delaney and Horgan were nominated for the Emmy Award for outstanding writing for a comedy series for their work.

As writers, Delaney and Horgan draw extensively from their own lives and the lives of those around them, lending the show a strong sense of authenticity. In one episode, for example, the character Sharon disposes of dirty sheets by throwing them out the window. "My mom did that when she was pregnant and I was a little kid," Delaney told Tim Lusher for the *Guardian* (16 Dec. 2015). "I had thrown up in my bed and she was tired so she just threw the sheets out the window and my dad came home to find them in the driveway." As a series that deals with the realities of pregnancy and parenting, *Catastrophe* draws heavily from the experiences of its creators, both of whom are parents.

In July 2016, Channel 4 announced that *Catastrophe* had been renewed for two more seasons. To some, the decision to continue on with the series may have been surprising, as the show's initial catalyst—the unexpected pregnancy—was by the second season firmly in the characters' pasts. For Delaney, however, the renewal provides further opportunities to tell a character-driven story. "I think what I like about the show isn't what's happening to the characters," he explained to Stephanie Van Schilt for *Junkee* (23 Nov. 2015). "It's more how Sharon and Rob deal with things, so I do feel like it could have life for quite a while."

PERSONAL LIFE

Delaney's personal life, particularly his struggle with alcohol abuse and depression, plays an essential role in his outlook as a comedian. Delaney has been sober since 2002, when he was involved in a serious car accident that occurred while he was driving under the influence of alcohol. Although he harmed no one but himself, breaking both arms, Delaney was forced to confront the consequences of his actions and vowed to stop drinking. Given the choice between prison and rehab, he chose the latter and completed a treatment program that proved effective. After leaving rehab, he also sought treatment for severe depression. Delaney has been open about his struggles with alcohol and depression since becoming a well-known comedian, with the goal of improving the lives of those dealing with similar challenges. "It's really important because depression kills people every day, you know? I can't let that happen if I have any means to combat it," he told Van Schilt. "I have to share what I've learned in living with my own depression with other people, so it's incredibly important. It's indispensably important. I have to do it because I know how painful that stuff is, and I know how fatal it is. . . . Shame on me if I don't share that at every opportunity, you know?"

Delaney met his wife, Leah, while they were volunteering at a camp for individuals with disabilities. They have three sons. A self-identified feminist, Delaney hopes to instill similar values in his children. "I am consciously thinking about, 'I have a greater responsibility now. I'm going to have to show feminism to my sons by the way I treat my sons' mom—my wife—and women in the world at large,'" he told West. Delaney lives with his family in London, where they settled while Delaney was filming *Catastrophe*.

SUGGESTED READING

Delaney, Rob. "A Conversation with Rob Delaney about Love, Sex, Marriage, and Waxed Vaginas." Interview by Patti Greco. *Cosmopolitan*. Hearst Communications, 20 July 2015. Web. 16 Aug. 2016.

Delaney, Rob. "An Interview with Rob Delaney . . . That We Did Because He Forgot to Write His Column." Interview by Rocco Castoro. *Vice*. Vice Media, 19 Sept. 2011. Web. 16 Aug. 2016.

Delaney, Rob. "Rob Delaney on 'Catastrophe,' Rape Jokes, and Winning Twitter." Interview by Phoebe Reilly. *Rolling Stone*. Rolling Stone, 17 June 2015. Web. 16 Aug. 2016.

Delaney, Rob. "Rob Delaney Is Back for a Second 'Catastrophe.'" Interview by Lindy West. *GQ*. Condé Nast, 9 Apr. 2016. Web. 16 Aug. 2016.

Delaney, Rob, and Sharon Horgan. "Rob Delaney and Sharon Horgan: 'He Rubs My Corners Off and I Try to Kick Some of the Sweetness Out of Him.'" Interview by Tim Lusher. *Guardian*. Guardian News and Media, 16 Dec. 2015. Web. 16 Aug. 2016.

Freeman, Hadley. "Rob Delaney: 'Twitter Has Rocketed Me to a Whole New Level of Standup.'" *Guardian*. Guardian News and Media, 17 Sept. 2012. Web. 16 Aug. 2016.

Van Schilt, Stephanie. "A Gloomy, Awkward (But Ultimately Lovely) Interview with Twitter's Favourite Comedian Rob Delaney." *Junkee*. Junkee, 23 Nov. 2015. Web. 16 Aug. 2016.

—Joy Crelin

Cara Delevingne

Born: August 12, 1992
Occupation: Model and actor

Photo by Asta1308 (Own work) [CC BY-SA 4.0 (http://creative-commons.org/licenses/by-sa/4.0)], via Wikimedia Commons

"Chances are that you've seen her face, with its distinctive caterpillar eyebrows, icy blue eyes, and button nose, somewhere in recent months, but you might not yet know her name," Karen Kay wrote for the *Guardian* (9 Feb. 2013). "From the giant Burberry billboards . . . to the stylized images of London street life captured for this season's Pepe Jeans campaign, Cara Delevingne is the hottest face on Planet Fashion. And she is on track to become—just like Jean Shrimpton, Twiggy, and Kate Moss before her—the latest British model to become a household name."

So accurate was Kay's prediction that fellow *Guardian* writer Imogen Fox penned a column just a few months later (7 Sept. 2013) in which she asserted, "The Cara Delevingne phenomenon is enough to make even the most seasoned fashion fan a little bilious. The onesie-wearing twenty-one-year-old is the darling of the glossies and tabloid catnip, a social media princess and a talented musician, best mates with Rihanna, parties with Prince Harry, and about to break into Hollywood."

Delevingne, who had her first starring film role in 2015 teen drama *Paper Towns* and who has also announced her intention to make a similar foray into the music industry, owes much of her fame to social media sites such as Twitter, where more than four million users read her posts, and Instagram, where more than twenty-two million followers view photos of her relaxing with celebrity friends.

EARLY LIFE

Cara Jocelyn Delevingne was born on August 12, 1992, in London and grew up in the exclusive neighborhood of Belgravia. Her family has been widely covered in media outlets on both sides of the Atlantic, particularly in England, because of their wealth and social connections. In an article for the *Evening Standard* (27 Apr. 2015), Joshi Herrmann describes the Delevingnes as "a long line of debutantes, party boys, and millionaires whose antics have set a high bar for their latest celebrity member."

Her paternal great-grandfather was Hamar Greenwood, a viscount who served in the British Parliament, and her paternal great-aunt Doris Delevingne was a socialite and close confidante of Winston Churchill. Delevingne's maternal grandfather, Sir Jocelyn Stevens, was the publisher of *Queen* magazine, and his wife, Janie Sheffield, served as a lady-in-waiting to Princess Margaret.

Delevingne's father, Charles, earned his fortune as a property developer in London, and her mother, Pandora, was a familiar figure on the London social scene of the 1980s. A close friend of Sarah, Duchess of York, Pandora battled a serious heroin addiction. Admitting that her mother's problems had severely affected her childhood, Delevingne told Rob Haskell for *Vogue* (19 July 2015), "You grow up too quickly because you're parenting your parents." Of the sparkling milieu of her youth, she said, "My family was kind of about that whole parties-and-horse racing thing. I can understand it's fun for some. I never enjoyed it."

Delevingne—who has two older sisters, Chloe and Poppy (also a model)—has been described as a brooding child. She was often sent to therapists and treated with various psychotropic drugs. As she entered her teen years, her problems intensified. "All of a sudden I was hit with a massive wave of depression and anxiety and self-hatred, where the feelings were so painful that I would slam my head against a tree to try to knock myself out," she recalled to Haskell. She began smoking marijuana and ultimately dropped out of Bedales School, a boarding school that she described to Haskell as "totally hippie-dippy."

She had started to play the drums a few years before in an effort to channel her energy, and she had some interest in drama and sent an audition tape to filmmaker Tim Burton, who was then directing a film adaptation of *Alice in Wonderland*. "I didn't get the part, but that experience lit a fire in me," she told Lynn Hirschberg for *W* magazine (12 Aug. 2013). She then turned her thoughts to modeling.

MODELING CAREER

Modeling seemed a natural path for Delevingne to take. She had appeared at age ten in a *Vogue Italia*, in a photo spread shot by the iconic fashion photographer Bruce Weber. Her sister Poppy had already been signed by Storm Model Management, an agency headed by the mother of a classmate, Sarah Doukas, who had been responsible for signing supermodel Kate Moss. "The Cara I know is cute, sexy, and more than a little unpredictable," Doukas told Kay. "But she's also very hard-working, unpretentious, gracious, and generous—and she has great empathy with the women of her generation."

Although Delevingne is now often compared to Moss for her waifish frame and elfin features, and the older model has become something of a mentor, Delevingne's career did not take off immediately. She was sexually harassed by male photographers taking test shots and turned away repeatedly from auditions for runway shows. She told Haskell, "The first time I walked into Burberry, the woman just said, 'Turn around, go away.' And all the test shoots with the pervy men. Never trust a straight photographer at a test shoot."

Then, at age eighteen, she was spotted by Burberry's chief creative officer Christopher Bailey and hired to appear in the 2011 spring campaign for the British fashion giant. Jobs for such brands as Fendi, DKNY, Saint Laurent, and H&M quickly followed. She has attributed much of her modeling success to her ability to channel a character in front of the camera. "I treat the camera like a person—I gaze into it," she explained to Hirschberg. "Photos are a flat thing, and you need to put life into them."

Others agree that her personality makes Delevingne a formidable force. "The thing about Cara is that she's more than just a model—she stands for something in her generation's eyes," designer Stella McCartney asserted to Haskell. "She has a fearlessness about projecting what she stands for, which is so rare. In a certain sense she's brought back some of that energy you saw in the supermodel era. . . . In our industry, people can be rather forced, not genuinely themselves. Cara would never pretend to be someone she's not, and she's not living her life for other people's approval." As Delevingne explained to Alexis Petridis for the *Guardian* (15 June 2014), "When I

started, the whole idea of the model was very different, it was a bit stuckup. Not stuckup, but no one was trying to have fun, or not even have fun, but be willing to smile." Delevingne was named model of the year at the British Fashion Awards in 2012 and 2014.

Despite walking the runway for several major designers and appearing on the covers of dozens of glossy fashion magazines, Delevingne eventually became disillusioned with the modeling world. "Modeling just made me feel a bit hollow after a while. It didn't make me grow at all as a human being," she told Shane Watson for the *Times Magazine* (16 Aug. 2015). "It is a mental thing as well because if you hate yourself and your body and the way you look, it just gets worse and worse." Reacting to the stress physically, she developed psoriasis, a skin condition that proved to be a challenge for makeup artists to cover.

HOLLYWOOD

Delevingne still harbored ambitions of acting, and she set her sights on a Hollywood career. She made her first big-screen appearance in 2012, in the costume drama *Anna Karenina*, taking on the small nonspeaking role of Princess Sorokina and attracting little notice from critics. In 2014 she appeared in the British thriller *The Face of an Angel*, loosely based on the true story of Amanda Knox, a young woman accused of murder. The film received mixed reviews when it was released in the United States the following year, although many critics praised Delevingne for her performance.

Delevingne's first high-profile Hollywood role came in 2015, when she starred as mysterious American teenager Margo Roth Spiegelman in the big-screen adaptation of John Green's popular young-adult novel *Paper Towns*. She received widely varying reviews for her portrayal, with Manohla Dargis writing for the *New York Times* (23 July 2015), "She's nice on the eyes, no doubt, but she doesn't have the tools to take this underwritten screen role and make it hurt, and you spend a lot of time watching her Groucho brows hold steady over her sunburst smiles." Peter Travers remarked in an article for *Rolling Stone* (23 July 2015), "Her flashing eyes and throaty voice indicate the star power to make it in pictures that move."

Also in 2015, Delevingne appeared as a mermaid in the hotly anticipated *Pan* (an adaptation of *Peter Pan* starring Hugh Jackman), and she has multiple other projects in various stages of completion, including the mystery-thriller *London Fields* (2015), the historical drama *Tulip Fever* (2016), the ensemble picture *Kids in Love* (2016), and the superhero caper *Suicide Squad* (2016).

Delevingne has expressed some interest in pursuing a career in music one day, although she has no immediate plans to release an album. The idea has been deemed by some industry insiders to be relatively realistic; Delevingne, who performed onstage with pop star Pharrell Williams in early 2015, is said to have demonstrable musical talent. However, despite her varied endeavors beyond modeling, she told Stephanie Chan for *Hollywood Reporter* (31 July 2015), "I'm not stopping modeling, I'm not retiring. I'm just doing film for the time being. . . . Maybe I'll do fashion sometimes, but at the moment I have no time to do anything."

PERSONAL LIFE

Delevingne began dating Grammy Award–winning singer Annie Clark, who goes by the stage name St. Vincent, in March 2015. Her previous high-profile partners include actor and DJ Michelle Rodriguez and musician Harry Styles.

Delevingne's friendships with such well-known pop culture figures as Selena Gomez and Rita Ora are exhaustively documented on her social-media accounts, as are her eating habits (she depicts herself as a voracious fan of hamburgers and other junk food) and grooming regimen. Of her famous eyebrows, she told David Colman for *Interview* (28 Mar. 2013), "You just don't pluck them. It's really simple. I mean, I do, obviously, a little bit, because otherwise I'd have a monobrow, but it's just about keeping them wild, keeping them free and woolly."

SUGGESTED READING

Fox, Imogen. "Six Degrees of Cara Delevingne." *Guardian*. Guardian News and Media, 7 Sept. 2013. Web. 1 Oct. 2015.

Haskell, Rob. "Cara Delevingne Opens Up about Her Childhood, Love Life, and Why Modeling Just Isn't Enough." *Vogue*. Condé Nast, July 2015. Web. 1 Oct. 2015.

Herrmann, Joshi. "The Divine Delevingnes." *Evening Standard*. Evening Standard, 27 Apr. 2015. Web. 1 Oct. 2015.

Hirschberg, Lynn. "The Anti-Role Model." *W*. Condé Nast, 12 Aug. 2013. Web. 1 Oct. 2015.

Jones, Ellen E. "Why Britain's Most Successful Model Cara Delevingne Is the Face of the Decade." *Independent*. Independent.co.uk, 21 Feb. 2014. Web. 1 Oct. 2015.

Kay, Karen. "Cara Delevingne: The Eyes Have It for Britain's Newest Supermodel." *Guardian*. Guardian News and Media, 9 Feb. 2013. Web. 1 Oct. 2015.

Watson, Shane. "Cara and the Truth about Sex Harassment in the Fashion Industry." *Times Magazine*. Times Newspapers, 16 Aug. 2015. Web. 1 Oct. 2015.   —*Mari Rich*

Elena Delle Donne

Born: September 5, 1989
Occupation: Professional basketball player

Elena Delle Donne is a forward for the Chicago Sky of the Women's National Basketball Association (WNBA). The six-foot-five, two-time WNBA All-Star was named most valuable player in the league in 2015. That season she became the fourth player in the history of professional basketball, male or female, with more than two hundred free-throw attempts to hit 95 percent of free throws. Delle Donne, who played in college for the University of Delaware Blue Hens, was the second pick of the 2013 WNBA Draft and was named rookie of the year in 2013. Even as a teenager playing for Ursuline Academy in Wilmington, Delaware, people spoke of Delle Donne as a young superstar, comparing her record to the high school careers of such standout players as LeBron James or Kobe Bryant in the National Basketball Association (NBA).

However, by the time she was only eighteen it appeared Delle Donne was burnt out. She had been slated to play for the University of Connecticut, the nation's powerhouse in women's basketball, but quit the team after just two days. It would be a year before she made a triumphant return to the sport, this time playing for the University of Delaware. Her sabbatical was unusual for an athlete of her caliber, but tied deeply to her life experience. The pressure to perform was phenomenal, and in Delle Donne's case—she suffers from Lyme disease—often painful. She temporarily quit basketball not because it was

difficult but because it took her away from her family, including her sister Lizzie, who was born blind and deaf, suffers from autism and cerebral palsy, and only communicates through hand-over-hand sign language. Even after turning professional Delle Donne turned down lucrative offers to play overseas during the WNBA off-season, as many other players do, so that she could remain close to her family. In 2015 she founded the Elena Delle Donne Charitable Foundation, which supports the Special Olympics and raises awareness about Lyme disease.

EARLY LIFE AND EDUCATION

Delle Donne was born on September 5, 1989, and raised in Wilmington, Delaware. Her parents, Ernest "Ernie" Delle Donne, who played basketball at Columbia University, and Joan Delle Donne, recalled how agile she was, even as a gawky young kid. Delle Donne grew up with her older sister, Elizabeth, or Lizzie, and her older brother, Gene. She was in the second grade when she begged her brother to let her tag along to his basketball practice. He relented and, after more pestering, let her join in. While they were playing, he threw a pass behind her, hoping to trip her up. She caught the ball behind her back and made a reverse layup. Gene was stunned.

Delle Donne soon began playing in earnest. She showed a remarkable talent so early that her mother recalls her signing her first autograph in the fifth grade. She won her first Amateur Athletic Union (AAU) national championship when she was twelve. The University of North Carolina offered her a scholarship when she was thirteen. At the suggestion of her basketball coach Steven Johnson, she completely reworked her free-throw strategy in order to reduce her motion to as few movements as possible. "It was horrific for probably a good year," Delle Donne said of her free throw to Tom Perrotta for the *Wall Street Journal* (25 Oct. 2015). Her hard work and willingness to experiment ultimately paid off, as in 2006 she set a national girl's high school record, making eighty consecutive free throws.

In the summer before her sophomore year at Ursuline Academy in Wilmington, Delle Donne attended a Nike All-American camp intended for the top eighty or so juniors and seniors in the nation. "There were long stretches daily where she was the best player on the floor," Geno Auriemma, head coach of the women's basketball team at the University of Connecticut, told Graham Hays for *ESPN*. "That's when it kind of was apparent to everybody that this isn't just some normal kid—that she had otherworldly kind of talents offensively. For a kid that young, that size, to be able to do what she was doing with the basketball, it was just fun to watch." Delle Donne was viewed as a prodigy in the manner of a young LeBron James or Kobe Bryant. Legendary

college coach Pat Summitt reportedly chartered a private jet to Wilmington just to see her play. Still, when Keith Pompey of the *Philadelphia Inquirer* (21 Jan. 2006) asked her about her future plans, she said that she hoped to become a special education teacher, so that she could help other kids like Lizzie. Delle Donne explained, "I feel like if I didn't do that, I would be wasting a talent of mine."

Delle Donne seemed an ideal player in every respect—she worked hard to perfect her game off the court and was driven to win on the court—but by her mid-teens, she was already starting to feel burnt out. In 2007, she took the summer after her junior year off and missed some of the next season after a bout of mononucleosis. During the illness, Delle Donne was surprised to discover that she missed her teammates more than the game itself. All told, Delle Donne led Ursuline to four state titles during her high school career and was recruited by the top schools in the sport, including the University of Connecticut (UConn), the leading institution for women's basketball in the National Collegiate Athletic Association (NCAA).

COLLEGE CAREER

Like many prospective freshmen, Delle Donne was conflicted about leaving home, but unlike other students, her decision was fodder for mass media speculation. She finally chose to play for the UConn. She missed her high school graduation ceremony to begin classes and training in June 2008. However, two days into her freshman year she appeared on her parents' doorstep after catching a ride from a friend in the middle of the night, announcing she was done with UConn and with basketball. Her abrupt departure made national headlines—but according to family and friends, Delle Donne was happy with her decision, rash though it appeared. She renounced her scholarship in August and later enrolled at the University of Delaware, where she joined the volleyball team.

Her new school's basketball team was aware of Delle Donne's presence, but Tina Martin, head coach of the university's Blue Hens women's basketball team, instructed players to avoid discussing basketball with Delle Donne if they came in contact with her. Martin did the same and was even careful not to say too much when Delle Donne's high school coach called her to set up a casual meeting with the young star. Martin knew that Delaware's program could not compete with those that Delle Donne had looked at a year earlier and left the decision of whether to play or not to play in Delle Donne's hands. "Bottom line is that she came home because of her family, so she needed to become comfortable with her family; she needed to be able to sort things out," Martin told Hays. "My thing was, 'She came home for a reason, so let her explore that reason.'"

About six months after Delle Donne left Connecticut, she began meeting with Martin for private training sessions. They met late at night long after the gym had emptied to avoid sparking rumors that the former prized recruit might return to basketball. The casual sessions, however, rekindled Delle Donne's love for the sport, and by the end of the school year she announced that she would join the Blue Hens for their 2009–10 season. On February 18, 2010, she set a school record when she scored fifty-four points in a game against James Madison University, racking up the highest point total of any player in women's college basketball that season. Later that year, she was named rookie of the year and was selected as the 2010 Colonial Athletic Association (CAA) player of the year. The Blue Hens made the NCAA tournaments in 2012— the year Delle Donne was named Academic All-American of the Year in Division I women's basketball—and again in 2013, when she helped lead the team to its first NCAA Sweet Sixteen appearance. Delle Donne majored in early childhood education with a focus in special education and graduated in 2013.

WNBA CAREER

Delle Donne was the second overall pick of the WNBA Draft in 2013. The first pick was Brittney Griner, a six-foot-eight center who had played for Baylor University in Texas. Between the two of them, Griner, who was selected by the Phoenix Mercury, and Delle Donne, who went to the Chicago Sky, generated considerable buzz for the league, which did not enjoy the same exposure as the NBA. When the two players soon faced off in the 2014 WNBA Finals, viewership jumped by 91 percent over the previous year.

In her first game with the WNBA, Delle Donne scored twenty-two points—the best Sky rookie debut in franchise history and the third best in the history of the league. She started in thirty-one games in 2013, was named rookie of the month four times, and became the first rookie to win the All-Star vote in WNBA history. She finished the season with the second-highest free throw percentage (.929) in the league and was named rookie of the year.

Delle Donne only played in sixteen games during the 2014 regular season due to a flareup of Lyme disease, but in 2015 returned to form. That year Howard Megdal wrote for *Vice* (17 July 2015), that "Delle Donne posted a 40.9 player efficiency rating over the first ten games of the WNBA season. No one else in the history of either the NBA or WNBA has ever topped 35 . . . . She is having, so far, something like the greatest individual basketball season anyone has ever seen." She led the league in scoring,

averaging 23.4 points a game, hit 95 percent of her free throws, and was named the league's most valuable player. Delle Donne's greatest strength lies in her multitude of talents. As Brian Kotloff remarked in an article for the WNBA website (14 Sept. 2015), "Star players have scored at spectacular rates in the WNBA before. They've been deadly accurate as a shooter or prolific as a shot blocker. Few have done all of the above."

Coaches, teammates, and fans however, often expressed frustration that Delle Donne's achievements have not been given the same recognition as those of her counterparts in the NBA, a trend that holds across women's basketball. The WNBA consistently struggled to bring in viewers and secure sponsorships, and additionally, as Delle Donne told Susan Rinkunas for *New York Magazine* (9 Mar. 2016), she and other players dealt with constant harassment. From social media trolls to the derogatory way commentators often talk about WNBA players (always "female basketball players," never merely "basketball players"), Delle Donne claimed that sexism in sports was not talked about nearly enough. "I just can't wait for the day where people want to talk about your skills on the court and not your looks," she told Rinkunas. Nevertheless, Delle Donne's game was a rebuke to all the sexist commentary she and the league faced. "Delle Donne's game functions as a direct refutation of every lazy trope about women's basketball," Megdal wrote. "Watch her pogo stick for rebounds or fly over from the weak side to protect the rim with one of her league-leading twenty-five blocks, and the myth of lesser athleticism disappears."

In April 2016 Delle Donne was named to the US Olympic Women's Basketball Team, whereby she would represent the United States at the 2016 Olympic Games in Rio de Janeiro.

SUGGESTED READING

Hays, Graham. "Finding Her Way Back Home." *ESPN*. ESPN Internet Ventures, n.d. Web. 30 Apr. 2016.

Kotloff, Brian. "How Elena Delle Donne's Spectacular 2015 Season Stacks Up in WNBA History." *WNBA*. NBA Media Ventures, 14 Sept. 2015. Web. 3 May 2016.

Megdal, Howard. "Elena Delle Donne Is Having the Best Season in Basketball History. Now What?" *Vice*. Vice Sports, 17 July 2015. Web. 3 May 2016.

Pompey, Keith. "A Well-Grounded Star." *Philadelphia Inquirer*. Philadelphia Media Network, 21 Jan. 2006. Web. 30 Apr. 2016.

Rinkunas, Susan. "The Sexist Garbage Women Athletes Face, According to a WNBA Star." *New York Magazine*. New York Media, 9 Mar. 2016. Web. 3 May 2016.
—*Molly Hagan*

Mac DeMarco

Born: April 30, 1990
Occupation: Musician

Mac DeMarco became the darling of the independent rock music scene as a singer-songwriter and the producer of his own records beginning in 2012, when he was just twenty-two years old. Onstage and offstage he became known for his pranks and eccentric behavior, but on his records his persona is more subdued. Although there is certainly humor and irony in his lyrics and tone, his albums deliver a dreamy, mellow musical world with groovy, guitar-driven songs and a voice influenced by Bob Dylan, Lou Reed, and John Lennon.

EARLY LIFE AND EDUCATION

Mac DeMarco, whose birth name is Vernor Winfield McBriare Smith IV, was born on April 30, 1990, in Duncan, British Columbia, Canada. He has a brother and a half-sister. His parents, who never married, were not together for long. His father, DeMarco has said, had problems with drugs and alcohol and was largely absent. When DeMarco was about five years old, his mother legally changed his name to McBriare Samuel Lanyon DeMarco, so that his father's last name would not be part of his name any longer. Mac has been his nickname since he was a little boy.

DeMarco primarily grew up in Edmonton, Alberta, Canada. He did not fit in well in Edmonton, DeMarco told Elliott Sharp for his profile on *RedBull.com* (29 Oct. 2013). The city was full of "jocks" and "juiced-up meathead dudes," guys who spent a lot of time working out or playing hockey, whereas DeMarco, though he liked soccer, mostly preferred to play video games. According to Sharp, DeMarco decided at the age of thirteen to become a computer programmer, which was an unusual choice in a family full of musicians. His grandfather played saxophone, his aunt sang with a brass band, and his grandmother sang opera.

High school was a mixed experience for DeMarco. Though he was a pretty good student, he told Sharp, he was always on the move—perpetually in need of activities or distractions or pranks that had nothing to do with school. His brother Hank, who is a ballet dancer, told Evan Minsker for *Pitchfork* (26 Mar. 2014) that when he and his brother were young, DeMarco would burst into the bathroom when Hank was taking a bath and "annoy him." DeMarco loved pranks, buffoonery, and just being a provocateur. "He's always been a kook since he was a little boy," Agnes DeMarco, his mother, told Minsker. "When I took him skating for the first time, he spun like a whirling dervish, fell down, and then got right back up to spin again."

Ralph Arvesen/CC BY 2.0/Wikimedia Commons

During his last year in high school, he began skipping school more often and playing more music. He played in a variety of bands, including Outdoor Miners and the Meat Cleavers, whose sound was inspired by lo-fi, punk, jam, and garage bands. He also played in Sound of Love, the name of which is a half-sincere nod to older R & B groups. Despite missing many classes his senior year, DeMarco managed to graduate.

MAKEOUT VIDEOTAPE

A few months after graduating from high school, DeMarco moved to Vancouver. In Vancouver he felt at home, comfortable with the independent rock scene. He went out to see indie bands such as Nü Sensae and White Lung in venues around the city and continued to make music of his own. To pay the bills, he briefly worked at Starbucks and then signed up to teach computer literacy classes to adults at a local community center. Due to a bureaucratic error, however, DeMarco was instead assigned to teach at a nearby high school, where he helped students make music with computer software.

Under the band name Makeout Videotape, DeMarco released a demo album called *Heat Wave!* of seven lo-fi songs in 2009. He made five hundred CDs and sold all of them. Due to increasing local popularity he started playing live, accompanied onstage by Alex Calder and Jen Clement. For the next two years or so, Makeout Videotape continued to perform in and around Vancouver, and DeMarco continued to release new material. Though he did not like the name Makeout Videotape, DeMarco continued to use it because it had become so well known in

Vancouver. However, he ended up leaving Vancouver for Montreal, where he began recording under his own name.

ROCK AND ROLL NIGHT CLUB

The songs that would soon become part of that album caught the attention of Mike Sniper, the founder of the record company Capture Tracks, which quickly signed DeMarco. In March 2012 Capture Tracks released DeMarco's *Rock and Roll Night Club* as an extended play record (EP), a recording that is not quite a full album. Like his previous recordings, *Rock and Roll Night Club* was recorded in a fairly lo-fi manner, with emphasis on style, oddness, and irony.

The cover of the album features DeMarco pouting, putting on lipstick, and staring into the camera, perhaps intentionally calling to mind the genre- and gender-bending Lou Reed album *Transformer* (1972). Reed was certainly an influence, as was Elvis Presley, but these influences, and others, manifest themselves in strange ways. In a review for *Pitchfork* (10 Apr. 2012), Evan Minsker wrote that on this album, compared to his previous project Makeout Videotape, DeMarco "gets weirder and churns out an unsettling brand of soft rock." In one song, wrote Minsker, DeMarco's voice sounds "deep, breathy, sleazy" and may make the listener feel "weirded out." But that is intentional. Sometimes, Minsker wrote, the tone is "both goofy and surreal." DeMarco is both a musician and a prankster, and in a sense *Rock and Roll Night Club* is an exercise in a postmodern twisting of influences that both conforms to and evades expectations. But the musicianship is there too; Minsker wrote that the album had some "lovely, shimmering melodies."

2

In October 2012, Capture Tracks released DeMarco's first full-length album, simply titled 2. This record was different and was the first indication of the new direction in which DeMarco was going to take his sound. On this album DeMarco does not overwhelm the listener with irony or silliness. There may be some of that in the lyrics, but the music is not played with a wink or a smirk. For the first time he offered some sense of vulnerability and an embrace of existential isolation and longing. For the music magazine *NME* (15 Oct. 2012), Louis Pattison noted, "Lyrically witty, full of neat turns of phrase, his songs recall the quirks and kinks of Jonathan Richman, the tale-telling and wit of Alex Turner (specifically the Arctics man's gentle, romantic work on the *Submarine* soundtrack), and the playful verbosity of Pavement's Stephen Malkmus."

The album received widespread critical acclaim. First, it sounded different than a lot of indie rock of the time. Second, it had a certain cohesive feel—it created its own atmosphere that drew in the listener, if the listener was willing to go to a strange new world. Luke Winkie, for the *Austin Chronicle* (15 Mar. 2013), observed that "DeMarco writes songs to figure out his own personal truth." He concluded his review by pointing out that the album is "nothing if not authentic." The album brought DeMarco not only more critical praise but also more fans. He began playing larger music venues.

SALAD DAYS

If DeMarco's *Rock and Roll Night Club* was the windup and his first full-length album was the pitch, then his next album, *Salad Days* (2014), was a definite home run. Here DeMarco more fully realized the vision and feel he had set out to establish on his previous album. For one, DeMarco is lyrically more focused on *Salad Days*. He made a sincere effort to write songs with more definite themes in mind. Furthermore, the instrumentation is both looser, in that it is more confident, and tighter, in that it is better produced. Certain psychedelic, audiophile concept albums such as the Beatles' *Sgt. Pepper's Lonely Hearts Club Band* (1967) and the Kinks' album *The Kinks Are the Village Green Preservation Society* (1968) are very much an influence. But there were others. The song "Chamber of Reflection" is reminiscent of indie duo Beach House in its exploration of a dreamy atmosphere, and "Let Her Go" is somewhat reminiscent of Jonathan Richman. And there certainly is a lightness to the album—it is worth noting that it was released on April 1, April Fools' Day.

For the most part, the album was well received by critics. Marc Hogan, who gave it 8.5 out of 10, wrote in his review for *Pitchfork* (1 Apr. 2014) that DeMarco's second full-length record "isn't a departure from its predecessor so much as a richer, increasingly assured refinement. For all its internal contradictions, *Salad Days* is no more or less than a great album in a tradition of no-big-deal great albums." If that seems paradoxical, it is intended to be. For *NME* (17 Apr. 2014), Alex Denney concluded his review by writing the following: "Sweet, soulful little man that he is, Mac knows better than to let his bellyaching get in the way of everyone else's good time—instead, he's simply dialed down the quirk and written his best record yet."

ANOTHER ONE

In August of the following year DeMarco released his next album, *Another One* (2015). Musically it continued the atmosphere he created with *Salad Days*, but lyrically it was even more focused. It is not a concept album per se but the theme of love—and its associated happiness, frustration, and jealousy—permeates the whole album. In large part it was inspired by his own romantic experiences. A notable exception is the last song of the album, titled "My House by the Water," inspired by the house he shares with his girlfriend, located in the Rockaway section of the New York City borough of Queens. The song mostly consists of wave sounds. In a typically odd move, at the end of the song DeMarco tells the listener his real address and invites any fan who is willing to make the trek to Rockaway for a cup of coffee.

Once again, *Another One* had a very positive reception. Paul MacInnes for the *Guardian* (6 Aug. 2015) called the album "odd, inimitable, and thoroughly charming." Mack Hayden for *Paste* (4 Aug. 2015) observed that "at no point throughout the whole outing does he lose out on poignancy because of his emphasis on simplicity." And Jeremy Gordon for *Pitchfork* (4 Aug. 2015) compared the album to a novella—small in size but full of substance. This substance is in the lyrics as much as in the music. Gordon observed that "DeMarco is an unusually sensitive songwriter, capable of ferreting out what someone else might be feeling even as he's absorbed in his own perspective."

PERSONAL LIFE

DeMarco lives in New York City.

SUGGESTED READING

DeMarco, Mac. "Mac DeMarco Explains His Mini-Album of Love Songs, Track by Track." Interview by Jacob Ganz. *All Songs Considered*. NPR, 31 July 2015. Web. 6 Sept. 2016.

Gordon, Jeremy. Rev. of *Another One*, by Mac DeMarco. *Pitchfork*. Condé Nast, 4 Aug. 2015. Web. 6 Sept. 2016.

Hayden, Mack. Rev. of *Another One*, by Mac DeMarco. *Paste*. Paste Media Group, 4 Aug. 2015. Web. 6 Sept. 2016.

Hoby, Hermione. "Mac DeMarco: 'I Live Like a Scumbag, But It's Cheap.'" *Guardian*. Guardian News and Media, 22 Mar. 2014. Web. 6 Sept. 2016.

Hogan, Marc. Rev. of *Salad Days*, by Mac DeMarco. *Pitchfork*. Condé Nast, 1 Apr. 2014. Web. 6 Sept. 2016.

Minsker, Evan. "Mac DeMarco: Mannish Boy." *Pitchfork*. Condé Nast, 26 Mar. 2014. Web. 6 Sept. 2016.

Winkie, Luke. Rev. of 2, by Mac DeMarco. *Austin Chronicle*. Austin Chronicle, 15 Mar. 2013. Web. 6 Sept. 2016.

SELECTED WORKS

Rock and Roll Night Club, 2012; *2*, 2012; *Salad Days*, 2014; *Another One*, 2015

—*Dmitry Kiper*

Neil Denari

Born: September 3, 1957
Occupation: Architect

For award-winning architect Neil Denari, the road from theoretical designs to physical structures has been a long one—but the journey has been all the more rewarding. After launching his career in the mid-1980s, Denari quickly became known for his innovative designs for buildings, which often featured modernist and machine influences yet were highly distinct from existing trends in experimental architecture. His work consisted of hand-drawn or computer-generated theoretical designs that existed only on paper until the first decades of the twenty-first century, when his unique architectural sensibility broke into the real world with the construction of notable projects such as HL23. A condominium building in the Chelsea neighborhood of New York City, HL23 features a distinctive design shaped out of both Denari's interest in experimenting with form and the daunting requirements of the building's unusual location. Dedicated to exploring form as well as materials and construction processes, he is similarly devoted to examining the areas in which design and function overlap and to tailoring his designs to specific cultural and local contexts. To Denari, an architect must be far more than a designer of visually interesting structures. "As architects, we have to create a louder voice within the existing power structure, so that architects aren't just perceived as artists, but partners in understanding scenario planning and demographics

John Sciulli/Stringer/WireImage/Getty Images

trending," he explained to Ting Pen for *ValuePenguin* (July 2013).

EARLY LIFE AND EDUCATION

Neil M. Denari was born to Muriel and Edward Denari in Fort Worth, Texas, on September 3, 1957. His father was an executive in the aerospace industry and an avid art collector who later pursued a career as an art broker. After graduating from Trinity High School in Euless, Texas, Denari enrolled in the University of Houston, where he studied architecture. He earned his bachelor's degree from the institution in 1980. Denari went on to pursue graduate studies at Harvard University, completing his master's degree in architecture in 1982. While a student, Denari was fascinated by the visual arts, particularly abstract and minimalist paintings. "The art that I studied most was color field painting," he told Sam Lubell for the *Architect's Newspaper* (5 Mar. 2012). "Robert Ryman and Barnett Newman and [Mark] Rothko—the classic stuff. And I had a voracious appetite for it. . . . The work was detail oriented and pure matter. It was never about form."

Denari also became interested in the intersections between architecture and other forms of art and design. "I wanted to know where ideas came from," he explained to Lubell. "If architecture is a medium, then I thought I should look at other things to spark the imagination. Maybe that's why people say sometimes my work looks like a building and sometimes it looks like industrial design or graphic design."

EARLY CAREER

After graduating from Harvard, Denari traveled to France, where he spent several months working as an intern for the aviation company Aérospatiale. Upon his return to the United States, he settled in New York and pursued a career in architecture, joining the established firm James Stewart Polshek & Partners (now Ennead Architects). He remained with the firm until 1986, filling the role of senior designer. He moved to Los Angeles two years later.

During his early years as an architect, Denari's designs existed solely on paper, as he created blueprints and renderings of theoretical structures that were never constructed. As examples of innovative modern architectural artwork, many of his pieces drew significant attention, and Denari himself quickly gained a reputation as a talented architect. A number of museums have exhibited his work or hold pieces in their collections, including the Cooper Hewitt, Smithsonian Design Museum in New York; the Heinz-Carnegie Museum in Pennsylvania; and museums of modern art in New York, California, and Australia. Many of Denari's pieces from the 1980s and 1990s, such as a 1992 design for a prototype architecture school held in the collection of the Museum of Modern Art in New York, feature designs that display mechanical and technological influences while demonstrating Denari's creative use of space.

NMDA

In 1998 Denari founded his own firm, originally known Cor-Tex Architecture and later renamed Neil M. Denari Architects (NMDA). Although he had been successful as an architect prior to founding the firm, doing so gave him further opportunities both to establish himself in the field and to develop and clarify his unique design sensibility. "It took some time to establish the firm, but a few people saw the value of it in the beginning, and I have built on it since," he told Pen of NMDA's early days. "Someone has to hire and take interest in you and your work first so that you can gain practical experience and have an opportunity to express yourself."

As the owner of his own firm, Denari continued to create the theoretical designs for which he had become known but also branched out into physical projects, including gallery installations and renovations to existing structures. NMDA's first major permanent project was commissioned by l.a.Eyeworks, a Los Angeles–based eyewear designer and retailer. The firm was tasked with transforming a commercial space in an existing building on Los Angeles's Beverly Boulevard into a functional yet architecturally distinct store that suited the funky eyewear sold within. Despite the space's relatively small size—the store measures less than 1,200 square feet—Denari and his colleagues took a year-and-a-half to complete their work, in large part because they sought to determine the best possible methods for bringing Denari's vision to life. Although relatively inexperienced when it came to physical projects, he found that working with clients who shared similar goals enabled his team to experiment with materials and techniques in order to make his designs a reality. "When the clients saw how much we were into the realization process, they knew that our lack of building experience would be superseded by intelligence," he told Gail Peter Borden for the book *Matter: Material Processes in Architectural Production* (2012). This long period of research and experimentation paid off. "Since we could completely control all aspects of the environment, it allowed us to make the project in its materiality and in its appearance look as close to the renderings as possible," he explained. Completed in 2002, the Denari-designed l.a.Eyeworks location has an open layout that encourages customer flow and features textured walls, cool tones, and eye-catching glass components.

MAJOR PROJECTS

Following the completion of the l.a.Eyeworks store, Denari took on a number of diverse projects, designing single-family residences, offices, and other spaces. While many of his projects consisted of interior renovations rather than new construction, one of his most famous accomplishments, the fourteen-story HL23, falls into the latter category. Located in New York's Chelsea neighborhood, HL23 was designed to fit around existing structures, most notably the High Line, an elevated park adjacent to the building. In light of its unique surroundings, HL23, which houses condominium units, eschews the traditional rectangle and square shapes of many multistory buildings in favor of a more abstract shape that is wider at the top than at the bottom, allowing the building to continue upward without cutting into the neighboring park, which was constructed on top of disused elevated rail tracks.

As his design of HL23 demonstrates, Denari is deeply concerned with designing structures that are not only visually compelling and innovative but also appropriate to the purposes they will serve and the locations in which they are built. This is in keeping with trends in the architectural field, which Denari described to Pen as becoming increasingly globalized. Those in the field must learn "how to think globally and act locally," he explained to Pen. "Rather than exporting ideas, architects have to devise designs that are appropriate and challenging in the right way to new environments." Denari has sought to take such considerations into account in his own work, tailoring his designs to the geographical and cultural contexts in which they will exist. One notable opportunity came in the form of a contest to design the New Keelung Harbor Service Building, a cruise ship terminal to be built in the port city of Keelung, Taiwan. Denari's firm submitted the winning proposal, designing a building that will meld the architect's vision of innovative form with the needs of the city and its people. The building will be "more than a functional transportation hub," as he told Pen. "The local context was to realize that this port terminal represented a gateway to country in terms of identity," he explained. "We designed a project that was very connected to its site. Due to the rainy local conditions, we envisioned a building that was very vivid, with bright colors and hues to make sure it stood out in the climate." Featuring a terminal as well as a connected office building, restaurant, parking garage, and public plaza, the New Keelung Harbor Service Building is set to be completed by the end of 2017.

Denari has received extensive recognition for his work, including honors from the American Institute of Architects (AIA) and the American Academy of Arts and Letters. He was inducted into the Interior Design Hall of Fame in 2010.

ARCHITECTURE EDUCATION

In addition to his work in the field, Denari has taught architecture since 1986, when he took a position at Columbia University. He has served as a visiting professor at a number of institutions, including the Shibaura Institute of Technology in Japan as well as Princeton University and the University of California at Berkeley. In 1988, Denari began to teach at the Southern California Institute of Architecture (SCI-Arc), and in mid-1997 he became its director. In that role, Denari sought to encourage innovation and promote new ways of thinking about the field. "What I want to do is try to raise the level of SCI-Arc's original mission, which was to be forward-thinking. And let's face it, if you're forward-thinking and you're dealing in concepts of new ideas, history has told us that new ideas are not always wanted by everyone," he told Nicolai Ouroussoff for the *Los Angeles Times* (17 Aug. 1997). "So SCI-Arc's mission is that we will be doing things that won't be readily understood or maybe consumable by the public, because we will be dealing with new ideas." After leaving SCI-Arc in 2001, Denari joined the department of architecture and urban design at the University of California at Los Angeles (UCLA), where he became a tenured professor. He was later named vice chair of the architecture program.

Denari has also contributed to a number of publications on architecture. He is the sole author of several books, including *Interrupted Projections*, published in 1996, and *Gyroscopic Horizons*, published in 1999. The former focuses on Denari's 1996 Japanese exhibition of the same name, while the latter presents some of Denari's designs as well as photographs and discussion of his architectural philosophy.

PERSONAL LIFE

Denari and his wife, Christine, live in Los Angeles.

SUGGESTED READING

Arcilla, Patricia. "Neil M. Denari to Complete Taiwan's New Keelung Harbor Service Building by 2017." *ArchDaily*. ArchDaily, 22 Feb. 2015. Web. 13 May 2016.

Denari, Neil. "Interview 2." *Matter: Material Processes in Architectural Production*. Eds. Gail Peter Borden, and Michael Meredith. New York: Routledge, 2012. 17–23. Print.

Denari, Neil. "Interview with Neil Denari." *Nooka*. Nooka, 9 Nov. 2010. Web. 13 May 2016.

Denari, Neil. "Neil Denari." Interview by Sam Lubell. *Architect's Newspaper*. Architect's Newspaper, 5 Mar. 2012. Web. 13 May 2016.

Denari, Neil. "UCLA Architecture and Urban Design: Interview with Neil Denari, Vice Chair." Interview by Ting Pen. *ValuePenguin*. ValuePenguin, July 2013. Web. 13 May 2016.

Ouroussoff, Nicolai. "Neil Denari." *Los Angeles Times*. Los Angeles Times, 17 Aug. 1997. Web. 13 May 2016.

Ouroussoff, Nicolai. "An Undulating Vision of the Future." *Los Angeles Times*. Los Angeles Times, 8 June 2002. Web. 13 May 2016.

—*Joy Crelin*

(Adam Bielawski/Wikimedia)

Jason Derulo

Born: September 21, 1989
Occupation: Singer

In a review of Jason Derulo's 2015 album *Everything Is 4* for the *New York Times* (2 June 2015), Jon Caramanica called the singer a "true chameleon" of the contemporary music industry. "Mr. Derulo may be the only true cross-genre pop star of the day, moving among styles with such fluidity that he barely leaves a lasting impression on any of them. He's not an R&B singer straining for pop acceptance, not a pop singer toughening up with hip-hop-inflected songs," he wrote.

Derulo's ability to choose versatile material and win fans has been confirmed by his album sales and chart performance; he has had several singles reach the number-one spot and crack the top ten on various Billboard charts, including "Whatcha Say," "Talk Dirty," and "Want to Want Me." Although Derulo has admitted to struggling against anonymity in the past even in the face of such chart-topping hits, he has continued to achieve success by straddling different musical modes.

EARLY YEARS

Jason Joel Desrouleaux was born in Miramar, Florida, on September 21, 1989. (He later changed the spelling of his name so that it would be easier for fans to pronounce.) His parents originally hailed from Haiti. His father, Joel Desrouleaux, is a Social Security administrator who still insists on working, even though his now-famous son has told interviewers that he would love to provide for his parents financially. Derulo's mother, Jocelyn Desrouleaux, worked as an immigration official; he often describes her to journalists in exceptionally loving terms and has said that of all the people in the world, he feels closest to her.

Derulo and his two older siblings were raised in the Miami neighborhood of Carol City. Although the close-knit family was positioned solidly in the middle class, the area (also home to hip-hop artists Rick Ross and Flo Rida) had pockets of crime and poverty. Suffering from asthma as a child, Derulo was also, by some accounts, relatively introverted. Although he is now known for his toned physique and six-pack abs, for a few years before hitting adolescence, he was somewhat overweight. "I had a lil' chub-chub moment from ages seven to eleven," he recalled to Chris Martins for *Billboard* (22 May 2015). "If somebody was teasing, they'd go straight to my fat. I was so insecure, I kept my shirt on in the pool, which is the worst because it sticks to your stomach anyway."

DISCOVERY ON THE BASKETBALL COURT

Displaying a propensity for music from an early age, Derulo often emulated the dance moves of Michael Jackson and MC Hammer as a preschooler and penned his first song—an ode to a girl he liked—at age eight. He also loved basketball, and one day on the court, he met Frank Harris, then a law student and skilled player who promised to help him better his game. When Derulo was slow to show improvement, however, he became frustrated. "Frank just kept beating me on the courts and finally I said to him, 'Basketball isn't my thing anyway, I'm a singer,'" Derulo recalled to Jo Piazza for Cable News Network (CNN) (23 Dec. 2009). Harris was initially unconvinced. "He said he was a singer and I was like, 'Uh huh, cool. This kid is probably in the chorus of his high school or something,'" the future entertainment manager told Piazza. "But then he sang and I realized he really had something, so I told him we would keep working on his basketball and I would talk to some people I knew in the music industry from New York."

In the meantime, Derulo—who gradually improved enough on the basketball court to help his high school team take home several state titles—also worked hard at school. He showed little interest in such pursuits as going to the prom or joining clubs, as he explained to Martins: "I didn't spend a lot of time doing things that I didn't think would make me great. I studied all kinds of dance, all types of music. I got good grades."

Later, Derulo attended the American Musical and Dramatic Academy in New York City, where he majored in musical theater. The two years he was at the school were lean ones, and he often subsisted on just bananas, which he could purchase for a quarter apiece from a street vendor. Offered a part in the Broadway show *Rent*, he turned it down for fear that he would be pigeonholed as a theater performer and diverted from obtaining a potential record deal.

BREAKING INTO THE MUSIC INDUSTRY

Thanks to Harris's industry contacts, while still in his teens, Derulo had also begun writing songs for high-profile performers, including P. Diddy, Danity Kane, Lil Wayne, and Pitbull. In 2007, Derulo wrote the single "Bossy" for a hip-hop artist known as Birdman and provided vocals on the track, proving his singing abilities and strengthening his case for being signed as a solo performer.

Two years later, managed by Harris and signed to Beluga Heights Records, a subsidiary of Warner Bros. Records, via producer J. R. Rotem, Derulo released his debut single, "Whatcha Say," which hit the top spot on the Billboard Hot 100 chart and was downloaded more than four million times. The track was the centerpiece of his self-titled debut album, released the following year. In a review of the album posted on AllMusic.com, David Jeffries expressed sentiments echoed by many other critics, writing that the single "was an infectious, slick, and on-point way to launch a career, but his debut album is less satisfying, even with plenty of the same well-crafted, futuristic R&B as his breakthrough tune." He continued, "Since Derulo seems entirely devoted to the song, the problem may lie with the album format itself. This one barely fits the definition at a scant nine songs, and there's little attention paid to the overall flow—but if what you're looking for is R&B that sparkles and dazzles, there are nine quick fixes here, each one just dying to get stuck in your head."

Derulo followed his debut with the 2011 album *Future History*, spawning such singles as "Don't Wanna Go Home," which peaked at number fourteen on the Billboard Hot 100; "It Girl," which reached the top ten in several countries;

"Breathing"; and "Fight for You." Again, critics gave his efforts middling reviews, with Jody Rosen, who characterized the work as "party-hearty robo R&B," writing for *Rolling Stone* (27 Sept. 2011), "Derulo doesn't travel light; on nearly every song he stuffs his suitcase until the seams split. . . . But Derulo is endearingly into it—he attacks the songs—and he can sing. . . . He's just a bit too overeager—too determined to please all of the people all of the time."

COMING BACK FROM AN INJURY

While rehearsing for the concert tour to promote *Future History*, Derulo landed on his head during a particularly acrobatic dance move and fractured his neck—an injury that could have left him paralyzed. "It was the craziest thing that's ever happened in my life," he recalled to a reporter for the Scottish *Daily Record* (13 Oct. 2013). "It's not something you ever think is going to happen to you. . . . I was pretty much humbled by the whole thing, due to not being able to do the simple things by myself, like tie my shoelaces or take a shower." The incident, he said, helped him grow as a person and reaffirmed how important it was to be surrounded by family and friends.

Wearing a neck brace and recuperating over the ensuing months, Derulo wrote songs for his third full-length album, *Tattoos*, which went on sale internationally in the fall of 2013. In the United States, however, he pared down the eleven tracks to just five and released the songs as an extended play (EP) of the same name. He has said that he got the idea for the title while contemplating the fact that life-altering experiences like his accident become an intrinsic part of a person, much like a tattoo. The United States finally got its version of Derulo's third full-length album the following year in the form of *Talk Dirty*, which included all of the singles from the international release—such as the hit "Talk Dirty"—as well as new original songs and featured collaborations with Snoop Dogg and Tyga.

Everything Is 4, Derulo's fourth full-length album, was released in 2015 and included the single "Want to Want Me." He arranged for the track's video to debut on the mobile dating app Tinder rather than via more conventional outlets. The album peaked in the top five of the Billboard Hot 200, and the single was added to the playlists of 156 US pop radio stations, shattering the previous record of 126 stations held by Justin Timberlake. In interviews regarding the new album, Derulo continued to emphasize his lifelong dedication to writing his own material. He explained to Daniel D'Addario for *Time* (2 June 2015), "For me, being a songwriter is, at the end of the day, the biggest gift. If you can't write a song, you're at someone else's beck and call, and you may never get another hit! And if someone doesn't write you one, you're kind of stuck."

In addition to his recording career, Derulo has appeared on television as a judge on the hit show *So You Think You Can Dance*, joining the panel during the competition's twelfth season in 2015. He quickly gained a reputation as a supportive figure, giving helpful advice even to those contestants he found severely lacking in talent.

PERSONAL LIFE

From 2011 to 2014, Derulo, who is known for his intense devotion to his fitness and nutrition regimen, dated singer Jordin Sparks. Sparks was featured in the duet "Vertigo," which was included as a track on *Tattoos* and *Talk Dirty*, and she appeared in the video for the single "Marry Me," which many fans took as a hopeful sign of their deepening relationship. Because of these collaborations—and because the two had appeared regularly in celebrity magazines discussing their intense love for each other—their acrimonious breakup came as a shock to many.

Along with his mother, he has launched Just for You, a charitable foundation. Building a hospital in Haiti has been one of the organization's central projects.

SUGGESTED READING

Caramanica, Jon. "Review: Jason Derulo Glides across Genres on '*Everything Is 4.*'" Rev. of *Everything Is 4*, by Jason Derulo. *New York Times*. New York Times, 2 June 2015. Web. 5 Nov. 2015.

Jackson, Eboyne. "Grit and Sacrifice Pay Off for Jason Derulo." *Amour Creole*. Amour Creole, 2011. Web. 5 Nov. 2015.

Martins, Chris. "Jason Derulo on Fitness Fanaticism, His Post-Jordin Sparks Love Life and All-Star-Filled New Album." *Billboard*. Billboard, 22 May 2015. Web. 5 Nov. 2015.

Piazza, Jo. "Jason Derulo: The Man behind the Hit." *CNN*. CNN, 23 Dec. 2009. Web. 5 Nov. 2015.

"R&B Star Jason Derulo on How Breaking His Neck Changed His Entire Outlook on Life." *Daily Record*. Media Scotland, 13 Oct. 2013. Web. 5 Nov. 2015.

SELECTED WORKS

Jason Derulo, 2010; *Future History*, 2011; *Tattoos*, 2013; *Talk Dirty*, 2014; *Everything Is 4*, 2015

—Mari Rich

Matthew Desmond

Born: ca. 1970
Occupation: Sociologist

When Matthew Desmond won a John D. and Catherine T. MacArthur Foundation Fellowship in 2015, the organization lauded him for "revealing the impact of eviction on the lives of the urban poor and its role in perpetuating racial and economic inequality" and for "shedding light on how entrenched poverty and racial inequality are built and sustained by housing policies in large American cities."

The sociologist is the author of the 2016 book *Evicted: Poverty and Profit in the American City*, which has been widely praised for its compelling narrative and accessibility to laypeople. "Desmond is an academic who teaches at Harvard—a sociologist or, you could say, an ethnographer," Barbara Ehrenreich wrote for the *New York Times* (26 Feb. 2016). "But I would like to claim him as a journalist too, and one who . . . has set a new standard for reporting on poverty." (This was high praise indeed coming from Ehrenreich; she was widely acclaimed for her 2001 book *Nickel and Dimed: On (Not) Getting By in America*, which examined the repercussions of the 1996 welfare reform act on the working poor.)

"I want my work to influence public conversation, to turn heads, and to bear witness to this problem that's raging in our cities," Desmond told Aditya Chakrabortty for the *Guardian* (11 Mar. 2016). "If journalism helps me with that I'll draw on journalism . . . and I'm not going to

John D. and Catherine T. MacArthur Foundation/CC BY 4.0/
Wikimedia Commons

worry too much if academics get troubled over that distinction."

EARLY LIFE AND EDUCATION

Matthew Desmond is the eldest of three children. He grew up in Winslow, a small city in the north of Arizona. His father was a nondenominational minister and prison chaplain, and, as Desmond wrote in the final section of *Evicted*, "my industrious mother worked everywhere." Money was frequently tight in Desmond's household, and on more than one occasion, the utilities were turned off when the bills were paid late. During those times, Desmond's mother prepared meals on a wood-burning stove. "She knew how to make do, having grown up across from a junkyard in Columbus, Georgia," he wrote. "She had done better for herself and expected us kids to do the same, to go off to college even if she and my father weren't able to help pay for it." Desmond's father also stressed the value of higher education and when driving past farms or construction sites would often point to the sweating, low-paid laborers as a form of cautionary tale.

Desmond took those entreaties seriously, and with the help of loans and scholarships, he entered Arizona State University. To earn money to cover the expenses that scholarships and loans did not, Desmond spent from early May to late August each year working with a firefighting crew stationed in the woods of northern Arizona. (Having taken copious field notes during those months, he would later write a book from a sociological perspective about fighting wildfires.)

As an undergraduate, Desmond studied history, justice, and communications, intending to pursue a career in law. "In those classes I began learning things that did not square with the image of America passed down to me from my parents, Sunday-school teachers, and Boy Scout troop leaders," he wrote. "Was the depth and expanse of poverty in this country truly unmatched in the developed world? Was the American Dream widely attainable or reserved for a privileged few?" At about this time, the bank foreclosed on Desmond's childhood home, and he has recalled the experience of returning to Winslow to help his parents move as both sad and embarrassing. In response, he began volunteering with the nonprofit group Habitat for Humanity and also befriended several homeless people who congregated on Mill Avenue, not far from his university's campus in Tempe. "The people I met living on the street were young and old, funny, genuine, and troubled," he wrote.

ENTERING ACADEMIA

Upon graduating summa cum laude with bachelor's degrees in justice studies and communication in 2002, Desmond entered the University of Wisconsin–Madison, where he earned a master's degree in sociology in 2004. He remained at the school for his doctoral studies, and it was during this time that he conducted the research that he later drew upon in *Evicted*.

Research may, however, be a pale and inaccurate description of Desmond's activities. Seeking to become immersed in the world he sought to study, in mid-2008, he moved into Milwaukee's most dilapidated trailer park; he later relocated to a decrepit rooming house in a predominately black neighborhood. Of that period, he wrote, as quoted by Elizabeth Gudrais for *Harvard Magazine* (Jan./Feb. 2014): "I sat beside families at eviction court; helped them move; followed them into shelters and abandoned houses; watched their children; ate with them; slept at their houses; attended church, counseling sessions, Alcoholics Anonymous meetings, and Child Protective Services appointments with them; joined them at births and funerals; and generally embedded myself as deeply as possible into their lives."

At times, Desmond felt a measure of guilt, writing in his journal, "I felt dirty, collecting these stories and hardships like so many trophies," as he recalled in *Evicted*. Once he had finished his fieldwork, those feelings intensified, and he sometimes found himself at university functions mulling over the fact that the cost of the wine being served would have paid a portion of someone's rent or grocery bill. "The work was heartbreaking and left me depressed for years," he wrote. "It leaves an impression, this kind of work. Now imagine it's your life."

While at the University of Wisconsin, Desmond launched the Milwaukee Area Renters Study (MARS), a comprehensive survey of tenants in the city's low-income private housing sector that provided new data on the causes and effects of eviction, urban poverty, and the low-income housing market. "Only after beginning his research did Desmond realize how socially significant—and how little studied—eviction was," Gudrais wrote. "No national data exist; he constructed the Milwaukee data himself by examining tens of thousands of Milwaukee County eviction records."

In 2010 Desmond—whose dissertation, "Eviction and the Reproduction of Urban Poverty," won the university's prestigious Lumpkin Dissertation Award—earned his doctoral degree and became a junior fellow at Harvard University. In 2012 he was named an assistant professor of sociology and social studies at that Ivy League university, and in 2015—the year he received his MacArthur Foundation Fellowship—he ascended to his current post, the John L. Loeb Associate Professor of the Social Sciences. Among his other titles at Harvard are codirector of the Justice and Poverty Project, faculty associate at the Weatherhead Center for International

Affairs, and steering committee member for the Kennedy School's Program on Inequality and Social Policy.

EVICTED

Evicted: Poverty and Profit in the American City was published in March 2016 to near-universal acclaim. It landed almost immediately on the *New York Times* Best Sellers list. The book follows the lives of several people, including Scott, a former nurse who has lost everything he owned because of his heroin addiction; Arleen, a single mother whose rent leaves her with just twenty dollars a month with which to feed and clothe her two children; and Lamar, who serves as a paternal figure to neighborhood boys despite having lost both legs to frostbite during a period of homelessness. Desmond also follows the fortunes of his subjects' landlords, including Sherrena, a former teacher who has discovered that "the hood is good" business for landlords who can afford to buy run-down rental properties.

Evicted was deemed "a regal hybrid of ethnography and policy reporting" by Jennifer Senior in a review for the *New York Times* (21 Feb. 2016) and "a magnificent, richly textured book with a Tolstoyan approach" by Jim Higgins for the *Milwaukee Journal Sentinel* (26 Feb. 2016). In her review of Desmond's book, Senior wrote: "The result is an exhaustively researched, vividly realized, and, above all, unignorable book—after *Evicted*, it will no longer be possible to have a serious discussion about poverty without having a serious discussion about housing. Like Jonathan Kozol's *Savage Inequalities*, or Barbara Ehrenreich's *Nickel and Dimed*, or Michelle Alexander's *The New Jim Crow*, this sweeping, years-long project makes us consider inequality and economic justice in ways we previously had not. . . . Through data and analysis and storytelling, it issues a call to arms without ever once raising its voice."

OTHER BOOKS

In addition to *Evicted*, Desmond is the author of *On the Fireline: Living and Dying with Wildland Firefighters* (2007), an ethnography for which he drew upon his experiences fighting fires as a student. (The volume was an adaptation of his master's thesis.) Although the book got only a modest degree of attention when it was first published, after nineteen Arizona firefighters died in 2013 while trying to extinguish the Yarnell Hill wildfire, media outlets called upon him for commentary. Desmond and Mustafa Emirbayer, a fellow University of Wisconsin scholar, cowrote *Racial Domination, Racial Progress: The Sociology of Race in America* (2009), which was republished as *Race in America* in 2015, and *The Racial Order* (2015). In the former, they discuss modern issues of social division that are more complex in

many respects than the segregation and bigotry of earlier decades. (One such major issue, for example, is the intersectionality of racism, sexism, homophobia, xenophobia, and other oppressive institutions.) The latter volume, as its publisher, the University of Chicago Press, describes it, "is a theoretical reconsideration of the fundamental problems of order, agency, power, and social justice."

PERSONAL LIFE

Desmond is married to Tessa Lowinske Desmond. She currently serves as an administrative director and lecturer for the Committee on Ethnicity, Migration, and Rights at Harvard, as well as the director of undergraduate studies for special concentrations. They have two sons.

Desmond admits that his studies have, at times, caused him to suffer from depression and have affected his personal relationships. Despite that, he remains in contact with many of his subjects. "On the one hand, you know you have something [a topic like eviction] that matters," he told Chakrabortty. "On the other hand, you have it because people you're close to suffered for it."

SUGGESTED READING

Chakrabortty, Aditya. "Matthew Desmond: 'I Want My Work to Bear Witness to This Problem That's Raging in Our Cities.'" *Guardian*. Guardian News and Media, 11 Mar. 2016. Web. 7 May 2016.

Ehrenreich, Barbara. Rev. of *Evicted: Poverty and Profit in the American City*, by Matthew Desmond. *New York Times*. New York Times, 26 Feb. 2016. Web. 7 May 2016.

Glauber, Bill. "'Genius Grant' Winner Matthew Desmond Made in Madison, Milwaukee." *Milwaukee Journal Sentinel*. Journal Media Group, 30 Sept. 2015. Web. 7 May 2016.

Gudrais, Elizabeth. "Disrupted Lives." *Harvard Magazine*. Harvard U, Jan./Feb. 2014. Web. 7 May 2016.

Pollitt, Katha. "*Evicted* by Matthew Desmond: What If the Problem of Poverty Is That It's Profitable to Other People?" Rev. of *Evicted: Poverty and Profit in the American City*, by Matthew Desmond. *Guardian*. Guardian News and Media, 11 Mar. 2016. Web. 7 May 2016.

Ramos, Dante. "In *Evicted*, a Problem Society Must Solve." *Boston Globe*. Boston Globe Media Partners, 17 Apr. 2016. Web. 07 May 2016.

Senior, Jennifer. "In *Evicted*, Home Is an Elusive Goal for America's Poor." Rev. of *Evicted: Poverty and Profit in the American City*, by Matthew Desmond. *New York Times*. New York Times, 21 Feb 2016. Web. 7 May 2016.

SELECTED WORKS

On the Fireline: Living and Dying with Wildland Firefighters, 2007; *Racial Domination, Racial Progress: The Sociology of Race in America*, 2009; *The Racial Order*, 2015; *Evicted: Poverty and Profit in the American City*, 2016

—*Mari Rich*

Genzebe Dibaba

Born: February 8, 1991
Occupation: Runner

Since the 1912 founding of the International Association of Athletics Federations (IAAF), track and field's world governing body, there has been a steady progression of new world records thanks to improved training methods, technological advances, and the rapidly evolving field of sports science. The progression of records in some athletic events, like the men's and women's marathons, has been significant, and the Ethiopian middle-distance runner Genzebe Dibaba has lived up to the credo that all records are meant to be broken. Dibaba made headlines in July 2015 when she broke the outdoor world record in the women's 1,500-meter race in Monaco. Her time of 3:50.07 was nearly four-tenths of a second faster than the previous record set by Qu Yunxia of China, which had stood for nearly twenty-two years and was long thought to be unbreakable.

Dibaba's record-setting feat was the culmination of a breakthrough 2015 season that also saw her win the gold medal in the 1,500-meter race at the IAAF World Championships in Athletics in Beijing, China. The younger sister of two professional distance runners, Dibaba had previously won world titles on the cross country and indoor circuits before her success in outdoor events. She also holds indoor world records in the 1,500-meter, 3,000-meter, 2-mile, and 5,000-meter races.

EARLY LIFE AND EDUCATION

The fifth of six children, Genzebe Dibaba was born on February 8, 1991, near Bekoji, a rural village in the Oromia region of Ethiopia's southern highlands. Bekoji has served as a breeding ground for world-class distance runners, including Fatuma Roba, the gold-medal winner in the women's marathon at the 1996 Atlanta Olympics, and Kenenisa Bekele, a triple Olympic champion who holds the world record in both the men's 5,000-meter and 10,000-meter events.

The Dibaba family supported themselves through subsistence farming. Dibaba's older sisters, Ejegayehu and Tirunesh, are both highly decorated distance runners. Ejegayehu won a

Augustas Didžgalvis/CC BY-SA 4.0/Wikimedia Commons

silver medal in the 10,000-meter event at the 2004 Olympics, and Tirunesh has won a combined three Olympic gold medals and five world titles in the 5,000- and 10,000-meter races. Dibaba's cousin, Derartu Tulu, meanwhile, is noted for being the first black African woman to win an Olympic gold medal after claiming victory in the 10,000-meter contest at the 1992 Olympics. Considered the doyenne of Ethiopian distance runners, Tulu has been credited with paving the way for Ethiopian women aspiring to pursue professional running careers.

Benefitting from the trailblazing path set by her cousin and sisters, Dibaba was positioned for distance-running greatness at a young age. She first enjoyed running success while competing in races at Bekoji Primary School. After receiving encouragement from a teacher there, Dibaba became determined to follow in her sisters' footsteps, a plan her parents supported. According to Dibaba, her mother was also a runner. "She was very strong because of her work but she never tried to have a career," she noted to Matthew Brown for the IAAF website (20 Nov. 2014).

During her formative years, Dibaba, like her sister Tirunesh, trained under legendary Ethiopian coach Sentayehu Eshetu, a former physical education teacher at Bekoji Primary School. Eshetu is responsible for steering the professional careers of the Dibaba sisters, Derartu Tulu, Kenenisa Bekele, and Tiki Gelana, the women's marathon gold medalist at the 2012 Olympic Games. Under Eshetu, Dibaba learned basic race strategies and tactics and built her strength through grueling hill workouts three times a week.

FIRST JUNIOR TITLE

As a teenager, Dibaba began running in regional competitions. In early 2005 she placed third at a meet held in the village of Asella, famed for being the hometown of Haile Gebrselassie, arguably the greatest distance runner of all time. Dibaba's third-place finish helped her earn a spot on the Oromiya team for the 2005 Ethiopian national championships, held in Addis Ababa, Ethiopia's capital. After an eighth-place showing there, Dibaba was recruited by Oromiya's Muger Cement Sports Club, which began offering her financial support.

In 2006 Dibaba captured a bronze medal in the 3,000-meter race at the national championships and had begun competing in international meets. In 2007, she qualified to represent Ethiopia's junior team at the IAAF World Cross Country Championships in Mombasa, Kenya. Dibaba finished fifth in the junior women's six-kilometer event, while her sister Tirunesh, running for Ethiopia's senior team, won the silver medal in the women's eight-kilometer. Later that summer Dibaba competed at the 2005 Reebok Grand Prix (now the Adidas Grand Prix) in New York, where she claimed tenth place in the 5,000-meter run, an event Tirunesh won.

Dibaba first came to the attention of the international track world in 2008, when she won her first junior title at the World Cross Country Championships, held at the Holyrood Park in Edinburgh, Scotland. Her victory helped inspire Tirunesh to win her third world cross-country title in the senior women's race. The Dibaba sisters became the first members from the same family to claim gold medals at the competition. "Genzebe is so young and talented," Tirunesh Dibaba explained to Brown for the IAAF website (30 Mar. 2008). "In time I expect she'll become even stronger and quicker than me."

BREAKING OUT OF HER SISTER'S SHADOW

Tirunesh's expectations proved true. Dibaba continued to distinguish herself on the cross-country, indoor, and outdoor circuits. She repeated her world junior champion win at the 2009 World Cross Country Championships in Amman, Jordan, becoming the second junior woman to win consecutive championships. Then, in August of that year, she won the 5,000-meter gold medal at the 2009 African Junior Athletics Championships in Mauritius. Later that month, in Dibaba's first major senior race, she placed eighth in the 5,000-meter at the IAAF World Championships in Athletics in Berlin, Germany.

Dibaba claimed her first senior cross-country title in November 2009 at the Cross Internacional de Atapuerca in Spain. She then defended the title in 2010, a year in which she also won the 5,000-meter gold medal at the World Junior Championships in Moncton, Canada. Running

on the senior team in 2011, Dibaba placed ninth at the World Cross Country Championships and eighth in the 5,000-meter race at the World Championships.

Entering the 2012 season, Dibaba decided to shift her focus from the 5,000-meter to the 1,500-meter race, winning her first world senior title in the event at the 2012 IAAF World Indoor Championships in Istanbul, Turkey. She followed that performance with a winning outdoor run over 1,500 meters at the Shanghai Golden Grand Prix, an annual IAAF Diamond League race, in May 2012. Two months later, she represented Ethiopia at the London Summer Olympics, where she failed to advance past the first round of 1,500-meter heats after suffering a hamstring injury, which then forced her to stop training for five months. "At times I thought my career was over," she admitted to John Aglionby for *Financial Times (FT) Magazine* (11 Dec. 2015).

TRANSFORMATION INTO WORLD RECORD BREAKER

It was during her recovery that Dibaba began working with Jama Aden, the national middle-distance coach of Qatar. Dibaba was introduced to Aden while he was conducting his annual winter running camp in Addis Ababa. In an effort to maximize Dibaba's performance in outdoor events, Aden overhauled her training methods, forcing her to focus less on mileage than on high-intensity runs, hill workouts, and biomechanical exercises. Dibaba later described Aden as "not just a coach" but "like a father to me," as she told Paul Gains for *Running World* (6 June 2014). "He always tells me that I can run fast and makes me believe in myself."

Dibaba's work with Aden paid immediate dividends. She opened her 2013 season with a victory in the three-kilometer pursuit at an IAAF Cross Country Permit meet in Edinburgh. She then returned to the 1,500-meter race for the indoor season, notching impressive wins at annual IAAF indoor permit meets in Germany and England. Dibaba's 1,500-meter success did not carry over to outdoor events, however, and she placed a disappointing eighth in the race at the 2013 World Championships in Moscow, Russia.

Nevertheless, the following February, Dibaba shattered three world indoor records. "In the space of fifteen days, Ethiopia's Genzebe Dibaba became the most talked about middle-distance runner on the planet," Gains wrote. On February 1, 2014, she set a new world record in the 1,500 meters, placing first in Karlsruhe, Germany, with a time of 3:55.17, topping the previous record by three seconds and her own personal best by nearly five seconds. Five days later, she shaved seven seconds off fellow countrywoman Meseret

Defar's 2007 world record in the 3,000-meter event at the XL Galan in Stockholm, Sweden, coming in first with a time of 8:16.60—the fastest mark in the event, indoor or outdoor, since 1993. Dibaba completed her trifecta one week later in her first two-mile race when she took nearly six seconds off Defar's 2009 world record in the event with a first-place time of 9:00.48 in Birmingham, England.

Dibaba next won the gold medal in the 3,000-meter event at the 2014 World Indoor Championships in Sopot, Poland. Despite a lackluster time of 8:55.04, she edged out second-place finisher and defending champion Hellen Onsando Obiri by more than two seconds to claim her second world indoor title. Dibaba suffered a minor back injury at the championships, which prevented her from continuing her run of dominance on the outdoor circuit. Still, she added another victory in the 3,000 meters at the IAAF Continental Cup, which was held in Marrakech, Morocco, in September 2014.

BREAKTHROUGH 2015 SEASON
One of Dibaba's goals entering the 2015 season was to break the world indoor record in the 5,000-meter race. She accomplished that goal in February with a blistering 14:18.86 time in the 5,000 meters at the XL Galan in Stockholm, again eclipsing a record previously set by Defar. Dibaba subsequently turned her attention outdoors and first enjoyed a trio of victories in the 5,000-meter event at Diamond League meets in Eugene, Oregon; Oslo, Norway; and Paris, France, achieving a personal-best time of 14:15.41 at the latter competition. She then returned her focus to the 1,500-meter discipline.

In July 2015 Dibaba set an African record in the 1,500 meters at a meet in Barcelona, Spain, with a first-place time of 3:54.11—the fastest mark in the world since 1997. One week later, she gained worldwide attention when she broke the world record in the 1,500 meters at a Diamond League meet in Monaco, with a time of 3:50.07. Her time bested Qu Yunxia's previous mark of 3:50.46, which had been set in her home country of China in September 1993. The record had long been considered unbreakable due to the rampant doping suspicions that surrounded it. Many Chinese athletes trained by Yunxia's coach, Ma Junren, have since received lifetime bans from the sport for using performance-enhancing drugs, with some later admitting that they were forced into taking them as part of state-sponsored doping programs.

Dibaba's record-breaking run was also called into question due to several doping scandals that marred the track world in 2015. Dibaba defended her time, explaining that after the race she felt like she was going to break the record and that her performance helped bring the idea of an untainted record-breaking time "back into the realm of believability," according to Emma Zehner for *Slate* (23 July 2015). "The situation [of doping in track and field] hasn't reached a point of no return," Dibaba said to Aglionby. "It can still recover and do well. The right decisions need to be made in a timely manner and the right actions need to be taken to manage the sport properly."

Dibaba followed up her Monaco triumph with a gold medal in the 1,500 meters at the 2015 World Championships in Beijing. Despite posting a markedly slower time of 4:08.09, she outlasted second-place finisher Faith Kipyegon of Kenya by nearly one second to claim her first world outdoor title. In Beijing, Dibaba also won a bronze medal in the 5,000-meter event, with a time of 14:44.14. Her accomplishments in 2015 earned her the IAAF women's athlete of the year award.

Dibaba entered the 2016 season with the goal of winning her first gold medal in the 1,500 meters at the Summer Olympics in Rio de Janeiro, Brazil. She lives in Addis Ababa with Tirunesh and Tirunesh's husband, the Ethiopian long-distance runner Sileshi Sihine. Dibaba often trains with her sister, whom she considers her idol.

SUGGESTED READING
Aglionby, John. "Women of 2015: Genzebe Dibaba, Athlete." *FT Magazine*. Financial Times, 11 Dec. 2015. Web. 18 Jan. 2016.

Brown, Matthew. "Monaco Press Points—Genzebe Dibaba." *IAAF*. Intl. Assn. of Athletics Federations, 20 Nov. 2014. Web. 18 Jan. 2016.

Gains, Paul. "Genzebe Dibaba Comes Out of Her Sister's Shadow." *Runner's World*. Rodale, 6 June 2014. Web. 18 Jan. 2016.

Zehner, Emma. "Push It to the Limit." *Slate*. Slate Group, 23 July 2015. Web. 18 Jan. 2016.

—*Chris Cullen*

Diplo
Born: November 10, 1978
Occupation: DJ, record producer

The American DJ, record producer, and music mogul Diplo can rightly be described as the electronic dance music (EDM) equivalent of the hip-hop icon Jay Z (formerly known as Jay-Z). Described as having "a businessman's mind with a creative soul," as his longtime friend, the music manager Scooter Braun, told Jonathan Ringen for *Billboard* (9 June 2016), Diplo emerged

mtheory LLC/[CC BY-SA 3.0]/Wikimedia Commons

A self-described "counterculture kid," Diplo grew up dreaming of dinosaurs and as a boy aspired to become a paleontologist. (His stage name, Diplo, derives from his favorite childhood dinosaur, the Diplodocus, one of the biggest sauropods of the late Jurassic period.) He also developed an early love of music, despite not coming from a musical family. Though it has been reported that he never learned how to play an instrument, his mother has said that he played the piano and started creating music in the second grade.

As a preadolescent, Diplo became particularly drawn to Miami bass, a raw, dance-oriented brand of hip-hop that is characterized by sustained kick-drum beats, fast tempos, and often sexually explicit lyrics. The genre, which rose to popularity in the late 1980s with artists such as 2 Live Crew, inspired Diplo to begin experimenting with turntables and would play a major role in the development of his eclectic sound.

In his teens, Diplo became an avid record collector and his musical tastes expanded to include reggae, rock, heavy metal, and breakbeat hardcore. At age seventeen, he landed his first DJ gig at a hotel in Daytona Beach, Florida. After graduating from Daytona Beach's Mainland High School in 1997, he enrolled at the University of Central Florida. He remained at the school for only a short time, however, before transferring to Temple University in Philadelphia, Pennsylvania, to study filmmaking.

HOLLERTRONIX AND PARTNERSHIP WITH M.I.A.

While attending Temple, Diplo began deejaying at Philadelphia's underground club circuit. In 2003, he and a friend, a local DJ named Low Budget, launched an underground party called Hollertronix, which quickly developed a strong following in Philadelphia. The party's success enabled the duo to release a mixtape that year titled *Never Scared*. Built around mash-ups of many different musical genres, from hip-hop to world music, the mixtape received critical acclaim and was named one of the top-ten albums of 2003 by the *New York Times*.

By then, Diplo had earned his undergraduate degree and had been working a number of jobs to support his music career, including doing social work and teaching in an after-school program. Earnings from deejaying and other mixtapes, however, allowed him to focus full time on creating music. In 2004, he released his debut solo album, *Florida*, which featured a collection of downtempo electronic tracks. He also traveled to Brazil to explore a local dance-music genre known as baile funk, an extension of Miami bass that was spawned in the rough-and-tumble favelas (slums) of Rio de Janeiro. The experience inspired him to release a mix of baile

from Philadelphia's underground DJ circuit to become one of the most in-demand producers in music. He first achieved international success in 2007, after cowriting and producing the hit single "Paper Planes" for the rapper M.I.A. Since then, he has, as Ringen noted, produced "for an entire MTV Video Music Awards' worth of artists," including Chris Brown, Beyoncé, Usher, Justin Bieber, and Madonna.

Diplo has recorded and performed professionally under a variety of aliases and is known for embracing many different styles of music, including pop, hip-hop, R & B, Jamaican dancehall, Miami bass, and Brazilian baile funk. "If I had a signature sound, I think that would be the end of me," he explained to Nolan Feeney for *Time* (19 Aug. 2015). He is a founding member of the Caribbean-influenced EDM group Major Lazer and makes up one-half of the Grammy Award–winning DJ duo Jack Ü, along with Skrillex. He also owns and operates the independent label Mad Decent.

EARLY LIFE AND EDUCATION

Diplo was born Thomas Wesley Pentz on November 10, 1978, in Tupelo, Mississippi, to Tom and Barbara Pentz. He had a peripatetic childhood, living at various times in Virginia, South Carolina, Tennessee, and Alabama, before his family settled in Fort Lauderdale, Florida. There, his father ran a bait shop and his mother worked as a grocery clerk. "We never had much money," he recalled to Jonah Weiner for *Rolling Stone* (22 Mar. 2012). "I had to borrow surfboards to go surfing. I never had a video game."

funk tracks titled *Favela on Blast* (2004), which brought him to the attention of the British-born Sri Lankan rapper M.I.A., the stage name of Mathangi "Maya" Arulpragasam.

Diplo collaborated with M.I.A., whom he met while spinning at a London club, on a well-received mixtape, *Piracy Funds Terrorism, Vol. 1* (2004), which helped increase M.I.A.'s profile outside of England. Meanwhile, it "boosted Diplo's reputation as a scene-spotter," Weiner wrote, "importing the mongrel pop of the global underclass to American clubs and blogs." He went on to work with M.I.A. on a series of other projects, including helping to produce the track "Bucky Done Gun" for her critically hailed solo debut *Arular* (2005). The pair would also become romantically involved for five years.

MAD DECENT AND MAJOR LAZER
Diplo's burgeoning reputation in the music industry helped him earn DJ of the year honors from *Spin* magazine in 2005. Later that year, he founded his own independent label, Mad Decent Records, which champions innovative global artists. The label's first signee was the Brazilian group Bonde do Role, who have been credited with helping to popularize baile funk in the United States. Mad Decent, which was headquartered in Philadelphia before moving to Los Angeles in 2010, releases dozens of recordings in a wide variety of formats from artists all over the world every year.

Diplo enjoyed his first international success in 2007, when he cowrote and produced M.I.A.'s downtempo rap ballad "Paper Planes," which samples the Clash's 1982 song "Straight to Hell." The song became a surprise runaway hit, reaching number four on the Billboard Hot 100 chart and earning a Grammy Award nomination for record of the year. In the wake of the song's success, Diplo was courted by major-label producers to make what he has described as "Paper Planes Part 2." He found it difficult to recreate the same magic in the studio, however, prompting him, in 2008, to form Major Lazer, an electronica-tinged Jamaican music project, or as Ringen put it, "his reggae-meets-EDM-meets-pop-meets-whatever crew." He founded Major Lazer with the British DJ Switch, whom he met through M.I.A. That same year, Mad Decent hosted its first block party, a street festival that would eventually turn into a popular, nationwide tour series held each summer.

The duo's first full-length album as Major Lazer, *Guns Don't Kill People . . . Lazers Do*, was released in 2009, featuring guest vocals by a number of Jamaican reggae and dancehall artists, including Turbulence and Vybz Kartel. In 2010, he tapped back into his interest in film-making and combined it with his passion for baile funk to direct the documentary *Favela on Blast*, hoping to make the rest of the world more aware of that still lesser-known Brazilian music scene. After Switch left Major Lazer in 2011, Diplo brought on Miami-based Jamaican MC Walshy Fire and the Trinidadian DJ and producer Jillionaire.

PRODUCER TO THE STARS
Concurrently, Diplo produced songs for a who's who of R & B, hip-hop, and pop. In 2011, he coproduced Chris Brown's "Look at Me Now," an infectious Southern hip-hop track featuring rappers Lil Wayne and Busta Rhymes that reached number six on the Billboard Hot 100 chart and received a Grammy nomination for best rap song. This fruitful collaboration led to production work for pop behemoth Beyoncé. He provided the sonic foundation for the songs "Run the World (Girls)" and "End of Time," both of which appeared on the singer's fourth studio album, *4* (2011).

In 2012, Diplo cowrote and produced "Climax," the hit lead single off Usher's seventh studio album, *Looking 4 Myself*. Also that year, he collaborated with Canadian pop sensation Justin Bieber on the song "Thought of You." Additionally, he helped produce singles for Santigold, Iggy Azalea, Snoop Lion, and Britney Spears, work that would earn him a Grammy nomination for producer of the year in 2013. Meanwhile, he and Major Lazer released their second album, *Free the Universe* (2013), which includes vocal contributions from such high-profile artists as Tyga, Bruno Mars, and Wyclef Jean.

While the production and deejaying aspects of his career continued to prosper, at this time he also admitted that Mad Decent had been struggling and was largely kept from folding by the success of giving away music and the viral spread of the YouTube video and Internet meme of people dancing to the Baauer single "Harlem Shake," which had boosted sales. "Honestly, that record was the thing that saved the label, because a year ago we were going to fold because we couldn't figure out how to make money," he shared with Kia Makarechi for the *Huffington Post* (25 Apr. 2013). "Then we just started giving music out for free and it worked out."

JACK Ü
In September 2013, Diplo teamed up with turntable titan Skrillex to form the EDM duo Jack Ü, debuting their first single, "Take Ü There," in 2014; it served as the lead single to their debut studio album, *Skrillex and Diplo Present Jack Ü*, released in February 2015. The duo's second single, "Where Are Ü Now," featuring Bieber, was released in conjunction with the album. Described by Ringen as "super-futuristic, vaguely tropical and built around top 40 hooks that would make [Swedish songwriter] Max

Martin blush," the song peaked at number eight on the Billboard Hot 100 chart. At the same time, Major Lazer released another album, *Peace Is the Mission* (2015), which includes the lead single "Lean On," which was coproduced by the French EDM artist DJ Snake and features vocals by the Danish singer MØ. The song became a major international hit, reaching number four on the Billboard Hot 100 chart and becoming the most streamed song of all time. In explaining the group's approach to the new album, Diplo told a staff member for *Billboard* (23 Apr. 2015), "If people hear a Major Lazer record, right away they're going to think, 'It's gotta be something I've never heard before.' That's how we always want it to be." He also served as a coproducer for pop icon Madonna's thirteenth studio album, *Rebel Heart* (2015).

At the 2016 Grammy Awards ceremony, Diplo accepted two Grammys for his work with Jack Ü, winning for best dance recording ("Where Are Ü Now") and best dance/electronic album. Working once again with Beyoncé, he coproduced the tracks "Hold Up" and "All Night" on her sixth album, *Lemonade* (2016).

OTHER VENTURES
Diplo has benefitted greatly from the worldwide EDM phenomenon that has taken place over the first decades of the 2000s. Instead of resting on his laurels, he has expanded his brand with myriad ventures that are closely tied into his music career, including a DJ residency in Las Vegas, Internet radio shows, film and television projects, and prescient investments in Tesla and Snapchat. In an article for *Fast Company* (17 Nov. 2014), he told Benjamin Svetkey, "I think one of the reasons I've been successful is that I can see things before other people do."

In 2015, Diplo was listed by *Forbes* magazine as one of the highest-earning DJs in the world, performing up to three hundred shows per year. He traveled with Major Lazer to Havana, Cuba, in March 2016, where they performed a free open-air concert to nearly five hundred thousand people. They became the first American musical act to play a concert in Cuba since the two countries reinstated diplomatic relations in 2014.

PERSONAL LIFE
Diplo lives in Los Angeles but spends only about one week each month there due to his busy touring schedule. He has two young sons, Lockett and Lazer, with his ex-girlfriend, Kathryn Lockhart. Since 2007, he has run Heaps Decent, a nonprofit arts organization based out of Sydney, Australia, that offers music workshops and programs for underprivileged youth.

SUGGESTED READING
Feeney, Nolan. "How Diplo Is Making Pop Music Weird." *Time*. Time, 19 Aug. 2015. Web. 18 Aug. 2016.
Marino, Nick. "Mad Genius." *Paste*. Paste Media Group, 21 July 2008. Web. 18 Aug. 2016.
Ringen, Jonathan. "Diplo on Why DJ Culture Is a 'Sinking Ship' and Wishing He Was Beyoncé." *Billboard*. Billboard, 9 June 2016. Web. 18 Aug. 2016.
Svetkey, Benjamin. "Why the World Is Moving to Diplo's Beat." *Fast Company*. Fast Company, 17 Nov. 2014. Web. 18 Aug. 2016.
Weiner, Jonah. "Diplo and the Search for the Perfect Beat." *Rolling Stone*. Rolling Stone, 22 Mar. 2012. Web. 18 Aug. 2016.

SELECTED WORKS
Never Scared, 2003; *Florida*, 2004; *Guns Don't Kill People . . . Lazers Do*, 2009; *Free the Universe*, 2013; *Peace Is the Mission*, 2015; *Skrillex and Diplo Present Jack Ü*, 2015

—*Chris Cullen*

Pete Docter
Born: October 9, 1968
Occupation: Director, screenwriter

There is a select list of directors who have won more than one Oscar for films they have helmed. Counted among them is an introverted, tall, lanky Midwesterner by the name of Pete Docter. While Docter had impressed audiences and critics as a writer and animator at Pixar for many years, after adding directing to his résumé, he accepted Oscars for best animated feature for the Pixar feature films *Up* (2009), about the adventures of an old man who floats his house away, and *Inside Out* (2015), about the various emotions vying for control inside an eleven-year-old girl's mind. The two films have grossed hundreds of millions of dollars worldwide and have added to Pixar's streak of producing high-quality computer-animated movies that are beloved by children and adults alike. Yet despite his success, Docter remains humble about his accomplishments—and even fearful that his work is a fluke. "I'm not the typical take-charge, silver-backed gorilla director," he said in an interview with Brooks Barnes for the *New York Times* (20 May 2015). "I often think I'm on the verge of getting fired. And then I'll think, well, maybe I should just quit: 'It's been nice, guys. I'll miss you.'"

Anthony Harvey/Getty Images

EARLY LIFE AND EDUCATION

Pete Docter was born in Bloomington, Minnesota, on October 9, 1968. He was raised in a musically inclined family, with his mother teaching music, his father directing a college chorus, and his two younger sisters growing up to become professional musicians. During his childhood, he had an active imagination. After visiting Disneyland in California, he wanted to turn his room into a version of a Disneyland attraction he had seen there—the Enchanted Tiki Room, where animatronic birds sing to visitors. He accomplished this feat by somehow convincing his parents to haul some bamboo harvested in California back to Minnesota on the top of the family van.

When not inside his magical room, he could be found near a creek not far from his family home, pretending to be Indiana Jones off on an adventure. His idyllic childhood, however, was in for a major change when his father decided to complete his doctorate in Danish choral music—in Denmark. In an interview with Terry Gross for National Public Radio (10 June 2015), Docter recalled, "When I was in fifth grade—so about eleven—my folks moved us to Denmark. And so not only did I have all new friends and all new surroundings, I didn't even understand what they were talking about, which was very difficult."

Though Docter had actually begun experimenting with animation by making his first flip-book out of a math textbook in the third grade, it was as he stepped back from that unfamiliar environment in Denmark and into himself that his love for drawing—and eventually

animation—truly developed. "I always felt this awkwardness and shyness, and so I kind of retreated into my own little world," he said to Barnes. "That's part of why I gravitated toward animation. It was easier to draw something that expressed how I felt than to say it out loud." Before long, he found it far easier to draw people than to talk to them.

The love of illustration never left him. For his undergraduate degree, Docter studied animation at the California Institute of the Arts (CalArts) in Valencia, California. Some of his short films were shown in the touring Spike & Mike's Festival of Animation, which allowed them to be seen by John Lasseter, the cofounder of Pixar. Upon graduating, Docter became one of the first employees at the fledgling Pixar Animation Studios, which, while just beginning to transition from being a computer company, would go on to not only pioneer computer animation but also become one of the most critically and commercially successful movie studios of the modern era.

WORKING FOR PIXAR

Pixar pioneered computer animation during the 1980s, when most cartoons were still drawn by hand. However, all of Pixar's early films were shorts, and though impressive, did not have the commercial draw of a full-length feature film. That all changed in 1995 when Pixar released *Toy Story*, the world's first computer-animated feature film. That groundbreaking film was also the first feature-length animated film that Docter worked on, primarily as a writer and animator.

The success of *Toy Story* put Pixar on the map by securing an audience for computer-animated films and by proving to critics that such films could be as compelling and as creative as their hand-drawn predecessors. Docter himself would work as a writer on many of the studio's major releases during this period, all of which achieved widespread critical and commercial acclaim. Included among these titles are *Toy Story 2* (1999), *Monsters, Inc.* (2001), and *WALL-E* (2008). *Monsters, Inc.*—about a scare factory in which nice-guy monsters use the energy from children's fears to power their world—is particularly notable on Docter's résumé as it was additionally the first full-length feature at Pixar that he also directed.

Docter credits his success in large part to the Pixar process, in which all of the writers, animators, and illustrators work together to produce the best possible final film. The director explained the Pixar process in his interview with Gross: "What we do is we have a script, of course, but for us, writing is also like storyboarding. It's drawing. And so we will cut all of those drawings together with music, sound effects and dialogue. And we screen this kind of stick-figure version of the film. . . . And then we go away into a room and we talk about what worked and what didn't."

WINNING THE OSCAR FOR *UP*

Docter has described each of his movies as being somewhat autobiographical in nature. In *Monsters, Inc.*, one of the main monsters, Sully, has his work life upended with the arrival of a young child, much the way Docter's own life was changed when his son was born. *Up* (2009), however, harkens back to the adventures of his childhood, when he (as Indiana Jones) left his ordinary world behind for a grand adventure. Additionally, the thought of a house flying away was partly inspired by Docter's introverted nature, as he explained to Brad Balfour for the *Huffington Post* (22 Apr. 2010): "I'd want to go crawl under my desk and just hide and rock by myself for a little while, so floating away from everything just seemed appealing."

In *Up*, which Docter both co-wrote and directed, a widower named Carl ties an enormous amount of balloons to his longtime home in order to fly his house to the jungles of Paradise Falls, which his childhood hero, Charles F. Muntz, explored. Carl does this in part to fulfill the wishes of his late wife, Ellie, but also because he feels he has missed out on the great adventures of his life. What he learns during his travels, however, is that his greatest adventures had been the lifelong one he had with his wife and now in making connections with new people, including a young stowaway on his balloon ride named Russell.

The film, which earned $731 million worldwide at the box office during its theatrical run, also impressed critics on both sides of the Atlantic. Writing for *Empire* (1 Oct. 2008), Ian Freer proclaimed, "For all its fantastical leanings, *Up* is that rare animated film that sees the world as real. Its pains feel real and its joys feel earned. That may be an obvious thing, but it lifts *Up* into a class by its beautiful self." *Up* would go on to earn Docter his first Oscar, when the film won the 2010 award for best animated feature.

MORE OSCAR GOLD FOR *INSIDE OUT*

Inside Out (2015), the next film Docter both co-wrote and directed, was largely inspired by his experience discovering that his daughter was growing up—transitioning out of childhood and becoming a young adult. The struggle, which he recalled so intimately from his own childhood, was one that he felt the need to capture on film. Unlike an ordinary coming of age story, this would be a cartoon taking place inside a girl's adolescent mind, with each of her emotions—joy, fear, disgust, anger, and sadness—personified as individual characters who guide the film's main character, Riley, from a control center inside her mind.

While every Pixar movie has an evolutionary process, Docter found this film's process particularly difficult. At one point he was so convinced that it was not working that he was ready to give up, perhaps even quit Pixar. A big problem was that the main plot point of having Joy and Fear getting lost together in Riley's mind just was not working. After a time, however, Docter realized that Sadness was the key—that it was okay for Riley to feel sad and through that experience grow as a human being. The change proved just what was needed to take the film into production. "He is a genius," actor Bill Hader, who voices Fear in the movie, said of Docter to Michael Cavna for the *Washington Post* (18 June 2015). "And he's incredibly modest—he's kind of like Jim Henson: Modest and very sweet, and he does this amazing thing of letting you do your thing. . . . He's very intuitive. He's not thinking: 'This is something the kids will love, and will get giant weekend box office.'"

Yet *Inside Out* did prove successful at the box office, raking in approximately $857 million worldwide. The film was also a hit with critics. Jonathan Romney, writing for the *Guardian* (26 July 2015), declared, "*Inside Out* is in the top rank of Pixar productions with its combination of audacity, intelligence, wit and emotional reward. Directed and co-written by Pete Docter (*Monsters, Inc.* and *Up*) and co-directed by Ronnie del Carmen, *Inside Out* starts from a boldly abstract premise. . . . Formidably ingenious, *Inside Out* hits an elusive sweet spot in terms of appealing to children and adults alike." Also well received by the film industry, *Inside Out* won the 2016 Academy Award for best animated feature, earning Docter his second Oscar statue.

PERSONAL LIFE

Docter and his wife, Amanda, have two children, Nicholas and Elie. Their family lives in a specially made home built into a private hillside in Northern California; the house is partly connected to a sixty-feet-tall artificial tree that indulges his childhood dream to live in a tree house. Docter—who is over six feet but enjoys driving a very small Smart car—is also a practicing Christian. In an interview for *Christianity Today* (26 May 2009), he discussed the intersection of art and faith with Mark Moring: "When people go to a movie, they want to see some sort of experience of themselves on the screen. They don't come to be taught. So in that sense, and in terms of any sort of beliefs, I don't want to feel as though I'm ever lecturing or putting an agenda forth."

SUGGESTED READING

Barnes, Brooks. "*Inside Out*, Pixar's New Movie from Pete Docter, Goes Inside the Mind." *New York Times*. New

York Times, 20 May 2015. Web. 10 June 2016.

Cavna, Michael. "Pete Docter's Inspiration behind Pixar's Mindful *Inside Out*? This One Goes to 11." *Washington Post*. Washington Post, 18 June 2015. Web. 10 June 2016.

Docter, Pete. "It's All in Your Head: Director Pete Docter Gets Emotional in *Inside Out*." Interview by Terry Gross. *Fresh Air*. NPR, 3 July 2015. Web. 10 June 2016.

Freer, Ian. Rev. of *Up*, dir. Pete Docter. *Empire*. Bauer Consumer Media, 1 Oct. 2008. Web. 10 June 2016.

Moring, Mark. "Pete Docter, Pixar's Star Director, Talks about His Christian Faith." *Christianity Today*. Christianity Today, 26 May 2009. Web. 10 June 2016.

Romney, Jonathan. "*Inside Out* Review—an Emotional Rollercoaster." Rev. of *Inside Out*, dir. Pete Docter. *Guardian*. Guardian News and Media, 26 July 2015. Web. 10 June 2016.

SELECTED WORKS

Toy Story 2, 1999; *Monsters, Inc.*, 2001; *WALL-E*, 2008; *Up*, 2009; *Inside Out*, 2015

—*Christopher Mari*

Keith Allison/Flickr/CC BY-SA 2.0/Wikimedia Commons

Josh Donaldson

Born: December 8, 1985
Occupation: Baseball player

Among the best all-around players in Major League Baseball (MLB), Josh Donaldson, the third baseman for the Toronto Blue Jays, has often been described as a "win-at-all-costs ballplayer," according to Robert MacLeod for the *Globe and Mail* (10 July 2015). Donaldson was drafted by the Chicago Cubs in the first round of the 2007 MLB Draft but was traded to the Oakland Athletics in 2008. He made his MLB debut with the Athletics as a catcher in 2010 and did not emerge as an everyday player until the 2012 season when he reinvented himself as a third baseman.

Driven by a relentless work ethic, Donaldson became one of the Athletics' most potent offensive threats and led the team to consecutive American League (AL) West Division titles in 2012 and 2013. In 2015, his first season with the Blue Jays, he won the AL Most Valuable Player (MVP) Award after leading the league in a number of offensive categories. He was named an AL All-Star starter in both 2014 and 2015.

EARLY LIFE

Joshua Adam Donaldson was born on December 8, 1985, in Pensacola, Florida, the only child of Levon Donaldson and Lisa French. Donaldson's parents divorced before he reached elementary school. He was raised primarily by his mother, who worked double shifts at her family's bar to make ends meet. Growing up Donaldson saw little of his biological father, a construction worker, who in 1992 was sentenced to prison for domestic violence and drug-related offenses. "A lot of stuff was going on that was not good," he recalled to Susan Slusser for the *San Francisco Chronicle* (23 May 2013). "I had to grow up pretty fast."

From an early age, Donaldson was steered toward sports so he would hopefully avoid his father's troubled path. A natural athlete, he was featured on television at the age of eighteen months because of his ability to drive golf balls. Although Donaldson had learned the game of golf from his father, his maternal uncle, Chuck Pyritz, introduced Donaldson to baseball.

Blessed with outstanding hand-eye coordination, Donaldson was a standout baseball player throughout his youth. His talent was matched only by his work ethic: he spent countless hours each day in his backyard honing his throwing and hitting skills. His on-field success was sometimes overshadowed, however, by his brash, cocky personality. "I wasn't scared to be a little flashier," Donaldson told MacLeod.

HIGH SCHOOL CAREER

Donaldson's flashy playing style put him at odds with his teammates on the varsity baseball squad at Pace High School in Pace, Florida. As a result,

Donaldson's mother enrolled him for his sophomore year at Faith Academy, a private Catholic school in Mobile, Alabama, located about sixty miles northwest of Pensacola. The school not only offered Donaldson a more disciplined environment but also better sports opportunities.

Donaldson earned a spot on Faith's highly regarded baseball team, which was coached by Lloyd Skoda. Skoda became another father figure, teaching Donaldson "not only how to play baseball but how to be a man," as Donaldson's mother put it to Jane Lee for MLB.com (10 May 2013). Skoda assigned Donaldson a mentor, Ben Daw, Faith's starting senior shortstop, to help temper Donaldson's bravado. "He was very guarded," Daw said of Donaldson to MacLeod. "He obviously had a lot going on in his life, and I think that's how he tried to protect himself, by trying to act tough."

With a strong support network in place, Donaldson shined, and as a senior, he batted .515 with twenty-one doubles, six triples, four home runs, and fifty-four RBIs. He was an all-state shortstop and pitcher and was named the Alabama high school player of the year. During his time at Faith, Donaldson was also a standout football player, setting a Faith single-season record with eleven interceptions as a cornerback.

AUBURN UNIVERSITY AND MLB DRAFT
After graduating from high school in 2004, Donaldson accepted a baseball scholarship at Alabama's Auburn University. After joining the team, he switched from shortstop to third baseman, and he performed solidly his freshman year, starting thirty-nine games and hitting .294 with seven home runs. He began splitting time as catcher during his sophomore season after the team's incoming freshman catcher signed a professional contract. He started thirty-six of fifty-six games behind the plate and led the Auburn Tigers with ten home runs, throwing out nearly 40 percent of runners trying to steal bases and recording seven pickoffs.

Donaldson began to come into his own as a player during the summer of 2006 when he played for the Harwich Mariners, part of the Cape Cod Baseball League. He earned an All-Star selection as catcher after hitting .302 with a team-best four home runs and carried his strong play into his 2007 junior season when he led the Tigers with a .349 batting average and fifty-four RBIs.

By this time Donaldson was being noticed by major-league scouts, who were intrigued as much by his power as they were by his versatility as a player. The Chicago Cubs ultimately drafted Donaldson as a catcher, and their then-general manager Jim Hendry told J. P. Morosi for Fox Sports (16 July 2014), "He was a hard-nosed kid with a lot of talent, a good-looking hitter.

We didn't know if he would be a catcher, so the backup plan was that he could play third."

ROAD TO THE MAJORS
Donaldson's professional career began auspiciously. After playing four games with the rookie-level Arizona League Cubs, Donaldson was assigned to the Cubs' short-season A affiliate, the Boise Hawks of the Northwest League, where he batted an impressive .346 with nine home runs and thirty-five RBIs. He failed to duplicate that success, however, during the first half of the 2008 season when he batted just .217 in sixty-three games with the Peoria Chiefs in the Midwest League. In July 2008 the Cubs traded Donaldson and three other players to the Oakland Athletics.

Donaldson, whose offensive struggles were largely attributed to the everyday rigors of catching, quickly returned to form as a member of the Athletics. He played the second half of the 2008 season with the advanced A-affiliate Stockton Ports, batting .330 with nine home runs and thirty-nine RBIs. He then spent the entire 2009 season with the AA Midland RockHounds of the Texas League, where he hit .270 with nine home runs and ninety-one RBIs in 124 games.

Donaldson opened the 2010 season playing with the Sacramento River Cats in the AAA Pacific Coast League. He played in eighteen games before earning his first call-up to the majors in April as a replacement for injured catcher Kurt Suzuki. He went on to appear in eight more games for the Athletics before returning to Sacramento. In eighty-six games with the River Cats that season, he posted a then career-high eighteen home runs but batted just .238.

Donaldson remained with the River Cats for the entire 2011 season and improved his average to .261, achieving seventeen home runs and seventy RBIs in 115 games. A lack of opportunities on the Athletics' roster led Donaldson to spend the winter of 2011 in the Dominican Winter League where he became dedicated to learning third base in order to broaden his marketability to the club. "He was always a guy we thought highly of," the Athletics' general manager Billy Beane explained to Morosi. "The biggest trick was finding an opportunity for him."

CATCHER AND ALL-STAR THIRD BASEMAN
Donaldson's big break came on the first day of spring-training camp in 2012, when starting third baseman Scott Sizemore suffered a season-ending knee injury. Donaldson opened the 2012 season but was relegated back to Sacramento because of offensive inconsistency. He remained there for much of the season before being recalled by the Athletics in mid-August when backup third baseman Brandon Inge was placed on the disabled list.

Donaldson regained his hitting stroke and batted .290 with eight home runs, eleven doubles, and twenty-six RBIs over the final forty-seven games of the season. He explained to Slusser that before the adjustments, he "was trying to hit everything—fastballs inside, sliders away, and it wasn't working." In the AL divisional series, Donaldson batted .294 before the Athletics lost to the Detroit Tigers in five games.

After intensifying his offseason training, Donaldson emerged as the team's top offensive player and a 2013 MVP candidate. He played in 158 games and batted .301 with twenty-four home runs and ninety-three RBIs, providing Gold Glove–caliber defense at third base. Putting Donaldson at catcher "was like caging a wild boar," Billy Owens, the director of player personnel, later told Eddie Martz for ESPN.com (26 Mar. 2014). "He was meant to run around on the field, do athletic things on the diamond, and play third base like a warrior."

The Athletics improved their record to 96–66 and clinched their second AL West title but lost to the Tigers in the division series. Donaldson was recognized for his regular-season performance, finishing fourth in the AL MVP voting and receiving MVP consideration in 2014 when he led the Athletics to a third consecutive playoff and earned his first All-Star selection as a starter for the AL squad. Donaldson led the Athletics in virtually every offensive category, finishing with twenty-nine home runs, ninety-eight RBIs, ninety-three runs, and seventy-six walks.

TORONTO BLUE JAYS AND 2015 MVP SEASON

Donaldson's fiery on-field intensity made him a fan favorite in Oakland, and the Athletics surprised many in November 2014 when they traded Donaldson to the Toronto Blue Jays in exchange for a third baseman, a shortstop, and two pitchers.

Donaldson solidified his status as an MLB "superstar," as Albert Chen noted for *Sports Illustrated* (12 June 2015), as he entered Toronto's 2015 season midpoint, hitting .293 with twenty-one home runs and earning his second straight All-Star selection as a starter. He also participated in the 2015 MLB Home Run Derby. "He's one of the best in the game," Blue Jays manager John Gibbons said to MacLeod. "He's not afraid to fail. If he fails it doesn't eat him alive. Some guys it eats them alive. So he goes out there and lays it out and gives it his best effort. . . . And usually the great ones, that's the way they are."

Donaldson carried his momentum into the second half of the season and finished among the league leaders in every major offensive category. He hit .297 with forty-one home runs and led the AL with 123 RBIs and MLB with 122 runs scored. He also led the AL in extra-base hits

(84) and ranked second in the league in slugging percentage (.568) and wins-above-replacement (8.7). Meanwhile, he continued to provide Gold Glove–worthy defense at third base, posting a strong .959 fielding average.

Donaldson helped bring stability to an already-potent Blue Jays team that won the AL East Division with a 93–69 record, reaching the postseason for the first time since 1993 and breaking MLB's longest playoff drought by advancing to the AL Championship Series. In eleven postseason games, Donaldson batted .244 with three home runs and eight RBIs.

In November 2015 Donaldson edged out Los Angeles Angels outfielder Mike Trout for the AL MVP Award. He became the second player in Blue Jays history to win the award. He was also named the MLB player of the year by *Sporting News* and won his first career AL Silver Slugger Award. Prior to the 2016 season, Donaldson signed a two-year contract extension with the Blue Jays worth nearly $29 million.

PERSONAL LIFE

Donaldson has earned attention around the league for his unique hairstyles. Toward the end of the 2015 season, he began sporting what many described as a cross between a faux-hawk and a samurai tail. Donaldson has said that the look was inspired by the Viking warrior character Ragnar Lothbrok from the History Channel series *Vikings*. He made a cameo appearance on the fourth season of the show in January 2016.

Donaldson spends the offseason in Daphne, Alabama, where he owns a home located two miles away from his mother.

SUGGESTED READING

MacLeod, Robert. "Donaldson's Turn: How a Troubled Kid Rose through Baseball to Become the People's All-Star." *Globe and Mail*. Globe and Mail, 10 July 2015. Web. 23 May 2016.

Matz, Eddie. "Safe at Third." *ESPN.go*. ESPN Internet Ventures, 26 Mar. 2014. Web. 23 May 2016.

Morosi, J. P. "He's Got Juice in His Hands: The Oral History of Josh Donaldson." *Fox Sports*. Fox Sports Interactive Media, 16 July 2014. Web. 23 May 2016.

Slusser, Susan. "A's Donaldson Takes Nothing for Granted." *SFGate*. Hearst Communications, 23 May 2013. Web. 23 May 2016.

—Chris Cullen

Adam Driver

Born: November 19, 1983
Occupation: Actor

"Adam Driver doesn't look like a movie star," Marlow Stern wrote for *Newsweek* (15 May 2013). "Below a jet-black mop of hair sits an array of incongruous features—squinty eyes, a long proboscis, prominent ears, and a wide mouth. His voice is guttural and prone to violent changes in pitch. When he moves his towering six-foot-three frame, he stalks like an explorer navigating treacherous terrain." Still, Driver, a former Marine and Juilliard-trained actor, has become something of an unconventional sex symbol during his run on the idiosyncratic HBO series *Girls*, on which he plays Adam Sackler, whom Stern described as the "oft-shirtless, emotionally incontinent carpenter . . . and antihero love interest of Hannah Horvath, played by the show's creator-star, Lena Dunham." Driver has received three Primetime Emmy Award nominations, in 2013, 2014, and 2015, for his performance as Sackler.

In addition to his star-making turn on *Girls*, Driver has appeared on the big screen in such films as *Frances Ha* (2012), *Inside Llewyn Davis* (2013), *While We're Young* (2014), and *This Is Where I Leave You* (2014). In 2015 he made a leap to big-budget blockbuster fare with his portrayal of villain Kylo Ren in *Star Wars: The Force Awakens*. In an article for the *Atlantic* (30 Aug. 2013), Jon Frosch explained the actor's versatility, writing, "Driver looks like a character actor . . . and his line delivery, at once slacker-ish and neurotic, makes him sound like one, too. But he has the charisma of a leading man."

EARLY LIFE AND EDUCATION

Driver was born on November 19, 1983, in San Diego, California, to Nancy (Needham) and Joe Douglas Driver. After his parents' divorce, he moved with his mother, who worked as a paralegal, to her hometown of Mishawaka, Indiana. "It's pretty archetypal," he recalled to George Gurley for *M Magazine* (2 June 2014). "Not small-town, really, but cheerleaders and homecoming and a brick high school. . . . There's not really anything to do. People like to cruise in front of Taco Bell."

Nancy married a Baptist minister, and although Driver sang in the choir he also possessed a streak of rebelliousness. "We would climb radio towers, set things on fire," he told Gurley. He and his friends sometimes also shot their own action videos, using fake guns and taking a perverse pride when police were called to investigate. At one point, inspired by the 1999 movie *Fight Club*, he cofounded his own such

group, whose members met in an empty field to beat each other up for fun.

While attending Mishawaka High School, Driver developed an interest in drama, appearing in productions of *The Odd Couple*, *Arsenic and Old Lace*, and *Oklahoma!*, among other such fare, and regularly winning lead roles. Upon graduating, he auditioned for the selective acting school Juilliard but was denied admission. Uninterested in attending a traditional college, he took a series of menial jobs, at various points mowing lawns, selling vacuums, and telemarketing.

Dissatisfied with the course of his life and recalling the many stories he had heard of penniless aspiring actors hitting the big time, one day he loaded his possessions into his car and headed to California. When the car broke down outside Amarillo, Texas, he spent almost all of his limited cash reserves getting it fixed, and after just two days at a youth hostel in Santa Monica, California, he was forced to head back to Mishawaka.

In the months following the terrorist attacks of September 11, 2001, his stepfather suggested he consider joining the military. In some interviews, Driver has described those conversations as acrimonious, but regardless, enlisting in the Marines in 2002 provided a clear career path and new sense of purpose. Much to his surprise, he loved it. "I never had the sports thing where I tested my manhood and was a guy and all that stuff before then," he told Vanessa Grigoriadis for *Vulture* (25 June 2012). "In retrospect, it's amazing acting training because you're locked with thirty guys your age living this Greek lifestyle, very aware of death, not feeling so immortal. It's an interesting atmosphere in which to learn a little bit about human behavior."

Driver, who quickly developed an intense sense of patriotism and a feeling of brotherhood with his fellow Marines, was devastated when he broke his sternum in a mountain-biking accident and could not go to Iraq with the rest of the Eighty-First Platoon Infantry. He was discharged for medical reasons in 2004 and enrolled in the University of Indianapolis on the GI Bill, spending much of his time writing to his military buddies and checking up on their families for them.

He ultimately decided to try again for admission to Juilliard. "I'd worked up a lot of confidence from the Marines," he explained to Grigoriadis. "Oh, I've been with the best, so I'll go to Juilliard because it's the best." This time, after performing a monologue from *Richard III*, he was accepted.

While there, Driver—who initially struggled to reconcile the seeming frivolity of acting with the sense of drive he had felt as a Marine—embarked on a project to bring theater to overseas military bases. He approached the United Service Organization (USO) with plans to mount Sam Shephard's play *True West*, but the organization rebuffed him, explaining that enlisted service members preferred to see high-wattage celebrities or pro cheerleaders rather than serious drama. Somewhat daunted, Driver narrowed the scope of his ambition, instead mounting a series of monologues stateside at Camp Pendleton, where he had been stationed. His efforts attracted favorable press, and Driver went on to stage a series of readings for veterans suffering from post-traumatic stress disorder.

EARLY ACTING CAREER

Driver graduated from Juilliard in 2009 and began amassing stage credits. He won praise that spring for portraying both a closeted high school student in an Off-Broadway production of *Slipping* and a young Jewish man who plans revenge on the Germans in the controversial play *The Retributionists*. Driver won other theater roles in such plays as *Mrs. Warren's Profession*, *Angels in America*, *Man and Boy*, and *Look Back in Anger*, many of them with the prestigious Roundabout Theater Company. Concurrently, he had occasional guest parts on such television shows as *The Unusuals* and *Law and Order*, and film roles began to come his way as well.

Driver made his big-screen debut with a bit part in the 2011 biopic *J. Edgar*, which starred Leonardo DiCaprio as the controversial Federal Bureau of Investigation (FBI) head J. Edgar Hoover. He came to more widespread critical attention in 2012 in *Frances Ha*, which followed the life of a free-spirited young woman faced with the task of growing up. At the time of the film's

US release, Driver had already begun appearing in *Girls*, which was generating excited buzz, and many critics included comparisons of the two projects in their reviews. Peter Bradshaw, for example, wrote for the *Guardian* (25 July 2013), "*Frances Ha* grew on me. It of course resembles that touchstone of contemporary cool, Lena Dunham's HBO TV comedy *Girls*, in the locations, the scene in which the befuddled single girl goes for a visit back home with her affectionately portrayed parents . . . and also in the appearance of that show's supporting star, the lugubrious Adam Driver, who plays Lev, a slightly preposterous artist with weird, faintly pugnacious and yet unreadable mannerisms."

GIRLS AND OTHER PROJECTS

While continuing to win roles in such films as *Lincoln* (2012) and *Inside Llewyn Davis* (2013), Driver acted steadily in *Girls*, becoming one of the ensemble comedy's most talked-about members. During the first season, his character, Adam Sackler, is obnoxiously self-involved and cruel to Dunham's character, Hannah Horvath, whom he is dating. As the series progressed over four seasons, he became more sympathetic, evolving into what many female fans considered ideal boyfriend material.

It was an arc that was not originally planned. The Adam Sackler character was initially meant to appear in only the pilot episode, but as one of the show's writers, Jennifer Konner, told Gurley, "Once you work with Adam Driver, you never want to stop. He has a naturalism to him, an instinctual side that is like one-eighteenth of a tiger or something. He's like a young De Niro." Richard Shepard, who directed several episodes of *Girls*, echoed those sentiments, recalling his first time working with Driver, "I said to Jenni and Lena, 'This guy is incredible.'" Shepard continued, "He's got that sort of odd look that is ultimately going to help him, because he's not a straight-ahead leading man, and the way he acts is not straight-ahead. He reminds me of stuff [Al] Pacino was doing in the early seventies." The fifth season of *Girls* is scheduled to air in 2016, and Dunham has predicted that she will end the show after seven seasons.

Driver's projects outside of *Girls* have included *Tracks*, a 2013 film starring Mia Wasikowska as a young woman on a 1,700-mile trek across the deserts of West Australia; the thriller *Hungry Hearts* (2014); the Noah Baumbach–helmed *While We're Young* (2014); and the dramedy *This Is Where I Leave You* (2014), in which he plays the youngest brother in a loving but dysfunctional family. Even in those cases where the films themselves earned lukewarm reviews, critics found much to like in Driver's performances.

THE FORCE AWAKENS AND BEYOND

Most commentators praised the news that Driver had been tapped for *Star Wars: The Force Awakens*, the highly anticipated seventh episode in the Star Wars franchise. The film was released in December 2015 to great box office success, grossing over $1.5 billion worldwide by the first weekend in January 2016. In the film Driver plays Kylo Ren, a masked villain reminiscent of the iconic character of his grandfather, Darth Vader. "It was a great joy to work with Adam Driver on this role, because he threw himself into it in a deep and remarkable way," the director, J. J. Abrams told Anthony Breznican for *Entertainment Weekly* (12 Aug. 2015). Reviewers praised Driver's strong performance as Ren, with *Rolling Stone*'s Peter Travers (16 Dec. 2015) writing, "Driver, masked and unmasked gives him hypnotic and haunting contours." *The Force Awakens* marks the beginning of the character's story arc in the franchise. Driver will appear as Kylo Ren in *Star Wars: Episode VIII*, which is due to be released in 2017.

Driver has said that he will continue to accept roles on the stage, screen, or television; the medium, he asserts, is less important to him than the quality of the writing. He once told Mark Kennedy for the Associated Press (14 Oct. 2011) that acting reminds him in some respects of his time in the military. "Acting is really about having the courage to fail in front of people," he said. "It is a dangerous thing and has the same rush as fast-roping from a helicopter."

PERSONAL LIFE

In 2013 Driver married longtime girlfriend Joanne Tucker, a fellow thespian. The two live in the New York City borough of Brooklyn. In addition to acting Driver runs his own nonprofit, Arts in the Armed Forces, whose mission is "to honor, educate, inspire, and entertain" active-duty military personnel, veterans, and their families.

SUGGESTED READING

Frosch, Jon. "The Surprising Star Potential of *Girls'* Adam Driver." *Atlantic*. Atlantic Monthly Group, 30 Aug. 2013. Web. 18 Oct. 2015.

Grigoriadis, Vanessa. "*Girls'* Adam Driver on Joining the Marines and Playing Lena Dunham's Boyfriend." *Vulture*. New York Media, 25 June 2012. Web. 18 Oct. 2015.

Gurley, George. "The Emergence of Adam Driver." *M Magazine*. Fairchild Fashion Media, 2 June 2014. Web. 18 Oct. 2015.

Pressler, Jessica. "The GQ Cover Story: Adam Driver." *GQ*. Condé Nast, 20 July 2014. Web. 18 Oct. 2015.

Ransbottom, Virginia. "Exploring Possibilities Mishawaka Grad Takes Challenging Path on Course to Broadway." *South Bend Tribune*. *South Bend Tribune*, 28 Dec. 2007. Web. 18 Oct. 2015.

Stern, Marlow. "Adam Driver on *Frances Ha*, His *Girls'* Audition, and Juilliard." *Newsweek*. Newsweek, 15 May 2013. Web. 18 Oct. 2015.

SELECTED WORKS

Frances Ha, 2012; *Girls*, 2012–; *Lincoln*, 2012; *Inside Llewyn Davis*, 2013; *While We're Young*, 2014; *This Is Where I Leave You*, 2014; *Star Wars: The Force Awakens*, 2015

—*Mari Rich*

Nicole Eisenman

Born: 1965
Occupation: Painter, sculptor, and printmaker

Nicole Eisenman is an award-winning painter, sculptor, and printmaker who uses her work to explore feminism, sexuality, and social issues. In 2015, she received a prestigious MacArthur Fellowship, which comes with a "genius grant" worth $625,000. Eisenman has been a professional artist for nearly thirty years. As an artisan and as a champion of queer and feminist artists, she is considered a major figure in the art world. She is also the cofounder with multimedia artist A. L. Steiner of the curatorial initiative *Ridykeulous: This Is What Liberation Feels Like*.

Eisenman is best known for employing the exaggerated forms of expressionism. She is a narrative painter, and her work tells stories that many feel are simultaneously funny, disturbing, and strange. As Mónica de la Torre wrote for *BOMB* magazine (2015), Eisenman creates "slant reflections of our contemporary world."

Eisenman's early work features cartoonish figures, which were a nod to her love of satirical cartoons. Though her aesthetic has broadened, her more recent works still retain a humorous quality. "Humor is an inlet," she told William Harris for the *New York Times* (10 Nov. 1996). "You can seduce people with it and make them happy, and then you can sort of slap them across the face and say, 'Look again.' Humor brings people into a piece, and then they'll scratch their head and think: 'Wow, what am I laughing at? Maybe this is really not so funny.'"

Eisenman's subjects are figures, faces, and bodies, and throughout her career she has stylistically referenced different art movements. In 2000, she presented a show that drew heavily from paintings of the early Italian Renaissance as well as celebrated queer and lesbian culture. Beginning in 2008, she presented a series of paintings of scenes from a New York

John D. & Catherine T. MacArthur Foundation/CC BY 4.0/
Wikimedia Commons

beer garden, which mimicked similarly constructed scenes of French life by impressionist painter Pierre-Auguste Renoir. In 2012, she abruptly shifted focus to produce a series of monotype portraits in the manner of one of her idols, early twentieth-century Norwegian painter Edvard Munch.

EARLY LIFE AND EDUCATION
Eisenman was born in 1965 in Verdun, France, where her father, Dr. Sheldon Eisenman, was stationed as an Army psychiatrist. She grew up in Scarsdale, New York, where her mother, Kay, served as a village trustee. Eisenman was interested in art from a very young age, and her parents recall her drawing startlingly lifelike pictures of her grandparents when she was four or five years old. Her great-grandmother, Esther Hamerman, was a Polish-born painter and folk artist.

Eisenman graduated in 1983 from Scarsdale High School where she was the art editor of the yearbook. She then went on to study painting at the prestigious Rhode Island School of Design (RISD), earning her master's degree in 1987. She moved to New York City the day after she graduated.

Eisenman took on odd jobs to make money, devoting weekends to her own work. She began to come into her own in 1992, exhibiting her work in a handful of group shows and "painting big, funny, irascible pictures of women in revolt," Holland Cotter wrote for the *New York Times* (25 Sept. 2014). In 1994, she presented a celebrated solo show titled *The Lesbian Museum:*

10,000 Years of Penis Envy. Her work was subsequently picked up by the Tilton Gallery in New York and the Shoshana Wayne Gallery in Santa Monica, California. "Once I started showing, things happened very quickly," Eisenman told Lisa Coleman Bradlow for the *Scarsdale Inquirer* (2 Oct. 2015).

In 1995, Eisenman was invited to participate in the Whitney Biennial, a well-known exhibition of contemporary art at the Whitney Museum of American Art in New York City. The exhibition usually features up-and-coming artists, and the museum had initially promised Eisenman a prominent space to feature her work. Organizers of the exhibition recanted at the last minute and relegated her to the basement. "I felt really annexed," she told Harris, "like I wasn't really in the show. One way to be more central would be to blow up the whole museum so that my wall would be the only one left. Everybody could stand around on the sidewalk and look down at it." Her frustration served as a springboard to create a piece that was a commentary on the show itself: a mural that she painted in ten days and called *Self-Portrait with Exploded Whitney*, which featured an artist, back to the viewer, painting while the museum lay in rubble all around her. The Whitney liked the piece so much that they bought it for its permanent collection. While the mural was displayed in the basement, Eisenman's larger installation—titled *The Whitney Buy Any Ol' Painting Sale 1995*—ended up receiving a more prominent space in the museum. Cotter, who is an early and ardent fan of Eisenman's work, praised the artist's "good humor" and her "amazingly inventive work" in his capsule review of the show (12 Mar. 1995).

MAJOR WORKS
By the late 1990s, Eisenman had become known as a provocative artist who explored sexual politics, gender, and "the joy, pain, embarrassment, and ecstasy of being human," Stephen Knudsen wrote for *Art Pulse* magazine (8 May 2014). In *Swimmers in the Lap Lane* (1995), for instance, Eisenman depicts what would normally be an orderly chain of lap swimmers as a teeming mass of flesh engaged in an aquatic orgy. In the satirical *Fishing* (2000), Eisenman depicts a group of artic Amazon women lowering a hogtied man into a hole in the ice. Similar send-ups of feminist and lesbian tropes include *Amazons Castrating Captured Pirates* (1992) and the less gruesome *Man Cloud* (1999), which depicts a writhing mass of men in the sky with an idyllic handful of nude women below on the grass. Cotter described the work in 2014 as "Sistine Chapel meets [American muralist] Thomas Hart Benton meets Classic Comics." But as another fan of Eisenman's work, *New York Magazine* art critic Jerry Saltz, noted, the artist abandoned her

cartoonish aesthetic for more painterly works around the turn of the millennium.

Eisenman's beer-garden series embraces the patrons of a Brooklyn watering hole. *Biergarten at Night* (2007) depicts drinkers squeezed into the frame, guzzling, canoodling, and socializing in an outdoor beer garden. Though not immediately noticeable, Eisenman has painted a death-like specter embracing a human figure, which changes the tone of the otherwise convivial scene. The painting is notable for the exaggerated facial expressions, the larger narrative that weaves through the characters depicted, and the androgyny or queerness of the figures themselves. Rather than focus on cartoon send-ups of gender roles, Eisenman chose in many of her beer-garden paintings to engage the viewer by painting the subjects as gender neutral or indeterminate.

One of Eisenman's best-known works, *The Triumph of Poverty* (2009), exhibits the techniques of her beer-garden paintings but also embraces her political roots. Painted in the midst of the global recession, it makes a pointed statement about greed and human suffering and is what Knudsen called a "twenty-first-century *Grapes of Wrath.*" In the painting, which is based on and named after Hans Holbein's 1533 painting, a group of men and women walking and riding in a car are heading in an unknown direction. Featured prominently among them is a top-hatted leader whose pants have fallen down to reveal that his buttocks is attached to the front of his body. He also leads a small and stumbling group, which is based on the characters in Pieter Brueghel the Elder's 1568 painting *The Blind Leading the Blind.*

2012 WHITNEY BIENNIAL AND A NEW DIRECTION

In 2011, Eisenman parted ways with her long-time partner, Victoria Robinson, and embarked on a new direction in her work: a serious foray into printmaking. She worked with several different artists to produce the prints, and she presented the resulting forty-five portrait prints at the 2012 Whitney Biennial. Colorful and arresting, Eisenman's work drew special praise for style and emotion from critic Peter Schjeldahl who wrote for the *New Yorker* (12 Mar. 2012), "Once nervously defiant, and often rather fey, Eisenman has acquired the confidence of an artist who is sure of our attention."

Around the same time, Eisenman also embraced plaster sculpture, a medium she had been hesitant to use since her art school days. She debuted her fives sculptures, which were larger-than-life figures in modern poses, at the Carnegie Museum in St. Louis where they were exhibited among classic statues of antiquity. One figure, *Prince of Swords* (2013), was placed

seated on a railing, legs dangling over the museum's first floor. The figure is slouched over and staring at a smartphone in his hands. Another 2013 sculpture, *Guy with Mugwart (Water Element)*, lies on the floor on its back with its head propped up against a pillar. The sculptures were presented as part of Eisenman's midcareer retrospective, *Dear Nemesis, Nicole Eisenman 1993–2013.* When asked why she chose the name, Eisenman told Knudsen, "Nemesis is the Greek god of retribution, specifically for the crime of indiscretion, of hubris. If you start to think you're a god, she's the one who will put you in your place." Eisenman added, "Maybe she pays extra attention to artists, since it is our job to create something out of nothing."

Eisenman's work has been exhibited at the Museum of Modern Art, the San Francisco Museum of Modern Art, the Carnegie Museum of Art, Kunsthalle Zürich in Switzerland, and the Museum Ludwig in Cologne, Germany. Over the course of her career, she received a Guggenheim Fellowship in 1996 and the Carnegie Prize in 2013.

PERSONAL LIFE

Eisenman lives in the Williamsburg neighborhood of Brooklyn, New York. She and former partner Victoria Robinson have two children: a daughter, George, born in 2007, and son, Frederick, born in 2009.

SUGGESTED READING

Bradlow, Lisa Coleman. "Artist's Genius Is Made Official with MacArthur Grant." *Scarsdale Inquirer.* S. I. Communications, 2 Oct. 2015. Web. 13 Mar. 2016.

Cotter, Holland. "A Career of Toasting Rebellions." *New York Times.* New York Times, 25 Sept. 2014. Web. 13 Mar. 2016.

Cotter, Holland. "A Critic's Dozen to Catch at the Biennial." *New York Times.* New York Times, 12 Mar. 1995. Web. 13 Mar. 2016.

De la Torre, Mónica. "Nicole Eisenman and David Humphrey." *BOMB.* Bomb Magazine, Summer 2015. Web. 13 Mar. 2016.

Harris, William. "Even the Art Museums Can't Escape Her Barbs." *New York Times.* New York Times, 10 Nov. 1996. Web. 13 Mar. 2016.

Knudsen, Stephen. "Nicole Eisenman: The Relevance of 21st-Century Expressionism." *Art Pulse.* ARTPULSE, 8 May 2014. Web. 14 Mar. 2015.

Schjeldahl, Peter. "Not Like the Other Ones." *New Yorker.* Condé Nast, 12 Mar. 2012. Web. 14 Mar. 2016.

SELECTED WORKS

Self-Portrait with Exploded Whitney, 1995; *The Whitney Buy Any Ol' Painting Sale 1995*, 1995;

Biergarten at Night, 2007; *The Triumph of Poverty*, 2009

—*Molly Hagan*

Canadian Film Centre from Toronto, Canada/CC BY 2.0/
Wikimedia Commons

Aunjanue Ellis

Born: February 21, 1969
Occupation: Actor

Over her twenty-year career, Aunjanue Ellis has shown great versatility as an actor, tackling a wide range of roles on film, television, and stage. Since making her theater debut in a Broadway revival of William Shakespeare's *The Tempest*, Ellis has built an impressive television résumé, often being cast as authority figures in legal and crime series, including ABC's *The Practice*, as well as the CBS shows *The Mentalist* and *NCIS: Los Angeles*. On the big screen she has garnered attention with her small but memorable portrayals of strong female characters, most notably in the Oscar-winning films *Ray* (2004), in which she played a spurned backup singer, and *The Help* (2011), in which she played Yule Mae Davis, a maid in 1960s Mississippi.

Ellis has since graduated to leading roles, landing her first starring role in the miniseries and female slave narrative *The Book of Negroes* (2015)—a project near to her heart. "I love telling Black folks' stories and how we deal with issues," she told Mekeisha Madden Toby for *Essence* (25 Sept. 2015). "I want to be part of things that set the record straight about who we are." Since 2015 the veteran actor has also headlined an ethnically diverse cast in the ABC drama *Quantico*.

EARLY LIFE AND EDUCATION

Aunjanue Ellis was born in San Francisco, California, on February 21, 1969. At age three she moved with her mother to her grandmother's farm in McComb, Mississippi. Ellis grew up in a devoutly religious family and frequently attended New Home Baptist Church, one of four that was headed by her late grandfather.

Growing up, Ellis displayed a natural affinity for performing. She would often make speeches, quote Scriptures, as well as participate in recitations and skits for the Easter and Christmas programs at her family's church. After graduating from South Pike High School in 1987, Ellis gained admission to Tougaloo College, in Jackson, Mississippi. Her first exposure to the theater came during her second year, when she first crossed paths with visiting Brown University professor James Barnhill, who cast Ellis in a student production.

At Barnhill's suggestion, the nineteen-year-old eventually transferred to Brown. There, she trained under drama teacher Lowry Marshall and witnessed firsthand the deep devotion to the performing arts. "When I was at Brown, they took [acting] very, very seriously. Some of these kids had actually acted professionally," she shared with *Backstage* (9 Nov. 2011). "My experience with that life was entirely through television. It was never personal. It was never that immediate. It was strange and life-changing."

Despite her burgeoning interest in acting, Ellis majored in African American studies at Brown. However, upon earning her Bachelor of Arts (BA) degree in 1992, she was accepted to the three-year graduate acting program at New York University's (NYU) Tisch School of the Arts. Ellis initially struggled before deciding to dedicate herself to the program. "I didn't see how the work that I was doing there was relevant until my third year," she admitted to *Backstage*. "I got so tired of losing roles. . . . After a while of that, I felt very bruised. I was like, 'Enough of this. This is not going to change in earnest unless I approach this differently.'"

DEBUTS ON BROADWAY

Ellis's hard work paid off. In the summer of 1994, she made her first professional appearance, alongside Patrick Stewart and Carrie Preston, in a revival of William Shakespeare's *The Tempest*, which premiered at the New York Shakespeare Festival, held at Central Park's Delacorte Theater. After completing her Master of Fine Arts (MFA) program in May 1995, Ellis reprised the role of Ariel five months later, when the George C. Wolfe production began a twelve-week run at the Broadhurst Theatre.

Ellis's Broadway debut did not go unnoticed. In a review for the *New York Times* (17 Dec. 1995), Susan Brenna hailed her for projecting "nearly as much force offstage as she does in character as Ariel. Slender and wiry with cheekbones out to here, Ms. Ellis plays the sprite without a trace of Tinkerbell, for she too has wrung her role dry of squishy girlishness." Also in October, she experienced another first: her television debut in an episode of the Fox detective drama *New York Undercover*.

CONQUERING THE BIG AND THE SMALL SCREENS

The following January, Ellis appeared in two movies that were screened at the 1996 Sundance Film Festival. Her first feature film was the coming-of-age indie drama *Girls Town* (1996), in which Ellis portrayed Nikki, an inner-city high-school senior whose suicide leads her three best friends on a journey of revenge and self-discovery. *Girls Town* captured the Filmmakers Trophy and Special Jury Recognition prize, while Ellis's other Sundance offering, the romantic comedy *Ed's Next Move* (1996), landed a distribution deal with Orion Classics.

In March 1996 Ellis played a California police officer on the ABC crime drama *High Incident*, which aired for two seasons before being canceled in May 1997. After appearing in the independent ensemble films *Side Streets* (1998) and *Desert Blue* (1998), she nabbed supporting roles in two higher profile films: the LL Cool J action thriller *In Too Deep* (1999) and the Julianne Moore drama *A Map of the World* (1999).

LEADING ROLES

Ellis returned to weekly television in 1999, with a recurring role on David E. Kelley's legal drama *The Practice*, followed by a two-episode guest stint on the NBC series *Third Watch* in 2000. She subsequently landed her largest film role yet in the big-budget Hollywood film *Men of Honor* (2000), costarring opposite Academy Award winners Robert DeNiro and Cuba Gooding Jr. as a part-time librarian and medical student whose husband (Gooding) becomes the first African American US Navy master diver. Her performance earned her an NAACP (National Association for the Advancement of Colored People) Image Award nomination.

Ellis followed that up with prominent roles in two independent features: the boxing drama *The Opponent* (2000) and the Samuel L. Jackson psychological thriller *The Caveman's Valentine* (2001). Next came smaller, more memorable parts, as a mentally ill woman in Sidney Lumet's courtroom television drama *100 Centre Street* and as a Big Sister volunteer in the female-centric indie *Lovely & Amazing* (2001). In 2002 Ellis took leading roles in the award-winning short *I Am Ali* and the blaxploitation parody *Undercover Brother*. She also became a series regular on the short-lived ABC medical drama *MDs* (2002).

Two years later, Ellis appeared alongside several Hollywood veterans, including Jamie Foxx, Kerry Washington, and Regina King, in the musical biopic *Ray* (2004). Ellis received her share of praise for her portrayal of blues singer Mary Ann Fisher, the first backup singer to join the legendary Ray Charles's band, from reviewers A. O. Scott for the *New York Times* (29 Oct. 2004) and Richard Corliss for *Time*. "The cast is terrific from top to bottom—Kerry Washington as Charles's wife; Regina King and Aunjanue Ellis as his singer-concubines," Corliss wrote (12 Oct 2004, on-line). "If there were an Oscar for ensemble acting, *Ray* would win in a stroll." At the 2005 Screen Actors Guild Awards, Ellis and her *Ray* costars were nominated for the award in outstanding performance by a cast in a motion picture category.

STEADY WORK IN TV AND FILM

For her next project—the independent film *Perception* (2005)—Ellis played the high-school friend of a woman who becomes paralyzed after being hit by a bus. Also in 2005, she landed the recurring part of a parole officer on the short-lived Fox crime drama *Jonny Zero* and was also cast as a high-ranking US Army officer in the Jerry Bruckheimer–produced military drama *E Ring*, which aired on NBC for one season (2005–6).

After reuniting with Jackson and Moore in *Freedomland* (2006), the movie adaptation of Richard Price's 1998 novel, Ellis took on the role of a jury consultant in another Bruckheimer production, the Fox legal series *Justice*, which ended in early 2007, after only twelve episodes. A year later she guest starred on the CBS crime drama *Numb3rs* as well as *The Border*, a Canadian police series, before turning up again on the big screen in *The Express* (2008), portraying the mother of Ernie Davis, the first African American Heisman Trophy winner.

FINDS HER PURPOSE WITH *THE HELP*

Ellis gained a new legion of fans in the fall of 2008, playing sexy, ruthless vampire Diane Hardwicke in a multi-episode arc during the first season of HBO's hit drama *True Blood*. Following appearances in the made-for-television movie *The Prince of Motor City* (2008) and the film *Notorious* (2009), as well as the independent films *I Love You Phillip Morris* (2009) and *Motherhood* (2009), Ellis reteamed with her *Men of Honor* costar Gooding for the TNT movie *Gifted*

Hands: The Ben Carson Story (2009), in which she played Carson's (Gooding) wife. She next costarred opposite Oscar winners Denzel Washington and John Travolta in the remake of *The Taking of Pelham 123* (2009) and guest-starred alongside Emmy Award–winner Julianna Margulies in a 2009 episode of the CBS drama *The Good Wife*. From 2009 to 2013, Ellis appeared in a recurring role on another CBS series, *The Mentalist*, in which she played a law enforcement agency head.

Following roles in a string of lesser-known films, including the straight-to-DVD Wesley Snipes action-adventure *Game of Death* (2010) and the Hilary Swank thriller *The Resident* (2011), Ellis was excited about returning to her home state of Mississippi to shoot her next project: the big-screen adaptation of *The Help*, based on Kathryn Stockett's 2009 bestselling novel about a group of African American housekeepers living in racially segregated Mississippi during the early 1960s. "Even though *The Help* is fiction, what it did was get conversations started—especially in Mississippi—about that way of life," she shared with Larry Nemecek for *Emmys.com* (26 Oct 2015). "So that's the stuff that excites me, and that's what I feel is my purpose."

Released in August 2011, *The Help* struck a chord with critics and audiences alike, earning Ellis and the rest of the cast best ensemble prizes at the National Board of Review, Screen Actors Guild (SAG), and Women Film Critics Circle Awards, among others.

TAKES THE LEAD

In July 2012, after a recurring supporting role as Mary Dresden in the short-lived Ashley Judd spy series *Missing*, Ellis was tapped to portray Ann Pettway in the Lifetime television movie *Abducted: The Carlina White Story* (2012). To prepare for the role of a child kidnapper, she adopted a different approach. "I didn't want to make her a villain at all,'" she told Melanie Yvette for *Ebony* (2 Oct. 2012). "If I was being honest, I couldn't do that, because in her mind, she was not a villain. She was a desperate woman . . . . She felt it was her responsibility to be a mother to this child." By the following month, Ellis reunited with LL Cool J on *NCIS: Los Angeles*, playing his character's wife, a CIA agent.

In late 2013 Ellis traveled back to Mississippi to play soul singer and James Brown collaborator Vicki Anderson in the biopic *Get On Up* (2014), another directorial effort by Tate Taylor. That fall she starred as a New Orleans street performer stricken with Alzheimer's in the independent drama *Of Mind and Music* (2014). The role hit close to home for the actor, whose aunt suffers from the illness and whose mother has Parkinson's. By mid-December—a month after guest-starring on the Fox mystery-adventure

series *Sleepy Hollow*—Ellis had wrapped up her NCIS stint.

In January 2015 Ellis successfully auditioned for the lead role in the six-part miniseries *The Book of Negroes* (2015), an adaptation of Lawrence Hill's 2007 novel and her third project alongside Gooding. After being abducted from her West African village and sold into slavery, Ellis's character, Aminata Diallo, spends most of her life in captivity in the United States. The actor was attracted to her character's individuality. "I think that's what people are going to relate to—that she's unlike anybody that we've seen in a very long time," she told Nsenga Burton for the *Huffington Post* (20 Apr. 2015). "A lot of times the stories about the struggle for freedom are told from the male perspective, and this is very much a woman's story."

The Book of Negroes premiered in Canada in January and made its US debut a month later. For her performance, Ellis earned a best actress in a movie/mini-series nomination from the prestigious Critics Choice Television Awards (2015). She returned to episodic television in the fall of 2015, as a member of the main cast in the ABC police drama *Quantico*, which was renewed for a second season. Ellis also has a supporting role in *The Birth of a Nation*, a historical drama about Nat Turner, the leader of an 1831 slave rebellion in Virginia. The film premiered at the 2016 Sundance Festival, where it claimed the Audience Award and the Grand Jury Prize, and will be released to a wider audience in October 2016.

PERSONAL LIFE

In July 2015 the Mississippi-based actor announced plans to relocate her film company, Miss Myrtis Films, from the Magnolia State to Louisiana, in protest over the Mississippi state flag's inclusion of the Confederate battle flag in its design. Ellis has been very vocal regarding this issue, even going so far as to don a white dress emblazoned with the words "Take It Down Mississippi" to the 2015 NAACP Image Awards. She also expressed the same sentiment in a June 25, 2015, op-ed piece for *Time*. On June 14, 2016, she was one of the leaders of the Take It Down Rally: X the X, held in Washington, DC.

SUGGESTED READING

Backstage Staff. "Successful Actors Talk about Their Training." *Backstage*. Backstage, 9 Nov. 2011. Web. 12 June 2016.

Brenna, Susan. "Up and Coming: Aunjanue Ellis and Carrie Preston; Two Young Performers Ride *The Tempest*." *New York Times*. New York Times, 17 Dec. 1995. Web. 12 June 2016.

Burton, Nsenga. "*The Book of Negroes*: Life, Liberty and Love." *Huffington Post*. TheHuffPost.com, 20 Apr. 2015. Web. 12 June 2016.

Corliss, Richard. "A Ray of Light on a Blue Genius." *Time*. Time, 12 Oct. 2004. Web. 12
June 2016.

Nemecek, Larry. "The Wisdom of a Child." *Em-
mys.com*. Academy of Television Arts & Sciences, 26 Oct. 2016. Web. 12 June 2016.

Scott, A.O. "Portrait of Genius, Painted in Music." *New York Times*. New York Times, 29
Oct. 2004. Web. 12 June 2016.

Toby, Mekeisha Madden. "Black Girl Magic:
Aunjanue Ellis Thrives on Telling Our Sto-
ries." *Essence*. Time, 25 Sept. 2015. Web. 12
June 2016.

Yvette, Melanie. "Aunjanue Ellis on *Abducted:
The Carlina White Story*." *Ebony*. Johnson, 2
Oct. 2012. Web. 12 June 2016.

SELECTED WORKS

The Practice, 1999; *Men of Honor*, 2000; *Ray*,
2004; *The Help*, 2011; *Abducted: The Carlina
White Story*, 2012; *NCIS: Los Angeles*, 2013–14;
Get On Up, 2014; *Of Mind and Music*, 2014;
The Book of Negroes, 2015; *Quantico*, 2015

—Bertha Muteba

Cynthia Erivo

Born: January 8, 1987
Occupation: Actor

Within a year of graduating from London's Royal
Academy of Dramatic Art (RADA), Cynthia
Erivo had already established herself as one of
the fastest-rising stars in British musical theater,
with supporting parts in *Marine Parade* and *I
Was Looking at the Ceiling and Then I Saw the
Sky*, as well as leading female roles in *The Three
Musketeers and the Princess of Spain* and *The
Umbrellas of Cherbourg*. Her profile increased
significantly in 2011, when she took on the role
of Deloris Van Cartier in the UK production of
Sister Act, a stage adaptation of the 1992 blockbuster film starring Whoopi Goldberg. However,
Erivo achieved her biggest breakthrough two
years later, when she played the principal role in
the London stage production of Alice Walker's
novel *The Color Purple* (1982). Her critically acclaimed turn as Celie earned her the opportunity
to reprise the role on Broadway. After *The Color
Purple* debuted on Broadway to critical praise in
2015, the relative unknown quickly became an
overnight sensation, and went on to win a Tony
Award the following year.

EARLY LIFE AND EDUCATION

Cynthia Erivo was born in London, England, on
January 8, 1987, and grew up in the South London district of Stockwell. After noticing Erivo's

Gary Gershoff/Getty Images

early love of performing, her mother enrolled
her in extracurricular arts activities. With her
mother's encouragement, Erivo also learned to
play several musical instruments, including the
clarinet, viola, and soprano sax.

Erivo first realized her gift for singing when
she was five. While making her stage debut in
her primary school's nativity play, she received
a standing ovation for her rendition of "Silent
Night." "You don't realize what that means or
what it is. I just knew that it felt good," she
shared with Scott Simon for National Public Radio (NPR) (12 Dec. 2015). "From that moment
on, I got the bug and realized that whatever
sound is coming out of my mouth when I sing
. . . makes people happy."

Singing was not Erivo's only talent. While
attending La Retraite Roman Catholic Girls'
School in southwest London, the fifteen-year-
old took part in a workshop at the Young Vic Theatre, England's renowned youth theater company, and nabbed the female lead in the troupe's
summer production of William Shakespeare's
classic *Romeo and Juliet*, under the direction of
Rae McKen. Upon completing her secondary
education, Erivo pursued a degree in music psychology at the University of East London (UEL)
but grew disenchanted quickly. "I was bored.
I was passing everything really easily," she revealed to Matthew Hemley for *The Stage* (26 July
2015). "I was getting the results I wanted, but
nothing else."

At the end of her second year at UEL, Erivo fatefully crossed paths with McKen, who
persuaded Erivo to apply for the three-year BA
degree in acting at London's Royal Academy of

Dramatic Art. "I said, 'Absolutely not. . . . I'm not going to get in—that's just ridiculous,'" she recalled to Emma John for the *Guardian* (27 July 2015). "But she wouldn't let it go. She forced me to put in the application form, and when I got in I realized that was where I was supposed to be."

ACTING CAREER BEGINS

Erivo subsequently transferred to the renowned drama school, where she wanted to refine both of her performance skills. "At RADA, I could keep the singing up and focus on the acting, so when I came out I would be able to combine the two," she told Hemley. While a student, Erivo worked for Thomas Pink, an upscale menswear designer, but after she graduated from RADA in 2010, she turned down a senior position from the company to launch a full-time acting career. "It would have been too comfortable and easy, so I said to myself, 'when you leave RADA you leave Thomas Pink,' and that's what I did," she shared with Theo Bosanquet for *What's on Stage* (19 Nov. 2014).

Erivo's first theater job came in May 2010 at the annual Brighton Festival, where she costarred as Ellie Jackson in *Marine Parade*, a musical celebrating love and loss among nine people spending the end of summer at a ramshackle, waterfront bed-and-breakfast. Two months later she played a social worker, in another song-filled ensemble, *I Was Looking at the Ceiling and Then I Saw the Sky*, which follows seven twentysomethings from various social and ethnic backgrounds whose lives intersect in the wake of the 1994 earthquake in Los Angeles. By year's end Erivo had assumed the role of Constance, d'Artagnan's love interest, in a touring production of *The Three Musketeers and the Princess of Spain*.

BREAKTHROUGH AND THE BIRTH OF A STAR

In the spring of 2011, Erivo had her breakthrough playing Madeleine in the stage adaptation of Jacques Demy's 1964 musical *The Umbrellas of Cherbourg*, in which every line of dialogue is sung. Although Erivo had only one singing line, she impressed associate casting director Will Burton and was invited to try out for the lead in *Sister Act*. Throughout the audition process, the relative newcomer appeared to be the frontrunner. "They put out a national call . . . but when I went in for my audition I found they'd already called my agent to ask if I could be seen," she told David Whetstone for the *Journal* (25 June 2013).

After meeting with *Sister Act*'s producers and director, Erivo was cast as Deloris Van Cartier/ Sister Mary Clarence, subsequently embarking on a yearlong tour of the United Kingdom and Ireland that lasted from September 2011 to October 2012. By November she had lined up

her next project: Craig Adams's *Lift,* a contemporary musical exploring the innermost thoughts of eight strangers from various backgrounds that connect during a shared ride in a London subway elevator. Erivo portrayed a lap dancer yearning to be a classically trained dancer during the production's month-long run in early 2013 at London's Soho Theatre.

In April 2013, two months after *Lift* ended, Erivo nabbed the coveted lead role in the London stage production of Alice Walker's Pulitzer Prize–winning 1982 novel *The Color Purple*. John Doyle's revival consisted of a stripped-down, minimalistic stage design and focused on the adversity experienced by the main character. When *The Color Purple* made its European premiere in July 2013 at the Menier Chocolate Factory, Erivo proved herself to be up to the task.

"Without attempting to show how Celie physically ages from 1914 to 1945, Erivo makes you believe you are seeing a naive girl's acquisition of self-belief, and hits every note dead-center," Michael Billington gushed for the *Guardian* (16 July 2013). In her review for *Time Out London* (23 Aug. 2013), Daisy Bowie-Sell wrote: "The petite Cynthia Erivo gives a deliberately slow-build performance. It's a superb turn with a spine-tinglingly great climax that betrays her beguiling and impressive talent." *The Color Purple* ended its limited run in September 2013.

A FIXTURE ON LONDON'S WEST END

Over the following year, Erivo headlined two West End productions: *I Can't Sing! The X Factor Musical*, in which she played Chenice, a contestant on the Simon Cowell singing competition series, and the historical drama *Dessa Rose*, in which she starred as the title character, a young runaway slave in the nineteenth-century American South. After making its world premiere in late March 2014 at the London Palladium, *I Can't Sing* closed less than two months later because of disappointing ticket sales. London's Trafalgar Studios played host to the European premiere of *Dessa Rose* in the summer of 2014.

Erivo returned to the West End in early October, tackling the dual roles of Poins and the Earl of Douglas in Phyllida Lloyd's all-female production of William Shakespeare's *Henry IV*. Set in a women's prison, this modern, condensed version of *Henry IV* ran for a month at the Donmar Warehouse in London. (Erivo's stint gave her the opportunity to do boxing and weightlifting.) By March 2015, Erivo was gracing the stage as Puck in another month-long Shakespeare revival: Nick Bagnall's dark, contemporary interpretation of *A Midsummer Night's Dream*, in which Erivo makes a memorable, acrobatic entrance in a top hat and tails while dangling upside down from a trapeze.

BROADWAY AND A TONY AWARD

Erivo was the lone cast member from the UK production of *The Color Purple* who reprised her critically acclaimed role of Celie in John Doyle's Broadway adaptation of *The Color Purple*. Also attached to the project were talk-show host and coproducer Oprah Winfrey; Danielle Brooks, from the television show *Orange Is the New Black*, who was recruited to play Celie's daughter-in-law, Sofia; and Academy and Grammy Award winner Jennifer Hudson, who made her Broadway debut alongside Erivo in the role of Shug Avery. The role of Shug was later filled by Heather Headley.

Much like the original 2005 production, Doyle's version was well received when it was unveiled at the Bernard B. Jacobs Theatre in December 2015. Ben Brantley for the *New York Times* (10 Dec. 2015) singled out Erivo's character's evolution, from "battered, invisible wife to determined, self-reliant businesswoman." "The greatest joy of all," he says, "is the ascendancy of Ms. Erivo. . . . Like the rest of the show, she never oversells herself; she asks us politely but compellingly to listen, even when she speaks in a whisper. By production's end, Celie has developed a muscular voice that reaches to heaven, and Ms. Erivo has emerged as a bona fide star who lifts the audience to its feet."

Equally complimentary was Charles McNulty for the *Los Angeles Times* (10 Dec. 2015): "Relatively unheralded, [Erivo] brings stark humanity—and an astonishing voice—to the role of the abused young woman dismissed as ugly and worthless who somehow manages to persevere long enough to have her radiant light recognized. It's hard to imagine that Erivo's heart-stirring Broadway debut, a portrayal that derives enormous power from humility, won't be recognized once award season arrives." McNulty's prediction proved true. In May 2016, Erivo received a Tony Award nomination in the category of best performance by a leading actress in a musical and walked away with the statuette a month later. She also made Tony Award history as one of the four African American actors who swept the musical acting categories.

Erivo hopes to parlay her Broadway success into a film career. "I genuinely want everything," she told Bosanquet. "I want to be an artist in my own right, writing and singing my own songs, I want to be in films, and I want to be on stage." As a songwriter, Erivo penned the tune "Fly before You Fall," which appeared on the soundtrack for the romantic drama *Beyond the Lights* (2014).

PERSONAL LIFE

Erivo is in a relationship with Dean John-Wilson, a fellow British actor whom she met while starring in *Sister Act*. She is a vegan and enjoys boxing and yoga.

SUGGESTED READING

Bosanquet, Theo. "Leading Ladies: Cynthia Erivo—'I Want to Do Everything.'" *What's on Stage*. WhatsOnStage.com, 19 Nov. 2014. Web. 10 Sept. 2016.

Brantley, Ben. "'The Color Purple' on Broadway, Stripped to Its Essence." Rev. of *The Color Purple*, dir. John Doyle. *New York Times*. New York Times, 10 Dec. 2015. Web. 10 Sept. 2016.

Erivo, Cynthia. "Cynthia Erivo: 'You Have to Drag Me off the Stage.'" Interview by Matthew Hemley. *Stage*. The Stage Media, 26 July 2015. Web. 10 Sept. 2016.

Erivo, Cynthia. "Interview With: Sister Act Star Cynthia Erivo." Interview by David Whetstone. *Journal*. Trinity Mirror East, 25 June 2013. Web. 10 Sept. 2016.

McNulty, Charles. "'Color Purple' Musical on Broadway Has a Divine, Moving Spirit." Rev. of *The Color Purple*, dir. John Doyle. *Los Angeles Times*. Los Angeles Times, 10 Dec. 2015. Web. 10 Sept. 2016.

—*Bertha Muteba*

Rick Famuyiwa

Born: June 18, 1973
Occupation: Film director, producer, and screenwriter

Mainstream African American filmmakers are often pigeonholed into making one of two films: the gritty urban drama or the light-hearted romantic comedy. The Nigerian American writer-director Rick Famuyiwa has tried to reverse that trend. An alumnus of the University of Southern California (USC) School of Cinematic Arts, Famuyiwa launched his professional film career in the late 1990s with *The Wood* (1999), a romantic comedy set in his hometown of Inglewood, California. The film enjoyed commercial success and led Famuyiwa into making two more conventional romantic comedies, *Brown Sugar* (2002) and *Our Family Wedding* (2010). However, Famuyiwa's next film, *Dope* (2015), a coming-of-age drama about three youths growing up in Inglewood, deliberately worked to subvert African American stereotypes. Premiering at the 2015 Sundance Film Festival, the film enjoyed both critical and commercial success and helped establish Famuyiwa as one of the most provocative African American filmmakers working today.

EARLY LIFE AND EDUCATION

Rick Famuyiwa was born on June 18, 1973, in Berkeley, California, to Nigerian immigrant parents, Idowu and Florence Famuyiwa. When

Amanda Edwards/Getty Images

Famuyiwa was four years old, his parents separated. Along with his younger brother, Kevin, Famuyiwa had a peripatetic upbringing, living in various parts of California and in North Carolina. They eventually settled with their mother in Inglewood, California.

Famuyiwa grew up in a diverse, middle-class Inglewood community. As a result, he developed varied interests, ranging from basketball and hip-hop music to ones that ran counter to the typical experience of an urban African American youth, such as science-fiction films, skateboarding, and surfing. A self-described geek, Famuyiwa admittedly had trouble fitting in as a student at Inglewood's La Tijera School, and later, at St. Bernard High School, a private Catholic school in Los Angeles's beachside Playa del Rey neighborhood.

The tall and athletic Famuyiwa did, however, fit in on the basketball court. Standing six feet four inches tall, he became a standout as the small forward on St. Bernard's varsity basketball team. He honed his basketball skills by spending countless hours on Inglewood's public courts playing pickup games with friends and strangers. Exposed to people from all walks of life, from drug dealers to doctors, Famuyiwa would "eavesdrop and file away their conversations for the movies he'd someday make," Amy Nicholson wrote for *LA Weekly* (27 May 2015).

After graduating from St. Bernard High in 1991, Famuyiwa enrolled at USC in Los Angeles. His mother worked at the school as a medical technician, which helped him get a discount on tuition. During his freshman and sophomore years, Famuyiwa was a walk-on member of USC's nationally ranked basketball team, then overseen by coach George Raveling.

FROM BASKETBALL PLAYER TO FILMMAKER

Famuyiwa had entered USC as a political science major, with the intention of becoming a lawyer. That plan changed, however, after Famuyiwa watched Oliver Stone's 1991 masterpiece *JFK*, which was released during his freshman year of college. Famuyiwa, who had grown up loving films such as *Back to the Future* (1985), became captivated by the enormous controversy and lasting cultural impact generated by Stone's three-hour-plus film, which reimagines, in hypnotic and visually arresting fashion, the events that preceded and followed the 1963 assassination of President John F. Kennedy.

Famuyiwa resolved to make films like *JFK*, but unique to his experience as a first-generation Nigerian American, that would challenge people to think differently about things. His decision to pursue film as a career was supported by his parents, "but it was definitely something that they were scared about," as Famuyiwa told Terry Gross for *Fresh Air* (1 July 2015), referring to their initial hope that he would become a doctor or lawyer.

Famuyiwa's road to becoming a filmmaker, though, required persistence. He twice applied unsuccessfully to USC's prestigious School of Cinematic Arts before being accepted on his third try during the second semester of his junior year. There, he studied under and became mentored by Todd Boyd, a nationally renowned critical studies professor. Boyd introduced Famuyiwa to works by influential African American filmmakers such as Warrington and Reginald Hudlin and served as an advisor on his senior thesis film *Blacktop Lingo* (1996).

The twelve-minute short, about characters Famuyiwa used to encounter on Inglewood's public basketball courts, was one of only twenty-nine films selected from more than one thousand submissions to be screened at the 1996 Sundance Film Festival. Famuyiwa became the first undergraduate from USC to have a film shown at the festival, which is held every January in Park City, Utah. He graduated from USC with degrees in critical studies and film and television production in May 1996.

THE WOOD

In the wake of his high-profile Sundance appearance, Famuyiwa landed an agent and began attending dozens of meetings with Hollywood production executives. No deals materialized after Famuyiwa pitched several screenplays, however, including one about a college basketball point-shaving scandal. He has recalled being urged to write spins on raucous Afro-centric comedies such as the Hudlin brothers' *House Party* (1990), gritty urban dramas such as John Singleton's *Boyz n the Hood* (1991), and "all these weird interpretations of blaxploitation," as he noted to Nicholson.

After a humiliating meeting with a high-profile producer, Famuyiwa started writing new scripts that dealt with subjects he believed in but that were also accessible for mainstream audiences. During this time, he worked full time at a Niketown store in Beverly Hills to earn a living. Famuyiwa eventually teamed up with Boyd to write *The Wood*, a male-bonding romantic comedy about African American friendship in 1980s Inglewood. The script won an admirer in Michelle Satter, the founding director of the Sundance Institute's feature film program. On the invitation of Satter, Famuyiwa attended the institute's annual summer workshop for directors and screenwriters, where he further developed his script.

The Wood was soon picked up by producers Albert Berger and Ron Yerxa, who subsequently sold the film to MTV Films and Paramount Pictures. Shot on a modest budget of $6 million and released in July 1999, *The Wood* follows three friends from middle school, named Mike, Slim, and Roland (portrayed by Omar Epps, Richard T. Jones, and Taye Diggs, respectively), as they humorously reminisce about their journey from adolescence into adulthood. The premise of the film, whose title refers to the nickname for Inglewood, revolves around Mike and Slim's frantic efforts to find Roland on the day of his wedding. Based on many of Famuyiwa's real-life experiences with his friends, *The Wood* helped portray Inglewood in a different light, and as Nicholson put it, "was quietly rebellious: an all-black movie where nobody dealt drugs or died." The film was also a box-office success, grossing approximately $25 million.

MAINSTREAM SUCCESS

The Wood's commercial success helped Famuyiwa land more directing opportunities. His second feature-length film, *Brown Sugar*, was released in 2002 and distributed by Fox Searchlight Pictures. Like *The Wood*, the film features a predominantly African American cast and explores the evolution of lifelong friendships. It centers on two hip-hop-loving childhood friends and music-industry professionals, portrayed by Diggs and Sanaa Lathan, who become romantically involved after a series of unforeseen circumstances. Though firmly situated within the conventions of the standard romantic comedy, *Brown Sugar* offered a fresh take on the genre with fully realized characters, a multilayered plot, and a pulsating hip-hop soundtrack. Many critics, in particular, singled out the quality of the acting in the film, which grossed an impressive $28 million on a budget of $8 million.

Famuyiwa next collaborated with Michael Genet on the screenplay for *Talk to Me* (2007), a biographical film about the pioneering African American radio personality Ralph "Petey" Greene (played by Don Cheadle), who was based in Washington, DC. The film, directed by Kasi Lemmons, chronicles Greene's friendship with manager Dewey Hughes and his rise to national prominence in the 1960s after overcoming a life of crime. Despite receiving flak from Greene's surviving family members for its loose handling of facts, *Talk to Me* earned a positive critical response for its direction, writing, and riveting performances. For his work on the film, Famuyiwa earned a National Association for the Advancement of Colored People (NAACP) Image Award for outstanding writing in a motion picture in 2008.

It was also in 2008 when Famuyiwa began working on *Our Family Wedding*, which drew inspiration from Barack Obama's historic presidential election in November of that year. "At the time the entire debate seemed to be around Hispanics voting for an African American," Famuyiwa explained to Megan Angelo for the *New York Times* (5 Mar. 2010). "We're all going to have to deal with each other culturally. It felt like a great opportunity to tell that story without being preachy."

Released in March 2010, Famuyiwa's third feature film again treads upon the theme of marriage, this time focusing on the planned union of an African American man (Lance Gross) and a Mexican American woman (America Ferrera). It follows the young couple as they struggle to accommodate their respective families' cultural differences and traditions. *Our Family Wedding* was tepidly received by critics, many of whom felt the film failed to live up to the promise of its cast, which included Academy Award–winning actor Forest Whitaker as the cantankerous father of Gross's character.

RETURNING TO HIS ROOTS WITH *DOPE*

Wanting to break away from Hollywood studio conventions, Famuyiwa returned to Inglewood in an attempt to rediscover his artistic voice. After *Our Family Wedding*, Famuyiwa explained to Lorraine Ali for the *Los Angeles Times* (12 June 2015), "it became more frustrating not being able to speak and say things I wanted to say. I wanted to rediscover something artistically that I felt I was losing and say things I never really had a chance to say."

Upon returning to Inglewood, Famuyiwa found inspiration in the form of avant-garde hip-hop artists such as Kendrick Lamar, Tyler the Creator, and A$AP Rocky. Intrigued by their unique interpretation of longstanding hip-hop traditions, Famuyiwa started working on a script that harked back to the harsh realism of films such as *Boyz n the Hood* and *Menace II Society* (1993) but that also offered an updated perspective on Inglewood youths. Famuyiwa aimed "to redefine that experience, the coming-of-age film, for a new generation," as he explained to Ronda Racha Penrice for the *Root* (17 June 2015).

Famuyiwa's resultant film, *Dope*, revolves around the story of Malcolm Adekanbi (Shameik Moore), a Harvard-bound high school senior and black hip-hop-loving "geek" living in Inglewood's rough-and-tumble "Bottoms" neighborhood. It follows Malcolm as he embarks on a series of wild exploits with his two best friends, Jib (Tony Revolori), an Indian nerd, and Diggy (Kiersey Clemons), a black lesbian. The three geek out on things such as 1990s hip-hop music and culture, vintage clothing, BMX riding, and Japanese comic books and front a punk-rock band called Awreeoh (pronounced "oreo"). When Malcolm unwittingly becomes mixed up in a drug deal, Jib and Diggy come to his aid.

Produced by Whitaker, Pharrell Williams (who also served as music supervisor), and Sean "Diddy" Combs, *Dope* premiered at the Sundance Film Festival in January 2015. There, the film became a sensation, sparking a bidding war among distributors. Open Road Films and Sony eventually bought the film for $7 million, in addition to a reported $15 million for marketing and promotion. Upon its nationwide release in June 2015, *Dope* received widespread acclaim from critics for its smart and fresh approach to subverting African American stereotypes. The film earned almost $18 million at the box office. "It's not a 'hood film or romantic comedy or Tyler Perry. It's like there's only two or three things black films can be, and it's none of those," Famuyiwa explained to Ali. Instead, Famuyiwa added, it can be looked at as a "*Risky Business* for the social-media generation." His next film, *Confirmation*, about the 1991 Supreme Court nomination hearings involving Clarence Thomas and Anita Hill, is scheduled to be released by HBO Films in 2016.

PERSONAL LIFE

Famuyiwa has been married to Glenita Mosley, whom he met at USC, since 1999. The couple has a daughter, Sade.

SUGGESTED READING

Ali, Lorraine. "The Comedy-Drama *Dope* Defies 'Black Film' Expectations." *Los Angeles Times*. Tribune, 12 June 2015. Web. 16 Feb. 2016.

Angelo, Megan. "Wedding Plan: Jump a Broom or Eat Goat?" *New York Times*. New York Times, 5 Mar. 2010. Web. 16 Feb. 2016.

Famuyiwa, Rick. "*Dope* Director on Geekdom, the N-Word and Confronting Racism with Comedy." Interview by Terry Gross. *Fresh Air*. NPR, 1 July 2015. Web. 16 Feb. 2016.

Nicholson, Amy. "The Fresh, New Comedy *Dope* Hopes to Redefine Inglewood." *LA Weekly*. LA Weekly, 27 May 2015. Web. 16 Feb. 2016.

Penrice, Ronda Racha. "Rick Famuyiwa: A *Dope* Director." *Root*. Univision, 17 June 2015. Web. 16 Feb. 2016.

Weddle, David. "The Path." *Los Angeles Times*. Los Angeles Times, 23 Mar. 1997. Web. 16 Feb. 2016.

SELECTED WORKS

Blacktop Lingo, 1996; *The Wood*, 1999; *Brown Sugar*, 2002; *Talk to Me*, 2007; *Our Family Wedding*, 2010; *Dope*, 2015

—Chris Cullen

Carmen Fariña

Born: April 5, 1943
Occupation: New York City schools chancellor

Carmen Fariña is the New York City schools chancellor—the top position in the New York City Department of Education, which serves the largest school district in the United States. A veteran New York City school teacher of twenty-two years, she was appointed to the post in 2013 by newly elected mayor Bill de Blasio.

EARLY LIFE AND EDUCATION

Carmen Fariña was born Carmen Guillén in New York City in 1943. She is the oldest of three children born to Spanish immigrants who fled the dictatorship of Francisco Franco in the 1930s. Her mother was a homemaker and her father was a maintenance worker at a New York City hospital.

As a child, she attended St. Charles Borromeo, a parochial school in Brooklyn, New York, where she was the only Spanish-speaking kindergarten student. Proud of her heritage even at a young age, she was once punished with suspension for arguing with a teacher who defended the Franco regime from which her family had fled.

It was as a sophomore in high school that Fariña decided to become a teacher, switching from a nonacademic courseload of typing and stenography classes to college-track math and language coursework. She attended Pace University as an undergraduate before embarking on a career as a teacher at New York Public School 29 (PS 29) in the Cobble Hill neighborhood of Brooklyn.

The reading curriculum designed by Fariña at PS 29 raised her profile among educators in

New York City. Rates of student achievement in the program were so high that the state Board of Education required it be expanded for grades five through nine.

Fariña later worked for five years as the core curriculum coordinator for District 15 of the New York Public Schools system.

SCHOOL ADMINISTRATOR

Beginning in 1991, Fariña spent ten years as principal of PS 6 on the Upper East Side of Manhattan, elevating the school from seventy-sixth in math and reading among New York City public elementary schools to a position in the top ten. In 2001, she became superintendent of New York School District 15 in Brooklyn.

In 2004, Fariña was appointed the city's deputy chancellor for teaching and learning. She utilized her time in the post to bolster the New York City school system's early education programs, allocating $40 million to teacher training, Saturday classes, study and organizational skills workshops, and parent counseling. Fariña spent two years in that capacity under Chancellor Joel Klein and Mayor Michael Bloomberg before her retirement in 2006.

Following her retirement, Fariña worked part time as an education advocate and was critical of the educational policies of the Bloomberg administration, namely its insistence on the use of standardized testing to rate schools.

She served as an unofficial consultant on the educational initiatives of Democrat Bill de Blasio's 2013 mayoral campaign. The two were first colleagues during de Blasio's tenure on the District 15 school board when Fariña was superintendent there.

After being elected to the mayoralty, de Blasio implored Fariña to accept an appointment as schools chancellor, a request she initially denied in preference to remaining retired and spending time with her grandchildren. Fariña ultimately decided to accept the post, officially taking the position in December 2013.

IMPACT

Carmen Fariña's impact on the nation's largest school system has been substantial in her brief tenure as chancellor. She has come to personify the de Blasio administration's attempt to dissolve tension between parents and the city's school system by improving methods of communication and fostering a relationship between school officials and the families of their students.

In addition to adopting the emerging educational benchmarks known as the Common Core standards, Fariña has also worked to expand access to early childhood education among New York City's youth, including supporting de Blasio's universal prekindergarten initiative.

With her success in creating contemporary education systems better adapted to the needs of modern students, Carmen Fariña has established a legacy as a major force in transforming the city's most troubled schools from those riddled with the inefficiency of antiquated policy to schools at the forefront of the nation's most progressive education movements.

Fostering student empowerment and enhancing the region's technology programs have also been a key part of the de Blasio administration's education initiative. Fariña has placed particular emphasis on the administration's efforts to transform public schooling as a training ground that prepares students for both secondary education and for careers in the city's future workforce.

PERSONAL LIFE

Fariña had been planning to move to Florida with her husband, Tony Fariña, prior to her appointment as schools chancellor. The couple has two daughters.

SUGGESTED READING

Fariña, Carmen, and Laura Kotch. *A School Leader's Guide to Excellence: Collaborating Our Way to Better Schools.* Portsmouth: Heinemann, 2008. Print.

Hartocollis, Anemona. "In School; A Principal with a Will of Steel Makes a Public School as Prestigious as a Private One." *New York Times.* New York Times, 24 Feb. 1999. Web. 11 June 2014.

Hernandez, C., Javier. "Veteran of City School System Is Said to Be Next Chancellor." *New York Times.* New York Times, 29 Dec. 2013. Web. 11 June 2014.

Layton, Lyndsey, and Michael Alison Chandler. "De Blasio Puts Education Reform at the Top of His Agenda as New York City Mayor." *Washington Post.* Washington Post, 8 Nov. 2013. Web. 11 June 2014.

Sullivan, Susan, and Jeffrey Glanz. *Supervision That Improves Teaching and Learning: Strategies and Techniques.* Thousand Oaks: Corwin, 2009. Print.

—*John Pritchard*

Stefan Fatsis

Born: April 1, 1963
Occupation: Journalist and author

Stefan Fatsis is a critically acclaimed sportswriter who has written extensively on professional sports for a number of major newspapers and magazines. He is also a popular voice on

Photo by 48states [CC BY-SA 3.0] or GFDL via
Wikimedia Commons

National Public Radio's (NPR's) show *All Things Considered*, for which he provides insights into the business and politics of professional sports, and on Slate.com's sports podcast *Hang Up and Listen*. He is the author of three books about competitive sports and continues to write about issues related to his passions, such as whether or not young children should be allowed to play football or if the editors of Merriam-Webster are doing the right thing by removing obscure or seemingly outdated words from the company's various dictionaries.

EARLY LIFE AND EDUCATION

Born on April 1, 1963, and raised in Pelham, New York, Stefan Fatsis is the son of Anita Fatsis and Michael T. Fatsis. His father had once been a ship's captain who went on to become the president of the Argonaut Trading Agency, a New York–based shipping agency. As a child at Prospect Hill Elementary School in Pelham, Fatsis, though small and light for his age, loved to play sports, particularly football; however, he quickly realized he would never become a professional player. Fatsis recalled his lack of childhood athleticism in the first chapter of his book *A Few Seconds of Panic: A 5-Foot-8, 170-Pound, 43-Year-Old Sportswriter Plays in the NFL* (2008): "In the fifth grade, I intercepted a pass and, with nothing but open space between me and the end zone, slipped and fell. . . . But I did play high-school soccer, not badly for 1976 to 1980 but badly enough to recognize that I had no chance of making my Division I college team. I played intramurals instead."

Fatsis studied at the University of Pennsylvania, where he earned a bachelor's degree in American civilization in 1985. While an undergraduate, he worked as a staff writer on the campus newspaper.

WORKING AS A SPORTSWRITER

Upon graduation, he got a job as a reporter for the Associated Press (AP), working out of Athens, Greece, and later Philadelphia, Boston, and New York City. In 1995, Fatsis joined the staff of the *Wall Street Journal*, where he worked as a sportswriter until 2006. Beginning in 1998 he also worked concurrently on the NPR show *All Things Considered*, where he has a weekly segment in which he discusses various professional sports and their businesses. He is also a featured reporter on *Hang Up and Listen*, a weekly sports podcast available on Slate.com.

Fatsis's writing had been published in a number of major periodicals, including the *Atlantic*, the *New Republic*, the *New Yorker*, the *New York Times*, *Slate*, *Sports Illustrated*, and the *Washington Post*. His work has also been collected in the following anthologies: *The Enlightened Bracketologist* (2007), *The Best Creative Nonfiction Vol. 2* (2008), *Anatomy of Baseball* (2008), and *Top of the Order: Twenty-Five Writers Pick Their Favorite Baseball Player of All Time* (2010), among others. He also maintains an active social-media presence on Facebook and Twitter.

BESTSELLING AUTHOR

Fatsis's first book, *Wild and Outside: How a Renegade Minor League Revived the Spirit of Baseball in America's Heartland*, was published to critical acclaim in 1995 and went on to become a best seller. In it, he describes the time he spent as a sportswriter following the Northern League, an independent six-team minor-league circuit that, unlike other minor leagues, has little financial support from any of the clubs in Major League Baseball (MLB). Centered in mostly the Midwest and Canada, the league provides the sort of intimate baseball experience for fans that is often missing in the corporate big leagues. The teams comprise mostly players of a caliber not quite at the major-league level, though some younger players seek to make the jump into the MLB and some older participants once played in the major leagues. The book's main thesis is that baseball should be a thrill for the fans—and that the maverick Northern League wants to keep it that way. A critic for *Kirkus Reviews* (15 Apr. 1995) described *Wild and Outside* as a "meticulous, heartfelt chronicle of a baseball minor league's struggle to return to the game the fun and intimacy that's all too often missing from the major league game."

Fatsis's next work of nonfiction, *Word Freak: Heartbreak, Triumph, Genius, and Obsession in* the *World of Competitive Scrabble Players*, was published in 2001 and also reached best-seller status. In this book, instead of just reporting on it, Fatsis became involved in the world of competitive Scrabble, which had been invented by an unemployed architect, Alfred Butts, during the Great Depression, but did not become popular until the 1950s. In addition to detailing the history of the game, he describes how he trained himself to become a competitive Scrabble player by not only memorizing lists of obscure words but also learning how to strategize and use the board most effectively. He eventually concluded that the experience was beneficial to him, both in the way in which it helped him to excise some of his own personal demons as well as to make new friends with a similar passion for Scrabble. Of *Word Freak*, a reviewer remarked in *Kirkus Reviews* (1 May 2001): "Despite an occasional overload of detail, this is a provocative look at the world of games and the way the mind works with words." An updated version of *Word Freak* was published for its tenth anniversary. Fatsis continues to play Scrabble competitively in tournaments.

A FEW SECONDS OF PANIC

Fatsis's third book, *A Few Seconds of Panic: A 5-Foot-8, 170-Pound, 43-Year-Old Sportswriter Plays in the NFL* (2008), is perhaps the one for which he is most famous. In it, Fatsis purposely sets out to write a sequel of sorts to George Plimpton's *Paper Lion* (1966), an account of the famed author's attendance at the Detroit Lions' NFL camp in 1963, to show how difficult it would be for an average person like himself to play with professional athletes. Unlike Plimpton, however, Fatsis wanted to at least attempt to train for the experience of playing in the National Football League (NFL) and began training as a kicker, believing that position was best suited to his meager athletic abilities. He also wanted to show how the league had changed in the forty or so years since Plimpton worked out with the Lions. In an interview with Scott Simon for NPR (26 July 2008), Fatsis recalled, "I spent a year with a personal trainer, gaining weight, getting into shape. I put on about a dozen pounds. And then I found Paul Woodside, a kicking coach nearby in Northern Virginia. And Paul drilled me for four or five months, and he taught me how to kick. And he taught me the emotional part of kicking, too. . . . By the end I was kicking 35- and 40-yard field goals, which I think is pretty good because if you stand on a football field 40 yards away from the goal posts, you'll realize just how far that is." (For comparison, in 1976, Ove Johansson set the current football field-goal record of 69 yards.)

The book not only depicts Fatsis's personal journey during the summer of 2006, when he trained as a placekicker with the Denver Broncos, but also gives a view to the experiences of dozens of players at training camp, many of whom will never make the final cut to play in the NFL. He describes the emotional and financial tolls these players endure in order to pursue their dreams of football glory. *A Few Seconds of Panic* became both a best seller and a critically acclaimed work. In a review for the *Washington Post* (27 July 2008), Steven V. Roberts wrote, "Fatsis might not be a real Bronco, but he's a real sportswriter, and this book tells you what brings real Broncos to tears."

PERSONAL LIFE

Fatsis has been married since 2002 to Melissa Block, the cohost of the radio show *All Things Considered,* which airs weekdays on NPR. The couple lives near Washington, DC, and has a daughter, Chloe, who is as passionate about sports as her father. Fatsis proposed to Block at a popular restaurant in Paris, France, as they finished dessert. The *New York Times* (3 Mar. 2002) described the setting: "Mr. Fatsis pulled out a bag containing a pair of Scrabble racks and two sets of tiles, which he then arranged in alphabetical order before Ms. Block. The first read, ILLOUWY; the second, AEMMRRY. Tears welling in her eyes, Ms. Block quickly unscrambled the letters and turned the racks around to face Mr. Fatsis. He then offered a more formal proposal, to which she nodded and cried out her approval."

SUGGESTED READING

"Catching Up with Author and Wannabe Broncos K Stefan Fatsis." *Sports Business Daily.* American City Business Journals, 8 July 2008. Web. 9 Nov. 2015.

Roberts, Steven V. "Paper Bronco." *Washington Post.* Washington Post, 27 Oct. 2008. Web. 23 Oct. 2015.

Simon, Scott. "Sportswriter Gets His Foot in the Door with Broncos." *NPR.* NPR, 26 July 2008. Web. 23 Oct. 2015.

Tone, Joe. "Ten Years of Scrabble Playing Later, Word Freak Author Stefan Fatsis Is Still Freaking." *Dallas Observer.* Dallas Observer, 9 Aug. 2011. Web. 9 Nov. 2015.

SELECTED WORKS

Wild and Outside: How a Renegade Minor League Revived the Spirit of Baseball in America's Heartland, 1995; *Word Freak: Heartbreak, Triumph, Genius, and Obsession in the World of Competitive Scrabble Players,* 2001; *A Few Seconds of Panic: A 5-Foot-8, 170-Pound, 43-Year-Old Sportswriter Plays in the NFL,* 2008

—*Christopher Mari*

Julian Fellowes

Born: August 17, 1949
Occupation: Screenwriter

Julian Fellowes is an Academy Award–winning screenwriter, novelist, and former actor best known as the creator and writer of the popular, Emmy Award–winning television series *Downton Abbey*, which aired in the United Kingdom on Independent Television (ITV) from 2010 to 2015 and in the United States on Public Broadcasting Service (PBS) from 2011 to 2016. As a storyteller, Fellowes's subject is typically the sometimes-sordid affairs of the English upper crust. His breakthrough script *Gosford Park* (2001), a murder mystery set on an English estate in the 1930s and directed by the late, legendary Robert Altman, earned him an Academy Award for best screenplay in 2002.

An English aristocrat himself, he followed an unlikely career path that began in a drama club in Cambridge in the 1960s. He was an intermittently employed character actor of the stage and screen for the next thirty years. Approaching sixty, Fellowes found that his encyclopedic knowledge of England's social culture was more valuable than his theatrical training. After being hired to pen *Gosford Park*, Fellowes has never looked back, though he has admitted to feeling wary of holding on to his successes: "I always feel that there's some giant hand about to lean in and snatch it all away from me, saying, 'That wasn't meant for you,'" he shared with Alex Witchel for the *New York Times* (8 Sept. 2011).

EARLY LIFE AND ACTING CAREER

Fellowes was born in Cairo, Egypt, on August 17, 1949, and raised largely in East Sussex, England. His father, Peregrine Fellowes, was a civil engineer who worked as a diplomat for the Foreign Office and later as an employee of the oil company Shell. His mother, Olwen Stuart-Jones, has been described as an independently minded and socially ambitious woman. Fellowes is the youngest of four boys; of his brothers, Rory Fellowes is a playwright and film animator and David Fellowes is an actor and writer. He grew up, thanks to his father's family, on the periphery of the stately and staid world he would become famous for describing, later recalling in interviews his days at boarding school and vacationing in the country. The characters played by actor Maggie Smith in *Downton Abbey* and *Gosford Park*—both of whom have a dry wit and firm views about English social tradition—are based on one of his real-life great-aunts.

Fellowes enrolled at Magdalene College in Cambridge in 1966, where he joined a comedic drama troupe called the Footlights. He also attended the Webber Douglas Academy

Mingle MediaTV (Julian Fellowes - DSC_0080)/CC BY-SA 2.0/ Wikimedia Commons

of Dramatic Art, where he earned money by writing romance and historical fiction under a pseudonym. After graduating in 1973, he made a name for himself as a character actor on television shows and in the theater. "I played horrible, corrupt conservative ministers in camel-hair coats, or I played lovable silly asses who fell over," he recalled to David Kamp for *Vanity Fair* (8 Nov. 2012).

After moving to Los Angeles in 1981, Fellowes narrowly missed out on joining the cast of the popular television series *Fantasy Island* after the French actor Hervé Villechaize was fired from the show. He appeared in a handful of made-for-television movies in the United States, including *Rita Hayworth: The Love Goddess* (1983), about the 1940s film siren. Fellowes played Hayworth's third husband's chauffeur, who served as a confidant for the famous actor. Lynda Carter, who played Hayworth, recalled that during filming, Fellowes served as her confidante as well. "Julian was one of those people you gravitated towards just because he was so . . . *nice*," she told Kamp. Returning to London in 1984, he later overcame initial network trepidation regarding the market value of period drama to successfully write adaptations of *Little Lord Fauntleroy* (1995) and *The Prince and the Pauper* (1996) for the BBC before appearing in several episodes of the sitcom *Monarch of the Glen* between 2000 and 2005.

EARLY WRITING CAREER AND *GOSFORD PARK*

Fellowes befriended American film executive Ileen Maisel in London in the 1990s. At the time, Maisel was working on an adaptation of the

John Fowles novel *Daniel Martin* (1977), about a man coming of age in England in the 1960s. During their weekly breakfasts, Maisel was surprised to find that Fellowes had strong opinions about the project. "Julian was smarter than any of the writers I was working with," she recalled to Kamp. The *Daniel Martin* project fizzled, but Maisel introduced Fellowes to the actor and producer Bob Balaban. The two men worked briefly on an adaptation of an Anthony Trollope novel. This project also never came to pass, but Balaban was deeply impressed by Fellowes and, around 2000, introduced him to the legendary auteur Altman. Balaban and Altman were in discussions to make an English murder mystery in the mold of Agatha Christie. According to Balaban, Fellowes, with his intimate knowledge of twentieth-century English country life, was a natural choice to write the script. It was an extraordinary coup for a budding screenwriter—especially one who was also already in his fifties. "Yes. I became the honorary president of the last-chance saloon. There was a feeling in Hollywood that if you had anything, it would manifest itself by your early to middle twenties, and that once you were fifty, if it hadn't happened, it clearly wasn't there. It was a nice thing to do, to make people think: ooh, perhaps I'd better not bin this script just because it's by a bald git," he joked to Rachel Cooke for the *Guardian* (25 Feb. 2012).

Gosford Park was a well-received marriage of Altman's anarchic style and Fellowes's love for historical detail as well as complex, multicharacter stories; Altman's influence makes *Gosford Park* the cynical cousin to Fellowes's later works about the same world. The film is a mystery but also, as Stephen Holden wrote for the *New York Times* (26 Dec. 2001), a "social satire" about wealth, class, and, unusually, the relationship between the English aristocracy and American Hollywood. The plot is complicated, but the central question of *Gosford Park* revolves around the murder of the lord of the manor at an English country estate in 1932. The large cast of characters includes an acerbic countess (Maggie Smith); a composer and film star named Ivor Novello (Jeremy Northam), a nonfictional character; a Hollywood producer (Bob Balaban) and his valet/bisexual lover (Ryan Phillippe); as well as a host of disaffected servants, with Helen Mirren playing the housekeeper. The late Roger Ebert, reviewing the film for the *Chicago Sun-Times* (1 Jan. 2002), called *Gosford Park* "a joyous and audacious achievement," describing it as "a comedy about selfishness, greed, snobbery, eccentricity, and class exploitation." Although the film was nominated for a handful of Academy Awards, Fellowes received the only one, for best screenplay.

DOWNTON ABBEY

In interviews, Fellowes has often divided his life into two radical sections: before and after *Gosford Park*. The Englishman's stunning turn as an Academy Award winner gave way to a host of writing opportunities. For the first time in his life, he was constantly in demand. In 2004, he cowrote the screen adaptation of William Makepeace Thackeray's *Vanity Fair*, starring Reese Witherspoon, and in 2005, he wrote and directed the British thriller *Separate Lies*. It was at this point that he also began to apply his writing talent and insight into English social classes to the novel form, publishing *Snobs* in the United Kingdom in 2004 and in the United States in 2005, which became a best seller. In 2009, in addition to writing the historical drama *The Young Victoria*, starring Emily Blunt, about the early years of Queen Victoria's reign in the 1830s, his second best-selling novel, *Past Imperfect*, was published in the United States. The following year, he cowrote *The Tourist*, a romantic thriller featuring Angelina Jolie and Johnny Depp.

His output during that period (and since) lends credence to the opinion of colleagues such as Balaban, who told Witchel, "He doesn't procrastinate. He doesn't hide. He works like a demon." Still, when producer Gareth Neame approached him with an idea for a serial drama about life on a country estate during the turn-of-the-century Edwardian period, Fellowes hesitated. To paraphrase Neame, Fellowes was worried that returning to a subject so closely related to *Gosford Park* might be a jinx. However, the material captured the writer and, within a few weeks, Fellowes sent Neame a detailed outline for the show's first season.

Downton Abbey premiered in late 2010 on ITV, a British television network. It first aired in the United States on PBS in early 2011 and proved almost immediately popular with American audiences as well. In attempting to explain the success of the show, aside from a possibly nostalgic yearning for a more stringent but predictable time, Fellowes told Witchel, "I think one of the things we got right with *Downton* was that we treat the characters of the servants and the family exactly the same. Some of them are nice, some of them are not nice, some of them are funny, some of them are not, but there is no division between the servants and the family to mark that."

The show begins in 1912 with the sinking of the *Titanic* (a topic Fellowes also explored further by writing the four-part miniseries *Titanic* in 2012), following its characters through World War I and the next twelve turbulent years of their lives. The series, which ran for six successful seasons, was noted for its heart in addition to captivating plotlines. Comparing it to Jane Austen and the Evelyn Waugh classic novel

Brideshead Revisited (1945), Meredith Blake, writing for the *A.V. Club* (9 Jan. 2011), deemed *Downton Abbey* a "playful, irresistible melodrama." It was nominated for a slew of awards throughout its run, and in 2011, Fellowes won an Emmy Award for outstanding writing for a miniseries. (The show was originally conceived as a miniseries.) *Downton Abbey* enjoyed a lesser popularity in England as it went on, which some have speculated could have had something to do with Fellowes's politics. A lifelong member of the Conservative Party, in 2011, Fellowes was given a seat in the House of Lords and the title Baron Fellowes of West Stafford. Although Americans were intrigued by the unusual social mechanisms of the English, the English themselves were more likely to view the show as an endorsement of outmoded class hierarchies.

Though *Downton Abbey* came to an end in 2015 in the United Kingdom and 2016 in the United States, Fellowes had accomplished his goal to finish the series on good terms: "I think it's good to leave when they're in mourning as opposed to intensely relieved," he stated to Alexandra Wolfe for the *Wall Street Journal* (11 Dec. 2015).

OTHER PROJECTS

Anticipating *Downton Abbey*'s eventual conclusion, Fellowes had continued working on other ventures. In 2015, he teamed up with Andrew Lloyd Webber, the musical theater maestro behind *The Phantom of the Opera* and *Cats*, to write the book for a musical adaptation of the 2003 film *School of Rock*. He was nominated for a Tony Award in 2016.

In 2016, Fellowes wrote a miniseries titled *Doctor Thorne*, adapted from an 1858 Trollope novel of the same name, that aired first in the United Kingdom before streaming on Amazon later in the year in the United States; the series inevitably drew comparisons to *Downton Abbey*. His most recent novel, *Belgravia*, is set in the 1840s and was released as a serial with audio on an app before being published in book form in the summer of 2016.

PERSONAL LIFE

Fellowes met Emma Kitchener in 1989, and they married in 1990. Kitchener-Fellowes, who is fifteen years Fellowes's junior, is the great-grandniece of the well-known Lord Kitchener, whose face adorned posters during World War I, urging young men to enlist. In addition to her philanthropic activities, Kitchener-Fellowes serves as a lady-in-waiting to Princess Michael of Kent. The couple has one son named Peregrine, after Fellowes's father. After his big break in 2002, Fellowes, who also owns an apartment in London, purchased a seventeenth-century manor house called Stafford House in Dorset.

SUGGESTED READING

Cooke, Rachel. "Julian Fellowes: Captain Invincible." *Guardian.* Guardian News and Media, 25 Feb. 2012. Web. 6 Sept. 2016.

Ebert, Roger. Rev. of *Gosford Park*, dir. Robert Altman. *RogerEbert.com.* Ebert Digital, 1 Jan. 2002. Web. 6 Sept. 2016.

Kamp, David. "The Most Happy Fellowes." *Vanity Fair.* Condé Nast, 8 Nov. 2012. Web. 6 Sept. 2016.

Witchel, Alex. "Behind the Scenes with the Creator of *Downton Abbey*." *New York Times.* New York Times, 8 Sept. 2011. Web. 6 Sept. 2016.

Wolfe, Alexandra. "Julian Fellowes's Class Act." *Wall Street Journal.* Dow Jones, 11 Dec. 2015. Web. 6 Sept. 2016.

SELECTED WORKS

Gosford Park, 2001; *Vanity Fair*, 2004; *Separate Lies*, 2005; *Past Imperfect*, 2008; *The Young Victoria*, 2009; *The Tourist*, 2010; *Downton Abbey*, 2010–15; *Doctor Thorne*, 2016

—Molly Hagan

Elizabeth Fenn

Born: September 22, 1959
Occupation: Historian

Elizabeth A. Fenn, a professor of history at the University of Colorado Boulder, was naturally gratified to win a Pulitzer Prize for her 2014 book, *Encounters at the Heart of the World: A History of the Mandan People.* "Academics are like everyone else—we love accolades," she told John Elmes for the *Times Higher Education* (28 May 2015). "But I don't know anyone who pursues their work with this in mind. Besides, prizes like this result from shared effort. Writing a book is a solitary experience, yet none of us works alone. My colleagues helped; the Mandan people helped; my husband, friends, family, and predecessors helped."

She hopes that the book, about a North Dakota tribe whose numbers plummeted precipitously following their encounter with European settlers in the 1830s, will serve a greater purpose. "I hope the Pulitzer is not so much an end as a beginning," she explained to Elmes. "The prize recognizes the central, foundational place of native peoples in American history. I'm not the first scholar to make a case for this, but the prize helps to move us all ahead."

EARLY LIFE AND EDUCATION

Elizabeth Anne Fenn was born on September 22, 1959, in Arlington, California. When she was five years old, her family settled in New Jersey, where she grew up. "New Jersey cultivated toughness and gave me a bit of an attitude," she told Elmes. "I learned how to look out for myself, but this came with an impatience and selfishness that I still struggle to shake."

An avid athlete who counted her father as one of her biggest supporters, she played field hockey in the fall, basketball in the winter, and softball in the spring and summer. Although Fenn has described herself as a lackluster student, she became passionately interested in history while attending Duke University in Durham, North Carolina. As an undergraduate, she lived for a time in a canvas teepee she erected on a tobacco farm on the outskirts of campus, showering at the school gym each morning rather than submitting to the constraints of dorm life. "It was fun until I ran out of firewood," she recalled to Emily Eakin for the *New York Times* (8 Sept. 2001). During the summers she worked as a landscaper and conservationist at Arches National Park in Utah.

Fenn wrote an honors thesis on Native Americans in the Hudson Bay fur trade, earned her undergraduate history degree from Duke in 1981, and then began graduate work at Yale University in New Haven, Connecticut. Along with fellow historian Peter H. Wood, she cowrote *Natives and Newcomers: The Way We Lived in North Carolina before 1770* (1983), but as she was preparing to write a doctoral dissertation on millenarianism in Native American culture, she found herself at a crossroad, unsure about continuing in academia. "I think I was just kind of bored," she explained to Eakin.

WORKING AS A MECHANIC

Somewhat fortuitously, her dilapidated Datsun began giving her trouble about this time, leading to an epiphany. "I took the valve cover off and for the first time in my life saw the inside of a car engine," she said. "It was a whole new world, all glistening and clean." Fenn enrolled at the Durham Technical Community College, where she studied automotive repair and then embarked on a new phase of life—fixing cars for a living at a series of local garages. "Most people would rather know a good auto mechanic than a historian," she quipped to Eakin.

Although she has joked that the best part of being a mechanic was getting to go home at night to drink beer and read whatever she liked, she found additional benefits. Working in "pretty much white, redneck" auto shops, as she told Clay Evans for *Colorado Arts and Sciences Magazine* (Dec. 2011), she came away with a valuable lesson. "It's okay to really love people with whom

I differ profoundly," she said. "You can disagree with someone, and that doesn't mean they are the devil incarnate. It made me very comfortable with difference." She kept that lesson in mind upon her return to academia, allowing students to freely speak their minds without worrying that they would alienate her.

That return to academia did not come for years, however. One day, while reading a French novel called *The Horseman on the Roof* (1951) by Jean Giono, which takes place in the midst of a cholera epidemic, she started thinking about epidemics and was reminded of her undergraduate research on fur traders, who had faced smallpox. "[After that] I felt compelled to write my dissertation," she told Sally Hicks for the Duke University website (30 Aug. 2002). "Could you write this story filled with the pathos and humanity this disease elicits?" After discovering that administrators at Yale would allow her to write her thesis without repeating any coursework or exams, she began writing up her proposal while working part time at Cross Creek BP and Auto Center on Guess Road in Durham.

CAREER AS A HISTORIAN

Fenn earned her PhD in history from Yale in 1999 and accepted a teaching post at George Washington University in Washington, DC. Her dissertation became her second book, *Pox Americana: The Great Smallpox Epidemic of 1775–82*, which was published in 2001 by Hill and Wang, a division of Farrar, Straus and Giroux that focused on works of historical nonfiction. (In the foreword of the book, she thanks Wayne Clayton, her boss at the Cross Creek BP and Auto Center, for allowing her a flexible work schedule.)

The volume discusses the smallpox epidemic that swept North America during the American Revolution, and it includes incendiary evidence that the British, who were for the most part immune to the disease because of previous exposure, used it as a biological weapon. "The book might have been just another scholarly monograph if it hadn't been for [the terrorist attacks of] Sept. 11 and the resulting fears about biological warfare," Hicks asserted. "It was published in October 2001, which made Fenn an obvious choice for media interviews in the aftermath of the terrorist attacks and subsequent anthrax scares." The volume ultimately won the 2002 James J. Broussard First Book Prize, the 2003 Longman-History Today Book of the Year title, and the 2004 Society of the Cincinnati Book Prize.

In the fall of 2002 Fenn began working as an assistant professor of history at Duke. There she reprised a course on the history of epidemics in America that she had taught at George Washington University. "I see it as an opportunity to educate people about our own history," she told Hicks. "Epidemics are catalytic moments in which society reveals itself."

Fenn left Duke in 2012 to accept an offer from the University of Colorado Boulder, where she serves as the Walter and Lucienne Driskill Professor of Western American History. Although she now enjoys the honor of holding an endowed chair, Fenn has said she rarely worried about her status in academia or career trajectory. "I've always thought if I don't get tenure, I can get by," she told Evans. "I look at my hands and think, 'These hands can do anything.' . . . I like knowing that I can fend for myself."

WINNING THE PULITZER
In 2014, after a decade of working on it, Fenn published *Encounters at the Heart of the World: A History of the Mandan People*. She had come across reference to the Mandan people while researching *Pox Americana* and was intrigued by the story of a once-flourishing culture that was nearly destroyed by what Fenn described to Evans as "catastrophic ecological change." In the book Fenn explains that Mandans had appeared in what is now South Dakota in about 1000 CE and that by the middle of the sixteenth century they had developed a thriving commercial trade with neighboring tribes. Within the next century, traders and explorers, including Lewis and Clark, had entered Mandan villages, bringing with them previously unknown diseases. The Mandans then had to cope with outbreaks of smallpox and whooping cough and infestations of Norway rats, which ate their stored food, leading to shortages. By the mid-nineteenth century, the Mandan population, once in the tens of thousands, had been reduced to only a few hundred. A reviewer for *Publishers Weekly* (18 Nov. 2013) wrote of the book, "Fenn brings to life and celebrates the customs and practices of the Mandans, while bemoaning the fate of this little-known North American tribe."

The volume won near-universal praise. In the notoriously discerning *Kirkus Reviews* (15 Jan. 2014), for example, a critic called the book "a nonpolemical, engaging study of a once-thriving Indian nation of the American heartland whose origins and demise tell us much about ourselves" and "an excellent contribution to the truth telling of the American Indian story."

From a competitive field that included Sven Beckert's *Empire of Cotton: A Global History* and Nick Bunker's *An Empire on the Edge: How Britain Came to Fight America*, Fenn's *Encounters at the Heart of the World* garnered the Pulitzer Prize in history. In awarding Fenn the $10,000 prize, the judges cited the book as an "engrossing and original narrative."

Fenn has said that she hopes her book contributes to a growing awareness of Native American culture and history, which she feels both education and academia have neglected in the past. "The case I make is that Native American history is American history," she told Harris. "I don't accept 1492 as the starting point of American history. American history begins with the people who occupied the continent. Throughout most of our past, those people were indigenous peoples, and their history is our history."

PERSONAL LIFE
Fenn married her onetime coauthor Peter Wood, a historian and emeritus professor at Duke University, in 1999. If she were to tire of being a historian, she has a list of other options: "I'd be a welder or a fiction writer, an engineer or a massage therapist, an actor or a race car driver, or maybe a high school coach," she wrote for *True West Magazine* (21 July 2015).

SUGGESTED READING
Eakin, Emily. "She Can Fix Your Engine, Too." *New York Times*. New York Times, 8 Sept. 2001. Web. 4 Feb. 2016.

Evans, Clay. "Former Auto Mechanic Makes Splash in the World of History." *Colorado Arts and Sciences Magazine*. U of Colorado Boulder, Dec. 2011. Web. 4 Feb. 2016.

Fenn, Elizabeth. "True Westerners." *True West Magazine*. True West, 21 July 2015. Web. 4 Feb. 2016.

Fenn, Elizabeth. "Q & A with Elizabeth Fenn." Interview by John Elmes. *Times Higher Education*. TES Global, 28 May 2015. Web. 4 Feb. 2016.

Fenn, Elizabeth. "2015 Pulitzer Prize Winner Elizabeth Fenn Talks American History before 1492." Interview by Kyle Harris. *Colorado Independent*. American Independent News Network, 22 Apr. 2015. Web. 4 Feb. 2016.

Hicks, Sally. "Scholar Trades Wrenches for Writing." *Duke University*. Duke U, 30 Aug. 2002. Web. 4 Feb. 2016.

SELECTED WORKS
Natives and Newcomers: The Way We Lived in North Carolina before 1770, 1983; *Pox Americana: The Great Smallpox Epidemic of 1775–82*, 2001; *Encounters at the Heart of the World: A History of the Mandan People*, 2014

—*Mari Rich*

Pauline Ferrand-Prévot

Born: February 10, 1992
Occupation: Professional cyclist

Pauline Ferrand-Prévot became one of the best professional cyclists in the world by the age of just twenty-four. In 2015 Ferrand-Prévot held simultaneous world titles in road cycling, cross-country mountain biking, and cyclo-cross, which covers courses featuring grass, dirt, pavement, gravel, and sand, as well as steep hills, mud pits, and other barriers that force riders to dismount and carry their bikes. She was the first racer, male or female, to achieve this feat. Her swift rise was without precedent in the sport, and she proved something of a swaggering, young talent in the world of cycling. Often referred to by her initials "PFP," she sports a diamond embedded in her left incisor and is not coy about her ambition to be the best.

After a relatively poor showing in the 2012 Olympic Games in London—she finished eighth in road race and twenty-sixth in cross-country—Ferrand-Prévot began training hard for the 2016 Games in Rio de Janeiro, Brazil. She plans to compete for titles in road race, time trial, and mountain bike. (There is no cyclo-cross event at the Olympics.) It is highly unusual for a cyclist to excel across disciplines, especially at the elite level, in the manner of Ferrand-Prévot. Each discipline presents its own particular mental and physical challenges. In road cycling, which takes place of course, on a road, cyclists race in a pack, or peloton, and must strategize as to when to sprint and break away. Road cycling is the most popular cycling discipline and has long enjoyed support in European countries such as France. Time trial cycling is a subdiscipline of road cycling in which cyclists race individually against the clock.

Cross-country mountain biking, which was introduced in the 1970s, is a relatively new sport, only becoming an Olympic event in 1996. Mountain biking requires a very different skill set than road cycling. Cyclists must be adept at handling their bikes on all kinds of terrain, much like in cyclo-cross. Ferrand-Prévot has said she enjoys the unique challenges of each discipline, and she refuses to specialize in one over any other. "People wanted to put me in one category, I think because it was easier for them," she told Tom Reynolds for *BBC (British Broadcasting Corporation) Sports* (24 Sept. 2015). "The French federation was not so happy because they wanted me to make a choice. But I said no. Now with all my world titles I am very happy because I can say to all those people that what I chose to do was good for me."

Bryn Lennon/Getty Images

EARLY LIFE

Ferrand-Prévot was born in Reims, two hours east of Paris, France, on February 10, 1992. Her parents, Daniel and Sylviane Dubau, were both competitive cyclists and owned a bicycle shop in town. Her older brother, Evan, and younger sister, Axelle, also became competitive cyclists. Ferrand-Prévot began riding a bike when she was five, and she took up mountain biking at eight. She warmed to the sport immediately thanks to her deep love of competition. Even in school she liked being the best, and in cycling she rode to win. "When I do something, I always have to be first. I like to be the best," she told Caley Fretz for *Velo* magazine (7 Dec. 2015). "At school, if I was not the best I was crying. My mother was the same. I think it's something in my family." She quickly decided she preferred the bike to her first love, ice dancing, because in cycling competitors have more control over their chance at victory. "In cycling you just race," she told Reynolds. "When you get to the finish you see the result. In ice dancing, you cannot decide your result. You just have to do your best and you can't decide if you win or not."

Ferrand-Prévot began entering local races as a child, but she quickly moved up to more elite cycling circles. She won her first junior national championship in 2005, when she was twelve years old. She went on to win four more national titles, as well as junior championship world titles in mountain biking in 2009 and 2010 and road cycling in 2010. Ferrand-Prévot turned pro in 2011, entering seven elite races and finishing in the top ten in all but one. In late 2011 she joined the Rabobank-Liv team at the behest of the team's captain, Dutch pro cyclist Marianne Vos.

In 2012 Ferrand-Prévot won her first national championship in time trial—which she won again in 2013 and 2014—and participated in the Olympic Games in London. As a first-time Olympian she made only a fair showing, and it has been suggested that the nonstop party atmosphere of the Olympic Village was to blame for her lackluster performance. She finished eighth in the road cycling event and a dismal twenty-sixth in mountain biking. Ferrand-Prévot spent the next several years preparing for the 2016 Games in Rio. She got a tattoo of the Olympic rings on her wrist and made at least one trip to Brazil to scope out her race routes and secure lodging, claiming she would not be staying in the athlete's village this time around.

THREE WORLD CHAMPIONSHIP TITLES

In April 2014 Ferrand-Prévot earned her first major elite victory in Wallonia, Belgium, at La Flèche Wallonne Féminine, but her breakthrough year was just beginning. That September she competed in the road cycling world championship in Ponferrada, Spain. Defending champion Vos was favored to win the race, or as Daniel McMahon put it for *Business Insider* (5 May 2015), "For many, the talk wasn't about *who* would win but about *how* Vos would win." A two-time Olympic gold medalist and twelve-time world champion, Vos had earned a spot as one of the greatest cyclists in the world. Despite Ferrand-Prévot's big win in Wallonia, insiders did not dream that the young protégé could so quickly dethrone the master. And from the beginning, the race appeared to fall in Vos's favor. "I thought the podium was lost, to be honest, when the group was away with Vos. I did not think our group would be able to catch them," she told Gregor Brown for *Cycling Weekly* (27 Sept. 2014). Ferrand-Prévot seemed to be flagging on the last climb of the last lap, but in the last three hundred meters, she managed to outsprint her teammate and win the race by mere inches. After the race, Ferrand-Prévot was euphoric but also surprised. "I sprinted and I didn't look back," she told Brown. "I didn't expect to win a sprint in the world championships."

Watching Ferrand-Prévot win her first world championship that day, McMahon wrote, "I felt as if I was witnessing not just the coronation of a new champion but a bona fide changing of the guard in women's cycling." Four months later, in January 2015, Ferrand-Prévot won the cyclo-cross world championship in Tábor, Czech Republic. Vos was suffering from a hamstring injury going into the race, and several cyclists hoped to claim victory in her stead. Among them was Italian champion Eva Lechner. For most of the first two laps of the race (out of

five), Lucie Chainel-Lefèvre of France held the lead over a small group that included Ferrand-Prévot, Vos, and World Cup champion Sanne Cant of Belgium. Halfway through the second lap, Ferrand-Prévot closed the gap on Chainel-Lefèvre. She held her lead until the final lap, when Cant managed to gain a tiny lead, but Ferrand-Prévot held on. Cant later said, as quoted by Brecht Decaluwé for *Cycling News* (31 Jan. 2015). "I attacked on the climb and hoped to get a gap but she was still on my wheel." Ferrand-Prévot took the lead, and in the final sprint, Cant was too spent to pass her. "She's simply superfast," Cant said. "It's stupid."

In September 2015 Ferrand-Prévot completed her historic trifecta, winning the cross-country mountain biking world championship in Vallnord, Andorra. Ferrand-Prévot had been surprised to win her first two races, but in Vallnord, she was more determined than ever to win. But the race's course was steep, tricky, and muddy from rain. "With the altitude, the climb, and the slippery downhill, it was so hard. I really gave it everything because I wanted this title," Ferrand-Prévot told Rob Jones for *Cycling News* (5 Sept. 2015). By the second lap (out of six), she shared the lead with Catharine Pendrel of Canada, and soon after that, she pulled away completely, ultimately winning the race by nearly one minute.

ROAD TO RIO

The same month, however, Ferrand-Prévot lost her world championship title in road cycling, coming in sixth after recovering from a crash early in a race in Richmond, Virginia. Lizzie Armitstead of Great Britain was crowned the new champion. A few months later, in November, Ferrand-Prévot suffered a tibial plateau fracture in training. She decided to pull out of cyclo-cross, which runs from fall to late winter, for the rest of the season and forgo defending her title at the cyclo-cross world championships in January 2016. The decision to claim extra recovery time was calculated toward improving her Olympic ambitions in Rio. She trained through the winter months and made plans to race at the Strade Bianche, a road cycling race, in Italy in March 2016.

Her expectations for her return performance were low, she told Peter Cossins for *Cycling News* (4 Mar. 2016). "Above all I just want to see where I am at the moment. The other girls have two more months' preparation behind them than me." Ferrand-Prévot placed eleventh in the race, which was won by Armitstead, who finished one minute and twenty-three seconds ahead of her and who will likely be one of Ferrand-Prévot's biggest rivals in Rio. Ferrand-Prévot plans to prepare for her dual Olympic races—road and mountain—by alternating training months on each discipline. In April she planned to focus entirely on road cycling while in May she would focus entirely on mountain biking. June would mark the beginning of her official ramp up for the Olympic Games, beginning in August. "I'm going to tackle the two disciplines head on," she told Cossins. "At the Games I'll need to switch from one bike to the other very quickly."

PERSONAL LIFE

In her personal life Ferrand-Prévot dated Vincent Luis, an up-and-coming French triathlete, and counted Vos as a personal mentor.

SUGGESTED READING

Brown, Gregor. "Pauline Ferrand-Prévot Celebrates an 'Unexpected' World Champs Win." *Cycling Weekly*. Time, 27 Sept. 2014. Web. 4 Apr. 2016.

Cossins, Peter. "Ferrand-Prevot Returns at Strade Bianche." *Cycling News*. Immediate Media, 4 Mar. 2016. Web. 4 Apr. 2016.

Decaluwé, Brecht. "Ferrand-Prévot Beats Cant to World Championship Title." *Cycling News*. Immediate Media, 31 Jan. 2015. Web. 4 Apr. 2016.

McMahon, Daniel. "Meet Pauline Ferrand-Prévot, the 23-Year-Old Who's the Most Dominant Cyclist in the World." *Business Insider*. Business Insider, 5 May 2015. Web. 4 Apr. 2016.

Reynolds, Tom. "Pauline Ferrand-Prévot: Why French Star May Be Greatest Cyclist." *BBC Sport*. BBC, 24 Sept. 2015. Web. 3 Apr. 2016.

—*Molly Hagan*

Deb Fischer

Born: March 1, 1951
Occupation: US Senator

During her two terms in Nebraska's unicameral legislature, Deb Fischer honed a distinctive political style. "Sometimes, she got her colleagues in the Nebraska Legislature to side with her by making assurances," John Eligon wrote for the *New York Times* (1 June 2012). "Other times, she would sway them with incredulity. . . . And on other occasions, [she] . . . would draw a line in the sand. . . . Senator Fischer got what she wanted."

When Fischer, a Republican, vied for a seat in the US Senate in 2012, she got that as well. Facing off in the primary against Attorney General Jon Bruning and State Treasurer Don Stenberg, she portrayed herself as a tough-minded individualist battling big-city lawyers. Despite the fact that a poll conducted a few months before the election showed that the majority of

United States Congress/Wikimedia Commons

Nebraskans had never even heard of Fischer, her campaign took off after she was endorsed by GOP favorite Sarah Palin, and she clinched the nomination. Fischer easily triumphed in her race against Democratic opponent Bob Kerrey to win the Senate seat that would be vacated by retiring Democrat Ben Nelson. Since then, Fischer has built a national reputation as a staunch conservative, although she does not lean as far to the right as some in her party might prefer.

Although Fischer is the third female senator from Nebraska and the first since 1954, she believes that her position as a rancher from a rural part of the state, rather than gender, is what sets her apart in the Republican caucus. She feels, however, "a special kinship to other senators from rural states," she explained to Betsy Woodruff for the *National Review* (8 Mar. 2013). "We're kind of blunt . . . we understand vastness."

EARLY YEARS AND EDUCATION

Debra Strobel Fischer was born on March 1, 1951, and grew up in the town of Lincoln, Nebraska. Matthew Hansen for the *Norfolk Daily News* (30 Sept. 2012) described Fischer's childhood as "seemingly ripped straight from a Norman Rockwell painting." Her father, Gerold "Jerry" Strobel, was Nebraska's state director of roads, and her mother, Florence Strobel, was a teacher. Fischer was the youngest of three children and competed regularly with older brothers Cory and Jim in board games, tag, and dodge ball. As a high school student, she read several newspapers each day, including the *Lincoln Journal* and the *Omaha World-Herald*. She regularly watched the news at night, and became engrossed in the coverage of the Vietnam War, which was then raging.

After graduating from high school in 1969, Fischer enrolled at the University of Nebraska–Lincoln, majoring in political science and thinking about a future career in local government. Those plans were derailed, however, when she met her future husband, Bruce Fischer, a rancher's son from an isolated rural area of north-central Nebraska. The couple married in 1972, and Fischer dropped out of college before earning her degree in order to move to his family's sprawling ranch in the town of Valentine, more than five hours from Lincoln.

Fischer's next phase of life involved helping run the Sunny Slope Ranch, giving birth to and raising three sons, gardening, and golfing. "We were starting a family and running (the ranch)," she recalled to Hansen. "We were doing what everybody does. We were making a home. We were making a life."

In 1987, when Fischer's mother retired from teaching and became available to help out with Fischer's household, the time seemed ripe for a new phase. Florence Strobel lived at the ranch during the week while Fischer lived at her childhood home in Lincoln in order to earn her needed credits to graduate from the university. The two women then switched places on the weekends. It was a grueling year, but Fischer received her bachelor's degree in education in 1988.

EARLY POLITICAL CAREER

Fischer began her life in public service on a local school board before being elected to the Valentine school board. She eventually ascended to the presidency of the Nebraska Association of School Boards and was appointed to the School Finance Review Committee while also serving on the oversight agency of the Nebraska Coordinating Commission for Postsecondary Education.

In 2004 Fischer ran for a seat in her state's unicameral legislature. Nebraska is unique among other states in the nation because it has a single-house system in the legislature. This form of government has been in place since 1937, and there are forty-nine members of the Unicameral, as it is generally known, each serving a four-year term. Nebraska is also unusual in having the only nonpartisan legislature in the country, which means that a candidate's political party is not listed on the election ballot; rather, the two candidates with the most votes in the primary face each other in the general election.

Running against six opponents in the primary to represent the Forty-Third legislative district, Fischer came in second and defeated front-runner Kevin T. Cooksley in the general

election by a margin of 50.4 percent to 49.6 percent. Fischer quickly won a reputation for being tough-minded and goal-oriented, and in 2008 she was unopposed for reelection.

SENATE CAREER

When term limits prevented her from running for a Unicameral seat in 2012, Fischer set her sights on the US Senate. Although she had relatively little money in her campaign coffers, she bested her better-funded primary opponents, Attorney General Jon Bruning and State Treasurer Don Stenberg, who were seemingly so engaged in attacking each other that they apparently underestimated the threat that Fischer posed. Voters were swayed by her reputation as a hard-working rancher, dedicated legislator, and solid conservative who had none of the political baggage of her opponents, and she was chosen to run against former Democratic senator Bob Kerrey in the general election. "I knew people and people knew me, and you shouldn't ever discount the friendships and the networking that a candidate has at the grassroots level," she told Woodruff. "You can still win a race in a state like Nebraska at the grassroots level."

During her Senate campaign, Fischer promised to work toward lowering taxes and balancing the federal budget by reducing the size and reach of the federal government and eliminating "ineffective agencies, such as the Federal Highway Administration." Kerrey tried portraying Fischer as a right-wing Tea Party favorite, but while she did have the endorsement of Palin, one of its most prominent members, the faction did not officially endorse her candidacy. "The Democrats didn't know what to do with me after the primary," she recalled to Woodruff. "I was their worst nightmare. I had nothing they could attack. So they immediately tried to portray me as a tea-party candidate, or to portray some of my views as extreme. I like to say that 58 percent of Nebraskans didn't think they were extreme views."

On the day of the election, Fischer triumphed over Kerrey by sixteen points to win the seat. Thus far in her term, which is set to expire in January 2019, Fischer has voted well within the mainstream of her party, opposing abortion except in cases of rape or incest, for example, and favoring gun rights. Among bills she has sponsored or cosponsored have been those aimed at exempting clinical and health software from regulation under the Federal Food, Drug, and Cosmetic Act; prohibiting the Internal Revenue Service from asking any taxpayer any information regarding religious, political, or social beliefs; increasing the maximum loan available in the Small Business Administration's microloan program; creating a tax credit for businesses equal to 25 percent of compensation paid to employees during vacation periods; and amending the Fair Labor Standards Act of 1938 to strengthen equal pay requirements.

Fischer currently sits on several Senate committees and their subcommittees. Her Senate committee assignments include the Committee on Armed Services; the Committee on Commerce, Science and Transportation; the Committee on Environment and Public Works; and the Committee on Small Business and Entrepreneurship.

OPPOSITION AND ACCUSATIONS
Several of Fischer's political opponents have attempted to derail her campaigns and sully her reputation by calling attention to the personal lives of her three sons, Adam, born in 1974; Morgan, born in 1977; and Luke, born in 1982. Each has at least one conviction for driving under the influence, but Fischer has repeatedly declined to comment, stating that her sons are private citizens and are not running for elected office.

During her campaign against Bob Kerrey for the Senate seat, Kerrey accused Fischer and her husband of making a land grab in the mid-1990s against elderly neighbors, Les and Betty Kime, through a legal argument called adverse possession. This tactic allows for the acquisition of another person's property by deliberately and in plain sight using the property with or without the owner's permission. The Kimes had allowed the Fischers to graze their cattle on Kime land over many years but had refused to sell or swap the land with the Fischers when approached to do so. The Fischers then sued the Kimes for ownership of the land under adverse possession. The judge ruled in favor of the Kimes, however, and when they died, their heirs considered selling the land to the Nebraska Game and Parks Commission. Kerrey accused Fischer in attack ads of subsequently backing a bill to defund the Nebraska Environmental Trust—thus effectively stymieing the bequest.

Many opponents have also targeted the Fischers for accepting what is termed "agricultural welfare" because for years the family grazed their cattle on federal land at below-market rates. While Fischer has expressed openness to changing the regulations that govern grazing on federal land, she has said, as reported by Margery A. Beck and Thomas Beaumont for the *Huffington Post* (14 Sept. 2012), "We pay the bill that they send us. We follow the rules that they put out there."

SUGGESTED READING
Eligon, John. "From Long Shot to GOP's Best Bet in Nebraska's Senate Race." *New York Times*. New York Times, 1 June 2012. Web. 10 Nov. 2015.

Hansen, Matthew. "Fischer's Unlikely Route to Politics Fueled by Grit and Determination." *Norfolk Daily News*. Norfolk Daily News, 30 Sept. 2012. Web. 10 Nov. 2015.

Warren, Mark. "The 2012 Senate Races: Nebraska." *Esquire*. Hearst Communications, 16 Oct. 2012. Web. 10 Nov. 2015.

Weiner, Rachel. "How Deb Fischer Pulled an Upset in Nebraska." *Washington Post*. Washington Post, 16 May 2012. Web. 10 Nov. 2015.

Woodruff, Betsy. "Deb Fischer: Rancher, Country Gal, Senator." *National Review*. National Review, 8 Mar. 2013. Web. 10 Nov. 2015.

Woodruff, Judy. "Sen.-Elect Deb Fischer on Spending, Gun Control and Bipartisanship." *PBS*. NewsHour Productions, 1 Jan. 2013. Web. 17 Feb. 2016.

—*Mari Rich*

FKA twigs
Born: January 16, 1988
Occupation: Singer

"While some critics have related [FKA] Twigs to Sade, Björk, Aaliyah, and trip-hop artists like SZA, her sound is uniquely her own—melismatic falsetto over beats that are equal parts spooky, and soothing," Dee Lockett wrote for *Slate* (11 Aug. 2014). "Twigs has also gone to great pains to construct an image that effectively communicates her identity in a way her music sometime can't." Nowhere is this more reflected than in her hypnotic, provocative, and artistic videos, particularly "Water Me," in which she resembles an anime-like doll; the bondage-themed "Papi Pacify" and "Pendulum"; and "Video Girl," an ode to her stint as a backup dancer. This also extends to her live performances, including her memorable US debut on the November 4, 2014, episode of *The Tonight Show Starring Jimmy Fallon*, during which she sang "Two Weeks" while manipulating an air sculpture.

FKA twigs also has a knack for pushing boundaries in her personal style, from her Josephine Baker–style slicked baby hairs and septum ring to her matte red lips and heavily decorated nails. Her innovative look has graced the pages of *Vogue*, *Elle*, and *Glamour UK*. The singer is among several celebrities slated to appear in Calvin Klein's spring 2016 underwear campaign.

EARLY LIFE
FKA twigs was born Tahlia Debrett Barnett on January 16, 1988, in Gloucestershire, a rural county in southwest England. Despite growing up poor without her biological father, Barnett, an

Anthony Harvey/Getty Images

only child, refers to the formative years spent in the sleepy countryside of Tewksbury as idyllic. "My early years of . . . [childhood] were pretty close to perfect; I couldn't really have wanted for much more," she recalled to *National Public Radio (NPR)* (29 Aug. 2015). "My mom was never worried about me going outside and playing in the street. In many ways, I was allowed a lot of freedom, which allowed for a lot of creative freedom as well."

Barnett was also a fan of black-and-white films; one of her childhood favorites was the 1948 ballet classic *The Red Shoes*. She acquired her love of dance from her mother, a former salsa dancer who often snuck her daughter to her DJ gigs at salsa nightclubs. She credited her stepfather, a jazz enthusiast, with introducing her to an eclectic array of music, including ska and African fusion.

When Barnett was young she convinced her mother and stepfather to enroll her in ballet and jazz classes at the local Coady Dance Studios despite her family's financial hardships. A talented student, she earned an academic scholarship to attend St. Edward's School, Cheltenham, a private, coeducational Roman Catholic school in the nearby town of Charlton Kings. Because of her heritage—her mother was part Spanish, her father Jamaican— the social aspect of school proved to be difficult for Barnett. "I was never the pretty girl at school. I'm tiny and mixed-race. I grew up in a white area," she confided to Carrie Battan for *Pitchfork* (1 Aug. 2013). "I was always the loner. I was always kind of off—a little weird." She also stood out for her various hairstyles, which ranged from ringlets to braids.

Barnett's growing interest in dancing led her to create her own innovative interpretive routines, including one that reenacted the life of a slave, set to Marvin Gaye's "Calypso Blues." By her early teens, she decided to follow in her mother's footsteps, becoming a regular presence at choreography competitions and often traveling to London for dance and modeling jobs. "In school I had a tough time fitting in and dancing was my way of being in my own element," Barnett revealed to Greg Kot for the *Chicago Tribune* (6 Nov. 2014). She also continued to expand her creative horizons and signed up for opera lessons.

BEGINNINGS OF A MUSIC CAREER

In her teens Barnett's love of music began to rival her passion for dance. She spent her weekends immersing herself in the local music scene. "There was a youth club . . . with a low-key studio, and they'd have guys rapping, and I'd put the chorus down on the track," she shared with Battan. "Eventually, people started saying, 'You've got a really nice voice, you should start doing your own stuff.'" She continued to focus on her first love, however, moving to south London on her own to attend dance school. However, the shy seventeen-year-old struggled to adjust to her new surroundings.

After a month, Barnett had a change of heart. She dropped out of dance school and briefly studied philosophy and sociology at Croydon College before she decided to pursue music full-time. But by then, her tastes—in both music and dance—had changed. "I went in the opposite direction," she recalled to Cedar Pasori for *Complex* (June/July 2015). "I liked punk music. I gave up ballet. I rejected the training I'd had."

When she was eighteen Barnett began collaborating in the studio with several London-based producers to find her own sound. It was during one of these sessions that she penned the song "I'm Your Doll." (She also experienced another milestone: meeting her biological father, a jazz dancer, for the first time.) At nineteen, Barnett traveled across the pond to Los Angeles, California, where she spent six months recording tracks with various producers. When the resulting demos yielded nothing, she returned to London and continued to work on her music while juggling stints as a shot girl at a Piccadilly Circus nightclub and as a jazz singer at a the Experimental Cocktail Club in Chinatown.

BACKUP DANCING AND *EP1*

Barnett also relied on her dancing talents to help pay the bills. During her early twenties, she worked at the London Urban Arts Academy, instructing disadvantaged youths on how to sing, dance, play music, and write poetry. With the help of an agent Barnett booked gigs as a backup dancer; over a two-year period, she appeared in a string of music videos for several high-profile British pop stars including Kylie Minogue, Cheryl Cole, Taio Cruz, and Ed Sheeran. Her most memorable appearances were in two Jessie J videos: the 2010 song "Do It Like a Dude" and the 2011 hit "Price Tag," in which she played a dancing marionette.

However, for her performances on London's cabaret scene, Barnett commanded center stage, dressing up as a 1940s seductress (which she described as Betty Boop-meets-Jessica Rabbit) and belting out Screamin' Jay Hawkins's "I Put a Spell on You." "My cabaret character was someone much harder than I am, someone that could go and steal someone's glass of wine . . . chuck it on them in rage, or . . . climb over a table," she told Emilie Friedlander for *The Fader* (22 Apr. 2014). "Someone that could just be really daring in a way that no one ever got angry at her . . . the side of womanhood that you would have always wanted to explore but rarely got the chance to."

Barnett was still committed to pursuing a music career. She continued to write her own material, eventually amassing enough confidence to release her first official recording, the four-track *EP1* (2012), under the moniker twigs—a reference to the loud, cracking sound her bones make when she dances. In the latter half of 2012 twigs garnered press for the record's accompanying videos, which she directed with Grace Ladoja. The provocative music video for twigs's first single, "Hide," made its debut in July.

For her second music video, "Ache," which premiered a month later, twigs went in a completely different direction, showcasing a member of the London-based dance crew Wet Wipez dancing to the song in slow motion. Interest surrounding twigs grew even more when she graced the cover of *i-D* magazine's pre-fall 2012 issue in a close-up shot donning two of her trademarks: the septum ring and Josephine Baker-inspired baby hairs (which were fashioned to spell the word "love" across her forehead). In December 2012 twigs released *EP1* on vinyl disc and digitally (via the music streaming service Bandcamp). She also unveiled her remaining videos on her YouTube channel: the colorful, 3D computer-generated "Weak Spot" and the black-and-white "Breathe," the latter featuring twigs wielding a hammer and destroying a car.

SIGNING WITH YOUNG TURKS AND *EP2*

In early 2013, following the strong critical reception of her self-released debut, twigs was relentlessly pursued by Tic Zogson, a producer and A&R representative at the British independent label Young Turks. "We met at some bondage party," she told Simon Vozick-Levinson for *Rolling Stone* (20 Nov. 2014). "Then over the next two months, he wouldn't leave me alone."

For her follow-up twigs entered the studio with producer Alejandro "Arca" Ghersi. Between May and September 2013 she released videos for four new tracks, including the breakout single "Water Me," which contains a close-up of the singer staring blankly into the camera and bobbing her head from side to side as her eyes become cartoonishly large and eventually a solitary tear falls.

In mid-September the singer digitally released the four songs as *EP2* (2013) in the United Kingdom under a newly adopted moniker—the result of a trademark lawsuit filed by the American alternative pop act The Twigs. "I was actually gonna be AFK twigs, but then somebody said to me, 'that stands for 'Away From Keyboard' . . . I know I'm aloof but that's pushing it a bit too far!" she joked to Tim Noakes for *Dazed* (19 June 2014). "I just swapped around two of the letters to FKA twigs." In the wake of the buzz generated by her EPs, FKA twigs appeared on British Broadcasting Corp.'s (BBC's) Sound of 2014 longlist and Billboard's "14 Artists to Watch in 2014." She launched a short North American tour in April 2014. A month later *EP2* reached the top five of the Billboard US Dance/Electronics Albums chart and barely missed the top ten of Billboard's US Heatseekers Albums category.

LP1 AND *M3LL155X*

For her first full-length studio album FKA twigs reteamed with Arca and worked alongside Grammy-winning producers Emile Haynie and Paul Epworth, among others. The result—*LP1* (2014)—was very well received by the music press. Critics praised the album for its aesthetic and genre risks as well as its wholly unique sound.

To promote her new disc, which topped the UK Independent Albums chart and Billboard's US Dance/Electronic Albums, FKA twigs played several summer dates in the United States and Canada before embarking on a more extensive fall tour across North America, the United Kingdom, and Europe. She ended 2014 on a high note as *LP1* was featured in the year-end lists of several notable publications, including *Time*, *Rolling Stone*, *Spin*, the *Huffington Post*, the *Guardian*, and the *Daily Telegraph*. Also that December she collaborated with Google Glass on a short film that she directed.

Not content to rest on her laurels, FKA twigs released another EP, *M3LL155X* (pronounced "Melissa"), in August 2015. Regarding her album title, she shared with Pasori, "The EP is called Melissa, and 'Melissa' to me is my personal female energy. . . . It's not a weird alter ego. It's just my way of separating it from myself." Along with the EP, which reached the top five of Billboard's US Independent and US Dance/Electronic charts, FKA twigs released a sixteen-minute short film that she directed containing clips from four of the EP's five tracks: "In Time," "Figure 8," "Glass & Patron," and a reworking of "I'm Your Doll." She also returned to the concert trail, including a sold-out, three-night residency at the Red Bull Music Academy and gigs at several worldwide music festivals including Coachella and Lollapalooza.

PERSONAL LIFE

The notoriously private singer began dating actor Robert Pattinson in 2014 and by April 2015 they were engaged. The couple made their red-carpet debut at the 2015 Met Gala.

SUGGESTED READING

Battan, Carrie. "Rising: FKA Twigs." *Pitchfork.* Condé Nast, 1 Aug. 2013. Web. 10 Feb. 2016.

Friedlander, Emilie. "FKA Twigs: Power Play." *Fader.* Fader, 22 Apr. 2014. Web. 10 Feb. 2016.

"'I'm Not Scared of Learning': FKA Twigs on Submission and Control." *NPR.* NPR, 29 Aug. 2015. Web. 10 Feb. 2016.

Kot, Greg. "FKA Twigs Danced Past Her Past into a New Sound." *Chicago Tribune.* Tribune, 6 Nov. 2014. Web. 10 Feb. 2016.

Lockett, Dee. "A Guide to FKA Twigs, Music's New It Girl." *Slate.* Slate Group, 11 Aug. 2014. Web. 10 Feb. 2016.

Noakes, Tim. "FKA Twigs: Future Shock." *Dazed.* Waddell, 19 June 2014. Web. 10 Feb. 2016.

Pasori, Cedar. "Under Control." *Complex.* Complex Media, June/July 2015. Web. 10 Feb. 2016.

—*Bertha Muteba*

Joe Flacco

Born: January 16, 1985
Occupation: Football player

Joe Flacco has been a quarterback for the Baltimore Ravens since 2008. In 2013, Flacco was named Most Valuable Player (MVP) after he led the Ravens to victory over the San Francisco 49ers in Super Bowl XLVII.

EARLY LIFE AND EDUCATION

Joseph Vincent Flacco was born in Audubon, New Jersey, in 1985 to Steve and Karen Flacco. He is the oldest of six children and has four brothers and one sister.

The Flaccos encouraged all their children to participate in sports, often practicing football and baseball with them. Growing up, Flacco was never a fan of a specific football team, opting instead to admire individual players

such as Joe Montana, quarterback for the San Francisco 49ers.

Flacco earned three varsity letters as an athlete for the Audubon High School Green Waves in wrestling, baseball, and football, though he particularly excelled at football. Named the team's starter his sophomore year, Flacco would go on to set all-time New Jersey state records for both career passing yards and single-game passing yards.

Flacco's success at Audubon led to several college scholarship offers. He chose the University of Pittsburgh, where he was offered a full scholarship and would be close to home. Flacco also wanted to play for former New York Jets quarterbacks coach Walt Harris who was head of the Panthers football program.

COLLEGE CAREER

Flacco was redshirted his freshman year with the Panthers. ("Redshirting" in athletics refers to an interruption or suspension in a player's involvement in the team, usually to extend that player's eligibility period.) Flacco sat out his freshman football season, despite sound health, in order to hone his skills and preserve roster positions for other players.

In his sophomore year, Flacco was relegated to the squad's third-string quarterback behind Tyler Palko and Luke Getsy. Disgruntled, Flacco ultimately opted to depart Pittsburgh and transfer to the University of Delaware. Despite the fact that the move represented a drop from National Collegiate Athletic Association (NCAA) Division I football to lesser Division I-AA, he was eager to switch to a school where he would have more opportunities to play. (In 2006 Division I-AA was renamed Football Championship Subdivision, or FCS.)

NCAA rules required Flacco to sit out the entire 2005 season and forgo his scholarship before he joined the University of Delaware Blue Hens in 2006 as a nonscholarship student athlete.

In two seasons as the Blue Hens starting quarterback, Flacco would become its most successful quarterback, setting records in twenty categories, most notably in career completions and total passing yards. Despite playing in a less competitive division, Flacco's excellence at Delaware caught the attention of numerous National Football League (NFL) scouts, who lauded his tremendous arm strength and game management skills. In 2008, the Baltimore Ravens selected Flacco as the eighteenth overall pick in the first round of the NFL draft.

NFL CAREER

Injuries to other quarterbacks on the Ravens roster thrust Flacco into the team's starting role for the 2008 NFL season. He responded to the pressure with aplomb, becoming the first rookie quarterback in NFL history to win two football playoff games before ultimately losing to the Pittsburgh Steelers in the 2009 AFC Championship game. Flacco received the 2008 NFL Rookie of the Year Award for his success.

The Ravens saw three more winning seasons with Flacco as starting quarterback leading the team through the playoffs. The 2012 season was no different, however, except that the Ravens advanced through the playoffs and reached the Super Bowl to play against the San Francisco 49ers in Super Bowl XLVII.

Flacco would complete over twenty passes for 287 yards and three touchdowns in the Ravens victory, a performance for which he earned Super Bowl XLVII's MVP award.

IMPACT

Joe Flacco is representative of a new generation of NFL quarterbacks in that, unlike a majority of his predecessors, he was drafted into the NFL from a relatively unknown college program and without the celebrity and fanfare that has been attached to many of the past NFL starting quarterbacks.

Flacco has gone to great lengths to keep his personal life private, opting to eschew lucrative commercial endorsements in order to concentrate on the job at hand. It is this dedication to his team and the Ravens organization that has earned him the respect of both his teammates and fans.

In a league where quarterbacks have been known for their running, Flacco is somewhat of a throwback to the quarterbacks he grew up watching and admiring: Flacco is a patient pocket-passer who relies on pregame preparation and a magnificent throwing ability to reach receivers far down the field.

PERSONAL LIFE

Flacco married his long-time girlfriend Dana Grady in June 2011. The couple, who met as students at Audubon High School, has two sons, Stephen and Daniel.

SUGGESTED READING

Cacciola, Scott. "Flacco Keeps His Profile Low, Save for One Day." *New York Times*. New York Times, 27 Jan. 2013. Web. 23 Feb. 2014.

Cook, Ron. "Ron Cook: Not Fair to Give Pitt Flak about Flacco." *Pittsburgh Post-Gazette*. PG Publishing, 29 Jan. 2013. Web. 8 Apr. 2014.

"Joe Flacco: Biography." *Joe Flacco*. JoeFlacco5.com, n.d. Web. 23 Feb. 2014.

Miller, Randy. "Average Joe: Audubon's Flacco Famous, but Still Grounded." *USA Today*.

Gannett Satellite Information Network, 20 July 2013. Web. 23 Feb. 2014.

Mink, Ryan. "Five Things You May Not Know About Joe Flacco." *Baltimore Ravens*. Baltimore Ravens, 10 July 2013. Web. 23 Feb. 2014.

Nagelhout, Ryan. *Joe Flacco*. New York: Stevens, 2014. Print.

Van Valkenburg, Kevin. "Joe Flacco Is Anything but Average." *ESPN NFL*. ESPN Internet Ventures, 23 Aug. 2013. Web. 23 Feb. 2014.

Wilson, Aaron. "With New Offense around Him, Ravens QB Joe Flacco Knows He Has a Chance 'To Do New Things.'" *Baltimore Sun*. Tribune Interactive, 5 Apr. 2014. Web. 8 Apr. 2014.

—*John Pritchard*

LaToya Ruby Frazier

Born: January 1982
Occupation: Artist

LaToya Ruby Frazier is an award-winning photographer, best known for capturing the decay of her hometown, Braddock, Pennsylvania, through the eyes of her family members. Frazier has been compared to Depression-era photographers such as Dorothea Lange and Walker Evans, but her personal inspirations are more diverse: she cites as influences the Mexican painter Frida Kahlo and photographer Francesca Woodman, a prodigy who captured arresting images of herself and other young women before committing suicide at the age of twenty-two in 1981. Frazier was also inspired by contemporary artists whose work engages with African American experience and invisible communities such as in Braddock, including Bronx-born installation artist Abigail DeVille, whose site-specific *Harlem Stories* explores the ways in which gentrification is erasing the face of the historic African American neighborhood. Frazier also told Greg Lindquist for the magazine *Art in America* (19 Mar. 2013) that she looked to seventeenth-century Dutch painter Johannes Vermeer when capturing portraits like those of her mother and grandmother. The "body language and gestures" of Vermeer's female subjects, she said, "convey larger social and cultural meanings." She added, "Concepts of family, privacy, intimacy, comfort, and luxury are as present in my portraits as they are in Vermeer's paintings."

In 2014 Frazier became an assistant professor of photography at the School of the Art Institute of Chicago (SAIC), but for Frazier, who began taking photographs when she was a teenager, photography served as more than a career.

John D. and Catherine T. MacArthur Foundation/CC BY 4.0/
Wikimedia Commons

"I used my camera to fight for my survival," Frazier told Maurice Berger for the *New York Times* (14 Oct. 2014). "It provided me with an education and with funds to provide food and shelter for my family. Without my camera I would not have been able to resist the systematic oppression and racism my family continues to face in Braddock, Pittsburgh and in this country."

EARLY LIFE AND EDUCATION

Frazier was born in Braddock, Pennsylvania, in January 1982. Braddock is a suburb of Pittsburgh located on the banks of the Monongahela River and was the location of Andrew Carnegie's first steel mill. Frazier's family migrated to the town from the South in the early twentieth century, and her great-grandfather took a job at the steel mill. Her grandmother Ruby, who helped raise her and appears in many of Frazier's photographs, grew up in the 1930s, when the town's mills were active and the population was relatively diverse. However, by the 1960s, when Frazier's mother was a child, Braddock's white residents were beginning to flee to newly built suburbs. By the time Frazier was born, the mills began to close.

Frazier grew up in the town's poorest section, a neighborhood called the Bottom, one of low elevation that abutted the steel mill. She lived with her grandmother in a three-story house directly next to the mill. Their proximity to the factory spawned generations of health problems. After a long battle with pancreatic cancer, Frazier's grandmother died in 2009. Her mother suffered from a variety of ailments, including an unidentified neurological disorder, and Frazier herself was diagnosed with lupus, an autoimmune disease exacerbated by pollutants.

Despite, and perhaps because of, her harsh surroundings, Frazier was drawn to art from an early age. She drew and painted with watercolors. However, it was in high school that she came into the possession of a disposable camera, an event that changed her life. She began taking pictures of her family, and when she was sixteen, she left Braddock to study photography at the Edinboro University of Pennsylvania. In 2004 she earned her bachelor of fine arts (BFA) in applied media arts, and in 2007 she earned a master of fine arts (MFA) in art photography from Syracuse University. In 2010 she participated in the Whitney Museum of Art Independent Study Program and in 2013 she was a Guna S. Mundheim Fellow for visual arts at the American Academy in Berlin. Before becoming an assistant professor at the School of the Art Institute of Chicago in 2014, she served in academic and curatorial positions at the Yale University School of Art, Rutgers University, and Syracuse.

EARLY CAREER AND INSPIRATIONS

In 2009 Frazier's work was featured in a group exhibition called *The Generational Triennial: Younger than Jesus* at the New Museum in New York City. (The title refers to the age of the artists, all of whom were thirty-three or younger.) In 2010 her work was featured in a series called *Greater New York* at the Museum of Modern Art's PS1, and in 2012 her photographs appeared in the Whitney Biennial. Her first solo exhibition, *A Haunted Capital*, opened at the Brooklyn Museum in 2013. The forty photographs on display captured ten years in the life of Frazier's family. As Andrew Russeth wrote in his review for the New York *Observer* (16 July 2013), Frazier "manages, with almost preternatural ease, to capture herself, her family and her surroundings as they display mixtures of strength and vulnerability that feel disarmingly candid. Carefully documenting the lives of one small group of people, the show also evinces—and addresses—grave American traumas." In 2014, another solo exhibit, *LaToya Ruby Frazier: Born by a River*, opened at the Seattle Art Museum. The title references a lyric from the Sam Cooke civil-rights-era anthem "A Change Is Gonna Come." Among black-and-white photographs of Frazier's family, the exhibition also featured large color aerial photographs of Braddock taken in 2013 and a video that Frazier made for the PBS series *Art21*.

The images in Frazier's PBS video refer to a 2010 Levi's advertising campaign, shot in Braddock, which glorified the city's revitalization campaign, led by Mayor John Fetterman, who opened the city to artists and films. That program had some notable success; the films *Out of the Furnace*, a 2013 thriller, and *The Road* (2009), based on Cormac McCarthy's Pulitzer Prize–winning novel of the same name, were both shot in Braddock, for example. However, according to Frazier and others, the gentrification campaign did little to address the poverty or pervasive health problems suffered by Braddock's existing residents. In Frazier's video, the artist stands in front of a Levi's pop-up store in New York, tearing her Levi's jeans by scraping her legs on the sidewalk. "On one level, the performance counters Levi's romanticized view of work and of Braddock as an icon of blue-collar fortitude and solidarity," Berger wrote for the *New York Times* (21 Feb. 2014). "On another, it speaks to the insidiousness of gentrification, which can tear a community apart by driving up rents and property values and displacing its poorest residents."

THE NOTION OF FAMILY

Braddock once boasted more than twenty thousand residents, but after the steel industry took a nosedive in the 1980s that number dwindled to about two thousand by 2010. Unemployment, addiction, disease, and health problems caused by pollution and toxic waste ravaged the community and shaped the crumbling wasteland that became such an integral part of Frazier's identity. In 2008 Mayor Fetterman told Jim Straub and Bret Liebendorfer for *Monthly Review*, that even among other Rust Belt cities, Braddock had fared poorly. "Statistically speaking, Braddock is an outlier among outliers," he said. "I don't know of any other place in the Rust Belt that had a 90 percent population loss." But Braddock's losses, described in this manner, tell only half the story. The town's woes have historically and disproportionately affected its black residents. Even during its heyday, Braddock's African Americans were barred from senior positions at the mill and were not extended the same beneficial housing policies as their white neighbors. When the mills went bust, most of Braddock's white residents fled, leaving black residents to pick up the pieces. "This continued omission, erasure, invisibility and silence surrounding African-American sacrifices to Braddock and the American grand narrative," Frazier told Maurice Berger for the *New York Times* (14 Oct. 2014), inspired her to take up her camera and produce her first book of photos, called *The Notion of Family*, in 2014.

In making *The Notion of Family*, Frazier told the novelist Teju Cole for the *New York Times* (10 Feb. 2016), she "spiraled out" in terms of viewpoint. Frazier noted that photographers such as Walker Evans, who had captured images of steel mills, viewed the mills with an outsider's perspective. In contrast, Frazier's own photographs begin on the inside, with her own

family, and move outward to landscapes and aerial views. *The Notion of Family* spans twelve years and includes some of Frazier's best known images including, "Momme (2008)," which features Frazier's mother's profile in the foreground, with Frazier, looking directly at the camera, behind her. This photograph is posed, but others, such as a blurry photograph in which Frazier's grandfather stands from his wheelchair to let Grandma Ruby wipe his bottom, are not.

More so than poverty, illness is a pervasive theme of the book. Frazier recalled her mother, an enthusiastic participant in Frazier's ongoing project, calling her after various operations and surgeries, asking her to come home and document them in photos. Frazier's work documents abuses against her family while actively reclaiming her voice as an African American woman who grew up in poverty. "One of my goals is to disrupt the privileged point of view that only educated and elite practitioners can create work about the poor or disenfranchised," Frazier told the artist Dawoud Bey in an interview for the book, as quoted by Jane Harris for the *Paris Review* (7 Oct. 2014). "My mother did not have to read Roland Barthes to understand death in a photograph."

Frazier's raw and powerful photographs earned her many accolades including a fellowship from the John Simon Guggenheim Memorial Foundation (2014), the Gwendolyn Knight & Jacob Lawrence Prize of the Seattle Art Museum (2013), the Theo Westenberger Award (2012), the Louis Comfort Tiffany Foundation Award (2011), and Art Matters grant (2010). In 2015 Frazier was awarded a prestigious MacArthur Foundation "genius" grant.

SUGGESTED READING

Berger, Maurice. "Born by a River, Watching the Change." *New York Times*. New York Times, 21 Feb. 2014. Web. 3 Apr. 2016.

Berger, Maurice. "LaToya Ruby Frazier's Notion of Family." *New York Times*. New York Times, 14 Oct. 2014. Web. 2 Apr. 2016.

Cole, Teju. "The Living Artist." *New York Times*. New York Times, 10 Feb. 2016. Web. 3 Apr. 2016.

Frazier, LaToya Ruby. Interview by Greg Lindquist. "Haunted: Q&A with LaToya Ruby Frazier." *Art in America*. Art in America, 19 Mar. 2013. Web. 3 Apr. 2016.

Harris, Jane. "The Notion of Family." *Paris Review*. Paris Review, 7 Oct. 2014. Web. 3 Apr. 2016.

Russeth, Andrew. "'LaToya Ruby Frazier: A Haunted Capital' at the Brooklyn Museum." *Observer* [New York]. Observer, 16 July 2013. Web. 3 Apr. 2016.

Straub, Jim, and Bret Liebendorfer. "Braddock, Pennsylvania Out of the Furnace and Into the

Fire." *Monthly Review* 60.7 (2008). Web. 2 Apr. 2016.

—*Molly Hagan*

Katherine Freese

Born: February 8, 1957
Occupation: Physicist

Dr. Katherine Freese has dedicated her career to uncovering some of the universe's deepest secrets. An accomplished researcher specializing in the fields of theoretical cosmology and astroparticle physics, she is a longtime member of the faculty at the University of Michigan in Ann Arbor, where she holds the position of George Eugene Uhlenbeck Professor of Physics. In September 2014 Freese took a leave of absence from the University of Michigan to fill the post of director of NORDITA, the Nordic Institute for Theoretical Physics in Stockholm, Sweden.

At NORDITA, founded by Nobel Prize–winning Danish physicist Niels Bohr in 1957, scientists from all over the world research some of the most cutting-edge concepts in theoretical physics, among them dark matter, one of Freese's chief research concerns. "The dark matter problem is almost one hundred years old," she told Graihagh Jackson for the University of Cambridge–based *Naked Scientists* podcast (2 June 2015) of the scientific community's attempts to identify the invisible particles that may compose much of the mass in the universe. "This is maybe the longest outstanding problem in all of modern physics. So, this is a big one and we really want to nail it. The good news is that we have ideas for what it could be and we think that discovery is around the corner. So, I'm predicting in the next ten years that we'll know."

EARLY LIFE AND EDUCATION
Katherine Freese was born on February 8, 1957, in Freiburg, Germany, one of two children born to Ernst and Elisabeth Bautz Freese. The family moved to the United States when Freese was still a baby. Her parents were both biologists who taught at the University of Wisconsin and later worked for the National Institute of Neurological and Communicative Disorders and Stroke, part of the National Institutes of Health (NIH). Growing up as the child of professors fostered an interest in academia in Freese, who excelled academically, beginning college at the age of sixteen.

Freese attended the Massachusetts Institute of Technology (MIT) for a year before transferring to Princeton University, where she studied physics. She had first become interested in the

Dr. Katherine Freese, University of Michigan Department of Physics

subject at the age of fifteen, when she took a class in physics at the prestigious Phillips Exeter Academy's summer school. "I [thought] physics was a kind of broad field that could open many possibilities, and then I was good at it," Freese told Serena Nobili for the blog of the Oskar Klein Centre for Cosmoparticle Physics (28 Sept. 2012). "I think this is the way many people choose what to study, by exclusion, if you are good at something and not everyone else is, you have to go for it."

GRADUATE STUDIES
Freese graduated from Princeton in 1977 with a bachelor's degree in physics. Unsure of her career path but planning to attend graduate school, she took a break from her academic studies to travel. While living and working in Tokyo, Japan, she developed appendicitis and was eventually hospitalized for an emergency appendectomy. Recovering in the hospital, she read the book *Spacetime Physics* by Edwin Taylor and John Wheeler, which deals with Albert Einstein's theory of special relativity. Inspired by what she read, Freese became newly devoted to physics and resolved to continue her studies in the field. The topics discussed in the book, and Einstein's work in general, would remain of special significance to Freese throughout her career. "I work with Einstein's equations or their immediate consequences every day," she wrote for Princeton University Press's blog (21 Nov. 2015). "I'm a theorist. I invent things and hope they turn out to match reality. All my work lies within the

framework of modern cosmology, which began with Einstein's work in relativity in 1915."

Upon her return to the United States, Freese enrolled in Columbia University, from which she earned her master's degree in 1981. While at Columbia, she began working at the Fermi National Accelerator Laboratory, or Fermilab, outside of Chicago, where she conducted research related to neutrino oscillations. While at Fermilab, Freese traveled to Chicago twice each week to take a cosmology course with David Schramm, a professor at the University of Chicago. Intrigued by Schramm's course, she changed fields and schools to pursue a PhD in cosmology, focusing particularly on the problem of dark matter, with Schramm as her advisor. She earned her PhD from the University of Chicago in 1984.

DARK MATTER

The term dark matter refers to a hypothetical form of matter that some physicists theorize makes up a large portion of the mass of everything in the universe. This matter is referred to as dark because it cannot be detected, as it emits neither light nor energy. Exactly what kind of particles might make up dark matter is a subject of debate, and it was that question that Freese sought to investigate early in her career. While studying under Schramm, she began her study of dark matter by investigating neutrinos; however, she ultimately determined that they were not candidates for dark matter. She moved on to weakly interacting massive particles, or WIMPs, particles that weigh "anywhere between the same mass as a proton or a thousand times as much," she explained to Tom Siegfried for *Quanta Magazine* (22 July 2014), and interact weakly with one another. "The reason that we think this is such a compelling candidate for dark matter is that if you postulate this one thing, these weak interactions, you can explain the amount of dark matter in the universe," she told Siegfried. "These particles are their own antimatter, so whenever they encounter one another, they annihilate, meaning they turn into something else. So when the WIMPs are gone, they turn into photons or other particles. In the early universe we can compute how many there were, and how they accomplished this annihilation among themselves, and then we can ask how many are left today, and you get the right abundance left today to explain the dark matter."

Over the years, Freese also became interested in dark energy, a theoretical form of energy that would affect the universe's rate of expansion. Although regular matter and energy have the ability to convert into one another, dark matter and dark energy are not related in that way; rather, scientists tend to group them together because they are both considered dark, or invisible to normal detection methods.

Another of the intriguing concepts Freese studied is that of dark stars, which Freese believes may have formed only 200 million years after the Big Bang. The term "dark" in this case refers not to the visibility or color of these theoretical stars but to the means by which they are powered. Whereas typical stars are powered by nuclear fusion of hydrogen atoms, Freese and her colleagues suggest that some stars may be powered instead by the annihilation of dark matter. "The products of dark matter annihilation, the photons, electrons, positrons, could get stuck inside this collapsing cloud and heat it up. So it's annihilation power, it's annihilation heating, dark matter heating," she told Siegfried. "These things would be very diffuse, puffy. Their radii are about as large as the distance between the Earth and the Sun, or even ten times that. Their surface temperatures are very cool. Dark matter power is evenly spread out throughout the whole star—unlike in fusion, the power source is not concentrated at the center. But it's a real star." Freese has noted that the James Webb Space Telescope, slated to be launched into space in 2018, will likely be able to detect such stars if they truly exist.

POSITIONS AND PUBLICATIONS

After completing her PhD, Freese completed a postdoctoral fellowship at the Harvard Center for Astrophysics as well as fellowships at the Kavli Institute for Theoretical Physics in Santa Barbara, California, and at the University of California at Berkeley. In 1987 she joined the faculty at MIT as an assistant professor of physics, remaining at the university until 1991. Freese next moved to the University of Michigan in Ann Arbor, where she became an associate professor and gained tenure. She was promoted to full professor in 1999 and was named George E. Uhlenbeck Professor of Physics ten years later.

Over the course of her career, Freese served as a visiting professor at various institutions, including the California Institute of Technology and the European Organization for Nuclear Research (CERN). She also served on many boards, including the international advisory board of the Oskar Klein Center for Cosmoparticle Physics and the executive board of the American Physical Society. The author of more than one hundred papers, Freese has written extensively about numerous concepts, including dark matter, dark stars, and Cardassian expansion, a model of the expansion of the universe that she and coauthor Matthew Lewis named after aliens from the Star Trek franchise. In 2014 she published her first book, *The Cosmic Cocktail: Three Parts Dark Matter*. The book, written primarily for a lay audience, chronicles the history of the search for dark matter, defining the key concepts at play and also detailing Freese's personal involvement in dark matter research.

NORDITA

In September 2014 Freese took a leave of absence from the University of Michigan to fill the position of director at NORDITA, the Nordic Institute for Theoretical Physics in Stockholm, Sweden, for a three-year term. At the institute, scientists carry out research in numerous areas of theoretical physics, including cosmology, astrophysics, and high-energy physics. NORDITA also hosts a variety of conferences and educational programs. "This opportunity to direct one of the major institutes on the planet is exciting," Freese told Siegfried of the directorship. "It's a leadership position that I look forward to trying out."

PERSONAL LIFE

Freese was married to Fred Adams, a theoretical astrophysicist and professor at the University of Michigan, for a number of years. She and Adams have a son, Douglas. When not in residence in Stockholm, Freese divides her time between Ann Arbor and New York. In her free time, she enjoys playing a variety of sports.

SUGGESTED READING

Freese, Katherine. "Big Think Interview with Katie Freese." Interview by David Hirschman. *Big Think*. Big Think, 7 May 2010. Web. 8 Jan. 2016.

Freese, Katherine. *The Cosmic Cocktail: Three Parts Dark Matter*. Princeton: Princeton UP, 2014. Print.

Freese, Katherine. "The End of Darkness?" Interview by Graihagh Jackson. *Naked Scientists*. U of Cambridge, 2 June 2015. Web. 8 Jan. 2016.

Freese, Katherine. "Interview with Katherine Freese." Interview by Serena Nobili. *Oskar Klein Centre for Cosmoparticle Physics*. Oskar Klein Centre for Cosmoparticle Physics, 28 Sept. 2012. Web. 8 Jan. 2016.

Freese, Katherine. "Quick Questions for Katherine Freese, Author of *The Cosmic Cocktail: Three Parts Dark Matter*." Interview by Betsy Blumenthal. *Princeton University Press Blog*. Princeton UP, 17 June 2014. Web. 8 Jan. 2016.

Freese, Katherine. "#ThanksEinstein: Katherine Freese on How Relativity Rejuvenated Her Career." *Princeton University Press Blog*. Princeton UP, 21 Nov. 2015. Web. 8 Jan. 2016.

Siegfried, Tom. "In Search of Dark Stars." *Quanta Magazine*. Simons Foundation, 22 July 2014. Web. 8 Jan. 2016.

—*Joy Crelin*

Ron Funches

Born: March 12, 1983
Occupation: Comedian

"Ron Funches delivers non sequiturs and absurdist observations in a sleepy sing-song, a style that melds surprisingly well with subjects like neck tattoos, Humane Society pamphlets, and the ethnic demographics of the tuba-playing population," Erik Adams wrote for *A.V. Club* (10 July 2014). Funches, who began his career as a stand-up comic, is now perhaps best known for portraying Shelly, a friendly oddball on the popular NBC sitcom *Undateable*. He is reportedly just as quirky and appealing in real life. Describing him as "jolly with a soft-spoken sincerity about him," Blair Socci wrote for *Splitsider* (5 Aug. 2013), "It's hard to find a more likeable person than comedian Ron Funches. . . . He also has one of the top five best laughs in the universe."

Belying conventional wisdom, Funches believes "being nice can be funny," as he explained to Kristi Turnquist for the *Oregonian* (29 July 2012). "My comedy is kind of a counteraction to some of the comedy I don't like. Or things I don't like. Fear-based things, like homophobia or sexism. I like to go the other way with it."

EARLY LIFE

Funches was born on March 12, 1983, in California and moved as an infant with his mother and sister to the Chicago neighborhood of Woodlawn, where, as Funches recalled to Turnquist, there was "a fair amount of shootings and robberies and whatnot."

Nan Palmero/CC BY 2.0/Wikimedia Commons

His mother, a social worker and a fan of comedy, first introduced Funches to television shows such as *I Love Lucy*, which became a particular favorite, and the British skit-based show *Benny Hill*. In those days of VCRs and video-rental stores, she sometimes brought home tapes of popular comedians performing stand-up routines. Funches learned from an early age that if he or his sister were in danger of getting in trouble with their mother, making her laugh was a surefire method to distract her from doling out punishment. Although Funches had a well-honed sense of humor, he was never considered a class clown by his parochial school teachers or friends. He was so shy and soft-spoken that if he thought of a funny line, he merely whispered it to whomever was sitting nearby.

When Funches was thirteen, his mother explained that she could no longer afford to send him to Catholic school, and the thought of attending the local public high school, which featured metal detectors at the school's entrances, caused Funches some trepidation. His father, a pipefitter who was then living in Salem, Oregon, agreed that Funches should come live with him in the Pacific Northwest in order to attend high school.

Salem's McKay High School required some adjustment on Funches's part who was one of the very few black students. He thrived at McKay, however, especially when he was assigned to the advanced-placement English class and introduced to literature by J. D. Salinger and William Faulkner. Funches explained to Turnquist that he "was finally reading something that wasn't boring." Although his parents hoped that he would earn a college degree, Funches lasted just three weeks at a local community college before dropping out. (He now realizes the imprudence of that decision, and he recently costarred in a humorous public service announcement with voice actor and fellow comic Phil LaMarr for a nonprofit group called Get Schooled, which aims to prepare high-school students to attend college.)

Funches embarked on a series of odd jobs, including grocery-store cashier and call-center operator. "The worst job I ever had was working as a Lady Liberty sign-twirler for a tax services place, where I'd just dance and have fun," he recalled to Adams. "The way I talk about it makes it sounds like a fun job—but then I got a staph infection from the costume." His living situation was also sometimes unstable; during one rainy season in Oregon, he slept on a futon in a friend's damp basement for several months, listening to daily threats from the friend's mother that she was going to kick Funches out.

COMEDY CAREER

When Funches was twenty-two years old, a new father, and worried that he might be stuck in dead-end jobs forever, he decided to finally pursue his long-held dream of performing stand-up comedy. He researched local venues that might allow him to perform, and, forcing himself to find his courage, he began participating in open-mic nights.

His initial goals were admittedly modest. "With comedy I just wanted to make enough money . . . where I wouldn't have to work any other job," he told Socci. Thanks to his unusual delivery and engaging persona, Funches gradually found himself winning more and more major gigs. He counts comics Mitch Hedberg and Dave Chappelle as inspirations. Jason Zinoman for the *New York Times* (26 Aug. 2014) described his jokes as having "a melodic, stop-and-go style so laid-back that it's easy to miss how polished they are." Zinoman described Funches as having a "puppy dog persona" and being "naturally adorable," but Zinoman also pointed out that Funches obviously "works at it" because "his brand of cute doesn't just happen."

Zinoman, who was charmed when the comedian threw a handful of candy into the seats during a show, characterized Funches as "a subtle, savvy performer [who] toys with the assumptions of the audience, using them to create tension and set up his jokes." For instance, Zinoman described one routine in Funches's act where Funches addressed an audience member in the front row and said, "Oh hello, Mr. White Face. I mean you no harm. So please don't come at me." He then delivers what at first appears to be the punch line: "That's a conversation I had with a kitty cat several day ago," but Funches is not finished, and he delivers the true punchline, "It's also now the slogan for Black History Month."

Not every audience member has been appreciative of Funches or his humor. One day early in his career, he was performing at a restaurant on the East Coast, when a pair of patrons began making racist comments that included derogatory references to watermelon and Oprah. Funches has explained to journalists that although he was then too surprised to respond effectively, he has since learned to "read" hecklers, discerning which are merely aiming for a little attention and which need to be dealt with more assertively.

ACTING CAREER

In 2012 Funches, who was by then doing his stand-up routines across the country, decided to move to Los Angeles. He had been picking up occasional minor roles on such television shows as the satirical sketch comedy *Portlandia* (on which he portrayed a baseball player), and he knew that if his career was going to continue progressing, he had to place himself at the center of the entertainment industry. He explained to Socci that shortly after the move he realized he needed further training. "People started to become interested in me for acting and I didn't have any type of background. I didn't know how to do any of it," he said. "It's taken a lot of crash courses and acting classes and a great acting coach. It's been a lot of hard work."

That work paid off in 2014, when, after a series of bit parts on a handful of little-seen shows, he was cast as Shelly on *Undateable*, which stars fellow stand-up comic Chris D'Elia who advises his circle of quirky friends on their love lives while being unable to commit to a stable relationship himself. In a review for the *Chicago Tribune* (4 June 2014), Courtney Crowder called Funches's character "the most lovable of the losers, the sweetness at the center of the *Undateable* Tootsie Pop." She continued, "While Funches may not have the most lines or screen time, he's easily the show's most memorable character. His cool, calm delivery and winning one-liners balance out the largeness and plentiful physical comedy of his costars."

Funches continues to perform stand-up shows when his schedule allows, and he appears regularly on such late-night television programs as the *Tonight Show* and *Conan*. Thanks to his distinctive vocal style—he often describes his laugh as being similar to that of an Asian princess—he has done voiceover work on animated shows such as Netflix's *BoJack Horseman* and *The Adventures of Puss in Boots*, FOX network's *Bob's Burgers*, and Cartoon Network's *Adventure Time*. In 2015 he appeared on the big screen in the film *Get Hard*, a comedy starring Will Ferrell and Kevin Hart. Among his upcoming projects is another big-screen comedy, *Killing Hasselhoff*, which is due to appear in 2016 and is about a struggling nightclub owner who must pay off a vicious loan shark.

PERSONAL LIFE
Funches and his wife are no longer together, though Funches speaks highly of her. "I give her much respect and love for making it as far as she did," the comedian told Turnquist, explaining that their marriage was under great stress because he traveled so often when he was performing stand-up comedy full time.

The two have a son, Malcolm, who was diagnosed with autism at the age of two. Funches does not shy away from lovingly joking about Malcolm during his act or discussing Malcolm's autism with journalists. Funches told Theis Duelund for *Los Angeles Magazine* (28 May 2014) that "generally it's easier to tell a joke over and over again when it's something you truly care about. A lady e-mailed me that her child had been diagnosed with autism and that hearing my material on the subject had helped her. To me, it

just means that I'm making the right decision in talking about this." He has also explained to interviewers that his move to Los Angeles to seek higher-profile work was motivated in large part by his determination to provide Malcolm with the best resources and caregivers possible.

Of his future career, he told Crowder, "I want to try as many things that I never tried before as I can. . . . Seeing my face on a billboard or a bus is crazy. I used to be in the bus and now I am outside the bus looking at my face on it."

SUGGESTED READING
Adams, Erik. "Comedian Ron Funches Answers Our 11 Questions." *A.V. Club*. Onion, 10 July 2014. Web. 20 Jan. 2016.

Crowder, Courtney. "Funny How Funches Gets the Laughs in NBC's 'Undateable.'" *Chicago Tribune*. Tribune, 4 June 2014. Web. 20 Jan. 2016.

Duelund, Theis. "7 Things You Need to Know about Comedian Ron Funches." *LAMag*. Emmis, 28 May 2014. Web. 20 Jan. 2016.

Socci, Blair. "Talking to Ron Funches About Standup, LA, and His First Sitcom Acting Gig." *Splitsider*. Awl, 5 Aug. 2013. Web. 20 Jan. 2016.

Turnquist, Kristi. "Rising Star, Comedian Ron Funches Outgrows Portland, Leaves for Los Angeles." *Oregonian*. Oregonian Media Group, 29 July 2012. Web. 20 Jan. 2016.

Zinoman, Jason. "Purrs Like a Kitty Cat, Stings Like a Bee". *New York Times*. New York Times, 26 Aug. 2014. Web. 20 Jan. 2016.

—*Mari Rich*

John Lewis Gaddis

Born: April 2, 1941
Occupation: Historian

John Lewis Gaddis's career as a historian has spanned four decades. In addition to being one of the world's preeminent experts on U.S. foreign policy and the Cold War, he won the 2012 Pulitzer Prize for his official biography of American diplomat and political scientist George F. Kennan.

EARLY LIFE AND EDUCATION
John Lewis Gaddis was born in 1941 in Cotulla, Texas, a small town of 3,600 people in the southeastern part of the state. After graduating Cotulla High School, he enrolled at the University of Texas at Austin, where he earned a bachelor of arts in 1963. Gaddis remained at the university for his graduate work and doctoral work, earning a master's degree in 1965 and a PhD in 1968.

In 1969, Gaddis took a position on the faculty at Ohio University. Over the course of his career, he has also taught at Indiana University, the Naval War College, Princeton University, and the University of Oxford. In 1980, he taught as a Fulbright Scholar at the University of Helsinki.

COLD WAR HISTORIAN

Gaddis's first book, *The United States and the Origins of the Cold War, 1941–1947*, came out in 1972 to significant acclaim, and the Cold War became the central focus of his career. Gaddis published *Containment: Documents on American Foreign Policy and Strategy 1945–1950*, with colleague Thomas H. Etzold in 1978. The book features essays by Gaddis and Etzold and a collection of declassified documents related to America's policy of containment during the Cold War. In *Russia, the Soviet Union, and the United States: An Interpretive History* (1978), Gaddis traces the ideological and political history of the two countries from the eighteenth century to the twentieth century.

Gaddis was awarded a Guggenheim fellowship in 1986. He went on to coauthor *Containing the Soviet Union: A Critique of US Policy* and *The Long Peace: Inquiries into the History of the Cold War*, both published in 1987. In 1992, Gaddis was selected to serve one year as president of the Society for Historians of American Foreign Relations. The collapse of the Soviet Union, which began in 1989, was largely unanticipated by foreign policy analysts and international relations experts. Gaddis's 1992 book, *The United States and the End of the Cold War: Implications, Reconsiderations, Provocations*, presents an analysis of changes in American foreign policy in the years after the founding of the Russian Federation. The Soviet Union's fall afforded Gaddis access to previously classified archives of information in Eastern Europe. This expanded perspective caused Gaddis to reanalyze much of his earlier work, an effort he summarizes in his 1997 book *We Now Know: Rethinking Cold War History*. He served along with colleagues Phillip H. Gordon, Ernest R. May, and Jonathan Rosenberg as coeditor of the 1999 compendium *Cold War Statesmen Confront the Bomb: Nuclear Diplomacy Since 1945*.

In 2005, Gaddis published *The Cold War: A New History*. The work explores the development of relations between the United States and the Soviet Union and their transition from allies during the Second World War to bitter, nuclear-armed rivals. *The Cold War* synthesizes Gaddis's career-long effort to understand and explain the economics and political ideology behind the geopolitical rivalry that greatly informed the creation of the twenty-first century's global political landscape.

GEORGE F. KENNAN: AN AMERICAN LIFE

Gaddis was awarded the 2012 Pulitzer Prize for biography for his book *George F. Kennan: An American Life* (2011). The work is a culmination of a relationship between Gaddis and Kennan that began with a series of interviews in 1981. Kennan—a political scientist, diplomat, and foreign policy advisor to numerous American presidents—is considered one of the founders of the American Cold War–era policy of containment. The term *containment* refers to the economic and security policies undertaken by the American government to deter the spread of communism and the political influence of the Soviet Union throughout the second half of the twentieth century. Communications made by Kennan to colleagues in the United States during the years he served as a diplomat to the Soviet Union helped further the notion among American policy makers that the Russians sought to expand the reach of communist ideology across the globe. *An American Life* was also awarded the 2011 National Book Critics Circle Award and the 2012 American History Book Prize, which is presented annually by the New-York Historical Society.

IMPACT

In May 1997, Priscilla Johnson McMillian of the *New York Times* referred to Gaddis as "the respected dean of Cold War historians." His work has been published in a variety of journals and magazines pertaining to the fields of foreign policy and international relations, including *Diplomatic History, Ethics & International Affairs, Foreign Policy, Foreign Affairs*, and the *American Interest*. In 2005, President George W. Bush presented him with a National Humanities Medal.

PERSONAL LIFE

Gaddis married Barbara Sue Jackson on September 4, 1965. The couple had two sons John Michael Gaddis and David Matthew Gaddis and later divorced. Gaddis married his second wife Toni Dorfman, a theater director, in 1997.

SUGGESTED READING

"Historians Will Debate Cold War." *Lewiston Daily Sun*. Lewiston Daily Sun, 23 Jan. 1989. Web. 8 Apr. 2014.

Italie, Hillel. "Cold War Historian Finishes Epic on George Kennan." *Washington Times*. Washington Times, 19 Apr. 2012. Web. 8 Apr. 2014.

"John Lewis Gaddis on George Kennan." *Wilson Center*. Woodrow Wilson Intl. Center for Scholars, 6 May 2012. Web. 8 Apr. 2014.

Kaplan, Fred. "America's Cold War Sage and His Discontents." *New York Times*. New York Times, 22 Nov. 2011. Web. 8 Apr. 2014.

McMillan, Priscilla Johnson. "Cold Warmonger." *New York Times.* New York Times, 25 May 1997. Web. 8 Apr. 2014.

"Professor John Gaddis, Alumni Win Pulitzer Prizes." *Yale News.* Yale U, 16 Apr. 2012. Web. 8 Apr. 2014.

Thompson, Nicholas. "A Pulitzer for Kennan's Biographer." *New Yorker.* Condé Nast, 16 Apr. 2012. Web. 8 Apr. 2014.

SELECTED WORKS

The United States and the Origins of the Cold War, 1941–1947, 1972; *Containment: Documents on American Foreign Policy and Strategy 1945–1950,* 1978; *Russia, the Soviet Union, and the United States: An Interpretive History,* 1978; *Containing the Soviet Union: A Critique of US Policy,* 1987; *The Long Peace: Inquiries into the History of the Cold War,* 1987; *The United States and the End of the Cold War: Implications, Reconsiderations, Provocations,* 1992; *We Now Know: Rethinking Cold War History,* 1997; *The Landscape of History: How Historians Map the Past,* 2002; *The Cold War: A New History,* 2005; *George F. Kennan: An American Life,* 2011

—*Joshua Pritchard*

Appalachian Encounters (Rhiannon Giddens)/CC BY 2.0/ Wikimedia Commons

Rhiannon Giddens

Born: February 21, 1977
Occupation: Musician

Rhiannon Giddens is one of the founding members of the African American string band Carolina Chocolate Drops, which received a great deal of acclaim and recognition for continuing the string-band tradition after the group won a 2010 Grammy Award for best traditional folk album for *Genuine Negro Jig.* The group played folk music from the nineteenth and early twentieth centuries in a way that breathed new life into it. After the Carolina Chocolate Drops put out their next album, *Leaving Eden* (2012), which was also praised for its vivacious take on old folk tunes, Giddens started working on other projects. The famous roots music producer T Bone Burnett took her under his wing, and in 2015 Giddens released her first solo album, *Tomorrow Is My Turn,* on which she sang the songs of some of her favorite female performers, including Dolly Parton, Patsy Cline, Odetta, and Nina Simone. Thanks to her passion and classically trained voice, the album was very well received.

EARLY LIFE

Rhiannon Giddens was born in 1977. She was raised in Piedmont, North Carolina. Her father is white, and her mother is of African American and Native American ancestry. From a young age Giddens was interested in history, reading, and music. Her taste in music was broad, but it did not yet include the original recorded performers of traditional folk music. She would listen to 1960s folk revival musicians such as Joan Baez and Peter, Paul and Mary rather than old blues and folk musicians such as Lead Belly or Blind Lemon Jefferson. In an interview with *Soundcheck Magazine* (2013), Rhiannon said that in her younger days she had an "eclectic taste," and liked bands like Queen and They Might Be Giants. She also listened to instrumental classical music, such as the notable Spanish classical guitarist Andrés Segovia. By the time she was in high school, Giddens was taking some singing lessons and was in a choir.

CLASSICAL TRAINING

Giddens attended Oberlin College and Conservatory in Oberlin, Ohio. She turned down a full scholarship from Carnegie Mellon University because of its reputation for musical theater, she told David Menconi for *Oberlin* alumni magazine (Spring 2011). Giddens did not want to speak on stage; she only wanted to sing. At Oberlin she studied opera singing. Being insatiably curious, Giddens would do extensive research into the roles she performed. For example, she told Donald Gibson for *No Depression* magazine (26 Oct. 2015), when she was performing in an opera set in eighteenth-century France, she read about and researched that time period to understand "why this character would act the way she does." Giddens received her degree in vocal performance in 2000.

While at Oberlin, she discovered contra dance—a kind of old fashioned folk dance somewhat similar to square dancing. She initially expected it to be a dance in the style of the English countryside, but in fact she heard the band playing old American folk music. This piqued her interest in American folk music and inspired her to learn to play the banjo and the fiddle (a violin played in the folk style).

FORMING THE CAROLINA CHOCOLATE DROPS

Giddens continued to play, sing, and read about American folk music in the years following her graduation. Her love of that music brought her to the Black Banjo Gathering in Boone, North Carolina, in 2005. This convention, as the name suggests, was a gathering focused on the history of African American string bands. At the convention Giddens met the two other founding members of what would become the Carolina Chocolate Drops: fiddle player Justin Robinson and guitar player Dom Flemons. The name of the band is a tribute to the 1930s band Tennessee Chocolate Drops. Together, Giddens, Flemons, and Robinson developed their technique, learned more about American folk music history, and received mentorship from Joe Thompson, a renowned black fiddle player from North Carolina. Thompson, in his eighties by then, taught the band much of their initial repertoire.

The following year the Carolina Chocolate Drops put out their first album, *Dona Got a Ramblin' Mind* (2006). The record consisted of fourteen traditional American folk songs: old blues and country and various mixes thereof. Giddens played banjo and fiddle and sang. Robinson played fiddle, and Flemons played guitar, banjo, harmonica, percussion, and jug. The group's second album, *Heritage* (2008), was a collection of studio and live performances. Musically it was a continuation of the modern take on tradition that the band made in the first album. It featured such songs as "Another Man Done Gone" and "Sittin' on Top of the World," as well as an a cappella performance from Giddens in "Po' Lazarus." The song "Cornbread and Butter Beans," with its up-tempo, knee-slapping rhythm, would go on to become one of the concert audiences' favorites. The band performed the song at MerleFest in 2008, with their mentor Joe Thompson joining them as a fiddler and vocalist. The following year that performance was released on the album *Carolina Chocolate Drops & Joe Thompson* (2009).

GENUINE NEGRO JIG

Genuine Negro Jig (2010), the group's Nonesuch Records debut, was the album that made the name Carolina Chocolate Drops known to a wider audience. The album was produced by Joe Henry, who had worked with the likes of Allen Toussaint and Elvis Costello. It did not take long for the good to excellent reviews to start rolling in. Like the previous album, *Genuine Negro Jig* consisted mostly of traditional songs, with a few exceptions, like covers of Blu Cantrell's modern R & B song "Hit 'em Up Style (Oops!)" and Tom Waits's haunting, melancholy tune "Trampled Rose." There were also originals, like the song "Kissin' and Cussin'," which was written by Justin Robinson. Giddens's voice was certainly one of the stars of the album: it is deeply haunting on "Reynadine," fun and defiant on "Hit 'em Up Style," and beautifully sad on "Why Don't You Do Right?" Others sang as well, and the album was instrumentally supported primarily by banjos and fiddle.

"Erasing the gap between the 1930s and today," wrote Jon Young for *Spin* (23 Feb. 2010), "this striking North Carolina trio brings a modern sizzle to the legacy of classic African American string bands like the Mississippi Sheiks, with fiddles, banjos, and even kazoos sparking an electrifying ruckus." Though reviewers rarely failed to mention how unusual it was for a band with such young members to play such an old style of music, they also often mentioned how the Carolina Chocolate Drops have shed new light on old music without falling into the trap of imitation. "What they've also done is dust off a musical form seen today as either a novelty or the exclusive provenance of ethnomusicologists," wrote Corey duBrowa for *Paste Magazine* (24 Feb. 2010). "Several generations removed from the origins of their chosen idiom, the Carolina Chocolate Drops are nonetheless the genuine article." The album *Genuine Negro Jig* hit number 1 on the Billboard Top Bluegrass Albums chart and number 150 on the Billboard 200 chart. The group also received a 2010 Grammy Award for best traditional folk album.

LEAVING EDEN

The group's second album for Nonesuch Records was preceded by high expectations from both critics and fans. The high quality and sudden success of *Genuine Negro Jig* set a certain standard. *Leaving Eden* was released on February 27, 2012, only a week after the death of Joe Thompson. Prior to the recording of the album, the group suffered another loss of sorts, when Justin Robinson left the band to pursue solo projects. Hubby Jenkins, a multi-instrumentalist, was added on as a new member.

Leaving Eden was a strong record, even stronger than the previous one, some critics said. It was produced by the alternative-country guru Buddy Miller. In his review for Allmusic.com, Steve Leggett observed that as good as the band is, their studio albums up to this point had been "a bit encased in glass compared to the live performances." This time, however, Leggett wrote, they got it right: Miller recorded the album with the band in one room—as opposed to having the band members record separately so the other singers' or players' sound does not "leak" into different microphones—which made the performance sound and feel more like a live show. "The result," Leggett wrote, "is a wonderfully immediate album that feels like a Saturday night house party—complete with moonlight, dust flying from the carpet under the feet of dancers, and crickets and night bird calls out the open windows. The sound breathes, and the Drops shine."

A new voice that was featured on the album was that of Adam Matta, who is a beatboxer, making a surprising range of sounds with only his mouth and microphone. Will Hermes, in a review for *Rolling Stone* (28 Feb. 2012) concluded, "*Leaving Eden* is a lesson in twenty-first-century American folk—a tradition that's as miscegenated as ever, and stronger for it." The album reached number 1 on the *Billboard* Top Bluegrass Albums chart and number 123 on the *Billboard* 200 chart.

TOMORROW IS MY TURN

Giddens's path to recording her first solo album started when she met the respected music producer T Bone Burnett. In 2012 Burnett, who was supervising the making of the album *The Hunger Games: Songs from District 12 and Beyond*, asked the Carolina Chocolate Drops to create a futuristic folk song. The following year, in relation to the Coen Brothers film *Inside Llewyn Davis* (2012), Burnett organized a concert at New York City's Town Hall that had as a theme the 1960s folk revival and its inspirations. Giddens performed Odetta's version of "Water Boy," which got a standing ovation and once again caught Burnett's attention. In 2014 Burnett asked Giddens to join a group of many musicians—including Jim James of My Morning Jacket, Elvis Costello, and Taylor Goldsmith of Dawes—on a Bob Dylan tribute album called *Lost on the River: New Basement Tapes* (2014). Giddens performed a song on the album, and the experience inspired her to write a song of her own.

That song, "Angel City," a peaceful waltz of sorts, would serve as the closing track of *Tomorrow Is My Turn*, Giddens's 2015 solo debut. Burnett had asked Giddens to come up with an idea of what she felt would be her dream album, and she did: an album full of the songs of important and powerful female performers, including Dolly Parton, Patsy Cline, Elizabeth Cotton, Odetta, Nina Simone, Sister Rosetta Tharpe, and Geeshie Wiley, the latter certainly the most obscure. The album, the name of which comes from a song performed by Nina Simone, was definitely a Rhiannon Giddens album and not a Carolina Chocolate Drops album. It was her concept, her vision, and her voice. But it was still deeply steeped in American roots music.

The album received many positive reviews. "Over the past two years, Rhiannon Giddens has become one of the most promising voices in American roots music," was how Jonathan Bernstein began his review for *Rolling Stone* (10 Feb. 2015). Bernstein, who called the album a "feminist tour of the American roots canon," concluded that more often than not Giddens "imbues these classics with a freshness and vitality that feel right at home in 2015." Hal Horowitz for *American Songwriter* (10 Feb. 2015) proposed that it was Giddens's "golden, soulful voice that is the real attraction. She treats these songs respectfully but not overly so, allowing her own style to emerge in the process."

Though striking out on her own gained her additional attention and praise, Giddens remains adamant that she does not desire stardom. "It's not about me, it's about the music," she told Jon Pareles for the *New York Times* (23 Jan. 2015). "I don't do this because I want to be a star. I don't do this because I want to make a lot of money. . . . This is a calling, definitely."

PERSONAL LIFE

Giddens is married to the Irish musician Michael Laffan. They have two children, and have homes in both North Carolina and Ireland.

SUGGESTED READING

Bernstein, Jonathan. Rev. of *Tomorrow Is My Turn*, by Rhiannon Giddens. *Rolling Stone*. Rolling Stone, 10 Feb. 2015. Web. 11 Apr. 2016.

Giddens, Rhiannon. "Learning Curves and Musical Curiosities." Interview by Donald Gibson. *No Depression*. Freshgrass, 26 Oct. 2015. Web. 11 Apr. 2016.

Horowitz, Hal. Rev. of *Tomorrow Is My Turn*, by Rhiannon Giddens. *American Songwriter*. ForASong Media, 10 Feb. 2015. Web. 11 Apr. 2015.

Pareles, Jon. "A Solo Spotlight for a Powerful Voice." *New York Times*. New York Times, 23 Jan. 2015. Web. 11 Apr. 2016.

SELECTED WORKS

Heritage, 2008; *Genuine Negro Jig*, 2010; *Leaving Eden*, 2012; *Tomorrow Is My Turn*, 2015

—*Dmitry Kiper*

Domhnall Gleeson

Born: May 12, 1983
Occupation: Actor

Irish actor Domhnall Gleeson is perhaps one of the more unlikely household names in film. The son of successful character actor Brendan Gleeson, he was initially reluctant to follow his father into the field of professional acting, preferring to try his hand at screenwriting and directing instead. By the age of twenty-three, however, he had earned a Tony Award nomination for his featured role in the Broadway production of the play *The Lieutenant of Inishmore*. A decade later, he had appeared in two of the biggest cinematic franchises of all time—Harry Potter and Star Wars—as well as several Academy Award–winning films. For Gleeson, this dramatic career trajectory has been less a planned rise to prominence and more a side effect of the high caliber of the projects in which he feels fortunate to have appeared. "All I know is when you read a great script, you know it," he told James Mottram for the *Independent* (14 Dec. 2015). "And I've been lucky . . . I got to read a number of them and got to be in a few. So I'm hoping I can continue that."

EARLY LIFE AND EDUCATION

Domhnall Gleeson was born on May 12, 1983, in Dublin, Ireland, the first of four sons born to Brendan Gleeson and Mary Weldon. His mother worked as a community welfare officer, while his father was a teacher who left that career to pursue work as an actor when Gleeson was very young. Although he entered the realm of professional acting relatively late in life, embarking on his new career path while in his mid-thirties, the elder Gleeson soon established himself as a successful character actor, initially in television movies and later in major films such as *Braveheart* (1995), *Gangs of New York* (2002), *In Bruges* (2008), and several films in the Harry Potter series.

Gleeson and his brothers grew up in Malahide, a coastal town north of Dublin. As a child and teen, he was aware of his father's attempts to break into acting and subsequent work in the field but was largely unaware of any hardships the family faced during those early years. "You might know you didn't have the coolest trainers but you don't realise it was hard for your parents to get Christmas together some years," he explained to Ryan Gilbey for the *Guardian* (16 Aug. 2012). Despite his father's success as an actor and his own positive experiences acting in school plays, Gleeson was largely uninterested in acting professionally, preferring instead to pursue a career behind the camera. After graduating from Malahide Community School, he

Gage Skidmore/CC BY-SA 3.0/Wikimedia Commons

attended the Dublin Institute of Technology to study media arts.

EARLY CAREER

Gleeson's induction into the realm of acting was largely accidental. In 1999, Brendan Gleeson was awarded the Irish Film and Television Award (IFTA) for best actor for his role in the 1998 film *The General*. As his father was unable to attend the award ceremony, Gleeson, then sixteen years old, attended and accepted the award in his father's place. His father had given him several pages of notes, but facing a limited amount of time in which to deliver an acceptance speech, Gleeson was forced to improvise. "I wasn't really a showoff. I was quite shy," he told Donald Clarke for the *Irish Times* (15 Jan. 2016). "I made some stupid joke about how teachers know I'm really good at skimming. It got a lot of laughs. It was live on TV and it had been quite a somber ceremony. I lightened the mood." Following his appearance at the IFTAs, an agent contacted Gleeson and offered to represent him. Though reluctant to pursue acting work, he accepted the offer. "I said to the agent, 'I don't want to be an actor,'" he told Adam B. Vary for *BuzzFeed Entertainment* (21 Dec. 2015). "But it's cool to *have* an agent. Maybe some girl will be impressed—which didn't work."

For three years after his speech at the IFTAs, Gleeson largely avoided professional acting work, taking on only one role: a small part in the 2001 television miniseries *Rebel Heart*. While attending university, however, his agent alerted him to an opportunity that appealed to him, and Gleeson ultimately made his stage debut in *The*

Lieutenant of Inishmore, a new play by award-winning playwright and screenwriter Martin McDonagh that was performed in London in the summer of 2002. Gleeson later traveled to New York to perform in the play when it made its Broadway debut in 2006, appearing throughout its four-month run. He was nominated for the Tony Award for best featured actor in a play for his performance in the Broadway production. This first major role was a life-changing one for Gleeson, prompting him to consider a full-time acting career seriously. "I am pretty certain I wouldn't have been an actor if I hadn't read for *The Lieutenant of Inishmore*," he told Clarke. "If I hadn't gotten it, the path would have been very different."

FILM AND TELEVISION

In the years between the London and New York performances of *The Lieutenant of Inishmore*, Gleeson took on a number of roles in television and film, including parts in the 2005 horror comedy *Boy Eats Girl* and the television series *The Last Furlong* (2005). Among his most significant projects during that period was a small role in the Academy Award–winning short film *Six Shooter* (2004), which was written and directed by McDonagh and starred Gleeson's father. *Six Shooter* was the first of several projects in which Gleeson and his father would appear together, some of which would also feature his brother Brian, the second of the Gleeson children to pursue a career in the field.

For several years following *The Lieutenant of Inishmore's* run on Broadway, however, Gleeson took on no acting work, in part because of his own limitations as an actor at the time. "I found out very quickly that if I was going to work, I was going to have to work very hard to try to do different things, not just play a version of myself," he explained to Vary. "That would be the only way to keep interested in acting, but also, the only way to keep working." By 2009, however, Gleeson had returned to acting professionally, appearing in films such as *A Dog Year* and *Perrier's Bounty* that year. The following year brought supporting roles in the critically acclaimed films *Never Let Me Go* and *True Grit*. Gleeson also fulfilled his earlier goal of working behind the camera during that period, writing and directing the short films *What Will Survive of Us* (2009) and *Noreen* (2010) as well as writing for the television sketch comedy show *Your Bad Self*.

BREAKTHROUGH ROLES

In addition to steady work, the year 2010 brought what was perhaps Gleeson's most high-profile work to that point. Since 2005, Brendan Gleeson had appeared in the blockbuster Harry Potter film series, playing the dark wizard–hunter Alastor "Mad-Eye" Moody. In 2010's *Harry Potter and the Deathly Hallows: Part 1* Gleeson joined his father, filling the role of Potter ally Bill Weasley. He went on to reprise the role in part two of the film the following year. Although the role of Bill was a relatively small one, the global popularity of the Harry Potter series brought Gleeson to the attention of millions of viewers.

The next major shift in Gleeson's career came in 2012, when he appeared in a supporting role in *Anna Karenina*, an adaptation of the 1877 Leo Tolstoy novel directed by British filmmaker Joe Wright. Prior to that film, Gleeson had primarily been offered roles of "cowards, creeps, and sex pests," as Irish director Tom Hall put it to Gilbey. "I'm not built like a leading man," Gleeson explained to Gilbey. "Conventionally handsome is not really where I'm at." His role in *Anna Karenina*, however, cast him in a new light. As the aristocratic Konstantin Levin, a romantic figure in the film, Gleeson demonstrated his ability to play yet another type of character. "I had never played any romantic parts before Joe decided that I could," he told Vary. "That was a massive shift in my career, in terms of the jobs I was able to do." The actor further demonstrated his versatility in the 2013 romance *About Time*, about a young man who discovers that he has the ability to time travel. Gleeson went on to appear in a number of other major projects, including the 2014 films *Calvary*, in which he appeared alongside his father, and *Unbroken*. For the latter film, a World War II drama, Gleeson lost a significant amount of weight, so much that his contact lenses no longer fit his eyes.

A BUSY YEAR

If the years following Gleeson's appearance in *Harry Potter and the Deathly Hallows* were formative ones for his career, 2015 was the year in which he was seemingly everywhere. Of the four films in which he starred that year, two—*Brooklyn* and *The Revenant*—were nominated for the Academy Award for best picture, while the science-fiction thriller *Ex Machina* was well received by critics and audiences. It was his role in *Star Wars: The Force Awakens*, however, that made Gleeson a household name.

Gleeson plays General Hux in the film, the first of several planned sequels to the original Star Wars trilogy. A leader of the First Order, the successor to the Empire of the original films, Hux works closely with the villainous Kylo Ren (Adam Driver) and represents a significant threat to heroes Rey (Daisy Ridley) and Finn (John Boyega). Gleeson has admitted that despite the cultural influence of the Star Wars franchise, he was initially reluctant to take the role when it was offered, as he had not had the opportunity to read the script. When the filmmakers allowed him to read the script, however, it immediately won him over. His experience working on the film was a positive one, and though he had not been a devoted childhood fan of the Star Wars films, the enthusiasm surrounding the film was inescapable. "One thing [director JJ Abrams] is very good at doing is imbuing a whole set with a very positive atmosphere," Gleeson told Mottram. "Every time, before they called 'action,' if the adrenaline or energy had dropped a little bit, it would be like, 'Everybody—Star Wars! Stand up straight. Come on! How great is this!? Come on! Let's go, let's go! Action!' And then you barrel into it." Gleeson is set to reprise the role of Hux in the following Star Wars film, scheduled for release in December 2017.

PERSONAL LIFE
When not filming, Gleeson resides in Dublin.

SUGGESTED READING
Calia, Michael. "'Ex Machina' and 'Star Wars' Star Domhnall Gleeson Geeks Out about Sci Fi and Film Noir." *Wall Street Journal.* Dow Jones, 24 Apr. 2015. Web. 11 Mar. 2016.

Clarke, Donald. "Domhnall Gleeson: The Force Is Strong in This One." *Irish Times.* Irish Times, 15 Jan. 2016. Web. 11 Mar. 2016.

De Semlyen, Phil. "10 Things We Learnt about Domhnall Gleeson." *Empire.* Bauer Consumer Media, 19 Jan. 2016. Web. 11 Mar. 2016.

Gilbey, Ryan. "Domhnall Gleeson: 'Handsome Is Not Really Where I'm At.'" *Guardian.* Guardian News and Media, 16 Aug. 2012. Web. 11 Mar. 2016.

Gleeson, Domhnall. Interview by Angelina Jolie. *Interview.* Interview, 4 June 2015. Web. 11 Mar. 2016.

Mottram, James. "*Star Wars: The Force Awakens*—Domhnall Gleeson on Playing the Villain and How JJ Abrams Inspired the Cast." *Independent.* Independent, 14 Dec. 2015. Web. 11 Mar. 2016.

Vary, Adam B. "The Year We All Learned How to Pronounce Domhnall Gleeson." *BuzzFeed Entertainment.* BuzzFeed, 21 Dec. 2015. Web. 11 Mar. 2016.

SELECTED WORKS
Six Shooter, 2004; *A Dog's Year,* 2009; *Perrier's Bounty,* 2009; *Never Let Me Go,* 2010; *True Grit,* 2010; *Harry Potter and the Deathly Hallows: Part 1,* 2010; *Harry Potter and the Deathly Hallows: Part 2,* 2011; *Anna Karenina,* 2012; *About Time,* 2013; *Calvary,* 2014; *Unbroken,* 2014; *Ex Machina,* 2015; *Brooklyn,* 2015; *Star Wars: The Force Awakens,* 2015; *The Revenant,* 2015

—Joy Crelin

Renée Elise Goldsberry

Born: January 2, 1971
Occupation: Actor

Renée Elise Goldsberry was already a veteran of the stage and screen when, in 2014, she was cast as one of the leads in Lin-Manuel Miranda's groundbreaking Broadway musical *Hamilton,* which is inspired by historian Ron Chernow's 2004 eponymous biography of Alexander Hamilton, one of the founding fathers of the United States. Since its Off-Broadway debut in 2015, *Hamilton,* which fuses rap, hip-hop, and other varieties of music with traditional musical theater conventions, has become a cultural phenomenon, winning numerous awards and honors and garnering "the kind of worshipful press usually reserved for the appearances of once-in-a-lifetime comets or the births of little royal celebrities," as theater critic Ben Brantley wrote in his review of the musical for the *New York Times* (6 Aug. 2015).

Known for portraying strong and independent women, Goldsberry has won widespread praise for her performance in the play as Hamilton's sister-in-law, Angelica Schuyler Church. Among other awards, in 2016, she received her first Tony Award in the category for best featured actress in a musical.

EARLY LIFE AND EDUCATION
Renée Elise Goldsberry was born on January 2, 1971, in California. She grew up in Houston, Texas, and Bloomfield Hills, a suburb of Detroit, Michigan. Her father is a prominent chemist and

Walter McBride/Getty Images

businessman and her mother, an industrial organizational psychologist, is the president and owner of Humanomics, Inc., a business consulting firm based in Houston.

Despite her left-brained pedigree, Goldsberry became drawn to the performing arts at an early age. As a young girl, "I wasn't just playing with baby dolls," she noted to Karu F. Daniels for the NBC News website (8 May 2016). "I was standing in the mirror with brush in my hand as a microphone singing songs." She has said that her parents sang to her from the time she was an infant and that they always encouraged her to pursue her passions.

Goldsberry first got her start on stage at the age of eight when she appeared alongside her younger brother in a production of Frank Loesser's musical *Guys and Dolls* at a summer camp sponsored by the Houston International Theatre School. "I fell in love with it immediately and deeply. It created a monster," she told Andrew Dansby for the *Houston Chronicle* (11 June 2016).

That "monster" did not show itself, however, until Goldsberry's junior year at Cranbrook Kingswood High School in Bloomfield Hills, when she first began auditioning for the school's plays and musicals. After debuting in the lead role of Nellie Forbush in a production of the musical *South Pacific*, she established herself as one of the school's standout actors. At Cranbrook, she was also a four-year member of the Madrigals, an all-female chamber singing choir.

Upon completing high school, Goldsberry attended Carnegie Mellon University's prestigious School of Drama in Pittsburgh, Pennsylvania, where she earned a Bachelor of Fine Arts degree in musical theater in 1993 before earning a master's degree in vocal jazz performance from the University of Southern California's Thornton School of Music in 1997.

TELEVISION AND BROADWAY DEBUTS

The same year Goldsberry completed her formal schooling, she participated in the inaugural John Lennon Songwriting Contest, where she claimed the prize for best rock song. Also in 1997, she made her small-screen debut, landing a recurring role as a backup singer on FOX's hour-long legal dramedy series *Ally McBeal*. She would appear in more than forty episodes of the hit show, which aired for five seasons before being canceled in 2002.

Concurrently with her role on *Ally McBeal*, in 2001, Goldsberry made her feature-film debut in a starring role in the indie romantic comedy *All about You*, for which she received critical praise for her performance; she was additionally credited with cowriting several of the songs on the film's soundtrack. She also made guest appearances on a number of other television series,

including *Providence* (2002) and *Star Trek: Enterprise* (2002).

When she landed her first Broadway job as a replacement for the lead role of Nala in the award-winning musical production of Disney's *The Lion King* in 2002, Goldsberry moved to New York. The high-profile role opened the door to other acting opportunities, and in February 2003, she originated the role of defense attorney Evangeline Williamson on the long-running ABC soap opera *One Life to Live*.

Goldsberry appeared in more than 250 episodes of the show from 2003 to 2007. For her portrayal of Williamson, she was nominated for consecutive Daytime Emmy Awards for best supporting actress in 2006 and 2007. She also earned Image Award nominations from the National Association for the Advancement of Colored People (NAACP) for best actress in a drama series in 2004 and 2007. She credited her experience on the show with helping her learn about "the rooting factor" of the characters she portrays, as she put it to Victoria Myers for the theater website *The Interval* (26 Apr. 2016). Her job as an actor, she explained to Myers, is to get audiences "involved and invested in my character, so I have to fight for my character and pull off your idea."

BROADWAY AND OFF-BROADWAY MAINSTAY

During her four-year run on *One Life to Live*, Goldsberry remained actively involved in the theater. In the summer of 2005, she played the role of Silvia in the Shakespeare in the Park rock musical production of *Two Gentleman of Verona*, which was staged for a two-week run at the Delacorte Theater in New York's Central Park. She earned plaudits for her lively performance; in his review for the *New York Times* (29 Aug. 2005), Ben Brantley called her "the production's true find, a sparkplug of musical wit and vitality."

In December 2005, Goldsberry originated the role of Nettie in the Broadway musical production of *The Color Purple*, which is based on Alice Walker's 1982 Pulitzer Prize–winning novel of the same name. She left the production after only a month, however, to give birth to her first child. She would return to the stage in late 2007 to appear in an Off-Broadway revival of the musical *The Baker's Wife*.

Returning to Broadway in June 2008, Goldsberry replaced Tamyra Gray as the heroin-addicted stripper Mimi Marquez in *Rent*, the Pulitzer Prize–winning rock musical written by Jonathan Larson. She portrayed Mimi until the end of the play's run in September of that year, and appeared in the live film version of the final stage performance. At the time of its closure, *Rent* was the seventh-longest-running show in Broadway history. She also continued to supplement her stage work with television roles, and in

2010, she began appearing on the CBS legal drama *The Good Wife*, starring Julianna Margulies. Goldsberry portrayed the recurring character of assistant district attorney Geneva Pine, appearing in twenty-three episodes over the course of the show's seven-season run from 2009 to 2016.

In 2011, Goldsberry costarred with Frances McDormand and Tate Donovan in David Lindsay-Abaire's limited-run Broadway drama *Good People*, which offers a portrait of life in South Boston. Her portrayal of Kate, Donovan's character's wife, won her an Outer Critics Circle Award nomination. She next garnered strong critical notices for her turns in Off-Broadway productions of the Shakespeare comedies *Love's Labor's Lost* and *As You Like It*, in 2011 and 2012, respectively. She would also give "a dynamic and layered performance," Myers noted, as singer Heather Jones in a revival of the musical *I'm Getting My Act Together and Taking It on the Road*, which was presented as part of the inaugural season of the Off-Broadway musical series Encores! Off-Center in 2013. As for films, Goldsberry played a bereaved mother in the McDormand-produced crime drama *Every Secret Thing* in 2014 and had a small role in the Tina Fey/Amy Poehler comedy *Sisters* in 2015.

LIFE-CHANGING ROLE IN *HAMILTON*

Goldsberry was on "a self-imposed maternity leave" when she first heard about auditions for *Hamilton*, as she recalled to Pamela Jacobs in an interview for *Resident* magazine (Sept. 2015). Miranda's hip-hop musical traces the life and political career of Alexander Hamilton, the first US treasury secretary, who was killed in a famous 1804 duel with vice president Aaron Burr, his political rival and onetime friend. It draws focus to Hamilton's relationships with Burr and other real-life historical figures, including his wife, Eliza; her sister, Angelica; the French aristocrat and American Revolutionary War hero Marquis de Lafayette; and US presidents George Washington, Thomas Jefferson, and James Madison.

Goldsberry initially thought herself unsuited to play the intellectual Angelica, whose character was described as a cross between Trinidadian-born rapper Nicki Minaj and aging singer Desiree Armfeldt from the Stephen Sondheim musical *A Little Night Music*. However, after hearing Miranda's demo for Angelica's signature song, a rap solo titled "Satisfied," she auditioned for and eventually won the part. The song "was unlike anything I'd ever heard," she told Jacobs, adding that it was enough to convince her that *Hamilton* "was going to be a huge hit."

That instinct proved valid as *Hamilton* opened to rapturous reviews when it received its world premiere Off-Broadway at New York's Public Theater in February 2015. The nearly three-hour-long musical, which features a predominantly African American and Latino cast, enjoyed a wildly successful, sold-out three-month run, during which it was attended by numerous political luminaries, journalists, and celebrities. For her portrayal of Angelica, Goldsberry won the Drama Desk Award and the Lucille Lortel Award for best featured actress in a musical.

CULTURAL PHENOMENON

In August 2015, *Hamilton* moved to the Richard Rodgers Theatre on Broadway. Anticipation for *Hamilton*'s Broadway premiere was such that it pulled in upward of $57 million in advance ticket sales, the highest-ever figure for a Broadway show. Goldsberry and most of the musical's other original cast members, which, in addition to Miranda (Hamilton), included Leslie Odom Jr. (Burr), Daveed Diggs (Jefferson and de Lafayette), and Phillipa Soo (Eliza), reprised their roles from the Off-Broadway production.

As it had during its run at the Public Theater, *Hamilton* received nearly unanimous praise from critics, many of whom labeled it a zeitgeist-defining musical. Brantley observed that *Hamilton* offers "proof that the American musical is not only surviving but also evolving in ways that should allow it to thrive and transmogrify in years to come," and credited it with "changing the language of musicals" through its innovative use of hip-hop, rap, and R&B music as narrative storytelling devices. Jacobs called *Hamilton* "a perfect piece of art," Miranda "the Shakespeare of our time," and Goldsberry's performance "flawless, powerful, evocative, and just plain wonderful." Many reviewers singled out Goldsberry for her riveting portrayal of Angelica, who was believed by some to have been Hamilton's lover. David Cote, in his review for *Time Out New York* (6 Aug. 2015), commented that Goldsberry, who also takes the lead on songs titled "The Schuyler Sisters" and "It's Quiet Uptown," "will make you demand a spinoff musical all her own."

Goldsberry was featured on the forty-six-track original Broadway cast album for *Hamilton*, which, upon its release in September 2015, debuted at number twelve on the Billboard 200 albums chart, the highest entry for a cast recording since 1963. The album reached number three on the Billboard 200 chart and number one on the Billboard rap albums chart; in February 2016, it took home the Grammy Award for best musical theater album.

Two months after its Grammy win, *Hamilton* was awarded the 2016 Pulitzer Prize for Drama. It went on to earn a record-breaking sixteen Tony Award nominations, taking home eleven total awards, including the coveted trophy for best musical. Goldsberry captured her first Tony Award for best performance by a featured actress in a musical.

LIFE AFTER *HAMILTON*

As a member of the *Hamilton* company, Goldsberry has experienced a grueling schedule of
eight performances a week. In July 2016, following the departures of Miranda, Soo, Odom,
and Diggs, it was announced that she would be
leaving the musical that fall to play a lead role
in Netflix's ten-episode science-fiction drama
series *Altered Carbon*. She remains confident,
however, that *Hamilton*, which has spawned
a Chicago production and a US national tour,
will continue to flourish with new performers.
"It feels like there are pieces of art that need to
be in the world, and this [*Hamilton*] is one of
them," she told Dansby.

PERSONAL LIFE

Goldsberry resides in Manhattan with her husband, attorney Alexis Johnson. The couple have
a son, Benjamin, and an adopted daughter,
Brielle.

SUGGESTED READING

Brantley, Ben. "Review: *Hamilton*, Young Rebels
Changing History and Theater." Rev. of *Ham-
ilton*, dir. Thomas Kail. *New York Times*. New
York Times, 6 Aug. 2015. Web. 18 July 2016.

Dansby, Andrew. "Tony Nominee Bitten by
Acting Bug as Child in Houston." *Houston Chronicle*. Hearst Newspapers, 11 June
2016. Web. 18 July 2016.

Goldsberry, Renée Elise. "*Hamilton*'s Renée
Elise Goldsberry." Interview by Pamela Ja-
cobs. *Resident*. Resident, Sept. 2015. Web. 18
July 2016.

Goldsberry, Renée Elise. "An Interview with
Renée Elise Goldsberry." Interview by Vic-
toria Myers. *Interval*. Interval, 26 Apr. 2016.
Web. 18 July 2016.

SELECTED WORKS

Ally McBeal, 1997–2002; *The Lion King*, 2002–
3; *One Life to Live*, 2003–7; *The Color Purple*,
2005–6; *Rent*, 2008; *The Good Wife*, 2010–16;
Good People, 2011; *Hamilton*, 2015–16

—*Chris Cullen*

Paul Goldschmidt

Born: September 10, 1987
Occupation: Baseball player

Arizona Diamondbacks slugger Paul Goldschmidt has been affectionately referred
to by his teammates and fans as "America's
first baseman" for his combination of wholesome attributes and outstanding talent. One
of the best all-around players in Major League

David/Flickr/Ucinternational/CC BY 2.0/Wikimedia Commons

Baseball (MLB), Goldschmidt rose to the top
of the game through "the relentlessness of his
will," as Ben Reiter noted for *Sports Illustrated*
(19 Aug. 2015).

Despite an imposing six-foot-three,
225-pound physique, Goldschmidt was ignored
by major college programs coming out of high
school. Even after a strong performance at Texas
State University, he was only an eighth-round
choice of the Arizona Diamondbacks in the 2009
MLB Draft. Goldschmidt nonetheless rose rapidly through the Diamondbacks' farm system and
made his MLB debut during the 2011 season,
soon developing into one of baseball's most consistent and productive players. He was runner-
up in the voting for the National League (NL)
Most Valuable Player (MVP) Award in 2013
and 2015 and earned four consecutive All-Star
selections from 2013 to 2016. He also defied
detractors by transforming himself into one of
the game's best defensive first basemen, winning
Gold Glove Awards in 2013 and 2015.

EARLY LIFE

Paul Edward Goldschmidt was born on September 10, 1987, in Wilmington, Delaware, to
David and Kim Goldschmidt. He grew up with
two younger brothers, Adam and Robert. When
Goldschmidt was around five, his family moved
to The Woodlands, Texas, an affluent suburb
of Houston.

Goldschmidt's paternal great-grandparents
were Jews who left Germany in 1938 to escape persecution by the Nazis. They moved
to the United States, settling in Boston, Massachusetts, where they ran a luncheonette.

Goldschmidt's paternal grandfather, Ernie, owned a series of food-related businesses, while his father carried on his family's entrepreneurial spirit in the flooring industry.

Goldschmidt started playing baseball at the age of five at the urging of his father, who was a diehard fan of Boston's storied MLB franchise, the Red Sox. Despite initially enjoying soccer more than baseball, he immediately fell in love with the sport. Goldschmidt's father spent countless hours throwing to him during batting practice and built a soft-toss net in the family garage so he could spend extra time working on his hitting mechanics. The two often watched telecasts of Houston Astros games, with Goldschmidt's father using the opportunity to teach him about the fundamentals of the game by scrutinizing players' performances.

Growing up, Goldschmidt also played other sports, which, in addition to soccer, included football, basketball, and roller hockey. By the time he reached the eighth grade, however, he had settled on baseball. He was always one of the standouts on his youth baseball teams, despite not necessarily being the most naturally gifted. As his father put it to Reiter, "He was always a good athlete growing up, but there were always better players."

HIGH SCHOOL AND COLLEGE CAREER

Goldschmidt attended the Woodlands High School, where he played on the varsity baseball team. One of the smaller players on the team, Goldschmidt initially played second base and, despite having superb baseball acumen, showed little glimpses of the power he would eventually possess. Evaluators also considered his swing too long to work against higher-level pitching and his defense lacking. Following his freshman season, he began weight training and putting in extra hours on the field and in the batting cages to improve his all-around game.

During the summer after his sophomore season, Goldschmidt played for the elite Kyle Chapman travel-baseball program, during which he caught the attention of Trip Couch, then the Arizona Diamondbacks' Houston-area scout. Couch was as impressed by Goldschmidt's demeanor as he was by his then-burgeoning power. By that time, the young player had been moved to third base, thanks to a growth spurt and muscle development.

Goldschmidt showcased his power during his senior season in 2006, when he helped Woodlands High win a state title. He was, however, overshadowed by several of his teammates, particularly Kyle Drabek, a highly coveted pitcher who was selected in the first round of that year's MLB Draft by the Philadelphia Phillies. Goldschmidt was a forty-ninth-round pick by the Los Angeles Dodgers and was mostly overlooked by major college programs. "I think people undervalued how well he could hit," Couch explained to Seth Livingstone for *USA Today* (30 Aug. 2011). "He was a big kid who sometimes looked a little stiff playing third base."

Instead of entering the Dodgers' farm system, Goldschmidt opted to accept a scholarship to Texas State University (TSU), in San Marcos, Texas. In three seasons at TSU, he proved his critics wrong, establishing school records for home runs and runs batted in (RBIs). Goldschmidt emerged as a bona fide major-league prospect during his junior season in 2009, when he batted .352 with eighteen home runs and eighty-eight RBIs in fifty-seven games and led the team to the Southland Conference championship. Ty Harrington, his coach at Texas State, called him "the most organized, persistent, inspired worker I've coached in my career," as he told Bob Young for the *Arizona Republic* (9 July 2013). "That guy wakes up in the morning," Harrington added, "and he can tell you what he is going to do that day to get better."

ARIZONA DIAMONDBACKS

Despite concerns about Goldschmidt's defense and what was still considered to be a long swing, Couch ultimately convinced the Diamondbacks' management to draft him, thanks largely to his makeup, which was given a score of eighty, the highest grade allowed on a scouting report. Goldschmidt's "makeup is as good as any kid I've ever been around in twenty years of college and pro baseball," Jerry Dipoto, the Diamondbacks' former senior vice president of scouting and player development, asserted to Livingstone. "He never wants to talk about himself. He'll tell people it's about the team."

Still, the Diamondbacks selected five other corner infielders before selecting Goldschmidt in the eighth round, as the 246th overall pick, of the 2009 MLB Draft. Upon joining the Diamondbacks, Goldschmidt was moved to first base, which coaches felt better suited his tall, bulky frame. In an attempt to become more of a complete player, he began working in earnest on his defense, which up until that point had been considered the weakest part of his game. "I realized if I wanted to play baseball as a career, I needed to outwork everyone else," Goldschmidt explained to Livingstone.

Goldschmidt hit his way through rookie-level ball in 2009, batting .334 with eighteen home runs and sixty-two RBIs in seventy-four games for the Missoula Osprey. He again put up impressive offensive numbers during the 2010 season, when he racked up 35 home runs, 42 doubles, and 108 RBIs in 138 games for the Diamondbacks' advanced-A affiliate, the Visalia Rawhide of the California League. He was named the league's MVP and the Diamondbacks' organizational player of the year.

EARLY MLB CAREER

For the start of the 2011 season, the Diamondbacks assigned Goldschmidt to the Mobile Bay-Bears in the AA Southern League. Despite being in a more pitcher-friendly league, he continued to build on his success at the plate, hitting .306 with twenty-one doubles, thirty homers, and ninety-four RBIs in 103 games before being promoted to the Diamondbacks' big-league club in August 2011. At the time of his call-up, he was leading all minor leaguers in home runs and RBIs. (Goldschmidt was later named *USA Today's* minor league player of the year for 2011.)

Goldschmidt recorded a single in his first major-league at-bat and ultimately went one-for-four in a 5–2 Diamondbacks victory. Quickly thrust into an everyday starting role, he proceeded to collect five home runs and thirteen RBIs in his next twenty games. Goldschmidt finished his rookie season with a .250 batting average, a .474 slugging percentage, eight home runs, and twenty-six RBIs in forty-eight games, providing a spark down the stretch for a Diamondbacks team that captured its first NL West title since 2007.

In the 2011 playoffs the Diamondbacks lost in the first round to the Milwaukee Brewers in five games. Goldschmidt appeared in four games of the series, in which he batted a scorching .438 with two home runs and six RBIs. He became only the second rookie in MLB history to homer in his first two playoff games.

During his first full MLB season in 2012, Goldschmidt solidified his role as the Diamondbacks' starting first baseman. He batted .286 with forty-three doubles, twenty home runs, and eighty-two RBIs in 145 games. Many of Goldschmidt's home runs were of the tape-measure variety, the most notable of which came on May 27, when he hit a 471-foot shot against the Brewers at Chase Field, the longest at that ballpark that season.

Power displays aside, Goldschmidt also showcased other blossoming aspects of his game. He finished second among NL first basemen in stolen bases (18) and third among league first basemen in fielding percentage (.995). "People who hit like him are usually content with getting on base, hitting a homer here, driving in a run there," Diamondbacks center fielder A. J. Pollock told Reiter. "But if there's another element of the game out there, he's looking to gain an edge on it."

HUMBLE SUPERSTAR

Over the next three seasons, Goldschmidt proved to be a model of consistency for the Diamondbacks as he established himself as a perennial All-Star and MVP candidate. Prior to the 2013 season, the Diamondbacks signed Goldschmidt to a five-year, $32 million contract extension. Team president and CEO Derrick Hall called the first baseman "an organizational dream," as quoted by Young. "He's about as good a kid as you'll meet, and what makes him so special is his humility."

Goldschmidt rewarded the Diamondbacks' faith in him by earning his first All-Star selection and finishing second in the NL MVP voting in 2013, when he led the NL in home runs (36), RBIs (125), extra-base hits (75), slugging percentage (.551), on-base plus slugging percentage (OPS, .952), total bases (332), and intentional walks (19). He also received his first NL Gold Glove Award at first base, after finishing second in the league with a .997 fielding percentage, and his first NL Silver Slugger Award.

In 2014 Goldschmidt earned his second consecutive All-Star selection, this time as a starter for the NL squad. He hit .300 with thirty-nine doubles, nineteen home runs, and sixty-nine RBIs in 109 games before a hand injury cut short his season. He recovered in time for the 2015 season, in which he contended for the so-called Triple Crown of hitting, finishing second in the NL with 110 RBIs, third in the league with a career-high .321 batting average, and fifth in league with thirty-three homers. He also set new career highs in on-base percentage (.435), slugging percentage (.570), on-bases plus slugging (1.005), stolen bases (21), and walks (118). He was the only player in the majors that year to hit .300 or better with at least thirty home runs, one hundred RBIs, and twenty stolen bases.

Though the Diamondbacks missed out on the playoffs for the fourth straight season, Goldschmidt finished as runner-up in the NL MVP voting for the second time in three years, earned his third straight All-Star selection, and received his second career Gold Glove and Silver Slugger Awards.

2016 SEASON

Goldschmidt uncharacteristically got off to a slow start to the 2016 season, batting .223 with forty-five strikeouts and just thirty-one hits through the first forty games. He quickly bounced back, however, and entered the season's midpoint leading all NL first basemen in walks and on-base percentage, while ranking in the top three among league first basemen in average, RBIs, and OPS. He was selected to his fourth straight All-Star team, tying him with Hall of Fame pitcher Randy Johnson for the most selections in Diamondbacks franchise history. "He's a professional in all aspects of the word," Diamondbacks pitcher Daniel Hudson said of his teammate to Sarah McLellan for the *Arizona Republic* (10 July 2016).

PERSONAL LIFE

A perennial dean's list student at TSU, Gold-schmidt completed his Bachelor of Science Degree in Management from the University of Phoenix in September 2013. He and his wife, Amy, whom he met during his freshman year at TSU, had a son, Jake, in September 2015. The couple is active in charitable endeavors to benefit the Phoenix Children's Hospital.

SUGGESTED READING

Kahrl, Christina. "Out of Nowhere, Goldschmidt Now a Star." *ESPN.com*. ESPN Internet Ventures, 30 May 2014. Web. 9 Aug. 2016.

Livingstone, Seth. "Arizona's Goldschmidt Named Top Minor League Player." *USA Today*. USA Today, 30 Aug. 2011. Web. 8 Aug. 2016.

McLellan, Sarah. "Diamondbacks' Paul Gold-schmidt Heads to All-Star Game on a Roll." *AZCentral*. AZCentral.com, 10 July 2016. Web. 8 Aug. 2016.

Reiter, Ben. "How Paul Goldschmidt Turned Himself into a Perennial MVP Candidate." *Sports Illustrated*. Time, 19 Aug. 2015. Web. 8 Aug. 2016.

Young, Bob. "Arizona Diamondbacks' Paul Gold-schmidt No Fan of Spotlight." *AZCentral*. AZCentral.com, 9 July 2013. Web. 8 Aug. 2016.

—*Chris Cullen*

Alfonso Gomez-Rejon

Born: November 6, 1972
Occupation: Director

Alfonso Gomez-Rejon is a television and film director best known for his 2015 indie hit *Me and Earl and the Dying Girl*, and his Emmy-nominated work on the television series *American Horror Story*. For nearly twenty-five years, Gomez-Rejon cut his teeth working as a production assistant for major Hollywood directors Martin Scorsese and the late Nora Ephron. He made his first feature-length film, a remake of a 1970s low budget horror movie, in 2014, but tapped into his grief after the death of his father to make the widely-praised 2015 dramedy, *Me and Earl and the Dying Girl*. Earl premiered at the prestigious Sundance Film Festival where it won both the Audience Award and the Grand Jury Prize for dramatic feature. Gomez-Rejon has said that he connected with the material and knew it could be a special film after reading the script. (The film is an adaptation of a 2012 novel of the same title by Jesse Andrews.) "I thought that if I was able to take this journey with Greg [the main character] that I might come out a

Montclair Film Festival/CC BY 2.0/Flickr/Wikimedia Commons

different person after this," he told Jeremy Kinser for the Sundance Institute (16 June 2015). "I wanted to get this job and I fought for it. I thought I could really make this into a personal movie."

EARLY LIFE AND EDUCATION

The youngest of three children, Gomez-Rejon was born in Laredo, Texas, on November 6, 1972. Laredo is on the Mexican border. All of Gomez-Rejon's extended family live in Mexico and his parents were strict about speaking only Spanish at home so that he would not forget his roots. His father, Julio Cesar Gomez-Rejon, was a singer who became a psychiatrist and started the first mental health center on the border. His older brother is a musician and his sister is a sculptor and chef. Gomez-Rejon was a film buff from an early age, developing a particular fondness for the work of Academy Award–winning director Martin Scorsese. Gomez-Rejon devoured Scorsese's work on VHS, and later used the director's career trajectory as a template for his own. He credits one of Scorsese's early films, the 1973 crime drama *Mean Streets*, as a formative influence. When Gomez-Rejon was twelve, he and some friends shot a short film for English class in which a girl appeared to jump off of a bridge that overlooked a highway. Lacking any editing tools, the realistic one-take shot impressed his classmates. Gomez-Rejon made more films as a student at St. Augustine High School in Laredo. As a sophomore he made a horror film called *Death . . . My Hobby* with his friends, as he recounted to Barbara Chai for the *Wall Street Journal* (29 June 2015). His youthful enthusiasm for film reflects that of his characters in *Me and Earl and the Dying Girl* (2015).

After graduating from high school, Gomez-Rejon enrolled at the film school at New York University. He arrived at school two weeks early and happened upon the cast and crew of *Sesame Street* filming in Washington Square Park. Gomez-Rejon stopped and watched; eventually a producer asked him to help stop traffic around the shoot. This chance meeting led to work on the sets of a two music videos—all before Gomez-Rejon's first day of class. Gomez-Rejon was shy but determined; by Christmas break in his freshman year, he was working as a production assistant and getting paid to storyboard short films. In 1994, during his senior year, he got a job working in Scorsese's office. Gomez-Rejon was not allowed to meet Scorsese right away. The other assistants would send him away, often to Scorsese's mother's house where he would hang pictures or run personal errands. Eventually, the crew, and the director himself, warmed up to the newcomer. Gomez-Rejon was Scorsese's personal assistant during the Las Vegas filming of *Casino*, which was released in 1995.

EARLY CAREER AND MENTORS

Gomez-Rejon loved watching Scorsese work on set. Sometimes he would sketch out scenes scheduled for the day's shoot and stick the sketches in his back pocket in the hopes that Scorsese would see them. Though Scorsese never asked, comparing his own sketches to how Scorsese shot the scenes was a valuable learning tool. "I just learned to just be quiet, be a ninja and just be there—be there for whatever he needs and be invisible when you're not needed, but soak everything up and hoping that, in the future, you're armed with some of that knowledge," he told Anna Sale for *National Public Radio* (*NPR*) (23 June 2015). Gomez-Rejon also developed a friendship with Academy Award–winning film editor and longtime Scorsese collaborator Thelma Schoonmaker, and *Casino* screenwriter, Nick Pileggi, husband of Nora Ephron.

After graduating with a master's degree from the American Film Institute (AFI) in 1997, Gomez-Rejon found his next gig through Pileggi. Ephron hired him as her personal assistant while she was filming the romantic comedy *You've Got Mail* (1998). Like Scorsese, Ephron was very kind and respectful to her assistant. "She was incredibly generous and treated me like a colleague from day one," he told Kinser. In 2000, while shooting the film *Lucky Numbers*, Ephron pushed to hire Gomez-Rejon as a second unit director, or assistant director. "That's how I got into the guild so that as a member of the DGA [Director's Guild of America] I could technically call myself a director," Gomez-Rejon explained

to Kinser. "That just led to everything and changed my life."

Gomez-Rejon went on to work second unit director for Ephron's *Bewitched* (2005) and *Julie & Julia* (2009). He also worked, in the same capacity, for Academy Award–winning director Alejandro G. Iñárritu's *Babel* (2006), Kevin Macdonald's *State of Play* (2009), and Ryan Murphy's *Eat, Pray, Love* (2010). Murphy, the Emmy Award–winning creator of the television musical comedy *Glee* and the serial television drama *American Horror Story*, hired Gomez-Rejon to direct episodes of both shows. Gomez-Rejon directed eight episodes of *Glee* between 2010 and 2012, and twelve episodes of *American Horror Story* between 2011 and 2014. Murphy was very trusting of the young director. Gomez-Rejon drew up an entire storyboard for his directorial debut with *Glee*. Murphy barely glanced at the storyboard and simply told Gomez-Rejon to do what he wanted. Gomez-Rejon's work on *American Horror Story* earned him two Emmy Award nominations in 2011: one for best direction of a miniseries and another for best miniseries.

In 2014 Gomez-Rejon made his feature-length directorial debut with the horror movie—a remake on the 1976 film of the same name—called *The Town that Dreaded Sundown*. The film, which Murphy produced, was met with lukewarm reviews.

ME AND EARL AND THE DYING GIRL

Gomez-Rejon's hectic television shooting schedule helped to advance his career, but also distracted him from the grief of losing his father in 2010.When the script for *Me and Earl and the Dying Girl* came across his desk, the director was surprised to see parallels between the main character, a teenager named Greg, and himself. Greg (played by Thomas Mann) is forced to befriend a girl in his class named Rachel (Olivia Cooke) who has been diagnosed with leukemia. Greg prides himself on keeping an emotional distance from other people, even his only real friend, Earl (RJ Cyler), with whom he makes short parody films for fun. Greg and Earl make a film for Rachel, something they have never done before. The making of the film is a disaster, and Greg and Earl must reckon with their own relationship and their relationship with Rachel while also coming to terms with the fact that she will likely die. *Me and Earl and the Dying Girl* is about the power of friendship but also, as the boys' English teacher tells them, how a person's story can continue even after the person herself is dead.

The script, adapted by Jesse Andrews who wrote the 2012 novel, landed on the 2012 blacklist, an annual list of favorite unproduced movie scripts culled by production companies. Gomez-Rejon fought to make the film because he wanted to show a character who loved movies, like his young self, but also because he saw it as a tribute to his father. He wanted, he told Patrick Z. McGavin for Roger Ebert's website (2 Feb. 2015), to "treat it as if it was going to be my last film, and make it for my dad. It was pretty clear that is the reason I was going to make a film for him the way that Greg makes one for Rachel." With a minimal budget, Gomez-Rejon and cinematographer, Chung Chung-hoon, were able to conjure a world that was both realistic and surreal. It premiered at the 2015 Sundance Film Festival, where it won the Audience Award and the Grand Jury Prize for dramatic feature. Fox Searchlight purchased the film for $12 million. It premiered in limited release in June 2015. The film, premiering as it did soon after the release of the well-known cancer love story adaptation, *The Fault in Our Stars* (2014), pleasantly surprised most audiences and garnered good reviews. *New York Times* critic A. O. Scott wrote (11 June 2015), "While the filmmakers are not above trying to wring a few tears, they don't wage an all-out assault on your feelings. There is a notable absence of aggression and of the kind of manipulation that yanks adjectives like 'devastating' from the laptops of unwitting reviewers. The film is touching and small, but also thoughtful and assured in a way that lingers after the inevitable tears have been shed and the obvious lessons learned."

In March 2016, it was announced that Gomez-Rejon would direct a film based on Delia Ephron's upcoming novel, *Siracusa*. Other future projects include *The Foreigner*, a thriller slated to star Oscar Isaac of *Star Wars* fame, and a series for Hulu called *Citizen*, which Gomez-Rejon cocreated with writer and producer Josh Pate and writer Nicholas Schutt.

SUGGESTED READING
Chai, Barbara. "*Me and Earl and the Dying Girl* Director Recounts His Own High School Films." *Wall Street Journal*. Dow Jones, 29 June 2015. Web. 14 July 2016.

Gomez-Rejon, Alfonso. "'Me and Earl' Director Traces Path from Scorsese's Assistant to Sundance." Interview by Anna Sale. *NPR*. NPR, 23 June 2015. Web. 14 July 2016.

Gomez-Rejon, Alfonso. "Sundance 2015 Interview: Alfonso Gomez-Rejon of *Me and Earl and the Dying Girl*." Interview by Patrick Z. McGavin. *RogerEbert.com*. Ebert Digital, 2 Feb. 2015. Web. 15 July 2016.

Kinser, Jeremy. "Alfonso Gomez-Rejon on Scorsese, Loss, and His Sundance Winner *Me and Earl and the Dying Girl*." *Sundance Institute*. Sundance Institute, 16 June 2015. Web. 14 July 2016.

Scott, A. O. "Review: In *Me and Earl and the Dying Girl*, A Comfort Zone That Cannot Last." Rev. of *Me and Earl and the Dying Girl*, Dir. Alfonso Gomez-Rejon. *New York Times*. New York Times, 11 June 2015. Web. 15 July 2016.

SELECTED WORKS
Glee, 2010–2012; *American Horror Story*, 2011–2014; *The Town That Dreaded Sundown*, 2014; *Me and Earl and the Dying Girl*, 2015

—Molly Hagan

Gabriela González

Born: February 24, 1965
Occupation: Physicist

Gabriela González is a professor of physics and astronomy at Louisiana State University (LSU). She also serves as the spokesperson and leader of the Laser Interferometer Gravitational-Wave Observatory, or the LIGO Scientific Collaboration, in nearby Livingston, east of Baton Rouge. LIGO was devised in the 1970s as a class exercise to prove the existence of gravitational waves as predicted by Albert Einstein's theory of general relativity, but by 2015, it was a sprawling network of more than 950 scientists across the United States and fifteen other countries, working together to monitor two massive detectors located 1,865 miles apart in Livingston and Washington State.

On September 14, 2015, a postdoctoral student monitoring the LIGO detectors on his computer in Hanover, Germany, noticed a tiny disturbance. After close analysis, that disturbance was confirmed to be a signal created by gravitational waves, originating from a collision between two black holes more than one billion light-years away. To appreciate the significance of the discovery, one must understand the significance of gravitational waves. In 1915, Einstein described gravity as warps and curves in the fabric of space-time. In his theory of general relativity, he hypothesized that if space-time really did behave like fabric—if it could warp and curve like a piece of cloth—it should also be able to ripple when it was disturbed by a release of energy, such as from the merging of two black holes. These "ripples" are gravitational waves. Their discovery, author Brian Greene said in a video for the World Science Festival (11 Feb. 2016), is a "pivotal" moment in the history of science. It confirmed another of Einstein's ideas, he said, but more important it "marked a new era" of discovery, uncovering an entirely new medium with which to explore the universe, particularly black holes.

EARLY LIFE AND EDUCATION

González was born in Córdoba, Argentina, on February 24, 1965. Her mother was a math teacher. Growing up, González dreamed of following in her footsteps, but after enrolling in her first physics class in high school, González made other plans. "I was amazed at how we could 'explain' the world with physics and we could predict what objects would do," she told the American Physical Society (APS) for their website. "When I found out this also applied to stars and the universe, and that there were unknown phenomena waiting to be discovered, I decided I couldn't do anything else!"

González attended the University of Córdoba and earned her Licenciatura, comparable to an American master's degree, in 1988. In 1989, she moved to Upstate New York to attend Syracuse University. González studied with Peter Saulson, a physicist who came to the university in 1991. She conducted her doctoral research on the Brownian motion (a concept that describes the random movements of particles when they are suspended in fluids) of a torsion pendulum (rotating pendulum). Though it may not sound like it, the subject's application is similar to the work González does with LIGO. González and Saulson jointly published a paper on the subject in 1995, the same year that González earned her PhD. González joined the faculty of Pennsylvania State University in 1997 and LSU in 2001.

A BRIEF HISTORY OF LIGO

González's professor, Saulson, came to Syracuse from the Massachusetts Institute of Technology (MIT), where he had worked with a physicist named Rainer Weiss. Weiss had devised LIGO as a class exercise in the early 1970s. A few years earlier, a man named Joseph Weber had claimed to have discovered gravitational waves using special technology. Weiss's students were curious about Weber, so Weiss devised his own theoretical experiment to explain to them what Weber was doing. The more he talked about his experiment, the more he realized it might actually work. He began designing the massive instrument that would become LIGO around the same time Weber's findings were publicly debunked.

Weiss received military funding as well as funding from the National Science Foundation (NSF) to build several prototypes. In 1975, he partnered with Kip Thorne, a physicist at the California Institute of Technology (CalTech), and along with several other scientists, including Saulson, presented a proposal for LIGO to NSF in 1983. They began to receive funding—the most of any NSF-backed experiment ever—after crafting another proposal in 1989. They broke ground in 1994, and what the team dubbed Initial LIGO was up and running in 2001. In 2010,

the team stopped the experiment and spent the next five years improving the detector. Advanced LIGO, the new iteration of the project, was slated to begin working on September 18, 2015; the first gravitational wave was detected during a testing run four days before that.

The observatory itself consists of two four-kilometer, vacuum-sealed tunnels arranged in an L shape. As an instrument, it can be described as a super precise interferometer, with laser beams shooting through each tunnel that act as a "ruler," Nicola Twilley explained for the *New Yorker* (11 Feb. 2016), to measure the gravitational waves, using the speed of light as a constant. "Picture two people lying on the floor, their heads touching, their bodies forming a right angle," Twilley wrote. "When a gravitational wave passes through them, one person will grow taller while the other shrinks; a moment later, the opposite will happen. As the wave expands space-time in one direction, it necessarily compresses it in the other. Weiss's instrument [gauges] the difference between these two fluctuating lengths . . . The greater the mismatch, the stronger the wave."

WORK WITH LIGO

González began working with LIGO in 1993, when she was a graduate student and the project was still in its testing phase. She got involved through Saulson, she told Liz Kruesi for *Quanta Magazine* (22 Oct. 2015). "He talked about LIGO and how you could measure these distortions in space-time," she said. "And putting that together—the measurement of things that are happening here on Earth, next to you, that are a ripple in space-time and that bring you information from black holes millions of light-years away—it was irresistible. I said, that's what I want to do." In 1995, she joined LIGO at MIT as a staff scientist, and in 1997, she helped organize all of the LIGO scientists into the LIGO Scientific Collaboration. The collaboration began with fourteen member universities; by 2016 there were fifty, with more than nine hundred individual members. González was elected spokesperson for the group in 2011.

When Marco Drago, the Italian postdoc in Hanover, first saw a signal on his computer screen on September 14, 2015, he was excited but extremely cautious. The LIGO team had had a false alarm in 2010 and caught the mistake just before sending their findings to be published. The team also has a small group of scientists in their ranks whose job it is to create what Twilley called "blind injections," or fake evidence of a gravitational wave. In 2015, that group vehemently denied having faked the signal—though some, including Drago, wondered if their denials were part of the test. Others at LIGO suggested that the signal was created by a malicious party hoping to derail the experiment. González and others interrogated the four scientists they deemed capable of pulling off such a feat, but those scientists were quickly cleared. Only then did the scientists at LIGO begin to consider the possibility that the signal was real.

DETECTING GRAVITATIONAL WAVES

Groups within the Scientific Collaboration verified the signal from every possible angle and eventually confirmed, Twilley wrote, "that the detection met the statistical threshold of five sigma, the gold standard for declaring a discovery in physics. This meant that there was a probability of only one in 3.5 million that the signal was spotted by chance." Thus verified, the discovery yielded several important findings, including the existence of black hole pairs, which, like gravitational waves, had previously existed only in theory.

The signal also allowed LIGO scientists to calculate the masses of the black holes from which the gravitational wave emerged, their orbital speed, and the moment when the two holes first touched. As these measurements attest, gravitational waves allow scientists to "see" the universe without light. "This is a completely new kind of telescope," David Reitze, the executive director of the LIGO Laboratory in California, told Twilley. "Until now, we scientists have only seen warped space-time when it's calm," Thorne explained in an email to Dennis Overbye for the *New York Times* (11 Feb. 2016). "It's as though we had only seen the ocean's surface on a calm day but had never seen it roiled in a storm, with crashing waves."

The discovery was officially announced to the public on February 11, 2016, though in the scientific community, rumors had been circulating for months. In June, LIGO announced the verification of another signal, produced from the collision of two black holes approximately 1.4 billion light-years away, which they had detected in December 2015. This second discovery was equally significant, proving the credibility of LIGO's work, but its announcement did not capture the same enthusiasm as the original. On February 12, 2016, González gave a special lecture to explain the group's findings at the American Association for the Advancement of Science (AAAS) annual meeting. Most notably, she adjusted the frequency of the signal to produce a chirping sound that the scientists could hear. She described it as making "the black holes really sing," as quoted by Becky Ham for the AAAS website (15 Feb. 2016). "Isn't that amazing?" González said. "I can't stop playing it."

PERSONAL LIFE

González is married to fellow LSU physicist and Hearne Chair Professor of Physics Jorge Pullin.

The two met in Córdoba and moved in 1989 to Syracuse, where Pullin worked on his postdoctoral research. Two years later, Pullin took another position in Utah. Due to the unpredictable nature of short-term postdoctoral arrangements and teaching contracts, the couple spent the next six years living apart. They reunited at LSU in the early 2000s. "Living apart was a considerable emotional—and financial—strain, and we wouldn't recommend it to anyone," González told Valerie Jamieson for *Science* magazine (28 Mar. 2003), though she added: "In our case, it had a happy ending."

SUGGESTED READING

"Gabriela Gonzalez." *APS Physics*. Amer. Physical Soc., n.d. Web. 9 Aug. 2016.

Greene, Brian. "Brian Greene Explains the Discovery of Gravitational Waves." *World Science Festival*. World Science Foundation, 11 Feb. 2016. Web. 9 Aug. 2016.

Ham, Becky. "At AAAS, LIGO's González Describes Massive Effort to Detect Tiny Waves." *AAAS*. Amer. Assn. for the Advancement of Science, 15 Feb. 2016. Web. 9 Aug. 2016.

Jamieson, Valerie. "Love and the Two-Body Problem." *Science*. Amer. Assn. for the Advancement of Science, 28 Mar. 2003. Web. 9 Aug. 2016.

Kruesi, Liz. "Searching the Sky for Wobbles in Gravity." *Quanta Magazine*. Simons Foundation, 22 Oct. 2015. Web. 9 Aug. 2016.

Twilley, Nicola. "Gravitational Waves Exist: The Inside Story of How Scientists Finally Found Them." *New Yorker*. Condé Nast, 11 Feb. 2016. Web. 9 Aug. 2016.

—*Molly Hagan*

Eva Green

Born: July 6, 1980
Occupation: Actor

Eva Green struggled with shyness and stage fright during her younger years, but audiences would likely find few signs of either in her most famous film and television performances. The French-born actor gives off a sense of deep-seated confidence in many of her roles, from her breakout role in the James Bond reboot *Casino Royale* as Vesper Lynd, one of the few so-called Bond girls to be the famous spy's true equal, to her fierce commander Artemisia in *300: Rise of an Empire*, to the character of medium Vanessa Ives in the critically acclaimed television series *Penny Dreadful*. The daughter of French actor Marlène Jobert, Green grew up in an acting family and made her film debut in 2003, in

director Bernardo Bertolucci's *The Dreamers*. Although best known for taking on parts that commentators tend to identify as gothic, witch-like, or deadly, Green rejects the notion that her characters are solely in that mode, instead noting in interviews that she is more fascinated by qualities within each character. "I hope I'm not being reduced to the dark femme fatale, because it's almost a cartoon, one-dimensional, temptress kind of character," she explained to Mark Jacobs for *Interview* magazine (16 May 2011). "I like characters who have strong facades and then have secrets. They have cracks."

EARLY LIFE AND EDUCATION

Eva Green was born in Paris, France, on July 6, 1980. She was one of two girls, fraternal twins, born to Marlène Jobert and Walter Green. Acting ran in Green's family: her mother was a well-known actor in France and the recipient of an honorary César Award, France's most prestigious film award, while her father was a dentist who also appeared in the 1966 film *Au Hasard Balthazar*. Green and her sister, Joy, grew up in Paris.

Green was attracted to acting from an early age. However, she was very shy and struggled with stage fright while in school. After completing her secondary education, she decided to pursue studies in acting to see whether she was capable of pursuing a career in the field. "I didn't know if I could do it," she admitted to Jacobs. "So I did a workshop in England to improve my English and three months of acting to see if I liked it or not. I came back and did three years of drama school in Paris. That's when I realized

I really liked acting and that I was going to try to be an actress."

After returning to France, Green enrolled in the American University of Paris. Classes at the institution are primarily conducted in English, which gave Green further opportunities to master the language. She acted on stage during her time at the university before beginning to pursue work in film. Entering the world of film was a somewhat difficult process for Green: her mother had concerns about her daughter following in her footsteps, and Green wanted to avoid any allegations of nepotism. "The fact that my mum was so famous—I was embarrassed and self-conscious that people would think, 'Oh, my god, she wants to be an actress and it's going to be easy for her because her mum is famous,'" she told Jacobs, admitting that distancing herself from her mother's career was one of the benefits of working primarily outside of France.

EARLY CAREER

Green made her film debut in 2003, costarring in the drama *The Dreamers*. Directed by Italian filmmaker Bernardo Bertolucci, the film also featured French actor Louis Garrel and American actor Michael Pitt. Many of the people closest to Green, including her parents, cautioned her against taking the role of Isabelle, as it required significant nudity and could potentially have had a harmful effect on the development of her career. However, Green was not dissuaded by those warnings and chose to star in the film, which is set in the turbulent era of 1960s France. The film was nominated for several awards but did not gain much of a following until years after its release. "It's interesting because when it came out, it was not very successful," Green told Rebecca Nicholson for *Vice* (28 Apr. 2016). "In France, it died very quickly at the box office. It's really through the years that people have liked it. I mean, I love it. It was my first movie. I was such a fan of Bertolucci, and it's such a free movie. Very pure fun."

Despite the worries of her parents and others, Green's career did not suffer because of her role in the film, which was rated NC-17 in the United States. Rather, she followed her role in *The Dreamers* with an appearance in the French film *Arsène Lupin* in 2004. She made her English-language debut in the 2005 film *Kingdom of Heaven*, a historical drama set during the Crusades and directed by veteran filmmaker Ridley Scott.

A NEW KIND OF BOND GIRL

Green's breakout role in the English-speaking world came in 2006, with her role in *Casino Royale*, the first film in the James Bond franchise to star Daniel Craig as the titular spy. Green played Vesper Lynd, an employee of the British treasury who accompanies Bond on his mission. Over the course of the film, Lynd is revealed to have an agenda of her own. Green was initially reluctant to take on the role of a so-called Bond girl, as many such characters are little more than disposable playthings for Bond. "At first, when they approached me, I thought it would be me wearing a bikini and being beautiful, so I said I wouldn't audition," Green explained to Lynn Hirschberg for *W* (27 June 2016). "Then they sent me the script, and I saw that Bond was falling in love with my character—that she was sensitive and full of secrets. I could understand that."

The character of Lynd ultimately proved to be more nuanced than many of her Bond girl predecessors, in large part because of the depth Green gave to her performance. The film was received well by critics, as was the character, who some journalists have identified as one of the best female characters to appear in the Bond film franchise since its debut in 1962. The character of Vesper Lynd even continued to exert a strong influence over Bond in subsequent films in the series, a departure from the typical stand-alone nature of previous Bond films and Bond girls, though Green did not reprise the role.

DISTINCTIVE ROLES

Following her appearance in *Casino Royale*, Green became significantly better known in the United States and elsewhere, and she soon took on a number of major roles. In 2007 she played the witch Serafina Pekkala in *The Golden Compass*, an adaptation of the 1995 fantasy novel by British author Philip Pullman. She went on to appear in films such as *Franklyn* (2008) and *Perfect Sense* (2011). As an actor, Green tended to be very selective when it came to her choices of roles. "I'm very picky," she admitted to Jacobs. "I like to do things that I adore. It can't be in between. I really need to connect with the character to love it. I cannot do work just for the sake of it. . . . It's not a job. It's almost like a faith or a religion. Every time, I give a bit of my soul."

After several years in which Green appeared mostly in independent or lesser-known films, she made a dramatic return to the public consciousness in 2014. That year, she appeared in both *300: Rise of an Empire* and *Sin City: A Dame to Kill For*, playing very different yet similarly deadly women. Both action-oriented films featured extensive special effects, including widespread use of green screen technology. The process of making the films fascinated Green, who had typically appeared in less effects-oriented projects, and presented an enjoyable challenge for her as an actor. "There was nothing there," she told Emily Zemler for *Elle* (22 Aug. 2014) of the process of filming *Sin City: A Dame to Kill For*. "Sometimes you have props, but it's quite a weird world. The first day you're like, 'Oh my God.' I was lucky because I had real actors to interact with. I know some of the other actors did not have that chance. . . . You don't know how it's going to turn out. So the other actor is saving you. It's like theater."

PENNY DREADFUL AND OTHER WORK

In addition to her film work, Green has worked in television on several occasions. In 2011, she played the villainous character of Morgan in *Camelot*, a British-American coproduction loosely based on the legends of King Arthur. The series lasted only one season. Green returned to the small screen in 2014 with a costarring role in *Penny Dreadful*, likewise a British-American coproduction. Set in the Victorian Era and featuring both original characters and figures from literature, such as Mary Shelley's Dr. Frankenstein, the show follows a group of individuals with varying skills who join together to fight supernatural creatures. On the show, Green played medium Vanessa Ives, who, in addition to being one of the series' central characters, is a figure who particularly appealed to the actor. "I find playing Vanessa to be like taking a drug," Green told Hirschberg. "Sometimes exhausting, but also jubilating."

Penny Dreadful received positive reviews from critics over the course of its three-season run, earning numerous award nominations. In 2016, Green herself was nominated for the Golden Globe for best actress in a television drama for her performance as Vanessa. Despite the show's positive reception, the series came to an end with the conclusion of its third season, as its showrunners believed that the story it was meant to tell had ended.

In addition to the conclusion of *Penny Dreadful*, 2016 brought Green's second collaboration with director Tim Burton, with whom she worked on the 2012 film *Dark Shadows*. That earlier film, an adaptation of the 1960s television show of the same name that starred frequent Burton collaborator Johnny Depp, proved critically unsuccessful, though Green's performance was relatively well received. Green again worked with Burton on *Miss Peregrine's Home for Peculiar Children*, filling the title role. Released in September 2016, the film is based on a 2011 young adult novel by American writer Ransom Riggs.

PERSONAL LIFE

Green has claimed to not watch any of the films she performs in, finding it too self-conscious to do so. She has also expressed discomfort performing nude scenes, despite developing something of a reputation for them. She often describes herself in interviews as relatively reserved, even shy, in contrast to what might be expected of a famous actor, especially one who takes roles like hers. "I'm quiet—boring even—in real life," she told Stuart Jeffries for the *Guardian* (3 May 2016). "Nothing like the mad witches I play."

SUGGESTED READING

Green, Eva. "Eva Green." Interview with Mark Jacobs. *Interview*. Interview, 16 May 2011. Web. 12 Aug. 2016.

Green, Eva. "Eva Green: Femme Fatales Don't Have Cellulite." Interview with Emily Zemler. *Elle*. Hearst Digital Media, 22 Aug. 2014. Web. 12 Aug. 2016.

Green, Eva. "An Interview with Eva Green, Hollywood's Go-To Goth." Interview with Rebecca Nicholson. *Vice*. Vice, 28 Apr. 2016. Web. 12 Aug. 2016.

Green, Eva. "'Penny Dreadful' Star Eva Green Gets Real about Her Love of Goat Cheese and Mad Crossbow Skills." *Marie Claire*. Hearst Digital Media, 1 July 2015. Web. 12 Aug. 2016.

Green, Eva. "Q. and A. with Eva Green: Darkly, Demonically, Daringly 'Dreadful.'" Interview with Roslyn Sulcas. *New York Times*. New York Times, 5 May 2016. Web. 12 Aug. 2016.

Hirschberg, Lynn. "Tim Burton's New Muse Eva Green Swoops into the Spotlight." *W*. Condé Nast, 27 June 2016. Web. 12 Aug. 2016.

Jeffries, Stuart. "Eva Green: 'I Don't Want to Be Put in a Box Marked Weird Witch.'" *Guardian*. Guardian News and Media, 3 May 2016. Web. 12 Aug. 2016.

SELECTED WORKS

The Dreamers, 2003; *Kingdom of Heaven*, 2005; *Casino Royale*, 2006; *The Golden Compass*, 2007; *Camelot*, 2011; *Dark Shadows*, 2012; *300: Rise of an Empire*, 2014; *Sin City: A Dame to Kill For*, 2014; *Penny Dreadful*, 2014–16; *Miss Peregrine's Home for Peculiar Children*, 2016

—*Joy Crelin*

Beppe Grillo

Born: July 21, 1948
Occupation: Comedian

Beppe Grillo is an Italian comedian best known for his satirical humor and for being the founder of the Five Star Movement, an Italian political party.

Grillo has gone from being a satirical comedian to the founder of a prominent political party in Italy. His blog is one of the most visited in the world and he has used it to influence Italian politics and change how citizens are able to receive information about corruption within the political parties.

EARLY LIFE AND EDUCATION

Giuseppe Piero Grillo was born on July 21, 1948, in Genoa, Italy, a city on the country's western coast. His father owned a welding company. Grillo originally studied to become an accountant, but gave up his accounting studies in favor of pursuing a career in comedy. In Milan, he performed an improvised monologue in front of a committee of the Radiotelevisione italiana (RAI), the national public broadcasting company of Italy. The television presenter Pippo Baudo heard Grillo's monologue and subsequently helped him land spots on variety shows.

With appearances on shows like *Secondo voi* (1977–78) and *Luna Park* (1978), Grillo made a name for himself as a satirical comedian who had no interest in adhering to traditional Italian television standards. In 1979 he starred in the first season of the popular Saturday night variety show *Fantastico*. The show was a success and continued for several years with different actors and comedians.

In 1980 Grillo was involved in a car accident when the Jeep he was driving slipped on ice and went off the road, killing his three passengers. Grillo was convicted of manslaughter. The manslaughter conviction meant that Grillo was later unable to run for a seat in the Italian Parliament when his career turned toward politics.

COMEDY AND POLITICS

After the manslaughter conviction, Grillo returned to television with the travel shows *Te la do io l'America* (1981) and *Te lo do io il Brasile* (1984). The shows followed Grillo as he traveled through the United States and Brazil and commented on the culture and lifestyles he encountered. His popularity continued to grow: when he hosted the Sanremo Music Festival, twenty-two million viewers tuned in to watch.

During this time, Grillo began to address more social and political topics in his comedy routines. Although some television producers saw his comedy as risky, there was no denying his popularity, so he was consistently booked on shows. He even became the spokesman for a famous brand of yogurt, appearing in advertisements that won several marketing awards.

During an appearance on *Fantastico 7* (1987), he spoke out against the corruption of the Italian Socialist Party and its leader, Prime Minister Bettino Craxi. As a result, Grillo was effectively banned from public television and he began touring theaters instead. His live performances addressed issues such as consumerism, corruption, and freedom of speech.

He toured extensively for the rest of the 1990s. His show *Energy and Information*

(1995–96) was performed in over sixty cities in Italy and drew crowds of up to four hundred thousand. Grillo's other live shows include *Brain* (1997), *Soft Apocalypse* (1998), and *Discourse to Humanity* (1999).

Grillo continued to tour into the 2000s, and on January 26, 2005, he took to the Internet, launching his blog, *Blog di Beppe Grillo*. The website is updated frequently by Grillo, and by March 2006 it had become one of the top ten most-visited blogs in the world according to *Technorati.com*. He used the blog to further promote his political activism and expose corruption, particularly in the Italian government. In October 2005, *Time* magazine listed Grillo as one of their "European Heroes."

He used his popular blog and social media to organize a rally known as "V-Day" on September 8, 2007. Despite receiving no attention from the mainstream media, V-Day saw a tremendous amount of participation from Italian citizens. On V-Day, a petition calling for the removal of Italian parliamentarians who have been convicted of crimes collected more than three hundred thousand signatures in a few hours. A second V-Day was held on April 25, 2008. The focus of this second rally was freedom of information.

On October 4, 2009, Grillo launched the Five Star Movement (M5S), a political party aimed at unifying Italian citizens who believe in political honesty and direct democracy. The five stars in the title refer to what Grillo sees as the five key issues: public water, sustainable transport, development, connectivity through the Internet, and environmentalism. The group polled well in regional and local elections and, at the general election in February 2013, M5S won 25.56 percent of the popular vote—obtaining 108 deputies and 54 senators to represent them in the Italian Parliament.

M5S and Grillo have received much criticism over the years, particularly for what many see as a lack of clarity about the party's policies. Despite the criticism, however, Grillo and his party have become a major political force in Italy.

PERSONAL LIFE
Grillo married his second wife Parvin Tadjk in 1996. They have two children together as well as two each from previous marriages. They live in Marina di Bibbona in Bibbona, Italy.

SUGGESTED READING
Alderman, Liz, and Elisabetta Povoledo. "A Jester No More, Italy's Gadfly of Politics Reflects a Movement." *New York Times*. New York Times, 3 Mar. 2013. Web. 3 Mar. 2014.
Corcoran, Mark. "At Home with Beppe Grillo." *Australian Broadcasting Corporation*. ABC Online Services, 14 May 2012. Web. 4 Mar. 2014.

Jones, Gavin. "Beppe Grillo and the 5 Star Movement: An In-Depth Look at Italy's New Kingmaker." *Huffington Post*. TheHuffingtonPost.com, 7 Mar. 2013. Web. 3 Mar. 2014.
Mueller, Tom. "Beppe's Inferno." *New Yorker*. Condé Nast, 4 Feb. 2008. Web. 4 Mar. 2014.
"Profile: Beppe Grillo." *BBC News*. BBC, 26 Feb. 2013. Web. 4 Mar. 2014.

SELECTED WORKS
Secondo voi (According to you), 1977–78; *Luna Park*, 1978; *Fantastico* (Fantastic), 1979; *Te la do io l'America* (I give you America), 1981; *Te lo do io il Brasile* (I give you Brazil), 1984

—*Patrick G. Cooper*

Lauren Groff

Born: July 23, 1978
Occupation: Author

Lauren Groff has been called one of the best writers of her generation, with three best-selling, critically acclaimed novels and a collection of short stories to her name. Her first novel, *The Monsters of Templeton* (2008), received high praise from famed author Stephen King and was named to several "best of" annual lists, including those of Amazon.com and the *San Francisco Chronicle*. Her second novel, *Arcadia* (2012), won the Medici Book Club Prize and was a finalist for the Los Angeles Times Book Award. It also earned acclaim from a number of major newspapers and magazines and earned a place on the best books of the year lists for the *Christian Science Monitor*, the *Globe and Mail*, the *New York Times*, *Vogue*, and the *Washington Post*, among others. Like its predecessors, *Fates and Furies* found its way onto numerous "best of 2015" lists and was selected by Amazon.com as the best book of the year. It was also nominated for the National Book Award for fiction.

EARLY LIFE AND EDUCATION
Lauren Groff was born on July 23, 1978, to Jeannine and Gerald Groff and was raised in Cooperstown, New York. A town of about two thousand people, it is famous for being the home of the noted nineteenth-century American author James Fenimore Cooper, best known for the *Leatherstocking Tales*, and the Baseball Hall of Fame, which was established in 1939. Groff was a passionate reader, even as a child, and fantasized about becoming a writer at a very early age. "I've been a big reader all my life, and I always wanted to be a writer: I once thought being a writer meant serious spectacles and vast mahogany desks and rooms walled with books and

Ulf Andersen/Getty Images

a summer cottage in the Cotswolds with cows lowing out the window," she said in an interview with her alma mater, Amherst College (2008). "The reality is that I only dabbled at writing from the time I was little to the time I went to college."

After graduating from high school, Groff completed a gap year abroad in Nantes, France. She then enrolled at Amherst College, where she majored in French and English. It was there that she fell in love with writing short fiction after taking a workshop. In an interview with the *Millions* (15 Sept. 2015), Groff told Elizabeth Word Gutting: "I was a writer long before I wrote anything interesting. I went into college thinking I was a poet. But I'm a terrible poet!" At college, however, she was "quickly disabused of the idea" of being a poet and began writing fiction instead.

Groff earned her bachelor's degree from Amherst in 2001. She then took a three-year break from academia, during which time she worked a series of unenjoyable jobs as a bartender and telemarketer, before entering graduate school. She completed her master of fine arts (MFA) in fiction at the University of Wisconsin–Madison in 2006. For the 2006–7 school year, she was an Axton Fellow in Fiction at the University of Louisville.

EARLY WORKS
During her early writing career, Groff was able to place a number of her short stories with prestigious literary magazines, including the *Atlantic*, *Five Points*, *McSweeney's*, the *New Yorker*, and *Plowshares*. Her stories were also selected for inclusion in such anthologies as *Best New*

American Voices 2008, *Pushcart Prize XXXII*, and the 2007, 2010, and 2014 editions of *Best American Short Stories*.

Shortly after earning her graduate degree, Groff completed and was able to sell her first novel, *The Monsters of Templeton*, which was published in 2008. *The Monsters of Templeton* takes place in the fictional upstate New York town of Templeton, which is based on Groff's hometown of Cooperstown. Its main character, Willie Upton, returns home after having an affair with her married professor at Stanford University and nearly running over his wife, the dean of students. But instead of getting away from the complexities of her life, Willie finds herself being drawn into an even more confusing family drama: Her mother, Vi, an ex-hippie, tells her she now knows the identity of Willie's father—she was sure it had been one of three men—but she is not letting Willie in on the secret. This sends Willie on a journey of exploration into her family's past—as well as that of the town. Janet Maslin, in a review of *The Monsters of Templeton* for the *New York Times* (18 Feb. 2008), criticized the "overcrowding" of plot elements, asking, "Does the town really need a monster and ghosts and eerie Temple family portraits?" But, she concluded, "It speaks well for [Groff's] narrative talents that Willie Upton, disarming and smart, holds even more interest than the elaborate events that surround her." The novel went on to become Groff's first best seller.

Groff quickly followed her fiction debut with a critically acclaimed collection of stories, *Delicate Edible Birds* (2009). Of the nine stories that make up the collection, most of them take place in small-town upstate New York and many of them were previously published in prestigious literary magazines. A critic for *Kirkus Reviews* (15 Nov. 2008) declared: "The details make the difference in this sophomore effort. . . . Groff's skill makes commonplace occurrences seem compelling."

ARCADIA
Groff's next novel, *Arcadia* (2012), explores the life of Bit Stone, who grew up on a six-hundred-acre hippie commune in western New York in the late 1960s, and examines his life both during that time and afterward in four parts, jumping by about a decade each time. The novel begins with Bit at age five, living on the commune under the sway of a charismatic rock-star leader who will ruin their utopian dreams. The narrative then moves on to his years with his parents as a teenager, his own fatherhood, and eventually to his life in a postapocalyptic future in which the world is beset by plague outbreaks and people's movements are restricted by quarantines.

A critic for *Kirkus Reviews* (15 Jan. 2012) called it an "astonishing novel, both in ambition and achievement, filled with revelations that appear inevitable in retrospect, amid the cycle of life and death." Ron Charles, in his review for the *Washington Post* (13 Mar. 2012), agreed: "*Arcadia* offers something surprising: if not a redemption of utopian ideals, then at least a complicated defense of the dream. . . . *Arcadia* wends a harrowing path back to a fragile, lovely place you can believe in."

FATES AND FURIES

Groff followed this success with *Fates and Furies*, which received widespread critical acclaim in the United States upon its publication in 2015. The novel explores both sides of the decades-long relationship of a couple, Lancelot, nicknamed Lotto, and his wife, Mathilde. The story begins from Lotto's perspective. In this section of the novel, the reader learns of Lotto's privileged life as the son of a wealthy Florida family. He is sent to a boarding school in New England for his youthful misbehaviors and eventually goes to Vassar College, where he meets his future wife and discovers his love of the theater. After trying his hand at acting, Lotto eventually goes on to become a successful playwright. When the novel turns to Mathilde's perspective, the reader learns that their relationship is much more complex than as it appeared to be in Lotto's section, particularly as she is hiding traumas from her early childhood and young adulthood.

Reviewing the novel for the *Washington Post* (9 Sept. 2015), Ron Charles proclaimed: "Even from her impossibly high starting point, Lauren Groff just keeps getting better and better. . . . Swelling with a contrapuntal symphony of passions, *Fates and Furies* is that daring novel that seems to reach too high—and then somehow, miraculously, exceeds its own ambitions."

On the other side of the Atlantic, however, the book met with more tepid reviews. In the *Guardian* (28 Oct. 2015), Susanna Rustin wrote: "*Fates and Furies* . . . pivots on the shift in point of view. Everything we thought we knew in the first half comes undone in the second. . . . But the level of dishonesty in an ostensibly solid marriage is, to me, impossible to believe in." Rustin also criticized the introduction of murders and a private eye later in the book, calling it a "strange mashup of literary and pulp fiction." *Fates and Furies* was named a finalist for the 2015 National Book Award in the fiction category.

PERSONAL LIFE

Groff is married to Clay Kallman, whom she met at Amherst College. They have two sons. She and her family live in Gainesville, Florida.

SUGGESTED READING

Rev. of *Arcadia*, by Lauren Groff. *Kirkus*. Kirkus, 15 Jan. 2012. Web. 13 Apr. 2016.

Charles, Ron. "A Masterful Tale of Marriage and Secrets." Rev. of *Fates and Furies*, by Lauren Groff. *Washington Post*. Washington Post, 9 Sept. 2015. Web. 13 Apr. 2016.

Rev. of *Delicate Edible Birds*, by Lauren Groff. *Kirkus*. Kirkus, 15 Nov. 2008. Web. 13 Apr. 2016.

Groff, Lauren. "About the Author: Lauren Groff '01." Interview. *Amherst College*. Amherst College, 2008. Web. 13 Apr. 2016.

Groff, Lauren. "The Most Joyous Part: The Millions Interview Lauren Groff." Interview by Elizabeth Word Gutting. *Millions*. Millions, 15 Sept. 2015. Web. 13 Apr. 2016.

Murguia, Sophie. "Author Alum Writers Her Way to the Top." *Amherst Student*. Amherst Student, 18 Oct. 2013. Web. 13 Apr. 2016.

Ogle, Connie. "Interview: Lauren Groff, Author of 'Fates and Furies.'" *Miami Herald*. Miami Herald, 19 Nov. 2015. Web. 13 Apr. 2016.

SELECTED WORKS

The Monsters of Templeton, 2008; *Delicate Edible Birds*, 2009; *Arcadia*, 2012; *Fates and Furies*, 2015

—Christopher Mari

Rob Gronkowski

Born: May 14, 1989
Occupation: Football player

New England Patriots tight end Rob Gronkowski, affectionately known as "Gronk" by his teammates and fans, is one of the most dominant tight ends in the history of the National Football League (NFL). Ben Volin, writing for the *Boston Globe* (4 Oct. 2015), called the six-foot-six, 265-pound Gronkowski "a biohuman, wrecking ball of a Patriot who dominates opponents at will."

Gronkowski spent two seasons at Arizona State University before being drafted by the Patriots in the second round of the 2010 NFL Draft. In his first six seasons with the Patriots, he teamed up with perennial All-Pro quarterback Tom Brady to form the NFL's most potent quarterback–tight end tandem, amassing more receptions (380), receiving yards (5,555), and receiving touchdowns (65) than any tight end in the league. In 2011 he posted arguably the greatest season by a tight end in NFL history, when he set league single-season records for receiving yards and touchdown receptions. He has been named to the Pro Bowl four times and to the Associated Press (AP) All-Pro first team three times. He has played in two Super Bowls with the Patriots, winning a title in the 2014 season.

Tom Szczerbowski/Getty Images

Though Gronkowski has often drawn criticism for his wild exploits off the field, he has been lauded by teammates and coaches for his high football IQ and for an unrelenting work ethic that has helped him overcome a number of devastating injuries. "Rob's very attentive, very coachable," the Patriots head coach, Bill Belichick, commented, as quoted by Volin. "You tell him what you want him to do, he works very hard to do it the way you want it done. He's a smart football player."

EARLY LIFE

The fourth of five sons, Robert James Gronkowski was born to Gordon (known as "Gordy") and Diane Gronkowski on May 14, 1989, in Amherst, New York, a northern suburb of Buffalo. Gronkowski comes from an athletic pedigree. His great-grandfather was an Olympic athlete, while his father was a standout offensive lineman at Syracuse University.

Gronkowski and his brothers—Gordie Jr., Dan, Chris, and Glenn—grew up in a house dominated by sports. Mercilessly competitive, the Gronkowski brothers challenged each other to athletic competition on a daily basis. From an early age, Rob endured playful but painful beatings from his older brothers. Those physical brawls helped shape Gronkowski into the tough player that he eventually became. "Competing with my brothers at such a young age gave me a huge competitive advantage," he explained to Joe Wuebben for *Muscle & Fitness* (1 Oct. 2012).

Gronkowski's fearless nature complemented his outstanding natural athletic ability; he

excelled at every sport he played. He started playing football in the seventh grade, when his parents first allowed him to join the sport. In eighth grade, Gronkowski began lifting weights under the watchful eye of his father. Gordy Gronkowski put all of his sons on strict but safe strength-training programs and, in his spare time, ran them through myriad drills using tennis balls to improve their hand-eye coordination and mental toughness. Diane Gronkowski also played a pivotal role in her sons' athletic development, cooking all of their meals and shuttling them to their various practices and games.

Their tireless support and dedication helped breed a family of professional athletes. Gordie Jr. played professional baseball for six seasons before retiring in 2011. Dan and Chris, meanwhile, both had brief NFL careers, as a tight end and fullback, respectively. Rob's younger brother, Glenn, played fullback for Kansas State University from 2013 to 2015.

STAR ATHLETE

Conventional wisdom about the Gronkowskis holds that Rob was, unequivocally, the most talented athlete in the family. During his teenage years, he became "a legend in upstate New York, a Bunyanesque athlete who intimidated with his size, speed, and sports acumen," according to Jackie MacMullan for ESPN (12 Jan. 2012). Gronkowski attended Williamsville North High School in nearby Williamsville, New York, where he was a three-sport star in football, basketball, and baseball.

As a tight end and defensive end for Williamsville's varsity football team, Gronkowski routinely wowed his coaches and teammates. His athletic feats, however, were not just limited to football: He dunked with relative ease as a center on Williamsville's basketball team, once shattering an opposing team's backboard, and as a pitcher on the school's baseball team, his fastball consistently clocked in at ninety miles per hour. "Rob is just a freak athlete," his brother Dan told Wuebben.

Toward the end of his junior year, Gronkowski's parents separated, after which he moved with his father to Pittsburgh, Pennsylvania. (There, Gronkowski's father expanded his gym equipment company.) For his senior year, Gronkowski transferred to Pittsburgh's Woodland Hills High School, which has a nationally renowned football program. He immediately impressed the school's head football coach, George Novak, with his size. "He was so big," Novak recalled to Peter May for the *New York Times* (21 Jan. 2012), "I thought he was a college coach." Using that size to his advantage, Gronkowski continued to distinguish himself as a three-sport star at Woodland Hills, but none more so than on the gridiron. "He's one of the best to ever come out of this area, and there have been some pretty good ones," Novak affirmed to May.

ARIZONA TO NEW ENGLAND PATRIOTS

Gronkowski was reportedly recruited by at least sixty schools, but he chose to attend the University of Arizona. Gronkowski decided on Arizona after a family friend, former Wildcats linebacker Donnie Salum, persuaded him to attend the school. It also afforded him an opportunity to be reunited with his older brother Chris, who had transferred to Arizona from the University of Maryland.

With family by his side, Gronkowski excelled, and during his true freshman season at Arizona in 2007, he made twenty-eight receptions for 525 yards and six touchdowns. He eclipsed that performance during his sophomore season, when he recorded forty-seven receptions for 672 yards and a team-best ten touchdowns, all of which were school single-season records by a tight end. Gronkowski posted those numbers despite missing the first three games of the season with mononucleosis. He entered his junior season hoping to improve his game even further until a back injury forced him to undergo surgery.

Back surgery sidelined Gronkowski for his entire 2009 junior season. Upon returning to the field after a long rehabilitation, he decided to forgo his final two years of eligibility at Arizona and enter the 2010 NFL Draft. "It was a tough decision," he noted to May, "but I thought it was a good time to leave." Despite initial durability concerns and reservations about his carefree demeanor off the field, the New England Patriots traded up in the draft to select Gronkowski in the second round with the forty-second overall pick. Patriots head coach Bill Belichick had been convinced to draft Gronkowski after receiving a glowing recommendation from Gronkowski's Arizona coach, Mike Stoops, who praised his football intelligence, toughness, and competitive drive. Stoops recalled to MacMullan. "I told him that Rob might be the best tight end I've ever seen."

NFL SUPERSTAR

Stoops's assessment of Gronkowski proved prescient. As a rookie during the 2010 season, Gronkowski was quickly inserted into the Patriots' lineup and served as an integral cog in Belichick's innovative two tight end offense. Starting eleven of sixteen games, he recorded forty-two receptions for 546 yards and ten touchdowns, the latter of which were the second most by a rookie tight end in history (after Mike Ditka's twelve in 1961). Gronkowski's play helped power the Patriots to an NFL-best 14–2 record and an American Football Conference (AFC) East title.

Gronkowski proceeded to take the NFL by storm during the 2011 season. Starting all sixteen games for the Patriots, he set NFL single-season records for receiving yards (1,327 on a career-high ninety receptions) and touchdown receptions (seventeen) by a tight end. Gronkowski also became the first Patriots tight end to score a rushing touchdown and showcased his versatility as a blocker, with the analytics website Pro Football Focus grading him as the best run-blocking tight end in the league. Gronkowski earned his first Pro Bowl and AP All-Pro first team selections, and he played a major role in the Patriots advancing to Super Bowl XLVI, where the Patriots lost to the New York Giants, 21–17.

Meanwhile, Gronkowski became a cult figure in New England for his childlike on-field exuberance and for his "earth-moving spikes in the end zone," as May put it. He also caught national sports media attention for some of his questionable off-field antics, which included posing shirtless with a porn star for Twitter photos during the Patriots' bye week. Gronkowski was forced to apologize to Patriots owner Robert Kraft for the stunt, which nonetheless helped triple his Twitter following. Notwithstanding such indiscretions, the Patriots showed their faith in Gronkowski by awarding him a six-year contract extension worth $54 million in June 2012.

SIDELINED BY INJURIES

Much to the Patriots' delight, Gronkowski carried his dominant play into the 2012 season. He started all eleven games he played and made fifty-five receptions for 790 yards and eleven touchdowns. Gronkowski was on pace to match his performance from the 2011 season, but he was forced to miss five games after breaking his left forearm in the final minutes of the Patriots' blowout week-eleven victory over the Indianapolis Colts. He returned in time for the Patriots' AFC divisional playoff game against the Houston Texans but was then forced to leave the game after reinjuring his left arm in the first quarter. Despite his injuries, Gronkowski earned his second consecutive Pro Bowl and All-Pro first team selections. He also became the first tight end in league history to post three consecutive seasons with ten-plus touchdowns.

Nevertheless, Gronkowski continued to suffer setbacks with his left forearm, which, due to a lingering infection, required a total of four surgeries. Chronic back pain, meanwhile, forced him to undergo his second back surgery in June 2013. The surgery resulted in a delayed start to the 2013 season. Upon returning, Gronkowski played in just seven games before tearing two ligaments in his right knee against the Cleveland Browns. The injury prematurely ended his season and forced him to again undergo surgery, which made it "hard to stay motivated," he admitted to Volin in another article for the *Boston Globe* (16 Nov. 2014). "But you see your guys working around you, and you want to be back with them. I believe just going out and practicing hard and being around football every week just gets you better."

RETURN TO ALL-PRO FORM

After an off-season of rehabilitation, Gronkowski returned in time for the Patriots' summer training camp. Still, he was gradually eased back into the Patriots' offense. Gronkowski's role expanded as the season progressed, and he quickly reestablished himself as a force to be reckoned with. He played in fifteen games and led all tight ends with 1,124 receiving yards (on eighty-two receptions) and twelve touchdowns. He was named to his third Pro Bowl and earned a unanimous All-Pro selection.

Bolstered by Gronkowski's healthy return to form, the Patriots, after suffering AFC Championship Game losses in the previous two seasons, advanced to Super Bowl XLIX. The Patriots defeated the defending champion Seattle Seahawks, 28–24, to earn the franchise's fourth Super Bowl title. In the dramatic game, Gronkowski made six catches for sixty-eight yards and one touchdown.

Gronkowski further solidified his status as the NFL's best tight end in 2015, when he made seventy-two catches for 1,176 yards and scored eleven touchdowns in fifteen games. He earned Pro Bowl and All-Pro first team honors for the fourth time in his career. That season the Patriots won their seventh straight AFC East title and advanced to the AFC Championship Game, where they lost to the eventual Super Bowl champion Denver Broncos, 20–18.

PERSONAL LIFE

Off the field, Gronkowski is known for his jovial personality and party-boy reputation. He has parlayed that image into a successful brand that includes making paid appearances at numerous events and film cameos, hosting ladies-only football camps, sponsoring chartered party cruises, and running a website with his brothers called GronkNation.com, which sells bespoke T-shirts and autographed memorabilia.

In July 2015 Gronkowski published (with agent Jason Rosenhaus) a memoir, titled *It's Good to Be Gronk*, in which he states that he lives exclusively off his marketing money. Though Gronkowski has often been criticized for his partying ways, he has claimed that partying ultimately makes him a better player.

SUGGESTED READING

Ballard, Chris. "The Last Happy Man." *Sports Illustrated*. Time, 3 Sept. 2012. Web. 21 Jan. 2016.

MacMullan, Jackie. "It's Good to be Gronk." *ESPN*. ESPN Internet Ventures, 12 Jan. 2012. Web. 21 Jan. 2016.

May, Peter. "Gronkowski Earning Name for Scores and Spikes." *New York Times*. New York Times, 21 Jan. 2012. Web. 21 Jan. 2016.

Volin, Ben. "Rob Gronkowski Is More than a Fun-Loving Goof." *Boston Globe*. Boston Globe Media Partners, 4 Oct. 2015. Web. 21 Jan. 2016.

Volin, Ben. "Rob Gronkowski's Quick Return Truly Remarkable." *Boston Globe*. Boston Globe Media Partners, 16 Nov. 2014. Web. 21 Jan. 2016.

Wuebben, Joe. "Gronk'd: Getting Personal with the Gronkowskis." *Muscle & Fitness*. American Media, 1 Oct. 2012. Web. 21 Jan. 2016.

—*Chris Cullen*

Danai Gurira

Born: February 14, 1978
Occupation: Actor and playwright

In addition to her role as the dreadlocked, zombie-slaying Michonne on AMC's cult hit series *The Walking Dead*, Danai Gurira has distinguished herself as a playwright, with a unique point of view. "These plays comprise parts of a trilogy on Zimbabwe's coming of age from a feminine perspective," she told Darlene Donloe for *@This Stage Magazine* (18 Apr. 2012). "Stories of African women are scantily told. I don't know why that is. This is my calling . . . to tell the story from the feminine perspective."

Gurira's productions also reflect the culture and history of her parents' native Zimbabwe. They include *In the Continuum*, a two-women play dealing with the impact of AIDS across the United States and Africa; *The Convert*, a *Pygmalion*-like tale set in colonial-era Zimbabwe; and the comedy *Familiar*, about an upcoming Zimbabwean American wedding in Minnesota. Gurira's play *Eclipsed*, which revolves around five Liberian women held captive in a rebel camp, debuted on Broadway in 2016 to rave reviews. The groundbreaking drama features an all-black female cast headed by Academy Award–winner Lupita Nyong'o. *Eclipsed* earned six Tony nods, including one for best play.

EARLY LIFE AND EDUCATION

Danai Jekesai Gurira, a native of Grinnell, Iowa, was born to Josephine and Roger Gurira on Valentine's Day 1978, the youngest of five children. At the age of five, Gurira's family relocated to her parents' homeland of Zimbabwe, formerly the British colony of Southern Rhodesia, and settled

Tristan Loper/CC BY-SA 4.0/Wikimedia Commons

in the capital city of Harare. Her first exposure to the dramatic arts came when she joined the weekly Children's Performing Arts Workshop (CHIPAWO) as a thirteen-year-old. "It was getting a little endangered back then because we were being bombarded with Western music," she shared with Tim Sanford for the website Playwrights Horizons. "But then only in Chipawo I [learned] how to dance like my forefathers and foremothers. . . . The idea of creating a piece of work and performing it, and having it infused with the social issues was something I was doing in Chipawo." Gurira would continue to hone her performance skills, as a member of the Reps Theatre's youth theater company, Repteens, and the theater club at Dominican Convent High School.

After starring as Laertes in a production of William Shakespeare's *Hamlet*, Gurira experienced a turning point during senior year, while memorizing the Lady in Red monologue for her school's adaptation of Ntozake Shange's *For Colored Girls Who Have Considered Suicide When the Rainbow Is Enuf*. "I played with it in my living room," Gurira recalled to Donloe. "It's that whole thing when you get lost in time and space. You're in your calling, you're in your zone, you don't notice the clock. That was the first moment. I was eighteen."

Following her 1997 high school graduation, Gurira returned to the United States to pursue an undergraduate degree in social psychology at Macalester College, in St. Paul, Minnesota. "I was really looking at race, population, gender and how we psychologically function in a way that affects societal outcomes around

those issues," she shared with David Peisner for *Rolling Stone* (17 Oct. 2013). "I wanted to bring some voice to issues that concerned me. I couldn't see how the dramatic arts were going to make a huge change."

Gurira's outlook shifted during her junior year of college, when she spent a semester in South Africa. "That wasn't actually the program I initially wanted to be a part of," she recalled to Walter Bilderback for the website of the Wilma Theater (11 Oct. 2013). "But the irony was that it ended up being the one where I was exposed to a lot of great African artists who had used their craftsmanship and their voices against the injustice of apartheid. And so that was actually something that propelled me to step into really saying I'm going to make this my life work."

IN THE CONTINUUM

Upon earning her BA in 2001, Gurira was accepted to the master of fine arts program at New York University's (NYU) Tisch School of the Arts. The budding playwright's first effort—and final thesis project—was initially conceived as a one-character play about a woman living with AIDS. At a teacher's suggestion, Gurira collaborated with fellow NYU grad Nikkole Salter, who was also writing a similar play. The outcome was *In the Continuum*, a piece that focused on two black women of different backgrounds (a teenager from South Central Los Angeles and a married, middle-class newscaster from Harare) with one glaring similarity: both are expectant mothers who are HIV positive.

Gurira was not only influenced by the surge of HIV cases among black women across the United States and Africa, but also by her desire to change the Western media's portrayal of developing countries. "The story of the African can be one-dimensionalized, can be told from a very flimsy perspective . . . taking a story that's very dire and making it something light and trite," she told Scott Feinberg for the *Hollywood Reporter* (8 June 2016). "I just want something rich and full and multi-dimensional."

In 2004, after receiving her MFA degree, Gurira continued her collaboration with Salter. The duo spent the summer refining *In the Continuum* at the annual Ojai Playwrights Conference festival, with the help of Tony Award–nominated actor and playwright Charlayne Woodard. After conducting fully rehearsed workshops at the Mud/Bone Collective, a nonprofit performing arts organization in South Bronx, New York, *In the Continuum* eventually caught the attention of Andrew Leynse, Primary Stages' artistic director, in September 2004. Robert O'Hara was subsequently enlisted as director, and after several rewrites, *In the Continuum* made its Primary Stages debut the following October. "In raw, astonishing [performances], Gurira and Salter create two continents' worth of memorable people, but it's as the leads that they truly reveal their gifts," Mark Blankenship wrote in his *Variety* review (3 Oct. 2005).

Gurira and Salter reprised their roles in December 2005, for a thirteen-week Off-Broadway run at the Perry Street Theatre, followed by engagements in Zimbabwe, South Africa, and Scotland, before embarking on a US tour, with stops at Washington, DC's Woolly Mammoth Theatre and Los Angeles's Kirk Douglas Theatre, among others. *In the Continuum* earned critical acclaim from the *New York Times, New York Magazine*, and *Newsday*, among others, as one of the best plays of 2005. A year later it won an Obie Award, an Outer Critics Circle Award, and a Pulitzer Prize nomination. Gurira's performance earned her a 2006 Drama League Award nod and the 2007 Helen Hayes Award for lead actress.

ACTING CAREER AND *ECLIPSED*
Gurira's first big-screen appearance came in Tom McCarthy's *The Visitor* (2007), a post–September 11 indie flick in which she played a Senegalese jewelry designer—and illegal immigrant—found squatting with her Syrian boyfriend in a Manhattan apartment. Aided by a grant from the Theater Communications Group's (TCG) New Generations program, Gurira traveled to Liberia in 2007 to research her next play, interviewing former female soldiers, sex workers, and peace activists. She drew inspiration from a 2003 *New York Times* article about Black Diamond, an infamous Liberian rebel commander, as well as an accompanying image of female freedom fighters during Liberia's civil war. "I was raised in Africa and I had never seen anything like it, women with AK-47s, dressed very hip and looking formidable," Gurira recalled to Adam Rathe for *DuJour* (14 Oct. 2015).

Meanwhile, Gurira continued to amass film and television credits. A year after playing a spirit in Ricky Gervais's big-screen romantic comedy *Ghost Town* (2008), Gurira guest-starred on the short-lived ABC time-travel drama *Life on Mars*, an American remake of the award-winning BBC series of the same name. In mid-April 2009 she made her Broadway debut as Martha Pentecost, an ex-con's long-missing wife, in a revival of the August Wilson play *Joe Turner's Come and Gone*, which enjoyed a limited sixty-one-performance run at the Belasco Theatre.

In the fall of 2009, Gurira debuted her next production, *Eclipsed*, which chronicles the lives of five Liberian women held captive in a rebel camp. *Eclipsed* had its world premiere at Woolly Mammoth from August 31 to September 27, with subsequent month-long runs at the Kirk Douglas Theatre and the Yale Repertory Theatre in New Haven, Connecticut. After capping off the year with an appearance on NBC's

long-running crime drama *Law & Order*, Gurira costarred in 3 *Backyards*, winner of the directing prize at the 2010 Sundance Film Festival. She then landed a recurring gig on the critically acclaimed HBO series *Treme*, followed by minor roles, as an undercover agent and as a paramedic, in the Fox drama *Lie to Me* and Wes Craven's thriller *My Soul to Take* (2010), respectively. Gurira also spent part of the year traveling to Zimbabwe on another TCG grant–funded trip to research her next play, which is set in 1890s Southern Rhodesia.

In January 2011 Gurira returned to Sundance with Andrew Dosunmu's feature-film debut *Restless City*, which centered on African immigrants in New York City. That summer critics were raving about her work in another project: Shakespeare in the Park's repertory production of *Measure for Measure*. "Ms. Gurira . . . brings a thrilling intensity to her portrayal of the Catholic novice Isabella, one of Shakespeare's tougher-to-love heroines," Charles Isherwood wrote for the *New York Times* (30 June 2011). Equally effusive was Joe Dziemianowicz for the *New York Daily News* (1 July 2011): "This largely unknown actress is unequivocally captivating, and the stakes are at their highest and feelings most impassioned whenever she's on stage." Gurira's performance earned her the Actors' Equity Foundation's Joe A. Callaway Award (2011).

THE CONVERT AND THE WALKING DEAD
For her third play, *The Convert*, about a young southern African woman who finds refuge with a black Catholic missionary after fleeing an arranged marriage to an older man, Gurira drew inspiration from George Bernard Shaw's *Pygmalion*. "There was something that so bothered me about it that I wanted to adapt *Pygmalion* to the Zimbabwean perspective because it's real and such a part of the colonial experience," she told Sergio Mims for *Ebony* (3 Mar. 2012). "It's colonizing somebody. It's a way of saying, 'What you are isn't quite right.'"

The critically acclaimed historical drama made its world premiere at New Jersey's McCarter Theatre in January 2012, before eventually heading to Chicago's Goodman Theater and Los Angeles's Kirk Douglas Theater in the spring.

Gurira's acting career also began to take off. In March she was cast as Michonne, a dreadlocked, sword-wielding zombie killer in *The Walking Dead*, AMC's adaptation of the postapocalyptic comic book series. To prepare for the role, Gurira trained for a month with a stuntman/sword master and studied samurai movies. The season three premiere of *The Walking Dead*, Gurira's debut on the show, attracted 10.9 million viewers, making it the highest-rated episode in series history and the most-watched drama telecast in cable history.

The following January, Gurira reunited with Dosunmu for *Mother of George*, which premiered to critical raves at Sundance. *The Walking Dead* finished strong, drawing record audiences for the March 31, 2013, season finale, among both total viewers (12.4 million) and adults ages eighteen to forty-nine (8.1 million). The show also ranked as television's top series among the coveted eighteen to forty-nine demographic. *The Convert*, which had a month-long run at Woolly Mammoth and Philadelphia's Wilma Theater in 2013, eventually earned a Los Angeles Outer Critics Circle prize and six Ovation Awards. Gurira's television career continued on an upward trajectory. *The Walking Dead* remained the top-rated show among adults ages eighteen to forty-nine during the next two seasons; by season five, the series was averaging nearly 14.5 million total viewers.

Gurira's next play, a culture-clash comedy, debuted in January 2015. Set in modern-day Minneapolis, *Familiar* revolves around an upper-middle-class Zimbabwean American couple, whose eldest daughter, a first-generation American is marrying into a white family, and wants to hold a traditional dowry ceremony.

ECLIPSED GOES TO BROADWAY

In July 2015 Yale alum Lupita Nyong'o, who had served as understudy in the 2009 production, was tapped to headline the Public Theater's production of *Eclipsed*. On October 14, after two weeks of previews, Gurira's ensemble piece opened Off-Broadway, establishing her as a force to be reckoned with. "It . . . signals Gurira as a playwright of uncommon ambition," David Rooney wrote for the *Hollywood Reporter* (14 Oct. 2015). *Eclipsed* moved to Broadway's John Golden Theater in February 2016, around the same time that *Familiar* debuted Off-Broadway at Playwrights Horizon. *Walking Dead*, whose sixth season was highlighted by an onscreen kiss between fan favorite Michonne and series protagonist Rick Grimes, capped off a fourth consecutive season at number one in the eighteen to forty-nine demographic.

In May 2016, on the same night that Gurira attended the Met Ball, *Eclipsed* earned six Tony Award nominations, including Gurira's first nod for best play. Despite being honored at the Lilly Awards and the Drama Desk Awards, Gurira failed to win a Tony. *Eclipsed*, which won the Tony for best costume design, ended its Broadway run on June 19, 2016.

Gurira will appear as Afeni Shakur, rapper Tupac's mother, in the biographical drama *All Eyez on Me*, scheduled to be released in November 2016. She has been cast opposite Nyong'o in Marvel Studios' adaptation of *Black Panther*.

PERSONAL LIFE

Gurira, who speaks four languages (English, French, Shona, and Xhosa), is the cofounder of Almasi Arts Alliance, a nonprofit organization dedicated to promoting collaborations between African and American artists.

SUGGESTED READING

Donloe, Darlene. "The 'Zamerican' Danai Gurira Examines *The Convert*." *@This Stage Magazine*. LA Stage Alliance, 18 Apr. 2012. Web. 16 Aug. 2016.

Dziemianowicz, Joe. "Actress Danai Gurira Makes Star Turn Look Like a Walk in the Park." Rev. of *Measure for Measure*, dir. David Esbjornson. *New York Daily News*. NYDailyNews.com, 1 July 2011. Web. 16 Aug. 2016.

Feinberg, Scott. "Awards Chatter Podcast—Danai Gurira ('Eclipsed')." *Hollywood Reporter*. Hollywood Reporter, 8 June 2016. Web. 16 Aug. 2016.

Gurira, Danai. Interview by Walter Bilderback. *Wilma Theater*. Wilma Theater, 11 Oct. 2013. Web. 16 Aug. 2016.

Gurira, Danai. Interview by Tim Sanford. *Playwrights Horizons*. Time Warner Foundation, n.d. Web. 16 Aug. 2016.

Rathe, Adam. "War Stories." *DuJour*. Dujour Media, 14 Oct. 2015. Web. 16 Aug. 2016.

Rooney, David. Rev. of *Eclipsed*, dir. Liesl Tommy. *Hollywood Reporter*. Hollywood Reporter, 14 Oct. 2015. Web. 16 Aug. 2016.

SELECTED WORKS

In The Continuum, 2005; *The Visitor*, 2007; *Ghost Town*, 2008; *Eclipsed*, 2009; *Lie to Me*, 2010; *My Soul to Take*, 2010 *The Convert*, 2012; *Familiar*, 2015

—Bertha Muteba

Simona Halep

Born: September 27, 1991
Occupation: Tennis player

At five feet six, the Romanian tennis player Simona Halep stands half a foot shorter than many of her elite contemporaries. Nevertheless, through a combination of talent, determination, and on-court savvy, Halep has risen to the top of women's tennis. "She punches above her weight," Ian Chadband wrote for *FedCup* (12 Mar. 2015), "with a singular game full of speed, variety, and a touch of daring as she darts around the court with delightful quietness." Meanwhile, Louisa Thomas, in an article for *Grantland* (29 May 2014), described Halep as a player who is "astonishingly fast" with "uncanny anticipation"

si.robi/CC BY-SA 2.0/Wikimedia Commons

and groundstrokes that are "compact, beautiful, [and] unreadable."

Halep turned professional in 2006 and made her debut on the Women's Tennis Association (WTA) Tour in 2009. During her first several seasons on the tour, she was dogged by injuries, struggled to perform well in big tournaments, and was better known for undergoing breast-reduction surgery than for her tennis game. Halep's fortunes shifted during the 2013 season, when, after changing her mindset and approach to the game, she won her first six WTA titles and reached the top twenty of the WTA singles rankings. Halep achieved her breakthrough in 2014, when she reached her first Grand Slam final at the French Open. She finished the 2015 season with a number-two singles ranking.

EARLY LIFE

Simona Halep was born on September 27, 1991, to Stere and Tania Halep in Constanta, Romania, which lies on the western coast of the Black Sea. Her father was a semiprofessional soccer player, competing for Romania's now-defunct Săgeata Stejaru club, before becoming the owner of a dairy factory. She started playing tennis at the age of four, following her older brother, Nicolae, into the sport.

Endowed with natural mobility, Halep quickly exhibited an aptitude for tennis, and by age six, she was playing the sport every day. At age eight she started competing in and winning tournaments. Halep has credited her first coach, Nicusor Ene, with playing an important role in her development as a tennis player. Ene kept her on a strict training regimen and taught her

how to conduct herself in a professional manner. Meanwhile, Halep's parents provided her with the necessary, albeit expensive, resources to further her career.

Early in her playing career, Halep modeled her game after her childhood idol, Belgian star Justine Henin, a former number-one-ranked player. Listed at only five feet five, Henin overcame her small size with speed, technique, and an all-court style of play. She retired in 2011 with forty-three WTA singles titles, including seven Grand Slam championships.

As a teenager coming up through the junior ranks, Halep, like Henin, was discouraged from pursuing a professional tennis career because of her diminutive frame. "I didn't trust them," she said of her detractors to Kaitlyn McGrath for the Toronto *National Post* (15 Aug. 2015), explaining that Henin made her realize that it was "not very important to be very tall to play tennis." Some, though, recognized Halep's potential, including Corneliu Idu, a Romanian businessman who began sponsoring her when she was fifteen. Idu, who owns a tennis club in Constanta, covered all of her travel and training expenses for two years.

A CAREER-ALTERING DECISION

When Halep was sixteen, she moved to Bucharest, Romania's largest city and capital, to take her game to the next level. Because Constanta lacked adequate competition and coaching, Halep did not feel she could stay there, she explained to Paul Newman for the London *Independent* (28 May 2014). By then, Halep had turned professional and begun competing in futures tournaments on the International Tennis Federation (ITF) circuit, a developmental platform for the WTA Tour.

Halep had already won a handful of ITF singles titles when, in 2008, she captured the French Open junior singles title and became the number-one-ranked junior women's tennis player in the world. After her French Open victory, Halep stopped playing on the junior circuit to focus exclusively on professional tournaments. In 2009, she won an ITF singles title in Maribor, Slovenia, and played in her first two WTA tournaments as a qualifier.

As Halep turned her attention to her professional career, she made the difficult decision to have breast-reduction surgery. Throughout her teens, Halep suffered from chronic back pain resulting from the extra weight on her chest, which also limited her mobility and slowed her reaction time on the court. In July 2009, despite receiving criticism from fans and unwanted media attention, she underwent a procedure to reduce her breast size from a 34DD to a 34C, in order to improve her game and prevent future injuries. "I don't like them in my everyday life," Halep said at the time, as quoted by Simon Briggs for the

Telegraph (28 May 2014), adding that she "would have gone for surgery even if I hadn't been a sportswoman."

FIRST WTA SINGLES TITLES

Halep's breast reduction proved to be a boon to her career. In 2010, she performed well in two outdoor clay tournaments, advancing to her first WTA quarterfinal at the Andalucia Tennis Experience in Marbella, Spain, and then reaching her first WTA final at the Grand Prix SAR in Fez, Morocco. Halep also represented Romania in the Fed Cup, the largest annual women's international team competition. (She played again for the Romanian Fed Cup team in 2014 and 2015.) She finished the season at eighty-one in the WTA singles rankings, marking the first time in her career that she cracked the top one hundred.

Over the next two seasons, Halep enjoyed a gradual rise up the WTA year-end rankings, climbing to fifty-three in 2011 and forty-seven in 2012. During the 2011 season, she reached the final of the Grand Prix SAR for the second straight year and recorded her first win over a top-ten player by defeating Li Na in the first round of the US Open. During the 2012 season, Halep advanced to the final of the Brussels Open, a premier-level WTA tournament in Belgium, after shocking former world number one Jelena Jankovic in the first round. That season she also made her Olympic debut at the Summer Games in London, where she lost in the first round.

Despite showing steady improvement, Halep tended to perform poorly in Grand Slams, often losing in the first or second round, due to injuries or a lack of mental toughness. Entering the 2013 season, she resolved to reverse that trend by becoming more aggressive on the court. Halep's new approach first showed results at the 2013 Italian Open in Rome, Italy, when, after entering the tournament as a qualifier, she overcame three top-twenty players en route to the semifinals. In the semifinals, Halep was defeated by Serena Williams, the world's top-ranked player and a twenty-one-time Grand Slam winner, in straight sets, but her performance helped set the tone for what would become a breakout season. "What changed was that I allowed myself to be relaxed on the court by taking the pressure off," she explained to Louisa. "I told myself to enjoy it and play with pleasure."

In a seven-month span following the Italian Open, Halep won the first six WTA singles titles of her career. In June 2013, she claimed her first two WTA titles in back-to-back fashion, winning the Nürnberger Versicherungscup, in Germany, and the Topshelf Open, in the Netherlands, and in the following month, she won the Budapest Grand Prix in Hungary. She then won the New Haven Open in Connecticut, the Kremlin Cup in Moscow, and the WTA Tournament of Champions in Sofia, Bulgaria.

Halep's six titles were second only to Williams's eleven on the WTA Tour in 2013. Halep, however, was the only player to notch victories on all four court surfaces (clay, grass, hard, and indoor). She was named the WTA's most improved player of the year and rose to number eleven on the WTA rankings.

FIRST GRAND SLAM FINAL

Hoping to build on her success, Halep approached the 2014 season with two goals in mind: to remain in the top twenty and to reach a Grand Slam quarterfinal. Despite opening the season without a coach, Halep wasted little time in achieving one of those goals when she reached the quarterfinals of the 2014 Australian Open. Notwithstanding that achievement, she was handily defeated by eventual finalist Dominika Cibulková in straight sets.

Overcome by unmanageable emotions in her quarterfinal match, Halep sought out the help of highly regarded Belgian tennis coach Wim Fissette, best known for his work with four-time Grand Slam winner Kim Clijsters. Fissette called it "an offer I couldn't refuse," as quoted by Briggs. "She has the complete game, and she is very intelligent on the court." To aid Halep's transformation into an elite player, Fissette persuaded her to switch from a defensive to a more offensive style of play and to have confidence in her game. As Fissette put it to Thomas in another article for *Grantland* (26 Aug. 2014), "I told her, technically, her serve was very good . . . but she had to believe in it."

Not long after she started working with Fissette, Halep showcased newfound confidence at the 2014 Qatar Open in Doha. There, she beat three top-ten players en route to the final, where she defeated Angelique Kerber in straight sets to win her first premier-level WTA title. Halep then finished as runner-up to Maria Sharapova at the 2014 Madrid Open, another premier tour event.

Halep carried her momentum into the 2014 French Open, where she cruised to her first Grand Slam final without dropping a set. In the championship match, she again squared off against Sharapova, battling for over three hours before losing in three sets "in what was the best Grand Slam women's final in the past decade," Thomas wrote. Halep became the first Romanian to reach a Grand Slam final since her manager Virginia Ruzici in 1980. Her finals match against Sharapova, meanwhile, was the first Grand Slam women's final to go to three sets since 2001.

Halep followed up her breakthrough French Open performance by reaching the semifinals of the 2014 Wimbledon Championships, where she lost to Canadian phenom Eugenie Bouchard. After notching another victory at the inaugural 2014 Bucharest Open and advancing to the finals of the year-end WTA championships, Halep ascended to number three in the WTA rankings and became the first Romanian to break into the world's top five.

2015 SEASON

Prior to the 2015 season, in an effort to get reacquainted with her Romanian tennis roots, Halep parted ways with Fissette and began working with countryman Victor Ionita. She opened the season by winning the 2015 Shenzhen Open in China, before advancing to her second consecutive quarterfinal at the 2015 Australian Open. She then earned the tenth and eleventh WTA titles of her career at the 2015 Dubai Tennis Championships in the United Arab Emirates, and the prestigious 2015 BNP Paribas Open in Indian Wells, California.

In the face of mounting pressure and expectations, Halep struggled mightily in her next two Grand Slam events, losing in the second round of the 2015 French Open and the first round of the 2015 Wimbledon Championships. She bounced back, however, at the 2015 US Open, where she advanced to the semifinals for the first time. One of Halep's most impressive wins at the tournament came during a three-set quarterfinal victory against the six-foot Belarusian player Victoria Azarenka, a former number-one ranked player. Responding to a comment about the seeming power disparity between her and Azarenka, Halep said in a post-match press conference, "I'm not very strong. . . . I don't have big muscles. I'm not tall. I have power inside. I fight," as quoted by Peter Bodo for ESPN (10 Sept. 2015).

Despite falling in the round-robin stage of the 2015 WTA championships in Singapore, Halep ended the season at number two in the WTA rankings. In January 2016, she began working with noted Australian tennis coach and ESPN commentator Darren Cahill.

In addition to singles tournaments, Halep, who resides in Constanta, has occasionally played in women's doubles and mixed-doubles competitions. Her on-court success and humble demeanor have made her one of the most popular players on the WTA Tour and an icon in her native Romania. "It's my dream to win a Grand Slam and I will keep trying harder," she affirmed to Chadband. "It is important for me to make the people in my country proud."

SUGGESTED READING

Bodo, Peter. "Simona Halep Packs a Powerful Punch." *ESPN.com*. ESPN Internet Ventures, 10 Sept. 2015. Web. 17 Dec. 2015.

Briggs, Simon. "French Open 2014: How a Breast Reduction Helped Simona Halep Unleash Her Full Potential." *Telegraph*. Telegraph Media Group, 28 May 2014. Web. 17 Dec. 2015.

Chadband, Ian. "Simona Halep, Modest but Brilliant." *FedCup*. ITF Licensing, 12 Mar. 2015. Web. 17 Dec. 2015.

Thomas, Louisa. "Match Striker: The Increasingly Unclassifiable, Increasingly Unstoppable Simona Halep." *Grantland*. ESPN Internet Ventures, 29 May 2014. Web. 17 Dec. 2015.

Thomas, Louisa. "Mind Games." *Grantland*. ESPN Internet Ventures, 26 Aug. 2014. Web. 17 Dec. 2015.

—Chris Cullen

Han Kang

Born: 1970
Occupation: Author

Although Han Kang has been a renowned writer of both poetry and prose in her native South Korea since the 1990s, she gained international acclaim with the publication of her surreal, psychological novel *Ch'aesikchuuija* in 2007. Almost a decade later, in 2015, she received new acclaim for the novel after it was translated into English as *The Vegetarian* and then again the following year when she won the coveted Man Booker International Prize for fiction. She followed that with another novel, *Sonyŏn i onda* (2014), translated into English as *Human Acts* (2016), which explored the human side of a massacre by government troops in South Korea in 1980. Han also teaches creative writing at the Seoul Institute of the Arts.

EARLY LIFE AND CAREER

Han Kang was born in the city of Gwangju, South Korea, in 1970. Her father, Han Seung-won, was a novelist, although he had a hard time making a consistent living from his writing, which led the family to move often. Perhaps the most significant move the family made was from Han's hometown of Gwangju to Seoul in 1980, when Han was nine years old. At Yonsei University, a private research university in Seoul and one of the most prestigious universities in the country, Han studied contemporary Korean literature. In 1993, she first published five poems in a South Korean magazine called *Munhak-gwa-sahoe* (Literature and society). The following year Han published fiction, in both long and short forms, and in 1998, she spent a semester at the famed

Jeff Spicer/Getty Images

International Writing Program at the University of Iowa, in the United States.

More than a decade before most English speakers had even heard of her, Han had begun to receive acclaim in her native South Korea. She continued to receive recognition for her literary writings through the 1990s and 2000s. According to a short biography the author provided to *Korean Literature in Translation* (11 June 2013), Han won the Korean Novel Award for her novella *Ah ki bu chuh* (Baby Buddha) in 1999, the Today's Young Artist Award in 2000, the 2005 Yi Sang Literary Award for the novella *Mong go ban jum* (Mongolian spot), and the 2010 Dongri Literary Award for the novel *Barami bunda, gara* (Breath fighting). *Baby Buddha* and *The Vegetarian* were both subsequently made into films. The latter played at the Sundance Film Festival in 2010.

THE VEGETARIAN

When *The Vegetarian* was first published in South Korea, in 2007, it was somewhat of a sensation. Han was already known for her poetry and fiction, but she had never before released a book quite like it—sexual, violent, surreal, and psychological, all in one. Eventually, the book became a cult hit, and not only in South Korea: The publication rights to the book were sold in more than a dozen countries. The story of how the book came to be translated into English begins in the United Kingdom, at the University of London's School of Oriental and African Studies. PhD student Deborah Smith was in her mid-twenties at the time she happened to come across the Korean-language version of *The Vegetarian*. She loved the vividly visual and poetic prose, so she tried to translate the book into English. However, her first attempt was less than successful, mostly because she was still new to the Korean language. But about a year later she sent a ten-page sample translation to a publisher in the United Kingdom. The submission was accepted, and Smith finished her translation of what became *The Vegetarian*. Smith went on to translate Han's next book into English as well. *The Vegetarian* was published in the United Kingdom in early 2015 and published in the United States in early 2016.

In *The Vegetarian*, Han combines surreal and poetic prose with language that is meant to hit the reader in the gut. The novel is written in three parts, all about the central character named Yeong-hye, a wife who decides to become a vegetarian. She is depressed and haunted by troubling dreams, and everyone seems to think that she is, at least somewhat, mentally unstable. She does indeed seem to unravel, ultimately wanting to become a tree. All three parts of the book are told from different perspectives of people in her life: Part one is told from the point of view of her husband, part two from the point of view of her brother-in-law, and part three from the point of view of her older sister. Occasionally, the reader does get direct access into the mind of Yeong-hye via italicized passages. Ultimately, the story is one of humanity on a small scale.

The critical reception for the book was nearly unanimously positive. In a review for the *Guardian* (24 Jan. 2015), Daniel Hahn wrote that Han's English-language debut was a "bracing, visceral, system-shocking addition to the Anglophone reader's diet. It is sensual, provocative, and violent, ripe with potent images, startling colors, and disturbing questions." In the pages of the *New York Times Sunday Book Review* (2 Feb. 2016), Porochista Khakpour noted that "there is no end to the horrors that rattle in and out of this ferocious, magnificently death-affirming novel." Khakpour went on to warn readers against a Western-focused, simplistic "ethnographic and sociological" interpretation of the book. "Han's glorious treatments of agency, personal choice, submission, and subversion find form in the parable," Khakpour wrote. "There is something about short literary forms—this novel is under 200 pages—in which the allegorical and the violent gain special potency from their small packages."

Although the book is specific to South Korean culture, it is also philosophically and emotionally relevant on a universal level. Laura Miller, writing for the online magazine the *Slate Book Review* (5 Feb. 2016), concluded as much in her review of the book. Miller also observed that the effect of Han's prose is "difficult to convey." There was not a specific passage in the text to which she could easily point. "*The Vegetarian* has an eerie universality that gets under your skin and stays put irrespective of nation or gender," wrote Miller. "But exactly what its business is there, I would not presume to say." A few months after the book's release in the United States, Han won the prestigious Man Booker International Prize for fiction, in May 2016.

HUMAN ACTS
By the time Han received the Man Booker Prize, her second English-language book, *Human Acts* (also translated by Smith), had been published in English. Unlike her previous novel, this one delves into modern Korean history and politics from only a few decades ago. Because Western readers would likely not be familiar with the historic moment referenced in the book, Smith wrote an introduction, in which she explained the 1980 massacre in Gwangju, South Korea. After the assassination of dictator Park Chunghee in 1979, army general Chun Doo-hwan took power in South Korea and put the country under martial law. His control of life in South Korea was ferocious, and he sought to quash any dissent. Various demonstrators—especially students and workers—took part in a protest in 1980 in Gwangju, where Han had been born a decade prior. The demonstrators were attacked and fired upon by state police; the protests continued, and the cycle of violence only got worse. In the end, according to official government estimates, at least two hundred—the number could be as high as two thousand—demonstrators were dead.

This massacre made a deep impression on Han when she was only twelve years old, which was only about two years after the event itself. On her father's bookshelf, she happened to find a book of gruesome photos of some of the victims: faces of dead protesters, some severely beaten and injured. This frightened young Han and, essentially, made her afraid of the human capacity for horrific acts.

In many ways *Human Acts* is about the terrible things people are capable of doing—yet it is also about the potential for human dignity to shine some light, at least in part, through so much darkness. Han explores deeply this difficult paradox of human nature. Like her previous novel, *Human Acts* has several narrators, including the "soul" of one of the victims; that victim's mother; and even, in the last section, Han herself—telling the reader why she felt compelled to write about this specific time in her country's history.

Like they were for *The Vegetarian*, the critical reviews for *Human Acts* were nearly unanimously positive. Writing for the *Financial Times* (30 Dec. 2015), Francesca Wade concluded that the book "portrays people whose self-determination is under threat from terrifying external forces; it is a sobering meditation on what it means to be human." Claire Armitstead for the *Guardian* (5 Feb. 2016) wrote that Han's prose is "grisly but never gratuitous in its struggle to apply an intrinsically humanist art form to the examination of industrial-scale butchery. As forensic as her observations are, she is also a formal innovator, whose work draws on her knowledge of poetry and on her interest in music and art." In addition to *The Vegetarian* and *Human Acts*, Han has published several award-winning novels in Korean.

SUGGESTED READING
Han Kang, and Deborah Smith. Interview by Mark Reynolds. "Han Kang: To Be Human." *Bookanista*. Bookanista, 2016. Web. 3 Aug. 2016.

Khakpour, Porochista. Rev. of *The Vegetarian*, by Han Kang. *Sunday Book Review*. New York Times, 2 Feb. 2016. Web. 3 Aug. 2016.

Miller, Laura. "'I'm Not an Animal Anymore': Han Kang's Mystifying, Ecstatic *The Vegetarian*." *Slate Book Review*. Slate Group, 5 Feb. 2016. Web. 3 Aug. 2016.

Wade, Francesca. Rev. of *Human Acts*, by Han Kang. *Financial Times*. Financial Times, 30 Dec. 2015. Web. 3 Aug. 2016.

SELECTED WORKS
Ah ki bu chuh (Baby Buddha), 1999; Ch'aesikchuuija, 2007 (The Vegetarian, 2015); Barami bunda, gara (Breath fighting), 2010; Sonyŏn i onda, 2014 (Human Acts, 2016)

—*Dmitry Kiper*

Yuzuru Hanyu
Born: December 7, 1994
Occupation: Figure skater

The Japanese figure skater Yuzuru Hanyu is known for his "profound mix of confidence and consistency" and for his deft combination of "artistry and athleticism," as Robert Samuels noted for the *Washington Post* (31 Mar. 2016). Since breaking out on the senior international circuit in 2010, Hanyu has established himself as one of the greatest male figure skaters of all time. In 2014 he won an Olympic figure skating gold medal and won his first career world title. A four-time Japanese national champion, Hanyu owns the world records for the short program, free skate, and combined total scores. He is the first male figure skater to break the 100-point barrier in the short program, the 200-point barrier in the

All Nippon Airways/CC BY-SA 4.0/Wikimedia Commons

free skate, and the 300-point barrier in the combined total score.

EARLY LIFE

Yuzuru Hanyu was born on December 7, 1994, in Sendai, the capital city of the Miyagi Prefecture in northeast Japan. Hanyu's first name means "bowstring" and represents "confidence, strength and straightness," as Hanyu explained to Tatjana Flade for *Golden Skate* (21 Apr. 2011). His father is a school administrator, and his mother is a homemaker.

Hanyu started skating at the age of four after his sister Saya, who is four years older, began taking skating lessons. He accompanied his sister to lessons at Sendai's indoor ice rink and became drawn to the challenge of learning and mastering new tricks. Hanyu's sister was taught by family friend Minoru Sano, a former world bronze medalist and a five-time Japanese national champion who worked as an instructor at the rink.

Though Hanyu enjoyed the acrobatic nature of figure skating, he disliked practicing and would often get bored after only five minutes on the ice. Hanyu, who suffers from asthma, initially preferred baseball to figure skating, a preference that was met with approval from his middle-class parents, who had no qualms about giving up the exorbitant costs associated with figure skating. He ultimately decided to stick with skating, however, because of his desire to succeed in the sport.

Hanyu first dreamed of becoming an Olympic figure skater when he was around seven years old. He fostered those dreams after watching the Russian skater Evgeni Plushenko compete at the 2002 Winter Olympics in Salt Lake City, Utah. Captivated by Plushenko's athletic, no-holds-barred skating style, Hanyu began working in earnest to master various jumps and spins. He grew up idolizing Plushenko, so much so that he even adopted the Russian's signature mushroom haircut.

JUNIOR CAREER

Hanyu's talent on the ice was evident early on, and what he lacked in size and strength he made up for in mental toughness. "I think there is no fear for anything," Hanyu told Flade. "That is my strong point." Hanyu's talent was such that his sister quit skating in the eighth grade so that the family would have the economic resources to further his career.

In 2004 Hanyu started competing nationally at the novice level, winning that year's Japan Novice Championships in the Novice B category. Around this time, Hanyu's home ice rink in Sendai was closed for financial reasons, which limited his training options. Hanyu did not devote himself full time to skating again until 2007, when the Sendai rink reopened. That year he won the Japan Novice Championships in the Novice A category and captured a bronze medal at the Japan Junior Championships.

During the 2008–9 season, Hanyu entered the junior ranks and started competing in events on the International Skating Union (ISU) Junior Grand Prix (JGP). In the fall of 2009, he won the gold medal at the junior national championships. That performance helped Hanyu qualify for the 2009 World Junior Figure Skating Championships in Sofia, Bulgaria. In his junior worlds debut, he placed eleventh in the short program and thirteenth in the long program, or free skate, to finish twelfth overall.

Hanyu enjoyed a dominant run on the junior circuit in 2009–10. He won JGP events in Croatia and Poland and then captured gold at the 2010 JGP Final in Tokyo, Japan. After the latter competition, he successfully defended his title at the Japan junior national championships. Hanyu was also invited to compete at the senior-level 2009–10 Japan Figure Skating Championships, where he placed sixth. Hanyu reached international prominence in 2010, when he won the gold medal at the World Junior Figure Skating Championships in The Hague, Netherlands. He finished ahead of silver medalist Song Nan of China by more than ten points.

OVERCOMING ADVERSITY

After winning the junior worlds, Hanyu began to transition to the men's senior international circuit. Adding a quadruple toe loop jump to his repertoire, he impressed in his senior debut, finishing fourth at the 2010 NHK Trophy, a Grand Prix event. Hanyu then placed seventh at his next Grand Prix event, the 2010 Cup of Russia, before notching a fourth-place finish at the Japan championships. Hanyu's first senior season culminated at the 2011 ISU Four Continents Figure Skating Championships in Taipei, Taiwan, where he won bronze medals in both the short program and the free skate.

Hanyu was training at his home rink in Sendai when, on March 11, 2011, the Tōhoku earthquake and tsunami struck northeast Japan. "The earth was shaking so violently," he recounted to *International Figure Skating* (Dec. 2011), "that I could hardly stand on my skates." Hanyu was forced to spend the next three days at an evacuation center with his family, whose home was damaged during the earthquake. His rink, meanwhile, was closed down for months after water pipes beneath it ruptured and caused the ice to melt.

Consequently, Hanyu moved his training base three hours north to Yokohama City, which was located a safe distance from the earthquake's epicenter. At the time of the tsunami and subsequent earthquake, which claimed more than eighteen thousand lives and caused an estimated $300 billion in damage, Hanyu was attending Tōhoku High School, the alma mater of the Japanese champion skaters Takeshi Honda and Shizuka Arakawa. He was nevertheless relegated to taking correspondence courses after relocating.

In April 2011 Hanyu took part in a charity show for earthquake victims and subsequently spent that summer skating in ice shows around Japan to stay in shape. "I seriously thought about quitting skating," Hanyu admitted to Jere Longman for the *New York Times* (14 Feb. 2014). "I had my hands full making a living to stay alive."

ROAD TO THE OLYMPICS

In July 2011, Hanyu returned to training in Sendai when his home rink reopened. In December of that year, he won the bronze medal at the Japan championships, helping him realize his goal of qualifying for the 2012 World Figure Skating Championships in Nice, France. In his first senior-level worlds, he won the bronze medal after placing seventh in the short program and second in the free skate.

In April 2012, Hanyu left his longtime coach and choreographer Nanami Abe to train with Brian Orser, a two-time Olympic silver medalist who had previously coached the South Korean figure skating champion Yuna Kim. Hanyu moved with his mother to Orser's home base of Toronto, Canada, and began training with Orser at the Cricket Skating and Curling Club. "When I first got him, it looked like he had 16 arms and legs," Orser recalled to Philip Hersh for the *Chicago Tribune* (13 Feb. 2014). "But there was a certain spirit I liked about him, even if it was a little bit out of control. I needed to get him a little more guided but not take away his spirit."

Under the guidance of Orser, Hanyu polished his raw skills and soon developed into one of the top male skaters in the world. He opened his 2012–13 season in auspicious fashion with a gold-medal victory at the 2012 Finlandia Trophy. After medaling and achieving record-breaking performances in two Grand Prix events, Hanyu qualified for that season's Grand Prix Final in Sochi, Russia, where he won the silver medal. He then claimed his first national title at the 2012–13 Japanese championships before ending his season with a fourth-place finish at the 2013 World Championships.

FIRST OLYMPIC AND WORLD TITLES

Hanyu entered the 2013–14 season with the goal of winning the gold medal in the men's singles event at the 2014 Olympics in Sochi. In the run-up to the Olympics, he defended his title at the 2013 Finlandia Trophy, won silver medals in his two Grand Prix events, captured his first Grand Prix Final title, and won his second consecutive national title.

Hanyu carried his dominant skating into Sochi, where he broke his own world record in the men's short program by achieving a score of 101.45 points. He became the first male skater in history to score more than 100 points in a short program. He then achieved a score of 178.64 points in the free skate for a combined score of 280.09, which was enough to secure the gold medal. At nineteen years old, Hanyu became the youngest men's Olympic champion since American Dick Button in 1948. "He's so explosive, and he does the most difficult things in such a way that you feel it's simple for him," Scott Hamilton, the 1984 Olympic men's figure skating champion, told Longman. "That gets incredible respect."

Following the 2014 Olympics, Hanyu competed at the 2014 World Championships in Saitama, Japan, where he narrowly overcame fellow countrymen Tatsuki Machida to win his first world title. He became the first male skater to win both Olympic and World championships in the same year since Russian Alexei Yagudin in 2002.

2014–15 AND 2015–16 SEASONS

Hanyu was hampered by several injuries during the 2014–15 season. He skated well enough, however, to qualify for the 2014–15 Grand Prix Final, where he won his second straight title after winning both the short and free skate programs. He then placed first in the short and free skate at the 2014–15 Japan Championships, to earn his third consecutive national title.

After the Japan Championships, Hanyu underwent surgery to correct a bladder problem.

He spent a month off the ice recovering; he was forced to stay off the ice for another two weeks after suffering a sprained ankle in practice. Hanyu's lack of adequate training ultimately affected his performance at the 2015 World Championships in Shanghai, China, where he claimed the silver medal behind his training partner, Spain's Javier Fernández. Assessing his performance during the season, Hanyu told Wei Xiong for *Golden Skate* (20 June 2015), "Whether this season was a failure for me depends on how you see it, but I believe failure is the stepping stone for success. . . . You won't realize some problems unless you fail."

Hanyu returned to dominant form in 2015–16, when he won his fourth straight Japanese title and established new world records for short program, free skate, and total scores. At the 2015 NHK Trophy, a Grand Prix event, he won the short program with a world record score of 106.33. He then set world records in the free skate and total score, with 216.07 points and 322.04 points, respectively.

Hanyu broke all three world records again at the 2015–16 Grand Prix Final in Barcelona, Spain. He won the short program with 110.55 points and the free skate with 219.48 points for a combined score of 330.43, helping him become the first male skater to win three consecutive Grand Prix Final titles. He finished ahead of silver medalist Fernández by 37.48 points, which broke the record for largest margin of victory at the competition.

At the 2016 World Championships in Boston, Massachusetts, Hanyu won the short program with a near-record 110.56 points. He lost out on winning his second world title, however, after faltering in the free skate, ultimately settling for the silver medal behind Fernández. Afterward, Hanyu took two months off from skating to recover from a nagging foot injury.

PERSONAL LIFE

One of Japan's most popular athletes, Hanyu has appeared in numerous commercials and advertising campaigns in his home country. He has also been involved in many philanthropic endeavors to assist victims of the 2011 Tōhoku earthquake and tsunami.

In 2012 Hanyu released an autobiography in Japan, translated as *Blue Flames*, part of the proceeds of which went to repairing the Sendai ice rink. He made his feature-film debut as a feudal lord in the 2016 Japanese samurai comedy *The Magnificent Nine*.

SUGGESTED READING

Flade, Tatjana. "Hanyu Shoots for the Top." *Golden Skate*. Golden Skate, 21 Apr. 2011. Web. 27 May 2016.

Hersh, Philip. "Japanese Figure Skater All Arms, Legs, and Achievement." *Chicago Tribune*. Chicago Tribune, 13 Feb. 2014. Web. 27 May 2016.

Kany, Klaus-Reinhold. "Yuzuru Hanyu Rises from the Ashes." *International Figure Skating*. Madavor Media, 8 Nov. 2011. Web. 27 May 2016.

Longman, Jere. "Yuzuru Hanyu of Japan Wins Men's Figure Skating Gold." *New York Times*. New York Times Company, 14 Feb. 2014. Web. 27 May 2016.

Samuels, Robert. "Men's World Figure Skating Championship Recap: The Reign of Yuzuru Hanyu." *Washington Post*. Washington Post, 31 Mar. 2016. Web. 27 May 2016.

Xiong, Wei. "Hanyu: 'Failure Is the Stepping Stone for Success." *Golden Skate*. Golden Skate, 20 June 2015. Web. 27 May 2016.

—*Chris Cullen*

James Harden

Born: August 26, 1989
Occupation: Basketball player

Since entering the National Basketball Association (NBA) in 2009, shooting guard James Harden has established himself as one of the league's most versatile and dangerous scorers. He first attracted attention while coming off the bench for the Oklahoma City Thunder. Despite playing in the shadow of his more heralded teammates Kevin Durant and Russell Westbrook, Harden thrived in that role, claiming the NBA Sixth Man of the Year Award in 2012. "It's about winning first," Harden told Jordan Ritter Conn for *Grantland* (29 May 2012), "but I want to be an All-Star, All-NBA, get individual awards. I know all that takes hard work and dedication."

In 2012, Harden was traded to the Houston Rockets, where he had the opportunity to be a starter. After Harden's arrival the team found consistent success and reached the Western Conference Finals in 2014–15. He fulfilled his wish for accolades with multiple All-Star team and All-NBA selections, a most valuable player award from the National Basketball Players Association (NBPA), and gold medals with the US national men's basketball team.

EARLY LIFE

James Edward Harden, Jr. was born to Monja Willis and James Harden, Sr. on August 26, 1989, in Bellflower, California. The youngest of three boys, Harden lived with his single mother in a mobile home in Rancho Dominguez, a working-class neighborhood in the city of Compton.

Tim Shelby/Flickr/CC BY 2.0/Wikimedia Commons

He had little contact with his absent father, a former US Navy seaman who served jail time for drug-related charges. Harden first learned to play basketball on a portable, adjustable hoop given to him by his mother, an AT&T maintenance administrator.

Growing up, Harden's favorite NBA team was the Los Angeles Lakers, and he idolized shooting guard Kobe Bryant. Despite having asthma, Harden continually honed his skills on the playground of Audubon Middle School. He stood out from his fellow students largely because of his physique. "He wasn't fat, but he was a bit on the chubby side. Not athletic at all. But everyone knew him," friend and former classmate Camilo Valencia told Abe Schwadron for *SLAM* (30 Nov. 2015).

HONING HIS FUNDAMENTALS
At age thirteen, while playing in an Amateur Athletic Union tournament, Harden caught the eye of Artesia High School basketball coach Scott Pera, who saw something special in the short, pudgy eighth grader. "He really loved basketball," Pera shared with Jenny Dial Creech for the *Houston Chronicle* (14 Feb. 2015). "And I knew he was a kid who would put in the work."

Determined to provide her youngest son with a safe environment and a good education, Harden's mother enrolled him at Artesia High School, located in the nearby suburb of Lakewood. Although Harden was the only freshman to play for the Pioneers varsity squad in 2003, his offense was one-dimensional and his work ethic was dismal. "I just stood in the corner," he admitted to Lee Jenkins for *Sports Illustrated*

(18 Feb. 2015). "I didn't dribble. I didn't move. I didn't do anything. I was lazy, really lazy."

Harden's high school coach resorted to unorthodox coaching tactics to motivate him to be more aggressive offensively. During practice drills, Pera donned an arm pad and relentlessly swarmed Harden, who had to make eight consecutive layups. Pera also engaged Harden in an ongoing bet involving free-throw attempts per game. If Harden converted at least six, Pera would buy him a hamburger; if he fell shy of that goal, he would have to perform extra sprints.

CONSECUTIVE STATE TITLES
Eventually, Harden's hard work paid off. By 2004–5, his sophomore year in high school, he was a starter, averaging 12.3 points and a league-tying 2.4 steals in twenty games for the Pioneers, who topped the Suburban League but were routed by the Santa Margarita Eagles at the 2005 California Interscholastic Federation Southern Section (CIF-SS) Division III-AA championship game. As a section finalist, Artesia advanced to the Division III Southern California regionals, where the St. Augustine Saints defeated them in the finals.

After the Pioneers suffered their first loss of the 2005–6 season, Pera encouraged Harden, a few inches taller than the previous season, to take more shots, but Harden was initially resistant. "He said: 'Coach, I don't want to be looked at as selfish. I don't want to be a ball hog,'" Pera shared with Howard Beck for the *New York Times* (26 May 2012). "I said: 'James, if you start missing or taking bad shots, I'll tell you to stop and readjust. . . . From that point on, he was unstoppable."

For the rest of the regular season the Pioneers went undefeated and were led by Harden, who averaged 18.6 points, 7.9 rebounds, 3.3 assists, and 3 steals per game as a junior. They exacted revenge on Santa Margarita in the finals of the 2006 CIF-SS playoffs and in the Southern California regional semifinals before defeating St. Mary's Stockton to capture the state Division III-AA title—Artesia's first since 1993. Harden was voted EA Sports Second-Team All-American and earned State Junior Player of the Year honors from CalHiSports.com.

Harden entered his final high school season without Pera, who had accepted a job as Arizona State University's (ASU) basketball-operations director. Under new coach Loren Grover, Harden posted similar numbers to his junior campaign—18.8 points, 7.9 rebounds, and 3.9 assists per game. The Pioneers ended the 2006–7 season with another division title and a second consecutive state championship. Subsequently, *Parade Magazine* named Harden to its All-American Second Team, and he was selected to play in the 2007 McDonald's All-American game.

FOLLOWING PERA TO ASU

Despite being recruited by a number of Pacific-10 (Pac-10; renamed Pac-12 in 2011) Conference schools such as UCLA, USC, and the University of Washington, Harden decided to attend Arizona State, where Pera was an assistant coach under Herb Sendek. "I didn't want to go to a high-powered-school. I wanted to blaze my own trail and start something and have my name in the rafters," Harden told Justin Verrier for *ESPN.com* (14 June 2012). "Put a program on the map."

Harden made an immediate impact as a rookie, averaging a team-leading 17.8 points per game for the Sun Devils, whose overall record improved from 8–21 to 21–13 in the 2007–8 season. Despite failing to make the NCAA tournament the Sun Devils received a berth to the 2008 National Invitational Tournament (NIT), losing to the University of Florida Gators in the quarterfinals. Harden, only the fifth freshman ever to lead the conference in steals (73), earned All-Pac-10 First Team honors and was voted to both the National Association of Basketball Coaches (NABC) and the United States Basketball Writers Association (USBWA) all-district teams.

After posting an overall record of 25–10 in the 2008–9 season the Sun Devils earned an NCAA berth (the team's first since 2003) behind the strong play of Harden, who led the Pac-10 in points (20.1 per game) and steals (1.69 per game). For his efforts, Harden was voted first-team all-American and was named Pac-10 Men's Basketball Player of the Year, becoming only the third ASU player—and third sophomore ever—to win this accolade.

ENTERING THE NBA

In April 2009, following his team's season-ending, second-round National Collegiate Athletic Association (NCAA) tournament loss to the Syracuse University Orange, Harden entered the NBA Draft. He became the third overall pick, drafted by the Oklahoma City Thunder, whose inaugural season (2008–9) after moving from Seattle, Washington, and changing their name from the SuperSonics had ended with a dismal 23–59 record. During his rookie season (2009–10) Harden, who had always been a starter, was suddenly thrust into the role of bench player on a squad teeming with young talent that included Durant, Serge Ibaka, and fellow Southern California native Westbrook.

Harden adjusted well, coming off the bench in seventy-six games and averaging nearly 10 points, 3.2 rebounds, and 1.8 assists per game en route to the NBA All-Rookie Second Team.

With fifty wins, the Thunder more than doubled their number of victories from the previous season, finishing fourth in the Northwest Division and earning the team's first-ever berth in the playoffs, where they suffered a first-round loss to the Lakers.

Harden resumed his bench role during the 2010–11 season with increased playing time. He appeared in all eighty-two games—starting five—and improved his scoring average to 12.2 points as the Thunder recorded their second straight 50-win season—and claimed the Northwest division title. Following first- and second-round wins against the Denver Nuggets and the Memphis Grizzlies, respectively, the team advanced to the NBA Western Conference finals, losing to the Dallas Mavericks in five games.

SIXTH MAN OF THE YEAR AWARD AND ON TO HOUSTON

Harden enjoyed a breakout season in 2011–12. Coming off the Thunder bench he averaged 16.8 points per game—third-best on his team and tops among all NBA reserve players—and was unanimously voted NBA Sixth Man of the Year, becoming the youngest-ever recipient. The Thunder captured their second consecutive division title and eliminated the Mavericks, the Lakers, and the San Antonio Spurs to reach the 2012 NBA Finals against the Miami Heat, who won the seven-game series.

Despite Harden's achievements he was unable to come to terms with the Thunder on a contract extension. In October 2012, Harden was part of a five-player trade to the Houston Rockets, who subsequently signed him to a five-year, $80-million deal. Harden quickly took to his new role as a starter alongside point guard Jeremy Lin and small forward Chandler Parsons. He earned Western Conference Player of the Week honors after scoring 37 points in his November debut against the Detroit Pistons and 45 points in the following game against the Atlanta Hawks. In January 2013, he was voted to his first NBA All-Star Game (held in Houston) and scored 15 points playing alongside former teammates Durant and Westbrook.

Harden ended the 2012–13 season averaging career highs in points (25.9), rebounds (4.9), and assists (5.8). He guided the NBA's youngest squad to a 45–37 regular-season record—and an NBA playoff appearance against his former team, the Thunder, who bested the Rockets in six games. Harden was also a third-team All-NBA selection.

TEAMING UP WITH HOWARD

The Rockets were expected to contend for the NBA title in 2013–14 with the addition of all-star center Dwight Howard. The offseason signing proved beneficial as the team improved their overall record (54–28) to claim the Western Conference's fourth seed and a postseason appearance. However, the team suffered another first-round defeat, this time against the Portland Trail Blazers. Harden, who appeared in his second All-Star Game and was voted to the 2014 All-NBA First Team, finished fifth in the league in scoring (25.4 points per game).

The team underwent another facelift for 2014–15 season following Lin's trade to the Lakers, the loss of Parsons to free agency, and the signing of Trevor Ariza. With Howard sidelined with persistent knee problems Harden took charge offensively, notching thirty-five 30-point games as well as two 50-point games to lead his club to a 56–26 record and their first division title. In postseason play, the Rockets reached the Western Conference Finals against the Golden State Warriors but were eliminated in five games.

Harden was among league leaders in several categories, including points per game (27.4), assists (565), field goals (647), free throws (715), and steals (154). Although Harden lost out to Warriors point guard Stephen Curry for the NBA's Most Valuable Player (MVP) award, he edged out Curry for the NBPA's inaugural MVP award.

After a 4–7 start to the 2015–16 season, the Rockets fired head coach Kevin McHale and promoted assistant J. B. Bickerstaff. However, midway through the season, the team still struggled to gel and had more losses than wins at the break for the All Star Game in mid-February. Much of the offense fell on a frustrated Harden, who struggled early as he recovered from an off-season ankle injury.

PERSONAL LIFE
Harden, who signed a thirteen-year $200 million contract with Adidas in August 2015, has made news off the court for his bushy beard, which has its own Twitter account. He also made headlines regarding his seven-month relationship with reality television star Khloe Kardashian, which ended in early 2016.

SUGGESTED READING
Beck, Howard. "Standing Out and Blending In." *New York Times*. New York Times, 26 May 2012. Web. 10 Feb. 2016.

Conn, Jordan Ritter. "The Many Faces of James Harden." *Grantland*. ESPN Internet Ventures, 29 May 2012. Web. 10 Feb. 2016.

Creech, Jenny Dial. "Harden's Ex-Coach and Longtime Mentor Watched Him Grow from 'Special' into Spectacular." *Houston Chronicle*. Hearst Newspapers, 14 Feb. 2015. Web. 10 Feb. 2016.

Jenkins, Lee. "James Harden, the NBA's Unlikely MVP." *Sports Illustrated*. Time, 18 Feb. 2015. Web. 10 Feb. 2016.

Schwadron, Abe. "Catch the Wave." *Slam*. Enthusiast Network, 30 Nov. 2015. Web. 10 Feb. 2016.

Verrier, Justin. "James Harden Growing Into His Game." *ESPN.com*. ESPN, 14 June 2012. Web. 10 Feb. 2016.

—Bertha Muteba

Serge Haroche
Born: September 11, 1944
Occupation: Physicist

Serge Haroche is one of two scientists awarded the 2012 Nobel Prize in Physics for discoveries regarding the study of quantum phenomena and the use of quantum mechanics in computing.

EARLY LIFE AND EDUCATION
Serge Haroche was born in 1944 in Casablanca, Morocco, into a small and tightly organized community of Russian Jewish families in North Africa. Haroche's father was born in Morocco and worked as a lawyer, while his mother's family emigrated from Russia after the Bolshevik Revolution. Haroche's family left Morocco after the country gained independence in 1956 and settled in Paris, France.

Haroche studied at the Lycée Louis-le-Grand, a preparatory school and then passed his examinations to enter the Parisian *grandes écoles*, the prestigious business, engineering, and science schools in the French system. Haroche entered the École normale supérieure (ENS) in 1963 where he first gained an interest in physics and began working at the ENS physics laboratory. He finished his undergraduate studies in 1967 and completed a PhD program at the University of Paris VI under Nobel Prize–winning physicist Claude Cohen-Tannoudji.

EARLY CAREER
Haroche codeveloped with Cohen-Tannoudji an approach to the dressed atom formalism, which explains the behavior of atoms that have been exposed to special types of energetic fields. In essence, these experiments were aimed at studying the interaction of matter and light in the form of light particles known as photons.

Following the completion of his PhD in 1971, Haroche completed postdoctoral research with Arthur Schawlow at Stanford University, where he concentrated on laser-guided studies of photons. Haroche returned to Paris in 1973 and worked at the French National Centre for Scientific Research (CNRS) before taking a position at the University of Paris VI in 1975. Haroche then began working with Rydberg atoms, which are atoms that have been excited by exposure to electrical fields.

With a group of researchers that included Michel Gross, Claude Fabre, Jean-Michel Raimond, Michel Brune, and Philippe Goy, Haroche performed microwave experiments on atoms using lasers to excite them into Rydberg states and then irradiating the sample with a microwave field. The field was contained within a structure made from copper mirrors, creating a trap for the excited atoms.

CAVITY QUANTUM ELECTRODYNAMICS
While the team's experiments initially used samples of billions of atoms, Haroche's team began attempting to reduce the size of their atomic sample in an effort to study one atom at a time. The field of research involving the study of atoms in a mirror trap was named cavity quantum electrodynamics (cavity QED) by MIT physics pioneer Daniel Kleppner in 1980.

From 1984 to 1993, Haroche divided his time between ENS and Yale University, where he was offered a part-time professorship in the physics department. In 1993, Haroche returned full-time to ENS as his team began to make major strides toward developing a nondestructive method of studying single atoms. That same year, Haroche was honored with the Michelson Medal from the Franklin Institute in Philadelphia.

In 1996, Haroche and his team achieved single atom studies within their open mirror atomic trap. In order to study photons, the team used rubidium atoms prepared with lasers and radiofrequency excitation. Using microwave pulses, Haroche's team was able to place the atoms in a state of superposition, which is an unusual physical condition predicted by quantum mechanics in which the atom simultaneously exhibits properties of both a particle and a wave. Quantum theory predicts that particles, like photons and electrons, exist as both particles and waves until measured by an observer at which time the particle collapses into one of the two states. Haroche's experiments, along with similar work from the laboratory of David J. Wineland, were the first to demonstrate the ability to "freeze" an atom in a superposition state.

Haroche and colleague Jean-Michel Raimond collaborated on a comprehensive instructional text about cavity QED, called *Exploring the Quantum*, which was published in 2006. That same year, Haroche's laboratory reached a major milestone when they were able to observe a photon transitioning between the classical and quantum states. Haroche and his colleagues quickly published a series of papers detailing the team's research over the previous fifteen years—from the nondestructive counting of photons to the preparation of superposition particles to the observation of quantum decoherence, or switching between states. The results of the team's observation of decoherence was published in 2008.

In 2009 Haroche received the CNRS Gold Medal, one of the most prestigious scientific prizes awarded in France. This preceded a major advanced research grant from the European Research Council (ERC) that same year. In 2012 Haroche accepted a position as an administrator for the Collège de France, shortly before he learned that he had been chosen to share the 2012 Nobel Prize in Physics with physicist David J. Wineland.

IMPACT
The experimental demonstration of quantum phenomena is one of the most groundbreaking developments in modern physics and is an important step in the development of quantum logic systems. Quantum logic systems are computational models that use the quantum behavior of atoms to perform calculations similar to the electronic impulses used in computers.

PERSONAL LIFE
Serge Haroche is married to Claudine Haroche (née Zeligson), a sociology and anthropology researcher at the French National Centre for Scientific Research. They first met as children in Casablanca and met again fifteen years later while both were students in Paris. They live in Paris and have two children.

SUGGESTED READING
Grenoble, Ryan. "2012 Nobel Prize in Physics, Awarded to Serge Haroche and David Wineland, Explained as Simply as Possible." *Huffington Post*. TheHuffingtonPost.com, 15 Oct. 2012. Web. 25 Apr. 2014.

Haroche, Serge. "Nobel Lecture: Controlling Photons in a Box and Exploring the Quantum to Classical Boundary." *Nobelprize.org*. Nobel Media, 8 Dec. 2012. Web. 25 Apr. 2014.

Haroche, Serge. "The Secrets of My Prizewinning Research." *Nature* 490.7429 (2012): 311. Print.

"Serge Haroche–Biographical." *Nobelprize.org*. Nobel Media, 2012. Web. 25 Apr. 2014.

"Serge Haroche, Quantum Physics: Biographic Note." *Collège de France*. Foundation Collège de France, n.d. Web. 25 Apr. 2014.

—*Micah Issitt*

Lalah Hathaway

Born: December 16, 1968
Occupation: Singer

Despite persistent comparisons to her father—the late, legendary soul singer Donny Hathaway—singer Lalah Hathaway has defied categorization throughout her career, working with artists from various genres, including gospel act the Winans, R&B diva Mary J. Blige, and hip-hop artist Kendrick Lamar. "So the best that I've found is to follow my own path because at the end of the day if I don't get the bonuses that I want, I've still done the thing that best suits me, which is being myself," she told Lesley Mahoney for Berklee.edu (16 Feb. 2012).

Hathaway's collaborations with jazz sensations Snarky Puppy and Robert Glasper earned her consecutive Grammy Awards in 2014 and 2015. She added another Grammy to her mantle in 2016 for the track "Little Ghetto Boy" from her seventh album and first-ever live disc, which was recorded at the same venue where her father recorded his seminal 1972 album.

Barry Brecheisen/WireImage for The Recording Academy/
Stringer/Getty Images

EARLY LIFE AND EDUCATION

Lalah Hathaway was born Eulaulah Donyll Hathaway on December 16, 1968, in Chicago, Illinois. She and her younger sister, Kenya, hail from a musical family. Her late father is best remembered for his 1970s duets with Roberta Flack, including the Grammy Award–winning "Where Is the Love" and "The Closer I Get to You." Her mother and namesake, Eulaulah, is a classically trained vocalist. Therefore, Hathaway's musical training started at an early age. "As the child of two musicians . . . there was never actually a start date. It was always the natural trajectory of my life," she shared with Chris Becker for *CultureMap Houston* (25 June 2011).

Although she did attend a high school for the performing arts in Chicago, Hathaway also cited mainstream radio as a major influence. Her life was forever changed in 1979 when her father suffered a fatal fall from the fifteenth-floor window of the Essex House, a New York City highrise hotel. His death would eventually be ruled a suicide.

After graduating from high school in 1986, Hathaway decided to pursue music and applied to only one school. "My mom wanted me to go to Howard University where my parents had met. We went to visit Howard and then came to visit Berklee. . . . When I got off the Amtrak train in Boston, I knew almost immediately that there was something there for me," she told Mark Small for *Berklee Today* (Fall 2014). While attending Berklee, Hathaway often traveled from Boston to Los Angeles, where she was recording her first demo. The tape eventually found its way into the hands of Jeff Forman at Virgin Records, who signed her to the label in 1989.

MAKING A NAME FOR HERSELF IN THE MUSIC WORLD

Hathaway spent her final semester recording her self-titled debut album, which she released in 1990. Combining elements of R&B, jazz, and pop, her freshman effort spent time on the Billboard Top R & B/Hip-Hop Albums chart and also spawned three hits on the Billboard Hot R & B Songs chart: the top-five song "Heaven Knows" and the subsequent singles "Baby Don't Cry" and "Somethin'."

Following the release of her debut, Hathaway relocated to Los Angeles at the suggestion of label executives. She quickly came to the attention of renowned, Grammy Award–winning jazz bassist Marcus Miller. "Everyone was talking about her and telling me I had to check out Donny's daughter," Miller told Shelah Moody for the *San Francisco Chronicle* (20 Oct. 2005). "I had a gig in Japan at a festival and I wanted to bring in something new, so I asked her to perform." A year after touring with Miller, she scored her fourth top-forty hit on the Hot R&B Songs chart by appearing in the song "Love Like This," the lead single from legendary jazz instrumentalist Grover Washington Jr.'s *Next Exit*.

For Hathaway's anticipated sophomore effort, *A Moment* (1994), Virgin Records executives enlisted the help of several rising R & B producers (Chuckii Booker and Keith Crouch, among others) in an attempt to revamp her sophisticated, mature vocal style and appeal to a younger audience. Although the album peaked at number forty of Billboard's Top R & B/Hip-Hop Albums chart, it contained the lead single "Let Me Love You," her fifth top-forty R & B hit.

After the somewhat disappointing performance of *A Moment*, Hathaway left her label, citing creative differences. "As black music was moving toward hip-hop, no one at Virgin Records knew what to do with me," she explained to Small for *Berklee Today* (Fall 2005). "There's this huge gap between hip-hop music and smooth jazz, and I'm kind of in the middle ground . . . the music industry has a hard time figuring out how to sell your records if you don't fit neatly into a category." This frustration marked the beginning of a ten-year hiatus in which, although she continued to write and work, she had trouble finding a suitable label and did not release any new solo records.

A WORKING HIATUS AND A NEW SOLO EFFORT

In 1999, Hathaway joined contemporary jazz imprint GRP Records to release the collaborative disc *The Song Lives On* (1999) with iconic contemporary jazz pianist Joe Sample. The album of jazz standards became her highest-charting record to date, reaching number two on Billboard's Top Contemporary Jazz Albums chart. She also collected multiple honors at the inaugural Billboard/BET Jazz Awards, including those for contemporary jazz vocalist and contemporary jazz vocal album.

Still trying to find her solo footing again, Hathaway continued to make appearances on other musicians' albums, including Meshell Ndegeocello's *Cookie: The Anthropological Mixtape* (2002) and Miller's two-disc set of live performances *The Ozell Tapes: The Official Bootleg* (2003). Also in 2003, she and her younger sister, Kenya, appeared in the star-studded music video for the title song of Luther Vandross's final recording, *Dance with My Father* (2003), before she was recruited to sing on a Vandross tribute record the following summer, topping the Billboard Adult R & B Songs chart with her rendition of "Forever, for Always, for Love".

In the fall of 2004, *Outrun the Sky* (2004) was released on the Mesa/Bluemoon label as Hathaway's first solo album in ten years, and her fourth overall. Her "Forever, for Always, for Love" remake was selected as the lead single and she received songwriting credit for eight of the album's songs, including "Boston," which she dedicated to her late father. Meanwhile, she embarked on the Daughters of Soul European tour, joining the daughters of R&B legends Chaka Khan and Nina Simone, as well as Nona Hendryx, Joyce Kennedy of Mother's Finest, and Sandra St. Victor of The Family Stand.

SELF PORTRAIT AND GRAMMY RECOGNITIONS

In 2008, not long after Hathaway had signed with the newly revived Stax Records, "Let Go," the first single from her fifth album, debuted at number sixteen on Billboard's Hot Adult R & B chart. *Self Portrait*, her first album for Stax, was unveiled two months later and peaked at number six on the Billboard Top R&B/Hip-Hop Albums chart. With this success, she hoped to continue illustrating the importance of the R & B and soul genres. "Rhythm and Blues music, soul music, it really was the beginning, in popular culture, of telling the story of black Americans in this country. Then it became telling the story of Americans in this country. That music never dies," she explained to Tre'vell Anderson for the *Los Angeles Times* (22 Apr. 2015).

To promote her latest album and impressive body of work, in July 2008, Hathaway embarked on a two-month US summer tour that included appearances at the Omaha Jazz and Blues Festival and the Detroit International Jazz Festival. By the end of the year, she had released her second single off of the album, "That Was Then," which reached number thirty-two on the Billboard Adult R & B chart. She continued to promote the album in 2009, with summer performances at Capital Jazz Fest in Columbia, Maryland, and Essence Fest in New Orleans, Louisiana.

In December 2009, the critical and commercial success of the album was solidified when Hathaway achieved a milestone with her first-ever Grammy Award nomination in the best female R & B vocal performance category for "That Was Then." When the fifty-second Grammy Awards ceremony occurred in January 2010, she attended for the first time as a nominee, ultimately losing the trophy to Beyoncé's "Single Ladies." Following the Grammy nod, her vocal talents were in high demand. She sang lead on four of the tracks from Kirk Whalum's double-live album *The Gospel According to Jazz Chapter III* (2010). Thanks to that work, she capped off the year with her second Grammy nomination, for best gospel performance ("He's Been Just That Good").

Though Hathaway had clearly made a name for herself in the industry and had often stated that she did not want to cover her father's work, she never stopped trying to identify with his legacy, which was illustrated in her cover of his single "You Were Meant for Me" on her album *Where It All Begins*, released in 2011. At the same time, further proving her versatility and popularity, she teamed up on projects with rising jazz sensations such as Esperanza Spalding over the ensuing years. Her next significant collaborative effort came in 2013, following an invitation from Snarky Puppy drummer Robert "Sput" Searight to join his jazz-fusion band's recording session. Asked to contribute a song to rework in a new arrangement, she brought her old hit "Something." "We rehearsed it once or twice and recorded it . . . in front of a live audience, who were arrayed around the band on the stage like after a family dinner," she recalled to Roy Trakin for Grammy.com (3 Mar. 2014). "The hook was that I was able to sing multiple chords at once." Hathaway's multiphonic vocal technique—a skill she first learned in her early teens—was featured on *Family Dinner, Volume 1* (2013), Snarky Puppy's live CD/DVD, and the accompanying YouTube video, which has amassed more than five million views.

TAKING GRAMMYS HOME

Hathaway's collaboration with Snarky Puppy also proved to be a hit with their industry peers, earning her, along with the band, her first Grammy win of her career for best R & B performance in 2014. Following this feat, unsigned at the time, Hathaway then set her sights on another first: recording her own live album. By August, not only had she raised the necessary funds (via the crowdfunding platform Pledge Music), but she had also appeared on Al Jarreau's tribute CD *My Old Friend: Celebrating George Duke*. She ended her year on a positive note, when "Jesus Children," her recent Glasper collaboration—and Stevie Wonder remake—was nominated for a Grammy. Not only did Hathaway perform the song at the fifty-seventh Grammy Awards ceremony in February 2015, but she also took home her second statuette, this time for best traditional R & B performance. She was also among the artists featured on Kendrick Lamar's sophomore disc *To Pimp a Butterfly*, providing vocals on three songs, including "Momma," which sampled her 2008 single "On Your Own."

In April, Hathaway recorded her first live album at the legendary West Hollywood nightclub Troubadour—the site of her late father's recording more than four decades earlier. *Lalah Hathaway Live* (2015) debuted at number two on Billboard's Top R & B/Hip-Hop Albums chart and gave her the highest first-week sales of her career (fifteen thousand copies). Her cover of her father's 1972 hit "Little Ghetto Boy" earned her the third Grammy trophy of her career, which she is most proud of out of all of her wins. "The first two were on records that I featured on. While they're me, they're not actually under my name in that way. This award is so much of me, and who I am and how I've grown up. It really makes a statement for me because it's my father's song," she explained to Joe Walker for SoulTrain.com (14 Mar. 2016).

PERSONAL LIFE

Outside of performing and recording, Hathaway has served as a national ambassador for the Circle of Promise, which promotes breast cancer awareness, particularly for African American women.

SUGGESTED READING

Hathaway, Lalah. "Lalah Hathaway: Multiphonic Renaissance." Interview by Mark Small. *Berklee Today*. Berklee College of Music, Fall 2014. Web. 12 Aug. 2016.

Hathaway, Lalah. "Lalah Hathaway '94: Charting Her Own Course." Interview by Lesley Mahoney. *Berklee.edu*. Berklee College of Music, 16 Feb. 2012. Web. 12 Aug. 2016.

Hathaway, Lalah. "Q&A: Lalah Hathaway Records Live Album at the Troubadour." Interview by Tre'vell Anderson. *Los Angeles Times*. Los Angeles Times, 22 Apr. 2015. Web. 12 Aug. 2016.

Hathaway, Lalah. "Singer's Singer Lalah Hathaway Has Lots of Stories to Share with Her Music." Interview by Chris Becker. *CultureMap Houston*. CultureMap, 25 June 2011. Web. 12 Aug. 2016.

SELECTED WORKS

Lalah Hathaway, 1990; *A Moment*, 1994; *The Song Lives On*, 1999; *Outrun the Sky*, 2004; *Self Portrait*, 2008; *Where It All Begins*, 2011; *Lalah Hathaway Live*, 2015

—Bertha Muteba

Sarah Hay

Born: 1987
Occupation: Dancer and actor

Sarah Hay is a ballet dancer and a Golden Globe–nominated actor. In 2014, Hay, a soloist at the Semperoper Ballett in Dresden, Germany, took a leave of absence to appear in the Starz miniseries *Flesh & Bone* (2015). She played Claire Robbins, a young ballet dancer from Pittsburgh struggling to make it at a cutthroat New York City ballet company. Billed as a story about the dark underbelly of the dance world, the eight-episode show explored psychological and physical abuse, prostitution and sexual exploitation, and incest. It has been compared to *Black Swan* (2010), Darren Aronofsky's Academy Award–winning ballet drama, but creator Moira Walley-Beckett, a former dancer and an Emmy Award–winning television writer, wanted *Flesh & Bone* to feel more realistic than that film. Walley-Beckett combined her own experiences and the gothic, tragic tone of ballets themselves to write the show. To increase the show's authenticity, she decided to cast real ballet dancers in the lead roles. Before *Flesh & Bone*, Hay

D Dipasupil/FilmMagic/Getty Images

appeared in two films as a dancer—one was a children's television special when she was nine and the other was *Black Swan*—but had never acted on camera. In 2016 she was nominated for a Golden Globe and a Critics' Choice Award.

EARLY LIFE AND EDUCATION

Hay was born to an artistic family in Princeton, New Jersey, in 1987. Her grandmother was an art dealer in New York City and her grandfather played for the New York Philharmonic. Her parents are psychologists; she has an older brother and an older sister, who aspired to become a dancer but later became a prosecutor.

Hay began dancing when she was three years old and enrolled as a student at the School of American Ballet (SAB) at Lincoln Center when she was eight. It was a serious step for the young dancer, and socially, the transition was not easy. Hay was the "loser," she told Amy Spencer for the *New York Post* (3 Dec. 2015), because her family was not wealthy. "I didn't have the Chanel butterfly clip everyone else did," she said. When she was nine, she was cast in the short children's movie *You're Invited to Mary-Kate and Ashley's Ballet Party* (1997), with *Full House* stars Mary-Kate and Ashley Olsen. Her friends were jealous, Hay recalled, though she cried because the directors made her wear pink clothes.

EARLY DANCE CAREER

As Hay got older, she became a "troublemaker," she told Spencer, only getting serious about ballet in her late teens, after leaving SAB. Her professors there suggested she was not cut out for ballet and that she should try modern dance instead. The suggestion devastated Hay, but she stuck with ballet and began attending open classes, through which she found a mentor in Susan Jaffe at the Princeton Dance and Theater Studio. On Jaffe's advice, Hay auditioned for and won a spot in the Jacqueline Kennedy Onassis School (JKO) through the American Ballet Theatre (ABT) in New York City, where she spent three years. She told Candice Thompson for *Pointe Magazine* (1 Oct. 2015), "I learned nuance and musicality at SAB, but my technical aspects developed later at JKO." Hay hoped to earn a slot dancing for the school's parent company, ABT, but was told she lacked focus. Other ballerinas were promoted in her stead, and Hay went back to open classes.

At one of those classes, Hay was spotted by Jean-Pierre Bonnefoux, the artistic director of the Charlotte Ballet in North Carolina. He offered her a contract with the second company. The Charlotte Ballet creates and produces contemporary work, an aspect of dancing there that Hay at first enjoyed. But after two years, she felt restless and began auditioning again. This time she landed a spot with the Pennsylvania Ballet (PAB), where she spent two years in the second company and another two years as an apprentice. She gained weight and struggled with body image issues. After four years with the company, Hay resigned. She was barely into her twenties yet starting to burn out. She decided to return to an element of dance she truly enjoyed.

Hay enrolled in a workshop in Dresden, Germany, to learn more about the award-winning choreographer William Forsythe. Hay had performed Forsythe's piece *In the Middle, Somewhat Elevated* at PAB and enjoyed the exacting technique his choreography requires. "Sarah was an instant standout when I staged Bill's work," Jodie Glass, a coach at PAB, told Thompson. "She has strong technique, keen musicality, and the willingness to take risks, such key elements for a contemporary ballerina."

In Dresden, Hay met Aaron S. Watkin, the artistic director of the city's Semperoper Ballett. She returned to New York and began auditioning for Broadway shows, but a month later, she received a call from Watkin, offering her a slot in the first company. She accepted and moved to Dresden at the age of twenty-three. There, she has said, she felt celebrated for her individuality—and her body type. "I have had to work on loving myself," she told Thompson. "When you feel at a loss all of the time you start to wonder if it's you, but for me it was the place. I felt thrown away by some people who had treated me horribly, but now I just try to see my imperfections as what make me who I am."

ACTING CAREER AND *FLESH & BONE*

In 2010, Hay appeared as a background dancer in *Black Swan*. Acting, or rather dancing on film, was always on her radar, but when she was contacted to audition for a new show about ballet called *Flesh & Bone*, she was hesitant to leave her successful career in Dresden, even temporarily. But the names attached to the project—Walley-Beckett, an Emmy Award–winning writer from the hit show *Breaking Bad*, and famed Quentin Tarantino producer Lawrence Bender—made her reconsider. She sent the casting team an audition video, expecting to never hear from them again. Instead, they contacted her asking for another video; the one she gave them was shot from too far away. Unbeknownst to Hay, the team was nearing the end of a worldwide search to cast Claire. Hay was invited to New York for a three-day final audition and won the role. Watkin enthusiastically granted her a six-month leave of absence from the company.

"It was really important that we show the dancers doing what they do and put the camera anywhere," Walley-Beckett told Gia Kourlas for the *New York Times* (30 Oct. 2015). "So that we would have the ability to breathe and sweat and bleed and soar with them." In addition to its twisting plot, *Flesh & Bone* emphasizes the artistry of dance. (Ethan Stiefel, a former dancer who appeared in the 2000 film *Center Stage*, served as the show's choreographer.) Hay, who worked with an acting coach for the first few days of filming, recalled the grueling days on set. "There were like twelve-hour dance days on set where you're doing the same thing twelve hours, over and over," she told Carly Valentine for *Nylon* magazine (6 Nov. 2015). "Your body just gives up, but you just have to keep going because you don't know which part they are going to use." Hay was most nervous shooting the dancing sequences—more so than the more dramatic moments of the show—because she wanted her technique to be perfect.

Flesh & Bone also stars Irina Dvorovenko, a dancer with the ABT in New York, and Sascha Radetsky. Until 2014, Radetsky was a soloist at ABT; he also starred in *Center Stage*. The show begins when Claire, escaping an abusive father and—as viewers discover by the end of the first episode—an incestuous relationship with her older brother, moves to New York City to start a new life as a ballet dancer. (Hay interviewed her psychologist parents to prepare for the role.) She auditions for the prestigious (and fictional) American Ballet Company. Despite withering looks from fellow dancers and the intimidating stare of the artistic director Paul (Ben Daniels), Claire performs exquisitely, winning a spot in the company. Hay told Emma Brown for *Interview* (6 Nov. 2015) that Walley-Beckett told her to think of Claire as a "fish out of water who's

been thrown into the shark tank." As the series progresses, this certainly appears to be the case. Claire encounters intense competition but also a sex trafficking ring, and runs out of the club where she works as a stripper.

Flesh & Bone was originally conceived as a multiseason show, but Starz nixed the plan, changing it to a limited series due to the high production costs. It premiered in November 2015 and was nominated for a Golden Globe Award for best limited series or made-for-television movie, but it received middling to poor reviews from critics who found it contrived and melodramatic. Critic Mike Hale went so far as to write for the *New York Times* (6 Nov. 2015) that the show was "impossible to take seriously." Yet most reviewers had only good things to say about Hay, whose performance was praised for its subtlety. Alissa Wilkinson, writing for *Vulture* (16 Nov. 2015), was more magnanimous in her critique of the show, viewing it through the lens of ballet itself. She described *Flesh & Bone* as a gothic horror story about obsession, domination, and desire. Wilkinson noted similarities between the show and famous ballets such as *Giselle*, in which the titular character commits suicide after discovering that the man she loves is engaged to another woman, while another character narrowly avoids being forced to dance until he dies. *Flesh & Bone*, Wilkinson writes, "is a contemporary twist on these familiar tropes."

PERSONAL LIFE

When not filming, Hay lives in Dresden. She has a pet turtle and enjoys watching cartoons in her spare time.

SUGGESTED READING

Hale, Mike. "Review: 'Flesh & Bone,' a Ballet Drama with Strippers." *New York Times*. New York Times, 6 Nov. 2015. Web. 13 June 2016.

Hay, Sarah. Interview by Emma Brown. *Interview*. Interview, 6 Nov. 2016. Web. 13 June 2016.

Kourlas, Gia. "In 'Flesh & Bone,' Moira Walley-Beckett Leaps Darkly into Ballet." *New York Times*. New York Times, 30 Oct. 2015. Web. 13 June 2016.

Spencer, Amy. "'Flesh & Bone' Star Refused to Get a Breast Reduction." *New York Post*. NYP Holdings, 3 Dec. 2015. Web. 13 June 2016.

Thompson, Candice. "A Star Is Born." *Pointe Magazine*. DanceMedia, 1 Oct. 2015. Web. 13 June 2016.

Valentine, Carly. "Sarah Hay Channels Her Real Life to Bring the Dark Side of Ballet to TV on the New Starz Mini-Series 'Flesh and Bone.'" *Nylon*. Nylon Media, 6 Nov. 2015. Web. 13 June 2016.

Wilkinson, Alissa. "*Flesh and Bone* Is a TV Show Structured Like an Actual Ballet." *Vulture*.

New York Media, 16 Nov. 2015. Web. 13 June 2016.

—*Molly Hagan*

Mary Kay Henry

Born: 1958
Occupation: President of SEIU

As president of the Service Employees International Union (SEIU), Mary Kay Henry has more than two million people, most of them health care workers, depending on her. Henry told Don Gonyea for National Public Radio (*NPR*) (12 May 2010), "There is a deep sense, I think, on the part of our members and all working people, that there is a crisis in this country for working people, that we've had it with trying to make ends meet and not have our work rewarded." She was selected as one of *Modern Healthcare*'s Top 25 Women in Healthcare in 2009.

EDUCATION AND EARLY CAREER

Henry was the third of ten children and the first girl born to a Catholic family; her mother was a substitute teacher and her father was a salesman. Henry told Steven Greenhouse for the *New York Times* (8 May 2010) that she began as an organizer when she was a child. "I was always asked to get everybody organized to get on the bus and to get everyone to the dinner table on time."

The family lived in a middle-class neighborhood outside Detroit, Michigan. There she saw how unions, particularly United Auto Workers (UAW), made a middle-class life possible. She attended Marian High School run by the Sisters, Servants of the Immaculate Heart of Mary. Among other things, she imbibed a sense of social justice from the sisters. Her Catholic roots have continued to inform her career. She earned a degree in urban studies and labor relations at Michigan State, graduating in 1979. That same year she was hired by SEIU as a researcher.

BEGINNING AT SEIU

Henry had never held a position in a local union when she took the job at SEIU. She was elected an International Executive Board member in 1996, and was the chief health care strategist on the board. Henry went on to hold a total of eighteen different jobs within the organization over the years. She organized health care workers in California at Tenet Healthcare and Beverly Enterprises. She also advised the US Conference of Catholic Bishops' Catholic Health Care & Work Subcommittee on health care issues. In 2004,

Chip Somodevilla/Getty Images

she was elected to the position of International Executive Vice President. In this position, she spent much of her time traveling around the country, meeting with hospital executives and health care providers, making the case for them to unionize.

TAKING ON THE PRESIDENCY

The SEIU underwent a period of transition during the mid-2000s that resulted in Henry's election as union president. In 2005 the SEIU, under then president Andy Stern, split off from the American Federation of Labor and Congress of Industrial Organizations (AFL-CIO). Stern had pushed for more union mergers, which the AFL-CIO rejected. Although Stern had doubled SEIU membership during his fourteen years in office, he had also been controversial in several respects. Chief among Stern's mistakes was alienating union leaders, putting his own aides in positions of power in local unions, and spending too much time lobbying in Washington.

The union's secretary-treasurer, Anna Burger, was Stern's handpicked successor. Henry was head of the SEIU health care division at the time and an unlikely candidate, but she drew significant support quickly. Burger withdrew her candidacy in April 2010 and Henry was unchallenged for the top position. Stern had resigned with two years left in his term, which Henry saw out.

Following her election, Henry determined to take a different approach to power than her predecessor and refocus the union. She told Jim O'Sullivan for *National Journal* (13 July 2012), "I think of myself as a channel for the 2.1 million members that we represent, and their influence is what I wield." She stated that she did not plan to rejoin AFL-CIO, as some union members hoped. Although she vowed to draw her focus away from politics, she did not abandon politics or the union's clout completely, and sought to increase the already hefty amount the union donated to political campaigns. As John Fund reported for *American Spectator* (2010), when she took the helm, Henry said the union would be "moving forward in an even bigger way on organizing, politics, and restoring our relationships throughout the American labor movement." She stated that she planned to further expand membership of the union with big spending on organizing, particularly in the private sector. She also earmarked $4 million for organizing minority workers.

POLITICS

The SEIU has been a strong supporter of Democratic Party candidates and issues, and is a powerful voice among Democrats in Washington. Henry's predecessor as president became known for bolstering this position for the union.

In 2010, when Arizona passed a tough anti-immigration law, Henry and others in her organization took on the issue of immigration. As she told James Barnes for *National Journal* (2010), "We don't believe that unemployment and the economic crisis can be addressed without fixing our broken immigration system." Although the union does not track citizenship, some members of the union are known to be undocumented workers.

Unions took some of the credit for President Barack Obama's 2012 reelection. Union leaders in Ohio, Nevada, and Wisconsin were able to deliver those states' combined thirty-four electoral votes for Obama. SEIU members canvassed an estimated five million homes prior to the election; some 3.7 million contacts were in battle-ground states. More than one hundred thousand SEIU members across the nation were involved in the effort. In celebrating Obama's victory, Henry stated that she hoped Obama would focus on immigration reform, and the SEIU would back any efforts made to that end. In May 2012 she was reelected unanimously at the union's twenty-fifth Convention.

FIGHT FOR 15

Part of that move forward is the Fight for 15 push to adjust the minimum wage (particularly for fast food workers) to fifteen dollars an hour, considered a living wage, as well as for the right to unionize. That jump in salaries would be a 67 percent raise; most fast food workers make about nine dollars per hour. After fast food workers went on strike during the summer of 2013,

Henry appeared on the *Colbert Report* to speak out in support of the strikers.

Some industry leaders predicted that such an increase in pay would result in higher consumer costs and lower rates of employment. It could also encourage automation of basic processes, leading to cuts in employment. As Steven Greenhouse reported for *New York Times* (4 Dec. 2013), however, Henry countered that argument, saying, "In our 90-year history as a union, I've never seen a time when workers got a wage increase that put people out of business. It's in our interest to make sure we secure our employment, not to reduce employment."

Union members wanted to dispute the increasingly common refusal of employers to increase their wages on the grounds that others were waiting for those jobs, and those others would accept a lower wage. As Henry explained to Claire Zillman for *Fortune* (2013), "[A]s long as that dynamic exists, we're going to continue to see a shrinking middle class because not many workers are standing up against multinational corporations that are employing low wages."

Although fast food workers are difficult to unionize because of the high turnover and resistance of corporations, supporting them is perceived as the right thing to do. California and New Jersey have passed laws increasing the minimum wage as a result of the pressure these protests have brought to bear.

In addition, the protests were a method of demonstrating unions' relevance at a time when union membership continues to decline. In 2012 only 11.3 percent of workers belonged to a union, the lowest figure in ninety-seven years. Judicial policy has generally favored employers over workers, and state right-to-work laws have weakened the labor movement. The SEIU membership is growing, however.

CALIFORNIA CONFLICT

One of the difficulties that arose on Stern's watch was the alienation of health care workers in Northern California. They formed their own union, the National Union of Healthcare Workers (NUHW), led by a former SEIU executive, Sal Rosselli. Tensions between the two groups continued as Henry took leadership, though she assured members that she would not attempt a merger. Henry told Barnes, "My goal is to change working people's lives in some measurable way."

In 2015 Henry proposed splitting a United Healthcare Workers local in California, the largest union in the state, into two segments, with 70,000 members going to a new SEIU local 2015. The move would create an SEIU chapter larger than that of the United Healthcare Workers. Complicating the situation is the fact that the leader of the local UHW is Dave Regan, a vice president of SEIU's Executive Board.

Central to the debate is the issue of whether health care workers are better represented by broad organizations or by special units.

A SUPREME COURT RULING

In June 2014 the Supreme Court stated in *Harris et al. v. Quinn* that union membership could not be mandated, even if the union negotiated on behalf of the worker. Although the case referred to a situation in Illinois, the ruling was expected to have effects in California and other states and affect hundreds of thousands of health care workers.

This ruling is a blow for the continued growth of SEIU, as well as of other unions. The concern is that once health care workers do not have to pay dues, they may drop membership as well. This happened in Michigan once home health aides were no longer classified as public employees required to become union members; nearly 80 percent of those workers dropped union membership. One argument is that many health care workers do not make a great deal of money; paying dues simply is another expense they would happily avoid. About one-fifth of SEIU's members are health care workers. This portion of the union members was expected to grow, based on projections from the Bureau of Labor Statistics that during the decade of 2012 to 2022, health care workers would grow 48 percent.

The SEIU is concerned with not only potentially diminishing revenues but also a decreased level of professional care. Without the protection of a union, wages tend to go flat and benefits are nonexistent. Workers under that system tend to quit more frequently than do union members.

The SEIU planned to continue its efforts to unionize thousands of home health aides who are without union representation. As Alana Semuels reported for *Los Angeles Times* (30 June 2014), Henry said, "No court case is going to stand in the way of home care workers coming together to have a strong voice for good jobs and quality home care."

PERSONAL LIFE

Henry was a cofounder of the SEIU's Lavender Caucus for gay and lesbian members. For nearly thirty years, Henry has been with her partner, Paula Macchello, a senior organizer with the Teamsters. She has been an outspoken advocate for gay marriage and is an occasional contributor for the *Huffington Post*.

SUGGESTED READING

Barnes, James A. "SEIU Chief on Changing Working People's Lives." *National Journal* (2010): n.p. Web. 5 Nov. 2015.

Fund, John H. "Goon Democrats." *American Spectator*. American Spectator, July–Aug. 2010. Web. 10 Dec. 2015.

Gonyea, Don. "SEIU's First Female President Sets Out to Heal Rifts." *NPR*. NPR, 12 May 2010. Web. 5 Nov. 2015.

Greenhouse, Steven. "$15 Wage in Fast Food Stirs Debate on Effects." *New York Times*. New York Times, 4 Dec. 2013. Web. 4 Dec. 2015.

Greenhouse, Steven. "New Union Leader Wants Group to Be More of a Political Powerhouse." *New York Times*. New York Times, 8 May 2010. Web. 4 Dec. 2015.

National Journal Staff. "Washington's Most Influential Women." *Yahoo! News*. Yahoo-ABC News Network, 13 July 2012. Web. 10 Dec. 2015.

Zillman, Claire. "Fast-Food Workers: Labor Movement's New Lease on Life." *Fortune*. Time, 5 Dec. 2013 Web. 5 Nov. 2015.

—*Judy Johnson*

Isaac Herzog

Born: September 22, 1960
Occupation: Israeli politician

Isaac Herzog is a longtime Israeli politician who has held key leadership roles in various national governments since winning a seat in the Israeli parliament, known as the Knesset, in 2003. He serves as both the opposition leader in the Knesset and as the leader of the Zionist Union, a center-left coalition party that was defeated by Benjamin Netanyahu's Likud Party in the 2015 elections. Herzog is also part of a family well connected to Israeli national politics for decades; most notable is his father, Chaim Herzog, who served as an Israeli general and later as the country's president. Unlike his political rival, Netanyahu, who is often described in the press as a bully, Herzog presents himself as a political realist. "He appears to be this wimpy guy with the voice a bit too high, who has no security experience. But what Herzog offers us, what he is selling, is that he is in reality the master political manipulator," Yossi Alpher, a former officer in the Mossad, the Israeli intelligence agency, told William Booth for the *Washington Post* (21 Feb. 2015).

EARLY LIFE AND EDUCATION

Isaac Herzog was born in Tel Aviv, Israel, on September 22, 1960, into Israel's equivalent of the Kennedys or the Bushes—a family with multigenerational ties to national politics. In an article published in *Haaretz* (9 Mar. 2015), Alona

Sebastian Widmann/CC BY-SA 2.0/Wikimedia Commons

Ferber called Herzog the "scion of a family described as the closest Israel comes to aristocracy or a royal family. . . . His family tree is comprised of a long line of impressive relatives." Herzog's mother was Aura Herzog, who served as an officer in the Science Corps during the Arab-Israeli War of 1948; she later became an art critic and author and also founded Israel's International Bible Contest in 1959 and the Council for a Beautiful Israel in 1968. Herzog's father, Chaim Herzog, was a lawyer, author, diplomat, and general, who was Israel's ambassador to the United Nations (UN) from 1975 to 1978; served as a member of the Knesset beginning in 1981; and was Israel's president from 1983 to 1993.

Herzog's paternal grandfather, Isaac Halevi Herzog, was the first chief rabbi of Ireland, before serving as chief rabbi of Israel, beginning in the prestate years in 1936 and serving until his death in 1959. Herzog's grandmother, Sarah Herzog, was the volunteer head of the Ezrat Nashim Hospital, which is today named for her: the Sarah Herzog Hospital. Other notable relatives include an American cousin, Sidney Hillman, who was a US labor leader and adviser to President Franklin D. Roosevelt. Herzog's brother Michael, retired in 2010 as a brigadier general in the Israel Defense Forces (IDF); his other brother Joel, is a businessman who works out of Geneva, Switzerland; and his sister, Ronit, is a clinical psychologist in Tel Aviv.

During the period Herzog's father was serving as Israeli ambassador to the United Nations, Herzog lived with his family in New York City and attended the Ramaz School, a private Jewish prep school. He later studied at Cornell University and New York University (NYU). In 1978 he returned to Israel to begin his mandatory service in the IDF. Upon completing his service in the Intelligence Corps, he studied law at the University of Tel Aviv. He subsequently worked as an attorney at Herzog, Fox & Neeman, a firm that his father founded. During this period of his life he was involved with various volunteer organizations and served as secretary of the Economic-Social Council from 1988 to 1990.

EARLY POLITICAL CAREER

Herzog began his political career in 1999, serving as a secretary in Prime Minister Ehud Barak's government until 2001, when Barak was succeeded by Ariel Sharon. He also served as chair of the Israel Anti-Drug Authority between 2000 and 2003. During the 2003 parliamentary elections, he ran as a Labor candidate and won his first seat in the Knesset. He then became a member of Prime Minister Sharon's cabinet when the Labor Party joined Sharon's coalition government in 2005. Under Sharon, he served as minister of construction and housing until Labor left the coalition in November 2005.

Following the 2006 parliamentary elections, Herzog first served as minister of tourism in Prime Minister Ehud Olmert's coalition government, a position he held until March 2007, when he was reassigned, serving as both minister of welfare and social services and as minister of the Diaspora, society and the fight against anti-Semitism. After the 2009 elections, he again became minister of welfare and social services, this time in the cabinet of Prime Minister Benjamin Netanyahu; he resigned his post when Labor leader Ehud Barak left to form a new party, Independence, in January 2011.

OPPOSITION LEADER

In 2011 Herzog ran for the Labor leadership but finished in the voting behind Shelly Yachimovich and Amir Peretz. He then won the Labor leadership in 2013 by defeating Yachimovich. At the same time, he became leader of the opposition, a title traditionally held in parliamentary systems by the leader of the political party that is not part of the ruling government and has the most seats in the legislature. As opposition leader Herzog was outspoken about what he perceived to be the failings of the Netanyahu government, including an unwillingness to address socioeconomic issues facing Israelis; an inability to resolve the decades-old Israeli-Palestinian conflict through the two-state solution that had been mediated by the United States; and a distrust of the administration of President Barack Obama in securing a nuclear-arms deal with Iran that would prevent the Islamic republic from getting nuclear weapons with which it could threaten Israel.

Two days after his 2013 election as opposition leader, Herzog met with Mahmoud Abbas, the Palestinian president, to affirm his dedication to the peace process. In the *Times of Israel* (6 June 2014), Herzog harshly criticized Netanyahu's lack of diplomatic progress with the Palestinians: "Israel will lose the support of the international community and the ability to preserve [Israel] as a Jewish and democratic state." He also remained outspoken against Netanyahu's approach to the Iranian nuclear crisis, particularly the prime minister's unwillingness to work with Obama, but remained firmly against allowing Iran to acquire nuclear weapons. "I agree that a nuclear Iran is extremely dangerous, and I believe that it must be prevented," Herzog said in an interview, as quoted by Booth. "No Israeli leader will accept a nuclear Iran. All options for me are still on the table," including air strikes by Israel.

2015 ELECTION AND BEYOND

After Netanyahu's governing coalition dissolved in early 2015, many Israeli pundits believed that Herzog stood a chance of replacing the long-serving Netanyahu as prime minister, particularly after he and Tzipi Livni agreed to form a new center-left faction, the Zionist Union. In many polls leading up to the March 2015 election, Herzog seemed poised for victory. During the campaign Herzog and his party continued to hammer away at social and economic concerns that they felt would appeal to average Israeli voters, while Netanyahu continued to warn about the impending danger that would come from the Iranian nuclear deal, which would allow the Iranians to keep peaceful nuclear facilities in exchange for a promise not to enrich nuclear materials to weapons-grade. During the campaign, Herzog presented himself as the candidate of hope and change—similar to the way Obama ran during his first presidential election in 2008—and depicted his opponent as having been too long in his role as prime minister and too inflexible in dealing with the Iranian issue or the peace program with the Palestinians.

In the end, however, Herzog's Zionist Union added just three seats in the Knesset, for a total of 24 out of 120, and Netanyahu was able to retain his premiership by building a coalition government of conservative and religious parties. Despite the loss, Herzog remained upbeat about his prospects of building a centrist government in the future. "I have huge respect for the left— the left is bold, the left is very focused and is very ideological—but most of the rank and file of the Israeli public wants something more pragmatic," Herzog said to Jodi Rudoren of the *New York Times* (27 Mar. 2015). "I moved my party to the center and I will continue forcefully to stage my party to the center. The only way to win in Israel is by being in the center." He also resisted calls to join the Netanyahu government, believing he can be a more effective voice for change as opposition leader. "I made it clear time and again that we are an alternative to Netanyahu," he said, as quoted by Rick Gladstone for the *New York Times* (11 Nov. 2015), "and I also made clear in some very harsh speeches that I feel that Netanyahu . . . bears a responsibility and he has to make a historic change." However, Herzog's Zionist Union will face competition from other centrist Israeli political parties, including Yesh Atid, led by Yair Lapid, and Kulanu, led by Moshe Kahlon, who broke with the Netanyahu–led Likud Party just prior to the 2015 election.

After the elections, Herzog began striking a different tone on a number of issues, most notably the Iran nuclear treaty. He now considers it a bad deal, although he once felt that Obama would get a deal that was good for Israel's security. The Iranian nuclear deal has been seen in a poor light by most of the Israeli public, who believe that Iran would, at the very least, use some of the money it will receive after the lifting of international economic sanctions to fund anti-Israeli groups such as Hezbollah in Lebanon and Hamas in the Gaza Strip. At worst, many Israelis believe, the Iranian government will finds ways to circumvent the deal in order to build nuclear weapons to threaten Israel.

In an interview with Jeffrey Goldberg for the *Atlantic* (16 July 2015), Herzog remarked of the Iranian nuclear deal: "Most of the Israeli body politic is worried about the agreement, and people need to understand our worries. The world doesn't fully understand the fact that we are left here alone in this neighborhood. . . . But I don't intend to clash with the administration. We're very glad for all that the Obama administration has done for us. We have respect for the United States, for this great ally and friend, and we don't want to be in a confrontation or clash. But we have to let people know that we think this is a dangerous situation."

PERSONAL LIFE

Isaac Herzog lives in Tel Aviv and is married with three children. His wife, Michal, is a lawyer. He speaks both Hebrew and English and has published numerous articles in both the Israeli and foreign media.

SUGGESTED READING

Booth, William. "Meet the Underdog Israeli Candidate Who Might Dethrone 'King Bibi.'" *Washington Post.* Washington Post, 21 Feb. 2015. Web. 6 Jan. 2016.

Ferber, Alona. "The Herzog Family Tree: Israel's Answer to the Kennedys." *Haaretz.* Haaretz, 9 Mar. 2015. Web. 11 Jan. 2016.

Gladstone, Rick. "Israeli Opposition Leader Withholds Judgment on Netanyahu's Visit." *New York Times.* New York Times, 11 Nov. 2015. Web. 11 Jan. 2016.

Goldberg, Jeffrey. "Israeli Opposition Leader: Iran Deal Will Bring More Chaos to the Middle East." *Atlantic.* Atlantic Monthly Group, 16 July 2015. Web. 11 Jan. 2016.

"Netanyahu 'Loathes' Obama, Israel's Opposition Leader Charges." *Times of Israel.* Times of Israel, 6 June 2014. Web. 6 Jan. 2016.

Rudoren, Jodi. "Israeli Center-Left Seeks Path Forward." *New York Times.* New York Times, 27 Mar. 2015. Web. 6 Jan. 2016.

—*Christopher Mari*

Hugh Hewitt

Born: February 22, 1956
Occupation: Radio host

Gage Skidmore/CC BY-SA 2.0/Wikimedia Commons

Hugh Hewitt is an Emmy Award–winning conservative radio host, lawyer, author, and constitutional law professor at the Chapman University School of Law in Orange County, California. He has been the host of a radio program called *The Hugh Hewitt Show*, broadcast on Salem Radio Network, since 2000. The program enjoys a small but loyal band of followers. Hewitt is widely respected in conservative circles as an antidote to more reactionary figures such as Rush Limbaugh, whose own program boasts ten times the audience of *The Hugh Hewitt Show*. Without referring to Limbaugh by name, Hewitt told Nicky Woolf for the *Guardian* (13 Sept. 2015), "The point about talk radio that many people don't understand: they think it's just screaming, yelling, emotional, when in fact I believe it's educational, informative, and persuasive if done well."

Hewitt is a tough interviewer but not an overly aggressive one; he is vocal about his conservative beliefs—he often describes himself as "center right"—but enjoys speaking with guests across the political spectrum. David Axelrod, a former campaign strategist for President Barack Obama, described him to Todd S. Purdum for *Politico Magazine* (15 Sept. 2015) as "challenging at points, but fair," adding: "He is also clearly serious about public policy issues and doesn't merely treat your answers as a necessary interlude between his turns to speak." Hewitt was a fervent Mitt Romney supporter when the Massachusetts governor and billionaire ran for president in 2008 and 2012, and he even wrote a book about him called *A Mormon in the White House? 10 Things Every American Should Know About Mitt Romney* (2007). Hewitt has authored more than a dozen other books—including a critique of former secretary of state Hillary Clinton called *The Queen: The Epic Ambition of Hillary and the Coming of the Second "Clinton Era"* (2015)—and countless columns for the *Washington Examiner* and *Townhall.com*. When Salem Radio Network and Cable News Network (CNN) partnered to host three of the Republican primary debates, Hewitt served as a debate panelist for the first time in September 2015. Purdum described the seemingly tireless Hewitt as a "one-man mini media empire."

EARLY LIFE AND EDUCATION

Hewitt was born on February 22, 1956, in Warren, Ohio. His father was a lawyer who was largely apolitical but voted Republican. Hewitt was raised in a Catholic and Presbyterian household. When he was in the sixth grade, Hewitt read *One Day in the Life of Ivan Denisovich*, a 1962 novel about a prisoner in a Soviet prison camp by Aleksandr Solzhenitsyn. The book, Purdum wrote, was Hewitt's "political awakening." His revulsion for communism pushed him to explore the political right. After graduating from John F. Kennedy Catholic School, Hewitt attended Harvard University where his first professor was the Pulitzer Prize–winning historian and author Doris Kearns Goodwin, and his tutor was Alan Keyes, a conservative activist who ran for president three times during the 1990s and early 2000s. His roommates at Winthrop House, a residence hall, were liberal Democrats: Mark Gearan, who would go on to work in the Clinton administration and head the Peace Corps, and Dan Poneman, deputy energy secretary for

President Barack Obama. The threesome remain close despite their ideological differences. As a senior in 1978, Hewitt failed to gain entry to any of the law schools that he had hoped to attend, and through Ray Price, President Richard Nixon's speechwriter, he got a job as a research assistant to David Eisenhower, author and grandson of President Dwight D. Eisenhower.

Hewitt moved to California, where Eisenhower was writing a book called *Eisenhower at War* (1986) about his grandfather's campaigns during World War II. Hewitt's work with Eisenhower ended after a few months, and he moved to San Clemente to work as an assistant for Eisenhower's father-in-law, Richard Nixon. Nixon had resigned from the presidential office following the Watergate scandal in 1974. In 1978 he was writing a book called *The Real War*, about geopolitics and the Cold War. It became a best seller when it was published in 1980. Hewitt relished his two years with the former president, spending "hundreds, if not thousands of hours sitting and talking with him at the age of twenty-two and twenty-three," he told Purdum, and he thinks of Nixon as his mentor.

After two years working for Nixon, Hewitt enrolled at the University of Michigan Law School. After graduating in 1983, he clerked for several judges on the circuit court of Washington, DC, including future Supreme Court justices Antonin Scalia and Ruth Bader Ginsburg, and held several positions in the Reagan administration, including a stint in the White House counsel's office alongside future chief justice John Roberts. In 1989 Hewitt moved back to California to serve as the first executive director of the Nixon presidential library in Yorba Linda. "You don't say no to the guy who made your bones," he told Woolf. In 1990 he made headlines when he told a *Los Angeles Times* reporter, "I don't think we'd ever open the doors to Bob Woodward"—one of the journalists responsible for breaking the Watergate story—"He's not a responsible journalist." After his job there ended, Hewitt entered private practice with a law firm in Newport Beach. He continues to practice law part time with Arent Fox, where he specializes in endangered species law, representing private interests such as golf clubs.

RADIO CAREER AND *THE HUGH HEWITT SHOW*

Hewitt began his radio career in 1990 with his own weekend show on KFI, a Los Angeles AM radio station. In 1992 Hewitt became the cohost of a nightly public affairs show called *Life and Times*, broadcast on the Public Broadcasting Service (PBS) member station KCET. For his work on the show, Hewitt won three Emmy Awards. After a brief foray into television with PBS, the conservative Salem Radio Network offered Hewitt his own syndicated daily radio

show. *The Hugh Hewitt Show*, a three-hour daily public policy program, premiered in the summer of 2000. Hewitt was live on the air the morning of the terrorist attacks on September 11, 2001; the show now airs in the afternoon.

Hewitt is known for asking hard-hitting questions about foreign policy but eschews questions about social issues. He refuses to ask guests questions about contraception for example, because such social issues, he has said, fall under the category of personal belief. "I don't believe in asking about personal belief," he told Shane Goldmacher for the *National Journal* (13 Mar. 2015). "It's so antithetical to the founding." He is much more interested in talking to guests about national defense. "Have more of everything than anyone, and no one will mess around with you," he told Goldmacher, summing up his personal philosophy on defense. In a 2015 interview with former governor Jeb Bush, Hewitt was perturbed when the Republican presidential candidate said he was unsure of the size of the Navy's submarine fleet. "I am a national security guy, first and foremost," he told Goldmacher. There are two questions that Hewitt asks every guest: the first is if they have read *The Looming Tower* (2006), a comprehensive history of al-Qaeda by Lawrence Wright. The second, which he believes tells him all he needs to know about a person, is whether or not Alger Hiss—a US State Department official convicted of perjury in 1950—was a Soviet spy.

Regular guests on Hewitt's show include Erwin Chemerinsky, a liberal constitutional law professor and dean at the University of California, Irvine; liberal *Washington Post* columnist E. J. Dionne; Chuck Todd, the current host of *Meet the Press*; Jonathan Alter, a journalist for the *Daily Beast*; and John Eastman, Hewitt's colleague at the Chapman University School of Law. Hewitt is particular about posting complete transcripts of his interviews—a valuable resource and rarity in talk radio—because he is distrustful of mainstream media outlets and their ability to accurately quote his guests. When journalists ask to write about him, he agrees on the condition that they agree to be interviewed on his show. When Nicholas Lemann, then the dean of the Columbia University Graduate School of Journalism (now dean emeritus), asked to write a profile about him for the left-leaning *New Yorker* in 2005, Hewitt asked if he could write a profile about Lemann for the conservative *Weekly Standard*. Hewitt used the piece to write about what he called, as quoted by Goldmacher, "the collapse of credibility of the mainstream media."

THE REPUBLICAN 2016 PRESIDENTIAL CAMPAIGN

Despite his ubiquity on air and in print, Hewitt rarely makes the news himself. But in September

2015 he drew conservative ire after stumping Republican presidential candidate and real estate mogul Donald Trump with questions about foreign policy on his show. Trump, who blustered his way through an answer that confused Hamas, a Palestinian Islamic group, and Hezbollah, a Shia Islamist militant group, later called Hewitt a "third-rate announcer" who set out to make him look foolish. The altercation between Trump and the conservative mainstay was indicative of the gulf between political newcomers and experienced politicians that has threatened to split the Republican Party on the campaign trail for the 2016 presidential election. On his show, Hewitt has interviewed almost all of the Republican candidates. Despite his enthusiastic support of Romney in past elections, he had yet to endorse a Republican candidate by the beginning of 2016. Hewitt has also become a frequent guest of the Sunday morning political talk show *Meet the Press*.

In 2015 the Salem Radio Network partnered with CNN to sponsor three Republican primary debates, two of which Hewitt served as panelist posing questions to candidates. His strategy for asking questions, he told Purdum, was similar to the strategy for interviewing guests on his show. "If the candidates are debating among themselves, we're doing a good job," he said. "And the more we're talking, the less we're doing a good job. You gotta listen. I've been doing this for twenty-five years. If something comes up that's emotionally riveting and satisfactory and revealing, don't step on your story."

PERSONAL LIFE
Hewitt, who has written extensively about his Christian faith, attends Catholic mass on Saturday nights and Presbyterian services with his wife, Betsy Hewitt, on Sunday mornings. Hewitt met Betsy at a political fundraiser in San Diego, and they married in 1982. On his radio show and in his books he refers to her as "The Fetching Mrs. Hewitt," or simply "FMH." The couple live in Orange County and have three children: Will, Diana, and James, who is the deputy press secretary for the Republican National Committee (RNC).

SUGGESTED READING
Goldmacher, Shane. "How Did Hugh Hewitt Become the GOP's Go-To Pundit?" *National Journal*. Atlantic Media, 13 Mar. 2015. Web. 8 Jan. 2016.
Lemann, Nicholas. "Right Hook." *New Yorker*. Condé Nast, 29 Aug. 2005. Web. 6 Jan. 2016.
Purdum, Todd S. "Donald Trump's Grand Inquisitor." *Politico Magazine*. Politico, 15 Sept. 2015. Web. 5 Jan. 2016.
Woolf, Nicky. "Hugh Hewitt: Is He Donald Trump's Arch Nemesis—or the Antidote to Fox News?" *Guardian*. Guardian News and Media, 13 Sept. 2015. Web. 6 Jan. 2016.

SELECTED WORKS
A Mormon in the White House? 10 Things Every American Should Know About Mitt Romney, 2007; *The Happiest Life: Seven Gifts, Seven Givers, and the Secret to Genuine Success*, 2013; *The Queen: The Epic Ambition of Hillary and the Coming of the Second "Clinton Era"*, 2015

—*Molly Hagan*

Michael Daniel Higgins
Born: April 18, 1941
Occupation: President of Ireland

Michael Daniel Higgins was elected president of Ireland in October 2011, after serving as a member of parliament for several decades. A veteran of Irish politics, he was the first person to have served at all three levels of the Irish government.

EARLY LIFE AND EDUCATION
Michael Daniel Higgins was born on April 18, 1941, in Limerick, Ireland. When he was five, family expenses related to his father's health problems prompted his parents to send him and his younger brother to live on their aunt and uncle's farm in County Clare. Higgins would later cite the poverty-induced separation of his family as a major influence in his political career, fostering a keen desire to help the less fortunate.

He received a scholarship to attend University College Galway (now the National University of Ireland, Galway), where he studied sociology. Upon graduation, Higgins became a political science lecturer at the school. He maintained an intense interest and involvement in Ireland's political climate while spending time abroad as a student at Indiana University Bloomington in the United States, where he earned a master's degree in sociology in 1967.

POLITICAL CAREER
Higgins orchestrated two failed campaigns for election to the Dáil Éireann, the lower house of Irish parliament, in the late 1960s and early 1970s. He was appointed to the Seanad Éireann, the upper house, by Taoiseach (Prime Minister) Liam Cosgrave in 1973, serving until 1977. He won election to the Dáil Éireann in the 1981 general election but held on to his seat for just one year. Higgins twice served as the mayor of Galway, from 1982 to 1983 and from 1991 to 1992. He returned to the Seanad on the National University of Ireland constituency from 1983 to 1987. Higgins was elected to the Dáil Éireann

242 Michael Daniel Higgins

again in 1987, serving as one of that body's most prominent politicians until 2011.

Higgins's passion for politics was rivaled by an equal enthusiasm for the arts. Throughout his time as a politician, Higgins acted in several films and authored four poetry collections as well as numerous essays on Irish culture and politics. In 1993, Higgins was appointed Ireland's minister for arts, culture, and the Gaeltacht. Higgins's fervent work in this role led to some of the most impactful and lasting successes of his political career. His decision not to renew the highly controversial section 31 of the Irish Broadcasting Acts, a rule that gave the minister for posts and telegraphs the power to issue a ministerial order not to broadcast certain material, which was used principally to bar interviews with spokespersons for Sinn Féin from the air during the Troubles, was seen as a landmark victory over censorship in Irish political media.

In 1993, cognizant of the potential revenue available to federal coffers by promoting the country as a viable filming location for international production studios, Higgins reestablished the Irish Film Board, an organization that had been dormant since the mid-1980s. The decision was seen as a boon in the presentation and preservation of Irish culture and a much-needed boost to the nation's creative professionals. Since its reestablishment, the Film Board has funded numerous Irish film productions that were critically and popularly acclaimed, including *Intermission* (2003), *The Magdalene Sisters* (2003), and *Man about Dog* (2004).

The permanent establishment of a government-funded Irish-language television station had long been a goal of the nation's progressive political figures, and Higgins's nomination as arts minister made him a key figure in that venture. He was instrumental in the logistical and infrastructural work needed to found the Irish-language public television network Teilifís na Gaeilge, later known as TG4. The station presents news, documentaries, and feature films in Irish.

In addition to his successes on the Irish cultural and political landscape, Higgins remained a prominent voice in human rights advocacy throughout his tenure in the Dáil. He was one of the most prominent European politicians who spoke of the need for global intervention in the decade's social crises in Somalia, Cambodia, and Iraq. In 1996 he was elected president of the Council of European Culture Ministers.

In 2011, Higgins sought and won the Labour Party's nomination for the Irish presidency. Citing his breadth of experience on the national and international levels, Higgins's campaign centered on a rejuvenation of civic engagement and a rebirth of Ireland's cultural standing and political influence in both Europe and the world.

Higgins's chief rival in the presidential election was prominent Irish businessman Seán Gallagher, who had risen to national prominence as a panelist on the entrepreneurial-based reality show *Dragon's Den*. Despite trailing Gallagher in the polls in the weeks leading up to the election, Higgins defeated his main rival soundly, receiving nearly 40 percent of first-preference votes.

Upon his election, Higgins set forth a detailed agenda despite expressing his desire to serve only one seven-year term in office. The Higgins administration sought to champion the creative endeavors of Irish people while attempting to reestablish the country as a premier tourist destination. Higgins went on to hold a series of seminars dedicated to young Irish men and women both at home and abroad in the hope of generating interest in the nation's political future among younger generations.

IMPACT

Over the course of his political career, Higgins has dedicated himself to promoting Irish arts and culture as well as fostering an interest in politics among Ireland's youth. A supporter of affordable housing initiatives, Higgins became the official patron of Habitat for Humanity Ireland, an organization that works to provide homes to people in need, in 2012.

PERSONAL LIFE

Higgins married Sabina Coyne in 1974. The couple has four children.

SUGGESTED READING

Dalby, Douglas. "Labour Party Leader Set to Win Ireland's Presidential Election." *New York Times*. New York Times, 28 Oct. 2011. Web. 3 Mar. 2014.

"Michael D. Higgins." *Áras an Uachtaráin*. Áras an Uachtaráin, n.d. Web. 3 Mar. 2014.

"Michael D. Higgins Wins Irish Presidential Election." *Telegraph*. Telegraph Media Group, 28 Oct. 2011. Web. 3 Mar. 2014.

O'Leary, Jennifer. "Who Is Michael D. Higgins?" *BBC News Europe*. BBC, 28 Oct. 2011. Web. 3 Mar. 2014.

Seminara, Dave. "A Conversation with Michael D. Higgins, the President of Ireland." *Gadling*. AOL, 13 Aug. 2012. Web. 3 Mar. 2014.

—*John Pritchard*

Judith Hill

Born: May 6, 1984
Occupation: Singer

Some artists are overnight successes; others, like R & B–soul singer and pianist Judith Hill, take a little bit longer to find fame. Despite her powerhouse voice, impressive stage presence, and ability to sing in a variety of genres, Hill spent many years jobbing as a background singer for many superstar artists—including Elton John, Stevie Wonder, Gregg Allman, and Barry Manilow—instead of being on center stage. She received her first serious notice as an artist while serving as a duet partner for Michael Jackson shortly before Jackson died unexpectedly in 2009; she went on to record a soundtrack for a Spike Lee film and compete on the singing contest series *The Voice*. Now, with a Prince-produced solo album, *Back in Time* (2015), under her belt, she seems poised—finally—for superstardom. In her interview with Lourdes Garcia-Navarro for NPR's *Weekend Edition* (11 Oct. 2015), Hill compared life as a backup singer to her blossoming career as a solo artist: "I think the thing that I loved about being a background singer was the community. It's always great to get with the girls and travel around the world and you have this sisterhood when you're a background singer. When you're an artist, it's very much you're the boss and you've got people working for you. So there's a lot more responsibility and, of course, this is my dream and this is what I love. But I do miss those days where—the girls, we would just go out on the town and we would just have fun and the responsibility was on artist, not us. We just had to come in and sing."

EARLY LIFE AND EDUCATION

Judith Hill was born on May 6, 1984, and raised in Los Angeles, California. Her African American father, Robert "Pee Wee" Hill, is a session musician who played with a number of funk bands in the 1970s, including Sly and the Family Stone; her mother, Michiko, is Japanese and a classically trained pianist. "I was kind of an outcast growing up. I grew up in a mainly white community and I was the only one girl with big hair and biracial," Hill said in an interview with *CBS News* (13 Nov. 2015). "And a lot of times, kids would be like, 'Can you please move. I can't see the chalkboard, your hair's too big,' and all these things, so I felt a bit awkward in my own skin."

If she felt out of place in school, Hill always felt at home around music; it was part of her life from the time she was born. In interviews she recalls writing her first song, "God Is Made," with her mother when she was just four years old. Her parents, both respected session musicians,

David Livingston/Getty Images

maintained a recording studio in their home. Her childhood bedroom even doubled as the vocal room. Often very famous musicians came in to record there. Because of Hill's early interactions with so many recording artists, she was exposed to a wide range of musical styles, especially pop, funk, soul, and R & B. In talking with Garcia-Navarro, Hill recalled the influence of various musicians who came to record at her parents' home studio: "Rose Stone was a great mentor to me. She was a vocalist that would always come through the house. And my dad played with Billy Preston, and sometimes he'd come to the house and play the organ and that was always a treat to see. I thought that was normal life but as I am here now looking back, I realize what a treasure that was to have."

THIS IS IT

In 2005 Hill graduated from Biola University in La Mirada, California, with a degree in music composition. Two years later she was performing as a backup singer for Michel Polnareff, a French singer-songwriter, and toured the world with him. This stint with Polnareff was the beginning of her long career as a backup singer. During these years she toured and recorded as a background singer with such music stars as Gregg Allman, Taylor Hicks, Carole King, Barry Manilow, Rod Stewart, Stevie Wonder, and Elton John. In an interview with Mandalit del Barco for NPR's *Morning Edition* (11 June 2013), Hill said that background singing "adds so much charm to the record. You can feel it when you've got [a] group of singers. It adds a whole other quality rather than the one person tracking [a] million times."

But it was her fateful experience with Michael Jackson that would profoundly change her life. In 2009 Hill was selected to be Jackson's duet partner for his upcoming comeback tour, *This Is It*. She practiced with him for a number of months before the King of Pop unexpectedly died on June 25, 2009, at the age of fifty. Hill, along with the rest of the musicians who would have accompanied Jackson on the tour, then performed at his memorial concert at the Staples Center in Los Angeles on July 7, 2009. Her performance of the song "Heal the World" wowed viewers worldwide. Hill described her experience with Michael Jackson in an interview with Michele McManmon for *LA Weekly* (20 Feb. 2016): "We were part of the band he was going to take out; it was a very shocking, unexpected death. It was one of those experiences where, I don't know how I was asked to sing at his memorial, but I was deeply honored. It was a surreal, spiritual experience. I didn't really get to know him. Every time he came to rehearsal he was very kind, fun to work with and in bright spirits, so it was wonderful." Hill also appeared in the documentary *Michael Jackson's This Is It*, a compilation of behind-the-scenes and rehearsal footage from the preparation for the Jackson's comeback tour that never happened.

A BREAKOUT YEAR
In the years after her aborted tour with Michael Jackson, Hill sought to make a name for herself while continuing to work as a backup singer, both on record and on tour. In 2012 a number of her songs were featured on the soundtrack to the 2012 Spike Lee film *Red Hook Summer*, which premiered at the Sundance Film Festival that year. Notable among these songs was the ballad Hill penned, "Desperation."

Hill returned to national prominence in March 2013, when she auditioned for and won a spot on *The Voice*, a singing contest on NBC. On the show, all four celebrity judges blindly listen to a singer and based on the strength of his or her vocal performance, a judge turns around and asks the singer to be on his or her team. In Hill's case, all four judges turned around, but she ultimately chose judge Adam Levine of the band Maroon 5 to be her coach in competition. Of her experience being coached by Levine on *The Voice*, Hill told McManmon: "He was fun! He knows how being on a television show works, the emotional response that people have to what you say, sing; it was all very interesting. It was cool, educational—like being on *The Hunger Games*, where I'm this character and there are certain things that happen inside that show."

Hill made it through five more rounds of competition before being eliminated by popular vote in the Live Top 8 round—a shocking turn of events as Hill was considered an odds-on favorite to win. "Everyone's like, 'Man, I'm so shocked,'" Hill said shortly after her elimination in her interview with Del Barco. "It seems now it's a country show. Middle America was watching the show that day. The demographic's different from my audience."

Although disappointed by her loss, Hill looked forward to new opportunities. Later in 2013 she was featured in *20 Feet from Stardom*, a documentary depicting the lives and careers of backup singers. The film won a 2014 Oscar for best documentary, as well as a 2015 Grammy Award for best music film. The documentary featured not only Hill but also talents such as Merry Clayton, who performed on the Rolling Stones' song "Gimme Shelter"; Darlene Love, who recorded the 1963 song "Christmas (Baby Please Come Home)"; and Lisa Fischer, who parlayed her background singing into the solo hit single "How Can I Ease the Pain," which won the 1992 Grammy Award for best female R & B vocal performance.

SOLO SUCCESSES SINCE *THE VOICE*
In 2013, Hill signed a record deal with Sony Music but ultimately never recorded an album with that label. Toward the end of 2013, Hill teamed up with Josh Groban, both to record backing vocals for his album *All That Echoes* and to accompany him as the opening act for the North American leg of his tour. She then went on to tour with John Legend during the fall of 2014. Yet the most notable thing to have occurred to her during 2014 may have been something that seemed inconsequential at the time: an interview she did with REVOLT TV, during which she named Prince as her dream collaborator. Shortly after doing the interview, she received a call from an unknown number on her cell phone. "I say, 'Hello,' and he says, 'Judith, this is Prince.' I was like, 'Oh, hi Prince.' Like real calm but really, going crazy in my living room," Hill recalled in her interview for *CBS News*. "And we shared our love for funk music and that's kind of how it all started."

Hill went to Prince's Paisley Park studio in Minneapolis at his invitation to jam. After performing for a time with members of his band, the New Power Generation, Prince asked Hill to show him some of the songs she had written. She did and they began jamming on them, eventually coming up with some new arrangements. Before long he was convinced that she had enough material available to record a solo album, on which Prince served as the producer. Using their common love of funk as a bridge, Prince and Hill recorded an album's worth of music in relatively short order with an eye toward maintaining the spontaneous feel of their initial sessions.

Back in Time, Hill's debut solo album, was released on October 23, 2015, to positive reviews. Jon Pareles declared in an article for the *New York Times* (18 Nov. 2015): "Judith Hill has the grit of vintage soul and gospel in her voice, and her producer—the hands-on funk historian named Prince—revels in it on her official debut album, 'Back in Time.'" Pareles added, "Backing her up, Prince and the New Power Generation sound like they're having sheer fun—sinewy, in-the-pocket fun, whether they're playing snappy funk for 'Wild Tonight' or going bluesy and inspirational on 'Cry, Cry, Cry.' Flesh and fingers drive the music, not programming. And as prominent as Prince is on these songs, they clearly belong to Ms. Hill."

Shortly after Prince unexpectedly died on April 21, 2016, Hill took to Twitter to describe her sense of loss: "Still waiting to wake up from this terrible nightmare. Can't believe this." Following Prince's death, Hill toured the United States to promote her debut album throughout the summer of 2016.

SUGGESTED READING

"Backup Singer Judith Hill Makes Long-Awaited Solo Debut." *CBSNews*. CBS Interactive, 13 Nov. 2015. Web. 6 June 2016.

del Barco, Mandalit. "Spotlighting Background Singers in *Twenty Feet from Stardom*." *Morning Edition*. NPR, 11 June 2013. Web. 30 May 2016.

Hill, Judith. "Zero Feet from Stardom: Judith Hill Grabs the Mic." Interview by Lourdes Garcia-Navarro. *Weekend Edition*. NPR, 11 Oct. 2015. Web. 30 May 2016.

McManmon, Michele. "Judith Hill Has a Grammy and a Prince-Produced Debut Album—But She Almost Quit Music." *LA Weekly*. LA Weekly, 20 Feb. 2016. Web. 30 May 2016.

Pareles, Jon. "Soul and Gospel Grit, Caribbean Strains and Denver Roots Rock." *New York Times*. New York Times, 18 Nov. 2015. Web. 30 May 2016.

—*Christopher Mari*

Amy Hood

Born: 1971 or 1972
Occupation: CFO of Microsoft

In May 2013, Amy Hood became the first woman to serve as Microsoft Corporation's chief financial officer (CFO). Responsible for managing more than $83 billion in revenue, she was listed in 2014 among *Forbes* magazine's World's 100 Most Powerful Women.

EARLY LIFE AND EDUCATION

Amy Hood earned a bachelor's degree in economics from North Carolina's Duke University. Following graduation in 1994, she worked as an associate in the investment banking and capital markets group of Goldman Sachs, a major multinational investment banking, securities, and investment management firm. In 1997, while still employed at Goldman Sachs, Hood enrolled in Harvard Business School. She graduated in 1999 with a master's degree in business administration.

Hood left Goldman Sachs in November 2002 to join Microsoft Corporation as director of investor relations, a position she held for the next eighteen months. Following that she served in various roles, including chief of staff of the server and tools division, and in January 2010 she served as CFO of Microsoft's business division. It was in this position that Hood oversaw the division's financial strategy, management, and reporting. She was also instrumental in facilitating the introduction of and transition to Microsoft's Office subscription service, Office 365. Hood was also a key player in the company's 2011 acquisition of Skype, an online communication tool, and the 2012 acquisition of Yammer, an internal communication system used by organizations and businesses.

It was during Hood's time in lead managerial roles in both the server and tools group and in the business division that both departments were major growth areas for Microsoft. At the time of Hood's promotion from CFO of the business division to CFO of Microsoft Corporation in 2013, the business division had generated over $24 billion during that fiscal year, which was approximately one-third of the company's total revenue at the time.

CAREER AT MICROSOFT

Amy Hood has worked in the banking, capital markets, and technology sectors, and much of her career has focused on maximizing shareholder value through sound management practices and strategic innovation and investment. Her work at Goldman Sachs laid the foundation for this strategy by providing opportunities for Hood to work closely with a variety of clients in a number of investment and financial growth scenarios.

During her time at Microsoft, Hood has been instrumental in moving the company to cloud computing, initiating subscription pricing for software in the Microsoft Office Suite, and acquiring assets such as Skype and Yammer. All of these advancements with Microsoft have the consumer experience at their core, yet were developed and pursued to bring a return on investment for shareholders as well as to ensure Microsoft's continued growth.

As she took her position as CFO of Microsoft, Hood voiced her appreciation for predecessor, Peter Klein, and her respect for Microsoft Corporation: Klein had developed a first-rate team of financial experts and with them created a collaborative and congenial environment. Such a culture has been a significant help to Hood in maintaining Microsoft's expenditures while enhancing the corporation's value for shareholders.

From her time with the server and tools group and the business division, Hood brings to the position of CFO a familiarity with financial statements and corporate health as well as an expertise in investment and capital markets. These qualities give Hood the background necessary to successfully lead the financial side of Microsoft.

Hood has also played a significant role in envisioning a new business model for Microsoft, which is built on a perception of the company and its products as solution providers and innovators. For example, when Microsoft began to see a decline in revenue that was directly related to the decline in customer demand for desktop computers and consumer software, Hood was instrumental in the move to subscription software and services model in its new product Office 365, which provides immediate access to updated software and applications anywhere the consumer might log on. Subscriptions also benefit corporate revenue, since they help safeguard against economic downturns and market fluctuations. By combining a customer focus with an understanding of the financial statements behind meeting consumer needs, Hood has made a successful career in the very demanding technology sector, and her work addresses consumer needs in innovative ways that are profitable to the solution provider.

PERSONAL LIFE

Amy Hood lives in Seattle, Washington, with her husband and daughters.

SUGGESTED READING

McCarthy, Bede. "Amy Hood to Take on Chief Financial Officer Role at Microsoft." *Financial Times*. Financial Times, 9 May 2013. Web. 20 June 2014.

"Microsoft Names Corporate Vice President Amy Hood as New Microsoft Chief Financial Officer." *Microsoft*. Microsoft, 8 May 2013. Web. 20 June 2014.

"Power Women." *Forbes*. Forbes.com, n.d. Web. 20 July 2014.

Tu, Janet I. "Microsoft Names Amy Hood as New Chief Financial Officer." *Seattle Times*. Seattle Times, 8 May 2013. Web. 20 June 2014.

Warren, Tom. "Microsoft Selects Amy Hood as New CFO: A Key Insider Who Helped Seal the Skype Deal." *The Verge*. Vox Media, 8 May 2013. Web. 20 June 2014.

—*Gina Hagler*

Katinka Hosszú

Born: May 3, 1989
Occupation: Swimmer

Hungarian swimmer Katinka Hosszú had already competed in two Olympics and held one world title when she entered the 2012 Summer Olympic Games in London. She was widely expected to win a medal at those Games, but the closest she came to the podium was a fourth-place finish in the 400-meter individual medley, her signature event. Drained by the pressure of trying to win an Olympic medal, Hosszú, then twenty-three years old, considered walking away from swimming for good.

After partnering with Shane Tusup, "her all-in-one husband, coach and agent," as Rachel Lutz put it for NBC Olympics (22 July 2016), Hosszú regrouped, changed her approach, and developed the kind of self-confidence needed to shine on the world stage. Earning the nickname the "Iron Lady" for her grueling race programs, Hosszú has since enjoyed a late-career resurgence rarely seen in the world of swimming and has emerged as one of the most dominant female swimmers in the world. She has collected four more world championship gold medals, won four overall World Cup series titles, and earned more

Ian MacNicol/Getty Images

World Cup prize money than any swimmer in history. She was named Fédération internationale de natation (FINA) Swimmer of the Year in 2014 and 2015.

Hosszú redeemed herself in historic fashion at the 2016 Games in Rio de Janeiro, Brazil, where she claimed her first career Olympic gold medal by shattering the world record in the 400-meter individual medley. She also won gold medals in the 200-meter individual medley and 100-meter backstroke events, and added a silver medal in the 200-meter backstroke. "Nobody can argue right now that she's not the most versatile swimmer in the world, male or female," the NBC Olympics swimming analyst Rowdy Gaines said, as quoted by Lutz.

EARLY LIFE

The middle child of Istvan Hosszú and Barbara Bakos, Katinka Hosszú was born on May 3, 1989, in Pécs, a city located on the slopes of the Mecsek Mountains in southwest Hungary. Hosszú grew up in a family of athletes. Her father is a former professional basketball player who is enshrined in Hungary's basketball Hall of Fame. Hosszú's older brother, Gergely, plays professional basketball in Germany, while her younger brother, Adam, is a forward for the Hungarian national futsal team (indoor soccer).

Hosszú's interest in swimming was largely influenced by her grandfather, who was a swim coach. When Hosszú was about four years old, her grandfather started taking her to a local six-lane, 25-meter pool. The idea of becoming an Olympic champion was first planted in Hosszú's mind after her grandfather recognized her natural ability to glide in the water. Hosszú recalled to Lutz, in another article for NBC Olympics (30 Mar. 2016), that it did not take her long at all to learn how to swim. "I was always really comfortable in the water."

Early in her swimming career, Hosszú was encouraged by her father to drop swimming in favor of basketball because he felt the latter offered better odds for future success. She remained dedicated to swimming, however, and enjoyed a decorated youth career under the direction of her grandfather, who served as her coach until she was thirteen.

Strict and demanding, Hosszú's grandfather once threw one of his sandals at her during a workout and her father would speed her to practice if they were running late. "She was his only athlete," Istvan Hosszú explained to Karen Crouse in a profile of Hosszú for the *New York Times* (3 Aug. 2016). "He was the grandparent, but not at the pool."

OLYMPIC DEBUT AND EARLY SWIMMING CAREER

Hosszú attended Bela III High School, a sports-centered school in the city of Bafa, where she developed into one of the best young swimmers in Hungary, which "has a huge tradition in swimming," as she told Lutz. "Pretty much if you're not an Olympic medalist [there]," she added, "then you probably shouldn't be swimming anymore."

Hosszú achieved her first major swimming milestone at the 2004 European Junior Swimming Championships in Lisbon, Portugal, where she won a gold medal as a member of the 800-meter freestyle relay team. There, she also captured bronze medals in the 200-meter freestyle and 400-meter individual medley events. One month after that competition, Hosszú made her Olympic debut at the 2004 Summer Games in Athens, Greece. Just fifteen years old at the time, she placed thirty-first in the 200-meter freestyle.

Following the Olympics, Hosszú competed at the 2004 European Short Course Swimming Championships in Vienna, Austria, where she won a bronze medal in the 400-meter individual medley and placed sixth in the 200-meter individual medley. She notched fifth- and eighth-place finishes in those events, respectively, at the following year's edition of that competition, which was held in Trieste, Italy.

Over the next few years, Hosszú would start to focus primarily on the 400- and 200-meter individual medley events, which consist of equal lengths of the four main competitive swimming strokes: butterfly, backstroke, breaststroke, and freestyle. At her first World Championships in 2007, she came in eleventh in the 400 individual medley and twelfth in the 200 individual medley. Then, in 2008, she took home a silver medal in the 400-meter individual medley at the long-course European Championships, which are held every two years.

That summer Hosszú swam in her second Olympic Games, in Beijing, China. Despite dropping the 200 freestyle from her Olympic program, she achieved mixed results in her individual events, finishing twelfth in the 400 individual medley and seventeenth in the 200 individual medley.

COLLEGE CAREER AT USC

In the fall of 2008, Hosszú enrolled at the University of Southern California (USC), in Los Angeles, California, after being recruited by the school's internationally renowned swim coach Dave Salo. Marking her first time in the United States, Hosszú considered leaving the school after only two weeks due to homesickness and an inability to speak English fluently. Her mother nonetheless convinced her to stay.

During her freshman year at USC, Hosszú began dating her future husband and coach Shane Tusup, a fellow swim team member who helped ease her adjustment to life in the United States. Tusup reportedly had to ask Hosszú out four times before she relented, after which "we were together like 24/7," as Tusup noted to Nick Zaccardi for *NBC Sports* (15 Apr. 2015).

Under Salo, who has steered the careers of many Olympic swimmers, Hosszú quickly became a standout on a top-ranked Trojans team. As a freshman during the 2008–9 season, she notched second-place finishes in the 400-yard individual medley at both the National Collegiate Athletic Association (NCAA) and Pac-10 championships. Hosszú then competed for Hungary at the 2009 World Championships, where she claimed her first world title, winning the 400-meter individual medley with a time of 4:30.31, then the third-fastest time in history. She also earned bronze medals in the 200-meter individual medley and 200-meter butterfly.

Over the next three seasons, Hosszú, who was named the 2009 Hungarian Female Athlete of the Year, would become one of the most versatile swimmers in the NCAA. During her sophomore 2009–10 season at USC, she won her first Pac-10 title in the 200-yard butterfly while finishing second in that event and third in the 400-yard individual medley at the NCAA championships. On the international circuit, Hosszú won gold medals in the 200-meter butterfly and 200-meter individual medley, and as a member of Hungary's 800-meter freestyle relay team at the 2010 European Championships.

In 2011 Hosszú established herself as the top collegiate female swimmer when she swept the 200 individual medley, 400 individual medley, and 200 butterfly events at both the NCAA and Pac-10 championships. She did not fare as well, however, at the 2011 World Championships, where she placed sixth, fifteenth, and nineteenth in those events, respectively.

Hosszú, who served as a senior cocaptain for the Trojans, added two more NCAA titles, and three more European titles during the 2011–12 season, after which she turned professional. In the spring of 2012, she graduated from USC with a degree in psychology.

HEARTBREAK AT THE 2012 OLYMPICS

Expectations were extremely high for Hosszú at the 2012 Games in London, where she set her sights on winning her first Olympic medal. She arrived in the English capital as the favorite to win the 400-meter individual medley, but failed to medal in the event, placing fourth after leading the field over the first 200 meters. She finished with a time of 4:33.49, nearly six-tenths of a second behind bronze medalist Li Xuanxu of China.

Devastated, Hosszú immediately considered withdrawing from her other two individual events, the 200-meter individual medley and the 200-meter butterfly. "My Olympics was pretty much done," she told Zaccardi. "I wanted to go home." Still, Hosszú soldiered on, finishing eighth in the medley and ninth in the butterfly.

Following the Olympics, Hosszú retreated to her native Hungary, where she fell into depression. She considered quitting swimming altogether until Tusup intervened with sage advice. "I told her, you've experienced the worst, basically, for a swimmer, to be .5 away from a medal," Tusup recalled to Zaccardi, adding that his pep talk ended up being the "turning point" in what would become a career resurgence.

HUNGARY'S "IRON LADY"

In the fall of 2012, Hosszú parted ways with Salo and adopted Tusup as her full-time coach. The two began experimenting with an approach that placed a greater emphasis on weightlifting and racing. On the advice of Tusup, Hosszú increased the individual event loads of her competitive programs, which offered her unconventional conditioning and the opportunity to reap greater prize earnings. "It was a perfect two years to really test, retest and then really figure our stuff out," Tusup explained to Lutz. "And then just make a big long push."

Hosszú debuted her ambitious new programs, which included the addition of backstroke events, on the 2012 World Cup circuit. (The World Cup consists of a series of two-day meets in Europe and Asia where the top three finishers in each event are awarded prize money.) After competing in eight individual events and winning five gold medals at a World Cup meet in Beijing, Hosszú was bestowed with the nickname the "Iron Lady" by the Chinese media. She won the 2012 World Cup title as the series' top female earner, and again captured World Cup titles in 2013, 2014, and 2015, becoming the first swimmer to surpass more than $1 million in prize money on the circuit.

At the 2013 World Championships, Hosszú swept the 200- and 400-meter individual medleys to claim her second and third career world titles. Then, in 2014, she collected six medals at the European Championships and another eight at the short-course World Championships. At the latter competition, Hosszú broke short course world records in the 100- and 200-individual medleys and in the 100- and 200-meter backstroke events. That season she also set seventeen Hungarian records, helping her earn FINA Swimmer of the Year honors.

Hosszú was again named FINA Swimmer of the Year in 2015, after she took home two more gold medals, in the 200- and 400-meter individual medleys, and a bronze, in the 200-meter backstroke, at the 2015 World Championships in Kazan, Russia. There, she set her first long-course world record, breaking the 200-meter individual medley world record with a time of 2:06.12.

2016 OLYMPICS

Hosszú entered the 2016 Olympics expecting to contend for medals, but did so without being burdened by the pressure to win. That relaxed mindset proved to be the difference for her, and she redeemed herself in the 400-meter individual medley by taking home the gold medal with a world-record time of 4:26.36. Hosszú's time was nearly two seconds faster than the previous record of 4:28.43, set by Ye Shiwen of China at the 2012 Olympics, which was impressive enough to prompt speculation that she used performance-enhancing drugs. (Hosszú has vehemently denied such accusations since her resurgence began in 2012.)

Hosszú also won gold medals in the 200-meter individual medley and 100-meter backstroke, setting an Olympic record in the former event with a time of 2:06.58. In addition, she won a silver medal in the 200-meter backstroke. Hosszú said to Barry Svrluga for the *Washington Post* (3 Aug. 2016): "I'm already thinking how I can get faster. I definitely want to. . . and I think I can."

Hosszú has already announced her intention to compete at the 2017 World Championships, which will be held in the Hungarian capital of Budapest. She has also not ruled out the possibility of competing at the 2020 Olympics in Tokyo, Japan.

PERSONAL LIFE

Hosszú and Tusup married in August 2013. The two run an international sports management agency and have taken advantage of the "Iron Lady" nickname by launching a website that sells brand-related merchandise, including T-shirts, hats, and posters.

Though Tusup has developed a polarizing reputation in the swimming world for his verbally aggressive coaching style and at times brusque demeanor, Hosszú has credited him with much of her success. "He's pretty hard as a coach," she told Crouse, "but at home he's super sweet and loving and really funny."

SUGGESTED READING

Crouse, Karen. "Katinka Hosszú and Her Husband Raise Eyebrows at the Pool." *New York Times*. New York Times, 3 Aug. 2016. Web. 8 Aug. 2016.

Hosszú, Katinka. "Q & A with Katinka Hosszú." Interview by Rachel Lutz. *NBC Olympics*. NBCUniversal, 30 Mar. 2016. Web. 8 Aug. 2016.

Lutz, Rachel. "Olympic Alchemy: Turning Hungary's 'Iron Lady' Katinka Hosszú into Gold." *NBC Olympics*. NBCUniversal, 22 July 2016. Web. 8 Aug. 2016.

Svrluga, Barry. "Katinka Hosszú, Swimming's Iron Lady, Is Raising All Kinds of Eyebrows." *Washington Post*. Washington Post, 7 Aug. 2016. Web. 8 Aug. 2016.

Zaccardi, Nick. "Katinka Hosszú Emerges from Depression to Become Swimming's Iron Lady." *NBC Sports*. NBCUniversal, 15 Apr. 2015. Web. 8 Aug. 2016.

—Chris Cullen

Greg Howard

Born: April 4, 1988
Occupation: Journalist

Greg Howard is a journalist and David Carr Fellow at the *New York Times*. Previously a writer for the New York *Village Voice* and the sports and culture website *Deadspin*, Howard joined the staff of the prestigious newspaper in 2016. He has also written for *Esquire*, *Slate*, and the *Dallas Observer*. Howard, who was a college soccer star, began his career as a sportswriter, and often wrote about the intersection of sports and race. In 2015 he wrote a withering critique of well-known African American sports journalist Jason Whitlock after the two had a falling-out over an entry in another article Howard wrote, "The Big Book of Black Quarterbacks." The two men, who up to that point had shared a comfortable mentor-mentee relationship, have very different views about structural racism and how it shapes the African American community. Whitlock, for example, attributed the paltry number of black sportswriters to a lack of ambition on the part of individuals rather than a flawed system that favors white voices in 2013. A longtime provocateur, Whitlock expressed his views more pointedly in 2007, after white radio personality Don Imus referred to the black players of the Rutger's women's basketball team as "nappy-headed hoes." Amid the resulting uproar and Imus's suspension, Whitlock penned an article blaming Imus's slur not on Imus, but on the black community itself and what he deemed its single corroding force—rap music. Defending that article, Whitlock referred to Rev. Al Sharpton and civil rights activist Jesse Jackson, both of whom had spoken out against Imus, as domestic terrorists. In his critique, Howard described Whitlock in *Deadspin* (20 June 2014) as "the most hated sportswriter in the black community." Whitlock's story—and his polarizing views—inform Howard's own career because Howard very nearly worked for Whitlock, but also because Howard, after making a name for himself through his very public feud with Whitlock, is now best known as a cultural critic, espousing views about race and racism that make him, in many ways, Whitlock's intellectual foil.

EARLY LIFE AND EDUCATION

Gregory Sterling Howard II was born in Washington, DC, on April 4, 1988, to parents Gregory and Karla Howard. He, his older sister, Nicki, and his younger brother, Malcolm, were raised in Bowie, Maryland. Howard was a talented soccer player at Eleanor Roosevelt High School in Greenbelt, where he was named first-team All-Prince George's County twice, first-team All-Met, first-team All-State and first-team All-South Region. He served as team captain during his senior year. After graduation, he played for the Loyola Greyhounds at Loyola University Maryland. As a student, he studied journalism and writing, though as a self-described "college jock," he wrote in an article for *Deadspin* (20 June 2014), he did not seriously consider writing as a profession until his junior year. After that he was a columnist for the *Greyhound*, Loyola's student newspaper, and briefly interned with Baltimore *Style Magazine*. Howard graduated with a BA degree in creative writing in 2010. The same year, he enrolled as a graduate student at New York University's Arthur L. Carter Journalism Institute. During his time there, he wrote for a local *New York Times* syndicate blog, served as an editorial intern for *Esquire* magazine, and wrote for the newsblog the Slatest at *Slate*. He earned his MA degree in magazine journalism in 2011.

EARLY CAREER AND *DEADSPIN*

In 2012, Howard joined the staff of the weekly *Dallas Observer* where he wrote 5,000-word cover stories as an editorial fellow. A few months later he transferred to the *Observer*'s sister publication, the *Village Voice*, as a staff writer. He became a freelance writer for *Deadspin*, a sports and culture website owned by Gawker Media, in early 2013. That year he developed a professional relationship with Whitlock, who was, at the time, building an editorial team for an ESPN website about sports and race called The Undefeated. Whitlock was impressed by Howard and offered him a job, though the website had yet to launch. In the interim, *Deadspin* offered Howard a staff writing position. With Whitlock's blessing—and with the intention of soon quitting—Howard accepted the job at *Deadspin* in early 2014.

That February, Howard published an article for *Deadspin* called "The Big Book of Black Quarterbacks." The project, an exhaustive list of every black quarterback that ever played for the National Football League (NFL), was a months-long labor of love for Howard. The article, published in two parts, chronicles the rise of forgotten stars like Frederick Douglass "Fritz" Pollard, who played for the league in the early 1920s, and offers commentary on the careers of contemporary players like Cam Newton of the Carolina Panthers. It went live just after the Super Bowl, while Howard was confined to a hospital room, suffering from a severe allergic reaction to a medication. An angry Whitlock called Howard to express his displeasure with the piece. At issue was Howard's entry for Robert Griffin III, or RGIII, then quarterback for the Washington, DC, NFL team. In it, Howard sharply criticized Whitlock and another African American sports journalist, Rob Parker, for their coded comments—directed at a largely white audience—about RGIII's blackness. Parker, citing Griffin's white fiancée and his stated desire to be "more than a black quarterback," suggested that the quarterback had betrayed his community. Whitlock, meanwhile, wrote that Griffin lacked humility for deciding to stay in a game when he was hurt. Whitlock attributed this lack of humility to the influence of rap music, essentially arguing that Griffin was a product of an element of black culture that Whitlock abhorred. Howard found both men's arguments extreme, belabored and willfully reductive. "There was nothing particularly elevating about the RGIII discussion," Howard wrote. "It *was* wrongheaded, and it rested on the old, stale demands that a black celebrity in a white world be an exemplar of blackness."

Whitlock was hurt by Howard's criticism, and never contacted the young writer again. But their association did not end there; on June 10, 2014, Howard published a long article for *Deadspin* about Whitlock in which he characterized the elder writer's core beliefs as both morally and journalistically reprehensible. He accused Whitlock of peddling an inflammatory view of black culture, displaying willful ignorance of systemic racism, and largely throwing black people—most notably those who do not enjoy a national following—under the bus to make money. In light of these criticisms, he also took ESPN to task for hiring him to run a website for and about African Americans. "[Whitlock] rose to a position where he gets to speak for black people largely by being the kind of commentator black people would never want speaking for them," Howard wrote.

Whitlock vehemently disagreed with Howard's assessment, and took to his own blog to defend himself. A war of thousands of words followed, and escalated after Whitlock suggested in a tweet that Howard had once been arrested in 2010. Whitlock was removed as the creator of The Undefeated in June 2014. The site went live in May 2016. The feud dominates Howard's body of work at *Deadspin*—and arguably, made his name in online sports writing—though he also led the site's coverage of the 2014 World Cup and, in February 2016, wrote an extensive report on how the major sports news outlet *SB Nation* came to publish a (quickly rescinded) article sympathetic to convicted rapist, and former football player, Daniel Holtzclaw.

NEW YORK TIMES DAVID CARR FELLOW

In February 2016, the *New York Times* named Howard one of its inaugural David Carr fellows. (Carr was an author and beloved media journalist who died in 2015.) The newspaper announced that Howard would spend the next two years as a contributor to the *New York Times Magazine*. He joined the *Times* staff in March, and his first piece, a cover story about civil rights activist and political candidate DeRay Mckesson, was published on April 11, 2016. Mckesson, one of the most visible leaders of the Black Lives Matter movement, announced that he would run for mayor of Baltimore, his hometown, in February 2016. As Mckesson was beloved by celebrities, media figures and even President Barack Obama, his last-minute decision to become a political candidate won widespread support very quickly. After the announcement, Howard wrote a piece for *Deadspin* (5 Feb. 2016), in which he argued that Mckesson's candidacy might be the next step for the movement, and was cautiously optimistic about his chances at winning. Howard's *Times* article, for which he interviewed Mckesson and trailed him around Baltimore, was published a few months later and titled, "DeRay Mckesson Won't Be Elected Mayor of Baltimore. So Why Is He Running?" Howard chronicled Mckesson's failure to adapt his message for local office and his unpreparedness for the daily slog of a campaign, but also wrote about how far the movement had come since its early days in Ferguson, Missouri, in 2014. Mckesson might not have understood the intricacies of Baltimore's waste management program, Howard wrote, but he was responsible in part for the profusion of Black Lives Matters signs in the city.

On June 17, 2016, in the wake of the deaths of Prince and Muhammad Ali, and, more specifically, a documentary television series about O. J. Simpson, Howard wrote an article called "Why 'Transcending Race' Is a Lie." In it, he criticized the phrase, which is often used by white people to describe the aforementioned men. To say that a person "transcended" their race suggests that being black is something that must be overcome, he wrote, and "is anchored in the fallacy that the handicap is blackness itself, rather than a society that terrorizes and undermines blacks at every turn." It denies racism, he wrote, "through the denial of race itself."

A few days after the deaths of Alton Sterling and Philando Castile at the hands of police officers in July 2016, Howard wrote an article called "How Police See Us, and How They Train Us to See Them." In the article, Howard continued to develop threads inherent in his earlier writings. "Black people are approached as though inherently violent, and so any interaction with a police officer can end violently," Howard wrote. He further argued that police, like occupying soldiers in a war zone, often put the onus of safety on the black people with whom they interact. In such cases, he wrote, "the burden of not killing is lifted from the soldiers, and local people are tasked with the burden of not provoking death."

SUGGESTED READING

Howard, Greg. "A Conversation on Sportswriting and Race with *Deadspin's* Greg Howard." Interview by Laura Wagner. *Code Switch*. NPR, 26 Oct. 2015. Web. 14 July 2016.

O'Donnell, Jake. "Jason Whitlock Goes All-In on *Deadspin*, Greg Howard Responds with Pure Fire." *SportsGrid*. SportsGrid, 15 Oct. 2015. Web. 14 July 2016.

Somaiya, Ravi. "*New York Times* Awards David Carr Fellowships to 3 Journalists." *New York Times*. New York Times, 23 Feb. 2016. Web. 14 July 2016.

SELECTED WORKS

"How Police See Us, and How They Train Us to See Them," *New York Times*, 8 July 2016; "Why 'Transcending Race' Is a Lie," *New York Times*, 17 June 2016; "DeRay Mckesson Won't Be Elected Mayor of Baltimore. So Why Is He Running?" *New York Times Magazine*, 11 Apr. 2016; "Can Jason Whitlock Save ESPN's 'Black Grantland' From Himself?" *Deadspin*, 10 June 2014; "The Big Book of Black Quarterbacks," *Deadspin*, 6 Feb. 2014

—*Molly Hagan*

Armando Iannucci

Born: November 28, 1963
Occupation: Screenwriter and director

If one has only a passing familiarity with Armando Iannucci's most famous works and no knowledge of the man himself, one might imagine him to be a foul-mouthed fiend with nothing but disdain for politicians and all they represent. However, this could not be further from the truth. Although his political comedy series *The Thick of It* and *Veep* are notoriously profane, journalists who have met with Iannucci almost inevitably describe him as quiet and bookish in manner.

Despite his predilection for poking fun at politicians, Iannucci displays a perhaps

Armando_Iannucci_and_the_Thick_of_It_writing_team/
RanZag/CC BY 2.0/Wikimedia Commons

surprising amount of sympathy for the government figures he lampoons. "I think they show their real character when they're left to their own devices," he explained to June Thomas for *Slate* (20 Apr. 2012). "It's frustrating that they can't say what they really want to say or that they're misinterpreted. In many ways, I sympathize with them, because we as a public, and we as a media, put extraordinary pressure on them to get it right all the time." A critically acclaimed writer of television as well as films, Iannucci brings his unique sensibility to each of his projects, casting the memorable characters he creates—from news broadcasters to government ministers and White House staffers—in a new and often absurd light.

EARLY LIFE AND EDUCATION

Armando Giovanni Iannucci was born in 1963 in Glasgow, Scotland, the second-youngest of four children born to Armando and Gina Iannucci. His father, the owner of a pizza factory, had been a member of the Italian resistance during World War II and immigrated to Scotland after the war. His mother, a hairdresser, was born in Scotland but was also of Italian descent. Iannucci has noted that he sometimes felt like an outsider because of his Italian ancestry, particularly when he attended university in England, where he stood out for being both Italian and Scottish. "I felt doubly outside," he explained to Teddy Jamieson for *HeraldScotland* (18 Oct. 2013), "Then you realize everyone else feels that when they go to Oxford. They always feel that they are

the outsider, that they'll be found out, and then you realize we're all in the same boat."

The young Iannucci was an avid reader and was fascinated by politics; he was engrossed by election coverage and enjoyed reading parliamentary transcripts. Over the years his unique sense of humor was shaped by the work of comedic writers such as Douglas Adams and television shows such as *Yes Minister*, a political comedy that has had a strong influence on his later work. After graduating from St. Aloysius' College, a Jesuit day school in Glasgow, Iannucci attended University College, Oxford, during which time he considered pursuing a career as a civil servant. Following the completion of his bachelor's degree in English, Iannucci began to work toward a PhD, focusing on the works of seventeenth-century English poet John Milton. However, he ultimately left university without completing his thesis.

EARLY CAREER

Iannucci began his career in entertainment on the radio, working initially for Radio Scotland, one of the stations operated by the British Broadcasting Corporation (BBC), and soon joining the BBC's Radio 4. In 1991, he collaborated with several colleagues to create the radio program *On the Hour*, which parodied radio news broadcasts. In addition to being one of Iannucci's first major projects, the program was notable for being the origin of the character of Alan Partridge, a correspondent played by comedian and actor Steve Coogan. Coogan would become one of Iannucci's most frequent collaborators, and the two have created numerous projects featuring the character of Partridge, including *The Day Today*, a 1994 television show based on *On the Hour*, and the 2013 film *Alan Partridge*.

Having established himself as a talented writer, Iannucci wrote for a number of television shows during the 1990s and early 2000s, including *I'm Alan Partridge*, *Gash*, and *Time Trumpet*. In 2001, Channel 4 aired the *Armando Iannucci Shows*, an eight-episode series that Iannucci starred in as well as wrote. He also appeared as himself in a number of documentaries and panel shows during that period.

THE THICK OF IT

In 2004, Iannucci began developing the series that would be his most successful to date, the political comedy *The Thick of It*. Drawing from both previous political television comedies and his youthful fascination with politics, he collaborated with a number of writers—including Ian Martin, who told Ian Parker for the *New Yorker* (26 Mar. 2012) that he had been consulted because of his "talent for a certain kind of stupid, overblown, bombastic, baroque swearing"—to bring his vision to life. The show's first season, consisting of only three episodes, was made with a limited budget, which in many ways shaped the overall tone and feel of the show going forward. "I was given a sum of money and asked what I could do with it," Iannucci explained to Eamonn Forde for the *Big Issue* (20 Apr. 2015). "I worked out I could shoot three half-hours in an empty building over the course of seven or eight days—providing we just confined it to a couple of offices. That determined the way we shot it as we had to shoot fast and be able to move from room to room. It was good because it forced a new style and it forced a freneticism."

Premiering on BBC Four in May 2005, the first season of *The Thick of It* chronicles the mishaps of a newly appointed government minister and his staff as they navigate various challenges, including formulating policies and dealing with the press. Perhaps the most iconic character introduced during the show's first season was Malcolm Tucker, played by Peter Capaldi, the foul-mouthed and short-tempered director of communications for the British prime minister. The character is widely thought to be based on Alastair Campbell, the notorious director of communications and strategy for former prime minister Tony Blair, although Iannucci himself denies this.

The Thick of It proved popular among viewers, and Iannucci and his team followed the first season with three more seasons as well as several specials. A spin-off film, *In the Loop*, was released in 2009. Iannucci directed and cowrote the film, which features several characters from *The Thick of It* as well as a number of original American characters. *In the Loop* was nominated for numerous awards, including the Academy Award for best adapted screenplay.

VEEP

Although an established television writer in the United Kingdom, Iannucci made few inroads into the United States during the first two decades of his career. A pilot for an American adaptation of *The Thick of It* was produced in 2007, but Iannucci had little involvement with the project, which proved unsuccessful. He spent several years in talks with HBO in an attempt to develop a series for the premium channel, eventually pitching a show called *Couldn't Be Better*, about the young creators of an Internet startup; however, the show did not make it past the script stage. Finally, in 2011, HBO announced that it had ordered a first season of Iannucci's new series, *Veep*.

A satirical take on the US government that follows vice president Selina Meyer, played by *Seinfeld* actor Julia Louis-Dreyfus, and her staff, *Veep* is conceptually similar to *The Thick of It* but is not a direct adaptation. This is partly because of the differences between the British and American political systems. Iannucci has noted that much of the show's humor is derived from the essential powerlessness of the position of vice president. "The dynamic of the job is you're so close, and yet you're excluded," he explained to Parker. "You know that people are slightly disrespecting you behind your back. But they can't disrespect you to your face, because you could be the most powerful person in the world one day. So everyone has to guard themselves when they speak to you, but you know that outside—in all of the restaurants and cocktail parties—you're a joke."

Premiering on HBO in April 2012, *Veep* was a critical success. The show has been nominated for numerous awards and in 2015 won the Emmy Award for outstanding comedy series. Iannucci stepped down as showrunner in April 2015, just prior to the airing of the show's fourth season, noting that spending several months in the United States each year while working on the show was preventing him from being able to spend time with his family. David Mandel, who had previously worked on the HBO series *Curb Your Enthusiasm*, took over as showrunner for the show's fifth season.

FUTURE PROJECTS

In May 2015, Iannucci announced that he was writing the screenplay for *The Death of Stalin*, based on the graphic novel *La mort de Staline* (2010) by French comics writer Fabien Nury. He also announced that he would be directing the film. Although its topic is a serious one, Iannucci has noted that he will be bringing his own comedic sensibilities to the project. "It's bleak humor rather than farce," he told Charlotte Edwardes for *Evening Standard* (8 Oct. 2015). "I'd like people to realize they've laughed a lot during it while also being tense and uncomfortable."

PERSONAL LIFE

Iannucci met his wife, a speech therapist, while attending Oxford. They live in Hertfordshire, in southern England, and have three children, Emilio, Marcello, and Carmella.

Because of the political nature of much of his work, particularly *The Thick of It*, Iannucci's personal political views are often a subject of interest among journalists. Indeed, he is open about a number of his political beliefs, including his opposition to the Iraq War and distaste for US businessman and political candidate Donald Trump. However, in general he is less partisan than he is troubled by the political system as a whole. "My natural instinct is to waver between Labour and the Liberal Democrats, but I just worry that politics is failing. And I think people are baffled by it," he explained to Bryony Gordon for the *Telegraph* (23 Oct. 2009). Despite frequently satirizing the British political establishment, he has been recognized by that same body for his contributions to British media and was named an officer of the Order of the British Empire (OBE) in February 2013.

SUGGESTED READING

Edwardes, Charlotte. "King of Satire: Armando Iannucci on *Veep*, Jeremy Corbyn, and His New Film about the Last Days of Stalin." *Evening Standard*. EveningStandard.co.uk, 8 Oct. 2015. Web. 8 Jan. 2016.

Forde, Eamonn. "Armando Iannucci Interview: 'I Hope *The Thick of It* Didn't Put Young People Off Politics.'" *Big Issue*. Big Issue, 20 Apr. 2015. Web. 8 Jan. 2016.

Gilbert, Gerard. "Armando Iannucci: 'How I Conquered America.'" *Independent*. Independent.co.uk, 23 June 2012. Web. 8 Jan. 2016.

Gordon, Bryony. "Armando Iannucci Interview." *Telegraph*. Telegraph Media Group, 23 Oct. 2009. Web. 8 Jan. 2016.

Iannucci, Armando. Interview by June Thomas. "A Conversation with Armando Iannucci." *Slate*. Slate Group, 20 Apr. 2012. Web. 8 Jan. 2016.

Jamieson, Teddy. "The Herald Magazine Cover Story: Armando Iannucci Interview." *Herald-Scotland*. Herald & Times Group, 18 Oct. 2013. Web. 8 Jan. 2016.

Parker, Ian. "Expletives Not Deleted." *New Yorker*. Condé Nast, 26 Mar. 2012. Web. 8 Jan. 2016.

SELECTED WORKS

The Day Today, 1994; *Knowing Me, Knowing You with Alan Partridge*, 1994; *The Armando Iannucci Shows*, 2001; *I'm Alan Partridge*, 1997–2002; *The Thick of It*, 2005–2012; *In the Loop*, 2009; *Veep*, 2012– ; *Alan Partridge*, 2013

—*Joy Crelin*

Andre Iguodala

Born: January 28, 1984
Occupation: Basketball player

When the Golden State Warriors clinched the 2015 National Basketball Association (NBA) championship—their first title in forty years—Andre Iguodala was named series most valuable player (MVP) for his strong defensive play against Cleveland Cavaliers forward LeBron James, who was held to under 40 percent shooting. Iguodala, who was inserted at Game 4, has the distinction of being the first player to win this award without starting every game.

Keith Allison/CC BY-SA 2.0/Wikimedia Commons

Although Iguodala had previously been a starter during his stints with the Philadelphia 76ers and the Denver Nuggets, he was willing to accept a reserve role with the Warriors. "I think everybody wants to be great," former 76ers teammate Aaron McKie told Baxter Holmes for *ESPN.com* (17 June 2015). "I think everybody wants to be the superstar, but Andre, he's always been comfortable being in his own skin being the player that he is."

EARLY LIFE

Andre Tyler Iguodala was born to an African American mother and a Nigerian father on January 28, 1984. The Springfield, Illinois, native traces his early love of hoops to his childhood. "I started basketball when I was around four or five years old, pretty much my whole family played," he told Motez Bishara and Junko Ogura for *CNN.com* (6 Nov. 2015). Growing up, Iguodala frequented the local Boys & Girls Club and actively participated in other sports, including karate, swimming, and football. "I kept [Andre] real busy, just didn't give him a lot of idle time," his mother Linda Shanklin, an administrator for the Springfield Housing Authority, shared with Joe Juliano for the *Philadelphia Inquirer* (26 June 2004). "Finally, he came into his niche [basketball] and said, 'This is what I want to do.' I shot around in the backyard with my brother all the time, so he took to that."

HIGH SCHOOL CAREER

During the late 1990s, Iguodala played basketball and was on the track and field team at

Lanphier High School, where his competitive streak was evident, especially after a disappointing third-place result in the high jump at the qualifying meet for the 1999–2000 Illinois High School Association (IHSA) track and field state finals. "He was sure he was going to states," Mike Garcia, Iguodala's track coach, told Kate Fagan for the *Philadelphia Inquirer* (12 Apr. 2009). "That caught my attention."

Despite playing in the shadow of Lions teammate Richard McBride, Iguodala eventually turned heads on the basketball court. As a junior, playing point guard for the varsity team, he averaged 13.1 points and 6.2 rebounds per game while also shooting nearly 58.8 percent from the field. During the semifinals of the 2001 Amateur Athletic Union (AAU) Junior Boys' Basketball National Championship, Iguodala's game-winning shot against Maryland-Mount Royal earned his Illinois Warriors a berth in the finals, where he scored 22 points en route to the AAU national title—and MVP honors. In November 2001, heavily recruited, Iguodala signed a national letter of intent to play for Nolan Richardson at the University of Arkansas.

During Iguodala's senior year, the Lions compiled a 32–2 record and reached the finals of the 2002 IHSA Class AA boys' state tournament. When the University of Arkansas fired Richardson in 2002, Iguodala successfully petitioned for permission to transfer to another school, without sitting out the mandatory one-year penalty period. By April he had committed verbally to attend the University of Arizona. That summer Iguodala won bronze at the COPABA (Confederation of PanAmerican Basketball Associations) Men's Junior World Championship Qualifying Tournament in Venezuela.

During high school, Iguodala was a National Honor Roll student and three-time letterman in track. He also earned accolades as the Chicago Sun-Times Player of the Year, a Nike All-American, and a second-team Parade All-American. Furthermore, he competed in the Jordan Brand Classic, an annual showcase of the country's elite high school basketball players.

TWO SEASONS IN ARIZONA

In 2002–3, his first season at the University of Arizona, Iguodala came off the bench for a talent-rich squad, captained by senior Luke Walton—an unlikely role model. "I had all the intangibles, but I just didn't know how to get them out of myself," Iguodala shared with Holmes. "Then this slow white dude is killing me every day in practice, getting position, making the right plays. . . . Just seeing that for the whole year, I kind of absorbed everything." Iguodala made the Pacific-10 (Pac-10) All-Freshman Team playing for the Wildcats, who advanced to the 2003 Elite Eight of the National Collegiate Athletic Association (NCAA) Tournament. Despite his solid numbers, Iguodala never seriously considered pursuing a professional basketball career—until he spotted his name on an NBA draft site.

Subsequently, Iguodala dedicated himself to honing his skills. "Everything was basketball," he recalled to Jonathan Abrams for *Grantland* (1 Dec. 2013). "It was all about 'How do I get to a place I hadn't even dreamed about?'" The effort paid off for the sophomore, who nearly doubled his previous season's output for points and assists. However, the Wildcats did not fare as well, suffering a first-round loss in the 2004 NCAA Tournament.

PLAYING FOR THE SIXERS

In April 2004, Iguodala left school and entered the NBA Draft. After signing with sports agent Rob Pelinka, he was selected ninth by the Philadelphia 76ers. During his rookie season (2004–5), Iguodala joined a veteran lineup that included Allen Iverson (AI) and Chris Webber. Nicknamed "AI2," Iguodala started all eighty-two games for the 76ers, who finished second in the Atlantic Division but failed to advance past the first round of the playoffs.

During his first season, Iguodala took part in the 2005 Rookie Challenge (now known as the Rising Stars Challenge), an exhibition game held during NBA All-Star Weekend between a team of rookies and a team of second-year players or sophomores. At the end of the season, Iguodala's team finished fourth in the Rookie of the Year voting and earned All-Rookie First Team honors. In 2005–6, the 76ers failed to make the playoffs, after posting a 38–44 record and a second-place finish in the Atlantic Division. However, Iguodala was the Rookie Challenge MVP as a sophomore.

After a poor start to the 2006–7 season, the 76ers made two big salary-clearing moves: trading the disgruntled Iverson to the Denver Nuggets and buying out Webber's multimillion dollar contract a month later. Both decisions paid off, as the 76ers compiled a winning record for the remainder of the season. Iguodala became the go-to guy, logging about forty minutes per game and scoring a team-leading 18.2 points per game, though the 76ers missed the playoffs for the second consecutive year.

Despite having a losing record in 2007–8, the team returned to the postseason for the first time in three years, behind a solid effort from Iguodala—the team leader in minutes, points, and steals per game. In August 2008, Iguodala re-signed with the team for six-year $80-million contract. For the 2008–9 season, the rest of the 76ers roster underwent a transformation. The team signed several free agents, including All-Star forward Elton Brand, center Theo Ratliff, and forward Donyell Marshall. In December

2008, following a 9–14 start, the 76ers fired Coach Maurice Cheeks. Despite Brand's season-ending injury two months later, Iguodala and his teammates clinched a berth in the 2009 NBA playoffs but suffered another first-round loss, this time to the Orlando Magic.

BECOMING AN ALL-STAR, WINNING GOLD, AND LEAVING PHILLY

Under new head coach Eddie Jordan, who implemented an up-tempo offensive system, Philadelphia struggled early in the 2009–10 season. In December 2009, the 76ers, who were twenty-ninth out of thirty teams in attendance, tendered a one-year, non-guaranteed free-agent deal to former player and fan favorite Iverson. However, Iverson's second stint with his original club lasted until only March 2010, when his daughter's health issues abruptly ended his comeback.

Iguodala stepped up, scoring 17.1 points per game while averaging career highs in rebounds and assists. However, Iguodala's play was not enough to turn things around for the 76ers, who finished the season with a 27–55 record and failed to make the playoffs, resulting in Jordan's firing. During the offseason, Iguodala was a member of the US men's national basketball team that captured the gold medal at the 2010 International Basketball Federation (FIBA) World Championship.

In 2010–11, under new coach Doug Collins, Iguodala became team captain. He led the team in minutes, assists, and steals per game and earned NBA All-Defensive Second Team honors. His 14.3 points per game were second-best on the team (behind Brand). The 76ers advanced to the postseason but lost to LeBron James–led Miami Heat in the first round of the playoffs. With a league-wide lockout looming, Iguodala traveled to New York, where he spent a week shadowing a venture capitalist and visiting the New York Stock Exchange (NYSE) as part of his Merrill Lynch summer internship. He also contemplated interning with a hedge fund or clothing company. However, the start of the 2011–12 NBA season was delayed only until Christmas—a month after an agreement was reached.

Iguodala, whose contract was expiring, made the most of the shortened 2011–12 season. He not only averaged 12.4 points, 6.1 rebounds, 5.5 assists, and 1.7 steals per game but also made his first All-Star Game appearance, as a reserve player. Another highlight included the 76ers clinching the final Eastern Conference playoff spot. They upset the Chicago Bulls in the first round but lost a thrilling seven-game conference semifinals against the Boston Celtics.

That summer, Iguodala was part of the gold-medal-winning US men's basketball team at the 2012 London Olympics. He made headlines back home, when he was traded to Denver. In his first season under Coach George Karl, Iguodala did not disappoint, averaging 13 points, 5.3 rebounds, and 5.4 assists in eighty games. The Nuggets ended the 2012–13 season with a franchise-record fifty-seven wins, earning coach of the year honors for Karl and advancing to the Western Conference first round, where the team was favored over the Golden State Warriors. After barely winning the first game and then losing the next three, the Nuggets escaped elimination in Game 5 before losing the series in six—the team's ninth first-round loss in its previous ten seasons—and costing Karl his job.

A NEW HOME IN GOLDEN STATE AND A FINALS MVP AWARD

Although the Nuggets offered Iguodala a five-year, $60-million deal, he opted out of his final contract year to test the free-agent waters. In July 2013, he signed a four-year, $48-million contract with the Golden State Warriors. In 2013–14, Iguodala averaged 9.3 points, 4.7 rebounds, 4.2 assists, and 1.5 steals in sixty-three starts and earned 2014 All-NBA Defensive Team honors for the 51–31 Warriors, who were eliminated in a thrilling seven-game playoff series against the Los Angeles Clippers.

The next season (2014–15), Steve Kerr, the new head coach of the Warriors, approached Iguodala, who had been a starter his entire career, about coming off the bench—a daring move that Iguodala accepted. Kerr's experiment worked; Golden State posted the league's best record (67–15) and also set a franchise record for wins. Iguodala, whom Kerr designated as co-captain, played a career-low 26.9 minutes per game. Former college teammate and Warriors assistant coach Luke Walton told Holmes, "He's unbelievable at seeing what the team needs and giving the team that on certain nights. . . . That's an uncommon ability in this league, because . . . everybody wants their stats."

Following a first-round sweep of the New Orleans Pelicans, the Warriors lost only three games on their way to the NBA Finals against LeBron James and the Cleveland Cavaliers. After the Warriors lost two of the first three games in the seven-game championship series, Kerr made another bold decision in Game 4: He inserted Iguodala into the starting lineup to defend against James. Iguodala not only held James to 20 points but also scored 22 points of his own in Golden State's dominating 103–82 victory. Iguodala remained a starter for the rest of the series, contributing a team-high 7 assists, a game-high 3 steals, and 14 points in the Warriors' Game 5 win.

In Game 6, Iguodala's had 25 points, 5 assists, and 5 rebounds, capping off the series clincher for the Warriors, who nabbed their first NBA title in four decades. Although James was the first player to lead both teams in points, assists, and rebounds for an entire Finals series, Iguodala held him to less than 40 percent shooting while averaging 16.3 points, 5.8 rebounds, and 4 assists per game—an effort that earned Iguodala seven out of eleven first-place votes for Finals MVP.

In 2015–16, the Warriors picked up where they left off, clinching the Pacific Division title for the second straight year and approaching the record for most regular-season wins ever, a mark held by the Michael Jordan–led Chicago Bulls, who won seventy-two games in 1995–96. Coming off the bench, Iguodala averaged 7.3 points and 4.1 rebounds in sixty games before being sidelined by a sprained left ankle in March 2016.

PERSONAL LIFE

Iguodala has a son, Andre Jr., with his wife, Christina Gutierrez, and a daughter, London, from a previous relationship. He gives back to the community via the Andre Iguodala Youth Foundation and also serves as style director of the Twice menswear brand. He lives in Berkeley, California.

SUGGESTED READING

Abrams, Jonathan. "Andre Iguodala: The New Pippen." *Grantland*. ESPN Internet Ventures, 1 Dec. 2013. Web. 14 Mar. 2016.

Bishara, Motez, and Junko Ogura. "Andre Iguodala: NBA 'Chef' Cooks Up Championship-Winning Recipe." *CNN.com*. Turner Broadcasting System, 6 Nov. 2015. Web. 14 Mar. 2016.

Fagan, Kate. "Looking into the Life of the Sixers' Andre Iguodala." *Philadelphia Inquirer*. Philadelphia Media Network, 12 Apr. 2009. Web. 14 Mar. 2016.

Holmes, Baxter. "Iguodala NBA's No-Stats Finals MVP." *ESPN.com*. ESPN Internet Ventures, 17 June 2015. Web. 14 Mar. 2016.

Juliano, Joe. "Versatile Iguodala Is Happy He's in Philadelphia—And So Is His Mom, Who Kept Him Busy with Sports." *Philadelphia Inquirer*. Philadelphia Media Network, 26 June 2004. Web. 14 Mar. 2016.

—*Bertha Muteba*

Oscar Isaac

Born: March 9, 1979
Occupation: Actor

For much of his career thus far, actor Oscar Isaac has devoted himself to playing characters whom he described to Brett Martin for *GQ* (15 Dec. 2015) as possessing a "sense of melancholy, anger, [and] displacement." Having gained some critical attention for his roles in films such as 2011's *Drive*, in 2013 he earned widespread acclaim for his performance as the titular folk singer of Joel and Ethan Coen's *Inside Llewyn Davis*, a role that identified Isaac as a capable and compelling leading man. However, it was an entirely different kind of role, that of decidedly upbeat pilot Poe Dameron in *Star Wars: The Force Awakens*, which would bring Isaac the greatest renown to date. Although the science-fiction epic, perhaps the most anticipated film of 2015, differed tremendously in scope and tone from Isaac's usual dramas, he nevertheless brought his signature artistic commitment to the final product. "Oscar is a far more sophisticated actor than one might get for a role that could be looked at as just a daring, kick-a——pilot," the film's director, J. J. Abrams, told Martin. "But I needed a great actor—not just a great-looking guy who also acts."

Where Isaac's performance in *Inside Llewyn Davis* made him a critical darling, his scene-stealing role in *The Force Awakens* made him an international household name. To Isaac, however, his success in both quiet dramas and science-fiction blockbusters is more the result

Gage Skidmore/CC BY-SA 3.0/Wikimedia Commons

of good fortune than any calculated moves on his part. "You can't really plan that stuff out," he told Kevin Jagernauth for the *Playlist* (31 Aug. 2015). "I was just fortunate enough that things came around when they did, and they seemed cool enough for me to want to get involved with them. I like acting, so it was just fun to try different styles, and I definitely like a good challenge, so I look for stuff that I haven't done before."

EARLY LIFE AND EDUCATION
Isaac was born Oscar Isaac Hernández Estrada on March 9, 1979, in Guatemala. One of three children born to a Guatemalan mother, María, and a Cuban-born father, Oscar, Isaac moved to the United States with his family as a baby. The devoutly Christian family lived for a time in Maryland and Louisiana before eventually settling in Country Walk, a suburb of Miami, Florida. In August 1992, when Isaac was thirteen, Hurricane Andrew made landfall in southern Florida, causing widespread destruction in the region. Although he and his family were unharmed, the category 5 storm destroyed their home as well as many others in the neighborhood. Following the hurricane, the family moved to the city of Delray Beach.

Isaac attended a number of schools around Miami, including Westminster Christian Middle School, from which he was expelled for spray-painting some of the school's fire extinguishers, among other infractions. He later attended Santaluces Community High School but failed his senior year because of frequent tardiness from his first-period gym class.

As a child and young man, Isaac struggled with some of the more restrictive aspects of his upbringing, which he has attributed in part to growing up around Miami. "It has always felt kind of conservative, culturally and politically; it was a bit rigid for me growing up. It wasn't a flourishing place for the arts," he explained to his brother, Mike Hernández, for the *Miami New Times* (15 Dec. 2015). Despite this perceived lack of support for artistic pursuits in his home region, Isaac developed a passion for music, which his parents in many ways encouraged. His father, a pulmonologist, "was a bit of a frustrated artist so we grew up listening to Bob Dylan and Jimi Hendrix, all the singer-songwriters," he told Bernadette McNulty for the *Telegraph* (6 Jan. 2014). He played guitar and bass in a number of bands as a teenager, playing genres such as ska and punk. His primary band after high school, Blinking Underdogs, found some local and regional success, at times serving as the opening act for well-known bands such as Green Day. At that time, Isaac also seriously considered enrolling in the military but was dissuaded by his parents. Instead, he remained in the greater Miami area, playing in bands and taking courses in the performing arts at Miami Dade College.

EARLY CAREER
In addition to performing music, Isaac began to establish himself as a stage actor. He appeared in various plays in southern Florida and secured his first film role, a small part in the 1998 independent crime drama *Illtown*. During a trip to New York City to perform in a play there, he began to consider studying performing arts at the prestigious Juilliard School; he ultimately decided to enroll in the institution. While attending, he appeared in the film *All about the Benjamins* (2002), before graduating in 2005. Following his time at Juilliard, he continued to work as a stage actor, notably starring in Shakespeare in the Park productions of *Two Gentlemen of Verona* and *Romeo and Juliet*.

Isaac also did not begin seriously pursuing work in film until after completing his degree. His first major role during that period was that of the biblical Joseph in the 2006 film *The Nativity Story*. He went on to appear in films such as the 2008 biopic *Che: Part One* and the 2010 adventure film *Robin Hood*. The year 2011 saw a significant increase in his profile as an actor, as he played supporting roles in the action film *Sucker Punch* and the critically acclaimed crime drama *Drive*. He was initially reluctant to take the role in the latter film, as he considered the character of Standard, as portrayed in the original script, to be the sort of stereotypical character that he had long sought to avoid. However, after he discussed his concerns with director Nicolas Winding Refn and screenwriter Hossein Amini, the filmmakers reworked the character of Standard to be more nuanced, and Isaac signed on to the film.

INSIDE LLEWYN DAVIS
Although Isaac had gained some critical and popular attention for his work in films such as *Drive*, it was his starring role in 2013's *Inside Llewyn Davis* that proved to be his breakout performance. Written and directed by veteran filmmakers Joel and Ethan Coen, the film was loosely inspired by the life of Dave Van Ronk, a guitarist and singer who lived in New York in the 1960s. Isaac, who plays the titular folk musician, was drawn to the film in large part because of the Coen brothers' involvement.

The Coens, in turn, were drawn to Isaac because of his demonstrated musical ability. Davis sings and plays guitar throughout the film, so the role demanded an actor capable of doing so. To prepare for the role, Isaac studied the style of guitar playing known as Travis picking, taking lessons from Erik Frandsen, a musician and actor who had played with Van Ronk. He also worked extensively with

T Bone Burnett, a veteran musician and the film's executive music producer. The film was ultimately well received by critics, and Isaac was nominated for the Golden Globe for best actor as well as a number of other awards for his performance.

LEADING ROLES

The success of *Inside Llewyn Davis* brought Isaac significant notice and in turn opened up a variety of new opportunities. Having demonstrated his ability to carry a film as a lead actor, he went on to costar in the 2014 drama *A Most Violent Year* alongside Juilliard classmate Jessica Chastain. Set in New York City in 1981, the statistically most violent year in the city's history, the film chronicles a family's attempts to survive and thrive amid widespread unrest.

The following year, Isaac costarred in the science-fiction thriller *Ex Machina* as well as in the television miniseries *Show Me a Hero*. In the miniseries, which aired on HBO beginning in August 2015 and is based on real events, Isaac plays Nick Wasicsko, a city council member and later mayor of Yonkers, New York, who faces issues related to desegregation and public housing in his city during the 1980s. The role of Wasicsko was only Isaac's second television role—the first was a small role in a 2006 episode of *Law and Order: Criminal Intent*—and he found the process of shooting the miniseries to be somewhat more difficult than shooting a film, in large part because of its longer time and condensed shooting schedule. "I remember being in a van, memorizing huge chunks of very dense political dialogue because things had shifted around and we lost a location or it was going to rain," he recalled to Martin. "We shot a six-hour movie in three months." The cast and crew's hard work paid off: *Show Me a Hero* was nominated for several awards, and Isaac won the Golden Globe for best actor in a limited series for his performance.

STAR WARS

Prior to late 2015, Isaac was primarily known for his work in dramas and period pieces. However, that changed for good in December of that year with the premiere of *Star Wars: The Force Awakens*. The long-awaited seventh installment in the Star Wars series, *The Force Awakens* takes place several decades after the events of the original trilogy of films. Isaac plays Poe Dameron, a daring resistance pilot who plays a crucial role in the fight against the villainous First Order. A fan of the Star Wars films since childhood, Isaac was initially unsure whether he was suited for a role in the franchise. "I didn't know if I could make it interesting," he explained to Martin. "I didn't know why me and not anybody else." A meeting with director Abrams, however, convinced him.

The process of filming *Star Wars: The Force Awakens* was in many ways on an entirely different scale than Isaac's previous projects, a fact of which he was acutely aware. "I actually felt the most green and insecure that I had in a long time," he told Martin. Nevertheless, he soon found his place alongside actors Daisy Ridley and John Boyega as one of the franchise's newest heroes. Abrams was impressed by Isaac's performance. He told Martin, "Oscar's concerns about making the character feel alive and authentic is the exact reason he's a great actor. . . . And he gave the role a nuance that I think made it one of the strongest in the movie." Isaac even made an unexpected mark on the franchise when he suggested that his character could have been born on the moon Yavin 4, a location that appeared in 1977's *Star Wars: A New Hope* in scenes filmed in Guatemala. This detail was later incorporated into the character's official history through tie-in media.

Although little is known about the eighth installment in the Star Wars series, scheduled for release in December 2017, Isaac has confirmed that he will reprise the role of Poe in that film. In addition to the Star Wars films, he appears as the villainous Apocalypse in the comic-book adaptation *X-Men: Apocalypse* (2016) and is set to costar in the historical drama *The Promise* (2016) alongside veteran actor Christian Bale. He has likewise remained active in the theater and is scheduled to star in an Off-Broadway production of *Hamlet* in the summer of 2017. As for the types of roles he looks for, his philosophy has not changed, as he explained to Claire Black for the *Scotsman* (24 Jan. 2015): "I'm drawn to characters who don't show all their cards right off the bat. It takes time to understand who they are and where they're coming from."

PERSONAL LIFE

When not filming, Isaac lives in Brooklyn, New York. He continues to play music, occasionally for an audience. One of his prized possessions is the 1924 Gibson guitar he played in *Inside Llewyn Davis*, which the filmmakers gave him after the end of filming. "I had to figure out if it was going to be a museum piece," he told Paulette Cohn for *Paste* (30 Aug. 2015). "But, no, I take it on tour. I play it in coffee shops. It is meant to be played, so I play it all the time."

SUGGESTED READING

Black, Claire. "Actor Oscar Isaac on Why He Prizes Anonymity." *Scotsman*. Johnston, 24 Jan. 2015. Web. 11 Apr. 2016.

Hernández, Mike. "Before *Star Wars: The Force Awakens*, Actor Oscar Isaac Was Just a Miami Kid." *Miami New Times*. Miami New Times, 15 Dec. 2015. Web. 11 Apr. 2016.

Isaac, Oscar. "Oscar Isaac Interview for *Inside Llewyn Davis*: 'I Had No Interest in Going off the Rails.'" Interview by Bernadette McNulty. *Telegraph*. Telegraph Media Group, 6 Jan. 2014. Web. 11 Apr. 2016.

Martin, Brett. "Oscar Isaac Talks *Star Wars: The Force Awakens*." *GQ*. Condé Nast, 15 Dec. 2015. Web. 11 Apr. 2016.

SELECTED WORKS
Robin Hood, 2010; *Sucker Punch*, 2011; *Drive*, 2011; *Inside Llewyn Davis*, 2013; *A Most Violent Year*, 2014; *Ex Machina*, 2015; *Show Me a Hero*, 2015; *Star Wars: The Force Awakens*, 2015; *X-Men: Apocalypse*, 2016

—Joy Crelin

Vijay Iyer

Born: October 26, 1971
Occupation: Musician

Ben Gabbe/Getty Images

Of all the paths Vijay Iyer could have taken in life, becoming a jazz pianist and composer is perhaps one of the more surprising ones. Iyer spent his childhood and adolescence playing classical violin, not piano, and his undergraduate and graduate-level studies were in mathematics and physics rather than music. For Iyer, however, his background in math and science has been key to his understanding of the intersections between music and cognition, the subject of his doctoral research. His journey as a self-taught pianist has been similarly formative, significantly influencing his development as a creative, innovative musician and composer.

Perhaps most of all, however, Iyer's varied background provided the foundation for his career as a musician who largely disregards the boundaries of genres and musical traditions. Although his music is typically categorized as jazz, some of his work also incorporates elements from genres such as hip-hop and classical Indian music. "All the choices I make as an artist are inspired by the history of this music and this musical community that I'm a part of," he explained to Visi Tilak for the India Ink blog of the *New York Times* (31 Oct. 2013). "It's always been a space for collaboration and creation that is irrespective of marketplace notions of genre." It seems clear that Iyer's musical experimentation has paid off; a critically acclaimed artist, Iyer has been nominated for numerous awards, including a Grammy, and in 2013 he was awarded the prestigious MacArthur Fellowship, or genius grant.

EARLY LIFE AND EDUCATION
Vijay Iyer was born Vijay Raghunathan on October 26, 1971, in Albany, New York. The last name Iyer is a clan name used by some members of his extended family; Iyer began using it himself in the early 1990s. His parents, Raghu and Sita, immigrated to the United States from India in the 1960s so that Raghu could pursue a doctorate in pharmacology. The family moved to Rochester, New York, when Iyer was a toddler and later settled in the suburb of Fairport, where he and his older sister, Pratima, grew up.

Music played an important role in the Raghunathan household: Pratima studied piano, and Iyer began violin lessons at the age of three. Introduced to piano through his sister, he began to teach himself to play that instrument as well. In high school, Iyer continued to study violin and also joined the school jazz band, in which he initially played the vibraphone, a percussion instrument. During this time he discovered the work of self-taught jazz musician Thelonious Monk. "When I heard Thelonious Monk, it was a revelation," he told Nate Chinen for *JazzTimes* (June 2005). "Something about it just seemed so close to home for me—maybe partially as a self-taught pianist. Because of the way I was dealing with the piano, it wasn't on any formal terms." Iyer also excelled academically, skipping a year of middle school and graduating from Fairport High School at the age of sixteen.

Although Iyer enjoyed playing music, he was initially unsure of his career path. "I was still figuring things out," he explained to Alec Wilkinson for the *New Yorker* (1 Feb. 2016). "I didn't know that I would, or even could, be a musician." He enrolled in Yale University to study mathematics and physics, earning his bachelor's degree from the college in 1992. At Yale he began to play piano in the school dining hall for fun and also experimented with writing music. After graduating he moved to California to attend the University of California, Berkeley, from which he earned a master's degree in physics in 1994. Four years later he earned his PhD from the institution, having designed an interdisciplinary program focusing on the intersections of music and cognitive science under the guidance of Professor David Wessel, then head of the university's Center for New Music and Audio Technologies. Iyer's thesis was titled "Microstructures of Feel, Macrostructures of Sound: Embodied Cognition in West African and African American Musics."

EARLY CAREER

While at Berkeley, Iyer began playing keyboard as part of the house band at an Oakland club called the Bird Kage. He later met bandleader and saxophonist Steve Coleman, who asked him to travel to Europe as part of his band. After taking Coleman up on his offer, Iyer traveled to Paris with the band in 1995. The experience was a daunting yet educational one for him. "These are some of the best musicians in the world, I thought, so I better step up. It's not a hobby anymore," he told Wilkinson. "I was in way over my head, and I felt like I was always messing up—I think I had something like impostor syndrome. But seeing what [Coleman] worked on, how he worked on it, the scope of his knowledge was a tremendous education for me."

Iyer also began recording albums while at Berkeley. His first, *Memorophilia*, was released in 1995 and featured contributions by a number of fellow musicians, including Coleman. He followed that album with *Architextures* (1998), a similarly collaborative record that featured traditional Indian elements as well as Iyer's many jazz influences. Iyer moved to New York City in 1999 and has noted in interviews that this move brought about a musical shift for him in addition to a geographical one; albums released after *Architextures* have been identified as quite different from Iyer's first two releases.

For Iyer, the process of making music has been a highly collaborative one. Although he released several albums solely under his own name in the ensuing years—among them *Memorophilia* and *Architextures* as well as *Panoptic Modes* (2001), *Reimagining* (2005), and *Tragicomic* (2008), the term solo album feels like a misnomer when applied to his work. Iyer's albums occasionally include solo piano pieces, but in many cases, the pianist is accompanied by a host of other musicians. His frequent collaborators on his records include saxophonist Rudresh

Mahanthappa, drummer Marcus Gilmore, and bassist Stephan Crump.

At the same time, Iyer recorded two albums with experimental hip-hop and spoken-word artist Mike Ladd: *In What Language?* (2003) and *Still Life with Commentator* (2007). Both works are politically and socially conscious.

THE VIJAY IYER TRIO AND FURTHER CRITICAL ACCLAIM

Perhaps the most critically acclaimed and popular of Iyer's albums have been those recorded by the Vijay Iyer Trio. This musical trio includes bassist Crump and drummer Gilmore, who appear on several of Iyer's other albums. On the Vijay Iyer Trio's recordings, the three musicians have equal billing, and bass and drums are prominent. The group's first album, *Historicity*, was released in 2009 to significant critical acclaim and earned a nomination for the Grammy Award for best jazz instrumental album. With that nomination, Iyer became the first artist of Indian descent to have a work nominated in that category.

While Iyer continued to work on albums released under his own name, including his first true solo effort, *Solo*, in 2010, he also strove to work with other artists who would enable him to incorporate diverse musical influences into his work, mingling jazz with elements of other genres. For the 2011 album *Tirtha*, he collaborated with musicians Prasanna and Nitin Mitta—who play the guitar and the tabla, respectively—to play music that merges modern jazz with multiple genres of classical Indian music. For Iyer, however, their musical endeavors are about far more than the mingling of genres. "I've been trying to learn about aspects of Carnatic and Hindustani music for twenty years," he told Tilak. "Not to become a practitioner of it but to just learn about it so I can work with it, work with the elements in it, and so that I can collaborate with Indian musicians. . . . The fact is that all three of us, in the Tirtha group, are kind of cosmopolitan global citizens. It's really more about that than it is about someone mixing jazz with Indian music."

The Vijay Iyer Trio eventually followed *Historicity* with the album *Accelerando* in 2012. The next year, Iyer recorded his third collection with Ladd, one that he has claimed to be most valuable to him, titled *Holding It Down: The Veterans' Dreams Project*; this work has a social and political nature similar to the duo's earlier collaborations by exploring the experiences of veterans of the Afghanistan and Iraq wars. "Art can heal, and we can be a part of a larger conversation," Iyer told Jeff Spevak for the *Democrat & Chronicle* (19 June 2014) of his collaborations with Ladd. "We can put ourselves in the middle of it."

Iyer has received significant recognition for his work, both within and outside of the jazz community. In 2013 he was awarded the prestigious MacArthur Fellowship, sometimes known as the genius grant, from the John D. and Catherine T. MacArthur Foundation. To further showcase his diverse approach, he also accepted an offer to sign with the German label ECM Records.

TEACHING AND COMPOSING

In addition to performing and recording music, Iyer has taught at a number of colleges and universities, including the New School and New York University. In 2014, along with the release of his first ECM album *Mutations*, he became the first individual to hold the title of Franklin D. and Florence Rosenblatt Professor of the Arts at Harvard University. "I'm very excited because in a lot of ways this is a new step," he told Peter Reuell for the *Harvard Gazette* (25 Sept. 2013) upon the announcement of his appointment prior to his first semester at the university. "It's not that I'm a stranger to academia. But I've spent the last fifteen years mostly outside of it. . . . When I arrive at Harvard, I look forward to wading in deeper—mentoring student composer-performers, illuminating new currents in American music, and convening conversations with some of the stellar thinkers on campus. And I especially look forward to connecting all of what we do to the world beyond the university, because a life in the arts means a life of service to those around us." As a professor in Harvard's Department of Music, Iyer works with individual students and ensembles and teaches seminars.

In early 2015 Iyer took on the yearlong position of artist in residence at the Metropolitan Museum of Art in New York, where he staged a number of performances over the course of the year. That same year, the Vijay Iyer Trio released *Break Stuff* (2015), which received positive attention from critics as well as fans of Iyer's work.

In addition to performing music himself, Iyer works as a composer, creating pieces for a variety of other performers. His compositions have been premiered by various musical groups, including the Silk Road Ensemble, the International Contemporary Ensemble, and the Brentano String Quartet.

PERSONAL LIFE

Iyer married computational biologist Christina Leslie in 1999. They have a daughter and live in New York. During the school year, Iyer spends a few days each week in Cambridge, Massachusetts, while teaching at Harvard.

SUGGESTED READING

Chinen, Nate. "Vijay Iyer: Othering." *JazzTimes*. JazzTimes, June 2005. Web. 16 Feb. 2016.

Iyer, Vijay. "A Conversation with: Jazz Pianist Vijay Iyer." Interview by Visi Tilak. *India Ink*. New York Times, 31 Oct. 2013. Web. 16 Feb. 2016.

Iyer, Vijay. "An Interview with MacArthur 'Genius,' Jazz Pianist, and Composer Vijay Iyer." Interview by Peter Margasak. *Reader*. Sun-Times, 21 Oct. 2014. Web. 16 Feb. 2016.

Reuell, Peter. "A Professorship and a MacArthur." *Harvard Gazette*. Harvard U, 25 Sept. 2013. Web. 16 Feb. 2016.

Spevak, Jeff. "Fairport's Vijay Iyer Coming Home for Jazz Fest." *Democrat & Chronicle*. USA Today Network, 19 June 2014. Web. 16 Feb. 2016.

Wilkinson, Alec. "Time Is a Ghost: Vijay Iyer's Jazz Vision." *New Yorker*. Condè Nast, 1 Feb. 2016. Web. 16 Feb. 2016.

SELECTED WORKS

Memorophilia, 1995; *Architextures*, 1998; *Panoptic Modes*, 2001; *In What Language?*, 2003; *Historicity*, 2009; *Solo*, 2010; *Tirtha*, 2011; *Holding It Down: The Veterans' Dreams Project*, 2013; *Mutations*, 2014; *Break Stuff*, 2015

—*Joy Crelin*

Chris Jackson

Born: ca. 1971
Occupation: Editor and publisher

Since 2006, Chris Jackson has been the vice president of Spiegel and Grau, an imprint of Random House, and he has edited and published several critically acclaimed and best-selling books on race, including Ta-Nehisi Coates's *Between the World and Me*, which won the 2015 National Book Award for nonfiction, and Bryan Stevenson's *Just Mercy: A Story of Justice and Redemption*, which won the 2015 Carnegie Medal for nonfiction. "To the extent that twenty-first-century literary audiences have been introduced to the realities and absurdities born of the phenomenon of race in America, Jackson has done a disproportionate amount of that introducing," Vinson Cunningham wrote for the *New York Times Magazine* (2 Feb. 2016). Cunningham explained that "Jackson has ushered into being the works of category-defying novelists like Victor LaValle and Mat Johnson, polemicist-experientialists like Coates and the civil rights attorney Bryan Stevenson and pop-cultural vanguardists like the chef-memoirist Eddie Huang and the rapper-entrepreneur Jay Z."

In a laudatory piece for *Ebony* (14 Apr. 2016), Adrienne Samuels Gibbs explained why Jackson has attained such stunning success in the publishing world, whose upper ranks are overwhelmingly populated with white editors and executives. "Jackson is a rare bird because of his background and understanding of how to take Black stories and turn them into something that the entire market should—and could—appreciate," she wrote. "Literary folk know that Jackson knows how to pick 'em. From Edwidge Danticat to Aaron McGruder to Victor LaValle, the editor has an eye for great stories and how said stories will be accepted by the larger book-buying population."

Jackson has been open about the racism that he has faced in the publishing industry. It has come in forms both subtle and overt and both personal and institutional. He has been asked to fetch coffee for lower-level colleagues, fielded assertions that the sales figures of books about rappers are inflated by counting shoplifted books, and been forced to ask white staffers to stop mimicking black vernacular in an offensive manner. "It fuels your desire to not just do good work, but to beat them in a way that changes the game, that uproots some of that stupidity and blindness," he told Cunningham. "What unites this generation of black writing [is a desire] not just to be accepted or included or even to define our work in opposition to the mainstream, but to go our own way with some kind of integrity, rigor, and honesty. And to win."

EARLY LIFE

Jackson, one of three siblings, grew up in the New York City neighborhood of Harlem during the 1970s and 1980s. When he was little, his family lived in the Grant Houses, a public housing project. Even after they had moved into a privately owned tenement building, the setting remained dangerously crime-ridden. "Our downstairs neighbor was murdered, a shooting happened right around the corner while my sister was coming home from school, and another neighbor turned his apartment into a crack den," Jackson recalled to Cunningham.

Jackson was four years old when his father died, leaving his mother to raise Jackson and his siblings alone. A devout Jehovah's Witness, she leaned heavily on her faith as a single mother. Jackson had a more complicated relationship with the church—leaving it in his early teens and then returning at his mother's request when she was fighting cancer. (She died when he was just eighteen.) He renounced the religion permanently when he was in his twenties, precipitating a deep rift with his siblings.

He became, as he described it to Cunningham, a "depressed orphan who lost his family to a crazy religion and consoled himself almost exclusively with books." As a result, Jackson did not feel fully at home in his own predominantly black neighborhood—nor did he feel particularly at ease at the predominantly white Hunter College High School, an elite institution on the Upper East Side. Despite having won admission by passing the school's famously rigorous entrance exam, Jackson often felt that his classmates and teachers held him in low esteem and believed that he did not belong in that rarified setting.

One experience in high school, however, set him on the path to his current career: an internship at James Charlton Associates, a book packager. (Packagers hire writers, edit their text, and design the books before sending them to a publisher to market and sell—essentially acting as a middleman and expediting the process of book production.)

EDUCATION AND EARLY CAREER

After graduating from Hunter, Jackson entered Columbia University, an Ivy League institution in Upper Manhattan, but he has not discussed his time there at any length with interviewers. He has discussed in great detail, however, the lifeline he found in literature as a young person. In a guest essay for the *Atlantic* (14 Jan. 2011), he described himself as "a Harlem kid whose life had been transformed by black books and who believed in their power with an evangelist's zeal."

Among Jackson's first jobs in the publishing industry was a stint at Paragon House. He then took a job as an editorial assistant at John Wiley and Sons, where he was assigned to a department focused on science, health, and self-help books. Although those areas of focus were not of great interest to him, he took every opportunity to learn and network. He was active in PEN—a national organization of writers, editors, translators, agents, and other publishing figures—and one of its subcommittees called the Open Book Committee, which was devoted to helping young industry professionals of color connect with older mentors. Through the group he met legendary agent Marie Brown; editor Janet Hill, who later founded the Harlem Moon imprint at Doubleday; literary agent and editor Manie Barron; and others. "None of these people defined themselves solely as publishing professionals. They all believed that they were engaged in literary activism that transcended their job titles," he wrote in his essay for the *Atlantic*. "They were on a mission."

During the early 1990s, the book industry was making an attempt to diversify, fueled in part by the popularity of black authors such as Toni Morrison, Alice Walker, Terry McMillan, and E. Lynn Harris. Some major publishers created new imprints (such as Hill's Harlem Moon) specifically to appeal to black audiences and actively sought out new black authors.

STEP INTO A WORLD

Advancing through the ranks at Wiley, Jackson acquired an anthology compiled by hip-hop journalist and activist Kevin Powell. *Step into a World: A Global Anthology of the New Black Literature*, published in 2000, contained essays, fiction, poetry, criticism, and journalism from more than one hundred young writers of color, including Malcolm Gladwell, Junot Díaz, Edwidge Danticat, and Victor D. LaValle. In a review for the *Houston Chronicle* (17 Dec. 2000), Joshunda Saunders opined, "*Step into a World* is the most important collection of post-civil-rights-movement, post-colonial writing since *The New Negro*," referencing the famous 1925 anthology edited by Alain Locke that captured the early creative output of the Harlem Renaissance movement.

In his lengthy profile of Jackson, Cunningham also mentioned *The New Negro*, which included a piece by Jessie Fauset, who served for almost a decade as the literary editor of the National Association for the Advancement of Colored People's magazine the *Crisis* and who has been credited with fostering the Harlem Renaissance movement. "Fauset corresponded widely with Renaissance figures, and her letters reveal a deft, coaxing way with writers. She folds criticism seamlessly into flattery, identifying the writer's most consequential gift and encouraging its cultivation," Cunningham explained. "Jackson fills a similarly multifaceted role today—gatekeeper, encourager, cool-but-kind appraiser of talent—and might be the first twenty-first-century example of a twentieth-century type: the black editor as not only acquirer, tweaker, and disseminator but also as movement-shaper." The year of the anthology's publication, Jackson made a move to Crown Publishing, where he was charged with expanding the imprint's African American publishing program.

SPIEGEL AND GRAU

In 2006 he was hired as an executive editor at Spiegel and Grau, a newly created Random House imprint whose mission was to publish thought-provoking but entertaining works. There, Jackson acquired and edited such books as Bryan Stevenson's *Just Mercy* (2014), a memoir about the unfairness of the US criminal justice system, and Jill Leovy's critically acclaimed *Ghettoside: A True Story of Murder in America* (2015), which examines why the homicide rate is so disproportionately high for black men.

Many of his releases had a measurable societal impact. Discussing *Decoded*, a 2011 volume in which the rapper Jay Z gives a close reading of his lyrics, for example, Cunningham asserted that the volume had been partially responsible for prompting the venture capital firm Andreessen Horowitz to invest in the website Rap Genius, which analyzes the cultural references and word play in rap lyrics. "Jackson's role, then, is to perform nothing less than a kind of magic," Cunningham wrote. "He stands between the largely white culture-making machinery and artists writing from the margins of society, as well as between the work of those writers and the largely white critical apparatus that dictates their success, in both cases saying: This, believe it or not, is something you need to hear."

Perhaps no other Spiegel and Grau release made a bigger splash on the literary scene than Ta-Nehisi Coates's 2015 volume, *Between the World and Me*.

WORKING WITH TA-NEHISI COATES

Jackson and Coates had met when Coates was working at the *Village Voice*, a New York City–based alternative paper, and was trying to find a publisher for a book about the history of hip-hop he hoped to write. Although Jackson rejected that proposal, the two remained in touch, and one day, when Coates was chatting about his relationship with his father, Jackson recognized the germ of an idea for a book. The result was Coates's debut memoir, *The Beautiful Struggle: A Father, Two Sons, and an Unlikely Road to Manhood*, which Spiegel and Grau published in 2008 to great acclaim.

The attention paid to Coates's debut was dwarfed, however, by that given to his 2015 memoir, *Between the World and Me*. Written in the form of a letter to his adolescent son, the slim volume addresses what it is like to live in the United States as a black man and how best to free oneself from the burdens of history. The book spent months atop the *New York Times* Best Seller List and earned the National Book Award. Although the notoriously conservative white columnist David Brooks disagreed with many of Coates's assertions in his review of the book for the *New York Times* (17 July 2015), he nevertheless called it "a mind-altering account of the black male experience. Every conscientious American should read it." Coates has been effusive in crediting Jackson for his help and input. "I know that it's my name on the book," he admitted to Cunningham. "But I could not have written that book alone. Somebody had to pull it out of me."

Following the release of *Between the World and Me*, Random House announced that it would be revitalizing its One World imprint, which had originally been launched in 1991 with the aim of promoting multicultural literature. Jackson was named the vice president, publisher, and editor-in-chief of the imprint. "In recent months, we've watched with awe as Chris has had a run of books that have been acutely, urgently, brilliantly of our time," publisher Julie Grau wrote in a memo announcing his promotion, as quoted by Andrew Albanese for *Publishers Weekly* (4 Dec. 2015). One World will release its first books following the imprint's relaunch in the fall of 2017.

PERSONAL LIFE

In 2004 Jackson married Sarah McNally, a former editor at Basic Books whose family own a chain of independent bookstores called McNally Robinson in Canada. Shortly after their wedding, she opened a McNally Robinson bookstore on Prince Street in Manhattan, where it quickly became a beloved local institution. In 2008 the couple had a son and rechristened the store McNally Jackson Books in his honor. They later divorced.

SUGGESTED READING

Albanese, Andrew. "PW Notables of the Year: Chris Jackson." *Publishers Weekly*. PWxyz, 4 Dec. 2015. Web. 30 June 2016.

Cunningham, Vinson. "How Chris Jackson Is Building a Black Literary Movement." *New York Times Magazine*. New York Times, 2 Feb. 2016. Web. 30 June 2016.

Gibbs, Adrienne Samuels. "Clap for Him! Chris Jackson Lands New Role at Random House Imprint." *Ebony*. Johnson, 14 Apr. 2016. Web. 30 June 2016.

Hoffman, Jan. "Her Life Is a Real Page-Turner." *New York Times*. New York Times, 12 Oct. 2011. Web. 30 June 2016.

Jackson, Chris. "R.I.P. Manie Barron." *Atlantic*. Atlantic Media Group, 14 Jan. 2011. Web. 30 June 2016.

Laymon, Kiese, Rachel Kaadzi Ghansah, Harmony Holiday, and Chris Jackson. Interview by Manjula Martin. "Publishing while Black." *Scratch Magazine*. Toast, 28 Oct. 2014. Web. 30 June 2016.

Pride, Felicia. "Chris Jackson: Converting the World—One Book at a Time." *Publishers Weekly*. PWxyz, 16 June 2008. Web. 30 June 2016.

—*Mari Rich*

Abbi Jacobson

Born: February 1, 1984
Occupation: Comedian

Abbi Jacobson, along with her friend and writing partner Ilana Glazer, is the star, writer, and creator of one of the funniest and boldest shows on television, *Broad City* on Comedy Central. The show is about two young women in their twenties who are exaggerated versions of Jacobson and Glazer. With a combination of absurd physical comedy and thoughtful explorations of identity, the show delves into race, gender,

iDominick/CC BY-SA 2.0/Wikimedia Commons

sexuality, and other issues, all without being heavy-handed.

Broad City premiered on Comedy Central in 2014, with substantial help from executive producer Amy Poehler, who is best known for her acting work on *Saturday Night Live* and *Parks and Recreation*. In an interview with Nick Paumgarten for the *New Yorker* (23 June 2014), Poehler said, "The rule is: Specific voices are funny, and chemistry can't be faked. There's something about them [Jacobson and Glazer] that's really watchable and organic and interesting. There aren't enough like them on TV: confident, sexually active, self-effacing women, girlfriends who love each other the most."

EARLY LIFE AND EDUCATION

Abbi Jacobson was born in 1984. She grew up in Wayne, Pennsylvania, just outside of Philadelphia. Her father, Alan Jacobson, worked as a graphic designer. Her mother, Susan, worked as an artist, focusing on found objects. She has a brother and a sister. Her parents divorced when she was thirteen years old. According to Paumgarten, while Jacobson was in eighth grade at Valley Forge Middle School, she would, as her homeroom's representative during student council meetings, read the official minutes of the meetings as Linda Richman, the flamboyant Jewish lady character played by Mike Myers on the comedy sketch series *Saturday Night Live*. That would get a big laugh from her fellow students. "That was my first taste," Jacobson told Paumgarten. "I thought, 'Maybe I'm a comedian.'"

Jacobson went on to attend Conestoga High School. During that time she dabbled in acting at a local theater, and even auditioned for several musicals at her high school. However, she could not sing well, so she rarely got any major roles. During her junior year in high school, she did land a role as one of the hosts of a cabaret, which gave her another opportunity to perform in front of an audience. But acting, although enjoyable, was not her dream. She wanted to pursue visual arts.

After graduating from high school in 2002, Jacobson attended the Maryland Institute College of Art (MICA), in Baltimore, where she majored in general fine arts and minored in video. Although she continued to pursue drawing, painting, and design, her interest in film, acting, and screenwriting continued to grow. In fact, her interest in becoming an actor took her out of MICA when she transferred to Emerson College in Boston, Massachusetts. However, she did not like Emerson College and transferred back to MICA after only a single semester in Boston. Jacobson graduated from MICA in 2006, after which she moved to New York City.

UCB

When Jacobson arrived in New York City, she was very serious about becoming an actor, so she enrolled at the Atlantic Theater Company, a rigorous and respected training ground for actors, but she did not last more than a week. She wanted more freedom and did not want to follow the school's technique. She simply wanted to experience more joy and fun in acting. Her roommate at the time told her about the Upright Citizens Brigade—fully called the Upright Citizens Brigade Theatre and Improvisational and Sketch Comedy Training Center and commonly referred to as UCB. It was founded by comedians Matt Besser, Amy Poehler, Ian Roberts, and Matt Walsh. (Poehler would go on to play a crucial role in Jacobson's career.) Beginner classes in improvisation or sketch writing at UCB were, and still are, open to anyone, regardless of whether they have ever acted, improvised, or written comedy skits before. Jacobson instantly loved UCB. It was just what she was looking for. Those improv and sketch comedy classes also led Jacobson to meet many funny, like-minded people. With some of those people she formed improv comedy groups, and that is where she met Ilana Glazer, who would become her writing and acting partner for what would turn out to be a popular Web series titled *Broad City*.

Abbi Jacobson and Ilana Glazer developed an especially close friendship, and they decided to use that friendship as the foundation of a Web series, which they started to write together in late 2009. "They pulled ideas from their own lives," wrote Paumgarten, "from their diaries, their phones, and their everyday experiences getting battered around by the city: the indignities of aborted booty calls, crowded office bathrooms, birthday brunches, and laundry-sex breakups." They used not only their experiences but those of their friends. The characters they played, also named Abbi and Ilana, found themselves in various absurd, uncomfortable, fun, and weird situations all over New York City.

ONLINE SUCCESS

Jacobson and Glazer made a total of thirty-three episodes, each a few minutes long, a common length for a comedy skit. Provocatively titled *Broad City*—"broad" is an outdated and sexist way to refer to a woman—the show explored gender, race, sexuality, dating, and various high and low points of urban life. *Broad City* began to get more and more viewers and soon became a cult hit. Then it began to get coverage on late-night comedy shows as well as in mainstream publications such as the *Wall Street Journal* and the *New York Times*. Writing for the *Wall Street Journal* (14 Feb. 2011), Megan Angelo praised the series for its "sneak-attack feminism."

Through a teacher at Upright Citizens Brigade, Jacobson and Glazer got in touch with Amy Poehler, who by this point had found fame as a former cast member of *Saturday Night Live* and the star of the comedy series *Parks and Recreation*. Jacobson and Glazer asked Poehler to appear on the last Web episode of *Broad City*. Already a fan of the Web series, Poehler agreed. Later they asked her if she would consider being the show's executive producer and helping them pitch it to television networks. Again Poehler agreed. After the FX television network passed on the show, Poehler took it to Comedy Central. Brooke Posch, the development executive who gave the show the green light, told Paumgarten that upon meeting Jacobson and Glazer, "the chemistry was sitting there right in front of me."

BROAD CITY

Broad City premiered on Comedy Central in 2014. Jacobson and Glazer hired four other writers for the show, but they essentially called all the shots. They not only wrote the series, they also had a say in how the series was shot and edited. Like in the Web series, they played characters also named Abbi and Ilana, and they, like in real life, were close friends. The chemistry between the two seemed to almost come off the screen, it was that palpable. But it was not a documentary in any sense of the term. The show exaggerated their personalities and occasionally had surreal elements—at times because of Abbi and Ilana's continuous marijuana smoking on the show. (Although they are avid marijuana enthusiasts in real life, they have both stated repeatedly that during the making of the series they are completely sober—otherwise, they say, they would not be able to do it.) Both characters—like Jacobson and Glazer in real life—are also Jewish, of the secular, liberal New York City variety. That fact is in one way or another revisited throughout the series, starting in the very first episode: Ilana, in an attempt to raise money so she and Abbi can go see rapper Lil Wayne in concert, decides to place the following ad on Craigslist: "We're 2 Jewesses trying to make a buck."

The show was critically acclaimed from the start. The television critic Emily Nussbaum for the *New Yorker* (10 Feb. 2014), placing *Broad City* in the context of such TV shows as *Girls*, *30 Rock*, and *Inside Amy Schumer*, called the show a "tiny, oddball series on Comedy Central with its own dank flavor of stoner surrealism." She observed that "for a new sitcom, it's also unusually confident, and appealingly detached from the boring constraints of realism." She noted that the show must be somewhat influenced by the FX comedy series *Louie*, created by and starring the comedian Louis C.K. Undeniably, one of the most compelling aspects of the show is the deep friendship between Abbi and Ilana. As Megan Garber wrote in an article for the *Atlantic* (17 Feb. 2016), the show does not "simply portray" or even "simply celebrate" their friendship. It actually explores their friendship as "life partners," not as though they are placeholders for a future romantic partner, but like they *are* that partner—only in a platonic way. "Abbi and Ilana spend most of their free time together," wrote Garber. "They are dedicated to each other, wholly. They love each other, passionately—often illogically."

When *Broad City* began its third season, Emily Nussbaum again reviewed the show for the *New Yorker* (7 Mar. 2016). The show had by that point become part of the popular culture discussion about women, sexuality, race, gender, and identity. In her review Nussbaum touched on two crucial aspects of the show. One, what she called the "genius slapstick," the show's "elaborate sequences of physical comedy." The second aspect of the show Nussbaum delved into was more complicated: "Jacobson and Glazer's take on identity politics—and their characters' well-intentioned but barely informed fourth-wave, queerish, anti-rape/pro-porn intersectional feminism—is a more intricate matter, both a part of the show's philosophy and a subject of its satire."

But part of the complex, smart humor of the show is how Jacobson and Glazer combine exaggerated physical comedy with ideas of fourth-wave feminism, in which personal identities are not only complicated but fluid. One example is the second episode of the third season, in which Abbi has to impersonate Ilana so that Ilana will not get in trouble at her food co-op. Nussbaum complimented the "sheer anarchic strangeness

of Jacobson's performance, as she masturbates an eggplant and falls backward into a display of bulk beans, mid-twerk." Comedy Central renewed the series for two more seasons in 2016.

OTHER PROJECTS

Jacobson has also appeared on other TV shows, such as *Inside Amy Schumer* (2015), and she voiced a character on the third season of the Netflix original animated series *BoJack Horseman* (2016). She will also costar in the film *Human People*. In addition to her film and television work, Jacobson has published two coloring books for adults, *Color This Book: New York City* (2013) and *Color This Book: San Francisco* (2013), and an illustrated book called *Carry This Book* (2016) that imagines what various celebrities and fictional characters might carry in their bags. Jacobson lives in New York City.

SUGGESTED READING

Garber, Megan. "*Broad City* and the Triumph of the Platonic Rom-Com." *Atlantic*. Atlantic Monthly Group, 17 Feb. 2016. Web. 15 Aug. 2016.

Nussbaum, Emily. "Laverne and Curly." *New Yorker*. Condé Nast, 7 Mar. 2016. Web. 15 Aug. 2016.

Paumgarten, Nick. "Id Girls." *New Yorker*. Condé Nast, 23 June 2014. Web. 15 Aug. 2016.

SELECTED WORKS

Broad City, 2014– ; *Inside Amy Schumer*, 2015; *BoJack Horseman*, 2016

—*Dmitry Kiper*

Marlon James

Born: November 24, 1970
Occupation: Author

Marlon James is the 2015 winner of the United Kingdom's most prestigious literary award, the Man Booker Prize, which was first awarded in 1969 and has recently been opened to any novel written in English and published in Great Britain. James won for his searing epic novel, *A Brief History of Seven Killings* (2014), which uses the real-life attempted assassination of legendary reggae singer Bob Marley as a jumping-off point to explore Jamaica's violent past. In an interview with Arun Rath for National Public Radio (NPR) (5 Oct. 2014), James described how he perceived his generation of Jamaican authors, which is the generation after the so-called "postcolonial" generation of Caribbean authors such as V. S. Naipaul and Derek Walcott: "Post-post-

Eamonn M. McCormack/Stringer/GettyImages

colonial . . . [is a] newish generation of writers where we're not driven by our dialogue with the former mother country [the United Kingdom]. The hovering power for us when growing up in the '70s and '80s was not the UK. It was the States. It was America. And it wasn't an imperialistic power. It was just a cultural influence. . . . For us, for example, identity is not necessarily how to define ourselves in the relation of colonial power—colonial oppressor. So now it's a matter of defining who you are, as opposed to who you are not."

EARLY LIFE

Marlon James was born in Kingston, Jamaica, on November 24, 1970, one of eight children in his family. During his childhood, Jamaica was facing rising internal tensions in the postcolonial period, as violence and gang warfare ensnared the island nation and the capital of Kingston in particular. (Jamaica had received its independence from the United Kingdom in 1962.) As crime spiraled out of control and the economic situations worsened, many Jamaicans fled their country to live in the United States—a policy that was encouraged by the ruling government, which was looked on by many as unable to handle the numerous crises facing the nation.

Although Jamaica struggled, James was insulated from the worst of the violence and had a middle-class upbringing. His parents were both on the police force at one time; his mother eventually retired as a police detective, while his father left the force in 1973 in favor of a career as a criminal lawyer and later as a judge. James recalled in an interview with Christopher

John Farley for the *Wall Street Journal* (2 Oct. 2014): "They worked in Kingston. We all lived in Portmore. Portmore wasn't as volatile . . . My upbringing was very middle class almost to the point of dull. . . . Sometimes writers overplay their hard background. My background wasn't hard at all. A crisis for me was deciding who I liked better, Starsky or Hutch."

Growing up, James read widely, due to his parents' love of reading. His father was greatly devoted to poetry, particularly the works of William Shakespeare and the Romantics, whereas his mother enjoyed literature like the short stories of O. Henry. His mother also collected the *Reader's Digest* condensed versions of classic novels, which James devoured, not knowing they had been condensed. But James's own personal childhood literary influences were comic books. "A lot of what shaped my literary sensibilities were things like comics: Batman, Superman, X-Men. The sort of cheap pulp fiction," James told Farley. "Comics suggest possibility. That's our magical realism. The idea that storytelling can still be a world of wonder is something I think we got from comics. Even when I describe a scene, the details I pick first, I realize I'm still doing it comic style even though I'm writing it."

EARLY CAREER AND FIRST NOVEL

James studied literature at the University of the West Indies, then went to work in advertising for more than ten years. Because of his generation and his middle-class upbringing, he had no expectations of becoming something as romantic and as financially unstable as a writer. So instead he plugged away in advertising, first as a copywriter, and later as an art director and graphic designer. Yet the idea of writing never left him. He then wrote his first novel, *John Crow's Devil*, which was eventually published in 2005 by Akashic Books, a publisher based in Brooklyn, New York. That first novel, however, did not have an easy road to success. It was rejected more than seventy times. The process so frustrated James that he deleted every copy of the manuscript from every single one of his devices, and he stopped writing altogether for a year. When Kaylie Jones, a writer visiting Jamaica, offered to edit the novel for free, however, he managed to recover the manuscript from his e-mail outbox.

The novel takes place in Jamaica in 1957 and centers on a rivalry between two preachers, Bligh, an alcoholic, and York, the newcomer who curses Bligh as the devil's spawn. Caught between the two are the local villagers, who come to believe that Bligh has brought witchcraft to their homes when the village is overrun by vultures, known in Jamaica as "John Crows." In a review for the *Independent* (27 Oct. 2005), Ian Thompson remarked: "James ratchets up the violence as he heaps on Jamaican local colour.

The prose is wildly overheated ('Promise was a pink ray in the morning sky and a silent twinkle on unopened flowers'). At times, though, it has real vigour and energy. . . . In its lavish cruelty, *John Crow's Devil* encourages the foreign view of Jamaica as a place of exotic oblivion, rum-fuelled assaults and vendetta." The novel was named a New York Times Editor's Choice, and was a finalist for both the Commonwealth Writers Prize and the Los Angeles Times Book Prize.

THE BOOK OF NIGHT WOMEN

Although his debut novel met with success, James still did not consider himself a writer. It was not until he completed work on his second novel, *The Book of Night Women* (2009), that he came to understand that being an author of serious fiction was his life's calling. In his sophomore effort, he returns to Jamaica, this time in the nineteenth century, to a sugar plantation where sadistic abuse of the field slaves was common. The main character is a very young slave woman named Lilith, whose green eyes and dark skin suggest that she is of mixed-race heritage. Lilith is asked to join a group called the Night Women, which is organizing a revolt against their slave owners across the island. Lilith, however, believes herself to be better than her fellow slaves because her father, she is sure, was a white man. She refuses to join the group, certain that she can get more out of life without them. Her vanity and her refusal to accept her subservient place in this brutal society finds her clashing with both her slave masters and fellow slaves.

In the *New York Times Book Review* (26 Feb. 2009), Kaiama L. Glover cheered: "Marlon James's second novel is both beautifully written and devastating. . . . Writing in the spirit of Toni Morrison and Alice Walker but in a style all his own, James has conducted an experiment in how to write the unspeakable—even the unthinkable. And the results of that experiment are an undeniable success." For 2010, the novel went on to win the Dayton Literary Peace Prize and the Minnesota Book Award (Novel & Short Story), and was named as a finalist for the National Book Critics Circle Award.

A BRIEF HISTORY OF SEVEN KILLINGS

A Brief History of Seven Killings, James's ambitious third novel, was published in 2014. It uses the attempted assassination of renowned reggae singer Bob Marley (simply called "The Singer" in the novel) in 1976 to explore various aspects of Jamaican society, from the 1970s to the 1990s, through the stories of seven different murders and in the voices of a number of narrators. When he began writing, James believed he had a simple crime story on his hands, but he soon came to realize that the tale he wanted to relate was far more complicated than that. In order to tell

it, he would use a number of styles and dialects. As he worked and plotted, he kept a chart on his wall of characters' personalities and motivations over the course of the novel. *A Brief History of Seven Killings* met with immediate rave reviews upon its publication. Connie Ogle wrote for the *Miami Herald* (13 Nov. 2015), "*Seven Killings* is a crime novel echoing Roberto [Bolaño's] epic *2666* and William Faulkner's classic *As I Lay Dying*, a remarkable examination of Cold War intrigue and the personal and global cost of nation building."

On October 13, 2015, *A Brief History* was named the winner of the prestigious 2015 Man Booker Prize. Winning the Man Booker Prize has proved a boon to James's literary career, with a significant increase in book sales—and also considerably more media attention. James told Ogle: "What I find is the nonliterary media person will come sniffing around for dirt, but there's no real dirt. It's quite hilarious." In addition to the Man Booker Prize, *A Brief History* won a host of literary awards, including the 2015 Anisfield-Wolf Book Award for Fiction, the 2015 OCM Bocas Prize for Caribbean Literature (Fiction), and the 2015 Green Carnation Prize, and was a 2014 finalist for the National Book Critics Circle Award.

PERSONAL LIFE

James lives in Minneapolis, Minnesota, and has been a professor in the English department at Macalester College in St. Paul since 2007. In 2013 he received the Silver Musgrave Medal from the Institute of Jamaica.

SUGGESTED READING

Alter, Alexandra, and Kimiko De Freytas-Tamura. "Marlon James, Jamaican Novelist, Wins Man Booker Prize." *New York Times*. New York Times, 13 Oct. 2015. Web. 14 Dec. 2015.

Glover, Kaiama L. "Womanchild in the Oppressive Land." Rev. of *The Book of Night Women*, by Marlon James. *New York Times Sunday Book Review*. New York Times, 26 Feb. 2009. Web. 14 Dec. 2015.

James, Marlon. "Writer Marlon James Reimagines a Watershed in Jamaica." Interview by Christopher John Farley. *Wall Street Journal*. Dow Jones, 2 Oct. 2014. Web. 14 Dec. 2015.

Ogle, Connie. "Interview: Marlon James, Author of 'A Brief History of Seven Killings.'" *Miami Herald*. Miami Herald, 13 Nov. 2015. Web. 14 Dec. 2015.

Rath, Arun. "A 'Post-Post-Colonial' Take on the Violent Birth of Modern Jamaica." *NPR.org*. NPR, 5 Oct. 2014. Web. 15 Dec. 2015.

Thomson, Ian. Rev. of *John Crow's Devil*, by Marlon James. *Independent*. Independent. co.uk, 27 Oct. 2005. Web. 14 Dec. 2015.

SELECTED WORKS

John Crow's Devil, 2005; *The Book of Night Women*, 2009; *A Brief History of Seven Killings*, 2014

—*Christopher Mari*

Jamie xx

Born: October 28, 1988
Occupation: British DJ, record producer, and multi-instrumentalist

The British DJ, record producer, and multi-instrumentalist Jamie Smith, better known by his stage name Jamie xx, is widely considered one of the most inventive and respected producers in pop music. He forms the sonic backbone of the critically acclaimed, London-based indie-pop trio the xx, which has been hailed as one of the most forward-thinking bands of the twenty-first century. Since bursting onto the scene in 2009 with their Mercury Prize–winning debut album, *xx*, the band has been known for Smith's minimalist musical production and the intimate boy-girl vocals of Oliver Sim and Romy Madley Croft. Their second album, *Coexist*, was released in 2012.

Concurrently with the xx, Smith launched a solo career as a DJ, producer, and remix artist. Since 2009 he has produced and remixed songs for such artists as Jack Peñate, Florence + the Machine, Adele, Radiohead, Gil Scott-Heron, and Drake. Smith cemented his burgeoning reputation in the music world in 2015 when he released his Mercury Prize– and Grammy Award–nominated debut album *In Colour*. In an interview with Carrie Battan for *Grantland* (13 May 2015), the former BBC Radio 1 DJ Zane Lowe described Smith's music as "tasteful, tough, and heavy at once . . . . He understands the lineage of UK dance music, but he's pushing it forward."

EARLY LIFE

Jamie Smith was born on October 28, 1988, in the London, England, suburb of Putney. He developed a passion for music at an early age while listening to his parents' vinyl record collection of mostly folk, jazz, and soul music. Smith recalled to Philip Sherburne for the music website *Pitchfork* (19 May 2015) that songs by soul legend Otis Redding "would just kill me."

Smith discovered dance music through the influence of two uncles who were both DJs. One lived in New York and played Latin music in bars around the city. The other had his own show on a radio station in Sheffield, England,

kate fisher/Flickr/CC BY 2.0/Wikimedia Commons

that specialized in hip-hop, R&B, and electronic dance music.

When Smith was ten years old, his Sheffield-based uncle gave him a pair of turntables. "I wasn't even aware of what they were for," he admitted to Greg Kot for the *Chicago Tribune* (9 July 2015). "I was just interested in the actual physical objects and being able to play with them in my bedroom." Smith had received piano, saxophone, and drum lessons as a youth, but it was the music from the turntables that captivated him.

As Smith got older, he started amassing a record collection of his own, and as a regular listener of UK pirate radio, he developed a keen interest in electronic dance music and its many subgenres. At fifteen, Smith began work as a DJ at bars around the London borough of Camden, playing his "own brand of electronic and hip-hop music with soul samples," he explained to Kot.

FORMATION OF THE XX

Romy Madley Croft and Oliver Sim had known each other since they were toddlers. They attended the same primary school and both came from music-loving families. Madley Croft taught herself the guitar, Sim learned the bass, and unbeknownst to each other, they each began writing and recording songs separately in their respective bedrooms. In secondary school, the teenagers eventually decided to meld their talents, and in June 2005, they formed a boy-girl duo they named "the xx."

Smith had been best friends with Madley Croft and Sim since age eleven when they met at the Elliot School in southwest Putney, England.

He had initially turned down an opportunity to join their band as a drummer. "I didn't think I was good enough," he explained to John Colapinto for the *New Yorker* (30 June 2014), "and I didn't want to be onstage." As a result, when Madley Croft and Sim began playing small gigs in and around Putney, they would perform their sets to prerecorded drum tracks on a CD. After attending some of their shows, however, Smith agreed to work on drum tracks for them. By then he had begun experimenting with a Music Production Center, or MPC, which Colapinto described as a "combined recorder, sampler, and drum machine."

Smith, Madley Croft, and Sim were eventually joined by another classmate, Baria Qureshi, who came on as a second guitarist and keyboard player. After the quartet graduated from Elliott School, they began writing songs and performing in earnest. By 2007, the xx had caught the attention of Caius Pawson, founder of the British independent label Young Turks, a subsidiary of XL Recordings. Pawson became their manager, found them a rehearsal space, and started lining up paid gigs for them. The xx then signed a record deal with Young Turks in 2009.

BREAKTHROUGH DEBUT ALBUM

The xx spent more than a year working on the songs that would be included on their 2009 debut album, *xx*. During the recording process, Pawson brought in several big-name music producers such as Diplo, Kwes, and Paul Epworth to work with the band. Each producer, however, "injected their own style into what we were doing," Smith explained to Kot. "It took that experience to make us realize we had our style, our own sound, and should stick with that." Smith subsequently produced the album and perfected the band's sound, which would come to be characterized by sparse, minimalist production, the hushed vocal interplay between Madley Croft and Sim, and a mélange of styles from soul and R&B to post-punk, gothic rock, and ambient electronica.

Released to the public in August 2009, *xx* received widespread critical acclaim. The thirty-eight-minute album showcased the band's broad range of musical influences, earning them comparisons to such artists as the Cure, Joy Division, Cocteau Twins, New Order, and Interpol. It featured eleven songs that Sasha Frere-Jones described for the *New Yorker* (25 Jan. 2010) as "intimate" and the kind "to be sung inches from someone's ear, preferably with the lights off." In a profile of the xx for the *Independent* (1 Dec. 2012), Craig McLean called their self-titled debut "a wonder: an album of space and beauty and atmosphere, of spidery guitar lines and echoey electronics and simple soul, but also of indelible pop hooks."

The album also enjoyed gradual commercial success and eventually reached platinum status. The opening instrumental track on the album, "Intro," was used by the BBC in its coverage of the 2010 British general election and by NBC in its coverage of the 2010 Winter Olympic Games, and was also sampled by singer-songwriter Rihanna on her 2011 song "Drunk on Love." Other songs, meanwhile, were featured in television shows, movies, and commercials. In September 2010, *xx* received the much-coveted Mercury Prize, England's top musical honor. It has since been regarded as one of the best albums of the 2000s.

IN-DEMAND PRODUCER AND REMIXER

In support of their debut album, the xx toured extensively for two years. In October 2009, shortly after the tour began, Qureshi left the band due to internal conflicts with her bandmates. Despite such difficulties, the tour provided Smith with an outlet to channel his passion as a DJ. A devotee of London's vibrant club scene since his late teens, he had already begun performing DJ sets, and during stops along the xx tour, he began hosting DJ parties at local bars and clubs under the moniker Jamie xx.

As the xx grew in popularity, Smith suddenly found himself in demand as a producer and remixer. In 2009 he remixed songs for two British artists, singer-songwriter Jack Peñate's "Pull My Heart Away" and indie rock band Florence + the Machine's cover of Candi Staton's 1986 "You Got the Love." Smith's work on the latter song impressed XL Recordings head Richard Russell, who enlisted him to remix Gil Scott-Heron's final studio album, *I'm New Here* (2010). After receiving Scott-Heron's approval, Smith reworked the late rap pioneer's autobiographical introspective album in its entirety to reflect modern dance music trends. The result was the album *We're New Here*, which was released in February 2011 to critical acclaim. In a review for the BBC (21 Feb. 2011), Ele Beattie called the album "not merely a rehash of the original, but a cohesive, considered masterpiece in its own right."

Later in 2011 Smith collaborated with the Canadian rapper Drake on his hit single, "Take Care." The song sampled Smith's remix of Scott-Heron's "I'll Take Care of You" and featured guest vocals from Rihanna; it reached number seven on the US *Billboard* Hot 100 singles chart. Also that year Smith released a well-received two-track single, "Far Nearer/Beat For," remixed songs for Adele ("Rolling in the Deep") and Radiohead ("Bloom"), and coproduced the Alicia Keys song "When It's All Over," which appeared on the Grammy Award–winning singer's fifth studio album *Girl on Fire* (2012).

COEXIST AND *IN COLOUR*

In between his high-profile solo collaborations, Smith returned to the studio to produce the xx's long-awaited second studio album *Coexist*, which was released in September 2012. The album debuted at number one on the UK albums chart, but it was not as critically well received as the band's debut album. Contrary to the spontaneity that surrounded the making of *xx*, Smith, Madley Croft, and Sim approached their sophomore album with the aim of recapturing their "artfully spartan sound," as McLean put it. Consequently, *Coexist* stripped down the band's sound even further and was hampered by "an airless mood and fussy production," according to John Colapinto.

Still, *Coexist* received a number of laudatory reviews, some of which hailed the album as a masterpiece. The xx had also attracted a fan base large enough to begin headlining major music festivals around the world. In late 2013 the band held an intimate, high-profile performance at Manhattan's Park Avenue Armory; they returned to the venue for a second series of shows in March 2014. During the xx's busy touring schedule, Smith continued to work as a DJ, producer, and remixer. In 2014 he released two dance-inspired singles, "Girl/Sleep Sound" and "All under One Roof Raving," the latter of which used samples from Mark Leckey's 1999 short film *Fiorucci Made Me Hardcore*.

Smith's desire to complete other tracks he had been working on ultimately led him to release a solo album, *In Colour*, which was released by Young Turks in May 2015. Featuring collaborations with Madley Croft, Sim, and electronic musician Four Tet, the up-tempo album draws inspiration from London's club culture and contains elements from a wide array of dance music styles. It debuted at number three on the UK albums chart and reached the top spot on the *Billboard* dance/electronic albums chart; it peaked at number twenty-one on the *Billboard* 200 album chart. In addition to "Girl" and "Sleep Sound," the album featured the singles "Gosh," "Loud Places," and "I Know There's Gonna Be (Good Times)." It was shortlisted for the 2015 Mercury Prize and received a 2016 Grammy Award nomination for best dance/electronic album.

In Colour was one of the best-reviewed dance music albums of 2015. Battan called *In Colour* "a vivid album that puts Smith at the forefront of experimental dance music. . . . Whereas the xx treat quietude like a competition, the albums hovering deliberately on the brink of silence, Smith is more comfortable working with dynamics." Meanwhile, Sherburne called the album "a polychrome riot of [Smith's] varied influences. Shouting jungle MCs, dulcet doo-wop harmonies, trance arpeggios, snippets of crowd noise, and rough-hewn breakbeats all get thrown into Smith's mid-tempo rock tumbler."

OTHER PROJECTS

In addition to his solo career and work with the xx, Smith has scored the music for a contemporary ballet production, titled *Tree of Codes*. Based on the novel of the same name by Jonathan Safran Foer and featuring a set designed by the Danish-Icelandic installation artist Olafur Eliasson, the ballet premiered at the Manchester International Festival in July 2015. It received its New York premiere at the Park Avenue Armory in September of that year.

Smith and his xx bandmates have already begun working on their third studio album, which is slated to be released in 2016.

SUGGESTED READING

Battan, Carrie. "Jamie xx Is All Ears." *Grantland*. ESPN Internet Ventures, 13 May 2015. Web. 18 Jan. 2016.

Colapinto, John. "Shy and Mighty." *New Yorker*. Condé Nast, 30 June 2014. Web. 18 Feb. 2016.

Kot, Greg. "For Jamie xx, the Dancefloor Can Be a Melancholy Place." *Chicago Tribune*. Chicago Tribune, 9 July 2015. Web. 18 Feb. 2016.

McLean, Craig. "Mood Music: The xx Are Looking on the Glossier Side of Life as They Begin a Tour." *Independent*. Independent.co.uk, 1 Dec. 2012. Web. 18 Feb. 2016.

Sherburne, Philip. "Jamie xx: Taking Shelter in Loud Places." *Pitchfork*. Condé Nast, 19 May 2015. Web. 18 Feb. 2016.

SELECTED WORKS

xx, 2009; *Coexist*, 2012; *In Colour*, 2015

—*Chris Cullen*

Sally Jewell

Born: February 21, 1956
Occupation: United States Secretary of the Interior

Sally Jewell is an engineer, business executive, and Democratic politician who assumed the office of United States Secretary of the Interior on April 12, 2013.

EARLY LIFE AND EDUCATION

Sally Jewell was born Sarah "Sally" Margaret Roffey on February 21, 1956, in London, England, to Peter and Anne Roffey. In 1960, her family moved to Seattle, Washington, for her father's fellowship at the University of Washington

(UW) Medical School as an anesthesiologist. He had issues with England's class system as well, which helped catalyze their move.

Peter Roffey was an avid camper and member of Recreational Equipment Inc. (REI), a corporation that specializes in outdoor recreational equipment. Coincidentally, Jewell would later become chief executive officer (CEO) of REI. She took up mountaineering at a young age—she climbed Mount Rainier in Washington at the age of sixteen, and has since completed several major climbs. Jewell's mother, Anne Roffey, was a nurse practitioner whose area of expertise was in women's health.

Jewell graduated from Renton High School in Renton, Washington, in 1973. She continued her education at UW, graduating in 1978 with a degree in mechanical engineering. At the time, there was a shortage of professional engineers, so Jewell was able to select from several job offers.

OIL AND BANKING INDUSTRIES

Jewell took a position at Mobil Oil, which relocated her to southern Oklahoma. She worked there for three years before accepting a bigger opportunity with Rainier Bank in Seattle as a petroleum engineer. Her job there consisted of estimating the value of oil deposits. She became known for rejecting unsafe loans to the oil and gas sector, which helped save the bank when the oil business in Oklahoma and Texas began to fail. Eventually, Rainier Bank was acquired by Security Pacific Bank. Jewell stayed on after the acquisition to run their business-banking endeavors.

In 1991, Jewell helped found the Mountains to Sound Greenway Trust, a foundation focused on preserving a 1.5 million-acre stretch of land that reaches from Seattle to Central Washington. She left Security Pacific Bank in 1992 when she began work at West One Bank in Washington. She left that position in 1995, and then worked for Washington Mutual from 1995 to 2000. This was her last job in the banking industry.

REI

Jewell became the chief operating officer of REI in 2000, where she was previously a board member since 1996. In 2005, she was promoted to CEO. She helped the outdoor recreation equipment company become sustainable following a year in the red and a failed venture in Japan. Under her leadership, REI was regularly noted by *Fortune* magazine as one of the best companies to work for. Jewell received the 2009 Audubon Society's Rachel Carson Award for Environmental Conservation.

In addition to serving as the CEO of REI, Jewell's love of the outdoors led her to serve on the board of the National Parks Conservation Association. She was also a board member of Premera Blue Cross, a nonprofit health insurance company headquartered in Washington, and the University of Washington's Board of Regents.

In 2012, REI donated almost $4 million to protect public trails and parks. Jewell spoke at the 2011 White House conference on the America's Great Outdoors initiative. In her introduction of President Barack Obama at the conference, she stated that the outdoor-recreation industry is worth $289 billion and helps support 6.5 million jobs.

SECRETARY OF THE INTERIOR

On February 6, 2013, Obama nominated Jewell to become the US Secretary of the Interior. This made her the first woman chosen to be a part of Obama's cabinet during his second term as president. The Senate Energy and Natural Resources Committee approved her nomination in March 2013. The Senate confirmed Jewell as Secretary of the Interior on April 10, 2013.

As Secretary of the Interior, Jewell is tasked with managing numerous environmental and economic concerns in the United States. She administers sustainable development of energy supplies on public lands and waters, upholds obligations to the federally recognized American Indian tribes, and supervises national parks, wildlife refuges, and other public lands. These responsibilities also cover about 30 percent of US oil and gas production, which comes from land overseen by the Department of the Interior.

IMPACT

Jewell has taken her passion for the outdoors all the way to the White House. She used her role as CEO for REI to promote the protection of national parks and other public recreational areas. As Secretary of the Interior, Jewell plays an important role in crucial issues such as sustainable energy and land preservation. Her experience in the oil and banking industries provides her with a unique perspective on these and related topics.

PERSONAL LIFE

Jewell met her husband, Warren Jewell, while the two were engineering students at UW. They married in 1978, a week after graduation. They have two children, Peter and Anne. Jewell lives in Seattle and still enjoys mountain climbing and kayaking in her spare time.

SUGGESTED READING

Bernstein, Lenny. "Sally Jewell At a Different Kind of Summit: Head of the Department of the Interior." *Washington Post*. Washington Post, 25 Dec. 2013. Web. 16 Apr. 2014.

Broder, John M. "New Interior Chief Savors a Steep Learning Curve." *New York Times*. New York Times, 29 Apr. 2013. Web. 16 Apr. 2014.

Daly, Matthew. "Sally Jewell Picked to Be Interior Secretary by Obama." *Huffington Post*. TheHuffingtonPost.com, 6 Feb. 2013. Web. 16 Apr. 2014.

Krasny, Ros. "Obama Taps REI Chief Sally Jewell for Interior Secretary." *Chicago Tribune*. Tribune, 6 Feb. 2013. Web. 16 Apr. 2014.

Ouchi, Monica Soto. "A Profile of REI's Sally Jewell: Team Player at Her Peak." *Seattle Times*. Seattle Times, 23 Mar. 2005. Web. 16 Apr. 2014.

—*Patrick G. Cooper*

Gage Skidmore/CC BY-SA 3.0/Wikimedia Commons

Michael B. Jordan

Born: February 9, 1987
Occupation: Actor

Michael B. Jordan has become one of the young actors to watch in the millennial generation. Having come of age on such celebrated television dramas as *The Wire* and *Friday Night Lights*, he has now come into his own as a leading man, particularly through his acclaimed performances in such recent films as *Fruitvale Station* (2013) and *Creed* (2015), both of which were collaborations with another young talent in Hollywood, director Ryan Coogler. As an actor of color, Jordan believes that he has a particular role to play as he advances in his chosen field of endeavor. "I'm just trying to shine lights on little situations that I feel are the problem and telling it through art. I think that's my part. To have people receive something that inspires thought and conversation, and maybe you can change the way someone thinks. I think that's where it starts," Jordan said to Cara Buckley for the *New York Times* (28 Oct. 2015). "If you can change the way you think, the way you receive somebody, and not be intimidated by the way they look, or the color of their skin, or what they have on, it's a step."

EARLY LIFE

The second of three children, Michael Bakari Jordan was born in Santa Ana, California, on February 9, 1987, and raised in Newark, New Jersey. His father, Michael A. Jordan, was a caterer; his mother, the former Donna Davis, was a high school guidance counselor and artist. The family, though never rich, possessed a strong work ethic and a belief that hard work eventually pays off. "It comes from my parents," Jordan said of his own work ethic to James Mottram for the *Independent* (3 Jan. 2016). "They've always worked hard their entire lives and it's something

that's rubbed off on me. And yeah, man, you've got to sacrifice. It can't be fun and games all the time. You work hard for a certain amount of time and then you'll be able to relax a little bit, as time goes on, as you grow up, as you get older. That's always been my motto."

Jordan and his family were close during his childhood. And his extended family wasn't far away—cousins lived across the street and one of his grandmothers lived nearby. "We had seven or eight houses on the block that were friends of the family for decades," Jordan recalled of his Newark childhood in an interview with Camille Augustin for *Vibe* (23 Nov. 2015).

Opportunity knocked early for Jordan. During a routine trip to the doctor's office, the receptionist suggested to Donna Jordan that Michael could work as a model, just as two of the receptionist's sons were then doing. A short time later Jordan began modeling, which led to his getting small parts on such television shows as *The Sopranos* (1999) and *Cosby* (1999), as well as in the films *Black and White* (1999) and *Hardball* (2001).

FINDING SUCCESS ON TELEVISION

Jordan's breakout performance came in the first season of *The Wire*, the critically acclaimed HBO crime drama set in and around Baltimore, Maryland, which debuted in 2002. On *The Wire*, Jordan played Wallace, a sixteen-year-old drug dealer who became a favorite character during the 2002 season. Many credit Wallace's popularity to Jordan's terrific acting. "He was so focused back then—he just wanted to win," Idris Elba, Jordan's costar from *The Wire*, said to

Amy Kaufman for the *Los Angeles Times* (11 July 2013). "It's funny—his name is Michael Jordan—and on *The Wire* we used to laugh about that, because he was that good but in a different arena."

According to interviews with the actor, having the same name as one of the greatest basketball players in history has always given him something of a competitive chip on his shoulder. "He set the bar so high of success and his accomplishments and just respecting his own craft," Jordan said of the NBA legend to Augustin. "I always wanted to have my name mean something based upon the work that I put in. It wouldn't be just a comparison to that guy; I would have my own legacy."

After leaving *The Wire*, Jordan played the part of Reggie Montgomery on the long-running daytime soap opera *All My Children* from 2003 to 2006. He then made a number of guest appearances on other television shows, including *Without a Trace* (2006), *Cold Case* (2007), and *Burn Notice* (2009) before landing his next steady gig as Vince Howard on the acclaimed television series *Friday Night Lights*, a high school football drama that ran from 2006 to 2011. Jordan played the star quarterback from 2009 until 2011.

BECOMING A LEADING MAN

Jordan eventually became uncomfortable with the roles that his agents were sending him, most of which were young inner-city black men who had trouble with the law or who came from broken homes. To avoid typecasting and stereotyping, he began asking his agents to bring him movie parts written originally for white actors. One of the first to get his attention was a role in Josh Trank's sci-fi drama *Chronicle* (2012), about three teenagers who develop telekinetic powers. Although the part had originally been written with a Jewish teenager in mind, Trank took to Jordan immediately and revised the part to fit him. "Michael has had a SAG [Screen Actors Guild] card since he was eleven. He's been holding down the responsibility of making a career for himself in a very competitive environment since before he hit puberty," director Josh Trank told Amy Kaufman for the *Los Angeles Times*. "Fame and success can turn anybody into a monster—but he's not like, 'My movie won prizes at Sundance and got into Cannes and now I can finally break windows and beat people up!' He's having all this success, yet he's dealing with it so professionally."

Jordan's next role came as the lead actor in *Fruitvale Station* (2013), director Ryan Coogler's critically acclaimed feature-length film debut about the real-life shooting of Oscar Grant, a young African American man killed in 2009 by a police officer in Oakland, California. The film received considerable critical acclaim for both its star and director, who made a personal and artistic connection while working together. Both were especially proud of the work they did together on *Fruitvale Station*. "I'm trying to . . . [do] films that get people to think about the things we have in place: our systems, education, judicial, police brutality with *Fruitvale Station*," Jordan said to Augustin. "I want to tell the contemporary black male experience today of those situations of how we're treated."

Jordan's next major role came as the superhero Johnny Storm, also known as the Human Torch, in Josh Trask's *Fantastic Four* (2015). That film, which was based on the long-running Marvel comic series created by Stan Lee and Jack Kirby in 1961 about a quartet of astronauts, who gain remarkable powers, was a reboot of the Twentieth Century Fox film series, which had had two entries in the 2000s. Prior to Jordan's take on the role, every version of Johnny Storm, either in print or in animated cartoons or live-action films, had been white. Initially, public reaction on Jordan's casting was decidedly mixed. Upon the film's release, however, most people agreed that Jordan's great performance was the highlight of a very weak film. In addition to receiving a critical drubbing, making it one of the worst-reviewed comic book movies ever, *Fantastic Four* generated just $168 million worldwide; it had cost $120 million to make. "It was tough, because it was the first time I ever went through that," Jordan said of *Fantastic Four's* negative critical and commercial response to Cara Buckley for the *New York Times*. "Some things are out of your control, even if you show up and give everything you've got, even if you give 110 percent."

CREED

Perhaps Jordan's biggest role to date was his gripping portrayal of the young boxer Adonis Johnson in Ryan Coogler's 2015 film, *Creed*. Adonis is the son of Apollo Creed, the rival and later friend of Rocky Balboa, who is the title character in the Rocky film series. Each of those six films—which began in 1976 with *Rocky*—was either written or written and directed by actor Sylvester Stallone, who also portrayed *Rocky*. The films have been beloved by generations of filmgoers, including Coogler and his father, who used to watch them together during the director's formative years.

Coogler believed there was still life in the Rocky series. He began writing a script in which Rocky was the mentor and trainer to Jordan's character Adonis. Though initially hesitant about returning to the series because he believed it had finished out well with *Rocky Balboa* (2006), Stallone eventually agreed to reprise his signature role under Coogler's direction. Jordan, who underwent a rigorous training regimen to portray a light heavyweight fighter (and who often took real hits while filming the fight scenes), was particularly impressed with Stallone during production. Talking with Mottram, Jordan noted: "Sly did the biggest thing for me, which was to take that pressure off me, and not worry about competing or trying to live up to what the Rockys were—just to be myself and do what we were going to do."

Creed went on to become a critical and commercial hit, grossing about $110 million in North America and $174 million worldwide on a $35 million budget. Critics were impressed not only with Coogler's deft direction but also with the performances of Jordan and Stallone, which were quickly ranked among the best of their careers. Reviewing the film for *Variety* (18 Nov. 2016), Andrew Barker declared, "Cut and spry, Jordan looks every inch a fighter, and the physicality of his performance is matched by some well-rounded internal gymnastics: Adonis bears a chip on one shoulder from his group-home past, and one on the other from his treatment as a sort of legacy admission into the boxing world, and Jordan manages to make his character's fiery temper empathetic rather than alienating."

SUGGESTED READING

Augustin, Camille. "Michael B. Jordan: Black Star Rising." *Vibe*. SpinMedia, 23 Nov. 2015. Web. 9 Apr. 2016.

Barker, Andrew. Rev. of *Creed*, dir. Ryan Coogler. *Variety*. Variety Media, 18 Nov. 2015. Web. 10 Apr. 2016.

Buckley, Cara. "Michael B. Jordan Gives Millennials Their 'Rocky' with 'Creed.'" *New York Times*. New York Times, 28 Oct. 2015. Web. 9 Apr. 2016.

Kaufman, Amy. "'Fruitvale Station' Star Michael B. Jordan Feels the Heat." *Los Angeles Times*. Los Angeles Times, 11 July 2013. Web. 10 Apr. 2016.

Mottram, James. "Michael B. Jordan: Star of Rocky Sequel Creed on Why He Goes for Roles Written for White Characters." *Independent*. Independent.co.uk, 3 Jan. 2016. Web. 9 Apr. 2016.

SELECTED WORKS

The Wire, 2002; *All My Children*, 2003–6; *Friday Night Lights*, 2009–11; *Chronicle*, 2012; *Fruitvale Station*, 2013; *Fantastic Four*, 2015; *Creed*, 2015

—*Christopher Mari*

Megyn Kelly

Born: November 18, 1970
Occupation: News host

Conservative news host Megyn Kelly has been affiliated with the Fox News Channel since 2004, and in 2014 she became the only female media figure on *Time* magazine's list of the year's one hundred most influential people.

EARLY LIFE AND EDUCATION

Megyn Kelly was born on November 18, 1970, in the suburbs of Syracuse, New York. Her father, Edward, was a professor at the State University of New York's School of Education in Albany, and her mother, Linda, was a nurse. Kelly, who has two older siblings, enjoyed, by all accounts, a stable middle-class upbringing. She was a solid student, a player of basketball and field hockey, and a valued member of the cheerleading squad.

Her formative years were not entirely happy, however. When she was a sophomore at Bethlehem Central High School, her father unexpectedly died of a heart attack, just days before Christmas.

Kelly, who worked as an aerobics teacher to supplement the family's income after her father's death, had long harbored ambitions to be a reporter, but after graduating from high school in 1988, she was rejected by the journalism program at Syracuse University. Instead, she studied political science there, earning her bachelor's degree in 1992. Kelly next entered Syracuse University Albany Law School, where she served as associate editor on the Albany Law Review and graduated in 1995 with honors.

Upon graduation, Kelly worked for the Chicago office of law firm Bickel and Brewer LLP. She later joined Jones Day, a prestigious international law firm, and gained a reputation as a gifted corporate litigator. Despite her widely acknowledged talents in the field, within a decade she had become disillusioned and unhappy with her grueling schedule.

Remembering her youthful dream, Kelly started sitting in on journalism classes and, with the help of a cameraman she knew, produced an audition tape.

CAREER IN JOURNALISM

After moving to Washington, DC, in 2003, Kelly approached Bill Lord, the vice president and station manager of WJLA-TV, a local ABC affiliate. Taking a chance on an inexperienced but passionate applicant, he hired her for a weekly freelance assignment that netted her about $17,000 a year. (Her day rate as a freelancer, she has joked, was about the same as her hourly rate as a corporate attorney.)

In that capacity she came to the attention of Brit Hume, then a Washington-based managing editor for Fox News. Impressed by her on-screen energy and classic beauty, he advocated for her with Roger Ailes, the head of the network. Although there were no openings at the time, Ailes created a spot for her as a Washington reporter in the fall of 2004.

Hume's instinct proved correct. Kelly's reporting on such major stories as the 2004 presidential election, the Duke rape case in 2006, and the mass shooting at Virginia Tech in 2007 were widely watched, and Fox audiences responded well to her blunt, no-nonsense style—and her good looks.

In 2007 Kelly began cohosting the morning program *America's Newsroom* alongside Bill Hemmer. Airing each weekday from nine o'clock to eleven o'clock in the morning, the show featured a mix of general news reporting, point-counterpoint discussions of current affairs, and feel-good human-interest stories. It also regularly featured a popular segment called "Kelly's Court," during which she drew upon her legal training to discuss celebrities' legal woes, government court cases, and other such topics.

In 2010 Kelly became the solo host of *America Live*, which appeared on Fox from one o'clock to three o'clock in the afternoon. During the highly rated show, Kelly delivered the top news of the day and moderated debates about various controversial issues. She also reprised "Kelly's Court," bringing in a panel of legal experts for serious discussions of stories related to the judicial system.

America Live had taken over the time slot held by a show called *The Live Desk*, and the wisdom of Fox officials quickly became apparent: total viewers increased by 20 percent by the end of the year, including a big boost in the sought-after demographic of twenty-five- to fifty-four-year-olds. (Cynics posited that the increase had largely been the result of the steamy photo shoot Kelly had done for *GQ* right before her program debuted.)

In 2013 Kelly—who had been a centerpiece of Fox's 2012 election coverage as cohost of *America's Election HQ*—made a highly publicized move to prime time. *The Kelly File*, as her new program is called, airs in the coveted nine o'clock to ten o'clock slot on weekday nights. On the highly rated show, Kelly, who, like almost all of Fox News's on-air personalities, leans right politically, covers breaking news, conducts in-depth investigative reports, and interviews public figures.

IMPACT

Although commentator Bill O'Reilly's Fox show consistently remains the top-rated in total viewers, Kelly's ranks a very close second. Although she has millions of fans, Kelly also has fervent detractors, who lament her conservative views and deride some of her more strident pronouncements. They point, for example, to her assertion that pepper-spraying by the police is not a harsh means of crowd control because the spray is food based, and her declaration that both Santa and Jesus are known to be Caucasian.

PERSONAL LIFE

Kelly's first marriage, to a doctor, ended in divorce in 2006. (For a time, she used her married name, Kendall, professionally.) In 2008 she married Douglas Brunt, an Internet security expert who left the business world to write novels. They have three children: Edward Yates, Yardley Evans, and Thatcher Bray.

SUGGESTED READING

Conger, Bryan. "On the Rise: Megyn Kelly." *Washington Examiner*. Washington Examiner, 4 Sept. 2013. Web. 9 June 2014.
Heller, Jake. "Megyn Kelly's Viral Feminist Moment." *Newsweek*. Newsweek, 5 June 2013. Web. 9 June 2014.
Hill, Erin. "Fox News Channel's Megyn Kelly on Politics and Parenting." *Parade*. Condé Nast, 24 Jan. 2014. Web. 9 June 2014.
Kurtz, Howard. "Megyn Kelly, Fox News's Fast-Rising Anchor." *Washington Post*. Washington Post, 14 Apr. 2008. Web. 9 June 2014.
Reed, Julia. "Outspoken Fox News Anchor Suffers No Fools, Gladly." *Harper's Bazaar*. Hearst, 1 Feb. 2013. Web. 9 June 2014.
Zak, Dan. "Megyn Kelly, Fox News's (Quickly) Budding Star." *Washington Post*. Washington Post, 11 Dec. 2013. Web. 9 June 2014.

SELECTED WORKS

America's Newsroom, 2007–10; *America Live*, 2010–13; *The Kelly File*, 2013–

—Mari Rich

Tori Kelly

Born: December 14, 1992
Occupation: Musician

Tori Kelly, as Bobby Olivier wrote for the website NJ.com (25 Apr. 2016), performs "under the guise of a gleaming, industry-certified 'pop star,'" with a "mainstream breakthrough jam" cowritten and produced by perennial Billboard chart topper Max Martin—the man responsible for number-one hits by such industry superstars as Taylor Swift, Britney Spears, and Pink. At the same time, however, Olivier cautioned against taking the singer at face value: "Kelly's

GabboT (Kringle 11)/CC BY-SA 2.0/Wikimedia Commons

perspective is wonderfully layered, and through effortlessly exquisite vocal control—and an unwillingness to hide her faith in secular pop—she's become the substantive radio songstress who deserves a closer listen."

Despite her youth, Kelly's success has been far from overnight. After well-received childhood appearances on the relaunched *Star Search* (in 2003) and *America's Most Talented Kids* (in 2004), she was signed briefly to a record deal, which fell through when producers could not agree on an artistic direction for her. In 2010, while still a teenager, she appeared on the widely watched televised singing competition *American Idol* and was told by the show's famously acerbic judge Simon Cowell that her voice bordered on annoying.

It was not until videos she posted of herself on YouTube began to go viral that the music industry truly opened its doors. Signed to a deal with Capitol Records largely on the strength of her social-media popularity, Kelly has released a best-selling full-length album, received a Grammy nod, and earned the admiration of many critics. "While her breaking into the mainstream has been a few years coming now," Hugh McIntyre wrote in his interview with Kelly for *Forbes* (11 Feb. 2016), "Tori Kelly is still one of the most exciting new names in music."

EARLY LIFE

Victoria Loren Kelly was born on December 14, 1992, in Wildomar, California. Her mother, Laura Carlson Kelly, is a nurse, and her father, Allwyn Kelly, is a construction worker who played bass guitar and sang in a variety of bands

in his younger years. Journalists frequently mention Kelly's mixed heritage: Allwyn is half Jamaican and half Puerto Rican, and Laura hails from an Irish and German background. Kelly also has a younger brother, Noah, an avid soccer player with whom Kelly reportedly enjoys a close relationship; he often posts photos of her and messages of support on his own social media accounts.

Kelly's parents loved music, and Kelly has told journalists that no genre was off-limits in their household when she was growing up. She was influenced by a wide variety of artists, including Jeff Buckley, Lauryn Hill, and Michael Jackson, as well as by the gospel music that Laura, a devout Christian, often played. Kelly began singing at the age of three. "I was almost kind of shocked when I went to kindergarten. I thought that all of the kids would love music just as much as I do," she told Alan Sculley for the *Virginian-Pilot* (21 Apr. 2016). "That was normal. And they're raising their hands saying they wanted to be a firefighter, a police officer, and I would always just, I just really wanted to be a singer."

Kelly, who also began playing the guitar at a young age, graduated from high school in 2011, but she had begun trying to get her music career off the ground well before then.

EARLY CAREER ATTEMPTS

In 2003, Kelly, then ten years old, competed on the newly relaunched television talent show *Star Search*, hosted that season by comedian Arsenio Hall. Competing in the junior vocalist category, she sang the tune "Blessed," by contemporary Christian star Rachael Lampa. Although she was well received by the judges, Kelly ultimately lost the grand championship to Tiffany Evans, who garnered perfect scores in all her performances and who went on to find moderate success after signing with Columbia Records.

The following year, Kelly appeared on *America's Most Talented Kids*, competing in the eight-to-twelve age group with her rendition of Christina Aguilera's "Keep on Singin' My Song." This time she triumphed, beating out Hunter Hayes (who, despite that loss, went on to receive the Country Music Association Award for new artist of the year in 2012, as well as numerous Grammy nominations).

Kelly's win attracted the attention of executives at Geffen Records, who signed her to a deal but quickly dropped her when they could not agree on what songs she should be playing or image she should be cultivating. Kelly found the discussions distressing and has said that from that point forward she decided to simply remain herself, singing only the songs she wanted and not allowing anyone else to dictate how she looked or sounded.

She did, however, make one last attempt at a televised singing competition, auditioning at the age of sixteen for season nine of *American Idol*. For that high-profile show, she performed John Mayer's hit "Gravity," and while the other judges praised both her performance and "look," Simon Cowell deemed her voice "almost annoying" and asserted that her long sundress made her look like "a big orange." Regardless, she made it through the round but was cut before the live semifinals.

Kelly has told interviewers that her experience on *American Idol* was difficult but valuable. "Deep down, I knew I was good, and I knew I could do it," she recalled in an interview for *Seventeen* (4 Jan. 2016). "I needed to get knocked down and to build up a thick skin. Who knows what I would have been singing about otherwise? You have to go through things in order to inspire others with your story." She later told Olivia Fleming for *Elle* (26 Feb. 2015) that if she had a chance to talk to Cowell again, she would say, "Thank you for not putting me on your show. Everything happens for a reason and I probably wouldn't be who I am now if I had made it on that show."

THE POWER OF SOCIAL MEDIA

In 2007 Kelly began posting on the video-sharing website YouTube, which had launched just two years before. Her first video showed her performing a version of the traditional hymn "Go Tell It on the Mountain," and she went on to upload acoustic covers of hits by such artists as Rihanna and Michael Jackson. She told Olivier, "The whole image of just me and my guitar was kind of an accident. I wasn't really going for that. But I fell in love with it, and I love to strip down a song and be able to perform it really raw." She gained particular attention for a version of Frank Ocean's "Thinkin Bout You" that she recorded with fellow aspiring artist Angie Girl, the latter serving as human beatbox.

As word spread online about Kelly's videos, her YouTube channel gradually amassed almost 1.5 million followers, and by July 2016 the Ocean cover had been viewed more than 25 million times. She acknowledges that her success is due almost wholly to social media. "I started writing music when I was fifteen in my bedroom, and I'd post them on MySpace and from there it shifted to doing covers on YouTube, and building my Twitter," she told Fleming. "It was like, 'Oh, people actually care what I have to say now.' And then there was Instagram, and then Vine and Snapchat even. It means I get to be really close to the people who are supporting my music, and it's also cool because they feel close to my journey. We're kind of going through it together."

In May 2012 she released a six-song digital EP, *Handmade Songs by Tori Kelly*, which she wrote and recorded entirely by herself, in her bedroom. Her growing online fan base responded by downloading it enough times to send it to number nine on the Billboard Heatseekers chart and number six on Nielsen SoundScan's new artist chart.

MAINSTREAM MUSICAL SUCCESS

Kelly soon found herself playing live to packed crowds at local venues. At one such performance, she was approached by music manager Scooter Braun, whose clients have included pop stars Justin Bieber and Ariana Grande. Although Kelly was initially skeptical because of her previous experiences in the mainstream music industry, she ultimately agreed to work with Braun. At first, her fears seemed founded; the outspoken manager did not shy away from being harsh. "But it was me and my manager, one on one," she recalled to Allison Stewart for the *Chicago Tribune* (4 May 2016). "We have these talks where we go into what people are saying, and he told me he was hearing things within the industry. His peers were questioning me: 'She's kind of plain.' 'She's vanilla.' 'What are you going to do with her?' It took me back to that little girl who was so insecure. It put a fire under me, for sure. I felt like I had something to prove. At the same time, I felt, why should I have to prove anything?"

Kelly decided to put her trust in Braun. "In our very first meeting, he said, 'I don't want to change you, I want to get behind what you're already doing. Your style is already there,'" she told Stewart.

In September 2013 Kelly signed with Capitol Records; in October of that year, the label released *Foreword*, an EP of her original songs, which debuted at number sixteen on the Billboard 200 chart and sold sixteen thousand copies in its first week alone. She followed up with 2015's *Unbreakable Smile*, her full-length debut, which sold seventy-five thousand copies within one week and leapt immediately to the number-two spot on the Billboard 200. Cowritten and executive produced by Max Martin, who has worked with many of the chart-topping pop artists of the last decade, the album included the tracks "Nobody Love" and "Should've Been Us," which quickly became massive hits.

The year 2015 turned out to be a banner one for Kelly. The newly minted pop star was awarded the Breakthrough Artist honor at Billboard's Women in Music event in December and was nominated for both Artist of the Year at VH1's Big Music in 2015 event (held in November) and Favorite Breakout Artist at the People's Choice Awards (held in January 2016).

In 2016 Kelly was nominated for a Grammy Award for best new artist. Although she lost the award to Meghan Trainor, her performance at the Grammy ceremony—a duet with fellow nominee James Bay—was met with thunderous applause and was later widely acknowledged as a highlight of the televised show.

PERSONAL LIFE

Despite rumors surrounding Kelly's relationship with pop star Ed Sheeran, with whom she collaborated on the single "I Was Made for Loving You," Kelly has told journalists that she considers Sheeran to be only a friend and mentor. She shares her mother's strong faith and has said that some of her songs that sound romantic on first hearing them are, in reality, love songs to God.

In February 2016, Keds sneakers named Kelly as a member of its Keds Collective, a group of successful women from various entertainment industries whom the company enlisted to commemorate its hundredth anniversary. Kelly appeared in an ad campaign for the brand and designed her own custom pair of sneakers.

SUGGESTED READING

Kelly, Tori. "Tori Kelly Finally Kicks the Door Open, after Years of Knocking." Interview by Allison Stewart. *Chicago Tribune*. Tribune, 4 May 2016. Web. 6 July 2016.

Kelly, Tori. "Tori Kelly Is 'Speechless' about Her Best New Artist Grammy Nomination." Interview by Hugh McIntyre. *Forbes*. Forbes Media, 11 Feb. 2016. Web. 6 July 2016.

Kelly, Tori. "Tori Kelly May Be Music's Brightest New Star, but She's Far from an Overnight Success." Interview by Julian Mitchell. *Forbes*. Forbes Media, 21 Jan. 2016. Web. 6 July 2016.

Kelly, Tori. "Tori Kelly Might Just Be the Next Britney Spears/Katy Perry/Taylor Swift." Interview by Olivia Fleming. *Elle*. Hearst Communications, 26 Feb. 2015. Web. 6 June 2016.

Kelly, Tori. "Tori Kelly Says the Secret to Success Is Giving Up." Interview by Charles Manning. *Cosmopolitan*. Hearst Communications, 6 May 2016. Web. 6 July 2016.

"Tori Kelly on What It Feels Like to Have Simon Cowell Call Your Voice 'Almost Annoying.'" *Seventeen*. Hearst Communications, 4 Jan. 2016. Web. 6 July 2016.

—*Mari Rich*

Ellie Kemper

Born: May 2, 1980
Occupation: Actor

Michael Arbeiter admitted for *Bustle* (22 Jan. 2015) that "adorability" is Ellie Kemper's "shtick," adding that "anyone who's seen her projects definitely knows it well: Her roles are endearingly merry, treading just deep enough into childlike whimsy to allow for a doting preciousness over her every deed." He grudgingly admitted, "And it works. . . . As the image of impeccable sweetness, unfettered positivity, and impossible purity, Kemper has been a real joy to watch and a habitual riot to boot."

Winning over curmudgeonly critics is all in a day's work for the Princeton-educated Kemper, who is said to be as pleasant and personable in real life as she is on the screen. "Ellie Kemper is—let's not mince words here—*nice*," Mark F. Bernstein wrote for the *Princeton Alumni Weekly* (8 Feb. 2012). "Upbeat. Positive. Easy to work with. Patient with autograph seekers. . . . She is, in fact, the first to acknowledge that Erin [from the hit sitcom *The Office*] . . . is pretty much just 'an exaggerated version of myself.' Sometimes life imitates art, but it works the other way, too."

EARLY LIFE AND EDUCATION

Elizabeth Claire Kemper was born on May 2, 1980, in Kansas City, Missouri. She was the second of four children born to Dorothy Jannarone Kemper and David Woods Kemper, who is the

Josephine Sittenfeld/GNU Free Documentation License/
Wikimedia Commons

CEO of Commerce Bancshares, a holding company that was founded by his great-grandfather William Thornton Kemper Sr. Her younger sister, Carrie, became a comedy writer, and the two worked together on *The Office*.

When Kemper was about five years old, her family moved to St. Louis. As children, Kemper and her sister wrote their own skits and performed them for their parents. After the family purchased a video camera, the two girls enlisted the help of their younger brother and a neighborhood friend to appear in increasingly ambitious skits, which they then filmed and edited their work in a rudimentary studio they had set up in the basement.

Kemper attended John Burroughs School in St. Louis, where she appeared in numerous school plays and musicals. In eighth grade, Kemper took an improvisational comedy class that was taught by actor Jon Hamm, who had attended Burroughs as a teenager and had returned to his alma mater as a guest instructor. Although Kemper, then fourteen, has recalled that the future star of *Mad Men* was very handsome, and many of the girls harbored crushes on him, at twenty-three, he appeared old to her. For his part, Hamm remembered his former pupil fondly. "[She] was a preternaturally confident and prepared student," he told Curtis Sittenfeld for *Vanity Fair* (31 Dec. 2014). "She was easily one of the youngest (and smallest) in the class, but on stage was clearly miles ahead in confidence and ability."

After graduating from Burroughs in 1998, Kemper entered Princeton University, where her mother had also attended. Kemper played field hockey and—also like her mother—joined the Triangle Club, which creates and performs professional-caliber, original musical comedies. Additionally, Kemper became a member of Quipfire!, Princeton's improvisational comedy group.

After graduating from Princeton in 2002, Kemper studied English literature at England's Oxford University for a year with vague plans of becoming a teacher. She changed her focus, however, after her return to the United States and deciding instead to move to New York City to try her hand at earning a living as a comic actor.

ACTING CAREER
Kemper initially took acting classes and performed with the Upright Citizens Brigade Theatre (UCB) and the Peoples Improv Theater (PIT). She soon found an agent and landed a string of jobs in radio and television commercials for such companies as Dunkin' Donuts and Kmart. The income from those jobs provided her with enough money to live on, and she continued performing in small venues at night,

often teaming up with her friend and roommate Scott Eckert, whom she knew from her days at Princeton. It was during this time that Kemper also accepted an unpaid writing internship with late-night host Conan O'Brien, who occasionally assigned her a small role in a comedy sketch. Within a few years, she began winning small roles in television movies and shorts, but her big break came after she moved to Los Angeles, where in 2009 she fortuitously landed a role on *The Office*, a quirky show with a large following.

Kemper had auditioned to be a cast member on *Saturday Night Live* in 2008 but had been turned down. An audition for the sitcom *Parks and Recreation* was similarly disappointing, but casting agents on the show were impressed enough to recommend her to their counterparts at *The Office*, a comedy set at the fictitious Scranton-based headquarters of paper company Dunder Mifflin. Starring Steve Carell as regional manager Michael Scott, the show premiered in the United States in 2005. By 2009 its creators were looking for an actor to play a temporary receptionist at the company because the original receptionist had been promoted to the Dunder Mifflin sales department.

So appealing was Kemper's portrayal of sweet-natured Erin Hannon that her story arc was expanded from four episodes to six, and the writers ultimately decided to make the character a regular on the show. "It definitely felt like the next stage has started," Kemper recalled to Sittenfeld. "The idea of watching *The Office* and then being on it felt like a huge leap." Describing the taping of an episode that featured Carell and guest star Will Ferrell, she explained to Sittenfeld, "I was like, Oh my gosh, what is happening? These are two of the funniest men on the planet—and this is a job?"

The Office gave Kemper increased visibility in the industry, and she began to be tapped for big-screen roles. She had a small part in the Russell Brand film *Get Him to the Greek* (2010), and in 2011 she was a member of the ensemble cast of the popular comedy *Bridesmaids*, which surprised many critics by grossing over $26 million its first weekend in theaters and becoming a sleeper hit. Then, in 2012 she played a teacher in the movie adaptation of *21 Jump Street*, which was originally a popular late-1980s television show. In 2014, once *The Office* had ended, Kemper became the only guest-host in the history of *The Ellen DeGeneres Show*, filling in when DeGeneres was sick.

UNBREAKABLE KIMMY SCHMIDT
High-profile comedy writer and actor Tina Fey was also a fan of Kemper's work. "My first impression was, 'That girl's funny, but maybe she's too pretty to be on *The Office*,'" Fey told Sittenfeld. "But she grew on me because she's good at

downplaying her prettiness." Fey and her writing partner Robert Carlock began thinking of a project for Kemper and came up with the idea for *Unbreakable Kimmy Schmidt*, a comic series about a young woman who was held in an underground bunker for years by a crazed cult leader (Reverend Richard Wayne Gary Wayne, played by Jon Hamm), only to find upon her escape that the world is a very different place. "I didn't know if it was a prank at first, because you know, the premise doesn't necessarily sound like a comedy," Kemper told Patricia Garcia for *Vogue* (4 Mar. 2015) of seeing a script for the first time. "So at first I wasn't sure if they were serious or not. . . . But I think comedy is a very useful tool in dealing with a terrible situation."

Critics raved about the show (which was originally slated for NBC but ultimately aired on Netflix instead). "There never was any doubt that Ellie Kemper could anchor her own comedy series," Verne Gay wrote for *Newsday* (6 Mar. 2015). "She's all lightness, charm, vitality, and teeth— big bright ones that have a character all their own. Here she's Pippy Longstocking meets Amelia Bedelia. . . . As a character with a sartorial preference for canary yellow, Kemper's Schmidt comes into focus intensely and immediately. She pops off the screen, and pleasingly so."

Some, although praising Kemper's positivity, examined the darker implications of the series. "Kimmy's ugly history comes through, in inference and in sly, unsettling jokes about trauma, jagged bits that puncture what is a colorful fish-out-of-water comedy," Emily Nussbaum wrote for the *New Yorker* (30 Mar. 2015). "The backstory that emerges combines elements from a number of familiar tabloid stories: those of Katie Beers (abducted from her abusive family, kept in an underground bunker), Elizabeth Smart (snatched from her bedroom by a self-styled messiah), Jaycee Dugard (abducted from her front yard), and the three women who were rescued . . . after having been beaten and raped for years."

Netflix released the entire series all at once, and many fans admitted via social media that they had watched each of the thirteen episodes during marathon viewing sessions. The show and its actors received several Emmy nominations in 2015, and Netflix agreed to purchase a second season of the hugely popular show, which it plans to air in the spring of 2016.

PERSONAL LIFE

In 2012 Kemper married comedy writer Michael Koman, whom she had met while interning for Conan O'Brien's show. She divides her time between Los Angeles and New York and has written regularly for the online satirical publications *Timothy McSweeney's Internet Tendency* and the *Onion*. She is slated to provide the voice for one of the main characters in *The Secret Life of Pets*, an animated feature scheduled for release in 2016.

SUGGESTED READING

Arbeiter, Michael. "Is There a Problem with Ellie Kemper's 'Adorbs' Shtick?" *Bustle*. Bustle. com, 22 Jan. 2015. Web. 20 Oct. 2015.

Bernstein, Mark F. "Funny Girl." *PAW*. Trustees of Princeton U, 8 Feb. 2012. Web. 20 Oct. 2015.

Garcia, Patricia. "*Unbreakable Kimmy Schmidt* Star Ellie Kemper on Her David Letterman Toaster and Filming with Tina Fey." *Vogue*. Condé Nast, 4 Mar. 2015. Web. 20 Oct. 2015.

Gay, Verne. "Ellie Kemper Shines on Netflix." *Newsday*. Newsday, 6 Mar. 2015. Web. 20 Oct. 2015.

Heisler, Steve. "Ellie Kemper." *AV Club*. Onion, 20 Apr. 2010. Web. 20 Oct. 2015.

Pennington, Gail. "From VP Queen . . . to 'The Office.'" *StL Today*. StLToday.com, 13 Dec. 2009. Web. 20 Oct. 2015.

Sittenfeld, Curtis. "Ellie Kemper, Star of *Unbreakable Kimmy Schmidt*." *Vanity Fair*. Condé Nast, 31 Dec. 2014. Web. 20 Oct. 2015.

SELECTED WORKS

The Office, 2009–13; *Get Him to the Greek*, 2010; *Bridesmaids*, 2011; *21 Jump Street*, 2012; *Unbreakable Kimmy Schmidt*, 2015–

—Mari Rich

Dallas Keuchel

Born: January 1, 1988
Occupation: Baseball player

While many sports commentators remark that the vast majority of pitchers in Major League Baseball (MLB) rely on techniques such as blistering fastballs to strike out opposing batters, Houston Astros left-hander Dallas Keuchel has built a career around finesse and craftsmanship on the mound. Since making his debut with the Astros in 2012, Keuchel has been known as a command pitcher who generates most of his outs through the strategic placement of his pitches, which include a two-seam fastball, a changeup, and a slider. Despite a less than ninety-mile-per-hour fastball, Keuchel has become one of baseball's best at forcing ground balls. "He doesn't have high-velocity numbers," Astros manager A. J. Hinch told Tyler Kepner for the *New York Times* (27 Feb. 2016). "But what he is exceptional at is finding a way to get guys out."

Keith Allison/Flickr (Original version) UCinternational (Crop)/
CC BY-SA 2.0/Wikimedia Commons

After posting lackluster numbers in his first two seasons with the Astros, Keuchel had a breakout year in 2014 when he won twelve games and recorded a 2.93 earned run average (ERA). The following year, he earned his first career All-Star selection and received the coveted American League (AL) Cy Young Award after leading the league in a number of pitching categories and propelling the Astros to their first playoff berth since 2005. One of the game's best fielding pitchers, Keuchel won Rawlings Gold Glove Awards for defensive excellence in both 2014 and 2015.

EARLY LIFE

Dallas Keuchel was born on January 1, 1988, in Tulsa, Oklahoma, to Dennis and Teresa Keuchel. He has an older sister, Krista. His father spent twenty-five years in the horticulture industry, and his mother works as a cardiology referral specialist at a Tulsa hospital.

Keuchel grew up playing sports, starting with baseball, football, and basketball year-round as a kindergartener. From the time he was little, Keuchel was a "workhorse," as his mother put it to Evan Drellich for the *Houston Chronicle* (9 May 2015). "If he was out there playing, he played with his all." Keuchel inherited a strong work ethic from his parents, both of whom took turns playing catch with him in the family backyard.

Originally an outfielder and first baseman, Keuchel switched to pitching when he was eight years old at the suggestion of a youth coach. Despite only having average arm strength, he demonstrated pinpoint control from the beginning. Keuchel "could dot you between the eyes if he wanted to," his father told Ed Godfrey for the *Oklahoman* (27 Jan. 2016). "He didn't throw real fast but he threw strikes."

Growing up, Keuchel's exceptional command of the strike zone and his natural hitting ability helped to earn him spots on elite baseball travel teams. He has not only credited his parents for playing an instrumental role in his baseball development but also his paternal grandfather, Joseph, an obstetrician in Tulsa who helped fund many of his costly travel tournament trips.

HIGH SCHOOL AND COLLEGE BASEBALL

Keuchel was also influenced by his parents' friend Charlie O'Brien, a former MLB catcher from 1985 to 2000. Keuchel was teammates with O'Brien's son, Chris, now a catcher for the Baltimore Orioles, on Tulsa's Bishop Kelley High School varsity baseball team. Keuchel helped lead the team to state championships during his sophomore and senior seasons, and as a senior, he went 10–0 with a remarkable 1.57 ERA. Despite those numbers and being a standout football and basketball player, Keuchel was passed over on all-state recognition. He was also overlooked by professional baseball scouts because of his underwhelming physical gifts. Still, Keuchel was a "locked-in individual" who "knew what he wanted," as his high-school coach, Tony Scardino, told Mark Cooper for *Tulsa World* (14 July 2015). "He knew what he had to do to get there [to the majors], and nothing was going to stand in his way."

Following his 2006 graduation, Keuchel accepted a scholarship to play baseball at the University of Arkansas in Fayetteville where he struggled at first with a 5.88 ERA but steadily improved over his next two seasons. In 2009 he helped propel the Razorbacks to the semifinals of the College World Series.

By the end of his junior season, Keuchel had caught the attention of major-league scouts, including Houston Astros scout Jim Stevenson who ultimately convinced the Astros to draft Keuchel in the seventh round of the 2009 MLB Draft. As Stevenson explained to Drellich, "If you didn't know him and didn't catch him on a regular basis, you could not appreciate what he did week after week after week."

HOUSTON ASTROS

When Keuchel joined the Astros, he already had what was deemed a major-league-ready, two-seam sinking fastball. He also threw a highly deceptive changeup and a big, looping curveball. Nevertheless, he was not rated among the team's top twenty prospects after the 2009 season, in which he posted a solid 2.70 ERA in eleven games with the Tri-City ValleyCats, the team's Class A Short Season affiliate.

Keuchel remained an under-the-radar prospect over the next two seasons, and after achieving a combined 17–22 with a 3.95 ERA in 2010 and 2011, he entered the 2012 season ranked as the twenty-first-best prospect for the Astros. He opened that season with the Oklahoma City RedHawks (now called the Oklahoma City Dodgers) in the AAA Pacific Coast League, where he posted a subpar 4.26 ERA over 80.1 innings before earning his first call-up to the majors on June 17, 2012.

Keuchel had an auspicious major-league debut, allowing just one run on four hits over five innings against the Texas Rangers. He was even more impressive in his second career start, pitching a complete game against the Cleveland Indians to record his first major-league win. Keuchel struggled the rest of his rookie season, finishing with more walks (39) than strikeouts (38) and a bloated 5.27 ERA in sixteen starts. He continued to perform poorly in 2013, and his struggles mirrored those of the Astros, who lost more than one hundred games for the third consecutive season, finishing with a major-league and franchise-worst 51–111 record. Keuchel's lackluster early-career numbers derived from his inability to consistently command his pitches and "trying to be too fine" with them, as he explained to Zach Schonbrun for the *New York Times* (5 Oct. 2015).

EMERGENCE AS THE ASTROS' ACE
During the 2014 off-season, Keuchel worked with Astros pitching coach Brent Strom and catcher Jason Castro to make several adjustments to his pitching, among them abandoning his curveball, which had largely been ineffective at the major-league level. In its place, Keuchel began to develop a slider-curveball hybrid pitch, or "slurve," which he had first experimented with in high school. He also adopted a more aggressive mindset by focusing on a strategy that emphasized pounding the strike zone.

With these adjustments, Keuchel enjoyed a breakout 2014 season. He narrowly missed out on an All-Star selection; despite the disappointment, he worked to transform himself and his pitches. He soon emerged as one of the game's best groundball pitchers and led the majors with a groundball rate of 64.4 percent, which was the highest single-season rate for a left-hander since 1987. Brent Strom explained to Kepner how Keuchel has learned to dictate how his pitches are hit: "He always presents to the hitters a strike, whether it's a strike or not, as it crosses the strike zone."

Keuchel finished the season with a 12–9 record and a 2.93 ERA in two hundred innings, to go along with an AL-best five complete games.

On the defensive side of the ball, Keuchel led all major-league pitchers in total chances (66) and assists (47) and recorded just one error for a .985 fielding percentage, helping him earn his first career AL Gold Glove Award.

Thanks in part to Keuchel's transformation, the Astros enjoyed a nineteen-game improvement from the previous season, finishing fourth in the AL West Division with a 70–92 record. Nevertheless, one month before the end of the season, second-year manager Bo Porter was fired as part of efforts led by general manager Jeff Luhnow to rebuild the team's culture. He was replaced by former MLB catcher A. J. Hinch, who would name Keuchel as the 2015 opening-day starter.

CY YOUNG AWARD WINNER
In 2015 Keuchel began to look like one of the best pitchers in the game, dominating the opening season and earning AL Pitcher of the Month honors for April and May. By the season's midpoint, he was leading all major-league pitchers in innings pitched (137.1), tied for first in the league in wins (11) and ranked second in the league in ERA (2.23). He was selected to the All-Star team and was named the AL starting pitcher.

Keuchel carried his momentum into the second half of the season, winning Pitcher of the Month for August, making him the first Astros pitcher to win the award three times in one season and the first major-league pitcher to achieve that feat since Jake Peavy in 2007.

Keuchel finished the season with a record of 20–8, a 2.48 ERA, and 216 strikeouts in 232 innings. He led the majors in groundball rate (62.3 percent) and led the league in wins, innings, shutouts, and wins-above-replacement (WAR), while finishing second in the league in ERA and opponent batting average (.217). He recorded a perfect 15–0 record in home games, becoming the first pitcher to achieve the most wins at home with zero losses. The left-hander attributed much of his success to "working on the plate, making balls look like strikes and strikes look like balls," as he told Robert Sanchez for *ESPN. com* (2 June 2016). "I was in the zone."

Anchored by Keuchel's dominant pitching, the Astros emerged as one of the biggest surprises of the 2015 MLB season. The team won twenty-three of Keuchel's thirty-three starts and finished with an 86–76 record overall to advance to the playoffs for the first time since 2005. Keuchel started in and won the wild-card game against the New York Yankees, despite pitching on only three days' rest. He also won his second career postseason start, defeating the Kansas City Royals in game three of the AL Division Series, which the Astros ultimately lost in five games.

For his regular-season performance, Keuchel was awarded the 2015 Cy Young Award, becoming only the third Astros pitcher to receive the honor. He also won his second straight Gold Glove Award after leading all major-league pitchers in defensive runs saved (13) and all AL pitchers in assists (53) and total chances (72).

2016 SEASON

Expectations were high for Keuchel and the Astros as the 2016 season opened. Dogged by command issues, reduced pitching velocity, and what many observers regarded as fatigue, Keuchel regressed mightily during the first half of the season in which he struggled to a 6–9 record and a 4.80 ERA. Meanwhile, the Astros—who were early-season favorites to represent the American League in the World Series—got off to a poor 17–28 start before bouncing back to enter the midseason break with a 48–41 record. Keuchel remained confident that he would regain his form, explaining to Sanchez, "I am where I am because of changes. It's a constant evolution . . . . As much as I want to dwell on my own undoing, I have to move forward. That's the way baseball works."

PERSONAL LIFE

Keuchel spends the bulk of the off-season in Tulsa, where he enjoys spending time with friends and family.

SUGGESTED READING

Cooper, Mark. "Making of an All-Star: Dallas Keuchel's Journey to All-Star Game Starter Began in Tulsa." *Tulsa World*. BH Media Group, 14 July 2015. Web. 23 June 2016.

Drellich, Evan. "Growing Up Keuchel: How the Astros' Ace Developed His Attention to Detail, Success." *Houston Chronicle*. Hearst Newspapers, 9 May 2015. Web. 23 June 2016.

Godfrey, Ed. "How Dallas Keuchel Makes a Bunch of Old Oklahoma Prep Baseball Players Feel Better about Themselves." *NewsOK*. NewsOK.com, 27 Jan. 2016. Web. 23 June 2016.

Kepner, Tyler. "Guile Sharpens Perpetual Thorn in Yankees' Side." *New York Times*. New York Times, 27 Feb. 2016. Web. 23 June 2016.

Sanchez, Robert. "Has the Pressure Ever Been Greater for the Astros' Dallas Keuchel?" *ESPN.com*. ESPN Internet Ventures, 2 June 2016. Web. 23 June 2016.

—*Chris Cullen*

Sadiq Khan

Born: October 8, 1970
Occupation: Mayor of London

Sadiq Khan's election as mayor of London on May 5, 2016, has been widely considered a groundbreaking moment in British politics. The London-born son of Pakistani immigrants, Khan is both the city's first Muslim mayor and its first mayor to belong to an ethnic minority group. His victory was also a significant one for the Labour Party, as Khan defeated his closest competition, Conservative candidate Zac Goldsmith, by a substantial margin, in addition to replacing incumbent Conservative mayor Boris Johnson, who chose not to stand for reelection. For Khan, however, his rise to the position of mayor represents something far more personal. "The Khan story is a London story," he said in an interview for the *Economist* blog *Bagehot's Notebook* (4 Feb. 2016). "My grandparents left India to go to Pakistan. My parents left Pakistan to come to London. I will be in the first generation of Khans not to be an immigrant. London gave me and my family a chance to fulfill our potential." Assuming the role of mayor has put Khan in the position to give back to the city that granted his family so many opportunities.

Khan began his career as a human-rights lawyer, handling cases related to discrimination and civil liberties and serving for several years as chair of a human-rights advocacy organization. He began his political career as a councillor for Tooting, a ward in the London Borough of Wandsworth, and went on to serve as a member of Parliament

Katy Blackwood/CC BY-SA 4.0/Wikimedia Commons

for the area. As mayor, he has said that he intends to address issues such as housing, transportation, and infrastructure in his home city, as well as work to foster understanding and acceptance among London's diverse residents.

EARLY LIFE AND EDUCATION

Sadiq Aman Khan was born on October 8, 1970, in London, England, the fifth of eight children. His parents, Amanullah and Sehrun, had immigrated to the United Kingdom from Pakistan; their own parents were likewise immigrants, having moved from India to Pakistan following the partition of British India in 1947. In London, Khan's father found work as a bus driver, while his mother worked from home as a seamstress. Amanullah Khan was a member of a labor union, and Khan's observations of the benefits of union membership would shape much of his later views on the importance of labor organization.

Khan and his seven siblings grew up in a three-bedroom council house, part of Greater London's supply of affordable public housing, in Earlsfield, a Wandsworth ward adjacent to Tooting. Over the years, his parents worked to save up for a home while also providing financial assistance to their extended family. "My mum and dad would send money to their relatives back in Pakistan," Khan said to George Eaton for the *New Statesman* (11 Mar. 2016). "My mum still does, because we're blessed being in this country."

Growing up, Khan attended state-run schools in Tooting, including Fircroft Primary School and Ernest Bevin School (now Ernest Bevin College), a comprehensive secondary school. The latter institution had a somewhat rough reputation, but Khan has noted that he received an excellent education from the local schools. He completed his final year of secondary schooling at the Burntwood School, a girls' secondary school that is coeducational for students in their final (sixth form) year. Khan was an avid fan of soccer, but the racial intolerance he and his siblings encountered while attending games made a lasting impression on him, and he ultimately stopped supporting some of his once-favorite teams because of the behavior of their fans. In addition to keeping up with soccer matches, Khan began working at a young age, taking on a paper route and later working on construction sites and at local stores.

After leaving Burntwood, Khan attended the University of North London, now part of London Metropolitan University. Although he initially intended to become a dentist, Khan decided instead to study law, a field that appealed to him in part because of its depiction in media; he was especially a fan of the American program *LA Law*, which debuted on television while he was a teenager. "*LA Law* was about lawyers in LA who do great cases, act for the underdog, drove nice cars, look great, and I wanted to be [Victor] Sifuentes," he recalled to Jeremy Wilson for *Business Insider* (30 Jan. 2016), referring to the character portrayed by American actor Jimmy Smits. He concluded, "So I did a law degree rather than dentistry and loved law." Khan graduated from the university in 1992 and completed his education at the College of Law (now the University of Law) in Guildford, just southwest of London.

EARLY CAREER

Khan's firsthand experience with racial discrimination sparked in him a passion for human rights and social justice at an early age. In light of that long-standing interest, he entered the field of human-rights law in 1994, joining the firm Christian Fisher as a trainee solicitor. He proved to be a valuable employee and was made partner after three years. Several years later, after the departure of firm cofounder Mike Fisher, Khan was made an equity partner, and the firm was renamed Christian Khan. Khan worked closely with the firm's other named partner, human-rights lawyer Louise Christian, during his tenure there.

As a human-rights lawyer, Khan worked on numerous cases related to racial discrimination, police brutality, and other such issues. At times, it was necessary for him to represent controversial figures, a practice that his political opponents would take notice of and criticize later in his career. In 2001, for instance, he represented American activist Louis Farrakhan, who had been banned from entering the United Kingdom since the 1980s, in seeking the end of that ban. The leader of the political and religious group the Nation of Islam, Farrakhan is a polarizing figure who is considered by some to be anti-Semitic. Although Khan at times objected to the actions and rhetoric of his clients, he believed strongly in the right to equal treatment under the law, regardless of one's personal stance. "One of the great things about this country is we've got the rule of law, we've got due process, everyone's entitled to, you know, good representation," he said to Wilson.

In addition to his legal work, Khan served for several years as chair of the advocacy group Liberty, which focuses on promoting human rights and civil liberties. Khan abruptly departed Christian Khan in 2004, seeking to focus his energies on establishing himself as a politician.

ENTERING POLITICS

A member of the center-left Labour Party, Khan first entered politics in 1994, when he ran for the position of councillor for London's Tooting district and won. Only twenty-three years old when he first took the position, he would continue to represent Tooting as a councillor for twelve years. Although Khan balanced his political career with his work in human-rights law for more than a decade, he eventually determined that making more significant progress would require him to devote his attention fully to politics. "Although I'd won cases at the European Court of Human Rights, and I'd won cases in the House of Lords and the Court of Appeal, I still couldn't escape the fact that if you're part of the legislature and the executive, you can make legislation that improves the quality of life for literally millions of people," he told Esther Webber for *BBC News* (7 May 2016).

Following his departure from his law firm, Khan turned his attention toward Parliament, running for the office of member of Parliament (MP) for Tooting. He won the election in May 2005 and was reelected twice, first in 2010 and then in 2015. However, he resigned from the post a year into his third term, after being elected mayor of London.

As MP for Tooting, Khan focused particularly on issues such as transportation, the justice system, and the environment. He voted in favor of marriage equality in 2013, a move that angered some of his more socially conservative constituents. He also served for a time as a member of the shadow cabinet, the secondary cabinet set up by the leader of the opposition party, following the 2010 election of Conservative Party leader David Cameron to the office of prime minister. Under the leadership of Labour politicians Harriet Harman and Ed Miliband, Khan worked to promote Labour stances on a number of key issues.

MAYORAL CAMPAIGN

In 2016, though still representing Tooting in Parliament, Khan set his sights on a new political office: mayor of London. The city was then under the leadership of Conservative mayor Boris Johnson, who had held the position since 2008. Johnson had decided not to run for reelection, as had frequent Labour candidate and former mayor Ken Livingstone. This opened up the election to a wide range of candidates, with twelve ultimately vying for the office. Khan's chief opponent was Zac Goldsmith, a Conservative MP who was also a native Londoner. The two candidates could not have seemed more different: Khan was from a working-class immigrant family, while Goldsmith came from a wealthy, aristocratic background. Over the course of the campaign, many commentators called attention to the differences between the two, who seemed to represent two very different visions of London's future.

Although both leading candidates initially expressed a desire to keep the campaign professional, it soon took on a more personal note. Goldsmith's campaign began to attack Khan on grounds that some observers considered to be both racist and Islamophobic, attempting to draw connections between the politician and Islamic extremists. Khan's previous work as a human-rights lawyer and as chair of Liberty in some ways provided fuel for such assertions, as both jobs had sometimes put him in contact with controversial individuals and groups. Khan, however, rejected this line of attack, frequently reiterating that he was dedicated to combating extremism in Britain while also noting that Muslims were not solely responsible for dealing with the issue. "We've got to defeat radicalization and extremism by all of us working on this—this isn't a uniquely Muslim problem," he told Eaton. "There's a great saying, which is, 'It takes a village to raise a child.' Similarly, it will take a village to defeat terrorism and extremism." Largely, however, Khan sought to focus on the issues faced by London's residents in their everyday lives—issues that he, as mayor, would specifically address. "The problem with today's London is that there are too many Londoners who aren't able to fulfill their potential, they haven't got a secure affordable home, they haven't got a good local state school, they don't go to university based on their grades, they can't get good quality apprenticeships," he told Wilson.

Khan's focus on concrete problems and solutions paid off. On May 5, 2016, he was elected mayor of London, winning more than 56 percent of the second-round vote.

MAYOR OF LONDON

In his first months as mayor, Khan has worked to address a number of the problems he had identified as a candidate. One such issue was the cost of public transportation, which affected many of London's residents. During his first week in office, Khan announced that a new "hopper fare" would be introduced to the city's bus system in September, allowing riders to transfer from one bus to another for free, provided that they do so within one hour of paying their original bus fare. Riders may make only one transfer under this system; however, new technology that will allow riders to make multiple transfers within an hour is scheduled to be introduced in the relatively near future.

Although focusing significantly on city infrastructure and related areas, Khan has not lost his devotion to human rights. He is particularly interested in building bridges among London's populations and combating intolerance. Khan opposed the United Kingdom's exit from the European Union, popularly referred to as "Brexit," and has expressed concerns about the anti-immigrant rhetoric used by some Brexit proponents.

PERSONAL LIFE

Khan married fellow lawyer Saadiya Ahmed in 1994. They have two daughters, Anisah and Ammarah. A sports enthusiast, Khan is a fan of soccer and cricket, among others, and ran in the 2014 London Marathon.

SUGGESTED READING

Cowood, Fiona. "The Grazia Interview: Sadiq Khan." *Grazia Daily*. Bauer Consumer Media, 6 May 2016. Web. 12 Aug. 2016.

Eaton, George. "The Pugilist: Sadiq Khan's Quest to Become Mayor of London." *New Statesman*. New Statesman, 11 Mar. 2016. Web. 12 Aug. 2016.

Khan, Sadiq. "An Interview with Sadiq Khan." *Bagehot's Notebook*. Economist Newspaper, 4 Feb. 2016. Web. 12 Aug. 2016.

Khan, Sadiq. "London's New Mayor Sadiq Khan on Faith, London's Housing Crisis and His Favourite Joke." Interview by Alastair Campbell. *British GQ*. Condé Nast UK, 4 May 2016. Web. 12 Aug. 2016.

Sands, Sarah. "As He Launches His Bid for City Hall, Sadiq Khan Says 'I Won't Be a Zone One Mayor.'" *London Evening Standard*. Evening Standard, 13 May 2015. Web. 12 Aug. 2016.

Webber, Esther. "London Mayor: The Sadiq Khan Story." *BBC News*. BBC, 7 May 2016. Web. 12 Aug. 2016.

Wilson, Jeremy. "We Asked Sadiq Khan Why He Should Be Mayor of London (and He Gave Us His Cute Baby Pictures)." *Business Insider*. Business Insider, 30 Jan. 2016. Web. 12 Aug. 2016.

—*Joy Crelin*

Elle King

Born: July 3, 1989
Occupation: Singer

A wide audience first heard Elle King's distinctive rasp when "Playing for Keeps," the lead track of her eponymous debut EP, was chosen in 2012 as the theme song for the VH1 reality show *Mob Wives Chicago*. That audience grew wildly upon the 2014 release of her single "Ex's & Oh's," which was featured in heavy rotation on radio stations across the dial and reached the top spot on the *Billboard* rock chart. It also hit number one on the alternative chart.

"Ex's & Oh's" was released as the lead single off King's full-length debut album, *Love Stuff* (2015). Arianna Davis, in her description of the album for *O Magazine* (Mar. 2015), wrote that she found hints of Billie Holiday and Johnny Cash in King's foot-tapping songs. "It's a jumble

Levi Manchak/CC BY 2.0/Wikimedia Commons

of rock, country and R&B," King told Davis. "I used to be afraid to use the word pop to describe my music, but underneath my tough, bad-girl sound, there's some fun."

She described her sound more fully to Andrew Bevan for *Teen Vogue* (May 2013) as "a hot mess of Southern soul, with a little bit of rock 'n' roll, country, and R&B. I can't choose just one genre, so I'm going to play all of them." The result, Bevan opined, "is an authentic and deeply personal arsenal of songs about heartache, disillusionment, and kicking some serious butt that walk an emotional line with a been-there-done-that swagger."

King's lyrics often pertain to her former romantic relationships and past exploits. "I flip the turntables," she explained to Bevan. "I write a lot from the male perspective, but as a female. That's how I live my life. I can roll with the boys."

EARLY YEARS

The singer was born Tanner Elle Schneider on July 3, 1989, in Los Angeles, California to Rob Schneider, a comedian and actor best known for the *Deuce Bigalow* film franchise and his stint on *Saturday Night Live*, and London King, a former model. The couple had eloped just days after meeting, and they divorced shortly after the singer's birth.

King's mother, who ultimately left modeling to become a doula, raised King largely in southern Ohio, and she remarried when King was about nine years old. King credits her stepfather, musician Justin Tesa, with setting her on her career path. He was supposed to purchase a new Shaggy CD for her, but brought home a record by the punk band The Donnas. "When I heard the badass riffs on [their] *Rock 'N' Roll Machine*, I was hooked," she told Davis. Her introduction to The Donnas was a turning point for King's musical taste.

Tesa continued to influence her tastes. "He let me go through his records, and I started getting into Blondie and the Runaways, and then I would kind of go down a different avenue, and I got really into soul music," King recalled to Brittany Spanos for *Rolling Stone* (12 Feb. 2016). "I fell in love with Otis Redding. . . . And then I got three female heroes: Aretha Franklin, Dolly Parton, and Wanda Jackson."

While she expresses only deep affection for her mother and stepfather, King admits that as a teen, she often caused them trouble. "[All] my parents were really beautiful and wonderful and charming, and I didn't know where I fit into that spectrum," she told John Jurgensen for the *Wall Street Journal* (21 Feb. 2015). "I was chubby and goofy looking and the class clown [and I had] a really loud mouth."

GETTING AN EDUCATION AND CAUSING TROUBLE

When she got her tongue pierced without permission at age thirteen, her mother sent her to live for a time with Schneider. King had had a cameo role in Schneider's 1999 big-screen comedy, *Deuce Bigalow: Male Gigolo*; playing a seemingly cherubic door-to-door cookie salesperson who breaks into a disgusted tirade when she spies a pornographic film on the main character's television. King accompanied Schneider when he filmed the sequel *Deuce Bigalow: European Gigolo* in Amsterdam.

At about this time, she also learned to play the guitar, and she was soon using fake IDs to get into New York City clubs to play. Whenever her mother discovered the false documents and destroyed them, King simply had new ones made. "I did some stupid things when I was younger, but I got a lot out of my system," she recalled to Bevan. "Every time, my mom was waiting there with an 'I told you so.' Moms are usually right."

King dropped her father's last name when she turned eighteen to avoid professional associations with him. Despite her eventual name change, King maintains a good relationship with her father and has told journalists that she has learned a great deal from him. "We'd travel around the world I would see how he would interact with fans who would stop [him] in the street," she recalled to Garrett Kamps for *Billboard* (31 Aug. 2015). "He would give anything for his fans. At the end of the day those are the people who keep us doing what we're doing."

After finishing high school in New York City, King entered the University of the Arts, in Philadelphia, Pennsylvania. Her interest in the banjo was piqued there. "I saw a cute boy playing one," she remembered to Rob Copsey for the online British publication *Official Charts* (26 Jan. 2016). "The banjo is a beautiful instrument. I know it's not the sort of instrument many people my age pick up, but I thought, I've played the guitar for eight years–I can do that! Turns out it's a completely different instrument and it took me ages."

College did little to help King change her behavior. She often skipped classes to hang out at a local park with other aspiring musicians, and she soon dropped out altogether to follow a boyfriend to Denmark. The relationship did not last and King eventually returned home broken hearted.

SINGING CAREER

King subsequently lived for a time in Los Angeles, where she joined an ill-fated pop group overseen by former *American Idol* judge Randy Jackson. Fueled by her romantic disappointments, she began penning songs on the banjo, and one of them, "Good to Be a Man," caught the attention of a manager, who helped her ink a publishing deal with EMI. As a result of that fortuitous break, she soon found herself performing in the office of RCA Records Chairman and CEO Peter Edge. Signed to the label, she released her four-track EP in June 2012. In addition to "Good to Be a Man," the compilation included "Playing for Keeps," which was chosen as the theme song for VH1's *Mob Wives Chicago*, a short-lived spin-off of the channel's New York-based series *Mob Wives*.

Following the EP's release, RCA arranged for King to cowrite and record with a variety of other artists. "It's like a blind date," she told Spanos, explaining that it was not a satisfying period. "When I write music, it's a very personal thing to me." She began touring widely in an attempt to expand her fan base, and over the next two years she appeared at such festivals as South by Southwest (SXSW) and opened for more established artists like James Bay and Ed Sheeran. In 2013 King started working with producer Dave Bassett and her album started to fall into place.

In September 2014 she released the single "Ex's & Oh's," which quickly climbed the charts and primed fans for the February 2015 release of the full-length album *Love Stuff*. Although the name is taken from that of a Florida sex shop she drove past one day, King told Copsey, "I don't actually go into those kind of shops, honestly. I'm a little more prude than people think."

Discussing Bassett, she told Jurgensen, "The songs we wrote together made my sound. That was an amazing turning point in my life and my career." Critics agreed. Reviewing the album for the *Guardian* (10 Oct. 2015), Kitty Empire wrote: "Imagine if you crossed Dolly Parton with

Beth Ditto, or slipped Meghan Trainor into the skin of Amy Winehouse. You would get a caricature, yes–a bad girl with big retro pipes–but that caricature would not waste a second of your time. The songs would strip paint from the walls, and the talk in between them wouldn't pull many punches." At the 2016 Grammy Awards, "Ex's & Oh's" received nominations in two categories: best rock song and best rock performance.

King provided a single, "Good Girls," for the soundtrack of the 2016 remake of the film *Ghostbusters*. King also teamed up with country star Dierks Bentley for a duet titled "Different for Girls."

PERSONAL LIFE

Interviewers often mention King's larger-than-life personality and earthy appeal. "Sometimes I'm too loud and sometimes I get too drunk and sometimes I'm not very ladylike, but I'm myself," she said, as quoted by Jonathan Ringen for *Billboard* (5 Nov. 2015).

In February 2016, King became engaged to Andrew Ferguson, whom she calls Fergie. A native of Scotland, Ferguson had reportedly known King for only a few weeks before proposing during a boat ride under the Golden Gate Bridge. Although American news outlets knew little about Ferguson initially, Scottish papers reported that he had been a clerk at an upscale clothing boutique before moving to the United States to be with King.

SUGGESTED READING

Bevan, Andrew. "Elle King on Her Debut Album and Rolling with the Boys." *Teen Vogue*. Condé Nast, May 2013. Web. 5 June 2016.

Davis, Arianna. "How Elle King Became Rock's Rising Star." *O Magazine*. Hearst, Mar. 2015. Web. 5 June 2016.

Empire, Kitty. "Elle King Review—Dirt, Depth, and Attitude." *Guardian*. Guardian News and Media, 10 Oct. 2015. Web. 21 July 2016.

Jurgensen, John. "Rocker Elle King's Gritty Debut." *Wall Street Journal*. Dow Jones, 21 Feb. 2015. Web. 5 June 2016.

King, Elle. "Singer-Songwriter Elle King Gets Real about Her Hit 'Ex's & Oh's: 'The Best Music Is Honest Music.'" Interview by Garrett Kamps. *Billboard*. Billboard, 31 Aug. 2015. Web. 5 June 2016.

King, Elle. "Elle King Interview: 'I Might Curse and Drink Too Much, but I'm Not Afraid of Hard Work.'" Interview by Rob Copsey. *Official Charts*. Official UK Charts, 26 Jan. 2016. Web. 5 June 2016.

Spanos, Brittany. "Elle King Talks Shock of Grammy Nods." *Rolling Stone*. Rolling Stone, 12 Feb. 2016. Web. 5 June 2016.

—Mari Rich

Regina King

Born: January 15, 1971
Occupation: Actor

"Regina King has had the kind of slow and steady career arc that should prove as an inspiration for any actor willing to play the long game in a business that often overemphasizes youthful flashes in the pan," Robert Ham wrote for *Paste* magazine (9 Oct. 2015). That arc began in 1985 when King was a teenager and began as a series regular on the long-running situation comedy *227*; her career continued as she made favorable impressions on critics and audiences in such films as *Boyz n the Hood* (1991), *Jerry Maguire* (1996), *How Stella Got Her Groove Back* (1998), and *Daddy Day Care* (2003). More recently, King has appeared on such popular shows as *Southland*, *The Leftovers*, and *American Crime*.

King won a 2015 Primetime Emmy Award for outstanding supporting actress in a limited series or a movie for her work on *American Crime*. As Nsenga K. Burton wrote for the *Root* (26 Sept. 2015), "Regina King has finally arrived. . . . The woman who has been earning major roles in television, film, and television again has slowly but surely been building a body of work that rivals any A-list superstar in Hollywood."

Because King, on occasion, also tries her hand at directing and producing projects, she is sometimes compared to Angelina Jolie, the A-list actor who has found success behind the camera as well as in front of it. "It's a really great time for black actresses right now, but there's

a small number of those who also can direct," Cori Murray, the entertainment director for *Essence* magazine, explained to Kelley L. Carter for *Buzzfeed* (18 Mar. 2015). "She's a celebrity, but she's willing to take that step back and guide a whole new generation of actors. You think about what Angelina Jolie is able to do; know that Regina has been quietly doing those same things all along too."

EARLY YEARS

Regina King was born on January 15, 1971, and grew up in a middle-class area of Los Angeles, California. Her father, Thomas, was an electrician, and her mother, Gloria, was a special education teacher. King's older sister, Lavelle, died of a heart attack in 2010. Her younger sister, Reina, is also an actor.

King's parents divorced in 1979. When being interviewed, King often expresses great admiration for her mother, who subsequently raised the girls on her own. "Our mother was preaching and teaching us all the time," King recalled to Luaine Lee for the *Bend Bulletin* (7 Oct. 2015), explaining that Gloria was a practitioner of Religious Science, which is a movement that draws upon idealistic and pantheistic philosophies to form its teachings. King explained to Lee that her mother instilled in her daughters a belief that "if you can see it, you can achieve it" and that "love and fear are the same energy, just one applied negatively and one applied positively." King went on to explain to Lee that she felt she had "been lucky enough to have a mother that instilled, at a very young age, your value is not in what others think. It's how you feel about yourself."

Gloria willingly made the financial sacrifices necessary so that King could take classes in tap dancing, ice skating, and a host of other extracurricular activities. From age nine through fourteen, King took acting lessons from Betty Bridges, the mother of child actor Todd Bridges, who shot to stardom in the late 1970s as Willis Jackson on the television sitcom *Diff'rent Strokes*.

EARLY ACTING CAREER

King began appearing in local theater productions at the age of twelve. King first came to widespread attention in 1985, when she was cast as Brenda Jenkins, the daughter of the main character played by Marla Gibbs on *227*. The show, which was set in an apartment building bearing the titular number, ran until 1990, airing more than one hundred episodes. So popular was her portrayal of Brenda Jenkins—a boy-crazy but studious girl-next-door—that King, who attended regular public high school during her run on the show, feared she might be forever typecast.

King's next major role, as the tough-talking Shalika in John Singleton's critically acclaimed urban drama *Boyz n the Hood* (1991) was far from portraying a girl-next-door. Her performance in the role won her praise. "Fortunately, I've never had serious trauma. I haven't had somebody die from drugs. I haven't been caught up in drugs, and I don't have a mother or father who didn't have jobs or education," King told Joan Morgan for *Essence* (Oct. 1998). "The *Boyz n the Hood* story was not my story." Despite that, Singleton was impressed by the grit and realism King brought to the film, which featured several other future stars, including Cuba Gooding Jr. and Ice Cube, and he cast her in his subsequent projects *Poetic Justice* (1993) and *Higher Learning* (1995).

In 1996 King reunited with Gooding in the blockbuster film *Jerry Maguire*, which starred Tom Cruise as a sports agent at a crossroads in his career. King played the wife of Gooding's character, Rod Tidwell, a wide receiver whose exhortations to "show me the money!" became one of the picture's most-quoted lines. Thanks to the solid notices she received for her portrayal, King began auditioning for more high-profile roles.

In 1998 alone, she appeared in three films: *How Stella Got Her Groove Back*, a big-screen adaptation of a novel by Terry McMillan, who had high praise for King's work as the main character's wise-cracking sister; the political thriller *Enemy of the State*, in which she played the wife of Will Smith's character; and *Mighty Joe Young*, in which she broke away from the usual wife and sister roles to portray a wildlife researcher.

GAINING PROMINENCE

Although not winning high-profile major roles, King found herself in steady demand over the next several years. She acted in such big-screen comedies as *Daddy Day Care* (2003), *Legally Blonde 2: Red, White & Blonde* (2003), and *Miss Congeniality 2: Armed and Fabulous* (2005), and she received her best reviews to date for her work in the 2004 biopic *Ray*, which starred Jamie Foxx as Ray Charles, the iconic soul musician. King played Charles's back-up singer and mistress Margie Hendricks in a performance that Peter Travers for *Rolling Stone* (20 Oct. 2004) called "dynamite." A. O. Scott, a movie critic for the *New York Times* (29 Oct. 2004), similarly praised King for "matching Mr. Foxx's feints and weaves with bouncing pugnacity."

Although her film career was going well, King ultimately sought a return to television work in order to spend more time with her family. In 2007 she was featured in nine episodes of the political thriller series *24*, playing attorney Sandra Palmer who represents the Islamic-American Alliance and is the sister of President Wayne Palmer, whom she advises on Muslim relations. From 2009 to 2013 she starred as the strong but flawed Detective Lydia Adams in the police drama *Southland*. "It's incredibly hard out there for women of color. That's why I do love being a woman of substance on *Southland*," she told Allison Samuels for the *Daily Beast* (29 Jan. 2012). "Someone who isn't a caricature and isn't a stereotype. But remember she wasn't written as a black character and that makes a big difference in how she can be portrayed." After a four-episode guest stint during the 2013 and 2014 seasons of the comedy *The Big Bang Theory*, King appeared in the HBO dramatic series *The Leftovers* in 2015. She played Dr. Erika Murphy, the matriarch of a seemingly perfect family that is in reality hiding dark secrets.

AMERICAN CRIME

Early in 2015 King began appearing in the critically acclaimed anthology series *American Crime*, which follows the participants in a racially charged murder trial. During its first season, she portrayed Aliyah Shadeed, an African American convert to Islam and the sister of the prime suspect in the crime. "I felt like it was important to stay rooted and confident in the choice that this woman made to change her name, to welcome Allah into her heart," King, who interviewed several Muslim women while preparing for the role, told Ham of her character. "This was a woman who was probably born and raised Baptist. . . . What was it about this religion that made her change? There has to be something beautiful about it. I felt like if I always remember . . . that any thoughts that she may have that may be perceived as radical . . . are still rooted from a really beautiful place." King's portrayal garnered her a Primetime Emmy Award, an honor that critics have nearly universally characterized as well deserved.

King has returned for the second season of the show, as have many of the other actors, although the story arc is entirely new and each actor plays a different character. Set at a Midwest high school, the plot revolves around a sexual assault, and King portrays the parent of one of the students involved.

ANIMATION VOICE-OVERS AND TELEVISION DIRECTING

King can be heard in one of the most attention-getting series on her résumé: *The Boondocks*, which is an animated show based on a comic strip by Aaron McGruder. It follows the adventures of African American brothers Huey and Riley Freeman who live in a predominantly white suburb. After it premiered in 2005, the show was lauded and disparaged for its unflinching look at the issues of race and culture. King provides the voices for both brothers and has won praise for her ability to transition smoothly between the

two characters, as well as for the warmth and humanity she brings to them.

King's directing credits include a 2013 episode of *Southland*, a 2015 episode of the hit show *Scandal*, and several episodes of the 2015 BET (Black Entertainment Television) series *Being Mary Jane*, about the life and loves of an attractive young talk-show host.

PERSONAL LIFE

King was married to Ian Alexander Sr., a music-industry executive, from 1997 to 2007. They had one child, Ian Jr., before their acrimonious split. At the insistence of King, who remembered the trauma of her parents' divorce, they later recaptured some semblance of friendship for the sake of their son.

Much to the delight of tabloid readers, King went on to date actor Malcolm Jamal Warner, who played Theo Huxtable in the hit television comedy *The Cosby Show* (1984–92). The pair split in 2013, and although occasional dating rumors surface, King has told interviewers that she is more focused on her work, son, and close friends than on her romantic life.

SUGGESTED READING

Burton, Nsenga K. "Emmy Award-Winning Actress Regina King Talks HBO's *The Leftovers*." *Root*. Univision Communications, 26 Sept. 2015. Web. 11 Dec. 2015.

Carter, Kelley L. "How Regina King Has Stayed Relevant—and Happy!—in Hollywood for 30 Years." *Buzzfeed*. Buzzfeed, 18 Mar. 2015. Web. 11 Dec. 2015.

Ham, Robert. "Regina King Talks *The Leftovers*, *American Crime*, and Getting in the Director's Chair." *Paste*. Paste Media, 9 Oct. 2015. Web. 11 Dec. 2015.

Lee, Luaine. "Regina King Has Endured Ups and Downs." *Bend Bulletin*. Bulletin, 7 Oct. 2015. Web. 11 Dec. 2015.

Samuels, Allison. "Regina King: *Southland* Star Defies TV Stereotypes of Black Women." *Daily Beast*. Daily Beast, 29 Jan. 2012. Web. 11 Dec. 2015.

SELECTED WORKS

227, 1985–90; *Boyz n the Hood*, 1991; *Jerry Maguire*, 1996; *How Stella Got Her Groove Back*, 1998; *Enemy of the State*, 1998; *Ray*, 2004; *24*, 2007; *Southland*, 2009–13; *The Leftovers*, 2014–15; *American Crime*, 2015–

—*Mari Rich*

Ezra Klein

Born: May 9, 1984
Occupation: Journalist

Ezra Klein is best known for his work as a blogger for the *Washington Post*. His widely acclaimed *Wonkblog* specializes in covering policy formation, including health-care policy and budgetary issues. In addition to his work as a journalist, Klein also makes regular television appearances to discuss politics and policy. In 2014, he became the editor in chief of the news website *Vox*.

EARLY LIFE AND EDUCATION

Ezra Klein was born on May 9, 1984, in Irving, California. His father worked as a math professor, and his mother worked as an artist. Although Klein graduated from high school with a low GPA, he was accepted at the University of California, Santa Cruz (UCSC), and he later transferred to the University of California, Los Angeles (UCLA).

Klein developed an interest in blogging after several unsuccessful attempts to secure writing internships and a position on the UCSC student newspaper. During this time, he also developed a passion for politics, becoming a Democratic Party activist and an active supporter of Gary Hart's short-lived presidential campaign. In 2004, Klein covered the Democratic National Convention as a blogger, a type of journalistic coverage that was still novel at the time. He earned a bachelor's degree in political science from UCLA in 2005.

By the time Klein was twenty years old, he had been published in the *Washington Monthly* and *LA Weekly*. Having developed a large reading audience and a reputation as a skillful political writer and media critic in a variety of Internet forums and newspapers, Klein took a writing fellowship at the *American Prospect* and began blogging for the magazine in 2005. He was promoted to staff writer the following year and to associate editor in 2007.

Although Klein maintained his liberal political perspective at the *American Prospect*, his work became more nuanced, focusing on the details of policy development and implementation. Covering issues ranging from health care to financial regulation reform, Klein used the blog format to his advantage, writing copiously and posting content regularly in order to follow the nuances of the political process.

WONKBLOG

Klein remained with the *American Prospect* until 2009, when he joined the staff of the *Washington Post*. His move to the paper was representative of a larger trend in mainstream media: the increased acceptance of blogging and digital media as a reputable and effective method of journalism. Klein and his colleague Melissa Bell helped introduce a new journalism workflow to the *Washington Post*, one better adapted to the demands of the digital space. They introduced new content-management technologies in order to provide readers with content, video, and images within turn times that far exceeded traditional print-based methods.

At the *Washington Post*, Klein blogged primarily about economic issues and domestic policy. His *Wonkblog*, for which he served as writer and editor, developed into a key feature of the newspaper's digital offerings. Under Klein's direction, the blog gained a reputation for producing clear explanations of multifaceted policy debates and providing cogent overviews of various federal policies. Klein also offered tongue-in-cheek deconstructions of the mainstream media's coverage of major policy debates.

Throughout the early 2010s, *Wonkblog* provided detailed coverage and analysis of the debate surrounding federal health-care reform. It offered readers historical context, reviewing the successes and failures of various health-care plans proposed by previous administrations and members of Congress and comparing health-care systems around the world. Klein and his staff worked to simplify for their readers the complex issues surrounding the larger health-care debate, including employer coverage regulations, insurance requirements, federal and state funding commitments, and the individual mandate provision of the Patient Protection and Affordable Care Act of 2010.

In addition to health-care reform, *Wonkblog* also covered such issues as immigration reform, national security, and domestic policy. It became one of the most widely read political blogs in the United States, popular with voters, journalists, and legislators alike. In combination with *Wonkblog*'s offerings, Klein penned a daily policy review entitled *Wonkbook* that was delivered to readers as a blog page and in the form of a daily e-mail. Included with *Wonkbook*'s daily issues summary were regularly appearing short-form features that provided links to expanded coverage elsewhere on the web.

By 2013, *Wonkblog* was drawing more than four million monthly views, increasing to as many as ten million during peak months. *Wonkblog*'s efficient and thorough writing style and centrist political perspective helped solidify its popularity and establish it as a significant revenue source for the *Washington Post* during a period of dwindling print subscriptions.

Beyond his work as a writer, which has included long-form pieces for the *New Yorker* and a column for *Bloomberg View*, Klein began making regular television appearances. He has appeared as a political commentator on such programs as the *Rachel Maddow Show, Countdown with Keith Olbermann,* and *Hardball with Chris Matthews.* Taking advantage of Klein's ability to deliver efficient explanations of complex topics, the *Rachel Maddow Show* designed a recurring feature specifically for Klein called "The Ezra Klein Challenge."

VOX MEDIA

Klein left the *Washington Post* with two of his colleagues in 2014 to start a new venture with the digital-media company Vox Media. (The *Washington Post* retained ownership of and continues to produce content for *Wonkblog.*) Klein undertook his new project with *Slate* columnist Matt Yglesias and former *Washington Post* colleagues Melissa Bell and Dylan Matthews. He has stated that he seeks to create a new digital journalistic model aimed at moving beyond traditional print and television media's focus on new information, focusing instead on providing background and contextual information in order to improve comprehension. The website, simply titled *Vox,* debuted in April 2014.

IMPACT

Through his determined attention to detail, Klein became one of the first major stars of the journalist blogosphere and helped establish the blog format as a new force in political journalism. The *Week* magazine named Klein the blogger of the year in 2010. In 2011, *GQ* magazine named him one of the fifty most powerful people in Washington, DC. Klein received the American Political Science Association's Carey McWilliams Award for political journalism in 2013.

PERSONAL LIFE

In October 2011, Klein married Annie Lowrey, an economic correspondent for the *New York Times* and *New York* magazine.

SUGGESTED READING

Butterworth, Trevor. "The End of the Wunderkind." *Awl.* Awl Network, 24 Jan. 2014. Web. 23 July 2014.

Byers, Dylan, and Hadas Gold. "Why Ezra Klein Left the Washington Post." *Politico.* Politico, 21 Jan. 2014. Web. 23 July 2014.

Friedersdorf, Conor. "How Will Ezra Klein's 'Project X' Add Context to News?" *Atlantic.* Atlantic Monthly, 5 Feb. 2014. Web. 23 July 2014.

Ioffe, Julia. "Ezra Klein: The Wise Boy." *New Republic.* New Republic, 12 Feb. 2013. Web. 23 July 2014.

Pierce, Charles P. "Ezra Klein Gets It Very Wrong." *Esquire.* Hearst Communications, 11 Mar. 2013. Web. 23 July 2014.

Wallace, Benjamin. "Here, Let Ezra Explain." *New York.* New York Media, 2 Feb. 2014. Web. 23 July 2014.

—*Joshua Pritchard*

Lisa Kron

Born: May 20, 1961
Occupation: Actor, playwright

Playwright Lisa Kron has often used her own life and family as sources for her work. A cofounder of the writing and acting team Five Lesbian Brothers, she achieved major success with her Tony Award–winning musical *Fun Home,* which premiered in 2013. She has received playwriting fellowships from many sources, including the Sundance Theater Lab and the Guggenheim Foundation, and has taught at the Yale School of Drama. Kron explained to Gary Garrison for *Dramatist* (Mar./Apr. 2012), "The operating principle of theatre is based on the most universal and inescapable fact of human experience, which is that none of us, no matter who we are or in what ways we are privileged, knows what will happen in the coming moment. I believe that inescapable truth is theatre's animating force and our principal tool as theatre makers."

EARLY LIFE AND EDUCATION

Kron was born to Jewish parents in 1961 and grew up in Lansing, Michigan. Her father, Walter, fled Nazi Germany at the age of fifteen in

D Dipasupil/FilmMagic/Getty Images

1937, but his parents were killed in a concentration camp; these family memories would help shape Kron's worldview. Her mother, Ann, was a local activist, determined that her children should live in a racially diverse neighborhood. Ann also suffered from poor health including episodes of severe fatigue. After later using both parents as subjects of plays, Kron admitted to Beth Stevens for *Broadway.com* (11 May 2015), "There's something slightly indefensible about writing about other people who are alive. . . . I think writers do it because they believe they have an imperative that's greater than the imperative to let people control their own image."

As a young girl in 1960s and 70s Kron was often frustrated by her social status. "I was consciously waiting to be an adult," she told Stevens. "I was someone who was a mini adult trapped in a child's body waiting to be set free. I was painfully shy as a kid." That shyness caused her to feel invisible, and she developed a sense of humor in part to become visible.

Kron did not attend theater as a young person, but she listened to cast albums of popular musicals such as *Fiddler on the Roof, Camelot,* and *My Fair Lady.* She graduated from Everett High School in 1979 and attended Kalamazoo College as a theater major. She suffered from severe allergies, leading to a stay in an allergy hospital while in college, as well as chronic fatigue syndrome similar to her mother. These conditions developed her interest in health and wellness issues.

NEW YORK CITY AND THE FIVE LESBIAN BROTHERS

In the mid-1980s, after touring with a theater repertory company, Kron went to New York City, where she was drawn into the East Village performance art milieu. She found a home at the WOW Café Theater, a collective dedicated to empowering women and offering lesbian performers a voice. The experience not only upended her more traditional understanding of theater but also offered sexual freedom. Of those early years Kron told Garrison, "I just kept moving forward wherever there were open doors. I was scared of everything but I was more scared of looking back and realizing I had not done the things I was afraid of . . . and regretting that."

Kron honed her craft going from one club to another, learning what worked and what did not. She told Wendy Weisman for *American Theatre* (Mar. 2006) that this served as a "vaudevillian education." While performing solo shows—mainly improvised comedy—she ultimately determined that what most interested her was the nature of drama. Once she felt she understood the dramatic action of a solo show she moved on to other forms.

Kron joined four other lesbian writers and performers—Maureen Angelos, Babs Davy, Dominique Dibbell, and Peg Healey—in an effort to write a play to tour. *Voyage to Lesbos* (1990) was the result, and the process of learning to write together and giving up complete control formed the women into a cohesive group. They playfully named themselves after the 1938 children's book *Five Chinese Brothers.* The company would go on to numerous accolades, including Obie and Bessie Awards.

Joining the group was a means for Kron to transition from improvisational solo shows to writing. Yet collaboration did not come naturally to her, as she explained in an interview with John Dias for *Dramatist* (2006): "I assumed I would still be in charge, but I was quickly disabused of that, and it took a long time for me to get to a true collaboration. The Brothers don't write for their own characters. We don't cast a play until it's done, so we're not writing the lines we want to say. We're writing for the play. We're not writing for ourselves." The experience changed her mind about collaborative work to the extent that she later required students to collaborate while teaching at Yale.

2.5 MINUTE RIDE

Kron continued collaborating with the Brothers but also began writing new works on her own. Her play *101 Humiliating Stories* (1993) and the Brothers production *The Secretaries* (1994) were both well received. But it was the 1996 debut of her play *2.5 Minute Ride* that showcased her true gift for manipulating dramatic form. The work examines her relationship with her father, an emotionally distant survivor of the Holocaust. The show braids three strands: her father's love of roller coasters, the trip the two of them made to the Auschwitz concentration camp, and her brother's orthodox wedding to a Jewish woman. It opened in New York City Off-Broadway at the Joseph Papp Theater in 1999 and won an Obie Award.

As Kron told Simi Horwitz for *Back Stage* (1999), "I wanted to raise the question of how we see the past. The actual event and the memory of it are two different things. I also wanted to look at my relationship to my father's history as a way of coming to terms with his—and my mother's—impending death." To challenge the idea of memory, Kron's narrator operates a slide projector showing no images, only rectangles of light. The work also changed Kron's ideas about autobiographical pieces versus fiction pieces. She learned that in contrast to her presuppositions, the former was not easier. She told Horwitz, "I used to feel that acting in an autobiographical work was less scary than appearing in a fictional piece because I'd be able to control what audiences see about me. I've changed my mind about the safety of the autobiographical piece"

WELL AND *IN THE WAKE*

Kron's next work, *Well*, debuted in 2004 and also had its roots in autobiography. It is a play about a dramatist named Lisa Kron writing a play and trying to find its central concerns. It is also about Kron's mother, Ann, a character in the play who is ill and yet upstaging everyone else and questioning the version of events the playwright is trying to offer. Kron explained the disruptions to Weisman, "*Well* really is about how we create narrative to make sense of our lives, and how each of our own individual narratives is not necessarily true for someone else. We each make sense of the world in a different way."

Well opened on Broadway in 2006 with Kron playing herself, actor Jayne Houdyshell playing her mother, and Leigh Silverman directing. Dias noted that the show's fragmented narrative and examination of health suggest that "wellness lies in our ability to embrace the complexities and contradictions of life." Kron found it gratifying that the show, written by a woman and with mainly women in the cast, could make it to the male-dominated world of Broadway. Both Kron and Houdyshell were nominated for Tony Awards for their performances.

Although the Broadway run closed after six weeks, it received critical acclaim and opened new opportunities for Kron. She was invited to facilitate writing workshops in Italy in 2007. Her next show, *In the Wake*, premiered in 2010, and was her first work in which she did not also act. The show concerns a woman, Ellen, whose life is shaped by the events of the early twenty-first century. Although still retaining some autobiographical elements, *In the Wake* saw Kron make a conscious effort to create a main character of universal appeal. In doing so she addressed large, often political themes both directly and through allegory. Kron explained that the spark for writing the show was the number of people who kept asking how the September 11, 2001, terrorist attacks could have happened to America. As she told Kate Taylor for the *New York Times* (17 Oct. 2010), "There were many people, like me, who found that an appalling question. Why *not* us? What does that mean? You really think there's logic to that kind of pain or tragedy?"

FUN HOME

In addition to writing Kron continued acting in other works, including a highly praised production of Bertolt Brecht's *Good Person of Szechwan* by the Foundry Theater in 2013. Yet her acting career would continue to be overshadowed by her writing with the premier of her next play later that same year. The musical *Fun Home*, based on the graphic memoir of the same name by Alison Bechdel, took Kron in a new direction and soon became her most successful work. She wrote the book and lyrics of the adaptation to go with a score by Jeanine Tesori, balancing the writing, rewriting, and production process with her other acting duties. Of her dashing from one role to another, Kron told Eric Grode for *New York Times* (24 Oct. 2013), "It's deliciously overwhelming to leave this one totally immersive world, take the elevator and come out into this other world."

Bechdel's story relates the difficulty of coming out to her parents and the suicide of her closeted gay father. Kron worked to create an original piece from the graphic novel. Her experience working with material inspired by real-life events helped her work out the adaptation despite it being her first musical. She and Tesori checked with Bechdel on the changes in the script, earning the author's strong approval. The original production at New York City's Public Theater was met with rave reviews, earning several extensions, and a Broadway production opened in March 2015. The show was nominated for a Pulitzer Prize and a host of other high-profile awards. It eventually won five Tony Awards out of ten nominations, including best musical, best book of a musical, and best original score, which Kron shared with Tesori. They made history as the first all-female writing team to win the latter award. Other prizes included three Lucille Lortel Awards, the New York Drama Critics' Circle Award for best musical, and two Obie Awards.

PERSONAL LIFE

In 2015 Kron married Madeleine George, another playwright and cofounder of the 13 Playwrights theater company. They had been together for nearly two decades when they married. Kron does not have formal academic training in playwriting. Instead, as she told Dias, "I don't see a play's structure on paper, but I can feel it when I'm in front of people and saying it out loud. I feel it reflected back to me from the audience."

SUGGESTED READING

Grode, Eric. "A Quick Trip from Playwright to Player: Lisa Kron Juggles Two Shows at Public Theater." *New York Times*. New York Times, 24 Oct. 2013. Web. 21 Jan. 2016.

Horwitz, Simi. "Going Solo." *Back Stage* 40.19 (1999): 28. Print.

Kron, Lisa. "The Importance of Being Lisa Kron." Interview by Wendy Weisman. *American Theatre* 23.3 (2006): 34–37. Web. 2 Feb. 2016.

Kron, Lisa. "*Fun Home* Scribe Lisa Kron on the 'Slightly Questionable' Act of Writing about Real People and Her Quest Not to Be Invisible." Interview by Beth Stevens. *Broadway.*

com. Broadway.com, 11 May 2015. Web. 22 Jan. 2016.

Kron, Lisa, Jayne Houdyshell, and Leigh Silverman. "On Well." Interview by John Dias. *Dramatist* 8.5 (2006): 44–47. Print.

Smith, Anna Deavere, Lisa Kron, Sarah Jones, and Mike Daisey. "Solo Actor/Writer Round Table." Interview by Gary Garrison. *Dramatist* 14.4 (2012): 8–17. Print.

Taylor, Kate. "Pushing the Spotlight Away From Herself." *New York Times*. New York Times, 17 Oct. 2010. Web. 25 Jan. 2016.

SELECTED WORKS
2.5 Minute Ride, 1996; *Well*, 2004; *In the Wake*, 2010; *Fun Home*, 2013

—*Judy Johnson*

Gage Skidmore/CC BY-SA 3.0/Wikimedia Commons

Brie Larson

Born: October 1, 1989
Occupation: Actor

Award-winning actor Brie Larson has been performing her craft for the better part of her life. As she told Jenelle Riley for *Variety* (13 Oct. 2015), "I was born with a clear idea of what I wanted to do. It has not always been easy for me because of it." First appearing regularly on television in 2001, she continued to make a name for herself in Hollywood, diligently working her way up to her most intense and widely praised role to date in the independent film *Room* (2015), which moved her into the ranks of A-list actors. At the same time, she has become interested in other parts of the industry, such as directing, helping to create and enter the award-winning film *The Arm* at the 2012 Sundance Film Festival.

Despite receiving the Academy Award for best actress in 2016, she explained to Jack Smart for *Backstage* (21 Oct. 2015) that she still struggles with the process of separating her self-identity from her film personas: "It's impossible, when you're playing a character for twelve hours a day, to assume that's not going to rewire some aspects of your brain. It just will. . . . But then you have to spend an equal amount of time undoing those neurons you're wiring together, to make sure you're back to yourself."

EARLY LIFE AND EDUCATION
Brie Larson was born Brianne Sidonie Desaulniers in Sacramento, California, on October 1, 1989, to parents who both worked as chiropractors. She and her younger sister, Milaine, were homeschooled. At age six, following a declaration to her mother as she washed dishes one day that she was determined to become an actor and despite being shy and wary of eye contact, Larson became the youngest person ever to enter the program at the American Conservatory Theater in San Francisco.

Soon after relocating with her mother and Milaine to Los Angeles in pursuit of her dream, Larson began acting under her more pronounceable stage name when she was seven, appearing in a commercial for a phony "Malibu Mudslide" Barbie broadcast on *The Tonight Show with Jay Leno*. Although she had been told the trip was only temporary, she eventually learned that her parents had decided to divorce before they left Sacramento, leaving the three to settle permanently in a small studio apartment, an experience that helped prepare her for her star turn in *Room* years later.

Though she did land minor roles in television shows such as *Touched by an Angel* (1999), her big breakout role on the small screen came when she was cast in 2001 as one of the daughters of Bob Saget's character on the WB sitcom *Raising Dad*. While the show was canceled by 2002, the following year she starred in the Disney Channel film *Right on Track*. Even at that age, however, Larson knew she did not want to become a Disney kid. As she told Riley, "I just couldn't do it. I always had this attraction to holding up a mirror to the world, and this didn't feel like real life. I wondered what would be the point." While still young, Larson became adept at turning down roles that did not fit her vision.

Meanwhile, after spending just a day-and-a-half at a traditional high school before deciding she did not fit in, Larson opted for another way to get her education. She explained to Amy

Nicholson for *BoxOffice Pro* (16 Mar. 2012), "It was also that I didn't feel like the teachers were cultivating anything. And I was already working and already immersed in this other world—and loving every second of it—and staying in a high school wasn't really conducive to that. They wanted my butt in a seat. They weren't going to put things aside for me because I couldn't be in class when I was working. So it wasn't the right fit." At one point, famed music executive Tommy Mottola saw enough potential in her as a teenage pop singer to sign her, and together they produced the album *Finally out of P.E.* in 2005. However, Larson quickly lost interest in producing music commercially.

FINDING HER FOOTING

Larson resumed auditioning and was eventually cast in her second regular television role on cable channel Showtime's *United States of Tara* in 2009, costarring as the daughter of veteran actor Toni Collette's character. During the show's run, she also performed a small but often scene-stealing role as the main character's ex-girlfriend in the film *Scott Pilgrim vs. the World* (2010). Though she would come to feel comfortable on the set of *United States of Tara* as she remained with the show until its end in 2011, she also expressed gratitude at having the opportunity to use that experience to further her career, as she explained to Matthew Jacobs for the *Huffington Post* (16 Oct. 2015): "I was there from eighteen to twenty, such an important time in my life and such a safe place where I was so loved and understood and nurtured. . . . I still miss it, but it was a great opportunity for me to find myself again and not just stay in a safe place, but to go back out in the world and see what was there for me."

Her exposure on *United States of Tara* earned Larson more parts in mainstream films, such as that of the teenage punk-rock daughter of Woody Harrelson's lead character David Douglas Brown in the drama *Rampart* (2011). Additionally, as part of her efforts to achieve a greater sense of self, she decided to branch out into writing and directing, submitting her codirected and cowritten film *The Arm* at the 2012 Sundance Film Festival, which won the short film special jury award for comedic storytelling. With the 2012 film *21 Jump Street*, she moved into a comedy role as Molly, a high school student and the romantic interest of undercover police officer Morton Schmidt (Jonah Hill).

TAKING THE LEAD

In 2013, Larson landed her first starring role in the independent film *Short Term 12* as a supervisor of troubled teenagers in a group home. The film, heavily lauded by critics, was nominated for three Film Independent Spirit Awards and won two awards at the South by Southwest Film Festival. Larson, who also received critical praise and even comparisons to Jennifer Lawrence's breakout role in *Winter's Bone* (2010), won the Gotham Independent Film Award for best actress.

That film brought her to the attention of Irish director Lenny Abrahamson, who had been working for a year on a script for *Room* with the author of the 2010 novel of the same name, Emma Donoghue. She had been reworking her novel into a film and had already written a first draft, looking for the right collaboration. Abrahamson wrote Donoghue a moving letter asking to assist with her project. The writer was impressed with his understanding of how the film should look, as she told Riley, "He had such confidence with aspects of the project other directors found scary, like the first half being set in a locked room. Other directors suggested ways around it—flashbacks, animation, fantasy sequences. He would have none of that." After watching her performance in *Short Term 12*, Abrahamson put Larson on the short list of actors he would consider for the lead role and then cast her.

After appearing alongside Mark Wahlberg in *The Gambler* (2014) and knowing that she was going to be working on *Room*, an intense film, Larson determined to become involved in a more lighthearted project in the meantime. She accepted a role in the comedic Judd Apatow film *Trainwreck* (2015), playing the younger sister of comedian Amy Schumer's main character. She told Laurie Sandell for *Hollywood Reporter* (20 Jan. 2016), "I thought, 'Before I go away and be a monk, I'll do this fun thing, laugh . . . and eat whatever I want.'"

ROOM

Larson won critical and commercial acclaim for her complex role as Ma in *Room*, netting both an Academy Award and a Golden Globe Award for best actress in a drama. The indie film, shot in forty-nine days in Toronto, Canada, is a gripping drama that was also awarded the Grolsch People's Choice Award at the Toronto International Film Festival. For seven years, Ma—who was kidnapped and raped at seventeen—and her son, born two years later, are kept in a shack in the backyard of the man who took her innocence. Larson told Smart, "It's very draining to play somebody with that type of emotional charge inside of her." To understand the effects of claustrophobia and lack of light, she met with therapists, finding relief during the intense work in caring for her costar, Jacob Tremblay, who plays Ma's son and was eight years old at the time.

Larson had the luxury of eight months between being cast and filming to acclimate herself to playing a woman with bad teeth and an in-jured wrist who also has a vitamin D deficiency and is understandably depressed. She worked with a trainer, ate six small, protein-rich meals daily, and lost fifteen pounds to gain the gaunt look required. Staying out of the sun to achieve the pallor of a captive, she remained in her home for a month, also warning family and friends that she could be extra sensitive while filming.

Working on the film, rather than depressing Larson, gave her a sense of gratitude. She called her mother every few days during filming to apol-ogize for yet another remembered unkindness from her childhood. She also realized that her mother had made their isolation and poverty fun following the divorce. In addition, she was kept from darkness by the attitude of Tremblay, who found being in a film—even one so difficult—to be a delight, which was infectious. The two both enjoy *Star Wars* and *Legos*, another connection, and Larson's ability to name all of the Teenage Mutant Ninja Turtles helped as well.

By the end of the shoot, Abrahamson knew that he had chosen his lead actor well and highly praised her talents as a refined and versatile per-former. "Brie has this very special quality, which is that she can go to these very dark and emo-tionally raw places, but she does it with such simplicity and grace," he shared with Jane Mulk-errins for the *Telegraph* (23 Feb. 2016). Her per-formance catapulted her from supporting roles to being an A-list bankable star.

IN DEMAND
Two films starring Larson were scheduled for release in 2016: the musical romantic com-edy *Basmati Blues* and the British crime drama *Free Fire*. Additionally, following her star turn in *Room*, she was cast in the latest King Kong film, *Kong: Skull Island*, which is scheduled for a 2017 release; costars include Samuel L. Jack-son and John C. Reilly. Her ability to do both comedy and drama had attracted the attention of the film's director, Jordan Vogt-Roberts. He told Sandell, "She weaves and slaloms between com-edy and drama in a seamless way."

Larson has also been cast in a film adapta-tion of Jeannette Walls's 2005 memoir *The Glass Castle*, in which she will again costar with Harrelson.

PERSONAL LIFE
Larson is engaged to Alex Greenwald, the lead singer for Phantom Planet. She finds the suc-cess she has achieved comes with a price. As she explained to Riley, "The hardest pill for me to swallow has been receiving recognition, getting dressed up, going to events. That's the part that has always terrified me. You can see dozens of photos where I have zero hair and makeup and I'm wearing my own jeans and T-shirt, because I

was not that interested in that side of it." Serv-ing on the board of Los Angeles–based nonprofit Cinefamily, she has started Women of Cinefam-ily, which highlights films written, directed by, or starring women.

SUGGESTED READING
Manly, Lorne. "Brie Larson Finds a Hectic Life after *Room.*" *New York Times.* New York Times, 31 Dec. 2015. Web. 7 July 2016.

Mulkerrins, Jane. "Oscar Nominee Brie Larson: '*Room* Was Exhausting to Shoot.'" *Telegraph.* Telegraph Media Group, 23 Feb. 2016. Web. 7 July 2016.

Riley, Jenelle. "Brie Larson Opens Up on the 'Emotional Marathon' of *Room.*" *Variety.* Vari-ety Media, 13 Oct. 2015. Web. 7 July 2016.

Sandell, Laurie. "Brie Larson's 20-Year Climb to Overnight Stardom: I'm 'Totally out of My Comfort Zone.'" *Hollywood Reporter.* Hol-lywood Reporter, 20 Jan. 2016. Web. 7 July 2016.

Smart, Jack. "Make 'Room' on Your Oscar Short-list for Brie Larson." *Backstage.* Backstage, 21 Oct. 2015. Web. 7 July 2016.

SELECTED WORKS
Raising Dad, 2001–2; *United States of Tara,* 2009–11; *Rampart,* 2011; *21 Jump Street,* 2012; *Short Term 12,* 2013; *The Gambler,* 2014; *Train-wreck,* 2015; *Room,* 2015

—*Judy Johnson*

Katie Ledecky
Born: March 17, 1997
Occupation: Swimmer

Maryland native Katie Ledecky is the "best swimmer in the world today," Jeff Metcalfe de-clared for the *Arizona Republic* (13 Apr. 2015). Widely considered the best female distance free-style specialist of all time, Ledecky has enjoyed an unprecedented run of success since burst-ing onto the international swimming scene in 2012, when at age fifteen she unexpectedly won the gold medal in the 800-meter freestyle event at the Summer Olympic Games in London. A product of the renowned Nation's Capital Swim Club, Ledecky is the world record holder in the 400-, 800-, and 1,500-meter freestyle events and has held a stranglehold on those events since the 2012 Games. She has also consistently es-tablished herself among the world's best in the 200-meter freestyle. Ledecky, who is known for her humble demeanor and unrelenting work eth-ic, has won a total of fifteen gold medals in major international competitions.

Freed Photography/CC BY-SA 4.0/Wikimedia Commons

EARLY LIFE

Kathleen "Katie" Genevieve Ledecky was born on March 17, 1997, in Washington, DC, the younger of the two children of David and Mary Gen Ledecky. Ledecky grew up in a family of swimming enthusiasts. Her late maternal grandfather, Edward Hagan, was an avid swimmer who helped spearhead the development of an indoor pool in Williston, North Dakota, where he raised his family. Ledecky's mother, a former hospital administrator, swam on the pool's swim team and later became a standout swimmer at the University of New Mexico (UNM).

Ledecky was drawn to swimming through her mother, who was nationally ranked in the 200 freestyle during her time at UNM. Ledecky then began swimming competitively at age six after following her brother Michael, who is three years older, onto a summer swim team called the Palisade Porpoises. The same year, Ledecky and her brother joined the Nation's Capital Swim Club (NCAP, then known as the Curl-Burke Swim Club).

A natural in the water, Ledecky demonstrated "real promise in her ability to understand how to do each stroke," as her mother noted to Dan Friedell for the *Washington Times* (18 Apr. 2012). Competitive and with an eagerness to succeed, Ledecky embraced the discipline required of an elite swimmer and began training in earnest. She played other sports growing up, such as soccer and basketball, but ultimately gave those up to focus on swimming.

GROOMED FOR SUCCESS

Throughout her youth Ledecky dominated her peers in age-group races, or as her father put it to Friedell, "blew away the field." Though exceptionally proficient in each of the four competitive swimming strokes, Ledecky stood out early on in the freestyle, which complemented her tall, lean frame and naturally long arm stroke. By age nine, she was already competing in distance freestyle events.

Ledecky's early development as a swimmer was fostered by Yuri Suguiyama, who coached the NCAP for six years before becoming an assistant coach at the University of California, Berkeley, in 2012. Suguiyama, a former standout distance freestyler at the University of North Carolina, recognized Ledecky's potential for greatness and optimized her training by cycling in fresh male swimmers to challenge her during workouts. "The one thing that worked with Katie," he explained to Karen Crouse for the *New York Times* (26 Apr. 2014), "is we never put expectations on her because she usually blew those out of the water."

Ledecky was driven toward success by her parents, who took turns shuttling her to weekday morning and afternoon club practices. Her mother kept her well-nourished and encouraged her to approach races with a sprinter's mindset. Meanwhile, Ledecky's father, an attorney, handled the logistics of her demanding year-round swimming commitments. According to family friend Ted Leonsis, majority owner of the Washington Capitals, Wizards, and Mystics, Ledecky was raised in an environment that "promoted excellence but didn't stringently demand it," as he said to Dave Sheinin for the *Washington Post* (4 Feb. 2015).

UNLIKELY OLYMPIC CHAMPION

Ledecky first rose to national attention in the summer of 2010, when, at age thirteen, she outperformed senior-level swimmers in a sectional competition in Buffalo, New York. There, she swept the 200-, 400-, 800-, and 1,500-meter freestyle events in addition to winning titles in the 400-meter individual medley and as a member of the 800-meter relay team. It was then, her father recalled to Friedell, "when we realized we were on to something."

By the time she entered her freshman year at the Stone Ridge School of the Sacred Heart, in Bethesda, Maryland, Ledecky had established herself as one of the top freestyle distance swimmers in the country. She became, at fifteen, one of the youngest swimmers to attend the 2012 US Olympic Trials in Omaha, Nebraska. Despite her age, Ledecky earned a spot on her first Olympic team after placing first in the 800-meter freestyle, with a trials record time of 8:19.78. She also barely missed qualifying in the 400-meter freestyle with a third-place finish in the event. Her time of 4:05 flat nonetheless broke a twenty-four-year-old national age group record held by distance swimming legend Janet Evans.

As the youngest member of the 2012 US Olympic swim team, Ledecky was not expected to contend for a medal at the London Games. She surprised many, however, by winning the gold medal in the 800-meter freestyle with a time of 8:14.63, breaking another long-standing American record held by Evans. Attacking the race "as if it were an eight-minute sprint," as Crouse noted, Ledecky finished more than four seconds ahead of second-place finisher Mireia Belmonte García of Spain and posted the second-fastest overall time in the event. She would go on to win best female performance of the year and breakthrough performer of the year honors at the 2012 Golden Goggles Awards.

WORLD DOMINANCE

Following her Olympic breakthrough, Ledecky returned to NCAP and began training under Bruce Gemmell, who took over coaching duties from Suguiyama. Gemmell, whose son Andrew was also a member of the 2012 Olympic team, acknowledged that Ledecky won a gold medal in the 800-meter "without swimming the race particularly well," as he told Sheinin. Gemmell began working with Ledecky on pre-race strategies so she would avoid running the risk of going out too fast and tiring out in future events. "She focuses better than a lot of people," Gemmell explained to Metcalfe. "She's willing to try new things and expose herself to failure."

Ledecky started to show glimpses of her extraordinary potential in 2013 when she captured four gold medals at the World Championships in Barcelona, Spain. At that meet, she established world records in the 800-meter and 1,500-meter freestyle events and set an American record in the 400-meter freestyle. She became the first woman to win all three events at a World Championships since Germany's Hannah Stockbauer in 2003. Following her performance at the championships, Ledecky was recognized as the World Swimmer of the Year and the American Swimmer of the Year by *Swimming World* magazine.

Upon returning home from Spain, Ledecky devised a strict workout and competition plan with Gemmell that would set her up for optimum success at the next world championships in Kazan, Russia. Over the next two years, she would make a strong case for being the best female distance freestyler of all time. That reputation crystallized for Ledecky in the summer of 2014 when she set five world records during a nine-week span.

Ledecky's most notable performance that summer came at the 2014 Pan Pacific Swimming Championships in Gold Coast, Australia, where she won five gold medals. She swept the 200-, 400-, 800-, and 1,500-meter freestyle events, becoming the first woman to win four individual golds at the meet. She won her other gold as a member of the 800-meter freestyle relay team and set world records in the 400- and 1,500-meter freestyles.

One day after taking almost half a second off her 400-freestyle world record, Ledecky shaved six seconds off her 1,500-freestyle mark. She lapped three swimmers in her timed-final heat and finished more than twenty-seven seconds ahead of second-place finisher Lauren Boyle. Speaking to Sheinin in the *Washington Post* article, USA Swimming national team director Frank Busch called Ledecky's 1,500 performance "the most impressive race I've ever seen" and said that she is "blazing a completely different trail than anyone who has come before."

2015 WORLD CHAMPIONSHIPS

After the 2014 Pan Pacific Championships, Ledecky took a break from international competition to complete her studies at Stone Ridge. As a team cocaptain during her senior year, she shattered the American record in the women's 500-yard freestyle, with a time of 4:26.58, at the Washington Metropolitan Interscholastic Swimming and Diving Championships. In addition to the 500-yard freestyle, she twice set the national high school record in the 200-yard freestyle. Upon graduating from Stone Ridge in June 2015, Ledecky held every school swimming record except for the 100-yard breaststroke. She has said that her high-school coach, Bob Walker, worked closely with her club team coaches throughout her prep career to accommodate scheduling conflicts.

One month after her high-school graduation, Ledecky realized her two-year plan with Gemmell by turning in another dominating performance at the 2015 World Championships in Kazan, Russia. There, she became the first swimmer in history to win the 200-, 400-, 800-, and 1,500-meter freestyles at the same world championships. She won five gold medals in total, including one again as a member of the 800-meter freestyle relay team. Meanwhile, Ledecky again beat two of her own world records, taking almost three seconds off her mark in the 1,500-meter freestyle (15:25.48) and almost four seconds off her time in the 800-meter freestyle (8:07.39).

During the world championships, eleven-time Olympic medalist Ryan Lochte called Ledecky "one of the best distance freestylers I've ever seen," as quoted by Crouse for the *New York Times* (3 Aug. 2015). Ledecky was named World

Swimmer of the Year and American Swimmer of the Year for the third consecutive year.

2016 OLYMPICS

Ledecky committed to Stanford University but deferred her enrollment to the school until after the 2016 Olympics in Rio de Janeiro, Brazil. In the fall of 2015, she took two classes at Georgetown University as a visiting student. She did not return there, however, for the spring semester, instead deciding to focus solely on her training for the Olympics.

In January 2016 Ledecky swam at an Arena Pro Series event in Austin, Texas, where she reset her own mark in the 800-meter freestyle, with a time of 8:06.68. She also won the 200- and 400-meter freestyles and placed second in the 100-meter freestyle, with a personal-best time of 53.75.

Ledecky is the favorite to win the 200-, 400-, and 800-meter freestyles at the 2016 Olympics, where she is also expected to swim on the 800-meter freestyle relay team. Because the 1,500-meter event is not included in the Olympics, Ledecky has honed in on the 100-meter freestyle as a possible fourth individual event. "I don't know exactly what the future holds for me," she told Metcalfe. "You have to have a plan and work with your coaches and do what's best for you based on the timing."

SUGGESTED READING

Crouse, Karen. "Unrelenting Will toward Victory Drives Teenager." *New York Times*. New York Times, 26 Apr. 2014. Web. 30 Mar. 2016.

Friedell, Dan. "Katie Ledecky, 15, Pools Talents in Bid to Make US Team." *Washington Times*. Washington Times, 18 Apr. 2012. Web. 30 Mar. 2016.

Metcalfe, Jeff. "Katie Ledecky Emerges as World's Best Swimmer." *Arizona Republic*. Azcentral.com, 13 Apr. 2015. Web. 30 Mar. 2016.

Sheinin, Dave. "Katie Ledecky Finishes High School Career with Olympics, More World Records in Sight." *Washington Post*. Washington Post, 4 Feb. 2015. Web. 30 Mar. 2016.

—*Chris Cullen*

Michelle K. Lee

Born: 1965
Occupation: Director of the US Patent and Trademark Office (USPTO)

The first US patent was issued in July 1790, three months after the first Federal Patent Act was passed by Congress. It was not until the

United States Patent and Trademark Office

early 1800s, however, that an official Patent Office was established in Washington, DC. By the 1990s, hundreds of thousands of applications for patents were presented to the USPTO each year—a trend that has continued into the twenty-first century.

Michelle Kwok Lee is the undersecretary of commerce for intellectual property and the director of the United States Patent and Trademark Office (USPTO). Lee, who was officially sworn in as director of the USPTO in 2015, is the office's first female head. In this capacity she serves as the US president's primary advisor on intellectual property. An engineer and patent attorney, Lee headed the intellectual property legal team at Google after joining the company in 2003, and in 2012 she was the first director of the USPTO's satellite office in California's Silicon Valley.

Her dual background in law and engineering made her the perfect candidate to lead the USPTO, which is poised to address the ever-changing concepts of ownership in the digital age. Problems have plagued the patent system in recent years, such as the rise of patent trolls—individuals or companies that do not make or develop products but instead hold patents and earn money by suing other companies for violating their patents. Ending such abuses in the current system is complicated, though Lee hopes that the Leahy-Smith America Invents Act of 2011, which went into effect in 2013, will go a long way toward that end. The law is widely considered the most significant shakeup at the USPTO in decades.

In addition to its implementation and the need to mediate between the competing interests of the tech industry and the pharmaceutical industry, Lee has launched an initiative called All in STEM, which encourages young women to pursue careers in the STEM subjects—science, technology, engineering, and mathematics. As part of that initiative, the USPTO partnered with the nonprofit group Invent Now to create a summer program called Camp Invention. Lee has even reached out to the Girl Scouts of America and has lobbied them to create a merit badge for intellectual property. She is also the cofounder of Chief Intellectual Property Counsels, or ChIPs, a network of female patent attorneys.

EARLY LIFE AND EDUCATION

Michelle Lee was born in 1965 to Chinese immigrant parents in Santa Clara, California. She grew up in nearby Saratoga. Her father was a Silicon Valley engineer and encouraged his daughter to tinker at his workshop in the family's home and build handheld radios and a television set. "I was not aware that was not what most girls grew up with," Lee told Rick Schmitt for *Stanford Lawyer*, the Stanford Law School alumni magazine (11 Nov. 2015). Lee was also a dancer. She spent sixteen years studying classical ballet, but ultimately her love for science and technology dictated the course of her studies.

After high school, Lee attended the Massachusetts Institute of Technology (MIT), where she earned a bachelor of science degree in electrical engineering in 1988 and a master's degree in electrical engineering and computer science in 1989. After graduation, she interned at Hewlett-Packard Research Laboratory and worked the MIT Artificial Intelligence Laboratory. Lee finished her master's thesis—which Jessica Alpert for the *MIT Technology Review* (20 Oct. 2015) described as "a program to qualitatively characterize the behavior of nonlinear electrical circuits"—much earlier than she had expected. With the extra time on her hands, she decided to sit in on a lecture at nearby Harvard Law School.

The topic of the lecture was the 1984 Betamax case, in which the US Supreme Court overruled the US Ninth Circuit Court of Appeals and declared that Sony Corporation, Betamax, and any other home video tape recording (VTR) devices could not be liable for copyright infringement. Broadly speaking, the Supreme Court ruled that it was allowable under the law to sell recording devices that could record programs for the purpose of later viewing, even if the technology had the potential to be used illegally, such as in recording a television show or movie and then selling the recording for a profit. The Betamax case paved the path for future recording and viewing technologies such as VCRs, DVDs, TiVo, and online sites such as YouTube. "There was a spark there," Lee told Alpert, though she likely had little inkling of just how important such cases might be in 1989. "Having to apply old case law to new facts—that was fascinating to me." What is clear, however, is that this case and others like it were shaping the future of intellectual property rights and patent law.

APPLE V. MICROSOFT

Although she had been selected as a National Science Foundation Fellow and had planned to pursue her PhD in computer science at MIT, the lecture at Harvard and the Betamax case fascinated Lee and inspired her to change her career focus and path. She applied to law school and decided to attend California's Stanford Law School to study intellectual property law. While there, she served as editor of the *Stanford Law Review* and earned her degree in 1992.

After law school, Lee clerked for US District Court Judge Vaughn Walker in the Northern District of California. Walker was hearing arguments in *Apple Computer, Inc. v. Microsoft Corp,* a copyright infringement lawsuit case in which Apple was hoping to prevent Microsoft from using elements of a graphical user interface (more commonly known as GUI) that Apple claimed were very similar to GUIs used in several of its products. The first GUIs were introduced by Apple Macintosh in 1984. Desktop icons such as a pen to represent a writing program made personal computers easier to use and more accessible to consumers who realized they did not need to be computer experts to use the product. Apple's GUI was so successful that when Microsoft released a version of its Windows software in 1988, the interface appeared quite similar. Apple sued Microsoft for copyright infringement, arguing that Microsoft illegally copied the "look and feel" of Apple's interface. The case was tied up in the legal system for so long that Lee had read a brief of the case as a master's student at MIT, and four years later she worked with Walker as he decided the case.

The court was asked to consider two specific points: does a product's copyright apply to a computer's interface? And if so, to what degree? Walker and the court ruled that copyright protection for software must be limited in order to "make it easier for software developers to create new programs," Jonathan Weber explained in an article for the *Los Angeles Times* (11 Aug. 1992). In other words, Apple retained the rights to certain icons, but they did not own the exclusive right to the overall use of icons. The case had wide-ranging implications on innovation in Silicon Valley and on the industry's interpretation of intellectual property.

GOOGLE

After working with Walker on the *Apple* case, Lee clerked for Judge Paul R. Michel of the US Court of Appeals for the Federal Circuit. She then joined the San Francisco law firm of Keker & Van Nest in 1994. In 1996 she began work with Fenwick & West in Silicon Valley, where she worked with big tech firms such as Cisco Systems, Logitech, Apple, and Sun Microsystems. She made partner before leaving the firm in 2003 to work for Google.

Lee joined Google as deputy general counsel and head of patents and patent strategy, essentially building their intellectual property legal team from the ground up. "It was not entirely clear that Google would have the path that it now has, but it seemed like an exciting opportunity," Lee told Diana Samuels for the *Silicon Valley Business Journal* (1 Mar. 2012) of her reasoning at the time. "The company was very innovative, and I thought I could always go back to partnership at the law firm I was at." When she arrived, Google had only a handful of patents, but by the time she left the company in 2012, they held over 10,500 patents. During her nine-year tenure, Lee oversaw Google's acquisition of YouTube and its $12.5 billion acquisition of Motorola Mobility in 2011. "Michelle is an incredibly action-oriented leader and not afraid of taking on challenging projects and problems," Megan Smith, a former Google vice president, told Schmitt. "Getting different people to the table and working through complex solutions with multiple dimensions—that is where she has great strengths. She pushed teams to work quickly but with great perspective."

UNITED STATES PATENT AND TRADEMARK OFFICE

While working for Google, Lee served two terms on the US Patent and Trademark Office's (USPTO) Patent Public Advisory Committee, and in November 2012, she accepted a position as the head of the USPTO's Silicon Valley satellite office. In January 2014, she was appointed deputy director of the USPTO, essentially running the office's day-to-day activities. The top position of director had remained vacant since February 2013, and it was difficult to find a replacement who would satisfy the competing pressures of the tech and pharmaceutical industries—the two sectors with the most to gain by having an insider in the patent office.

Pharmaceutical companies have long lobbied for stricter patent laws, reasoning that the longer a company can keep exclusive rights to a particular drug, the more money that company will make. Tech companies take the opposite view and have called for patent reform. They cite the hundreds of thousands patent applications that seemingly languish in the USPTO's backlog as a reason they feel the patent process should be faster and easier to navigate.

Despite reports in July 2014 that the Obama administration was ready to nominate Phil Johnson, the senior vice president for intellectual property policy and strategy at Johnson & Johnson, a pharmaceutical company, Lee was officially nominated for the directorship by President Barack Obama on October 16, 2014. Lee found supporters in both political parties and was easily confirmed by the Senate on March 9, 2015. As the USPTO director, Lee oversees one of the largest intellectual property offices in the world, with more than twelve thousand employees and an annual budget of more than three billion dollars. "We all benefitted when she made the decision to go into public service. I cannot imagine anyone more qualified," Mallun Yen, the executive vice president of RPX Corporation, told Schmitt of Lee's appointment.

PERSONAL LIFE

Lee is married to Christopher Shen, a lawyer for Intel. The couple has a daughter named Amanda Mavis.

SUGGESTED READING

Alpert, Jessica. "The Jack of All Trademarks." *MIT Technology Review*. Massachusetts Institute of Technology, 20 Oct. 2015. Web. 14 Jan. 2016.

Samuels, Diana. "General Counsel Winner (IP Lawyer): Lee Leads Google's Efforts to Improve Nation's Patent System." *Silicon Valley Business Journal*. American City Business Journals, 1 Mar. 2012. Web. 14 Jan. 2016.

Schmitt, Rick. "Michelle K. Lee: First Woman to Head USPTO Sets Innovation Agenda." *Stanford Lawyer*. Stanford U, 11 Nov. 2015. Web. 14 Jan. 2016.

Weber, Jonathan. "News Analysis: Apple Case Ruling to Aid Software Developers." *Los Angeles Times*. Los Angeles Times, 11 Aug. 1992. Web. 14 Jan. 2016.

—*Molly Hagan*

Robin Coste Lewis

Occupation: Poet

Rarely does a poet's first book win a national award; yet Robin Coste Lewis did so with her collection *Voyage of the Sable Venus*, published in 2015. That year, the collection won the National Book Award for poetry at the sixty-sixth annual presentation. No poet's debut book of poems had received the award since Marilyn Hacker's *Presentation Piece* in 1974. The citation for the

Steve Sands/WireImage/Getty Images

award praises Lewis's achievement: "Juxtaposing autobiography with art-historical constructs of racial identity, she defines and creates self. In poems that consider the boundaries of beauty and terror, Coste Lewis intimately involves us with all that has formed her." Her work has also been a finalist for the National Rita Dove Prize, the International War Poetry Prize, and the Discovery Prize. She is a fellow of the Los Angeles Institute for the Humanities.

EARLY LIFE AND EDUCATION

Although Lewis's family is from New Orleans, she was born and raised in Compton, California. Her father worked as a janitor and was focused on his daughter's education. The town in which she grew up did not have a library for many of her childhood years; nevertheless, her mother and father gifted her many books.

Like others in her family and neighborhood, Lewis carried a switchblade as a child for her own protection. Police brutality was a lived reality. Growing up in the 1960s, Lewis struggled, as she told Dana Isokawa for *Poets & Writers* (15 Dec. 2015), "We all had a profound sense of injustice growing up. It was impossible not to feel that, watching profound degradation so common it felt like air. Our education was a travesty. So just holding a pencil when I was younger was very difficult for me. No one took our minds seriously." Because of her surroundings, Lewis has noted that she did not realize that aspirations beyond being a nurse or postal worker were possibilities.

When she was six, Lewis told her Aunt Patrice, who was visiting the family, she wanted to be a writer. Her aunt walked with her to the store and bought her pencils and a notebook. As she explained to Angela Chen for the *Guardian* (21 Dec. 2015), "I thought that if one wanted to be a writer, one had to write novels because I didn't know that one could be a poet."

Lewis now thinks that had she been presented the options of being a visual artist or an art historian, she might have pursued those careers instead. It was writing, however, that claimed her. This was especially so after reading Lorraine Hansberry's *To Be Young, Gifted, and Black* when in junior high. She took Advanced Placement English courses in high school, one of two African American students in those classes. She attended Hampshire College in the 1980s. Until then she had never read anything assigned for school that had been written by a black author.

Lewis earned a master of fine arts (MFA) from New York University (NYU), where she was a Goldwater Fellow. She then went on to obtain a master of theological studies in Sanskrit and comparative religious literature from the Harvard Divinity School. As one of the oldest extant languages and the source of many other Western languages, Sanskrit interested her.

From 1999 until 2002, Lewis was an assistant professor of creative writing at her undergraduate alma mater. She held other teaching jobs at Hunter College and Wheaton College. She also taught in Paris for New York University's low-residency MFA program.

A LIFE-CHANGING ACCIDENT

Lewis decided to become a poet after she was in a horrific accident—she fell through the floor of a restaurant in San Francisco—that left her bedridden for two years, with permanent brain damage. It took her a year to learn the alphabet again. She was forbidden to read or write more than one sentence daily. Writing made her sick, though thinking did not. She underwent extensive speech and language therapy.

The accident took on the nature of a blessing, however, as Lewis explained to Isokawa, "All those skills artists must acquire—stillness, concentration, discipline, compression, wrestling with the ego, all of it—walked in the door, hand in hand, with brain damage." As she explained to Chen, "I would sit there for eight hours a day thinking of one line and it became delicious. It was this huge epiphany—'Oh, this is what poetry is! You can put an entire essay into one line!' It was odd but it was the greatest gift, and I never looked back."

VOYAGE OF THE SABLE VENUS AND OTHER POEMS

Lewis's first collection of poetry features the title poem, a seventy-nine-page work that was inspired by Thomas Stothard's etching "The

Voyage of the Sable Venus." Stothard imitated the famous "Birth of Venus" by Sandro Botticelli, replacing the blond Venus with an African woman bound for slavery in the Americas. Neptune's trident in Botticelli's painting was replaced by the British flag, making the etching a pro-slavery piece. Stothard in turn had been inspired by a poem by Isaac Teale: "The Sable Venus, an Ode," which concerns the raping of slave women.

The prologue of the poem describes it as "a narrative poem comprised solely and entirely of the titles, catalogue entries, or exhibit descriptions of Western art objects in which a black female figure is present, dating from 38,000 BCE to the present." Lewis arranges these chronologically in the poem. She uses the titles, catalog entries, or exhibit descriptions as the poem, changing only the punctuation. In cases where the language had been sanitized, Lewis returned to the original language, such as *slave* or *colored*.

She knew this would be a major piece of writing and so waited until she was working on her MFA at NYU to begin. Her project advisor was the Pulitzer Prize–winning poet Sharon Olds. Lewis sometimes wrote from early evening until one in the morning, completing a draft during the first semester.

Her initial intent was not to cover so much historical ground. With her background in Sanskrit, however, she glanced at the ancient world and found more of the same. Finding black women depicted in every culture, she determined her research was an epic poem rather than an essay. As she told Jeffrey Brown in an interview for *PBS* (Public Broadcasting System) *NewsHour* (29 Dec. 2015), "Epic is one of the oldest forms we have as human beings. And I thought that it would be really helpful and also mirror the history itself if I showed, if I tried to capture, this history of how we have looked at black women visually in epic form."

CHANGE OF PLANS

Lewis's debut book, which took her five or six years to write, is structured as a triptych, a three-part work in which the centerpiece is larger, with "wings" on either side. Lewis brackets the long poem with autobiographical poems on either side. That structure was the idea of her editor, Deb Garrison. The initial idea had been to print just the single epic poem. Garrison asked Lewis to send her other poems she had written. At first reluctant, over the course of a year's conversations with Garrison, Lewis decided that including them was the right idea. She told Nicole Sealey for National Book Foundation's website that she published the poems "because I did not want to hide from my reader and I do not want to waste my reader's time by strutting before them in a mask. If the reader is going to be generous with their attention, I mustn't just pretend

to feed them. I must give them something real to eat."

The poems comment on each other. As Jay Deshpande wrote for the *Slate* (20 Nov. 2015), Lewis's poetry "erases the line between confessional, identity-based poetry and conceptual poetry—a line that has been problematically racialized for far too long." He goes on to reference the work of other writers of color who are invigorating poetry, placing Lewis's work in a larger literary context. Lewis has been compared to other African American writers, such as Gwendolyn Brooks and Rita Dove.

The collection's cover is a photograph of a young African American woman staring into a shop window, taken in the late 1930s by writer Eudora Welty. It serves to put the reader on notice that the gaze on African American women, particularly by white observers, will be at the heart of this book. In November 2015, Robin Coste Lewis was announced as the winner of the National Book Award for poetry.

NEXT STEPS

Lewis is revising earlier manuscripts that she wrote while she was at NYU. One, about Arctic exploration and colonialism, focuses on Matthew Henson, the black explorer who co-discovered the North Pole. As she explained to Isokawa, "I use this history as an allegory for postcolonial desires for subjectivity." The second project is an erasure of a 1931 children's book *The Pickaninny Twins*. Lewis is calling her version *The Pickaninny Wins!*

In addition, as part of her program at the University of Southern California (USC), she is making a series of short films from old photographs—from daguerreotypes to Polaroids—she found in a suitcase after her grandmother's death. She is interspersing these with written text.

PERSONAL LIFE

Lewis lives in Los Angeles and has a son. A member of Cave Canem, an association for black writers, she is also a Provost Fellow at USC, where she is seeking a doctoral degree in poetry and visual studies. She describes herself as hypergraphic—she cannot stop writing and does not have the problem of writer's block that sometimes plagues other writers. As she told Chen, "I am an artist through to my marrow, which might be a curse and not necessarily a good thing."

SUGGESTED READING

Brown. Jeffrey. "Poet Robin Coste Lewis Evokes the Black Female Form across History." *PBS NewsHour*. NewsHour Productions, 29 Dec. 2015. Web. 8 Mar. 2016.

Chen, Angela. "Poet Robin Coste Lewis: 'I Am an Artist through to My Marrow.'" *Guardian*.

Guardian News and Media, 21 Dec. 2015. Web. 7 Mar. 2016.

Chiasson, Dan. "Rebirth of Venus." *New Yorker*. Condé Nast, 19 Oct. 2015. Web. 1 Mar. 2016.

Deshpande, Jay. "Robin Coste Lewis' National Book Award Marks a Shift in How the Literary World Regards Black Poets." *Slate*. Slate Group, 20 Nov. 2015. Web. 8 Mar. 2016.

Isokawa, Dana. "Fractures through Time: our Eleventh Annual Look at Debut Poets." *Poets and Writers*. Poets and Writers, 15 Dec. 2015. Web. 9 Mar. 2016.

Sealey, Nicole. "Interview with Robin Coste Lewis, 2015 National Book Award Winner, Poetry." *National Book Foundation*. Natl. Book Foundation, n.d. Web. 11 Mar. 2016.

—*Judy Johnson*

Wojciech Migda (Wmigda)/CC BY-SA 3.0/GNU Free Documentation License/Wikimedia Commons

Stacy Lewis

Born: February 16, 1985
Occupation: Golfer

"I've been the underdog my whole life," the American professional golfer Stacy Lewis told Steve DiMeglio for *USA Today* (14 Nov. 2012). By "underdog," Lewis was referring to the slim chances she was given of ever becoming a professional golfer. Diagnosed with scoliosis at age eleven, she was forced to wear a back brace for six and a half years before undergoing spinal fusion surgery that threatened to end her golf career before it even began. Against all odds, Lewis recovered and went on to attend the University of Arkansas, where she enjoyed a highly decorated four-year career. She turned professional in 2008 and soon emerged as one of the best players on the Ladies Professional Golf Association (LPGA) Tour.

A two-time major champion and former world number one, Lewis truly caught the attention of the golfing world in 2014, when she became the first American in twenty-one years to win the Rolex Player of the Year award, the Vare Trophy, and the money list title. The three honors are known as the triple crown of women's golf.

EARLY LIFE

Stacy Lynn Lewis was born on February 16, 1985, in Toledo, Ohio, to Dale and Carol Lewis. She grew up with an older sister, Beth, and a younger sister, Janet. When Lewis was two her family moved to Anderson, South Carolina. They remained in Anderson until Lewis was eleven, when they moved to The Woodlands, Texas, a suburb of Houston.

Lewis developed an early affinity for sports and other competitive activities. "She always liked to be in control, even when she was a kid," her father recalled to Mechelle Voepel for *espnW* (12 Feb. 2013). "If we were riding bikes or going out on a hike, she wanted to be the one in front." Lewis inherited her passion for golf from her father and grandfather, Al Lewis, who were both golf enthusiasts. She began accompanying her father, a low-handicap player, to local golf courses at the age of eight.

Along with her sisters, Lewis swam competitively throughout her youth. Her interest in swimming waned, however, after moving to The Woodlands, a master-planned community that "more or less was created around golf," as Lewis said in an interview with Guy Yocom for *Golf Digest* (4 June 2013). Taking advantage of the area's temperate climate and world-class golf courses, Lewis started playing golf every day after school, and by her early teens, she was regularly competing in junior tournaments.

CAREER-THREATENING CONDITION

For Lewis, golf also served as an outlet to overcome adversity. The same year her family moved to The Woodlands she was diagnosed with scoliosis, a potentially debilitating condition that causes an abnormal curvature of the spine. To correct the condition, Lewis began wearing a hard plastic, corset-like back brace eighteen hours a day. She was, however, allowed to take the brace off when she played golf, which helped her further gravitate to the sport.

When Lewis attended The Woodlands High School, she faced yet another obstacle. The school had a highly competitive women's golf team divided into four different squads (freshman, junior varsity, varsity B, and varsity A). Only five players could qualify to represent the varsity team in tournaments, in which the top four scores are counted. Undaunted by the competition, Lewis earned a spot on the team and emerged as a standout, helping lead her school to three consecutive Class 5A state titles.

Still, Lewis was mostly overlooked by college golf programs because of her small size and relative lack of power. By her own account, she was "average," as she told Rich Polikoff for the *Arkansas Democrat-Gazette* (3 Mar. 2013), and was not even the best player on her high school team. Lewis's scrappy style nonetheless caught the attention of Kelly Hester, then the head women's golf coach at the University of Arkansas, who recruited her. Hester was also impressed with Lewis's academic success, which allowed her to receive a merit scholarship even as she was not initially offered athletic scholarship money.

In the fall of her senior year, Lewis signed a letter of intent to attend Arkansas, which "felt like the perfect place for me," as she put it to Tim Letcher for SECSports.com (3 July 2014). It was also around this time that Lewis was informed by doctors that she could remove her back brace, which she had tried to conceal from her high-school peers by wearing oversized clothes. Three months later, however, Lewis discovered that the curvature in her spine had gotten worse and that she would be forced to have career-threatening surgery. "I thought that I would never play golf again," she admitted to Letcher.

In June 2003 Lewis underwent a spinal fusion procedure, which required doctors to deflate her left lung and remove one of her ribs to insert a titanium rod and five screws in her spine. After successful surgery, Lewis, who consequently gained two inches in height, was ordered to abstain from playing golf for three months. That was followed by another six-month rehabilitation period, where she was prohibited from lifting or carrying anything over five pounds. "Coming out of my surgery, I just wanted to play golf," Lewis said to Voepel. "I didn't care how I played or where I played, I just wanted to be able to do it."

ARKANSAS TO THE LPGA
As a result of her spinal surgery, Lewis redshirted during her freshman 2003–4 season at Arkansas. Allowed to chip and putt during her recovery, she worked tirelessly on her short game and also underwent training sessions to increase her core strength and flexibility. "I watched a lot of golf," Lewis noted to Letcher, "watched my teammates play and got to see, from my coach's perspective,

what they were doing wrong and how to manage my game better."

Despite entering the 2004–5 season with low expectations, Lewis surprised many by winning three titles, including the Southeastern Conference (SEC) championship, and earning SEC freshman player of the year honors. She went on to not only become Arkansas' top player but also the most decorated golfer in program history. In her four-year career at Arkansas, Lewis won a total of twelve titles and was a four-time first-team All-American. She won the coveted National Collegiate Athletic Association (NCAA) individual championship in 2007 and her second SEC title in 2008.

After graduating from Arkansas with a double major in accounting and finance, Lewis closed out her amateur career by representing the United States in the 2008 Curtis Cup, the top team competition for women amateur golfers. She went undefeated in five matches, helping lead the United States to victory over Great Britain and Ireland. In the process, she became the first player in history to go 5–0 in a single Curtis Cup tournament.

Following the Curtis Cup, Lewis competed in the 2008 US Open Qualifying Tournament, where she turned professional. After winning that tournament by four strokes, she played in the 2008 US Women's Open in Edna, Minnesota. She led her first major tournament through the first fifty-four holes before eventually finishing tied for third. Lewis competed in several other tournaments that season, but failed to win or make enough money to automatically qualify for the 2009 LPGA Tour. As a result she attended the notoriously difficult LPGA Qualifying Tournament, also known as Q-School. She won the tournament, ensuring her a LPGA Tour card for the 2009 season.

Lewis entered her rookie season on the LPGA Tour with high expectations, but she struggled somewhat and finished forty-seventh on the LPGA Tour earnings list. "I was kind of lost," she told Adam Schupak for the *New York Times* (11 Sept. 2012). "But I knew this much: I didn't want to be somebody who just makes cuts."

FIRST LPGA TITLES AND TOP AMERICAN PLAYER
To guide her in the right direction, Lewis began working with Professional Golfers' Association (PGA) instructor Joe Hallett, who helped tighten her golf swing. When Lewis returned to the golf course in 2010, her swing had become "smooth, efficient, repeatable, powerful, rhythmic, and beautiful," according to Schupak. That year she notched four top-ten finishes, including a season-best runner-up finish at the 2010

Tres Marias Championship, and rose to number thirty-four on the earnings list.

Lewis's work with Hallett began to crystalize during the 2011 season, when she won her first LPGA title at the Kraft Nabisco Championship, one of the LPGA's five majors. Lewis won the 2011 edition by three strokes, edging third-round leader and defending champion Yani Tseng, then the number one-ranked female golfer in the world. That season Lewis recorded ten more top-ten finishes, including a runner-up showing at the 2011 Evian Masters, and finished fourth on the earnings list, with more than $1.3 million. She also represented the United States at the 2011 Solheim Cup, marking her debut at the biennial international team competition.

Prior to the 2012 season, Lewis set out to become the top-ranked American in the world rankings. She accomplished that feat after capturing her second and third career LPGA titles, at the Mobile Bay LPGA Classic and the ShopRite LPGA Classic, respectively. Lewis then effectively established herself as one of the top players in the world after winning two more titles in 2012, at the Navistar LPGA Classic and the Mizuno Classic. She finished the season with sixteen top-ten finishes, took home over $1.8 million in prize earnings, and led the tour in wins, birdies, eagles, and rounds in the sixties. For her performance, Lewis received the LPGA's prestigious Rolex Player of the Year award, becoming the first American to receive the award since Beth Daniel in 1994. In the wake of receiving the honor she told DiMeglio, "I've never been the longest, the tallest, the biggest, or the most athletic. I just had to work and figure out a way to get it done."

LPGA TRIPLE CROWN WINNER

Lewis continued her ascendance in 2013, when she became the number-one ranked player in the world. She unseated Tseng from the top spot after winning back-to-back titles at the 2013 HSBC Women's Champions and the 2013 RR Donnelley LPGA Founders Cup. Lewis held the position, though, for only four weeks before relinquishing it to South Korea's Inbee Park. She did, however, prevent Park from winning four majors in a row when she won the 2013 RICOH British Open, edging out the competition by two strokes to win her second career LPGA major title. At the end of the season, Lewis won the Vare Trophy for having a tour-best and career-low scoring average of 69.484.

Lewis's 2014 season was even more historic. She won three titles, recording a six-stroke victory at the LPGA Shootout, a five-shot win at the ShopRite LPGA Classic, and a one-shot triumph at the Walmart NW Arkansas Championship. Meanwhile she led the tour in scoring

average for the second straight year and also led in top-ten finishes, rounds under par, and birdies. In addition to again winning the Vare Trophy, Lewis earned her second Rolex Player of the Year award and finished first on the year-end money list with over $2.5 million in earnings. By capturing all three honors she became the first American in twenty-one years to win the LPGA's triple crown.

Lewis did not win any titles in 2015, despite placing third on the tour in top-ten finishes, scoring average, rounds under par, and earnings and first in birdies. In April of that year, she narrowly missed winning her third career major title when she lost to Brittany Lincicome in a sudden-death playoff at the 2015 ANA Inspiration. Despite the somewhat disappointing year, Lewis remained confident in her skills and positive about her career. "I never had aspirations of playing professional golf, and to play it at the highest level, it's like a fairy tale," she told Polikoff. "It doesn't seem real."

PERSONAL LIFE

Lewis resides in Palm Beach Gardens, Florida. She became engaged to her boyfriend, Gerrod Chadwell, the head women's golf coach at the University of Houston, in November 2015.

SUGGESTED READING

DiMeglio, Steve. "Underdog Stacy Lewis Now at Top of LPGA." *USA Today*. USA Today, 14 Nov. 2012. Web. 27 Dec. 2015.

Letcher, Tim. "SEC 40/40: Lewis Fights Back to Become Elite Golfer." *SECSports.com*. SEC Digital Network, 3 July 2014. Web. 27 Dec. 2015.

Polikoff, Rich. "Stacy Lynn Lewis: Iron Will." *Arkansas Democrat-Gazette* 3 Mar. 2013: 1D–2D. Print.

Schupak, Adam. "Women's Golf Money Leader Could End U.S. Drought." *New York Times*. New York Times, 11 Sept. 2012. Web. 27 Dec. 2015.

Shipnuck, Alan. "Leading Lady." *Sports Illustrated* 18 Mar. 2013: G4. Print.

Voepel, Mechelle. "Stacy Lewis Is Where She Wants to Be." *espnW*. ESPN Internet Ventures, 12 Feb. 2013. Web. 27 Dec. 2015.

—*Chris Cullen*

Damian Lillard

Born: July 15, 1990
Occupation: Basketball player

The Portland Trail Blazers' Damian Lillard is "a point guard for the new age, a ferocious

Thearon W. Henderson/Getty Images

competitor who can score as well as he passes and puts pressure on the defense as soon as the ball is in his hands," Marc Stein wrote for *ESPN.com* (2 July 2015). Though overlooked for much of his early basketball career, the six-foot-three Lillard has emerged from little-known Weber State University to become one of top players in the National Basketball Association (NBA).

The Trail Blazers' 2012 first-round pick, Lillard has established himself as an all-around force since his 2012–13 rookie season. He was the unanimous selection for the 2013 NBA Rookie of the Year. A prolific scorer and savvy floor leader, Lillard earned back-to-back All-Star selections during the 2013–14 and 2014–15 seasons and played a pivotal role in the Trail Blazers earning playoff berths in each of those years. He again led the Trail Blazers to the play-offs in 2015–16, in which he posted career highs in most statistical categories and was named to the All-NBA Second Team.

EARLY LIFE

Damian Lamonte Ollie Lillard was born on July 15, 1990, in Oakland, California. He is the old-est of the three children born to Houston Lillard Sr. and Gina Johnson, who separated when he was in high school. He has an older brother, Houston Jr., and a sister, LaNae.

Despite his parents' separation, Lillard had a stable upbringing. He was introduced to basket-ball by his father, who, when he was not working for a local box company, would run him through drills that placed a special emphasis on the fun-damentals of the game. "We would have a court,

and he would never let me lower my [adjustable rim]," Lillard recalled to Sam Amick for *Sports Illustrated* (7 June 2012). "Everybody else would lower their court and dunk, and he wouldn't let us. He would make us keep it up and shoot the ball."

For a time during his youth, Lillard regularly attended Golden State Warriors games at what is now Oracle Arena. His father was a Warriors season-ticket holder and would take him and his brother early to games so they would be able to watch and analyze players during their pregame warmups. Both of Lillard's parents made sure he was actively involved in sports in an effort to keep him cocooned from the ever-present violence that existed in his rough-and-tumble Brookfield Village neighborhood.

At thirteen Lillard made a promise to his mother, who worked for an Oakland-based medical insurance company, that he would at-tend and graduate from college. Afterward, he predicted that he would play in the NBA, win league Rookie of the Year honors, and, eventu-ally, become an all-star. "And everything he said he was going to do in that speech, he did," Lil-lard's mother told Ian Thomsen for *NBA.com* (12 May 2015).

HIGH SCHOOL CAREER

Lillard's road to realizing those lofty goals began at Arroyo High School, located in nearby San Lorenzo. As a five-foot-five freshman, Lillard earned a spot on Arroyo's varsity team, but he opted to leave the school after the head coach was let go. During his sophomore year, he trans-ferred to St. Joseph Notre Dame High School, a nationally recognized basketball powerhouse in Alameda. He made the varsity team there, too, but was benched by coach Don Lippi in favor of upperclassmen. Lippi "wasn't a fan of the way I played," Lillard noted to Kerry Eggers for the *Portland Tribune* (7 Apr. 2016). "He told me I passed the ball too soft, wasn't fast enough, didn't shoot fast enough."

Consequently, prior to his junior season, Lillard transferred to Oakland High School, where "it all started to happen for me," as he told Eggers. Under coach Orlando Watkins, he flourished, expanding what was mostly an offensive-minded game into one that placed an equal emphasis on defensive play. As a senior, Lillard averaged more than 28 points per game and was named First Team All-League for the second consecutive season.

It was during Lillard's senior season that his bright basketball future was almost taken away from him: while waiting at a bus station after practice one night, he was robbed at gunpoint by three men. The men took the ten dollars in his pocket before running off to evade the po-lice. "I was in so much shock that I don't think it even processed all the way," Lillard recalled to Thomsen. "All it took was to pull the trigger and I would have been dead on the spot."

WEBER STATE TO PORTLAND TRAIL BLAZERS

Lillard was not heavily recruited coming out of high school, receiving offers from only midmajor schools (Division I schools not part of the "power five" conferences). Among them was Weber State University, in Ogden, Utah. The school's head coach, Randy Rahe, had recruited Lillard after being told about him by his friend Raymond Young, Lillard's AAU (Amateur Athletic Union) coach. Rahe nonetheless told Lillard that he would have to continue to work hard and do well in school for the chance to develop into an NBA-caliber player. "He wanted to be an NBA player," Watkins explained to Max Stephens for *MaxPreps.com* (8 Jan. 2014). "And that gave him a chance. . . . He was built to want to be the best."

Taking Rahe's advice to heart, Lillard made an immediate impact for the Wildcats as a freshman, averaging 11.5 points on 43.4 percent shooting and earning Big Sky Conference Freshman of the Year honors. Then, during his sophomore season, he was named Big Sky Conference Most Valuable Player (MVP) after leading the conference in overall scoring at 19.9 points per game. That off-season, Lillard took his training "to the next level," as he put it to Amick, in an effort to improve his game even further.

Lillard's fast-rising career came to a halt nine games into his junior season in 2010–11, however, when he suffered a season-ending foot injury. Undaunted, he returned in 2011–12 to have one of the greatest seasons in Weber State history. Lillard led the nation in scoring for most of his redshirt junior season and finished second in the country with an average of 24.5 points per game. He also increased his production in virtually every other offensive category. He received Big Sky MVP honors for the second consecutive year and became the first player in conference history to be named to the Associated Press (AP) All-America team.

By the end of the 2011–12 season, Lillard had established himself as the top point guard prospect in the country. He opted to forgo what would have been his redshirt senior season and entered the 2012 NBA Draft. Impressed by his combination of athleticism and scoring prowess, the Portland Trail Blazers selected him with the sixth overall pick in the draft. (Lillard would receive a professional sales degree from Weber State in May 2015.)

NBA ROOKIE OF THE YEAR

Upon joining the Blazers, Lillard was immediately designated the team's floor leader by the team's first-year coach, former NBA player Terry Stotts. Showcasing his all-around game, Lillard did not disappoint as a rookie, playing in all 82 regular-season games and leading all first-year players in points (19), assists (6.5), and minutes (38.6) per game. He established an NBA rookie record for three-point field goals in a season, with 185, and played more minutes than any other player in the league (3,167). Meanwhile, he became only the third rookie in league history to record at least 1,500 points and 500 assists in a season.

Lillard won all six of the Western Conference Rookie of the Month honors during the season, en route to winning the 2013 NBA Rookie of the Year Award. He received all 121 first-place votes, making him only the fourth unanimous selection in league history. He was also a unanimous selection to the NBA All-Rookie First Team. In an article for the *Sporting News* (15 Feb. 2014), Stotts said to Sean Deveney, "Any rookie, no matter the position, you have to be willing to play through mistakes and accept the learning curve, but Damian was just special. . . . I did not have the same concerns a lot of coaches might have had when you're relying on a rookie point guard."

NBA ALL-STAR

Lillard followed up his spectacular rookie season with an even better sophomore campaign, in which he averaged 20.7 points, 5.6 assists, and 3.5 rebounds per game, and earned his first career All-Star selection. During the 2014 NBA All-Star Weekend, Lillard became the first player to participate in five events: the Rising Star Challenge, Skills Challenge, Three-Point Shootout, Dunk Contest, and All-Star Game.

Lillard's dazzling play helped the Trail Blazers finish fifth in the Western Conference with a surprising 54–28 record. They advanced to the playoffs for the first time since the 2010–11 season, reaching the Western Conference semifinals, where they lost to the eventual NBA champion, the San Antonio Spurs, in five games. That result notwithstanding, he was named to the All-NBA Third Team for the first time in his career.

Lillard again earned an All-Star selection during the 2014–15 season, when he averaged 21 points, 6.2 assists, and 4.6 rebounds per game. He played in all 82 games for the third consecutive season and posted a career-high .434 field goal percentage. The Trail Blazers finished with a 51–31 regular-season record, helping them advance to the postseason for the second straight year. They were eliminated in the first round, however, losing to the Memphis Grizzlies in five games.

FACE OF THE FRANCHISE

During the 2015–16 off-season, the Blazers lost starters LaMarcus Aldridge, Wesley Matthews, Nicolas Batum, and Robin Lopez to trades and free agency. The Blazers nonetheless locked up Lillard for the long term with a five-year, $120-million contract extension, making him the face of the franchise. Still, many basketball observers looked at the 2015–16 season as a rebuilding year for the team.

Defying expectations, Lillard galvanized a Blazers team with the NBA's lowest payroll and the third-youngest roster in the league. In 75 games, he averaged 25.1 points, 6.8 assists, and 4.0 rebounds, and teamed up with third-year guard C. J. McCollum to form the third-highest-scoring tandem in the NBA. Though the Westgate Las Vegas SuperBook projected the team to win only 26.5 regular-season games, the Blazers finished with a 44–38 record and advanced to the Western Conference semifinals for the second time in three seasons.

Throughout the 2015–16 season, Lillard achieved a number of career milestones. During an October game against the New Orleans Pelicans, he recorded his 600th career three-point field goal, making him the fastest NBA player in history to accomplish the feat, doing so in 247 games. In that game, he also reached 1,500 career assists, making him the second-fastest Trail Blazer to reach that milestone.

On February 19, 2016, Lillard had the best game of his NBA career, when he scored a career-high 51 points in a dominant 137–105 Trail Blazers' win over the defending NBA champion Golden State Warriors. He also added 7 assists and 6 steals while committing no turnovers, making him the first NBA player in history to put up those numbers in a game. He became the first Trail Blazer to amass more than 400 assists in each of his first four seasons and also surpassed Wesley Matthews's franchise record for three-pointers. At the end of the season, he was named to the All-NBA Second Team.

Personal accomplishments aside, Lillard has expressed his desire to turn the Trail Blazers into a perennial title contender. "All my life," he explained to Eggers, "I've dreamed about being 'the biggest.' Once we get in the playoffs, I'm not playing just to be there. I'm playing to win it all."

PERSONAL LIFE

Lillard "carries himself with an uncommon combination of sturdiness and humility," Kevin Arnovitz wrote for *ESPN.com* (11 May 2016). "He's both serious and accessible, the guy at the bar secure enough to nurse a drink by himself, but completely sociable if his solitude is interrupted." Widely known for his humble and caring nature, Lillard has taken part in the annual antibullying campaign "Respect, Pass It On," since his rookie season.

Among Lillard's favorite endeavors off the basketball court is rapping, and in 2013, he launched a weekly social media trend called "4Bar Friday," in which fans and other NBA players are offered the chance to submit videos of themselves rapping on Instagram. In 2015, Lillard released a full-length single, "Soldier in the Game," through the online audio distribution platform SoundCloud.

Lillard has a lucrative endorsement deal with the German sportswear company Adidas and owns a six-bedroom home in a suburb of Portland, Oregon, which he shares with his mother and sister.

SUGGESTED READING

Amick, Sam. "Tough-Minded Lillard Leaps from Mid-Major to Potential Top-10 Pick." *Sports Illustrated*. Time, 7 June 2012. Web. 29 Aug. 2016.

Arnovitz, Kevin. "Lillard's Inclusive Leadership Could Make Portland a Destination." *ESPN.com*. ESPN Internet Ventures, 11 May 2016. Web. 29 Aug. 2016.

Deveney, Sean. "From Oakland to Ogden to Oregon, Lillard Has Had Helping Hands." *Sporting News*. Sporting News Media, 15 Feb. 2014. Web. 29 Aug. 2016.

Eggers, Kerry. "Damian Lillard: The Face of the Blazers." *Portland Tribune*. Pamplin Media Group, 7 Apr. 2016. Web. 29 Aug. 2016.

Stein, Marc. "Damian Lillard Agrees to 5-Year, $120 Million Extension with Trail Blazers." *ESPN.com*. ESPN Internet Ventures, 2 July 2015. Web. 29 Aug. 2016.

Stephens, Max. "Damian Lillard's High School Coach Saw the Skill and Chip." *MaxPreps.com*. CBS Interactive, 8 Jan. 2014. Web. 29 Aug. 2016.

Thomsen, Ian. "Lillard Carries Family Affair from Oakland to Portland." *NBA.com*. NBA Media Ventures, 12 May 2015. Web. 29 Aug. 2016.

—*Chris Cullen*

Joanne Liu

Born: April 11, 1965
Occupation: President of Doctors Without Borders

Joanne Liu, the president of the international aid group Médecins Sans Frontières (MSF), known in the English-speaking world as Doctors Without Borders, has cited *The Plague* by Albert Camus as one of her favorite books. The 1947

Andrew Toth/GettyImages

novel describes an epidemic in the Algerian city of Oran. Its narrator, a physician named Rieux, is an empathetic character who tries to contain the outbreak with little cooperation from either the authorities or other doctors. He perseveres, he says, because he has never become accustomed to seeing people suffer and die. "I think today it's one of our problems," Liu told Alice Fishburn in an interview for the *Financial Times* (12 Dec. 2014), in the midst of a major Ebola outbreak in Africa. "Somehow we got used to death and then we dehumanized it. We account for conflicts in figures. Ebola is 13,500 infected, 5,000 people have died. . . . People are losing their sense of empathy, their sense of wanting to do something."

Liu, however, is at the forefront of those both empathetic and proactive enough to do something about the humanitarian and medical crises that arise around the globe. Affiliated with the Nobel Peace Prize–winning group since 1996 and its president since 2013, Liu has cared for patients in refugee camps in Mauritania and Kenya, treated rape victims in the Democratic Republic of the Congo, and aided tsunami survivors in Indonesia and earthquake victims in Haiti. She dismisses the notion that she is heroic, although it is not uncommon for her to work in the midst of shelling or gunfire. "My life is so comfortable compared to Syrians who have lived under the threat of attack for the last three years," she asserted to Charlotte Clarke for the *Financial Times* (19 Jan. 2014). "I have nothing to complain about, even if I am busy, or have moments when things get tough. . . . When I see a mother who has walked

for three weeks to come to a MSF clinic, with two kids on her back and her belongings on her head, facing intimidation and physical abuse on her way, I am inspired by her resilience."

EARLY YEARS AND EDUCATION
Liu was born on April 11, 1965, in Quebec, Canada. Her parents—immigrants from the province of Guangdong (formerly known as Canton) in the southernmost region of China's mainland—operated China Garden, one of the first Asian restaurants in Quebec City. She was often bullied both verbally and physically by her predominantly white classmates. "It shapes your mind, consciously or unconsciously," she told Les Perreaux for the *Globe and Mail* (20 Oct. 2014). "I always made a huge deal of being good at everything. That's how I coped with it. You react by overperforming, or underperforming."

When she was young, Liu read the book *Et la paix, docteur?* (1985) by Jean-Pierre Willem, an account of a physician working with Doctors Without Borders during the Soviet invasion of Afghanistan. Her imagination was sparked. "This doctor was all by himself in the lonely mountains and this experience had made him feel useful," she recalled to Sylvie Arvanitakis for *Montréal enSanté* magazine (Winter 2014). "I thought this was the kind of meaning I'd like to have in my life."

After high school, Liu joined Katimavik, a Canadian youth program that arranges for its members to do volunteer work in their communities. She then signed on with Canadian Crossroads International, taking part in an exchange program that sent her to Mali to volunteer for three months.

Liu attended a CEGEP (Collège d'enseignement général et professionnel or "general and vocational college"), as publicly funded preuniversity programs are known in Quebec. She then entered McGill University, a large research university in Montreal, where she earned her medical degree in 1991. (She told Clarke that if she had to do it all over again, "I would probably do an undergraduate degree before going to medical school. Perhaps in arts and sciences, for the creativity.")

Upon graduating from McGill, she undertook a residency in pediatrics at the University of Montreal from 1991 through 1995 and also completed a two-year fellowship in emergency pediatrics at a medical facility connected to New York University from 1994 to 1996.

DOCTORS WITHOUT BORDERS
Doctors Without Borders was started in 1971 by a group of French doctors and medical journalists, with the goal of providing needed medical care to the victims of war, natural disaster, and epidemic, regardless of gender, race, religion,

creed, or political affiliation. Dismayed by events in southern Nigeria, where military forces were targeting hospitals and blockading supplies to the tiny secessionist state of Biafra, the founders based their group on the premise that the needs of people outweighed respect for any national boundaries.

In 1996 Liu embarked upon her first mission for the organization, fulfilling a longstanding goal. She signed on to go to Mauritania, an African nation located between Senegal and Western Sahara that was home to tens of thousands of refugees from the unstable neighboring country of Mali. The only physician caring for fifty thousand Malians in a massive refugee camp, she became used to practicing medicine with no running water or electricity. Since then, she has been brutally honest in conveying her experiences to aspiring volunteers. "There's nothing romantic about doing a mission overseas, so you need to be clear on your motivations to do this," she explained to Arvanitakis.

Subsequent trips found her dealing with cholera epidemics in Bulgaria, assessing medical needs in high-conflict areas of the Middle East, monitoring premature infants amidst the wreckage of a Haitian earthquake, and caring for victims of a devastating tsunami in Indonesia, among other such missions.

Liu performed those missions by using vacation days from her primary job as a pediatric emergency doctor at the Sainte-Justine Hospital for Children in Montreal. She also took time to work as a program manager for Doctors Without Borders from 1999 to 2002, overseeing missions in a dozen countries and an annual budget of five million Euros. From 2004 to 2009, she served as president of MSF Canada.

Liu occasionally became frustrated by the inefficiencies and injustices of the humanitarian-aid world. She told Fishburn of her dismay at the conditions in a camp for displaced persons in the Central African Republic: "People were talking to me with their two feet in mud. And I said, 'This is not possible, that in the twenty-first century we still have to see that.' And that for me is really a call for how can we do better? Can I stand on a spot where I don't have my two feet in water?"

PRESIDENT OF MSF

In October 2013 Liu became president of the international organization, which by then had 32,000 staff members working in some seventy countries. Almost immediately she was faced with the task of responding to a deadly Ebola outbreak in West Africa. In an interview with Audie Cornish for *All Things Considered* (19 Aug. 2014), Liu explained, "The reality is all of us who are dealing with Ebola in this particular epidemic are breaking new grounds. We never

faced an epidemic of Ebola of that kind of magnitude and that much spread in the past. . . . What was applied in some isolated remote villages in the past, you cannot do a cut and paste right now of what is going on in an urban area like Monrovia."

Liu received widespread praise for her handling of the crisis and was named one of the most important leaders of the year by the editors of both *Fortune* and *Time* magazines, among other such honors. The past recipient of a Teasdale-Corti Humanitarian Award from the Royal College of Physicians and Surgeons of Canada, Liu has also received accolades for her development of an innovative telemedicine project that connects Doctors Without Borders physicians in 150 remote locations with a collective of some 300 specialists around the world, allowing medical experts who are unable to travel to still lend help.

Liu has always stressed, however, that Doctors Without Borders could not operate without the help of local medical personnel. She continually reminded journalists that for every one of the Doctors Without Borders volunteers sent into affected regions, ten local staffers, most of whom had lost family members and friends, were working zealously.

The dangers in which Doctors Without Borders workers willingly place themselves was brought to stark light in October 2015, when a hospital in the Afghan city of Kunduz was devastated by an aerial attack that killed twenty-two people, including several of the group's staff members. US officials confirmed that the US military had conducted an airstrike in the vicinity of the hospital, prompting Liu to post a series of distressed messages to her Twitter account, including one that read, "In the Intensive Care Unit six patients were burning in their beds," and another that said, "MSF demands full account from the Coalition regarding aerial bombing activities over Kunduz—independent investigation needed."

PERSONAL LIFE

Liu, who in 2014 attended the Desautels Faculty of Management at McGill University and participated in the specialized International Masters in Health Leadership Program, is now based in Geneva. She has announced her intention to travel back to Montreal to work at the Sainte-Justine Hospital for Children at least once a year in order to keep her clinical skills sharp. Her husband, an engineer, divides his time between Geneva and Canada.

SUGGESTED READING

Arvanitakis, Sylvie. "The Good Doctor." *Montréal enSanté*. McGill U Health Center, Winter 2014. Web. 4 Oct. 2015.

Cornish, Audie. "Doctors Without Borders: What We Need to Contain Ebola." *All Things Considered*. NPR, 19 Aug. 2014. Web. 4 Oct. 2015.

Fishburn, Alice. "Women of 2014: Joanne Liu." *Financial Times*. Financial Times, 12 Dec. 2014. Web. 4 Oct. 2015.

Frieden, Tom. "Time 100 Leaders: Joanne Liu." *Time*. Time, 16 Apr. 2015. Web. 4 Oct. 2015.

Gordon, Andrea. "Montreal Doctor Becomes Second Canadian to Lead Médecins Sans Frontières." *Toronto Star*. Toronto Star Newspapers, 8 Nov. 2013. Web. 4 Oct. 2015.

Liu, Joanne. "Women at Business School—Joanne Liu." Interview by Charlotte Clarke. *Financial Times*. Financial Times, 19 Jan. 2014. Web. 4 Oct. 2015.

Perreaux, Les. "Vacations Out for Canadian Chief of Aid Group Doctors Without Borders." *Globe and Mail*. Globe and Mail, 20 Oct. 2014. Web. 4 Oct. 2015.

—*Mari Rich*

Lorde

Born: November 7, 1996
Occupation: Musician

EARLY LIFE AND EDUCATION

Lorde was born Ella Marija Lani Yelich-O'Connor in Auckland, New Zealand, in 1996. She was the second of four children born to Sonja Yelich, a poet, and Victor O'Connor, a civil engineer. She was raised in the Auckland suburb of Devonport.

She developed an interest in performance at an early age, participating in musical theater productions from the time she was five years old. Thanks to her poet mother, she also had a love of books and began reading Raymond Carver and Kurt Vonnegut by the time she was twelve.

Lorde attended Belmont Intermediate School, where, at age twelve, she won the school's talent show with a performance of a cover song. Impressed by her unique voice and mature stage presence, a friend's father sent a recording to manager Scott Maclachlan, who helped her to secure a record deal.

Signed by Universal Records at age thirteen, she began work on her debut EP, *The Love Club*. Due to a lifelong fascination with royalty and aristocracy, she considered performing under the stage moniker Duke but eventually decided that it was too masculine. She ultimately opted to adopt the name Lord, adding an e to the end to make the name appear more feminine.

RISE TO STARDOM

The Love Club was released as a free download on the music site SoundCloud in November 2012 and quickly reached over sixty thousand downloads. An official digital release followed in March 2013, and Universal released a CD in May of that year. *The Love Club* debuted in the number-two position on the New Zealand Top 40 album chart.

The EP's first single, "Royals," debuted at number one on the New Zealand Top 40 chart and remained there for three weeks. In August 2013, "Royals" reached the top of the US Billboard Alternative Songs chart, making Lorde the first female artist in seventeen years to reach that position. "Royals" also made Lorde the first solo artist from New Zealand to top the US Billboard Hot 100 and the youngest artist to do so in more than twenty-five years.

Lorde's second EP, the *Tennis Court EP*, was released in June 2013. Its lead single, "Tennis Court," debuted at number one on the New Zealand Top 40 chart, giving Lorde a record high of four tracks on the chart simultaneously.

Lorde's full-length debut, *Pure Heroine*, was released in September 2013 to widespread critical and commercial success. Driven by the continued success of the single "Royals," the album propelled the singer-songwriter to international stardom and a bevy of live performances, including on television shows such as *Later. . . with Jules Holland* and *Late Night with Jimmy Fallon*. Numerous critics lauded the record as a welcome deconstruction of its pop music contemporaries and a more serious and thought-provoking play on the genre.

Pure Heroine was nominated for Grammy Awards in four categories, including record of the year and best pop vocal album. The song "Royals" won Grammys in the categories of song of the year and best pop solo performance. Lorde capped her two-award victory with a live performance of the song at the awards ceremony.

IMPACT

Despite her youth, Lorde has emerged as one of several artists in the pop music genre who have challenged previous conceptions of female pop artists as carefree starlets. She has dealt with her critical and commercial success with aplomb, stating in several interviews that she remains unsure if music in fact will be her major pursuit in life. She has also made no qualms about her stance as a vocal feminist, embracing her role as a musical role model for women throughout the world. Lorde has separated herself from many contemporaries due to her embrace of subject matter beyond the typical pop milieu of love and relationships, opting instead to explore more existential and critical themes, a maturity made more profound by her stage presence and evocative range as a vocalist.

SUGGESTED READING

Fleming, Olivia. "Discovery: Lorde." *Interview.* Brant Publications, 2013. Web. 20 Mar. 2014.

Liedel, Kevin. "Lorde: Pure Heroine." *Slant.* Slant, 29 Sept. 2013. Web. 20 Mar. 2014.

Lipshutz, Jason. "The New Queen of Alternative." *Billboard* Sept. 2013: 26. Print.

Ryan, Charlotte. "Lorde: Behind the Success Story." *New Zealand Herald.* APN New Zealand, 2 May 2013. Web. 20 Mar. 2014.

Stern, Marlow. "Meet Lorde, the 16-Year-Old Singer Poised to Take Over Pop Music." *Daily Beast.* Daily Beast, 2 July 2013. Web. 20 Mar. 2014.

Symonds, Alexandria. "Lorde." *Interview.* Brant Publications, 2013. Web. 20 Mar. 2014.

Weiner, Jonah. "Lorde's Teenage Dream." *Rolling Stone.* Wenner Media, 28 Oct. 2013. Web. 20 Mar. 2014.

SELECTED WORKS

The Love Club EP, 2013; *The Tennis Court EP,* 2013; *Pure Heroine,* 2013

—*John Pritchard*

Flying Lotus

Born: October 7, 1983
Occupation: Musician

The Los Angeles–based musician and producer Flying Lotus has earned the title "the electronic Jimi Hendrix," a designation given to him by music journalist and British Broadcasting Corp. (BBC) DJ Mary Anne Hobbs for his effortless ability to craft lushly constructed, genre-bending musical soundscapes on computers. Flying Lotus's music is "tumultuous," Andy Beta wrote for *Fader* (Oct./Nov. 2014), "taking daredevil risks and embracing chaos, smashing together disparate sounds yet retaining a firm sense of control."

Since launching his music career in the mid-2000s, Flying Lotus has distinguished himself as one of the leading practitioners of Los Angeles's progressive beat movement, which is characterized by the melding of electronic music and hip-hop with the free-flowing nature of jazz. He has released five critically acclaimed solo albums: *1983* (2006), *Los Angeles* (2008), *Cosmogramma* (2010), *Until the Quiet Comes* (2012), and *You're Dead!* (2014). He is the founder of the independent label Brainfeeder and has collaborated with the likes of such artists as Thundercat, Thom Yorke of Radiohead, Erykah Badu, and

Simon Fernandez/CC BY 2.0/ Wikimedia Commons

Kendrick Lamar. He also raps under the alias Captain Murphy.

EARLY LIFE

Flying Lotus was born Steven Ellison on October 7, 1983, in Los Angeles, California. He grew up in Winnetka, a middle-class neighborhood in the west-central part of Los Angeles's San Fernando Valley. His great-aunt, Alice Coltrane, was a celebrated jazz harpist, pianist, and composer and was the second wife and collaborator of the legendary saxophonist John Coltrane. His grandmother, Marilyn McLeod, is a former Motown songwriter who wrote songs for the likes of Diana Ross and Smokey Robinson.

Flying Lotus was raised by his mother, Tammy, who helped oversee the John Coltrane estate, and his grandmother. His father, who died in early 2000, was largely absent from his life. In an interview with Simon Vozick-Levinson for *Rolling Stone* (7 Nov. 2014), Flying Lotus recalled, "There were times when the money was there and times when we were broke as f——. Sometimes we didn't have a phone or good food." Music was the unifying force that tied his family together. The family spent every Sunday at Alice Coltrane's ashram in Agoura Hills, California, where they would spend hours singing and playing music.

Flying Lotus has recalled attending his family's Los Angeles–area John Coltrane festivals as a boy and playing Coltrane's signature instrument, the saxophone, throughout his youth. Still, it "wasn't my instrument," as he explained in an interview with Patrick Sisson for the music website *Pitchfork* (13 June 2010). "It was fun and I was decent at it, but I wasn't learning the kind of things I wanted to play."

FINDING HIS PLACE

Enamored with West Coast gangsta rap and inclined toward technology, Flying Lotus was drawn early on to synthesizers and drum machines. He started creating hip-hop soundscapes at age fifteen when his cousin, Alice and John's youngest son Oran Coltrane, gave him a Roland MC-505 Groovebox. "That opened up everything for me," he told Chris Martins for *LA Weekly* (13 May 2010). Up until that time, he added, "I didn't really know my place in the family legacy."

For Flying Lotus, creating music helped him cope with the alienation he felt while growing up in a community devoid of art and culture. He had trouble fitting in at his public high school and started experimenting with drugs and fell in with a like-minded crowd of teenagers. Things came to a head during his junior year, when he was kicked out of school for telling an undercover police officer where to buy marijuana. As part of his probation, Lotus was sent to Henry David Thoreau High School, a continuation school in Woodland Hills for juvenile offenders. "It was an exposure to the real," he told Vozick-Levinson. "I got a crash course in diversity."

After competing high school, Flying Lotus briefly drifted away from music to study film, which had been a passion of his since childhood. He first attended Hollywood's Los Angeles Film School before spending a year at the Academy of Art University in San Francisco where he met and befriended David Wexler, the grandson of Oscar-winning cinematographer Haskell Wexler. Wexler, now a video artist who goes under the name Dr. Strangeloop, showed Lotus how to program music on a laptop, which renewed Lotus's interest in beatmaking.

FIRST TWO STUDIO ALBUMS AND BRAIN-FEEDER

In 2004 Flying Lotus returned to Los Angeles to launch his music career. Around this time, he started interning at Stones Throw Records, a groundbreaking Los Angeles–based hip-hop label that helped launch the careers of Madlib and the late J Dilla, the forefathers of instrumental-driven rap music. Lotus immersed himself in the city's then-burgeoning beat scene and began crafting material inspired by his many creative influences, which included video games and comic books and electronic music pioneers like Aphex Twin and Squarepusher.

Lotus's big break came after he was hired to create bumper music to transition between programs during Cartoon Network's *Adult Swim* programming block. Some of that music would later appear on his debut full-length album,

1983, which was released in 2006. The album showcases the multilayered electronic- and jazz-based hip-hop for which Lotus would become known. Also in 2006, Lotus became a regular attendee of DJ, producer, and label head Daddy Kev's highly influential Low End Theory party, a now-famous weekly "producer's lounge" held at the Los Angeles club Airliner.

Lotus soon developed a close relationship with Kev, whose party served as the nerve center for the Los Angeles beat scene. "Lotus is kind of like Neo from *The Matrix*,'" Kev, who has served as chief engineer on many of Lotus's releases, told Mike Rubin for the *New York Times* (28 May 2010). "He is 'The One.'" Lotus's "chosen-one" status brought him to the attention of record labels, and he signed with the prestigious London-based label Warp Records in 2007 and released a six-track EP called *Reset* later that year.

Flying Lotus's second studio album, *Los Angeles*, was released on Warp in 2008. The seventeen-track album pays homage to the golden age of hip-hop and expands on the genre-bending compositions of his debut. The album also paved the way for a series of *Los Angeles*–influenced EPs that Lotus released throughout the year. Lotus also established his own independent record label, Brainfeeder, in 2008. Distributed by Kev's Alpha Pup Records, the label is home to bass virtuoso Thundercat, who is Lotus's close friend, and many other local beat scene practitioners, including Ras G, Samiyan, Daedelus, and the Gaslamp Killer.

BREAKTHROUGH WITH *COSMOGRAMMA*

Flying Lotus spent over eighteen months working on his next album, *Cosmogramma* (2010), which was inspired by the loss of his mother, who died suddenly of complications from diabetes on October 31, 2008. Wanting to create an album that would capture the grieving process, Lotus resolved to make ambitiously complex arrangements with a wide array of collaborators. He also hoped to include elements that would connect to his musical lineage, particularly that of his great-aunt Alice, who died in 2007.

The seventeen-track *Cosmogramma* is "a marriage of twenty-first-century technology and 1960s West Coast psychedelic experimentation, sounding at times like a futuristic take on free jazz," Rubin wrote. Heavily influenced by Alice Coltrane's 1972 symphonic masterpiece *Lord of Lords*, the album features recorded sounds of Lotus's mother's life-support machines and live instrumentation from Thundercat, string arranger Miguel Atwood-Ferguson, harpist Rebekah Raff, and Grammy Award–nominated saxophonist Ravi Coltrane, Oran's older brother. It also includes guest vocals by Radiohead's Thom Yorke and frequent Lotus collaborator Laura Darlington.

Cosmogramma was widely praised by music critics and helped catapult Flying Lotus to international fame. Martins called the album "a potential game-changer for electronica, instrumental hip-hop and jazz" and proclaimed it "a magnum opus, imbued with a tangible mysticism." Meanwhile, Hobbs explained to Rubin, "In the same way that Jimi Hendrix was completely reinventing what you could do with a guitar, Lotus is reinventing what you can do with electronic tools."

In the wake of *Cosmogramma's* success, Flying Lotus embarked on a fruitful creative partnership with Thundercat. In 2011 he produced the bassist's solo debut, *The Golden Age of Apocalypse*, which was released to critical acclaim, and he went on to serve as a producer on Thundercat's next two studio albums, *Apocalypse* (2013) and *The Beyond/Where the Giants Roam* (2015). Thundercat explained to Martins that recording with Flying Lotus is like "playing with a classical musician. . . . Steve knows his craft. There's no hesitation and he's great at what he does. He's in a class of his own."

UNTIL THE QUIET COMES AND YOU'RE DEAD!
Flying Lotus adopted a minimalist approach in his fourth studio album, *Until the Quiet Comes* (2012), which draws its influence from dreams. Most of the album's nineteen songs were recorded with an Ableton Live sequencer and various digital and analogue instruments and feature contributions from Thundercat, Atwood-Ferguson, Yorke, and Darlington. Neo-soul singer Erykah Badu, composer Johnny Greenwood, and the late pianist Austin Peralta are also featured. A short film of the same name was directed by Indian actor Kahlil Joseph and was released in conjunction with the introspective album, which debuted at thirty-four on the US Billboard 200 album chart.

Flying Lotus's fifth studio album, *You're Dead!*, was released by Warp in 2014. It was originally conceived as a jazz album before evolving into a hyper-fusion concept album about mortality. Comprised of nineteen tracks spanning a brisk thirty-eight minutes, it features guest appearances by A-list rappers Kendrick Lamar and Snoop Dogg as well as an appearance of Lotus's rap alter ego Captain Murphy. Jazz legend Herbie Hancock contributed piano arrangements to several songs, and Thundercat and a bevy of other artists also contributed to the album.

You're Dead! became Lotus's first album to crack the top twenty on the US Billboard album chart and was hailed by critics as the most ambitious effort of his career. In a review for AllMusic, Andy Kellman put Flying Lotus in the company of Alice and John Coltrane, concluding that, like them, Lotus has "created exceptionally progressive, stirring, and eternal art." Meanwhile, Will Hermes proclaimed for *Rolling Stone* (21 Oct. 2014) that *You're Dead!* was "the boldest, most fully engaged fusion of the hip-hop-laptop era."

In 2016 Flying Lotus received a Grammy Award nomination for best dance recording for "Never Catch Me," a feverish, electronic-tinged jazz number on which Lamar provided vocals. He also earned a nomination for album of the year for his production work on Lamar's critically acclaimed third studio album, *To Pimp a Butterfly* (2015).

OTHER WORK
Flying Lotus is known for his energetic live performances, which are accompanied by psychedelic improvised projections. He has appeared at a number of world-renowned festivals, including the Bonnaroo Music and Arts Festival, the Coachella Valley and Arts Festival, and the Glastonbury Festival.

In the summer of 2012, Lotus, who has also written several film scores, began rapping under the alias Captain Murphy, which is based on a character of the same name from *Sealab2021*, an Adult Swim program. His debut rap mixtape as Captain Murphy, *Duality*, was released on Brainfeeder in November 2012. Lotus has announced plans to release a full-length Murphy album sometime in late 2016 or 2017.

SUGGESTED READING
Beta, Andy. "Cover Story: Flying Lotus Confronts Death." *Fader*. Fader, Oct./Nov. 2014. Web. 30 Apr. 2016.

Martins, Chris. "Flying Lotus Rising." *LA Weekly*. LA Weekly, 13 May 2010. Web. 30 Apr. 2016.

Rubin, Mike. "Lost, with Laptops, in Psychedelic Space." *New York Times*. New York Times, 28 May 2010. Web. 30 Apr. 2016.

Sisson, Patrick. "Flying Lotus." *Pitchfork*. Condé Nast, 13 June 2010. Web. 30 Apr. 2016.

Vozick-Levinson, Simon. "Flying Lotus: Inside the Mind of a Mad Beat Scientist." *Rolling Stone*. Rolling Stone, 7 Nov. 2014. Web. 30 Apr. 2016.

SELECTED WORKS
1983, 2006; *Los Angeles*, 2008; *Cosmogramma*, 2010; *Until the Quiet Comes*, 2012; *You're Dead!* 2014

—Chris Cullen

Wesley Lowery

Born: July 9, 1990
Occupation: Journalist

Wesley Lowery is an award-winning journalist for the *Washington Post* who helped direct national attention to the killing of Michael Brown, and the protests that followed Brown's death, in Ferguson, Missouri, in August 2014. Lowery himself made headlines while covering the Ferguson uprising when he and Ryan Reilly of the *Huffington Post* were arrested while dining at a local McDonalds. Lowery, who used to write for the *Boston Globe*, has also covered the Boston Marathon bombings, the Aaron Hernandez murder case, the killing of unarmed teenager Trayvon Martin, and the 2012 presidential election. In 2014 the National Association of Black Journalists (NABJ) named him their emerging journalist of the year.

Lowery has consistently been at the forefront of major news stories; he became a verified reporter on Twitter after live-tweeting the Boston Marathon bombings and the manhunt that followed. As a college senior at Ohio University, he e-mailed George Zimmerman, the man accused of murdering Trayvon Martin. Zimmerman wrote back, and Lowery was invited on Cable News Network (CNN) to break the news. Lowery has successfully harnessed the power of the Internet, particularly social media outlets like Twitter, to tell stories as they happen. The late David Carr, a media reporter for the *New York Times*, wrote about Lowery's arrest on August 17, 2014, emphasizing the particular value of Twitter as a news medium. "In and of itself, Twitter is not sufficient to see clearly into a big story; it's a series of straws that offer narrow views of a much bigger picture," he wrote. "But as a kind of constantly changing kaleidoscope, it provides enough visibility to show that something significant is underway." Lowery's work, more than that of many of his colleagues, embodies this on-the-ground approach to storytelling.

EARLY LIFE AND EDUCATION

Lowery was born on July 9, 1990 in Woodbridge, New Jersey, but grew up in Teaneck. His family moved to Shaker Heights, a suburb of Cleveland, Ohio, before Lowery entered high school. He traces his interest in journalism back to middle school, though his father was a journalist who instilled in his son the importance of the field. Lowery attended Shaker Heights High School, where he was editor-in-chief of the school's award-winning newspaper, the *Shakerite*. He graduated in 2008 and entered the E. W. Scripps School of Journalism at Ohio University in Athens, Ohio. As he told Chris Manning for student-run *Backdrop Magazine* (10 July

Gary Gershoff/Stringer/Getty Images

2014), Lowery was strategic about getting a leg up in media even as a freshman, starting at the university newspaper, the *Post*, on his first day and working there "every day of college." That kind of effort was necessary to succeed in journalism, he told Manning: "What I wrote today will be better than what I wrote yesterday and what I wrote the day before, so you need to be writing every day." In 2011 Lowery became editor-in-chief of the *Post*. He also reported for *Loop 21*, a news website that focuses on African American issues. During his tenure at Ohio University, Lowery held internships at the *Boston Globe*, the *Wall Street Journal*, the *Columbus Dispatch*, and the *Detroit News*. The most memorable, he told Manning, was his internship with the *Dispatch*. "It was really trial by fire," he said. "They really threw me in." Lowery was also a METPRO Reporting Fellow at the *Los Angeles Times*. In January 2012 he contributed an op-ed to the *New York Times* about how young voters felt about President Obama during his reelection campaign.

Lowery was in his senior year in February 2012, when George Zimmerman shot and killed an unarmed black teenager named Trayvon Martin in Sanford, Florida. Zimmerman was a self-appointed neighborhood watch captain who claimed that he killed Martin, who was walking from the convenience store to his father's house, in self-defense. Invoking Florida's controversial "Stand Your Ground" law, he said that Martin had threatened his life, but details soon emerged that complicated Zimmerman's version of events. Martin, who was seventeen, was carrying only a bag of Skittles and a bottle of iced tea, and had told his girlfriend over the phone that he was being followed by a strange man. Zimmerman said that Martin looked "suspicious," but many pointed to the veiled racism of the description: Martin was a black man in a predominantly white neighborhood. After weeks of public pressure, authorities arrested Zimmerman in March 2012, but he was acquitted of second-degree murder in July. Martin, and the hoodie sweatshirt he was wearing when he was killed, quickly became an emblem of the burgeoning civil rights movement, Black Lives Matter, which Lowery has spent much of his career reporting on.

While the case was unfolding, Lowery began investigating a website that Zimmerman had set up to raise money for his defense. Lowery tracked the website back to the domain from which it had been purchased and discovered a contact address. On a hunch, Lowery reached out to see if the e-mail address belonged to Zimmerman. "I knew there was a chance [that Zimmerman would respond] so as a journalist, it's my job," he later recalled to Allie Harris, a student reporter for Lowery's own *Shakerite* high school newspaper (25 Apr. 2012). Lowery received a response from Zimmerman twenty minutes later. Lowery and Zimmerman exchanged several e-mails, though Zimmerman stopped responding when Lowery began to ask him more probing questions. Still, the contact was a huge coup for Lowery, who was still a student at the time. Lowery wrote a blog post about the e-mails for *Loop 21*, and appeared on the Jane Velez-Mitchell show on Headline News the next day, April 11, to discuss the story.

BREAKING NEWS IN BOSTON

After graduating in 2012, Lowery joined the *Boston Globe* as a general assignment and political reporter in 2013. It was a big year for news in Boston, and Lowery hit the ground running. Lowery was not working on April 15, the day of the Boston Marathon bombing, but after the attacks occurred he volunteered to cover the story. A few days later, in the early morning on April 19, Lowery and a few of his colleagues were at a concert when they got news of a shooting at the Massachusetts Institute of Technology (MIT). Lowery immediately headed to the campus in Cambridge, where he met up with a photographer named David Yang. The men followed police cruisers when they abruptly peeled out of the crime scene. Although the reporters did not know it at the time, the police were chasing the Tsarnaev brothers, suspects in the bombing, who had shot a campus police officer at MIT and were on the run. The chase ended in a shootout that claimed the life of Tamerlan Tsarnaev; his brother, Dzhokhar Tsarnaev, was found hiding in a boat in Watertown around 8 p.m. that night.

Dzhokhar was later convicted and sentenced to death.

Lowery followed the story through the day, signing off of Twitter around 5 a.m. on April 19 and jumping back into the fray to report Dzhokhar Tsarnaev's capture. The number of people that followed his account tripled that week, from 3,000 to 15,000. (By 2016, he had more than 300,000 followers.) A journalist liaison for the site awarded him the coveted blue checkmark of verification. Lowery's reporting proved a valuable contribution to the work of his colleagues, who won a Pulitzer Prize for their coverage of the bombing in 2014.

In June 2013, former New England Patriots tight end Aaron Hernandez was arrested and charged with the murder of Odin Lloyd. Lowery was at the courthouse the morning of the arraignment along with a number of other reporters, many of them sports reporters who had never covered a murder case. Lowery arrived early and realized that the there was no cell phone reception in the eighteenth-century building. When the judge read the charges against Hernandez, every reporter went for their phone, but Lowery's was the first tweet to go through. "At that time the live feed wasn't up yet on TV and so I was the first person to break the news that he was charged with murder because I figured out Twitter wasn't going to work and so I tweeted via text and it went through," Lowery recalled to Manning. As the trial went on, Lowery became the go-to source for sports websites like *Deadspin* and the now-defunct *Grantland*. Hernandez was eventually convicted of first-degree murder for killing Lloyd at an industrial park near his house.

SHOOTING IN FERGUSON

Lowery joined the *Washington Post* as a politics and congressional reporter in January 2014, though he later switched to covering law enforcement and justice for the newspaper. On August 9, 2014, an unarmed African American teenager named Michael Brown was shot and killed by a white police officer named Darren Wilson in Ferguson, Missouri, a suburb of St. Louis. While the details of the altercation were unclear, the result left Brown, with multiple bullet wounds, dead in the street. His body lay uncovered for four hours. Ferguson residents, outraged by the gruesome killing and its botched aftermath, took to the streets in protest. Social media drew more protestors, and the police response to the crowds escalated quickly. Officers met protestors with riot gear, flash grenades and tanks; as Carr wrote, photos on social media painted a surreal picture of war that looked more like Iraq or Gaza than an American suburb.

Lowery was assigned to cover Ferguson two days after the shooting. Social media continued to be the driving force behind the protests, but also the coverage of those protests. News channels like CNN were focused on other news events until the sheer number of people engaged with #Ferguson on Twitter became too great to ignore. This is the atmosphere into which Lowery arrived in Ferguson.

On August 13, Lowery and Ryan Reilly, a reporter for the *Huffington Post*, were at a McDonald's restaurant a few blocks away from where Brown had been killed. The restaurant, with its Wi-Fi connection and power outlets, had served as a makeshift staging area for reporters since the protests began. A crowd of police officers entered the restaurant and asked Lowery and Reilly for their press identification. Lowery produced his, though Reilly refused, asking why it was necessary. The officers left but returned moments later, asking the men to leave the restaurant. Lowery began recording video on his cell phone. What happened next, as Lowery wrote in a detailed article for the *Washington Post* (14 Aug. 2014), was complicated. The officers asked him to stop recording, although doing so was not illegal, and then gave him conflicting information on which door he was supposed to exit through. Lowery was still recording when his bag began to slip from his shoulder. When he went to adjust it, telling them as he did so, they converged on him and put him in handcuffs. "Multiple officers grabbed me," Lowery wrote. "I tried to turn my back to them to assist them in arresting me. I dropped the things from my hands. 'My hands are behind my back,' I said. 'I'm not resisting. I'm not resisting.' At which point one officer said: 'You're resisting. Stop resisting.' That was when I was most afraid—more afraid than of the tear gas and rubber bullets."

Later, the officers told Lowery he had been arrested for trespassing. He and Reilly were released later that night without charges. The arrests made headlines the next day, and the *Washington Post* and other news outlets responded with anger. The *Post* released a statement that read in part: "That behavior [of the officers] was wholly unwarranted and an assault on the freedom of the press to cover the news." Lowery spent the next three months in Ferguson, and returned a year later to cover the anniversary of Brown's death. Around the same time, he received a summons from the St. Louis County court. He was charged with trespassing and interfering with a police officer.

SUGGESTED READING

Carr, David. "View of #Ferguson Thrust Michael Brown Shooting to National Attention." *New York Times*. New York Times, 17 Aug. 2014. Web. 14 Mar. 2016.

Harris, Allie. "Lowery Reaches Zimmerman Via Email." *Shakerite*. Shaker Heights High School, 25 Apr. 2012. Web. 14 Mar. 2016.

Lowery, Wesley. "Q&A: Wes Lowery." Interview by Chris Manning. *Backdrop Magazine*. Backdrop Magazine, 10 July 2014. Web. 14 Mar. 2016.

Lowery, Wesley. "In Ferguson, *Washington Post* Reporter Wesley Lowery Gives Account of His Arrest." *Washington Post*. Washington Post, 14 Aug. 2014. Web. 14 Mar. 2016.

SELECTED WORKS

"Obama's Challenge Will Be Mobilization," *New York Times*, 10 Jan. 2012; "A Long Night in Watertown: Reporter's Account of the Standoff with Marathon Bomb Suspect," *Washington Post*, 17 Apr. 2014; "Aaron Hernandez Is Charged with Murder," *Boston Globe*, 27 June 2013; "In Ferguson, *Washington Post* Reporter Wesley Lowery Gives Account of His Arrest," *Washington Post*, 14 Aug. 2014

—*Molly Hagan*

Kyle Lowry

Born: March 25, 1986
Occupation: Basketball player

Kyle Lowry, point guard for the National Basketball Association (NBA) team the Toronto Raptors, has often been described as a "pit bull" for his toughness and tenacious style of play. Drafted by the Memphis Grizzlies in the first round of the 2006 NBA Draft, Lowry struggled to gain his footing as a starter during his first seven seasons in the league, largely due to injuries and a reported bad attitude as well as deep-rooted problems with authority. He began to come into his own as a player after the 2011–12 season when he was traded from the Houston Rockets to the Toronto Raptors.

Since then, Lowry has overhauled his approach to the game and has developed into one of the best point guards in the NBA. He helped the Raptors increase their regular-season win totals in each of his first four seasons with the team and has led them to three consecutive playoff berths from 2014 to 2016. He has earned two All-Star selections (2015, 2016) and one All-NBA Third Team selection (2016).

EARLY LIFE

Kyle Lowry was born on March 25, 1986, in Philadelphia, Pennsylvania, to Lonnie Lowry Sr. and Marie Holloway. He and his older brother, Lonnie Jr., grew up in a North Philadelphia neighborhood that was plagued by drugs,

Keith Allison from Hanover, MD, USA (Kyle Lowry)/CC BY-SA 2.0/Wikimedia Commons

homelessness, and the ever-present threat of violence. From the time he was born, Lowry had very little contact with his biological father and has stated that he was seven years old the last time he saw his father.

Lowry was raised by his mother and grandmother, both of whom pushed him into sports at an early age in an attempt to keep him off the streets. Marie Holloway worked two jobs to make ends meet for the family. Growing up, Lowry and his brother were "scared" of his mother and grandmother, as he admitted to Adam Figman for SLAM Online (14 Apr. 2014). "We were the kids where everybody would be playing, and it's 8 o'clock, and you can hear my grandma screaming our names out down the street to come in the house."

Strict rules notwithstanding, Lowry developed a particularly close bond with his older brother, who stepped in as a father figure. Lowry's brother showed him how to play basketball and made him dribble a basketball around the neighborhood with his off hand and play pickup games against older boys; he also shuttled young Lowry to tryouts for Amateur Athletic Union (AAU) teams. Lowry spent much of his childhood and adolescence honing his basketball skills at the Hank Gathers Recreation Center in North Philadelphia.

As a youth Lowry dreamed early on of playing professionally in the NBA. He modeled his game after one of his childhood idols, former Philadelphia 76ers great Allen Iverson, a perennial All-Star shooting guard who was known for his toughness and hard-nosed style of play. Though

Lowry, like Iverson, was undersized compared to his peers, "I was always faster than everybody, and stronger," he recalled to Marcus Hayes for the *Philadelphia Daily News* (18 Jan. 2012).

A PHILADELPHIA KIND OF PLAYER

At Philadelphia's Northeast High School, Lowry stood out from his teammates for his unrelenting desire to win. After leading Northeast High to the Public League finals as a sophomore point guard in 2002, he transferred to Cardinal Dougherty High School, a now-defunct Catholic school in North Philadelphia's Olney neighborhood.

Lowry adjusted well to the Catholic League's more physical style of play, leading Dougherty to back-to-back league title games during his junior and senior seasons. "A Philly player is what a basketball player is," he told Jonathan Abrams for *Grantland* (23 Sept. 2014). "It doesn't matter if you're six feet and they put you at power forward or if you're seven-feet-two and they put you at point guard, you'll get it done because you're mentally tough."

Lowry's transition to the more disciplined atmosphere at Cardinal Dougherty High also proved seamless, thanks to the guidance of head coach Mark Heimerdinger and assistant coach Dave Distel, the latter of whom helped recruit him to the school and became another father figure for Lowry.

During his senior year, a number of Division I schools showed interest in Lowry, but all of them wound up signing other recruits. At Distel's suggestion, Lowry looked into attending Villanova University, located in the wealthy Philadelphia suburbs. Although at first uninterested in the school, Lowry decided to attend after talking with Villanova Wildcats head coach Jay Wright. "I knew he was really smart even though he wanted to act like a tough street kid and act like he didn't like anybody," Wright told Abrams, referring to Lowry's former antiauthoritarian attitude.

VILLANOVA TO MEMPHIS GRIZZLIES

Lowry got off to a rocky start at Villanova, first with homesickness and then he tore the anterior cruciate ligament (ACL) in his left knee in a pickup basketball game, putting his basketball career on hold. The injury sidelined Lowry for only four months, during which time he impressed coaches with his ability to quickly grasp the Wildcats' playbook. "When I see a play one time, I've got it," Lowry explained to Hayes. "When I see it twice, I master it. When I see it three times, I know where the loopholes are."

After missing the first few games of his freshman season, Lowry performed solidly as the Wildcats' backup point guard, averaging 7.5 points, 3.2 rebounds, 2 assists, and 1.3 steals in twenty-four games. He was named to the Big East All-Rookie team and Philadelphia's Big Five Rookie of the Year. As a sophomore, he earned a starting spot in Wright's four-guard system and led the Wildcats to the Elite Eight of the National Collegiate Athletic Association (NCAA) tournament. He received All-Big East Second Team honors after averaging 11 points, 4.3 rebounds, and 3.7 assists per game.

With his sights still on the NBA, Lowry chose to skip his junior season at Villanova and enter the 2006 NBA Draft. Despite concerns from some teams about Lowry's injury history and his attitude, the Memphis Grizzlies selected him with the twenty-fourth overall pick in the draft's first round.

After playing on the Grizzlies' 2006 Summer League team, Lowry entered his rookie 2006–7 season as a backup to the team's veteran point guard Damon Stoudamire. His rookie campaign lasted just ten games, however, after he broke his left wrist in the second quarter of a game against the Cleveland Cavaliers.

WAITING HIS TURN

Despite recovering from his injury, Lowry was again relegated to a backup role during the 2007–8 season with the Grizzlies, despite playing in all eighty-two games for the only time in his career.

In February 2009 the Grizzlies traded Lowry to the Houston Rockets, putting him behind the Rockets' then newly christened starting point guard Aaron Brooks for the remainder of the 2008–9 season and for the entire 2009–10 season. Lowry's long-awaited opportunity to prove himself as a starter came early into the 2010–11 season when Brooks suffered an ankle injury during a game against the San Antonio Spurs. Lowry shined in his absence and after his eventual trade, starting in seventy-one games and averaging 13.5 points, 6.7 assists, and 4.1 rebounds in 34.2 minutes.

At the conclusion of the 2010–11 season, the Rockets fired head coach Rick Adelman and replaced him with former Hall of Fame power forward and Minnesota Timberwolves coach Kevin McHale. Lowry, who had grown to trust Adelman, quickly clashed with McHale, who had adopted a stricter, more no-nonsense approach that was grounded in a team-first philosophy. Reflecting on this period in his article for the *Players' Tribune* (11 Feb. 2016), Lowry has said that "During my time with [McHale], I was immature. I didn't handle things the right way."

Lowry, nevertheless, solidified his role as a starter during the 2011–12 season before being sidelined for a month due to a bacterial infection. He played in a total of forty-seven games and averaged 14.3 points, 4.5 rebounds, 6.6 assists, and 1.55 steals. Lowry was then traded to the Toronto Raptors in July 2012 and has said that his unwillingness to adapt to McHale's coaching also played a role in his departure from the team.

EMERGENCE AS STAR PLAYER WITH THE TORONTO RAPTORS

With the Raptors, Lowry once again found himself as back-up for a starting point guard, veteran José Calderón, and any chances to usurp Calderón as starter were thwarted by several early-season injuries. Lowry nonetheless returned to a starting role in January 2013 when the Raptors traded Calderón to the Detroit Pistons.

After the 2012–13 season, in which he averaged 11.6 points, 4.7 rebounds, and 6.4 assists in sixty-eight games, Lowry met with Raptors' management to discuss his future with the team. He initially planned to leave after the 2013–14 season when he became eligible for free agency. However, after being challenged by the Raptors' first-year general manager Masai Ujiri, Lowry resolved to change his attitude and take on more of a leadership role with the team. He explained in his *Players' Tribune* article that "to be a great player, I had to grow up and be more mature. . . . I had to learn to be the face of the franchise. To be a leader. To be *that* guy."

Lowry and the Raptors struggled to a 6–12 record to open the 2013–14 season, but with Raptors' forward Rudy Gay's trade in early December 2013, Lowry was given the opportunity to assume control of the Raptors' offense and reestablish himself as an All-Star–caliber player. He started in a career-high seventy-nine games and averaged what were then career bests in points per game (17.9), assists per game (7.4), and three-point field goal percentage (38.0).

Lowry helped lead the Raptors to an unlikely Atlantic Division title with a 48–34 record and advance to the playoffs logic since 2008. The Raptors lost to the Brooklyn Nets in the first round.

RAPTORS' FRANCHISE PLAYER

Lowry was offered a four-year, $48 million contract extension with the Raptors in July 2014. In the 2014–15 season he earned his first career All-Star selection, and despite missing twelve games in the season's second half due to injury, Lowry closed out the regular season averaging 17.8 points, 6.8 assists, and 4.7 rebounds on 41 percent shooting.

The Raptors, meanwhile, won a franchise-best forty-nine games but were swept in the first round of the playoffs by the Washington Wizards. Lowry averaged only 12.3 points and 4.8 assists in the series after being plagued by fouls and what many observers regarded as fatigue. In an effort to be more effective in the long term for the Raptors, Lowry overhauled his diet and workout program during the 2015–16 off-season, losing fifteen pounds of his normal playing weight. His slimmer physique paid immediate dividends for him on the court when he enjoyed the best season of his ten-year career, earning career highs in points per game (21.2), minutes per game (37.0), steals per game (2.1), and three-point field goal percentage (38.8).

Lowry was named an All-Star starter for the second consecutive season and helped the Raptors establish a new franchise mark for regular-season wins (56) for the third straight year. The Raptors advanced to the Eastern Conference Finals for the first time in franchise history. Though they lost to the Cleveland Cavaliers in a hard-fought six-game series, Lowry was recognized for his performance and was named to the All-NBA Third Team. "I still feel like I can be better," he explained to Mike Mazzeo for *ESPN. com* (22 Jan. 2016). "I'm never satisfied. . . . I think the best I can be is a champion. There is no other goal in basketball."

During the summer of 2016, Lowry participated in the Olympic Games in Rio de Janeiro, Brazil, as a member of the US men's national basketball team.

PERSONAL LIFE

He and his wife, Ayahna, a former college basketball star, have two young sons, Karter and Kameron.

SUGGESTED READING

Abrams, Jonathan. "You Can Count on Me." *Grantland*. ESPN Internet Ventures, 23 Sept. 2014. Web. 30 July 2016.

Ebner, David. "Kyle Lowry Ready to Lead Raptors to Greater Heights." *Globe and Mail*. Globe and Mail, 2 Oct. 2014. Web. 30 July 2016.

Figman, Adam. "Aphillyated." *SLAMonline*. Enthusiast Network, 14 Apr. 2014. Web. 30 July 2016.

Hayes, Marcus. "Ex-Villanova Star Lowry Fueling Rockets." *Philly.com*. Philadelphia Media Network (Digital), 18 Jan. 2012. Web. 30 July 2016.

Lowry, Kyle. "Growing Pains." *Players' Tribune*. Players' Tribune, 11 Feb. 2016. Web. 30 July 2016.

Mazzeo, Mike. "Kyle Lowry Lifted Up His Game by Dropping the Pounds." *ESPN.com*. ESPN Internet Ventures, 22 Jan. 2016. Web. 30 July 2016.

—*Chris Cullen*

Frank Luntz

Born: February 23,1962
Occupation: Political consultant and pollster

"It's not what you say. It's what they hear." That is the frequently repeated slogan of Frank Luntz, who is best known as a Republican political consultant and pollster. Luntz played an important role—as pollster and consultant—for the Republican Contract with America, a platform coauthored by Newt Gingrich, who led the 1994 Republican takeover of Congress. Luntz is known for his ability to turn a phrase to lessen its negative impact on the listener. For example, he began calling the estate tax the "death tax," referred to school vouchers as "opportunity scholarships," softened the impact of the ominous-sounding global warming by introducing the more neutral phrase "climate change," and called drilling for oil a more optimistic-sounding "American energy exploration."

Despite Luntz's success as a pollster and wordsmith, his work has been controversial and has come under fire from both Republicans and Democrats. He has been criticized by nonpartisan groups on occasion for bending the truth with his creative use of language, as well as for flat-out lying. Luntz, as Michelle Cottle wrote for the *New Republic* (27 Jan. 2010), has been "reprimanded (by the American Association for Public Opinion Research (AAPOR)), and censured (by the National Council on Public Polls (NCPP)) for the questionable methodology and interpretation of

Michael Kovac/GettyImages

his polling." Few argue with the success of his strategies, however.

Luntz is the chief executive officer (CEO) of Luntz Global, which performs polling, consulting, crisis management, ad creation, and product development for corporations such as the National Broadcasting Corp. (NBC), British Broadcasting Corp. (BBC), Continental Airlines, Facebook, Google, General Motors (GM), Coca Cola, the National Football League (NFL), National Hockey League (NHL), Merrill Lynch, and Citi Bank.

EARLY LIFE AND EDUCATION

Frank Luntz was born in 1962 and raised in West Hartford, Connecticut. He attended the University of Pennsylvania, receiving a bachelor of arts degree in history and political science in 1984. He then went to the University of Oxford in England to pursue his graduate-school education. He received his PhD in politics in 1987, at the age of twenty-five. In 1988, he served as a political consultant in Israel to the Likud Party. He then returned to the United States, where he taught at various universities, primarily his alma mater, the University of Pennsylvania, serving as an adjunct professor from 1989 to 1996. He also taught classes at George Washington University and Harvard University.

His role as a political player in the United States began in 1992 and gained national significance in 1994. In 1992, he conducted polls for Pat Buchanan's primary campaign for president, and he also did political polling for Ross Perot, a billionaire who ran for president as an independent. In 1993, he interviewed with New York City Republican mayoral candidate Rudy Giuliani, because Giuliani's political consultant had recommended him. He got the job, and in 1993 and 1997, he served as a pollster for Giuliani. In an interview on the Public Broadcasting System (PBS) program *Frontline* (conducted on December 15, 2003), Luntz said that while working for Giuliani, he had one main job: "explain to the campaign what the public wanted and to help explain to the public that that's exactly what [Giuliani] was offering."

ON THE NATIONAL STAGE

In 1994, a group of Republicans, led by Newt Gingrich, decided they needed a fresh strategy to win a majority in Congress in the November midterm elections. They created what they called the Contract with America, a statement of their agenda. Hired by the Republican National Committee, Luntz helped draft the contract and then conducted polls about it. In his *Frontline* interview, Luntz said that in 1994, he insisted that the following sentence be in the document: "If we break this contract, throw us out. We mean it." He insisted that the sentence not

only be included but also that it should be at the bottom of the "contract," because, he reasoned, most people may not read the whole document, but they will read the beginning and end; only if they liked what they had read in those two sections would they read the rest.

Aside from conducting surveys for either politicians or corporations, Luntz began using dial sessions, a type of real-time polling. In these sessions, people watch a politician speak—during a debate, for example—and use a small device with a dial that allowed them to turn a knob to immediately register their approval or disapproval of what they saw and heard. He told David Horovitz in an interview for the *Jerusalem Post* (16 July 2010) that the dial went from zero to one hundred, with fifty as neutral, zero as the lowest rating, and one hundred as the highest. In the PBS interview, Luntz said that the dial technology is "like an X-ray that gets inside your head, and it picks out every single word, every single phrase [that you hear], and you know what works and what doesn't. And you do it without the bias of a focus group. People are quiet as they're listening, and they're reacting anonymously. The key to dial technology is that it's immediate, it's specific, and it's anonymous." He elaborated by adding that "politics is instantaneous" and "not intellectual; it is gut." Throughout his career as a pollster and consultant, Luntz has insisted on the primary importance of appealing to people's emotions instead of their reason. Luntz also said that the dial measures intensity. One cannot understand public opinion or behavior, he said, without understanding the intensity of people's feelings.

LIE OF THE YEAR AWARD

In 2009, Luntz put together a twenty-eight-page memo titled "The Language of Health Care," which he sent to congressional Republicans, suggesting they use it as a sort of playbook to attack the health care reform bill on which Democrats were working under the leadership of President Barack Obama. He encouraged Republicans to attack the plan using evocative words and phrases, most notably calling the plan "a Washington takeover" or a "government takeover of health care." In an interview with Deborah Solomon for the *New York Times* (21 May 2009), Luntz said: "'Takeover' is a word that grabs attention." When Solomon followed up and pointed out that a government takeover was "not at issue" and that Democrats wanted the public to be able to decide between public and private health insurance plans, Luntz said, "I'm not a policy person. I'm a language person."

The following year, Bill Adair and Angie Drobnic Holan wrote an extensive analysis of Luntz's "takeover" claim for the nonpartisan website PolitiFact.com (16 Dec. 2010), in which they gave him PolitiFact's Lie of the Year Award for calling Obamacare "a government takeover of health care." (PolitiFact's reporters and editors gave the award, but the website's readers also selected Luntz's statement as the "most significant falsehood" of the year.) After PolitiFact reporters studied the 906-page health care bill, they concluded that the "government takeover" statement was false because the plan relied primarily on the "existing system of health coverage provided by employers." Furthermore, the conclusion that a relative increase in regulation of the health-care industry was a "government takeover" was untrue; the government regulates many industries, such as airline and electric-utility companies. "The memo," wrote Adair and Holan, "is about salesmanship, not substance." The nonpartisan fact-checking site FactCheck.org also debunked the "takeover" claim originated by Luntz.

WORKING FOR THE KOCH BROTHERS

After spending approximately $400 million for election and advocacy purposes in 2012 and not getting the results they wanted, prominent conservative donors the Koch brothers started looking for someone to help them improve the language of their campaigns, wrote Peter Stone for *Mother Jones* (8 Dec. 2014). In his focus groups, Luntz found that appeals to emotion as opposed to those of ideology were more effective, and that women were "more effective anti-Obamacare spokespeople than men." As a Fox News commentator, Luntz also praised the effectiveness of ads using this information. "Luntz, however, is coy about his involvement with any of these efforts," wrote Stone. When Stone asked Luntz for some details on his work for the Koch brothers, Luntz said he would not discuss it and insisted that "98 percent of my work is corporate"—meaning not for political causes.

Though the level of Luntz's involvement with certain campaigns or causes has not always been known, after the 2012 election he was a changed man. According to a profile of him by Molly Ball for the *Atlantic* (6 Jan. 2014), Luntz became "profoundly depressed" after the 2012 presidential election. He was haunted by the divisiveness and negativity he encountered while speaking to and polling voters, a negativity he understood he "had helped create," wrote Ball. But mostly Luntz blamed President Obama. Luntz said, "We have now created a sense of dependency and a sense of entitlement that is so great that you had, on the day that he was elected, women thinking that Obama was going to pay their mortgage payment, and that's why they voted for him. And that, to me, is the end of what made this country so great." In 2015, Luntz was involved in polling for the Republican presidential debates, conducting a question-and-answer session with Donald Trump supporters.

PERSONAL LIFE

Luntz is single and divides his time among four residencies: a mansion in Los Angeles, a house in Virginia, an apartment in New York City, and, most recently, a home in Las Vegas. He is also the author of three books. His first book, *Words That Work: It's Not What You Say, It's What People Hear* (2007), featured chapters such as "The Ten Rules of Successful Communication" and "The 21 Words and Phrases for the 21st Century."

SUGGESTED READING

Ball, Molly. "The Agony of Frank Luntz." *Atlantic*. Atlantic Monthly Group, 6 Jan. 2014. Web. 3 Nov. 2015.

Solomon, Deborah. "The Wordsmith." *New York Times*. New York Times, 21 May 2009. Web. 3 Nov. 2015.

Stone, Peter. "How Newt Gingrich's Language Guru Helped Rebrand the Kochs' Message." *Mother Jones*. Mother Jones, 8 Dec. 2014. Web. 3 Nov. 2015.

SELECTED WORKS

Words That Work: It's Not What You Say, It's What People Hear, 2007; *What Americans Really Want . . . Really: The Truth about Our Hopes, Dreams, and Fears*, 2009; *Win: The Key Principles to Take Your Business from Ordinary to Extraordinary*, 2011

—*Dmitry Kiper*

Helen Macdonald

Born: 1970
Occupation: Author

Helen Macdonald, a British poet, nature writer, and falconer, is the author of the highly popular and critically acclaimed *H Is for Hawk* (2014), a book that defies easy categorization. It is a memoir by a woman who channels the grief she feels in the wake of her beloved father's death into training a goshawk, an extremely difficult bird to tame, while studying the failed attempt by the renowned novelist T. H. White to train the same kind of bird. In an interview with Aditi Sriram for *Guernica* (15 July 2015), Macdonald recalled how she envisioned the book as being connected to more than one specific genre: "I wanted it to be a memoir about grief, certainly. . . . But I also wanted it to be nature writing, and I wanted it to be a biography. Having all those three genres in one book was a very definite decision I made. What grief does is shatter narratives: the stories

Anthony Harvey/Stringer/Getty Images

you tell about your life, they all crumble at this point. Things become very confused, your agency is called into question, you're not really sure who you are or what you're facing, and I wanted that confusion to be in the text."

Macdonald's book has met with considerable praise from both book lovers and critics in the United States and in her native United Kingdom, and it has become an international best seller. It has also earned a number of awards, including the 2014 Samuel Johnson Prize for Nonfiction and the 2014 Costa Book Award, two very well-regarded prizes presented to authors in the United Kingdom.

EARLY LIFE AND EDUCATION

Helen Macdonald was born in 1970 and grew up in Surrey, a county in the southeast of England outside London, with her brother, mother, and father. Her father, Alisdair Macdonald, was a respected photojournalist; one of his best-known shots is the famous photo of Princess Diana and Prince Charles kissing on the balcony of Buckingham Palace in Westminster on their wedding day in 1981. As a young girl, after going on numerous nature walks with her father to nearby forests, fields and heaths, Macdonald became immensely fascinated with hawks and read everything she could about them. She dreamed of becoming a biologist when she grew up and even slept like a hawk, with her arms folded behind her back. "My poor parents, I must have been a nightmare. All I could think about was hawks. I would talk about them incessantly, and they never told me to shut up, bless them," Macdonald recalled in her interview with Emma

Higginbotham for the *Cambridge News* (7 Sept. 2014). "I've always just thought they were the most beautiful, perfect things. There's a line in [the 1969 film] *Kes,* which I always found very moving: it's when little Billy Casper says that when they fly, everything goes silent. And I think that captures it: there's a kind of awe about them. They seem a little bit other-worldly."

From 1990 to 1993 Macdonald studied at New Hall at the University of Cambridge, where she earned her bachelor's degree in English literature. She had initially wanted to study biology, but lacked the necessary math skills. After finishing her degree she worked, from 1995 to 1999, in the field of falcon conservation. During this period she was involved with various breeding projects in Wales. She then returned to school and earned her master of philosophy (MPhil) in the history of philosophy and science at Cambridge.

SHALER'S FISH AND FALCON
Since 2000 Macdonald has worked as a teacher, poet, freelance writer, and college research fellow. Her first book, *Shaler's Fish*, was a collection of poems first published in 2001 and reissued in 2016 after the success of *H Is for Hawk.* Although the collection covers a wide variety of topics, each poem in the collection is thematically linked by an author who uses her trained, watchful eye to find interconnections in natural world. In a review for *Publishers Weekly* (18 Jan. 2016), a critic wrote of Macdonald's debut collection of poetry: "Macdonald employs her knowledge of the natural sciences as she deftly works scientific discoveries into poems on such subjects as love, politics, solitude, death, and more. . . . The rich and heady language calls to mind the tradition of the English Romantic poets while offering wholly new and original constructions."

Macdonald's second published work, *Falcon* (2006), is an expansive survey about the falcon, covering both the evolutionary history of the bird and its varied meanings and representations in human culture. She delves into topics ranging from how the falcon was worshipped as a god in ancient Egypt, to how the Nazis used them for military projects during World War II (1939–45), to their connection to the US space program. In a review for the *Washington Post* (21 May 2006), Rachel Hartigan Shea proclaimed, "This beautifully designed book offers a natural history of this fastest of all the animals as well as the story of how these birds' lives have long intertwined with those of humans."

H IS FOR HAWK
In March 2007, as Macdonald was finishing up her college research fellowship at Jesus College, Cambridge, her father died unexpectedly of an

unknown heart condition while photographing storm-damaged buildings. The loss of her father, to whom she was extremely close, upended Macdonald's life and the grief overwhelmed her. She found it very difficult to let go of him, particularly because his death was so sudden. Six months after his death, she found herself in Scotland purchasing a juvenile goshawk, with the idea of training it in her Cambridge home. Her experience with the goshawk, which she names Mabel, forms the backbone of her book *H Is for Hawk*, which is both a natural history and a grief memoir, while a biography of the troubled but gifted author T. H. White, who is best known for his novel *The Once and Future King* (1958). White had also attempted to train such a bird and described his misbegotten experience in *The Goshawk* (1951).

In her book Macdonald attempts to escape her grief by becoming more and more like Mabel. In fact, after a point she begins to feel as if she were seeing the world through Mabel's eyes. Yet while using Mabel to attempt to escape her grief, she also finds that Mabel helps to link her to the world. She now believes that the absorption she had in caring for Mabel, despite the exhaustion involved, ultimately helped to bring her through her father's loss. At the end of the training period, Macdonald gives Mabel to a friend who owns a large aviary and she finds herself able to again return to human companionship, changed by the experience, but better for it. In interviews, she has described Mabel's training as something akin to an addiction because she attempted to do this very difficult thing in an almost compulsory way, despite suffering from depression, vertigo, and outright clumsiness, breaking dishes as frequently as she dented her father's car.

H Is for Hawk received outstanding reviews upon its publication in 2014. When it was released in the United States in March 2015, it became a best seller on both sides of the Atlantic, including topping the *New York Times* Best Sellers list for more than two months. Christian House, reviewing the memoir for the *Telegraph* (27 Jan. 2015), declared: "This book is a soaring triumph. It is a joy to follow Mabel and Macdonald's flight out of such disconsolate scenes as one settles into a new roost and the other gradually comes to realise that 'hands are for other human hands to hold. They should not be reserved exclusively as perches for hawks.'" For the *New York Times* (19 Feb. 2015), Vicki Constantine Croke called the book "breathtaking," writing, "Helen Macdonald renders an indelible impression of a raptor's fierce essence—and her own—with words that mimic feathers, so impossibly pretty we don't notice their astonishing engineering. . . . Although 'animal as emotional healer' is a familiar motif, Macdonald's journey clears its own path—messy, muddy and raw."

AWARDS AND ACCOLADES

Macdonald has earned numerous awards for her best-selling *H Is for Hawk*, including the 2014 Samuel Johnson Prize for Nonfiction, which is presented annually in the United Kingdom for the best nonfiction writing in English and carries a stipend of £25,000. On the prize's website, Claire Tomalin, the chair of judges, noted of Macdonald's work: "Congratulations to Helen Macdonald, who has written a book unlike any other, about an obsession with a wild creature, brought to life in prose sometimes technical and always striking, and set in English landscapes observed with a visionary eye. Writing about wild life and the environment has never been better or better informed than this."

Macdonald is also the winner of the 2014 Costa Book Award, which carries with it a cash award of £30,000 and is presented to authors of English-language books who are based in Great Britain and Ireland. *H Is for Hawk* also made more than twenty-five best books of the year lists for a number of periodicals, including *Time*; *O, The Oprah Magazine*; *Vanity Fair*; the *Washington Post*; the *Boston Globe*; the *Chicago Tribune*; the *San Francisco Chronicle*; the *Miami Herald*; the *St. Louis Post Dispatch*; the *Minneapolis Star Tribune*; *Library Journal*; *Publishers Weekly*; and *Kirkus Reviews*, among others.

SUGGESTED READING

Croke, Vicki Constantine. Rev. of *H Is for Hawk*, by Helen Macdonald. *New York Times*. New York Times, 19 Feb. 2015. Web. 17 Mar. 2016.

Higginbotham, Emma. "Cambridge Author Helen Macdonald on Grief, Goshawks, and Her Best-Selling Book, *H Is for Hawk*." *Cambridge News*. Local World, 7 Sept. 2014. Web. 17 Mar. 2016.

House, Christian. "A Soaring Triumph." Rev. of *H Is for Hawk*, by Helen Macdonald. *Telegraph*. Telegraph Media Group, 27 Jan. 2015. Web. 17 Mar. 2016.

Macdonald, Helen. Interview by Caroline Sanderson. *Bookseller*. Bookseller Media, 29 May 2014. Web. 17 Mar. 2016.

Macdonald, Helen. "In Full Flight." Interview by Aditi Sriram. *Guernica*. Guernica, 15 July 2015. Web. 17 Mar. 2016.

Rev. of *Shaler's Fish*, by Helen Macdonald. *Publishers Weekly*. PWxyz, 18 Jan. 2016. Web. 17 Mar. 2016.

Shea, Rachel Hartigan. "New in Paperback." *Washington Post*. Washington Post, 21 May 2006. Web. 17 Mar. 2016.

SELECTED WORKS

Shaler's Fish, 2001; *Falcon*, 2006; *H is for Hawk*, 2014

—*Christopher Mari*

Rami Malek

Born: May 12, 1981
Occupation: Actor

Rami Malek is an Egyptian American television and film actor who plays Elliot Alderson, a troubled cybersecurity hacker, on the surprise hit TV drama *Mr. Robot*, which premiered in the summer of 2015 on the USA network. Before his breakout starring role in the series, for which he earned nominations for both a Screen Actors Guild (SAG) Award and a Golden Globe Award, Malek was best known for his part in the World War II miniseries *The Pacific* in 2010. His one-of-a-kind look—he has won legions of admirers for his striking eyes—made him a familiar bit player in films such as *The Twilight Saga: Breaking Dawn—Part 2* (2012), *Short Term 12* (2013), and *Need for Speed* (2014), in which he famously strips naked in an office building. After winning his first role on the popular television series *Gilmore Girls* in 2004, he also earned a nod from the Gay and Lesbian Alliance Against Defamation (GLAAD) for his role on the short-lived Fox sitcom *The War at Home* (2005–7) and landed a reprised role in all three of the films in the Night at the Museum franchise.

Several critics have specifically lauded Malek's ability to effectively portray the complex lead character in *Mr. Robot* as a significant factor contributing to the show's overall success. In interviews, Malek has expressed feeling a subsequent sense of validation regarding this appreciation of his work after years in the industry. "I've had a lot of casting directors say to me recently it's nice that you've turned a corner and we've been hoping for this to happen for you for quite some time," he told Emma Brown for *Interview* magazine (26 Aug. 2015). He added, "It's hard work to actually survive and flourish in this business, and to feel like I'm having a moment where I'm able to display a few things I think I'm capable of, it really fills me with pride and at the same time I'm consistently humbled by it."

EARLY LIFE AND EDUCATION

Rami Said Malek was born in Los Angeles, California, on May 12, 1981. Both of his parents are Egyptian. His father was a tour guide in Cairo, who began selling insurance door to door when he moved to the United States. He encouraged

Sleepindaroof/CC BY-SA 4.0/Wikimedia Commons

his children to do something "special" with their lives, Malek recalled to Neil Drumming for the *New York Times* (25 Aug. 2015), which Malek interpreted to mean "looking at the world and seeing how I can affect it." Malek's older sister became an emergency room doctor, and his identical twin brother, Sami, became a teacher.

Malek attended Notre Dame High School in Sherman Oaks, where he had a crush on classmate and future actor Kirsten Dunst. Upon graduation in 1999, he knew that he wanted to be an actor, but decided, unusually, that he did not want to spend his college years training in big industry cities such as Los Angeles, New York, or Chicago. Instead, he studied theater at the University of Evansville in southern Indiana, where he cut his teeth performing Shakespeare before graduating in 2003.

When Malek then returned to Los Angeles, he worked delivering pizza and making falafel sandwiches while trying to jumpstart his acting career. After a year and a half of papering production houses with his résumé, he got a call from a producer, Mara Casey. She wanted to know who Malek's manager was, and when he told her that he did not have one, she almost hung up on him. However, he persuaded her to see him anyway, and he landed a small part on an episode in the fourth season of the hit television series *Gilmore Girls* in 2004.

EARLY CAREER

Malek's bit role in *Gilmore Girls*—he played a student at a Seventh-day Adventist college named Andy—helped launch his career. In 2005, he landed guest roles on the dramas *Over*

There and *Medium* as well as an extended guest role on the Fox sitcom *The War at Home*; he earned the show a GLAAD Media Award nomination for his portrayal of a gay teenager named Kenny. In 2006, he appeared as the pharaoh Ahkmenrah in the comedy *Night at the Museum*— a role he would later reprise in two additional installments, including *Night at the Museum: Battle of the Smithsonian* in 2009.

In 2010, Malek played Private Merriell "Snafu" Shelton in the HBO miniseries *The Pacific*. Produced by Steven Spielberg and Tom Hanks, it was marketed as the companion project to *Band of Brothers*, a lauded 2001 HBO miniseries that told the true story of the 101st Airborne Division through their training, participation in the D-day invasion, and subsequent trek through Europe during World War II. *The Pacific*, which focuses on three soldiers fighting in the American military campaign on various Japanese islands in the Pacific, cost over $200 million and took several years to shoot, but it did not enjoy the same success as its predecessor. True to its disparate source material, the miniseries followed three different men in three different units, their stories leapfrogging through episodes at random. Most reviewers found the show's arc confusing and that the stakes of its narrative were unclear. Nevertheless, Malek won accolades for his portrayal of Snafu, a New Orleans native and battle-scarred foil to one of the sensitive main characters. He comes into *The Pacific* in the fifth episode, but Hank Stuever, writing for the *Washington Post* (12 Mar. 2010) called his performance a "standout" of the series. "A drawling and creepy angel-of-death figure, Snafu feels like he's been reassigned from a 'Nam flick—a necessary antihero among fallen heroes," he wrote.

THE PACIFIC LEADS TO FURTHER ROLES

Malek recalls viewing his role in *The Pacific* as the pinnacle of his career. "When I did *The Pacific* and I played Snafu, I walked away and I said, 'Ahhh, it's never gonna get better than that,'" he told Nic Screws for *Bloomberg Business* (26 Aug. 2015). Instead, Snafu was merely the beginning of Malek's ascension to more high-profile roles. Shortly after, Hanks, impressed by Malek's work in *The Pacific*, cast him in his comedy *Larry Crowne* (2011). The film, which also stars Julia Roberts, revolves around Hanks's character, who enrolls at a community college after losing his job. Malek plays one of Hanks's mean-spirited classmates. The following year, he was cast in the Paul Thomas Anderson film *The Master*, starring the late Philip Seymour Hoffman and Joaquin Phoenix. Set in the 1950s, the drama follows Freddie (Phoenix), a convert to a cult-like religion called the Cause led by Hoffman's character, Lancaster Dodd. Malek plays

Dodd's son-in-law, Clark, a loyal follower who is suspicious of Freddie and his influence within the cult. *The Master* was widely praised for the nuance of its storytelling and the strength of its cast. Phoenix, Hoffman, and costar Amy Adams (who played Lancaster's wife, Peggy Dodd) were all nominated for Academy Awards.

Meanwhile, writer and producer Sam Esmail had never written for television before, but in the summer of 2014, USA green-lit his dramatic series *Mr. Robot*, about a socially anxious but gifted hacker named Elliot Alderson. It was an enormous leap of faith for the cable network, best known for comedies such as the long-running *Monk* (2002–9), starring Tony Shalhoub, and serviceable procedural dramas such as *Covert Affairs* (2010–14). An edgy, complicated, episodic thriller about vigilante hackers—one that speaks directly to income inequality and movements such as Occupy Wall Street—was definitely "off-brand" for USA, Josef Adalian wrote for *Vulture* (27 Aug. 2015); but then again, that was the intention. Executives at the network were looking to draw younger viewers and compete with other networks churning out prestigious dramas, most notably AMC and HBO. Esmail—a bit like Matthew Weiner, creator of AMC's first original series *Mad Men* (2007–15), before him—benefitted from being USA's first foray into serious drama. USA threw its support behind the show, launching a massive marketing campaign and ordering a second season before a single episode had aired. According to statements he has given in interviews, Malek, who had given his third turn as Ahkmenrah in 2014's *Night at the Museum: Secret of the Tomb*, was brought in to audition for the part of Elliot upon a recommendation made by actor Emmy Rossum, who had been dating Esmail (the two are now engaged) and had admired Malek's work in *The Pacific*.

STARRING IN A SURPRISE HIT TELEVISION SERIES

After securing the lead role in *Mr. Robot*, Malek was diligent in his research. He and Esmail— who is also of Egyptian descent—had "marathon conferences," Noel Murray reported for *Rolling Stone* (26 Aug. 2015), discussing every aspect of Elliot's strange persona. Malek also had extended conversations with the show's cinematographer, Tod Campbell (*Mr. Robot* has been widely praised for its cinematography), and offered up his own worn black hoodie as the template for Elliot's trademark look. Playing a hacker, Malek is required to memorize a great deal of technical jargon. "I just have to research everything," he told Melanie McFarland for the technology news website *GeekWire* (18 Aug. 2015). "If I don't understand it, there's no way an audience member is going to understand it."

Mr. Robot is a drama built around subverting hegemony. Malek plays a lonely, pill-popping, hoodie-ensconced youth named Elliot, who works for a cybersecurity firm called Allsafe by day and leads a vigilante band of hackers by night. Esmail originally conceived of the story as a movie, but quickly realized that Elliot's story was too large for such a small frame. Elliot is an antihero in the mold of Walter White, the chemistry teacher turned drug kingpin on the popular AMC drama *Breaking Bad* (2008–13), and Tony Soprano, the Mafioso of the genre-defining HBO drama *The Sopranos* (1999–2007). "For all of Elliot's foolishness and mistakes, he does have this desire to have an effect on society and to help others," Malek told Alison Willmore for *Buzzfeed* (26 Aug. 2015) of his character. "He may go about it in the worst ways at times, but at least he's giving it a shot—and I think that's something people can respect." But Elliot, who provides voice-over narration to the on-screen action, is also an unreliable narrator—a narrator that cannot be trusted to tell the truth. Much of the action in the series is derived from the tension between what is true and what may or may not be occurring only in Elliot's mind.

Critics embraced the show as well as Malek's performance. Alessandra Stanley wrote for the *New York Times* (23 June 2015) that Malek "is both touching and unnerving as a brilliant misanthrope in a hoodie." Erik McClanahan, writing for the site *Indiewire*, (8 Sept. 2015) was more effusive. "Not enough can be said for Malek's work here," he wrote. "He understands this character in a way that makes it impossible to imagine anyone else in the part. . . . If you don't already remember him from smaller roles . . . then you will after seeing this star-making turn." In addition to Malek's SAG Award nomination for best outstanding performance by a male actor in a drama series and Golden Globe Award nomination for best actor in a television series in the drama category, *Mr. Robot* won the coveted Golden Globe Award for best television series in the drama category in 2016.

In 2015 Malek landed his first starring role in a feature film. The indie mystery, titled *Buster's Mal Heart*, in which he plays a mountain man, is scheduled to be released in 2016. To date, he has kept the details of his personal life private.

SUGGESTED READING

Drumming, Neil. "Looking Back on *Mr. Robot* and a Season of Hacker Drama." *New York Times*. New York Times, 25 Aug. 2015. Web. 17 Feb. 2016.

Malek, Rami. "The Many Mysteries of *Mr. Robot*." Interview by Emma Brown. *Interview*. Interview, 26 Aug. 2015. Web. 17 Feb. 2016.

McFarland, Melanie. "Interview: *Mr. Robot* Star Rami Malek on Getting Inside the Mind of a Hacker." *GeekWire*. GeekWire, 18 Aug. 2015. Web. 17 Feb. 2016.

Murray, Noel. "*Mr. Robot*: Meet the Show's Breakout Star Rami Malek." *Rolling Stone*. Rolling Stone, 26 Aug. 2015. Web. 17 Feb. 2016.

Screws, Nic. "Rami Malek, Star of *Mr. Robot*, Is Ready to Start Dressing Like a Grown-Up." *Bloomberg Business*. Bloomberg, 26 Aug. 2015. Web. 17 Feb. 2016.

Willmore, Alison. "The Summer TV Heartthrob No One Saw Coming." *Buzzfeed*. Buzzfeed, 26 Aug. 2015. Web. 17 Feb. 2016.

SELECTED WORKS

The War at Home, 2005–7; *Night at the Museum*, 2006; *Night at the Museum: Battle of the Smithsonian*, 2009; *The Pacific*, 2010; *Night at the Museum: Secret of the Tomb*, 2014; *Mr. Robot*, 2015–

—*Molly Hagan*

Marcus Mariota

Born: October 30, 1993
Occupation: Football player

Professional football players born in Hawaii are often assumed to be big, heavy linemen. Marcus Mariota, quarterback of the Tennessee Titans of the National Football League (NFL), has helped change that perception. Blessed with a rare combination of speed and arm strength, the six-foot-four, 215-pound Mariota has used his athletic gifts to become one of the most accomplished quarterbacks in college football history. Over a three-year career at the University of Oregon, he won more games than any other Oregon player and broke numerous school records. Mariota's career at Oregon culminated in 2014, when he became the first Hawaiian-born player to win the Heisman Memorial Trophy Award, college football's top honor.

Selected by the Titans with the second overall pick in the 2015 NFL Draft, Mariota entered the league with many doubters, as football observers wondered whether his success in college would translate to the professional ranks. He answered his detractors, however, with a solid debut season for the Titans that saw him break several franchise rookie passing records. Veteran Titans receiver Harry Douglas said of Mariota, who is often misunderstood for his quiet, introverted nature, to Jim Wyatt for TitansOnline.com (11 Sept. 2015), "I love his demeanor, how

Wesley Hitt/GettyImages

cool, calm and collected he is. . . . His future is so bright."

EARLY LIFE

Marcus Ardel Taulauniu Mariota was born on October 30, 1993, in the Hawaiian capital of Honolulu on the island of Oahu. His brother, Matt, is four years younger than him. His father, Toa, hailed from American Samoa, and his mother, Alana, was of German lineage and raised in Alaska and Hawaii. Mariota grew up in an affluent Honolulu neighborhood and lived within walking distance of Sandy Beach, a world-famous surfing destination on Oahu's south shore. He developed a natural affinity for the water and spent much of his youth boogie boarding and bodysurfing at Sandy.

From an early age, Mariota also was drawn to football. As a boy he rooted for the Dallas Cowboys and idolized such Cowboys stars as quarterback Troy Aikman and running back Emmitt Smith. Mariota was initially only allowed to play organized flag football because his father wanted to reduce his chances of getting physically injured. He played flag football for several years before his mother persuaded his father to allow him to transition to helmets and shoulder pads.

Tall, lean, and nimble, Mariota first played wide receiver in flag football and during his first year of Pop Warner football. He became quarterback, however, after coaches took notice of his arm strength and natural throwing ability. Welcoming the opportunity to "get the ball every play," as he told Wyatt, Mariota made a seamless transition to his new position and emerged as a standout for his Pop Warner team, the Kalani

Falcons. It was during his time with the Falcons that Mariota first displayed the poise for which he eventually became known. "Kids trusted him," his mother noted to Aaron Fentress for the *Oregonian* (30 Aug. 2012). "If a play fell apart he would always take care of the ball and always do something."

WAITING HIS TURN

Mariota's football prowess was matched only by his talent in soccer, which he also played throughout his youth. He was a prolific goalscorer as a forward and midfielder for the elite Honolulu Bulls Soccer Club. Mariota eventually stopped playing for the Bulls to focus on football, but he continued to play soccer at Saint Louis School, the private all-boys school in Honolulu he attended from middle school through high school. He played on Saint Louis School's varsity soccer team and earned all-state honors as a defender during his junior year.

Mariota's football career at Saint Louis, however, began unremarkably. After serving as a second-string quarterback on the school's junior-varsity team as a freshman, Mariota spent his sophomore and junior seasons backing up all-state quarterback Jeremy Higgins, who was a grade ahead of him, on the school's varsity squad. Despite Higgins's all-state status, Mariota routinely outperformed him in practice, so much so that he considered transferring from Saint Louis after his sophomore year so he could have the opportunity to showcase his skills to college scouts.

Undaunted, Mariota persevered and dedicated himself even more to improving his game. Among those who guided Mariota's development as a quarterback was Vinny Passas, Saint Louis's long-established quarterbacks coach. Mariota was always "the first guy out on the practice field and the last to leave," Passas told Wyatt. "And once he got the chance, I think we all knew he was going to be special because of his attitude and athletic ability." When Mariota's chance finally arrived during his senior season, he did not waste it: he threw for 2,597 yards and thirty-two touchdowns while leading Saint Louis to an 11–1 record and the 2010 Hawaii state championship.

UNIVERSITY OF OREGON

Following his junior season at Saint Louis, Mariota's parents sold their home to help send him to football camps on the US mainland. Among the camps he attended was the University of Oregon's in Eugene, Oregon. Mariota had dreamed of playing at Oregon since 2009, when former Saint Louis standout Jeremiah Masoli led the University of Oregon Ducks to the Rose Bowl. He verbally committed to Oregon after attending their summer camp and was then offered a scholarship to the school before his senior season.

Despite his stellar senior campaign Mariota was largely ignored by other major college football programs due to his small body of work as a starter and doubts about his skill set. At the time most Samoan players being recruited out of Hawaii were burly offensive or defensive linemen, not agile dual-threat quarterbacks. Mariota ultimately honored his commitment to Oregon, choosing the school over the University of Memphis, the only other program to offer him a scholarship.

Mariota was initially disappointed that he would have to compete with another coveted dual-threat prospect, future Heisman Trophy winner Johnny Manziel, for Oregon's starting quarterback spot, but Manziel retracted his commitment to Oregon to play for Texas A&M University. Still, when Mariota began his freshman season at Oregon in the fall of 2011, he was listed as the school's third-string quarterback behind returning starter Darron Thomas, who had led the Ducks to a national championship game, and backup sophomore Bryan Bennett, a former four-star recruit. As a result Mariota redshirted that year to develop his frame and learn coach Chip Kelly's fast-paced spread offense.

Following the 2011 season, Thomas declared for the 2012 NFL draft, clearing the way for a new starter. Mariota subsequently beat out Bennett in an open quarterback competition that off-season, during which Oregon coaches acclimated to the Hawaiian's stoic, low-key personality. "Some of the coaches on our staff didn't like him because he literally didn't say a word," Mark Helfrich, then Oregon's offensive coordinator and quarterbacks coach, admitted to Tim Rohan for the *New York Times* (23 Aug. 2014). "He just kind of deferred to the elders on the team from a leadership standpoint."

HEISMAN TROPHY

As the first freshman to start a season-opener for Oregon in twenty-two seasons, Mariota showcased the inner fire and competitiveness that belied his calm exterior and the dual-threat abilities that made him dangerous as a passer and runner. Starting all thirteen games during the 2012 season, he passed for 2,677 yards and thirty-two touchdowns and rushed for 752 yards and five touchdowns, leading the Ducks to a 12–1 record and a number-two national ranking. Following that season, Helfrich took over head coaching duties from Kelly, who left Oregon for the NFL. "He's got a gift for playing football," Kelly later said of Mariota, as quoted by Phil Sheridan for ESPN (11 Dec. 2014). "He can throw the ball, he can run. He's the most talented kid I coached in college."

Over his next two seasons at Oregon, Mariota used his exceptional talent to become what many considered "the best player in college football," as Lindsay Schnell wrote for *Sports Illustrated* (12 Dec. 2014). He led the Ducks to an 11–2 record and another top-ten national ranking during his redshirt sophomore season in 2013 and then guided them to a 13–2 overall record and a national championship game runner-up finish as a redshirt junior in 2014. In fifteen starts during his redshirt junior season, Mariota passed for 4,454 yards and forty-two touchdowns, rushed for 770 yards and fifteen touchdowns, and led the nation with a passer efficiency rating of 181.7. Among his many end-of-season honors included becoming the first Hawaii native and first Oregon player to win the prestigious Heisman Trophy.

Shortly after the 2015 national championship, Mariota, who earned a general science degree from Oregon, decided to skip his senior season for the NFL Draft. He finished his career at Oregon as the most decorated quarterback in school history, winning a school-record thirty-six games and setting all-time school marks for passing yards (10,796), touchdown passes (105), and rushing yards by a quarterback (2,237), among many others. He became one of just four players in Division I Football Bowl Subdivision (FBS) history with at least 10,000 passing yards and 2,000 rushing yards in a career.

TENNESSEE TITANS

Many scouts and analysts expected Mariota to be either the first or second quarterback taken in the 2015 NFL Draft. Those predictions proved true when the Tennessee Titans selected Mariota as the second overall pick in the draft. Mariota was selected after the Tampa Bay Buccaneers used the top pick on Florida State quarterback Jameis Winston, who was deemed more NFL-ready due to his experience of running a pro-style offense for the Seminoles. Still, Mariota became the highest picked Hawaiian-born player in NFL draft history. In July 2015 he signed a four-year contract with the Titans worth $24 million.

Mariota was the centerpiece of a rebuilding effort for the Titans, who had just come off a fourteen-loss season and missed the postseason for the sixth consecutive year. The team believed Mariota could revive a stagnant offense that had finished thirtieth in the league in both total yards per game (311.8) and points per game (15.9) during the previous season, and the Titans used six of their next eight draft picks on offensive players to help complement him. Meanwhile, to ease Mariota's transition to the NFL, the Titans' second-year head coach Ken Whisenhunt adjusted his offensive system to accommodate his strengths.

ROOKIE SEASON

Named the Titans' starting quarterback in training camp, Mariota quickly put to rest any questions about his ability to adapt to a pro-style offense. In his professional debut with the Titans, he threw for 209 yards and four touchdowns in a 42–14 blowout victory over the Winston-led Buccaneers. He became only the second quarterback in history (after Fran Tarkenton) to throw four touchdowns in his NFL debut and the first to record a perfect passer rating (158.3) in his debut. Mariota started twelve games overall as a rookie and set Titans rookie records for passing yards (2,818), touchdowns (19), and completions (230). He also rushed for 252 yards and two touchdowns, one of which came on a dynamic eighty-seven-yard run against the Jacksonville Jaguars.

Despite encountering typical rookie struggles and missing four games due to a pair of knee injuries, Mariota's rookie season was regarded as a success. The Titans' season, however, was marked by turmoil. The team fired Whisenhunt after a 1–6 start and replaced him on an interim basis with tight ends coach Mike Mularkey. Under Mularkey the team did not fare much better, as they finished with a 3–13 overall record, which tied for the worst record in the league. "You have to stay the course, no matter what happens," Mariota explained to Jim Wyatt in another article for TitansOnline.com (23 Dec. 2015). "Prepare each and every single day. Enjoy the process, and find ways to get better."

Shortly after signing his rookie contract, Mariota purchased a $1 million condominium in downtown Nashville, Tennessee. Known for his generous and humble nature, he established the Marcus Mariota Scholarship Fund, which awards an annual four-year scholarship to an incoming student-athlete at Saint Louis High School.

SUGGESTED READING

Chapman, Don. "Leader of the Quack Attack." *Midweek Kaua'i*. Midweek Kauai, 22 Oct. 2012. Web. 21 Dec. 2015.

Fentress, Aaron. "Marcus Mariota: Focused, Laid-Back Leader Oregon Ducks Are Ready to Follow." *Oregonian*. Oregon Live, 30 Aug. 2012. Web. 21 Dec. 2015.

Rohan, Tim. "A Star's Bumpy Trail to Oregon." *New York Times*. New York Times, 23 Aug. 2014. Web. 21 Dec. 2015.

Schnell, Lindsay. "From Hawaii to Eugene, How Oregon's Marcus Mariota Rose to Become a Star." *Sports Illustrated*. Time, 12 Dec. 2014. Web. 21 Dec. 2015.

Wyatt, Jim. "Marcus Mariota Motivated to Please Titans, Fan Base." *TitansOnline.com*. Tennessee Titans, 11 Sept. 2015. Web. 23 Dec. 2015.   —*Chris Cullen*

Laura Marling

Born: February 1, 1990
Occupation: Musician

Laura Marling released her debut album, *Alas I Cannot Swim,* in 2008, just days after her eighteenth birthday, and many critics praised not only the music's virtuosity but the artist's preternatural precocity. In a review for the *Guardian* (7 Feb. 2008), Caroline Sullivan echoed the sentiments of many when she called the recording "unnervingly grown-up" and deemed it "remarkable, coming from someone so young." Later, John Pareles wrote for the *New York Times* (4 Sept. 2011), "Three albums into her career . . . it's no longer news that Ms. Marling, now twenty-one, sounds startlingly grown up, with a dusky voice and songs that conjure fables and revelations alongside piercing human insights."

In addition to making frequent mention of her youth, music journalists often invoke Marling's similarities to female singer-songwriters of past eras. In a piece for *T Magazine* (29 Mar. 2015), for example, Rachel Syme opined, "Her lilting vibrato is similar to Joni Mitchell's, a haunted, fragile warble," while Sharon O'Connell of *Quietus* (19 Mar. 2015) praised her "cleverly structured but unfussy, modernist songs that draw on the Laurel Canyon acoustic folk scene of the late 60s and early 70s" and her "sweetly resonant voice and trademark immaculate phrasing."

While many are misled by her haunting lyrics and palely ethereal appearance into thinking

that Marling, who was named best British female solo artist at the 2011 Brit Awards, is evocatively baring her soul, she told Pareles: "I'm quite private. I wouldn't be able to get up and play the songs every night if they really jabbed a piece of glass into my eye every night. They are personal. But they're not confessional."

EARLY LIFE AND EDUCATION
Marling, the youngest of three daughters, was born on February 1, 1990, in the Hampshire village of Eversley, in southern England. Her mother, Judi, was a music teacher and an avid gardener, and her father, Charles, was a baronet. Her family tree includes "High Sheriffs, lancers, Liberal MPs and a VC noted for his bravery during the Mahdist revolt," Tom Lamont wrote for the *Guardian* (27 Apr. 2013). Charles established a recording studio on the family's farm near the market town of Wokingham, and Marling has told journalists that she recalls crawling around tangles of speaker wires and other equipment as a youngster. Syme described Marling's childhood as "a Brontë novel crossed with a Led Zeppelin song."

Charles taught Marling to play the guitar when she was three years old and often had her listen to the music of his own formative years, including Joni Mitchell and Neil Young. That was, she explained to Pareles, "a bit of a blessing and a bit of a curse [because] I couldn't slot myself into the age-appropriate genre." Marling began playing local music gigs while still in her early teens, and she has recalled to interviewers that a bouncer once refused her entry to a venue where she was scheduled to perform, on the grounds that she was underage; she ended up playing that night on the sidewalk outside the club for anyone who cared to come out and listen.

By her own accounts, Marling was a somewhat troubled young woman, prone to panic attacks, obsessions, and poor self-esteem. Still, she was talented and well connected enough to sign a deal with Virgin Records at sixteen, and with her parents' blessing, she left Leighton Park Quaker School to move to London and forge her career. She soon became associated with a group of bands (including Mumford & Sons and Noah and the Whale) that the press ultimately labeled "nu-folk," for their use of acoustic instruments and love of traditional melodies.

MUSIC CAREER
"I came [to London] completely naively, with unbelievably high spirits, ready to take on anything," Marling recalled to Alice Fisher for the *Guardian* (25 Oct. 2008). "I toured with Noah and the Whale and it was incredibly exciting, but I got this sense that my heart was beating just a little too fast." She calmed some of her nervousness by writing the songs that would become

Alas I Cannot Swim, which was shortlisted for the prestigious Mercury Prize. Marling was among the youngest artists ever to be nominated for the prize, which was established in 1992 to promote the best of British and Irish music and which has been called the musical equivalent of the Booker Prize for literature and the Turner Prize for art. Her second and fourth albums were also nominated for the Mercury Prize.

In her review of *Alas I Cannot Swim*, Sullivan asserted, "If [this album] doesn't install her as the heir to the likes of [Venezuelan-American singer-songwriter] Devendra Banhart, there's no hope for folk-pop," adding that the most impressive feature of the album was Marling's "ability to articulate heartbreak" and calling her "a lyricist to watch."

Marling followed her auspicious debut with *I Speak Because I Can* (2010), which entered the UK album charts at number four. Most critics felt that the sophomore effort lived up to its promise. "*I Speak Because I Can* delivers on nearly every level," James Christopher Monger wrote in an undated review for the *AllMusic* website. "Love, death, and heartbreak are hardly new subjects when it comes to folk music, but they refresh themselves so often in our lives that their relevance becomes tenfold with each new bite, scrape, or blow to the head, a notion that Marling explores with both guarded wisdom and elegant petulance."

Her next releases were equally well received. Of 2011's *A Creature I Don't Know*, Joshua Love wrote for the influential music magazine *Pitchfork* (13 Sept. 2011), "Marling may spend the majority of these songs . . . struggling to find wisdom and peace in the face of trials brought on by lust, money, and death, but she almost always sounds like she already has all the answers." In a review of the 2013 release *Once I Was an Eagle* for that same publication (3 June 2013), Rachael Maddux wrote, "Marling is twenty-three; at first, the amount of time she had spent on this earth seemed relevant because nobody in her peer group was making albums like this. With *Once I Was an Eagle*, it's because nobody of any age is making albums like this."

HIATUS AND *SHORT MOVIE*
Although she had been writing and recording steadily during the period following her move to London and had purchased an old townhouse on a cobblestone street in the city's East End, Marling began in her early twenties to experience what many music journalists characterized as a quarter-life crisis. She told Syme, "I became suddenly aware of the crushingly high-structured environment which I lived in, one record after the other. I kind of ... unraveled. I wondered, what is my life if I'm just living it to write songs about it? I'd always lived outside

the normal, isolated. And I was pulling these exhausting songs from my stomach every night. I wanted to run away."

She embarked on a solo tour of the United States, performing songs from *Once I Was an Eagle*, and decided to remain on the West Coast after the tour was over. She initially wanted to live in a remote, rural area in southern Oregon or northern California, but, she told Lamont, she realized she "had to be sort of contactable" and instead ended up in Los Angeles. There she took a complete break from writing and playing music for six months. She took the opportunity to experience some of the things she felt she had missed out on as a teenager, such as going to bars and clubs for fun rather than to perform, and filled her time with a variety of hobbies, including camping, gardening, yoga, and learning to read tarot cards. Eventually, however, she returned to performing.

One night, in a bar in a town on the border of California and Oregon, she met an old hippie who engaged her in a long conversation; she invited him to a gig and the two remained in touch. The man frequently described life as "a short f——ing movie," words that stayed with Marling after she returned to songwriting. In 2015 Marling, who had by then moved back to England, released *Short Movie*, which she composed using her father's old Gibson electric guitar, rather than her usual acoustic instrument. "It's not a drastic change, as Marling's up-tempo tracks have always had muscle, but it's palpable nevertheless," Katherine St. Asaph wrote for *Pitchfork* (27 Mar. 2015). "[The album contains] vocals that curl words into secretive murmurs, and lyrics that tiptoe up to confessions then stop just short. Mythology and formal allusions swirl around even her candid moments, assuring that any autobiography is lost in the fog."

PERSONAL LIFE

Marling described herself to Syme as always being "the girl who ran away with a boy." She was involved early in her career in a relationship with Noah and the Whale's front man, Charlie Fink. He went on to write several songs about their difficult breakup and included them on the band's second album.

She told Lamont, "I live on this delicate balance between normality and the bizarre world of music. I sit with my toes curled over the edge. And though that's very nice, because I can have the best of both worlds, it can be difficult to place oneself."

SUGGESTED READING

Fisher, Alice. "Little Gal with a Full-Grown Talent." *Guardian*. Guardian News and Media, 25 Oct. 2008. Web. 3 May 2016.

Lamont, Tom. "Laura Marling: 'Americans—They're Just a Lot More Poetic.'" *Guardian*. Guardian News and Media, 27 Apr. 2013. Web. 3 May 2016.

Marling, Laura. "Become Undisguised." Interview by Sharon O'Connell. *Quietus*. Quietus, 19 Mar. 2015. Web. 3 May 2016.

Marling, Laura. "Stay Vulnerable." Interview by Laura Snapes. *Rookie Magazine*. Lauren Redding, 20 Mar. 2015. Web. 3 May 2016.

Pareles, John. "Goddesses and Beasts in a Dusky, Lilting Roar." *New York Times*. New York Times, 4 Sept. 2011. Web. 3 May 2016.

St. Asaph, Katherine. Rev. of *Short Movie*, by Laura Marling. *Pitchfork*. Pitchfork Media, 27 Mar. 2015. Web. 3 May 2016.

Syme, Rachel. "Laura Marling Bids Goodbye to All That." *T Magazine*. New York Times, 29 Mar. 2015. Web. 3 May 2016.

SELECTED WORKS

Alas I Cannot Swim, 2008; *I Speak Because I Can*, 2010; *A Creature I Don't Know*, 2011; *Once I Was an Eagle*, 2013; *Short Movie*, 2015

—Mari Rich

Moncef Marzouki

Born: July 7, 1945
Occupation: President of Tunisia

Moncef Marzouki was elected president of Tunisia in December of 2011. Emerging from an extensive background in medicine and public health, Marzouki entered the Tunisian political landscape in 1991 as a prominent opposition figure to President Zine El Abidine Ben Ali. Marzouki's rise to power occurred during the period of democratic uprisings in the Middle East that became known as the Arab Spring.

EARLY LIFE AND EDUCATION

Moncef Marzouki was born in the northern Tunisian city of Grombalia on July 7, 1945. An accomplished student as a child, he developed a passion for human rights at an early age. As a young man he was particularly inspired by the work of Indian civil rights leader Mahatma Gandhi.

While in his twenties, Marzouki left Tunisia to enroll in the University of Strasbourg in France, where he studied general medicine and public health. He graduated from the university in 1973. Marzouki returned to Tunisia in 1979, where he immersed himself in the country's fractured political sphere, aligning himself with groups seeking human rights reforms.

In 1981, Marzouki took a post teaching medicine at the university in the costal Tunisian city of Sousse. In addition to joining the Tunisian League for the Defense of Human Rights, he cofounded Sousse's Center for Community Medicine in an attempt to improve health care access for those living in the city's slums. While in Sousse he also helped cofound the African Network for the Prevention and Protection against Child Abuse and Neglect.

Following the rise to power of President Zine El Abidine Ben Ali in 1987, Marzouki became even more involved in Tunisian politics. The Ben Ali administration's decades of rule in Tunisia were plagued by accusations of human rights violations, hard-line economic policies that created widespread poverty and unemployment, and government-sponsored oppression of rival political factions. As a member of the opposition, Marzouki established himself as one of the nation's preeminent civil rights advocates as well as a champion of human rights and medical care for all Tunisians.

FROM POLITICAL PRISONER TO PRESIDENT

In 1992 President Ben Ali called for a new round of presidential and parliamentary elections to be held in March 1994. Tunisia's six major opposition parliamentary parties, which had boycotted national elections in 1989, citing inappropriate influence by Ben Ali, were invited to participate. Marzouki chose to run publicly against Ben Ali. However, he was unable to collect the necessary signatures that would allow him to appear on the ballot before being imprisoned by the Ali administration for his political activism. Marzouki remained imprisoned for several months but was released after Nelson Mandela, the newly elected president of South Africa, spearheaded an international campaign against his incarceration. Following his release he went into exile, living primarily in France. During his time away from Tunisia, Marzouki taught at universities in France and continued his human rights work.

As the Ben Ali regime drew increasingly negative international attention, Marzouki returned to Tunisia in the late 1990s. By that time, he had garnered increased anti–Ben Ali support from his fellow Tunisians, some of whom joined him in the founding of a new political party, the Congress for the Republic (CPR). The party's aim was to bring about democratic change in the nation's political system. Though Marzouki and his fellow party members were forced into exile after the CPR was banned by the Tunisian government, they continued their work against the Ben Ali regime abroad throughout the remainder of the decade.

In December of 2010, Mohamed Bouazizi, a produce seller from the central Tunisian city of Sidi Bouzid, committed suicide by self-immolation in front of the city's municipal offices after government officials confiscated his wares following his refusal to pay bribes. Bouazizi's death became a rallying point for many Tunisians, who, frustrated by years of poverty and oppression under Ben Ali's rule, began to organize protests against the regime. The ensuing revolt, dubbed the Jasmine Revolution by Western commentators, gained the attention of the international media and sparked a series of protests and revolutions throughout the Arab world in what came to be known as the Arab Spring.

After weeks of violent clashes between protesters and pro–Ben Ali security forces led to mounting casualties, Ben Ali attempted to maintain power by making limited concessions in the first weeks of 2011. However, this effort was ineffective. A state of emergency was declared, and in mid-January 2011 Ben Ali fled to Saudi Arabia. Shortly afterward, Marzouki returned to Tunisia.

The National Constituent Assembly formally elected Marzouki president of Tunisia in December of 2011. He continued to serve in the role as Tunisian lawmakers developed a new constitution, which was ultimately adopted in January of 2014.

IMPACT

Although Tunisia's Jasmine Revolution and the ensuing Arab Spring marked a triumph for supporters of democracy throughout the world, seasoned politicians and activists such as Marzouki have been cautious to deem their young rebellion complete. Marzouki frequently speaks of the more than three hundred Tunisians who died during the country's political transformation and has continued to encourage his country to draw on its strong, well-educated middle class to strengthen its democracy. As president of Tunisia, Marzouki has sought to present a strong example of the potential of a free society to other states in the region struggling under oppressive rule.

PERSONAL LIFE

Moncef Marzouki is married to Beatrix Rhein, a French physician. He has children from a previous marriage.

SUGGESTED READING

Gerges, Fawaz A., ed. *The New Middle East: Protest and Revolution in the Arab World*. New York: Cambridge UP, 2014. Print.

Perkins, Kenneth. *A History of Modern Tunisia*. New York: Cambridge UP, 2014. Print.

"President Mohamed Moncef Marzouki of Tunisia Visits NYU Law." *NYU Law*. New York University School of Law, 27 Sept. 2007. Web. 14 Feb 2014.

Rand, Dafna Hochman. *Roots of the Arab Spring: Contested Authority and Political Change in the Middle East*. Philadelphia: U of Pennsylvania P, 2013. Print.

"Tunisia Installs Former Dissident Moncef Marzouki as President." *Al Arabiya*. Al Arabiya, 12 Dec. 2012. Web. 14 Feb. 2014.

—*John Pritchard*

Tatiana Maslany

Born: September 22, 1985
Occupation: Actor

When director John Fawcett and screenwriter Graeme Manson, the creators of the hit television series *Orphan Black*, set out to cast the show's lead role, they faced a tough challenge. The science-fiction show follows a group of clones as they seek to learn about their origins and avoid those who mean them harm, and as such, the lead actor must play not one role but many. Embodying multiple clones, each with her own distinct personality, would be a daunting proposition for many actors—but not for Tatiana Maslany. A Canadian actor then best known for her roles in a string of television movies as well as independent films such as *Grown Up Movie Star* (2009) and *Picture Day* (2012), Maslany stunned *Orphan Black*'s creators with her ability to transition between the outwardly similar but inwardly very different characters and won the role in the series, which premiered on both the Canadian television channel Space and BBC America in March 2013.

In some ways, Maslany seems an unlikely star: she avoids many of the trappings of show-business life, remaining close to her roots in improvisational and community theater. "I never wanted fame. I've never sought it out," she told Rachel Heinrichs for *Flare* (2 Mar. 2015). "I just want to work with good directors and cool characters." Nevertheless, her performance as *Orphan Black*'s clones, from the streetwise Sarah to the unstable Helena, has earned her critical acclaim and made her name a household one among many fans of science-fiction media.

EARLY LIFE AND EDUCATION

Tatiana Gabrielle Maslany was born on September 22, 1985, to Renate and Dan Maslany. Her father was a woodworker, and her mother was a translator. Both spoke German fluently, and Maslany learned to speak the language at a young age; she would later draw on that skill for *Orphan Black* and the 2015 film *Woman in Gold*. She and her two younger brothers, Daniel

Wikimedia/Flickr/Gage Skidmore/CC BY-SA 2.0

and Michael, grew up in Regina, the capital of the Canadian province of Saskatchewan.

Maslany began acting early in life, making films with her brothers in their backyard, and started to pursue it in earnest at the age of nine. Her earliest performances were in community theater and improv, the latter of which gave her valuable experience in immersing herself in numerous different characters. Maslany attended Dr. Martin LeBoldus Catholic High School in Regina but often left school to appear in films or television shows. "Being in high school was weirder to me than being on set," Maslany confessed to Lili Loofbourow for the *New York Times Magazine* (2 Apr. 2015). "I'd go away for two months and shoot something and be totally at home, and then come back to school and be like, How do I talk to people?" Among the various jobs Maslany took on while still in high school were roles in the children's science-fiction show *2030 CE* and the 2004 film *Ginger Snaps 2: Unleashed*.

EARLY CAREER

After graduating from high school in 2003, Maslany opted not to enroll in university, instead choosing to continue to develop her acting career. She toured for a time with General Fools, a Regina-based improv troupe, and at the age of twenty she moved to Toronto to pursue work in film and television. "It was horrible," she told Heinrichs about the move. "I cried all the time from the shock of being alone in my apartment with only two pieces of Ikea furniture."

As difficult as the move to Toronto was for Maslany, the decision ultimately turned out to be the correct one, as she soon found work in numerous projects. She found particular success in made-for-television films and miniseries, appearing in productions such as *Dawn Anna* (2005), *The Robber Bride* (2007), and *The Nativity* (2010). Maslany likewise found work in various television series, including *Instant Star* and *Heartland*.

In addition to her television work, Maslany took on roles in a number of Canadian independent films. In 2009 she starred in the film *Grown Up Movie Star*, about a troubled teen's coming of age. For her performance, she was awarded a special jury prize at the 2010 Sundance Film Festival. "I didn't even know there was a performance [award] possibility at awards night," she recalled to Susan G. Cole for *NOW Toronto* (30 Aug. 2012). "I had a big cold—my nose was bright red—and I just sat there when they announced the prize. I vaguely remember somebody telling me I had to say something, so I went up, burbled garbage, and then vibrated offstage." After that first brush with critical acclaim, Maslany continued to win roles in films, including *Picture Day* (2012) and the Hollywood film *The Vow* (2012).

ORPHAN BLACK

In 2013, Maslany began to star in the television show *Orphan Black*, a science-fiction series that airs in both Canada and the United States. The show focuses on British con artist Sarah Manning, who discovers that she is one of numerous clones created by a mysterious scientific institute. By the end of the first season, which aired between March and June 2013, the show had revealed the existence of numerous clones, including Canadian suburban mother Alison Hendrix, American graduate student Cosima Niehaus, and Ukrainian assassin Helena.

Maslany plays all of those clones, a task that is both difficult, given the myriad differences between the characters, and exhilarating. "The writers are incredible, and I was definitely drawn to the piece because of the specificity and complexity of the writing; that none of the women on the page read as the same woman. They feel like different people with different life goals and different upbringings and worldviews," she told James Ostime for *Interview* magazine (31 May 2013). "It was about physicalizing and embodying that, putting it my body, walking differently depending on how I look at the world."

Orphan Black proved popular with viewers and was renewed for a second and third season, which began in April 2014 and 2015, respectively. The show received acclaim from many critics and was nominated for a number of awards, including numerous Canadian Screen Awards and the speculative media–focused Hugo Award.

GETTING INTO CHARACTER

Playing *Orphan Black's* many similar yet dramatically different clones is a difficult task in and of itself, and the needs of the show's plot render Maslany's job even more difficult. Immersed in a dangerous scientific conspiracy, individual clones must at times impersonate their counterparts; Maslany, then, must, on occasion, play a clone pretending to be another clone. To create such layered performances and to fill her many roles in general, Maslany draws heavily from her improv background. "The thing about the characters in improv is that you can create hundreds of them, and then you have to remember those that came out of the previous scene. You call them back," she explained to Anthony D'Alessandro for *Deadline* (27 Aug. 2015). "There's no props, no costumes, and on *Orphan Black*, improv serves me. Improv has given me strength. My favorite improvisers are courageous and those who say yes to things in a scene. The notion of saying yes helps me every day on set, especially when I have to switch characters halfway through the day or play characters off the top of my head."

In addition to her improvisational work, Maslany uses some even less conventional methods for getting into character. She is known for creating customized playlists for each character, using music and dance as a means of connecting with them as individuals. When preparing to embody the assassin Helena, for instance, she listens to American singer-songwriter Tom Waits, and while when getting into character as con artist Sarah, she listens to the British electronic group the Prodigy. Maslany also works extensively with a dialect coach, drawing from her existing skill with languages.

As the critical reception of her performance suggests, Maslany's techniques for getting into character have been highly effective. She was nominated for a Golden Globe Award for best performance by an actress in a television drama in 2014 and for the Emmy Award for lead actress in a drama in 2015. Fueled by her many intriguing characters, in 2015 *Orphan Black* was renewed for a fourth season, which is set to air in the spring of 2016.

OTHER PROJECTS

Mostly known within Canada during the first decade of her career, Maslany became an internationally recognized actor thanks to her work on *Orphan Black*. This recognition led to extensive opportunities for Maslany, from guest roles in popular television shows such as *Parks and Recreation* and the animated Netflix series *BoJack Horseman* to roles in major films. In 2015, Maslany appeared in the film *Woman in Gold*, which starred veteran British actor Helen Mirren. Based on true events, the film tells the story of Maria Altmann (Mirren), an Austrian Jewish woman who, decades after World War II, attempts to reclaim a painting that belonged to her family and had been stolen by the Nazis during the war. Maslany plays the younger version of Mirren's character, appearing in flashbacks to Altmann's youth, and speaks German exclusively in the film. Although Maslany did not appear in any scenes with Mirren due to the nature of her role, she was enthusiastic about the opportunity to play the same character as the critically acclaimed actor, who had previously won the Academy Award for best actress for her role in the 2006 film *The Queen*.

Despite her success as an actor, Maslany considers herself to be a work in progress and continues to take acting classes to expand her horizons and challenge herself. Indeed, ongoing challenges are, for Maslany, a way of life. "I never want to be one thing," she told Heinrichs. "As an actor, I never want to be the girl who was that. Which is why *Orphan Black* is so exciting. I'm never going to be typecast because I get to play all of these different characters."

PERSONAL LIFE

Maslany lives in Toronto. She is in a long-term relationship with Welsh actor Tom Cullen, whom she met while filming the 2012 miniseries *World without End*. The two are set to costar in the independent romantic drama *The Other Half*, scheduled for release in 2016.

SUGGESTED READING

Cole, Susan G. "Tatiana Maslany Is All Grown Up." *NOW Toronto*. NOW Communications, 30 Aug. 2012. Web. 11 Dec. 2015.

Heinrichs, Rachel. "Meet Our April Cover Star, Tatiana Maslany!" *Flare*. Rogers Media, 2 Mar. 2015. Web. 11 Dec. 2015.

Loofbourow, Lili. "The Many Faces of Tatiana Maslany." *New York Times Magazine*. New York Times, 2 Apr. 2015. Web. 11 Dec. 2015.

Maslany, Tatiana. "Orphan Black's Tatiana Maslany on Female Empowerment in TV and Her Favorite Clones." Interview by Anthony D'Alessandro. *Deadline*. Penske Business Media, 27 Aug. 2015. Web. 11 Dec. 2015.

Maslany, Tatiana. "Q&A: 'Orphan Black's' Tatiana Maslany: 'Honored' for Emmy Nod; Surprised by Internet's 'Nutty' Reaction." Interview by Meredith Blake. *Los Angeles Times*. Los Angeles Times, 15 Aug. 2015. Web. 11 Dec. 2015.

Maslany, Tatiana. "Tatiana Maslany, Beside Herself." Interview by James Ostime. *Interview*. Interview, 31 May 2013. Web. 11 Dec. 2015.

Maslany, Tatiana. "Tatiana Maslany on *Orphan Black* Season 3 and Filling Helen Mirren's Shoes." Interview by Jessica Goldstein.

Esquire. Hearst Digital Media, 2 Apr. 2015. Web. 11 Dec. 2015.

SELECTED WORKS

Grown Up Movie Star, 2009; *Picture Day*, 2012; *Cas & Dylan*, 2013; *Orphan Black*, 2013– ; *Woman in Gold*, 2015

—Joy Crelin

Natalie Massenet

Born: May 13, 1965
Occupation: Founder of Net-a-Porter

By the time Natalie Massenet departed the online designer-fashion retailer Net-a-Porter in 2015, it was clear that many consumers were not only comfortable shopping for clothing online but that they often preferred online shopping over visiting stores. At the time she founded the company in 2000, however, that was not the case. At that time, the luxury clothing and accessories that she would soon make available online were typically sold in specialty stores and were generally unavailable to the majority of consumers, even those who could easily afford them, and Massenet knew that many consumers would eagerly purchase such items from the comfort of their own homes. Although Net-a-Porter faced significant skepticism during its early days, Massenet did not become discouraged. "I was completely confident. I never thought it wouldn't work. I never once thought it wouldn't be huge," she told Addy Dugdale for *Fast Company* (2 Apr. 2010).

Massenet's belief in her idea was well founded. Within four years of the website's debut, it was financially profitable. Over the following years, the Net-a-Porter brand expanded significantly; the company launched the Outnet, an online retailer specializing in clothing from previous seasons, as well as the men's clothing site Mr. Porter and the print magazine *Porter*. Although Massenet left the company following its merger with the Italian-based Yoox Group in 2015, she set off to explore new possibilities with the tremendous success of Net-a-Porter under her belt.

EARLY LIFE AND EDUCATION

Natalie Massenet was born Natalie Sara Rooney on May 13, 1965, in Los Angeles, California. Her father, Robert Rooney, was an American journalist who later became a film publicist. Her mother, Barbara Jones, was a British model and film stand-in. Massenet spent her early childhood in Paris, France, but moved back to Los Angeles following her parents' divorce, remaining with her

Jeff Spicer/Getty Images

father. She and her father were close, and she credits him with giving her the courage to take risks in her professional life. "My dad taught me never to be afraid of what's on the other side of the mountain," she told Dugdale.

In Los Angeles, Massenet attended St. Bernard High School, from which she graduated in 1983. She went on to enroll in the University of California, Los Angeles, which her father had also attended. She earned her bachelor's degree in English from the university in 1987.

EARLY CAREER

Massenet worked a series of jobs early in her career, including stints at a men's clothing store and as a receptionist. She spent a year working as a model in Tokyo, Japan, and later described her work there to Kate Reardon for *Vanity Fair* (31 Aug. 2012) as "really bad."

Building on her interest in fashion, Massenet soon turned her attention to fashion journalism, taking a position with the Italian magazine *Moda*. While working for the magazine, she served as an assistant to photographer Mario Testino. In 1991 she joined the magazine *Women's Wear Daily*, for which she became West Coast editor. Massenet moved to the United Kingdom in the late 1990s and took a position at *Tatler*, a British lifestyle, fashion, and society magazine. At the magazine, she worked with renowned fashion director Isabella Blow.

While working in fashion journalism, Massenet began to identify a problem in the existing designer fashion marketplace: often, the fashionable clothing items and accessories featured in high-profile fashion magazines were not available for purchase by the magazines' readers, either because they were sold only in a select few stores or were produced in very small, limited production batches. Massenet also noted that such items generally were not available for purchase online, a shopping medium that appealed to her, as she was pregnant with her first child at the time. She began to imagine a retailer that would sell a curated collection of designer clothing online where consumers could shop from the privacy of their own homes or offices. Massenet named the fledgling business Net-a-Porter, a play on the French term prêt-à-porter, or ready to wear. In the fashion industry, the term is used to distinguish designer clothing available off the rack from the more expensive and exclusive haute couture.

NET-A-PORTER

At first, many in the fashion industry viewed Massenet's idea with skepticism, as did a number of the potential investors whom she contacted during Net-a-Porter's early days. The Internet was not yet an omnipresent fixture in consumers' lives, and the concept of e-commerce—and especially fashion e-commerce—was in many ways still in development. "There were a lot of unimaginative private-equity people who said that women would never shop online," Massenet recalled to Dugdale. "I think about those people a lot. I'm sure their wives are having Net-a-Porter bags delivered to their homes every day."

Despite encountering such naysayers, Massenet was convinced that her idea was a good one. Net-a-Porter launched on a small scale, initially operating out of Massenet's home. "When we launched in 2000, we used American English to make us sound international and signed all our correspondence from 'the Editors,' even though it was really just me and a couple of others packing the black boxes with clothes and ribbon bows," she told Karen Kay for the *Guardian* (10 July 2015) of the company's early days. "We were serving women who had access to a computer Monday to Friday: there would be a surge on Monday lunchtimes, then again last minute on a Friday. In those days, you had to unplug your home phone to get online, and you could drink a whole cup of coffee while a webpage uploaded. I do feel like I am reminiscing about a time when we had to milk our cows and make our own cheese."

Although many other web-based businesses struggled amid the dotcom crash of the early 2000s, Net-a-Porter rose out of it, weathering the difficult economic time just as it would later weather the global recession that began in 2007. Massenet has frequently told journalists that she views bad times such as those economic downturns as opportunities, a viewpoint in line with her notoriously positive attitude. As the decade progressed, Net-a-Porter began to find financial success, becoming profitable in 2004.

DISRUPTING FASHION RETAIL

As online shopping increased in popularity and Net-a-Porter grew as a business, the retailer became a prominent force both in the fashion industry and in retail. By choosing to stock clothing by particular designers, it served as a tastemaker, influencing the fashion industry through its curated inventory. Net-a-Porter also became well known for its luxury packaging, which featured signature gift boxes and ribbons that harkened back to an earlier era of retail.

Although much of the company's business revolved around innovative design, Massenet believed that the shopping experience itself should be kept simple. "Our consumers don't like gimmicks," she explained to Kay. "They don't want things to spin around the screen or pop up. We've discovered they want good, honest words and really great photos that show full-length details." Presenting shoppers with options also became an important facet of Net-a-Porter's business model. The company began to offer to ship items in brown paper packaging to buyers hoping to be discreet about their purchases, and it also offered shoppers the ability to browse the site on their own or enlist expert help. "The majority want to be left alone and like self-service, but a small percentage of women treat technology as a conduit to old-world service and use our trained personal shoppers and customer care team as they might do in a traditional bricks-and-mortar boutique," Massenet told Kay.

Over the years, Massenet and her colleagues expanded the company's offerings through the creation of affiliated sites such as the Outnet and Mr. Porter. The former sells discounted clothing and accessories from previous seasons, while the latter is the menswear counterpart to the main Net-a-Porter site. In 2014, the company moved in a direction that was seemingly inconsistent with its origins in e-commerce, launching the print magazine *Porter*. With the frustrations that had sparked the creation of Net-a-Porter still fresh in her mind, Massenet stressed in interviews that every clothing item featured in Porter would be available for purchase rather than remaining out of the reach of readers. She also noted that although Net-a-Porter's primary focus was digital, the creation of a print product perfectly suited its status as a multimedia company. Still, she viewed the Internet as the true future of commerce and socialization. "Look at the way eleven-year-olds are living their day-to-day lives already," she told Dugdale. "More things will take place virtually. They won't be meeting in public. They won't be going to stores. We haven't even begun to see just how many transactions are going to take place online. I attend Internet conferences all the time and they literally make the hairs on the back of my neck stand up."

DEPARTURE FROM NET-A-PORTER

Although Massenet remained with Net-a-Porter for more than a decade, she eventually stepped back from its everyday operations but remained the company's chair. The Swiss company Richemont, a major investor in Net-a-Porter, bought a majority stake in the company in 2010. In March 2015, Richemont announced that Net-a-Porter would be merging with Yoox Group, an Italian-based clothing retailer, to form the Yoox Net-a-Porter Group. Although Massenet was initially set to remain with the company in the position of executive chair, she ultimately decided to move on, announcing her departure in September 2015. Within the fashion and e-commerce industries, rumors suggested that her departure was in part the result of conflicts with Yoox management. However, Massenet remained characteristically positive about the move, telling reporters that the merger came at a good time for her to explore new opportunities.

Following her departure from Net-a-Porter, Massenet continued to serve as chair of the British Fashion Council, a role to which she was appointed in 2013. In recognition of her services to fashion, she was given the title of dame by Queen Elizabeth II in early 2016. She was previously named a member of the Most Excellent Order of the British Empire in 2009.

PERSONAL LIFE

Massenet married investment banker Arnaud Massenet in 1997. They had two children, Isabella and Ava, before divorcing in 2011. Massenet later began a relationship with photographer Erik Torstensson. She lives with her family in the South Kensington neighborhood of London.

As her work with Net-a-Porter might suggest, Massenet is an avid online shopper. "Very few of my purchases are made offline, because I don't have time to walk round stores, and I hate going into stores in my raggedy jeans and seeing an assistant sneer at me," she explained to Kay. "I love the way the Internet has democratized shopping."

SUGGESTED READING

Dugdale, Addy. "Crib Sheet: Natalie Massenet, Founder of Net-a-Porter." *Fast Company*. Mansueto Ventures, 2 Apr. 2010. Web. 15 July 2016.

England, Lucy. "The Spectacular Life of Net-a-Porter Founder Natalie Massenet." *Business Insider*. Business Insider, 3 Sept. 2015. Web. 15 July 2016.

Friedman, Vanessa. "Why Natalie Massenet's Departure from Net-a-Porter Matters." *New*

York Times. New York Times, 3 Sept. 2015. Web. 15 July 2016.

Hyland, Véronique. "The Backstory behind Natalie Massenet's Departure from Net-a-Porter." *Cut.* New York Media, 3 Sept. 2015. Web. 15 July 2016.

Massenet, Natalie. "CEO Talk: Natalie Massenet, Chairman and Founder of Net-a-Porter." Interview by Imran Amed. *Business of Fashion.* Business of Fashion, 13 Nov. 2008. Web. 15 July 2016.

Massenet, Natalie. "Natalie Massenet: We Must Never Fall in Love with the Way We Are Doing Things." Interview by Karen Kay. *Guardian.* Guardian News and Media, 10 July 2015. Web. 15 July 2016.

Reardon, Kate. "Natalie Massenet." *Vanity Fair.* Condé Nast, 31 Aug. 2012. Web. 15 July 2016.

—*Joy Crelin*

Christine McCarthy

Born: ca. 1955
Occupation: Media executive

Christine M. McCarthy worked her way up the Walt Disney Corporation structure for fifteen years before becoming a senior executive vice president and chief financial officer (CFO) of Disney in June 2015. McCarthy will manage annual revenues in the range of $50 billion. She reports directly to Bob Iger, the chairman and chief executive officer (CEO) of Disney. As Joseph Pimentel reported for the *Orange County Register* (30 June 2015), Iger praised McCarthy, saying, "Christine has done an incredible job as Disney's treasurer over the past fifteen years, and her strong leadership and keen financial acumen make her an ideal chief financial officer. She is highly respected in the finance sector, and in this new role she will have even more impact on creating value for Disney shareholders."

EARLY LIFE AND EDUCATION
Born in Winthrop, Massachusetts, McCarthy is a third-generation Irish American. She graduated in 1977 from Smith College, one of the so-called Seven Sisters colleges, with a bachelor's degree in biological science. While there, she received an award for excellence in botany. Although not many would see the connection between biology and finance, McCarthy does. As she told Hilary Johnson for *Treasury and Risk* (27 June 2011), "Applying the scientific method to problem-solving doesn't have to be restricted to lab experiments. . . . When you're going through

problems, you quickly throw out irrelevant factors, and focus on the things that really make a difference. That training early on in your career can really be well-applied in business."

In 1981, McCarthy earned her master's degree in business administration, with specializations in finance and marketing, from Anderson School of Management at the University of California, Los Angeles (UCLA).

Before moving to Disney McCarthy worked in the banking industry, serving from 1981 to 1996 as an executive vice president at First Interstate Bancorp. She moved on to the role of CFO for Imperial Bancorp, a regional bank, in April 1997. She left that job to take a post at Disney in 2000, around the same time that Comerica purchased Imperial Bancorp.

STARTING AT DISNEY
The move to Disney from a regional bank made sense to McCarthy, as she explained to Johnson, "What was appealing is that it's not a narrow treasury function, and never has been at Disney." She went on to state, "I am never bored. . . . On any given day, I can be switching around pretty quickly." For five years, from 2000 to 2005, McCarthy served as senior vice president and treasurer at Disney before moving to executive vice president of corporate finance, real estate, and treasurer for another five years. In that role, she oversaw more than 18 million square feet of warehouses and corporate office space in forty countries.

McCarthy offered a press statement on her promotion, as Pimentel reported, "I am humbled and honored to be entrusted with the role of CFO of this incredibly dynamic company. . . . Under Bob's leadership, Disney has delivered record results, and I look forward to working with our talented senior management team as we build on the company's financial strength and strong balance sheet to deliver shareholder value." Her responsibilities include overseeing investor relations, corporate planning, and corporate real estate. Her annual salary is more than $1 million, with eligibility for stock awards and bonuses that would quadruple that sum. McCarthy is the company's liaison to Wall Street and creator of its financial strategy.

FACING CHALLENGES
In light of the declining number of television viewers, Disney and other entertainment companies are struggling to find their balance. The value of Disney's stock shares fell during the second quarter of 2015, during the months just prior to McCarthy's appointment, and earnings fell short of the goal. Income increases were mainly due to two divisions: Disney Parks and Resorts and Consumer Products.

According to John Buckingham for *Forbes* (19 Aug. 2015), even as companies such as Disney experience the effect of "cord-cutting," or consumers moving from paid cable television, Disney has a "diverse revenue stream, loyal fan base and solid portfolio of franchises," which will allow it to weather the storm of the shift in how media is consumed. About 46 percent of Disney income results from cable channels, such as ESPN (Entertainment and Sports Programming Network), Disney Channel, and ABC Family.

Cord-cutting has adversely affected ESPN, one of Disney's biggest revenue sources. The sports channel offers exclusive content from the National Basketball Association (NBA) and college football playoffs. McCarthy downgraded projections of ESPN's high single-digit growth to mid-single digit growth in light of changes in the options for online content delivery. To cut costs, ESPN has dropped some of its big-name announcers, such as Keith Olbermann and Bill Simmons, and has also lost advertising dollars.

DISNEY IN CHINA

Like many multinational corporations, Disney was interested in expanding into China, where Disney films were banned in 1999 after Disney released a film on the Dalai Lama. The ban was eventually lifted, and McCarthy was instrumental in paving the way for Shanghai Disney, working with Shanghai Shendi Group on financing for the $5.5-billion park and with contractors and suppliers. Ownership of the park is split between Shanghai Shendi, a state-owned investment group with 57 percent controlling interest, and Disney, with the other 43 percent ownership.

The sixth Disney resort and the first in mainland China, the nearly one thousand–acre park is scheduled to open in 2016. As reported by Maggie Hiufu Wong for CNN (Cable News Network) (15 July 2015), company president Iger, displaying the design of the newest theme park, stated, "We are building something truly special here in Shanghai that not only showcases the best of Disney's storytelling but also celebrates and incorporates China's incredibly rich heritage to create a one-of-a-kind destination that will delight and entertain the people of China for generations to come."

Shanghai Disney is the third Disney theme park in Asia, joining parks in Tokyo and Hong Kong. It will be the first Disney theme park to open in ten years. The castle, the largest among all the parks, will house all of the Disney princesses. Six theme lands and a Disneytown shopping and dining experience will await guests. At the Walt Disney Grand Theatre, visitors will be able to enjoy the first Mandarin Chinese–language production of "The Lion King." Despite the fact that China expects to add fifty-nine theme parks by 2020, Disney expects high numbers of visitors. About 330 million people live within a three-hour drive or train ride from Shanghai.

FORECASTING THE FUTURE

Disney's future success will partly hinge on its first *Star Wars* film, which was released in December 2015. The company also continues to rely on merchandise with movie tie-ins. The Disney film *Frozen* (2013) was so successful both at the box office and as a merchandising tool that Disney's Epcot Center in Orlando, Florida, plans a "Frozen Ever After" ride, as well as enhancements to the Norway Pavilion.

In projecting 2016, McCarthy stated in *Forbes*, "The strength of the U.S. dollar versus a number of key foreign currencies is expected to adversely impact our operating income in 2016 by approximately $500 million." Disney was unable to purchase currency hedges for the same attractive rate as in fiscal year 2015. For a company that generated more than $13 billion in one fiscal quarter, that is not a huge sum of money. However, McCarthy was being transparent about the challenge that Disney faces.

Iger, head of Disney, announced his resignation, effective in 2018, and some pundits have speculated that McCarthy will be considered to fill his shoes as the next president of Disney. In September 2015, McCarthy was elected to the supervisory board of Euro Disney SCA, now commonly known as Disneyland Paris. It is the most often visited theme park not only in France but also throughout all of Europe.

PERSONAL LIFE

McCarthy is married to Michael McCormick. The couple has two children, Daniel and Kelsey. McCarthy and her husband have served as trustees of and donors to the college preparatory Westridge School for Girls, in Pasadena, California. McCarthy is also a mentor for the STEM (Science, Technology, Engineering, and Math) program of the National Math and Science Initiative. The initiative was begun to address both the shortage of workers proficient in math and science and the fact that the United States has fallen behind other developed nations in these areas. McCarthy serves as a director of Phoenix House California, a treatment facility for substance abuse serving both adolescents and adults. She was also a board member of the Los Angeles Philharmonic Association from 1998 to 2001. An active Smith alumna, she has been a member of the Smith College Investment Committee and was a director and treasurer for her alma mater's alumni association until 2002. In addition, she and McCormick have donated to

UCLA Anderson's School of Management. She is a governor of the UCLA Foundation.

Treasury and Risk named McCarthy one of the one hundred most influential people in finance in both 2003 and 2011. In 2015 she was *Treasury Today*'s woman of the year, an award given at the eighth annual Adam Smith Awards, which recognizes achievement at the highest level of treasury. The woman of the year award honors inspiration as well as achievement and innovation.

SUGGESTED READING

Buckingham, John. "Video Games and the Happiest Place on Earth: What Do They Have in Common?" *Forbes.* Forbes, 19 Aug. 2015. Web. 12 Oct. 2015.

Fritz, Ben. "Disney Defends ESPN in an Age of Cable Cord-Cutting." *Wall Street Journal.* Dow Jones & Company, 4 Aug. 2015. Web. 13 Oct. 2015.

Johnson, Hilary. "No Small World of Finance." *Treasury and Risk.* Summit Business Media. 27 June 2011. Web. 13 Oct. 2015.

Palmeri, Christopher. "Disney Promotes Christine McCarthy as First Female CFO." *Bloomberg Business Week.* Bloomberg, 30 June 2015. Web. 12 Oct. 2015.

Pimentel, Joseph. "Disney Names Its Treasurer, Christine McCarthy, as New Chief Financial Officer." *Orange County Register.* Orange County Register, 30 June 2015. Web. 8 Oct. 2015.

—*Judy Johnson*

Tom McCarthy

Born: 1969
Occupation: Author

For all those commentators who have declared the novel is dead as a literary form, many critics, both in the United States and the United Kingdom, would ask that they give their attention to Tom McCarthy, an author whose work has been compared to the great Irish novelist James Joyce, long considered to be one of the masters of the novel. McCarthy, unlike many modern novelists, does not hail from the literary world of academia or the literary establishment; his work instead grew out of the European art scene. His celebrated first novel published, *Remainder*, was put out by a small art press in 2005 after it had been rejected by numerous established, traditional publishing houses. Since that time, McCarthy has gone on to pen an acclaimed work of literary criticism and three additional novels, including,

most recently, *Satin Island* (2015), which was short-listed for the Man Booker Prize.

In an interview with Tim Martin for the *Telegraph* (19 Mar. 2015), McCarthy discussed the continuing importance of literature in modern life: "I don't think we need to abandon the form of the book just because the Internet has been invented." He explained, "Most other media formats work: you get an iPhone and it does something, and if it doesn't do that thing, you take it back for a repair. But the book is deliberately set up not to perform a certain function, to systematically frustrate. It's always been a dysfunctional medium, and since it never works, it never stops working. So I'm perfectly happy writing books."

EARLY LIFE AND EDUCATION

Tom McCarthy was born in London, England, in 1969 and attended Dulwich College, an independent boys' school in southeast London, for his primary education. He then studied English literature at the University of Oxford, where he earned his undergraduate degree. An avid reader, he developed a passion for writers such as Joyce, William S. Burroughs, Jacques Derrida, and Claude Lévi-Strauss. In interviews, he has admitted that he always thought of himself as a writer, although his route to becoming a published author would prove circuitous.

From 1991 to 1993, McCarthy lived in Prague, in the Czech Republic, primarily because it was an inexpensive place to live. He was then living on a British government program called the Government Enterprise Allowance Scheme, which registered artists as small businesses and allowed them to receive a small stipend, keeping unemployment figures down. From there, he moved to Berlin and then to Amsterdam before returning to London in 1996. During this time, he was writing continually. He published book reviews for local periodicals and wrote a novella, but none of these efforts proved particularly lucrative. In order to make money, he worked a series of odd jobs as a bartender, a life model, and a picture framer. At the same time, he began his first novel, *Men in Space*, which he quickly found a publisher for—who just as quickly turned around and said they could not actually publish it. Putting his first effort aside, he eventually wrote another novel, *Remainder*, finishing it in 2001. Many editors also liked that novel, but still no publisher was willing to print and sell it.

INVOLVEMENT IN THE ART WORLD

While working on his fiction, McCarthy became deeply involved with the modern art scene. In an interview for *BOMB* magazine (Spring 2015), McCarthy recalled how he began his immersion to Frederic Tuten: "During my early twenties— I started hanging out with visual artists. These people generally had a much more dynamic engagement with literature than most 'literary' people. They were into Burroughs and [Georges] Bataille and [Maurice] Blanchot, and other people whose names didn't even begin with B; and their work seemed to be actively addressing the whole legacy of literary modernism. . . . So I fell into that world. It's still really my home territory. I'm a writer through and through, but the art world—to a large extent—provides the arena in which literature can be vigorously addressed, transformed, and expanded."

McCarthy was particularly interested in the ways reading and writing intersected within an art space. He described one such project to Tuten: "I did this project with Rod Dickinson, in which we 'corrected' the French anarchist Martial Bourdin's attempt to blow up the Greenwich Observatory in 1894. . . . It's what [Joseph] Conrad's *The Secret Agent* is all about. We reprinted all the newspapers from the time, altering a sentence here and there to make the Observatory actually 'have been' destroyed; doctored photographs; and even made a short film on a hand-cranked camera which we post-produced to show the building burning. . . . It's about fictions and the real."

At the same time, McCarthy cofounded the International Necronautical Society (INS) with his friend, the philosopher Simon Critchley. The INS is a tongue-in-cheek, avant-garde organization that uses old-fashioned manifestos, declarations, and denunciations to demonstrate how an art platform can be a literary form.

EARLY WRITING CAREER
In 2004, due to McCarthy's increased presence in the art world, Clémentine Deliss and Thomas Boutoux offered to publish *Remainder* through their Parisian art press, Metronome, and sell it in galleries and museums, not through bookstores. Although just 750 copies of that 2005 edition of *Remainder* were ever printed, it earned considerable attention and was eventually republished by Alma, an independent mainstream British publisher, and Vintage, an American publisher, shortly thereafter.

The book is about an unnamed protagonist who survives a rather mysterious accident involving something falling onto him from the sky, spends months in a coma, and subsequently receives a multimillion-pound payout, which he then uses to obsessively restage and reenact vaguely remembered events from his past in an attempt to achieve a sense of authenticity. The novel wowed critics on both sides of the Atlantic. Patrick Ness reviewed *Remainder* for the *Guardian* (11 Aug. 2006), observing, "This is a refreshingly idiosyncratic, enjoyably intelligent read by a writer with ideas and talent. . . . It's a novel that could so easily have missed out on

being published here. It's a forgotten axiom that pre–Harry Potter no one was looking for books about boy wizards. One publisher took a chance, et voilà, the biggest success in modern publishing history." In 2008, *Remainder* earned the Believer Prize, which is presented by the editors of the *Believer*, an American literary magazine.

The year after publishing his first novel, McCarthy followed that success with his first book of literary criticism, titled *Tintin and the Secret of Literature* (2006), which discusses, with considerable thought and intelligence, whether or not *The Adventures of Tintin*—the beloved comic collections created by Belgian cartoonist Georges Remi, who wrote under the pen name Hergé—are actually literature. The work was largely praised as an especially creative example of literary criticism.

MEN IN SPACE
In 2007, McCarthy published *Men in Space*—the first novel he had written—in the United Kingdom, after trimming it down and reworking it some because, with the insight of being years removed and officially a published author, he felt it had been too unwieldy in its original form. The novel, set in Prague shortly after the overthrow of its communist government, centers on the forgery of a stolen religious painting depicting a hovering saint. The forger is a bohemian painter named Ivan Manasek who quickly becomes deeply involved with a number of questionable characters. Comprised of thirty-six sections with many interlocking episodes involving seven main characters and numerous secondary ones, *Men in Space*, like its predecessor, was met with cheers in the United Kingdom upon its publication, which were echoed when it was finally published in the United States in 2012. Stephen Burn wrote of *Men in Space* for the *New York Times* (24 Feb. 2012), "Reading the novel is like entering an echo chamber where minor details in localized scenes resonate across the larger text. . . . *Men in Space* is sometimes overly caught up in fine details, and occasionally characters are implausibly slow at reading the signals that surround them—but the novel is an intellectually voracious cross section of a historical moment, and a thrilling indication of the vitality of the contemporary British novel."

A THIRD NOVEL: C
In McCarthy's third novel published in the United Kingdom (it was published before *Men in Space* in the United States), *C* (2010), Serge Carrefax comes of age in the early years of the twentieth century surrounded by his eccentric father's wireless inventions and in the midst of a school for deaf children, which his father supervises. After Serge's sister, Sophie, kills herself, he gets involved with World War I as well as in the

postwar hedonism of London in the 1920s; during this time, he develops a drug habit and even makes his way to an archeological dig in Egypt. His life serves as a mirror of the times, reflecting the changes in society that brought England from the Victorian age into the modern era.

"*C* is a 1960s-style anti-novel that's fundamentally hostile to the notion of character and dramatizes, or encodes, a set of ideas concerning subjectivity. On the face of it, though, it's a historical fantasy, sometimes witty and sometimes eerie, built around the early years of radio transmission," Christopher Tayler wrote of the book in a review for the *Guardian* (30 July 2010). "The near-Joycean scale and density of all this is truly impressive, as is McCarthy's ability to fold it into a cleanly constructed narrative, which has its boring stretches but also moments of humor and weird beauty." In addition to receiving considerable critical acclaim, *C* was short-listed for the 2010 Man Booker Prize and won the inaugural Windham-Campbell Prize from Yale University in 2013.

SATIN ISLAND

McCarthy's most recent novel is *Satin Island*, which was published in both the United States and the United Kingdom in 2015. In it, McCarthy returns to the modern era by describing the life and work experiences of U., the narrator of the novel who serves as an "in-house ethnographer" for a consulting firm in London. The firm—and U.—help their corporate and governmental clients develop a better understanding of consumers' desires and anxieties in order to better target their goods and services to a now-worldwide market. The book is a study of both how narratives are created and how the digital world has transformed human society into a single global tribe of consumers.

Numerous critics were impressed by McCarthy's slim, powerful novel. Jeff Turrentine wrote of *Satin Island* for the *New York Times* (20 Feb. 2015), "McCarthy isn't a frustrated cultural theorist who must content himself with writing novels; he's a born novelist, a pretty fantastic one, who has figured out a way to make cultural theory funny, scary, and suspenseful—in other words, compulsively readable." That same year, *Satin Island* was short-listed for the Man Booker Prize and the Goldsmiths Prize.

PERSONAL LIFE

McCarthy has two young daughters and lives with his family in London.

SUGGESTED READING

Bollen, Christopher. "Tom McCarthy Is No Longer a Well-Kept Secret." *Interview*. Interview, 13 Mar. 2012. Web. 13 July 2016.

Martin, Tim. "Tom McCarthy: A Kafka for the Google Age." *Telegraph*. Telegraph Media Group, 19 Mar. 2015. Web. 13 July 2016.

Tuten, Frederic. "Tom McCarthy." *BOMB*. BOMB, Spring 2015. Web. 13 July 2016.

SELECTED WORKS

Remainder, 2005; *Tintin and the Secret of Literature*, 2006; *Men in Space*, 2007; *C*, 2010; *Satin Island*, 2015

—*Christopher Mari*

Sheri McCoy

Born: 1959
Occupation: Chief executive officer and director of Avon Products

McCoy is one of a relatively small number of female chief executive officers (CEOs) of a *Fortune 500* company. She was ranked among the most powerful women in business by *Forbes* in 2012 and has been on *Fortune* magazine's list of the most powerful women in business every year since 2008.

EARLY LIFE AND EDUCATION

Sheri McCoy was born in 1959 in Quincy, Massachusetts, and grew up in nearby Braintree. In high school, she enjoyed science, math, and problem solving. Entering Southeastern Massachusetts University (now University of Massachusetts, Dartmouth), McCoy knew she was interested in doing research but had no specific career plan. During her senior year, a textile chemistry professor encouraged her to apply to Princeton University. He also arranged for her to receive a full scholarship through the Textile Research Institute.

She graduated with a bachelor's degree in textile chemistry in 1980 from Southeastern Massachusetts University. She then enrolled in the chemical engineering master's program at Princeton and received a master's degree in chemical engineering in 1982. In 1988, she earned a master's degree in business administration from Rutgers University.

CAREER AT JOHNSON & JOHNSON

In 1982, following her graduation from Princeton, McCoy joined Johnson & Johnson, a corporate giant with companies in the consumer health, biologics, pharmaceuticals, and medical devices and diagnostics sectors. Her first position was as an associate scientist in the research and development unit for the personal products division.

McCoy quickly rose through the ranks, managing businesses in every key product division, including the medical devices, consumer, and prescription medicines groups. She had responsibility for companies worldwide, including key markets in China, Brazil, and Latin America.

She held a variety of positions. She was the vice president of marketing for the skin-care business, including brands such as Neutrogena, Aveeno, and Johnson's Baby Oil. She also served as the vice president of research and development for the personal products worldwide division and the global president for the baby and wound care division of the consumer sector. In addition, she was in charge of BabyCenter, a leading online community for new and expectant mothers.

In 2005, McCoy was appointed chair of Johnson & Johnson's medical devices and diagnostic group. She served in that position until 2008, when she became the worldwide chair of the surgical care group.

From 2009 to 2011, McCoy was the worldwide chair of the pharmaceuticals group. This was a difficult period for Johnson & Johnson, as the company had lost patent protection on several of its largest revenue-generating drugs. McCoy met these challenges by spending more than $950 million to acquire a start-up biotechnology firm, a risk that later proved advantageous when its prostate cancer drug was approved by the US Food and Drug Administration, with estimated annual sales of $800 million.

In December 2010, McCoy was named one of Johnson & Johnson's two vice chairmen, becoming the vice chairman of the executive committee at the beginning of 2011, with responsibility for sixty thousand employees in the consumer, pharmaceutical, information technology, and corporate office of science and technology divisions. Once again, she faced great challenges as recalls of key products such as Tylenol had eroded consumer confidence and caused the company to lose over $1 billion in sales.

McCoy helped to turn around the consumer products division and was considered a top contender to succeed CEO Bill Weldon when he retired. In late February 2012, Johnson & Johnson announced that position would go to McCoy's fellow vice chairman, Alex Gorsky.

MOVE TO AVON

On April 23, 2012, McCoy joined Avon Products Inc. as its CEO. In May 2012, she was elected to its board of directors.

At Avon, McCoy faced challenges similar to those she had overcome during her thirty-year career with Johnson & Johnson. She was tasked with resolving issues resulting from criminal and civil investigations of bribery in China and other countries by the US Department of Justice and the Securities and Exchange Commission. Among these tasks was helping to regain consumer confidence that had been lost after the widely publicized bribery charges and corporate scandal. She was also charged with reversing declines in sales and restructuring sales and operations. Within her first year as CEO, McCoy cut spending, cut employees, and cut unprofitable units. She pulled out of Vietnam and South Korea and set a goal to reduce operating expenses by $400 million within two years. She is working to develop long-term growth initiatives and strengthen earning opportunities for the company's six million representatives. She has invested heavily in Avon's information systems, hoping to better utilize digital and social media tools to reach consumers and restore the Avon brand to its former stature.

OTHER ACHIEVEMENTS

McCoy serves on several boards. She is the director of the US Foundation for Inspiration and Recognition of Science and Technology (FIRST), a nonprofit organization dedicated to increasing young people's interest in science and technology. She is also a member of the Partnership for New York and the Stonehill College and Catalyst boards.

McCoy holds four US and one European patents.

IMPACT

Over the course of her career in business, McCoy has helped to lead two global conglomerates through challenging social, economic, and legal difficulties. As a vice chairman of Johnson & Johnson, McCoy was instrumental in gaining new business opportunities, reversing declining sales due to lost patents, and restoring consumer confidence. As CEO and director of Avon, McCoy has made significant headway in restructuring the company, investing in new markets, and, once again, helping a company regain its reputation and market share.

PERSONAL LIFE

McCoy married Terence Patrick McCoy, a fellow student at Southeastern Massachusetts University. They have three sons: Ryan, Matthew, and Patrick. She resides in New Jersey.

SUGGESTED READING

Brady, Diane. "Can Big Pharma's Sheri McCoy Give Avon a Makeover?" *Business Week.* Business Week, 9 Apr. 2012. Web. 5 July 2014.

"Questions for Sheri McCoy." *ISSUU—UMass Dartmouth Magazine* (Spring 2011): 15–16. Web. 5 July 2014.

Sellers, Patricia. "Why the Guy Got the CEO Job at J&J." *Fortune.* Fortune, 24 Feb. 2012. Web. 8 July 2014.

"Sheri S. McCoy: Chief Executive Officer." *Avon*. Avon Products, 2014. Web. 3 July 2014.

"Sheri S. McCoy." *Rutgers Business School*. Rutgers, 2014. Web. 3 July 2014.

"UMass Dartmouth Holds Undergraduate Commencement." *Chancellor's Office of University of Massachusetts, Dartmouth*. University of Massachusetts, Dartmouth, 12 May 2013. Web. 5 July 2014.

Voreacos, David, and Tom Schoenberg. "Avon Will Pay $135 Million to Settle Bribe Investigation." *Bloomberg*. Bloomberg, 1 May 2014. Web. 8 July 2014.

—*Barb Lightner*

Denis McDonough

Born: December 2, 1969
Occupation: White House Chief of Staff

After having served as the head of strategic communication for the National Security Council, Denis McDonough was appointed White House chief of staff in January 2013.

EARLY LIFE AND EDUCATION

Denis Richard McDonough was born on December 2, 1969, in Stillwater, Minnesota, to William and Kathleen McDonough. He has ten siblings. McDonough attended Saint John's University in Collegeville, Minnesota, from which he earned degrees in history and Spanish.

While at Saint John's, McDonough played on the school's football team under college football Hall of Fame coach John Gagliardi. McDonough has credited Gagliardi with instilling in him a sense of competition, which he says has helped him get ahead in politics. He has also credited former university president Dietrich Reinhart with getting him interested in the world beyond the Midwest. McDonough graduated summa cum laude in 1992.

After graduating, McDonough traveled throughout Latin America and taught high school in the Central American country of Belize. When he returned to the United States, McDonough continued his education at Georgetown University in Washington, DC, where he studied at the Edmund A. Walsh School of Foreign Service, a school specializing in international affairs education. He graduated in 1996 with his master's degree.

EARLY CAREER

Shortly after graduating from Georgetown, McDonough entered politics and took a staff position with the House International Relations Committee (later renamed the House Committee on Foreign Affairs). The committee is overseen by the House of Representatives and reviews, debates on, and presents foreign-policy legislation to the US Senate. Due to his extensive knowledge of Latin America, McDonough's work with the committee focused on that facet of international relations.

In 1999 McDonough left the committee to serve as a senior foreign policy adviser for South Dakota senator Tom Daschle, the former Senate majority leader. Daschle was a strong early supporter of Illinois senator Barack Obama, and this connection would help McDonough later in his career. McDonough eventually became Daschle's senior foreign policy adviser before Daschle lost his Senate seat after his reelection defeat in 2004.

McDonough then became legislative director for newly elected senator Ken Salazar, a Democrat from Colorado. He also began working under Daschle as a senior fellow at the Center for American Progress, a progressive organization where McDonough helped research health care policy.

OBAMA ADMINISTRATION

In 2007, presidential candidate Barack Obama's chief foreign policy adviser, Mark Lippert, was deployed to Iraq. McDonough had previously met Lippert while working for Daschle, and the two remained friends. When Lippert was deployed, McDonough was chosen to replace him as foreign policy adviser on Obama's presidential campaign.

Once Obama's election campaign was in full swing in 2008, McDonough was promoted to senior foreign policy adviser. He was in charge of twenty sets of experts who were grouped together based on districts and issues. He was also part of a team of thirteen senior campaign advisers and facilitated dialogue between his group of foreign advisers and Obama.

Following Obama's inauguration on January 20, 2009, McDonough became the head of strategic communications for the National Security Council (NSC). The role of the NSC is to act as a forum for the president when national security and foreign policy issues are being considered. When Lippert was deployed to Iraq again, McDonough took over his position as NSC chief of staff.

McDonough received another promotion in October 2010, when President Obama announced his appointment as principal deputy national security adviser, replacing Thomas E. Donilon, who became chief national security advisor. In this position, McDonough helped develop policy changes for the president to consider. He also helped plan troop withdrawals from Iraq and Afghanistan and helped enforce internal administration discipline within the

White House. In May 2011, while McDonough was serving as principal deputy at the NSC, al-Qaeda leader Osama bin Laden was killed by US Navy Seals in Pakistan in a Central Intelligence Agency–led operation.

On January 25, 2013, Obama named Mc-Donough his new White House chief of staff, succeeding former chief of staff Jack Lew. As chief of staff, McDonough is charged with overseeing all White House operations from a managerial, negotiatory, and advisory position. Since becoming chief of staff, McDonough has worked to unify the clashing members of government. McDonough has also become known for personally visiting members of government in order to address any issues or concerns they may have.

IMPACT

McDonough is considered to be President Obama's most trusted foreign policy adviser and one of his closest confidantes, which has given McDonough a great amount of influence within the administration. He has played an essential role in national security decisions during Obama's presidency and has helped unite partisan members of government.

PERSONAL LIFE

McDonough is married to Kari McDonough, and together they have three children: Addie, Liam, and Teddy. They reside in Maryland. In his spare time, McDonough enjoys fishing.

SUGGESTED READING

Cooper, Helene. "The Advisor at the Heart of National Security." *New York Times.* New York Times, 9 July 2010. Web. 21 Feb. 2014.

Cooper, Michael. "The New Team: Denis Mc-Donough." *New York Times.* New York Times, 23 Nov. 2008. Web. 21 Feb. 2014.

Eisele, Albert. "At Home in the West Wing: An Interview with Denis McDonough '92." *Saint John's Magazine* Winter 2009: 22–23. Print.

Horwitz, Sari, and David Nakamura. "Obama Taps McDonough as Chief of Staff, Says Goodbye to Longtime Adviser Plouffe." *Washington Post.* Washington Post, 25 Jan. 2013. Web. 21 Feb. 2014.

Hunt, Albert. "Obama Chief of Staff Emerges as Strong Leader." *Waco Tribune.* BH Media Group Holdings, 11 Feb. 2014. Web. 21 Feb. 2014.

—*Patrick G. Cooper*

DeRay Mckesson

Born: July 9, 1985
Occupation: Activist

"I want to believe there is a way to protest that is more than marching but not bloodshed," De-Ray Mckesson told Sandhya Somashekhar for the *Washington Post* (11 Nov. 2014). Mckesson began attending and organizing protests after the fatal shooting of unarmed black teenager Michael Brown by police in Ferguson, Missouri, on August 9, 2014, and since then, he has been at the forefront of a twenty-first-century civil rights movement. "The protest campaign, which emerged out of the riots that followed Brown's killing, lacks a single charismatic leader or direction from a national organization," Somashekhar wrote. "But at the front lines, an influential contingent of organizers including Mckesson is giving the movement a sense of identity and shaping how the American public sees it." Thanks in great part to Mckesson's efforts, millions of Americans have taken up the rallying cry that Black Lives Matter—a slogan and hashtag that had been coined by other activists following the 2013 acquittal of George Zimmerman, a neighborhood-watch volunteer in Sanford, Florida, who shot and killed Trayvon Martin, an unarmed black teen.

Along with his fellow activist Johnetta Elzie, with whom he publishes the online newsletter *This Is the Movement* and organizes the group We the Protestors, Mckesson was named to *Fortune* magazine's list of the fifty greatest leaders in the world in 2015. He modestly told the editors

Joe Kohen/Stringer/GettyImages

of the publication, "My role here is just to amplify the message."

EARLY LIFE AND EDUCATION

Mckesson was born on July 9, 1985, and grew up with his sister, TeRay, in Baltimore, Maryland. Their mother was addicted to drugs and abandoned the family when Mckesson was three years old. Although their father also struggled with addiction, he eventually got clean and was able to raise the two children with the help of his grandmother.

In sixth grade, Mckesson was elected to his school's student government, and he won reelection each year until he graduated from college. Describing his high school years to Sofiya Ballin for the *Philadelphia Inquirer* (4 Nov. 2015), he said, "There were adults who cared about me and pushed me when they didn't have to, and a lot of them were teachers."

Seeking to follow in their footsteps and get a teaching degree, Mckesson attended Bowdoin College, a small liberal-arts college in Brunswick, Maine. He earned part of his tuition by working in the mailroom, and during quiet times there he assiduously studied the labels on the mailboxes, hoping to learn the name of every other person on campus so that he could campaign more effectively for student government posts. (He was ultimately elected president of the Bowdoin Student Government and of his graduating class.) He also volunteered to give school tours to prospective students and parents, and when he realized that his audience was not responding well to his patter, he tweaked it over and over again until it met with a more enthusiastic reception. "There was a whole generation of Bowdoin students who came to the college because of the campus tours DeRay would do," Barry Mills, president of the college, told Jay Caspian Kang for the *New York Times Magazine* (4 May 2015). "He's always known how to inspire a group of people, so it doesn't surprise me that he's become a thought leader for what's going on out in Ferguson." Mckesson was eventually made head tour guide, served as a head proctor of one of the residence halls, spearheaded numerous initiatives aimed at student involvement and social justice, and became a well-known and much-liked figure on campus.

EARLY CAREER IN EDUCATION

After graduating from Bowdoin in 2007, Mckesson joined Teach for America, a nonprofit organization dedicated to sending recent college graduates who are passionate about education to teach in underserved schools. Mckesson was assigned to Frederick Douglass Academy VIII, a middle school in the New York City borough of Brooklyn, where he taught sixth-grade math. While in New York City, he also served as a

program advisor at the Harlem Children's Zone, a nonprofit organization that provides parent education, preschool programs, tutoring, and after-school programs to poor families.

In 2009, when his two-year Teach for America job had ended, Mckesson returned to Baltimore, where he accepted a post as center director at the educational nonprofit Higher Achievement, leading the organization's recruitment and retention efforts. In 2010 he joined TNTP (formerly known as The New Teacher Project), a nonprofit focused on eliminating educational inequity for poor and minority students, as a training and resource manager. In 2011 he became a human capital strategist in the Baltimore public school system and quickly gained a reputation for being fervent in the service of the city's students, eagerly courting the best hires and terminating any teacher whose skills he found to be subpar. In 2013 he was offered a post as a senior director of human capital for the public schools of Minneapolis, Minnesota, and moved from his hometown.

PROTESTS AND REPORTING

It was in Minneapolis that Mckesson was watching television on August 9, 2014, and learned of the shooting of Michael Brown, an unarmed African American teenager who had been preparing to start his first year of college. Brown had been killed by a white Ferguson police officer, who suspected him of robbing a nearby convenience store. Distraught protesters were soon streaming to the site of the shooting. Mckesson became determined to join them. He explained to Kang that as devoted as he was to educational causes, "I kept thinking, Kids can't learn if they're dead."

He set out from Minneapolis on August 16 and headed to Missouri, live-tweeting the trip along the way. (He had been inspired by those on the scene already tweeting and was especially struck by the disparity between their reports of trying to protest peacefully and the televised images of police in riot gear swinging batons.) Initially, his tweets were prosaic: "I should've gotten gas in Iowa. Much more expensive in St. Louis." Once he arrived in the thick of the protests, he found weightier material. "I just couldn't believe that the police would fire tear gas into what had been a peaceful protest," he recalled to Kang. "I was running around, face burning, and nothing I saw looked like America to me."

Mckesson began tweeting steadily, telling readers of the tanks and heavily armed police that were becoming fixtures on the streets of Ferguson. When he had to return to Minneapolis to work, he traveled back to the St. Louis area each weekend to protest and tweet from the front lines of the protests there. He befriended fellow protester Johnetta Elzie, and the pair later joined forces with Brittany Packnett, the executive director of St. Louis's Teach for America program, and Justin Hansford, a law professor at St. Louis University, to publish *This Is the Movement*, a newsletter that contained news out of Ferguson and criticized the mainstream media's coverage of the protests. *This Is the Movement* attracted a wide range of readers, with more than fourteen thousand subscribers, including officials from the US Department of Justice. Its fans included several professional journalists, and Mckesson and Elzie were soon being invited to appear on local and national news shows. Although they had not intended to do so, they became the unofficial faces of the protest movement. "I see myself as a protester who is also telling the story as it happens. . . . The goal was to create a space where people could go to get true news," Mckesson said of the newsletter in an interview with Noah Berlatsky for the *Atlantic* (7 Jan. 2015). "Now the movement has spread beyond St. Louis, we cover stories from around the country. So the goal was to be a hub of information." In 2015 Elzie and Mckesson received PEN New England's Howard Zinn Freedom to Write Award for their reporting and activism.

ACTIVISM

The group began organizing their own protest actions, tweeting a time and place to followers, who showed up en masse. (At times, the police, who were also following them on Twitter, showed up even before members of the public.) As Kang wrote, "Together, Mckesson and Elzie were developing a model of the modern protester: part organizer, part citizen journalist who marches through American cities while texting." It has been a highly effective model in many respects. Kang remarked, "Their innovation has been to marry the strengths of social media—the swift, morally blunt consensus that can be created by hashtags; the personal connection that a charismatic online persona can make with followers; the broad networks that allow for the easy distribution of documentary photos and videos—with an effort to quickly mobilize protests in each new city where a police shooting occurs." As of January 2016, Mckesson had amassed more than 270,000 followers on Twitter.

Several high-profile political figures have called upon Mckesson and his associates to learn more about the issues concerning them, and in the fall of 2015 he met with Democratic presidential candidates Hillary Clinton and Bernie Sanders to push for police reform as part of an initiative called Campaign Zero, which seeks to end police violence. He also urged the candidates to address such pressing matters as racial bias in the workplace and access to housing, child care, and education.

On the one-year anniversary of Brown's killing, some two hundred activists joined Mckesson to hold a march in St. Louis. When he and several others crossed police barriers in an attempt to stage a sit-in, they were arrested.

CRITICISMS

In addition to the danger of arrest, Mckesson's work has put him squarely in the crosshairs of opponents. He often receives tweets containing offensive, racist language and threats of violence. A frequent charge is that he is a "race-baiter" or is simply fomenting discontent to advance his own purposes. In mid-2015, after nine black parishioners were killed by a white shooter in Charleston, South Carolina, and Mckesson announced his intention to organize protests in that city, a new hashtag began trending among mostly white Twitter users from outside the state of South Carolina: #GoHomeDeRay.

Even among fellow African Americans, there has been some disagreement about his strategies. He has criticized longtime activist Al Sharpton over the older man's more traditional (and, in Mckesson's mind, less effective) tactics, and prominent media personality Oprah Winfrey publicly criticized the movement for its lack of clear leadership. Winfrey explained to Mary Green for *People* magazine (3 Jan. 2014), "What I'm looking for is some kind of leadership to come out of this to say, 'This is what we want. This is what has to change, and these are the steps that we need to take to make these changes, and this is what we're willing to do to get it.'" In response to that charge, Mckesson tweeted (2 Jan. 2015), "Stand with us. There are many 'leading.'"

Additionally, Mckesson is openly gay, which raises the ire of some. He has firmly stated, however, that he will not be dissuaded from his work by those who oppose him, whatever their reasons. When he is ready to return to a less-public life, he envisions himself teaching middle-school math. "[At that age] they still believe in magic," he told Ballin. "It was still a space of wonder, and I really appreciate that."

SUGGESTED READING

Berlatsky, Noah. "Hashtag Activism Isn't a Cop-Out." *Atlantic*. Atlantic Monthly Group, 7 Jan. 2015. Web. 7 Jan. 2016.

Casey, Garrett. "DeRay McKesson '07 Participates in 'Principled Protesting' in Ferguson." *Bowdoin Orient Express*. Bowdoin Orient Express, 26 Sept. 2014. Web. 7 Jan. 2016.

Kang, Jay Caspian. "Our Demand Is Simple: Stop Killing Us." *New York Times Magazine*. New York Times, 4 May 2015. Web. 7 Jan. 2016.

Pearce, Matt, and Kurtis Lee. "The New Civil Rights Leaders: Emerging Voices in the 21st

Century." *Chicago Tribune*. Chicago Tribune, 5 Mar. 2015. Web. 7 Jan. 2016.

Somashekhar, Sandhya. "Ferguson Protest Organizers: 'I Sleep, Eat and Breathe This.'" *Washington Post*. Washington Post, 11 Nov. 2014. Web. 7 Jan. 2016.

—*Mari Rich*

Kate McKinnon

Born: January 6, 1984
Occupation: Actor

Kate McKinnon has amused and amazed *Saturday Night Live* (SNL) viewers ever since her debut on the NBC sketch comedy show in 2012. She so deeply embodies each character she plays that they seem real, even when they are ridiculous, silly, or overeager. Some of her most famous impersonations include the politician Hillary Clinton, pop star Justin Bieber, and German chancellor Angela Merkel. Prior to joining *SNL*, McKinnon performed with the sketch and improvisational comedy group Upright Citizens Brigade, in New York City. Prior to that she was a cast member of *The Big Gay Sketch Show* on the cable channel Logo. (She is, in fact, the first openly gay female cast member of *Saturday Night Live*.) In 2016 McKinnon costarred—and some critics would say stole the show—in the all-female film remake of the comedy classic *Ghostbusters*. Having been nominated for multiple Emmy Awards for her performances on *Saturday Night Live*, McKinnon won her first Emmy in 2016.

EARLY LIFE

Kathryn McKinnon Berthold, who would later simply go by her shortened first name and middle name, was born and raised in Sea Cliff, New York, on Long Island. From a very young age she was interested in various kinds of performance: dressing up in costumes, performing in dance recitals, and playing music. She began playing piano around the age of five and she would, about six years later, pick up cello and guitar. Her father worked as an architect, and by the time McKinnon was in high school, her mother worked at the school as the president of the drama club. McKinnon was so obsessed with performing and costumes that she would go to preschool dressed up as Peter Pan, according to a profile of McKinnon by Yelena Shuster for *Columbia College Today* (Mar./Apr. 2007). The next year McKinnon took to dressing up as Pippi Longstocking, and the following year as Snow White,

David Livingston/Getty Images

before her teachers made her stop around second grade.

McKinnon and her younger sister, who was also into playing dress-up and doing voices, watched *Saturday Night Live* together as children. They would also record the show on videotape so that they could rewatch it, and McKinnon would even transcribe some of her favorite skits so she and her sister could reenact them exactly as written. McKinnon was particularly inspired by the *SNL* female cast members, most notably Ana Gasteyer, Molly Shannon, and Cheri Oteri. Though quite different and talented in their own way, the three actors shared a combination of sensitivity and fearlessness, the latter of which especially would become a notable attribute of McKinnon's performances. McKinnon's parents, who also had a talent for doing voices, were very encouraging of their daughters' extracurricular activities. The girls took fun seriously. In addition to her creative and musical pursuits, however, McKinnon had another side to her curiosity: she was obsessed with science. She was particularly fascinated by astrophysics and quantum mechanics. She would take apart and put together circuit boards and other electronics, though, as she said later, she gave up any ambition of becoming a scientist by the time she was in high school because she was not very good at math.

Her high school years were at times difficult. During freshman year, she told Shuster, McKinnon realized she was gay, but she told almost no one in school. She told her parents when she was fifteen, and her sister three years later. She told Schuster that no one was openly gay at her school. Students freely used "gay" as a derogatory term, and teachers sometimes even "made fun of gay people" themselves, McKinnon said, so it didn't feel safe for her to come out, and she wanted to protect her younger sister from ridicule. She graduated from high school in 2002, after which she went to study acting in New York City.

COMEDY AT COLUMBIA

McKinnon majored in theater at Columbia University, where over the course of four years she played dozens of characters in various stage productions. In college McKinnon began to express herself even more—not just as an actor but also as an out gay person. She found the environment more open, and unlike high school, she met other lesbian, gay, bisexual, or transgender (LGBT) people. She learned a lot about sketch comedy and improvisation during her years performing in the *Varsity Show*, an annual university production that satirizes various aspects of life at Columbia University. For her thesis, she created a one-woman show called *The Samantha Show*, which she put on during the early part of her senior year. The show was a combination of her thoughts, feelings, and many diverse characters. Her last semester at Columbia was even busier. Not only did she cofound the comedy troupe Tea Party, she also auditioned for the television sketch comedy show *The Big Gay Sketch Show*.

THE BIG GAY SKETCH SHOW

The Big Gay Sketch Show was produced by Rosie O'Donnell and ran for three seasons on the Logo network, which was created by MTV to appeal particularly to those who identified themselves as LGBT. Starting in April 2007, the show ran for three seasons. "It was an important milestone to have a gay sketch show," McKinnon told Schuster. "Comedy is important to me and to have a show that is just about how funny it is to be gay seems like a good thing. I was desperate to be involved in that." McKinnon got a chance to show off her uncanny ability to do impressions with her own twist. Among others, she did such sketches as "40 Dollars a Day with Rachel Ray," in which she went around New York City as celebrity chef Rachel Ray, "Gay Boy at Christmas," in which she played a young British royal who wants a vagina for Christmas, "Girls Gone Wilde," featuring her as one of the wild girls of Oscar Wilde, "Lesbian Speed Dating," in which she and another gay woman get along so well during a speed-dating session that they decide to move in together, and "War on War," in which McKinnon is part of a folk duo that sings such lines as, "We'll start an army of understanding, and drop hope bombs from above," all while smiling sweetly and sincerely.

UPRIGHT CITIZENS BRIGADE

For about two years, starting in 2010, McKinnon performed in New York City at the sketch and improv comedy group Upright Citizens Brigade (UCB), cofounded by Amy Poehler before her days as a cast member on *Saturday Night Live*. McKinnon once again got to demonstrate her talent, performing in sketches in which members of the *Jersey Shore* reality show explain the novel *The Catcher in the Rye*; another sketch in which she plays a calm radio announcer who gets overly specific about what to do in various emergencies, such as an earthquake; and one in which she played musician and poet Patti Smith in a VH1 *Behind the Music* parody about the Hard Rock Café. In addition to appearing in dozens of recorded sketches, McKinnon also had three one-woman shows at UCB: *Disenchanted*, *Best Actress*, and *Kate McKinnon on Ice*.

SATURDAY NIGHT LIVE

McKinnon's debut on *Saturday Night Live*, the popular NBC sketch comedy show, was in April 2012. It didn't take long for viewers to notice her great talent for—seemingly very easily—being able to manipulate her voice, facial expressions, and body language to suit a particular character. After a few years on the show, McKinnon gained special attention and recognition for her impersonation of Hillary Clinton, who started her second campaign for the presidency of the United States in April 2015. As Ian Crouch of the *New Yorker* (13 Apr. 2015) noted, *Saturday Night Live* has seen many cast members impersonate Clinton over the course of her career as First Lady, US senator from New York, secretary of state, and presidential candidate—among them Janeane Garofalo, Ana Gasteyer, Amy Poehler, and Vanessa Bayer. Yet McKinnon's impersonation, the way she embodied Clinton's seriousness and attempts at lightheartedness, was very special: her Clinton, wrote Crouch, is simultaneously "stiff and robotic" yet also "full of sexuality and swagger." In fact, wrote Crouch, McKinnon's Clinton impression is "already among the best impersonations of a politician ever to appear on the show—joining a list of greats that includes Dana Carvey as George H. W. Bush, Phil Hartman and Darrell Hammond as Bill Clinton, Will Ferrell as George W. Bush, and Tina Fey as Sarah Palin."

McKinnon has played dozens of characters, some famous (or infamous) and some not. Examples of the former include tennis champion Billie Jean King, pop star Justin Bieber, and German chancellor Angela Merkel. McKinnon's Merkel is very different from the German chancellor's public persona—serious, confident. Her Merkel is a bit sad and lonely and deeply envious of how cool US president Barack Obama is. McKinnon's parody of Justin Bieber had her impersonating the pop star's real ad for Calvin Klein: that was in a sense a double (or even triple) impersonation, because she had to impersonate someone with a very affected public persona acting in an ad, which is itself a kind of performance. Some of McKinnon's other notable performances include the buddy-cop parody "Dyke & Fats" and the tongue-in-cheek music video "(Do It on My) Twin Bed," which has several female *SNL* cast members singing about bringing their boyfriends home for the holidays and then having sex on what used to be their childhood bed. In that video, McKinnon's seductive over-the-top sincerity is infectious. And as the cowriter of the lyrics for the song in the sketch, McKinnon received her first Emmy Award nomination, in 2014, for outstanding original music and lyrics. Also that year, as well as the following year, McKinnon received Emmy Award nominations for outstanding supporting actress in a comedy series for her work on *SNL* before winning the award in 2016.

GHOSTBUSTERS

In 2016, McKinnon costarred in the remake of the film *Ghostbusters*. She played nuclear engineer Jillian Holtzmann alongside fellow *SNL* cast member Leslie Jones, who played Patty Tolan, as well as *SNL* alumna Kristen Wiig, who played Erin Gilbert; and Melissa McCarthy, who played Abby Yates. Yet despite playing the Ghostbuster with the fewest lines and simplest backstory, wrote Kyle Buchanan for the website *Vulture* (12 July 2016), McKinnon actually gives the best performance. "The remarkable thing is that on paper," wrote Buchanan, "it wouldn't appear that McKinnon has much to do. The other three Ghostbusters . . . all have actual character arcs, and each proves to be a crucial plot-mover. Holtzmann, on the other hand, is mostly consigned to reaction shots and non sequiturs. No matter: McKinnon makes a banquet of them." She manages to be goofy, funny, sexy and charming—all at once. "Nearly everything turns her on," wrote Buchanan, "including dangerous weaponry and her fellow Ghostbusters, and her free-floating sexual swagger is likely to inspire ardor from the audience, too." In her review of the movie for the *New York Times* (10 July 2016), Manohla Dargis wrote that although no one of the four female leads "dominates" the movie, McKinnon "comes close." McKinnon, wrote Dargis, "makes for a sublime nerd goddess (she brings a dash of the young Jerry Lewis to the role with a glint of Amy Poehler)."

SUGGESTED READING

Buchanan, Kyle. "Why Kate McKinnon Is the *Ghostbusters* Breakout." *Vulture*. New York Media, 12 July 2016. Web. 15 Sept. 2016.

Crouch, Ian. "Kate McKinnon's Genius Hillary Impersonation." *New Yorker*. Condé Nast, 13 Apr. 2015. Web. 15 Sept. 2016.

Itzkoff, Dave. "Kate McKinnon on 'Ghostbusters,' 'S.N.L.' and Hillary Clinton." *New York Times*. New York Times, 3 Aug. 2016. Web. 15 Sept. 2016.

Shuster, Yelena. "One Funny Voice at a Time." *Columbia College Today*. Columbia University, Mar./Apr. 2007. Web. 15 Sept. 2016.

SELECTED WORKS

The Big Gay Sketch Show, 2006–10; *UCB Comedy Originals*, 2010–11; *Saturday Night Live*, 2012– ; *Ghostbusters*, 2016; *Masterminds*, 2016

—Dmitry Kiper

Steve McQueen

Date of birth: October 9, 1969
Occupation: Director, producer, and screenwriter

Steve McQueen is a British film director, producer, and screenwriter best known for his films *Hunger* (2008), *Shame* (2011), and *12 Years a Slave* (2013).

EARLY LIFE AND EDUCATION

Steven Rodney McQueen was born on October 9, 1969, in Ealing, England, a working-class area outside of London. His parents had immigrated to England from Trinidad and Grenada. He attended Drayton Manor High School in Ealing, where he excelled at soccer and got along well with his peers, although he struggled with schoolwork because he is dyslexic. Due to a lazy eye, he wore an eye patch, which he believes stigmatized him early on, causing him to be placed in slower classes in school.

McQueen became interested in the arts as a child, despite his father's wishes that he focus on becoming an electrical engineer. McQueen took advanced-level art classes at Ealing's Hammersmith and West London College, and he was later accepted into the Chelsea College of Arts in London to study painting. He then moved on to the Goldsmiths College of Art of the University of London, where he first began experimenting with film on a Super 8 camera. He graduated from Goldsmiths in 1993.

McQueen took his passion for film to the United States, where he enrolled in New York University's Tisch School of the Arts in New York City. He dropped out after three months, however, because he was discouraged with the school's emphasis on the technical rather than the creative aspects of film.

FILM CAREER

McQueen directed several short, experimental films during the 1990s and early 2000s, which he used to address controversial themes such as race, homosexuality, and aggression. The black-and-white silent short film *Bear* (1993) depicts two naked men, one of whom is McQueen, circling each other in an aggressive yet seductive manner. *Just above My Head* (1995) features the top of McQueen's head as he walks up a street and is a reference to American writer James Baldwin's novel *Just above My Head* (1979), which confronts the issues of homosexuality, individuality, and racism.

The Museum of Modern Art in New York commissioned his short film *Deadpan* (1997), which is an homage to comedic actor Buster Keaton's silent film *Steamboat Bill, Jr.* (1928). In *Deadpan*, a barn's gable wall collapses on top of McQueen, who emerges unharmed because he was standing where a window would be. The short received critical acclaim, and McQueen won the 1999 Turner Prize, which is awarded to a British visual artist under the age of fifty.

In 2006 McQueen became an official war artist and spent six days in Basra, Iraq, documenting the Iraq War. This experience inspired his project *Queen and Country*, which depicts the portraits of 155 dead British soldiers on sheets of stamps. McQueen campaigned for them to become official stamps, but the British Royal Mail denied the petition. He explained that it was not a political statement but a way for the effects of war to enter people's everyday lives.

McQueen then wrote and directed his first feature-length film, *Hunger* (2008), which presents a dramatization of the 1981 hunger strikes in the Maze Prison of Northern Ireland. Bobby Sands, a volunteer with the Provisional Irish Republican Army (IRA), led the strikes in the hope of regaining political prisoner status. After sixty-six days of striking, Sands died.

Hunger debuted at the Cannes Film Festival on May 15, 2008, and received critical acclaim, winning the Camera d'Or award for best first feature film. The film appeared on many Top Ten lists for the year and received numerous awards and nominations. Many critics applauded a seventeen-minute take in the film, one of the longest in cinema history.

McQueen reunited with *Hunger* star Michael Fassbender for his next film, *Shame* (2011). Fassbender plays a successful New York executive struggling with sex addiction. The majority of critics praised the film, which went on to win and be nominated for numerous awards. McQueen was appointed Commander of the Order of the British Empire in 2011.

For his next film, McQueen adapted the autobiography of Solomon Northup, a free African American during the time of slavery in the United States who was abducted and sold into slavery in the South. *12 Years a Slave* (2013) was praised by critics for its acting, direction, and unflinching look at the brutality endured by slaves. The film was nominated for and won many awards, including the Golden Globe for best picture.

IMPACT

McQueen likes to take his time making films and is a sought-after director for actors and others in the industry. With his first three feature films, he garnered numerous accolades from critics and award associations. His short films and artwork have been exhibited around the globe. In a relatively short amount of time, he has proven himself a crossover talent who successfully transitioned from the art world to the film industry.

PERSONAL LIFE

In 1997 McQueen relocated from London to Amsterdam, where he lives with his partner, cultural critic Bianca Stigter. They have a son, Dexter, and a daughter, Alex. He has stated that he gets some of his best ideas while cooking or cleaning his house.

SUGGESTED READING

Horn, John. "*12 Years a Slave* Has Meant Sacrifice and Rewards for Director Steve McQueen." *Los Angeles Times*. Tribune Company, 21 Feb. 2014. Web. 15 Apr. 2014.

Kino, Carol. "Intense Seeker of Powerful Elegance." *New York Times*. New York Times, 28 Jan. 2010. Web. 15 Apr. 2014.

Palmer, Alun. "Steve McQueen: Struggle to Succeed of Golden Globe Winner Tipped to Be Britain's Most Successful Movie Director." *Mirror*. MGN, 15 Jan. 2014. Web. 15 Apr. 2014.

Sooke, Alastair. "Venice Biennale: Steve McQueen Interview." *Telegraph*. Telegraph Media Group, 29 May 2009. Web. 15 Apr. 2014.

Weiner, Jonah. "The Liberation of Steve McQueen." *Rolling Stone*. March 2014: 44–47. Print.

SELECTED WORKS

Bear, 1993; *Five Easy Pieces,* 1995; *Just above My Head,* 1996; *Deadpan,* 1997; *Hunger,* 2008; *Shame,* 2011; *12 Years a Slave,* 2013

—*Patrick G. Cooper*

K. Michelle

Born: March 4, 1982
Occupation: Singer

The singer Kimberly Michelle Pate, better known by her stage name K. Michelle, gained attention and notoriety as the star of VH1's reality television series *Love & Hip Hop: Atlanta*, from 2011 to 2013. She was blunt, ambitious, and ready to fight, which drew attention. In 2014 she returned to reality television as the star of her own VH1 spin-off series, *K. Michelle: My Life*. However, she is also an accomplished singer who has put out two genre-crossing albums: *Rebellious Soul* (2013) and *Anybody Wanna Buy a Heart?* (2014), both of which peaked in the top ten of multiple Billboard album charts. Though generally considered an R & B singer, K. Michelle has also been influenced by classical, soul, and country music. In reference to the latter, her forthcoming album is tentatively titled "I Ain't White but I Hope You Like." True to herself, she seeks to provoke and to grab people's attention.

EARLY LIFE AND EDUCATION

Kimberly Michelle Pate grew up in Memphis, Tennessee, showing both a talent and a strong interest in music and the performing arts from a young age. In the first few years of schooling she took gymnastics and swimming classes, as well as piano. Pate was also an aspiring singer: from the age of two or three, she was already trying to sing. She went on to train with the vocal coach Bob Westbrook, who was well known as a children's vocal teacher (some of his other pupils included Britney Spears and Justin Timberlake). As a child Pate had a room with a large walk-in closet, which her parents envisioned she could use to practice her singing, a kind of miniature "soundproof" studio.

Pate attended Overton High School, which has a strong focus on performing and creative arts. According to Khari Bowman of *Teen Appeal* (5 May 2015), the school newspaper, Pate was a member of the show choir and the student government association; she was also crowned Miss Overton High School during one of the school's annual beauty pageants.

Upon graduating from high school in 2000, Pate attended Florida Agricultural and Mechanical University, commonly known as Florida A&M University, in Tallahassee, Florida. During her audition for the school, she did some yodeling—a fact that she has mentioned often throughout her career—and got a scholarship as a result. At the university she minored in music and majored in psychology. She was also a member of the Delta Sigma Theta sorority. During her time in college, Pate became pregnant,

Therealdee/CC BY-SA 4.0/Wikimedia Commons

but she continued to go to class. Once her baby boy, Chase, was born, Pate continued to study and work hard. Only during the last few months of her time at Florida A&M did she have her parents come pick up her newborn so that she could focus on finishing her bachelor's degree. She graduated in 2004.

FIRST SINGLES AND PERSONAL STRUGGLES

Pate was discovered by Mickey "MempHitz" Wright, a Jive Records executive, and was signed to the record label in 2009. During her time at Jive Records, Pate put out two swaggering, sassy singles: "Self Made" and "Fakin' It." The latter featured a guest appearance by the rapper and singer Missy Elliott. Also, soon after signing with Jive Records, Pate was introduced to the R & B star R. Kelly, someone she had idolized for a long time; Pate admired R. Kelly as not only a singer but also a songwriter. She appeared as a singer (in a duet) on R. Kelly's song "Love Is," from his album *Love Letter* (2010), but the duet did little to seriously advance her career.

Pate had bigger issues to deal with, and they intertwined both her personal and professional lives. She had become romantically involved with Wright, but after a few years the relationship fell apart. Pate accused Wright of domestic violence. (He denied it, was never charged, and ultimately ended up suing Pate for defamation, though he eventually dropped the lawsuit.) Pate's debut album, tentatively titled *Pain Medicine*, was to be released on Jive Records, but the deal fell through.

Pate found herself at a low point. She decided she had to do something, so she joined the VH1 reality show *Love & Hip Hop: Atlanta*, which followed a cast consisting mostly of women who wanted to make it in the music business. She explained why she joined the show to Yolanda Sangweni for *Essence* magazine (21 Aug. 2013): "I wanted something. I had nowhere to be. I was sleeping on my manager's couch, didn't have any money. . . . I was worried about my brand and Marlon [Wayans] said, 'What brand? You ain't got no brand.' That was a real saving. I had nothing to lose. And I needed the money." Being on that show did indeed bring her some attention, even notoriety. By the time her first album debuted, the name K. Michelle was associated in pop culture with someone short-tempered and quick to fight, but also driven and ambitious.

REBELLIOUS SOUL

When Pate put out her first singles in 2009, she was often compared to the singers Keyshia Cole and Mary J. Blige. She welcomed these comparisons, but when it came time to put out her debut album, she wanted to show that her musical tastes and styles were her own and that she was a unique performer. In an interview that appeared on YouKnowIGotSoul.com (1 Feb. 2013), Pate had some personal and characteristically blunt things to say about her new album and the musical environment in which it was released. She named her debut album *Rebellious Soul* (2013), because, she said, that describes her personality. Also, her approach to songwriting, she insisted, is totally her own: "I'm definitely not following the latest trends on this album, because I don't even listen to the radio. It's going to stick to some R & B roots, but I am a classically trained pianist and I do play guitar and I'm a very musical person as far as different sounds and different things I love to hear. I don't like people handing me a track and saying to write to it, everything is being created and centered around me. I'll get a piano and I'll start to sing and I'll hand it over to a producer to produce."

For those, critics and fans both, who had been following K. Michelle's career as either a singer or reality star, few were likely surprised by the directness and honesty of her first album. The album showed a variety of musical influences, given both Pate's experience and passion. It mixes elements of not only R & B and soul music but also classical and country music. (She has stated that she likes the storytelling aspect of country music.) The songs ranged from the soulful "V.S.O.P." to the confessional "I Don't Like Me," which delves into feelings of self-hatred and doubt. In his review of the album for the *Guardian* (8 Aug. 2013), Alex Macpherson observed that *Rebellious Soul*, though it does not "have quite the impact" of K. Michelle's 2010 mixtape, has "enough to confirm the emergence of a vital voice." Jon Caramanica, for the *New York Times* (12 Aug. 2013), reminded his readers that despite K. Michelle's reputation for having a "quick temper" on the reality show *Love & Hip Hop: Atlanta*, the singer has a "boatload of genuine talent." "Unlike her earlier singles," wrote Caramanica, "her debut record was less about swagger and more about 'the confidence of survival.'" The album quickly rose to number one on the Billboard top R & B albums chart and to number two on the Billboard Top 200 chart. The record also led to the creation of *Rebellious Soul Musical*, a musical directed by renowned Golden Globe–winning actor Idris Elba.

ANYBODY WANNA BUY A HEART?

Pate's second album, also under the stage name K. Michelle, was titled *Anybody Wanna Buy a Heart?* (2014). Like her debut album, the record combined several influences, such as R & B, soul, and country music. She successfully collaborated with the duo Pop & Oak, Eric Hudson, and Lil' Ronnie. The album also had a range of approaches, from the more upbeat and erotic "Something about the Night" to the big ballad "How Do You Know?" and the country infused "God I Get It." In 2014, *Rolling Stone* magazine put the album on its twenty best R & B albums list, noting that this "Southern queen proves she's more than a one-sound emoticon," referring to her multigenre approach. Michael Arceneaux, in a review for *Complex* (11 Dec. 2014), offered this paradoxical conclusion: "Despite [*Anybody Wanna Buy a Heart?*] not packing as hard a punch as we're used to hearing from K. Michelle, she's never been more impactful." He then added, "It is an excellent album, and while it may have taken her longer than she'd like to make this known, it cannot be denied any longer: K. Michelle is leaps and bounds ahead of many of her peers." The album rose to number six on the Billboard Top 200 chart and to number two on the R & B albums chart.

Despite finding success in the music world, Pate decided not to leave the world of reality television behind. In the fall of 2014 she appeared as the star of the VH1 spin-off reality TV series *K. Michelle: My Life*. The following year the series was renewed for another season. During its first season, the series was ranked the number-three new cable reality show for women between the ages of eighteen and forty-nine, according to *Variety*.

SUGGESTED READING

Bowman, Khari. "Overton High Visited by Former Student K. Michelle." *Teen Appeal*. U of Memphis Dept. of Journalism, 5 May 2015. Web. 12 Jan. 2016.

Caramanica, Jon. "CDs from K. Michelle and Leo Genovese." *New York Times*. New York Times, 12 Aug. 2013. Web. 11 Jan. 2016.

Michelle, K. Interview by Yolanda Sangweni. "Exclusive: K. Michelle Talks New Image, New Album, and Why Keyshia Cole Told Her to 'Get off Twitter.'" *Essence*. Essence Communications, 21 Aug. 2013. Web. 11 Jan. 2016.

Michelle, K. Interview. "K. Michelle Talks 'Rebellious Soul', Winning Once She Stopped Caring, Reality TV." *YouKnowIGotSoul.com*. YouKnowIGotSoul.com, 1 Feb. 2013. Web. 11 Jan. 2016.

—*Dmitry Kiper*

Ruthie Ann Miles

Born: 1983
Occupation: Actor

Walter McBride/WireImage/Getty Images

Stage actor Ruthie Ann Miles made her Broadway debut in the spring of 2015, and won her first Tony Award a few months later. She won the Tony Award for best featured actress in a musical for her role as Lady Thiang in the revival of the classic Rodgers and Hammerstein musical, *The King and I*. Miles, who is half Korean and half white, has spoken about the difficulties that confront actors of Asian descent seeking success on the stage. "We have a lot of amazing, talented people who just don't have a platform," Miles told Carey Purcell of *Playbill* (8 June 2015) about the community of Asian actors. "They don't have an opportunity. But they are working. They are going to class. They are hitting those auditions and doing readings, and they are striving and working so hard. But there's no place to practice, which is on the stage. There aren't enough roles. There aren't enough opportunities." Miles herself has been extraordinarily lucky, landing the role of Imelda Marcos, the former first lady of the Philippines, in the first readings of *Here Lies Love*, an immersive musical composed by artist and musician David Byrne and British DJ Fatboy Slim. Miles went on to originate the role in the show's Off-Broadway run in 2013, earning both a Lucille Lortel Award and a Theatre World Award for her work. Miles drew on her experience playing the power-hungry Marcos when she was cast as Lady Thiang, the King's chief wife, in *The King and I*, but she looked to the spirit of her maternal grandmother, Wang HeeSook, for emotional inspiration.

EDUCATION AND EARLY CAREER

Miles was born in Arizona in 1983 and spent her early years in Korea. She and her mother, Esther Wong, a church pianist, settled in Honolulu, Hawaii, when Miles was in the second grade. Miles attended Jefferson and Kaahumanu elementary schools, then entered Washington Intermediate before entering Kaimuki High School in the late 1990s. Under the guidance of a few teachers, Miles developed a love for music and theater that she nurtured through after-school programs. "I had a single mom, so extracurricular activities were my life," she told Yu Shing Ting for *MidWeek*, a Honolulu weekly (23 June 2013). "And the more I keep in touch with my band directors and theater directors, and listening to their programs die, it really saddens me." Miles was an aspiring music teacher—she and her mother used to listen to the radio and try to harmonize their voices with the singers—but after she landed the role of a showgirl named Linda Low in the Rodgers and Hammerstein musical *Flower Drum Song*, she changed her mind. "That was *the* moment," she told Marc Snetiker for *Broadway.com* (10 May 2013). Miles had been bitten by the acting bug. After graduating from Kaimuki in 2001, Miles enrolled at Southern Oregon University in Ashland before transferring to Palm Beach Atlantic University in Florida. She graduated with a degree in musical theater and moved to New York City to attend New York University in 2005. She earned her master's degree in musical performance in 2007.

Like most musical theater actors, Miles got her start performing as an understudy and touring on the national circuit, appearing in *Annie* and *Sweeney Todd*. In the latter, Miles played rival barber Adolfo Pirelli, a role that required her to play the piano, accordion, and flute onstage. In 2009 she was an ensemble member and understudy for the adult puppet show *Avenue Q*. She also appeared in the 1970 musical *Two by*

Two, based on the Clifford Odets play *The Flow-ering Peach*, but in 2011, when she began work-shops for a musical written by Talking Heads musician David Byrne and DJ Fatboy Slim, she was still taking whatever roles came her way to keep working.

HERE LIES LOVE

Here Lies Love, an immersive disco musical about the life of former first lady of the Philip-pines Imelda Marcos, was originally conceived in 2010 as a concept album. "I read that Imelda Marcos loved going to discos and that she had a mirror ball in her New York apartment and turned the roof of the palace in Manila into a disco," Byrne told Allan Kozinn for the *New York Times* (4 Apr. 2013). "Here's a kind of music that's hedonistic and transcendent, that transports you to another world, and to me that captures some of what a powerful person is feeling. So it seemed like a natural soundtrack to this particular megalomaniac's story." Mar-cos, wife of the late Ferdinand Marcos, is best known for her prodigious shoe collection, which became a symbol of her husband's wasteful and brutal rule. Miles signed onto *Here Lies Love* early on in the project, and for two years, Byrne reworked the story and score while the cast performed for private audiences. In 2012 an early version of the show enjoyed a run at the Massachusetts Museum of Contemporary Art.

Byrne contacted Oskar Eustis, the artistic director of New York's Public Theater, and ar-ranged for the theater to produce the musical in 2013. The trappings of the production, directed by Alex Timbers, were a bit unusual: the theater was transformed into a 1970s disco, and the au-dience was invited to stand for the whole ninety-minute show and dance to the music. The action took place at various places in the room, so the audience had to be in constant motion to follow the story. *Here Lies Love* might have been physi-cally taxing for actors and audiences alike, but it was a critical and popular hit, as was Miles's por-trayal of Marcos. "Miles is a knockout as Imelda, never allowing us to lose sight of that needy girl desperate to be loved as she makes her way from beauty pageant winner to politician's wife and ruthlessly ambitious, self-professed 'people's star—star and slave,'" Adam Green wrote in his review for *Vogue* magazine (24 Apr. 2013). "Avoiding any hint of camp or condescension, she brings such disarming sincerity and simplic-ity to the role that she allows us to feel both re-pelled and sympathetic." Ben Brantley, for the *New York Times* (24 Apr. 2013), wrote that Miles was the "ideal" Marcos.

THE KING & I

Soon after the first run of *Here Lies Love*, Miles landed the role of Lady Thiang in the classic 1951 Rodgers and Hammerstein musical *The King and I*. Based on a true story, the musical follows a British widow named Anna Leonowens who travels to the court of the king of Siam (pres-ent-day Thailand) in the 1860s to serve as a tutor for the king's children. The 2015 revival was di-rected by Bartlett Sher, a 2008 Tony Award win-ner for best director of a musical for his revival of *South Pacific*. Kelli O'Hara, who played the lead in that production, was cast as Anna, and Ken Watanabe, the famous Japanese actor, made his American stage debut as King Mongkut. Miles played Lady Thiang, the king's first wife. Lady Thiang loves the king so much that she rejects Anna's efforts to convince her of her own power-lessness within the kingdom. Lady Thiang's role in the musical is small—though her solo bal-lad, "Something Wonderful," is one of the most popular songs in the Rodgers and Hammerstein oeuvre—but Miles used that slightness to her advantage, imbuing those moments when she is not speaking with her watchful presence. Lady Thiang is a judicious diplomat whom Miles once compared to former first lady and secretary of state Hillary Clinton, but she is also a woman of surprising emotional depth who is capable of rendering her "Something Wonderful" ode to the king as an "exquisite expression of romantic real-ism that could be the show's anthem," Brantley wrote in his review for the *Times* (16 Apr. 2015).

Sher's production of *The King and I* won four Tony Awards in 2015, including trophies for Miles (best performance by an actress in a featured role in a musical) and O'Hara (best performance by an actress in a leading role in a musical) as well as best costume design in a musical and best revival of a musical. When her name was announced at the awards ceremony, a flustered Miles read a prepared speech from her cell phone in which she thanked everyone from her costars to several high school teach-ers. The same year, she earned the Outer Critics Circle Award for featured actress in a musical. In preparation for the role, Miles looked to the spirit of her grandmother who lived through the Korean War. "She lived through hunger and dis-ease. She took care of my grandfather and basi-cally sacrificed her whole life to help the family survive," Miles told Harry Haun for *Playbill* (7 Aug. 2015). But like Lady Thiang, Miles's grand-mother led the family "in a way that was not loud but very passionate."

PERSONAL LIFE

Miles is married to Jonathan Blumenstein, an economic consultant, and they have a daugh-ter named Abigail. Miles was pregnant with Abigail during the early run of *Here Lies Love*. Miles and her family, including her mother, live in Brooklyn.

SUGGESTED READING

Brantley, Ben. "A Rise to Power, Disco Round Included." Rev. of *Here Lies Love*, by David Byrne and Fatboy Slim. Public Theater, New York. *New York Times*. New York Times, 23 Apr. 2013. Web. 16 Feb. 2016.

Brantley, Ben. "'The King and I,' Back on Broadway." Rev. of *The King and I*, by Richard Rodgers and Oscar Hammerstein II. Lincoln Center—Vivian Beaumont Theatre, New York. *New York Times*. New York Times, 16 Apr. 2015. Web. 16 Feb. 2016.

Haun, Harry. "Learn How Ruthie Ann Miles' Grandmother Helped Guide Her to a Tony-Winning Turn in *The King & I*." *Playbill*. Playbill, 7 Aug. 2015. Web. 16 Feb. 2016.

Kozinn, Allan. "Imelda Marcos, With a Beat." Rev. of *Here Lies Love*, by David Byrne and Fatboy Slim. Public Theater, New York. *New York Times*. New York Times, 4 Apr. 2013. Web. 16 Feb. 2016.

Miles, Ruthie Ann. "Ruthie Ann Miles on Playing Imelda Marcos in *Here Lies Love*, Being a New Mom and the Future of Theater." Interview by Marc Snetiker. *Broadway.com*. Broadway.com, 10 May 2013. Web. 16 Feb. 2016.

Purcell, Carey. "'There Aren't Enough Roles,' Says Tony Winner Ruthie Ann Miles on Diversity in the Theatre." *Playbill*. Playbill, 8 June 2015. Web. 16 Feb. 2016.

Ting, Yu Shing. "Taking Imelda to the Big Apple." *MidWeek*. MidWeek, 23 July 2013. Web. 16 Feb. 2016.

—*Molly Hagan*

George Miller

Born: March 3, 1945
Occupation: Director and screenwriter

George Miller's body of work is perhaps one of the more eclectic ones in Hollywood. A director, screenwriter, and major figure in Australian cinema, Miller first gained attention as the winner of an Australian short film contest in the early 1970s and burst onto the film scene later in the decade with *Mad Max* (1979), the first of several films featuring the titular character's adventures and struggles in a brutal, dystopian world. Although best known for the *Mad Max* films and their postapocalyptic aesthetic, Miller has never shied away from dramatically different projects, which have been as wide ranging as the comedic film *The Witches of Eastwick* (1987) and the medical drama *Lorenzo's Oil* (1992). Perhaps even more surprising, Miller is also well known for his family films, which include installments in the Babe and Happy Feet franchises. Indeed,

Gage Skidmore/CC BY-SA 3.0/Wikimedia Commons

Miller's eclectic résumé has raised a few eyebrows. "People do look at me weirdly," he told Terry Gross for National Public Radio (8 Feb. 2016). "Even my mother said, 'When you started making the *Babes* and *Happy Feet*s I thought you were calming down, in some way,' but then she saw the latest, *Fury Road*, [and] she said, 'Sometimes I wonder what goes on in your head.'"

For Miller, though, his unusual career trajectory makes perfect sense, as it has changed and shifted alongside the trajectory of his life. Timing is everything. A return to the world of *Mad Max*, for instance, could not happen until Miller was fully ready. "I definitely wasn't interested in making another *Mad Max* movie," he told Adam Sternbergh for *Vulture* (12 Feb. 2016) of his decision to make his critically acclaimed 2015 installment in the series, *Mad Max: Fury Road*. "But there was some strong gravitational pull to this story, and to the exercise of this film, which was to see whether we could take one continuous chase and see how much the audience could apprehend, moment to moment, about the characters, their relationships, and the world they were invited into. And I also wanted to see if I'd learned anything about making films in the interim."

EARLY LIFE AND EDUCATION

George Miller was born on March 3, 1945, in the state of Queensland, Australia. One of four sons born to Jim and Angela Miller, he has a fraternal twin brother named John. Miller and his brothers grew up in the town of Chinchilla, where their parents, both Greek immigrants, ran a general store.

The landscape and culture of Chinchilla made a lasting impression on Miller. "Completely flat roads. Loamy soil. Heat haze. Burnt land," he recalled to Paul Byrnes for *Australian Screen*. "And with a very intense car culture. I mean the main street of town and Saturday night were just the kids in the cars. By the time we were out of our teens, several of our peers had already been killed or badly injured in car accidents. And there was just those long flat roads where there was no speed limit and people would just go." Miller's observations of his surroundings in Chinchilla, as well as his memories of playing outdoors there as a child, played a key role in the development of the setting of his later *Mad Max* films. His interest in cinema, also developed during his childhood in Chinchilla, would likewise be formative.

The family eventually moved to the city of Sydney, where Miller attended Sydney Boys High School. After graduation, he enrolled in the University of New South Wales to study medicine. Although intent on becoming a doctor, he remained interested in film and experimented with making short films with his brother. Their short film *St. Vincent's Revue Film*, made in 1971, won a local contest and enabled Miller to attend a film workshop at the University of Melbourne. At the workshop Miller met Byron Kennedy, a fellow budding filmmaker who became one of his greatest creative partners. Miller and Kennedy collaborated on a short film titled *Violence in the Cinema, Part 1*, which premiered at the 1971 Sydney Film Festival. Although beginning to find success as a filmmaker, Miller nevertheless completed his medical residency at St. Vincent's Hospital in Sydney and worked for a while as a doctor. He was especially struck by his time working as an emergency doctor, in which role he became acutely aware of the injuries and deaths that frequently resulted from motorcycle and car accidents. "It kind of disturbed me quite a bit," he told Byrnes. Much like his childhood memories of Chinchilla, Miller's work as a doctor helped to shape the roots of the *Mad Max* series.

MAD MAX

Beginning in the mid-1970s, Miller and Kennedy worked to develop the film that would become *Mad Max*. The two developed the story together, and Miller went on to cowrite the screenplay with James McCausland and direct the film himself. After several years of development and fundraising, the filmmakers managed to scrape together the film's very low budget, which came to less than 400,000 Australian dollars.

Released in Australia in 1979 and in the United States early the following year, *Mad Max* stars then unknown Australian actor Mel Gibson as the titular Max Rockatansky, a police officer who confronts the marauding gangs of near-future, postapocalyptic Australia, where gasoline is scarce and fast vehicles are prized. "Basically they're allegorical stories in the same way that the classic Western was that," Miller told Gross of the *Mad Max* films. "Max . . . is that sort of wanderer in the wasteland, looking for some sense of meaning in a very stark world." Although polarizing among critics, the film proved financially successful thanks to both its positive public reception and its exceedingly low budget. It had a lasting influence on both Australian and global cinema, introducing Miller as a talented director and screenwriter, Gibson as a leading man, and *Mad Max*'s dystopian aesthetic as the model for countless pieces of media to come.

After the success of their first film, Miller and Kennedy teamed up to create the company Kennedy Miller Entertainment, which worked to develop a variety of films as well as television miniseries in Australia. The two collaborated once again on 1981's *Mad Max 2*, known in the United States as *Mad Max 2: The Road Warrior*. In 1983, however, prior to the filming of the third installment in the series, *Mad Max: Beyond Thunderdome* (1985), Kennedy was killed in a helicopter accident. The incident was deeply upsetting to Miller, who told Scott Foundas for *Variety* (2015) that he had considered Kennedy his "movie twin." Because of that, Miller hired director George Ogilvie to codirect *Mad Max: Beyond Thunderdome* and remained somewhat detached from the process himself.

BRANCHING OUT

Although best known for the Mad Max films, Miller began branching out significantly as a director and screenwriter in the mid-1980s and particularly began to explore television. Working as a director, screenwriter, or producer, depending on the project, he contributed to television miniseries such as 1984's *Bodyline* and *The Last Bastion*. Miller enjoyed directing and writing for television, as the medium granted him opportunities that film often did not. "It was a great thing to do because as a director I got to work with a lot of other directors, producers, and actors," he explained to Sternbergh. "The great thing about television is it has to be done quickly. You have to work fast."

Continuing to work in film as well, Miller gained further international attention with *The Witches of Eastwick* (1987), based on a novel by American writer John Updike, and *Lorenzo's Oil* (1992). The latter film is based on the true story of a young boy who developed the degenerative disease adrenoleukodystrophy and his parents' attempts to find a cure. Miller and cowriter Nick Enright were nominated for an Academy Award for best original screenplay for their work.

FAMILY FILMS

Based on the bulk of his work between 1979 and the early 1990s, Miller might have seemed an unlikely director and writer of family films. However, he proved successful in that subgenre beginning in 1995, when the film *Babe*, based on a screenplay by Miller and fellow writer Chris Noonan, was released. Adapted from a book by Dick King-Smith, the live-action film follows the adventures of a talking pig who learns to herd sheep. Miller and Noonan were nominated for an Academy Award for their screenplay, and the film itself was nominated for the award for best picture. Miller went on to cowrite and direct the film's 1998 sequel, *Babe: Pig in the City*. Miller further established himself as a talented creator of family films with the 2006 release of *Happy Feet*, an animated film about a dancing penguin that won an Academy Award for best animated feature film. He also directed the film's sequel, *Happy Feet 2* (2011).

RETURN TO THE WORLD OF *MAD MAX*

Following the release of *Mad Max: Beyond Thunderdome*, Miller's signature saga was presumed finished, and for over a decade Miller had little interest in revisiting the world of films. That began to change in the late 1990s, when Miller began to think about the concept that eventually became *Mad Max: Fury Road*, the fourth installment in the series. The process of developing the film was a lengthy one, subject to a number of delays and changes to the potential cast. Miller ultimately chose actor Tom Hardy to replace Gibson as Max and recruited Charlize Theron to play the warrior Furiosa. Although a variety of issues, including weather-related changes to the intended filming locations, delayed the film's production, the film was ultimately released worldwide in mid-2015, more than fifteen years after Miller began working on it.

In making the film, Miller sought to experiment with the possibilities of medium and genre. Essentially consisting of a lengthy car chase, *Mad Max: Fury Road* contains significantly less dialogue than many of its contemporaries. "Its basic antecedents are in silent cinema, which is something I became very interested in when I started making movies," Miller told Sternbergh. "The real [visual] language was defined during the silent cinema, which brought all the action and chase movies, the real Westerns, and particularly Harold Lloyd and Buster Keaton. So one of the things that drew me to *Fury Road* was to be able to go back into that area, and see what we can do now with all the tools that are available." Much like many modern action films, *Mad Max: Fury Road* heavily features visual effects. However, Miller and his team emphasized the use of practical effects work when possible in an attempt to give the film a greater feeling of authenticity. "It's a film in which we don't defy the laws of physics. It's real people in a real desert," he told NPR. "We chose to do it old school and that means going out to a remote location with endless deserts and have real vehicles and human beings in that landscape."

Mad Max: Fury Road met with significant critical acclaim. The film was nominated for ten Academy Awards, including the award for best picture, and won six of them, the most of any film that year. Miller announced in the spring of 2015 that he planned to follow the film with a sequel, tentatively titled *Mad Max: The Wasteland*.

PERSONAL LIFE

Miller married actor Sandy Gore in 1985. The two had a daughter prior to divorcing. He later married film editor Margaret Sixel, with whom he has two sons. Sixel has edited a number of Miller's films, including *Babe: Pig in the City*, *Happy Feet*, and *Mad Max: Fury Road*. She won an Academy Award for film editing for her work on *Fury Road*.

SUGGESTED READING

Calvert, Alana. "By George, He's Still One of Us—Chinchilla's George Miller." *Chinchilla News*. Australian Regional Media, 28 May 2015. Web. 15 June 2016.

Foundas, Scott. "Mad George." *Variety*. Variety, 2015. Web. 15 June 2016.

Maddox, Garry. "On the Set of *Mad Max: Fury Road* with Director George Miller." *Sydney Morning Herald*. Fairfax Media, 25 Apr. 2015. Web. 15 June 2016.

Miller, George. "George Miller." Interview by Andrew Denton. *Enough Rope with Andrew Denton*. Australian Broadcasting Corp., 20 Oct. 2008. Web. 15 June 2016.

Miller, George. "George Miller." Interview by Paul Byrnes. *Australian Screen*. Natl. Film and Sound Archive, n. d. Web. 15 June 2016.

Miller, George. "'Mad Max' Director George Miller: The Audience Tells You 'What Your Film Is.'" Interview by Terry Gross. *Fresh Air*. Natl. Public Radio, 8 Feb. 2016. Web. 15 June 2016.

Miller, George. "*Mad Max: Fury Road* Director George Miller on His Unlikely Oscar Contender and Even Unlikelier Career." Interview by Adam Sternbergh. *Vulture*. New York Magazine, 12 Feb. 2016. Web. 15 June 2016.

SELECTED WORKS

Violence in the Cinema, Part 1, 1971; *Mad Max*, 1979; *Mad Max 2: The Road Warrior*, 1981; *Mad Max: Beyond Thunderdome*, 1985; *The Witches of Eastwick*, 1987; *Lorenzo's Oil*, 1992; *Babe*, 1995; *Babe: Pig in the City*, 1998; *Happy Feet*, 2006; *Mad Max: Fury Road*, 2015   —*Joy Crelin*

Federica Mogherini

Born: June 16, 1973
Occupation: Politician

A virtual unknown outside of Italy, Federica Mogherini first came to international attention in February 2014, when she was appointed Italy's foreign minister. Six months later, Mogherini made headlines again for her election as the European Union's (EU) head of foreign affairs. The latter nomination drew sharp criticism from a number of EU Eastern member states, who were concerned by Mogherini's pro-Russian viewpoint. Her detractors also questioned her previous lack of foreign policy experience, which was limited to representing Italy in the parliamentary assemblies of both the North Atlantic Treaty Organization (NATO) and the Council of Europe (CoE).

However, Mogherini has her share of staunch defenders, including Chiara Moroni, a fellow member of the Italian parliament. "Federica is something rare in Italian politics: she got to where she is entirely on merit," she shared with James Panichi for *Politico* (24 Aug. 2014).

AN EARLY START IN POLITICS

Federica Mogherini was born on June 16, 1973, in Rome, Italy. Mogherini's father, Flavio Mogherini, was a renowned production designer-turned-film director who passed away when she was ten. Although she hailed from an artistic family, she grew up as more of an academic. In addition to attending a local high school that specialized in foreign languages, she joined the Federazione Giovanile Comunisti Italiani (FGCI), also known as the Federation of Young Italian Communists, in 1988. At Rome's Sapienza University, Mogherini studied political science and became a member of the European Community Organization of Socialist Youth (ECOSY). As part of the Erasmus student exchange program, she spent time abroad in Aix-en-Provence, France, at the Institute for Research and Studies on the Arab and Muslim World (IREMAM), where she wrote her thesis about the connection between Islamic politics and religion.

After graduating with honors in 1994, Mogherini embraced political activism. She volunteered with the Italian Recreational and Cultural Association (ARCI), promoting racial tolerance in cooperation with the Council of Europe's "All Different, All Equal" and "Nero e non solo!" (translated as "Black and not alone" or "Black and beyond") youth campaigns. Mogherini was subsequently elected to the Sinistra Giovanile in 1996, the youth wing of the Democratic Party of the Left (also known as the Partito Democratico della Sinistra or PDS); she also sat

Union Europea En Perù/Flickr/CC BY 2.0/Wikimedia Commons

on the European Youth Forum's board, in charge of welfare and social affairs.

EARLY CAREER IN FOREIGN AFFAIRS

Mogherini continued to climb up the party ranks in 2001, with her election to the national council of the Democrats of the Left (Democratici di Sinistra or DS), Italy's former Communist Party. Within two years Mogherini, who speaks French and English fluently, was handling foreign policy for the party. From 2003 to 2007 she supervised its European and international affairs division, under party leader, Piero Fassino. Mogherini's responsibilities involved preserving ties with other parties (the Party of European Socialists (PES), the Socialist International (SI), and the US Democratic Party), as well as overseeing relations with international peace movements in Afghanistan, Iraq, and the Middle East.

In 2007 she became a fellow of the German Marshall Fund of the United States, which fosters leadership and transatlantic relations development. That same year, Walter Veltroni, the former mayor of Rome and recently elected head of the newly founded Democratic Party (PD), formed by the union of the DS and Daisy (Margherita) parties, tapped Mogherini for a leadership post. She served on Veltroni's staff for the new political party.

JOINING THE ITALIAN PARLIAMENT

In 2008 Mogherini won her first election—to the Italian parliament's lower house, the Chamber of Deputies, where she represented the constituents of Veneto. During her first term, Mogherini was appointed secretary of the parliament's defense committee and represented her country in the Parliamentary Assembly of the Council of Europe (PACE), the council's advisory body on human rights and democracy. She also sat on the lower house committee on foreign affairs. In 2008 she also became a member of the Italian Institute for Foreign Affairs (IAI). In 2009 Dario Franceschini took over as chairman of the PD and Mogherini was given a position on his staff as well, with responsibilities pertaining to equal opportunities.

At the end of her first term, Mogherini was subsequently reelected to the Chamber of Deputies in February 2013. However, instead of representing Veneto, she served as a representative for the Emilia-Romagna constituency. In August Mogherini was voted in as head of the Italian delegation to the NATO Parliamentary Assembly, as well as vice-president of its political committee. Once again she occupied seats on the defense and foreign affairs committees. In December the newly elected Democratic Party leader Matteo Renzi—and former mayor of Florence—selected Mogherini to join his cabinet, where she oversaw European and international relations.

ITALY'S FOREIGN PRIME MINISTER
On February 14, 2014, amid a stagnating economy, high unemployment, and a growing debt crisis, Enrico Letta was ousted as Italy's prime minister. He was succeeded by revolt leader and fellow party member Renzi, who became the youngest minister in the history of the country—but also one lacking political experience on the national stage. Renzi's new center-left cabinet consisted of eight women, including Mogherini, whom he designated as minister of foreign affairs and international cooperation.

Mogherini was sworn in on February 22 and two weeks later, she traveled to Paris, France, to attend a gathering of diplomats from the West and Russia regarding Russia's military takeover of Crimea in Ukraine. Mogherini adopted a pro-Russian stance (due in part to Italy's heavy reliance on gas imports from Russia), calling for negotiations between Russia and its Ukrainian counterpart, while urging other European countries to be supportive of Kiev's new government. Reconciliation was also Mogherini's rallying cry at a March international conference supporting the future development of politically unstable Libya that she hosted. In front of a delegation of about forty fellow foreign ministers, including Libyan prime minister Ali Zeidan, Mogherini encouraged Libya's transition toward a democratic government and parliamentary elections.

Diplomacy was once again on the agenda during the March 2014 Nuclear Security Summit at The Hague in the Netherlands. Mogherini rubbed shoulders with President Obama at the conference, where the Italian delegation

agreed to dispose of its stockpile of uranium and plutonium. In March 2014 Mogherini played host once again to Lebanese foreign minister Gebran Bassil in preparation for an international conference later that year, recommending political support and military training for Lebanese armed forces to strengthen border security and prevent conflicts in Syria and Iraq from spreading into Lebanon. Mogherini played a part in negotiating the July 2014 release of Sudanese-born Meriam Ibrahim from prison in Sudan. Ibrahim had been sentenced to death for converting from Islam to Christianity—her husband's religion.

BECOMING THE EU'S FOREIGN POLICY CHIEF
Prior to the EU's summit in mid-July, Mogherini was mentioned as the top candidate to succeed the United Kingdom's Catherine Ashton as the high representative of the Union for Foreign Affairs and Security Policy. However, her lack of experience and pro-Russian stance prompted Poland and three Baltic member states to block Mogherini's appointment. Despite the opposition, Renzi increasingly lobbied for Mogherini.

In early August, Renzi sent a letter to EU Commissioner-elect Jean-Claude Juncker, formally nominating Mogherini as Italy's representative for EU Commissioner. Mogherini defended her eligibility for the position, Catherine Dunn of *International Business Times* (30 Aug. 2014) reported: "I'm a foreign minister of a G7 country. . . It's this year [been] twenty years I've been involved in European and foreign issues." Opposition waned once Donald Tusk, the former Polish prime minister and a hard-liner on Russia, was named European Council president. Ultimately, Mogherini impressed leaders with her focus on human rights and prevention, instead of mere crisis control, in foreign policy. By the end of the month, the PES had approved Mogherini's nomination and European Council head Herman Van Rompuy officially announced her as the new high representative and vice-president of the European Commission. At her press conference, Mogherini underscored the need for a diplomatic agreement between Russia and the Ukraine.

TAKING THE REINS
After taking office on November 1, 2014, Mogherini hit the ground running, visiting the West Bank, Gaza, and Israel to resurrect stalled Middle East peace talks. A month later she designated Ashton as her special advisor on nuclear negotiations with Iran. Mogherini also traveled to Kiev and Brussels, in an effort to tackle the ongoing Ukrainian crisis (the pro-Russian rebel occupation in the east) and recommend necessary economic, political, and judicial reforms. However, in January 2015 Mogherini courted

controversy for her proposal to lift Russia's economic sanctions and reengage with Russia—but only on the condition that it withdraw troops from the Ukrainian border. The approach drew criticism from several of EU's eastern European members (the United Kingdom, Poland, and the Baltic states, among others), who regarded it as too soft.

Mogherini's efforts against global terrorism would prove more successful. In July 2015 Mogherini announced the successful negotiation of a peaceful agreement between Iran and six world powers (China, France, Russia, Britain, the United States, and Germany) regarding Iran's nuclear program. In August she played mediator between former foes Serbia and Kosovo, reaching a landmark agreement to normalize relations.

By September 2015 Mogherini's focus had expanded to include the refugee crisis in both Africa and Europe, the latter of which she largely attributes to conflicts in Syria and Libya. She partnered with international companies and nongovernmental organizations (NGOs) to provide financial assistance to Syria, south Sudan, and the Central African Republic. Mogherini ended the year on a hopeful note, with the signing of the Skhirat Agreement, which seeks to unite the rival factions of Libya into one governing body.

For 2016 Mogherini's agenda includes strengthening Libya's political agreement; focusing on the Syrian and Middle East peace talks; as well as dealing with the refugee crisis and the war against global terrorism.

PERSONAL LIFE

Mogherini is married to Matteo Rebesani, with whom she has two children. She is quite active on social media. In addition to her blog, she keeps in touch with her constituents via Facebook and Twitter.

SUGGESTED READING

Agnew, Paddy. "New Foreign Affairs Chief Inexperienced." *Irish Times*. Irish Times, 1 Sept. 2014. Web. 12 Jan. 2016.

Dunn, Catherine. "Who Is Federica Mogherini, The 41-Year-Old Italian in Charge of the EU's Foreign Policy?" *International Business Times*. IBT Media, 30 Aug. 2014. Web. 13 Jan. 2016.

Milasin, Ljubomir. "Mogherini: Italy's Young Rising Star." *Yahoo! News*. Yahoo, 30 Aug. 2014. Web. 7 Jan. 2016.

Panichi, James. "Federica Mogherini—Italy's Scapegoat." *Politico*. Politico SPRL, 24 Aug. 2014. Web. 7 Jan. 2016.

—*Bertha Muteba*

Ernest Moniz

Born: December 22, 1944
Occupation: US Secretary of Energy

Ernest Moniz has served as the thirteenth United States secretary of energy since 2013 and is regarded by Democrats and Republicans alike as the most qualified person to have ever held that office. Because much of the energy secretary's role involves directing the handling and uses of nuclear materials, it helps tremendously that Moniz is a nuclear physicist with decades of experience. He is also adept at and experienced in maneuvering within political circles. Moniz has been praised for his ability to explain complex issues in a way that makes it easy for the average person to understand. He has also served on the faculty of the prestigious Massachusetts Institute of Technology (MIT) since 1973.

Although he has some critics, many quarters have praised him for helping Secretary of State John Kerry develop the framework of a nuclear nonproliferation treaty aimed at curtailing Iran's ambitious nuclear program. Many Western nations see Iran's nuclear program as extremely dangerous if left unchecked. "Now, if we are able to obtain a final deal that comports with the political agreement . . . then I'm absolutely positive that that is the best way to prevent Iran from getting a nuclear weapon," President Barack Obama explained in a news briefing, as quoted by Steven Mufson for the *Washington Post* (30 Apr. 2015), before the deal was signed on July 14, 2015, in Vienna, Austria. "And that's not my opinion, that's the

US Department of Energy

opinion of people like Ernie Moniz, my secretary of energy, who is a physicist from MIT and actually knows something about this stuff."

EARLY LIFE AND EDUCATION

Ernest Moniz was born in 1944 in Fall River, Massachusetts. Both his maternal and paternal grandparents were Portuguese immigrants from the Azores Islands. His father worked at the rubber manufacturing plant Firestone, and his mother was a homemaker. Fall River was a blue-collar town, a place from which a future physicist seemed unlikely to spring. Luckily for Moniz, MIT, one of the great scientific universities in the United States, was providing funds to local high schools in order to improve their physics curricula following the Soviet Union's successful launch of the world's first artificial satellite, *Sputnik*, in 1957. "Fortunately the physics teacher at the high school decided that the high school would be one of the pioneers, one of the guinea pigs," Moniz recalled to Matt Viser for the *Boston Globe* (22 Feb. 2014). "That's when I got hooked on physics."

Moniz attended Durfee High School in Fall River, where Moniz not only became devoted to physics but also played basketball and tennis. After graduating in 1962, he attended Boston College, a highly respected Jesuit Catholic research university, on a scholarship he received from his father's labor union. While there he edited the science journal, *Cosmos*, before going on to graduate summa cum laude in 1966 with a Bachelor of Science degree. He then attended Stanford University in California, one of the leading educational institutions in the country, where he earned his doctorate in theoretical physics in 1972.

PROFESSOR AT MIT

Since 1973 Moniz has been a faculty member of the Department of Physics at MIT. He served as department head from 1991 to 1995 and worked as the director of the Bates Linear Accelerator Center (now the Bates Research and Engineering Center), which is a multipurpose laboratory run by MIT researchers who conduct a number of experimental projects on the campus, including those in the areas of nuclear and particle physics. In 2006, Moniz became the founding director of the MIT Energy Initiative, and he has also served as the director of the MIT Laboratory for Energy and the Environment. In these positions, he looked for ways in which government policies and technologies could be improved to bring humanity closer to a low-carbon world through a mix of traditional fuels such as coal, oil, and natural gas as well as through innovative technologies such as nuclear power and wind and solar energy.

Moniz has also been widely praised by his MIT colleagues for his intellectual contributions as well as other positive attributes. "He has this marvelous sense of humor," former MIT president Susan Hockfield explained to Viser. "You don't feel as though you're getting browbeaten by him. You feel like he's teaching you. And he's a master teacher."

ENTERING THE POLITICAL ARENA

Moniz's first major role in government came during President Bill Clinton's first term. He first served as the associate director for science in the Office of Science and Technology Policy in the Executive Office of the President from 1995 to 1997. He was then promoted to undersecretary at the Department of Energy, where he served from 1997 until Clinton left office in January 2001. In this position Moniz had three major responsibilities: leading the science and energy programs at the department, working as the secretary's special negotiator on all matters related to the disposal of Russian nuclear weapons and materials, and reviewing and assessing all US nuclear stockpiles.

After leaving the Clinton administration and returning to MIT, Moniz continued to advise individual political leaders and members of Congress. For instance, he was among a group of experts who advised John Kerry during Kerry's presidential campaign for the 2004 election. He was also asked to testify before Congress, which did not make him popular among many environmentalists, who criticized Moniz for being too comfortable with using fossil fuels for interim periods. In a 2011 hearing before Congress, for example, Moniz described natural gas as a "bridge fuel" and "one of the most cost-effective means by which to maintain energy supplies while reducing CO_2 emissions," according to David J. Unger for the *Christian Science Monitor* (11 Feb. 2013). Moniz, however, bristles at the idea that he is not a good steward of the environment. "I frankly don't care what the mix of technology is, as long as it gets us to low carbon," Moniz said to Viser. "And I think we need every arrow in the quiver. . . . I have been out there as a climate warrior. But it's not good enough because we refuse to exclude part of the portfolio."

SECRETARY OF ENERGY

In March 2013, President Obama nominated Moniz to replace Steven Chu, the outgoing secretary of energy and a Nobel Prize–winning physicist. Although Moniz's nomination earned some grumbling among environmentalists, it was generally met with considerable praise. In *Forbes* (9 Mar. 2013), James Conca wrote, "There are not many who are better qualified, few with as much experience, and none with more chutzpah than Ernie Moniz. And he will need all three if he is to accomplish anything in a job that has been a standing nightmare for decades."

The US Senate confirmed Moniz's appointment with a unanimous vote on May 16, 2013. After being sworn in on May 22, Moniz officially took charge of the Department of Energy (DOE). In order to improve the department's functionality, he created a new position, undersecretary of management, and began recruiting top people from a score of backgrounds to fill key posts within the department. Two-thirds of the department's budget is devoted to the maintenance of the US nuclear weapons stockpile and the cleanup of radioactive materials from former sites of weapons development, yet that it not the department's only job. In addition to helping the nation develop cleaner alternative energy sources than those derived from fossil fuels, the DOE has a significant role in the nonproliferation of nuclear weapons around the world.

CONFRONTING IRAN'S NUCLEAR PROGRAM

For more than a decade, the international community has perceived the Iranian nuclear program as a threat to peace. Not only would the development of nuclear weapons by Iran destabilize the entire Middle East because it would motivate neighboring countries to build their own nuclear weapons, a nuclear-capable Iran would also be a threat to Israel, a key US ally and a nation that Iranian leaders have periodically threatened.

Since taking office in January 2009, President Obama has used diplomacy in efforts to prevent Iran from obtaining a nuclear weapon, which has been challenging because the United States and Iran have not had solid diplomatic relations since the late 1970s when the US embassy in the capital of Tehran was seized and fifty-two US citizens were held hostage from November 4, 1979, until January 20, 1981. After a series of sanctions and United Nations (UN) resolutions demanding that Iran stop enriching uranium, however, the Iranian government finally began a series of talks with the US government in March 2013.

After a September 2013 phone call between Obama and Hassan Rouhani, the newly elected Iranian president, the two sides began formal talks, with Secretary of State John Kerry leading the US delegation. At Kerry's side for much of the negotiations was Secretary Moniz, who negotiated with Dr. Ali Akbar Salehi of the Atomic Energy Organization of Iran. As Kerry and Iranian representatives discussed other aspects of the nuclear deal, including sanctions relief for Iran, Moniz and Salehi hammered out the technical aspects of the deal. During the negotiations, Moniz used teams of experts at the eight US national laboratories, which are part of the Department of Energy, to verify calculations pertaining to, for example, Iran's "breakout time"—the period needed for Iran to accumulate enough nuclear material to build a weapon. "Basically, our job was to address issues with major technical dimensions," Moniz said to Mufson. "What would an Iranian nuclear program look like over quite a few years to meet our requirements of confidence . . . to be able to identify quickly if in fact activity were not in the bounds of the agreement and to provide enough time in that eventuality that we and our partners could respond appropriately?"

In April 2015, a framework deal was announced: In exchange for sanctions relief, the Iranians agreed to curtail their nuclear program and allow inspections to ensure that no nuclear weapons would result from it. On July 14, 2015, after additional weeks of intense negotiations, the two sides signed a nonproliferation deal in Vienna, Austria, ending more than a decade of tensions over the Iranian nuclear program.

PERSONAL LIFE

Moniz has garnered quite a bit of attention on the Internet, due in large part to his hairstyle, which is longish and somewhat curled at the ends and has often been compared to George Washington's. Moniz explains that no one but his wife, Naomi Hoki, has cut his hair in decades. Moniz and his wife, who married in 1973, have an adult daughter, Katia, and at least two grandchildren. The Moniz family resides not in Washington but in Brookline, Massachusetts.

Moniz has appeared on numerous television programs, including *The Daily Show*, to discuss issues pertaining to energy, and he is notable for serving as the "designated survivor" for Obama's 2014 State of the Union Address—a practice put in place during the Cold War to allow for the continuance of government in case something catastrophic should happen while the president is addressing this joint session of Congress.

SUGGESTED READING

Conca, James. "Will Secretary Moniz Put Energy Back into the Department of Energy?" *Forbes*. Forbes.com, 9 Mar. 2013. Web. 9 Nov. 2015.

Moniz, Ernest. "A Nuclear Deal That Offers a Safer World." *Washington Post*. Washington Post, 12 Apr. 2015. Web. 9 Nov. 2015.

Mufson, Steven. "Energy Secretary Moniz Emerges as Obama's Secret Weapon in Iran Talks." *Washington Post*. Washington Post, 30 Apr. 2015. Web. 9 Nov. 2015.

Siegel, Robert. "U.S. Energy Secretary: Deal Keeps Iran Further Away from a Nuclear Weapon." *All Things Considered*. NPR, 16 July 2015. Web. 9 Nov. 2015.

Unger, David J. "Will Ernest Moniz Be the Next Energy Secretary?" *Christian Science Monitor*. Christian Science Monitor, 11 Feb. 2013. Web. 9 Nov. 2015.

Viser, Matt. "As Energy Chief, Ernest Moniz Is Man in the Middle." *Boston Globe*. Boston Globe Media, 22 Feb. 2014. Web. 13 Nov. 2015.

—*Christopher Mari*

Sy Montgomery

Born: February 7, 1958
Occupation: Writer

Sy Montgomery has written more than twenty books for adults and children about exotic animals and their habitats. "Montgomery has been chased by an angry silverback gorilla in Zaire and bitten by a vampire bat in Costa Rica, worked in a pit crawling with 18,000 snakes in Manitoba and handled a wild tarantula in French Guiana," according to her website. "She has been deftly undressed by an orangutan in Borneo, hunted by a tiger in India, and swum with piranhas, electric eels, and dolphins in the Amazon. She has searched the Altai Mountains of Mongolia's Gobi for snow leopards, hiked into the trackless cloud forest of Papua New Guinea to radio collar tree kangaroos, and learned to scuba dive in order to commune with octopuses."

Among her most popular books was her best-selling 2006 memoir, *The Good Good Pig*, about her experiences raising an ordinary piglet who eventually grew to 750 pounds and became a beloved figure in the close-knit New Hampshire town where she lived "All my books, all my articles, all my commentaries are all the same love letter repeated over and over," Montgomery told an interviewer for *Reading Rockets*, a website devoted to literacy and children's books. "I'm trying to reconnect us with the rest of our family. They may not look like us, they may have more legs than us, or fewer. . . . It's trying to reestablish this connection that humans I think naturally have with the rest of animate creation." Her writing aims to inspire both adults and children to treat the environment and all of its creatures with more care. "The problems that animals face in this world, they're all, almost all of them, of our making. Inadvertently," she explained to *Reading Rockets*. "As a writer, you can show people what's happening, and hand their power back to them to protect this sweet, green world."

EARLY LIFE AND EDUCATION

Montgomery was born on February 7, 1958, in Frankfurt, West Germany, where her father,

(Photo taken by: Sam Marshall)
http://symontgomery.com/about-sy/

Austin James Montgomery, a career military man, was then stationed. (He eventually spent thirty-five years in the service and rose to the rank of brigadier general, in which capacity he commanded the Brooklyn Army Terminal, then one of the largest US military supply bases in the world.) Referring to her father in one passage of *The Good Good Pig*, she described him as "a hero I so adored that I had confessed in Sunday school that I loved him more than Jesus."

Montgomery was by all accounts an unusual child. As soon as she could talk she began telling people that she was a dog rather than a human, and later she professed to be a horse. Her father cooperated by nicknaming her "Pony," but her glamorous Southern mother, who hailed from a small town in Arkansas, sometimes despaired. Montgomery refused to wear the frilly dresses her mother insisted on sewing for her, and when given a doll, she ignored it. She did, however, use doll clothing to dress the caiman reptiles her father bought her as pets, and she has recalled horrifying a group of military wives having cocktails with her mother by pushing a doll carriage full of the clothed reptiles into the gathering. Montgomery was sent home from kindergarten on her first day there because she bit a classmate; her explanation that the boy had been pulling the legs off of a helpless daddy longlegs on the playground fell on deaf ears. "Even then I knew: the daddy longlegs and his kin were my tribe; the cruel little boy was not," she wrote in *The Good Good Pig*.

Montgomery said in her interview for *Reading Rockets*, "When I was growing up, I naturally felt attracted to other animals. I didn't have a lot of other children in my life growing up. But that was fine, because I had lots of other friends. They just happened to be squirrels and crickets." She also had a Scottish terrier named Molly, whom she considered almost a sister, since she was an only child. "By having friends who were members of other species, I kind of hooked into this wider world," she told the *Reading Rockets* interviewer.

Active in the Girl Scouts, Montgomery harbored an early ambition to be a veterinarian until a teacher encouraged her to be a writer. Upon graduating from high school in 1975 Montgomery entered Syracuse University, where she worked on the school newspaper and embarked on a demanding triple major. In 1979 she earned degrees in magazine journalism from the university's S. I. Newhouse School of Public Communications and in psychology and French language and literature from the College of Arts and Sciences.

EARLY WRITING CAREER

Montgomery initially took a job as a business reporter at the *Buffalo News* in New York, but she had little interest in business. She thus jumped at the opportunity when a smaller publication in Bridgewater, New Jersey, offered her a job covering science, medicine, and the environment, and she later began writing a regular column, "Nature Journal," for the *Boston Globe*. "It gave me the autonomy to write about what I love—the natural world, which had always fascinated me," she told Frederic Golden for the *Los Angeles Times* (19 Apr. 1995). Her first book, *The Curious Naturalist: Nature's Everyday Mysteries* (1991), was a collection of those columns, which looked at the miracles of nature—such as dragonfly larvae crawling out of their shells or ordinary houseflies cleansing their eyes with their hands—that readers could find right in their own backyards, local parks, and beaches.

In 1991 Montgomery also published the ambitious volume *Walking with the Great Apes: Jane Goodall, Dian Fossey, Biruté Galdikas*, which covered the lives and research of three iconic female primatologists. In order to afford the travel involved in preparing the book, Montgomery scrimped and saved for over a year, reportedly subsisting on little more than water and rice. During the trip, she was forced by her meager budget to stay in unsafe lodgings and consume just one small meal a day, was robbed by her own tour guide in Rwanda, and traveled on rickety buses that were as likely to leave her stranded on the side of the road as get her to her destination. Reviewers almost universally agreed, however, that the result was a triumph, and the book has since been reissued multiple times. *Walking with the Great Apes* was named a 1991

New York Times Notable Book of the Year, won the nonfiction prize from the New Hampshire Writers' and Publishers' Project, and was a finalist for a *Los Angeles Times* Book Prize for science and technology.

SUCCESS

Montgomery's next book for an adult audience was *Spell of the Tiger: The Man-Eaters of Sundarbans* (1995), for which she journeyed to the swamps of West Bengal and Bangladesh. She has said the trip was ample proof of the wisdom of listening carefully to the native inhabitants of a region rather than to scientists. "In the giant mangrove swamp known as Sundarbans, I was researching these strange man-eating tigers who swim out after your boat and eat you," she explained to Jeannine Stronach in an interview for PaperTigers.org (Mar. 2007). "Nobody knows why the tigers are so aggressive. I wanted to find out. It's hard to study something that is trying to eat you, so I turned to the local people for answers. They told me tales that sounded impossible. 'The tiger flies through the air,' they said. 'The tiger can become invisible!' But what they were saying was completely true: a tiger can't flap its wings like Tinkerbell, but it certainly can leap for twenty feet—and that's flying. The tiger can't go see-through, like Casper the Friendly Ghost. But because of its exquisite camouflage, it can hide behind a single blade of grass—completely invisible." She explained, "It turned out the local people understood completely the mystery of why these tigers are so unlike tigers elsewhere. The scientists just didn't understand what they were saying."

Montgomery subsequently wrote *Journey of the Pink Dolphins: An Amazon Quest* (2000), *Search for the Golden Moon Bear: Science and Adventure in Pursuit of a New Species* (2002), and *The Wild Out Your Window* (2002). Her most beloved book for the adult market was the best-selling *The Good Good Pig* (2006), which chronicles not a rare or exotic species but the life and death of Christopher Hogwood, a sickly piglet whom Montgomery nursed back to health and then named for a conductor and musicologist she admires. She recalled to the interviewer for *Reading Rockets* that writing about her cherished porcine friend was the hardest assignment she ever completed. "For other books I've gotten dengue fever and laid in some cockroach-infested hut and been hunted by tigers and bitten by a vampire bat and all these things," she said. "But writing about someone who I'd loved and lost was miserable."

THE SOUL OF AN OCTOPUS

In 2011 Montgomery published an article in *Orion Magazine* titled "Deep Intellect" (25 Oct. 2011), in which she described her relationship with an octopus named Athena at the New England Aquarium in Boston, Massachusetts. That article went viral and, inspired by its popularity, she subsequently wrote a book-length study of octopuses titled *The Soul of an Octopus: A Surprising Exploration into the Wonder of Consciousness*, which was published in 2015. Her research for this book prompted her to earn her scuba diving certification and travel to the reefs of Moorea and Cozumel National Marine Park. "This miraculously insightful and enchanting book expands our understanding of consciousness and sheds light on the very notion of what we call a 'soul,'" Maria Popova wrote in a review for *BrainPickings* (14 Dec. 2015). "*The Soul of an Octopus* is an astoundingly beautiful read in its entirety, at once scientifically illuminating and deeply poetic." The book was a finalist for the National Book Award and was named a notable book for 2016 by the American Library Association (ALA).

In addition to her work for adults, Montgomery has written prolifically for children. Many of her books are created in collaboration with respected nature photographer Nic Bishop, with whom she launched the award-winning Scientists in the Field series, which includes *The Snake Scientist* (1999), *The Tarantula Scientist* (2004), *The Tapir Scientist* (2013), *The Octopus Scientists* (2015), and *The Great White Shark Scientist* (2016), among many others. Her book *Quest for the Tree Kangaroo: An Expedition to the Cloud Forest of New Guinea* (2006) earned the Orbis Pictus Award for outstanding nonfiction for children, a Henry Bergh Children's Book Award, and a Robert F. Sibert honor citation.

PERSONAL LIFE

Montgomery, who has scripted and narrated multiple documentaries for National Geographic, told the *Reading Rockets* interviewer that unless she is dressed up to give a lecture or appear on television, she generally looks like she "woke up beneath piled leaves." She has been a vegetarian for decades.

Montgomery married fellow writer Howard Mansfield, whose areas of expertise are American history and preservation. The two met while working on the student newspaper at Syracuse University. Her parents, she admitted, were unhappy that she was dating a Jewish man, and after she married him—in a wedding ceremony they refused to attend—they formally disowned her. (They later reconciled.) The couple live in rural Hancock, New Hampshire, where they keep a large menagerie that includes a border collie and assorted chickens.

SUGGESTED READING

Golden, Frederic. "Captured by the Law of the Jungle." *Los Angeles Times*. Los Angeles Times, 19 Apr. 1995. Web. 2 Apr. 2016.

Montgomery, Sy. Interview. "Transcript from an Interview with Sy Montgomery." *Reading Rockets*. WETA Public Broadcasting, n.d. Web. 2 Apr. 2016.

Montgomery, Sy. Interview by Jeannine Stronach. *PaperTigers.org*. PaperTigers, Mar. 2007. Web. 2 Apr. 2016.

Montgomery, Sy. Interview by Laura Clark Rohrer. *National Book Foundation*. Natl. Book Foundation, n.d. Web. 2 Apr. 2016.

Thatcher, Leslie. "Discovering the World with Sy Montgomery." *Truth Out*. Truthout, 26 Oct. 2009. Web. 2 Apr. 2016.

SELECTED WORKS

The Curious Naturalist: Nature's Everyday Mysteries, 1991; *Spell of the Tiger: The Man-Eaters of Sundarbans*, 1995; *Journey of the Pink Dolphins: An Amazon Quest*, 2000; *The Wild Out Your Window: Exploring Nature Near at Hand*, 2002; *Search for the Golden Moon Bear: Science and Adventure in Pursuit of a New Species*, 2002; *The Good Good Pig*, 2006; *The Soul of an Octopus: A Surprising Exploration into the Wonder of Consciousness*, 2015

—*Mari Rich*

Robby Mook

Born: December 3, 1979
Occupation: Clinton campaign manager

At thirty-six, Democratic campaign strategist and manager Robby Mook has a lot more experience in politics than his age would suggest. He is the campaign manager for Hillary Clinton's 2016 presidential bid, and he was also involved with Clinton's first attempt to become the Democratic Party's presidential nominee, in 2008. In 2013, Mook managed the gubernatorial campaign for Democratic candidate Terry McAuliffe in Virginia. From 2009 to 2013, he served as the political director for the Democratic Congressional Campaign Committee (DCCC), helping put Democrats in the US House of Representatives. Mook is the sort of political strategist who keeps his cool, hires politicos to do jobs he cannot, and stays away from the press. He generally avoids social media and doing interviews, leaving that to the politicians he manages. Nonetheless, the press and the political world continue to be fascinated with Mook because of both his age and approach. In 2015, he was named one of *Fortune's* "40 Under 40," the magazine's list of young

Douglas Graham/Roll Call via Getty Images

and influential people in business. One of the many intriguing facts about him is that his list of highly loyal political operatives is called the "Mook Mafia," something about which he has unsurprisingly said nothing.

EARLY LIFE AND EDUCATION

Robert Mook, who goes by "Robby," was born on December 3, 1979 and grew up in Vermont, first in Sharon and then Norwich, where he spent most of his early years. His mother worked as a hospital administrator at the Dartmouth-Hitchcock Medical Center, and his father worked as a physics teacher at Dartmouth College. Mook attended Hanover High School, where during his freshman year he auditioned for a part in Molière's play *The Imaginary Invalid*. However, the play's director noticed that Mook's primary interests lay outside the world of acting. At the time, Matt Dunne was a state representative, running for reelection, and also happened to be the high school's theater director. "Robby was fantastic in the play," Dunne later recalled in an interview with Paul Heintz of the Vermont newspaper *Seven Days* (18 Sept. 2013), "but what he was really interested in was the political thing." That "thing" was Dunne's reelection campaign, for which Mook volunteered. Thus, at the age of fourteen, Mook began his involvement in politics, his passion for which only grew during his college years.

Mook attended Columbia University in New York City, where he was a classics major. As profiles of Mook have pointed out, he never took a political-science course, which is ironic given his passion and chosen profession. During the

summer following his freshman year, he returned to Vermont, where Dunne hired him as the first paid staffer for the Vermont House Democrats, the state legislature's Democratic caucus. Mook lived in Burlington, Vermont, organizing fundraisers and going door-to-door. Back in Columbia University, Mook got involved with the College Democrats and became active in launching the school political organization's first electronic records of volunteers and voters. At the time this kind of political strategizing was forward thinking. "Robby was one of those students at Columbia you just knew was going to change the world, and you felt proud to know him," Sam Arora, who was a year younger than Mook at Columbia and would go on to become a Maryland state delegate, told Jonathan Lemire for *Columbia College Today* (Spring 2012). "With his powerful combination of heart and mind, I think all of Robby's friends knew he would rise quickly." Mook graduated from Columbia in 2002.

NATIONAL STAGE

After graduating from college, Mook returned to Vermont, where he delved deeper into politics. In 2002, he served as field director for Vermont Democrats' coordinated campaign. Later on, Mook worked for the 2004 presidential primary campaign of Howard Dean, the former Democratic governor of Vermont. Mook initially served as Dean's deputy field director in New Hampshire and then in Wisconsin. Also, according to Lemire, Mook helped coordinate the Dean campaign's use of the Internet to help organize support—a novel idea at the time. "That was a national campaign very early on," Mook told Lemire. "We had to bottle lightning, as we knew there was a lot of energy and excitement in the campaign." However, Dean lost New Hampshire and Wisconsin, and ultimately lost the support of Democrats after a particularly impassioned speech that ended with a yell that became known as the "Dean Scream." The media perceived this as a major gaffe; it was replayed numerous times, and it ultimately brought down the Dean campaign. Mook, however, learned from the experience. "That campaign taught a very important lesson to me early on: The winds can blow quickly in a very different direction, and when you have support, lock it in," Mook told Lemire. "Sometimes you learn more from losing than from winning."

After the Dean campaign, Mook worked for John Kerry, the 2004 Democratic Party's presidential nominee. Mook served on the Democratic National Committee as the get-out-the-vote director for the state of Wisconsin leading up to the 2004 presidential election, which Kerry lost to the incumbent George W. Bush. In 2005, Mook managed Democrat Dave Marsden's successful bid in a state delegate race in Virginia, and in 2006, he ran a successful coordinated campaign in Maryland to get two Democrats—Martin O'Malley and Benjamin Cardin—elected to the Senate.

HILLARY CLINTON, TAKE ONE

In 2007, when he was still in his late twenties, Mook began work on the 2008 Democratic presidential primary campaign for Hillary Clinton. He started out as her state director in Nevada, then moved on to Ohio, Indiana, and New Hampshire. Even though Mook was young, his passion and expertise was both noticeable and admired, not only inspiring passion and dedication but also leading some to perceive him as a kind of political idol. According to a profile of Mook by Noah Davis for *Vice* (20 Feb. 2015), "Former campaign vets remember that during the 2008 Nevada primary, Mook [w]as treated like a cult figure whenever he stopped by the dive bar where Hillary staffers would spend what limited free time they had." Recalling that time, the veteran Democratic campaign organizer Teresa Vilmain told Davis, Mook "takes time to get to know people. He invests in relationships. He's not afraid to ask questions. He knows what he doesn't know and hires people who are smarter than him in those areas."

MOOK MAFIA

In 2008, Barack Obama, not Hillary Clinton, became the Democratic Party's presidential candidate, so Mook moved on to other projects. In 2009, he became the political director for the Democratic Congressional Campaign Committee (DCCC), the official campaign wing of the Democratic Party in the House of Representatives. Mook's job involved the complicated task of moving around campaign funds to allocate money for polling, direct mail, television advertising, and strategizing for specific congressional campaigns. At the time Mook was only thirty years old, but he had the respect of many political veterans, whether politicians or campaign strategists. During the next presidential campaign year, 2012, when President Obama was running for a second term, Mook helped Democrats in the House of Representatives gain eight seats—though not control of the House.

The following year Mook served as the campaign manager of Democratic candidate Terry McAuliffe in the Virginia gubernatorial election. In a profile for the *New York Times* (14 July 2013), Albert R. Hunt called Mook a "33-year-old political wunderkind." Under Mook's campaign management, McAuliffe won the Virginia race for governor, beating Republican and state attorney general Ken Cuccinelli, but the campaign was hard-fought and often bitter. As Davis observed in his *Vice* profile, Mook's effectiveness in negatively defining the opposing politician—a move Mook has been known to employ often—is essential but can have "unintended consequences." Benjamin Tribbett, a Virginia strategist and political blogger, told Davis that McAuliffe did not so much run on his merits, on what he could do, as on who he is not—the Republican Cuccinelli. The result of the negative campaign, Tribbett suggested, was that it made things difficult for McAuliffe to work with the Republican state legislature. Another potential challenge for Mook came in November 2014 when *ABC News* posted leaked e-mails about the e-mail LISTSERV of about 150 Democratic campaign veterans called the "Mook Mafia." Although there was nothing incredibly damning or surprising in the leaked e-mails, Davis pointed out that wanting to "smite Republicans mafia-style," and in general comparing himself to a mafia boss, was the kind of technique a future Hillary Clinton campaign would likely find damaging.

HILLARY CLINTON, TAKE TWO

On the other hand, Mook's ability for "avoiding drama," as Davis noted, could be a major asset for the Clinton presidential campaign. When Hillary Clinton declared in 2015 that she would run for president, she eventually asked Mook to be her campaign manager (he was first brought on as a consultant). Mook was highly experienced and had earned Clinton's trust, as well as that of her husband, former president Bill Clinton. "By all accounts," wrote Jay Newton-Small for *Time* (2 Feb. 2016), "Mook was hired as much for his easygoing nature as for his expertise in ground game and harnessing the latest technology to get out the vote. He also was apparently hired for his talent for self-restraint. He refuses to criticize Clinton's 2008 operation, simply saying that the times and the campaigns were different."

Mook's poise and maturity have been noted by a variety of political journalists and insiders, and, as Amy Chozick wrote for the *New York Times* (14 Mar. 2015), these attributes are a major reason that many former aides for President Obama have joined the Clinton presidential campaign in several senior positions. Chozick cites one particularly illustrative example: during the 2008 Democratic primary when Clinton was running against Obama, competing to become the party's presidential nominee, the Obama campaign's offices were vandalized in Indiana. In a symbolic gesture, though certainly not without political considerations, Mook reached out to the Obama campaign and offered them use of the Clinton campaign's office space. Political strategist Ellen Qualls told Chozick that she believes that Mook, in the 2016 presidential campaign, will be the "King of avoiding distractions and shiny objects." For that reason alone, he is an essential part of Clinton's 2016 presidential campaign.

SUGGESTED READING

Chozick, Amy. "A Young Manager for Clinton Juggles Data and Old Baggage." *New York Times*. New York Times, 14 Mar. 2015. Web. 9 May 2016.

Davis, Noah. "Walk Softly and Carry a Big E-mail List." *Vice*. VICE Media, 20 Feb. 2015. Web. 9 May 2016.

Hunt, Albert R. "Virginia Campaign Could Lift Strategist to Stardom." *New York Times*. New York Times, 14 July 2013. Web. 9 May 2016.

Lemire, Jonathan. "Robby Mook '02 Works to Turn the Country Blue." *Columbia College Today*. Columbia University, Spring 2012. Web. 9 May 2016.

—*Dmitry Kiper*

Paul Moravec

Born: November 2, 1957
Occupation: Composer

A composer of classical music that has been described as both accessible and engrossing, Paul Moravec received the 2004 Pulitzer Prize for Music in honor of his work *Tempest Fantasy*.

EARLY LIFE AND EDUCATION

Paul Moravec was born in Buffalo, New York, on November 2, 1957. After graduating from the prestigious Lawrenceville School in New Jersey, he enrolled at Harvard University. As a student of music at Harvard, he performed with the Harvard-Radcliffe Collegium Musicum, one of the three university-affiliated choral groups known collectively as the Holden Choirs. Moravec earned a Bachelor of Arts in composition from Harvard in 1980. Upon completion of his undergraduate work, Moravec was awarded the Rome Prize Fellowship (Prix de Rome)—a scholarship to study music at the American Academy in Rome, Italy.

Moravec attended graduate school at Columbia University, earning a master of music degree in 1982 and a doctorate of musical arts in composition in 1987. In 1987, he started teaching at Dartmouth College. He remained at Dartmouth until 1996, when he took a position at Hunter College, part of the City University of New York. During this time, Moravec struggled with severe depression. At part of his treatment, he received electroshock therapy. Moravec did not speak publicly about his experience with mental illness until the late 2000s, but has since stated that the experience caused him to reinvent his career and life.

MUSICAL CAREER

Over the course of his career as a composer, Moravec has written over one hundred works of music, including music for orchestras, chamber ensembles, and choirs. He composed one of his first orchestral works, *Streamline*, in 1988. Moravec's other orchestral compositions include *Spiritdance* (1989), *Aubade* (1990), *Ancient Lights* (1994), and *Adelphony* (1997). Moravec has composed a number of works for chamber ensembles, including several pieces for string quartet. His earliest chamber pieces include *The Open Secret* (1985), *The Kingdom Within* (1989), and *Circular Dreams* (1991). He produced a variety of chamber pieces during the 2000s, including *Octocelli* (2000), *Quatrocelli* (2000), and *Cool Fire* (2001).

A prolific composer, Moravec has also created pieces for brass quintets, solo performances for various instruments, works for solo piano, and works for piano and voice. Among his works for brass are *Quintessence* (1998) and *Hampshire Harmony* (1993). He created numerous works for solo instrument and piano during the early years of his career, including *Lyric Dances* (1981) and *Timepiece* (1984). Later works in this vein include *Epithalamion* (1993) for trumpet and piano and *Protean Fantasy* (1997) for violin and piano. He released three works for piano and solo instrument in 2001, including *Ariel Fantasy*, *Autumn Song*, and *Zu-Zu's Petals*. Moravec's solo piano works include *Music Reminders* (1983), *Characteristics* (1995), *Impromptus* (1999), and *Vai!* (2002).

Moravec's music has been associated with a genre described by music critic Terry Teachout as "new tonalism"—a return to the tonal tradition that has characterized Western music from at least the seventeenth through the mid-twentieth century, and which was interrupted by a postwar avant-garde modernism that experimented with atonal and minimalist composition that tended to be off-putting to the public at large. Writing in *Commentary* magazine in 1997, Teachout placed Moravec among a group of new tonalists of the 1980s who were creating serious music that appeared in conventional forms such as symphonies, chamber music, and film scores, and was accessible to common listeners.

In 2003, Moravec released *Tempest Fantasy*, an ensemble piece for violin, cello, piano, and clarinet. The work premiered on May 2, 2003, at the Morgan Library in Manhattan, performed by clarinetist David Krakauer and the string ensemble Trio Solisti. Inspired by Shakespeare's play *The Tempest*, the work is organized into five sections: "Ariel," "Prospero," "Caliban," "Sweet Airs," and "Fantasia." In 2004, Moravec was awarded the Pulitzer Prize in Music in recognition of *Tempest Fantasy*. That same year, he took a teaching position at Adelphi University.

Moravec's work has been recorded by musicians worldwide and released in various collections. These include *Time Gallery* (2006), *Moravec: Useful Knowledge* (2011), and *Paul Moravec: Northern Lights Electric* (2012). A pianist, Moravec has also released recordings of his own musical performances. He appears on the track "Vita Brevis" on the album *New American Song Cycles* (2004), a collection of music featuring tenor Paul Sperry. Moravec also appears on soprano Melanie Mitrano's 2006 release *Songs in Transit: An American Expedition.* Moravec's first opera, *The Letter,* with a libretto by Teachout, was commissioned by the Santa Fe Opera and premiered in July 2009. He composed a second opera with a libretto by Teachout, *Danse Russe,* which premiered in 2011.

IMPACT

In addition to receiving the Pulitzer Prize, Moravec has been the recipient of several awards and distinctions over the course of his career. His 1999 work *Mood Swings* was named the year's best classical composition by the *Washington Post.* In 2006, he was selected as a member of the New York Composers Circle. The American Academy of Arts and Letters presented him with their Arts and Letters Award in 2012. In 2013, he was named a Guggenheim Fellow. He has received grants from the National Endowment for the Arts, the Rockefeller Foundation, the New Hampshire State Council on the Arts, and the Camargo Foundation. Moravec has served as a panelist at events held for the National Endowment for the Arts and the American Society of Composers, Authors, and Publishers.

PERSONAL LIFE

Moravec's wife, Wendy Lamb, is a publishing executive.

SUGGESTED READING

Johnson, Daniel Stephen. "Paul Moravec: Mining Tonality for New Intricacies." *WQXR.* New York Public Radio, 1 Feb. 2012. Web. 15 June 2014.

Mead, Julia C. "Music; Living Out the Pulitzer Fantasy." *New York Times.* New York Times, 30 May 2004. Web. 15 June 2014.

"Paul Moravec Wins Pulitzer Prize for Tempest Fantasy." *New Music Box.* New Music Box, 5 Apr. 2004. Web. 15 June 2014.

Shattuck, Kathryn. "A Composer Who's Weathered Some Tempests of His Own." *New York Times.* New York Times, 22 Apr. 2007. Web. 15 June 2014.

Zinko, Carolyne. "Like Melancholy Prince of His Musical 'Fantasy,' Moravec Used Imagination to Overcome Despair." *SFGate.* Hearst Communications, 22 Mar. 2005. Web. 15 June 2014.

SELECTED WORKS

Streamline, 1988; *Spiritdance,* 1989; *Aubade,* 1990; *Ancient Lights,* 1994; *Adelphony,* 1997; *Mood Swings,* 1998; *Tempest Fantasy,* 2003; *Northern Lights Electric for full orchestra,* 2008; *The Letter,* 2009; *Danse Russe,* 2011

—*Joshua Pritchard*

Wagner Moura

Born: June 27, 1976
Occupation: Actor

Wagner Moura is a Brazilian actor best known for his role on the Netflix crime drama *Narcos,* which began streaming in 2015. Moura plays the infamous Colombian drug kingpin Pablo Escobar, and after the show's first season was released, he was nominated for his first Golden Globe Award for best actor in a television drama in 2016. Before *Narcos,* he appeared in the 2013 science-fiction thriller *Elysium,* about a dystopian future in which the rich live on a luxury space station while the poor fight for resources on a ruined Earth; however, he is best known in Brazil for his role in the film *Elite Squad* (2007) and its sequel, *Elite Squad: The Enemy Within* (2010). The latter was Brazil's highest-grossing movie in the country's cinematic history. Though as a young man Moura had actually dreamed of becoming a journalist, he has admitted that he was not cut out for the life of a reporter; he found that he could still pursue his passion for social justice through his celebrity. Recently becoming a goodwill ambassador for the International Labor Organization (ILO), he has been working with the United Nations (UN) to end forced labor. "Brazil was the last country in the world to abolish slavery, so slavery is part of our history, of our soul," he told Emma Brown for *Interview* (27 Aug. 2015). "I am willing to do anything [the ILO wants] me to do because this is something that resonates a lot with me."

EARLY LIFE AND EDUCATION

Wagner Maniçoba de Moura was born on June 27, 1976, and grew up in a rural town in Brazil's northeastern state of Bahia. He graduated with a degree in journalism from the Federal University of Bahia, but quickly became disillusioned with the work itself. He was not talking to politicians or sending corrupt people to jail, but instead knocking on doors, interviewing people about blocked streets—"things that I didn't really care about," he told Brown. He quit, and decided to pursue a career as an actor, as his acting impulse had always been strong and he had already participated in theater groups and school

Zé Carlos Barretta from São Paulo, Brasil (stk_001938)/CC BY 2.0/Wikimedia Commons

productions; he also became the lead vocalist of a band called Sua Mãe (Your Mother). In 2000, he performed in the play *A Máquina* (To Machine), a production that toured throughout many cities and further exposed him to the possibility of acting outside of the theater.

ELITE SQUAD FILMS

Moura appeared in a small supporting role in the 2000 romantic comedy *Woman on Top*, starring Penelope Cruz, as well as the 2001 drama *Behind the Sun*, which was nominated for a Golden Globe for best foreign language film, and *The Three Marias* (2002). Additionally, he landed television roles in series such as *Sexo Frágil* (Fragile Sex) (2003–4) and *Paraíso Tropical* (Tropical Paradise) (2007).

However, Moura's big break came in 2007, when he was cast in writer-director José Padilha's action drama *Elite Squad*, or *Tropa de Elite*, as it was released in Brazil in the original Portuguese. The film follows the story of Capitão Nascimento (Moura), a captain of the elite Battalion of Police Special Operations, or BOPE, in Rio de Janeiro. (Moura reportedly trained with the real Rio police force to prepare for the role.) Nascimento and BOPE are the only forces keeping the city in order, though their methods are ethically fuzzy. Nascimento hopes to retire—his wife is pregnant—and must train a replacement before an upcoming visit from the pope, to rule over Rio as brutally as he does. David Edelstein, who reviewed the film for *New York* (2008), compared it to *The French Connection*, a gritty thriller about New York City from 1971. *Elite*

Squad is a "classic tragedy," he wrote, told from an unusual angle. The violence is gratuitous in an effort to emphasize the complex web of enemies and alliances in Rio and the larger world; the police collude with the gangs and there are "lefty college kids who denounce cops while smoking (and dealing) dope—unconcerned with the blood shed for their high."

The film, which was leaked shortly before its release, was enormously popular with audiences, raising a national debate about how best to deal with organized crime in the slums of Rio while also making Moura a star in Brazil. A sequel, *Elite Squad: The Enemy Within (Tropa de Elite 2: O Inimigo Agora e Outro)*, was released in 2010. Taking place thirteen years after the first film, which was set in 1997, it begins with Nascimento having to deal with a prison rebellion. The police want, and believe they can achieve, a peaceful resolution, but one of Nascimento's officers thinks that the mutiny might give them the perfect opportunity to kill an important gang member. Plans to execute the latter coup go poorly, but make Nascimento a popular hero. As the film progresses, he renounces his lawless policing ways, and *Elite Squad: The Enemy Within* becomes less a complex portrait of its hero than an indictment of the Brazilian government and its failure to break the cycle of corruption. In interviews, Moura has expressed a sense of fulfillment at having been involved in a film that exposes such issues: "It's a film about not only the corrupt relationship of the police with the militia, drug dealers, but more than that the relationship with the politicians and the way politicians in Brazil use the police force in order to maintain the power they have here," he explained to Brown. "I am really proud of that film."

Elite Squad: The Enemy Within became the highest-grossing film in Brazilian history. American critics praised the film, though they also often found it to be more didactic than its anarchic predecessor. "This is a good film, not great," the late Roger Ebert wrote for the *Chicago Sun-Times* (30 Nov. 2011). "Too little attention is paid to the complexities and personalities of the characters. We're always aware they stand for something."

BECOMING PABLO ESCOBAR

The success of the Elite Squad films brought Padilha to Hollywood, where he directed the 2014 blockbuster *Robocop*. At the same time, he approached Moura with a different idea, one more in line with the work they had done together in Brazil, in 2013. Padilha asked his friend—who had experienced his own Hollywood turn that same year in the role of a human smuggler opposite stars such as Matt Damon and Jodie Foster in the science-fiction film

Elysium—if he would ever consider portraying Pablo Escobar. Moura was initially taken aback; he was the last person he would have thought of to play the Colombian drug lord, as he did not even speak Spanish and was approximately forty pounds thinner.

Still, Moura was intrigued. Not long after their conversation—before Padilha even officially offered Moura the role—he hopped on a plane to Medellín, Colombia, to begin preparing. Escobar had been born into poverty, but became one of the richest men in the world as the leader of the Medellín cartel, shipping cocaine into the United States. A criminal who ruthlessly executed thousands, at his peak in the 1980s, he was worth an estimated $30 billion. He was one of the world's most famous outlaws, but he was ostentatious with his wealth, presiding over Colombia like an emperor; he owned mansions, a private zoo, and an army of criminals to carry out his bidding. Still, Escobar, who was gunned down by police in 1993 at the age of forty-four, was a complicated figure. He gave away large sums of money to the poor, earning himself comparisons to the folk hero Robin Hood, and even more than twenty years after his death, some people in Medellín have pictures of Escobar hanging in their homes.

In Medellín, Moura began taking Spanish classes at a university after it was decided that the show would be done in both English and Spanish. He later said it was one of the hardest things he had ever done. Outside of class, he read books about Escobar. *"Everybody* wrote a book about him," Moura told Lisa Liebman for *Vulture* (11 Sept. 2015), "the waiter, the guy who fixed his car." He spoke with locals—studying their accents and listening to their stories—though he told them that he was an exchange student because he was nervous to reveal that he would be playing their most provocative national figure. "Everyone knows someone who knew Pablo, or who died [as a result of him]," he told Liebman. "So I was able to really understand who this guy was. . . . And then I forgot all that; I threw [it] in the garbage in order to create my own Pablo." Focusing on the fact that Escobar was not an entirely black-and-white villain, citing examples such as the former kingpin's alleged devotion to his family, Moura has chosen to portray the real-life character as more of an ambiguous antihero.

NARCOS

Narcos, created by Carlo Bernard, Chris Brancato, and Doug Miro, premiered on Netflix in August 2015. To play Escobar, who was quite large, Moura gained over forty pounds—something he vows never to do again, shirking praise for the physical transformation. Still, critic Neil Genzlinger of the *New York Times* (27 Aug. 2015) called Moura's lead performance "prize-worthy." He wrote, "The further into the show you get, the more you realize that although the structure is classic good-guys-versus-bad-guys, the heart of the piece is its study of Escobar, portrayed as a man whose grandiose appetites aren't satisfied by the incredible amounts of money his business brings in."

Beginning in 1989, the show follows the intersecting stories of Escobar and American Drug Enforcement Administration (DEA) agent Steve Murphy, who was sent to Colombia to ensnare and kill him. *Narcos* illustrates the rise of Escobar's empire, relying on familiar tropes from famous crime films such as *The Godfather* (1972), *Scarface* (1983), and *Goodfellas* (1990). It draws most heavily upon the latter, by filmmaker Martin Scorsese, employing copious voice-over narration to provide historical context and keep the plot moving. As the series progresses, it touches on the same ethical questions raised by Padilha's Elite Squad films. As Scott Tobias for the *New York Times* (28 Aug. 2015) put it in the context of Murphy's quest to capture Escobar, "How far is too far in pursuing justice when it comes to Escobar? If following procedure is so laughably ineffectual, then when do you realize where the line is drawn? And does that line keep moving?" *Narcos* was nominated for a Golden Globe Award for best television series—drama, and Moura himself was nominated for an individual Golden Globe Award for best performance by an actor in a television drama. "[T]he greatest thing honestly about doing *Narcos* was feeling that I was part of something bigger than just being Brazilian. . . . Being in Colombia and feeling that the story I was telling resonated with me," he told Brown about being part of the show. A second season is set to premiere on Netflix in the fall of 2016.

As of early 2016, Moura also planned to step behind the camera for the first time to serve as director for a biopic about Brazilian revolutionary Carlos Marighella.

PERSONAL LIFE

Moura is married to photographer and journalist Sandra Delgado. They have three children: Bem, Salvador, and José. The family lives in Rio de Janeiro.

SUGGESTED READING

Brown, Emma. "Wagner Moura and the Politics of Pablo Escobar." *Interview*. Interview, 27 Aug. 2015. Web. 14 June 2016.

Ebert, Roger. Rev. of *Elite Squad: The Enemy Within*, dir. José Padilha. *RogerEbert.com*. Ebert Digital, 30 Nov. 2011. Web. 14 June 2016.

Edelstein, David. Rev. of *Elite Squad (Tropa de Elite)*, dir. José Padilha. *New York*. New York Media, 2008. Web. 14 June 2016.

Genzlinger, Neil. "Review: *Narcos* Follows the Rise and Reign of Pablo Escobar." Rev. of *Narcos*, dir. José Padilha. *New York Times*. New York Times, 27 Aug. 2015. Web. 14 June 2016.

Liebman, Lisa. "*Narcos's* Wagner Moura on Playing Pablo Escobar and Why He Learned Spanish before He Got the Part." *Vulture*. New York Media, 11 Sept. 2015. Web. 14 June 2016.

Tobias, Scott. "*Narcos*' Episode 2 Recap: Death to Kidnappers." *New York Times*. New York Times, 28 Aug. 2015. Web. 14 June 2016.

SELECTED WORKS

Elite Squad, 2007; *Elite Squad: The Enemy Within*, 2010; *Elysium*, 2013; *Narcos*, 2015–

—*Molly Hagan*

The *Washington Post*/GettyImages

David Muir

Born: November 8, 1973
Occupation: Journalist

As a young boy in upstate New York, broadcast journalist David Muir did not fantasize about playing football or basketball. "Every evening, I would excuse myself from playing in the backyard and go inside to watch the evening news," he confided to Verne Gay for *Newsday* (1 Sept. 2014). "I wanted to get out there and see the world." Showing early promise, he cut his teeth at the local television station—first as an intern and then as a weekend anchor—before moving on to a bigger market, Boston's WCVB. His raw, natural talent caught the attention of executives at ABC News, where he quickly made a name for himself as an anchor of the overnight news show *World News Now*.

Becoming a mainstay at the network, Muir covered breaking news while juggling a coanchor stint at the newsmagazine *Primetime Live* with the eventual weekend anchor duties of *World News*. In 2014 he followed in his idol Peter Jennings's footsteps when he was tapped to replace Diane Sawyer as the sole anchor of *World News Tonight*; at age forty, he was the youngest anchor to hold the role of evening news anchor in half a century. "He's the epitome of what a modern anchor needs to be," James Goldston, the president of ABC News who appointed Muir to the coveted position, told Roger Yu for *USA Today* (18 Oct. 2015).

EARLY LIFE AND EDUCATION

David Muir was born in Syracuse, New York, on November 8, 1973, to Pat Mills, a legal secretary, and Ronald Muir, a steamfitter. Growing up in Onondaga Hill, Muir, whose parents eventually divorced, dreamed of becoming a journalist and idolized Peter Jennings, ABC's *World News Tonight* anchor from 1983 to 2005. "I thought [he] was the James Bond of evening news," he shared with Emily Strohm for *People* (10 Nov. 2014).

As a fifth grader, Muir would climb inside a cardboard box and stage mock news broadcasts in the family living room. Even Linda DeSaw, Muir's sixth-grade teacher, was impressed at how he already had his future mapped out. "He would say to me, 'I'm either going to be a newscaster and take Matt Lauer's job (on the *Today* show at NBC), or I'm going to have a real estate agency and you can work for me,'" she told Donnie Webb for *Syracuse.com* (23 July 2014).

At age twelve, the budding journalist wrote to Ron Curtis, a longtime anchor at Syracuse's WTVH, a local CBS affiliate, requesting advice on how to break into the television news industry. Muir recalled to Stephen Battaglio for *TV Guide* (19 Mar. 2013) that he was encouraged by Curtis's typewritten response of, "Competition in television news is keen, but there is always room for the right person." Within a year, Muir had joined WTVH as an intern.

While attending Onondaga Central High School, Muir juggled a part-time job bagging groceries at Wegmans supermarket with summer internships at WTVH, where his duties ranged from hauling giant tripods for field reporters and camera crew to delivering vending machine sodas to the station's anchorpersons. He also found time to read the school's morning announcements, which he would report like a newscast.

CLIMBING THE RANKS AND REPORTING FROM BOSTON

Upon receiving his high school diploma in 1991, Muir studied journalism at Ithaca College's Roy H. Park School of Communications. During his senior year, he accepted WTVH's weekend news anchor position. He traveled between Ithaca and the station until 1995, when he graduated magna cum laude with a Bachelor of Arts degree.

Shortly after being promoted to full-time anchor and reporter, Muir had his first real taste of international reporting, broadcasting from Tel Aviv, Jerusalem, and the Gaza Strip in the wake of Israeli prime minister Yitzhak Rabin's 1995 assassination. He also covered President Bill Clinton's 1999 impeachment trial during his five-year stint at WTVH (1995–2000). Muir's accomplishments earned him best local newscast accolades from the Syracuse Press Club as well as recognition from *Syracuse New Times* readers, who voted him as one of the city's best news anchors.

In 2000 Muir sent a demo reel of his news stories and anchor work to WCVB, an ABC affiliate and Hearst Television flagship station in Boston, Massachusetts. It was not long before his tape caught the attention of Candy Altman, the station's news director. "He was still not polished yet as an anchor. But there was just something about the way he communicates and his reporting," Altman recalled to Yu. "Getting people to trust you and open up to you is a skill, and David has that skill." Muir joined the station that May.

Muir's raw talent would prove to be an asset to WCVB. In just three short years, while performing double duty as a weekend anchor and general assignment reporter, he was part of a news team that received the regional Edward R. Murrow Award for investigative reporting as well as accolades from the Associated Press (AP) for their coverage tracking the timeline of the hijackers who crashed four planes, including two into New York City's World Trade Center, on September 11, 2001. Not long after the attack, he was reporting on the events and the aftermath from Logan International Airport. In retrospect, Muir has commented to journalists that working in Boston gave him great opportunity to hone his skill: "At that time, Boston was one of the greatest markets to cover. . . . It was a great training ground," he told Brian Steinberg for *Variety* (26 Sept. 2014).

BEGINNING A LONG TENURE WITH ABC NEWS

It was Muir's reporting on the Iraq and Afghanistan wars while stationed in Doha, Qatar, that most directly caught the attention of ABC

network news officials. "I'm sure I was being watched and scrutinized," Muir confided to Yu. His suspicions turned out to be accurate when, in August 2003, he was named an anchor of ABC's overnight program *World News Now*, returning him to his home state of New York and bringing him onto the national stage.

From the start of his ABC News tenure, Muir was entrusted with coverage of high-profile and volatile stories, including the two-day Northeast blackout of 2003 and a series of tributes commemorating the sixtieth anniversary of D-day on June 6, 2004. Muir, who also began a correspondent stint for the network's investigative newsmagazine program *Primetime Live*, further distinguished himself in 2005 while reporting from New Orleans in the aftermath of Hurricane Katrina. His firsthand accounts for *World News* and 20/20 not only exposed the deplorable conditions within the Convention Center and Charity Hospital but also offered viewers an unflinching look at the hardest-hit hurricane victims. "I remember wanting to slouch down in the back seat because it felt like an invasion of their suffering," he told Jonathan Mahler for the *New York Times* (1 Sept. 2014). "But as difficult as it is . . . that camera lens in the window is going to give them a voice."

Muir also spent the latter part of the decade covering international news as one of the network's lead correspondents. During the summer of 2006 and 2007, Muir traveled to the Middle East, where he reported on the thirty-four-day war between Israel and Hezbollah fighters in Lebanon as well as Hamas's takeover of the Gaza Strip. He was assigned to cover the 2007 Peru earthquake—the deadliest in nearly four decades—and rushed to the scene of another quake in China's Sichuan Province in 2008. That same year, he visited the Ukraine on the twenty-second anniversary of the Chernobyl disaster.

At the time, ABC was also expanding Muir's role at the network. Along with being promoted to *Primetime Live* coanchor and anchor of the Saturday broadcast of *World News* in 2007, he was named to the broadcast team for the Beijing 2008 Summer Olympics and the 2008 presidential election night coverage. His reporting during Barack Obama's historic presidential inauguration in 2009 helped the ABC News crew win a News and Documentary Emmy Award (2010). He also tackled social hot button issues in 2009, joining Sawyer as cohost of an hour-long 20/20 special on gun control.

ANCHORING HIS OWN SHOW

Despite the increased responsibilities, Muir continued to cover breaking news stories for ABC. In 2010 he was front and center for the network's coverage of the BP oil spill, one of the biggest environmental disasters in US history, and the earthquake in Port-au-Prince, Haiti's capital. He also served as part of the 2010 Winter Olympics broadcast team.

Muir's hard work paid off the following February, when ABC News tapped him to anchor both weekend editions of *World News*, which were renamed *World News with David Muir*. That spring, he launched "Made in America," a *World News* segment highlighting American companies creating jobs that would go on to become a renowned staple of the program and receive an Emmy nomination. In June Muir landed a coveted interview with Michelle Obama during the First Lady's week-long visit to Cape Town, South Africa. By August, the total audience for Muir's program had increased by 9 percent and the demographic of viewers aged twenty-five to fifty-four had improved by 3 percent.

In 2011 Muir had the distinction of logging more airtime than any other network journalist while covering several high-profile stories, including the near-fatal shooting of Congresswoman Gabrielle Giffords in Tucson, Arizona; the earthquake and tsunami in Fukushima, Japan; the tornado that struck Joplin, Missouri—the costliest in US history; the Arab Spring protests in Egypt's Tahrir Square; and the ongoing famine in Mogadishu, Somalia (he was the first American anchor to report from the scene of the humanitarian crisis).

JOINING *20/20* AND SUCCEEDING SAWYER

As ABC News's lead correspondent, Muir contributed to network coverage of the 2012 US presidential election, which included a sit-down with Republican candidate Mitt Romney, as well as the mass shootings in Aurora, Colorado, and Newtown, Connecticut. Muir, who amassed the most airtime for a second straight year, extensively reported on Hurricane Sandy, one of the nation's most expensive and destructive storms, and its impact on New York City.

In early 2013, while covering the nuclear talks between Iran and the United Nations, Muir offered ABC viewers an unprecedented look inside Tehran, Iran's capital. Two months later, he added yet another achievement to his already crowded résumé, replacing Chris Cuomo as cohost of *20/20* alongside Elizabeth Vargas. At the close of the 2013–14 season, the show would record its highest ratings in five years. However, a crowning moment came when it was announced that Sawyer would be stepping down as *World News Tonight* anchor and managing editor in August 2014, and Muir, her chief substitute, was announced as her successor, meaning that he had landed one of his dream jobs.

Muir quickly proved himself worthy of the network's trust. In November—only two months after his debut on Labor Day—*World News Tonight* edged out NBC's *Nightly News* among adults twenty-five to fifty-four to notch its first ratings sweep in that demographic in eighteen years. The first week of April 2015 marked the first time since September 2009 that Muir's program had bested *Nightly News* and claimed the crown as the most-watched evening newscast. One month later, *World News Tonight* recorded a May sweep victory among adults eighteen to forty-nine and twenty-five to fifty-four—its first in eight years. In the fall of that year, Muir conducted a unique satellite interview with Pope Francis inside of the Vatican. Often commenting in interviews on his dedication to connecting and relating with the audience, he has also shared that he takes advantage of social media platforms, mainly Twitter, during commercial breaks to engage in immediate conversations and feedback with viewers. "This is the most competitive evening news race in a decade, and it's upping everyone's game," he explained to Yu.

PERSONAL LIFE

Muir, who lives in Manhattan, is notoriously private about his personal life. In 2014 he was included in *People*'s list of sexiest men alive.

SUGGESTED READING

Mahler, Jonathan. "The Anchor as Buddy, Confessional but Chill." *New York Times*. New York Times, 1 Sept. 2014. Web. 12 Jan. 2016.

Muir, David. "The Biz: The News about ABC's David Muir." Interview by Stephen Battaglio. *TV Guide*. CBS Interactive, 19 Mar. 2013. Web. 12 Jan. 2016.

Muir, David. "David Muir on His Move to ABC's *World News Tonight*." Interview by Verne Gay. *Newsday*. Newsday, 1 Sept. 2014. Web. 12 Jan. 2016.

Webb, Donnie. "David Muir: Syracuse Native Was Always on a Path to the Top of Network News." *Syracuse.com*. Syracuse Media Group, 23 July 2014. Web. 12 Jan. 2016.

Yu, Roger. "ABC News Evolves with Anchor Muir amid Stiff Competition." *USA Today*. USA Today, 18 Oct. 2015. Web. 12 Jan. 2016.

SELECTED WORKS

World News with David Muir, 2011–14; *20/20*, 2013– ; *World News Tonight with David Muir*, 2014–

—*Bertha Muteba*

Randall Munroe

Born: October 17, 1984
Occupation: Cartoonist and writer

Randall Munroe makes weird and wonderful things happen. A former NASA employee turned cartoonist, Munroe is the creator of *xkcd*, a self-described "webcomic of romance, sarcasm, math, and language" that has, since its genesis in 2006, inspired its ever-expanding fan base to smuggle chessboards onto roller coasters, semi-spontaneously converge on parks, and pose questions about science that are both absurd and pressing. Unabashedly geeky, often quite heartfelt, and at times highly innovative in scope, *xkcd* is one of a wave of online comics that have demonstrated the viability and versatility of the form in the first decades of the twenty-first century. For Munroe, *xkcd*'s presence on and deep ties to the Internet have been essential to its success. "It used to be if you wanted to do a newspaper comic, you had to appeal to a pretty big chunk of the newspaper's readership for them to want to keep you around," he told Gavin Edwards for *Rolling Stone* (2 Sept. 2014). "*Dilbert* would be office humor, but even that is pretty widely experienced. One of the nice things about the Internet is you can do a comic that's just for PhD students, or for truck drivers, and you get to reach all of them without having to satisfy the other 99 percent."

In addition to his popular comic, Munroe is the author of the books *What If? Serious Scientific Answers to Absurd Hypothetical Questions* (2014) and *Thing Explainer: Complicated Stuff in Simple Words* (2015), essentially offshoots of projects he initially began under the *xkcd* banner. The former uses real scientific data to answer bizarre questions such as "What would happen if you were to gather a mole (unit of measurement) of moles (the small furry critter) in one place?" (the response to which begins, "Things get a bit gruesome"), while the latter explains complex scientific and technological topics using only the thousand (or "ten hundred"—as "thousand" is not one of the words) most commonly used words in the English language. Both books feature illustrations in Munroe's typical stick-figure style as well as a significant amount of his signature humor. They also represent Munroe's interest in improving the communication of scientific ideas to the general public. "I think there are a lot of issues where people are recognizing that we need an in-between role," he told Lee Hutchinson for *Ars Technica* (7 Dec. 2015). He continued, "Even the stuff that we think is clear public communication isn't always having the effect we want, and maybe relying on scientists to also be communicators is a bad strategy, because they're busy being scientists."

EARLY LIFE AND EDUCATION

Randall Patrick Munroe was born in Easton, Pennsylvania, on October 17, 1984. The oldest of three sons born to Julie Crum and Michael Munroe, he lived in several states when he was young but grew up primarily in Chesterfield, Virginia, where his family settled when he was ten years old. Munroe was interested in math and science from an early age. An inquisitive child, he enjoyed understanding and explaining topics that intrigued him. "I'm a chronic explainer—when I was five years old, I was very shy, but show-and-tell was my favorite!" he told Hutchinson. "I've been a chronic explainer from a very young age." Munroe also enjoyed contemplating unusual questions; in his introduction to *What If?*, he recalls that once, at age five, he attempted to determine the number of hard and soft objects in the world. He ultimately decided that there were about five billion of the former and three billion of the latter, although he has admitted that he is not quite sure how he came to that conclusion.

As a child, Munroe was an avid reader and often got in trouble at school for reading in class, to the point that his teachers at times had to take his books away. After graduating from the Mathematics and Science High School at Clover Hill in Midlothian, Virginia, he attended Christopher Newport University, earning his bachelor's degree in applied physics in 2006.

While in college, Munroe took an internship at the National Aeronautics and Space Administration (NASA) Langley Research Center, where he worked on virtual-reality systems. After finishing his degree, he returned to Langley, this time as a contractor with the robotics navigation lab. "It was nothing glamorous; I was just tasked with making code compile for obscure projects, and I wasn't very good at it," he told Farley Katz for the *New Yorker* (14 Oct. 2008). "Now I spend most of my time drawing pictures and looking at funny things on the Internet, which in retrospect is largely what I did at my old job, too." When Munroe's most recent contract ended in 2006, he decided not to pursue further work in robotics, instead opting to move to Massachusetts and focus on the web comic he had started earlier that year.

XKCD

Although drawing pictures may not have been the most socially acceptable use of Munroe's time at the Langley Research Center, it was ultimately a life-changing one. A decade after leaving NASA behind, Munroe is best known for his web comic *xkcd*, the title of which is an unpronounceable nonsense word that he originally used as his America Online (AOL) screen name. The comic originated as a collection of sketches and comic strips that Munroe had drawn in high school and college, and later while at work. Wanting to preserve his drawings, he scanned them and posted the comic strips on his personal website. After readers started showing interest in his comics, he and his roommate created a separate website to host them.

Among the first forty-four images on the new site, all of which were posted on January 1, 2006, were a series of strips featuring a boy in a floating barrel and a variety of sketches drawn on graph paper. Other drawings serve as early examples of what would become Munroe's signature style, with simple stick-figure drawings making humorous, often obscure references rooted in math, science, and history. As Munroe started to add new work, *xkcd* began to gain significant popularity among users of websites such as Boing Boing and Reddit, and he began to sell merchandise, including T-shirts and prints of some of his more popular comics. By 2007, the comic had become so successful that Munroe decided to devote himself to it full time.

Although *xkcd* primarily consists of short, humorous comic strips, Munroe has created a number of more ambitious projects over the years. One, the comic "Click and Drag," presents a vast world that the reader can explore by clicking and dragging on the image. Another, "Time," features a cohesive narrative told through an animated sequence that was posted frame by frame over the course of about four months. "I thought about how there was the in-between space between animation, where you get many frames per second, and a daily comic, where you're getting updates every day," Munroe explained to Edwards. "I couldn't think of anything that had

been done in the in-between space, partially because it's really hard to reach people every hour without the Internet. You have to show up at their house—'All right, here's the frame for this hour'—and they're like, 'Please leave me alone.' I wasn't sure how people would consume it, but it's fun to have something where people are figuring out how to read it. Sometimes making something a little bit less accessible and more of a puzzle can make it more appealing." "Time" received significant acclaim from critics and readers and earned Munroe the 2014 Hugo Award for best graphic story.

UNEXPECTED INFLUENCE

One of the most intriguing aspects of *xkcd* is its ability to inject some of its signature whimsy into everyday life. The 249th comic posted to the site, created in April 2007, was titled "Chess Photo" and featured characters gluing chess pieces to a chessboard so that they could take a picture of themselves appearing to play chess while on a roller coaster. Fans of *xkcd* were amused by the idea, and a surprising number of people successfully reenacted the comic in real life, populating a gallery on *xkcd*'s website with fan-submitted photographs of their own roller-coaster chess matches. Munroe's comics have likewise inspired readers to photograph themselves playing guitar in the shower, set up ball pits in their homes, and, in September 2007, descend en masse on a park in Cambridge, Massachusetts, after Munroe included its coordinates and a date and time in the comic "Dream Girl." The comic has also influenced the wider Internet: Munroe's suggestion in the comic "Listen to Yourself" that YouTube comments be read aloud to their writers before being posted has been credited with inspiring the implementation of YouTube's audio preview feature.

Although *xkcd*'s significant influence among its readers is obvious in retrospect, Munroe was initially caught off guard by the unexpected ways that influence manifested. "I keep being surprised seeing the ideas in the comic leak out into real life," he told Katz. "It's tempting to just write a comic called 'EVERYONE MAIL RANDALL MUNROE TWENTY BUCKS'—maybe it would work, and I could just close down the *xkcd* store and sit on a beach and draw pictures and make snarky Reddit posts for the rest of my life."

WHAT IF? AND THING EXPLAINER

In addition to *xkcd*, Munroe is the author of two books that merge his humor and art with his lifelong interest in explaining things. *What If?*, published in 2014, was inspired by Munroe's experience delivering a lecture to high school students who visited the Massachusetts Institute of Technology (MIT) in 2009. The teenagers were not engaged by his discussion of energy, so he turned to popular culture to capture their interest, making physics more approachable through discussions of pop-culture mainstays such as *Star Wars* and the *Lord of the Rings*; one of the questions posed concerned the amount of energy released when the eye of *Lord of the Rings* villain Sauron explodes. Munroe later created a page on *xkcd's* site dedicated to collecting such questions from his readers, and he published the answers to some of the most interesting questions in book form, along with accompanying illustrations.

Munroe's second book, *Thing Explainer*, was inspired by his comic "Up-Goer Five," in which he labeled a drawing of the *Saturn V* rocket using only words included among the thousand most commonly used English words. Expanding on that concept, *Thing Explainer* explains a variety of complex topics using common words and illustrations. In March 2016, Munroe's publisher, Houghton Mifflin Harcourt, announced that it would include portions of *Thing Explainer* as well as similar new material in some of its high school textbooks.

PERSONAL LIFE

Munroe married in 2011. He and his wife live in Somerville, Massachusetts. In his interview with Katz, Munroe described *xkcd* as "about three-fourths autobiographical."

SUGGESTED READING

Chang, Kenneth. "He's Glad You Asked." *New York Times*. New York Times, 3 Nov. 2014. Web. 8 Apr. 2016.

Hutchinson, Lee. "A Brief Chat with *XKCD's* Randall Munroe—the *Thing Explainer* Explainer." *Ars Technica*. Condé Nast, 7 Dec. 2015. Web. 8 Apr. 2016.

Munroe, Randall. "Cartoon-Off: *XKCD*." Interview by Farley Katz. *New Yorker*. Condé Nast, 14 Oct. 2008. Web. 8 Apr. 2016.

Munroe, Randall. "A Conversation with Randall Munroe, the Creator of *XKCD*." Interview by Megan Garber. *Atlantic*. Atlantic Monthly Group, 26 Sept. 2012. Web. 8 Apr. 2016.

Munroe, Randall. "Dropping Science: *XKCD* Cartoonist Randall Munroe on His New Book." Interview by Gavin Edwards. *Rolling Stone*. Rolling Stone, 2 Sept. 2014. Web. 8 Apr. 2016.

Munroe, Randall. "*What If* There Were an Entire Book Devoted to Absurd Hypotheticals?" *NPR*. NPR, 7 Sept. 2014. Web. 8 Apr. 2016.

Tupponce, Joan. "A Cartoonist's Mind." *Richmond Magazine*. Target Communications, 24 Nov. 2009. Web. 8 Apr. 2016.

SELECTED WORKS

xkcd, 2006–; *What If? Serious Scientific Answers to Absurd Hypothetical Questions*, 2014; *Thing Explainer: Complicated Stuff in Simple Words*, 2015

—Joy Crelin

James Murphy

Born: February 4, 1970
Occupation: Musician, producer

James Murphy began performing as a musician and DJ in the 1980s, but remained relatively unknown until serving as front man of the alternative dance band LCD Soundsystem. The band first gained notoriety in 2002 with the song "Losing My Edge."

EARLY LIFE AND EDUCATION

James Murphy was born in Princeton Junction, New Jersey, on February 4, 1970. A passionate music fan from a young age, he attended West Windsor-Plainsboro High School South. Working with friends and colleagues, Murphy taught himself guitar, sound engineering, and deejaying. As a teenager, he listened to a wide variety of musical genres and would later cite artists such as David Bowie, The Smiths, Can, The Fall, The Beatles, The B-52s, Violent Femmes, Yes, and Harry Nilsson as influences on his own music.

In addition to music, Murphy was also interested in comedy writing and combat sports. After graduating from high school, he trained as a kick boxer for a year before moving to New York where he enrolled at New York University. Murphy excelled as a student, earning a degree in English while immersing himself in the city's music scene. From 1988 to 1989, Murphy played guitar in a band called Falling Man and worked part-time as a sound engineer. He also earned regular work deejaying at various dance clubs throughout New York, playing audience selections by artists such as Donna Summer, Kraftwerk, and Public Image Ltd. His work as a DJ led him to begin creating his own dance music. In 1991, Murphy entered talks with the producers of *It's Garry Shandling's Show* about a writing position for a new sitcom. In what became something of a notorious moment in Murphy's career, he turned down the position, which he later learned was for the sitcom *Seinfeld*. In 1999, Murphy and his friend Tim Goldsworthy founded the label that became known as DFA Records.

LCD SOUNDSYSTEM

Murphy formed the electronic dance group LCD Soundsystem in 2001. One of the group's early singles, "Losing My Edge," became popular in the New York underground club scene.

The song, which is almost eight minutes long, features sardonic, tongue-in-cheek lyrics about record collecting and music fandom. The band gained a global audience following the release of the album *LCD Soundsystem* in 2005, which featured "Losing My Edge." The two-disc record, which was released on DFA Records, features sixteen tracks that are an eclectic mix of musical genres, including post-punk, house music, alternative rock, and psychedelic pop. The widespread success of the album, which also includes the singles "Give It Up" and "Yeah," resulted in the band generating large audiences at their performances. Beyond its commercial success, *LCD Soundsystem* was also well received by critics when the album received two Grammy nominations in 2005: best dance recording for the song "Daft Punk Is Playing at My House" and best electronic/dance album.

LCD Soundsystem released its second album, *Sound of Silver*, in March 2007. The record met with instant critical acclaim, earning a rating of 9.2 out of 10 from the alternative music website Pitchfork. *Sound of Silver* became a commercial success on the heels of the singles "North American Scum" and "All My Friends." LCD Soundsystem toured widely with the Canadian alternative rock band Arcade Fire in support of the record. The two bands released a joint single, with LCD Soundsystem performing a cover of British dance punk band Joy Division's "No Love Lost" and Arcade Fire performing a cover French pop sensation France Gall's 1965 song "Poupée de cire, poupée de son." *Sound of Silver* received a 2007 Grammy Award nomination for best electronic/dance album. The album was also named as one of the best albums of the year by the *Guardian*.

The band's third album, *This Is Happening*, was released in May 2010. The release of the record was complicated by online leaks of the tracks, which Murphy protested. The album features a multi-instrumentalist performance by Murphy, who plays—in addition to performing vocals—the synthesizer, bass guitar, guitar, drums, and keyboards. Like its two predecessors, the album received critical acclaim, earning praise from a litany of music publications, including *Pitchfork*, *Spin*, *Paste*, *AllMusic*, and *Consequence of Sound*. The album's single "Drunk Girls," was popularized by a music video directed by filmmaker Spike Jones. LCD Soundsystem toured throughout Europe in support of the album from April to September 2010.

Murphy announced the end of LCD Soundsystem in February 2011. The band performed a final show in New York City at Madison Square Garden on April 2 that year.

IMPACT

With LCD Soundsystem, Murphy helped to popularize a genre-blending style of dance music. The band was also one of the first to achieve widespread commercial success in the era of digital music—when downloads of albums and single tracks began to displace sales of hardcopy recordings. Since finishing his work with LCD Soundsystem, Murphy has worked as a music producer and served as producer on the 2013 Arcade Fire album *Reflektor* and the 2013 Yeah Yeah Yeahs' album *Mosquito*.

SUGGESTED READING

Bailey, Rachel. "LCD Soundsystem Releases In-Studio Video, Announces European Tour Dates." *Paste*. Wolfgang's Vault. 25 Jan. 2010. Web. 10 Apr. 2014.

Bowen, Rebecca. "Arcade Fire, LCD Soundsystem Add Gigs, Split 7." *Paste*. Wolfgang's Vault. 13 Aug. 2007. Web. 10 Apr. 2014.

Dombal, Ryan. "James Murphy Talks *Greenberg* Soundtrack, New LCD Soundsystem." *Pitchfork*. Pitchfork Media. 3 Mar. 2010. Web. 10 Apr. 2014.

"I Speak as a Lifetime Failure." *Guardian*. Guardian Media Group. 29 Oct. 2004. Web. 10 Apr. 2014.

"James Murphy Chats about LCD Soundsystem Split. Reunion Prospects. Wacky Store." *Spin*. Spin Media. 9 July 2012. 10 Apr. 2014.

Klosterman, Chuck. "LCD Soundsystem's Last Stand." *Guardian*. Guardian Media Group. 23 Apr. 2010. Web. 10 Apr. 2014.

"LCD Soundsystem Beg Crowd Not to Leak Album at New York Show." *NME*. IPC Media. 13 Apr. 2010. Web. 10 Apr. 2014.

SELECTED WORKS

LCD Soundsystem, 2005; *Sound of Silver*, 2007; *This Is Happening*, 2010

—Joshua Pritchard

Satya Nadella

Born: 1967
Occupation: CEO of Microsoft

As CEO of one of the world's largest computer technology companies, Satya Nadella is charged with reshaping Microsoft into a company that can compete with innovators such as Google and Apple.

EARLY LIFE AND EDUCATION

Bukkapuram Nadella Satyanarayana was born in Hyderabad, India, in 1967 to Prabhavati Nadella and Bukkapuram Nadella Yugandhar. His father was a civil servant in the elite Indian Administrative Service. Nadella spent his early years in the Bukkapuram village in the Anantapur district in Rayala Seema, where his paternal grandparents lived. He then attended Hyderabad Public School, a prestigious boarding school in the Begumpet neighborhood of Hyderabad, from 1978 to 1984.

In secondary school, Nadella was an above-average student who engaged in many extracurricular activities, including his school's cricket, football, and debating teams. As an adult, Nadella remains passionate about cricket and credits the skills he learned as part of the cricket team with being instrumental in shaping his leadership and teamwork skills.

After being denied admission to his first-choice school due to an average entrance test score, Nadella enrolled in the Manipal Institute of Technology, then part of Mangalore University and now part of Manipal University. He received his bachelor's degree in electrical engineering in 1988. Nadella then traveled to the United States and completed a master's degree in computer science from the University of Wisconsin–Milwaukee. He would later earn a master's degree in business administration from the University of Chicago's Booth School of Business.

ENGINEERING, TECHNOLOGY, AND LEADERSHIP

Nadella began his career working on the technology side of Sun Microsystems. He joined Microsoft in 1992 as a program manager in the Windows developer relations group, where he helped develop many client-server platforms. He was soon promoted to general manager for the commerce platforms group. Over the next few years, he played significant roles in developing the Microsoft Commerce Server, the BizTalk Server, and the technology behind interactive television and digital rights management.

Nadella became vice president of the Microsoft bCentral online service for small businesses in 1999. Two years later, he was named corporate vice president of Microsoft Business Solutions, where he helped create software such as the Microsoft Office Small Business products and Microsoft Dynamics CRM. In 2007, he advanced to senior vice president of research and development for the online services division. His work included developing the MSN, Live Search, and advertising platforms.

In 2011, Nadella became president of the server and tools division, where he led the move from client-server software to Windows Azure (now Microsoft Azure), Microsoft's cloud platform and services. In 2013, he took on the role of executive vice president of the cloud and enterprise group, a position he held until February 4, 2014, when he was chosen to become the new CEO of Microsoft.

Nadella has been instrumental in building and growing many of Microsoft's newer offerings, including its computing platforms, developer tools, Xbox gaming system, Bing search engine, Surface line of tablets, and cloud infrastructure and service. After becoming CEO, he said that while he would continue to grow these areas of the company, he would also focus heavily on increasing the company's market share in mobile devices.

As the third CEO of a major multinational company, Nadella stepped into a challenging situation. Between 2000 and 2014, Microsoft underwent significant struggles, losing ground to competitors such as Apple and Google, which forced the company to quickly shift its focus to mobile and cloud computing in order to keep up with a changing market. Microsoft founder and former CEO Bill Gates believed Nadella to be up to the task, citing his engineering and computer skills, business vision, leadership, and people skills.

One of Nadella's early actions as CEO was to ask Gates to stay on as a technology adviser, which Gates accepted. In his first six months as CEO, Nadella announced the acquisition of smartphone manufacturer Nokia, released a version of Microsoft Office for Apple's iPad, and made policy changes to gain inroads for Windows in the mobile market.

In addition to working at Microsoft, Nadella is on the board of many companies. As of 2014, he was the director of supply-management software company BravoSolutions US and a member of the advisory board of financial software company Nirvaha, among others.

IMPACT

Satya Nadella is the first CEO of Microsoft who is not a founder or original employee. He also has the distinction of being tasked with moving Microsoft away from its roots into areas that founders Bill Gates and Paul Allen could never have envisioned when they started the company in 1975.

PERSONAL LIFE

In 1992, Nadella married Anupama Priyadarshini, a fellow student at Hyderabad Public School and Manipal University. They have three children: two daughters, Tara and Divya, and a son, Zain. They live in Bellevue, Washington, and travel to India at least once a year to visit their parents and families.

SUGGESTED READING

Dutt, Ela. "Satya Nadella: Our Man at Microsoft." *News India Times.* News India Times, 7 Feb. 2014. Web. 15 July 2014.

Krishna, S. Rama. "Nadella Is Still Rooted to His Village in AP." *Sunday Guardian* [Delhi]. MJP Media, 8 Feb. 2014. Web. 15 July 2014.

Nadella, Satya. "'Never, Ever Stop Learning': Satya Nadella." Interview by Anisha Dhiman. *Deccan Chronicle*. Deccan Chronicle, 29 July 2013. Web. 15 July 2014.

Sharf, Samantha. "It's Official: Microsoft Names Satya Nadella Its Third CEO." *Forbes*. Forbes. com, 4 Feb. 2014. Web. 15 July 2014.

Tu, Janet I. "'He Knows His Stuff': CEO Satya Nadella Is Well-Liked, Low Profile." *Seattle Times*. Seattle Times, 4 Feb. 2014. Web. 15 July 2014.

Williams, Rhiannon, and Katherine Rushton. "Bill Gates Quits as Microsoft Chairman and Satya Nadella Is Named Chief Executive." *Telegraph*. Telegraph Media, 4 Feb. 2014. Web. 15 July 2014.

Wingfield, Nick. "Microsoft's Profit Dips Less Than Expected as It Reshapes Itself." *New York Times*. New York Times, 25 Apr. 2014. Web. 1 July 2014.

—*Barb Lightner*

László Nemes

Born: February 18, 1977
Occupation: Director and screenwriter

Since the culmination of World War II, there have been numerous films made about the Holocaust. Few directors, however, have tackled the delicate subject as viscerally and realistically as László Nemes, whose debut feature, the Hungarian Holocaust drama *Son of Saul* (2015), delves into the devastating reality of a Sonderkommando member at the infamous Auschwitz-Birkenau concentration camp. Known as the "bearers of secrets," Sonderkommandos were squads of Jewish male prisoners who were forced to assist the Nazis in the gas chambers and disposing of bodies. They worked for only a few months before being killed themselves, in order to make room for new Sonderkommando teams and to ensure that the Nazis' heinous crimes would be kept secret.

Nemes had only previously directed three short films when *Son of Saul* premiered in the main competition at the 2015 Cannes Film Festival. The film won the prestigious festival's second-highest honor, the Grand Prix, and achieved worldwide critical acclaim, propelling Nemes from relative obscurity into the international spotlight. He has been hailed for eschewing the conventions of the Holocaust film by providing a harrowingly immersive portrait of life in a concentration camp. In 2016 *Son of Saul*

Lenke Szilágyi/CC BY-SA 3.0/Wikimedia Commons

became the first Hungarian film to win the Golden Globe Award for best foreign language film and only the second to win an Academy Award in that category. "When you hear 'Holocaust film,' you immediately see what that is, and we wanted to make another kind of movie. We wanted to make a visceral kind of film," Nemes told Kate Taylor for the *Globe and Mail* (23 Dec. 2015).

EARLY LIFE

László Nemes was born on February 18, 1977, in Budapest, Hungary. He comes from a family whose history is inextricably linked to the Holocaust. Nemes's maternal great-grandparents were among the more than four hundred thousand Hungarian Jews who were deported to and killed at Auschwitz in 1944. His maternal grandmother, meanwhile, fled Nazi-occupied Hungary to what is now Ukraine and his father's family waited out the war in hiding. "A big part of the family never returned," he noted to Taylor.

Nemes was first made aware of his family's Holocaust horrors when he was around five years old. "I always had this sense of being unable to understand it and being angry," he explained to Lisa Klug for the *Times of Israel* (18 Dec. 2015). "That's always been a defining feeling." Growing up Jewish in Communist-era Hungary also shaped Nemes's world view. Classmates derogatorily referred to him as "the dirty Jew," which was "something that defined my perceptions of humans," as he told Shevaun Mizrahi for *Filmmaker* (28 Oct. 2015). "I was pretty much scared throughout my childhood."

Nemes found solace from his fear in film, which he developed a passion for at an early age.

His father, András Jeles, is a prominent Hungarian film and stage director whose film *Why Wasn't He There?* (1993) was among the first to address the Nazis' deportation of Hungarian Jews. Nemes spent a lot of time on film sets as a child, but has seldom spoken of his father in interviews. He was raised by his mother, who taught philosophy. In 1989 the two immigrated to Paris, France, to build a new life.

LEARNING FROM A MASTER

As a teenager, Nemes started making short horror films in his Paris basement. He hoped to attend film school but when that option was not available, he decided to study history at Paris's Institut d'Études Politiques (Sciences Po). Upon graduating, he took classes in cinema studies at the Sorbonne in Paris. Much of his film education, however, came through independent study.

In 2003, Nemes returned to Budapest to launch his film career. Eager to gain hands-on filmmaking experience, he reached out to another major influence, Béla Tarr, arguably Hungary's most acclaimed director, about the possibility of offering him his services. Tarr, then three years removed from directing his post–World War II, apocalyptic masterpiece *Werckmeister Harmonies* (2000), subsequently hired Nemes to assist him on the "Prologue" segment of the European anthology film *Visions of Europe* (2004). He then served as an assistant director on Tarr's eighth feature, *The Man from London*, which premiered in competition at the 2007 Cannes Film Festival.

After wrapping filming on *The Man from London*, Nemes enrolled in the graduate film program at New York University's prestigious Tisch School of the Arts. He left Tisch, however, after only a year. "It didn't bring anything rewarding or usable," Nemes explained in his interview with Mizrahi. "My time in film school reaffirmed the idea that it is better to learn directly from a master . . . Béla Tarr was my film school."

The knowledge Nemes gained from working with Tarr served him well during the making of his first short film *With a Little Patience* (2007), which follows a young German office clerk who, while going about her mundane daily routines, bears witness to Nazis herding a group of Jewish civilians into the forest to be executed. The chilling, thirteen-minute short premiered at the 2007 Venice International Film Festival and won a number of awards, including top honors at the 2008 Drama International Short Film Festival, held in northern Greece.

REINVENTING THE HOLOCAUST FILM

Following *With a Little Patience*, Nemes directed two more award-winning short films, titled *The Counterpart* (2008) and *The Gentleman Takes His Leave* (2010). The former is a wartime drama that focuses on a tryst between two male officers from opposing armies. The latter, meanwhile, is based on a story by Russian author Fyodor Dostoyevsky.

By 2010 Nemes had already begun developing his first feature-length film *Son of Saul*. He initially conceived the idea for the film after discovering a collection of texts written by members of the Sonderkommando called *Des voix sous la cendre* (Voices from beneath the ashes). Commonly known as the "Scrolls of Auschwitz," the texts offer a glimpse into the harrowing day-to-day realities of Auschwitz Sonderkommandos. The texts were buried and hidden before the Sonderkommando revolt that took place at Auschwitz on October 7, 1944, but were recovered after the war. "I never knew there were voices coming directly from the dead like that. I had the feeling I was thrown into the middle of it," Nemes said to Geoffrey Macnab for *Screen Daily* (13 Nov. 2015).

Nemes teamed up with his friend Clara Royer, a French novelist, and the two began working on a script about the Sonderkommando experience in Auschwitz. From the outset, Nemes and Royer aimed to break away from the so-called "code" of the Holocaust film genre, which, as exemplified by Oscar winners such as Steven Spielberg's *Schindler's List* (1993) and Roberto Benigni's *Life Is Beautiful* (1997), has largely focused on uplifting, broad-context survival stories with clearly drawn heroes and villains. "All these older films establish a safe road for the viewer, and at the end, some kind of liberation," Nemes explained to Andrew Pulver for the *Guardian* (14 Apr. 2016). "But that's not the story of the Holocaust. That's the story of how we want the Holocaust to be. It's not the story I wanted to tell."

Wanting to create a film that would "give back dignity to the dead and the dying," as he explained to Taylor, Nemes settled on the fictional story of a single prisoner, Saul Ausländer, a Hungarian Jewish member of the Sonderkommando. In 2011 Nemes developed the script while participating in the Cannes Cinéfondation residency program in Paris.

SON OF SAUL

Nemes had initially envisioned *Son of Saul* being a French production with a French main character. He scrapped that idea, however, after failing to secure financing in France and Israel. Nemes was eventually persuaded by the film's producers, Gábor Sipos and Gábor Rajna, to make the film a majority Hungarian production, and in 2013, the Hungarian Film Fund agreed to finance most of its budget. Partial funding was also provided by the New York–based Conference on Jewish Material Claims against Germany.

Shot in twenty-eight days on an old military base outside of Budapest, *Son of Saul* takes place during a thirty-six-hour period at Auschwitz in

October 1944. The 107-minute film follows Saul, portrayed by Hungarian poet and former punk rocker Géza Röhrig, as he embarks on a mission to provide a proper burial for a young boy who may or may not be his son. As Saul frantically searches for a rabbi to preside over the boy's clandestine burial, he runs into conflict with a disparate group of Sonderkommandos who stage an armed rebellion modeled after the real-life one. Almost the entire film features Saul in extended, shallow focus close-ups, rendering much of the atrocities around him blurry and out of focus. "I wanted the viewer to be within the experience," Nemes explained to Klug. "That is something that makes it unique."

Son of Saul was originally intended to premiere at the 2015 Berlin Film Festival, which Nemes thought would have been a good setting for the seventieth anniversary of the liberation of Auschwitz. When the festival failed to grant the film a competition slot, he and his producers turned their attention to Cannes. There, the film not only landed a competition berth, which is a rarity for a debut feature, but also won the prestigious Grand Prix.

CRITICAL ACCLAIM AND ACCOLADES FOR *SON OF SAUL*

At Cannes, Son of Saul elicited strong responses from critics. In a representative review for *Variety* (14 May 2015), Justin Chang called the film a "terrifyingly accomplished first feature," and wrote that it was "as grim and unyielding a depiction of the Holocaust as has yet been made" on the subject, praising Nemes's "unstintingly realistic approach." Meanwhile, Manohla Dargis, in her review for the *New York Times* (20 May 2015), pointed out Nemes's "technical virtuosity" but described the film as being "radically dehistoricized" and "intellectually repellent" for its decision to focus on a single individual rather than the larger, terrorized whole.

For the most part, though, Son of Saul received overwhelmingly positive reviews as well as praise from filmmakers such as Claude Lanzmann, whose landmark nine-hour documentary *Shoah* (1985) was among the first to address the existential plight of the Sonderkommando. In June 2015, Son of Saul was released in Hungary, where it sold over one hundred thousand tickets, the most ever for an independent film there. The film subsequently screened at festivals all over the world, taking home best foreign language film honors at several of them.

After its US release in December 2015, Son of Saul became the first Hungarian film to win the award for best foreign language film at the Golden Globe Awards. The film's run of success culminated in February 2016, when it won the Oscar for best foreign language film at the eighty-eighth Academy Awards; it became the second Hungarian film to win the award (after István Szabó's 1981 film *Mephisto*). Just days before its Oscar win, Paul Byrnes, in a laudatory review for the *Sydney Morning Herald* (24 Feb. 2016), proclaimed Son of Saul "one of the greatest films ever made. Just when it seemed that cinema was spent . . . László Nemes has revived it by tackling the hardest story anyone could tell, in a way that has never been done—and in his first film."

Nemes served as a jury member for the main competition at the 2016 Cannes Film Festival, and he had already begun work on his next feature film, titled *Sunset*, which will center on a young female protagonist in pre–World War I Budapest.

SUGGESTED READING

Chang, Justin. Rev. of *Son of Saul*, dir. László Nemes. *Variety*. Variety Media, 14 May 2015. Web. 16 May 2016.

Dargis, Manohla. "At the Cannes Film Festival, Some Gems Midway Through." Rev. of *Son of Saul*, dir. László Nemes. *New York Times*. New York Times, 20 May 2015. Web. 16 May 2016.

Macnab, Geoffrey. "Lazlo Nemes Talks Hungary's Oscar Submission *Son of Saul*." *Screen Daily*. Media Business Insight, 13 Nov. 2015. Web. 16 May 2016.

Nemes, László. "Hell on Earth: László Nemes on *Son of Saul*." Interview by Shevaun Mizrahi. *Filmmaker Magazine*. Filmmaker Magazine, 28 Oct. 2015. Web. 16 May 2016.

Nemes, László. "In Devastating *Son of Saul*, Jewish Director Goes Where Few Others Dare." Interview by Lisa Klug. *Times of Israel*. Times of Israel, 18 Dec. 2015. Web. 16 May 2016.

Pulver, Andrew. "Laszlo Nemes: 'I Didn't Want *Son of Saul* to Tell the Story of Survival.'" *Guardian*. Guardian News and Media, 14 Apr. 2016. Web. 16 May 2016.

Taylor, Kate. "Nemes's *Son of Saul* Aims to 'Give Back Dignity' to Auschwitz Work Brigade." *Globe and Mail*. Globe and Mail, 23 Dec. 2015. Web. 16 May 2016.

SELECTED WORKS

With a Little Patience, 2007; *The Counterpart*, 2008; *The Gentleman Takes His Leave*, 2010; *Son of Saul*, 2015

—Chris Cullen

Joanna Newsom

Born: January 18, 1982
Occupation: Musician

As arguably the most prominent harpist in American indie music, soprano Joanna Newsom is an anomaly: a contemporary musician with roots in the Renaissance who plays in rock clubs. Her music is filled with rich language. Words such as *poetaster* and *grammerie* appear in her songs, which are themselves unusually long and reminiscent of the ballad traditions of centuries past. She has been compared to other idiosyncratic artists such as Tori Amos and Björk. Yet she is aware of her limitations, telling Claire Suddath for *Time* (15 March 2010), "As a composer, I require assistance. I have ideas, and I have an album in mind, but I'm limited. I need help making the record." Newsom has appeared on television with hosts David Letterman and Stephen Colbert as well as on the show *Portlandia*. She also modeled for the Armani label in 2009. She made her film debut with a brief appearance in *Inherent Vice*, the 2014 Paul Thomas Anderson film. Anderson also directed two of her music videos.

EDUCATION AND EARLY CAREER

Joanna Caroline Newsom grew up in Nevada City, California. She had a progressive upbringing in Nevada City, which is known as a countercultural hub of Northern California. Her parents, William and Christine, were both musical and were both physicians—her father was an oncologist, while her mother was an internist. They were also birdwatchers, and taught Joanna and her siblings (older brother, Pete, and younger sister, Emily) how to identify various species. She began playing the harp as a child; she asked for lessons at age four, but was told she was too young. After a few years of piano lessons, her teacher accepted her in the study of the harp.

When Newsom was twelve, she attended Lark Camp in Mendocino Woodlands, a weeklong folk camp. Diana Stork was the harp teacher, and impressed with Newsom's ability. She told Jody Rosen for *New York Times* (3 March 2010), "Joanna had a great imagination, and a beautiful lyrical sense, a very nice sense of chordal accompaniment. The one thing that I really thought I could share with her was polyrhythms." Stork taught Newsom to use different rhythms with each hand, a technique of the West African *kora* players. The left hand represents earth with a steady one-two-three-four beat. At the same time, the right hand plays a one-two-three beat that does not resolve, representing heaven. Every twelve beats, earth and heaven come together.

d&e/CC BY 2.0/Wikimedia Commons

By the time Newsom was a young teenager she was fearful of sounding too much like anything that had already been done, and so began to study various kinds of music, including those from other cultures. She also started to develop her own unique process for writing her songs. She told Roy Harper for *Bomb* (2011), "A song's structure builds outward, for me, from the idea of tension rising up between the syllabic emphases in the lyrical line, and the rhythmic and melodic emphases in the metric line."

Newsom attended Mills College in Oakland, studying creative writing and music composition. She left Mills in 2002 before completing a degree, finding the dissonance favored there not in line with her love of melody. She did take creative writing classes to sharpen her writing skills. In them, she found Walt Whitman, Vladimir Nabokov, and Cormac McCarthy to be inspirations.

Also in 2002, the singer Bonnie Prince Billy (real name Will Oldham) heard recordings Newsom had made for friends and invited her to tour with him. In 2004, Newsome released her first album on the Drag City independent label. Entitled *The Milk-Eyed Mender*, it featured the lush storytelling and rich lyricism for which Newsom would become known. The album sold two hundred thousand copies, an impressive number for a release from an independent label.

YS

Touring in America and Europe in 2005, Newsom premiered a few longer songs that would become part of her second album, *Ys*. The album, pronounced "ees," is named for an island in Breton mythology. Newsom's 2006 album differs from her first in the orchestral arrangement that Van Dyke Parks provided. (Parks is perhaps best known for working with Randy Newman and arranging for the Beach Boys.) Writing for the *New Yorker* (4 Dec. 2006), Sasha Frere-Jones described the album as "a series of complex, through-composed songs that have more in common with Kurt Weill's long-form ballads than with contemporary pop music." Newsom herself likened it to William Faulkner's 1929 novel *The Sound and the Fury*.

The five songs on the album range in length from seven to seventeen minutes. Asked why the songs were so much longer than typical for indie music, Newsom told Emma Pearse for *New York* (20 Nov. 2006), "They're an attempt to respond to a year in my life, to organize four events, all of which were pretty massive and after which I was never the same again. There was a death, and it was a very, very huge one for me. I am exploring a whole collection of human tendencies that creep up in reaction to mortality and loss, among which are decadence." The album sold 250,000 copies.

Newsom took the album and other songs on tour to several cities. The touring band she put together for *Ys* became the Ys Street Band (a nod to Bruce Springsteen and his E Street Band). Together with four members of the Ys Street Band, Newsom recorded an extended play (EP) that was released in 2007 under the title *Joanna Newsom and the Ys Street Band*. The three-song EP featured two stripped-down recordings of old songs, as well as a new one called "Colleen."

HAVE ONE ON ME

When Newsom released two singles on Drag City's website, bloggers and fans began to hope it signaled a new forthcoming album. Indeed, the tracks were part of her third album, *Have One on Me*. Released in 2010, it was a three-disc set more than two hours long. Newsom intended it as a narrative to be heard in one sitting, and has compared it to a book with multiple chapters. The songs cover one day: morning, day, and night. Critics praised the album, stating that it was the most accessible of her albums to date.

Newsom had developed a severe case of vocal nodules while on tour for *Ys*; she took a month-long vow of silence to heal, then worked with a trained vocal coach. Because of this, her voice on *Have One on Me* was deeper than her usual soprano. The album has eighteen songs, averaging seven minutes each. Ryan Francesconi did the arrangements; he used some instruments from the Balkans to add texture. He praised Newsom's technical skill to Rosen, saying that her "rhythms are so subtle—so subtly off the beat all the time. And that's a really interesting thing, because her harp is very precise, yet the

vocal floats on top, and has a really separate feeling. The things she can do independently while playing the harp are humbling."

The title track is about Lola Montez, a musician who lived in the Nevada City area during the mid-nineteenth century and with whom Newsom somewhat identifies. She told Rosen, "To be a woman and to be a performer at that time meant something very different than it does now, but I'm also interested in what the similarities are. I was interested in the fact that she was constantly traveling and constantly having to start over and make a new life for herself. And her connection to this town is very important to me."

For years Newsom continued to use the student-level harp her parents bought for her when she was young, renting other instruments to use on tour or for recording. She finally purchased a Lyon & Healy Prince William Concert Grand harp for herself after her third album was released. It weighs eighty-three pounds and is more than seventy-four inches tall.

DIVERS

Newsom released a video single in August 2015, "Sapokanikan," which became the harbinger of her fourth album, *Divers*, released in October 2015. It opens and closes with the sound of hooting owls. Birds were one of the inspirations for the album, as Newsom told Jonah Weiner for *Rolling Stone* (15 Oct. 2015). She spent time "just watching birds fly, especially these loose-bodied, inefficiently flapping, joyful birds that just fling themselves at the sky, like the swallows you'll see a lot around this town."

She deals with a multitude of themes and influences on the album, ranging from oyster harvesting to Percy Bysshe Shelley's poem "Ozymandias." She lived in Greenwich Village for a time, and became interested in the Native American tribe that had once lived in the area, the Lenape. The album's lead single, "Sapokanikan," is named for the Lenape trading village that existed in the present-day location of New York City's Washington Square Park.

The album has eleven tracks but is less than an hour in length. Newsom again branched out and varied her instrumentation—keyboards and synthesizers are included among more classical instruments. On some tracks medieval instruments such as clavichords are used. In addition, she worked with composers Dave Longstreth of Dirty Projectors and classical composer Nico Muhly. Newsom's voice had by this time recovered and returned to her normal soprano range.

The work focuses on water, but its lyrical content is complex. The songs take various viewpoints, with Newsom inhabiting different characters rather than speaking as herself. The writing required about two years, with a few months to do the basic vocal tracks. Then came the process of trying to convey to her collaborators what she heard in her head, which required another year or two. As she told Zach Schonfeld for *Newsweek* (2015), "I'm so glad no one told me when I started it how long this particular idea was going to take. I would have been really discouraged. As it was, I was bright-eyed, idealistic and really excited about this idea and forging ahead and it just happened to take a really long time to finish."

During its first week of sales the album bested her previous record, selling fourteen thousand copies. That put it number one on both the Billboard Alternative Albums and Folk Music charts. It was her first number one in the former and second in the latter.

SETTING HER LIMITS

Newsom and her recording company agreed that her work would not be available on the online music-streaming service Spotify. She told Schonfeld, "It's a business that's literally built from the ground up to circumvent labels having to pay artists."

Another limit Newsom set was on her social media presence, refusing to cultivate a fan following. She remained a private person despite her success. She claimed not to read articles about her work, having been frustrated by coverage portraying her as some kind of delicate, fantastical creature or labeling her music as childlike. However, she did come to accept that her music and image does project a certain quality that she cannot control. She told Rosen, "I think that there's always going to be an element of my experience of the world—as much as I feel this as a deficiency—that is unprotected, unbuffered."

PERSONAL LIFE

In 2013 Newsome married actor and former *Saturday Night Live* cast member Andy Samberg in Big Sur, California. The following year they purchased Moorcrest, an estate in Beachwood Canyon previously inhabited by actors Mary Astor and Charlie Chaplin. Newsom's younger sister, Emily, an astrophysicist who became a geophysicist, sometimes joins her background vocals. Her brother, Pete, is also a musician.

SUGGESTED READING

Frere-Jones, Sasha. "String Theory." *New Yorker*. Condé Nast. 4 Dec. 2006. Web. 16 Feb. 2016.

Newsom, Joanna. Interview by Roy Harper. *Bomb*. Bomb, 2011. Web. 16 Feb. 2016.

Newsom, Joanna. Interview by Claire Suddath. *Time*. Time, 1 Mar. 2010 Web. 16 Feb. 2016.

Pearse, Emma. "The Mysterious Diva of Folk Music." *New York*. New York Media, 2006 Web. 16 Feb. 2016.

Rosen, Jody. "Joanna Newsom, the Changeling." *New York Times*. New York Times, 3 Mar. 2010. Web. 20 Feb. 2016.

Schonfeld, Zach. "Joanna Newsom's High Dive." *Newsweek*. IBT Media, 21 Oct. 2015. Web. 15 Feb. 2016.

Weiner, Jonah. "Joanna Newsom on Andy Samberg, Stalkers, and Latest Harp-Fueled Opus." *Rolling Stone*. Rolling Stone, 15 Oct. 2015. Web. 1 Mar. 2016.

SELECTED WORKS

The Milk-Eyed Mender, 2004; *Ys*, 2006; *Joanna Newsom and the Ys Street Band*, 2007; *Have One on Me*, 2010; *Divers*, 2015

—*Judy Johnson*

Kim Ng

Born: November 17, 1968
Occupation: Major League Baseball executive

Kim Ng is possibly the most powerful woman in professional baseball. The senior vice president of baseball operations for Major League Baseball (MLB) since 2011, she began her career by handling salary arbitration for the Chicago White Sox and followed that with a stint in the offices of the American League. Ng made history in 1998 when she became the first woman hired as assistant general manager for the New York Yankees and the second woman ever to fill that role in any baseball team. She later worked for the Los Angeles Dodgers in the same capacity, spending nine years with the team before joining MLB leadership.

During her decades in baseball operations, Ng settled numerous salary disputes, helped teams recruit and retain key players, and impressed baseball insiders and fans with her skills and devotion to the sport. Her qualifications made her a strong contender for a number of open general manager positions, and over the years numerous sports media outlets speculated that she could one day become the first woman to serve in that capacity. Although Ng has admitted that reaching that position is an aspiration of hers, she prefers to live and work in the present and take the next steps in her career as they come. "I never look too far ahead in terms of my career," she told Yael Kohen for *Marie Claire* (18 July 2012). "I think if you do a good job, people will recognize that."

Linda Cataffo/NY Daily News Archive/Getty Images

EARLY LIFE AND EDUCATION

Kimberly Ng was born on November 17, 1968, in Indianapolis, Indiana. She was the oldest of five daughters. Her parents, Jin and Virginia, worked in finance. The family moved to the Queens borough of New York City when she was a child, and she began her schooling there. They later moved to Long Island and then again to New Jersey, where they settled in the suburban community of Ridgewood. Ng attended Ridgewood High School, from which she graduated in 1986.

Ng developed a love of baseball early in life. The game was a passion of her father's, and it soon became one for Ng as well. "I have always loved the game," she told the University of Chicago's *College Report* (June 1998). "No one needed to teach me to like it, it was just natural to me." She grew up playing stickball, among other sports, and was an avid fan of the New York Yankees. As a teenager, she played on the Ridgewood High School softball team.

After graduating from high school, Ng enrolled in the University of Chicago, where she studied public policy. She also played on the university's softball team, winning an award for most valuable player during her time there. She earned her bachelor's degree from the university in 1990.

EARLY CAREER

Ng began her career in professional baseball shortly after graduating, taking a position with the Chicago White Sox in 1991. While with the team she worked alongside Dan Evans, who later became the general manager of the Los Angeles

Dodgers. Upon joining the White Sox organization, Ng began work as a special project analyst responsible for dealing with contracts and arbitration. In professional baseball, arbitration is the process of determining a player's pay through a hearing. Teams prefer to avoid arbitration hearings and thus hire employees dedicated to negotiating with players and coming to compromises without the need for official hearings.

Despite being a lifelong fan of baseball, the behind-the-scenes operations of a professional team were largely new to Ng. "I had some analytic skills, having come from University of Chicago," Ng told Jonah Keri for *Baseball Prospectus* (18 Nov. 2003). "But I didn't know about arbitration exhibits, negotiating contracts, or anything like that." Despite her unfamiliarity with some of those processes, her new responsibilities presented a challenge that was more exciting than insurmountable. "In some ways it was sink or swim," she told Keri. "It's not real tough to figure out though—if you have a feel for baseball, it's not rocket science. You just need to be analytical enough, driven enough to be good at it." Having proven her adeptness at handling negotiations and contracts, Ng was eventually promoted, becoming assistant director of baseball operations for the team.

Ng remained with the White Sox until 1997 when she left to take the position of director of waivers and records in the New York–based offices of the American League. One of the two professional baseball leagues in the United States, the American League encompasses teams such as the White Sox, the Yankees, and the Boston Red Sox. Although the position meant that she was no longer deeply involved with the operations of a specific team, she viewed working for the league as a major opportunity to meet numerous baseball executives and gain a better understanding of the finer points of baseball operations. "I felt that I'd be able to interact with other clubs, with GMs and assistant GMs a lot," she explained to Keri. "It was also a way to delve into the rules, to learn how they're enforced. When you're in the league office, you might get calls from four or five teams about one rule. The lessons get hammered in, and you improve your contacts at the same time."

JOINING BASEBALL MANAGEMENT

Ng left her position with the American League after about a year in favor of a job in a professional baseball front office. Joining her favorite team from her childhood, the Yankees, she was hired as assistant general manager under Brian Cashman. Taking the position represented a major step for Ng, as it brought her not only into baseball management but also within sight of the general manager position, one of the most important in any baseball organization. Ng's hiring was also a significant moment in baseball history for several other reasons, among them that she was the youngest assistant general manager working and one of the few Asian American baseball executives. What received the most attention, however, was that Ng was only the second woman to serve as assistant general manager, after Elaine Steward, who became assistant general manager of the Red Sox in 1990. With Ng now proving her ability as assistant manager, sports media began to speculate on how long it would be before a woman—most likely Ng—would attain the general manager position.

Ng preferred to disregard such speculation and downplayed the historic nature of her position, instead focusing on her work. "I take the gender issue out of the equation entirely. There is not a best male or female way to do my job. The best is simply the best and that's what I aim for," she told the *College Report*. "You have to decide what you want and work hard to get it. This advice goes for everyone. If you're looking to work in the major leagues, you're usually going to have to start out in the minor leagues and make very little."

While working for the Yankees, Ng dealt with player trades, contracts, and other key operational duties. Among other deals, she worked to secure contracts with notable players such as Mariano Rivera and Derek Jeter, who were major assets to the team. Although Ng and her fellow staff members worked largely behind the scenes, they remained deeply immersed in the sport of baseball itself. "We are always with the players, the balls, and the bats during batting practice," she explained to the *College Report* (June 1998). "We watch every single game the Yankees play, and we form our own opinions about the players' styles and skills." During Ng's years with the Yankees, the team performed well in both the regular season and the postseason, advancing to the World Series three years in a row. The team won the series in 1998, 1999, and 2000, defeating the San Diego Padres, Atlanta Braves, and New York Mets, respectively.

LOS ANGELES DODGERS

Ng left New York in 2002 and relocated to Los Angeles, California, where she joined the Los Angeles Dodgers as assistant general manager and vice president. She was recruited to the organization by general manager Dan Evans, with whom she had worked in Chicago. As assistant general manager, Ng again brought her skill at handling negotiations, helping the team's management avoid arbitration hearings and reach workable compromises with players. She was also responsible for many elements of player acquisition, including trades and scouting.

In 2005, following the departure of Evans and his successor, Paul DePodesta, Dodgers ownership sought a new general manager for the team. Ng made headlines when it was announced that she would interview for the position, becoming the first woman to do so. The team's owners ultimately selected veteran baseball executive Ned Coletti for the position. Although Ng had not yet achieved her goal of becoming a general manager, she remained positive about her chances. "The difference between an assistant GM and a general manager is huge," she told James Klatell for *CBS Evening News* (8 July 2006). "I think having to pay your dues is a big part of it—and that's what I am doing." She would later interview for general manager positions with a number of other teams, including the Philadelphia Phillies and the San Diego Padres.

MLB EXECUTIVE

In 2011, Ng left the Dodgers to take the position of senior vice president of baseball operations for Major League Baseball. Working under former Dodgers manager Joe Torre, who initially served as MLB's executive vice president of baseball operations and was later named chief baseball officer, she is responsible for working with the various US professional teams as well as overseeing a number of international initiatives, including those related to drafting international players. "This is a chance for me to contribute in a very meaningful way to the game," she explained to Ken Gurnick for *MLB.com* (8 Mar. 2011). Despite her commitment to her work for MLB, however, she remained interested in one day holding a general manager position. "As far as long-term aspirations, they're still there," she told Gurnick. "If anything, this makes me a more fully qualified candidate."

PERSONAL LIFE

Ng is married to Tony Markward. The two met while they were both attending the University of Chicago. In addition to baseball, Ng enjoys playing golf.

SUGGESTED READING

Eng, Sherri. "Dodgers Assistant General Manager Kim Ng Ready to Make the Jump to Top Job." *SABR.* Soc. for Amer. Baseball Research, 2011. Web. 15 July 2016.

Gurnick, Ken. "Ng Leaving Dodgers to Join Torre with MLB." *MLB.com.* MLB, 8 Mar. 2011. Web. 15 July 2016.

Klatell, James. "Baseball's Female Pioneer." *CBS Evening News.* CBS, 8 July 2006. Web. 15 July 2016.

Kohen, Yael. "Game Changer." *Marie Claire.* Hearst Communications, 18 July 2012. Web. 15 July 2016.

"Making It in the Majors: Kimberly Ng, AB'90." *College Report*. U of Chicago, June 1998. Web. 15 July 2016.

Ng, Kim. "Prospectus Q&A." Interview by Jonah Keri. *Baseball Prospectus*. Baseball Prospectus, 18 Nov. 2003. Web. 15 July 2016.

O'Connor, Ian. "League of Her Own: Yanks Tab Kim Ng as Assistant GM." *Daily News*. New York Daily News, 5 Mar. 1998. Web. 15 July 2016.

—Joy Crelin

Trevor Noah

Born: February 20, 1984
Occupation: Television host

In 2015 *Comedy Central* surprised longtime fans of *The Daily Show* when it announced that Trevor Noah, a South African comedian who had appeared on the show just a handful of times, would be replacing Jon Stewart, the beloved fake newscaster who had so effectively anchored the show for sixteen years with a remarkable blend of political commentary and comedy. Unlike other late-night programming moves around the same time that had replaced longtime hosts with well-known personalities (for example, popular comedian Jimmy Fallon replacing long-running *Tonight Show* host Jay Leno), Noah was young and relatively unknown in the United States, although he had been immensely popular not just in his native South Africa but on the entire African continent for more than a decade. Some critics questioned whether or not a non-American could deliver the sort of incisive political commentary on a program that approximately 12 percent of the nation relies on as its primary news source. Noah, however, believes his being the first nonwhite host of the program will aid him considerably—and bring a much-needed outsider's edge to his new role. "I may not be American, but I am black," Noah said in an interview with Zach Baron for *GQ* (21 July 2015). "It's not like I had to learn how to be black."

EARLY LIFE

Trevor Noah was born on February 20, 1984, in Johannesburg, South Africa, to Patricia Nombuyiselo Noah, a South African Xhosa of Jewish descent, and Robert Noah, a native of Switzerland. At the time, South Africa was still a decade away from ending the brutal national system of racial segregation known as apartheid, which had kept the white ruling minority separate from the black majority since its formal institutionalization in 1948. The system began to break down in 1990, when the longtime political

Brad Barket/Stringer/GettyImages

activist Nelson Mandela was freed from prison after twenty-seven years of incarceration and began negotiating with the white government for an end to the institution. (Mandela became the first black president of South Africa in 1994, and served until 1999.) Noah joked of South Africa's history of racism, as quoted by Joseph P. Williams for *U.S. News & World Report* (16 Oct. 2015): "We've produced the finest racism in the world—hand-crafted, artisanal."

Noah, who is biracial, was in essence an illegal child. Although the white South African government had a designation for mixed-race individuals—"colored"—marriages and sexual relations between individuals of different races were illegal. In order to keep his parents safe, Noah told neighborhood kids that he was an albino throughout his childhood. When he and his mother visited his father, she had to dress as a maid. The family could not even walk down the street together; his father would have to stay on one side whereas he and his mother walked down the other. Recalling those visits to his father, Noah said to Zach Baron for *GQ*: "So I would see my dad's life, but it's like visiting Disney World. Even though you visit Disney World, you don't go, 'That's how life is.' You go, 'No, I live my normal life, and Disney World exists.'"

Noah and his mother lived with other relatives in a two-room house in the black township of Soweto in Johannesburg, which saw numerous uprisings against the white government. At the end of apartheid in 1994, his father moved to Cape Town. He and his mother lived in Soweto until she married Ngisaveni Shingange, around the time Noah was nine. Noah had little love for his stepfather from the outset. When he became abusive to Noah, his mother, and the two sons he and Noah's mother had together, Noah began looking for a way to escape. At seventeen, he did just that, leaving his mother and brothers in favor of a roach-infested apartment.

Noah's mother and Shingange divorced in 1996 but continued to live together until 2002, when Shingange's abuse finally proved too much for her. At first, she and her two younger sons lived in a shack next to the family home, but then she ultimately moved herself and her two sons away from Shingange.

EARLY CAREER IN SOUTH AFRICA

While all of this was going on, Noah was taking the first steps in his comedy career, doing stand-up in any dive that would give him an opportunity. He came to comedy by accident; he gave his first performance on a dare from his friends. At the time, South African comedy was dominated by older white comedians who did not like Noah or his tendency to poke fun at apartheid and racism. In 2008 he was discovered by an American documentary filmmaker named David Paul Meyer, who had come to South Africa to explore the local stand-up scene. This meeting would lead to a number of future collaborations between Noah and Meyer.

In 2009, he toured his one-man show "The Daywalker," which was filmed and released the same year as his first stand-up special, *Trevor Noah: The Daywalker* (2009). While preparing to film the special, his mother was nearly killed by her estranged ex-husband, after he learned of her engagement to another man. She was shot in the torso and in the head. She survived only because Noah's fifteen-year-old half-brother had been able to drive her to the hospital in time. Noah recalled visiting his mother's bedside in the hospital for Zach Baron: "She says, 'No, no. Please, look at the bright side. I'm still here. Just be grateful that I'm still here.' I'm like, 'Yeah, but still.' She says, 'And on an even brighter side . . . look at my nose. I've got half a nose now. So now you're officially the best-looking person in the family. There's no contest.' And then I start crying. Everyone's laughing and crying. You know? But that's who we were as people; that's who we've always been."

The exposure of his stand-up helped make him the most popular comic in South Africa, and before long, all of Africa. He made television appearances and at twenty-four hosted the South African Film and Television Awards. He also hosted South Africa's music awards and the South African Comedy Festival. He then parlayed his enormous popularity and talent into a new high profile gig as the host of South Africa's version of *The Daily Show—Tonight with Trevor Noah* (2010–11). The first of Meyer's

documentaries featuring Noah, *You Laugh But It's True*, was released on the international film circuit in 2011 and won best documentary at two festivals. Filmed in 2009, the film provided a snapshot of Noah's early career and his struggle to succeed against the complicated backdrop of the South African racial climate.

COMING TO AMERICA

When it became clear that after two seasons serving as host of *Tonight with Trevor Noah* he had achieved all he could possibly achieve in South Africa, Noah decided to see if he could further his success in the United States. Virtually unknown stateside, Noah joined Gabriel Iglesias's *Stand-Up Revolution* tour, which brought him to obscure parts of the country. It was a lonely time for Noah, but he continued to write new jokes and perfect his material—and the audiences responded. "Trevor was such a natural," tour veteran Shaun Latham told David Tobia of the *New Republic* (26 Sept. 2015) in a phone interview. "It was amazing to watch how quickly he could write and adapt. . . . Each city we went to he would write new jokes."

His breakthrough came in 2012, when he was asked to perform on *The Tonight Show*, then hosted by Jay Leno. National American audiences got to see for the first time the material Noah had spent more than a decade perfecting. His *Tonight Show* performance also demonstrated the personality he would bring to his later role as host of *The Daily Show*—an extremely bright immigrant bewildered by American society. His performance in front of Leno was hailed as a success. As Noah's career has progressed, he has been critical of his earlier performances, including the performance on *The Tonight Show*. He told Zach Baron for *GQ*: "You show me half my jokes from even two years ago, three years ago— I hate them. Because you see, like, a young version of yourself. You're like, 'Why would you say that? You idiot! That makes no sense.' Or, 'That's just stupid.' Or, 'Ahh, I can't believe I said that about a woman.' You should not like what you did back then, because that shows that you've grown. If you're still doing it, that's a scarier place to be."

THE DAILY SHOW

On February 10, 2015, Jon Stewart, the anchor of Comedy Central's *The Daily Show*, announced that he would be leaving the program after a successful sixteen-year run. Finding a replacement for Stewart, who was beloved by his audience, proved no easy task for *Comedy Central's* management. Ultimately, they found Stewart's successor in Trevor Noah, who had appeared as a correspondent on *The Daily Show* only three times and was just thirty-one years old at the time of the announcement in March

2015. *Comedy Central*, however, was certain it had found the right anchor for its audience and demographics. Michele Ganeless, the *Comedy Central* president, said in an interview, as quoted by Dave Itzkoff of the *New York Times* (30 Mar. 2015): "We talked to women. We talked to men. We found in Trevor the best person for the job. . . . You don't hope to find the next Jon Stewart—there is no next Jon Stewart. So, our goal was to find someone who brings something really exciting and new and different."

Outgoing host Stewart also hailed the decision, and joked that he would rejoin the show as a correspondent just to be a part of it. There was some initial backlash over *Comedy Central's* choice after several of Noah's older jokes, which were posted on Twitter and portrayed women and Jews in a way some found offensive, resurfaced. Noah's *Daily Show* debuted to mixed reviews, though he has begun to find his groove in his new role. Reviewing Noah's version of the show for the *Washington Post* (29 Sept. 2015), Amber Phillips proclaimed: "Smartly, Noah also doesn't try to imitate Stewart's unique brand of comedy. The new host seems to rely on one-liners more than Stewart, whose go-to was often presenting the irony of the world in mash-up form and then giggling or ranting about it. Also apparently gone are the dramatic, staring-into-the-camera-with-eyes-bulging pauses Stewart favored; Noah is faster-moving and faster-talking than his predecessor."

SUGGESTED READING

Baron, Zach. "Trevor Noah on His Surreal Journey to the *Daily Show*." *GQ*. Condé Nast, 21 July 2015. Web. 20 Dec. 2015.

Itzkoff, Dave. "Trevor Noah to Succeed Jon Stewart on *The Daily Show*." *New York Times*. New York Times, 30 Mar. 2015. Web. 20 Dec. 2015.

Phillips, Amber. "Trevor Noah's *Daily Show*: Still Very Political, Still Very Snarky, Still Very Jon Stewart." *Washington Post*. Washington Post, 29 Sept. 2015. Web. 20 Dec. 2015.

Tobia, David. "Trevor Noah Didn't Come from Nowhere." *New Republic*. New Republic, 26 Sept. 2015. Web. 20 Dec. 2015.

Williams, Joseph P. "A Fresh Take on Politics." *U.S. News & World Report*. U.S. News & World Report, 16 Oct. 2015. Web. 20 Dec. 2015.

SELECTED WORKS

Trevor Noah: The Daywalker, 2009; *You Laugh but It's True*, 2011; *Trevor Noah: That's Racist*, 2012; *Trevor Noah: It's My Culture*, 2013; *Trevor Noah: Nationwild Comedy Tour*, 2015; *Trevor Noah: Lost in Translation*, 2015; *The Daily Show*, 2015–   —*Christopher Mari*

Sara Nović

Born: 1987
Occupation: Author

Sara Nović is the celebrated author of *Girl at War*, a novel published in 2015 that portrays the coming of age of a girl soldier from Croatia who fought during the Yugoslav Wars of the 1990s. During these brutal civil wars, from which the independent republics of Slovenia, Croatia, Bosnia and Herzegovina, Serbia, Montenegro, and Macedonia emerged, more than 100,000 died in the worst fighting seen on the European continent since the end of World War II (1939–45). Nović has earned considerable praise from critics on both sides of the Atlantic for her gripping depiction of her main character's harrowing wartime experiences and her life afterwards.

In interviews, Nović frequently describes herself as amazed that she is able to pursue writing as a career, something that she never imagined she could do. "I guess I never considered writing to be a career that a person could have," she told Katrina Medoff for the *Queens Chronicle* (2 July 2015). "It was just a thing that I always did, but I thought it was a nerdy thing that I always did that I wasn't supposed to be sharing with others." In addition to her work as an author, Nović, who has experienced progressive hearing loss throughout much of her life, is also a writing teacher and the founder of a magazine pertaining to deaf people's issues.

EARLY LIFE

Sara Nović was born in New Jersey in 1987, the daughter of parents of Croatian ancestry. As a young girl, she loved to read and write, but never showed anything she wrote to anyone, apart from her younger sister. In an interview with Catherine LaSota for *Electric Literature* (15 May 2015), Nović recalled, "I was always an avid reader, but it never occurred to me that people were writing these books! . . . I was always writing stuff like terrible poetry or whatever—stories too—as a kid, but, like, hiding them under my bed. They weren't things that I showed people."

In 2005, at age seventeen, she visited Croatia for the first time. The country was then about a decade removed from the Croatian War of Independence, which lasted from 1991 to 1995. By the time of Nović's visit, Croatia had become something of a resort country in the general public's mind. During her visit, she was guided around the country by two friends. They introduced her to many people, both in the coastal cities and in Zagreb, the country's capital, which is farther inland. Everyone was very willing to talk about the war, including some of its more horrible aspects, like the systematic raping of

Croat women by Serbian Chetnik soldiers so they could have Serbian children. Nović told Meredith Turtis for *Vanity Fair* (27 May 2015): "The war had been technically over for almost ten years . . . but people there felt abandoned by the West at that point, and they were really keen to talk about it."

EDUCATION

When Nović returned to the United States, she entered Emerson College in Boston, Massachusetts, as an undergraduate. While there she wrote a short story about a child growing up during the war, which led directly into the writing of her first novel, *Girl at War*. Nović recalled how this happened in her interview with LaSota: "I wrote a short story when I was in undergrad that pretty much still exists as the end of Part One of *Girl at War*. It's this very violent thing that happens. I gave it to a professor, and he was like, oh good, go write a book! . . . But then I just started writing chunks, and I think you can kind of see that in the structure, how it was kind of vignettes, and there is different stuff in all directions. I was writing those for years, but not really figuring out the direction."

Much of her writing was inspired by disappointment: so many people knew so little about Croatia, even the professor who had suggested she develop her story into a novel. He had encouraged her, in large part, because he had read very little about Croatia and its violent war for independence. Nović found that she was met with similar blankness when she mentioned Croatia to other people as well, and she felt that perhaps she could do something to remedy this situation. "I don't think it's fiction's job to educate people," she told Medoff. "It can't do that—it would be a really boring book if you wrote a book like a textbook. But I think it can make people curious to find out about stuff." She continued working on the novel as she pursued her MFA in fiction and translation at Columbia University in New York City. While there, her hard work paid off: she signed a contract with Random House to publish her debut novel.

GIRL AT WAR

Girl at War used many of the stories Nović had learned during her visit to form the background of her main character's life, and was also influenced by the writings of Bosnian author Izet Sarajlić, whose poetry she was translating while working on the novel. Ana Jurić, the ten-year-old girl at the heart of the story, leads a normal life of play and school in the city of Zagreb in Croatia in the months leading up to the breakup of Yugoslavia. Before long, however, the city begins to be divided on ethnic lines. As the war intensifies, with trips to air raid shelters becoming more frequent, Ana and her friends' childhood games

begin to take on a new level of intensity. Her life changes irrevocably when her parents try to get her sickly sister to safety on a flight to the United States and are taken to the woods and killed by Serb forces. Ana then becomes a child soldier.

The narrative shifts from Ana's past in 1991 as a child soldier in Croatia to 2001 in America with her sister and her adoptive family, who live in the suburbs outside Philadelphia. Tensions mount between Ana and her sister, who lived in the United States and experienced none of the war's tragedies, as well as between Ana and her boyfriend at New York University's New School, who seems unable to deal with her past.

The novel received mostly superlative reviews upon its publication; well-known literary critic Eileen Battersby panned it for the *Irish Times*, but most responses were positive. Turtis wrote in *Vanity Fair*, "[Nović's] dive into the conflict's gray areas—both its subtleties and emotional side effects—is what makes *Girl at War* masterfully layered and, at times, wrenching." Similarly, in the *New York Times* (27 May 2015), Anthony Marra remarked: "Nović builds the inner world of Ana's childhood—as both puberty and paramilitaries loom just over the horizon—with the same vivid detail she gives the blockaded city. . . . Throughout, 'Girl at War' performs the miracle of making the stories of broken lives in a distant country feel as large and universal as myth. It is a brutal novel, but a beautiful one."

ON BEING A "DEAF WRITER"

Nović is deaf, something that proves a challenge for a writer in a culture that often describes writing in terms of sound: musical, lilting, flowing. In an article she wrote for the *Guardian* (23 May 2015), Nović noted: "I frequently see advice from famous authors—Stephen King among them—that you absolutely must read your own work aloud in order to edit it properly. Without listening to your words in your own voice, you can neither fully understand what you've written nor hear how to fix it. At best this kind of advice leaves me feeling a little left out, but at worst, I wonder: am I making mistakes a hearing writer wouldn't?"

Nović, however, does not see her condition as a handicap; far from it, she sees it as a boon. Because she is able to tune out the hearing world, she is able to write without distraction. She wrote the majority of her first novel on the New Jersey Transit while commuting two hours each way from Philadelphia, where she was then living, to her classes at Columbia. She has also set out to dispel many of what she sees as myths about deaf people—that they are handicapped or desire to be more than what they are. She describes Deaf culture as rich and meaningful, and loves American Sign Language (ASL) for its directness. In fact, she says she dreams in

ASL, though her written language of preference is English (her first language), and she is fluent in Croatian.

PERSONAL LIFE AND OTHER WORK

Nović lives in the Queens neighborhood of Sunnyside in New York City with her sister. She teaches writing at Columbia University and the Fashion Institute of Technology in Manhattan, and also serves as the fiction editor at *Blunderbuss Magazine*. She is also the founding editor of *Redeafined*, a magazine devoted to providing more accurate information about deaf people and Deaf culture, which she believes are often inaccurately depicted.

In addition to publishing *Girl at War*, Nović has written for a wide variety of publications, including the *Believer, Vice, TriQuarterly*, the *Massachusetts Review, Blunderbuss*, and the *Minnesota Review*, among others. She is also a translator of Serbian and Croatian authors, and in 2014 received a prestigious travel fellowship from the American Literary Translators Association. In 2015 she began writing a work that is set in a school for the deaf in Boston, Massachusetts. "It's just kind of a short story that gets longer and longer instead of ending, which I eye with suspicion because that's what happened when I was writing ['Girl at War']," she explained to Medoff.

SUGGESTED READING

Battersby, Eileen. "Notes from a Phony War-Torn Childhood." Rev. of *Girl at War*, by Sara Nović. *Irish Times*. Irish Times, 9 May 2015. Web. 23 Jan. 2016.

Marra, Anthony. Rev. of *Girl at War*, by Sara Nović. *New York Times*. New York Times, 2 June 2015. Web. 23 Jan. 2016.

Medoff, Katrina. "Sunnyside Woman Talks Novel Set in Croatia During War." *Queens Courier*. Schneps Communications, 2 July 2015. Web. 23 Jan. 2016.

Nović, Sara. "What It's Like to Be a Deaf Novelist." *Guardian*. Guardian News and Media, 23 May 2015. Web. 23 Jan. 2016.

Nović, Sara. "A Capacity for Empathy." Interview by Catherine LaSota. *Electric Literature*. Electric Lit, 15 May 2015. Web. 25 Jan. 2016.

Turtis, Meredith. "This War Happened: A Wrenching New Novel Relives the Disastrous Croatian War." Rev. of *Girl at War*, by Sara Nović. *Vanity Fair*. Condé Nast, 27 May 2015. Web. 23 Jan. 2016.

—*Christopher Mari*

Emily Nussbaum

Born: February 20, 1966
Occupation: Television critic

Emily Nussbaum, television critic for the influential magazine the *New Yorker*, won not only a National Magazine Award (popularly known as the Ellie Awards) in 2014 but also a Pulitzer Prize in 2016. She earned both awards as a result of essays she wrote for the *New Yorker*. Nussbaum chose to become a television critic because of the show *Buffy the Vampire Slayer*; as she explained to Lisa French for the *Conversation* (18 Aug. 2014), "Buffy was the first show where I was just transformed by becoming a super-fan in a slightly insane way." She began championing the show, even though it was about a teenage girl and on a cable channel. She refers to herself as a "hoppy-brained" person, which suits her career path.

EARLY LIFE AND EDUCATION

Emily Nussbaum was born to a political power couple, Bernard and Toby Nussbaum. Her father, a lawyer, was White House counsel to President Bill Clinton in 1993 and 1994. Politically active her entire life, Toby was a member of the 1992 Electoral College, voting for President Clinton. Nussbaum has two brothers, Peter and Frank.

In 1988, Nussbaum graduated from Oberlin College in Ohio, where she read old issues of *Esquire* for the quality of the writing, she admits. Although she was interested in magazines,

Marla Aufmuth/Getty Images for Massachusetts Conference for Women

she was not planning on writing for them for her career. Her various early jobs included working at a battered women's shelter and secretarial roles through a temporary agency. She lived in Atlanta for a time, as well as in Providence, Rhode Island.

After earning a master's degree in poetry, Nussbaum began graduate school at New York University (NYU), planning to pursue a doctoral degree in literature with a focus on Victorian literature. She thought she would become a professor, but she dropped out due to ill health. While studying poetry, she wrote book and poetry reviews for the *New York Times*. She stopped reviewing poetry, because, as she told Anaheed Alani for *Rookie* (9 Apr. 2014), "Since poetry is something that makes the people who are writing it zero money, it's one person's creation, and it goes out to a tiny audience, if you give even a *mixed* review on a huge platform like the *New York Times*, it's like crushing a puppy. There is actually a quality of brutality to it that I felt emotionally uncomfortable with."

WORKING IN NEW YORK

Nussbaum was in her late twenties when she began writing criticism. A friend had become an editor of *Lingua Franca*. Nussbaum began writing short articles for the magazine, then longer pieces. While still in graduate school at NYU, she began to edit pieces at the online site *Nerve*, which led to her being recommended to an editor at the online site *Slate*. Nussbaum wrote for that publication as well. She eventually landed a full-time job at *Nerve*.

Nussbaum found her inspiration in not only the critics she read but also the online world, as she told French. There was "often online digital conversation about TV, which I found wildly stimulating and also global; . . . [it is] a way to talk with an audience of television viewers that otherwise I wouldn't have had access to."

When Jodi Kantor, who had been Nussbaum's editor at *Slate*, went to the *New York Times* to head its Arts & Leisure section, she hired Nussbaum as a freelancer for the *New York Times Magazine*. There Nussbaum wrote photo captions, did research, and looked for places to photograph.

Later, when Adam Moss, who had edited the *New York Times Magazine*, became editor in chief at *New York Magazine*, he hired Nussbaum as culture editor, a position she held for seven years. As Nussbaum told an audience at Yale University, as Larry Milstein reported in *Yale Daily News* (10 Oct. 2013), "Never disbelieve that knowing people helps. . . . It is important to have a political sense of what is going on in the journalism world." As culture editor, Nussbaum had the task of redesigning and producing the magazine's Culture Pages. She became the television critic after the death of John Leonard.

One of her most noted accomplishments at *New York Magazine* was developing the Approval Matrix, which debuted as a feature in 2004 and was inspired by a similar chart in *Wired*. Designed as a quadrant for locating where various cultural events and items fit, its four sides are labeled "highbrow," "lowbrow," "despicable," and "brilliant." For example, a 2004 Approval Matrix rated the new jazz space at Lincoln Center both highbrow and brilliant, while a Paris Hilton sex tape was lowbrow and despicable. Nussbaum explained the terminology to Myles Tanzer for *BuzzFeed* (13 Aug. 2014), "It's outrageous to say something is despicable. It's snotty but it sets the whole tone. I do think that despicable is so important and people love to talk about it." The feature replaced the magazine's back page crossword puzzle in 2009.

NEW YORKER

In 2011, Nussbaum was hired as television critic at the *New Yorker* after Nancy Franklin retired. She makes it a point to vary the shows about which she writes, moving from comedy to drama and from network to cable shows.

Part of Nussbaum's task as a television critic is to raise the level of respect for the medium. She told Yale University students, as Milstein recorded, "Television is a form that is historically condescended to—it is graded on a curve because people do not take it as seriously as they should. . . . Being critical of a TV show . . . raises the quality of television as a whole."

Nussbaum sees the value of DVD and TiVo as means of curating and rewatching television programs, making criticism possible as shows are viewed more than once. As a result, criticism is taken more seriously, and literary writers as well as entertainment reporters are paying attention. Commenting on the new critical attitude, Nussbaum told Claire Zulkey for *Zulkey.com* (12 July 2013), "I'd say that it's a group of critics who aren't interested in the old defensive/condescending approach to the medium, or in endless comparisons to movies and books, and who are trying to forge new ways to talk about television as its own fantastic thing."

PRODUCT PLACEMENT IN A "GOLDEN AGE" OF TELEVISION

Nussbaum is among viewers and critics who regard contemporary television programming, with scripted, well-written shows, as a "golden age" of television. Along with a return to smart scripts, however, shows are also returning to an earlier model of programming that includes product placement. Food and drink items are especially seen in shows, in part because of the financial difficulties that network television is experiencing.

With the advent of devices such as TiVo, viewers are forwarding past traditional advertisements. In addition, broadcasting television on a variety of platforms has diluted the television-viewing population, which has splintered as some people choose to watch online providers such as Netflix, Hulu, or Amazon Prime rather than a limited number of broadcast channels. To recoup revenue, television has turned to product placement, inviting sponsors to pay for screen time.

Nussbaum opposes this subtle maneuvering, as she explained to Robert Siegel for NPR's *All Things Considered* (7 Oct. 2015), "I want to be able to believe the stories that are happening before me. I want to be a partner to the artist telling me something and not to the advertiser cleverly hiding, flacking for their product." The lack of disclosure as to whether a company has paid for product placement bothers Nussbaum, who fears that television programs cannot be critical about certain issues because the corporations funding them also help the networks and other platforms stay in business.

Nussbaum's original *New Yorker* article (12 Oct. 2015) on this topic expressed her dismay at the slick use of products into television narratives. "The cleverer the integration, the more harmful it is. It's a sedative designed to make viewers feel that there's nothing to be angry about, to admire the ad inside the story, to train us to shrug off every compromise as necessary and normal."

ELLIES AND THE PULITZER

Since 1966, the American Society of Magazine Editors, along with the Columbia School of Journalism, has sponsored the National Magazine Awards. In 2014, more than fifteen hundred works were submitted. Nussbaum won in the category of Columns and Commentary, which included both political and social commentary, as well as news analysis, criticism, and reviews. *New Yorker*'s editor David Remnick submitted three Nussbaum essays—reviews of *Shark Week*, *Difficult Women*, and *Private Practice*—to the judges, comprising more than three hundred magazine editors, photography editors, journalism educators, and art directors.

In 2016, Nussbaum won the Pulitzer Prize for criticism, which included a $10,000 stipend. Remnick submitted ten of Nussbaum's essays to the prize committee; most were written in 2015. In the citation to the award, the Pulitzer judges wrote it was given in recognition of "television reviews written with an affection that never blunts the shrewdness of her analysis or the easy authority of her writing."

Interestingly, one year earlier, Mary McNamara, a television critic for the *Los Angeles Times*, won the same honor. A Pulitzer Prize for criticism in television had not been given since 1988. As Alyssa Rosenberg wrote for the *Washington Post* (18 Apr. 2016), "It's notable that great writing about television by women is getting recognized at a moment when female characters and artists are ascendant in a medium that seemed to break through when creators started telling a very specific kind of story about men."

Nussbaum's award brought recognition to the *New Yorker* as well, making it the first magazine to win a Pulitzer Prize for journalism. The publication took two awards for feature writing as well. In 2015, the first year that magazines were included for consideration, the *New Yorker* was a two-time finalist in the category of feature writing.

PERSONAL LIFE

Nussbaum is married to journalist Clive Thompson; they have two sons, Gabriel and Zev. She watches television on various devices—a flat-screen television, her phone, and her computer. She considers TiVo a great advance; she began using it as soon as it came out. She begins her day by checking her Twitter account on her phone. She is active on Twitter, where she has more than 120,000 followers, regarding it as a way to exchange ideas across the globe—and to help her procrastinate, as she says. After checking Twitter, she moves on to the *New York Times*, reading the book section first. She reads several online blogs and zines, as she told Esther Zuckerman for the *Wire* (5 Oct. 2012), "I love how swashbuckling and varied the voices can be online, as opposed to the more conventional structures of print magazines." However, she and her husband do subscribe to several print magazines.

SUGGESTED READING

Milstein, Larry. "Nussbaum Talks Technology, Journalism." *Yale Daily News*. Yale Daily News, 10 Oct. 2013. Web. 19 July 2016.

Nussbaum, Emily. "Speaking with: The New Yorker TV Critic Emily Nussbaum." Interview by Lisa French. *Conversation*. The Conversation, 18 Aug. 2014. Web. 6 July 2016.

Nussbaum, Emily. "In the 'Golden Age of Television,' Advertising Intersects with Programming." Interview by Robert Siegel. *All Things Considered*. National Public Radio, 7 Oct. 2015. Web. 1 Aug. 2016.

Nussbaum, Emily. "The Price Is Right: What Advertising Does to TV." *New Yorker*. Condé Nast, 12 Oct. 2015. Web. 1 Aug. 2016.

Rosenberg, Alyssa. "Why People Are Freaking Out over Emily Nussbaum's Pulitzer Prize for Criticism." *Washington Post*. Washington Post, 19 Apr. 2016. Web. 6 July 2016.

—*Judy Johnson*

Lupita Nyong'o

Born: March 1, 1983
Occupation: Actor

Lupita Nyong'o is an actor best known for her Academy Award–winning performance in *12 Years a Slave* (2013).

EARLY LIFE AND EDUCATION

Lupita Amondi Nyong'o was born on March 1, 1983, in Mexico City, Mexico, where her father, Peter Anyang' Nyong'o, was a visiting lecturer in political science. She is the second of six children. Both of her parents are descended from the Luo people of western Kenya; Nyong'o has dual citizenship and identifies herself as Mexican Kenyan.

A year after Nyong'o's birth, her father was appointed a professor at the University of Nairobi and her family returned to Kenya. Nyong'o's father was later elected to represent the Kisumu Rural Constituency in the Kenyan Senate, where he promoted democratic reform.

Nyong'o attended a girls' school in Nairobi, where her interest in acting began to flourish—her first stage appearance was in a minor role in a school production of *Oliver Twist*. At age fourteen she played Juliet in a production of *Romeo and Juliet* with the Phoenix Players, a Nairobi-based repertory theater company. She also appeared in the Phoenix Players' productions of *On the Razzle* and *There Goes the Bride*.

When she was sixteen years old, her parents sent her back to Mexico to learn Spanish. She stayed there for seven months, studying at the Universidad Nacional Autónoma de México's Learning Center for Foreigners in Mexico City.

Nyong'o attended Hampshire College in Amherst, Massachusetts, from which she graduated in 2003 with a bachelor's degree in film and theater studies. While at Hampshire, Nyong'o worked as a production assistant on the film *The Constant Gardener* (2005). She also worked as a postproduction intern on *The Namesake* (2006) and as an art intern on *Where God Left His Shoes* (2007).

ACTING AND DIRECTING

During her final year at Hampshire College, Nyong'o began working on a senior thesis project focusing on albinism in Kenya, inspired by her friendship with a Kenyan albino and news of the tragic albino killings in the neighboring country of Tanzania. This project became a feature-length documentary, *In My Genes*, which was screened at several festivals in 2008 before its official release in 2009. Nyong'o wrote, directed, and edited the film, which follows eight albino Kenyans and illustrates the discrimination and superstitions to which their society subjects

them. In 2008, *In My Genes* won awards at the Five College Film Festival, an annual event organized by a consortium of American colleges, and at the Festival de Cine Africano de México, a Mexico City–based festival for African films. *In My Genes* was also selected as the opening night film of the 2010 New York African Film Festival.

After starring in the independent short film *East River* (2008), Nyong'o returned to Nairobi in August 2008. The same year she directed a music video for the song "Little Things We Do" by musicians Wahu and Bobi Wine. The video was nominated for the award for best video at the MTV Africa Music Awards in 2009.

Nyong'o made her television debut on the Kenyan MTV series *Shuga* (2009–12), which she also codirected. The show premiered in November 2009 as part of a multimedia campaign to spread awareness about sexual health and AIDS prevention. *Shuga* centered on the lives and romantic entanglements of a group of young Kenyans; Nyong'o starred as Ayira, a vivacious college student who has a disastrous affair with an older man. The series won a Gold award for public relations in health at the 2010 World Media Festival in Hamburg, Germany, and the best overall edutainment award at the 2012 Edutainment Africa Awards.

Nyong'o then pursued a master's degree in acting at the Yale School of Drama at Yale University in New Haven, Connecticut. While at Yale, she appeared in several school productions such as *The Really Big Fat Show*, *Uncle Vanya*, and *The Taming of the Shrew*. For her outstanding acting abilities, Yale awarded her the 2011–2012 Herschel Williams Prize.

Not long before she finished her degree in 2012, Nyong'o landed her breakthrough role in the historical drama *12 Years a Slave* (2013), in which she starred alongside Chiwetel Ejiofor and Michael Fassbender. The film is based on the 1853 autobiography of Solomon Northup, a freeborn African American who was abducted and sold into slavery in Louisiana in 1841. Directed by acclaimed British filmmaker Steve McQueen, *12 Years a Slave* was lauded as an unflinching look at the brutal treatment of slaves in the United States. Nyong'o's character, Patsey, is a slave working on the same plantation as Northup where she is the subject of the unwanted attentions of her master and the jealous cruelty of his wife.

Nyong'o's performance was widely praised by critics. She won over twenty awards for the role, including the 2014 Academy Award for best supporting actress. Her acceptance speech was celebrated as gracious and moving, for both her acknowledgment of the history behind her role as Patsey and for her positive affirmation that goals can be achieved. Uhuru Kenyatta, the president of Kenya, posted a message on his official website congratulating Nyong'o on her nomination.

Wanting to do something lighter after the grueling filming of *12 Years a Slave*, Nyong'o next took on a role as a flight attendant in the 2014 action thriller *Non-Stop*. The film starred Liam Neeson and received mixed reviews. Nyong'o also appeared in fashion magazines as one of the faces of the fashion house Miu Miu's spring 2014 campaign, and was featured on the cover of *New York* magazine's 2014 spring fashion issue. Her personal style has garnered much public attention, for both her new role as a fashion icon and for challenging standards of beauty as a black woman.

IMPACT

Nyong'o went from an unknown to one of the most talked-about actors of 2014 after only one role in a feature film. She received numerous awards for her role in *12 Years a Slave* and became the first Kenyan to ever win an Academy Award. Nyong'o has been praised as a positive role model for black girls and women around the world.

PERSONAL LIFE

Nyong'o moved to Brooklyn, New York, after wrapping up her work on *12 Years a Slave*. In addition to English and her mother tongue, Luo, she is fluent in Spanish and Swahili, and can also speak conversational Italian.

SUGGESTED READING

Herndon, Jessica. "Lupita Nyong'o Is Hollywood's New Fixation." *Associated Press*. Assoc. Press, 18 Feb. 2014. Web. 10 Mar. 2014.

Nyong'o, Lupita. Interview by Jada Yuan. "Lupita Nyong'o on *12 Years a Slave*, Getting into Character, and 'Impostor's Syndrome'". *Vulture*. New York Media, 2 Oct. 2013. Web. 11 Mar. 2014.

Odula, Tom, and Jason Straziuso. "Pride of Africa: Kenya Celebrates Nyong'o's Oscar." *Associated Press*. Assoc. Press, 3 Mar. 2014. Web. 11 Mar. 2014.

Okoro, Enuma. "What Actor Lupita Nyong'o Can Teach Us About Beauty." *Guardian*. Guardian News and Media, 17 Jan. 2014. Web. 11 Mar. 2014.

Williams, Sally. "Lupita Nyong'o: Interview with a Rising Star." *Telegraph*. Telegraph Media, 10 Jan. 2014. Web. 12 Mar. 2014.

SELECTED WORKS

East River, 2008; *In My Genes*, 2009; *12 Years a Slave*, 2013; *Non-Stop*, 2014; *Shuga*, 2009–12

—*Patrick G. Cooper*

Chigozie Obioma

Born: 1986
Occupation: Author

Chigozie Obioma's debut novel *The Fishermen* has garnered an impressive amount of praise in literary circles on both sides of the Atlantic since its publication in 2015. The novel, about a quartet of young Nigerian brothers who disobey their father's orders and go fishing in a forbidden river, was shortlisted for the Guardian First Book Award, the Center for Fiction's First Novel Prize, and the Man Booker Prize for Fiction. On October 5, 2015, it was announced that *The Fishermen* had won the inaugural 2015 FT/OppenheimerFunds Emerging Voices Prize for African and Middle Eastern Fiction. In a review for the *New York Times* (14 Apr. 2015), critic Fiammetta Rocco declared that "Chigozie Obioma truly is the heir to Chinua Achebe," the celebrated Nigerian author who, like Obioma, was not yet thirty years old when his debut novel, *Things Fall Apart*, was published in 1958 and subsequently became a classic of world literature. Although Obioma's novel is often compared to Achebe's *Things Fall Apart*, he has cited Amos Tutuola's *The Palm-Wine Drinkard* (1952) as one of his greatest literary influences.

Obioma, who has been overwhelmed by the praise his work has received, remains humble about his accomplishments, which he credits to his focus on what he believes makes fiction valuable. The author told Nathan Go in an interview for the *Michigan Quarterly Review* (9 Apr. 2015): "For me, for a work of fiction to be successful, it

Mireya Acierto/Getty Images

should satisfy three things: one, it should have something definite to say; two, it should be constructed in an effective plot that has an arc, a beginning and end that can be told orally; and three, it should be grounded in some form of a philosophical framework."

EARLY LIFE

Chigozie Obioma was born into a middle-class family in Akure, in the southwestern part of Nigeria, in 1986. He has seven brothers and four sisters. Nigeria is a prosperous African nation of about 180 million people, with more than 60 percent of the population under the age of twenty-five years old. Despite large oil reserves and an educated middle class, Obioma has said he believes that Nigeria has not made as much progress as it should have due in large part to the fact that the state of Nigeria and its borders are an artificial construct, put together from disparate tribal groups by the British when it was part of their colonial empire. The nation remains divided between its largest two tribal groups, the Igbo and Yoruba, and has struggled through a civil war and numerous military juntas. Although a period of democratization has been taking place since 1999, Obioma believes the country could do more with what it has. Speaking to Lorien Kite in the *Financial Times* (6 Oct. 2015), Obioma commented on the problems facing Nigeria: "We're one of the richest countries by earnings in the world, but in all the years we've been amassing all of this wealth from the oil, we've made nothing out of it."

For Obioma, one of Nigeria's great blessings is that it maintains a rich oral storytelling culture, one that he has been attuned to since his early childhood. He spent much of his early years listening to tales told by his grandmother, mother, and father. "When I was about eight or nine I was sick in hospital with malaria or something, and my dad would sit by my bedside and tell me stories. Then when I was well, one day he came back from work and I asked him to tell me a story, and he said, 'Go and read it yourself,' and he gave me a book and I went and read it and discovered that one of the most fascinating stories he'd ever told me was inside it," he recalled in an interview with Mark Reynolds for *Bookanista*. "That was a secret before then, so that was a pivotal moment. Prior to that I had always seen my dad as this great man who had this vast reserve of stories, but then I saw I could actually get this thing from books, and I started reading voraciously. And then I began to replicate the stories in written form, so that was the point where I moved from a storyteller to a writer."

EDUCATION AND EARLY WRITING CAREER

The idea that whole worlds could spring from one person's imagination led Obioma to think

he could perhaps become a professional writer. However, while there was a firm oral tradition in Nigeria, reading was not as popular there when he was growing up. "It is an unfortunate situation but literary culture is almost zero, you are an anomaly if you engage with books. . . . Reading is seen as a taxing experience," he explained to Reynolds. Many of his friends and family members simply did not think his aspirations to become a writer were such a good idea. So instead he studied economics at a Nigerian college before deciding to try his hand at writing. "When I was growing up I would say I wanted to be a writer. I wasn't necessarily discouraged, but people would be sad or afraid for me: 'You're going to end up in penury, why not just be a lawyer or something and write on the side?'" he recalled to Reynolds. "But I wanted to study the tradition of literature, and with some luck I was able to convince my parents to let me go. London was of course where I wanted to come, but the UK border control wouldn't give me a visa, so Cyprus somehow came up as the next viable option."

Beginning in 2007, he studied literature at Cyprus International University. While there, he called home one day in 2009, feeling rather homesick. He spoke to his father, who, during the course of their conversation, told him how his two older brothers, who had once been such fierce rivals as children, had grown much closer and were now almost inseparable. Obioma began to wonder what factors could possibly drive a family apart irrevocably. The germ of this idea became the foundation for his debut novel, *The Fishermen*, which first appeared as a short story titled "Fishermen" in a 2011 issue of the *Virginia Quarterly Review*. Obioma earned his bachelor's degree in 2011, graduating at the top of his class and giving the university's commencement speech that year. He remained at Cyprus International University for an additional year to complete a master's degree and work as a research assistant.

In 2012 Obioma moved to the United States to earn his master of fine arts (MFA) degree at the University of Michigan. While studying there, he published a number of critically acclaimed works, including another short story, "The Great Convert," which was published in *Transition* magazine in 2014. In 2015 his poem "The Road to the Country" was published in an issue of the *Virginia Quarterly Review*, as well as an essay, "Audacity of Prose," in the online literary magazine the *Millions*. Obioma won the university's Hopwood Award for the novel and for poetry in 2013 and 2014, respectively. He completed his MFA degree in 2014.

THE FISHERMEN

Obioma had entered his MFA program with his novel complete and a literary agent who wanted to publish *The Fishermen*, which was released in February 2015 by ONE, an imprint of Pushkin Press, in the United Kingdom and by Little, Brown and Company in the United States and Canada. The novel is told from the point of view of the youngest of four brothers, Benjamin, who recalls how, during his childhood in the 1990s, he and his brothers, Ikenna, Boja, and Obembe, decided to go fishing in the Omi-Ala River one day behind their mother's back while their father, who works for the Central Bank of Nigeria, is away in another town. During the weeks their father is gone, the brothers skip school and visit this forbidden and polluted river. There, they come across a deranged homeless man named Abulu, who prophesies that the eldest of them, Ikenna, will be murdered by a fisherman. This prediction sets in motion a chain of events that irrevocably alters the brothers' relationships with one another and brings all of their father's plans for them—to become successful, educated men—to ruin.

During the course of the novel, Obioma switches between Benjamin telling the story as an adult to his experiencing the events as a child, in order to build narrative tension. He also makes use of imagery taken from the natural world, often describing characters as animals—for example, the father of the four brothers is described as an eagle guarding over his young eagles.

The novel met with near universal praise and has been translated and published in seventeen languages. Helon Habila, in a review for the *Guardian* (13 Mar. 2015), cheered, "*The Fishermen* mixes the traditional English novel form with the oral storytelling tradition, dramatizing the conflict between the traditional and the modern. But *The Fishermen* is also grounded in the Aristotelian concept of tragedy, which mostly goes: a good and noble-minded man shows hubris and is brought down by the gods for it. . . . *The Fishermen* is an elegy to lost promise, to a golden age squandered, and yet it remains hopeful about the redemptive possibilities of a new generation." Eleanor Catton, author and winner of the 2013 Man Booker Prize, praised the book in an advanced review: "Awesome in the true sense of the word: crackling with life, freighted with death, vertiginous both in its style and in the elemental power of its story. Few novels deserve to be called 'mythic,' but Chigozie Obioma's *The Fishermen* is certainly one of them."

PERSONAL LIFE

In August 2015 Obioma took up a position as an assistant professor of literature and creative writing at the University of Nebraska–Lincoln. He is also at work on a second novel, currently titled *The Falconer*, which takes place in the mid-nineteenth century at the time when Africans were first coming into direct contact with the British, who would ultimately occupy large sections of Africa. Like his previous effort, Obioma is continuing to explore how memory plays into storytelling, specifically how people remember events as opposed to how things may have actually happened. Of memory and writing, Obioma told Go: "The novelist has to think of a structure that would effectively deliver what he's trying to say and the philosophy behind it. I do think that the subject of memory, of telling a story has a very fascinating dimension."

SUGGESTED READING

Habila, Helon. "Four Brothers and a Terrible Prophecy." Rev. of *The Fishermen*, by Chigozie Obioma. *Guardian*. Guardian News and Media, 13 Mar. 2015. Web. 14 Dec. 2015.

Kite, Lorien. "Chigozie Obioma—Emerging Voices 2015 Fiction Winner." *Financial Times*. Financial Times, 6 Oct. 2015. Web. 14 Dec. 2015.

Obioma, Chigozie. "Tangled Lines." Interview by Mark Reynolds. *Bookanista*. Bookanista, n.d. Web. 14 Dec. 2015.

Obioma, Chigozie. "Of Animal Metaphors and the British Legacy." Interview by Nathan Go. *Michigan Quarterly Review*. Michigan Quarterly Review, 9 Apr. 2015. Web. 14 Dec. 2015.

Rocco, Fiammetta. Rev. of *The Fishermen*, by Chigozie Obioma. *New York Times*. New York Times, 14 Apr. 2015. Web. 14 Dec. 2015.

—*Christopher Mari*

Ayman Odeh

Born: January 1, 1975
Occupation: Politician

Ayman Odeh is a lawyer and Arab Israeli politician. In 2015, he was elected to the Knesset, Israel's parliament, and ran as a member of the Joint List, a coalition of four small Arab-backed parties that formed in January 2015. Arabs account for approximately 20 percent of Israel's population, and 80 percent of Arab Israelis are Muslim, while most of the remaining 20 percent are Christian or Druze. Their representation within the Israeli government, however, is not proportional to these numbers. As a population, Arab Israelis are considered a marginalized minority in Israel. They face discrimination and higher levels of unemployment and poverty than Israeli Jews. As conflict intensifies in Gaza, the Israeli-occupied Palestinian territory between Israel and Egypt, violence against Arabs in Israel has been on the rise. A recent poll revealed that one-third of Israelis think that Arab Israelis such

as Odeh should not even be allowed to vote. "Why did you come to this studio and not to a studio in Gaza?" former foreign minister Avigdor Liberman asked Odeh in a televised debate shortly before the March 2015 elections, as quoted by Elhanan Miller for the *Times of Israel* (4 Mar. 2015). "Why aren't you standing for election in Ramallah [in the West Bank] rather than in the Israeli Knesset? Why are you even here? You're not wanted here."

Odeh is a former member of the socialist Hadash Party and served as a city councilman in the Israeli port city of Haifa, where he also practiced law before becoming the leader of the Joint List. As a politician, Odeh has lobbied for partnership between Jews and Arabs and has called for an "alliance of the disadvantaged" that would focus on economic differences between Israeli citizens rather than on their religious or ethnic differences. He recently proposed a ten-year plan to eradicate structural discrimination and close the country's widening socioeconomic gap.

Odeh counts as supporters Jewish Israelis as well as Arabs who are disillusioned by the harsh rhetoric of Prime Minister Benjamin Netanyahu's right-wing Likud Party. Even conservative Israeli president Reuven Rivlin, also a member of the Likud Party, has called for an end to hate speech and violence against Arab Israelis and Palestinians. "I'm not asking if we've forgotten how to be Jewish," he told David Remnick for the *New Yorker* (17 Nov. 2014), "but if we've forgotten how to be human."

EARLY LIFE AND POLITICAL CAREER
Odeh was born in Haifa, a port city in northern Israel, on January 1, 1975. Haifa is a diverse city, where Jews and Arabs live among one another. Growing up, Odeh was the only Muslim student at his Christian school. When he was twenty-three and had graduated from law school, Odeh was elected to the municipal council of Haifa. As a young politician, he was inspired by the US civil rights movement of the 1960s. He compared his own ideals first to Malcolm X, a Muslim leader and black nationalist, and then to Martin Luther King Jr., a Baptist minister and social activist. "When I began my political career, I identified with Malcolm X. After two or three years, I evolved . . . because of my service on the council in the city of Haifa," he told Marc Schulman for *Newsweek* (6 Mar. 2015). "As a result of that experience I was transformed from being someone who believed that either the Jews or the Arabs could survive here, to someone who thought that Arabs and Jews must work together."

Odeh recalls many occasions when as a young man he was interrogated by the Israel security agency, Shin Bet. He felt bullied and paranoid, but even in his fear he realized that coexistence was the only feasible way to achieve Arab equality. If the Jewish majority was afraid of him, he reasoned, he would show them they had nothing to fear. He preached safety and prosperity through peace, and extending an olive branch became an integral part of his political agenda.

CREATION OF THE JOINT LIST
Odeh became the secretary-general of the Jewish Arab socialist Hadash Party in 2006. Hadash, the former communist party, was one of four Arab-backed political parties in Israel, the others being the progressive Balad Party, sometimes called the National Democratic Alliance; the right-wing, Arab-nationalist Ta'al Party; and the Islamic Party. The parties tried to join forces in the past but any suggested coalition broke down under the weight of ideological differences. The passage of the Governance Law in March 2014, which threatened to do away with the parties altogether, made their union urgent and necessary.

The group—an unlikely coalition of communists, Islamists, and feminists—owes its existence to Foreign Minister Liberman who sponsored the Governance Law in what was widely believed to be an effort to push Arab-backed parties out of the Knesset altogether. Instead, the four small parties banded together to form the Joint List and in 2015 won 13 seats in the 120-seat Knesset. The Joint List is now the third largest political party in Israel. There has been an Arab presence in the Israeli government since the state's inception, though Arab Israelis have never held significant power. "Uniting the Arab political forces is of historical importance," Mohammad Darawshe, a political analyst and an advocate for cooperation between Arabs and Jews, told Diaa Hadid for the *New York Times* (15 Mar. 2015). "No minority has ever been able to make any strategic accomplishment without uniting first."

PROMOTING ARAB ISRAELI EQUALITY

In January 2015, the politically disparate parties agreed to an eight-point platform. The platform called for equal rights for women and raising the minimum wage. It also demanded an end to the Israeli-Palestinian conflict and called for a two-state solution, as well as an end to the Israeli occupation of the West Bank and Gaza, which began in 1967 after the Six-Day War. Most Arab Israelis have powerful ties to the occupied areas and therefore have a strong interest in seeing them liberated. But Odeh and the Joint List, while still technically advocating for such an outcome, are operating from a more politically pragmatic point of view by first focusing on equality for all Arabs within Israel. The Arab-backed parties of the past lost support among Arab Israeli citizens for their single-minded focus on Palestinian nationalism.

Before the 2015 election, voter turnout among Arabs was lower than the national average. One voter, a young man named Mohammed Yehya, explained to Hadid, "[My family and I] never voted before, because we didn't believe Arab Knesset members could achieve any goal while they stayed fragmented." Citing a desire for a better life in his own country, he added, "We want to have our influence in politics," he said. "We want to be treated like Jews."

THE 2015 ELECTION

Odeh, who was practicing law in Haifa at the time of the election, seemed a perfect choice to become the face of the Joint List. Schulman compared Odeh's folksy and amiable demeanor to former US president Bill Clinton. He "has the personality of a natural politician," Schulman wrote. "He immediately put me at ease." Odeh acquired more supporters a week before the election when he smiled through a personal attack from Liberman, who, according to Karen Laub for *People's World* (16 Mar. 2015), baited Odeh by "claiming Arab politicians 'represent terror groups' . . . and berating him as a 'fifth column'" who was trying to destroy Israel from within. Odeh, perhaps referencing Liberman's unintentional role in the formation of the Joint List and in Odeh's political career, quoted the Old Testament in response: "He who digs a pit (for others) will fall into it."

On the day of the election on March 17, 2015, two-thirds of Arab Israelis turned out to vote, most of them supporting the Joint List, which won thirteen seats in the Knesset. Israelis also voted to reelect conservative Prime Minister Netanyahu, making Odeh and the Joint List's goals all the more difficult. Several months into his first term, political analysts continue to express cautious enthusiasm for Odeh. The success of Arab equality in Israel will depend on keeping together the fragile coalition that makes up the Joint List.

CIVIL RIGHTS ACTIVIST

Odeh's belief in equal treatment for all groups within Israel is seen in his support of Bedouins. The Palestinian Arab Bedouin are indigenous to the Negev region in southern Israel, and in a 2008 report for Human Rights Watch, Lucy Mair called on Israel to change its policies regarding the tens of thousands of Bedouin inhabitants of the region: "Discriminatory land and planning policies have made it virtually impossible for Bedouin to build legally where they live and also exclude them from the state's development plans for the region. The state implements . . . punitive measures disproportionately against Bedouin as compared with actions taken regarding structures owned by Jewish Israelis that do not conform to planning law." Conditions had not improved for Bedouins by 2015, and a few days after the election, Odeh embarked on a four-day march to Jerusalem to show his support for the unrecognized Bedouin villages. Though the plight of the Bedouin is well documented, it was nevertheless an unexpected move.

Around the same time, Odeh expressed solidarity with Ethiopian Israelis who were protesting racism and police brutality. Through his actions, he has made clear that he is a champion of the disenfranchised of Israel. Like Martin Luther King before him, Odeh expressed optimism for a better future, citing the United States as an example. He told Dalia Hatuqa for *Al Jazeera* (16 Mar. 2015) that if change "could have happened in such a segregated country as the United States—where there was actual slavery of African Americans, as well as ethnic cleansing of the Native Americans—then why can't it happen here?"

PERSONAL LIFE

Odeh is married to Nardine Aseli, who is a gynecologist. They have two children, one of whom is named for Nardine's brother Aseel, who was killed in 2000 during the second Palestinian intifada, an uprising against the Israeli occupation of the West Bank and the Gaza Strip, when he was just seventeen years old.

SUGGESTED READING

Hadid, Diaa. "Arab Alliance Rises as Force in Israeli Elections." *New York Times*. New York Times, 15 Mar. 2015. Web. 16 Nov. 2015.

Hatuqa, Dalia. "Q&A: Ayman Odeh, Head of the Joint List." *Al Jazeera*. Al Jazeera Media Network, 16 Mar. 2015. Web. 16 Nov. 2015.

Mair, Lucy. "Off the Map: Land and Housing Rights Violations in Israel's Unrecognized Bedouin Villages." *Human Rights Watch*. Human Rights Watch, Mar. 2008. Web. 16 Nov. 2015. PDF file.

Miller, Elhanan. "After Uniting Arabs behind Him, Ayman Odeh Looks to Lead Opposition." *Times of Israel*. Times of Israel, 4 Mar. 2015. Web. 16 Nov. 2015.

Remnick, David. "The One-State Reality." *New Yorker*. Condé Nast, 17 Nov. 2014. Web. 16 Nov. 2015.

Schulman, Marc. "Israeli Election: What Do Israeli Arabs Want?" *Newsweek*. Newsweek, 6 Mar. 2015. Web. 16 Nov. 2015.

—*Molly Hagan*

Brad Barket/Stringer/Getty Images

Leslie Odom Jr.

Born: August 6, 1981
Occupation: Actor and singer

Leslie Odom Jr. is an award-winning singer and film and stage actor who stars in the popular rap Broadway musical *Hamilton*, about the life of founding father and Treasury secretary Alexander Hamilton. Odom won a Drama Desk Award in 2015 for his role as Aaron Burr, vice president to Thomas Jefferson and the man who challenged Hamilton to a duel and then shot him dead in 1804.

Odom was already a Broadway veteran when he accepted the role in *Hamilton*, but the explosive success of the production propelled him into the national limelight: Not since the musical *Rent* in the 1990s—which also included Odom in its 1998 Broadway cast—has a piece of theater so thoroughly captured the nation's attention. *Hamilton*, with its hip-hop score, multiethnic cast, and story of a young immigrant tenaciously shaping his own destiny, is believed to be a contender for several 2016 Tony Awards. The musical has already won a 2016 Grammy Award for best musical theater album. In March 2016, the cast performed at the White House, where First Lady Michelle Obama called it "the best piece of art in any form that I have ever seen in my life."

Odom joined the cast of *Hamilton* in 2013 while it was still in its early stages. He recalled to Daoud Tyler-Ameen for National Public Radio (NPR) (21 Dec. 2015) that prior to joining the cast he first heard the song "Wait for It" at a theater workshop at Vassar College. When the actor playing Burr finished the song, which combines R & B with a dance beat, Odom felt as if he had "never heard a song quite like that on Broadway" and "whoever was going to get to sing 'Wait for It' eight shows a week was going to be a lucky actor."

EARLY LIFE AND EDUCATION

Odom was born on August 6, 1981, and grew up in Philadelphia, Pennsylvania, near the Baptist church where he sang in the choir. When he was ten, his fifth grade teacher at Masterman Middle and High School signed him up for a contest to write and perform speeches. Odom liked performing and found he was a talented actor. A slew of arts scholarships, including one at Philadelphia's historic New Freedom Theatre, and roles in local productions followed. "I grew up in Philadelphia in a time where we took it for granted that we were supposed to be young and gifted and black," Odom told Aubrey Whelan for *Philly.com* (28 Dec. 2015). "It was a culture of excellence—and all my friends were more talented than I was." As a teenager, Odom was drawn to the urgency of performances such as those of HBO's *Def Poetry Jam*. In an interview with Charlie Rose that aired August 12, 2015, Odom explained that *Hamilton* creator and star Lin-Manuel Miranda captured a similar urgency in his Tony Award–winning 2008 musical *In the Heights*, about life in New York City's Washington Heights neighborhood.

Odom was similarly drawn to the raw rock-opera *Rent*, which dominated Broadway in the 1990s. Based on Puccini's tragic opera *La Bohème*, the musical follows the lives of a group of artists living in New York City in the early 1990s.

Rent, Odom told Ellen Gray for *Philly.com* (20 Mar. 2013), "was the show that opened my heart up," and he often stood listening to the entire cast album on headphones at a local music store. The show had already been running on Broadway for two years in 1998 when Odom saw an open audition to join the Broadway cast. Only seventeen at the time, he auditioned and won a small ensemble role. He was the youngest person to ever be in the cast, and the role earned him a salary, a union card, and the confidence to pursue acting full time. After graduating from Masterman in 1998, Odom won a scholarship to study acting at the Carnegie Mellon School of Drama in Pittsburgh. He graduated from there with honors in 2003.

EARLY CAREER

After graduation, Odom moved to Los Angeles where he quickly landed a recurring role on the television series *CSI: Miami* playing fingerprint specialist Joseph Kayle from 2003 to 2006. During those years he also appeared as a guest star on several other series, including *The Big House*, *Gilmore Girls*, and the sci-fi drama *Threshold*. In 2006, he appeared on several episodes of the Fox thriller *Vanished*, but the series lasted only one season—as did Odom's next project, the 2007 USA comedy series *Big Day*. From 2008 to 2012, Odom appeared in small roles on several series such as *Grey's Anatomy*, *NCIS: Los Angeles*, and *House of Lies*. His luck began to turn in 2012, however, when he was first cast as Declan "Winky" Hall in the film *Red Tails*, produced by Lucas Films and based on a true story of a crew of African American pilots during World War II. Next, Odom was cast in the much-hyped television series *Smash*, a fictional, behind-the-scenes drama about the cast and crew of a Broadway musical. Odom played a dancer named Sam Strickland, and despite early popularity, the show was cancelled after its second season. From 2013 to 2014, Odom appeared on the CBS sci-fi mystery series *Person of Interest*, and beginning in 2013, he appeared in the recurring role of Reverend Curtis Scott on *Law and Order: Special Victims Unit*.

Odom considered himself lucky to consistently book jobs after graduating from Carnegie Mellon, but something was not right. "I got very sad," he told Tyler-Ameen, "because one day I realized that other people's work was inspiring me, and my own was not." Although Odom had some theater roles in Los Angeles, landing a role in a production of the musical *Jersey Boys* at La Jolla Playhouse and earning an Astaire Award for outstanding male dancer in a Broadway show for his role in the short-lived musical *Leap of Faith*, he had yet to find a project that moved him in the same way that *Rent* had as a teenager. After seeing a new show by Lin-Manuel Miranda

called *Hamilton* when it was being workshopped in 2013, however, Odom explained to Michael Gioia for *Playbill* (11 Feb. 2015) it was the first time since he was a young teenager enthralled with *Rent* that a production had "opened up [his] heart and senses."

HAMILTON

When Miranda later offered Odom the opportunity to read for the role of Aaron Burr, he jumped at the chance. For actors at any show's early stages, there are no guarantees of keeping their part as a show develops, and for the first two years in his role of Burr, Odom continually reiterated his interest in the part to the show's creators. He even turned down a lucrative television offer in order to appear in *Hamilton*'s Off-Broadway run at the Public Theater in 2015.

Odom's character is the show's brooding antihero and its narrator, and he has several major songs throughout the production, including the haunting "Wait for It," in which Burr laments the loss of people in his life. The character, as created by Miranda and interpreted by Odom, is more than the show's villain. His complexities, which include pain, jealousy, and a slow-burning rage, draw the audience to him rather than repel them. "All I try to do is put as many colors as I can on the canvas every night," Odom told Alex Beggs for *Vanity Fair* (6 Aug. 2015) of developing Burr's character. "I also don't want to clean it up, either; he made horrible mistakes just like Alexander did. I want all of his beauty and ugliness up there every night. I want him to be a mirror of the people [in the audience]."

Hamilton premiered at the Joseph Papp Public Theater on February 17, 2015. Seemingly overnight, the show became the hottest ticket in town—even US president Barack Obama came to see it during this early run and saw it again on Broadway five months later. The Off-Broadway run was extended three times, and the production moved to Broadway and opened at the Richard Rodgers Theatre on August 6, 2015. In his first review of the production, Ben Brantley for the *New York Times* (17 Feb. 2015) wrote that *Hamilton* is "a show that aims impossibly high and hits its target." Brantley wrote that Odom played the role of Burr with "caressing silkiness" and that he "seethes enviously in the shadows, commenting and plotting, an Iago with an inconvenient conscience."

Critics have praised *Hamilton* for its seamless marriage of eighteenth-century intrigue and twenty-first-century music, but Miranda has often said that he was drawn to the story—which he first read in Ron Chernow's 2004 biography *Alexander Hamilton*—because Hamilton reminded him of the scrappy rapper-turned-mogul Jay Z. Taken from this point of view, the score is the truest expression of the spirit of its central character. *Hamilton* is also an immigrant story. Alexander Hamilton came from the island of St. Croix and may have been of mixed race. Likewise, most of the cast is African American, Latino, and Asian. "Before they were founding fathers, these guys were rebellious sons, moving to a new, fierce, liberating beat that never seemed to let up," Brantley wrote for the *New York Times* on August 6, 2015, comparing the American Revolution to a looming musical theater revolution. "*Hamilton* makes us feel the unstoppable, urgent rhythm of a nation being born."

PERSONAL LIFE
Odom married Nicolette Robinson, an actor, in 2012 and they live in New York City. The couple met while working on a production of the musical *Once on This Island* in Los Angeles. Odom was the assistant director, and Robinson, still a student at the University of California, Los Angeles (UCLA), was in the cast. For three months in 2015, Robinson played the role of Eden in the Off-Broadway production of *Invisible Thread*. In 2014, Odom released a self-titled, solo jazz album featuring show tunes and cover songs.

SUGGESTED READING
Beggs, Alex. "*Hamilton*'s Leslie Odom Jr. at the Scene of the Historic Duel." *Vanity Fair*. Condé Nast, 6 Aug. 2015. Web. 5 Apr. 2016.

Brantley, Ben. "'Hamilton,' Young Rebels Changing History and Theater." *New York Times*. New York Times, 6 Aug. 2015. Web. 5 Apr. 2016.

Brantley, Ben. "In 'Hamilton,' Lin-Manuel Miranda Forges Democracy Through Rap." *New York Times*. New York Times, 17 Feb. 2015. Web. 5 Apr. 2016.

Gioia, Michael. "Lin-Manuel Miranda and Leslie Odom Jr. Reveal How *Rent* Shaped History and *Hamilton*." *Playbill*. Playbill, 11 Feb. 2015. Web. 12 Apr. 2016.

Gray, Ellen. "Local Actor Gets His 'Smash' Close-Up." *Philly.com*. Philadelphia Media Network (Digital), 20 Mar. 2013. Web. 5 Apr. 2016.

Tyler-Ameen, Daoud. "Being Aaron Burr." *NPR*. NPR, 21 Dec. 2015. Web. 5 Apr. 2016.

Whelan, Aubrey. "Leslie Odom Jr.: Being Burr in 'Hamilton' Like Falling in Love." *Philly.com*. Philadelphia Media Network (Digital), 28 Dec. 2015. Web. 5 Apr. 2016.

—*Molly Hagan*

Of Monsters and Men
Occupation: Band

Nanna Bryndís Hilmarsdóttir
Born: May 6, 1989
Occupation: Lead vocalist/guitarist

Arnar Rósenkranz Hilmarsson
Born: April 6, 1987
Occupation: Drummer

Kristján Páll Kristjánsson
Born: December 1, 1989
Occupation: Bassist

Brynjar Leifsson
Born: September 11, 1990
Occupation: Lead guitarist

Ragnar "Raggi" Þórhallsson
Born: March 6, 1987
Occupation: Lead vocalist/guitarist

The Icelandic indie folk/chamber pop group Of Monsters and Men (OMAM) gained international fame in 2011 after their acoustic performance of the song "Little Talks" went viral. The song has been described as a sweet, upbeat duet that many listeners felt immediately drawn to and that quickly led to the band's rapid fame with OMAM soon being included in the line-up at music festivals and concerts across the United States and Europe. The group has been showcased on such US late-night television shows as *Late Night with Jimmy Fallon* and *Saturday Night Live*, and their song "Silhouettes" was included on *The Hunger Games: Catching Fire* soundtrack. Another song, "Sinking Man," was featured on volume 1 of the original soundtrack for *The Walking Dead*. Their first album, *My Head Is an Animal* (2012), is comprised of what Jonathan Bernstein for *Rolling Stone* (17 Apr. 2015) referred to as "stomp-drum choruses." Their second release, *Beneath the Skin* (2015), was immediately popular and is described by Bernstein as "an abrupt shift" in style from the band's debut album. Lead vocalist Nanna Bryndís Hilmarsdóttir explained to Bernstein that the second album represents the group's desire to be "completely, uncomfortably open, like an open book."

EARLY BEGINNINGS AND RISE TO THE TOP
The origins of the group Of Monsters and Men began in 2009 when lead singer, guitarist, and songwriter Nanna Bryndís Hilmarsdóttir decided to expand her solo project, Songbird. Bryndís Hilmarsdóttir had been playing mostly open mic nights in bars and cafés around Iceland's capital city, Reykjavik, and sometimes recruited her

The timing of "Little Talks" and the OMAM sound was also right. Many critics and listeners alike have compared OMAM to such well-established groups as Arcade Fire, Mumford and Sons, and the Decemberists. Þórhallsson agrees: When asked by Mossman why the band is so popular in the United States, he answered without hesitation, "Because of Mumford and Sons . . . other bands that sound like them got to America too."

SONG WRITING PROCESS

Although most agree that OMAM seems to draw their sound from popular and recognized indie rock bands, the group, especially its song writers Bryndís Hilmarsdóttir and Þórhallsson, is also influenced and inspired by nature, Icelandic countryside, and the mystical. Land and sea, animals, fables, and fairy tales are featured into many of OMAM's songs. Dave Simpson for the *Guardian* (23 Aug. 2012) writes that the songs "abound with joy but with a less tangible, mournful undercurrent that gives them an other-worldly magical quality."

Þórhallsson explained to Mossman the song writing process he and Bryndís Hilmarsdóttir share, "We found that we could bond better by telling each other fairy tales." *Interview Magazine* (19 Jan. 2012) included Bryndís Hilmarsdóttir's take on the song writing process and in particular how "Little Talks" was written: "How we usually make our lyrics is, Raggi and I, sometimes we come up with stories or situations. ["Little Talks"] is about a relationship. . . . It's about a couple and the husband passed away and [the song is] the conversation between the two of them. We don't know if she's going crazy or if someone's actually there." Both composers agree that they enjoy creating stories with their lyrics and allowing the listener to decide what exactly the story is about. Barry Walters for *Spin* (3 Apr. 2012) described their duets as "rare vocal alchemy."

MY HEAD IS AN ANIMAL

The group's debut album, *My Head Is an Animal*, which featured "Little Talks," was released first in Iceland by the label Record Records in September 2011. It quickly reached the top of the charts in that country and the band was signed by Universal Music Group in October. By December 2011, Universal released a four-song recording (referred to as an EP, or extended play recording) in anticipation of the album's international release. The EP, *Into the Woods*, included the songs "Little Talks," "Six Weeks," "Love Love Love," and "From Finner." Many people were already familiar with "Little Talks," and the acoustic guitars (even the bass for this performance was acoustic) along with the tambourine, minimal drum kit, accordion, and frequent shouts of

Bill McCay/WireImage/Getty Images

high school friend and future OMAM guitarist Brynjar Leifsson to play with her. They soon added Raggi Þórhallsson to help with vocals and guitar and then expanded even more with three additional band members—a bassist, a drummer, and an accordionist—and together they named the new group Of Monsters and Men. The band was initially frustrated when performing because, as Bryndís Hilmarsdóttir explained to Kate Mossman for the *Guardian* (11 Aug. 2012), "We were quiet, and people would talk louder than the music." To fight back, OMAM added more drums, a trumpet, and a xylophone to their sound to become what Mossman described as the "noisiest folk-rock band . . . ever heard." In 2010, the band decided to compete in Músíktilraunir, Iceland's annual music competition and nationwide battle of the bands, which is held in Reykjavik. After winning the contest, OMAM earned an automatic invitation to play at the Iceland Airwaves Festival later that year.

Despite winning a national competition, Of Monsters and Men were still unknown outside of Iceland. However, it was the group's casual, acoustic performance in Raggi Þórhallsson's living room of the song "Little Talks" that would launch them into pop music stardom. The Seattle, Washington, public radio station KEXP, which features alternative and indie rock music and live streams festivals from around the world, became interested in OMAM after hearing them perform at the Iceland Airwaves Festival. In October 2010, the station posted OMAM's living-room performance online, and "Little Talks" was soon noticed by the pop-folk-indie community and won fans across the globe.

"Hey!" made for a catchy song and widened the consumer interest in and appeal for *My Head Is an Animal*.

The album was released in the United States and internationally in April 2012 and within a few months, the band went on tour to promote the album. They began in the United States with the South by Southwest (SXSW) festival in Austin, Texas, and then played major cities such as Los Angeles, San Francisco, Portland, Seattle, Chicago, Boston, Philadelphia, and New York. They played in a wide range of international venues such as Australia, Japan, the Netherlands, and throughout Europe.

In addition to sold-out performances around the world, Of Monsters and Men's debut album was mostly well received by critics. Simpson described the album as "using everything from glockenspiels to Motown drums, chants and stomping feet" with "campfire singalongs [turned] into skyscraping anthems." Jody Rosen for *Rolling Stone* (24 Apr. 2012) observed that although some things about the album may sound familiar, the band members "put muscle behind their prettiness, turning songs from cute to grand," and some of the lyrics about birds and trees sound "mysterious, and vaguely menacing." Walters, however, offered a review that was mixed at best, saying the album is "sweetly benign in small doses." Walters also stated that the lyrics are simplistic and that the vocal delivery is somehow wrong—pointing out his belief that the vocals on the album show an awkward difference between the lyrical content and how that content is expressed.

The album would go on to peak at number 6 on the Billboard 200 in 2012 and in 2013. Also in 2013, and again in 2014, the album would peak at number 1 on the Billboard Top Rock Albums chart, and again at number 1 on that chart in 2014.

BENEATH THE SKIN

The group's second album, *Beneath the Skin*, was released in Iceland in June 2015. Because of the success and popularity of the band's debut album, expectations among critics and the public were high. As the sophomore album's title indicates, this was an attempt at something more personal, less about birds, bears, and woods and more about personal emotions and feelings. As a result of years of touring, the album was recorded by members of a band that had bonded and had become much closer over time—both musically and personally. The album opens with the upbeat, optimistic "Crystals"—the song "Empire" has a similar quality—and then goes to track two, titled "Human," which tries to embrace the group's slightly different focus on deeper human experiences.

Ken Capobianco for the *Boston Globe* (9 June 2015) opened his review by pointing out that someday Of Monsters and Men "will actually burrow beneath the skin and reveal genuine depth, but the pleasures of this, their second record, remain mostly on the surface." Citing the songs "Organs" and "Black Water," Capobianco, though liking the album's polished production, observes that the "best tracks explore heartache, anger, and loneliness directly, peeling back the layers of pretension to find the humanity." In a representative negative—or at least deeply skeptical—review, Killian Young, for the online music magazine *Consequence of Sound* (1 June 2015) concluded that the listener's enjoyment of the new album, which is quite similar to the first one, "may largely hinge on whether you hear their animalistic motifs as gimmicky or as a legitimate narrative vehicle." Bryndís Hilmarsdóttir acknowledged to Bernstein that the album is the "polar opposite" of *My Head Is an Animal* and that much of her songwriting this time around was inspired by other women artists: "I find that I'm inspired by other women making music. . . . I've been listening to women." The record peaked at number 2 on several Billboard charts, including Top Rock Albums and Top Digital Albums. It also peaked at number 3 on the Billboard 200 chart.

SUGGESTED READING

Bernstein, Jonathan. "Of Monsters and Men on 'Uncomfortably Open' New LP: 'It Demands a Reaction.'" *Rolling Stone*. Rolling Stone, 17 Apr. 2015. Web. 15 Feb. 2016.

Capobianco, Ken. "Of Monsters and Men, 'Beneath the Skin.'" *Boston Globe*. Boston Globe, 9 June 2015. Web. 15 Feb. 2016.

Mossman, Kate. "Of Monsters and Men: 'We Found We Could Bond Better by Telling Each Other Fairytales.'" *Guardian*. Guardian News and Media, 11 Aug. 2012. Web. 15 Feb. 2016.

Walters, Barry. "Of Monsters and Men, 'My Head Is an Animal.'" *Spin*. SpinMedia, 3 Apr. 2012. Web. 15 Feb. 2016.

Warner, Andrea. "Of Monsters and Men: How One of the Biggest Bands in the World Almost Never Happened." *CBC Music*. CBC, 21 May 2013. Web. 15 Feb. 2016.

—*Dmitry Kiper*

Chinelo Okparanta

Occupation: Writer

Chinelo Okparanta is a celebrated young Nigerian American author whose published works, the short-story collection in *Happiness, Like Water*

(2013) and her debut novel, *Under the Udala Trees* (2015), have been praised for their explorations of the intersections of sexuality, religion, family, and society. She has received acclaim from fellow authors, critics, and book lovers on both sides of the Atlantic for both the beautiful cadences of her writing and her ability to write thoughtfully and honestly on such personal subjects as sexuality and religion. Her work also provides a keen insight into everyday life in Nigeria, a country often beset by religious strife, particularly between its Christian and Muslim populations, as well as by human rights abuses such as child abuse and exploitation, female genital mutilation, domestic violence, and various forms of discrimination. When asked by Celeste Headlee for National Public Radio's (NPR) *Tell Me More* (14 Aug. 2013) if she was concerned about her stories being too critical of her native country, Okparanta replied, "As much as people would like to say that, oh, you're portraying, you know, Nigeria in such negative light . . . they all know, deep inside, that all I'm doing is saying the truth, and sometimes what you need to do is just show things as they are so that maybe, collectively, we will all decide to do something differently. . . . This is my experience of Nigeria and that's all I'm doing is just writing."

EARLY LIFE AND EDUCATION

Chinelo Okparanta was born in Port Harcourt, Nigeria, and was raised as a Jehovah's Witness. In an interview with Rae Winkelstein-Duveneck for the *Iowa Review* (19 Mar. 2013), she confirmed that the communal, multifamily experience of Nigerian childhood depicted in several of her stories "was somewhat [her] childhood experience—at least in an idealized version of [her] childhood." She has recalled in interviews pleasant memories of listening to her mother and her aunts talking in the kitchen, having large family dinners, and attending church services together on Sundays—all aspects of her life that have been incorporated and described in keen detail in her writings.

Yet Okparanta has dark memories from this time as well, due in large part to religious upbringing, which is also reflected in her fiction. "Growing up a Jehovah's Witness was never a humorous subject to me," she said to Winkelstein-Duveneck. "There was so much fear associated with it that it was never something I took lightly. . . . We were reminded repeatedly that Armageddon was coming. We were reminded of this with very vivid imagery in our *Watchtower* and *Awake* magazines, images of cataclysmic conflagrations—the sky all blown up in flames, orange and yellow and red. We were told that it would be a global war. . . . You can imagine the fear such imagery instills in a child." As an adult, after studying religion on her own,

she "made a conscious decision to continue as a Christian, though not as a Jehovah's Witness," she told Winkelstein-Duveneck.

When Okparanta was ten years old, her father moved to the United States to attend a graduate engineering program at Boston University, and she immigrated with him. While an undergraduate at Pennsylvania State University, she took some classes that made her realize she enjoyed writing, but it was not until she was studying for her master's degree at Rutgers University that she "gave [her]self permission to think seriously about writing fiction," she told Yuka Igarashi for *Granta* magazine (10 Feb. 2012). After completing her Master of Arts degree, she attended the prestigious Iowa Writers' Workshop, where, in addition to earning her Master of Fine Arts degree, she also acquired a literary agent and a publisher.

HAPPINESS, LIKE WATER

Okparanta's first published short stories, "America" and "Runs Girl," appeared in *Granta* in winter 2012. She continued publishing her short fiction in numerous prestigious publications, including the *Southern Review*, the *Iowa Review*, and the *Kenyon Review*. Notable among these early stories was her story "Fairness," which appeared in the literary journal *Subtropics* in spring 2012 and was included in the 2014 O. Henry Prize collection of the twenty best short stories of the year. A number of these stories—which deal with a wide range of issues, including sexuality and love, domestic abuse, and psychology, as well as broader topics such as religion, globalization, colonialism, and capitalism—found their way into her debut collection, *Happiness, Like Water* (2013); in fact, only one story in the collection, "Wahala!," had not been previously published. Echoing Okparanta's own life, the stories in the first half of the collection are set in Nigeria, while those in the second half are set in the United States.

Happiness, Like Water earned Okparanta the 2014 Lambda Literary Award for lesbian fiction, in addition to being nominated for the 2015 Nigerian Writers Award for motivational writer of the year, long-listed for the 2013 Frank O'Connor International Short Story Award, and short-listed for the 2013 Caine Prize for African Writing (for "America"), the 2013–14 Society of Midland Authors Award for adult fiction, the 2014 New York Public Library Young Lions Fiction Award, the 2014 Etisalat Prize for Literature, and the 2014 Rolex Mentor and Protégé Arts Initiative. It also was named as one of the notable books of the year by the editors of the *New York Times* and the *Guardian* and received impressive reviews from both fellow authors and critics. In a review for the *New York Times Book Review* (13 Sept. 2013), Ligaya Mishan observed, "The stories in Chinelo Okparanta's first collection are quiet, often unnervingly so, in the manner of a stifled shriek. Hints of menace—a reference to a robbery, an illness, a drop of blood on peeling linoleum—are delivered blandly, matter-of-factly, as if resisting the urge to dramatize were a kind of survival mechanism. This is deceptive, for the plots in *Happiness, Like Water* are heated where the prose is not."

Discussing the collection with Headlee, and in particular her depiction of mother-daughter relationships, Okparanta said, "A lot of it did come from experiences that I've had in my own life and in, you know, the mothers around me, for example, my aunts. I am from a family of many, many women, and so clearly that opens up my eyes to the issues that, you know, women have with their mothers. And so I do have a very close relationship with my mother. And so it makes sense that some of the issues that come up in these stories will be things that are from my own personal experience."

UNDER THE UDALA TREES
In 2015 Okparanta published her first novel, *Under the Udala Trees*. The book is set in Nigeria in the late 1960s, when the Nigerian state of Biafra was waging a civil war against the central government for its independence. That horrific failed rebellion provides the backdrop to a love story between two women: Ijeoma, who is a Christian Igbo, and Amina, a Muslim Hausa. The women meet when Ijeoma goes to work as a servant in another town after her father is killed in an air raid and her mother is unable to take care of her. The friendship between the two quickly develops into a passionate love affair, but their relationship must be kept secret, as homosexual relationships were (and still are) taboo in Nigeria. After the couple is torn apart upon being discovered together, Ijeoma's mother does her best to make her daughter live a more "normal" life, even forcing her to marry a man she does not love. Throughout the book, Okparanta explores the relationship of the individual to society and the various ways in which society influences individual thinking.

Upon its publication, *Under the Udala Trees* received overwhelmingly positive reviews. *Guardian* reviewer Anjali Enjeti (24 Sept. 2015) wrote, "Okparanta deftly negotiates a balance between a love story and a war story, each of which threatens to eclipse the other. Though it has to work on many levels at once, *Udala Trees* delivers a delicate study of the competing forces that pull at Ijeoma: her gay identity, the defeat of independent Biafra, the taboo of Igbo and Hausa relationships, and Ijeoma's demotion from upper-middle-class student to poor house-girl." Carol Anshaw wrote in the *New York Times* (23 Oct. 2015), "The book operates in a storytelling

mode, a looping reminiscence by an adult Ijeoma. A few times she even steps forward to address the reader in a confidential tone. There are few stylistic flourishes; Okparanta prefers to step aside and allow Ijeoma to plainly tell her story, giving the novel an intimate feel."

Like *Happiness, Like Water*, Okparanta's debut novel received considerable literary recognition. Editors at numerous media outlets and publications, including NPR, the *New York Times*, the *Los Angeles Times*, and the *Wall Street Journal*, named it to various "recommended" and "best of" lists for 2015. In June 2016, *Under the Udala Trees* earned Okparanta her second Lambda Literary Award for lesbian fiction. Among its other accolades, the book was also nominated for the 2015 Kirkus Prize for fiction, long-listed for the 2015 Center for Fiction's First Novel Prize and the 2016 Chautauqua Prize, and short-listed for the 2016 National Association for the Advancement of Colored People (NAACP) Image Award for outstanding literary work (fiction) and the Publishing Triangle's 2016 Ferro-Grumley Award.

TEACHING CAREER
In addition to her writing, Okparanta has taught at a number of colleges and universities as a fellow or a visiting professor, including Columbia University, Howard University, Middlebury College, the University of Iowa, Southern New Hampshire University, and the City College of New York. She told Igarashi that when she started writing seriously, it was "always in conjunction with [her] career as a teacher," adding, "I knew what everyone said, you know, the whole idea of a starving artist. I didn't want to starve." For the 2012–13 school year, she was the Olive B. O'Connor Fellow in Fiction at Colgate University; in 2013 she was a visiting professor of English and creative writing at Purdue University; and in fall 2016, she will begin her first semester as a tenure-track assistant professor of English and creative writing at Bucknell University in Lewisburg, Pennsylvania.

SUGGESTED READING
Anshaw, Carol. Rev. of *Under the Udala Trees*, by Chinelo Okparanta. *New York Times*. New York Times, 23 Oct. 2015. Web. 9 June 2016.

Enjeti, Anjali. "Love in the Time of Biafra." Rev. of *Under the Udala Trees*, by Chinelo Okparanta. *Guardian*. Guardian News and Media, 24 Sept. 2015. Web. 9 June 2016.

Mishan, Ligaya. "How She Left." Rev. of *Happiness, Like Water*, by Chinelo Okparanta. *New York Times*. New York Times, 13 Sept. 2013. Web. 9 June 2016.

Okparanta, Chinelo. "*Happiness, Like Water* Based on Nigerian-American Writer's

Reality." Interview by Celeste Headlee. *NPR*. NPR, 14 Aug. 2013. Web. 9 June 2016.

Okparanta, Chinelo. Interview by Yuka Igarashi. *Granta*. Granta, 10 Feb. 2012. Web. 9 June 2016.

Okparanta, Chinelo. "Religion, the Bible, and Personal Morality: An Interview with Chinelo Okparanta." Interview by Rae Winkelstein-Duveneck. *Iowa Review*. U of Iowa, 19 Mar. 2013. Web. 9 June 2016.

—*Christopher Mari*

Mallory Ortberg

Born: November 28, 1986
Occupation: Writer and cofounder of the *Toast*

Mallory Ortberg is a humor writer best known as the cofounder of the website the *Toast*—an eclectic mix of pop culture, Western art, literature, and feminism—and the author of the book *Texts from Jane Eyre: And Other Conversations with Your Favorite Literary Characters* (2014). Ortberg also writes the advice column "Dear Prudence" for *Slate*. She got her start writing for popular sites such as *Gawker* and the *Hairpin*, teaming up with fellow writer Nicole Cliffe to launch the *Toast* in 2013. Ortberg is a book lover who satirizes the Western literary and artistic canon through a contemporary, feminist lens. As an example of a character she has satirized, Ortberg told Lidia Jean Kott for the *Huffington Post* (3 Nov. 2014) that William Shakespeare's Hamlet "is a distant character who represents questions about life and mortality," but he is "also a person who [would] yell at his mom to bring him sandwiches but not come into his room."

EARLY LIFE AND CAREER

Ortberg was born in Los Angeles, California, on November 28, 1986. She lived in Southern California until she was eight years old, spending the rest of her formative years in Illinois. Ortberg's parents are well-known evangelical Christian pastors John and Nancy Ortberg. She has two siblings, including sister Laura Ortberg Turner, a religion and culture writer. Her upbringing was steeped in biblical teachings, and Ortberg, already an avid reader, considered becoming a pastor with a scholarly bent, like both of her parents. After high school, Ortberg attended Azusa Pacific University, a Christian university in suburban Los Angeles. She studied English and grappled with her faith. By the time she graduated, she had decided to leave the church and also came out as gay. For a number of years, Ortberg described herself as an atheist, though she told Catherine Woodiwiss for *Sojourners* (19 Apr.

2016), a Christian magazine, that she adopted a kind of spirituality after getting sober in 2013.

In 2009, Ortberg moved to San Francisco and worked as a server at a restaurant before landing a job with an academic publisher. About a year-and-a-half into her job, she began taking on freelance writing assignments, usually for free. After another year of building up her body of work, she began writing for larger media outlets—for money—and got second and third jobs as the weekend editor for both *Gawker* and the women's site the *Gloss*. While exhausting, the experience was invaluable. Ortberg learned how both to write headlines and to engage with readers; but most important, she learned how not to be precious about her own work.

LAUNCHING HER OWN WEBSITE

After a total of three years working full time in publishing, she quit her job to pursue a career as freelancer. She landed a job as a copy editor at Yelp, but two weeks later, she was offered a staff writing position with the *Atlantic*. It was a dream job, but by this time, Ortberg was seriously pursuing an opportunity to create her own website—she could not do both. Ortberg turned down the *Atlantic* job, and the *Toast* launched in the summer of 2013.

Ortberg met Nicole Cliffe, a writer and editor, when they were both freelancing for the *Hairpin*, a website focused on women's interests. The two shared a similar sense of humor and discussed the possibility of joining forces to start their own site. Ortberg had considered starting her own site before. As a freelancer and prolific site commenter, she had met a lawyer from Chicago named Nicholas Pavich, who told her that he liked her writing and suggested that, were she to ever start her own site, he would help fund it. The two had never met in person, but as enthusiasm for what would become the *Toast* grew between Ortberg and Cliffe, the women decided to invite Pavich onboard as a third partner.

Thanks to Cliffe and her husband's previous jobs—they met working at a hedge fund—the *Toast* was able to launch with a good amount of capital. Ortberg and Cliffe have talked openly about their financial beginnings. In a series of tweets from October 2015 Cliffe made clear her husband's role as benefactor: "You honestly can't start an indie site without VC [venture capital] money or a rich husband or a check from a Real Company." With a sizable account going in, the *Toast* was able to pay freelancers, though not a significant amount immediately, and Ortberg was able to draw a salary. The site began turning a profit through ads within three months.

THE *TOAST*

Though the *Toast* works with a number of freelance writers, Ortberg remains the driving voice of the site, writing three to five posts a day. "It's always been 'The Mallory Ortberg Show,' to me, and it's her voice and tone that I think of when I think of the *Toast*," Cliffe told Rebecca Greenfield for *Fast Company* (1 Oct. 2014). Content ranges from discussions of cult-classic films, such as the post that discussed the lesbian undertones in the 1978 film *Grease*, to literature—from the Bible to the pulpy paperback *Flowers in the Attic*.

One popular post—and one particularly representative of Ortberg's voice—was called "Women Listening to Men in Western Art History." In it, Ortberg combines images of classic paintings with contemporary captions that focus on the woman's expression in the piece. "I saw an image online and thought how interesting it is that many paintings throughout Western art history are called *The Conversation* or *Two People Flirting* or *The Couple*. You're clearly meant to see this as a pleasant interaction, but the look on the woman's face is so clearly, 'Someone, please, for the love of God, get me out of here. I wish I were dead,'" Ortberg told Sarah Galo for the *Guardian* (3 Nov. 2014) of the genesis of the article, and subsequent ones like it. "I love the idea that basically for six hundred years of Western European art, male artists were thinking, 'That's the look women always have on their face when you talk to them. That's not boredom, that's just their listening face.'" Other posts satirize male politician-speak ("As a Father of Daughters, I Think We Should Treat All Women like My Daughters") or imagine famous historical and literary figures as jerks ("Dirtbag Ethan Frome").

In 2014, Ortberg launched a sister site called the *Butter* with the novelist and essayist Roxane Gay. The project was initially successful but, because of Gay's various commitments, the website shuttered in 2015. The same year, Ortberg launched the "Convert Series," a series of interviews discussing religion and religious conversion.

TEXTS FROM JANE EYRE
In 2012, Ortberg wrote an article for the *Hairpin* called "Texts from Scarlett O'Hara," in which she imagined the tempestuous heroine of *Gone with the Wind* dogging Ashley, the object of her affection, via smartphone. The idea came from a reader who commented on an article that Cliffe wrote for the Awl about *Gone with the Wind*, a romance novel set during the Civil War. The reader, who had grown up in the South, suggested that life was the same there, except with cell phones—Ortberg ran with it, imagining egotistical Scarlett texting Ashley to meet her at the mill because she was not wearing a corset. The article proved enormously popular, and Ortberg continued the series, focusing on characters in books ranging from *Don Quixote* to the

young-adult series *Sweet Valley High*, first at the *Hairpin* and then at the *Toast*. The joke is not merely that King Lear, for example, has a phone, Ortberg explained in an article for the *Guardian* (30 Oct. 2015), it is how King Lear would have used it given his intense insecurities. "Think of the thousands of messages Heathcliff and Cathy [of *Wuthering Heights*] would have flung back and forth to one another," she wrote. "What makes so many of these literary characters compelling and memorable is the same thing that would make them terrible, impossible-to-live-with roommates, friends, employers, lovers, and parents. They're often treated with great seriousness; it's more fun to refuse to do so."

A few weeks after the Scarlett O'Hara post, Ortberg found a literary agent and wrote up a proposal for a book. The two women shopped the proposal, but no publishing company seemed to take the idea as Ortberg envisioned it—one wanted her to write a young-adult novel, another asked her to drop the literary references. Soon after Ortberg revived the series at the *Toast*, Henry Holt and Company expressed an interest in the concept. After several drafts, the book was published in 2014. In her review for the *Los Angeles Review of Books* (6 Nov. 2014), Sarah Mesle praised the book for its effective feminist satire, skewering the sanctity of the conceptual "great male novelist." Strange though it may seem, Mesle wrote that *Texts from Jane Eyre* functions both as "a major work of bathroom humor reading" and "a significant contribution to feminist literary criticism."

In November 2015, *Slate* magazine announced that Ortberg would replace longtime advice columnist Emily Yoffe and assume the helm of the popular "Dear Prudence" column. "Mallory is one of the most distinctive and exciting writers working today: wise, big-hearted, and devilishly funny," Julia Turner, editor in chief of *Slate*, wrote in an article announcing the news (9 Nov. 2015).

SUGGESTED READING
Galo, Sarah. "Mallory Ortberg: 'If Men Show Up That's Great, But We Don't Need Them.'" *Guardian*. Guardian News and Media, 3 Nov. 2014. Web. 28 Apr. 2016.

Greenfield, Rebecca. "The Toast's Recipe for Bootstrapping a Profitable Media Business." *Fast Company*. Mansueto Ventures, 1 Oct. 2014. Web. 29 Apr. 2016.

Ortberg, Mallory. "'Heathcliff whr r u:' Literary Classics by Text Message." *Guardian*. Guardian News and Media, 30 Oct. 2015. Web. 29 Apr. 2016.

Ortberg, Mallory. Interview by Lidia Jean Kott. "Mallory Ortberg and Her (Small) Media Empire." *Huffington Post*. TheHuffingtonPost. com, 3 Nov. 2011. Web. 28 Apr. 2016.

Ortberg, Mallory. Interview by Catherine Wood-
    iwiss. "The Toast's Mallory Ortberg on Death,
    Faith, and Why It's So Easy to Make Fun of
    Christians." *Sojourners*. Sojourners, 19 Apr.
    2016. Web. 28 Apr. 2016.
Turner, Julia. "Meet Our New Dear Prudence
    Columnist." *Slate*. Slate Group, 9 Nov. 2015.
    Web. 19 Apr. 2016.

SELECTED WORKS
"Texts from Scarlett O'Hara," *Hairpin*, 12 June
2012; "As a Father of Daughters, I Think We
Should Treat All Women like My Daughters,"
Toast, 11 Sept. 2014; "Women Listening to Men
in Western Art History," *Toast*, 23 June 2014;
"Dirtbag Ethan Frome," *Toast*, 23 Mar. 2016

—*Molly Hagan*

(Wikimedia/Flickr) "David Oyelowo" by usbotschaftberlin
[Public Domain] via Wikimedia Commons

David Oyelowo

Born: April 1, 1976
Occupation: Actor

Shortly before moving to the United States in
2007, British actor David Oyelowo had a vision
as he was first reading a script of the film *Selma*
that he would play Dr. Martin Luther King Jr.
"God told me I would play the part," he told Jada
Yuan for *Vulture* (2 Dec. 2014). "The director
at the time didn't agree with God." It would be
another seven years before Oyelowo would realize his dream. During that time, he went from
a virtual unknown to an up-and-coming and in-
demand actor, landing supporting parts in several critically acclaimed feature films, including
The Help (2011), *The Paperboy* (2012), *Lincoln*
(2012), and *The Butler* (2013). His dream finally
became reality in 2014, when Oyelowo was cast
as King, the Nobel Peace Prize–winning civil
rights leader, and he subsequently delivered a
breakthrough performance that earned him a
Golden Globe Award nomination for best actor.

EARLY LIFE AND EDUCATION
The oldest of three boys, David Oyelowo was
born to Nigerian immigrants on April 1, 1976,
in Oxford, England. His father worked for British Airways before it was privatized, and his
mother worked for British Rail. At age six, Oyelowo, whose surname means "A King Deserves
Respect," moved with his parents from south
London to Nigeria. Upon arriving in Lagos, he
discovered that his grandfather was the ruler of
Awe, part of Oyo State, in southwestern Nigeria.
"We were met at the airport by this line of cars
and driven to Oyelowo Street," he recalled to Gerard Gilbert in an interview for the *Independent*
(8 Feb. 2013). "It sounds way more impressive

than it actually is. There are so many royal families in Africa." Over the next seven years, Oyelowo attended a strict boarding school.

When Oyelowo was thirteen, he and his
family returned to the United Kingdom following a military coup in Nigeria. They settled into
a two-bedroom home in the London borough of
Islington, and Oyelowo was enrolled at a local
all-boys comprehensive school, where he was
bullied by other black students. "They called
me 'coconut'—white on the inside and black
on the outside—simply because I had lots of
white friends and wanted to work hard and get
on," he told James Rampton for the *Independent*
(17 Jan. 2007).

Oyelowo's introduction to acting came at age
fourteen, when his pastor's daughter invited him
to join a youth theater group, an invitation he
mistook for a romantic date. "It was so embarrassing. . . . I turned up at Finsbury Park tube
station with a rose and as I walked towards her I
could just tell I'd got this wrong," he recounted
to Gilbert. After a subway strike stranded two
actors in the Royal National Theatre, Oyelowo
agreed to read a scene from an upcoming production, *The Disposables*. His impressive reading convinced the play's director to offer him the
male lead.

Although his parents wanted him to study
law, Oyelowo fell deeper in love with acting after
attending City and Islington College, where he
took an A-level course in theater studies. Under
the guidance of his theater studies teacher, Oyelowo applied to several drama schools.

MAKING HISTORY AT THE ROYAL SHAKESPEARE COMPANY

After graduating from City and Islington College in 1994, Oyelowo completed a yearlong art foundation course at the London Academy of Music and Dramatic Art (LAMDA) before being offered a drama scholarship at the renowned institution. In 1998, upon completing three years of classical training, Oyelowo quickly landed parts in two BBC shows: the crime series *Maisie Raine* and the drama *Brothers and Sisters*. A year later he was invited to join the Royal Shakespeare Company (RSC), amassing stage credits in Aphra Behn's *Oroonoko*, Ben Jonson's *Volpone*, and William Shakespeare's *Antony and Cleopatra*.

Oyelowo made history in 2000 when he became the first black actor to portray an English ruler in an RSC production. Although his nontraditional casting as the lead in *Henry VI* drew criticism, Oyelowo remained unfazed. "Not that long ago white actors were playing Othello in Shakespeare plays in the UK," he told Terry Gross for NPR's *Fresh Air* (29 May 2015). "So it sort of didn't hold any water, really. . . . But the play very quickly dulled those voices." Oyelowo's performance earned him the 2000 Ian Charleson Award for best newcomer in a classic play as well as his father's approval. "[It] just blew my dad away," Oyelowo recounted to Rampton. "He'd experienced a lot of racism here in the 1960s, and he felt witness to a great change in his lifetime."

EARNING RECOGNITION IN *MI-5*

Following his groundbreaking stint in *Henry VI*, Oyelowo became a small-screen fixture with his supporting role as Danny Hunter in the popular British spy thriller *Spooks* (known in the United States as *MI-5*). He remained with the show for three years (2002–4) until his character met an untimely end in the season three finale—at the actor's request. Next came a cameo in the 2005 two-part reunion special of the Judi Dench sitcom *As Time Goes By*, followed by appearances alongside several other big-name actors, including Ben Kingsley in *A Sound of Thunder* (2005) and Jennifer Aniston in *Derailed* (2005). Oyelowo returned to the stage in a 2005 revival of Aeschylus's Greek tragedy *Prometheus Bound* at the Sound Theatre in London.

In 2006 Oyelowo had prominent roles in the Bollywood comedy *American Blend*, as well as the BBC dramas *Shoot the Messenger* and *Born Equal*, both which featured fellow Nigerian actor Nikki Amuka-Bird. In addition to guest-starring in a 2006 episode of *The Gil Mayo Mysteries*, he was part of the all-star ensembles of *The Last King of Scotland* (2006), Kenneth Branagh's unique adaptation of Shakespeare's comedy *As You Like It* (2006), and *Five Days* (2007), a five-part BBC crime thriller.

MOVING TO HOLLYWOOD

Oyelowo made the fateful decision in 2007 to move to Los Angeles, California. "I had a very nice career in the UK, but heroes of mine are Daniel Day-Lewis, Sidney Poitier, Denzel Washington, and when I looked at the zenith of what they do, it came out of Hollywood," he told Andy Warhol for *Interview* (5 Jan. 2015). "So my wife and I took the risk in 2007 of leaving the UK, coming here, and hoping that I could scale those heights." The gamble paid off for Oyelowo, who subsequently revisited his role in *Prometheus Bound* in the spring of 2007, during a critically acclaimed Off-Broadway run with the Aquila Theater Company.

By 2008 the actor had emerged as a fast-rising star, with supporting parts in several high-profile projects, including the small-screen version of Lorraine Hansberry's play *A Raisin in the Sun* and the pilot episode of *The No. 1 Ladies' Detective Agency* (2008). A devout Christian, Oyelowo appeared in the BBC miniseries *The Passion* (2008), portraying Joseph of Arimathea, the man who buried Jesus's crucified body in his own tomb. He then tackled the role of legendary blues musician Muddy Waters in the independent biopic *Who Do You Love* (2008).

GAINING PROMINENCE

After appearing opposite Naomie Harris in the 2009 two-part television movie *Small Island*, an adaptation of Andrea Levy's 2004 novel about Jamaican immigrants in post–World War II Britain, Oyelowo reunited with Harris for *Blood and Oil* (2010). A year later he began amassing big- and small-screen credits, opposite some of Hollywood's heavyweights. His guest-starring stint as a judge in an episode of the Julianna Margulies legal drama *The Good Wife* preceded his first major supporting role as a corporate villain in the summer blockbuster *Rise of the Planet of the Apes* (2011), which grossed more than $480 million worldwide. But that was not Oyelowo's only box-office triumph that summer; he costarred alongside Viola Davis and Jessica Chastain in the sleeper hit *The Help*, an adaptation of Kathryn Stockett's best-selling 2009 novel about racial tensions in the 1960s Deep South during the burgeoning civil rights movement.

Oyelowo's next big role was as an overconfident, emotionally charged Tuskegee airman, battling discrimination in and out of the cockpit, in the George Lucas–produced *Red Tails* (2012). He was openly critical of the lack of support by Hollywood to promote the film, which featured a predominantly black cast. "A film centered around the Second World War with a predominantly white cast would not have the pressure on it that *Red Tails* has," he told Christian Blauvelt for *Entertainment*

Weekly (16 Jan. 2012). "I don't think it's a film that would've gotten made without George self-financing it, because there's no 'white savior' role."

Oyelowo then joined Matthew McConaughey and Nicole Kidman in Lee Daniels's adaptation of Pete Dexter's 1995 novel *The Paperboy*, in which Oyelowo portrayed an ambitious Miami reporter investigating the case of a death-row inmate. The 1960s film noir thriller debuted to mixed reviews at the 2012 Cannes Film Festival, where it received a nomination for the prestigious Palme d'Or.

Oyelowo switched gears, playing the romantic lead in *Middle of Nowhere* (2012)—his first collaboration with writer, director, and producer Ava DuVernay. He was eager to appear in the independent drama after receiving her screenplay. Oyelowo's performance as a charismatic bus driver earned him a nomination for the 2013 Independent Spirit Award for best supporting male. He ended the year on a high note, appearing as a cavalryman opposite his idol Daniel Day-Lewis in Steven Spielberg's biopic *Lincoln* and playing a detective in the action flick *Jack Reacher*, starring Tom Cruise in the title role.

SELMA AND BEYOND

A year later Oyelowo reunited with Daniels for *The Butler* (2013), a fictionalized account inspired by longtime White House butler Eugene Allen. To prepare for his role as civil rights activist Louis Gaines, Oyelowo, whose character ages from seventeen to sixty-eight, exercised vigorously and made sure to sleep ten hours a night to appear younger; he ate salty foods, drank more water, and scaled back significantly on his hours of sleep to look older. *The Butler*, which took four years to make due to lack of funding, went on to gross over $176 million, propelled by an all-star ensemble that included Forest Whitaker and Oprah Winfrey. The BBC spy thriller *Complicit* and the short *206* were also among Oyelowo's 2013 credits.

In 2014 Oyelowo realized his seven-year dream to play Martin Luther King Jr. with the release of *Selma*, which chronicled the civil rights leader's epic 1965 march from Selma to Montgomery, Alabama. After Daniels backed out of the project, Oyelowo was instrumental in getting the film made, recruiting Winfrey as producer and recommending DuVernay as director. He fully embodied the lead role, shaving his hairline, gaining thirty pounds, and adopting King's mannerisms and trademark Southern drawl. Despite earning a 2015 Golden Globe nomination for best actor, Oyelowo was snubbed by the Oscars.

Another 2014 highlight was Oyelowo's tour de force solo performance as a psychologically troubled war veteran in the HBO drama *Nightingale*, which earned him his second Golden Globe nomination, his first Primetime Emmy Award nomination, and a Critics' Choice Television Award. After reuniting with McConaughey in *Interstellar* and Chastain in *A Most Violent Year*, both released in 2014, Oyelowo continued to challenge himself with his lead role in *Captive* (2015), portraying a real-life escaped convict who breaks into a woman's home and holds her hostage.

The actor welcomes the opportunity to play various and diverse roles but refuses to accept stereotypical parts. "A degree of self-fulfilling prophecy comes with being constantly told that there's something problematic about you and your section of society. But during my formative years, that wasn't continually drummed into me, so there were no limits on my expectations," he told Rampton. "No prejudice has held me back because I haven't let it. There is a monster to be fed, but I've left it safely in its cave." In an interview with Ryan Gilbey for the *Guardian* (1 Feb. 2015), Oyelowo explained his method for selecting his roles, saying, "I'm in this for the long haul. I truly believe in cinema's potential for cultural impact. I have a clear idea what I want to do—to enrich people's lives. . . . For me, it's a very conscious decision to follow my heart rather than the dollar."

PERSONAL LIFE

Oyelowo lives in Sherman Oaks, California, with his wife, Jessica, and their four children.

SUGGESTED READING

Blauvelt, Christian. "*Red Tails*: Rising Star David Oyelowo Talks George Lucas Decades-in-the-Making Tuskegee Airmen Epic." *Entertainment Weekly*. Time, 16 Jan. 2012. Web. 16 Dec. 2015.

Gilbert, Gerard. "Upwardly Mobile: David Oyelowo on Going from Tooting Bec to Tom Cruise's Jet." *Independent*. Independent.co.uk, 8 Feb. 2013. Web. 16 Dec. 2015.

Gilbey, Ryan. "David Oyelowo: 'No One Says to Oliver Stone: White Characters Again?'" *Guardian*. Guardian News and Media, 1 Feb. 2015. Web. 16 Dec. 2015.

Gross, Terry. "David Oyelowo on Acting, His Royal Roots and the One Role He Won't Take." *Fresh Air*. NPR, 29 May 2015. Web. 16 Dec. 2015.

Oyelowo, David. "Q & Andy: David Oyelowo." Interview by Andy Warhol. *Interview*. Brant, 5 Jan. 2015. Web. 16 Dec. 2015.

Rampton, James. "David Oyelowo: An Actor's Life." *Independent*. Independent.co.uk, 17 Jan. 2007. Web. 16 Dec. 2015.

—*Bertha Muteba*

Kevin Parker

Born: January 20, 1986
Occupation: Musician

Kevin Parker is the musical brain behind the contemporary psychedelic rock group Tame Impala, which entered the world stage in 2010 with the release of their first album, *Innerspeaker*. That album and the group's two subsequent records, *Lonerism* (2012) and *Currents* (2015), were written and produced by Parker. He also played every instrument, which included drums, bass, guitars, keyboards, and sang vocals. The only time Tame Impala play as a group is when they are live on stage; otherwise, it is essentially a one-man band, and that format does not seem likely to change.

The nearly unanimous critical perception of Tame Impala, and therefore Parker, is that the band not only sounds great in terms of mixing and production, but also that their music is unique and surpasses its influences as well any attempt at simple categorization of its sound. Tame Impala's two most recent albums were each nominated for a Grammy Award for Best Alternative Music Album.

EARLY LIFE AND EDUCATION

Kevin Parker was born on January 20, 1986, in Sydney, Australia, to Zimbabweans Jerry and Rosalind Parker. He has one brother, Steve, and the boys grew up primarily in the capital city of Perth. Their parents divorced when Parker was very young, and in an interview with Nosheen Iqbal for the *Guardian* (5 Oct. 2012), Parker explains that his parents were from very different economic backgrounds, which he speculated contributed to their divorce. In an interview with Mark Dapin for the *Sydney Morning Herald* (27 June 2015) Parker describes his mother as "one of the spirits in life" who "spends half her time up mountains [and] hiking." His father, as he described to Iqbal, is an accountant and a "closet musician at heart." The boys initially lived with their mother, stepfather, and half sister. Within a few years, however, Steve chose to live instead with their father and his family. When Parker was about to enter high school, he decided to also move in with his father, whose home was near the beach and provided Parker with more stability.

Parker learned to play a variety of instruments when he was very young. His father bought him his first guitar and taught him a few basic chords, and by the time Parker was twelve, he had learned to multitrack himself—record himself playing individual instruments and then putting it together as one recording—by using two tape recorders. He would first record the drums, then the keyboard, then the bass, and he

C Flanigan/WireImage/Getty Images

would continue to add various instruments depending on what he felt the song called for. (This technique, although with higher quality equipment, would become his recording method when he formed Tame Impala.) His father noticed what he was doing and bought him an 8-track recording machine for his sixteenth birthday, which made it easier to record multiple tracks. Parker's father also influenced his son's musical taste through his vast record collection of mostly artists from the 1960s and 1970s—bands like the Beatles, the Beach Boys, the Shadows, and Supertramp.

Parker was a rebellious teenager, who by the age of thirteen was smoking marijuana, drinking, and shoplifting. He was sent to a private Catholic high school, which is where he met fellow musician and future Tame Impala guitarist Dom Simper. Perth's vibrant music scene provided the environment for Parker and Simper to perform the covers of songs inspired by his father's record collection. After high school, Parker enrolled in college and, on the insistence of his father, majored in engineering. He then changed his major to astronomy but did not make it to many classes. He got a job working for a Perth law firm delivering documents to people around town, which gave him a chance to walk, be alone, and think about his songs.

TAME IMPALA IS BORN

Parker and Dom Simper continued to play together, and Parker continued to make home recordings in his bedroom. When he was about twenty, he and Simper began performing with drummer and backup vocalist Jay Watson, and the live Tame Impala act was formed. From the beginning, the live set was very different from the recorded material: Parker, when in complete control of the music and how it is played and performed, has often been labeled a perfectionist by the music press. Around 2007 the band began to receive more attention online after many of their songs were posted on Myspace, a once popular social networking website where many new artists and musicians shared their work. In 2008 the group was signed by the relatively small label Modular Recordings, and they released a self-titled EP. As word continued to spread, Tame Impala became more and more of an indie rock sensation, and they were booked to open for such bands as MGMT, You Am I, and the Black Keys—all before they had officially released a full-length album.

INNERSPEAKER

Tame Impala's first full-length studio album, *Innerspeaker*, was released in 2010 to rave reviews. The album showcased a new band, a new voice, a master craftsman of music and sound, and a contemporary twist on psychedelic (psych) rock. Several well-known influences were evident: Pink Floyd, the Kinks, the Beatles, Cream, and more contemporary bands like the Flaming Lips. Many critics and fans noted an almost eerie resemblance between Parker's vocals and those of John Lennon during the Beatles' psychedelic rock stage on songs such as "Tomorrow Never Knows" and "A Day in the Life," where Lennon's vocals are somewhat nasally, surreal, and distorted.

In his review of the album for the music website *Pitchfork* (28 May 2010), Zach Kelly echoed what many other music critics were writing about Tame Impala's sound and music: "By all accounts, fixing their gaze so intently on established influences should play as either disingenuous or forced. It's difficult to be so plugged-in to a vintage feel without the music seeming time-capsuled, but the band's vibrance helps these songs sound very much alive." He noted that Flaming Lips collaborator Dave Fridmann helped mix the sonically rich album along with Parker and pointed out how well the various instruments were blended, "cultivating a uniform feel."

LONERISM

Parker spent the next two years recording and mixing the group's second album, *Lonerism* (2012). Telling Iqbal about the creation of the record, Parker explained that "[*Lonerism*] almost drove me insane. In fact, it pretty much did; it was two agonizing years, one in Perth, one in Paris." Parker said that although song ideas come to him fairly quickly and "in flashes," the construction of the sounds of the song and having

to select guitar effects and drum sounds and then mixing the record takes him an unbearably long time. Even after mixing a song, he explains that he sometimes feels as if it is horrible and sometimes feels the complete opposite—that it is brilliant. *Lonerism* was just as layered and sonically sophisticated as the group's first album, though there were fewer guitars and more synthesizers. The album reached number 30 on the Billboard 200 chart.

Ian Cohen for *Pitchfork* (8 Oct. 2012) observed that what makes *Lonerism*—and Tame Impala in general—better than what he called "revivalist" bands is that they "tap into the progressive and experimental spirit of psychedelic rock, and not just [its] sound." Not that sound is in any way unimportant for Cohen; it is simply a part of a bigger musical context. "You could spend," he wrote, "the entirety of opener 'Be Above It' letting your ears luxuriate in the diversity of tactile sensations—the subliminal whisper of the title becomes a rhythm track, a barreling drum break is severely tweaked to sound like an oncoming rush of bison, a flanged guitar wobbles like neon Jello, and Parker's laconic, slightly echoed vocals pulls the whole thing together." Alexis Petridis for the *Guardian* (4 Oct. 2012) elaborates on the sometimes simplistic comparisons of Tame Impala to psych rock bands of the late 1960s by explaining that, "Tame Impala just sound like Tame Impala: delving into the past in order to drag it into the future."

CURRENTS

If the second album stepped away from guitars and moved more toward synthesizers, the third album, *Currents* (2015) took a great leap. It was notably different both conceptually and musically from anything Parker and Tame Impala had ever produced and was musically more in line with soul and R & B than it was psychedelic rock. Along with the ubiquitous presence of synthesizers and up-tempo drums, there were various stylistic changes: the influence of dance, pop, funk, and R & B was noticeable throughout the album though a classic rock influence was still present. More specifically, there was an undeniable influence of popular artists who in the 1980s also sought to combine genres, namely Prince and Michael Jackson. Critics and fans who were caught off-guard by the shift in sound and style expressed disappointment. Generally, however, the album was still very well reviewed. "The new album," wrote Corban Goble for *Pitchfork* (14 July 2015), "feels more insular and personal while exuding a newfound sexiness."

In various interviews Parker was quite outspoken about the meaning and significance of the album and Tame Impala's ever-evolving sound. Speaking to Steven Hyden for *Grantland* (10 June 2015), Parker explained that, "*Lonerism* is such an insular, detached album. I got that out of the way, and now I want to join the world." Jon Pareles for the *New York Times* (15 July 2015) wrote of *Currents* that "Parker has maintained his studio obsessiveness. But now, instead of piling up countless layers, he continuously tweaks fewer tracks; the timbres keep changing on vocals, drums, and instrumental lines, smudging each one just so. He also blurs the distinction between electronic and organic." In fact, blurring distinctions, whether in sound, feel, or genre, has become something that should be expected of Parker. *Currents* peaked at number 4 on the Billboard 200 chart, which was Tame Impala's highest chart position to date.

PERSONAL LIFE

Parker has been dating Australian Sophie Lawrence since 2014, and they share a home southwest of Perth in Western Australia. Despite a 2016 world tour with Tame Impala in 2016, Parker continued to write new music in his Perth recording studio when he was home during tour breaks. He was unsure, however, whether the music would be produced for future Tame Impala albums or whether he is writing for another artist to record.

SUGGESTED READING

Dapin, Mark. "Why Tame Impala Are Out of This World." *SMH*. Fairfax Media, 27 June 2015. Web. 16 May 2016.

Goble, Corban. "Cosmic Neurotic: The Heady Perfectionism of Tame Impala's Kevin Parker." *Pitchfork*. Condé Nast, 14 July 2015. Web. 16 May 2016.

Hyden, Steven. "Tame Impala Let It Happen." *Grantland*. ESPN Internet Ventures, 10 June 2015. Web. 16 May 2016.

Iqbal, Nosheen. "Tame Impala: A Trip Inside the Head of Main Man Kevin Parker." *Guardian*. Guardian News and Media, 5 Oct. 2012. 16 May 2016.

Kelly, Zach. "*Innerspeaker*." *Pitchfork*. Condé Nast, 28 May 2010. 16 May 2016.

Pareles, Jon. "Review: Tame Impala's New Album Clears the Haze." *New York Times*. New York Times, 15 July 2015. Web. 16 May 2016.

SELECTED WORKS

Innerspeaker, 2010; *Lonerism*, 2012; *Currents*, 2015

—*Dmitry Kiper*

Teyonah Parris

Born: ca. 1987
Occupation: Actor

Teyonah Parris has appeared in two conversation-inspiring films and one of the most critically acclaimed television shows ever aired. After graduating from the Juilliard School in 2012, she got her first break on the AMC series *Mad Men*, playing the first black employee in the ad agency featured in the series, and, in real life, becoming the first black actor to have a recurring role on the show. Parris then played the fiery, ambitious Coco in the thought-provoking satirical film *Dear White People* (2014) and Lysistrata in the Spike Lee–directed *Chi-Raq* (2015), which addresses gun violence in Chicago's South Side, an impoverished, largely black section of the city. Parris has also become a beauty and fashion icon. In February 2016, she appeared on the cover of *Essence* magazine.

EARLY LIFE

Teyonah Parris was born around 1987 in Hopkins, South Carolina. She was the middle of three children and the only girl. She has spoken fondly of her Southern upbringing. "For the summers, I would go down to my grandparents' house," Parris told Stefania Marghitu for the *Hairpin* (10 Oct. 2014). "We climbed trees and cut grass; there were rabbits and pigs. I really just got to be a kid. I think that's one of the pluses of growing up 'down south': being outside for hours and just running around. . . . It fostered adventure and creativity."

Frazer Harrison/Getty Images

In addition to what she calls "tomboy" activities such as climbing trees and wrestling with her brothers, she played softball, though even at a young age she began to develop an interest in performing. Parris appeared in various beauty pageants. The family did not have much money, so her beauty pageant outfits were often homemade, sometimes reconstructed from her brothers' hand-me-downs.

ACTING BUG

Around the age of ten Parris became interested in becoming an actor. She wanted to study acting and to be in films. Pageants did not satisfy that desire. For two years she attended Lower Richland High School in Columbia, South Carolina, after which she auditioned for, and got into, the South Carolina Governor's School for the Arts and Humanities, a boarding school in Greenville, South Carolina, with a strong emphasis on the performing arts. Parris lived on campus at the high school, performed in plays, and received an intense, strong education in acting.

When the time came to search for colleges, she applied to about twenty, according to Rebecca Haithcoat's profile for the magazine *Complex* (20 Aug. 2015). In 2005, the year she graduated from high school, Parris was accepted to the Juilliard School, in New York City, one of the most respected and prestigious schools for performing arts. Before getting into Juilliard's acting school, Parris had to audition. She and her father drove from South Carolina to New York, where she auditioned several times. A few months later, she was accepted to the school. Parris took part in Juilliard's four-year drama conservatory program in actor training and received a bachelor of fine arts degree in drama.

EARLY STAGE AND SCREEN ROLES

After graduating from Juilliard, Parris appeared in the Broadway play *A Free Man of Color*, which is about a wealthy black man living—and living it up—in New Orleans in 1801. Also around this time Parris appeared in the film *How Do You Know* (2010), playing a character named Riva. The comedy failed to make a serious impact with either audiences or critics, however. Prior to *How Do You Know*, Parris had never been in a film or on a television show, so while on set, she tried to learn as much as possible. Around 2011, she moved to Los Angeles, California, and tried to make it in Hollywood as an actor. For about eight months, Parris went on audition after audition but did not get a callback.

Eventually, she decided to move back to New York City. But first she planned a trip to India, thinking it would do her good to have such an adventure. During this time, she received a chance to audition for a part on the award-winning, critically acclaimed series *Mad Men*, which, by this point, had aired for four seasons. The show focused on an advertising agency in the 1960s in New York City as the private lives of its central characters.

MAD MEN

In an interview by Mina Hochberg posted on AMC's website (Aug. 2012), Parris said that she knew little about the role she would be playing on the show. "I went in [to the audition] just thinking it was a very small part," Parris said. "I could have been opening a door for all I knew. I had no clue." *Mad Men* was often praised for its attention to detail and, staying within the context of historical accuracy, it did not initially feature any black employees in the ad agency. However, Parris performed well during her audition and was called back to meet with series creator and showrunner Matt Weiner, star Jon Hamm, and two of the show's casting directors. Parris got the part of Dawn Chambers, the ad agency's first African American employee. Parris told Marghitu that after shooting her first episode, she took her planned trip to India. Upon returning to Los Angeles, she was told that her character Dawn—the new secretary of Hamm's character, Don Draper—would be appearing in more episodes.

This was a huge break for Parris, who eventually appeared in twenty-two episodes. The character of Dawn first appeared on *Mad Men's* fifth season, which takes place between 1966 and 1967, long before Parris was born. Therefore, she talked with her grandmother, who happened to live in New York City in the 1960s and worked as a secretary. In an interview with Jai Tiggett for the website *Shadow and Act* (23 Oct. 2014), Parris said, "I remember asking about her experiences and thinking that I was going to get this story that it was so hard and everybody was so mean. And she was just like, 'It was fine. Some [people] were nice, some weren't. But I did the work and went home.' It just showed me that one person can't represent the whole race. So when I took on Dawn I thought, she can't be the spokesperson for the entire black community in the '60s, so what is her story going to be?"

In fact, the character of Dawn is a humble, hardworking, and modestly dressed young woman trying to get by in the working world. Later in the series the ad agency hires another black secretary—Shirley, who, unlike Dawn, has an afro and wears short dresses. The characters of Shirley and Dawn have a funny, yet profound, scene in which they call each other by the other's name. The scene illustrates that, though the two women look so different, some people in the office mix them up simply because they are young black women. This was an important scene for Parris's character, because, as Linda Holmes explained for the blog *Monkey See* on the National

Public Radio (NPR) website (21 Apr. 2014), it "subtly realigned the show's consideration of race from one that was primarily about the experiences of white people to one that was at least curious about, if not yet diving deeply into, the experiences of black people, and specifically black women."

DEAR WHITE PEOPLE
In 2014, Parris costarred in the thought-provoking satirical film *Dear White People*. The plot revolved around several black college students on a primarily white campus. One of those black students has a college radio show called "Dear White People," which is meant to call out white people on subtle (and often unintentional or, at least, subconscious) forms of racism. The two female leads exemplify opposite ends of the film's comments about identity and race. Parris plays Coco Conners, who uses black stereotypes to gain fame on the Internet, while her counterpart Samantha White (Tessa Thompson), the host of the "Dear White People" radio program, goes out of her way to address racism and fight the system. Stuck in the middle is Lionel Higgins (Tyler James Williams), a skinny, gay, black nerd—although he despises such categories and considers himself simply a person who wants nothing to do with the positions (and affectations) of either Coco or Samantha. That he—and others in the film—continue not to be seen as a person but as a collection of labels underlies the film's focus on identity.

The film received critical acclaim, launching another national conversation about race. In his review of the film for the *New York Times* (16 Oct. 2014), A. O. Scott called it "as smart and fearless a debut as I have seen from an American filmmaker in quite some time." Scott added: "It's a clever campus comedy that juggles a handful of hot potatoes—race, sex, privilege, power—with elegant agility and only an occasional fumble." In an interview with Logan Hill for the *New York Times* (4 Sept. 2014), Parris said, "Sometimes, we see a shallow version of the African American experience, which is so vast and deep. I was excited that the film speaks on issues that never get spoken about and isn't banging you up against the head with them, but making you laugh and feel a little uncomfortable."

CHI-RAQ
In 2015, Parris starred in the film *Chi-Raq*, an adaptation of the ancient Greek play *Lysistrata* by Aristophanes, directed and cowritten by Spike Lee. The film's title refers to Chicago, where the film takes place, and Iraq, which the United States invaded in 2003, equating the latter with the extremely dangerous and violent world of Chicago's South Side, parts of which are predominantly black, impoverished, and troubled by gang violence. As in the Aristophanes play, the women eventually get so tired of the violence that, led by Lysistrata (played by Parris), they stage a "sex strike"—they refuse to have sex with their boyfriends until they put down their guns and end the violence. The film is highly stylized: aside from the fact that lines of dialogue are in verse, there are musical numbers and various sorts of exaggerated shots. As a contrast to that, the film has scenes in which real-life victims of gun violence speak to the camera.

Chi-Raq received many positive reviews but also no shortage of mixed and negative ones. In *Vulture* (4 Dec. 2015), David Edelstein praised the film and Parris's performance, noting that she plays Lysistrata "with all cylinders firing. She stares down the camera. She swings her derrière while eyes explode all over, like Jayne Mansfield in *The Girl Can't Help It*. It's hard to believe she is the actress who played Don Draper's secretary Dawn Chambers on *Mad Men*, who kept most of her thoughts (and private life) to herself—but she did, after all, go to Juilliard."

PERSONAL LIFE AND OTHER PROJECTS
Parris has appeared as a recurring character, Missy Vaughn, on the TV series *Survivor's Remorse* (2014–15), a behind-the-scenes look at the world of professional basketball. She also appeared in the television show *The Good Wife* in 2010 and the television movie *The Miki Howard Story* (2016). She lives in New York City.

SUGGESTED READING

Haithcoat, Rebecca. "Challenges Welcome: A Teyonah Parris Joint." *Complex*. Complex Media, 20 Aug. 2015. Web. 2 Mar. 2016.

Hill, Logan. "Breaths of Fresh Acting Talent." *New York Times*. New York Times, 4 Sept. 2014. Web. 2 Mar. 2016.

Parris, Teyonah. Interview by Julia Felsenthal. "Teyonah Parris on Sex Strikes, Chi-Raq, and Collaborating with Spike Lee." *Vogue*. Condé Nast, 5 Dec. 2015. Web. 2 Mar. 2016.

Parris, Teyonah. Interview by Stefania Marghitu. "Nothing but the Truth: An Interview with Teyonah Parris." *Hairpin*. Hairpin, 10 Oct. 2014. Web. 2 Mar. 2016.

Scott, A. O. "Advanced Course in Diversity." *New York Times*. New York Times, 16 Oct. 2014. Web. 2 Mar. 2016.

SELECTED WORKS
Mad Men, 2012–15; *Dear White People*, 2014; *Survivor's Remorse*, 2014–15; *Chi-Raq*, 2015

—*Dmitry Kiper*

Simon Pegg

Born: February 14, 1970
Occupation: Actor, writer

Simon Pegg was already an established television actor and writer in the United Kingdom when he gained international attention in *Shaun of the Dead* (2004), playing an unlikely hero who protects his loved ones from a zombie apocalypse. With its modest $4 million budget, the romantic zombie comedy, or "romzomcom," also cowritten by Pegg, became an unlikely hit. Not only did the film's breakthrough spawn two other collaborations with *Shaun of the Dead* director Edgar Wright and costar Nick Frost in their Three Flavors Cornetto trilogy—*Hot Fuzz* (2007) and *The World's End* (2013)—but it also led to more prominent, scene-stealing roles in two blockbuster franchises: the Mission: Impossible and Star Trek series. Wright attributes much of Pegg's success to his relatable charm. "A lot of great British comic actors have a talent that means they tend to play grotesques, whether it's Peter Sellers or Steve Coogan or John Cleese," Wright told Craig McLean for *British GQ* (8 Feb. 2011). "But Simon has a slightly different quality, in that he can be a really funny Everyman—and that's really rare. People take it for granted when somebody has the ability to be the centre of something."

A LOVE OF PERFORMING

Simon John Beckingham was born on February 14, 1970, in Brockworth, a village in Gloucestershire, a rural county in Southwest England. Pegg comes from a family of performers. His father, John Henry Beckingham, was a piano salesman by day and a musician at night. But it was his mother's involvement in the local amateur dramatic troupe that sparked his interest. "I grew up around a really passionate group of people who were doing theatre . . . simply for the sake of doing it," he told John Walsh for the *Independent* (12 July 2013). "And that's where I got my love of it from."

When he was seven, his parents divorced, and his mother, Gillian, largely raised him. She later remarried shoe shop–owner Richard Pegg; Simon changed his last named from Beckingham to Pegg. The youngster displayed a penchant for comedy. Pegg's father recounted to McLean, "From the time he could talk, Simon has been able to absolutely crack me up. One Christmas he made me laugh so much that I strained my intercostal muscles."

At nine years old, Pegg discovered another passion: science fiction. He quickly fell in love with the animated version of the original *Star Trek* television series, which aired weeknights on

(Paul Hudson/Wikimedia) By Paul Hudson (Simon Pegg) [CC BY 2.0], via Wikimedia Commons

BBC2 (British Broadcasting Company 2). "I was already a big sci-fi fan, since *Star Wars* had already hit and it opened me up to the possibilities of the sci-fi world," Pegg recounted to Jean Trinh for the *Daily Beast* (13 May 2013). "*Star Trek* always seemed like a slightly more grownup, intellectual, and philosophical version of the genre." Pegg's fixation with science fiction, as well as the horror and action genres, would carry into adulthood and help shape his career. Another BBC2 (British Broadcasting Company 2) show that captured Pegg's attention was the offbeat British sitcom *The Young Ones*, whose lead actor, Rik Mayall, inspired his other great love: comedy.

After attending local schools—Castle Hill Primary School, Brockworth Comprehensive School, and the King's School, Gloucester—the sixteen-year-old moved away from home and lived with strangers to pursue his A levels in English literature and theater studies at Stratford-upon-Avon College. (A levels are the highest exams a student must pass in the United Kingdom to complete their secondary education.) Two years later he eschewed drama school in favor of attending Bristol University. "Drama schools would tend to shape you," he shared with McLean. "And I didn't really want to be ridden roughshod over. I wanted to be my own person." While studying at Bristol, Pegg joined the campus comedy troupe David Icke and the Orphans of Jesus and began performing stand-up gigs on the local circuit.

LAUNCH OF AN ACTING CAREER

In 1993, two years after receiving his bachelor's degree in film, theater, and television, Pegg embarked on a stand-up comedy career in London. He quickly became a fixture on the small screen, earning his first acting and writing credits while appearing alongside Jessica Hynes in Independent Television's (ITV's) short-lived sketch comedy show *Six Pairs of Pants* (1995). After reuniting with Hynes in the 1996 sitcom *Asylum*—also his first collaboration with director Edgar Wright—Pegg subsequently joined the second season of the half-hour comedy *Faith in the Future* (1996), replacing Charlie Creed-Miles as Jools.

Over the next two years, Pegg was a regular in the sketch comedy series *We Know Where You Live* (1997) and *Is It Bill Bailey?* (1998). In 1998, after *Faith in the Future*'s third and final season, he joined the cast of another BBC program, the Monty Python–esque television series *Big Train*. A year later, he made his film debut with a minor role in *Tube Tales*, followed by another small part in the Rik Mayall dark comedy *Guest House Paradiso*.

Pegg received his first starring role as Ray Purbbs, a 1960s underground magazine publisher in the BBC sitcom *Hippies* (1999), which only had a six-episode run. For his next television project, Paramount Comedy Channel executives proposed developing a comedy costarring Pegg and Hynes. Pegg agreed; he and Hynes wrote the script and Wright was brought in to direct.

The result was the slacker comedy *Spaced* (1999–2001), in which the duo played twenty-something strangers who impersonate a professional couple to rent an affordable apartment. The show also featured Nick Frost in his acting debut. Frost is Pegg's close friend and frequent collaborator whom he first met in the early 1990s when Pegg's then girlfriend worked with Frost at a North London Mexican restaurant. *Spaced* utilized references to popular science fiction and horror films, as well as the themes of extended adolescence and friendship that would come to characterize his future work with Frost and Wright. The show ran for two seasons and received considerable critical praise.

SUCCESS WITH *SHAUN OF THE DEAD*

Pegg's growing popularity led to appearances in high-profile projects including Steven Spielberg's World War II miniseries *Band of Brothers* (2001) and two big-screen comedies starring fellow British comedian Steve Coogan: *The Parole Officer* (2001) and *24-Hour Party People* (2002). By then, Pegg had begun collaborating with Wright on *Shaun of the Dead*, about a down-on-his-luck electronics salesman who becomes an unlikely hero when zombies attack unsuspecting Londoners. His first-ever screenplay was initially inspired by a *Spaced* dream sequence that features zombies. The film's plot (and title) also pay homage to *Dawn of the Dead*, George A. Romero's 1978 cult classic. "They create this amazing little bourgeois paradise in this shopping mall, and it's hilarious, because the world was falling apart," Pegg told Carolyn Kellogg for the *Los Angeles Times* (16 June 2011), discussing *Shaun of the Dead* and *Dawn of the Dead*. "*Shaun of the Dead* was about living in a city, and becoming so immune to what was going on around you that you literally don't notice the world ending."

Shaun of the Dead filmed on location over nine weeks and premiered in March 2004. It features Pegg in the title role, alongside Nick Frost. The self-described "romantic zombie comedy" was an instant hit in the United Kingdom and the United States, and would become a cult classic in its own right.

HOLLYWOOD COMES CALLING

Pegg's starring role in *Shaun of the Dead* earned him the attention of the film's numerous fans, many of whom were film directors and actors. In 2005 he appeared as a villain in an episode of the popular science-fiction series *Doctor Who* and narrated the first season of *Doctor Who Confidential*, a behind-the-scenes documentary that chronicled the reboot of the long-running British show. It was not long before Hollywood took notice of Pegg; American filmmaker JJ Abrams cast him in *Mission: Impossible III* (2006). "I was just blown away by Simon's sense of humour," Abrams recounted to McLean. "He was also surprisingly emotional and convincing. I remember thinking . . . 'this guy can probably do anything.'"

International audiences were equally charmed by Pegg's performance as Benji Dunn, Tom Cruise's sidekick. By July 2006, two months after the US release of *Mission: Impossible III*, Pegg had completed filming on the follow-up to *Shaun of the Dead* and his second collaboration with Wright and Frost. Released in February 2007, *Hot Fuzz* starred Pegg as a highly decorated London cop banished to a seemingly sleepy town, where he and his inept partner (Frost) investigate several mysterious deaths.

STAR TREK STRIKES BOX-OFFICE GOLD

Pegg reunited with Abrams for a big-screen revival of *Star Trek*. Although Pegg was the first choice to play Montgomery "Scotty" Scott, he was not as quick to accept the role as one might think. "At first, it felt too huge to just give an arbitrary reply to," Pegg confided to Yvonne Villareal for the *Los Angeles Times* (28 Apr. 2009). "JJ said the worst thing that could happen is that every couple of years, with any luck, we get to have fun in outer space. And I just thought, of course, it's a no-brainer."

Critics hailed the casting decision. In a review for the *Boston Globe* (5 May 2009) Ty Burr remarked that "What lifts the Abrams film into the ether is the rightness of its casting and playing, from [Zoe] Saldana's Uhuru . . . to Simon Pegg's grandly comic Scotty, the movie's most radical reimagining of a *Star Trek* regular." With a domestic gross of $257 million, the film ranked seventh among 2009's highest-grossing movies in North America. However, *Star Trek* was not Pegg's only blockbuster film; he also voiced the character of Buck, a weasel, in *Ice Age: Dawn of the Dinosaurs*, which was that year's highest-grossing animated film.

NEW PROJECTS WITH FROST AND ABRAMS

Over the next few years, Pegg would return to franchises and collaborators, all while branching out with smaller films. Pegg's next starring role came in John Landis's dark romantic comedy *Burke and Hare* (2010). He then replaced Eddie Izzard as the voice of sword-wielding mouse Reepicheep in *The Chronicles of Narnia: The Voyage of the Dawn Treader*.

In 2011 Pegg and Frost reunited professionally on several projects, without Wright for the first time. They collaborated on their first screenplay, *Paul*, a science-fiction road film about two alien-obsessed, comic-book fans who encounter an extraterrestrial while touring UFO sites in the American Southwest. Pegg and Frost were asked by Steven Spielberg to play the Thompson Twins in *The Adventures of Tintin: The Secret of the Unicorn* (2011), Spielberg's 3-D adaptation of the popular Belgian comic-strip character. For *Mission: Impossible—Ghost Protocol* (2011), Pegg's character graduated from computer hacker to full-fledged agent.

Next, Pegg played Jack in the low-budget thriller *A Fantastic Fear of Everything* (2012). Pegg then rejoined the crew of the USS *Enterprise*—for *Star Trek Into Darkness* (2013); its $462 million worldwide gross made it the franchise's highest-earner internationally. He capped off 2013 with the release of *The World's End*, another collaboration with Frost and Wright; the comedy follows the reunion of five childhood friends who battle alien invaders during a hometown pub crawl.

A DIFFERENT DIRECTION

In 2014 Pegg changed gears, starring in two romantic comedies: *Hector and the Search for Happiness*, about an unfulfilled psychiatrist on a journey of self-discovery, and *Man Up*, in which he played a divorced, middle-aged man who finds love with a woman he mistakes for his blind date. The following year Pegg returned to more familiar territory, reprising his role in *Mission: Impossible Rogue Nation*. Pegg assumed the lead role in the science-fiction comedy *Absolutely Anything* (2015)—Robin Williams's final movie.

Pegg, a *Star Trek* and *Star Wars* junkie, is making his mark on both franchises. He served as Abrams' creative consultant and also has a cameo in *Star Wars: The Force Awakens*, released in mid-December 2015. He has also cowritten the script for *Star Trek Beyond*, the upcoming third installment of the *Star Trek* film series, which will be released in July 2016.

PERSONAL LIFE

Pegg lives in Hertfordshire with his wife, Maureen (McCann) and their daughter, Matilda.

SUGGESTED READING

Burr, Ty. "Star Trek." Rev. of *Star Trek*, dir. JJ Abrams. *Boston.com*. Globe Newspaper, 5 May 2009. Web. 12 Nov. 2015.

Kellogg, Carolyn. "Simon Pegg Riffs on *Dawn of the Dead*, Zombie Consumers and Popular Culture." *Los Angeles Times*. Tribune, 16 June 2011. Web. 12 Nov. 2015.

McLean, Craig. "When GQ Met Simon Pegg." *British GQ*. Condé Nast, 8 Feb. 2011. Web. 12 Nov. 2015.

Pols, Mary. "The New *Star Trek* Movie: It Will Leave Fans Beaming." Rev. of *Star Trek*, dir. JJ Abrams. *Time*. Time, 6 May 2009. Web. 12 Nov. 2015.

Trinh, Jean. "Simon Pegg on His First *Star Trek* Memories, Playing Scotty, and More." *Daily Beast*. IAC, 13 May 2013. Web. 12 Nov. 2015.

Villareal, Yvonne. "Great Scott, Simon Pegg Is Engineering a *Star Trek* Career." *Los Angeles Times*. Tribune, 28 Apr. 2009. Web. 12 Nov. 2015.

Walsh, John. "Simon Pegg Profile: Everyone's Favourite Lad." *Independent*. Independent Print, 12 July 2013. Web. 12 Nov. 2015.

SELECTED WORKS

Spaced, 1999–2001; *Shaun of the Dead*, 2004; *Mission: Impossible III*, 2006; *Hot Fuzz*, 2007; *Star Trek*, 2009; *Paul*, 2011; *Mission: Impossible—Ghost Protocol*, 2011; *Star Trek Into Darkness*, 2013; *The World's End*, 2013; *Mission: Impossible Rogue Nation*, 2015

—*Bertha Muteba*

Salvador Pérez

Born: May 10, 1990
Occupation: Baseball player

Salvador Pérez of the Kansas City Royals is regarded as one of the toughest and most durable catchers in Major League Baseball (MLB).

Arturo Pardavila III/Flickr/CC BY 2.0/Wikimedia Commons

Signed by the Royals at age sixteen in 2006, the Venezuelan-born Pérez has drawn comparisons to such catching greats as Hall of Famer Johnny Bench and perennial All-Star Sandy Alomar Jr. for his powerful arm, quick release, and large, rangy frame. Standing six feet three and weighing 240 pounds, Pérez has matched his defensive prowess behind the plate with above-average offensive numbers since making his major-league debut with the Royals during the 2011 season.

During the 2013 through 2015 seasons, Pérez caught more games and innings than any catcher in baseball and amassed more hits than any catcher in the American League (AL). He earned All-Star Game selections in each of those three seasons, as well as Rawlings Gold Glove Awards for defensive excellence. Pérez has served as a major catalyst for the Royals' resurgence as a playoff contender, helping them earn back-to-back World Series berths in 2014 and 2015. In the 2015 World Series, Pérez batted .364 to lead the Royals to their first world championship since 1985. He was unanimously named the series' most valuable player (MVP), making him just the second Venezuelan in history to receive the honor (Pablo Sandoval was the first, winning the award while with the San Francisco Giants in 2012).

EARLY LIFE

Salvador Johan Pérez was born on May 10, 1990, in Valencia, the capital of the state of Carabobo in northern Venezuela. His biological father deserted the family when Pérez was four years old, after which he was raised by his mother, Yilda Diaz. When Pérez was eight, the two moved in with Yilda's mother, Carmen de Diaz, who also helped raise him. Pérez's mother supported the family by working as a housecleaner and selling homemade Venezuelan food.

Pérez started playing baseball at the age of four when his mother, a former softball pitcher, signed him up for a baseball school in Valencia. His mother believed baseball would help him "keep busy in his spare time and stay away from bad influences," as she told Dick Kaegel for MLB.com (22 Sept. 2011). Diaz taught her son how to hit by pitching bottle caps or corn kernels to him in the family living room. Pérez would try to hit them with a broomstick, which helped him develop strong hand-eye coordination.

Pérez quickly developed a love for the sport, and by age six, he was already drawing attention for his catching, throwing, and hitting skills. He honed those skills playing pickup baseball games with his friends on Valencia's all-dirt fields. Among his friends was José Altuve, now an All-Star second baseman for the Houston Astros, who grew up in nearby Maracay, Venezuela. The two were frequent teammates on youth squads that competed in state and national tournaments.

Pérez pitched and played the infield before settling in at the catcher position. By the time Pérez reached high school, his major-league-caliber talent was evident. His mother became intimately involved in his baseball development, helping with administrative matters, assembling equipment, and attending various meetings for his youth-league teams. "My mom is my support," Pérez explained to Kaegel. "She has been with me every step of the way."

KANSAS CITY ROYALS

Pérez first started receiving attention from professional scouts when he was sixteen. By then, he had reached his full height of six feet three and "already looked like a major leaguer," as Altuve noted to Matt Snyder for CBS (Columbia Broadcasting System) Sports (14 July 2014). Among those who saw Pérez play was Orlando Estevez, the Royals' Latin America scouting coordinator. Estevez invited Pérez to a Royals' tryout camp in Venezuela and worked him out as catcher after watching him perform inauspiciously at third base. In September 2006, after being impressed by his infectious personality and his unique combination of size and skills, the Royals signed Pérez to a contract that included a $65,000 signing bonus.

When Pérez joined the Royals, the only question about him was whether he would be able to hit at the major-league level. Still, Pérez made an immediate impression. "He had the cannon-caliber arm, and he had the ballet dancer's feet, and he possessed the natural leadership skills," as Rustin Dodd noted for the Kansas City Star

(2 Nov. 2015). Not long after Pérez reported to the Royals' Rookie League team in Surprise, Arizona, in 2007, Bill Fischer, a senior adviser with the team, likened him to a Venezuelan version of Hall of Fame catcher Johnny Bench. Pérez's big frame and strong defensive skills also earned him comparisons to former MLB catcher Sandy Alomar Jr., a six-time All-Star during his career.

RISE TO THE MAJOR LEAGUES

Pérez spent parts of three seasons playing rookie-level ball, during which he filled out his frame and developed his power. He advanced to A-level ball during the second half of the 2009 season and was then promoted to the Royals' advanced-A affiliate, the Wilmington Blue Rocks of the Carolina League, for the 2010 season. Pérez put to rest any doubts about his hitting abilities that season, batting .290 with seven home runs and fifty-three runs batted in (RBIs) in ninety-nine games with the Blue Rocks. Royals left fielder Alex Gordon, who played with Pérez during a brief injury rehabilitation assignment with the Red Rocks in 2010, recalled to Tyler Kepner for the *New York Times* (21 Oct. 2014), "I kind of knew, when I was watching him, that this guy was going to be pretty special."

In the spring of 2011, Pérez attended the Royals' annual training camp as a nonroster invitee. There, he impressed Royals manager Ned Yost and other coaches with his quick release and strong throws to second base, ability to block errant pitches, and game-calling acumen. Afterward, Pérez was sent to play with the Northwest Arkansas Naturals in the AA Texas League, where he batted .283 with eight home runs and forty-three RBIs in seventy-nine games. He was then promoted to the Omaha Storm Chasers, in the AAA Pacific Coast League.

After batting .333 in twelve games with the Storm Chasers, Pérez was deemed ready for the major leagues. He was called up to the Royals on August 10, 2011, when backup catcher Brayan Peña went on paternity leave. In his major-league debut, against the Tampa Bay Rays, Pérez collected one hit in three at-bats and showcased his defensive prowess, picking off two runners and catching five pop-ups. He remained with the Royals for the rest of the 2011 season, batting .331 in thirty-nine games.

FRANCHISE CORNERSTONE

In February 2012, Pérez and the Royals agreed to terms on a five-year, $7-million contract that included a club option for three additional years. On the day the contract was announced, Yost said of Pérez, as quoted by Bob Dutton for the *Kansas City Star* (27 Feb. 2012): "He's a very rare find. . . . He's the total package. I've never seen anyone who compares to him."

With his new contract in tow, Pérez was expected to become the Royals' starting catcher during the 2012 season. Pérez's progress was slowed, however, after he tore the meniscus in his left knee during warm-ups before a spring-training game. The injury required Pérez to undergo surgery and sidelined him for the first three months of the season. As a result, Pérez appeared in just seventy-four games. Nonetheless, his .301 batting average, eighty-seven hits, and sixteen doubles were tops among AL catchers with a minimum of seventy games caught during the span after his return in late June 2012. Meanwhile, he also finished with the second fewest strikeouts (27) among MLB players with at least 250 at-bats and led the majors with five pick-offs.

During his first full season as a starter in 2013, Pérez established himself as a Royals franchise cornerstone while emerging as one of the best dual-threat catchers in the league. He caught in 137 of the 138 games in which he appeared and batted .292 with 13 home runs and 79 RBIs. He amassed 145 hits, which led all AL backstops and were the most by a catcher in Royals history. On the defensive side, Pérez threw out 35.2 percent of runners trying to steal, which was the second highest percentage among AL catchers with at least one hundred games. He earned his first career All-Star selection, becoming the first Royals catcher to receive the honor since Darrell Porter in 1980. He also won his first Gold Glove Award.

After gradually improving their win-loss record in each of the previous four seasons, the Royals became a legitimate playoff contender in 2013. Anchored by a nucleus of young talent, which in addition to Pérez, included center fielder Lorenzo Cain, first baseman Eric Hosmer, and third baseman Mike Moustakas, the Royals finished third in the AL Central Division with an 86–76 record, clinching their first winning season since 2003.

LEADING THE ROYALS' RESURGENCE

Pérez continued to play an integral role in the Royals' success in 2014. He entered that season's midpoint batting .283 with eleven home runs, eighteen doubles, and thirty-six RBIs in eighty-five games, helping him earn his second consecutive All-Star Game selection and first as a starter. The rigors of being an everyday catcher for the Royals, however, cooled his production during the second half of the season, in which he hit just .229 in sixty-five games. Pérez nonetheless led all AL catchers in hits (150) and finished the season batting .260 with seventeen home runs and seventy RBIs. He played 146 games behind the plate, which led all major-league catchers and established a Royals record. He also tied for the major-league lead with four pick-offs and his solid all-around defense landed him a second consecutive Gold Glove Award.

Pérez's durability behind the plate proved key in the Royals securing their first trip to the playoffs in twenty-nine years. After finishing second in the AL Central with an 89–73 record, the Royals faced the Oakland Athletics in a one-game AL Wild Card playoff. They defeated the Athletics, 9–8, in a dramatic back-and-forth, twelve-inning contest that was decided on a walk-off single by Pérez. The Royals carried their momentum through the next two rounds of the playoffs, sweeping both the Los Angeles Angels of Anaheim and the Baltimore Orioles, in the AL Division Series and AL Championship Series, respectively, to advance to their first World Series since 1985.

In the World Series, the Royals lost to the San Francisco Giants in seven games. In those games, Pérez hit .333 with a double, a home run, and four RBIs. He started all of the Royals' fifteen postseason games and caught every inning. His 161 games caught in 2014 were the most ever by a major-league catcher. "I love to catch every day," Pérez said during the Royals' postseason run, as quoted by a reporter for *USA Today* (28 Oct. 2014). "I know I need to rest now and again but I hate when I'm not playing."

WORLD SERIES MVP

Pérez again led the majors in games caught (139) in 2015. That season, Pérez duplicated his batting average (.260) and RBI total (70) from the previous year and hit a career-high twenty-one home runs. He led AL catchers in hits (137) and doubles (25) and ranked third among league backstops in homers and RBIs. He also led the majors with four pick-offs and threw out twenty-four would-be base stealers, which was third in the AL. He earned his third consecutive All-Star Game selection, starting at catcher for the AL squad for the second consecutive year, and received his third consecutive Gold Glove Award.

The Royals finished with an AL-best ninety-five wins en route to winning their first AL Central title and first division crown since 1985. In the playoffs, Pérez battled through various physical ailments to help the Royals advance to the World Series for the second consecutive year. They defeated the National League champion New York Mets in five games to claim the franchise's second world championship and first since 1985. Pérez was unanimously named World Series MVP after posting a .364 batting average in the series, to go along with two doubles, two RBIs, and three runs scored. He became the first catcher to win MVP honors since Pat Borders in 1992 and only the second Venezuelan-born player to receive the honor, after Pablo Sandoval in 2012.

During the 2015–16 off-season, the Royals signaled their faith in Pérez, signing him to a five-year, $52.2-million contract extension. The contract overrode the one Pérez signed in 2012, which had earned him the dubious distinction of being one of the lowest-paid catchers in the league. During the 2014 and 2015 seasons, Pérez caught 2,724 innings, which are the most innings caught over a two-year span since 1914. Royals center fielder Lorenzo Cain told David Waldstein for the *New York Times* (2 Nov. 2015), "He's a beast. . . . That guy gives everything he has. Without him, we aren't here right now."

PERSONAL LIFE

In addition to playing for the Royals, Pérez has spent some of his off-seasons playing winter ball in Venezuela. Two days before Pérez signed his new contract with the Royals, his mother was carjacked at gunpoint in Valencia. His mother was unharmed, and her vehicle was later recovered by national police. In the wake of the incident, Pérez condemned violence in Venezuela in a message posted on the social-media site Instagram. He also has a young son.

SUGGESTED READING

Dodd, Rustin. "Royals' Salvador Perez Has Made Journey from Young Catcher in Venezuela to World Series MVP." *Kansas City Star*. KansasCity.com, 2 Nov. 2015. Web. 21 Mar. 2016.

Dutton, Bob. "Royals Sign Catcher Perez to Five-Year Extension Worth $7 Million." *Kansas City Star*. KansasCity.com, 27 Feb. 2012. Web. 21 Mar. 2016.

Kaegel, Dick. "Mom's Support Has Perez on Royals' Fast Track." *MLB.com*. MLB Advanced Media, 22 Sept. 2011. Web. 21 Mar. 2016.

Kepner, Tyler. "Lights, Catcher, Action!" *New York Times*. New York Times, 21 Oct. 2014. Web. 21 Mar. 2016.

"Salvador Perez the Rock behind Royals' Pitching Staff." *USA Today*. USA Today, 28 Oct. 2014. Web. 21 Mar. 2016.

Waldstein, David. "This Time Around, Royals Catcher Salvador Perez Goes Out as the MVP." *New York Times*. New York Times, 2 Nov. 2015. Web. 21 Mar. 2016.

—*Chris Cullen*

Phil Plait

Born: September 30, 1964
Occupation: Astronomer

Phil Plait is the Bad Astronomer—not an evil or unskilled astronomer, but a gifted popular

(Wikimedia/Flickr) "Neil Armstrong-Apollo-11-spacesuit and Phil Plait" by Gazebo - Licensed under CC BY-SA 2.0 via Wikimedia Commons

science writer and blogger who under that moniker has used his experience as a research astronomer to dismantle pseudoscience and popular misconceptions about science in the wider media. In each of the thousands of pieces he has posted to his blog, *Bad Astronomy*, since he launched it in the 1990s, he has used humor, scientific facts, and his natural gifts as an educator to dispel wrong-minded popular beliefs, such as an egg being able to stand on its end only on the first day of spring or that the manned moon landings were faked. In addition to penning two popular science books, he has also appeared on numerous television documentary series to explain scientific theories and facts, as well as dispel popular inaccuracies.

Plait does this work not only because he loves astronomy but also because he recognizes its appeal to the average person. "There's something about astronomy. Of all the sciences, it seems to be the most popular. It may be the pictures. It may be the gee-whiz stuff. Astronomy touches on the kind of questions religions try to get to: Why are we here? How did we get here? Was there a beginning? Will there be an end?" Plait noted in an in-depth profile written by Jim Doyle for the *San Francisco Chronicle* (29 Mar. 2002), "Astronomy has a chance to answer these questions. We can make intelligent guesses about—maybe not why we got here, but how we got here. We know how stars formed, how our sun and planets formed. We don't know the specifics of how life started, but we know many ways life can get started and how it can evolve."

EARLY LIFE AND EDUCATION

Philip Cary Plait was born on September 30, 1964, in the Washington, DC, area. He was raised in Springfield, Virginia, by his father, who was an engineer, and his mother, who was a jeweler. He recalled his first experience with astronomy in the biography published on the *Bad Astronomy* website: "When I was maybe four or five years old, my dad brought home a cheapo department store telescope. He aimed it at Saturn that night. One look, and that was it. I was hooked."

Plait used that telescope for several years to look at the planets in our solar system and to study sunspots. At the age of thirteen, having saved enough money from his newspaper route, he purchased a better telescope, one with a ten-inch lens, which his parents allowed him to keep in the living room of their home. Before long he found himself becoming devoted to the study of astronomy and physics, so that by the time he entered the University of Michigan as a freshman, he knew he would major in astronomy and work his way toward becoming an astronomer.

Plait continued his education at the University of Virginia, where he earned his master's degree in astronomy in 1990 and his doctorate in 1994. During his time as a doctoral student he was part of a large research team that used the orbiting Hubble Space Telescope (first launched in 1990) to observe a ring of gas around Supernova 1987A. He also taught introductory astronomy courses, discovering a passion for science education. It was during his graduate studies that he first became interested in dispelling astronomy myths. His first webpage, posted in March 1993, debunked the belief that eggs will stand on end on the vernal equinox; Plait was inspired to spread the truth after watching a local news broadcast that propagated the myth.

RESEARCH AND OUTREACH

Plait's early career had two phases: the first as a research scientist; the second in educational outreach. Beginning in 1995 he worked as a private contractor at the National Aeronautics and Space Administration's (NASA) Goddard Space Flight Center in Maryland, studying faint, distant stars known as red dwarfs, which are the most common stars in our Milky Way galaxy. (Proxima Centauri, the closest star to our own sun at a distance of 4.22 light years, is a red dwarf.) He remained involved with the Hubble Space Telescope, working on its software and camera calibrations and helping to process the many images it captured. "The Hubble telescope has revolutionized the way we present astronomy to the public, which loves to see pictures of planets and stars," Plait told Doyle. "Hubble is taking incredibly high-resolution pictures."

While pursuing his research Plait also continued to update his website, adding pages explaining the truth behind topics such as what causes the seasons, why only one side of the moon is visible, and what makes the sky blue. He expanded his interest in education and outreach by speaking at schools and astronomy clubs, and soon became a frequent interviewee for local television and radio programs on astronomy content. His website steadily grew more popular and his public profile increased.

These developments led Plait to rethink his career path. "I'm just not cut out to be a research scientist," he told Doyle. "I was OK at it, but not great. But I am good at writing about this kind of stuff and talking about it." He left his work at Goddard to take up a position at Sonoma State University, where he worked in the Education and Public Outreach Group. While there he oversaw outreach programs that gave the public a better understanding of astronomical endeavors, such as the development of the Fermi Gamma-Ray Space Telescope, which was launched into orbit in 2008 and provides scientists with a better understanding of gamma radiation, dark matter, and micro black holes, among other research objectives.

BAD ASTRONOMY

In 1998 Plait's website adopted the name "Bad Astronomy," and its popularity increased along with that of the Internet itself. The site began receiving even more visitors that same year when Plait posted reviews dismantling the pseudoscience in two blockbuster movies, each about an asteroid hitting the Earth: *Deep Impact* and *Armageddon*. The former he accepted as relatively realistic; the latter he lambasted for being riddled with scientific inaccuracies. By 2001 Plait's website was receiving 4.5 million hits annually, boosted by a popular post that year in which Plait disparaged a FOX television program that suggested the moon landings were faked.

Plait's success with science education and outreach and his online popularity enabled him to try his hand as an author, continuing to debunk pseudoscience and myths while explaining scientific facts in a straightforward but humorous way. His first book, published in 2002, was named after his website, and *Bad Astronomy: Misconceptions and Misuses Revealed, from Astrology to the Moon Landing 'Hoax,'* like its namesake, helps to clear up falsehoods. Among other subjects, it accurately examines the Big Bang, meteors, and eclipses. The reviewer for *Publishers Weekly* (25 Feb. 2002) called the book a "knowledgeable, lighthearted volume," noting that "With avuncular humor, [Plait] points out the ways advertising and media reinforce bad science and pleads for more accuracy in Hollywood story lines and special effects." The book sold well and won Plait many new fans.

Plait's website eventually spawned a Bad Astronomy blog, which began in 2005 and eventually became the Bad Astronomer's main outlet. Across thousands of blog posts, Plait—with great good humor—demonstrated how astrology does not predict one's future, how there is no such thing as a face on Mars, how aliens have not visited Earth to impregnate women or mutilate livestock, and many other scientific facts. The success of his book and the ever-growing visibility of his blog led Plait to leave his position at Sonoma State University and pursue writing and other outreach projects full-time.

DEATH FROM THE SKIES! AND OTHER WORK

Plait's second book, *Death from the Skies!* (2008), uses humor to describe the ways in which life on Earth could come to an end, beginning with asteroid strikes, then continuing on to things like a hyperactive sun, supernovae, cosmic ray bursts, black holes, and invasions from aliens. Each of these potential disasters is then used to teach the reader something about science. A critic for *Kirkus Reviews* (20 Oct. 2008) called Plait's second book a "surprisingly upbeat look at all the ways the universe can destroy us. . . . Eminently readable basic science with an irresistible hook." *Death from the Skies!* was another popular success.

That same year Plait's blog came under the umbrella of *Discover* magazine's online publications. He also accepted the presidency of the James Randi Educational Foundation, a nonprofit organization founded by magician James Randi to promote scientific skepticism and debunk pseudoscientific and paranormal claims. He would hold the position until December 2009, when he stepped down in order to focus on his television projects.

In addition to blogging and writing numerous articles in scientific and general interest publications, Plait became involved in several works on television, beginning with guest appearances on various shows and a stint as a science consultant for the children's educational program *Zula Patrol* in 2007. In 2010 his three-part program *Phil Plait's Bad Universe* was released on the Discovery Channel, presenting highly relatable perspectives on topics such as asteroid strikes. He also made many appearances on the Discovery Channel's documentary series *How the Universe Works* (2010–15). During this period Plait also brought his blog—averaging 6 million annual hits—to a new audience beyond the scientific realm, moving from *Discover* to *Slate* magazine's stable of blogs in 2012. In 2015 he wrote and hosted a block of astronomy-themed episodes for the online video program *Crash Course*, developed in cooperation with PBS Digital Studios and made available free to the public on the video-hosting site YouTube.

Plait has also appeared on radio programs in his endless mission to dispel popular misconceptions. One frequent subject was the fear that life on Earth will be destroyed by an unseen gigantic meteor, such as the one that wiped out the dinosaurs, or battered by space junk. He asserted his belief that humanity has the technology and ability to prevent such disasters from happening. In a TEDx talk broadcast by Guy Raz on the "TED Radio Hour" (30 July 2014), Plait remarked: "The difference between the dinosaurs and us is that we have a space program and we can vote, and so we can change our future."

PERSONAL LIFE

Plait lives in Boulder, Colorado, with his wife, Marcella Setter, and their daughter, Zoe, who also enjoys astronomy considerably. "He's a pretty special guy," his wife told Doyle. "He's very passionate about astronomy and about putting good information out to replace the bad. He turns into a kid when he talks about astronomy. I tease him. I say, 'You're a rocket scientist, but you can't balance the checkbook.'" He has received numerous awards for his work, including a 2007 Weblog award, which named his blog the best science blog of the year, and the 2013 National Capital Area Skeptics Philip J. Klass Award. In 2008 the astronomer Jeff Medkeff named an asteroid after Plait. In 2009 the editors of *Time* named his blog one of the top twenty-five blogs on the Web.

SUGGESTED READING

Rev. of *Bad Astronomy: Misconceptions and Misuses Revealed, from Astrology to the Moon Landing 'Hoax,'* by Philip Plait. *Publishers Weekly.* 25 Feb. 2002: 52. Print.

Rev. of *Death from the Skies!*, by Philip Plait. *Kirkus Reviews.* Kirkus Media, 20 May 2010. Web. 10 Dec. 2015.

Doyle, Jim. "Profile/Phil Plait/Astronomer Works for Heavens' Sake/Rohnert Park Man Corrects Misconceptions." *SFGate.* Hearst Communications, 29 Mar. 2002. Web. 10 Dec. 2015.

"Dr. Phil Plait, AKA 'The Bad Astronomer' PR Kit: Biography." *Badastronomy.com.* Bad Astronomy, n.d. Web. 10 Dec. 2015.

Flatow, Ira. "Predicting When Space Junk Will Come Home to Earth." *NPR.* NPR, 21 Oct. 2011. Web. 1 Dec. 2015.

Raz, Guy. "How Can We Defend Earth from Asteroids?" *TED Radio Hour.* NPR, 30 July 2014. Web. 10 Dec. 2015.

—*Christopher Mari*

Rachel Platten

Born: May 20, 1981
Occupation: Singer-songwriter

Rachel Platten's hit tune "Fight Song" climbed the charts in 2015, and became one of the breakout pop hits of the year. For listeners, the song—"This is my fight song / Take back my life song"—seemed to become ubiquitous overnight, but for Platten, it was over twelve years in the making. "I grinded and worked so hard for so long and . . . I didn't think it was going to happen," Platten told Mike Wass for *Idolator* (20 Apr. 2015). "I thought I might need to figure something else out. That moment bred 'Fight Song.'" Platten, who studied international relations in college, had an epiphany that she should devote herself to music while interning in Trinidad during her senior year. Hundreds of original songs and countless late-night sets in small clubs later, Platten's big break came when "Fight Song" was played on an episode of *Pretty Little Liars* in late 2014. Today, Platten's gigs look a little different than they did ten years ago. She has performed at the Macy's Thanksgiving Day Parade, the MTV Video Music Awards, *Dick Clark's New Year's Rockin' Eve*, and the NFL (National Football League) Pro Bowl. In June 2015, she was a surprise guest on Taylor Swift's *1989* tour. (Swift was even spotted wearing a t-shirt that said, "This Is My Fight Song," which Platten had given her.) Her first studio album, *Wildfire*, was released through Columbia Records in January 2016, and that spring, Democratic presidential

DoD News Features (160512-D-dB155-010)/Wikimedia Commons

nominee Hillary Clinton used "Fight Song" as her unofficial anthem. In July, Elizabeth Banks directed a host of stars—including Platten, of course—in an a cappella version of "Fight Song" for a video at the Democratic National Convention in Philadelphia. "In a business that constantly trumpets overnight success," Kevin Alexander, Platten's college friend, wrote for *Elle* (11 Apr. 2016), "Rachel is proof that hard work isn't out of style, that grinding it out can still pay off."

EARLY LIFE AND EDUCATION

Platten was born in 1981 in New York City, and grew up in Newton Centre, Massachusetts. Her mother is a therapist. Her father has a doctorate in psychology, but works as a senior manager at a global consulting firm. She has a younger sister named Melanie. Platten was a musical child, always fiddling with the piano and singing Madonna songs. She attended Buckingham Browne and Nichols, a private school in Cambridge where she participated in musical theater, but did not make the cut to join the school's choir. "I was crushed," she recalled to Alexander. "Here was this thing I thought I was good at, and I can't even make the group." That letdown, Platten recalled, was a signal to her to pursue other goals. Her mother played the piano, but there was "no musical role model" in her life, she told Alexander. So she did what her friends were doing, and applied to a small liberal arts college after graduation. She ended up at Trinity College in Hartford, Connecticut, where she joined the school's a cappella group, the Trinitones. For Platten, as Alexander recalled, music appeared to be a hobby. Her senior year, she started a band with her political science professor's son.

Platten recalls feeling resigned to the fact that she would not be a professional singer or musician at that point. She was genuinely excited about pursuing a career in international relations, and dreamed of becoming a diplomat. As a college senior, she spent seven or eight months studying in Trinidad and Tobago, where she interned at a diplomat's office. She also snared an internship with a record label. During Carnival, a friend's band was playing in the International Soca Monarch contest. (Soca music is a style of Caribbean music specific to Trinidad and Tobago; it has been described as a mixture of calypso and soul.) The friend needed a keyboard player and back-up singer to perform. Platten volunteered, and because they did not have anyone else, she joked to Wass, they let her. Thus, at her first official gig, she performed for 80,000 people. Platten found the experience exhilarating. "It just felt like, 'Oh, this is what I'm supposed to do with my life,'" she told Wass. "This huge moment of clarity, so that was when I decided to switch."

EARLY CAREER

Upon her return to the United States, Platten recorded and self-released an album of songs she had written called *Trust in Me* with some friends. The learning curve was steep, she recalled to Alexander. "My first attempts at songwriting were overemotional and superwordy," she said. "Basically, English essays put to music. No concepts, just a lot of really bad metaphors." Platten graduated in 2003 and subsequently moved to Greenwich Village in New York City. She worked a slew of odd jobs to support herself while making the rounds at clubs on Bleecker Street. She worked as a temp followed by a brief stint as a waitress at a fondue restaurant called Dip. (She was fired after six weeks.) Later, she was an Estée Lauder salesperson, and wrote jingles. She began playing with a Prince and Sly and the Family Stone cover band called Dayz of Wild, though their repertoire was loose. Platten rapped and beatboxed on stage, admitting that she did not know all of the words to the songs. Still, she recalled to Alexander, the experience taught her a lot about music. One of the band members offered her piano and songwriting lessons in exchange for paying his phone bill. "I realized that if I was really going to take this seriously, I needed to put in the work," she told Alexander. For the next five years, she practiced six or seven hours a day.

Meanwhile, Platten continued to play gigs when she could. She even created a fake e-mail address to pretend to be her own agent. That masquerade helped her book her first national tour. In 2009 she signed a contract with a music management company called The Brain Music, run by a twenty-three-year-old songwriter named Freddie Wexler. Wexler was critical of Platten—he told her that her songs, Alexander wrote, "sounded like Regina Spektor rip-offs," referring to the Russian singer-songwriter. Still, he sent her to Stockholm to write with three Swedish producers who had worked with the boy band *NSYNC and 1980s pop superstar Cyndi Lauper. Platten and the producers wrote a piano-driven pop song called "1,000 Ships" in 2011. It peaked at number 23 on the Billboard adult pop songs chart in January 2012.

BIG BREAK

Her second album, *Be Here*, was released through the indie label Rock Ridge in the spring of 2011. The album included collaborations with *NSYNC's Fredrik Thomander and other artists. She soon landed a gig opening for singer-songwriter Andy Grammer on his first tour in 2012. Grammer's manager, Ben Singer, offered to represent her on the condition that she continue to write and improve her songs. She told Alexander that, under that directive, she wrote about 150 songs. One of them was an early version of "Fight Song;" it got Singer's attention, but he continued to urge her to fine-tune it. About a year later, during the summer 2013, she felt the song was finished. Platten was certain that "Fight Song" was something special. She put it on YouTube, and though it did not find any industry support through that medium, it garnered her a number of serious fans. One woman who heard it, Christine Luckenbaugh, had been in remission for fifteen years, but recently discovered that her cancer had returned. She made "Fight Song" her personal anthem. Luckenbaugh's friends reached out to Platten, and Platten surprised Luckenbaugh with a live performance—aided in vocals by Luckenbaugh's family and friends—before she passed away in 2014. Online, Platten curates a hashtag called #MyFightSong where fans with life-threatening illnesses share their stories as the song plays.

For Platten, the song was personally significant for a different reason. She had been working for over a decade, but even with her modest success, it appeared that true fame had eluded her. "Fight Song," she has said, "was her promise to herself that she would not give up on her dream." The song was picking up steam on the Internet, but it was not until it played on an episode of the teen drama *Pretty Little Liars* that it really caught on. Even then, Platten insists, its success seemed to happen in slow motion. The day after the show aired, Platten called her friend distraught. "Fight Song" appeared to sell a few more copies, but it did not catch on in the big way Platten had hoped. She decided to pick herself up—she sheepishly admitted to Wass that she had "collapsed" on the floor in anguish and disappointment—and move on. But then, as if by magic, the reaction Platten was looking for became manifest. Baltimore's Mix 106.5 radio station played it after one of Platten's friends played it for the station's program director. "Fight Song" moved into the top 100 songs on iTunes. As of July 2016, it had millions of downloads on iTunes, almost 200 million views on YouTube, and had topped both the US and UK Billboard charts.

WILDFIRE (2016)

A month after the *Pretty Little Liars* episode, Platten signed a deal with Columbia Records. It was a huge coup for the singer. Platten released her second single, "Stand by You," another anthem of empowerment, in fall 2015. The song was nearly as popular as her first, eventually hitting number 1 on Billboard's adult pop song charts in February 2016. Platten released her major label debut, *Wildfire*, in January 2016; the album reached number 4 on the Billboard top album sales chart. The album includes "Fight Song," "Stand by You," and "Hey Hallelujah," a

collaboration with her old tour-mate Grammer and other artists.

Wildfire received lukewarm reviews from both the *New York Times* and the *Boston Globe*, however. Many of Platten's critics find her earnest lyrics grating, and occasionally, a touch too cute. For another single from *Wildfire*, "Better Place," Platten asked couples and families to sit and look at each other while listening to her song, with the chorus, "It's a better place since you came along." But Platten, a self-help devotee, appears to be entirely sincere in her desire to inspire others. When Wass suggested that her music career was a stark departure from her early ambition to become a diplomat, Platten disagreed. "I thought about it and I was like, 'Are these so wildly different?'" she said. "But they're not because really what I want to do with music is bring people together. I want to travel the world, and I want to unite people, that was what I wanted to do in college too, in a different way."

PERSONAL LIFE

Platten met Kevin Lazan, a management consultant and entrepreneur, in 2006. They were married in 2012, and live in Santa Monica, CA.

SUGGESTED READING

Alexander, Kevin. "The Not-So-Overnight Success of Rachel Platten's 'Fight Song.'" *Elle*. Hearst Communications, 11 Apr. 2016. Web. 13 Sept. 2016.

Caramanica, Jon. "Review: Rachel Platten Experiments with 'Wildfire.'" Rev. of *Wildfire*, by Rachel Platten. *New York Times*. New York Times, 6 Jan. 2016. Web. 13 Sept. 2016.

Case, Wesley. "Rachel Platten Talks 'Fight Song' and Why She Owes Her Career to Baltimore." *Baltimore Sun*. Baltimore Sun, 9 Dec. 2015. Web. 13 Sept. 2016.

Donelson, Marcy. "Rachel Platten." *AllMusic*. AllMusic, 2016. Web. 13 Sept. 2016.

Johnston, Maura. "Album Review: Rachel Platten, 'Wildfire.'" Rev. of *Wildfire*, by Rachel Platten. *Boston Globe*. Boston Globe Media Partners, 7 Jan. 2016. Web. 13 Sept. 2016.

Wass, Mike. "Rachel Platten Talks 'Fight Song,' Making a Difference and Her Long Road to the Top: Idolator Interview." *Idolator*. SpinMedia, 20 Apr. 2015. Web. 13 Sept. 2016.

SELECTED WORKS

Trust in Me, 2003; *Fight Song*, 2014; *Stand By You*, 2015; *Be Here*, 2011; *Wildfire*, 2016

—Molly Hagan

Kristaps Porziņģis

Born: August 2, 1995
Occupation: Basketball player

Upon being selected by the New York Knicks in the first round of the 2015 National Basketball Association (NBA) Draft, Kristaps Porziņģis became only the third Latvian to be drafted into the NBA. One of the most-hyped international players to enter the league, Porziņģis, a seven-foot-three, 240-pound power forward, drew comparisons to superstars Dirk Nowitzki and Pau Gasol for his European background, exceptionally tall and slender frame, offensive versatility, mid- and long-range shooting ability, and superb passing skills. In an article for *The Cauldron* (18 June 2015), a blog run by *Sports Illustrated*, Yaron Weitzman wrote that "if God were to manufacture a big man tailor-made for today's pace-and-space NBA, Kristaps Porziņģis would be a pretty good factory model."

Like Nowitzki and Gasol, Porziņģis entered the NBA as an unknown entity after spending his first three professional seasons with Club Deportivo Baloncesto Sevilla, in Spain's Liga Asociación de Clubs de Baloncesto (ACB League), from 2012 to 2015. He was initially criticized for being "soft" due to his perceived lack of strength and lanky frame. Those criticisms notwithstanding, in his maiden NBA season Porziņģis made an immediate positive impact on a Knicks team that had finished with a franchise-worst 17–65 record during the 2014–15 season.

EARLY LIFE

The youngest of three brothers, Kristaps Porziņģis was born on August 2, 1995, in Liepaja, the third-largest city in Latvia. Porziņģis inherited his height and talent for basketball from his parents, Talis and Ingrida, who both stand over six feet tall. His father played semiprofessional basketball before becoming a bus driver; his mother played on Latvian national youth teams and later became a basketball coach. Porziņģis's older brothers, Janis and Martins, were also accomplished basketball players, with Janis playing professionally in Europe.

From the time Porziņģis was born, basketball formed the fabric of his existence. According to his mother, his first word was "ball." When Porziņģis was a toddler, he was already dunking balls on a miniature basketball hoop mounted to his bedroom door. He started playing organized basketball at the age of six, when his mother signed him up for a local youth team. During his first practice at Liepaja State Gymnasium, Porziņģis was admittedly reduced to tears after being given instructions by his demanding coach. Nonetheless, he quickly got a handle on

Ed/AIMG_1464/CC BY-SA 2.0/Wikimedia

basic basketball rules and became dedicated to the sport.

Porziņģis's shooting ability was apparent early on, but it was his height that made playing professional basketball a realistic endeavor. At age ten, he was the tallest player on his youth team. Despite his towering height, Porziņģis initially played point guard because of his unusual quickness, body control, coordination, and ball-handling skills. One of his biggest basketball influences was his father, who taught him toughness and strategy. "My dad was my first coach and still is my coach," Porziņģis told Weitzman. "Even now when I come back from games he'll start breaking down for me what I did right and what I did wrong."

Porziņģis's basketball development was hastened, in part, by a wooden basketball court his father built in the family's backyard. Each day after school, Porziņģis spent hours on the court with his father and brothers. "He was always sharp, even as a kid," his brother Janis recalled to Mike Gavin for *Newsday* (27 June 2015).

NBA DREAMS

Like many young basketball players, Porziņģis dreamed of playing in the NBA. However, as a boy growing up in Latvia, a former Soviet republic more known for producing hockey talent, those dreams remained elusive. For Porziņģis, the only homegrown NBA examples he had to follow were Gundars Vetra, a small forward who played just thirteen games for the Minnesota Timberwolves during the 1992–93 season, and Andris Biedrins, a seven-foot center who spent ten seasons in the league, from 2004 to 2014. As a result, Porziņģis turned his attention to American NBA stars, and throughout his childhood and adolescence, he routinely stayed up until the early hours of the morning to watch NBA broadcasts on television.

Porziņģis, who became a devoted fan of the Los Angeles Lakers and their superstar guard Kobe Bryant, familiarized himself with American culture by watching movies and cartoons in English. He excelled in English in school and further improved his grasp of the language through the help of a tutor his parents hired for him when he was ten. By age thirteen, he was nearly fluent in the language.

Porziņģis played for Liepajas Lauvas, his hometown's best-known team, until he was fifteen. By that time, he stood six feet eight inches tall but weighed barely 160 pounds. Despite his thin frame, Porziņģis was good enough skill-wise to catch the attention of a Latvian scout, who sent video of his games to several teams in Italy and Spain. He subsequently received a tryout with Baloncesto Sevilla (then known as Cajasol), which competes in Spain's ACB League, "widely regarded as the second-best professional basketball league in the world," as Josh Robbins noted for the *Orlando Sentinel* (20 June 2015). The team signed him to a long-term contract in late summer 2010.

BALONCESTO SEVILLA

Upon moving to Seville, Spain's fourth-largest city, Porziņģis experienced immediate culture shock. Despite being near-fluent in English, he spoke hardly any Spanish, making it difficult to communicate with teammates on Baloncesto Sevilla's junior squad. Consequently, Porziņģis considered returning home midway through his first season due to the language barrier and his homesickness. However, he ultimately decided to remain in Spain.

As Porziņģis immersed himself in basketball and the language and culture of Spain, he experienced an unexpected roadblock to his career: being diagnosed with anemia. The condition, which occurs when the body does not produce enough red blood cells, caused Porziņģis to suffer premature fatigue in practices and games. "I'd be on the court for one minute, then get tired," he recalled to Weitzman. "I was just feeling weak all the time." Through the help of a nutritionist, Porziņģis received proper treatment for his anemia and he quickly overcame the condition.

Porziņģis spent two seasons in Baloncesto Sevilla's junior ranks before rising to the club's senior team. He made his junior-squad debut at the 2011–12 Ciutat De L'Hospitalet, a prestigious regional qualifying tournament for the Nike International Junior Tournament. He then made his first appearances with Sevilla's senior team during the 2012–13 season, which saw him make his Eurocup debut. That season Porziņģis

also represented the junior team again at the L'Hospitalet tournament, averaging 16.6 points, 8.4 rebounds, and 2.6 blocks in five games.

Porziņģis first appeared on the radar of NBA scouts and general managers during the 2013 International Basketball Federation (FIBA) Europe Under-18 Championship. There, he led Latvia to a fourth-place finish after averaging 11.6 points and ten rebounds in nine games. For his performance, he was selected to the championship's All-Tournament Team.

THE NBA DRAFT

In his first full season with Sevilla's senior team in 2013–14, Porziņģis continued to show flashes of his potential, averaging nearly seven points and three rebounds in fifteen minutes per game. At the conclusion of that season, he declared himself eligible for the 2014 NBA Draft. Porziņģis drew interest from a number of NBA teams and was projected to be a top-fifteen pick. Less than two weeks before the draft, however, he decided to withdraw his name, instead opting to spend another season developing his game in the ACB League.

Porziņģis's decision to remain with Baloncesto Sevilla proved to be the right one. After spending his first two professional seasons playing under legendary coach Aíto García Reneses, he enjoyed a breakout year under his replacement, Scott Roth, a former NBA player and veteran assistant coach who helped teach him some of the finer points of the game, such as how to use screens and shoot on the run. Porziņģis also improved his post-up game and ball-handling under Sevilla assistant Audie Norris, who replaced Roth as manager midway through the 2014–15 season. He finished that season averaging eleven points, five rebounds, and one block in twenty-two minutes per game and earned the Eurocup Rising Star Award.

Porziņģis's breakout performance helped increase his draft stock. Many analysts expected him to be a top-five pick in the 2015 NBA Draft, as NBA scouts and executives regarded him as one of the most talented international players to come along in years with his rare combination of size and athleticism. In the run-up to the draft, ESPN basketball analyst and international draft expert Fran Fraschilla called Porziņģis "a potential mix of Dirk [Nowitzki], Pau Gasol from a body standpoint, and [Andrei] Kirilenko from an athletic standpoint in their primes," as quoted Robbins.

Despite Porziņģis's tremendous potential, Fraschilla and many other analysts, as well as NBA scouts and executives, expressed concerns about his lack of strength, his perceived aversion to a more physical style of play, and his ability to defend at the NBA level. Adding to that was the legacy of other European big men who failed to live up to their draft positions. As a result,

Porziņģis was labeled as "soft" entering the draft and seen as a considerable risk. That label notwithstanding, he was selected by the New York Knicks with the fourth overall pick in the first round, making him the highest drafted Latvian in NBA history.

THE NEW YORK KNICKS

Porziņģis arrived in New York as a mystery to Knicks fans, who greeted his selection with a resounding chorus of boos on draft day. Despite being one of the most storied franchises in basketball history, the Knicks had finished the previous season with a dismal 17–65 record, the second-worst mark in the NBA and the worst in franchise history. Since adding superstar forward Carmelo Anthony in 2011, the Knicks had failed to find a player to complement him. As a result, fans had hoped the team would go with a big-name pick out of a Division I college program rather than a mostly unknown prospect from Europe. Still, on the night of Porziņģis's drafting, Knicks president Phil Jackson, an eleven-time NBA championship–winning coach, predicted, as quoted by Marc Berman for the *New York Post* (25 June 2015): "I think our fans are going to like him. . . . This young man is an eye-opening athlete and a player."

Jackson's prediction proved true as Porziņģis emerged as a sensation for the Knicks during his rookie NBA season. Proving his detractors wrong, he made an immediate impact as the Knicks' starting power forward and became an instant fan favorite. In just his fourth NBA game, on November 2, 2015, he achieved his first career double-double after recording thirteen points and fourteen rebounds in a loss to the San Antonio Spurs.

Porziņģis officially marked his arrival to the league, however, on November 21, 2015, when he posted twenty-four points, fourteen rebounds, and seven blocks in a 107–102 Knicks win over the Houston Rockets. At 20 years and 111 days old, he became the youngest player in history to record single-game numbers that high in all three categories. Porziņģis's seven blocks also tied a franchise rookie record. "I think anytime he's on the floor, really good things can happen," Knicks' coach Derek Fisher said to Michael Lee for *Yahoo! Sports* (17 Nov. 2015). "He's really versatile on both ends, changing shots defensively, rebounding the ball well when he's around the paint. Offensively, he can do a lot of things."

Unfazed by the pressure of playing in New York, Porziņģis expressed hopes of leading the Knicks to their first NBA championship since 1973. "Right now, I want to be the best player I can be," he explained to Lee. "And obviously, as a team, we want to bring a championship here, and as I get better as a player and we get better as a team, there will be big things coming for us, for sure."

PERSONAL LIFE

Officially listed at seven feet three inches, Porziņģis is among the tallest players in the NBA. He has drawn comparisons to Dolph Lundgren's Ivan Drago character from the 1985 film *Rocky IV* for his height and spiky blond hairstyle. Physiognomic characteristics notwithstanding, Porziņģis has distinguished himself from other international players by his understanding and command of the English language and knowledge of American culture. These qualities have helped make him a burgeoning international star.

Porziņģis, who in July 2015 signed a four-year contract with the Knicks worth approximately $18.4 million, lives with his two brothers in an apartment in New York. He used part of his rookie contract to buy his parents a house in White Plains, New York, which is located ten minutes from the Knicks' training facility.

SUGGESTED READING

Armstrong, Kevin. "Knicks' Kristaps Porzingis' Many Gifts Take Him All the Way from Latvia to NBA's Brightest Stage." *Daily News*. NYDailyNews.com, 27 June 2015. Web. 8 Dec. 2015.

Berman, Marc. "Knicks Take Euro Stud, Who Gets Pau Gasol Comparison." *New York Post*. NYP Holdings, 25 June 2015. Web. 8 Dec. 2015.

Gavin, Mike. "Kristaps Porzingis Comes from a Basketball-Playing Family." *Newsday*. Newsday, 27 June 2015. Web. 8 Dec. 2015.

Lee, Michael. "Knicks Rookie Kristaps Porzingis Not Fazed by Big Apple Expectations: 'I Love Pressure.'" *Yahoo! Sports*. Yahoo Sports, 17 Nov. 2015. Web. 8 Dec. 2015.

Robbins, Josh. "Latvian Prospect Kristaps Porzingis Will Tempt the Magic in the NBA Draft." *Orlando Sentinel*. Tribune, 20 June 2015. Web. 8 Dec. 2015.

Weitzman, Yaron. "NBA Draft Watch: The Kristaps Porzingis Experience." *The Cauldron*. Sports Illustrated, 18 June 2015. Web. 8 Dec. 2015.

—*Chris Cullen*

Bel Powley

Born: March 7, 1992
Occupation: Actor

Bel Powley has quickly made a name for herself as a young actor to watch following her portrayal of Minnie, the lead character in the 2015 independent film *The Diary of a Teenage Girl*, which depicts the sexual awakening of a fifteen-year-old girl living in the bohemian San Francisco of the 1970s. The film, directed by Marielle Heller and based on a book by Phoebe Gloeckner, takes an honest and intimate look at Minnie's maturation following the loss of her virginity to her mother's boyfriend.

Powley, who has been acting on stage and screen in her native England since the age of twelve, now finds herself filming a slate of movies in Hollywood. "It's very surreal, and obviously really exciting," Powley said of her recent career boost in an interview with Sheryl Garratt for the *Telegraph* (24 July 2015). "That's what you want in any career: to move up to the next rung on the ladder. But also I feel it couldn't have happened to a better film. I'm not bigging myself up, but I feel so proud of it and what it's doing for young women. I want loads of girls my age to go and see it and share my experience."

EARLY LIFE AND CAREER

Bel Powley was born on March 7, 1992, in London, England. Her father, Mark Powley, is a British actor known for roles on British television dramas, and her mother, Janis Jaffa, is a casting director. Unlike many actors with parents who have jobs in the film industry, Powley grew up having little interest in acting. That began to change when Powley was around the age of twelve, when she and her friends began attending a drama group, the Young Blood Theatre Company, which met on Saturdays. There, she was discovered by a casting director, who wanted her and some of her friends to audition for a children's television show called *M. I. High*. Powley nailed her first professional audition and went on to work on the show for about two years, playing a spy named Daisy Millar.

Her parents, though initially appalled by the idea that their daughter would be following them into show business, ultimately allowed her to do the series, though still hoping she would attend college and have a more stable career. In a conversation with Emma Brown for *Interview* (22 Jan. 2015), Powley recalled, "I don't think I really had any idea what was going on. I think it's different when you start when you're young and you're still at school—there's not the pressure on you. It didn't feel like a job because I wasn't paying rent or supporting a family. It just felt like fun. I probably would have done it all for free."

Jamie McCarthy/Getty Images

After ending her run on that series, Powley continued to do television work, appearing in *The Bill* (2008), *Little Dorrit* (2008), *Murderland* (2009), and *The Cabin* (2011), while initially harboring plans to take a more traditional path and attend the University of Manchester. However, she explained to Brown why she never ended up making it to college: "I had a place to go to university; I was going to study history. I was in New York doing *Arcadia* and I suddenly thought, 'It feels a bit weird to go from a New York stage to Manchester University.' It didn't quite feel right. So I deferred it for a couple of years and kind of toyed with the idea of going and then I just ended up never going."

THE DIARY OF A TEENAGE GIRL

Following appearances on the British television series *Benidorm* in 2014, Powley received a significant career boost when she obtained a copy of the script for *The Diary of a Teenage Girl*, a screenplay written by Heller that is based on a 2002 autobiographical novel written and illustrated by Gloeckner. The novel focuses on a teenager growing up in the hedonistic, morally ambiguous San Francisco of the 1970s. Heller had first encountered Gloeckner's book as a Christmas present from her sister, becoming impressed by the raw honesty of the teenage main character, Minnie, whose diary Gloeckner based heavily on the sexual experiences she reported in her own teenage diaries. Unlike many depictions of teenage sexuality, which usually describe teenage boys' sexual urges, Gloeckner's book instead looks at a teenage girl's sexual desires in a straightforward and honest way.

After securing the rights to the story from its author, Heller, a stage actor, went about turning it into a stage play, which ended its run in New York in 2010. Although the play had been successful, Heller, believing it could reach a wider audience, decided to turn Minnie's story into a screenplay. She ultimately secured a spot in the Sundance Institute's screenwriting and directing lab programs, which support indie filmmakers.

The film, written and directed by Heller, opens on the day Minnie, played by Powley, loses her virginity to her mother's boyfriend, Monroe, who is played by Alexander Skarsgård. Minnie's mother, Charlotte (Kristen Wiig), inadvertently initiates the relationship when she suggests Monroe take her daughter out one night. During that evening, Minnie suggests to Monroe that she wants to sleep with him, and they soon begin meeting at his apartment to conduct their affair. Throughout the film, Minnie is portrayed as an eager participant in her sexual encounters with Monroe, as well as with teenage boys she becomes involved with. When asked by an audience member in a forum after a showing of the film if her intention had been to either condemn or glorify pedophilia, Heller answered, as quoted by Cara Buckley in the *New York Times* (29 July 2015), "Neither. I had one intention, which was to tell an honest story about a teenage girl and what it feels like to be a teenage girl."

LANDING HER BREAKOUT ROLE

Although Wiig and Skarsgård were easily cast, Heller looked at hundreds of young actors before finding Powley, whom she felt perfectly captured Minnie's sexual curiosity, innocence, earnestness, and humor in equal measure. To get the director's attention, Powell had submitted a passionate audition tape and, after conversing with Heller via Skype, had promised to work on a believable Californian accent. Their efforts soon paid off, as critics were particularly impressed with Heller's film debut and the choice to cast Powley in the lead role of Minnie.

In a review for the *New York Times* (6 Aug. 2015), Manohla Dargis observed, "The terrific actress Bel Powley was in her early twenties when 'Diary' was shot, but looks more like a teenager than most of the generically buffed and prettified adolescents who populate American screens. She has the wide-open look children have before life gets in the way." For her part, Powley was only too happy to take on a role that would finally provide her with the opportunity to portray a character she felt was always missing in the films that she had watched growing up. "When I was young," she explained to John Powers for *Vogue* (4 Aug. 2015), "there weren't any teenage girls I could relate to in film. They were

all put in boxes: the virginal good girl, the really sarcastic asexual one. I wanted to do something that represented how I felt then."

After premiering at the Sundance Film Festival to positive audience reviews, the film was picked up by Sony Pictures Classic. Overall, critics responded well upon its limited release in theaters, including praise for Powley's performance. Reviewing the film for the *Washington Post* (13 Aug. 2015), Ann Hornaday wrote, "With her Bettie Page bangs and watchful stare, Powley makes a transfixing Minnie, who ricochets from moon-faced naiveté to wry knowingness at the blink of a sea-green eye."

NEW AND UPCOMING PROJECTS

Since her star-making turn as Minnie, Powley has found herself as something of an in-demand actor in Hollywood, with multiple films debuting in 2015 and 2016. Her follow-up to *The Diary of a Teenage Girl* was *A Royal Night Out* (2015), a film imagining what happened on the night of V-E Day, when future British monarch Queen Elizabeth II (Sarah Gadon) and her sister Margaret (Powley) were allowed to roam the streets of London and mingle with ordinary Britons as they celebrated the Allied victory over Germany in World War II. In his review of the film for the New York *Observer* (4 Dec. 2015), Rex Reed declared, "*A Royal Night Out* is a film of enormous charm, texture, and good will. . . . Canadian actress Sarah Gadon makes a kind, wise, and dignified Princess Elizabeth, revealing some of the qualities her character would later become famous for as England's next monarch, and as the giddy, flighty Princess Margaret, Bel Powley lives up to her praise in *The Diary of a Teenage Girl*."

Her other recent and upcoming films include *Equals* (2015), *Carrie Pilby* (2016), *A Storm in the Stars* (2016), *Ashes in the Snow* (2016), *Wildling* (2016), and *Detour* (2016). In her interview with Garratt, she described *Equals* as a film by indie director Drake Doremus set in a future in which human emotions have been erased; *Detour* as a thriller in which she plays a pole dancer; and *A Storm in the Stars* as a story of the relationship between authors Percy Bysshe Shelley and Mary Wollstonecraft, which culminated in her writing *Frankenstein* (1818). In terms of future film roles, she has expressed a continued devotion to seeking out authentic, fully dimensional female characters. "I want to keep playing strong female roles. I don't mean superheroes, but women who are really alive," she said to Powers.

Despite her growing profile on both sides of the Atlantic, Powley also admits that as much as she enjoys making films, she longs to return to the theater. She told Garratt, "It grounds me; it brings me back to really concentrating on character development. It doesn't have to be the

West End or Broadway. I would happily do it in a studio theatre. I just want to do a play soon."

SUGGESTED READING

Dargis, Manohla. "A Hormone Bomb Waiting to Explode." Rev. of *The Diary of a Teenage Girl*, dir. Marielle Heller. *New York Times*. New York Times, 6 Aug. 2015. Web. 10 Mar. 2016.

Garratt, Sheryl. "Bel Powley Interview: 'I Want Loads of Girls to See *The Diary of a Teenage Girl* and Share My Experience.'" *Telegraph*. Telegraph Media Group, 24 July 2015. Web. 10 Mar. 2016.

Hornaday, Ann. "*Diary of a Teenage Girl* Is Funny, Forthright and Daringly Frank." Rev. of *The Diary of a Teenage Girl*, dir. Marielle Heller. *Washington Post*. Washington Post, 13 Aug. 2015. Web. 10 Mar. 2016.

Powers, John. "Nobody Puts Bel Powley in a Corner: The Diary of a Teenage Girl Star on Her Breakout Role." *Vogue*. Condé Nast, 4 Aug. 2015. Web. 10 Mar. 2016.

Powley, Bel. "Discovery: Bel Powley." Interview by Emma Brown. *Interview*. Interview, 22 Jan. 2015. Web. 10 Mar. 2016.

Reed, Rex. "Beyond Buckingham: Two Princesses Are on the Prowl in *A Royal Night Out*." *Observer*. Observer, 4 Dec. 2015. Web. 10 Mar. 2016.

SELECTED WORKS

M. I. High, 2007–8; *Little Dorrit*, 2008; *The Diary of a Teenage Girl*, 2015; *A Royal Night Out*, 2015; *Equals*, 2015; *A Storm in the Stars*, 2016

—*Christopher Mari*

Penny Pritzker

Born: May 2, 1959
Occupation: US Secretary of Commerce

For some, Penny Pritzker's appointment to the position of secretary of commerce may have seemed an unlikely one. Primarily an entrepreneur and philanthropist, Pritzker had never before held a government position, having previously been involved in politics primarily through her involvement with President Barack Obama's 2008 campaign as well as philanthropic efforts in her home city of Chicago. Indeed, upon taking charge of the Department of Commerce, she quickly had to become deeply familiar with the department's diverse responsibilities and the complex issues involved. As she explained to Melissa Harris for the *Chicago Tribune* (11 Nov. 2013), "It's this running start. . . . You're minding your business, and then all of a sudden you have

Department of Commerce/Wikimedia Commons

to be an expert on something, and you have to do it in four days."

It was a daunting challenge but one befitting both Pritzker's own career trajectory and the legacy of the Pritzker family. A successful entrepreneur who founded the Classic Residence by Hyatt brand of senior-living facilities (renamed Vi in 2010), Pritzker is a member of the prominent Pritzker family, one of the wealthiest and most successful business families in the United States since the mid-twentieth century. Inspired by her family's history of innovation in business, Pritzker has always sought out new challenges. "There is this voice and internal need to live up to the [family] expectations," she told Nina Easton for *Fortune* (2 June 2014). "And there are very big shoes involved."

EARLY LIFE AND EDUCATION

Penny Sue Pritzker was born in Chicago, Illinois, in 1959, the first child and only daughter of Don and Sue (Sandel) Pritzker. Her father's family was a prominent one in both the city of Chicago and the American business world, in large part due to the work of Pritzker's grandfather, father, and uncles. Her great-grandfather Nicholas Pritzker emigrated from what is now Ukraine to the United States in the late nineteenth century, settling in Chicago and eventually founding a successful law firm. His son Abram Nicholas "A. N." Pritzker became successful in real estate, and his sons in turn made profitable inroads into the hotel business, developing the Hyatt hotel chain into an international success. Pritzker's father played a crucial role in that family business, buying existing hotels and motels to expand the growing chain. To pursue further opportunities, he moved the family to Palo Alto, California, when Pritzker was a child. Pritzker's father died in 1972 when she was thirteen, and her mother struggled with depression, making Pritzker the de facto head of household. Her mother died a decade later in a car accident.

As a child, Pritzker was greatly influenced by her family's business endeavors. "I grew up in a household that revered building businesses," she recalled to Adam Bryant for the *New York Times* (21 Dec. 2013). "It wasn't thinking about leadership; it was more about building something. To build something, you ultimately have to lead." The family business had a more concrete influence on her as well, as she often accompanied her father to work and observed the day-to-day operations of the Pritzker-owned hotels. "I would play on the adding machine, and then we would walk across the street from the office to our motels," she told Bryant. "He'd send me into the ladies' room and he'd go in the men's room to make sure they were clean."

Pritzker attended the Castilleja School in Palo Alto, a preparatory middle and high school for girls. She graduated from the school in 1977. Pritzker went on to attend Harvard University, where she studied economics. She earned her bachelor's degree from the institution in 1981. She went on to receive degrees in both law and business from Stanford University in 1984.

JOINING THE FAMILY BUSINESS

Following her graduation from Stanford, Pritzker joined the family business in earnest, spending two years in a training program with Hyatt. Although she had been exposed to the hotel side of the business since her early childhood, she was more interested in pursuing opportunities in real estate. In 1987, despite her lack of experience in the area, she decided to start a senior-living company, launching herself directly into entrepreneurship. "I had never hired anyone. I'd never fired anyone," she told Bryant. "I had to put together a strategic plan, figure out the product, how to market it, and how to get it built. I learned by doing."

Pritzker's first business became Classic Residence by Hyatt, a chain of senior-living facilities geared toward seniors who preferred to live in upscale residences rather than nursing homes. Although the residences initially struggled to find tenants, they later became a success, with locations opening in numerous states. Having established herself as a successful entrepreneur in her own right, Pritzker continued to work in various family-owned businesses, including several businesses owned by the Marmon Group, a holding company founded by her uncles in the 1950s. She later founded additional businesses,

including the Pritzker Realty Group and the private investment company PSP Capital Partners. She resigned from her positions with both groups in 2013.

CAMPAIGN INVOLVEMENT

In addition to her many business endeavors, Pritzker was politically active on both local and national levels, spearheading fundraising efforts for a variety of politicians. Born and later based in Chicago, she played a particularly significant role in the success of a local politician in 2008, when then senator Barack Obama ran his successful presidential campaign. A key fundraiser for Obama and national finance chair for his campaign, she has been widely credited for helping raise the funds that enabled Obama to defeat Hillary Clinton in the 2008 Democratic primary. Following Obama's election to the presidency, Pritzker joined the President's Economic Recovery Advisory Board.

Following the 2008 election, it was widely reported that Pritzker was under consideration for the post of secretary of commerce. However, family obligations—primarily relating to the sale and dissolution of certain Pritzker family companies in order to settle a dispute—prevented her from taking the position at that time. Instead, the post of secretary of commerce was held, in either an official or an acting capacity, by a series of individuals, including Otto Wolff, Gary Locke, John E. Bryson, Rebecca Blank, and Cameron Kerry.

SECRETARY OF COMMERCE

Following Obama's reelection in 2012, Pritzker again became a leading contender to join the cabinet as secretary of commerce. She was ultimately appointed to the position and was sworn in as the thirty-eighth secretary of commerce on June 26, 2013. Although Pritzker had significant experience in business and a long history of successful entrepreneurial leadership, the role of secretary of commerce brought countless new experiences and challenges, including some of which she could not have even been aware prior to taking the post. "I was meeting with our Chinese counterparts, and you can't get briefed on that until you've been sworn in," she recalled to Harris. "Because there are things they're going to tell you that you're not allowed to know otherwise. So you start with that."

Despite such challenges, Pritzker resolved to learn by doing, taking the many responsibilities of her post in stride. One of her chief concerns was communicating with American businesses and promoting various endeavors to benefit both business and the American people. Her personal experience in business was essential, in part because of public perception of the Obama administration as anti-business. Pritzker's appointment served as a powerful suggestion that this is not, in fact, the case.

FROM JOB SKILLS TO TRADE

Among many other issues related to commerce, Pritzker has been particularly concerned with areas such as job creation and skills training during her tenure in office. "Skills training needs to be industry led," she told Paul Davidson for *USA Today* (19 Nov. 2013) of her stance on the matter. "Businesses need to define what they need so training providers can offer up the right training. That has not necessarily been the case. We have to train people for jobs that are open."

Pritzker is also a supporter of the Trans-Pacific Partnership (TPP), a proposed trade agreement among twelve Pacific Rim countries, including Asia-Pacific nations as well as those of North America. Among other provisions, the agreement would lower barriers to trade such as tariffs. The TPP has been met with opposition from politicians from across the political spectrum, and public opinion of it is mixed. However, while Pritzker acknowledges some of the arguments made by its opponents, she asserts that reducing the barriers to trade with the member countries will ultimately be beneficial to the United States. "You step back and you say to yourself: How can you possibly deny helping American companies have access to the fastest-growing markets in the world?" she explained in an interview with Richard N. Haass for the Council on Foreign Relations (4 Apr. 2016). "Our companies are at a disadvantage. How can you deny the fact 95 percent of customers are outside the United States? It's no longer sufficient to just sell within our own country."

DIVERSE RESPONSIBILITIES

Although the title of secretary of commerce might suggest that Pritzker deals exclusively with issues directly related to trade and business, a wide range of government bodies fall under the department's umbrella, and Pritzker thus has a degree of involvement in a diverse array of initiatives, from export control to infrastructure to economic development. Among numerous other bodies, the Department of Commerce oversees the Census Bureau, the National Institute of Standards and Technology (NIST), and the National Oceanic and Atmospheric Administration (NOAA). The latter body runs the National Weather Service, the importance of which Pritzker has highlighted in interviews. "We are the sensors, the satellites, the buoys, all the measurements that have to go on to produce the baseline weather information," she told Haass. "So every day we produce somewhere between 20 and 40 terabytes of data, which is about two to three Libraries of Congress [a] day, of information about the weather." During Pritzker's tenure

as secretary, the National Weather Service has particularly worked to coordinate with state and local leaders as well as with first responders in the hope of creating systems and processes that will enable the American people to be better protected during severe weather events. "We're becoming far more of a service organization, as much as a data organization," she explained to Haass.

PERSONAL LIFE AND PHILANTHROPY

Pritzker is married to Bryan Traubert, an ophthalmologist. They have two children, Donald and Rose. A committed philanthropist, Pritzker has been involved in a number of causes, supporting organizations such as the Chicago Public Education Fund, Skills for Chicagoland's Future, and the Pritzker Traubert Family Foundation, which is dedicated to funding educational, fitness, and cultural programs that benefit the children of Chicago.

SUGGESTED READING

Easton, Nina. "The Fascinating Life of Penny Pritzker (So Far)." *Fortune*. Time, 2 June 2014. Web. 9 Sept. 2016.

"Penny Pritzker, Secretary of Commerce." *Commerce.gov*. US Dept. of Commerce, 19 July 2016. Web. 9 Sept. 2016.

Pritzker, Penny. "Commercial Diplomacy: A Conversation with Penny Pritzker." Interview by Richard N. Haass. *Council on Foreign Relations*. Council on Foreign Relations, 4 Apr. 2016. Web. 9 Sept. 2016.

Pritzker, Penny. "Harris: Q&A with Penny Pritzker." Interview by Melissa Harris. *Chicago Tribune*. Chicago Tribune, 11 Nov. 2013. Web. 9 Sept. 2016.

Pritzker, Penny. "Penny Pritzker, on Hearing the Whole Story." Interview by Adam Bryant. *New York Times*. New York Times, 21 Dec. 2013. Web. 9 Sept. 2016.

Pritzker, Penny. "Q&A with Commerce Secretary Penny Pritzker." Interview by Paul Davidson. *USA Today*. USA Today, 19 Nov. 2013. Web. 9 Sept. 2016.

—Joy Crelin

Kevin Puts

Born: January 3, 1972
Occupation: Composer

EARLY LIFE AND EDUCATION

Kevin Matthew Puts was born on January 3, 1972, in St. Louis, Missouri. His parents raised him in Michigan and would often play orchestral music for him in his youth, including symphonies by Ludwig van Beethoven. This exposure fostered an early obsession with music. When he was about seven years old, he began practicing on a piano handed down from his grandparents. He took lessons but preferred improvising and playing by ear.

Puts practiced and studied piano seriously throughout high school and into college. Gradually his interest shifted from playing the piano to writing original compositions. He received his bachelor's degree from the Eastman School of Music in Rochester, New York, where he studied primarily under composers Samuel Adler and Joseph Schwantner. He continued his education with a master's degree from Yale University in New Haven, Connecticut. There, composers Jacob Druckman and Martin Bresnick were his instructors. After Yale, Puts returned to the Eastman School of Music, where he earned a PhD in musical arts. While earning his doctorate, Puts studied composition with composer Christopher Rouse and piano with instructor Nelita True.

In 1996, Puts was selected by the New York City–based nonprofit organization Young Concert Artists (YCA) to be a composer in residence. He composed two well-received works for performers of the YCA, titled *Canyon* (1996) and *Alternating Current* (1997). Puts also served as composer in residence for the California Symphony from 1996 to 1999.

CAREER IN COMPOSITION

From 1997 to 2005, Puts was an associate professor of composition at the University of Texas at Austin. Early in his professional career, Puts began receiving commission requests. In 1999 the New York Youth Symphony commissioned *Concerto for Everyone* (1999), which was performed at Carnegie Hall in New York City. Also in 1999, he was commissioned by the Vermont Symphony and Japan's Ensemble Kobe for the composition *Marimba Concerto* (1999).

Puts continued to produce a number of compositions that were performed by leading orchestras around the United States. In 2001, he was awarded a Guggenheim Fellowship grant for music composition. The American Composers Orchestra commissioned his *Falling Dream* (2002) for their twenty-fifth anniversary concert at Carnegie Hall. The same year Puts won the Barlow International Orchestra Competition, which led to a commission for his *Symphony No. 2 Island of Innocence* (1999). Several more commissions and compositions followed, including . . . *this noble company* (2003) and *River's Rush* (2004). In 2003, Puts was awarded the Benjamin H. Danks Award for Excellence in Orchestral Composition of the American Academy of Arts and Letters. He wrote his third symphony, *Symphony No. 3: ("Vespertine")* (2003),

after being inspired by the music of Icelandic singer Björk.

Puts produced three major works in 2006. His *Percussion Concerto* (2006) was performed by the Pacific Symphony and the Utah Symphony. The Minnesota Orchestra commissioned his composition *Sinfonia Concertante* (2006). To celebrate conductor David Zinman's seventieth birthday, Puts was commissioned by the Aspen Music Festival to compose *Vision* (2006), which was performed by acclaimed cellist Yo-Yo Ma.

In 2006 Puts left his position at the University of Texas and joined the Composition Faculty at the Peabody Institute, a preparatory school for musicians at Johns Hopkins University in Baltimore, Maryland. A year later, Puts premiered his fourth symphony—*Symphony No. 4: From Mission San Juan* (2007)—which was intended to be performed within the Mission San Juan Bautista, a Spanish mission in San Juan Bautista, California.

Puts continued to add to his prolific body of work while teaching at the Peabody Institute. In the summer of 2010 he performed his own work for the first time as a soloist with the Cabrillo Festival Orchestra. He was then commissioned by Minnesota Opera and Opera Philadelphia for the two-act opera *Silent Night* (2011). This was Puts's first time composing an opera. He collaborated on the project with librettist Mark Campbell. *Silent Night* is based on the screenplay of the film *Joyeux Noël* (2005), about the 1914 Christmas ceasefire between combatants in World War I. The opera is performed in English, French, and German, with bits of Italian and Latin as well.

Silent Night premiered on November 12, 2011 at the Ordway Theater in St. Paul, Minnesota. The majority of critics praised the opera, and its first run at the theater sold out. For his work on the opera, Puts was awarded the 2012 Pulitzer Prize in music.

IMPACT

Puts's work has been commissioned and performed by some of the United States' top symphonies, ensembles, and soloists, making him one of the most notable contemporary composers. His work has also been performed in Europe and Asia. Throughout his career he has been the recipient of numerous awards, including the Pulitzer Prize in 2012.

PERSONAL LIFE

Puts is married to Lisa GiHae Kim, a violinist in the New York Philharmonic. They have a son and live in Yonkers, New York.

SUGGESTED READING

Gazzola, Luiz. "Exclusive *Opera Lively* Interview with Kevin Puts, Pulitzer Prize-Winning

Opera Composer." *Opera Lively*. vBulletin Solutions, 13 Feb. 2013. Web. 31 Mar. 2014.

"Kevin Puts: Biography." *Musical World*. Musical World, n.d. Web. 31 Mar. 2014.

"Kevin Puts: Composition." *Peabody Institute*. Johns Hopkins U, n.d. Web. 31 Mar. 2014.

Puts, Kevin. "A Pulitzer Winner Asks: Why Write Symphonies?" *National Public Radio*. NPR, 5 Aug. 2013. Web. 31 Mar. 2014.

Smith, Tim. "The Engaging Voice of Composer Kevin Puts." *Baltimore Sun*. Tribune Interactive, 2 June 2012. Web. 31 Mar. 2014.

SELECTED WORKS

Symphony No. 1, 1999; *Symphony No. 2: Island of Innocence*, 1999; . . . *this noble company*, 2003; *Symphony No. 3: ("Vespertine")*, 2003; *Symphony No. 4: From Mission San Juan*, 2007; *Silent Night*, 2011

—*Patrick G. Cooper*

Julian Finney/Getty Images

Agnieszka Radwańska

Born: March 6, 1989
Occupation: Tennis player

Nicknamed "The Professor" for her intelligent approach to the game, Agnieszka Radwańska of Poland has been called "the most tactically sound, subtle tennis player in the world" by Tom Perrotta for the *Wall Street Journal* (2 July 2012), and "the tennis equivalent to a chess player" by Melenie Ambrose for *Perth Now* (2 Dec. 2013). Since turning professional and debuting on the Women's Tennis Association (WTA) Tour in 2005, the five-feet-eight Radwańska has made use of a wide variety of shots and tactics to overcome bigger and more physically imposing players.

Arguably the best tennis player to ever hail from Poland, Radwańska, who also occasionally competes in doubles competitions, has won eighteen career WTA singles titles and has consistently ranked among the top eight in the WTA season-ending singles rankings since 2011. She holds the distinction of being the first Polish player to claim a WTA singles title, the first in the Open Era (since 1968) to reach a Grand Slam singles final, and the first to win a WTA Tour Championships title, achieving the latter feat during the 2015 season.

EARLY LIFE AND EDUCATION

Agnieszka "Aga" Radwańska was born to Robert and Marta Radwańska on March 6, 1989, in Krakow, Poland. Not long after Radwańska was born, her father, a former tennis player, relocated the family to Gronau, Germany, where he worked as a teaching professional at the local tennis club. It was there that her sister, Urszula ("Ula"), who is twenty-one months younger and also on the WTA Tour, was born.

Along with her sister, Radwańska was introduced to tennis by her father when she was still a toddler. She started out hitting balloons before graduating to regulation-size balls. From the time she was five, Radwańska's father served as her full-time coach, and by age six, she had already won her first tournament. "I liked it from the beginning and so did Ula," she told Ambrose. "We enjoyed everything." It was around this time that Radwańska's family moved back to Poland so that she and her sister could attend school there.

One of Radwańska's heroes growing up was Swiss tennis star Martina Hingis, a former teenage prodigy who held the top spot in the WTA singles rankings for a total of 209 weeks during the course of her career. Listed at five feet seven, Hingis was known for using guile and inventiveness on the court to make up for her relative lack of size and power. She retired from singles play in 2007 with forty-three WTA titles, including five Grand Slam championships. (Hingis came out of retirement in 2013 to play on the WTA Tour doubles circuit, and as of July 2016, she was part of the top-ranked doubles team in the world.)

Recognizing early on that his daughter would never be able to go toe-to-toe physically with bigger and stronger opponents, Robert Radwańska instead focused on teaching her a more cerebral style of play that emphasized all aspects of the game. As a result, early in her career, Radwańska developed a tennis game that, like Hingis's, relied on tactics, strategy, and a wide arsenal of shots. She rounded out her game by participating in other sports, such as soccer and volleyball, which helped improve her balance and hand-eye coordination.

EARLY PROFESSIONAL CAREER

Radwańska has said that her tennis career occupied nearly all of her free time growing up. "Most of the time I was eating in the car," she recalled to Ambrose, "because I was going straight from school to the court." Radwańska's single-minded dedication to the sport was largely the work of her strict, demanding, and at times volatile father, who reportedly prohibited her and her sister from having boyfriends as teenagers in order to keep them focused on their careers.

This tough-love style of parenting nonetheless helped mold Radwańska into an elite player at a young age. A highly decorated junior player, Radwańska started competing in tournaments on the developmental International Tennis Federation (ITF) women's circuit in 2004. She turned professional the following year, playing in her first WTA tournament in April as a qualifier, in addition to winning one singles title and two doubles titles on the ITF circuit.

Radwańska first caught the attention of the tennis world in July 2005, when she captured the Wimbledon junior singles title. It marked her first time playing on grass courts, having been limited to playing on only indoor clay and carpet surfaces while growing up in Poland. She would go on to win the French Open junior singles title and become the top-ranked junior women's tennis player in the world in 2006.

During the 2006 season, Radwańska also represented Poland in the Fed Cup, the premier annual women's international team competition, for the first time. (She went on to play for Poland every year until 2015 but withdrew from the 2016 competition due to injury.) That season she rose from 381 to 57 in the WTA season-ending singles rankings, marking the first time that she cracked the top hundred.

Radwańska continued to climb up the WTA rankings in 2007, when she became the first Polish player to win a WTA singles title, recording a straight-set defeat against Russia's Vera Dushevina at the Nordea Nordic Light Open in Stockholm, Sweden. She also won her first career WTA doubles title, teaming up with her sister, who was that year's Wimbledon junior champion, to win the İstanbul Cup in Istanbul, Turkey. She reached the quarterfinals of three other singles tournaments, helping her achieve a year-end world singles ranking of 26.

RISE TO THE WTA ELITE

Over the next four seasons, Radwańska emerged as the best Polish player to come along since Wojtek Fibak, a former top men's player who achieved a career-high singles ranking of 10 in 1977. During the 2008 season, she won three more singles titles: the Pattaya Women's Open in Thailand, the İstanbul Cup in Turkey, and the International Women's Open in the United Kingdom. She also put in strong performances in each of the four Grand Slams, reaching the quarterfinals at the Australian Open and Wimbledon and the fourth round at the French Open and US Open, and made her Olympic debut at the 2008 Summer Games in Beijing, China, where she fell in the second round. She ended the year with a number-ten ranking.

Radwańska retained that ranking at the conclusion of the 2009 season, in which she notched a runner-up finish at the China Open in Beijing and reached the semifinals of both the Pan Pacific Open in Tokyo, Japan, and the Linz Open in Linz, Austria. During that season, in an interview with Christopher Clarey for the *New York Times* (20 June 2009), Fibak likened Radwańska to Hingis, calling her "a natural mover who understands the geometry of the court."

Radwańska's performance regressed slightly in 2010, when she dropped to fourteenth in the singles rankings. Some observers attributed this to growing tensions between Radwańska and her father, who openly berated her from the stands during a straight-sets second-round loss to unseeded Russian player Yaroslava Shvedova at the French Open. Radwańska nevertheless bounced back during the 2011 season, collecting three more singles titles and winning her second career doubles title, partnered with Slovakian player Daniela Hantuchová at the Sony Ericsson Open in Miami, Florida.

For the first time in her career, Radwańska qualified for the year-end WTA Championships. Despite falling in the round-robin stage of the championships, which were held in İstanbul, she finished the season in eighth place on the WTA singles rankings and won her first of five consecutive WTA Fan Favorite Awards for favorite singles player of the year. That season, the tension in Radwańska's professional relationship with her father came to a head when he again publicly criticized her following a straight-sets fourth-round loss to Russia's Maria Sharapova at the French Open.

FIRST GRAND SLAM FINAL

Prior to the 2012 season, Radwańska dropped her father as her full-time coach and began working with Tomasz Wiktorowski, the captain of Poland's Fed Cup team, and Borna Bikić, who had previously coached Serbian player Jelena Dokić. "He really taught me everything and, for sure, without him I wouldn't be here on the court," she said to Paul Newman for the *Independent* (1 Apr. 2012), "but sometimes it gets too much when you mix up your private life with tennis."

Radwańska's new coaching arrangement yielded immediate results. In February 2012 she won the Dubai Tennis Championships in Dubai, United Arab Emirates, defeating Julia Görges of Germany in straight sets. Then, in March, Radwańska achieved the biggest victory of her career, overcoming Maria Sharapova in straight sets to win the Sony Ericsson Open, which is regarded as the most prestigious non–Grand Slam tournament. In an article for *Tennis.com* (31 Mar. 2012), Pete Bodo observed that Radwańska used her entire arsenal of weapons to defeat the powerful six-feet-two Russian, including "seventy mile per hour serves, sliced forehands . . . , drop shots, and undercut backhands." Commenting on her style of play, Radwańska explained to Bodo, "I will never serve like a Serena [Williams], or even a Maria. I am different, and what I try to do is mix it up—everything—on the court."

Less than two months after the Sony Ericsson Open, Radwańska won her third WTA title of the season after delivering a straight-set defeat to Romanian Simona Halep in the final of the Brussels Open in Brussels, Belgium. She carried her momentum into the 2012 Wimbledon Championships, where she again showcased her all-around game en route to reaching her first Grand Slam final. In the championship match, Radwańska was defeated by Serena Williams, the world's top-ranked player, in three sets. She became the first Polish player to reach a Grand Slam final since the Open Era began in 1968 and rose to a career-high number-two world ranking before finishing the year ranked at number four.

WTA TOP FIVE FIXTURE
Radwańska remained firmly entrenched among the WTA's top five players. In 2013 she claimed two early-season victories, at the ASB Classic in Auckland, New Zealand, and then at the Apia International in Sydney, Australia, before closing out the year with another victory at the Korea Open in Seoul, South Korea.

One of the highlights of Radwańska's season came at the Sony Open (formerly known as the Sony Ericsson Open), when she won a point with a mesmerizing 360-degree spin backhand volley during her quarterfinal win over Kirsten Flipkens of Belgium. Though Radwańska failed to defend her title, losing to Williams in the semifinals, she received shot-of-the-year honors at the 2013 WTA Awards.

Radwańska opened the 2014 season by participating in her first Hopman Cup, an annual international mixed-team tennis event held in Perth, Australia. With her partner Grzegorz Panfil, she finished as the runner-up in the event, which marked her return to doubles play after a two-year hiatus. On the WTA singles tour, Radwańska put together a string of solid performances, including reaching the semifinals for the first time at the Australian Open. "Radwańska's lulling-but-lethal game allows for her to go on stealthy streaks of dominance that often leave opponents startled by how quickly their hopes can disappear," Ben Rothenberg wrote for the *New York Times* (22 Jan. 2014), in response to Radwańska's convincing three-set victory over Belarus's Victoria Azarenka in the quarterfinals of that tournament.

Radwańska's lone victory of 2014 came at the Rogers Cup in Montreal, Canada, where she defeated Venus Williams in straight sets. In her semifinal victory over Russia's Ekaterina Makarova, Radwańska again displayed her propensity for making difficult shots, scoring a point on an uncanny overhead backhand, which earned her the WTA Fan Favorite Award for shot of the year for the second consecutive year.

WTA FINALS CHAMPION
Prior to the 2015 season, Radwańska hired one of her other childhood idols, Martina Navratilova, an eighteen-time Grand Slam winner and arguably the greatest female tennis player of all time, to join her team of coaches. The two parted ways just four months into the 2015 season, however, after Navratilova was unable to commit to a full-time coaching role. During that time, Radwańska struggled mightily, amassing a 13–11 match record, reaching only one semifinal, and dropping to ninth in the world.

Though at one point Radwańska slipped to number fifteen in the rankings, she gradually improved as the season wore on. After a third-round exit at the US Open, Radwańska was three spots out of qualifying position for the season-ending WTA Championships in Singapore. She secured a place in the championships after notching victories at the Pan Pacific Open and the Tianjin Open in Tianjin, China.

During the round-robin stage of the championships, Radwańska lost her first two matches, against Sharapova and Italy's Flavia Pennetta, respectively, before defeating two top-five players to reach the final. In the championship final, Radwańska defeated fourth-seeded Petra Kvitová of the Czech Republic in a hard-fought three-set battle. She became the first player to win with the prestigious tournament after leaving the round-robin stage with a losing record. "It's the biggest day in my life," Radwańska said, as quoted by Sandra Harwitt for *ESPN.com* (1 Nov. 2015).

Radwańska won her third consecutive WTA Fan Favorite Award for shot of the year for pulling off a remarkable drop-shot winner during the third set of her championship match. She finished the year ranked at number five, after falling to sixth in 2014. After opening her 2016 season with a win at the Shenzhen Open in Shenzhen, China, and advancing to the semifinals at the Australian Open and the BNP Paribas Open in Indian Wells, California, she regained the world number-two ranking. As of July 2016, she had fallen back down to number four.

Radwańska has earned over $23 million in prize money, which currently ranks sixth all-time on the WTA Tour. Though consistently one of the most popular players on tour, Radwańska's popularity took a hit in 2013 when she posed nude for *ESPN the Magazine*'s annual "Body Issue." In response to critics, Radwańska told Melenie Ambrose, "They are always going to judge you and not always in a nice way. You have to be prepared for that. Not everyone is going to love you. You just do what you do."

SUGGESTED READING

Ambrose, Melenie. "Agnieszka Radwańska: Being Brave, Baring All and Bright Tennis Dreams." *Perth Now*. Nationwide News, 2 Dec. 2013. Web. 20 July 2016.

Bodo, Peter. "Born This Way." *Tennis.com*. Tennis Media, 31 Mar. 2012. Web. 20 July 2016.

Harwitt, Sandra. "Radwańska Hoping Year-End Title an Omen for 2016." *ESPN.com*. Disney, 1 Nov. 2015. Web. 20 July 2016.

Newman, Paul. "Triumphant **Radwańska** Goes Farther without Father." *Independent*. Independent.co.uk, 1 Apr. 2012. Web. 20 July 2016.

Perrotta, Tom. "The Subtlest Player at Wimbledon." *Wall Street Journal*. Dow Jones, 2 July 2012. Web. 20 July 2016.

"Radwanska Savors Her Moment of Success." *WTA Tennis*. WTA, 1 Nov. 2015. Web. 20 July 2016.

Rothenberg, Ben. "A Stealthy Approach Proves Best for Radwańska." *New York Times*. New York Times, 22 Jan. 2014. Web. 20 July 2016.

—*Chris Cullen*

Megan Rapinoe

Born: July 5, 1985
Occupation: Soccer player

Megan Rapinoe, a midfielder for both the US women's national soccer team (USWNT) and the Seattle Reign FC of the National Women's Soccer League (NWSL), is a "five-foot-seven, 133-pound package of dynamite," Ailene Voisin wrote for the *Sacramento Bee* (9 July 2012). Known for her bleached blonde

pixie hairstyle, free-spirited personality, and flamboyant goal celebrations, Rapinoe has established a reputation as one of the United States' most exciting and creative soccer players. As USWNT head coach Jill Ellis told Gwendolyn Oxenham for USSoccer.com (14 June 2015), Rapinoe "thrives in big games, big moments."

One of the most prominent openly gay professional athletes, Rapinoe made her national team debut in 2006 and her professional debut in 2009. She first burst into the national consciousness during the 2011 Fédération Internationale de Football Association (FIFA) Women's World Cup in Germany, where she fueled the USWNT to a runner-up finish. Rapinoe went on to help the team capture gold medals at both the 2012 Olympic Games in London and the 2015 World Cup in Vancouver, Canada. She has been a member of the Reign since 2013.

EARLY LIFE

The youngest of six children, Megan Anna Rapinoe was born on July 5, 1985, in Redding, California. She has a fraternal twin sister, Rachael. She grew up in Palo Cedro, California, a small town located eight miles east of Redding. Her father, Jim, was a construction worker, and her mother, Denise, worked as a waitress.

Growing up, Rapinoe shared an inseparable bond with her twin sister, who is older by eleven minutes. The two had an adventurous childhood and spent most of their time outdoors playing a wide variety of sports or fishing for crawfish. Extremely competitive, they frequently challenged each other to one-on-one basketball games, which Rachael usually won. "She was stronger and better," Rapinoe admitted to Jeré Longman for the *New York Times* (14 June 2015) about her sister, adding, "I was quite the late bloomer, always pushing, having something to fight for."

Rapinoe and her sister became drawn to soccer through their brother Brian, who is their next-closest sibling in age. Every day Brian took his sisters to a soccer field located across the street from the family home. There, he taught them how to play the game. Unlike her more reserved sister, Megan shared similar traits with Brian, who was witty and gregarious, and looked up to him with reverential admiration. "I idolized him," she told Oxenham. "I wanted to do whatever he did." Brian's life was derailed by drugs, however, and since his teens, he has been in and out of prison.

STRONGER TOGETHER

Brian's troubles ultimately brought Rapinoe and her sister closer together. They stayed out of trouble by throwing themselves headlong into soccer. Megan and Rachael's special athletic talents were apparent by their early teens, when they joined the Elk Grove United, an elite Sacramento-based club team that plays in the Women's Premier Soccer League, which is the second-highest tier of the US women's soccer league system.

Along with her sister, Rapinoe attended Junction School and Foothill High School in Palo Cedro. Unlike some of their professional peers, the Rapinoe sisters did not play high school soccer, instead opting to play club soccer full time for Elk Grove, which had training facilities that were located more than two-and-a-half hours away. They did, however, compete in both basketball and track at Foothill High, where Megan was also a perennial honor roll student.

While playing for Elk Grove, the Rapinoes developed into elite college prospects. Under head coach Danny Cruz, Megan honed the creative, free-flowing style for which she eventually became known. "I don't think he ever really told me how to play," she recalled to Grant Wahl in a profile for *Sports Illustrated* (6 Aug. 2012). "He was really good about letting us make mistakes and play free." That kind of freedom helped the Rapinoes flourish. As high-school juniors in 2003, they helped lead their Elk Grove team, which also included future USWNT member Stephanie Cox, to a number-one national ranking and a second-place finish at the US Youth Soccer National Championships in the under-nineteen division.

UNIVERSITY OF PORTLAND AND USWNT DEBUT

By the time they reached their senior year, the Rapinoes were being recruited by several colleges around the country. They ultimately accepted full scholarships to the University of Portland, which consistently has one of the top women's soccer programs in the country. They graduated from Foothill High School in 2004.

Unlike Rachael, Rapinoe did not play college soccer in 2004 due to her commitments with the US under-nineteen women's national team, which she had begun playing for during her senior year of high school. "I had to admit to myself that I was that good and that I deserved to be there with everyone else," she confessed to Lyndsey D'Arcangelo in an interview for the magazine *Curve* (Mar. 2013). Rapinoe proved herself at the 2004 FIFA U-19 Women's World Championship in Thailand. There, she helped the United States secure a third-place finish after scoring three goals in the tournament.

Rapinoe rejoined her sister at the University of Portland during the 2005 season. As a redshirt freshman for the Pilots that season, she emerged as a star, starting all twenty-five games as an attacking midfielder and notching fifteen goals with thirteen assists. She was named to the First Team All-America and was honored as a national freshman player of the year. Teaming up with her sister, Cox, and another future USWNT member, Christine Sinclair, Rapinoe led Portland to an undefeated season en route to winning the 2005 National Collegiate Athletic Association (NCAA) Division I Women's Soccer Championship.

Recognition of Rapinoe's outstanding play earned her an invitation to the US–WNT's residency training camp during the summer of 2006. That year she made her first four appearances with the team, scoring her first two career goals during a friendly match against Taiwan. Meanwhile, she continued to tear up NCAA competition during her sophomore season, in which she scored ten goals in the first eleven games.

INJURIES AND COMEBACK

Rapinoe was among the nation's leading scorers when, during a match against Washington State University, she tore the anterior cruciate ligament (ACL) in her left knee. The injury sidelined her for the remainder of the 2006 fall college season. Although she returned for the 2007 season, she only appeared in two games before suffering a second season-ending ACL tear in the same knee. The injuries forced her to take a hiatus from the US national team and ended her chances of competing at both the 2007 FIFA Women's World Cup and 2008 Olympic Games. "That was really hard," Rapinoe explained to Voisin, "but there was no sense feeling sorry for myself."

After fully recovering, Rapinoe returned for the 2008 season, which saw her reestablish herself as one of the top college players in the nation. She started all twenty-two games for the Pilots and recorded a team- and conference-best thirteen assists, in addition to five goals.

Rapinoe's comeback season was bittersweet, however. In just the third game of the season, her sister also tore her left ACL for a second consecutive year, which ultimately ended her playing career. Rachael went on to play briefly for an Icelandic professional team before retiring. She now runs soccer camps with her sister and works as a Darfur United coach ambassador.

PROFESSIONAL DEBUT AND THE 2011 WORLD CUP

Because of her injuries, Rapinoe was granted an extra year of college eligibility, but she opted not to return to Portland, instead deciding to enter the inaugural 2009 draft of Women's Professional Soccer (WPS), then the highest division of US women's soccer. She was selected second overall in the draft by the Chicago Red Stars. In her first professional season with the Stars, Rapinoe started seventeen of the eighteen games in which she appeared, scoring two goals with three assists, and was honored as a WPS First Team All-Star. She remained with the Stars through the end of the 2010 season, after which the team ceased operations.

Concurrent with her professional career, Rapinoe had returned to playing with the US-WNT. In addition to opening the 2011 season with the Philadelphia Independence, scoring one goal in four games, she was named to the USWNT's roster for that year's FIFA Women's World Cup. Heading into the Cup, she was relatively unknown outside of national soccer circles. Her profile, however, rose considerably after the USWNT's 3–0 group-stage win over Colombia. Coming in as a substitute shortly before the game's fiftieth minute, Rapinoe quickly scored to put the USWNT up 2–0. She celebrated the moment by singing Bruce Springsteen's "Born in the USA" into a field-level microphone, which catapulted her "from unknown reservist to YouTube-worthy fan favorite," D'Arcangelo wrote. "The whole point of soccer is to score a goal," Rapinoe explained to D'Arcangelo. "And there's no better feeling in the world."

Rapinoe achieved even more fame during the USWNT's quarterfinal victory over Brazil. In the 122nd minute of that game, she came on the field as a substitute and delivered a high-arching, left-footed cross to Abby Wambach to set up the game-tying goal in the waning seconds of overtime. The USWNT went on to defeat Brazil through a penalty-kick shootout. Though the team lost to Japan in the World Cup final, Rapinoe had etched herself into legend. *Sports Illustrated* later named Wambach's goal one of the ten most significant goals in US soccer history.

During the World Cup, Rapinoe was traded to magicJack, a team based in Boca Raton, Florida, that included superstars Wambach, Hope Solo, and Shannon Boxx. She helped them finish third in the WPS standings and reach the playoffs. The WPS folded after the 2011 season, however, largely due to a legal battle with magicJack owner Dan Borislow. The league was replaced by the NWSL, which formed in 2012.

AN "UN-AMERICAN" SOCCER STAR

It was during the USWNT's flight home from the 2011 World Cup when Rapinoe really considered revealing her sexual orientation to the public. "I had become more vocal for gay marriage and gay rights on social media," she explained to Sam Borden for the *New York Times* (10 Apr. 2013), "and at some point it just felt a little inauthentic." Rapinoe publicly announced her sexual orientation in an interview for *Out* magazine just before the 2012 Olympics.

In her first Olympic tournament, Rapinoe shined, starting all six games for the USWNT at the midfield position and recording three goals and a team-best four assists. She helped the team win their third consecutive gold medal, as they achieved redemption against Japan with a 2–1 victory in the Olympic final. During the Olympics, Wahl called Rapinoe "the most un-American player in US women's soccer" in his *Sports Illustrated* profile. "For decades the United States has thrived on strength and speed more than skill. Rapinoe is different. . . . Rapinoe relies instead on clever dribbling, fluid movement, and visionary passing."

Following the Olympics, Rapinoe signed a six-month contract with Olympique Lyonnais, a French club team that is widely regarded as one of the best in the world. She scored two goals in six matches for the team during the second half of the 2012–13 French league season and helped the team reach the 2013 Union of European Football Associations (UEFA) Champions League final. She returned to the team for the first half of the 2013–14 season. Meanwhile, in June 2013, Rapinoe made her NWSL debut as a member of the Seattle Reign. Despite only playing half of the 2013 NWSL season, she led the team with five goals in twelve games. The Reign, whose roster also features Solo and Cox, finished as runners-up to FC Kansas City in the NWSL championship final in both 2014 and 2015. At the 2015 FIFA Women's World Cup, Rapinoe helped the USWNT win their third World Cup title and first since 1999 with a 5–2 victory over Japan.

Rapinoe, who is sponsored by Nike and Samsung, became engaged to her longtime girlfriend, the indie singer-songwriter Sera Cahoone, in August 2015.

SUGGESTED READING

Borden, Sam. "A U.S. Soccer Star's Declaration of Independence." *New York Times*. New York Times, 10 Apr. 2013. Web. 16 Nov. 2015.

D'Arcangelo, Lyndsey. "Playing Out Loud". *Curve,* Mar. 2013: 70–73. Print.

Longman, Jeré. "Women's World Cup: First Opponents to Face the Fury of U.S. Players? Older Siblings." *New York Times*. New York Times, 14 June 2015. Web. 16 Nov. 2015.

Oxenham, Gwendolyn. "Pinoe's Biggest Fan." *USSoccer.com*. US Soccer, 14 June 2015. Web. 16 Nov. 2015.

Voisin, Ailene. "Redding Native Megan Rapinoe's Soccer Fortunes Keep Rising; Olympics Ahead." *Sacramento Bee*. Sacramento Bee, 9 July 2012. Web. 16 Nov. 2015.

Wahl, Grant. "Unquiet American." *Sports Illustrated*. Time, 6 Aug. 2012. Web. 16 Nov. 2015.

—*Chris Cullen*

Gordon Correll/CC BY-SA 2.0/Flickr/Wikimedia Commons

Eddie Redmayne

Born: January 6, 1982
Occupation: Actor

"The people that I play have to be extraordinary," Eddie Redmayne told Mark Jacobs for *GQ* (21 Dec. 2015). Indeed, the word "extraordinary" aptly describes many of the individuals the British actor has portrayed over the years, from fictional characters such as the revolutionary student Marius from the musical *Les Misérables* and the villainous Balem Abrasax from the 2015 science-fiction film *Jupiter Ascending* to real-life figures such as theoretical physicist Stephen Hawking and artist and transgender pioneer Lili Elbe. For Redmayne, his tendency to take on unique and powerful roles has paid off, bringing him both worldwide recognition and numerous awards, including the Academy Award for best actor for his portrayal of Hawking in 2014's *The Theory of Everything*. But while Redmayne has found acclaim as an actor since making his film debut in 2006, he does not actively seek it out. "If your dream is to tell stories, interesting stories, play interesting people, that's the bottom line," he explained to Jacobs.

EARLY LIFE AND EDUCATION

Edward John David Redmayne was born in London, England, on January 6, 1982. He was the second of three children born to Richard and Patricia Redmayne, and he also has two half siblings. His father was in finance, while his mother worked for a relocation business.

During Redmayne's childhood, his family lived in the Chelsea area of London. He attended primary school at Colet Court and went on to attend Eton College, a prestigious all-boys boarding school, where he was the classmate of numerous well-known British men of his generation, including Prince William and fellow actor Tom Hiddleston. As an adult, Redmayne has acknowledged the privilege inherent in attending such an institution but has noted that his greatest takeaways from his time at Eton were the relationships he formed with those around him. "It really is about friendship," he told Paul Flynn for *Out* magazine (11 Aug. 2015). "You live intensively with these people for five years, from the age of thirteen to eighteen, and those friendships are pretty solid."

Redmayne began acting early in life, performing in school plays and taking acting lessons. "Because I was at an all-boys school, I played a lot of girls' parts as a kid," he told Flynn of his early work. "I look identical to my mother. Everyone's always told me that, all my life." He made his first appearance on the professional stage in 1994 with a small role in the London production of the musical *Oliver!* He continued to act while at Eton but, despite his love of acting, opted not to enroll in drama school for university, instead attending Trinity College, Cambridge to study art history. He continued to appear onstage while at university and in 2002 gained significant attention for his performance as Viola, the heroine of William Shakespeare's comedy *Twelfth Night*.

EARLY CAREER

Redmayne began to receive widespread critical acclaim for his stage acting not long after leaving university. He appeared in the London production of the Edward Albee play *The Goat* in 2004 and in 2009 began acting in the play *Red*. Written by the playwright John Logan, *Red* starred veteran actor Alfred Molina as the twentieth-century American abstract-expressionist painter Mark Rothko, while Redmayne played the artist's assistant. The production later traveled to New York, and Redmayne ultimately won the Tony Award for best performance by a featured actor in a play for his work.

Although he spent much of his early career on stage, Redmayne also did some television work relatively early in his career, appearing in an episode of the series *Animal Ark* in 1998, while still at Eton, and in an episode of the soap opera *Doctors* in 2003. He followed these appearances with a larger role in the 2005 miniseries *Elizabeth I*, which starred acclaimed actor Helen Mirren in the title role.

Redmayne's on-screen debut came in 2006 when he played a lead role in the crime film *Like Minds*. He went on to have significant roles in films such as *The Good Shepherd* (2006), *Savage Grace* (2007), *Elizabeth: The Golden Age* (2007), and *The Other Boleyn Girl* (2008). He gained the most widespread attention to date, however, in 2012, with the premiere of the film *Les Misérables*. Based on the stage musical of the same name, which in turn is based on the work of nineteenth-century French novelist Victor Hugo, *Les Misérables* was a lavish musical that allowed Redmayne to display his singing ability for the first time on film. His portrayal of the revolutionary student Marius helped make Redmayne a better-known actor, particularly among American audiences.

THE THEORY OF EVERYTHING

Although he had long been experiencing a gradual increase in popularity, Redmayne was propelled into international stardom in 2014 with the release of the dramatic biopic *The Theory of Everything*. The film tells the story of noted British physicist Stephen Hawking, who in his early twenties was diagnosed with the disorder amyotrophic lateral sclerosis (ALS), also known as Lou Gehrig's Disease. *The Theory of Everything* explores Hawking's relationship with his first wife, Jane, as well as his academic achievements and experiences with ALS. Redmayne, who portrays Hawking, trained extensively for the role, which also presented a variety of significant costuming challenges. "I lost, like, fifteen pounds at the beginning of the film," he recalled to fellow actor Jennifer Lawrence for *Interview* magazine (13 Jan. 2015). "With the disease, Stephen did lose a lot of weight. But we couldn't

shoot chronologically, so we were having to jump between different time periods within the same day. Our extraordinary makeup artist, Jan [Sewell], and costume designer, Steven [Noble], did clever things like making the collars tight and my makeup look healthy in the morning, and then, if in the afternoon I was playing him older, they would mess with proportions—the collars would become bigger or they would use slightly oversized wheelchairs."

Perhaps the most daunting aspect of the role for Redmayne, however, was that he was to portray a living person and one of the world's most respected scientists. "The star power is almost indescribable," he told Jacobs of meeting Hawking for the first time. "It's the weird conflict between the fact that he can move next to nothing and yet he has the most expressive face you've ever seen. He can only move these tiny muscles and yet you can read so much from that." Hawking himself reportedly approved of Redmayne's performance, which ultimately earned him the Academy Award for best actor.

After starring in *The Theory of Everything*, Redmayne took a break from the dramatic and historical roles that had made up the bulk of his work and instead turned to the villainous role of the alien prince Balem in the 2015 science-fiction film *Jupiter Ascending*, written and directed by sisters Lilly and Lana Wachowski. The film was not nearly as well received as many of Redmayne's other works, and he even received the Razzie Award for worst supporting actor for his performance. He remained good humored about the award, the granting of which made him one of only a select few actors to have won both a Razzie and an Oscar.

THE DANISH GIRL

Redmayne's next project was the 2015 film *The Danish Girl*, directed by Tom Hooper. Hooper also directed Redmayne in *Les Misérables* and had passed *The Danish Girl* script to him during that production. "There's a certain gender fluidity about Eddie. He has this extraordinary translucency. This way his emotion can come through," Hooper explained to Nathan Heller for *Vogue* (18 Sept. 2015).

The Danish Girl is based on the life of Danish artist Lili Elbe, born Einar Wegener, one of the first people known to have undergone sex reassignment surgery. Elbe is an important figure in Lesbian, Gay, Bisexual and Transgender (LGBT) history, and Redmayne was well aware of the responsibility in portraying her. He researched the role extensively and reached out to *Jupiter Ascending* director Lana Wachowski, who is transgender. "This project had gone in and out and I didn't even think it would ever get made," Redmayne told Flynn. "But I did start talking to Lana about Lili and she told me how important the book, *Man into Woman* [an edited collection of Elbe's letters and journal entries], was to her. . . . She very kindly continued my education, pointed me to literature, and where I should be headed." Despite his extensive preparation and past experiences playing female characters, Redmayne found the experience of stepping out of his dressing room as Elbe to be a difficult one, telling journalists that he was acutely aware of all of the eyes on him. "It was a feeling that, apparently, women are substantially more used to," he told Heller. "That was incredibly nerve-racking, and yet it must be *nothing* like what it's like for a trans woman the first time she goes out."

The Danish Girl follows Elbe's first experiences presenting as a woman and her eventual transition, as well as the evolution of her relationship with her wife Gerda, played by Alicia Vikander, who painted many portraits of Elbe. Although some critics argued that the role of Elbe should have been played by a transgender actress, the film's reception was largely positive. Redmayne was nominated for the Academy Award for best actor, while Vikander took home the award for best supporting actress.

FANTASTIC BEASTS AND WHERE TO FIND THEM

It was announced during the summer of 2015 that Redmayne would star in the film *Fantastic Beasts and Where to Find Them*, a spin-off from the popular Harry Potter film and novel franchise. In British author J. K. Rowling's Harry Potter novels, *Fantastic Beasts and Where to Find Them* is a textbook used at the fictional Hogwarts School of Witchcraft and Wizardry. A tie-in book of the same name was published in 2001. The film builds on the existing source material and follows the adventures of fictional author Newt Scamander in the wizarding world of the 1920s. *Fantastic Beasts and Where to Find Them* is set to premiere in the fall of 2016.

PERSONAL LIFE

Redmayne met his future wife, public relations executive Hannah Bagshawe, while attending Eton. They married in the winter of 2014. Eddie Redmayne and wife Hannah welcomed baby Iris Mary together on Father's Day, 2016.

SUGGESTED READING

Dehn, Georgia. "Eddie Redmayne Interview." *Telegraph*. Telegraph Media Group, 23 Nov. 2009. Web. 10 June 2016.

Flynn, Paul. "Eddie Redmayne: An Education." *Out*. Here Media, 11 Aug. 2015. Web. 10 June 2016.

Heller, Nathan. "Eddie Redmayne on Transforming into *The Danish Girl*." *Vogue*. Condé Nast, 18 Sept. 2015. Web. 10 June 2016.

Jacobs, Mark. "Eddie Redmayne Shares His Theories on Life, the Universe, and, Well, Everything." *GQ*. Condé Nast UK, 21 Dec. 2015. Web. 10 June 2016.

Kellaway, Kate. "Eddie Redmayne: 'To Play Hawking I Had to Train My Body Like a Dancer.'" *Guardian*. Guardian News and Media, 7 Dec. 2014. Web. 10 June 2016.

Redmayne, Eddie. "Eddie Redmayne." Interview with Jennifer Lawrence. *Interview*. Interview, 13 Jan. 2015. Web. 10 June 2016.

Redmayne, Eddie. "Eddie Redmayne Interview: 'Love Is the Thing That an Equation Can't Be Made Of.'" Interview with Steven Mackenzie. *Big Issue*. Big Issue, 13 Jan. 2015. Web. 10 June 2016.

SELECTED WORKS

Elizabeth I, 2005; *The Good Shepherd*, 2006; *Savage Grace*, 2007; *Elizabeth: The Golden Age*, 2007; *The Other Boleyn Girl*, 2008; *Les Misérables*, 2012; *The Theory of Everything*, 2014; *Jupiter Ascending*, 2015; *The Danish Girl*, 2015; *Fantastic Beasts and Where to Find Them*, 2016

—Joy Crelin

Dawn Richard

Born: August 5, 1983
Occupation: Singer-songwriter

Dawn Richard, whose stage name is DΛWN, is a singer-songwriter who has won acclaim for her imaginative blend of R & B and electronica. In a review for *Pitchfork* (16 Jan. 2015), Andrew Ryce called Richard's 2015 album *Blackheart* a "singular, visionary work" of a "uniquely talented artist." *Blackheart* is the second album in Richard's Heart trilogy. The first, *Goldenheart* (2013), was a sprawling tale of love and loss told through a mythological lens. The third album, *RedemptionHeart*, is scheduled to be released in January 2017.

Richard got her start on the reality television show *Making the Band* 3, produced by Sean "Diddy" Combs. She appeared on three seasons of the show from 2005 to 2006 and was a part of the all-female R & B group Danity Kane, the show's product, until 2009. Richard was devastated by the band's breakup, but she quickly found her footing as a member of Combs's own Diddy-Dirty Money, a group that included Combs, Richard, and songwriter Kalenna Harper.

Influenced by myriad sources in art and literature, Richard's aesthetic exists proudly outside mainstream tastes, though her songs retain classic elements of popular R & B songs. Richard told Rachel Syme for *Pitchfork* (22 Jan. 2016) that she

Alexander Vaughn/Flickr: Dawn 24/CC BY 2.0/Wikimedia Commons

is happy to be producing independently because it allows her to exist in a sweet spot between the underground and the mainstream. "When either side doesn't know how to classify you, that's when you start to have some fun," she said.

EARLY LIFE AND EDUCATION

Dawn Angeliqué Richard (pronounced RUH-shard) was born on August 5, 1983. She was raised in New Orleans. Her father, Frank Richard, was the former lead singer of the 1970s funk band Chocolate Milk and later worked as a music teacher. Her grandmother was a librarian, and books were always an important part of her life. As a child, she read the popular Goosebumps series, but as she got older, she was attracted to horror writer Anne Rice, whose works draw on aspects of New Orleans culture, Greek mythology, and the works of William Shakespeare. Richard was inspired by not only the imagery of the books she read but also the experience of reading. Her love of book series led her to make her Heart albums a thematic trilogy.

Richard's mother owned a dance school, and Richard began dancing when she was just two years old. As a teenager she won a full scholarship to study marine biology at the University of New Orleans. She pursued that line of study concentrating on manatees and dolphins. Although she spent hours at the lab, she also worked as a dancer for the New Orleans Hornets (now the Pelicans). After three years, Richard ultimately graduated with a major in music marketing. It was a busy time for Richard, who was also launching her singing career. She performed

as an opening act for Grammy Award–winning R & B singer Anthony Hamilton and released her first solo album, *Been a While* (2005), with an independent label, under the name Dawn Angeliqué. Richard's career was just beginning to take off in 2005 when Hurricane Katrina destroyed her family's New Orleans home. The family lost everything and Richard was homeless for six months before moving to her parents' hometown in Baltimore. The Richards were gone for nearly ten years, moving back to the city in 2016. "We just moved into another neighborhood," Richard told Steve Knopper of the *Chicago Tribune* (21 Apr. 2016) of the family's bittersweet return. "Where we're from—it's gone."

MAKING THE BAND AND DANITY KANE

In 2004, Richard auditioned for a slot on the popular reality television show *Making the Band*. She beat out more than ten thousand women to appear on the show and even gave the group its name, "Danity Kane," the name of a manga character she was doodling at a rehearsal. The show was originally the brainchild of Lou Pearlman, the shady manager of popular 1990s boy bands NSYNC and the Backstreet Boys who was later convicted of running a multimillion dollar Ponzi scheme. In theory, the concept of the show was simple: assemble a commercially viable singing group; in reality, however, none of the four groups reached the heights that Pearlman's groups enjoyed during their heyday. Combs signed on as a producer of the show in its second season. Danity Kane, inarguably the most successful of the show's groups, was featured on the third season. Richard was excited to be a part of a group—other members included Aubrey O'Day, Wanita "D. Woods" Woodgett, Shannon Bex, and Aundrea Fimbres—but quickly realized that her creative suggestions were unwelcome. "So I had to appreciate other things about music, like the writing and the cadence and dealing with producers," she told Syme. "I became a student. I wanted to learn the actual idea of what this industry was before I could creatively speak a lot of the things that I wanted to speak."

In 2006, Danity Kane's self-titled first album debuted in the number-one slot on the Billboard charts. The album generated the Top 10 hit "Show Stopper." The group's second album *Welcome to the Dollhouse* (2008) also debuted at number one. Danity Kane was the first girl group to have its first two albums debut at number one. The second album contained the song "Damaged," which peaked at number ten on the Billboard singles chart. The group broke up in early 2009. According to Richard, only she and Fimbres showed up to tape parts of *Making the Band 4*, which continued to chronicle the group while Combs formed a boy band. Richard was frustrated by the unexpected rift among the group members. Referring to her and Fimbres, she told Jocelyn Vena for *MTV News* (28 Jan. 2008), "We're put in this position that we didn't ask to be in and we're being told to fix it." Richard, O'Day, and Bex reunited to record an album called *DK3* in 2014, but the group called it quits, for the last time, before the album was even released. The breakup reportedly came after Richard punched O'Day in the back of the head.

DIDDY-DIRTY MONEY

After Danity Kane broke up in 2009, Richard teamed with Combs and songwriter Kalenna Harper to form the electro-R & B group Diddy-Dirty Money. They released a debut album called *Last Train to Paris* in 2010. Sales were poor, though the album itself was widely praised. As Al Shipley wrote for the *Village Voice* (9 Apr. 2012), even Diddy's fans assumed his most innovative days—blending hip-hop and R & B with Notorious B.I.G. and Mary J. Blige—were behind him. *Last Train*, however, "turned out to be a masterpiece," Shipley wrote, "not so much adventurous as deliriously generous in its cornucopia of off-the-wall synth and percussion textures, and ruminations on heartache so intense they almost circled back around to celebratory."

In 2011, Dirty Money released a Valentine's Day mixtape called *LoveLOVE vs. HateLOVE*. It too was critically praised, but Combs disbanded the group soon after its release. In 2012, Richard asked to be released from her contract with Combs's Bad Boy Records and struck out on her own, without a label, with creative partner and manager, Andrew "Druski" Scott.

MIXTAPES, EPS, AND GOLDENHEART

In 2011, while Richard was still with Dirty Money, she made a free mixtape called *Prelude to a Tell Tale Heart*. It was downloaded one million times within the first month of its release and reached number one on the iTunes R & B chart. A year later, a newly independent Richard released an EP called *Armor On* exclusively on iTunes. It went to number one on the iTunes R & B chart and sold more than thirty thousand copies. Of its contents, Shipley wrote that *Armor On*, which included the popular single "Bombs," "is one of the most substantial records to ever be called an EP." The same year, Richard released an unconventional holiday EP, including some remixes of her 2011 iTunes single "December Sky," called *Whiteout*.

Expectations were high for Richard's solo debut album, *Goldenheart*, released in January 2013, but Richard met, and arguably exceeded, them. *Goldenheart* was one of the most critically lauded albums of the year, as well as one of the most unusual. It is a reflection on love and heartache cast as an epic battle on a scale more appropriate to Middle-earth, the setting of J. R. R. Tolkien's *The Lord of the Rings*, than to real life. Richard has said that she was inspired by fifteenth-century martyr Joan of Arc and aimed to blend medieval and futuristic imagery to construct metaphors about contemporary relationships. "It's a new version of these battles—age-old stories for *the now*," she told Marcus Holmlund for *Interview* magazine (25 Sept. 2012). "They're stories that have always been relatable, and I like to make people dream and think and imagine and learn and study."

Goldenheart incorporates R & B and electrodance beats like trance and dubstep. Its musical influences include Peter Gabriel—Richard's song "In Your Eyes" borrows heavily from Gabriel's famous song of the same name—and surrealist singer-songwriter Kate Bush. Richard's unique sound was created entirely with the help of one person, her partner and producer, Scott. The two parted ways before Richard's following album, *Blackheart*.

BLACKHEART

In 2015, Richard released *Blackheart*, the second album in her Heart trilogy. Richard said in multiple interviews that the album heralded her "Black Era," in which the music was darker and more personal than the bombastic songs that had preceded it. *Blackheart* is a deeply personal album. Thematically it explores Richard's frustrations with the music industry and family illnesses. Musically, it picks up where *Goldenheart* left off but "offers a sprawling and sometimes knotty take on songwriting," Ryce wrote, "sometimes doing away with verse and chorus structure altogether and settling on a stream-of-consciousness barrage instead." It is about falling down, to paraphrase Richard's interview with Daniel Montesinos-Donaghy for *Fact* magazine (30 Jan. 2015), but also about standing up. Asked if *Blackheart* was a feminist album, Richard told Montesinos-Donaghy, "Being a black woman in this industry, with two people"—she worked alone with producer, Noisecastle III—"able to have a number-one album with no label, no one to push us, and have some of the world's hardest critics praise us? . . . That's a feminist act."

SUGGESTED READING

Knopper, Steve. "Dawn Richard, Post Danity and Diddy, Is Satisfied." *Chicago Tribune*. Tribune, 21 Apr. 2016. Web. 4 May 2016.

Richard, Dawn. Interview by Marcus Holmlund. "Exclusive Song Premiere and Interview: '86,' Dawn Richard." *Interview*. Interview Magazine, 25 Sept. 2012. Web. 10 May 2016.

Richard, Dawn. Interview by Daniel Montesinos-Donaghy. "'There Is No Gender, No

Color, No Genre': Dawn Richard on Her Groundbreaking New Album Blackheart." *Fact*. Fact Magazine, 30 Jan. 2015. Web. 10 May 2016.

Richard, Dawn. Interview by Rachel Syme. "The Indivisible DAWN." *Pitchfork*. Condé Nast, 22 Jan. 2016. Web. 4 May 2016.

Shipley, Al. "Dirty Money Honeys: Dawn Richard and Kalenna Get Off the Bad Boy Train." *Village Voice*. Village Voice, 9 Apr. 2012. Web. 5 May 2016.

Vena, Jocelyn. "Danity Kane Are Over, Dawn Richard Says." *MTV News*. Viacom International, 28 Jan. 2016. Web. 4 May 2016.

SELECTED WORKS

Danity Kane (with Danity Kane), 2006; *Welcome to the Dollhouse* (with Danity Kane), 2008; *Goldenheart*, 2013; *Blackheart*, 2015

—*Molly Hagan*

CB NOV_Richie Ross_GettyImages-171165929

Ross Richie

Born: May 22, 1970
Occupation: Founder, BOOM! Studios

In the years since the debut of its first comic, the anthology *Zombie Tales*, in 2005, the comics publisher BOOM! Studios has become one of the biggest success stories in the American comics industry. Specializing in both comics based on licensed properties and wholly original works, the company has become known for publishing a wide array of comic books and graphic novels aimed at a variety of reader demographics, earning multiple industry awards along the way. In addition to the talent and hard work of its creators and employees, BOOM! Studios owes much of its success to its cofounder, Texas-born publisher Ross Richie.

Richie first entered the world of comic books in 1993, when he took a short-lived position with the publisher Malibu Comics. He later helped relaunch the comics publisher Atomeka before striking out on his own in 2005, cofounding BOOM! Studios with the goal of publishing innovative original and licensed comics. Over the following decade, he and his collaborators expanded the company's offerings through the creation of specialized imprints as well as through the acquisition of the established publisher Archaia Entertainment. "We're believers in classic voices," Richie told Cape Rust for *Pop Cults* (26 Apr. 2013) of BOOM! Studios' guiding ethos. "We believe licensed comic books can have heart and soul and don't have to be a cold cash-in. We believe that a company can have a positive, cooperative relationship with the talent that we partner with. We're a more diverse, more modern, forward-thinking group that's working every day to build the company of tomorrow."

EARLY LIFE AND EDUCATION

Ross Richie was born on May 22, 1970, in San Antonio, Texas. The younger of two brothers, he grew up in and around the city, where he attended Alamo Heights High School. As a student, he participated in sports and also developed a love of comic books. He was particularly drawn to the ongoing *X-Men* comic being published at the time, the heroes of which were "empowered by what [made] them weird," as he explained to Rust. "I might have played football, but the jocks would never embrace me. I might have been in some advanced classes in school, but the brains always thought I was a jock. And I scared the art school kids. I never fit in," he recalled. After graduating from high school in 1988, Richie attended the University of Texas at Austin. Although he initially enrolled with the intention of majoring in fine arts, he later moved to the university's film program.

EARLY CAREER

After graduating from the University of Texas, Richie moved to Los Angeles, California, to pursue work in the film and television industry. Like many aspiring media professionals, Richie worked a wide range of jobs over the following decade, including stints as a television production assistant and as a screenplay reader for the production company Trimark Pictures. Beginning in 1993, however, he began a brief but important tenure at the job that would shape much of his later career trajectory. While attending a comics convention that year, he had a fortuitous meeting with executives from the publisher Malibu Comics. Founded in 1986, Malibu was the publisher of original series as well as licensed comics based on existing properties. Richie soon joined the publisher's marketing department, where he worked to promote Malibu's various comics in retail stores and at conventions. He left the company in 1994 when it was acquired by the much larger Marvel Comics, but Richie has cited his job at Malibu Comics as the most influential of his early career and credits it with teaching him about the business side of comics publishing.

Richie worked a variety of jobs over the next decade and remained involved with comics, including as a writer. In 2003 Image Comics began publishing Richie's series *Dominion*, a collaboration with veteran comics artist and writer Keith Giffen. Although the series ended abruptly after two issues, Richie's work in comics was far from finished. The following year, Richie worked on the relaunch of Atomeka Press, a British comics publisher that had first operated between the late 1980s and 1990s. The relaunched Atomeka primarily published reprinted material. Richie considered leaving to found his own company with the hopes of publishing original comics as well. He was encouraged in that dream by Giffen, who was optimistic about Richie's chances of success. "Giffen . . . basically said to me, '*Publish comic books, stupid*,'" Richie told Rust. "I argued and told him it couldn't be done. He insisted that I do it and, boy, was he right." With Giffen's encouragement, Richie and cofounder Andrew Cosby founded their own publishing house, BOOM! Studios, in mid-2005. Cosby, a television writer and producer, had previously worked with Richie in the Malibu Comics marketing department.

BOOM! STUDIOS

Although Richie had more than a decade of experience in comics at that point, he remained initially unsure of whether an independent publishing venture would be successful, or even possible in the first place. "Even three months before the company started I didn't think I'd be doing it," he told Rust. "Me and my friends all joked in our social circle that anyone starting a comic book publishing business had a suicidal streak, the failure rate was so high. We had seen so many friends and colleagues lose their savings (or their house) on ventures like this."

Richie's worries proved to be largely unfounded. BOOM! Studios' first publication, *Zombie Tales*, debuted in June of 2005 as a copublication by BOOM! and Atomeka. An anthology comic, *Zombie Tales* featured content from comics creators such as Giffen and Mark

Waid, the latter of whom would go on to serve as BOOM! Studios' editor in chief and chief creative officer. The publication of *Zombie Tales* marked a strong start for the company, and BOOM! Studios would follow it with a number of additional *Zombie Tales* anthologies as well as countless other original comics works.

In addition to publishing quality work, Richie was focused on one of the key problems facing independent comics creators and publishers: visibility. "I've always been a big believer that you can have the world's greatest book, but if nobody knows it's there, it doesn't matter," he told Albert Ching for *CBR.com* (22 Dec. 2014). In a publishing world dominated by established companies such as Marvel Comics and DC Comics, it was often difficult for smaller businesses to establish a foothold in the highly competitive industry. Unlike many other independent publishers, however, Richie had the advantage of his marketing background and resolved to put his knowledge to work for the benefit of both his company and the creators of the works he published. "That was a big core value," he explained to Ching. "Let's not be obnoxious; let's not be that annoying marketing guy, but let's get the word out. That was always an objective for us."

EXPANDING PRODUCT LINE

Over the following decade, Richie and his coworkers at BOOM! Studios worked to expand the company's offerings, publishing a wide range of original comics. While many of the comics published in the company's early years were geared toward adults and older teens, BOOM! soon began to publish works targeted at younger readers as well, in part through specialized imprints such as BOOM! Kids, later renamed KaBOOM. Another imprint, BOOM! Box, publishes many comics oriented toward tweens and teens, including series such as *The Lumberjanes* and *The Backstagers*. While some of BOOM! Studios' publications are experimental in nature and therefore risky bets in the competitive comics market, Richie sees such creative and unique works as a benefit rather than a risk. "When we have opportunities like BOOM! Box to explore something that's different and unique and fun, we're going to go do that," he told Ching. "Sometimes it works, sometimes it doesn't. You know? You never bat a thousand. But it's such a gift to me to be in a place where you can explore that kind of creativity. My instinct is never to be conservative because it's such a squander of an opportunity if you are."

In addition to its many original publications, BOOM! Studios also became known as a publisher of comics and graphic novels based on licensed properties. That publication initiative began early in the company's existence, with the 2006 publication of the first comic in the

Warhammer: Damnation Crusade series, based on the Games Workshop property. Over the following years, BOOM! Studios published comics based on properties such as the film *Big Trouble in Little China*, the cartoon *Adventure Time*, and the card game Munchkin. Perhaps the most significant licensing partnership was with Disney, from which BOOM! Studios licensed the right to publish comics based on Pixar films such as *Toy Story*, *The Incredibles*, and *Monsters Inc.* as well as works featuring Disney characters such as Mickey Mouse and Donald Duck between 2008 and 2011. Although the company's deal with Disney ended and Cosby left in 2010, BOOM! Studios has remained a major publisher of licensed comics such as *Mighty Morphin Power Rangers* and *Sons of Anarchy: Redwood Original*, both based on television shows.

In 2013 BOOM! Studios acquired the independent comics publisher Archaia Entertainment, best known for publishing comics such as *Mouse Guard*. Rather than absorbing Archaia's titles into the main BOOM! Studios imprint, the company's leadership opted to create a dedicated imprint, known simply as Archaia, for those works.

FILM AND TELEVISION

In light of Richie's years of work in the film and television industry, it is little surprise that he would work to promote BOOM! Studios properties as potential sources for screen adaptations. The first major film based on a BOOM! Studios comic, *2 Guns*, was released by Universal Pictures in 2013. Starring actors Denzel Washington and Mark Wahlberg, *2 Guns* was based on the 2007 limited comic series of the same name, written by Steven Grant and illustrated by Mateus Santolouco. Richie served as one of the film's producers.

The success of *2 Guns* drew additional Hollywood attention to BOOM! Studios, and over the next years the company signed a variety of first-look deals relating both to film and television adaptations of its comics and comics adaptations of existing properties. Although the possibility of further film and television adaptations excites Richie, he is well aware that proceeding with caution is especially important when Hollywood is involved. "Having a comic book that garners Hollywood interest is very commonplace. It's how you control that process once it happens," he told Ching. "What people want to do—whether it's an agent, manager or producer—is to get in there, get their hands on your thing, and then they want to run with it, and they want it to service their agenda. That's not good for us, and it's not good for our creators, so that process needed to be handled and modulated, carried through to its best execution." In 2016, film studios announced proposed adaptation of

several BOOM! Studios properties, including *Mouse Guard*, *The Lumberjanes*, and *The Empty Man*.

PERSONAL LIFE

Richie is married to Johanna Stokes, a writer who has contributed to BOOM! Studios comics such as *Zombie Tales*, *Galveston*, and *The Calling: Cthulhu Chronicles*. They have two children. Richie lives with his family in California.

In addition to his work on the publishing side of the comics industry, Richie is first and foremost a devoted fan of the medium. "There has never been a time in comic book history when there's been so many good comics and they're coming from everyone," he told Russ Burlingame for *ComicBook.com* (15 Sept. 2013). "It's incredible. I love it as a consumer because I have a big reading stack and it's a lot of fun."

SUGGESTED READING

Burlingame, Russ. "BOOM! Studios CEO Ross Richie: There Has Never Been More Good Comics Than Now." *ComicBook.com*. ComicBook.com, 15 Sept. 2013. Web. 9 Sept. 2016.

Ching, Albert. "Ross Richie Forecasts BOOM! Studios' Busy Hollywood Slate." *CBR.com*. CBR.com, 22 Dec. 2014. Web. 9 Sept. 2016.

Gustines, George Gene. "Boom Box Comics Tell Stories of Teenagers, with a Light Heart." *New York Times*. New York Times, 15 May 2016. Web. 9 Sept. 2016.

Gustines, George Gene. "Sharing the Wealth as a Comic Book Goes to Hollywood." *New York Times*. New York Times, 27 July 2013. Web. 9 Sept. 2016.

Guzman, René A. "Double Firepower." *MySA*. Hearst, 6 Aug. 2013. Web. 9 Sept. 2016.

Phegley, Kiel. "Ross Richie and Jack Cummins on the BOOM!/Archaia Combination." *CBR.com*. CBR.com, 28 June 2013. Web. 9 Sept. 2016.

Rust, Cape. "20 Questions with Ross Richie of BOOM! Studios." *Pop Cults*. Pop Cults, 26 Apr. 2013. Web. 9 Sept. 2016.

—*Joy Crelin*

Daisy Ridley

Born: April 10, 1992
Occupation: Actor

On the morning of December 14, 2015, Daisy Ridley was largely an unknown actor, having secured only several small roles, primarily in British television shows, over the course of her fledgling career. By the end of the night, however, she was an international star. That day marked the

Gage Skidmore/CC BY-SA 3.0/Wikimedia Commons

world premiere of *Star Wars: The Force Awakens*, the seventh installment in the classic science-fiction series that had begun fifteen years before she was born. Playing the role of mysterious scavenger Rey in the film, Ridley was instantly propelled into the spotlight, impressing both longtime Star Wars fans and new audiences, as well as her more experienced costars. "Daisy is an incredible find," veteran Star Wars actor Harrison Ford told John Hiscock for the *Telegraph* (14 Dec. 2015). "She has not been in much—a couple of television things—but she is extraordinarily powerful on screen. She has strength and vulnerability and I think she is going to have an amazing career."

Speculation regarding Rey's origins, parentage, and significance within the Star Wars universe ran rampant prior to the film and continued long afterward, as *The Force Awakens* answered few of fans' most burning questions about the character and raised even more. Ridley, however, is far more interested in what her character is experiencing in the moment. "Rey is just living her life. She doesn't know what's going to happen later. So I tried not to think too much about everything that was coming," she told Dave Itzkoff for the *New York Times* (9 Dec. 2015). "The thing about 'Star Wars' is that every single person is important. Even though Rey is a big role, everyone influences everyone. If that wasn't so, why would so many people remember Admiral Ackbar?"

EARLY LIFE, EDUCATION, AND EARLY CAREER
Daisy Jazz Isobel Ridley was born on April 10, 1992, in the Westminster borough of London,

England. She was the youngest of three girls born to Chris Ridley and Louise Fawkner-Corbett, and she also has two older half sisters. Her father is a photographer, while her mother works as a publicist for the bank Barclays.

Ridley grew up in central London and initially attended local schools. However, in 2001 she enrolled in the Tring Park School for the Performing Arts, a boarding and day school in the county of Hertfordshire, north of London. While her later career as an actor might give the impression that she attended the school to advance that pursuit, that assumption could not be farther from the truth. "The reason I went was because I was naughty at my primary school," she confessed to Itzkoff. "So my mom thought if I was busy, then I wouldn't be. And it worked. . . . The school definitely taught me discipline." She remained a student at Tring Park until graduating in 2010. Although she did not initially attend the school for its performing arts programs, she eventually began to participate in theater programs there, particularly coming to enjoy musical theater.

After graduating from the Tring Park School, Ridley spent some time abroad, traveling in India before returning to the United Kingdom to find work as an actor. She worked a variety of day jobs during that period, including stints in retail and food service. In 2013, she made her film debut in the short film *Lifesaver*, following that role with parts in other short films, such as *Blue Season* (2013), as well as appearances in single episodes of television series such as *Casualty* (2013), *Youngers* (2013), and *Mr. Selfridge* (2014). *Scrawl*, an independent film created by students from England's Andover College for which she had filmed a role around 2012, was released at various film festivals in 2015.

Like many aspiring actors, Ridley at times struggled with the instability inherent in the profession. "I got an advertisement first, and then something else, which I got fired from," she recalled to Itzkoff. "It was soul-destroying. And then the next thing I got I thought was going to be my big break, and they cut the role." Despite such discouraging experiences, she persevered, continuing to pursue roles that interested her.

THE ROLE OF A LIFETIME
Ridley's persistence paid off. While continuing to look for work as an actor, she learned that the team behind the seventh film in the long-running Star Wars franchise were looking to cast a major part in the film. Over the course of more than half a year, she auditioned for the role multiple times, impressing the filmmakers with her powerful rendition of one of the film's pivotal scenes during her initial auditions. While her multiple callbacks suggested that the filmmakers enjoyed her performance, she was pessimistic

about her chances, doubting that an unknown actor such as herself would be able to obtain a major role in a film effectively guaranteed to be a blockbuster; however, she was wrong. While attending a play, she received a telephone call from director J. J. Abrams, who offered her the part of Rey, one of *Star Wars: The Force Awakens*'s protagonists. Stunned by the news, she continued to second-guess herself. "I didn't celebrate," she told Missy Schwartz for *Refinery29* (4 Dec. 2015). "I thought I was going to lose the part the whole time. Honestly, I was like, they've made a terrible mistake. I went for brunch the next day with my agents, and they were celebrating. I just felt sick and, like, I didn't want to be there. It's just so much to process."

Meanwhile, Abrams has explained in interviews that he had purposely sought out unknown actors to play the crucial lead roles, citing the fact that the original Star Wars trilogy had also included lesser-known actors in the cast at the time. Despite Ridley's hesitation to celebrate the role, Abrams has shared that casting her was almost instinctual: "I had this gut feeling that she was right," he told Emine Saner for the *Guardian* (28 Nov. 2015). "She showed a combination of vulnerability and strength which [sic] gave her a complexity, and there was an intelligence in her eyes that was an indicator she could play quite a complicated part. . . . There was a whole range where she could go with authenticity and conviction."

Having secured what was perhaps one of the most coveted film roles of the decade, Ridley next had to contend with a long period of keeping her role a secret. She was able to tell her immediate family, but she has noted in interviews that she found it somewhat difficult to keep the news secret from her friends and others in her life. In April 2014, however, the official *Star Wars: The Force Awakens* cast announcement revealed to the world what she had known for months: she was headed to a galaxy far, far away.

BECOMING REY

One of the central characters of *Star Wars: The Force Awakens*, Rey begins the film as a scavenger who lives alone on the desert planet of Jakku, fending for herself until an encounter with Finn, a defector from the villainous First Order, leads her into a life-changing adventure. During an interview with Tatiana Siegel for the *Hollywood Reporter* (4 Nov. 2015), Ridley explained her perspective on Rey and the character's appeal: "She's not a superhero. She's a normal girl thrust into extraordinary circumstances, so it's very relatable."

In preparation for playing the character, Ridley began an intensive training regimen that included weightlifting and a high-protein diet. While she initially struggled to grow accustomed

to this new routine, she later came to consider the exercise not only enjoyable but also therapeutic. Over the course of filming, she also formed a strong bond with her costars, especially fellow little-known British actor John Boyega, who plays Finn. She also had the opportunity to spend time with Ford, Carrie Fisher, and Mark Hamill, the stars of the original trilogy of Star Wars films, who reprised their iconic roles in *The Force Awakens*.

Although no stranger to filming, Ridley had never before been part of a project of that magnitude, and the process of creating such a high-profile film could have easily been intimidating and stressful. However, Ridley enjoyed her time on the set. "I used to steal the golf buggy which I wasn't allowed to do because I didn't have a driver's license so I wasn't insured so it was kind of illegal," she recalled to Hiscock. "There were dance offs, there was Funky Friday every Friday. . . . When we finished filming it was overwhelming emotionally for me because firstly I didn't want to finish and secondly to me it was more than filming a film. Just looking around the set on the last day and have everyone there and saying goodbye was a big moment."

STAR WARS: THE FORCE AWAKENS

Upon its premiere in December 2015, *Star Wars: The Force Awakens* became a tremendous success among filmgoers worldwide. The newest installment became one of the most financially successful films ever, earning more than two billion dollars at the box office worldwide. It was also a critical success, with many reviewers praising Ridley's performance as Rey as well as the work of her costars. Although plans for a still-untitled eighth film in the franchise had been in motion for some time, the success of *The Force Awakens* confirmed public demand for new Star Wars films and signaled the revitalization of the franchise. Ridley is set to reprise her role in the eighth film, along with many of her *Force Awakens* costars.

Despite *The Force Awakens*'s positive reception among fans and critics, Ridley herself finds it difficult to watch the film. "It's weirder than I ever could have imagined," she explained to Schwartz. "I was talking to Harrison [Ford] yesterday, and he said he still doesn't enjoy it, watching himself. He was saying, 'It's creative, so you enjoy the process, not the result.' And I was like, yes! Obviously, to see the finished result and see everyone's work that's gone into this incredible thing—that's amazing. But I'm looking forward to watching it again when I feel a bit more distant from it."

OTHER WORK

Since starring in *The Force Awakens*, Ridley has received an increasing number of film opportunities, including both live-action and voice roles. In 2016, she lent her voice to the English-language dub of the Japanese animated film *Only Yesterday*, a 1991 production by Studio Ghibli. Ridley provides the adult voice of protagonist Taeko, a young woman who reminisces about her earlier years throughout the film. Ridley also narrated the documentary *The Eagle Huntress*, about a thirteen-year-old Kazakh eagle hunter. In addition to her scheduled appearance in the eighth Star Wars film, Ridley has been linked to a number of films in preproduction, including the science-fiction thriller *Chaos Walking*.

PERSONAL LIFE

When not filming, Ridley lives in London. In addition to acting, she is pursuing studies in the social sciences and psychology. She has been in a relationship with British actor Charlie Hamblett for several years.

SUGGESTED READING

Hiatt, Brian. "Star Wars Strikes Back: Behind the Scenes of the Biggest Movie of the Year." *Rolling Stone*. Rolling Stone, 2 Dec. 2015. Web. 12 Sept. 2016.

Hiscock, John. "Star Wars: How New Kids John Boyega and Daisy Ridley Impressed Harrison Ford." *Telegraph*. Telegraph Media Group, 14 Dec. 2015. Web. 12 Sept. 2016.

Ridley, Daisy. "Daisy Ridley." Interview by Carrie Fisher. *Interview*. Interview, 30 Oct. 2015. Web. 12 Sept. 2016.

Ridley, Daisy. "Daisy Ridley Tells Us What It's Like to Hug Chewbacca." Interview by Missy Schwartz. *Refinery29*. Refinery29, 4 Dec. 2015. Web. 12 Sept. 2016.

Ridley, Daisy. "In New Star Wars, Daisy Ridley and John Boyega Brace for Galactic Fame." Interview by Dave Itzkoff. *New York Times*. New York Times, 9 Dec. 2015. Web. 12 Sept. 2016.

Saner, Emine. "How Daisy Ridley Went from Bit Parts to Lead in *Star Wars: The Force Awakens*." *Guardian*. Guardian News and Media, 28 Nov. 2015. Web. 12 Sept. 2016.

SELECTED WORKS

Casualty, 2013; *Youngers*, 2013; *Mr. Selfridge*, 2014; *Scrawl*, 2015; *Star Wars: The Force Awakens*, 2015; *Only Yesterday*, 2016

—*Joy Crelin*

Gina Rodriguez

Born: July 30, 1984
Occupation: Actor

When *Jane the Virgin* premiered in the fall of 2014, Gina Rodriguez became one of few Latina women leading a show on network television. Her portrayal of the titular character—a chaste, twenty-something woman whose pregnancy is the result of accidental insemination—earned her not only critical praise but also two Golden Globe nominations in 2015 and 2016.

The relative newcomer made Hollywood history in 2015, when she beat out more established performers to take home the statuette for best actress in a television comedy. With the victory, Rodriguez was catapulted into the spotlight and earned the distinction of being the CW network's first star to claim a Golden Globe award while also joining America Ferrera as the second Latina to ever win in this category.

A PERFORMER FROM A YOUNG AGE

Gina Rodriguez was born on July 30, 1984, in Chicago, Illinois, the youngest child of Magali, the interpreter services director for the Cook County Circuit Court, and Genaro, a boxing referee and Teamster organizer. While growing up with her two older sisters in the Belmont Cragin neighborhood on Chicago's Northwest Side, Rodriguez attended Andrew Jackson Language Academy (AJLA), an elite magnet school.

The self-admitted tomboy first fell in love with performing after attending the local Puerto Rican Day parade. "I remember being six years

Jason Merritt/Getty Images

old . . . and [seeing] these little girls in sequins outfits smiling and dancing," she shared with Patrick Gomez for *People* (19 Mar. 2015). "I was like, 'I want to be in those little sequin dresses.'" Within a year, the seven-year-old had joined the salsa dance troupe Fantasia Juvenil.

AN EDUCATION IN ACTING

Upon completing elementary school, Rodriguez was admitted to St. Ignatius College Prep, a private Catholic high school. She continued to hone her performance chops at salsa festivals across the United States and in Puerto Rico, with the Latin dance company Los Senores del Swing. Rodriguez discovered a newfound passion for acting, after appearing in a high school production of *A Chorus Line*. "I felt like [dancing] was limiting," she told Tomi Obaro for *Chicago* magazine (16 Dec. 2014). "I wanted to speak."

Determined to pursue an acting career, the sixteen-year-old Rodriguez participated in a prestigious, six-week intensive acting course called Theatrical Collaboration, one of the high-school summer programs offered at Columbia University. Following her 2002 graduation from St. Ignatius, Rodriguez attended the Tisch School of the Arts at New York University (NYU), with the help of her sister Ivelisse, an investment banker. While still in college, she made a handful of television appearances. In 2004 she made her television debut on NBC's long-running procedural *Law & Order*, followed by a guest appearance on Fox's short-lived crime drama *Jonny Zero* a year later.

STARTING WITH SMALL PARTS

After earning her degree from NYU in 2006, Rodriguez spent the next two years auditioning for roles while juggling odd jobs as a twin-specialist nanny, a waitress, and a masseuse. In 2008 she amassed a steady stream of roles, on the small and big screens. Following another guest appearance on *Law & Order*, in which she played a different character, Rodriguez landed small parts in the dramatic short *Ten: Thirty One* (2008) and the award-winning drama and festival-circuit favorite *Calling It Quits* (2008).

A year later Rodriguez won best actor at the First Run Film Festival in New York for the narrative short *Osvaldo's* and guest starred in an episode of CBS's *Eleventh Hour*. She continued to expand her profile and résumé in 2010, playing a bridesmaid alongside America Ferrera in the big-screen romantic comedy *Our Family Wedding*. On the small screen, Rodriguez appeared on an episode of the ABC sitcom *10 Things I Hate about You*, an adaptation from the 1999 teen film, and a multiepisode arc on *Army Wives*, Lifetime's longest-running series. She was also part of the ensemble cast of the TV movie *My*

Super Psycho Sweet 16: Part 2 (2010), the sequel to MTV's slasher flick. Despite the relatively slow start, Rodriguez remained hopeful. As she related to Gomez, "The [role models I saw on TV] weren't ever the color of myself or my siblings. I realized: Changing that is my mission."

FILLY BROWN

Following guest spots on the NBC sitcom *Happy Endings* and the CBS crime drama *The Mentalist*, Rodriguez gained about twenty pounds to portray the sassy best friend of an aspiring, underprivileged Latina dancer for her next feature film, *Go For It!* (2011). The performance not only earned her a 2011 Imagen Award nod for best supporting actress (the Imagen Awards honor Latinos in the entertainment industry). By November 2011 she had become a recurring fixture on the CBS soap *The Bold and The Beautiful* (2011–12).

Rodriguez drew the attention of producers of *Filly Brown*, an indie drama about a budding hip-hop artist from East Los Angeles. Despite not having a musical background, she was cast in the lead role, after dazzling producers with an impromptu rap during her audition. To lend credibility to the character, Rodriguez collaborated with the film's music producers to record several songs. "I was in their studio four days after booking *Filly Brown* and I was surrounded by all these Latin underground hip-hop artists— DJ Dominator, Medicine Girl, Lala Romero, Flo Pain, Chingo Bling, and Baby Bash," she recalled to Stephanie Goncalves for *Complex* (30 July 2013). "That was the greatest gift because, obviously, rapping over people's songs or imitating people was not going to work, especially for the story. Filly Brown had to discover her voice, and I had to discover mine too."

The film premiered at the 2012 Sundance Film Festival, where it earned a nod for the Grand Jury Prize. Rodriguez won an Imagen Award for best actress in a feature film for her role. Shortly after she was offered a holding deal with ABC and ABC Studios. However, she subsequently rejected a role in *Devious Maids*, a Lifetime series executive produced by Eva Longoria and Marc Cherry. "For the stories that Americans have, I feel like there's a perception that people have about Latinos in America specifically . . . that we are perceived in a very certain way," she shared with Ruben Navarrette for *CNN.com* (13 Jan. 2015). "Our stories have been told, and they're not unmoralistic. . . . but there are other stories that need to be told. And I think that the media is a venue and an avenue to educate and teach our next generation."

In February 2012 Rodriguez had a recurring role on the short-lived web comedy series *No Names* and was tapped to star in *Sleeping with the Fishes*, Nicole Gomez Fisher's directorial debut, by July. After Rodriguez was cast in the ill-fated Fox pilot *Wild Blue* the following March, *Sleeping with the Fishes* debuted in June at the 2013 Brooklyn Film Festival.

Rodriguez appeared in the dramatic shorts *California Winter* and *Una y Otra y Otra Vez* (*One Time and Another*) while also reuniting with Youssef Delara, *Filly Brown*'s director, for the big-screen psychological thriller *Enter the Dangerous Mind* (2013). Rodriguez followed those with small-screen roles in A&E's *Longmire* and TNT's *Rizzoli & Isles*.

JANE THE VIRGIN

Rodriguez's disappointment was short-lived. By January she had booked an audition for another pilot: the CW's adaptation of a Venezuelan telenovela about a driven, abstinent woman who becomes pregnant after being artificially inseminated by accident. Rodriguez instantly impressed series creator Jennie Snyder Urman. "Gina . . . was literally the third person that came in," Urman confided to Oliver Sava for the *A.V. Club* (8 Dec. 2014). "She knocked everything out of the park. After I [saw] her, I realized she gives me the most freedom as a writer . . . She can do drama, she can do comedy, she can do small moments and big moments." Rodriguez won a dream role when she was officially cast as the lead for *Jane the Virgin*. She was nominated for another Imagen Award, for best actress in a feature film, for her part in *Sleeping with the Fishes* around the same time.

When *Jane the Virgin* premiered in October 2014, she managed to equally enchant the critics. "Talented, magnetic, sexy and above all else extremely likable, Rodriguez is the glue that holds together the tonally difficult-to-pull-off *Jane the Virgin* series," Tim Goodman wrote for the *Hollywood Reporter* (13 Oct. 2014).

WINNING A GOLDEN GLOBE

In December 2014 Rodriguez was announced as a Golden Globe candidate, for best actress in a television comedy. The following month, the first-time nominee won the top prize, beating out veterans Edie Falco and Julia Louis-Dreyfus. Rodriguez, who has been outspoken in her support of the Latino community, dedicated her award to Latino viewers, saying that it was as much for her as for the Latinos who want to see themselves on television. After her Golden Globe win, *Jane the Virgin* was renewed for a second season. Lightning struck twice for Rodriguez a year later, with a second consecutive Golden Globe nod and a third-season renewal for her critically acclaimed series, despite ratings struggles.

Rodriguez, who was featured in *Time's* 100 Most Influential People list for 2016, is quickly becoming a hot commodity on the big screen.

She has two films scheduled for release in 2016: *Deepwater Horizon*, an action thriller costarring Mark Wahlberg and Kate Hudson; and the Ray Liotta drama *Sticky Notes*. Rodriguez has also signed on to appear in the sci-fi thriller *Annihilation*, slated for a 2017 release

ADVOCACY AND PERSONAL LIFE

In addition to her acting career, Rodriguez is involved with several causes and organizations. She has become an advocate of embracing a healthy body image—Rodriguez graced the cover of the May 2016 issue of *Women's Health*. She has also launched a social-media campaign that she called Movement Mondays to celebrate achievements by Latino performers in the television and film industry. Rodriguez, a boxing enthusiast and half-marathon runner, is collaborating with lingerie brand Naja to design an underwear line for women of all shapes and sizes. She is also a member of the board of directors for the Hispanic Scholarship Fund (HSF).

The Santa Monica, California resident has remained mum regarding her private life, following her September 2015 breakup with fellow actor Henri Esteve, her boyfriend of more than a year.

SUGGESTED READING

Gomez, Patrick. "*Jane the Virgin*'s Gina Rodriguez: My Inspiring Journey to Stardom." *People*. Time, 19 Mar. 2015. Web. 13 May 2016.

Goodman, Tim. "*Jane the Virgin*: TV Review." *Hollywood Reporter*. Prometheus Global Media, 13 Oct. 2014. 13 May 2016.

Navarrette, Ruben. "Gina Rodriguez, the Latina Meryl Streep?" *CNN*. Turner Broadcasting System, 13 Jan. 2015. Web. 13 May 2016.

Obaro, Tomi. "Gina Rodriguez Is Conquering Television in *Jane the Virgin*." *Chicago*. Chicago Tribune Media Group, 16 Dec. 2014. Web. 13 May 2016.

Rodriguez, Gina. "*Filly Brown* Actress Gina Rodriguez Talks Her FOX Pilot 'Wild Blue' and Shattering Hollywood Stereotypes." Interview by Stephanie Goncalves. *Complex*. Complex Media, 30 July 2013. Web. 13 May 2016.

Urman, Jennie. "Adapting a Telenovela with *Jane the Virgin* Showrunner Jennie Urman." Interview by Oliver Sava. *A.V. Club*. Onion. 8 Dec. 2014. Web. 13 May 2016.

SELECTED WORKS

Calling It Quits, 2008; *Go For It!*, 2011; *Filly Brown*, 2012; *Sleeping with the Fishes*, 2013; *Jane the Virgin*, 2014–

—*Bertha Muteba*

Pardis Sabeti

Born: December 25, 1975
Occupation: Geneticist

Pardis Sabeti, a computational geneticist, is one of the top scientists in the United States researching infectious diseases. Simply put, she uses math to understand the natural world, specifically the relationship between evolution and disease. In 2002, at the age of twenty-six, Sabeti had completed her doctorate in evolutionary genetics and was attending medical school at Harvard University when she created an algorithm that enables researchers and scientists to identify evidence of natural selection in the human genome, which had significant implications for such infectious diseases as Ebola virus disease.

In 2005 Sabeti received the Burroughs Wellcome Fund Career Award in the Biomedical Sciences. In 2014 she was named a person of the year by *Time* magazine, and the following year the magazine named her to its 100 Most Influential People list. Also in 2015 she was named as a Howard Hughes Investigator, which allowed her the financial freedom to continue her research. Sabeti is an associate professor of organismic and evolutionary biology at Harvard University's Center for Systems Biology and at the Harvard T. H. Chan School of Public Health. Sabeti is also a member of the Broad Institute, jointly run by Harvard and the Massachusetts Institute of Technology.

EARLY LIFE

Pardis Sabeti was born in Tehran, Iran, in 1975 where her father was a high-ranking member of the Iranian government. A few years prior to the Iranian Revolution of 1979, Sabeti's parents moved the family, including Sabeti and her older sister, Parisa, to the United States, where they eventually settled in Florida. Seth Mnookin for *Smithsonian Magazine* (Dec. 2012) explains that one summer in the early 1980s, Sabeti's mother brought home a few school supplies that included used textbooks, a chalkboard, and some school chairs in order to set up a "makeshift summer school" at home for her daughters. Sabeti's sister, who is two years older, played the role of teacher, and Sabeti was in charge of physical education and performing arts, according to Mnookin. "[Parisa] would teach me everything that she had learned the year before in school," Sabeti said of her sister, who also taught Sabeti addition, subtraction, division, and multiplication. "By the time I got to school," Sabeti told Mnookin, "I knew it all, and when we'd do the times tables, I was just focused on doing it faster than anybody else. I already had the information, so it just got me to focus on excellence."

Taylor Hill/GettyImages

Sabeti has always loved math, despite, as she explained in an interview for the Rhodes Project (2013), going "through the typical phases" as a child of deciding what to be when she grew up. She liked flowers, so she thought of owning a flower shop; she loved reading literature and writing short stories, so she wanted to become a novelist; after those dreams, she decided she wanted to become a doctor. And though she knew that all of these were actual careers and were things a person could be paid to do, as she said in her interview for the Rhodes Project, "What I always liked most was math. I just didn't know that there was a job in math at the time."

Sabeti was always a good student, and in high school she was a National Merit scholar and the recipient of an honorable mention on *USA Today*'s All-USA High School Academic Team.

UNDERGRADUATE YEARS

Sabeti attended the Massachusetts Institute of Technology (MIT), in Cambridge, Massachusetts, where she studied biology and worked in the laboratory of genomics pioneer Eric S. Lander, who in 1990 helped found the Whitehead/MIT Center for Genome Research. Lander was one of the principal leaders of the Human Genome Project, an international research effort to sequence and map every human gene. Lander, whom Sabeti referred to as "my main role model" in her Rhodes Project interview, became Sabeti's mentor and advisor in 1993. Sabeti further described Lander as an "incredibly good person as well as a great scientist." These qualities undoubtedly made a strong impression on Sabeti, who has expressed in interviews an earnest desire to not only be a great scientist but also a good person.

At MIT Sabeti started the Freshman Leadership Program regarding race relations, became the president of the class of 1997, played on the varsity tennis team, and served as a teaching assistant. Lawrence J. Vale, an associate professor of urban studies and planning who had known Sabeti since her sophomore year, served as her advisor with regard to her Rhodes Scholarship application. Vale told the MIT publication *The Tech* (10 Dec. 1996) that Sabeti has "a gentle confidence that never seems to cross into arrogance." Sabeti received her bachelor's degree in biology from MIT in 1997. But rather than going immediately to medical school, she decided to take a year off, and she applied to various programs. Sabeti was accepted as a Rhodes Scholar to the University of Oxford in England, which was a three-year program. She decided to take the scholarship and attend medical school later than initially planned. This decision ultimately created the foundation for her love for research.

A RHODES SCHOLARSHIP AND RESEARCH

Sabeti spent three years at the University of Oxford researching infectious diseases, their history and evolution, and the ways in which a disease's evolution impacts its present-day infectious manifestation. As reported by Mnookin, Sabeti "wanted to use the makeup of neighborhoods of genes (called haplotypes) to determine if a specific gene variation (called an allele) . . . had recently come to prominence . . . because it conferred an evolutionary advantage." To determine this, Sabeti used "genetic recombination—the breaking and rejoining of DNA strands—as a kind of clock to measure how long ago a given mutation had swept through a population." Mnookin referred to Sabeti's approach as "radical" with good reason; whereas nearly all research scientists were using "existing tools to analyze new data," Sabeti sought to create new tools to analyze data that was already available.

Her deep knowledge and love of math was undeniably an asset in her endeavor, but she still faced an uphill battle at Oxford in the actual challenges in her pursuit of her research and in convincing her colleagues and professors that her theories were worthy of pursuit and could be of value. Sabeti received her doctorate degree in evolutionary genetics in 2002 from the University of Oxford.

MEDICAL SCHOOL AND GENE RESEARCH

Following graduation from Oxford, Sabeti moved to Boston, Massachusetts, to attend medical school at Harvard University, where she continued her research. Mnookin describes a significant event in 2002 when late one night Sabeti "plugged a large data set related to the *DC40L*

gene, which she'd already linked to malaria resistance, into an algorithm she'd developed and watched results showing it was associated with a common haplotype—indicating it had recently been selected for." This meant that Sabeti had created an algorithm that would allow researchers and scientists to identify evidence of natural selection in the human genome. This finding helped launch Sabeti's research career to even greater heights. Late in 2002, she was the lead author of a paper in *Nature* titled "Detecting Recent Positive Selection in the Human Genome from Haplotype Structure." Sabeti graduated summa cum laude from the Harvard Medical School in 2006, becoming only the third woman in the medical school's history to graduate with such a high honor.

While at Harvard, Sabeti joined the Broad Institute, which was cofounded in 2003 by Harvard University and MIT and was headed by Sabeti's former MIT mentor and advisor Eric Lander. Sabeti went on to become a senior associate member of the institute in 2008 and also became an assistant professor at Harvard University that year. In 2012 Sabeti was promoted to associate professor of organismic and evolutionary biology.

Mnookin explains that Sabeti's next published paper in *Nature* appeared in 2007, and she was once again lead author. The paper, titled "Genome-Wide Detection and Characterization of Positive Selection in Human Populations," gave three examples of how "genes involved in a common biological process underwent selection in the same population." One pair of genes was involved in how Asians developed hair follicles; another pair had to do with European skin pigmentation; and the third pair had to do with the susceptibility of West Africans to getting infected by the deadly Lassa virus.

INFECTIOUS DISEASES RESEARCH

Sabeti has continued to research various prominent and deadly infectious diseases, despite the myriad challenges that such research presents. In 2012, for example, she coauthored a research paper for *Science*, titled "Epidemiology: Emerging Disease or Diagnosis?" The paper was controversial because it argued that infectious diseases such as Lassa and Ebola may not be new, but that scientists had only recently discovered them and the viruses had previously been overlooked, undetected, or thought to be something else. This presented the scientific community with a radically new evolutionary context with which to see the development of those infectious diseases.

In 2014 the world experienced the largest Ebola outbreak in recorded history, with more than 8,700 deaths and approximately 11,800 laboratory-confirmed cases since the outbreak started in late December 2013. According to the website of the US National Institutes of Health (29 Aug. 2014), Sabeti and her colleagues "discovered a number of mutations that arose as the outbreak spread. Some of these mutations, termed nonsynonymous mutations, alter the biological state of the virus and may allow it to continually and rapidly adapt to human immune defenses as the outbreak continues. This feature points to the need for improved methods that will allow for close monitoring of changes in the viral genome and the impact on vaccine targets." This kind of monitoring could both allow scientists to discover the spread and evolution of the virus as well as create better detection methods and perhaps even new drugs or vaccines. Of course, the key challenge with developing new drugs and vaccines is to stay ahead of the virus, which, like all living things, evolves and adapts. As Sabeti explained to Gina Kolata for the *New York Times*, "any change [in a virus] is one change too many, and we should stop this thing as quickly as we can."

PERSONAL LIFE

Sabeti started a rock band when she was at Oxford in the early 2000s and began performing music live. She loved it so much that when she returned to the United States, she started another band called Thousand Days when she was in medical school at Harvard. The band's website describes the group as a "guitar-heavy" alternative rock trio influenced by the likes of Liz Phair, Belly, Hole, and Throwing Muses. Sabeti is the band's lead singer, bassist, and songwriter. The group released its fifth album, *Turkana Boy*, in February 2015.

In 2012, Sabeti married John Rinn, an assistant professor of stem cell and regenerative biology at Harvard University. He is also a senior associate member of the Broad Institute.

SUGGESTED READING

Fung, Carina. "Three from MIT Named Rhodes, Marshall Scholars." *The Tech*. The Tech, 10 Dec. 1996. Web. 15 Nov. 2015.

Kolata, Gina. "The Virus Detectives: Sifting Through Genes in Search of Answers on Ebola." *New York Times*. New York Times, 1 Dec. 2014. Web. 15 Nov. 2015.

Mnookin, Seth. "Pardis Sabeti, the Rollerblading Rock Star Scientist of Harvard." *Smithsonian*. Smithsonian Inst., Dec. 2012. Web. 15 Nov. 2015.

"Profile with Pardis Sabeti." *Rhodes Project*. Rhodes Project, 2013. Web. 15 Nov. 2015.

—*Dmitry Kiper*

Sunjeev Sahota

Born: 1981
Occupation: Author

Sunjeev Sahota is an award-winning British novelist. His 2015 book, *The Year of the Runaways*, was shortlisted for the prestigious Man Booker Prize. His first novel, *Ours Are the Streets* (2011), is about a British Pakistani suicide bomber, and *The Year of the Runaways* is about a group of illegal migrants from India. "If novels can do anything," he told Andrew McMillan for the *Independent* (25 Sept. 2015), "it is shining a light into that dark tunnel, faces, histories, stories." Sahota did not read a novel until he was eighteen years old, but he published his first in 2011, when he was nearly thirty. His rose to prominence quickly after that. Based on an excerpt from his second novel, Sahota appeared on the respected literary magazine *Granta*'s 2013 list of the twenty best young British novelists, and his inclusion on the 2015 Man Booker shortlist garnered him international attention.

EARLY LIFE AND EDUCATION

Sahota was born in Derby, England, in 1981. His grandparents came to England from Punjab, India, in 1966. Many members of his extended family still live in India, and Sahota visits once or twice a year. He told McMillan that he has always had "a foot in both cultures." Sahota's grandfather worked at an iron foundry and his father was a TV engineer in Derby, where Sahota grew up in a community of fellow Sikhs. The family moved to Chesterfield, where his parents

Roberto Ricciuti/GettyImages

opened a convenience shop, when Sahota was seven. The town was quite different from Derby, Sahota recalled to McMillan. He and his younger brother, he said, were "the only brown kids" in school. Already shy and withdrawn, Sahota described these years as a "lonely experience."

Unlike most lonely children who ultimately become writers, however, Sahota did not seek comfort in books. In school, he read drama and poetry but mostly enjoyed math. He did not read a novel until he was eighteen years old. "I was in the airport, going to India and I bought *Midnight's Children*," he recalled to a journalist for the *Yorkshire Post* (14 Jan. 2011), referring to British Indian novelist Salman Rushdie's 1981 postcolonial epic. "I suddenly discovered this whole new world. I realized there was this storytelling language that I hadn't ever seen or heard before."

Rushdie's classic novel was a gateway drug for Sahota, who became a voracious reader. After *Midnight's Children*, he devoured Arundhati Roy's *The God of Small Things*, which won the Man Booker Prize in 1997; *A Suitable Boy* (1993), Vikram Seth's massive tome about post-partition India; and *The Remains of the Day* (1989), Kazuo Ishiguro's moving tale about an English butler after World War II. "It was like I was making up for lost time—not that I had to catch up, but it was as though I couldn't quite believe this world of storytelling I had found and I wanted to get as much of it down me as I possibly could," Sahota recalled in his interview for the *Yorkshire Post*.

Despite his growing interest in books, Sahota elected to study mathematics at Imperial College in London, though he continued to read about four novels a week. After graduation, he moved back to Chesterfield to be closer to his family. He took a job with an insurance agency and then a finance firm, both in Leeds. Sahota had always considered writing a novel in a distant way, but he set to work in earnest after Islamist terrorists launched an attack in London on July 7, 2005, killing fifty-two people and injuring approximately seven hundred more.

OURS ARE THE STREETS

When Sahota heard that one of the suicide bombers in the attack was from Leeds, he thought about his own experience growing up as a South Asian person in England and wondered what could make someone with a background similar to his own commit such a heinous crime. In 2006, he began writing a book about a young Muslim man, the son of immigrant parents, named Imtiaz Raina in an effort to explore that question. Sahota was cautious about his project, constantly worrying about being interrupted as he wrote in the upstairs bedroom of his family home in Chesterfield. "Being brought up in

the British Sikh community where shame and honor play such a big role and you don't air your dirty laundry, I felt I was exposing a lot, which is probably why I wanted to write it quite privately," he told Susanna Rustin for the *Guardian* (12 Dec. 2015).

Sahota went through five or six drafts of the novel over the course of about three or four years. *Ours Are the Streets* was published by Picador in 2011. The novel is written in the form of a journal that Raina hopes his wife and daughter will find when he is dead. Raina grew up in Britain, the son of Pakistani immigrants, but always felt at odds with the country of his birth. When he travels back to Pakistan after his father's death, his newfound sense of belonging leads to his radicalization and a plan to bomb a Sheffield shopping center. Sahota wanted to delve into Raina's life rather than merely explore his politics.

Our Are the Streets was generally well received. Arifa Akbar, in a review of the novel for the *Independent* (6 Jan. 2011), wrote that the book exhibited "great literary promise." Akbar remarked, "While Imtiaz is politicized, the book never takes on the angry, pedagogic tone of a newspaper column. It is a sad, nuanced, psychological meditation of the road to a fanaticism that resembles mental disorder." Other reviewers were positive but less enthusiastic, and one criticized Sahota's prose as that of a green writer, unsuccessfully mining his material for poetic imagery. Sahota continued to work in finance, writing his second novel on nights and weekends. In 2013, an excerpt of that novel earned him a coveted spot on *Granta*'s list of the twenty best young British novelists. One of the panelists, a veteran of the list himself, was none other than Sahota's literary hero Salman Rushdie. "I read this piece without knowing its title or the writer's name (both Top Secret at the time) but the talent couldn't be redacted," Rushdie wrote for the magazine (15 Apr. 2013). "There it is on every page, strong, fresh, and true. I look forward to reading more."

THE YEAR OF THE RUNAWAYS

Rushdie's encouragement came at the perfect time: Sahota had recently quit his job to write full time and his wife had just given birth to their first child. Sahota finished his second novel, *The Year of the Runaways*, and saw it published in 2015. The book takes place in 2003 and follows thirteen young Indian migrants living in England illegally. "There is a sizeable British Asian community in the UK that leads hidden lives," Sahota told Paromita Chakrabarti for the *Indian Express* (11 Aug. 2013). "It's a world that I am aware of and that interests me. More than the political questions of right and wrong, I am concerned about the interior lives of these characters."

One of the men in the novel, Randeep, is the son of an Indian bureaucrat and has a marriage visa. Another, Tarlochan, is a former rickshaw driver and member of the "untouchable" caste. Old prejudices surface in the men's new home, but they must rely on one another to get by. Sahota was more purposeful in the execution of his second novel, using classic storytelling techniques to paint a sweeping portrait of the men and the times in which they live. *The Year of the Runaways* was widely celebrated. *Granta*'s former editor John Freeman said reading it was like reading Sahota's "ninth novel, it's such a huge leap forward," as quoted by Charlotte Higgins for the *Guardian* (15 Apr. 2013). Lucy Daniel, in a review for the *Telegraph* (20 Aug. 2015), wrote that the narrative, which travels backward in time, "unfurls with an enormous variety of characters; when it reaches India, the story seems to burst out of its own framework with incredible confidence. Without flights of fancy, neither sensationalizing nor preachy, its greatest asset is that it doesn't oversimplify."

The Year of the Runaways was shortlisted for the Man Booker Prize alongside Hanya Yanagihara's best-selling *A Little Life* and Nigerian American novelist Chigozie Obioma's *The Fishermen*, among others. (The prize ultimately went to *A Brief History of Seven Killings* by Jamaican author Marlon James.) In 2015 Sahota began working on his third novel. He told Rustin that the book is inspired by South American magical realism, as exemplified by classic authors such as Gabriel García Márquez and Jorge Luis Borges, as well as a story from his own family history. His great-grandmother was married to one of four brothers, but because she and the other wives were required to keep their heads down and their faces covered, she did not know which brother she was married to. "When I read fiction, I read to understand the world," Sahota told Rustin. "But, for me, there's something about watching people go through their lives in this imagined space that enables me to go through life in a better way."

PERSONAL LIFE

Sahota, his wife, and their two children live in Sheffield, where his first two novels are set.

SUGGESTED READING

Akbar, Arifa. Rev. of *Ours Are the Streets*, by Sunjeev Sahota. *Independent*. Independent.co.uk, 6 Jan. 2011. Web. 10 Jan. 2016.

Chakrabarti, Paromita. "Sunjeev Sahota: The Accidental Author." *Indian Express*. Indian Express, 12 Aug. 2013. Web. 10 Jan. 2016.

Daniel, Lucy. Rev. of *The Year of the Runaways*, by Sunjeev Sahota. *Telegraph*. Telegraph Media Group, 20 Aug. 2015. Web. 10 Jan. 2016.

McMillan, Andrew. "Sunjeev Sahota Interview: Rise and Rise of the Man Booker Shortlisted Author." *Independent*. Independent.co.uk, 25 Sept. 2015. Web. 10 Jan. 2016.

Rushdie, Salman. "Salman Rushdie on Sunjeev Sahota." *Granta*. Granta, 15 Apr. 2013. Web. 10 Jan. 2016.

Rustin, Susanna. "Sunjeev Sahota: 'I Don't See Why I Should Benefit from Migration When Other People Don't.'" *Guardian*. Guardian News and Media, 12 Dec. 2015. Web. 10 Jan. 2016.

Sahota, Sunjeev. "Student of Maths Makes It All Add Up." Interview. *Yorkshire Post*. Johnston, 14 Jan. 2011. Web. 10 Jan. 2016.

—*Molly Hagan*

Ryuichi Sakamoto

Born: January 17, 1952
Occupation: Musician, composer

Ryuichi Sakamoto is perhaps one of the most influential musicians of the late twentieth century. One of the founding members of the band Yellow Magic Orchestra, he first came to prominence with that group in the late 1970s, winning over listeners both in his native Japan and abroad with his innovative take on electronic music. His three-decade solo career further cemented his place as a major figure in music history. Perhaps most far-reaching, however, has been Sakamoto's work as a composer of film scores. Having begun his career in that field with his score for the 1983 film *Merry Christmas, Mr. Lawrence*, he gained significant notice for his work on the score for 1987's *The Last Emperor*, for which he won an Academy Award. For a musician as creatively independent as Sakamoto, the need to adhere to the wishes and requirements of a film's creator may seem uncharacteristically limiting. However, he tends to view the process of working on a film score as an opportunity to accomplish things his own personal music cannot. "Working on the film is like a journey to an unknown place," he told Ruth Saxelby for *Fader* (4 Dec. 2015). "Each film is a big journey. And I cannot experience that or get that doing my own thing."

EARLY LIFE AND EDUCATION

Ryuichi Sakamoto was born in Tokyo, Japan, on January 17, 1952. His father worked as an editor, while his mother designed women's hats. A music lover from very early in life, he was introduced to a wide range of music by his uncle,

Joi Ito/Flickr/CC BY 2.0/Wikimedia Commons

who was an avid music listener and record collector. Sakamoto's uncle allowed the young music aficionado to borrow his records and also play his piano, an instrument that Sakamoto began studying at the age of three. Sakamoto initially developed a deep interest in European classical music by composers such as Johann Sebastian Bach. His early introduction to and experiences with music greatly shaped the ways in which he came to consider music later in life. "I always think about music horizontally and vertically at the same time," he explained to Spike Carter for *Vanity Fair* (29 Dec. 2015). "Also, to me, it's very important the connections of harmony in time which is two-dimensional. Because similar to language, a meaning would be totally different if you change the syntax. The same thing happens in music."

As a teenager, Sakamoto expanded his musical knowledge and tastes, playing in jazz bands while attending high school in the Shinjuku neighborhood of Tokyo. He soon developed a fascination with electronic music and all things connected with it, including the synthesizers frequently used in the genre. For Sakamoto, electronic music and its computerized instruments represented a potential for innovation that he found lacking in many forms of modern Western music. After completing high school, Sakamoto enrolled in Tokyo University of the Arts with the goal of specializing in electronic music. His studies at the university introduced him to a variety of new musical influences and gave him access to instruments and equipment that were otherwise out of reach. "I was thrilled when I saw three big synthesizers were sitting in

the classroom," he told Carter. "A new kind of palette and color and system—that's what I was eager to get."

YELLOW MAGIC ORCHESTRA

After graduating from Tokyo university, Sakamoto began to pursue music professionally, finding work as a producer and a session musician. He soon partnered with fellow musicians Yukihiro Takahashi and Haruomi Hosono to form the band Yellow Magic Orchestra. Sakamoto played keyboards, provided supporting vocals, and composed a number of songs for the band, which specialized in electronic music. Yellow Magic Orchestra was heavily inspired by the music of Kraftwerk, a German group that had emerged onto the electronic scene at the beginning of the 1970s, and its members sought to emulate and build upon that group's use of electronic instruments and distinctive vocals.

Yellow Magic Orchestra released its first album, a self-titled record, in 1978. Though unorthodox, Sakamoto and his bandmates' music was well received by Japanese listeners, and they found significant popularity in their home country. The band's music was released in the United States and Europe as well, introducing even more listeners to the possibilities of electronic music. The increasingly global nature of the band's popularity enabled them to tour outside of their home country as well as within it. "Playing in London in 1979 was exciting," Sakamoto recalled to Alex Hoban for the *Guardian* (19 May 2009). "It was at the start of new wave, the transition period after punk, and there were a lot of radical, fashionable young people on the streets and in the venues. I still remember clearly a fashionable new wave couple in a club going to the dancefloor when they played one of my songs, 'The End of Asia.' I just thought, 'Wow! They are so fashionable and cool . . . but we were the ones that made them dance . . . so, wow, we must be really cool too!'"

Over the following decades, Yellow Magic Orchestra released numerous studio albums, including *Solid State Survivor* (1979) and *Technodelic* (1981), as well as various other releases. The band separated in 1984; however, Sakamoto and his bandmates continued to collaborate upon occasion. In 1993, Yellow Magic Orchestra essentially reunited to release the album *Technodon*, but because of issues related to the ownership of the band's name, they were unable to sell the album under their usual moniker. In addition to their 1993 reunion, Yellow Magic Orchestra has reunited to perform live at various special events. A highly influential band, the group is credited with making substantial contributions to the development of genres such as techno and synthpop.

SOLO WORK AND COLLABORATIONS

As a solo artist, Sakamoto has released more than forty individual works, including studio albums, live albums, video albums, and other recordings. He made his solo debut in 1978 with the album Thousand Knives. Released while he was still performing as part of Yellow Magic Orchestra, that album and several subsequent records, including B-2 Unit and Left Handed Dream, provided Sakamoto with the opportunity to explore musically on his own while remaining part of a popular group. After Yellow Magic Orchestra's separation in 1984, he remained a prolific artist, releasing some fifteen full-length studio albums, along with numerous other records, over the following three decades.

In addition to recording as a solo artist and a member of Yellow Magic Orchestra, Sakamoto soon gained a reputation as a talented collaborator who thrived when working alongside fellow musicians. He began his collaborative work early in his career, playing with other musicians as early as the late 1970s. During the next decades, Sakamoto flourished as a collaborator, working with a wide range of artists from both Japan and elsewhere. In 1982, he collaborated with Japanese rock musician Kiyoshiro Imawano on the hit song "Ikenai Rouge Magic," and that same year, he worked with English vocalist David Sylvian on the song "Bamboo Music." Sakamoto worked extensively with Sylvian over the next decades and also collaborated with noteworthy musicians such as Japanese singer-songwriter Akiko Yano, to whom he was married for a time, and American rocker Iggy Pop.

FILM WORK

While Sakamoto's solo work, collaborations, and tenure with Yellow Magic Orchestra brought him significant fame over the course of his career, he has perhaps reached his widest audience through his work as a composer of film scores. He began his career in that field in 1983 with the score for Merry Christmas, Mr. Lawrence, a drama about World War II prisoners of war that stars English musician David Bowie as well as Sakamoto himself. The film's music was well received by critics, and Sakamoto was nominated for several awards for his work, winning the 1984 British Academy of Film and Television Arts (BAFTA) Award for best score.

His successful first outing as a film composer led Sakamoto to complete more than fifty additional scores over the subsequent decades, at times working in collaboration with other musicians. For his score for 1987's The Last Emperor, he worked alongside Chinese composer Cong Su and American musician and composer David Byrne; the three received the Academy Award for best score for their work on the film. Other films featuring scores by Sakamoto include The

Sheltering Sky (1990), the anime film Appleseed (2004), and the documentary Metamorphosis (2013). For Sakamoto, the process of working on film scores is both taxing and incredibly rewarding. "Each time I work on a film, I say to myself, 'This is it. This is the end.' Because it is so stressful, it's like torture," he told Saxelby. "But, you know, I still do it. Because I cannot get the same excitement or challenge or inspiration by doing my solo albums, my own music."

THE REVENANT

Sakamoto took a step back from his career in 2014 due to serious health concerns, but he was drawn back into the field in 2015 when he was asked to compose the score for The Revenant, the latest film from critically acclaimed director Alejandro González Iñárritu. "Alejandro used two pieces of my music in [the 2006 film] Babel," Sakamoto told Christopher R. Weingarten for Rolling Stone (17 Dec. 2015) of his introduction to the director's work. "At that time I had a phone conversation with Alejandro. Didn't meet him, but the way he used my music in the end of the film was very, very good, very impressive. Cinematic. I was so moved." The two later met for the first time in 2010, when Sakamoto visited Los Angeles to perform.

When first approached to work on The Revenant, Sakamoto, who was undergoing cancer treatment at the time, was unsure whether he was up to the task. "But working for Alejandro was maybe a once in a life thing," he told Weingarten. "Maybe twice." Having agreed to work on the score, he collaborated with composers Alva Noto (the stage name of Carsten Nicolai) and Bryce Dessner to create the dramatic, powerful, "gigantic" sound Iñárritu requested. The task was a significant challenge, but Sakamoto was undaunted. "Challenging is good," he told Weingarten. "At this age, you know, you need a challenge." The Revenant earned significant critical acclaim upon its release in the winter of 2015, and Sakamoto was nominated for numerous awards for his work on the score, including the BAFTA and Golden Globe awards.

PERSONAL LIFE

In the summer of 2014, Sakamoto announced that he had been diagnosed with throat cancer. In light of that news, he canceled his scheduled projects and appearances for the immediate future, opting to focus his time and energy on his treatment. Although undergoing cancer treatment was far from a pleasant experience, Sakamoto took his time away from work as an opportunity to recharge, both personally and as an artist. "It's the closest I've come to death during my lifetime," he told James Hadfield for the Japan Times (31 Mar. 2016) following his return to work. "I feel differently since I came back from that place, compared to before. I want to capture the mood I have now, post-cancer, in my music."

Sakamoto has been married twice and has three children, one of whom, his daughter Miu, is a pop singer in Japan. He lives primarily in New York. A devoted activist, Sakamoto is particularly outspoken about issues such as environmentalism and copyright reform.

SUGGESTED READING

Hadfield, James. "Ryuichi Sakamoto Offers His Thoughts on Politics, Japan, and How His Music Will Change 'Post-Cancer.'" *Japan Times*. Japan Times, 31 Mar. 2016. Web. 13 May 2016.

Sakamoto, Ryuichi. "In Conversation with the All-Knowing Ryuichi Sakamoto." Interview by Ruth Saxelby. *Fader*. Fader, 4 Dec. 2015. Web. 13 May 2016.

Sakamoto, Ryuichi. "*The Revenant* Composer Ryuichi Sakamoto Explains His Process." Interview by Spike Carter. *Vanity Fair*. Condé Nast, 29 Dec. 2015. Web. 13 May. 2016.

Sakamoto, Ryuichi. "Ryuichi Sakamoto Details 'Gigantic' Score to 'Birdman' Director's 'The Revenant.'" Interview by Christopher R. Weingarten. *Rolling Stone*. Rolling Stone, 17 Dec. 2015. Web. 13 May. 2016.

Sakamoto, Ryuichi. "Turning Japanese: The Philosophy of Ryuichi Sakamoto." Interview by Alex Hoban. *Guardian*. Guardian News and Media, 19 May 2009. Web. 13 May 2016.

SELECTED WORKS

Yellow Magic Orchestra, 1978; *Thousand Knives*, 1978; *Solid State Survivor*, 1979; *B-2 Unit*, 1980; *Technodelic*, 1981; *Merry Christmas, Mr. Lawrence*, 1983; *The Last Emperor,*1987; *Technodon*, 1993; *The Revenant*, 2015   —Joy Crelin

---

Catherine Samba-Panza

Born: June 26, 1954
Occupation: President of the Central African Republic

Catherine Samba-Panza, a former insurance broker and mayor of the city of Bangui, was elected interim president of the Central African Republic (CAR) in January 2014 during one of the most turbulent periods in the country's history. The CAR, a country in Africa's interior, is rich in natural resources such as diamonds, gold, oil, and uranium, but its citizens are extremely poor; its neighbors—Sudan and South Sudan among them—are mired in violent conflict, and since 2013, the CAR has been embroiled in its own bloody sectarian war. The CAR was a French colony called Oubangui-Chari before it gained its independence in 1960. An early president,

U.S. Department of State from United States/Wikimedia Commons

Jean Bedél Bokassa, a French war hero who enjoyed the support of the country's former colonial overlords, crowned himself emperor, and was finally deposed in 1979, after reportedly murdering schoolchildren for refusing to wear uniforms manufactured by his wife's clothing company.

The CAR suffered through several decades of dictators, including François Bozizé, who came to power in 2003 through a military coup. Bozizé, a Christian, sought support from the country's Muslim population, promising power to the minority group but delivering disenfranchisement and imprisonment. In response, rebels known as the Union of Democratic Forces Coalition (UFDR) formed a militia to overthrow Bozizé, leading to the three-year Bush War in 2004. The Bush War ended in a peace treaty in 2007, but discontent with Bozizé's leadership remained, and in 2012 six thousand men, almost all Muslim, formed a rebel group called the Seleka, meaning "alliance." The Seleka overran Bangui in March 2013 and installed the CAR's first Muslim president, Michel Djotodia. But the group continued to kill and pillage, even as Djotodia tried to disband them.

Christians and Muslims had coexisted peacefully in the region for years, but the violent Seleka unearthed buried resentments. Christians formed a counter rebel group called the antibalaka—the name derives from a combination of local terms meaning "anti-machete" and "anti-AK"—to fight the Seleka, and in December 2013, they entered Bangui. France sent troops to help quell the fighting, but the deployment was not large enough to have any significant effect in the conflict. Bent on vengeance, the antibalaka began a campaign to exterminate all of the Muslims in the CAR. As the balance of power shifted once again, Seleka president Djotodia stepped down and went into exile. Interim parliamentarians elected Samba-Panza to take his place. Samba-Panza, who is Christian, worked hard to reach out to Muslim citizens and bring peace through unity. "I am the president of all Central Africans, without exception," she said in her inaugural speech, as quoted by Andrew Katz for *Time* (23 Jan. 2014). Samba-Panza was meant to serve only one year as interim president, but ongoing violence forced the CAR to postpone the election to replace her until late 2015. By law, interim presidents are not allowed to run for permanent office.

EARLY LIFE AND EDUCATION

Samba-Panza was born in Fort Lamy (now N'Djamena) in the neighboring country of Chad on June 26, 1954. Her father was Cameroonian, and her mother was from the CAR. Samba-Panza moved to the CAR in 1972, when she was eighteen years old. She was active in women's rights groups and campaigned against female genital mutilation. "It's important to know your rights and to want to be able to defend them so your rights are respected," she told David Smith for the *Observer* (26 Jan. 2014). "The majority of my sisters and daughters in the Central African Republic don't know their rights, so they can't defend them. But we who know our rights can help them . . . the battle is always to promote and protect the rights of women. When they are victims of violence, notably sexual violence, it was a battle I always led." Samba-Panza studied law at the University of Panthéon-Assas in Paris, and practiced corporate law upon returning to the CAR. She also worked as an insurance broker.

POLITICAL ASCENSION

Samba-Panza entered politics in 2003 and was elected mayor of Bangui, the largest city in the CAR as well as its capital, in June 2013. Samba-Panza was a popular mayor, and developed a reputation, according to several sources, for being "incorruptible." With experience in conflict mediation and no ties to either the Seleka or the antibalaka, Samba-Panza seemed an ideal leader.

In December 2013 over one thousand people were killed in Bangui over the course of several days. By then, fighting between the antibalaka and the remaining Seleka forces had driven over one million people out of their homes; one hundred thousand of them were living in the Bangui airport, under the protection of French soldiers. Muslim president Djotodia was forced to step down on January 10, 2014, and an interim parliamentary body called the National Transitional Council (NTC) voted among seven candidates to replace him. Samba-Panza won in the second round of voting, earning seventy-five votes to her closest competitor Desire Kolingba's fifty-three. (Kolingba is the son of a former president.)

Samba-Panza was sworn in as interim president on January 23, 2014. Samba-Panza touted her gender, and her role as a mother, as an important component of her leadership. Her supporters, who dubbed her "Mother Courage" after the famous character from Bertolt Brecht's 1939 antiwar play, *Mother Courage and Her Children*, agreed. "Everything we have been through has been the fault of men," a community organizer named Marie-Louise Yakemba told Adam Nossiter for the *New York Times* (20 Jan. 2014). "We think that with a woman, there is at least a ray of hope." Generally speaking, the CAR is not an unusually progressive country when it comes to gender. In fact, nearly 60 percent of women in the CAR enter into forced marriages at a young age. But Minna Salami, a feminist commentator on Africa, told Smith that Samba-Panza's election fit a familiar pattern. "It is historically and globally the case that women are more prone to access institutions traditionally reserved for men during crises, for example the second world war, pan-African independence struggles, Burma, Liberia," she said. Samba-Panza specifically looked to Ellen Johnson Sirleaf, the woman who led Liberia out of civil war and was later awarded the Nobel Peace Prize, for inspiration.

INTERIM PRESIDENCY

On February 5 Samba-Panza addressed members of the newly reformed army assembled in Bangui, referring to the warring rebel factions as "my children" and calling for an end to violence. Not ten minutes after her speech ended, however, the army broke ranks to kill a man suspected of being a Seleka infiltrator, dragging his body through the streets before dismembering it and setting it on fire.

In addition to the daily violence, at the time of Samba-Panza's election approximately 90 percent of the country's 4.6 million citizens were underfed, eating only one meal a day. Schools were closed, and security services were provided by an inadequate number of international troops. "The state has essentially collapsed politically, legally, economically," Evan Cinq-Mars, a research analyst at the Global Centre for the Responsibility to Protect, told Katz. In a statement on January 20, 2014, UN Secretary General Ban Ki-Moon declared that the CAR was "in free fall." A few weeks later, Samba-Panza announced a plan to stop the fighting, and called on Europe to send soldiers to help the 1,600

French troops and nearly 5,000 African troops from various countries already in the CAR. Despite extra forces and financial aid, violence spread throughout the country. In May the government held talks with the Seleka, but no peace agreement emerged. Soon after that, in a soccer game between young Christians and Muslims, the antibalaka murdered three Muslim players. The killings spawned more killings at a Christian church; when Samba-Panza declared a national period of mourning for the people massacred at the church, Muslim citizens protested, accusing her of being sympathetic to the antibalaka. She denied this, though other members of the government were candid about their hatred for the Seleka. In July, Samba-Panza brokered a short-lived peace agreement, and in August, she fired her cabinet and appointed the country's first Muslim prime minister.

Elections to replace Samba-Panza and the interim government were scheduled for February 2015, though by fall 2014 Samba-Panza had already publicly commented that that date was likely unrealistic. Sure enough, the election was postponed until October 2015. In September, a new wave of violence engulfed Bangui. Samba-Panza, who was in New York meeting with UN officials and potential humanitarian donors, cut her trip short to return to the capital and address the crisis. Elections were postponed again. In late November, Pope Francis visited Bangui, pleading peace, and finally, on December 30, 2015, the first round of voting to elect a new president commenced. Nearly all of the country's 1.8 million registered voters journeyed to the polls to cast their vote. Most businesses were closed for the occasion, which was largely peaceful. "Many thought this day, this vote would not be possible for security and organizational reasons," Samba-Panza said, as quoted in an article for the *New Zealand Herald* (31 Dec. 2015). "But, you see, we are all voting in dignity and peace and I am proud." Of the thirty candidates running, there was no clear winner, and a second round of voting was scheduled for January 31, 2016.

PERSONAL LIFE

Samba-Panza is married to Cyriaque Samba-Panza, a former CAR politician. Together they have three children, two of whom reportedly live in France.

SUGGESTED READING

Anderson, Jon Lee. "The Mission." *New Yorker*. Condé Nast, 20 Oct. 2014. Web. 7 Jan. 2016.

Katz, Andrew. "Meet Catherine Samba-Panza, Central African Republic's New Interim President." *Time*. Time, 23 Jan. 2014. Web. 7 Jan. 2016.

Nossiter, Adam. "Woman Chosen to Lead Central African Republic Out of Mayhem." *New York Times*. New York Times, 20 Jan. 2014. Web. 7 Jan. 2016.

Smith, David. "After the Men Failed, 'Mother Courage' Fights to Bring Peace to Her Nation in Crisis: The Central African Republic's New President, Catherine Samba-Panza, Has Just a Year to Avert Civil War." *Observer* 26 Jan. 2014: 30. Print.

"Voters in Central African Republic Hoping for Stability." *New Zealand Herald*. NZME, 31 Dec. 2015. Web. 12 Jan. 2016.

—*Molly Hagan*

Romeo Santos

Born: July 21, 1981
Occupation: Singer

Romeo Santos is a Dominican American pop star. Formerly a member of the group Aventura, the Bronx-born Santos embarked on a solo career in 2011, leading many to dub him the king of bachata. Bachata is a percussive, guitar-driven form of Dominican music. Like the blues, the lyrics of bachata songs often deal with loneliness and heartache. Santos, who is bilingual, sings in Spanish but has collaborated with a number of English-speaking stars, including Lil Wayne, Nicki Minaj, Usher, and Drake. With Aventura he also collaborated with rappers Akon and Ludacris.

His bachata is one that could be described as classically New York, with elements of American hip-hop and R&B. Santos has achieved the unusual feat of becoming a global phenomenon despite being virtually unknown to non-Spanish-speaking Americans. The video for his 2013 single "Propuesta Indecente" ("Indecent Proposal"), has been viewed more than one billion times on YouTube; in Argentina, it was the most-watched video of the decade. He has sold out concerts at Madison Square Garden and Yankee Stadium (twice)—a feat Pink Floyd could not accomplish and one that Jay-Z pulled off only with the help of Justin Timberlake and Eminem. He made his acting debut in the franchise film *Furious 7* (2015) and lent his voice to the animated film *Angry Birds* (2016). In 2016, he teamed up with rapper Jay-Z to launch an arm of the mogul's Roc Nation entertainment company called Roc Nation Latino.

EARLY LIFE AND BACHATA MUSIC

Anthony Santos was born in the Bronx borough of New York City on July 21, 1981. His father, who is Dominican, worked in construction and

John Parra/WireImage/Getty Images

drove a cab. His mother is Puerto Rican. Santos attended PS 50 and Morris High School. When he was thirteen, he joined the church choir and began to hone his distinctive tenor voice and falsetto. He enlisted his cousin Henry Santos Jeter to form a band in 1993. The band, Los Tinellers or "Teenagers," also included two brothers, guitarist Lenny Santos and bassist and rapper Max Santos. Los Tinellers amassed a loyal, predominantly Dominican American, following playing a more traditional form of bachata at clubs, and sometimes corner delis, in New York and New Jersey. As the crowds got bigger, the group began to hire security guards. One guard, a New York City police officer named Johnny Marines, was particularly loyal to the band—so much so that Santos eventually made him their manager. Marines supposedly continued to work both jobs as the band became increasingly popular, sometimes making arrests while trying to book concert venues over the phone. Marines remains Santos's agent today.

In 1995, Los Tinellers released a self-produced bachata album called *Trampa de amor* (Love trap). Bachata, Isabela Raygoza explained for *Vice*'s music blog *Noisey* (8 Oct. 2015), was long considered the less loved cousin of the more popular merengue music. Once known as *amargue*, or "bitter music," bachata music is often about love and heartache but also the lives of ordinary people, much like American country music. In the Dominican Republic, the genre was considered the sound of the lower classes. Bachata stars such as Blas Durán and Antony Santos reoriented the genre in the late 1980s with the inclusion of electric guitars and

other pop influences. The rise in popularity also changed how the genre was culturally perceived. These bachata artists did not go unnoticed by Santos. "One day my father brings a cassette. He's showing me this, and he's like, 'Look at this guy, his name is Anthony Santos, like you," Santos recalled to Jasmine Garsd for NPR's *Weekend Edition* (18 Nov. 2011). "I popped it on and started hearing the songs, the music, and I was like, 'Wow, this sounds great.'" Santos went out and found all of the Antony Santos music he could, and before long he was performing bachata himself.

AVENTURA

In 1999, Los Tinellers signed with the indie label Premium Latin, who changed the group's name to Aventura (Spanish for "adventure"). They released their first album as Aventura, *Generation Next*, the same year. On their next album, *We Broke the Rules* (2002), Aventura experimented with the traditional bachata format. The stars of the previous generation, including Blas Durán and Antony Santos, may have added electric guitars to the genre, but Aventura pushed the boundaries of the genre further. According to Isabela Raygoza, the band added "flirtatious R&B vocals and a New York hip-hop attitude." With the band's sound and their boyish good looks, some considered Aventura the Latin answer to popular American boy bands such as *NSYNC. Aventura's fame went global after the group's 2002 single "Obsession," penned by Santos, became a surprise number-one hit in Europe.

As the front man of Aventura, the handsome Santos quickly became known for his amorous onstage persona and acquired the nickname Romeo. The band's 2007 live album, *Kings of Bachata*, was the second-best-selling Latin record of the year, and their 2009 album *The Last*—the title referred to Aventura's last record with Premium Latin, but it would also be their last album as a foursome—was the top-selling Latin album of that year. *The Last*, which continued the band's push to integrate bachata with more mainstream pop and hip-hop, was also a good indication of the direction Santos would pursue in his solo career. One single, "All Up 2 You," features the rap artist Akon and the reggaetón duo Wisin & Yandel. Another dance song on the record, "Spanish Fly," features Ludacris and a cameo from Wyclef Jean.

By 2009 Aventura had sold more than 1.7 million albums in the United States. They went on to perform four sold-out concerts at Madison Square Garden in 2010. Rumors surfaced that Santos wanted to leave the group, and according to Garsd, the breakup that came soon after was public and messy. "Santos claimed he carried the burden of the workload in Aventura," Garsd wrote. "His band members accused him of letting fame go to his head."

SOLO CAREER

Santos did not wait long to embark on his solo career; he released his first solo album, *Formula, Volume 1*, on Sony Latin in November 2011. Santos celebrated the success of *Formula, Volume 1* with three sold-out concert dates at Madison Square Garden in February 2012. The album peaked at number nine on the Billboard 200 chart and garnered the number-one singles "You" and "Promise," featuring Usher. Other guests on the album included Pitbull on the song "Aleluya" and Lil Wayne on the rare all-English song "All Aboard."

Santos has cited Latin stars such as Shakira, Marc Anthony, and Enrique Iglesias as influences but rejects their collective road to crossover mainstream English-language pop. When asked why, he told Larry Rohter for the *New York Times* (10 July 2014), "I believe in my culture, and I believe in my genre, because they are beautiful." Rohter went on to call Santos "a beacon for reverse crossover," attracting popular English-speaking artists to Latin audiences, not the other way around. He told Garsd that his goal was "for them to cross over into my world." On his 2014 album, *Formula, Volume 2*, both Drake and Nicki Minaj sang in Spanish. He also bridges a divide among Spanish speakers themselves, finding his style equally popular among those of Caribbean descent and Mexican and Central American descent. *Formula, Volume 2* was just as popular as its predecessor but also pushed Santos to new heights musically with new influences from varied genres. It includes a salsa song featuring Marc Anthony and a song called "Necio" (Foolish) featuring Latin legend Carlos Santana. The song "No Tiene La Culpa" (Not to blame) tells the story of a young man who is bullied for being gay. It led to rumors that Santos is gay, which the singer has denied.

Santos developed his image as a sex symbol as a member of Aventura and continues to hone that image as a solo artist. According to Jon Caramanica, who reviewed Santos's sold-out 2014 Yankee Stadium performance for the *New York Times* (13 July 2014), Santos is an "old pro" at performative seduction. Describing one successful and recurring bit, Caramanica wrote: "There will be a woman of ample proportions, and Mr. Santos will sing 'Un Beso' to her, then kiss her, then encourage her to let her hands roam free on his body. There will be admonishments to the men in the audience about how they aren't satisfying their women. There will be a microphone stand, parts of the stage and even the air itself that spend long stretches of time on the receiving end of Mr. Santos's gyrating pelvis."

Santos surprised the crowd at that same performance in 2014 by bringing out his old Aventura bandmates. In December 2015, Santos and Aventura announced that they would reunite to play twenty shows in the Washington Heights neighborhood of Manhattan in February 2016. Tickets for the shows sold out within hours. In a review of the first show, Krystyna Chavez wrote for *Billboard* (5 Feb. 2016) that the entire audience, most of them diehard fans, sang along "to hit after hit as if they had rehearsed."

PERSONAL LIFE

When Santos was twenty, his then-girlfriend became pregnant. At first Santos panicked. His career was just beginning to take off and he did not feel ready to be a father. Today, Santos is close with his teenage son, Alex, who has changed the singer's outlook on life. He has stated that as he has grown older, his son has helped to keep him focused and provided perspective about what is important. In all other regards, Santos keeps quiet about his personal life.

SUGGESTED READING

Caramanica, Jon. "The House That Romeo Built." *New York Times*. New York Times, 13 July 2014. Web. 17 July 2016.

Chavez, Krystyna. "Aventura Makes Bachateros & Washington Heights Proud at NYC Concert: Live Review." *Billboard*. Billboard, 5 Feb. 2016. Web. 17 July 2016.

Garsd, Jasmine. "Romeo Santos: Taking Bachata Mainstream." *Weekend Edition*. NPR, 18 Nov. 2011. Web. 15 July 2016.

Raygoza, Isabela. "Romeo Santos Da Gawd: How the King of Bachata Has Become a Crossover Pop Icon on His Own Terms." *Noisey*. Vice Media, 8 Oct. 2015. Web. 15 July 2016.

Rohter, Larry. "In the Language of Romance, Romeo Santos is a True Superstar." *New York Times*. New York Times, 10 July 2014. Web. 15 July 2016.

"Romeo Santos." *Sony Music Latin*. Sony Music, 2013. Web. 21 July 2016.

SELECTED WORKS

The Last (with Aventura), 2009; *Formula, Volume 1*, 2011; *Formula, Volume 2*, 2014

—*Molly Hagan*

Peter Sarsgaard

Born: March 7, 1971
Occupation: Actor

"Peter Sarsgaard always looks as if he has a secret. There's something in his almond-shaped eyes—a mix of withheld information, curiosity, and latent volatility," Lynn Hirschberg wrote for the *New York Times* (13 Nov. 2005). "There's a charged stillness about Sarsgaard's presence; even before he speaks, he communicates a kind of subterranean emotional range that commands interest."

Many of the characters Sarsgaard plays are murderers, rapists, and pimps. When told by Emine Saner for the *Guardian* (9 Aug. 2013) that she felt he brought a large measure of humanity to even the most reprehensible character, he replied, "It's not a matter of sympathy. I've always just been curious about people." He expanded on this, and on being repeatedly cast in bad-guy roles, to Dave Itzkoff for the *New York Times* (29 May 2013), "I'm an actor working and everybody's got their thing they do. . . . I'd rather be the guy in the black hat than the guy in the white hat any day."

Sarsgaard is known for such critically acclaimed films as *Boys Don't Cry* (1999), *Shattered Glass* (2003), *Garden State* (2004), *Kinsey* (2004), *The Dying Gaul* (2005), *Jarhead* (2005), *An Education* (2009), *Lovelace* (2013), and *Blue Jasmine* (2013). He has also made his mark in several television series, including *The Killing* (2013) and *The Slap* (2015).

EARLY YEARS AND EDUCATION

Peter Sarsgaard was born on March 7, 1971, at Scott Air Force Base, in Illinois, to the former Judy Lea Reinhardt and John Dale Sarsgaard, an Air Force engineer. The family moved frequently because of John's military career; Sarsgaard had already lived in a dozen different places by the time he entered college.

As a child, Sarsgaard was an avid soccer player. At the age of seven, he began taking ballet, believing that it would help him develop balance and strength. He has admitted to journalists that he was a mischievous child; at about age ten, he once went door-to-door in his neighborhood on the pretense of collecting money to support the local zoo, but then kept all the funds he raised.

Sarsgaard received a strict Catholic education at an all-boys Jesuit high school in Connecticut, which he has stated provided the foundation for his ability to act, beginning with learning about and becoming fascinated by transubstantiation: the process through which the bread and the wine offered during the sacrament of the Eucharist at a Catholic mass become the body and blood of Jesus Christ. He described it

to Matthew Marden and Rob Tannenbaum for *Details* (3 Apr. 2015) as "a kind of magic," and believing in it helps him with his craft because "if I'm acting and someone says, 'There's a giant star coming at you, and it speaks to you,' I can find a way to do that."

High school was also where he first became interested in movies, "The priests would screen films after school," Sarsgaard recalled to Hirschberg. "Some really racy Italian cinema, like Fellini." Explaining how his faith continues to inform his acting, he said, "You're supposed to love your enemy. That really impressed me as a kid, and it has helped me as an actor. I don't believe there are bad people. Just people who do bad things . . . [and] I view the characters I play as part of my religious upbringing. To abandon curiosity in all personalities, good or bad, is to give up hope in humanity."

Sarsgaard attended Bard College in upstate New York for two years before transferring to Washington University in St. Louis, Missouri, where he studied literature and history and was a member of the school's soccer team until he suffered several concussions during matches. Quitting the team, he turned instead to acting and later trained at a St. Louis–based satellite of the New York's Actors Studio. He also cofounded a campus improvisational group called Mama's Pot Roast.

EARLY CAREER

After graduating from college in 1993, Sarsgaard moved to New York with Malerie Marder, a classmate whom he later married. Trying to forge an acting career, he won a handful of small stage roles and a part in an episode of *Law & Order*. In 1995 he appeared in a brief flashback scene in *Dead Man Walking*, which starred Sean Penn as a murderer on death row. "In my first scene in any movie ever," Sarsgaard recalled to Hirschberg, "Sean Penn dragged me out to a swamp, threw me down in the mud, raped and killed me and my girlfriend. . . . And that was my big break." Soon after that, he and Marder moved to New Haven, Connecticut, so that she could earn a graduate degree in photography, and they later moved to Los Angeles. Never fully happy there, Sarsgaard returned to New York when his marriage to Marder broke up.

"I wasn't interested in getting stuck in any one thing, like a TV series," he explained to Hirschberg. "I never went out for commercials or long-running plays. I always knew what I didn't want." Sarsgaard soon found himself with the variety of acting roles he desired. In 1997 and 1998 he appeared in an episode of the television series *New York Undercover* and in the television movie *Subway Stories: Tales from the Underground*. He also appeared in a string of films, including *The Man in the Iron Mask*, *Another Day in Paradise*, *Desert Blue*, and *Minor Details*. He gained increased attention in the independent 1999 film *Boys Don't Cry*, which starred Hilary Swank as a young man named Brandon Teena whose friends (one of whom is portrayed by Sarsgaard) beat, rape, and murder him when they discover he is transgender.

STEADY FILM WORK

The next few years saw Sarsgaard appearing regularly in films, and in 2003 he won the most acclaim of his career to-date when he appeared in *Shattered Glass*, the story of a journalist who is discovered to be falsifying stories. Sarsgaard played the disgraced writer's editor, and his strong, multilayered performance was praised by several critics. His next big-screen efforts began to cement his reputation for portraying sometimes dark and troubled characters. In 2004 he appeared in *Garden State* as a drug-addled gravedigger and in *Kinsey* as Clyde Martin, an assistant to the 1940s sex researcher Alfred Kinsey (played by Liam Neeson). Although critics widely praised both the film and Sarsgaard's nuanced performance, much of the media attention centered on the fact that he appeared fully nude from a frontal angle and engaged in a kiss with Neeson's title character.

Sarsgaard next had a lead role in the independent film *The Dying Gaul* (2005), in which he played a screenwriter lured into a sexual relationship with a film executive and his wife. Critics agreed that it was among the finest acting of his career, but their praise became even more effusive when *Jarhead* (2005) was released.

Sarsgaard portrays Alan Troy, a US Marine serving in the Gulf War and the best friend and spotter for Anthony Swofford (Jake Gyllenhaal), a Marine sniper. "Unlike most of the actors in the film, I know this world," he asserted to Hirschberg. "I was born on an Air Force base in Illinois, my uncle was killed in Vietnam, and I have a cousin in a covert branch of the military who told me that he's using the same weapon, an M-203, that I'm using in *Jarhead*." Critics agreed with Sarsgaard's assessment of his performance and the level of realism he brought to the *Jarhead* part. "[It's] hard to believe," Stephen Hunter wrote for the *Washington Post* (4 Nov. 2005) "the same guy [who played Alan Troy] could play a redneck monster who could beat a girl to death in *Boys Don't Cry* and the editor of the *New Republic* in *Shattered Glass*, and seem perfect for each of the three roles." Sarsgaard won similar acclaim for his lead role in *An Education* (2009), which tells the story of a naïve sixteen-year-old who is seduced by a man twice her age. Critics widely commented on the blend of charm and revulsion that he brought to the part.

RECENT WORK

In 2013 Sarsgaard appeared in both the Woody Allen film *Blue Jasmine* and in a reoccurring role in the acclaimed television series *The Killing*. "When you sign up Peter Sarsgaard to be on a show like *The Killing*, it's probably safe to assume you don't want him to play the rigidly moral chief of police or the squeaky-clean neighbor next door," Itzkoff wrote. Sarsgaard explained to Melissa Locker for *Rolling Stone* (16 June 2013) that he felt his work in the series was "some of the best acting I have ever done in my life." His role as Chuck, the abusive husband of porn star Linda Lovelace, in the 2013 film *Lovelace*, gave Sarsgaard pause, however, despite his experience with playing reprehensible characters. "I have two little girls . . . and this material is incredibly disturbing for me," he told Emma Brown for *Interview* magazine (24 Jan. 2013). "I had a lot of resistance to playing this role, it's weirdly emotional for me, and I don't like playing [Chuck]. But obviously I needed to for some reason."

Sarsgaard's most recent films include *Pawn Sacrifice*, a 2014 film about chess prodigy Bobby Fischer; *Experimenter* (2015), in which he portrays controversial social psychologist Stanley Milgram; and the 2015 Whitey Bulger crime drama, *Black Mass*. He also appeared as Hector in the 2015 television series *The Slap*. Sarsgaard has several upcoming films in various stages of production, including one in which he plays Senator Robert Kennedy.

PERSONAL LIFE

Sarsgaard, a vegan who runs dozens of miles per week, is married to the actress Maggie

Gyllenhaal, whom he met in 2002. The couple has two daughters, Ramona and Gloria.

SUGGESTED READING

Brown, Emma. "Peter Sarsgaard Is a Good Person." *Interview Magazine*. Brant, 24 Jan. 2013. Web. 30 Jan. 2016.
Hirschberg, Lynn. "The Empathist." *New York Times*. New York Times, 13 Nov. 2005. Web. 30 Jan. 2016.
Hunter, Stephen. "'Jarhead': A Platoon Full of Sand and Grit." *Washington Post*. Washington Post, 4 Nov. 2005. Web. 14 Apr. 2016.
Itzkoff, Dave. "You Wouldn't Like Him When He's Angry: Peter Sarsgaard Joins 'The Killing.'" *New York Times*. New York Times, 29 May 2013. Web. 30 Jan. 2016.
Locker, Melissa. "Peter Sarsgaard on 'The Killing,' Death Row, and Woody Allen." *Rolling Stone*. Rolling Stone, 16 June 2013. Web. 14 Apr. 2016.
Marden, Matthew, and Rob Tannenbaum. "Peter Sarsgaard on *Hamlet*, Stage Fright, and Why He'd Rather Play the Bad Guy." *Details*. Condé Nast, 3 Apr. 2015. Web. 30 Jan. 2016.
Saner, Ermine. "Peter Sarsgaard: 'Being a Curious Person Leads You to Playing Villains.'" *Guardian*. Guardian News and Media, 9 Aug. 2013. Web. 30 Jan. 2016.

SELECTED WORKS

Dead Man Walking, 1995; *Boys Don't Cry*, 1999; *Jarhead*, 2005; *An Education*, 2009; *Lovelace*, 2013; *Blue Jasmine*, 2013; *The Killing*, 2013; *The Slap*, 2015

—*Mari Rich*

Caroline Shaw

Born: 1982
Occupation: Composer

Caroline Shaw is a musician and composer best known for her Pulitzer Prize–winning composition *Partita for 8 Voices*.

EARLY LIFE AND EDUCATION

Caroline Adelaide Shaw was born in 1982 in Greenville, North Carolina. Her mother, Jon, was a musician and singer who began teaching Shaw the violin when Shaw was two years old. Shaw has older brothers who also played the violin. Around age ten, Shaw began writing her own music. She would often attempt to emulate her mother and the work of renowned classical composers such as Wolfgang Amadeus Mozart and Johannes Brahms. She remained focused on the violin, however, throughout her youth.

When she was a teenager, Shaw formed a string quartet with her friends. She excelled at the violin, but she also learned the cello so that she could switch positions with others in the quartet. Singing at her local Episcopalian church helped shape her later compositions.

After graduating from high school, Shaw attended Rice University in Houston, Texas, where she graduated in 2004 with a Bachelor of Music degree. While attending Rice, Shaw was awarded a Thomas J. Watson Fellowship, which allowed her to explore Western musical aesthetics in the European gardens of France, Italy, Spain, and other countries. She presented a series of compositions based on the aesthetic elements of these gardens.

From there she continued developing her expertise with the violin at Yale University in New Haven, Connecticut, and performed with the Yale Baroque Ensemble. She received her master's degree in violin from Yale in 2007 and stayed in New Haven, where she accompanied dance classes on piano and violin. This taught her how to physically engage a live audience and experiment with music.

CLASSICAL PERFORMER AND COMPOSER

After living in New Haven, Shaw moved to New York City, where she began networking with various music ensembles. She sang in the style of Renaissance polyphony in the Choir of Trinity Wall Street in Manhattan. In an ensemble called Red Light New Music, Shaw played violin. She has also been a part of the chamber ensemble Alarm Will Sound, the Wordless Music Orchestra, and Ensemble Signal.

Many times a year, Shaw would visit her family in Greenville. During these trips, she would immerse herself in North Carolina's traditional bluegrass and gospel music. These experiences with local music heritage and her background in classical music led to Shaw becoming one of the founding members of Roomful of Teeth, a vocal ensemble that creates contemporary classical music, in 2009.

The following year, Shaw entered the PhD program in composition as a doctoral fellow at Princeton University in Princeton, New Jersey. Along with her studies, Shaw composed music for the percussion quartet So Percussion, which runs a summer institute on Princeton's campus.

Roomful of Teeth had a residency at the Massachusetts Museum of Contemporary Art (Mass MoCA) in North Adams, Massachusetts, where they studied and experimented with a plethora of vocal styles, including yodeling, Inuit throat singing, and Georgian singing. Their debut album, *Roomful of Teeth*, on which Shaw sang alto, won the 2014 Grammy Award for best chamber music or small ensemble performance.

Over the course of three summers, beginning in 2009, Shaw composed a four-movement a cappella piece for Roomful of Teeth called *Partita for 8 Voices*. The piece makes use of whispers, sighs, and wordless melodies. The work was inspired by texts from conceptual artist Sol LeWitt's "Wall Drawings," particularly his use of patterns and lines. The four movements of the work are also inspired by the baroque dance forms of allemande, sarabande, courante, and passacaglia. When composing the work, Shaw also considered the individual personalities of Roomful of Teeth's members. The four segments premiered individually from 2009 to 2011.

Shaw submitted *Partita for 8 Voices* to be considered for a Pulitzer Prize in hopes of providing Roomful of Teeth with more recognition. In April 2013 the piece was awarded the 2013 Pulitzer Prize for Music, making Shaw, at thirty years old, the youngest recipient. In 2014 the piece was also nominated for a Grammy Award for best classical contemporary composition.

In November 2013, *Partita for 8 Voices* made its live debut in New York. Shortly after that, Shaw premiered a vocal piece she had been commissioned to compose for a children's choir. Shaw also performs frequently with the American Contemporary Music Ensemble, a New York ensemble that focuses on classical masterworks and contemporary compositions alike. She is primarily a violin player for this ensemble.

IMPACT

At a young age, Shaw has amassed an impressive amount of accolades. She is the youngest person to win the Pulitzer Prize for Music since the award's inception in 1943. She has won one Grammy with her vocal group Roomful of Teeth and has been nominated for another. Her work has been featured at Mass MoCA as part of a permanent landscape installation called "The Expanded Field." She has also performed at the Manchester Chamber Music along with baroque violinist Robert Mealy.

PERSONAL LIFE

Shaw lives in Chelsea, New York, where she enjoys kayaking on the Hudson River. Besides music, she is also interested in painting and sculpture. She prefers being called a musician rather than a composer.

SUGGESTED READING

Lowder, J. Bryan. "The Strange, Beautiful Music That Won the Pulitzer This Year." *Slate*. Slate, 17 Apr. 2013. Web. 2 May 2014.

Menconi, David. "Awards, Accolades Continue for Greenville's Caroline Shaw." *The News & Observer*. NewsObserver.com, 25 Jan. 2014. Web. 2 May 2014.

Robin, William. "Caroline Shaw, a North Carolina Native Not Looking to be Called a Composer, Wins Music's Pulitzer." *Indy Week*. Indy Week, 8 May 2013. Web. 1 May 2014.

Tsioulcas, Anastasia. "Caroline Shaw, 30, Wins Pulitzer for Music." *NPR*. NPR, 15 Apr. 2013. Web. 3 May 2014.

Woolfe, Zachary. "With Pulitzer, She Became a Composer." *New York Times*. New York Times, 17 Apr. 2013. Web. 1 Apr. 2014.

SELECTED WORKS

Il cantico delle creature, 2007; *Partita for 8 Voices*, 2009; *Ritornello*, 2012; *Gustave Le Grey*, 2012

—Patrick G. Cooper

Claressa Shields

Born: March 17, 1995
Occupation: Boxer

Boxer Claressa Shields, nicknamed T-Rex, took home an Olympic gold medal as a seventeen-year-old in 2012, the first time women's boxing was included at the Games. Her prodigious talent and inspirational life story soon made her a favorite with fans and the media. An independent film, *T-Rex* (2015), was made about her path to the Olympics. After her victory Shields told Sonari Glinton for Nation Public Radio's *All Things Considered*, "I won on my family. I won on Flint's hope. I kind of blend them together, you know, and I just made myself happy. I wouldn't be able to live with myself if I hadn't got the gold medal because I worked so hard, so I wanted nothing but gold."

Shields would pursue more than that single gold medal, however. She continued her amateur career rather than immediately turning professional and won match after match. After claiming victories in the 2014 Elite Women's World Championships and the 2015 Pan American Games, she began training for her next shot at Olympic gold in Rio de Janeiro, Brazil, in 2016.

EARLY LIFE

Shields was born and raised in Flint, Michigan, a city suffering economically and socially from the decline of the automobile industry in the region. She did not speak until she was five years old due to the hardships of growing up in poverty. Her mother, Marcella Adams, struggled with drug and alcohol addiction, and the family often went hungry. Shields told Lisa Armstrong for *Essence* (Aug. 2012), "Growing up I could never get my mom to stop drinking. I lost that fight in that I wasn't even heard. Nobody ever listened

Thatcher Cook for PopTech/CC BY-SA 2.0/Wikimedia Commons

to me. I just felt like I was losing at life, period." To make matters worse she was sexually abused by acquaintances of her mother. When Shields finally told an aunt about the abuse, demonstrating with a doll, she then went to live with her grandmother until she was ten.

Shields's father, Clarence, had been an amateur boxer before he was imprisoned for breaking and entering. He spent seven of Shields's first nine years in prison, so she barely knew him. However, he told her about Laila Ali, one of the few women boxers to achieve fame. In 2006, when she was eleven, she went to coach Jason Crutchfield at a local gym and told him she was tired of losing and wanted to learn to box. A friend bet ten dollars that she would not last a week. After she proved the friend wrong, Crutchfield told Shields she needed a parent's approval to officially train. He was initially opposed to training a girl until he saw her potential.

Because he had seen how boxing could mar a person's face, Shields's father was at first opposed to her pursuing the sport, but he eventually gave in when he saw her determination. He observed how quickly she improved and how motivated she was; Crutchfield even used her to motivate young men who clowned around instead of training, telling them a girl could beat them. Shields never missed a practice and was always focused, in part as a way to handle her anger. As she told Armstrong, "Growing up I got hurt. It wasn't physically, it was more mentally. I was always angry, all the time. I think I was angry because I was so quiet. A lot of stuff I really held in."

TRAINING FOR THE OLYMPICS

As Shields learned the ropes she also juggled taking care of her younger siblings. Crutchfield acted as a father figure as well as a coach, and eventually she moved in with Crutchfield's family for summers, living with her aunt during the school year. By the time Shields was thirteen her talent was so apparent that Crutchfield began talking to her about the Olympics. In 2008 women's boxing was an exhibition sport in the Beijing Olympics and was to be officially included for 2012, raising the prospect of a medal run for the young boxer. Though she was originally misinformed that she would be too young to compete, she made the Olympics her goal. As she told Rick Maese for the *Washington Post* (9 Aug. 2012), Shields was especially motivated because competition was a potential way out of poverty. "When I used to go running, I used to see all these crackheads, these drug addicts. I just didn't want to be like them. I didn't want to be like them at all. I wanted to have a good life."

Shields trained vigorously, aided by the tough but constant support of Crutchfield. He established strict rules in order to keep her focused on the sport above all else. She took inspiration from boxing legends such as Sugar Ray Robinson and Joe Louis, watching videos of classic fights and picking up moves in the process. Shields's fighting style came to feature a seamless blend of both speed and power, which, together with her relentless determination to win, made her a formidable opponent. She began racking up win after win without a single loss, including national championships for the 2011 Junior Olympics and the 2011 National Police Athletic League (PAL) tournament.

At the trials for the first-ever US women's boxing team Shields dominated her competition with a combined total of 108 points to 64 points. Points are awarded when a boxer hits an opponent in the torso or head with a clean blow. Shields was accustomed to averaging thirty-one or thirty-two points per match and was disappointed to win one qualifying match with only twenty-three points. Still, she defeated many older and more experienced fighters, including five-time national champion Franchon Crews, and was named the tournament's outstanding boxer. She then went on to her first international competition, taking gold at the 2012 Continental Championship.

2012 OLYMPICS

Ranked number one in the United States in the middleweight class, Shields next needed to qualify for the Olympics at the May 2012 Women's World Boxing Championships in Qinhuangdao, China. She entered the tournament as a favorite despite being the youngest competitor. Yet there she faced the first setback of her young career, losing in an upset to Savannah Marshall of England—the first match she had ever lost. Shields was crushed. She told Armstrong, "I felt that without the Olympics, I would be living in Flint for four more years and I was thinking, I can't do it. I can't go back to living the way I was." Fortunately Marshall's ultimate performance in the tournament ensured that Shields earned a spot in the 2012 London Olympics.

At age seventeen Shields easily made it through the Olympic quarterfinals and semifinals. She knew that the final match would be against the thirty-three-year-old Russian boxer Nadezda Torlopova, and that night she barely slept. Yet when the match began Shields was ready. Knowing she was faster, Shields played to her strengths and defeated Torlopova, 19–12, winning the first-ever Olympic gold medal for women's boxing. It was the only gold for the US boxing team in London. When her victory was announced she began to laugh. She was the second-youngest boxer ever to win gold. As Maese reported, Shields said, "I earned this. This is my medal. I worked too hard. I worked really hard for this medal. I can't even explain all the pain that I had went through, all the people I had to do deal with. And just life, period."

Following her victory, Shields was recognized as the 2012 woman athlete of the year by the American Boxing Confederation. For Shields, though, the gold medal was also about lifting the rest of her family from poverty with whatever opportunities might now come her way. "I want it to be where my sister, my little brother, my mom, and them, they would never have to go without a meal again," She told Maese. "There's a lot of stuff that's going to be able to help my family out."

FURTHER VICTORIES

After the Olympics Shields was greeted by more than five hundred fans and her high school's marching band at the Flint airport as a local hero. The Michigan State Senate honored her. However, no major endorsements followed other than an advertisement for Audi and travel money from the Universal Kidney Foundation, a disappointment following her hard work and phenomenal success. The lack of guaranteed financial support and publicity contributed to Shields's decision to remain on the amateur boxing circuit rather than immediately compete professionally, which would have disqualified her from future Olympic consideration. Despite the potential for higher paydays and wider recognition, pro women's boxing typically offers less stability than amateur competition, and payouts are far below those of male pro boxers.

Shields completed her senior year at Flint Northwestern High School, becoming in 2013 the first member of her family to graduate from high school. She continued to box, winning more matches and being named the 2013 Youth World Champion, the 2014 USA Boxing National Champion, and the 2014 Pan American Olympic Festival Champion. When first asked about another Olympics, Shields told Chris Mannix for *Sports Illustrated* (9 Aug. 2012), "I don't know. I really can't say no, but I can't say yes. I like traveling for free. I like going to training camp. I really do love boxing. I want to be the best. If I can be two-time gold medalist, me and my coach have to talk about it."

Shields eventually decided to train for a second Olympic run and began preparing for the 2016 competition in Rio, despite a difficult split with Crutchfield. She avenged her previous world championship loss by winning the 2014 Elite Women's World Championships. She then took gold at the Pan American Games held in July 2015, winning all three bouts by unanimous decision. Following that victory Shields was chosen by her United States teammates to carry the flag in the closing ceremony of the games.

At the US Women's National Olympic Trials in October 2015, Shields won all four of her matches. Preparing for that competition, Shields devoted six to eight hours daily for seventy-two days of training with her new coach, Leon Lawson. Her focus was again squarely on winning, despite the media's obsession with her difficult early life. She told Linda Barnard for the *Toronto Star* (2 May 2015), "I want people when they hear Claressa Shields, I don't want them thinking of bad things. I want them to have hope, have faith in their future when they think about me. I came from . . . the bottom to where I am right now."

PERSONAL LIFE

Shields maintained somewhat strained relationships with her parents. Crutchfield became not only Shields's trainer but a father figure, and he forbade her to date, fearing she would get distracted. As he told Armstrong, "I tell her we ain't got time for boys. She's got the rest of her life for boys. Right now boxing is her boyfriend." This strictness contributed to the rift that grew between the trainer and his protégé after the 2012 Olympics. Against Crutchfield's wishes, Shields went to her high school prom with Ardreal Holmes Jr., a fellow boxer, and she continued dating him after the fallout with her coach.

In 2013 Shields matriculated at Olivet College, where she received a full scholarship. The school was attractive because it has a small boxing ring and punching bags, so she could continue to train. For eight months she fostered the baby of a cousin who could not afford a third child, intending to adopt it; however, the arrangement fell through. In her spare time, Shields bowls and enjoys karaoke. Before matches she listens to both rap and gospel music. She moved from Flint to Colorado Springs, Colorado, to train more intensely there at the US Olympic Center.

SUGGESTED READING

Armstrong, Lisa. "Undefeated." *Essence* 43.4 (2012): 110–15. Print.

Barnard, Linda. "Inside Ring and in Life, Champ Pulls No Punches." *Toronto Star* 2 May 2015: S5. Print.

Glinton, Sonari. "Medalist Claressa Shields Gets a Hero's Welcome." *All Things Considered*. NPR, 16 Aug. 2012. Web. 8 Feb. 2016.

Levy, Ariel. "A Ring of One's Own." *New Yorker*. Condé Nast, 7 May 2012. Web. 8 Feb. 2016.

Maese, Rick. "Claressa Shields Wins Only Gold Medal for US Boxing at London Olympics, and the First by a Woman." *Washington Post*. Washington Post, 9 Aug. 2012. Web. 8 Feb. 2016.

Mannix, Chris. "From Flint to Olympic Gold, Shields' Magical Journey Pays Off Royally." *Sports Illustrated*. Time, 9 Aug. 2012. Web. 8 Feb. 2016.

—*Judy Johnson*

Sia

Born: December 18, 1975
Occupation: Musician

Sia, the elusive star with a booming voice, has penned a number of major hit songs for herself and other artists, all while attempting to avoid the limelight. Tim Murphy, writing for *New York* magazine (20 June 2010), wrote that "Sia is almost pathologically afraid of fame." Often described as quirky or odd, Sia has had little choice but to deal with her fame, however, particularly since 2014, when her single "Chandelier" shot to the top spot on the pop charts and the accompanying video was viewed more than one million times within twenty-four hours of being posted.

Sia copes with the unwanted attention by rarely showing her full face in public, typically wearing a platinum blond wig so voluminous it hides her eyes or performing with her back to audiences. She has been known to negotiate unusual contracts with her record labels that stipulate that she will not be required to mount a live tour or to promote her music with the usual television and radio interviews. Her personal and professional quirks and her attempts to shield her privacy are frequently discussed in the press, yet serious critics instead focus on her undeniable musical talents. In a review of "Chandelier"

David Becker/GettyImages

for the influential music magazine *Pitchfork* (8 May 2014), for example, Jeremy Gordon wrote, "Sia's voice blasts off, the swelling strings propelling her past her contemporaries in the inspirational-pop stratosphere. It's a jaw-dropping vocal performance that's enough to convince you she could have a stadium-touring career of her own."

EARLY YEARS

The singer was born Sia Kate Isobelle Furler on December 18, 1975, in Adelaide, Australia. Her mother, Loene Furler, was an artist and teacher, and her father, Phil B. Colson, was a guitarist who played with a variety of local bands and was a close friend of Colin Hay, from the Australian rock group Men at Work. Because Sia has referred to the relatively well-known musician as "Uncle Collie," many sources have mistakenly assumed that Hay is a blood relation. Sia had a love of singing from a very early age.

Sia has told interviewers that she had a strained relationship with her father while she was growing up. Loene and Phil split up when Sia was ten, and he relocated to Sydney. (After she found success in the music industry, Sia did not speak to her father for several years, wondering whether he was envious of her career. They later reconciled and maintained a good relationship.) Sia, who has admitted to smoking large quantities of marijuana as a teen, attended North Adelaide Primary School and Adelaide High School, but she expressed few career goals except for making music.

START OF A MUSIC CAREER

Sia got her professional start in the mid-1990s as part of the Adelaide-based band Crisp. She appeared on two of the band's albums, *Word and the Deal* (1996) and *Delirium* (1997). Crisp disbanded in 1997. Later that year, she released a solo album, *OnlySee*, produced by Crisp bandmate Jesse Flavell and marketed under the name Sia Furler.

Dreaming of finding success on a larger stage, Sia began making plans to live in the United Kingdom. Her boyfriend, Dan Pontifex, was already living in London and was prepared to help her settle in. Just days before she was due to arrive, Pontifex was killed in a car accident. Devastated, she decided to go through with her plans anyway. Upon settling in London, Sia got her first big break when she was hired as a background singer for the popular funk band Jamiroquai. She later joined acclaimed electronica group Zero 7, providing vocals on the albums *Simple Things* (2001), *When It Falls* (2004), and *The Garden* (2006). Concurrently, however, she pursued a solo career, and in 2000 she signed a contract with Dance Pool records, which released *Healing Is Difficult* (2002). Prior to the album's release, the song "Taken for Granted" cracked into the top ten of the UK Singles Chart in June 2000. The album, mistakenly referred to as her solo debut by those unaware of *OnlySee*, featured the hit single "Drink to Get Drunk." The track "Little Man" was remixed by the garage artist Wookie and quickly became a favorite in London's dance clubs.

In 2004 Sia released *Colour the Small One*, an album that changed the trajectory of her career. It contained the haunting balled "Breathe Me." The song's lyrics exhort listeners: "Be my friend, hold me / Wrap me up, unfold me / I am small and needy / Warm me up and breathe me." The track was played during the final scene of the series finale of the hit HBO drama *Six Feet Under* and became an immediate viral phenomenon. In the United States, sales of the song ultimately surpassed 1.2 million.

Understandably, Sia's manager wanted to leverage her newfound popularity by sending her on tour, but the idea made the singer exceedingly nervous. She refused to travel without her two dogs (a demand that necessitated hiring an additional bus) and rebuffed the radio-station interviews that are generally obligatory for artists hoping to get airplay. Performing live, she began to don masks and dark clothing so that fans could not see her onstage. Still, the tour went well enough to result in her first live release, *Lady Croissant*, in 2007.

ADDICTION, RECOVERY, AND A NEW PHASE

While she was touring, Sia became deeply dependent on alcohol and the prescription drugs Xanax and OxyContin. "When you're in a different place every day, there's this kind of madness that sets in," she told Steve Knopper for the *New York Times Magazine* (18 Apr. 2014). "It's easy to get away with getting high, because everybody's drinking on the road. None of my friends thought I was an alcoholic, and neither did I." Despite her addictions and mental-health issues—she was diagnosed with bipolar disorder during this period—she continued to record albums, including *Some People Have Real Problems*, which was released in 2008 on the Starbucks-affiliated Hear Music label and reached number twenty-six on the Billboard 200 chart. The album received mixed reviews but gained her a wider audience, thanks to the coffee chain's marketing power. "With her old-school soul vocal style, with just a hint of roughness under her delicate high-register tones, set against the contemporary sophistication of her music, Sia is exactly the sort of artist a middle-aged Starbucks devotee who wants to remain at least tangentially hip would flock to," Stewart Mason wrote for *All Music*. "If Amy Winehouse did yoga instead of Jack Daniels, she'd sound a lot like Sia."

Sia followed that album with *We Are Born* (2010). "Aussie singer Sia got famous cooing moody tracks for Zero 7 and *Six Feet Under*, but there's a perky dance diva trapped behind her blond bob," Caryn Ganz wrote in a review for *Rolling Stone* (7 June 2010). "On her first album of up-tempo numbers, the thirty-four-year-old combines disco funk with the throwback soul of UK crooners like Adele. Her secret weapon: Strokes guitarist Nick Valensi, whose chugging riffs and loopy lines give her boogie-woogie real teeth."

Although those albums' tracks may have been upbeat, Sia's depression reached a new low. Later that year, she gathered all the drugs in her home and prepared a suicide note. Luckily, a friend intervened in time, and the singer entered a twelve-step program. Around this time, her manager hit upon an idea that allowed her to remain active in the music industry yet stay out of the limelight: he suggested she write songs for other artists.

PENNING POP HITS

Sia showed a remarkable ability to connect with her fellow musicians on a personal and emotional basis, befriending many of them. Among the hits she penned over the next few years were Christina Aguilera's "You Lost Me," Beyoncé's "Pretty Hurts," Britney Spears's "Perfume," David Guetta's "Titanium," Rihanna's "Diamonds," Ne-Yo's "Let Me Love You (Until You Learn to Love Yourself)," and Flo Rida's "Wild Ones." (She provided vocals for "Titanium" but did not appear on the video.)

Knopper remarked, "Writing for others allowed Furler to hide in plain sight for years." It also earned her the disrespect of some critics. "Within the industry, one often overhears Furler's name spoken with hushed reverence: her Midas touch when it comes to penning hits has made her one of the most bankable, in-demand back-room names," Alex Macpherson wrote in a piece for the *National* (24 July 2014). "Yet Furler is no chameleon. The writing style that she's built her reputation on is consistent and immediately recognizable, whether the backing track is a vulnerable piano ballad or a pumped-up dance floor anthem. It's also incredibly simple: Furler tends to take a single word or phrase as a foundational, nebulously 'inspirational' image, hammers it home via gigantic, blustery hooks and fills in the rest of the song around it as an afterthought." For her part, Sia seems unbothered by such criticism, unabashedly telling Knopper that she comes up with many tracks in under an hour and pointing out that royalties from those songs have allowed her to live very well.

In July 2014, however, Sia finally released a new solo album, *1000 Forms of Fear*, which immediately topped the charts in several countries, peaking at number one on the Billboard 200 chart. "On *1000 Forms of Fear*, it's clear that her time as a hitmaker for others not only brought her quirks into the mainstream but also made the songs she kept for herself catchier," Heather Phares wrote for *All Music*. Among the catchiest of these tracks was "Chandelier," and the song's music video features young dancer Maddie Ziegler in a flesh-toned leotard and platinum blond wig, performing modern interpretive moves in an eerily abandoned apartment. The result was an evocative piece that amassed more than one billion views on YouTube by December 2015. Sia received multiple Grammy nominations, including nods in the categories of music video of the year and song of the year for "Chandelier" and record of the year for *1000 Forms of Fear*. Ziegler appeared as Sia's proxy, sporting the same leotard and wig, in two subsequent videos from the album: "Big Girls Cry" and "Elastic Heart." Among the movie soundtracks to which Sia has contributed songs are *The Great Gatsby* (2013), *The Hunger Games: Catching Fire* (2013), *Annie* (2014), and *Fifty Shades of Grey* (2015). She was nominated for the 2015 Golden Globe Award for best original song for "Opportunity" from the *Annie* soundtrack.

PERSONAL LIFE

In 2014 Sia married filmmaker Erik Anders Lang, keeping news of the nuptials a secret until months later. In 2015 the couple announced that they were codirecting a documentary about her life. An avowed vegan, Sia has appeared in promotional ads for the animal-rights group People for the Ethical Treatment of Animals (PETA), despite her dislike of being in the public eye. She owns homes in Los Angeles and Palm Springs, California.

SUGGESTED READING

Furler, Sia. Interview by Kristen Wiig. *Interview*. Interview Magazine, 27 Mar. 2015. Web. 8 Dec. 2015.

Gallo, Phil. "Sia: The *Billboard* Cover Story." *Billboard*. Billboard, 25 Oct. 2013. Web. 8 Dec. 2015.

Ganz, Caryn. "Sia's Quiet Side." *Advocate*. Here Media, 26 Mar. 2008. Web. 8 Dec. 2015.

Gordon, Jeremy. Rev. of "Chandelier," by Sia. *Pitchfork*. Pitchfork Media, 8 May 2014. Web. 8 Dec. 2015.

Knopper, Steve. "Sia Furler, the Socially Phobic Pop Star." *New York Times Magazine*. New York Times, 18 Apr. 2014. Web. 8 Dec. 2015.

Macpherson, Alex. "Hidden Talents: Sia Furler and Her Formulaic Approach to Creativity." *National*. Abu Dhabi Media, 24 July 2014. Web. 8 Dec. 2015.

Murphy, Tim. "Sia, the Power Balladist Who Wants to Party." *New York*. New York Media, 20 June 2010. Web. 8 Dec. 2015.

SELECTED WORKS

Healing Is Difficult, 2002; *Colour the Small One*, 2004; *Lady Croissant*, 2007; *Some People Have Real Problems*, 2008; *We Are Born*, 2010; *1000 Forms of Fear*, 2014

—*Mari Rich*

Gayle Smith

Occupation: Administrator of the United States Agency for International Development

Gayle E. Smith became the head of the United States Agency for International Development (USAID) in 2015. In President Barack Obama's official White House press release (30 Apr. 2015) nominating Smith, who previously served other roles in his administration, he stated, "Gayle's energy and passion have been instrumental in guiding America's international development policy, responding to a record number of humanitarian crises worldwide, and ensuring that development remains at the forefront of the national security agenda at a time when USAID is more indispensable than ever." Though Smith's appointment faced some opposition in Congress, she was confirmed in November 2015.

USAID/Wikimedia Commons

EARLY LIFE AND EDUCATION

Smith was raised in Bexley, Ohio, near Columbus. She graduated in 1974 from Bexley High School, where she was a cheerleader. She earned a bachelor of arts degree from the University of Colorado at Boulder. After graduating she pursued a career in journalism.

As a journalist Smith focused on Africa and spent more than twenty years on that continent—primarily in Ethiopia, Kenya, and Sudan—covering economic, military, and political content for a number of publications. She reported for the BBC, *Christian Science Monitor, Boston Globe*, Associated Press, and others. Her work brought her recognition and honors including the World Affairs Council's World Journalism Award.

Smith also worked for several different nongovernmental organizations (NGOs) as she became a noted authority on international aid and development issues. During the 1980s one of her priorities while working for cross-border relief efforts was hunger alleviation in Eritrea and other areas. War and an economic embargo made hunger relief difficult. According to one of her colleagues, Alex de Waal, writing at *BostonReview.net* (15 June 2015), Smith "saw hunger—and worked to alleviate it—on par with any professional relief worker in modern times."

WORKING FOR CHANGE

Smith first became involved with the US Agency for International Development (USAID) in 1994 when she became the organization's chief of staff and administrator. She held that role until 1998, when she became the senior director for African affairs in the National Security Council

(NSC) in the administration of President Bill Clinton, also serving as a special assistant to the president. In 1999 she was presented with the Samuel Nelson Drew Award for distinguished contribution in pursuit of global peace by the National Security Council. She left the National Security Council in 2001 and resumed work with USAID and various NGOs as an adviser.

Smith was critical of US foreign aid efforts under the administration of President George W. Bush, arguing that they placed US economic interests and conservative cultural values above real positive change. Bush significantly increased aid to African nations, ostensibly to promote local economic development and fight HIV/AIDS. However, Smith noted that the administration specified that aid could not be given to organizations that provided abortion counseling or abortions and that as much as one-third of the funding for HIV/AIDS programs would be used to promote abstinence rather than comprehensive sex education. The policy led to the closure of abortion clinics in several African countries, and by 2004 USAID had stopped providing condoms to many developing nations. Meanwhile, African countries that were major oil producers were granted aid regardless of their reform efforts. In a critique published in *Index on Censorship* (Jan. 2004) Smith admitted that "the fact of the matter is that the allocation of US attention and resources derives directly from its perception of strategic interests," but suggested that such policies restricted progress in Africa.

In 2005 Smith joined the Clinton Global Initiative (CGI), an organization intended to bring together leaders from around the world to work together on problem solving. The initiative is part of the Clinton Foundation, which focuses attention on issues including health and wellness, girls and women, global health, economic development, and climate change. She served as the CGI's working group chair on global poverty until 2007. Smith also became a senior fellow at the Center for American Progress (CAP) in 2006 and continued to advocate for economic reform to advance various progressive goals. For example, in an article for *American Prospect* (Apr. 2006) she suggested that the United States should concentrate its agricultural expertise on biofuels, thus decreasing dependence on foreign oil while at the same time providing opportunities for small-scale farmers in developing nations. She concluded, "Our own prosperity, security, and moral credibility depend on a world united behind common principles and a global order that affords a majority of the world's people the right to live in dignity, earn a living wage, and offer better lives to their children."

DEVELOPMENT EXPERT AND ADVOCATE

In 2007 Smith was among the founders of the Enough Project, an arm of the Center for American Progress that attempts to end genocide and other crimes against humanity. The project focuses on abuses in Africa, mobilized in part by the failure of Western governments to respond to genocide in Rwanda in 1994 and subsequent crises in Sudan, Chad, and the Democratic Republic of the Congo. Enough works to end human rights abuses by governments, militant groups, and corrupt economic interests such as those that exploit natural resources. The group assists with campaigns in various African countries to create positive change through policy advice, support for social movements, and field research.

Smith was also a cofounder of the Modernizing Foreign Assistance Network (MFAN). The group sought to build a bipartisan consensus that the United States should assume a leading role in reducing poverty and encouraging economic growth globally. MFAN worked with the executive and legislative branches of the US government as well as the broader community of development workers in order to streamline and otherwise modernize US aid efforts. With US foreign aid spread among more than twenty separate agencies in 2008, MFAN called for the creation of a cabinet-level position for global development. Smith, as quoted by Caroline Preston for the *Chronicle of Philanthropy* (26 June 2008), voiced the goal, saying, "We now have the challenge and imperative to reshape the whole of our foreign-aid system and to craft a nimble, modern, and capable system." However, a cabinet-level development agency was not established, and MFAN had little success despite increased attention to aid efforts due to a worldwide food crisis driven by escalating costs.

NATIONAL SECURITY COUNCIL SENIOR DIRECTOR

Following his 2008 election President Obama appointed Smith to serve as senior director of the National Security Council, and she took office in 2009. She also served again as a special assistant to the president. Her areas of responsibility included democracy, global development, and humanitarian assistance issues.

In her new position Smith cultivated relationships with many world leaders, especially African governments, some of which dated back to her time in the Clinton administration. Her connections and expertise on Africa enabled her to closely direct the flow of US foreign aid. For example, in 2012 $580 million was directed to Ethiopia. Although some observers felt Smith was too accommodating to autocrats, such as Ethiopia's ruling political party, others believed

her many years of experience made her a strong fit for the job.

Among the issues Smith faced was a growing conflict in the African nation of South Sudan. The country was granted independence from Sudan in 2011 but almost immediately struggled with ongoing violent conflicts. Smith visited the country in 2014 after the United States facilitated a ceasefire between two leaders whose feuding led to thousands of deaths despite billions of dollars in US foreign aid. Voicing support for the goal of independence despite the state's fragility, Smith explained to Renee Montagne for National Public Radio's *Morning Edition* (30 Jan. 2014) how US involvement was making a positive difference and what further efforts were to come. "First and foremost, we will, with other donors, continue to meet humanitarian needs in South Sudan," she said. "Second, is there are a number of programs that we run in, for example, health and public heath that we think continue to be a wise investment."

USAID

In February 2015 the head of USAID, Rajiv Shah, stepped down. Two months later President Obama nominated Smith for the job. Shah had successfully established general bipartisan congressional support for the agency, a feat that Liz Schrayer, president of the US Global Leadership Coalition, believed Smith could replicate. As Schrayer told Helene Cooper for the *New York Times* (30 Apr. 2015), "Gayle supports prioritizing economic growth and making sure countries have skin in the game and are committed to real reform. That's where I think Republicans who have been supportive of Raj will be supportive of Gayle."

A Senate committee initially approved the nomination with no objections. However, Republican Senator Ted Cruz delayed Smith's confirmation by stalling on a full Senate vote as a protest against the Obama administration's nuclear agreement with Iran. When the vote did finally occur on November 29, 2015, Smith was confirmed by a 79–7 margin.

Upon taking office Smith immediately faced a number of ongoing humanitarian challenges that fell under USAID's responsibility. The 2014 Ebola virus outbreak in West Africa left the government scrambling to find ways to ensure that the world would be better prepared for the next such incident. Other issues included the Syrian refugee crisis and typhoon damage in the Philippines, in addition to regular development and foreign aid efforts.

One of Smith's first global tours took place in January 2016, when she led a delegation to the twenty-sixth annual African Union Summit. Senior government officials as well as members of the private sector gathered to discuss issues such as security and peace in the region. Peace in South Sudan was another agenda item, as were ways to provide funds to support the African Union in its activities to keep peace. After the summit she headed to Ethiopia, where officials from the United States were collaborating with local leaders to deal with drought and other extreme weather caused by the El Niño atmospheric pattern.

Smith took a positive approach in her first major policy speech to Congress on March 9, 2016, highlighting the progress made in education and economics. According to Jon Greenberg, writing for *PolitiFact* (24 Mar. 2016), Smith stated that since 1990 "every continent has seen substantial gains, with individual incomes growing by more than a third in every region of the developing world." She also touted the increase in children attending schools, though Greenberg noted that such gains do not reflect the potential disparity between rich and poor segments of society.

SUGGESTED READING

Cooper, Helene. "Obama Nominates Gayle Smith to Lead U.S.A.I.D." *New York Times.* New York Times, 30 Apr. 2015. Web. 9 May 2016.

"President Obama Announces His Intent to Nominate Gayle E. Smith to Lead the U.S. Agency for International Development." *White House.* WhiteHouse.gov, 30 Apr. 2015. Web. 9 May 2016.

Preston, Caroline. "Coalition Seeks Streamlined Approach to Foreign Aid." *Chronicle of Philanthropy* 20.18 (2008): 18. Print.

Smith, Gayle. "Old Wine in New Barrels." *Index on Censorship* 33.1 (2004): 60–65. Print.

Smith, Gayle. "The Politics of Aid." *Human Rights* 35.1 (2008): 1–4. Print.

Smith, Gayle. "US Maintains Humanitarian Assistance to South Sudan." Interview by Renee Montagne. *Morning Edition.* NPR, 30 Jan. 2014. Web. 9 May 2016.

Smith, Gayle. "A Win-Win Bargain." *American Prospect* 17.4 (2006): A28–A30. Print.

—*Judy Johnson*

Jill Soloway

Born: September 26, 1965
Occupation: Writer, director

Jill Soloway won an Emmy in 2015 for outstanding directing for a comedy series for her Amazon show *Transparent.* The show also won a Golden Globe for best comedy television series, a first for an Amazon original series. It was the first show

SolowayWiki/CC BY-SA 3.0

that Soloway created, preceded by a successful career as a writer, producer, showrunner, and director in both television and film. Of her characters in *Transparent,* Soloway told Terry Gross for National Public Radio's (NPR's) *Fresh Air* (31 Oct. 2014), "I don't really write these characters or do things with them. I feel more when I'm writing sort of like I'm a court stenographer and I'm listening to these characters." Soloway is happy that some people have used the show as a means of discussing their own transgender issues with family. Soloway was one of the 2015 *Time 100* and was one of six women honored in June 2015 at the Crystal + Lucy Women in Film Awards.

EARLY LIFE AND EDUCATION

Jill Soloway was born on September 26, 1965, in Chicago, to a public relations consultant, Elaine, and a psychiatrist then named Harry. Soloway and her older sister Faith, who are only eighteen months apart, grew up in Chicago where they attended Lane Tech High School. Her family was Jewish, something Soloway has said made her feel like an outsider all her life—in school, at summer camp, and in her college sorority.

The sisters grew up on Albert Brooks and Woody Allen comedies, which inspired them. Soloway was fascinated by storytelling at an early age. She told Gwen Ifill for *PBS NewsHour* (16 July 2015), "When I was a little kid, watching television, I was probably writing it in my head, pretending like I was inside the TV, instead of outside the TV, because that's where I wanted to be, on the other side of the glass."

As a teenager, she skipped school to follow bands and famous actors who came through Chicago. She attended college at the University of Wisconsin-Madison, where she realized that being a typical college girl was not what she wanted. She had a moment of insight when she encountered some women she described as feminists and hippies at Lake Mendota in Madison. She told Taffy Brodesser-Akner for *New York Times* (29 Aug. 2014), "I remember being really struck by the kind of fun they were having." She thought those students "didn't seem like they were being driven by how they looked." After taking a women's studies class, she was more aware of the difference in how men and women are regarded. This began a lifelong interest in portraying women as the subjects of their own stories.

After college Soloway went home to Chicago, where she worked in advertising, making commercials. Next she landed the job of associate producer on the documentary *Hoop Dreams* in 1994. Inspired by her work on *Hoop Dreams*, she developed a documentary on women's sexuality, but failed to get a grant to fund the project. That failure led her to turn her sights on making a documentary about the television show *The Brady Bunch* (1969–74).

As Soloway worked on the possible documentary, it became something else: a reenactment of the episodes of the show. Along with her sister Faith and their friends—some of whom were members of Annoyance Theatre, which Faith had cofounded—performed the resulting show, *The Real Live Brady Bunch*. The entertainment world noticed. After the show became a hit in Chicago, it also ran in New York for a year before moving to Los Angeles, where agents began to court the sisters. Faith later moved to Boston, but the sisters have worked on several projects together over the years, including *Transparent*.

EARLY TELEVISION WORK AND MORE

Soloway's early work in television included *The Oblongs* (2001), *Baby Blues* (2002), and *Nikki* (2000). She worked as a writer for a year on *The Steve Harvey Show* (1996–2002) before becoming a writer and a producer for the successful HBO drama *Six Feet Under* in 2002. She received that job offer after her agent sent a short story she wrote about actress Courteney Cox to Alan Ball, one of the producers of the show. *Six Feet Under* was nominated three times for an Emmy Award for best drama during the three years she worked on the show. Ball and Alan Poul gave the writers an unusual degree of freedom to critique and shape the show, even assisting with casting the characters.

Soloway's memoir *Tiny Ladies in Shiny Pants*, a series of linked essays focused on the roles and expectations of women, was published in 2005.

From 2008 to 2010 Soloway was showrunner for the Showtime series *United States of Tara*. The following year, she ran the show *How to Make It in America*. Soloway joined Shonda Rhimes's hit medical drama *Grey's Anatomy* during its fourth season as a consulting producer for the first thirteen episodes. In 2011 Soloway also made a short film about a Jewish woman who takes a Latino day laborer as a lover. Entitled *Una Hora Por Favora*, it was shown at the Sundance Film Festival.

Two years later Soloway and Rebecca Odes created Wifey.tv, an online video repository of material predominately by and about women and their point of view. Soloway wanted to create a place that focused on women as subjects and viewers, rather than as objects of the male gaze. The site states that its intended audience is "just about everyone" who is female and "men who are interested in seeing women as human beings," and accordingly has many categories of material. One of them, the documentary series *This Is Me* (2015), inspired by the television show *Transparent*, focuses on stories from the transgender community and was nominated for an Emmy Award.

AFTERNOON DELIGHT

Soloway's film *Afternoon Delight* is about a woman who takes a stripper to her home to live with her and her husband. Although Soloway originally set the action in Evanston, Illinois, ultimately the film was shot in Los Angeles. Soloway feared she would not get funding for the film and would need a low-budget option, so she chose to shoot in her own neighborhood, the trendy area of Silver Lake. About ten percent of the dialogue was improvised; Soloway is comfortable letting actors shape the story. The character of the stripper, McKenna, was partially based on a porn star and writer who attended an artist retreat with Soloway.

Afternoon Delight won a Sundance Film Festival directing award for Soloway in 2013. Soloway told Sasha Bronner for *Huffington Post* (29 Aug. 2013), "I feel like something made me want to go rescue my connection to my creative self. When I was working on this script, I was living in this creative place where I felt alive."

TRANSPARENT

Soloway's next project was a show produced by Amazon Studios and based loosely on her own parent, who came out as a transgender woman at age seventy-five. As Soloway told Terry Gross, "It just felt like the most perfect opportunity to tell a story about secrets, about boundaries, legacy, gender, family, all the things I'm obsessed with." *Transparent*, which debuted on Amazon Prime in February 2014, begins with Mort Pfefferman (Jeffrey Tambor) revealing his transgender identity to his ex-wife and three adult children and transitioning to openly living as a woman named Maura. While trying to understand their parent's new identity, each of the Pfefferman children also questions his or her own identity and sexuality.

The theme of secrets and their effects came up again in an interview with James Poniewozik for *Time* (27 Sept. 2014). Soloway said, "[G] rowing up in a house with a secret creates a certain environment that could potentially cause— I don't know. I don't know if the narcissism is personal, if it's psychological, if it's familial or if it's societal. I think it's a little bit of everything. We're a whole culture of people who have a really hard time seeing beyond themselves."

For Soloway, part of the thrill of the show is having much of the same technical staff as she'd had on *Afternoon Delight*. She was able to bring along the same hair and makeup personnel, cinematographer, and editor from the movie to the television show, which she considered rare. It also provided the opportunity to work again with her sister, Faith, who is a writer for the show. *Transparent* has also benefited from Soloway's determination to hire transgender consultants, crew, and cast. In total, Soloway had hired twenty transgender people for cast and crew and an additional sixty transgender people were featured as extras. Despite this inclusivity, Soloway drew some criticism for casting Tambor, a cisgender male, as Maura instead of a transgender actor.

The first season of the show was, by all accounts, a success. Critics hailed the show as one of the best shows of the year and the Lesbian, Gay, Bisexual, Transgender, Queer (LGBTQ) community overwhelmingly praised it for its frank portrayal of a family dealing with gender transition. The critical praise was equally reflected during the 2015 award season. The show won two Golden Globe Awards, including one for best comedy television series, and five Emmy Awards, including a directing award for Soloway and outstanding lead actor for Tambor. The show was also nominated for an additional six Emmys. The second season of *Transparent* started airing on Amazon in December 2015. Amazon announced in June 2015 that *Transparent* would be renewed for a third season. Soloway also signed a deal to exclusively develop future television content with Amazon Studios.

REACHING OUT

Soloway's focus on women's voices, comedy, and Judaism is not just present in her work in entertainment, but in the communities she helps to create and foster. Soloway told Gordon Haber for *Forward* (Jan. 2012), "My interest in community is what fuels my work as a writer, more than just wanting to write or just wanting to have a TV show, I like to create a community where people want to come and have a good time and do their best work." She has served as a mentor for WriteGirl, a program in Los Angeles designed to help adolescent girls express themselves through writing and other creative means. She also cofounded Object in 2007 with Lindsey Horvath, then president of the Hollywood chapter of the National Organization of Women (NOW). Through Object, Soloway and Horvath hosted events focused on women, sexuality, and power.

Though she grew up in a Jewish household, Soloway really reconnected with her faith after enrolling her older son in a Jewish preschool and later attending Reboot in 2005, an annual event that brings together Jews seeking new ways to express their heritage and culture. In 2011 she became a cofounder of East Side Jews, which seeks to provide a spiritual experience for Jews outside of the synagogue.

PERSONAL LIFE

Soloway married Bruce Gilbert, who is the music supervisor for *Transparent*, in 2011. They have one son, Felix, and, as of December 2015, are reportedly separating. Soloway has another son, Isaac, from a previous relationship.

SUGGESTED READING

Bianculli, David. "In 'Transparent,' A 70-Year-Old Divorced Dad Becomes A Woman." *NPR*. NPR, 27 Sept. 2014. Web. 10 Nov. 2015.

Brodesser-Akner, Taffy. "Can Jill Soloway Do Justice to the Trans Movement?" *New York Times Magazine*. New York Times, 29 Aug. 2014. Web. 11 Nov. 2015.

Bronner, Sasha. "Jill Soloway, 'Afternoon Delight' Filmmaker: I Should Have Written 'Girls' 10 Years Ago." *Huffington Post*. TheHuffingtonPost.com, 29 Aug. 2013. Web. 3 Dec. 2015.

Haber, Gordon. "Her Beachfront Home in Heaven." *Forward*. Forward Assn., 1 Jan 2012. Web. 19 Nov. 2015.

Soloway, Jill. "Funny, Dirty, Sad: The 'Holy Trinity' For 'Transparent' Creator Jill Soloway." Interview by Terry Gross. *NPR*. NPR, 31 Oct. 2014. Web. 3 Dec. 2015.

Soloway, Jill. "Q&A: Transparent Creator Jill Soloway on Transgender Stories and Indie TV." Interview by James Poniewozik. *Time*. Time, 25 Sept. 2014. Web. 10 Nov. 2015.

SELECTED WORKS

United States of Tara, 2008–10; *Afternoon Delight*, 2013; *Transparent*, 2014–; *This Is Me*, 2015

—*Judy Johnson*

Phillipa Soo

Born: May 31, 1990
Occupation: Actor and singer

Phillipa Soo is an actor and singer best known for playing Eliza Schuyler Hamilton, the wife of founding father Alexander Hamilton, in the hit Broadway musical *Hamilton*, which won ten Tony Awards and a Pulitzer Prize for Drama in 2016. The musical combines show tunes, R & B, and hip-hop to tell the story of Hamilton's life, from his penniless beginnings as an orphan in the Caribbean to his political rise, his eventual fall, and his untimely death by duel with politician Aaron Burr. Creator Lin-Manuel Miranda, who originated the titular role, employs a multiethnic cast to underscore the show's central theme about who controls the narratives of history. Presenting the story of white founding fathers with minority and multiethnic actors, Miranda—to paraphrase Michael Schulman for the *New Yorker* (6 Aug. 2015)—reclaims the history of those who have been erased. *Hamilton* challenges the traditional "great men" view of history in another way as well, ceding its final moment to Hamilton's wife, who endured her husband's infidelity while helping his political rise and, after his death, continued to protect his legacy while pursuing her own philanthropic goals.

After it debuted on Broadway in August 2015, *Hamilton* became a national phenomenon, pushing its stars into limelight of larger popular culture outside of theater and New York City. First Lady Michelle Obama, a huge fan of the show, even invited the cast to the White House. Soo, in an interview with Jeremy Gerard for *Deadline* (30 May 2016) described *Hamilton*'s success as both exhilarating and overwhelming, likening it to a hurricane: "You know it's strong. It's holding us up, but I look around and I see like chairs and trees and like large objects like flying around, this phenomenon, this hurricane. There's stuff going on but I feel relatively calm and if I just stay where I am and witness this phenomenon around me, that's the best thing for me to do at least."

EARLY LIFE AND EDUCATION

Phillipa "Pippa" Soo was born on May 31, 1990, and raised in Libertyville, Illinois. Her father, a doctor, is second-generation Chinese American; his parents came to the United States from China after World War II. Her Caucasian mother worked as a dramaturge for the European Reperatory Company in Chicago and then as an English professor. Unsurprisingly, Soo became interested in theater and the arts at an early age. When she was about three, she was enrolled in a dance class, but at her first recital she refused to appear onstage. At the end of the show, her

teacher convinced her to come out and take a bow, Soo told Emma Brown for *Interview* magazine (31 Aug. 2015). "I remember going out there and being like, 'Oh, this isn't so bad,'" she recalled. When she was eight or nine, her mother took her and her older brother to a production of *The Tempest*. The play, William Shakespeare's last, invokes the sorcery of its main character as a metaphor for the magic of making theater. The production, Soo remembered, was strange—the sprite, Ariel, wore a sparkling nude thong—but the young Soo was enchanted. After seeing the show, theater and dance became two distinct mediums in her mind. "Dance was awesome," she decided, as she told Brown, "but the theater was wild and crazy."

Soo taught herself to play the guitar and the ukulele and began taking voice lessons. At Libertyville High School, she appeared in student performances of *Oklahoma*, *Guys and Dolls*, and *Cats*. After graduation, she moved to New York City to study drama at the prestigious Juilliard School. There, as per the school's diverse curriculum, Soo studied acting in all of its various forms as well as singing. Among the shows in which she performed were *The World on the Moon*, an adaptation of Carlo Goldoni's eighteenth-century comedic opera, and Anton Chekov's drama *The Seagull*. Soo graduated with a bachelor's degree in 2012 and, within months, landed her first Off-Broadway role in a musical called *Natasha, Pierre & The Great Comet of 1812*.

NATASHA, PIERRE & THE GREAT COMET OF 1812

An adaptation of part of Leo Tolstoy's epic novel *War and Peace*, the play *Natasha, Pierre & The Great Comet of 1812* premiered at the small Off-Broadway theater Ars Nova in 2012. The pop opera by Dave Malloy was so successful in that space that it was revamped and presented a year later as a piece of immersive theater in a makeshift cabaret in Manhattan's Meatpacking District. Audience members were invited to partake of a Russian feast (with carafes of vodka available upon request) while the actors performed between the banquet tables of the cabaret's nineteenth-century Russian salon. Soo originated the role of Natasha, the show's ingénue. While her betrothed, Prince Andrey, is away at war, Natasha falls in love with the seductive Anatole. At the beginning of the show, however, she sings of her love for Andrey in one of the show's most famous songs, "No One Else." *New York Times* theater critic Charles Isherwood (16 May 2013) described Soo's performance as "luminous," while Lin-Manuel Miranda, the Tony Award–winning composer and lyricist of the hit musical *In the Heights* (2008), tweeted, as quoted by Adam Hetrick for *Playbill* (29 June 2016), "Took the missus to Natasha Pierre tonight. Phillipa Soo is a star."

Following that successful run, in the summer of 2014, Soo played Anne in Stephen Sondheim's musical *A Little Night Music* with the Berkshire Theatre Group at the Colonial Theatre in Pittsfield, Massachusetts.

HAMILTON

In 2009, Soo's friend showed her a video of Miranda performing a rap song at the White House, a piece that would become the opening number to *Hamilton*. Soo recognized Miranda from his role in *In the Heights*, but the video was the only context she had for *Hamilton* when she received a call from director Tommy Kail in December 2013. Kail, who had also been impressed by Soo's star turn in *Natasha, Pierre*, invited her to read the part of Eliza Schuyler Hamilton. Soo's reaction, she recalled to Brown, was, "Okay, great! Wait. . . . Who was she?" Miranda was still working on the script but wanted to do a read-through of the second act. When the first full draft of the script was finished in early 2014, Soo was called back again. She was officially in the cast.

To prepare for her role, Soo spoke with Ron Chernow, the Pulitzer Prize–winning historian and author of *Alexander Hamilton* (2004), the biography that inspired Miranda to pen the musical. *Hamilton* follows the life of the famous founder largely through his relationships with the women in his life. His future wife, Eliza Schuyler Hamilton (played by Soo), was the daughter of a Revolutionary War general and a senator from New York. While Alexander Hamilton (Miranda) enjoyed a lifelong intellectual relationship with Eliza's older sister Angelica (Renée Elise Goldsberry), he fell in love with and married Eliza. Eventually, she endured his political downfall, brought on by his affair with the opportunistic Maria Reynolds. After he was killed in 1804, Eliza weathered a series of personal tragedies all the while devoting herself to maintaining her husband's legacy. She also opened New York's first private orphanage and died in 1854—fifty years after Hamilton's death. The play, fittingly, ends with Eliza's words.

Hamilton premiered at the Public Theater in February 2015. Theater critic Ben Brantley, in a review for the *New York Times* (17 Feb. 2015), gave the show a rave review but also described it as the vanguard of a new kind of musical. "When one of the young rebels who populate this vibrant work says, 'History is happening in Manhattan,' you can only nod in happy agreement." Soo won a Lucille Lortel Award for outstanding lead actress in a musical in May 2015; the show, already gaining momentum thanks to stellar reviews and a visit from the Obamas, moved to Broadway at the Richard Rodgers Theatre in August. In 2016, Soo was nominated for, but did not win, a Tony Award for best leading actress in a musical. Soo retired from the show—at the same time as Miranda—on July 9, 2016.

BRANCHING OUT

While still working with the cast of *Hamilton*, Soo founded the Eliza Project, a charitable initiative to provide lessons in singing, dancing, and acting for underprivileged youth, in 2015. The teaching artist project—modeled on the one Soo saw at Juilliard—is partnered with the social service agency Graham Windham, whose roots go back to the Orphan Asylum Society that Schuyler Hamilton cofounded in 1806 and directed for twenty-seven years. The idea for the organization was born out of a pen-pal project between the show's cast members and children at the agency. Speaking of her character, Soo told Leslie Brody for the *Wall Street Journal* (29 Dec. 2015), "What better way to make a connection to her legacy?"

Soo left *Hamilton* to pursue other creative projects, foremost among them, the lead role in the musical adaptation of *Amélie*, the 2001 French romantic comedy by Jean-Pierre Jeunet. Soo had played the title role in its first workshops, though its first production at Berkeley Repertory Theatre in Berkeley, California, in summer 2015, starred Samantha Barks. The show is slated to open at the Ahmanson Theatre in Los Angeles in December 2016 under the direction of Tony Award winner Pam MacKinnon.

The show is anticipated to move to Broadway in the spring of 2017.

Also in 2016, Soo announced that she would be lending her voice to the Disney animated musical *Moana*, about a young Hawaiian princess, for which Miranda wrote some of the music. Soo will voice one of the villagers on Moana's island. The movie also features Dwayne "The Rock" Johnson as a demigod and Auli'i Cravalho, a Native Hawaiian teenager, as Moana. The movie will not be Soo's first brush with Hollywood. In 2013, she appeared in a number of episodes of a short-lived television musical drama about Broadway actors called *Smash*. Her *Hamilton* costars Miranda and Leslie Odom Jr. (who won a Tony Award for his portrayal of Aaron Burr) also appeared on the show.

PERSONAL LIFE

In 2015, Soo began dating actor Steven Pasquale, a theater and television veteran fourteen years her senior. Pasquale played Sean Garrity on the drama *Rescue Me* from 2004 to 2011, bigoted LAPD detective Mark Fuhrman in the 2016 miniseries *The People v. O.J. Simpson: American Crime Story*, and gentleman-thief Jamie Lockhart in a successful spring 2016 Off-Broadway production of Alfred Uhry's *Robber Bridegroom*.

The couple were engaged in February 2016. Soo and Pasquale live in New York City.

SUGGESTED READING

Brantley, Ben. "In 'Hamilton,' Lin-Manuel Miranda Forges Democracy through Rap." Rev. of *Hamilton*, dir. Tommy Kail. *New York Times*. New York Times, 17 Feb. 2015. Web. 8 Sept. 2016.

Brody, Leslie. "'Hamilton' Cast Helps Children in Need." *Wall Street Journal*. Dow Jones, 29 Dec. 2015. Web. 8 Sept. 2016.

Hetrick, Adam. "Lin, Phillipa and Leslie: The Pre- and Post-*Hamilton* History." *Playbill*. Playbill, 29 June 2016. Web. 8 Sept. 2016.

Isherwood, Charles. "Love Away from the Battlefield." Rev. of *Natasha, Pierre & The Great Comet of 1812*, dir. by Rachel Chavkin. *New York Times*. New York Times, 16 May 2013. Web. 7 Sept. 2016.

Schulman, Michael. "The Women of 'Hamilton.'" *New Yorker*. Condé Nast, 6 Aug. 2015. Web. 8 Sept. 2016.

Soo, Phillipa. "Hamilton's Good Wife Stands by Her Ham: Deadline Q&A with Phillipa Soo." Interview by Jeremy Gerard. *Deadline*. Penske Business Media, 30 May 2016. Web. 8 Sept. 2016.

Soo, Phillipa. "More than Mrs. Hamilton." Interview by Emma Brown. *Interview*. Interview Magazine, 31 Aug. 2015. Web. 7 Sept. 2016.

—*Molly Hagan*

Paolo Sorrentino

Born: May 31, 1970
Occupation: Director, writer

Paolo Sorrentino is an award-winning Italian screenwriter and director who is best known in the English-speaking world for his 2013 film *The Great Beauty* (*La grande bellezza*), a study of modern life in Rome through the eyes of an aged writer. It earned the 2014 Academy Award for best foreign language film, becoming the first Italian film to win an Oscar since 1998, and won or was nominated for many other notable awards. Sorrentino also gained attention for his films directed in English: *This Must Be the Place* (2011), his English-language debut starring Sean Penn, and *Youth* (2015), which featured Michael Caine and Harvey Keitel. Most of his feature-length films have been included in the prestigious Cannes Film Festival.

Sorrentino's films have consistently been well received by professional critics, and many see Sorrentino as one of the great European film directors of his era. Often compared to the renowned Italian director Federico Fellini, Sorrentino believes his own success is greatly due to the sense of humor he displays in his works. In an interview with David Gregory Lawson for *Film Comment* (4 Nov. 2013), Sorrentino remarked: "I believe that a sense of humor is vital to deal with everything. It is the best way to get away from heaviness and to reconnect with lightheartedness. And it is a formidable tool to focus on people's characteristics and unveil their secrets, and get in touch with truth and beauty."

Xavier Ganachaud/Flickr/CC BY-SA 2.0/Wikimedia Commons

EARLY LIFE

Little has been written in English of Paolo Sorrentino's early life, family and education. He was born on May 31, 1970, in Naples, Italy, and grew up there with his parents, sister, and brother. Sorrentino explained to Lawson how his hometown influenced his sense of humor, which is so prevalent in his films: "It is something that I think I inherited from the city I am from, Naples. The Neapolitan people grow up surrounded by this irony, 24 hours a day, so it's something that I've lived and breathed with my family, with the people around me, even just with shopkeepers who I interact with two minutes a day."

As a teenager Sorrentino lost his parents to an accident, and he would later credit famed soccer player Diego Armando Maradona with inadvertently saving his life in the incident. He was supposed to join his parents on a weekend trip to a home in the mountains they frequented, but, as he recalled in an interview with Nick Vivarelli for *Variety* (13 Dec. 2015): "I didn't go because I wanted to go watch Maradona and S.S.C. Napoli play a match." A malfunction with the cabin's heating system led to his parents' deaths. Sorrentino later attended university but studied economics—in fact, he never went to film school. He eventually dropped out of school in order to pursue filmmaking and writing. His first filmmaking experience came at the age of twenty when he created a short film with friends centered on a cooking contest. Sorrentino served as the fifty-minute film's director and also performed as an actor in two different roles.

FIRST FILMS

Inspired by his first taste of directing Sorrentino began work as a filmmaker in earnest, working with a friend as his producer. He began with short films, cowriting and codirecting *Un paradiso* (A Paradise) 1994) and taking sole writing and directing credit for *L'amore non ha confine* (*Love Has No Borders*) (1998). He also received a cowriting credit on director Antonio Capuano's film *Polvere di Napoli* (*The Dust of Naples*) (1998), a portrait of his native Naples, and two episodes of the television series *La squadra* (*The Team*) in 2000. Another short, *La notte lunga* (*The Long Night*) (2001), was completed the same year as his first feature-length film, *One Man Up* (*L'uomo in più*, 2001), a black comedy about the declining careers of a pop star and a soccer player.

One Man Up, which Sorrentino wrote and directed, earned him significant attention in the Italian cinema scene, including recognition as the year's best new director by the Italian National Syndicate of Film Journalists. It also marked his first collaboration with actor Toni Servillo, who would star in several of his subsequent works. Sorrentino followed this success with the critically acclaimed 2004 thriller *The Consequences of Love* (*Le conseguenze dell'amore*). The film, which again featured Servillo, earned a nomination at the 2004 Cannes Film Festival for the Palme d'Or, the highest prize awarded at the festival. This was his first collaboration with Luca Bigazzi, who would become his regular cinematographer and introduced the director to "an aesthetic of darkness," as Sorrentino told Vivarelli. In 2006 his next feature film, *The Family Friend* (*L'amico di famiglia*), was also nominated for the Palme d'Or at Cannes and added a nomination for best feature at the Chicago International Film Festival. It told the story of an old, money-obsessed man who falls in love with a young woman.

Sorrentino's following film, *Il Divo* (*The Celebrity*) (2008), was a fictionalized biopic about the life of the infamous Italian politician Giulio Andreotti, played by Servillo. It found great critical acclaim despite its controversial depiction of national corruption and elevated Sorrentino to new fame. The film received the Prix du Jury at Cannes, the third most prestigious prize of the festival behind the Palme d'Or (for which it was also nominated) and the Grand Prix. *Il Divo* also gained the director new recognition in the United States, even receiving an Oscar nomination for best makeup. Many critics began considering Sorrentino one of the most talented young directors in Italy and around the world.

THIS MUST BE THE PLACE AND THE GREAT BEAUTY

Sorrentino followed his breakthrough success with several short works before tackling his first English-language film. *This Must Be the Place* (2011) starred Sean Penn as an aging rock star named Cheyenne, with hair and makeup based on musician Robert Smith of the Cure. Cheyenne, who is burned out from substance abuse and emotional distress, is looking to track down a former Nazi guard at the Auschwitz concentration camp where his late father had been imprisoned. His search takes him all around the United States on a journey that reveals as much about his character as it does about modern America. In a review for *Variety* (20 May 2011) Jay Weissberg called the work "a film that brims with warmth, humanity and respect. . . . The pic may baffle but is certain to generate massive highbrow press and long-term cult status." *This Must Be the Place* earned Sorrentino yet another Palme d'Or nomination and won Cannes's Prize of the Ecumenical Jury, among other awards.

Sorrentino's next feature film, *The Great Beauty* (*La grande bellezza*, 2013), would bring even greater amounts of critical acclaim. The project once again reunited the director with Servillo, who plays Jep Gambardella, a journalist whose one published novel hints at an unfulfilled life. It is through Jep's eyes that the audience views modern-day Rome in all of its excesses and atmosphere of alienation. Also featured in the film are such colorful and varied characters as a bishop who talks more of food than God, a stripper who loves her job, and a nun who shames Jep with her simple yet profound statements.

The film received nearly universal accolades from critics and drew frequent comparisons to Fellini's masterpiece *La dolce vita* (*The Sweet Life*) (1960), considered by many film lovers to be one of the greatest movies of all time. Reviewing the film for *Variety* (20 May 2013) Weissberg declared: "Rome in all its splendor and superficiality, artifice and significance, becomes an enormous banquet too rich to digest in one sitting in Paolo Sorrentino's densely packed, often astonishing *The Great Beauty*." It continued Sorrentino's run of Palme d'Or nominations and also won the Academy Award for best foreign language film, the Golden Globe for best foreign language film, and the best non-English film award from the British Academy of Film and Television Arts (BAFTA).

YOUTH AND OTHER PROJECTS

After the success of *The Great Beauty* Sorrentino released several short works, including the short films *Sabbia* (*Sand*) (2014) and *The Dream* (2014). He returned to an English-language format for his next feature-length piece, *Youth* (2015). It featured Michael Caine and Harvey Keitel as two old friends and fellow artists (respectively a conductor and a director) who are looking to finish up their careers in two very different ways as they vacation at a Swiss spa. Caine's Fred Ballinger, now retired, resists returning to England at the queen's request to conduct a final concert of his most famous musical piece, while Keitel's Mick Boyle is working diligently with a team of young writers to finish a screenplay for what he believes will be his masterpiece. During their time at the spa, the duo trade old stories, particularly about their youthful womanizing, and encounter an eccentric cast of characters including a Miss Universe who enjoys walking around nude, a young American actor, an obese man, as well as Ballinger's daughter, played by Rachel Weisz.

Sorrentino explained to Vivarelli that *Youth* was intended to be "a warm, tender movie; sentimental in the good sense of the word." He went on to describe his growth as a filmmaker despite his lack of formal training: "Right from the start I pretended I knew what I was doing. Then, slowly, by working this assuredness became real." Critics once again found Sorrentino's work to be most assured, with many noting that his second work in English improved upon *This Must Be the Place* and approached the cinematic distinction of *The Great Beauty*. "*Youth* is a voluptuary's feast, a full-body immersion in the sensory pleasures of the cinema," Todd McCarthy wrote in a review for the *Hollywood Reporter* (20 May 2015). "It takes on potentially heavy material in a disarmingly whimsical, intelligent and keen-witted manner."

Youth brought Sorrentino a familiar Palme d'Or nomination as well as Oscar and Golden Globe nominations for best original song, among other accolades. In 2016 he was set to premiere *The Young Pope* (2016), an eight-part miniseries he wrote and directed. It stars Jude Law as the first American pope and Diane Keaton as the nun who helped to raise him.

PERSONAL LIFE

Paolo Sorrentino is married to Daniela D'Antonio, with whom he has two children, Anna and Carlo. In addition to his work as a screenwriter and filmmaker he is also the author of a novel, *Everybody's Right* (*Hanno tutti ragione*, 2011).

SUGGESTED READING

McCarthy, Todd. "'Youth': Cannes Review." Rev. of *Youth*, dir. Paolo Sorrentino. *Hollywood Reporter*. Hollywood Reporter, 20 May 2015. Web. 1 Feb. 2016.

Sorrentino, Paolo. Interview by David Gregory Lawson. *Film Comment*. Film Soc. of Lincoln Center, 4 Nov. 2013. Web. 2 Feb. 2016.

Sorrentino, Paolo. "'The Misery of Some People': Paolo Sorrentino on *The Great Beauty*." Interview by Sarah Salovaara. *Filmmaker*. Filmmaker, 7 Feb. 2014. Web. 2 Feb. 2016.

Sorrentino, Paolo. "Paolo Sorrentino on 'The Great Beauty' and Italian Alienation." Interview by Larry Rohter. *New York Times*. New York Times, 4 Dec. 2013. Web. 2 Feb. 2016.

Sorrentino, Paolo. "Paolo Sorrentino On Why Maradona Has a Special Place in His Heart." Interview by Nick Vivarelli. *Variety*. Variety Media, 13 Dec. 2015. Web. 12 Feb. 2016.

Weissberg, Jay. Rev. of *This Must Be the Place*, dir. Paolo Sorrentino. *Variety*. Variety Media, 20 May 2011. Web. 1 Feb. 2016.

Weissberg, Jay. Rev. of *The Great Beauty*, dir. Paolo Sorrentino. *Variety*. Variety Media, 20 May 2013. Web. 1 Feb. 2016.

SELECTED WORKS

Le consequenze dell'amore (*The Consequences of Love*), 2004; *L'amico di famiglia* (*The Family Friend*), 2006; *Il Divo*, 2008; *This Must Be the Place*, 2011; *La grande bellezza* (*The Great Beauty*), 2013; *Youth*, 2015

—*Christopher Mari*

Pete Souza

Born: December 31, 1954
Occupation: Photojournalist

Although presidents of the United States have been photographed since the mid-nineteenth century, it was not until the early 1960s, during the administration of John F. Kennedy, that the full-time position of official White House photographer was formally established. Since that time, when Army Signal Corps officer Cecil Stoughton began capturing the working-day life of President Kennedy, official White House photographers have trailed presidents from meeting to meeting, event to event—even continent to continent—to provide an historical record of the presidency. While typically the White House photographer's best and most flattering photos of the president are made available to the public during the president's time in office, the rest are preserved for the president's library and the National Archives.

Barack Obama's chief official White House photographer, Pete Souza, has decades of experience as a seasoned photojournalist. He has also served in the White House for two presidential administrations: Ronald Reagan's, from 1983 to 1989, and Obama's, beginning in 2009. In an interview with Renee Montagne and Steve Inskeep for National Public Radio's (NPR's) *Morning Edition* (15 Jan. 2009), Souza described the continuing importance of the official White House photographer's role in capturing arguably one of the most photographed people on Earth: "I think it's pictures that are going to be timeless. It's going to be pictures that were taken in sensitive meetings in the Oval Office, Cabinet room, Situation Room, the kind of pictures that the press photographers don't get." Souza added, "I'm also quite interested in making sure that my support staff are photographing events in a different way, showing the scene. For instance, you know, if the president has an event in the Rose Garden, you know, I might put one of my photographers on the roof of the West Wing, so that fifty years from now, people will be able to see what that scene looks like."

EARLY LIFE AND EDUCATION

Peter J. Souza was born in 1954 and grew up in South Dartmouth, Massachusetts. He received his undergraduate education at Boston University, where he graduated cum laude with a degree in public communications in 1976. He later earned his master's degree in journalism and mass communication at Kansas State University in 1979.

CAREER

Souza's early career in photojournalism began in the late 1970s at various local newspapers in the

MICHAEL KAPPELER / Staff/ GettyImages

Midwest. He worked for such Kansas newspapers as the *Hutchinson News* and the *Chanute Tribune* before he moved to Chicago in 1982 to serve as a photographer for the *Chicago Sun-Times*. Bill Luster, a fellow photojournalist and friend of Souza's, described Souza's talent as a photographer to Manuel Roig-Franzia for the *Washington Post* (1 Mar. 2009): "His pictures are very simple in terms of composition. At the same time, they are complex in terms of content."

Souza left his job with the *Sun-Times* in 1983 to join the White House Photography Office, where he served as an official photographer for President Ronald Reagan. He held this position until January 1989, after Reagan completed his second term in office.

THE REAGAN ADMINISTRATION

Reagan, a Republican, came to office in January 1981, promising to restore fiscal strength to the United States and to contain the Soviet Union's expansion of control over more of the world during the Cold War. (The Soviet Union had invaded Afghanistan in 1979 and would occupy that nation until February 1989.) A staunch, decades-long anticommunist, Reagan spent much of his first term as president building up the United States' military and nuclear capabilities as a deterrent to Soviet expansion and then spent much of his second term seeking ways to bring about an end to the Cold War. He found a ready partner in Soviet leader Mikhail Gorbachev, who, since taking office in 1985, had been pursuing a policy of *glasnost* (openness) with the West.

In these years just before the Soviet Union—and its satellite communist states in Eastern

Europe—collapsed, Souza had an inside look at this seminal moment in history. Souza recalled hearing a bit of conversation between Reagan and Gorbachev in Reykjavik, Iceland, in 1986, when they were at an impasse over a treaty to reduce stockpiles of a particular type of missile. As Souza recalled in an article for the *Chicago Tribune* in the days following Reagan's death (7 June 2004), Gorbachev said, "I don't know what else I could have done," to which Reagan responded, "You could have said yes."

As the official White House photographer, Souza captured many unique photos of Reagan, including some that did not seem significant at the time but that became historically significant later. Souza recalled one such picture to Inskeep: "[Reagan] was being escorted by Mikhail Gorbachev, and there were these different groups of, you know, quote/unquote, 'tourists,' set up around Red Square, and Gorbachev would escort him over, and they would ask President Reagan questions. . . . And I remember saying to the Secret Service agent, I said, I can't believe these tourists in the Soviet Union are asking these pointed questions. And the Secret Service agent said to me, oh, these are all KGB families. Now, what's really interesting is I have a picture in my Reagan book, and off to the left is this, one of these tourists with a camera around his shoulder, and it's been pointed out to me and verified that that was [Vladimir] Putin."

When Reagan died in June 2004, after a decade-long battle with Alzheimer's disease, Souza was asked by Nancy Reagan, the president's widow, to serve as the official photographer for Reagan's funeral. Some of Souza's best images of the fortieth president of the United States were collected in two volumes: *Unguarded Moments: Behind-the-Scenes Photographs of President Reagan* (1992) and *Images of Greatness: An Intimate Look at the Presidency of Ronald Reagan* (2004).

DOCUMENTING BARACK OBAMA'S RISE

After leaving the White House, Souza worked as a freelance photographer for nine years, from 1989 to 1997, and then joined the Washington, DC, bureau of the *Chicago Tribune* as its national photographer, a position he held from January 1998 to July 2007. Some of this work was collected in another book, *Plebe Summer at the U.S. Naval Academy* (2003), which captured the experience of naval cadets. But most significant, it was during this period that he came into contact with a rising star in the Democratic Party, Barack Obama. The young senator from Illinois and the seasoned photojournalist met first met on January 3, 2005, Obama's first day in the US Senate. His yearlong assignment with the *Tribune* was to record Obama's first year in office. One of Souza's most famous pictures from that

period adorns the cover of Souza's collection of photos, *The Rise of Barack Obama* (2008). In it, Obama is seen from behind jogging up the steps of the US Capitol, a moment that perfectly captured Obama's ascendance in the imaginations of political insiders.

Souza too was intrigued by the young senator and felt that Obama had the potential to become president, if he chose to do so. So, as he worked his assignment, he looked to capture moments in Obama's life and career that could potentially have historical significance. "I was looking for things that I knew that if he ever became president you would never see again," Souza told a reporter for *Time* (8 Oct. 2012). "[Obama was] walking down a sidewalk in Moscow in 2005 and no one recognized him. I realized that if he ever became president, you would never, ever see a photograph like that. The odds of becoming president are obviously pretty slim, but I knew he had the potential. And you can't say that about too many people."

Souza left the *Chicago Tribune* in July 2007 to take up an assistant professorship at Ohio University. There he briefly taught photojournalism before getting the call, once again, to serve as the official White House photographer, this time to a former young senator from Illinois.

RETURN TO THE WHITE HOUSE

Barack Obama was sworn in as the forty-fourth president of the United States in January 2009. Souza, who had established a good relationship with Obama while covering his Senate years, readily took on the opportunity to photograph the president in action. As the official White House photographer, Souza has been intimately involved with Obama's daily life, capturing him as he wrestled with passing health care reform, dealing with the devastating impact of the Great Recession, and winding down the wars in Afghanistan and Iraq. He has most notably shot the president's official portraits—the first official presidential portrait to be taken with a digital camera—as well as the now-famous photograph in the Situation Room, taken of Obama and his senior staff at the moment they learn that a US strike force has raided the compound where Osama bin Laden, the mastermind of the terrorist attacks that killed more than three thousand Americans on September 11, 2001, had been hiding. In his interview for *Time*, Souza reflected on his work during Obama's first term in office, "I tried to . . . not only to show some of the high points or low points of his presidency thus far but pictures that help people understand what he's like, not only as a president but as a human being. And how he relates to other people, how he relates to his family."

Souza continued to serve as Obama's official photographer in his second term, which began in January 2013, and he also serves as director of the White House photo office. An all-digital workflow has allowed Souza and his staff to produce upwards of twenty thousand photos of Obama and his staff each week. Steady streams of photos are directly uploaded to Souza's various social media accounts. Although well liked personally in Washington, DC, Souza has had a share of controversy during his time as Obama's official photographer. On Obama's first day in office in 2009, no outside photographers were allowed in to capture the moment; instead, Souza's photos were given to the media, and many outlets refused to run them. In 2013 the White House Correspondents' Association and other news organizations complained to Jay Carney, who was the White House press secretary at the time, that the White House was excluding outside press coverage in favor of Souza's photos, which presented the president in the most favorable light. In response to this criticism, Souza told Mark Landler for the *New York Times* (30 Nov. 2013): "It's legitimate for them to push for more access, and in some cases I think their arguments are valid, and in some instances I think their arguments aren't valid."

PERSONAL LIFE, AWARDS, AND EXHIBITIONS
Little has been written about Souza's private life. Even his marriage, to Patti Lease on October 19, 2013, was conducted in the most private of settings: the White House Rose Garden, a place where few weddings have traditionally taken place.

Souza's work has received numerous awards throughout his career, including the Pictures of the Year Annual Competition and the National Press Photographer's Award for best photojournalism. His photographs have been shown in solo exhibitions, including at the Smithsonian Museum of American History, the Corcoran Gallery of Art, Harvard University, Boston University, Ohio University, and Kansas State University, among others. He remains on an indefinite leave of absence from Ohio University's School of Visual Communication, where he is an assistant professor of photojournalism.

SUGGESTED READING
"Bio." *PeteSouza.com.* Pete Souza Photography, n.d. Web. 15 Oct. 2015.

Cillizza, Chris. "How Pete Souza Became President Obama's Secret Weapon." *Washington Post.* Washington Post, 19 Dec. 2012. Web. 13 Nov. 2015.

Landler, Mark. "Limit on Access Stirs Tensions between White House Photographer and Press Corps." *New York Times.* New York Times, 30 Nov. 2013. Web. 17 Oct. 2015.

Montagne, Renee, and Steve Inskeep. "A Front-Row View of Obama's White House." *Morning Edition.* NPR, 15 Jan. 2009. Web. 15 Oct. 2015.

"Pete Souza's Portrait of a Presidency." *Time.* Time, 8 Oct. 2012. Web. 18 Oct. 2015.

Roig-Franzia, Manuel. "White House Photographer Pete Souza Has the Country's Top Photo Op." *Washington Post.* Washington Post, 1 Mar. 2009. Web. 17 Oct. 2015.

SELECTED WORKS
Unguarded Moments: Behind-the-Scenes Photographs of President Reagan, 1997; *Plebe Summer at the U.S. Naval Academy,* 2003; *Images of Greatness: An Intimate Look at the Presidency of Ronald Reagan,* 2004; *The Rise of Barack Obama,* 2008

—Christopher Mari

St. Vincent

Born: September 28, 1982
Occupation: Musician

When multitalented musician St. Vincent won the Grammy Award for best alternative album in 2015, the event was the culmination of a decade-long career as perhaps one of the most intriguing musicians in the genre. A Texas native who dropped out of Berklee College of Music to pursue a career in music, first as a touring musician with acts such as the Polyphonic Spree and Sufjan Stevens and later as a solo artist, St. Vincent rose to prominence with a string of successful independent solo albums, beginning with 2007's *Marry Me.* The 2014 release of the eponymous *St. Vincent,* her first major-label record, propelled St. Vincent to new levels of popularity and critical acclaim, earning her significant recognition from longtime fans and new converts alike.

Known for her eclectic style and complex compositions, St. Vincent never shies away from trying new things, be they methods of composing or recording music, instruments, or genres of music; her full-length collaboration with former Talking Heads front man David Byrne, for instance, heavily features brass instruments, which are not typically found in her music. "That's the only way you grow," she told Geoffrey Himes for *Smithsonian* magazine (Dec. 2013) of her willingness to take musical risks. "When you have to try something you haven't done before, you're forced to take inventory of [your] strengths and weaknesses and see if you can update them."

Wikimedia/Flickr/Ralph Arvesen/CC BY 2.0

EARLY LIFE AND EDUCATION

Annie Erin Clark, better known as St. Vincent, was born on September 28, 1982, in Tulsa, Oklahoma. She and her siblings grew up primarily in the Lake Highlands area of Dallas, Texas, where they were raised by their mother, a social worker, following their parents' separation. St. Vincent was drawn to music at an early age, in part because it helped her process the anxiety she began to experience as a child. "When you're forced to deal with something big that you don't understand, you try to find ways to interpret the universe in a way that can make you feel safer or alleviate that crazy," she told Jonah Weiner for *Rolling Stone* (23 June 2014). "For me, it was music." As a child and teen, she became a fan of grunge bands such as Nirvana as well as various punk and classic rock groups.

Having learned to play guitar at the age of twelve, St. Vincent soon began composing her own songs and recording them using computer audio software. Technology would remain an important component of her writing process throughout her career, as it enabled her to transcend some of her own limitations as a musician. "I discovered I could write stuff that I couldn't play," she explained to Weiner. "My ears are smarter than my fingers." Although she worked alone much of the time, the young St. Vincent was no stranger to the collaborative nature of performance: she played in a metal cover band with her friends and also spent time as an assistant road manager for the jazz duo Tuck & Patti, which consisted of her uncle Tuck Andress and aunt Patti Cathcart. The latter experience was

a particularly influential one, teaching her many of the realities of life as a professional musician.

After graduating from Lake Highlands High School in 2001, St. Vincent enrolled in Berklee College of Music in Boston, Massachusetts. She continued to progress as a musician there, recording the three-song extended play (EP) *Ratsliveonnoevilstar*, released under her real name, and collaborating with fellow students on various projects. However, she found the school's emphasis on technique rather than artistry creatively stifling and ultimately dropped out before finishing her degree.

BECOMING ST. VINCENT

Although she completed brief stints as a hair model and an employee at a flower shop, St. Vincent concentrated primarily on music after leaving Berklee, establishing herself as a touring musician. She joined the symphonic rock band the Polyphonic Spree as a guitarist and vocalist, accompanying the group, fronted by vocalist Tim DeLaughter, on tour and playing on the 2007 album *The Fragile Army*. She left the touring band in 2006 and instead began to tour with singer-songwriter Sufjan Stevens. While on tour, she released the three-song EP *Paris Is Burning*, the first record to be released under the name St. Vincent.

The decision to take on the name St. Vincent was both a practical and an artistic one. "I didn't want to go under the name Annie Clark because to me it connoted a singer/songwriter, maybe acoustic, heart on sleeve thing that I wasn't doing," she explained to Brad Casey in an interview for the website of the WayHome music festival (2015). "It seemed like it would make sense to come up with a different name. I was asking myself, what could be it? Could it be something chameleon-like?" Inspired by a variety of sources, including her grandmother, a song by musician Nick Cave, a church in New York, and the hospital where poet Dylan Thomas died, the moniker St. Vincent came to suit the musician's work, which often features religious imagery.

UPWARD TRAJECTORY

St. Vincent released her first full-length album, *Marry Me*, in 2007. The album, the title of which was drawn from the television series *Arrested Development*, featured two of the songs from the *Paris Is Burning* EP as well as nine additional tracks. Released by the independent label Beggars Banquet Records, *Marry Me* earned favorable reviews and garnered St. Vincent fans, much to her surprise. "I had no expectations when *Marry Me* was released," she later told Nilina Mason-Campbell for *Pitchfork* (4 Mar. 2008). "I knew my friends and family would buy it, so that's six copies right there." Staying connected with her fans via her blog, MySpace page, and later Twitter account, St. Vincent cultivated a dedicated fan base that would help her later releases achieve high rankings on *Billboard* magazine's Independent Albums and Billboard 200 charts.

Her next two albums, *Actor* (2009) and *Strange Mercy* (2011), proved popular with critics as well as fans of alternative music, increasing her fame as an artist over the course of several years. For St. Vincent, her rise to prominence was the culmination of a decade's development as a musician and yet somewhat unexpected. "It doesn't feel like I crawled out of the woods and just kind of miraculously manifested on top of the pop charts. It's been a nice, steady, upward trajectory," she explained to Nell Alk for *Interview* magazine (3 Nov. 2011). "But, it feels great. You never know how these things are going to go. All you can do is make something that you like and feel proud of and then just hope for the best and try to get out of its way."

LOVE THIS GIANT

Even after beginning her solo career, St. Vincent continued collaborating with other artists; she performed on songs by a variety of acts, including Bon Iver, the New Pornographers, and Of Montreal. Perhaps her most productive collaboration, however, was with former Talking Heads vocalist David Byrne. The two first met at a 2009 benefit concert, but Byrne had been a fan of St. Vincent's music for several years. "When I first heard and saw Annie, I could see that she could write a memorable and beautiful melody—something a lot of younger artists shy away from, intentionally or not," he told Himes. "So I sensed she'd accepted that part of music—a part that is welcoming and inviting to us as audience members. But then she tempers that with fierce guitar playing and often dark and perverse lyrics delivered in an affectless tone. It's really quite disturbing, but in a good way."

After collaborating on a few songs for a one-time performance, St. Vincent and Byrne established a longer-term working relationship, cowriting and recording what would become the album *Love This Giant*. Released in 2012, the album featured alternating vocals and brass-band instrumentation, new features in St. Vincent's music. The duo toured North America, Europe, and Australia to promote the album and in 2013 released the EP *Brass Tactics*, which featured a mixture of new songs and remixes of tracks from *Love This Giant*.

ST. VINCENT

The year 2014 was a particularly significant one for St. Vincent. In February of that year, she released her fourth full-length solo album, the self-titled *St. Vincent*. Bolstered by the singles "Birth in Reverse" and "Digital Witness," the album rose to the number-twelve position on the Billboard 200 chart and hit numbers three and four on the Alternative Albums chart and the Top Rock Albums chart, respectively. *St. Vincent* proved to be a hit with critics as well, earning overwhelmingly positive reviews and featuring in numerous critics' lists of the best albums of 2014. Early the following year, St. Vincent won the Grammy Award for best alternative music album for the record.

The album's success and St. Vincent's increasing renown as a musician led to a number of unique opportunities for the artist. In addition to performing as the musical guest in a May 2014 episode of *Saturday Night Live*, she was selected to be one of four vocalists to perform alongside Dave Grohl and Krist Novoselic, the surviving members of Nirvana, at the band's induction into the Rock and Roll Hall of Fame. St. Vincent, who became a fan of the group as a child, was thrilled by the opportunity to join the band in a performance of the song "Lithium," from the 1991 album *Nevermind*. "*Nevermind* came out when I was nine, and it meant everything to me," she told James Montgomery for *Rolling Stone* (11 Apr. 2014). "I know I wouldn't be playing music if it wasn't for Nirvana."

PERSONAL LIFE

When not touring, St. Vincent lives in New York City's East Village. Although she grew up composing songs from her home, she often travels away from home to work on new material, in part to differentiate her working time from her everyday life. When writing songs for *St. Vincent*, for instance, she worked out of a friend's shed in Texas, going there each morning as if to an office. "I approach my work as I would a day job," she explained to Himes. "If you're a writer, you have to write. If you're a musician, you have to make music."

Notoriously private about her personal life, St. Vincent was thrust into a new kind of spotlight in early 2015, when her relationship with British model and actor Cara Delevingne became the subject of much speculation in the media. Although she has acknowledged that "there's been a little bit of enigma peeled back as of late" regarding her personal life, as she told Charlotte Cowles for *Harper's Bazaar* (19 Oct. 2015), she remains adamant that her music should remain the focus. "Ultimately what I make is what I want to be," she told Cowles. "It's my offering to the world."

SUGGESTED READING

Cowles, Charlotte. "Women Who Dare: St. Vincent." *Harper's Bazaar*. Hearst Communications, 19 Oct. 2015. Web. 11 Dec. 2015.

Himes, Geoffrey. "The Totally Original Sound of St. Vincent." *Smithsonian Magazine*. Smithsonian, Dec. 2013. Web. 11 Dec. 2015.

Montgomery, James. "Nirvana's Rock Hall Performance Had St. Vincent Profanely Excited." *Rolling Stone*. Rolling Stone, 11 Apr. 2014. Web. 11 Dec. 2015.

St. Vincent. Interview by Brad Casey. *WayHome*. WayHome Music and Arts, n. d. Web. 11 Dec. 2015.

St. Vincent. Interview by Nilina Mason-Campbell. *Pitchfork*. Condé Nast, 4 Mar. 2008. Web. 11 Dec. 2015.

St. Vincent. "A Glimpse of St. Vincent." Interview by Nell Alk. *Interview*. Interview, 3 Nov. 2011. Web. 11 Dec. 2015.

Weiner, Jonah. "The Dream World of St. Vincent." *Rolling Stone*. Rolling Stone, 23 June 2014. Web. 11 Dec. 2015.

SELECTED WORKS
Marry Me, 2007; *Actor*, 2009; *Strange Mercy*, 2011; *Love This Giant* (with David Byrne), 2012; *St. Vincent*, 2014

—*Joy Crelin*

Arturo Pardavila III/Flickr/CC BY 2.0/Wikimedia Commons

Giancarlo Stanton

Born: November 8, 1989
Occupation: Baseball player

There are few players in the history of Major League Baseball (MLB) who have hit baseballs harder and farther than Miami Marlins right fielder Giancarlo Stanton. With a six-foot-six, 245-pound physique that "resembles that of a Grecian god," as Christina De Nicola wrote for *FOX Sports* (21 June 2015), Stanton has wowed the baseball world with his prodigious power and tape-measure home runs since making his major-league debut with the Marlins in 2010. Adam Kramer, writing for *Bleacher Report* (29 Jan. 2016), said, "His at-bats are nightly spectacles—moments of raw power unmatched by anyone in the sport."

In his first five seasons with the Marlins, Stanton hit 181 home runs, the eleventh-highest total for a player through his age-twenty-five season in MLB history. In addition to being arguably the best power hitter in the game, he transformed himself into an all-around talent, capable of hitting for average and providing Gold Glove–caliber defense. An All-Star in 2012, 2014, and 2015, he emerged as a most valuable player (MVP) candidate in 2014, when he led the National League (NL) in a number of offensive statistical categories.

Stanton's MVP bid came to an abrupt end, however, when he suffered a horrific facial injury that forced him to miss the last three weeks of the 2014 season. It was just one of several injuries that plagued his relatively young career and prevented him from racking up even more impressive statistics. Despite his injury history, in November 2014 the Marlins signed Stanton to a thirteen-year, $325 million contract, the most lucrative deal in North American sports history.

EARLY LIFE
The son of postal workers, Giancarlo Cruz Michael Stanton was born on November 8, 1989, in the Panorama City neighborhood of Los Angeles, California. Stanton and his two siblings—brother Egidio and sister Kairice—were raised in the middle-class enclave of Sunland, located in the foothills of the San Gabriel Mountains. Stanton's father was of Irish heritage, while his mother was African American and Puerto Rican. His parents divorced when he was ten.

From an early age Stanton aspired to become a professional athlete. He grew up less than twenty miles from Dodger Stadium and dreamed of playing for the hometown Los Angeles Dodgers. His father began taking him to a baseball field at a Mormon church in Sunland for batting practice. "He'd throw buckets and buckets to me," Stanton recalled to De Nicola, "He'd have me sit there and think about where I want to hit the ball or what to do different in the next round." His father also ensured Stanton followed a high-protein and high-calorie diet to build strength and size to match his work ethic.

Stanton's herculean hitting ability was apparent from the time he picked up a bat. When he played Little League he routinely drew intentional walks because of his propensity to hit home runs. Stanton has said that he grew up idolizing and trying to emulate such sluggers as Mark McGwire and Ken Griffey Jr., both of whom he saw play while attending games at Dodgers Stadium as a youth.

MULTISPORT HIGH SCHOOL ATHLETE

By the time Stanton entered Verdugo Hills High School in Tujunga, California, in 2003, he was dominating not only in baseball but also in football and basketball. Stanton's athletic prowess was such that he chose to transfer to Notre Dame High School in Sherman Oaks, California, after his sophomore year for the chance to compete on nationally recognized sports teams.

In the year leading up to his arrival at Notre Dame, Stanton underwent a growth spurt that added six inches to his height, which helped transform him into a physically imposing three-sport athlete. During his junior year he did not perform well on the baseball diamond, however, as he struggled with plate discipline and hit only around .200. A two-way standout at wide receiver and cornerback for Notre Dame's football team and a top-scoring power forward on the school's basketball squad, Stanton was considered more likely to pursue professional football or basketball rather than baseball entering his senior season.

Motivated to prove he was as good as other top-rated area baseball players, Stanton spent the summer before his senior year working with a local hitting instructor, Phil Van Horn, who helped fine-tune his raw skills. That summer he put those honed skills on display at the Area Code Games in Long Beach, California, an annual showcase event featuring some of the top high school baseball prospects in the nation. Stanton's performance during a batting practice session, in which he hit a flurry of mammoth home runs, brought the otherwise unheralded player to the attention of Marlins' scout Tim McDonnell. "He's an athlete, a complete package of strength," McDonnell said of Stanton to Albert Chen for *Sports Illustrated* (2 July 2012). "I'd be shocked if I ever see another guy with that kind of raw power."

McDonnell kept close tabs on Stanton during his senior year. He did so discreetly, often watching games through binoculars from inconspicuous vantage points, so as not to reveal the Marlins' interest and put Stanton on the radar of other scouts. The secrecy proved unnecessary, however, as Stanton garnered little interest from other MLB teams despite hitting .393 with twelve home runs as a senior. This was largely a result of Stanton's continued commitment to football and basketball, which prevented him from playing on year-round baseball travel teams like other top prospects, limiting his exposure.

THE FLORIDA MARLINS

Stanton's relatively low profile proved a boon for the Marlins, who selected him with the seventy-sixth pick in the second round of the 2007 MLB Draft. He had been presented with a full scholarship offer to play football as well as baseball at the University of Southern California (USC), but he turned it down after being drafted. "I picked baseball over football because of the opportunity. I wanted to stick to one sport full time for the first time in my life," Stanton, who received a $475,000 signing bonus from the Marlins, explained to Kramer.

Stanton's first taste of professional baseball was humbling. In rookie-level ball for the Marlins during the 2007 season, he hit just .161 with one home run. Determined to regain his hitting form, Stanton spent that offseason working with John Mallee, then the Marlins' minor-league hitting coordinator, on his swing mechanics. He made his swing more compact by starting it with his hands closer to his right hip, which limited the distance his bat would have to travel through the hitting zone. "I think what he wanted to do more than anything was not just be known as a big, strong guy who can hit a ball a mile," the Marlins' scouting director Stan Meek told Ben Reiter for *Sports Illustrated* (25 Feb. 2015), "but to become a complete baseball player."

The adjustments quickly paid off, and in 2008 Stanton hit .293 with thirty-nine home runs for the Greensboro Grasshoppers, the Marlins' Class A affiliate. He went on to hit a combined twenty-eight homers in 2009, during which he split his time between the advanced-A Jupiter Hammerheads and the AA Jacksonville Suns.

In 2010 *Baseball America* ranked Stanton the top player in the Marlins' system and the third-best prospect in all of baseball. He returned to the Suns to open that season, but after batting .311 with twenty-one home runs in fifty-three games with the club, the Marlins deemed him ready for the majors. Stanton was promoted to the big-league club on June 8, 2010, for a game against the Philadelphia Phillies. He collected three hits in five at-bats and scored two runs in his debut, which was enough for him to be installed as the Marlins' everyday right fielder. Stanton finished his abbreviated rookie season with twenty-two home runs in one hundred games.

SLUGGER FOR A NEW ERA

By the time Stanton entered his first full MLB season in 2011 he had already built a reputation for hitting tape-measure home runs. That year saw him bolster that reputation: he hit thirty-four home runs that traveled at an average distance of 416 feet, with five traveling over 450 feet. Stanton's home-run total led the Marlins and ranked fifth in the NL, and his two-year career total of fifty-six home runs were the third-most for a player before his age-twenty-two season in the previous forty years.

During the 2012 season Stanton solidified his status as "perhaps the first great slugger of the poststeroid era," as Chen wrote. Despite being limited to just 123 games due to myriad injuries, he led the majors with a .608 slugging percentage, finished second in the NL in homers (thirty-seven), and batted a career-best .290, helping him earn his first career All-Star selection. Stanton again drew attention around the league for his monstrous homers, the most notable of which came on May 21, 2012, when he hit a grand slam off Colorado Rockies pitcher Jamie Moyer that traveled 462 feet and shattered a panel of lights on the left-field video scoreboard at Marlins Park. The ball's exit velocity set a record at 122.4 miles per hour.

Stanton's regular-season performance was one of the few bright spots for a Marlins team that finished last in the NL East Division with a 69–93 record. The disappointing showing overshadowed a season that had begun with optimism after a rebranding as the Miami, rather than Florida, Marlins, the construction of the $634 million, state-of-the-art Marlins Park, and several high-priced free-agent signings. Marlins owner Jeffrey Loria retaliated by firing controversial manager Ozzie Guillen with three years left on his contract and dumping more than $200 million in player salaries.

Stanton was the only star player retained and publicly expressed his dismay over Loria and the Marlins' history of knee-jerk moves and apparent willingness to field an uncompetitive team. Nonetheless, he entered the 2013 season hoping to build upon his breakthrough 2012 campaign. A recurring hamstring injury, however, derailed those hopes. The injury limited him to just 116 games, in which he hit twenty-four homers with sixty-two runs batted in (RBIs) and posted career lows in batting average (.249) and slugging percentage (.480). The Marlins struggled mightily in his absence, finishing with an NL-worst 62–100 record.

MVP CAMPAIGNS CUT SHORT BY INJURY

After returning to full health, Stanton helped bring the Marlins back to respectability in 2014, when he emerged as a viable MVP candidate. He batted .288 and led the NL in home runs (37), slugging percentage (.555), total bases (299), and intentional walks (24). He also finished second in the league in RBIs (105), walks (94), and on-base percentage (.395). He earned his second career All-Star selection, received his first career NL Silver Slugger Award, and was named an NL Gold Glove finalist for his defensive prowess in right field.

Energized by Stanton's play, the Marlins unexpectedly contended for a playoff spot and hovered at the .500 mark for the majority of the season before finishing with a 77–85 record. Stanton narrowly missed out on winning his first NL MVP Award, finishing as a runner-up to Los Angeles Dodgers pitcher Clayton Kershaw. Many baseball observers believed that Stanton would have won MVP if not for missing the last three weeks of the season due to a serious facial injury. On September 11, 2014, he was hit square in the face by a fastball from Milwaukee Brewers pitcher Mike Fiers, causing multiple facial fractures and dental damage. The injury forced him to undergo six surgeries and a lengthy period of rehabilitation. Still, "I got lucky," Stanton told Tim Keown for *ESPN the Magazine* (18 Mar. 2015). "I got hit in the best part of the worst place."

By the time of Stanton's injury, the Marlins had already set in motion plans to sign him to what they would describe as a "forever deal." Though some commentators worried that the devastating accident would affect Stanton's game, the Marlins shocked the sports world in November 2014 when they signed the slugger to a thirteen-year, $325 million contract extension. The immense deal was the largest contract with a team in the history of professional sports.

Stanton proceeded to put together another MVP-caliber season in 2015 before a broken bone in his left wrist thwarted his campaign. At the time of the injury, which limited him to just seventy-four games, he was leading the NL in homers (27) and RBIs (67), though the team continued to struggle and would finish at 71–91. Even with his shortened season Stanton became the Marlins' all-time leader in home runs and was named to his third career All-Star team. He also recorded the two longest home runs in the majors that season, with both traveling an estimated 484 feet.

PERSONAL LIFE

Stanton holds the distinction of being the first player in MLB history to have the first name Giancarlo. Up until the 2012 season he went by "Mike" because his birth name was too often mispronounced. His teammates, meanwhile, gave him the nickname "Bigfoot."

Stanton divides his off-seasons between Los Angeles and Miami. Unlike many other superstar athletes, he is known to largely eschew those cities' famous nightlife scenes, instead enjoying traveling, working out, and hanging out with friends and family.

SUGGESTED READING

Chen, Albert. "Name Changer, Game Changer." *Sports Illustrated* 2 July 2012: 46–49. Print.

De Nicola, Christina. "Walk Softly: Giancarlo Stanton's Mighty Path Inspired by Father." *FOX Sports*. Fox Sports Interactive Media, 21 June 2015. Web. 5 May 2016.

Keown, Tim. "What is Giancarlo Stanton Thinking?" *ESPN the Magazine*. ESPN Internet Ventures, 18 Mar. 2015. Web. 5 May 2016.

Kramer, Adam. "The Failed College Football Recruitment of Giancarlo Stanton." *Bleacher Report*. Bleacher Report, 29 Jan. 2016. Web. 5 May 2016.

Reiter, Ben. "Marlin Masterpiece." *Sports Illustrated* 2 Mar. 2015: 46–53. Print.

—Chris Cullen

Chris Stapleton

Born: April 15, 1978
Occupation: Musician

"Stapleton is a country musician who . . . has found a home in the genre while still setting himself apart from its current trends," Andrew Leahey wrote for *American Songwriter* magazine (22 Sept. 2015). "He doesn't sing about tailgates. He doesn't AutoTune his vocals. He doesn't rhyme 'Bacardi' with 'party.' Instead, Stapleton writes his own songs, plays his own guitar solos, and chases his muse wherever it leads him. In a town that's bound by tradition, he's a rare rule-breaker."

After more than a decade of penning songs for other musicians—including Luke Bryan, Kenny Chesney, Blake Shelton, Lee Ann Womack, and Tim McGraw—Stapleton released his first solo album in 2015 at the age of thirty-seven. *Traveller* swept the 2015 Country Music Association (CMA) Awards. *Traveller* received the CMA Award for album of the year and Stapleton took home the awards for male vocalist and new artist of the year.

"Stapleton's story is unique, heartening," Spencer Kornhaber wrote for the *Atlantic* (5 Nov. 2015). "He's neither a revered veteran with built-in acclaim nor an over-hyped newcomer but rather someone who has worked and worked behind the scenes and finally decided to make his own statement. Whatever factors went into his CMAs sweep, *Traveller*'s tales of struggle and misspent youth make his success seem especially poignant."

Despite the success of his solo career, Stapleton has announced his intention to continue writing songs for others. "It's all part of one wheel for me," he told Leahey. "Sometimes, you've gotta wear one hat more than you wear the other one. Sometimes, you just wear two hats at once. You have to make hay while the sun shines, so we're trying to do that. We're trying [to] figure out what life is now. That's always the case. You're just figuring out what life is."

EARLY LIFE

Stapleton was born on April 15, 1978, in Lexington, Kentucky, and raised in the nearby town of Staffordsville. His two grandfathers and his father all worked in the region's coal mines. His mother worked with the health department. His parents loved music, and his father bought himself a Gibson acoustic guitar, dreaming of having the time and energy to learn to play it at some point in the future. Finding the instrument stashed away one day when he was a teen, Stapleton taught himself to play.

Eastern Kentucky, where Stapleton grew up, had a vibrant musical tradition. "It's just part of the fabric of being from Kentucky," he told Walter Tunis for the *Lexington Herald-Leader* (2 May 2015). "Ricky Skaggs and Keith Whitley, Dwight Yoakam and Patty Loveless, the list goes on and on. Those names are just part of life in Kentucky. You can't help but be aware of them and be influenced by them. It's almost genetic in the sense that you don't have an existence that doesn't involve their music."

In 1996, after graduating from Johnson Central High School, Stapleton entered Vanderbilt University in Nashville, Tennessee, where he set out to study engineering. College, as he has recalled to several interviewers, "didn't take," and he dropped out after a year. He returned to

Kentucky and began working a series of odd jobs, including delivering pizza, and thanks to his guitar prowess, he found work playing in local bars at night.

Stapleton's living conditions were far from optimal. He lived with three other people in a small space with no air conditioning, paying eighty dollars a month. "It's since been condemned and torn down," Stapleton told Craig Shelburne for *American Songwriter* magazine (21 July 2014). "But we played bluegrass and I really got heavy into it. . . . We'd sit around and pick and have a good time every night." In 2001, Stapleton's friend Jesse Wells from the Kentucky Center for Traditional Music at Morehead State University introduced Stapleton to songwriter Steve Leslie, who recognized the young musician's promise and invited him to Nashville, the center of the country-music industry, to collaborate. "I moved to town with a chair, a sleeping bag, a sack full of clothes, a recorder, and my guitar," Stapleton told Shelburne. "I didn't want a cell phone. I didn't want someone to be able to get a hold of me, or know where I was, at any point in time. I wanted to be able to throw all my stuff in my car and leave."

SONGWRITING

Within a week of moving to Nashville, Stapleton had signed a publishing deal with Sea Gayle Music. "I didn't know that songwriting could be an actual job," he admitted to Leahey. "I didn't realize people did that for a living." He became intensely absorbed in his songwriting career, telling Leahey, "I was so fascinated with the culture of writing songs that for the first three or four years, the thought of actually performing didn't even cross my mind. I didn't really play live; I just wrote. I got to go to work every day, sit in a room, and make up songs. I was writing two or three songs or a day. That's all I wanted to do." Liz O'Sullivan, a senior vice president at Sea Gayle, recalled Stapleton's prolific output to Leahey: "Chris had this intense work ethic from the second he started. . . . We'd be sitting down in my office, and he would start scatting some lyrics and suddenly say, 'I've gotta leave and go write this song.' It was amazing to watch him. It was like nothing I'd ever seen."

O'Sullivan was blown away by Stapleton's incredible success, telling Leahey, "People were fighting over his songs. By the end of the first year, he'd gotten more cuts than some writers get in their whole career." Stapleton ended up writing songs for some of the biggest names in the country-music business, including Brad Paisley ("The Best Thing That I Had Goin'"), Lee Ann Womack ("There's More Where That Came From"), Tim McGraw ("Whiskey and You"), Blake Shelton ("100 Miles"), Darius Rucker ("Come Back Song"), Dierks Bentley ("Diamonds

Make Babies"), Thomas Rhett ("Crash and Burn"), Miranda Lambert ("Nobody's Fool"), Luke Bryan ("Drink a Beer"), and the legendary George Strait ("Love's Gonna Make It Alright"). In total, he has written more than one hundred songs—many of them chart-toppers—for other artists.

THE STEELDRIVERS AND THE JOMPSON BROTHERS

Stapleton began jamming in the evenings with Mike Henderson, a guitarist and mandolin player, and the two eventually formed a bluegrass-inspired band called the SteelDrivers, which also included bassist Mike Fleming, fiddler Tammy Rogers, and banjo player Richard Bailey. "I was writing songs about killing people and burying them," Stapleton recalled to Leahey. "That's what the SteelDrivers stuff was. It was a lot of tradition. But I was never gonna flat-pick a guitar as well as other bluegrass players could, and I was never gonna sing like other bluegrass singers could. I could only be me. I couldn't be anything else. And that's what the SteelDrivers stuff was, too. We were different."

The band released two albums (an eponymous debut in 2008 and *Reckless* in 2010) and garnered three Grammy nominations during the two years Stapleton was a member. By then a husband and father, he found the demands of touring difficult. Explaining his acerbically named song "The Devil Named Music," he told Leahey, "The band had played some horse farm gig in Wyoming, then rented a minivan and driven God knows how many hours to Billings, Montana, because that was the closest airport. We checked into an airport hotel to get an hour of sleep in our shared rooms. Then we got up, went to the airport, and checked in for a 5:30 a.m. flight, which was going to Salt Lake City." So fatigued and miserable was Stapleton—who then weighed an unhealthy three hundred pounds—that he barely remembered the plane ride. However, the agony of trying to breathe in Salt Lake City, at an altitude of 10,000 feet, remains fresh in his mind. "That's what that song is about," he explained to Leahey "I missed my kid and I missed my wife, and I was getting an idea of what it was like to be a touring musician."

Stapleton ultimately left the SteelDrivers and later launched a Southern rock–inspired band called the Jompson Brothers, which toured only in the vicinity of Nashville, traveling in Stapleton's truck. Although Stapleton did not stay with the band for long, he has described it as a fun project that honed his skills on electric guitar and forced him to expand his vocal range.

SOLO CAREER

In 2013 an executive from the Universal label approached Stapleton and signed him to a record deal with Mercury Nashville. Stapleton released his first solo single, "What Are You Listening To?," in the summer of 2013. The song peaked at number 46 on the Billboard Country Airplay chart. *Traveller*, Stapleton's debut solo album, appeared in May 2015. Leahey described the album as a collection of "country ballads about booze and breakups; roots-rockers about the grind of the road; folksy tributes to women, whiskey, and all points in between." Stapleton himself wrote twelve of the fourteen tracks, although it also includes covers of "Tennessee Whiskey" by Dean Dillon and Linda Hargrove and "Was It 26" by Don Sampson.

Most observers found the story behind the album's title track particularly compelling: Stapleton's father had died in 2013, and looking to clear his head, Stapleton flew to Arizona with his wife and a good friend. In Phoenix, they picked up a 1979 Jeep Cherokee that his wife had bought online and set out on a road trip back to Nashville. Watching the sun rise over the New Mexican desert one morning, he wrote the lyrics for "Traveller": "I'm just a traveller on this earth / Sure as my heart's behind the pocket of my shirt / I'll just keep rolling till I'm in the dirt."

Although many country-music fans had never before heard of Stapleton and the album had sold only modestly upon its release, more than thirteen million people watched him win a trio of major awards at the 2015 CMAs and perform a set that included "Tennessee Whiskey" with pop icon Justin Timberlake. Within a week, a video of their performance was trending on YouTube and "Chris Stapleton" had been the subject of more than two million Google searches. Sales skyrocketed, sending the album to the top of the Billboard 200 for two weeks.

Stapleton is now touring heavily and contemplating his next album. "It's not pressure," he told Joseph Hudak for *Rolling Stone* (18 Dec. 2015), discussing a follow-up album, "but I feel a responsibility to try to maintain the way we did it."

PERSONAL LIFE

Stapleton's facial hair has become something of a trademark for him. He explained to Jim Casey for *Nash Country Weekly* (26 Nov. 2015), "I've had a beard for at least a dozen years. My wife has never seen my chin. I had it long before *Duck Dynasty* was a thing or before anyone really went around buying beard products. I was covered in hillbilly facial hair long before it was cool."

In 2007, Stapleton married Morgane Hayes, a fellow songwriter who penned Carrie Underwood's chart-topping hit "Don't Forget to Remember Me." His wife regularly performs background vocals for Stapleton, both on stage and in the recording studio. They have two children.

SUGGESTED READING

Casey, Jim. "Chris Stapleton: The Trendsetter." *Nash Country Weekly*. Cumulus Media, 26 Nov. 2015. Web. 16 Mar. 2016.

Cooper, Duncan. "Chris Stapleton: Country Music Is Doing Just Fine." *Fader*. Fader, 22 Apr. 2015. Web. 16 Mar. 2016.

Geller, Wendy. "Chris Stapleton: Man of Few Words, Lots of Great Songs." *Rolling Stone*. Rolling Stone, 8 Aug. 2014. Web. 16 Mar. 2016.

Kornhaber, Spencer. "Chris Stapleton's Heartwarming Conquering of Country Music." *Atlantic*. Atlantic Media, 5 Nov. 2015. Web. 16 Mar. 2016.

Leahey, Andrew. "Chris Stapleton: The Natural." *American Songwriter*. ForASong Media, 22 Sept. 2015. Web. 16 Mar. 2016.

Shelburne, Craig. "The Unsung Heroism of Chris Stapleton." *American Songwriter*. ForASong Media, 21 July 2014. Web. 16 Mar. 2016.

Tunis, Walter. "Lexington Native Chris Stapleton, a Country Singer-Songwriter, Readies His Solo Debut." *Lexington Herald-Leader*. Kentucky.com, 2 May 2015. Web. 16 Mar. 2016.

—*Mari Rich*

Alan Stern

Born: November 22, 1957
Occupation: Planetary scientist, engineer

For more than a quarter century, planetary scientist and engineer Alan Stern has worked doggedly—some would say obsessively—to get an unmanned spacecraft to Pluto, which up until 2006 was considered the ninth planet in the solar system. In July 2015 he saw his longtime dream come true when *New Horizons*, a spacecraft that was engineered by a team he led, arrived at Pluto after a trip of nine years and more than three billion miles. The first close-up photos of Pluto and its moons wowed both members of Stern's team and the general public. Of the mission's success and Pluto's status, Stern remarked to Michael Lemonick in *Smithsonian* (June 2015): "It says something very deep about humans and our society, something very good about us, that we've invested our time and treasure in building a machine that can fly across three billion miles of space to explore the Pluto system. But it makes it hard to celebrate and appreciate that accomplishment in the context of a constant discussion about the demotion of Pluto."

Kris Connor /GettyImages

EARLY LIFE AND EDUCATION

The oldest of Leonard and Joel Stern's three children, Sol Alan Stern was born on November 22, 1957, in New Orleans, Louisiana. Even as a child, young Alan was fascinated by outer space. His father recalled how, when Alan was unable to sleep, he would take his son outside to look at the moon, which calmed him. "After many, many repeated applications of that, the first word out of his mouth was 'moon,'" Leonard Stern remarked to Eric Hand for *Science* (25 June 2015). "Not 'mama' or 'dada,' but 'moon.'"

Stern was born at the right time to be fascinated with space. During his early childhood, the first manned missions were sent into orbit and the first astronauts landed on the moon. Concurrently, the Stern family moved to Dallas, Texas, where Alan attended St. Mark's, a prep school that had its own planetarium and observatory. He was a member of the school's astronomy club as well. "That is all my brother ate, drank, slept, and breathed," his brother, Leonard "Happy" Stern, recalled to Eric Hand for *Science*. "Everything in his being was about how to be in space."

Stern even wrote a hundred-page book in the early 1970s, typed up by his grandfather's secretary, about a theoretical mission to a comet, and sent it to the National Aeronautics and Space Administration (NASA) headquarters. In response, a box filled with Apollo technical manuals arrived at his doorstep. He was hooked and was certain that he would someday become an astronaut.

ASTRONAUT IN TRAINING

Stern attended the University of Texas (UT) at Austin. He graduated from UT in 1978, then reenrolled there as a graduate student with a double major in aerospace engineering and planetary science. (He would receive his two master's degrees in 1980 and 1981.) At the same time he earned his pilot's license and became a flight instructor.

Stern applied for the astronaut corps multiple times. In 1988 he was one of just 130 astronauts called to interview out of thousands of applicants. But he came closest to his childhood dream of spaceflight just before Comet Hale-Bopp passed Earth in 1997. An instrument he had designed—the Southwest Ultraviolet Imaging System (SWUIS), used to observe the Hale-Bopp comet—would be on that *Discovery* shuttle flight. He was given a spot on the mission, called STS-85, after a committee of astronauts declared his expertise to be essential. At the last minute, however, Stern was pulled from the mission. "I was very upset because I realized . . . the time was running out. . . . it was all done. It was a done deal. It's the only time in my life I ever cried over something about work," he recalled for Michael Lemonick in *Smithsonian*. "I mean I just lost it."

PLUTO CALLING

During the years he was working to make the astronaut corps, Stern was also building instruments for astronauts' use. As an engineer at the University of Colorado, Boulder's Laboratory for Atmospheric and Space Physics (he served in various positions at the University of Colorado, Boulder from 1983 to 1991), he worked on two instruments designed to study Halley's Comet: the Spartan Halley satellite and a modified thirty-five millimeter camera for a crewmember to photograph the comet as part of the Comet Halley Active Monitoring Space Program. Both of these instruments perished along with the seven astronauts aboard *Challenger* when it exploded shortly after takeoff on January 28, 1986.

The loss of *Challenger* unnerved the space community and deeply troubled Stern, who knew many of the lost astronauts well. He channeled his energy toward useful endeavors, first by earning his doctorate in astrophysics and planetary sciences from the University of Colorado, Boulder in 1989, and also by pushing for an unmanned mission to Pluto, then the only planet that had not been visited by a remotely controlled spacecraft.

Stern had been fascinated with Pluto since at least 1978, when Charon, its major moon, was first detected. As Stern began working for Southwest Research Institute (SwRI) in 1991, first in San Antonio, Texas, and later in Boulder, Colorado, scientific interest in the icy distant world began to heat up. In 1992, it was confirmed that Pluto was part of the Kuiper Belt, a ring of icy objects orbiting at the edge of our solar system.

Scientists wanted to launch a probe to Pluto between the years 2001 and 2006, when the spacecraft could use Jupiter's massive gravity as an assist to get it there faster. Unfortunately, several proposals by various agencies, including the Jet Propulsion Laboratory (JPL), never got further than the planning stages because they were coming in painfully over budget. "It was incredibly frustrating," Stern told Michael Lemonick, "like watching Lucy yank the football away from Charlie Brown, over and over."

However, Stamatios "Tom" Krimigis, then head of the space department at Johns Hopkins University Applied Physics Laboratory (APL), believed he could win the mission from NASA with the right man leading it: Alan Stern.

CHARTING *NEW HORIZONS* TO THE DWARF PLANET

Stern, the APL team, and his associates at SwRI worked together to craft a mission—*New Horizons*—that would appeal to NASA's administrators. Stern's group won the contract by designing a mission that would employ off-the-shelf technology in order to keep down costs, yet still have seven different types of scientific instruments to study Pluto, its moons, and other objects in the Kuiper Belt. Because the end of the gravity-assist window was fast approaching, the group worked quickly to design and build the spacecraft so it could be launched on time. On January 13, 2006, *New Horizons*, powered by a plutonium core, launched aboard an Atlas V rocket, going supersonic in thirty seconds. It would arrive at Pluto in nine years. But long before Pluto would be changed in Earth's eyes by its first satellite contact, it was changed in a way that upset Stern and many members of the scientific community.

Just months after *New Horizons* launched, the International Astronomical Union (IAU) officially relegated Pluto to a new category of dwarf planets. When asked if he still believes Pluto is a planet, Stern told Joel Achenbach of the *Washington Post* (20 June 2015): "Of course I do! It has all the attributes of a planet. Screw the astronomers! Would you go to a podiatrist for brain surgery? They don't know what they're talking about!"

During the time it would take for *New Horizons* to reach Pluto, Stern kept busy on a wide variety of projects. Most notably, in 2007, he left his position as SwRI's executive director of the Space Science & Engineering Division after being tapped to serve as NASA's associate administrator for the Science Mission Directorate by then NASA Administrator Mike Griffin. Stern's job was to keep down costs in the $5 billion science division, including trimming down NASA's

various Mars missions. Stern, however, was accused of trying to cut off funds to two older rovers, *Spirit* and *Opportunity*, in favor of a newer one, *Curiosity*. After about a year of clashing with Griffin and Mars mission team leaders over cost overruns, Stern resigned.

Stern returned to SwRI in 2009 as associate vice president, a position he holds as of November 2015, but has also found time to embark on a number of other ventures. In 2009 he served briefly as an adjunct professor in the Department of Physics at the University of Central Florida. He was a member of the board of directors at the Challenger Center for Space Science Education from 2008 to 2012. For three years (2010–13), he served as the chief scientist and mission architect for Moon Express, a private company competing to win the Google Lunar XPRIZE, which will be given to the first company that safely lands a remote-controlled spacecraft on the surface of the moon. He also spent two years, from 2011 to 2013, serving as the director of Space Florida, which is the aerospace economic development agency of the State of Florida.

NEW HORIZONS ARRIVES AT PLUTO

New Horizons arrived at Pluto on July 14, 2015, for its flyby. The probe's first photos of Pluto and Charon stunned viewers around the world, as well as mission controllers. Shortly before the spacecraft's arrival at Pluto, Stern told Joel Achenbach for the *Washington Post*: "This—is a moment. People should watch it. They should sit their freakin' kids down and say, think about this technology. Think about people who worked on this for 25 years to bring this knowledge. . . . It's a long way to go to the outer edge, the very edge of the solar system."

Because of the distance of the spacecraft from Earth, it will take *New Horizons* sixteen months—until the fall of 2016—to transmit all of the information recorded during its flyby. As of July 2015, 95 percent of the data had yet to be reviewed by Stern's team. In a blog post written for *Sky & Telescope* (31 July 2015), Stern described some of the remarkable discoveries uncovered thus far: "[On] Pluto, we found a wonderland of diverse geological expression, with both old and young surfaces, mountain ranges, polygon-subdivided ice plains, flowing glaciers, and possibly even evidence for subsurface liquids. Pluto's mountains require strong materials to survive (and not slump) over time, indicating Pluto's crust is likely to be composed of water ice, rather than a deep layer of frozen nitrogen, which is soft and malleable to form long-lived mountains. We also found that Pluto was bigger—2,374 km in diameter—than most past estimates."

PERSONAL LIFE AND OTHER VENTURES

Alan Stern and his wife, Carole, have three children, the youngest of whom, Kate, was twenty-four years old when *New Horizons* reached Pluto. Shortly before its arrival, Kate told Michael Lemonick that she would be there with her father at mission control headquarters on the day of its encounter. "I can't imagine not being there. It's like if you're married and your wife gives birth and you don't show up."

In addition to his positions at SwRI and the *New Horizons* mission, Stern works as a consultant for a number of space-bound private companies including Blue Origin, Virgin Galactic, the NATSTAR Center and the Johns Hopkins University, among others. He is the cofounder of three companies. Uwingu, which was founded in 2012, raises money to fund space researchers, educators, and various scientific space projects by selling unofficial naming rights to celestial objects like exoplanets and Mars craters. The company's ventures were not without controversy, however; the International Astronomical Union publicly denounced the company. World View, a space-tourism firm founded in 2013, will send people into near low-Earth orbit via high-altitude balloons. Stern's third company, Golden Spike, a commercial venture founded in 2010, plans to someday provide private lunar missions to groups or individuals who want to visit the moon. As of 2015, he also serves as chief scientist at the Florida Space Institute (FSI). He is also the author of two books: *The US Space Program after Challenger: Where Are We Going?* (1987) and *Pluto and Charon: Ice Worlds on the Ragged Edge of the Solar System*, which he wrote with Jacqueline Mitton in 1997.

Stern continues to supervise the *New Horizons* mission, which is expected to make contact with an object in the Kuiper Belt designated 2014 MU69 in 2019. The object is in an orbit around the sun that is about one billion miles past Pluto.

SUGGESTED READING

Achenbach, Joel. "A Spacecraft Launched in 2006 Is About to Try for Our First Good Photo of Pluto." *Washington Post.* Washington Post, 20 June 2015. Web. 1 Nov. 2015.

Dunn, Marcia. "NASA's New Horizons on New Post-Pluto Mission." *Business Insider.* Business Insider, 22 Oct. 2015. Web. 1 Nov. 2015.

Hand, Eric. "How Alan Stern's Tenacity, Drive, and Command Got a NASA Spacecraft to Pluto." *Science.* Amer. Assn. for the Advancement of Science, 25 June 2015. Web. 1 Nov. 2015.

Lemonick, Michael. "One Man's Lifelong Pursuit of Pluto Is About to Get Real." *Smithsonian.* Smithsonian, June 2015. Web. 1 Nov. 2015.

Stern, Alan. "What We Found at Pluto." *Sky & Telescope.* F+W Media, 31 July 2015. Web. 1 Nov. 2015.

—*Christopher Mari*

Brad Stevens

Born: October 22, 1976
Occupation: Basketball coach

Brad Stevens is living proof that risky moves can pay off. The head coach of the Boston Celtics basketball team since 2013, Stevens was a high school basketball star who ultimately entered a career in marketing, rather than basketball, after graduation. His love of basketball remained, however, and Stevens soon made a career move that for many would be unthinkable, leaving his comfortable marketing job for a volunteer position in the basketball office of Butler University, a National Collegiate Athletic Association (NCAA) Division I school.

After working his way up through the ranks, Stevens ultimately spent six years as head coach of the Butler Bulldogs men's basketball team. A second stunning career shift came in 2013, when Stevens, who had never before coached a professional sports team, joined the Celtics as coach and became the youngest individual actively serving as head coach of a National Basketball Association (NBA) team. The Celtics' decision to hire a college coach rather than a seasoned NBA professional was soon

Jared Wickerham/Getty Images

demonstrated to have been a prudent one, as Stevens led the team to the NBA Playoffs in 2015 and 2016.

Despite his reputation as a risk taker in his professional life, Stevens has gained significant recognition for his calm demeanor and measured approach to coaching. "I'm not going to do cartwheels on the baseline very often," he explained to Keenan Mayo for *Men's Fitness*. "Hopefully I won't lose my mind very often. You're trying to stay measured, not necessarily to live up to that billing. It's more about thinking about the next play."

EARLY LIFE AND EDUCATION
Brad Stevens was born in Greenville, South Carolina, on October 22, 1976, to Mark and Jan Stevens. When he was about four years old, his family moved to Indiana, settling in the town of Zionsville, a suburb of Indianapolis. "It was a great place," Stevens recalled to Ray Compton for the *TownePost Network* (30 Mar. 2013). "I had great friends growing up. I still keep in touch with them. We would play basketball, then get on our bicycles and go to the Dairy Queen. I wouldn't trade those days in Zionsville for anything."

Stevens was a fan of basketball by the age of five and soon began practicing the game at home and with friends. When he was eight, his parents surprised him with a basketball hoop as a birthday gift, and Stevens soon began to spend much of his time shooting hoops outside and dribbling a basketball around the basement of his home. He later played on youth teams that belonged to the Amateur Athletic Union (AAU).

Stevens attended Zionsville Community High School, where he joined the varsity basketball team as a freshman. As a player, the teenage Stevens tended to be highly competitive and a prolific scorer. "I grew up with a maybe healthy—maybe a little unhealthy—fear of failure," he told Tony Rehagen for *Boston Magazine* (Nov. 2015). Basketball was a much-loved sport in Zionsville and throughout Indiana, and Stevens's attitude toward the sport and his performance on the court meant he fit right in. The importance of basketball to the area's residents was further underscored by the sheer size of the high school's varsity gym, in which Stevens played. "It was straight out of a movie, just like the gymnasium in [the 1986 basketball film] *Hoosiers*," he told Compton. "It could hold three thousand fans and the seating went all around the floor. It was like the fans were in the game with you."

In addition to basketball, Stevens played baseball, ran track, and served on the student council while in high school.

COLLEGE BASKETBALL
Although Stevens excelled as a player in high school, he opted not to pursue basketball at a high level in college, declining a scholarship offer from the Division I school Mercer University and instead enrolling at DePauw University, which belonged to the much less competitive Division III. As a member of the DePauw Tigers basketball team, Stevens struggled to balance his competitive style of play with the needs of the team as a whole, and during his junior and senior seasons with the Tigers, he spent an uncharacteristic amount of time on the bench while the team's coaching staff worked to develop the skills of younger players. Unhappy with this turn of events, Stevens seriously considered quitting the team. "I was about as down about basketball as I've ever been," he told Jackie MacMullan for *ESPN* (21 Nov. 2013). "I'd like to say it was just about the losing. I remember thinking, 'Do I want to keep doing this?'" However, he eventually determined that he would remain with the team for the rest of his college career. "I decided, 'Better finish this,'" he explained to MacMullan. "If I don't, I'm going to regret it."

Though he was at times disappointed and even hurt during his time on the DePauw Tigers, his time on the team played a critical role in his development as a both a basketball player and a coach. "I had the opposite of the traditional college career path. But I'm really thankful it happened," he told Shira Springer for the *Boston Globe* (23 July 2013). "It's allowed me to have a great pulse on guys who are going through difficult times individually with regard to playing time. It showed me how important it is to be a great teammate. It kind of started me on this path to coaching." As he told MacMullan, "College makes you grow up. My experience at DePauw was about as beneficial as any experience I've had." By the end of his four years with the Tigers, Stevens had earned four varsity letters and was recognized for his athletic performance by several bodies, including the Academic All-America program.

While attending DePauw, Stevens completed a summer internship at the pharmaceutical company Eli Lilly. After graduating from college in 1999 with a bachelor's degree in economics, he joined the company full time, taking a position as a marketing associate.

BUTLER UNIVERSITY
Although Stevens had found a comfortable job at Eli Lilly, he soon found that he missed basketball and wanted to return to the sport, this time behind the scenes. While still working at Lilly, he served as a volunteer assistant for the basketball team at Carmel High School, an assistant coach for the Municipal Gardens AAU team, and a coach at Butler University's youth

basketball camps. However, he still wanted to become even more involved in basketball. Having saved much of his pay during his time at Eli Lilly and determined that he could always fall back on that career if necessary, he left his job at the age of twenty-three to pursue his dream career in basketball. He held a volunteer position with the Butler University basketball team for the summer of 2000 and then was offered a full-time paying job, albeit one with a salary totaling less than half what he had earned in marketing. Not dissuaded by the low pay, Stevens took the position of director of basketball operations at Butler, a small university in Indiana that had achieved significant success in Division I athletics. In that role, he carried out a number of essential tasks for the team, including preparing scouting reports and making travel arrangements. He was later promoted to assistant coach, and in 2007, Stevens was named head coach of the Butler Bulldogs men's basketball team.

Stevens's experiences on his own college team were a strong influence on his outlook as a coach, and he worked to teach his players the importance of putting the team first, regardless of one's own ego. "I told our players at Butler, 'I hate to break it to you, but you aren't playing beyond here. That's reality. So why are you so concerned with yourself?'" Stevens told MacMullan. "It's a hard lesson, but I told them, 'How you handle your role on this team will be remembered by your coaches and your teammates. It will define you.'"

Over the course of his six-year tenure as head coach, Stevens's coaching efforts proved successful, and he led the team to the NCAA Final Four twice, in 2010 and 2011, becoming the youngest coach to do so. Over six seasons under Stevens's leadership, the Bulldogs won 166 games, marking the most wins of any Division I coach in the first six years of his career. Although the work of coaching was challenging at times, Stevens was ultimately proud of the rapport he established between himself and his players. "I've looked back on it many times," he told Mark Viera for the *New York Times* (1 Apr. 2011). "There have been many days in coaching where I've said, 'What was I thinking?' Because it is not the easiest job in the world. But it is very fulfilling, not because of the results you achieve but because of the relationships you build."

BOSTON CELTICS

Although he reportedly received job offers from multiple schools during his time at Butler, Stevens remained with the Bulldogs until 2013. That summer, he left the world of college basketball for the high-profile realm of professional sports, joining the NBA's Boston Celtics as head coach. Although the Celtics organization prefers to keep the details of its contracts secret, the sports media widely reported that Stevens had been offered a six-year, $22 million contract to coach the team. Only thirty-six years old at the time, Stevens became the youngest active head coach in the NBA.

Stevens initially struggled to lead the Celtics during his first season with the team, during which the Celtics lost fifty-seven games. Losing was a somewhat unfamiliar experience for Stevens, who had lost just forty-nine games during his entire tenure with the Butler Bulldogs. He resolved to turn the team around the following season, and he succeeded: the Celtics made it to the NBA Playoffs during Stevens's second season as coach, and they returned to the tournament the following year. Although the team did not make it past the first round of the Playoffs either time, Stevens was pleased with his players' performance. The Celtics organization was pleased as well, and in June 2016, the team's leadership announced that Stevens's contract had been extended.

While Stevens's future with the Celtics has been the subject of much speculation among basketball fans, he prefers to focus on the immediate challenges facing the team rather than worry about things to come. "I don't think about [the future]," he explained to Mark Murphy for the *Boston Herald* (2 May 2016). "I've said all along that if these guys want me to be around, I'll be around. It's not my choice. It's their choice. I've enjoyed the process of growth that we're on, I enjoy working here and the people I work with. I've got incredibly empowering leadership." Above all, Stevens is highly aware of how fortunate he is to have the opportunity to work in his beloved sport. "I'm thankful to be here," he told Murphy.

PERSONAL LIFE

Stevens met his future wife, Tracy Wilhelmy, while they were both in college. On their first date, they drove for more than an hour to attend a high school basketball game. Stevens and Wilhelmy married in 2003. They have two children, Brady and Kinsley, and live in Wellesley, Massachusetts.

SUGGESTED READING

Compton, Ray. "Brad Stevens: Home Town Hoopster Talks; Growing Up in Zionsville." *TownePost Network*. TownePost Network, 30 Mar. 2013. Web. 9 Sept. 2016.

Holmes, Baxter. "Indiana Roots Bound Brad Stevens to Basketball." *Boston Globe*. Boston Globe Media Partners, 27 Oct. 2013. Web. 9 Sept. 2016.

MacMullan, Jackie. "Brad Stevens' Story Isn't Storybook." *ESPN*. ESPN Internet Ventures, 21 Nov. 2013. Web. 9 Sept. 2016.

Murphy, Mark. "Brad Stevens on Evan Turner and His Own Future with Celtics." *Boston Herald*. Herald Media, 2 May 2016. Web. 9 Sept. 2016.

Rehagen, Tony. "Can Coach Brad Stevens Put the Celtics Together Again?" *Boston Magazine*. Metro, Nov. 2015. Web. 9 Sept. 2016.

Stevens, Brad. "Q&A with Celtics Coach Brad Stevens." Interview by Keenan Mayo. *Men's Fitness*. Weider, 2014. Web. 9 Sept. 2016.

Viera, Mark. "For Butler's Stevens, a Career Change Paid Off." *New York Times*. New York Times, 1 Apr. 2011. Web. 9 Sept. 2016.

—*Joy Crelin*

Sufjan Stevens

Born: July 1, 1975
Occupation: Musician

Musician Sufjan Stevens has never shied away from experimentation, whether with genre styles or even the form and function of music itself. A singer-songwriter who grew up playing classical piano and oboe but made the career-shaping decision to learn guitar in college, Stevens has spent more than a decade recording albums in a variety of genres, from folk to electronic and points in between. Incorporating wide-ranging influences, notably including the history and culture of the states of Michigan and Illinois, religious and spiritual references, and all-consuming emotions, Stevens's work is often intensely personal. At the same time, as an artist he is similarly capable of taking on ambitious projects that transcend both the personal and the boundaries between different forms of media. "I've never been too considerate about the distinction between a gallery and a club and an opera house," he told Brandon Stosuy for *Interview* (1 Dec. 2009) of his take on such arbitrary boundaries. "We bring misconceptions to these spaces, but those are grumpy, outdated grievances. There is no uptown/downtown conflict of aesthetics anymore. At least, none worth participating in."

A critically acclaimed artist, Stevens first found significant commercial success with the 2005 release of the album *Illinois* and continued to impress both fans and critics with his subsequent work. He returned to the spotlight once again in 2015 with the release of the album *Carrie & Lowell*, a powerful and moving record in which Stevens processes his feelings following the 2012 death of his mother, the titular Carrie. Although the process of recording the album and examining those feelings was a difficult one, the album in many ways serves to bring a sense of closure. "At the end I could speak for it, for the sadness," Stevens told author Dave Eggers for the *Guardian* (26 Mar. 2015). "It was dignified."

EARLY LIFE AND EDUCATION

Sufjan Stevens was born in Detroit, Michigan, on July 1, 1975. At the time of his birth, his parents, Carrie and Rasjid, were members of the Subud spiritual movement, the leader of which gave Stevens his first name. Carrie left the family when Stevens was a toddler, and Stevens and his siblings were raised primarily by their father and stepmother. In an interview with Eggers, Stevens described his family life during his youth as "a familial conglomerate mess."

Growing up in Michigan, Stevens was drawn to music from an early age, and he played and composed music for piano and oboe. Music was not a priority in his father's household, but he found a musical mentor of sorts in Lowell Brams, to whom his mother was married in the early 1980s. Brams played a key role in encouraging a relationship between the Stevens children and their mother, facilitating summer visits in Oregon for several years in a row, and introduced Stevens to music not present in his life before that point. Although Carrie and Brams divorced after several years, Brams and Stevens remained close, and the two would later cofound the independent record label Asthmatic Kitty.

Stevens attended Hope College, an institution based in Holland, Michigan, and affiliated with the Reformed Church in America, where he studied writing. He learned to play guitar while at the college, a development that would prove crucial to his evolution as a musician. "The guitar, because it's so personal and intimate and portable, lends itself to accompanying the human voice, and I think for me, the real revelation happened in discovering my own singing voice," he explained to Richard Harrington for the *Washington Post* (23 Sept. 2005). He played in various bands during college and experimented with a wide range of musical styles, from folk to garage rock. His background in classical music also remained influential during that period. Stevens graduated with honors from Hope College in 1998.

EARLY CAREER

Despite his love of music, Stevens did not initially consider pursuing a career as a singer-songwriter, instead focusing on creative writing. He was particularly inspired by the form of the short story. "For me, it was the perfect form in that it required an economy of ideas and of words, and a certain kind of editing and censoring and rendering," he explained to Harrington. "I always admired the brevity of an entire narrative in a few pages. That's what I was working at, and, ultimately, that would lead to a novel—but it never happened." Stevens moved to New York to attend the writing program at the New School for Social Research, and after graduating, he worked for a time as a graphic designer.

Although Stevens sought to focus on prose writing during this time, he began recording music as well, founding Asthmatic Kitty with Brams and releasing albums under that label. His first album, *A Sun Came*, was initially recorded while Stevens was a senior at Hope College and was finally released in 2000. Stevens composed all of the songs on the album, which mixes a number of genres, musical styles, and influences. He followed that album with *Enjoy Your Rabbit*, released in the fall of 2001. That album, which was inspired by the animals of the Chinese zodiac, fell primarily into the genre of electronic music. Although Stevens's first album had received mixed reviews, *Enjoy Your Rabbit*'s critical reception was largely positive, with music publications such as *Pitchfork* praising Stevens's songwriting and experimentation with genre and form.

THE FIFTY STATES PROJECT

Following the release of his initial albums, Stevens began work on the project that would bring him the most acclaim to date. With his so-called fifty states project, Stevens sought to create an album for each state in America, writing songs inspired by the history and local flavor of each. The first such album was *Greetings from Michigan: The Great Lakes State* (often referred to as simply *Michigan*), a tribute to his home state. In his prose writing, Stevens had long been interested in writing about Michigan, and this interest carried over into his music. "When I went back to songwriting, I was still preoccupied with the subject of Michigan, and I couldn't do away with it," he told Harrington. "It was kind of like a process of psychotherapy, bringing into realization these stories of place and geography and memory. It was definitely accidental, a slow discovery." Primarily a folk album, *Michigan* received significant critical acclaim following its release in 2003.

Stevens's next installment in the project, the 2005 album *Sufjan Stevens Invites You To: Come on Feel the Illinoise* (or *Illinois*), proved to be his most successful album to that point. *Illinois* was a critical and commercial success, garnering ample praise and reaching the position of 121 on the US Billboard 200 album chart. In addition to various references to Illinois history and culture, the album demonstrates the religious and spiritual influences for which Stevens's music would become known. Stevens released *The Avalanche*, an album of outtakes from *Illinois*, the following year. Despite the success of *Illinois* and its predecessor, however, Stevens ultimately decided not to continue with the fifty states project, which he later described in interviews as having been a promotional gimmick.

OTHER ALBUMS

In addition to the well-received *Michigan* and *Illinois*, Stevens released a number of additional albums. *Seven Swans*, for example, is a religiously influenced folk album that was well received by critics upon its 2004 release. The musician also recorded two Christmas albums, 2006's *Songs for Christmas* and 2012's *Silver & Gold*. He explored a somewhat new musical direction with 2010's *The Age of Adz*, an album that builds upon his previous experiments with electronic music. Although some fans and critics saw the album as a significant departure from Stevens's previous work, a number of venues named it as one of the best albums of 2010.

Perhaps Stevens's most ambitious project was *The BQE*, a 2009 album and multimedia art piece that originated as a live concern. *The BQE* was inspired by the Brooklyn-Queens Expressway and paired an album with a DVD featuring footage of the expressway as well as the *Super Teenager Hooper Heroes* comic book, written by Stevens.

CARRIE & LOWELL

Stevens's personal life and music took a turn in 2012, when his mother died. His relationship with his mother had long been a difficult one, in part because of his extended separation from her as a child and her struggles with mental illness. After Carrie's death, Stevens processed his feelings through music and in 2015 released the album *Carrie & Lowell*, named for his mother and Brams and inspired by both his feelings following Carrie's death and his memories of visiting his mother and stepfather in Oregon as a child. He initially considered naming the album *Oregon*, keeping it in line with his previous *Michigan* and *Illinois* albums. However, his friend Thomas Bartlett, a musician and producer who helped Stevens make sense of the album, convinced him not to do so, as he considered Stevens's attempts to create grand concept albums to be a form of "complicated misdirection and an architecture by which he could actually write about himself," Bartlett told Laura Snapes for *Uncut* (28 Apr. 2015). "I asked him to let go of the idea that this was an Oregon record and just allow it to be what it really feels like it is, which is a very, very personal record," Bartlett explained.

Carrie & Lowell received overwhelmingly positive reviews from critics, many of whom praised its emotional depth and artistry and deemed it Stevens's best work. The album was named one of the best albums of 2015 by several publications and was a commercial success as well, reaching the number-ten position on the Billboard 200 chart. For Stevens, recording *Carrie & Lowell* enabled him to process his complex feelings about his mother and brought him a sense of closure. "You can't change your history," he told Eggers. "But you can choose to relinquish the anger, and you can choose to recognize that there's no perfect way to cultivate a person."

PERSONAL LIFE

Stevens lives in Brooklyn, New York.

SUGGESTED READING

Beasley, Corey. "Tracing Sufjan Stevens's Intricate Ties to the Music of New York City." *Village Voice*. Village Voice, 30 Mar. 2015. Web. 8 Apr. 2016.

Eggers, Dave. "Sufjan Stevens Talks to Dave Eggers: 'I Was Recording Songs as a Means of Grieving.'" *Guardian*. Guardian News and Media, 26 Mar. 2015. Web. 8 Apr. 2016.

Harrington, Richard. "Sufjan Stevens's Musical States of Mind." *Washington Post*. Washington Post, 23 Sept. 2005. Web. 8 Apr. 2016.

Lewis, Tim. "Sufjan Stevens: 'I've Always Been Insecure about What I Do.'" *Guardian*. Guardian News and Media, 7 May 2011. Web. 8 Apr. 2016.

Roark, David. "How Sufjan Stevens Subverts the Stigma of Christian Music." *Atlantic*. Atlantic Monthly Group, 29 Mar. 2015. Web. 8 Apr. 2016.

Snapes, Laura. "Sufjan Stevens Interviewed: 'You Have to Cast Out Your Demons. . . .'" *Uncut*. Time, 28 Apr. 2015. Web. 8 Apr. 2016.

Stevens, Sufjan. "It's Sufjan Stevens's Way or the Highway." Interview by Brandon Stosuy. *Interview*. Interview, 1 Dec. 2009. Web. 8 Apr. 2016.

SELECTED WORKS

A Sun Came, 2000; *Enjoy Your Rabbit*, 2001; *Michigan*, 2003; *Seven Swans*, 2004; *Illinois*, 2005; *Songs for Christmas*, 2006; *The BQE*, 2009; *The Age of Adz*, 2010; *Silver & Gold*, 2012; *Carrie & Lowell*, 2015

—*Joy Crelin*

Noelle Stevenson

Born: December 31, 1991
Occupation: Artist, writer

Noelle Stevenson is an award-winning comic artist. Her young-adult graphic fantasy novel, *Nimona*, about a red-headed shapeshifter, was a finalist for the National Book Award for Young People's Literature in 2015, when Stevenson was just twenty-three years old. Stevenson's career began to take off while she was still a student at the Maryland Institute College of Art (MICA), thanks in part to the sizable following for her webcomics on the social networking site Tumblr. In 2012, Stevenson and a friend inadvertently launched a feminist meme known as the Hawkeye Initiative when they posted drawings of the male Marvel superhero Hawkeye in various sexy poses normally reserved for female comic characters. According to Stevenson and many of her fellow women artists and writers, the comic book world has long alienated women; from the historical lack of stories about female characters to the way the few female characters that do exist that are objectified as sexy sidekicks, they say the comic world has inadvertently fostered a hostile and overtly misogynist strain of readers.

Stevenson's work sidesteps existing comic tropes entirely. As a cocreator with Shannon Watters and Grace Ellis of the Eisner Award–winning series *Lumberjanes*, Stevenson wrote about the exploits of five female friends. Often, Stevenson explained to Joanna Robinson for *Vanity Fair* (15 July 2015), female characters are introduced in relation to male characters; for example, a woman may enter a room, a man insults her, and she punches him in the face. "Now we know she's tough and she's worthy of being here next to the men," Stevenson said of the intended message, adding of the men—"none of them have to punch anyone to prove that they can be here." In *Lumberjanes*, the female characters are introduced in relation to one another.

Jody Culkin/CC BY-SA 4.0/Wikimedia Commons

The first male character appears in the fourth issue. (Stevenson left the series after its seventeenth issue in 2015.) In 2015, Fox Animation and Twentieth Century Fox acquired the rights for *Lumberjanes*, and Stevenson's lauded web comic-turned-graphic novel *Nimona*.

EARLY LIFE AND EDUCATION

Stevenson was born and raised in Columbia, South Carolina. She is the middle of five children born to parents Hal and Diana Stevenson. Growing up, Stevenson and her siblings were homeschooled, and encouraged to pursue their own interests. Stevenson was interested in art, though not necessarily comic art. She recalled her first trip to a comic book shop when she was eleven years old, where she saw a cardboard cutout of Princess Leia from Star Wars, wearing her iconic metal bikini. A sign listing the shop's daily deals was taped over her bare midriff. "You get a message from that, you know? You get a message very loud and clear, and no one was throwing rocks at me and saying girls can't shop here, get out of here," she told Audie Cornish of National Public Radio's *All Things Considered* (13 May 2014). "You just kind of know when you're not supposed to be somewhere. And I wasn't even conflicted about it. I wasn't even like, I sure wish I could read comics; I just didn't even try."

As a teenager, Stevenson transitioned from homeschooling to attending Columbia's A.C. Flora High School, where she won a prestigious local art award from the Richland One's Visual Literary Festival during her senior year. After graduation, she enrolled at the Maryland Institute College of Art (MICA), but was unsure about what she wanted to do. During one summer break, while watching the *Lord of the Rings* movies with her family, Stevenson completed a series of sketches called "The Broship of the Ring," featuring the famous fantasy characters in a contemporary setting. She posted the drawings on her Tumblr—on the site she is known as Gingerhaze—where they were subsequently picked up by several larger sites like *i09* (owned by Gawker Media) in 2011. "That was the first thing I did that put eyes on me," she told Deena C. Bouknight for the *Columbia Metropolitan* (1 Oct. 2015), "but it was done strictly for enjoyment—not to sell or to market."

In the same spirit, Stevenson challenged other comic artists to join the Hawkeye Initiative, replicating existing images of female superheroes but replacing the woman with male hero Hawkeye. The challenge spawned its own Tumblr page in 2012. The same year, Stevenson completed an internship with BOOM! Studios, a comic publishing company in Los Angeles, and began a webcomic called *Nimona* after taking a graphic storytelling class. The comic became wildly popular; it earned her *Slate's* Cartoonist Studio Prize for Best Webcomic of the Year, a nomination for a Harvey Award for Best Online Comic, an agent, and a publishing contract with HarperCollins. (Her agent called to deliver the good news about the contract while Stevenson was in the middle of a class critique of *Nimona*.) In 2013, popular young adult author Rainbow Rowell asked Stevenson—who by then had gained acclaim as a prolific fan artist—to illustrate the cover of her 2013 novel about fan fiction, *Fangirl*. Stevenson graduated with a degree in illustration from MICA the same year.

NIMONA (2015)

Nimona, a comic about a shapeshifter and aspiring villain who bears a striking resemblance to her creator, was Stevenson's senior thesis. The project began for class, but Stevenson felt compelled to continue Nimona's story and to expand her world. The final product, published as a graphic novel in 2015, is both an action adventure story and a dark tale about identity and betrayal. Nimona, the character, is a mash-up of two different characters that Stevenson had created—the first a supervillain with an eye patch, and the other based on visual depictions of Joan of Arc. Nimona is a shapeshifter, Stevenson explained to Van Jensen for *Paste* magazine (4 June 2015), in part because the identity of a teenage girl is always in flux. "It's easy to feel like you don't have any control over yourself or your life or your body as a teen," she said. Of Nimona's villainy and penchant for violence, Stevenson said she has always been drawn to the complexity of so-called bad guys. Of Nimona herself she told Jensen, "I wanted her to be . . . difficult to love, but also lovable, in equal parts."

Nimona's world draws on fairy tale and superhero tropes and images, but is also futuristic. In the book, Nimona teams up with Lord Ballister Blackheart, a supervillain who yearns to best his nemesis, the ridiculous Ambrosius Goldenloin, in battle. Goldenloin is the figurehead of a shadowy, though purportedly "good" organization, called the Institution of Law Enforcement and Heroics. The story begins as comedy: Nimona is disappointed by Ballister's inadequate villainy, and their joint exploits occasionally go awry. The scope of Stevenson's story reaches much deeper into the true nature of Nimona, asking complex questions about good people who are capable of truly evil deeds. Faith Erin Hicks, who reviewed *Nimona* for the *New York Times* (10 July 2015), praised Stevenson, writing, "It is astonishing that 'Nimona'. . . is Stevenson's first solo, full-length work. Her voice is clear and precise, her drawings confident, her use of color growing in depth and assurance as the story progresses." *Nimona* is only the third graphic novel to be recognized by the National Book Awards. It was nominated for an Eisner Award for Best Graphic Album Reprint in 2016.

LUMBERJANES

In 2014, Stevenson teamed up with Shannon Watters, a woman for whom she had interned at BOOM! Studios, to create a new series called *Lumberjanes*. The two artists also reached out to Grace Ellis, a writer for a queer women's website, who had never written a comic before. The women were inspired to create a story about young girls that was neither boring nor cliché. Frustrated by sexualized images of women in adult comics and two-dimensional role model characters in comics for young people, the three women landed on the story of the Lumberjanes, a group of wilderness scouts who occasionally do battle with supernatural forces. The Lumberjanes are a diverse group of girls sharing a cabin at summer camp. As they vie for badges in activities like kayaking (like the Girl Scouts), they also find themselves wandering off into the woods, where a strange magic seems to have taken hold. The first issue of the *Lumberjanes* was published in 2014. Since then, the series has enjoyed a slew of collaborators and won Eisner Awards (the comic world's version of the Oscars) for Best New Series and Best Publication for Teens in 2015. Stevenson left the series to pursue other projects in 2015.

RUNAWAYS AND OTHER PROJECTS

In 2014, Stevenson contributed to Marvel's *Thor Annual*, and became a writer on the revived popular Marvel series *Runaways*, which was first published in 2003. In the new series,

Stevenson, working alongside artist Sanford Greene, created a world in which alternate versions of beloved Marvel characters do battle with a diabolical school headmaster. In 2015 Stevenson also became a writer for the second season of the animated Disney television series *Wander over Yonder*, about an intergalactic traveler named Wander. She is also working with screenwriter Todd Casey—the two met on *Wander over Yonder*—on a young adult book series for HarperCollins called 4 Wizards. In it, a wizard named Hugo takes on a sullen teenage apprentice named Ivy, who occasionally and unpredictably transforms into a demonic alter-ego named Nightshade. Stevenson told Andrew Wheeler for *Comics Alliance* (3 July 2015) that the two drew inspiration from some "wizard doodles" Stevenson was working on at the time. Basing the characters on the images, Stevenson and Casey imagined a world in which the deadpan comic actress Aubrey Plaza interned for Gandalf of *Lord of the Rings*—though Stevenson added that the series plans to tackle a larger world as well. "Fantasy is usually considered an escape, but it's also a way to deal with weighty real-world issues from a safe distance, and in a context where you usually have some kind of power that you don't have in real life." The first book will be published in 2017.

PERSONAL LIFE
Stevenson lives in Los Angeles.

SUGGESTED READING
Bouknight, Deena C. "Made in Cola Town." *Columbia Metropolitan*. Columbia Metropolitan, Oct. 2015. Web. 27 Apr. 2016.

Hicks, Faith Erin. Rev. of *Nimona*, by Noelle Stevenson. *New York Times*. New York Times, 10 July 2015. Web. 27 Apr. 2016.

Stevenson, Noelle. "How Noelle Stevenson Broke All the Rules to Conquer the Comic Book World." Interview by Joanna Robinson. *Vanity Fair*. Condé Nast, 15 July 2015. Web. 27 Apr. 2016.

Stevenson, Noelle. "'Nimona' Shifts Shape and Takes Names—In Sensible Armor, of Course." Interview by Audie Cornish. *All Things Considered*. National Public Radio, 13 May 2014. Web. 27 Apr. 2016.

Stevenson, Noelle. "Page One, Panel One: Creating Characters with Noelle Stevenson." Interview by Van Jensen. *Paste*. Paste Media, 4 June 2015. Web. 27 Apr. 2016.

Wheeler, Andrew. "Noelle Stevenson and Todd Casey Introduce '4 Wizards.'" *ComicsAlliance*. ComicsAlliance, 3 July 2015. Web. 27 Apr. 2016.

SELECTED WORKS
Nimona, 2015; *Lumberjanes*, 2014–15; *Runaways*, 2015

—*Molly Hagan*

Breanna Stewart

Born: August 17, 1994
Occupation: Basketball player

If women's basketball experts are correct, Breanna Stewart may be one of the most impressive players of her generation. Stewart, known to fans as Stewie, began her career playing on school and Amateur Athletic Union (AAU) teams and quickly impressed her coaches and fans with her dominance of the basketball court. Standing six feet four as an adult, she went on to play four successful seasons with the University of Connecticut Huskies, leading the team to four consecutive championships before being selected by the Seattle Storm as the first pick in the 2016 professional draft. Perhaps even more exciting for Stewart was the news that she had made the US women's basketball team that would compete in the 2016 Olympics in Rio de Janeiro, Brazil. All of that success is a lot for an athlete barely in her twenties, but Stewart remains undaunted. "I think the best way to deal with the pressure is to just not worry about it, just not think about it," she told Steve Serby for the *New York Post* (2 Apr. 2016). "If I was to focus on everything going on like outside the basketball court and surrounding me, then I'm sure yeah, I would feel a lot of pressure. But it's kind of like when you kind of let it go in one ear and out the other. You hear it, but you don't worry about it."

EARLY LIFE AND EDUCATION
Breanna Stewart was born on August 17, 1994, in Syracuse, New York. She was the oldest of two children born to Brian and Heather Stewart. Her family lived in Cicero, a suburb of Syracuse, until 2006, when they moved to nearby North Syracuse. An athlete from a young age, Stewart played a variety of sports during her childhood and teen years, including softball and volleyball. It was basketball, however, that truly captured her interest. When Stewart was about nine years old, her father began playing basketball for fun, participating in games at the YMCA in their town. Stewart often accompanied her father to games and watched him play, an experience that helped shape her devotion to the game. Her father also traces Stewart's love of the sport back to a particular day on which they watched a game on television together. "I can't remember the exact game, but I remember sitting here and

Sphilbrick/CC BY-SA 3.0/Wikimedia Commons

she wanted to watch with me and that was the beginning," he told Charlie Creme for *ESPN.com* (8 Feb. 2016). "From then on it was just basketball all the time." Although the family lived near Syracuse University, Stewart became a devoted fan of the University of North Carolina's basketball team.

EARLY CAREER
Stewart spent the early stages of her basketball career playing for AAU teams, beginning with the Syracuse Stars. Seeking a more competitive level of play, she would later go on to compete in AAU tournaments as a member of the Philadelphia Belles. Although she had reached six feet in height by the time she was twelve and had natural talent, some elements of her play needed work. To improve, she began an intense training regimen at home, dribbling laps around her neighborhood and even practicing her dribble in the basement of her family home during the winter. "Dribbling around the block definitely started things," Stewart explained to Creme. "It made me realize if I could get better at dribbling, I could get better at shooting and do other things that would make it tough to play against me."

The next step in Stewart's career came when she was in eighth grade, when coach Eric Smith recruited her to join the Cicero–North Syracuse High School varsity basketball team. Unlike many high schools, Cicero–North Syracuse accommodates grades ten through twelve; Stewart, then, joined the school's team two years before actually becoming a high school student. Although this was an unusual turn of events, it was the only correct course of action for Smith, who was impressed by Stewart's abilities and viewed the young player as an asset to his team. "Her mental ability is what sets her apart. She is so even-keeled, even when she isn't playing well," he later told Creme. "Nothing gets to her, which is why she is so good in pressure moments. She is so comfortable in her own skin." Stewart continued to play on the varsity team while attending Cicero–North Syracuse. In addition to playing for the school, she competed as a member of USA Basketball's under-eighteen team, among others, and also competed in the 2011 Pan American Games, becoming the youngest player to do so.

Although focusing on her high school and other competitions, Stewart also had to devote a great deal of thought to her options for her future career. As a resident of a suburb of Syracuse, it seemed obvious that she would consider attending nearby Syracuse University and playing for the school's women's basketball team, the Orange. However, she ultimately decided that she wanted to attend the University of Connecticut (UConn) in order to train under coach Geno Auriemma, who had led the women's basketball team to seven National Collegiate Athletic Association (NCAA) championships prior to Stewart's arrival at the school.

UCONN'S STAR PLAYER
After graduating from high school in 2012, Stewart enrolled in UConn, located in Storrs, Connecticut. As a new member of the UConn Huskies, she set challenging goals for her time on the team, telling reporters early in her college career that she hoped to win four consecutive NCAA championships. Although the women's basketball team had won quite a few championships, it had never won that many in a row; still, Stewart was determined to try.

Adjusting to playing on a college team was a bit of a process for Stewart, who had to become accustomed not only to the competitive college level of play, but also to Auriemma and his coaching techniques. To motivate Stewart throughout the course of her career, the coach at times would give her the silent treatment or say things to push her buttons. While such methods could easily backfire, for Stewart they were effective in motivating her to give the game her all. "He'll say something that you don't want to hear to make you work harder to reach towards it, to go towards it, to reach that goal," she told Serby of Auriemma.

Another challenge Stewart faced was meeting her own expectations. After a loss to Texas's Baylor University late in her freshman season, which Stewart has called the worst game of her career, she had a crisis of confidence that made her question whether she truly belonged at UConn. Despite her disappointment in herself,

Stewart soon pulled herself out of that funk, determined to improve her play so that such an upsetting loss would not happen again. "I think if I was someone who gave up when the going was tough, then I wouldn't be the type of person who wants to be a great player," she told Serby. Over the course of Stewart's time on the team, the Huskies lost only five games, four in her freshman season—including the Baylor game—and one in her junior season. During her sophomore and senior years, the team went undefeated in the regular season, further demonstrating Stewart and her teammates' dominance on the court.

NCAA CHAMPION
In addition to dominating the regular season for all four years of Stewart's college career, the Huskies continued to excel in the postseason. After rising through the ranks in the 2013 NCAA Tournament, the Huskies beat the University of Louisville's Cardinals to win the championship, the first for the team since 2010. During the following two years, the team twice defeated the University of Notre Dame Fighting Irish, the team that was responsible for two of Stewart's four regular-season losses, to win two more championships. Finally, in April of 2016, the Huskies faced off against the Syracuse Orange, Stewart's hometown team. Stewart and her teammates beat the Orange 82–51, securing the Huskies' fourth consecutive championship. For Stewart, the win represented the completion of the promise she had made to herself years before. "That was our goal coming in here when we were freshmen and to carry it out like this as senior is unbelievable," she told Sam Richmond for the NCAA's website (6 Apr. 2016). "We went out with a bang." In recognition of her performance in the NCAA championships, Stewart was named the player of the year by the Associated Press (AP) three years in a row, from her sophomore through senior years. She was also named the Final Four most outstanding performer all four years, the only player in NCAA women's basketball to have done so.

PROFESSIONAL PLAYER AND OLYMPIC CONTENDER
Less than two weeks after the Huskies' fourth championship win, the Women's National Basketball Association (WNBA) draft was held in Uncasville, Connecticut. The first player to be chosen in the draft, Stewart was selected by the Seattle Storm. She made her regular-season debut with the professional team on May 15, just over a week after her graduation from UConn. Although the Storm lost that game to the Los Angeles Sparks by thirty points, Stewart proved a key contributor to the team, scoring the most points in the game for the Storm. The team's performance during the beginning of the season

was mixed, with the Storm winning four out of the first ten games. Nevertheless, Stewart remained positive, viewing her rookie season as a valuable learning opportunity.

In late April of 2016, it was announced that Stewart would join the US basketball team and compete in the 2016 Olympics in Rio de Janeiro, Brazil. "It feels unbelievable to have the opportunity to play on the national team and play for a gold medal with this group is incredible," she told Chris Chavez for *Sports Illustrated* (27 Apr. 2016) when the news was made public. "You can't ask for a whole lot more coming out of college right away." In addition to the opportunity to compete on the international stage, Stewart was particularly excited to work with Auriemma once again. The Huskies coach had previously coached the United States' gold medal–winning 2000 and 2012 Olympic women's basketball teams. "One of the best parts upon realizing that I made the team is that I'll have one more opportunity to play for him," Stewart told Chavez. "My four years are done at UConn and that went by fast. It's going to be great to get back on the court with him." The 2016 Olympics is set to begin in August of this year, with the women's basketball competition beginning on August 6.

SUGGESTED READING

Altavilla, John. "Making of a Husky: Breanna Stewart; Tall on Talent, Short on Ego." *Hartford Courant*. Hartford Courant, 11 Nov. 2014. Web. 10 June 2016.

Berkman, Seth. "Breanna Stewart Is a Syracuse Fan but a UConn Star." *New York Times*. New York Times, 4 Apr. 2016. Web. 10 June 2016.

Creme, Charlie. "Childhood Home Is Where It All Started for Breanna Stewart." *ESPN.com*. ESPN, 8 Feb. 2016. Web. 10 June 2016.

Martin, Brian. "Great Expectations: Breanna Stewart's Test Starts Now." *WNBA.com*. NBA Media Ventures, 9 May 2016. Web. 10 June 2016.

Richmond, Sam. "UConn Women's Basketball: Breanna Stewart Makes Case She's the Greatest Ever with Fourth Title." *NCAA*. NCAA, 6 Apr. 2016. Web. 10 June 2016.

Stewart, Breanna. "Breanna Stewart on Durant Comp, Geno's Silent Treatment, and Going No. 1." Interview by Steve Serby. *New York Post*. NYP Holdings, 2 Apr. 2016. Web. 10 June 2016.

Stewart, Breanna. "Q&A: Breanna Stewart Discusses Making Her First Olympic Team." Interview by Chris Chavez. *Sports Illustrated*. Sports Illustrated, 27 Apr. 2016. Web. 10 June 2016.

—*Joy Crelin*

Lorenz Studer

Born: March 5, 1966
Occupation: Scientist

In 2015, Lorenz Studer, the director of the Center for Stem Cell Biology at the Memorial Sloan Kettering Cancer Center, was among the winners of the John D. and Catherine T. MacArthur Foundation Fellowships, or "genius" grants. For twenty-five years, Studer has been endeavoring to find treatments for Parkinson's disease, a degenerative disease of the brain and central nervous system that affects motor functions. Studer believes that the disease can be treated by creating and transplanting brain tissue into patients by genetically modifying stem cells to take the place of diseased cells. Studer's work has already demonstrated significant promise; clinical trials in human subjects may begin as early as 2017.

Studer hopes that the MacArthur Fellowship will aid him in his future research, but he admits to being totally surprised that he was named as a recipient. "I was sick with a 104-degree fever the day I received the phone call with the news that I got the MacArthur fellowship. By the end of the day, I wasn't even sure if the phone call had actually happened! But then I got an email, so I knew my mind had not made it up," Studer told Anna Azvolinsky for the *Scientist* magazine (1 Dec. 2015). "You don't even know that you were nominated, so it's a complete surprise. It's an amazing honor and it's encouraging because we do try to think outside the box and come up

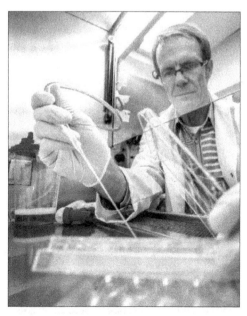

with nonlinear ideas. So it's very nice to be acknowledged for this."

EARLY LIFE AND EDUCATION

Lorenz Studer was born in the village of Hägendorf, Switzerland, located between the cities of Basel and Bern, on March 5, 1966. Even as a boy he had a passion for study and categorization, cataloging the specifications of his model-car collection in detail. An avid athlete, he competed in track and field and played a number of sports. "I was very excited about competition. I was very intense about anything that sparked my interest," Studer recalled to Azvolinsky.

From 1977 to 1985, Studer studied at Kanti Olten. During his teenage years, he developed an interest in medicine. In a 2008 piece published on the Memorial Sloan Kettering Cancer Center's website, Studer recalled: "My interest in medicine began when I was about 18. I had been in the hospital myself for an unusual type of bone infection and had also lost several close relatives to cancer." The deaths of an aunt and uncle profoundly impacted him, particularly because their deaths left his cousins orphaned. He became increasingly fascinated with the brain, in part because his relatives had died of brain tumors but also because of the ways hallucinogenic drugs such as LSD could put the mind in an altered state.

Studer studied medicine at the University of Fribourg from 1986 to 1988. While there, he was a student of Mario Wiesendanger, a neuroscience professor who stoked Studer's passion for brain research and neuroscience. Studer transferred to the University of Bern in 1988 to take advantage of Bern's university-based training hospital. At Bern he met Christian Spenger, a neurosurgeon fellow a little older than Studer, who introduced him to the idea of cell transplantation into the brain in order to treat neurodegenerative diseases similar to Parkinson's, a disease that affects about two in every one thousand people. With Parkinson's disease, the brain stops producing dopamine—a neurotransmitter that allows the brain to send messages properly to the body. When dopamine levels drop, functions such as motor skills and balance begin to suffer, leaving a person unable to perform even simple tasks.

EARLY RESEARCH IN FETAL AND STEM CELLS

The idea of replacing diseased or damaged brain cells with healthy ones fascinated Studer. After completing his MD in 1991, Studer stayed at Bern as a postdoctoral fellow, working alongside Spenger to develop further this revolutionary fetal-cell treatment. Over the course of four years, working out of a refitted broom closet, the duo began implanting fetal cells into animals as a way to treat Parkinson's. Their work culminated in the first clinical trials for Parkinson's sufferers in 1995.

Fetal cells, however, proved not to be ideal for the treatment of Parkinson's for a variety of reasons. One problem was that the pair procured fetal cells from aborted fetuses, which raised ethical concerns. The other reason was that fetal cells could not easily generate the mass quantities of cells needed to treat Parkinson's patients. In the end, it was a cumbersome and difficult process. "It was clear to me immediately that the use of fetal tissue was not going to be a good solution," Studer said to Rebecca Hiscott for *Neurology Today* (5 Nov. 2015).

From this setback, however, came a new opportunity. In 1995, Studer learned that an American researcher named Ronald McKay was working with stem cells, which are undifferentiated cells that can give rise to an endless number of cells of the same type or from which other cell types can develop through the process of differentiation. Studer believed he could grow stem cells into certain cell types needed for the brain. Specifically, he wanted to turn neural stem cells into mature brain cells called neurons. In 1996 Studer moved to the United States to work at the National Institutes of Health (NIH) in Washington, DC, where McKay's group was one of a handful then working with stem cells.

By 1998 Studer's work at the NIH had produced fruitful results: animal studies had shown that stem cells from the brain could be removed, grown in a culture and instructed by researchers to differentiate into specific types of cells. These cells were then implanted into the brains of mice suffering from Parkinson's disease. In short order the mice's brain functioning was partially restored. On Memorial Sloan Kettering Cancer Center's website, Studer recalled: "People were quite excited by this finding, and it is still the main paradigm for this kind of research. But we also realized that stem cells from the brain had limited potential, and that embryonic stem cells held more promise for differentiating into different cell types." The successful trial with mice was even mentioned in the US Congress as an example of the potential benefits of stem cells for treating diseases.

HEAD OF THE CENTER FOR STEM CELL BIOLOGY

Studer realized that brain stem cells were more limited in their potential than embryonic stem cells, which are taken from the inner cell mass of an early-stage preimplantation embryo, or blastocyst. Using embryonic stem cells—unlike using stem cells taken from adults or other parts of the body—has been considered ethically controversial for some time because it involves the destruction of the embryo, which if implanted in a womb and allowed to come to term, would develop into a human being. Despite the controversy, researchers like Studer believe that embryonic stem cells hold the key to curing a whole host of diseases as well as providing a better understanding of human physiology. "It's like the bread that never stops feeding people in the Bible," Studer said of embryonic stem cells, as quoted by Erin Blakemore for the *Washington Post* (5 Oct. 2015). "You can grow and grow and grow them. They can make millions and billions of cells. They could be anything."

While working at McKay's laboratory at the NIH, Studer met a fellow researcher named Viviane Tabar, whom he married in 1999. When Tabar applied for a research fellowship at Memorial Sloan Kettering Cancer Center in New York City, Studer decided to apply for a position as a faculty member there as well. In his piece for the Memorial Sloan Kettering Cancer Center's website, Studer wrote of how he came to head the Center for Stem Cell Biology: "I came to the Sloan Kettering Institute in 2000. My wife and collaborator . . . is a neurosurgeon and neuroscientist, and she had taken a position in Memorial Hospital. It may seem odd that a Parkinson's disease researcher would end up at a cancer center. But I knew the signals that guide stem cells are in many cases closely related to those that drive cancer growth."

Heading the Center for Stem Cell Biology, Studer has had a number of significant accomplishments. In 2001, he and his staff demonstrated that embryonic stem cells could be created from the skin cells of a mouse. By injecting the mouse's DNA into an egg with its nucleus removed, they created an early-stage embryo. In 2004 his team worked with human embryonic stem cells to make nerve cells. Three years later, they turned human embryonic stem cells into muscle cells; shortly thereafter, they showed how the nerve cells they had created from the skin cells of mice could be reimplanted into the mouse to treat Parkinson's disease. This latter achievement came with a large caveat: in order to repair brain function in mice with Parkinson's, the cells must match genetically.

In 2013 Studer's group received a five-year grant from the New York State Stem Cell Science program to develop dopamine neurons for the treatment of Parkinson's disease from human embryonic stem cells. As of 2015, his lab was able to produce some fifty different types of cells created from human embryonic stem cells, and it planned to begin clinical trials for Parkinson's disease as early as 2017.

Another remarkable accomplishment of Studer's lab derives from the work of the Nobel Prize–winning Japanese researcher Shinya Yamanaka, who developed a technique that could turn mouse fibroblasts (a type of cell that forms connective tissues in animals and plays a major role in the healing of wounds) back into stem cells. Remarking on the deaged cells, Studer told Rebecca Hiscott for *Neurology Today*: "If you make these cells, you cannot distinguish whether they came from a ninety-year-old or a five-year-old. It looks like the reprogramming process erases the age signature of the cell. That's really amazing, because it indicates that a big part of what makes cells aged is reversible. But it also posed a challenge, because if the cells are young, how do we make them old again to study a disease that happens only late in life, like Parkinson's disease?" Studer not only developed a way to turn various cells back into stem cells but also found a way to age the cells by adding progerin—a protein that is involved with the rare genetic disease called progeria, which causes children to age quickly. When the protein was added, the neuron that had once been an adult cell and then a stem cell was now demonstrating symptoms of Parkinson's.

MACARTHUR FOUNDATION FELLOWSHIP

In October 2015, Studer was one of twenty-four "thought leaders" presented with a MacArthur Foundation's Fellowship, given annually to individuals for their achievements in various fields, such as the arts and sciences. Studer plans to use the $635,000 he received to procure more investments for his laboratory, in the hopes of not only securing more clinical trials but also the talents of young minds able to push the research even farther. He believes that the more that is learned about how cells work, the more likely it will be that they can be manipulated to treat not only Parkinson's but also a whole host of diseases. "It's like a language or a piece of music," Studer said to Erin Blakemore for the *Washington Post*. "Cells constantly have to make decisions. If you figure out how to push the fate of cells toward one decision or the other, you get exquisite access to a high number of cell types."

SUGGESTED READING

"At Work: Center for Stem Cell Biology Director Lorenz Studer." *MSKCC.org*. Memorial Sloan Kettering Cancer Center, 2008. Web. 1 Apr. 2016.

Azvolinsky, Anna. "The Regenerator." *Scientist*. Scientist, 1 Dec. 2015. Web. 1 Apr. 2016.

Blakemore, Erin. "Ask a MacArthur Genius: Can Transplanted Brain Cells Cure Parkinson's?" *Washington Post*. Washington Post, 5 Oct. 2015. Web. 1 Apr. 2016.

Hiscott, Rebecca. "At the Bench: Lorenz Studer, MD, PhD: On Developing Stem Cell Therapies for Parkinson's Disease and Receiving a MacArthur 'Genius' Grant." *Neurology Today*. Amer. Acad. of Neurology, 5 Nov. 2015. Web. 1 Apr. 2016.

—*Christopher Mari*

Bhaskar Sunkara

Born: June 1989
Occupation: Editor and publisher

Bhaskar Sunkara is the editor and publisher of the socialist quarterly *Jacobin*. Sunkara was a sophomore in college—and only twenty-one years old—when he founded the magazine in 2009. "Looking back, I see it as a moment of creative ignorance," Sunkara told Jennifer Schuessler for the *New York Times* (20 Jan. 2013) of his own audacious decision. "You have to have enough intelligence to execute something like this but be stupid enough to think it could be successful." The term "Jacobin" refers to left-wing supporters of the eighteenth-century French Revolution, though Sunkara admits that the first time he heard the word was in reference to C. L. R. James's Marxist history of the Haitian Revolution, *The Black Jacobins* (1938). The bust of Toussaint L'Ouverture, the leader of that revolution, serves as the magazine's official logo.

In the wake of the Occupy Wall Street movement and the popular 2016 presidential campaign of democratic socialist Bernie Sanders, *Jacobin* has become very successful. Prominent fans include MSNBC host Chris Hayes and even, peculiarly, Reihan Salam, a conservative commentator for the *National Review*. By 2016, *Jacobin*'s website counted nearly a million readers and 20,000 print subscribers. In a profile of Sunkara for *Vox* (21 Mar. 2016), Dylan Matthews called *Jacobin* "the leading intellectual voice of the American left" and "the most vibrant and relevant socialist publication in a very long time." The magazine has a host of contributors, who write about political theory in clear, nononsense prose. Sunkara does not want to merely sell magazines; he wants to foster a political movement. "I'd actually be very happy if, by the time I die, there's an opposition current in the US of 5 to 7 percent that identifies as socialist or would support a socialist candidate," he told a reporter for the *New Left Review* (1 Nov. 2014).

EARLY LIFE AND EDUCATION

Sunkara, the youngest of five children, was born in June 1989 and grew up in Westchester County, New York. His parents are of Indian descent; his mother was born in Trinidad and his father moved there from India as a young man. They moved to the United States the year before Sunkara was born. His father was trained as a doctor but employed as a clerical worker. His mother was a telemarketer.

Both parents worked late, and young Sunkara spent most afternoons in the local library. He read *Animal Farm*, George Orwell's 1945 political satire, in the seventh grade. A reference to Leon Trotsky led him to the writing of the

Marxist theorist, which in turn led him to a number of other political writers, including Lucio Magri, a leader of Italy's Independent Left; British historian Perry Anderson; and the Polish British socialist intellectual Ralph Miliband. These thinkers and their books served as the bedrock of Sunkara's political ideology. "I'm lucky I didn't pick up Ayn Rand or Milton Friedman before I got to Trotsky," he joked in his interview with the *New Left Review*, referring respectively to the founder of objectivism and the Nobel Prize–winning libertarian economist, both influential right-wing thinkers.

He began taking the train into the city to attend antiwar rallies during the run-up to the Iraq War in the early 2000s, when he was still in middle school. He joined the New York chapter of the Democratic Socialists of America (DSA) when he was eighteen and began editing a blog called the *Activist* for the DSA's youth branch. Still, he told Virginia Fu for the *Blue and White*, a student magazine at Columbia University (1 Feb. 2016), "It was kind of like a dual consciousness where I was engaged day to day in left mainstream politics but I also had intellectual sympathies with the far left, and it was only in college that I started doing more activism explicitly as a socialist."

FOUNDING *JACOBIN*

Sunkara, who was voted "most likely to succeed" in high school, enrolled as an international relations student at George Washington University in Washington, DC, in 2008. During his freshman year, he continued his work as an editor for the *Activist* and began writing for *Dissent*, a popular political quarterly. In 2009, during the summer between his sophomore and junior year, Sunkara became seriously ill and was forced to spend the entire following school year on medical leave. The young student devised his own course of study, reading several books a week—most of them on Western Marxist and socialist thought—and took copious notes.

His studies engendered questions and those questions inspired him to conceive of founding his own magazine. He wanted to create a publication, he told the *New Left Review*, "that was uncompromisingly socialist, but that married some of the accessibility of the *Nation*," a long-running left-leaning weekly, "with the political seriousness of publications further to the left. A lot of what I was learning during the year I spent reading was how to convey these ideas in as simple a way as possible." Sunkara was turned off by Marxist jargon, which he saw as an intellectual "crutch," as he told the *New Left Review*, for talking about ideas that "are not actually very complex." *Jacobin*, he decided, would be both intellectually rigorous and readable.

Originally, Sunkara envisioned his project as web-based but quickly concluded that "it would have more impact if it was also a print journal," he told the *New Left Review*. It was an unusual decision for a young entrepreneur to make. Many older publications were and are being forced to move away from print entirely. For the young and inexperienced Sunkara, however, print was not a financial liability but a mark of distinction. A sleek, tangible product, he believed, lent his unknown magazine a certain amount of credibility.

JACOBIN'S GROWING INFLUENCE
The *Jacobin* website went live in September 2010, and its first issue came out in early 2011, the same year Sunkara graduated with a bachelor's degree in history. *Jacobin* began to gain national attention in September 2011, when it organized a speaking panel in Manhattan, several weeks after the Occupy Wall Street protests began at nearby Zuccotti Park. The panel encapsulated *Jacobin's* entire point of view: It was not enough to merely support the protest, Sunkara argued, one must understand what it meant and where it was headed. The panel was a turning point for the young magazine. It brought *Jacobin* to the attention of conservative personalities such as Glenn Beck and Andrew Breitbart, both of whom gave the magazine free publicity by denouncing it.

Meanwhile, the magazine itself took shape. In late 2011, Remeike Forbes, a graduate student from the prestigious Rhode Island School of Design (RISD) and fan of *Jacobin*, e-mailed Sunkara to offer his services. Forbes began designing the magazine's distinctive, graphic covers, and by 2016, as the magazine's creative director, he works closely with Sunkara to devise each issue's theme. The magazine, which is financially sustained through its subscribers and some donations, counts readers across the United States. In a handful of cities, conservative Salt Lake City among them, *Jacobin* has reader groups that serve as de facto socialist organizations. Sunkara encourages the groups by offering free magazines, syllabi, and help finding space. In Salt Lake City, the reader group meets at a Unitarian church.

The guiding principle of the magazine, Sunkara has said, is to publish stories that interest him and his small coterie of regular contributors. Often this formula works surprisingly well. In one issue, Sunkara published an article about the Carnation Revolution in 1974, "The Next Portuguese Revolution" by Mark Bergfeld (22 May 2014). It was a "surprise hit," Sunkara told the *New Left Review*, that taught Sunkara more about his readership and signaled to would-be contributors the breadth of *Jacobin's* interests.

Among the magazine's best-known pieces is Seth Ackerman's "Burn the Constitution" (1

Mar. 2011). (Sunkara came up with the title.) In it, Ackerman, a doctoral student candidate at Cornell University whom Sunkara met through the e-mail list of journalist Doug Henwood's newsletter *Left Business Observer*, argues that the US Constitution is an inherently conservative document. Citing Charles A. Beard, the influential Progressive Era historian, Ackerman argues in part that the Constitution affords the people very little control of their own government. The Progressive Era saw the rise of willingness to change the Constitution, engendering a conservative backlash to enshrine the document that continues in the modern Tea Party movement. Liberals argue that conservatives misunderstand the Constitution, Ackerman writes, without considering any problems inherent in the thing itself.

In 2014 *Jacobin* teamed up with Verso Books, an independent, radical publishing house, to begin publishing a series of books on topics ranging from the Chicago Teachers Union strike to sex workers' rights.

WRITING FOR OTHER PUBLICATIONS
In addition to his work with *Jacobin*, Sunkara has contributed to the progressive monthly *In These Times* and to *Vice*. In 2016, Sunkara and Sarah Leonard, of the *Nation* and *Dissent* magazine, edited a book of essays called *The Future We Want: Radical Ideas for the New Century*. A reviewer for *Kirkus* (9 Dec. 2015) wrote of the collection, "Piquant, irksome, challenging, head-turning, maddening—a collection that successfully endeavors to get your blood pumping."

Sunkara's own writing voice—like *Jacobin's* overarching style—is provocative. His acid-tipped pen often takes aim at a caste of center-left political commentators such as Ezra Klein of the *Washington Post*, whom he called, in an article for *In These Times* (18 Jan. 2013), "the archetype for the bankruptcy of modern liberalism." Sunkara is often funny and delights in controversial headlines, although he is careful not to make antagonizing people the *Jacobin's* raison d'être. In the same article about Klein, Sunkara outlines a larger argument about journalistic objectivity, an ideal that often leads well-intentioned journalists to limit debate and blur policy distinctions.

PERSONAL LIFE
Sunkara lives and works in Brooklyn.

SUGGESTED READING
Ackerman, Seth. "Burn the Constitution." *Jacobin*. Jacobin, 1 Mar. 2011. Web. 12 Sept. 2016.

Matthews, Dylan. "Inside Jacobin: How a Socialist Magazine Is Winning the Left's War of

Ideas." *Vox*. Vox Media, 21 Mar. 2016. Web. 12 Sept. 2016.

Rev. of *The Future We Want: Radical Ideas for the New Century*, ed. Sarah Leonard and Bhaskar Sunkara. *Kirkus*. Kirkus Media, 9 Dec. 2015. Web. 12 Sept. 2016.

Schuessler, Jennifer. "A Young Publisher Takes Marx into the Mainstream." *New York Times*. New York Times, 20 Jan. 2013. Web. 12 Sept. 2016.

Sunkara, Bhaskar. "Leaving a Marx." Interview by Virginia Fu. *Blue and White*. Columbia U, 1 Feb. 2016. Web. 12 Sept. 2016.

Sunkara, Bhaskar. "New Masses, New Media: Project Jacobin." Interview. *New Left Review*. New Left Review, 1 Nov. 2014. Web. 12 Sept. 2016.

—*Molly Hagan*

Raina Telgemeier

Born: May 26, 1977
Occupation: Comics artist

Raina Telgemeier is a comics artist, and the author of several best-selling comics books for young readers. She got her start in 2006 adapting several books from Scholastic's popular Baby-Sitters Club series into graphic novels and wrote her first original work, *Smile*, a graphic memoir, in 2010. The book won that year's Boston Globe/Horn Book Nonfiction Honor, and landed on the *New York Times* Best Seller list. It is perhaps unsurprising that *Smile*, as well as 2014's *Sisters*, are autobiographical works. Growing up, Telgemeier kept a comics journal in which she drew a comic about her day, every day, from when she was about eleven years old until the age of twenty-five. Telgemeier uses dialogue and drawing to capture both the comedy and tragedy of adolescence; in *Sisters*, her most recent book, Telgemeier and her younger sister bicker on an ill-fated road trip as they come to realize that their parents are drifting apart.

Telgemeier has created her own niche in an industry dominated by superhero stories that cater to the interests of male readers. According to Jennifer Maloney for the *Wall Street Journal* (31 Dec. 2014), young girls are becoming an important part of a booming market for graphic novels and comic books. "Graphic-novel sales are outpacing the overall trade-book market," Maloney wrote, "and their audience has expanded to include more women and younger readers." Telgemeier's work has won two prestigious Eisner Awards—a high honor in the comics industry—and a Stonewall Book Award for LGBT (Lesbian, Gay, Bisexual, Transgender) literature. *Ghosts*,

Telgemeier's upcoming graphic novel about two sisters who move to a strange and spooky new town, will be released in fall 2016.

EARLY LIFE AND EDUCATION

Telgemeier was born on May 26, 1977, and grew up in San Francisco alongside two younger siblings: a sister, Amara, and a brother, Will. Telgemeier started reading comic strips in the *San Francisco Chronicle* when she was nine. She loved strips like *Calvin and Hobbes* and *For Better or for Worse*. She tried to emulate what she saw, but was frustrated by the four-panel structure. She also tried making flipbooks, after she was dazzled by the animation in the Walt Disney film *The Little Mermaid*—but found that it could take hours to draw just a few seconds worth of cartoons. Later, she started reading comic books like Adrian Tomine's *Optic Nerve*, an alternative, self-published comic from the early 1990s, and the fantastical *Bone* by Jeff Smith, and realized she was better suited to the longer comic book form. Telgemeier was also inspired starting around age ten or eleven by cartoonist Lynda Barry, whose dark comic books often dealt with weighty issues. "I loved her raw honesty, and her characters were way worse than my life. It was a window into someone whose life was really tragic," she told Rebecca Huval for *Bitch Media* (8 Sept. 2014). "It's weird to say how helpful that is, but it was cathartic. Her characters are ugly and covered in weird marks, but also really funny and moving."

After graduating high school, Telgemeier worked several minimum wage jobs while taking art classes at a community college. She also worked briefly for a Top 40 radio station, an experience she described to Ashley Baylen for the Jewish daily *Shalom Life* (8 Nov. 2012) as "really bizarre." At twenty-two, she moved to New York City to attend the School of Visual Arts in Manhattan, and graduated with a degree in illustration and cartooning in 2002. Telgemeier honed her distinct style throughout her twenties, drawing inspiration from Disney cartoons, the Muppets, and Scooby Doo. She continued to self-publish short comics, or mini-comics, while working for a publishing company.

In 2004, one of her mini-comics was published in an anthology called *Broad Appeal*. At the release party for the book, Telgemeier met an editor from Scholastic who invited her to pitch an idea for the company's new comic book imprint, Graphix. At the meeting, Telgemeier mentioned that she was a huge fan of the Baby-Sitters Club books, a long-running series published by Scholastic. The editors at Graphix jumped at the chance to adapt the books as graphic novels, and hired Telgemeier in 2005. Telgemeier's first Baby-Sitters Club book, *Kristy's Great Idea*, was published in 2006, followed by *The Truth about Stacy, Mary Anne Saves the Day*, and *Claudia and Mean Janine* in 2008. (The series was first published in black and white; color was added, and the series was republished beginning in 2015.) It was a valuable crash course in long-form storytelling, Telgemeier told Christopher Irving for the blog *NYC Graphic Novelists* (16 Feb. 2010). "Drawing eight pages was all I'd ever tackled," she said. "So, jumping to 192 pages for the books was at first scary." She recalls hitting a turning point with the second novel, *The Truth about Stacy*. She was required to write the entire book in six months—her fastest turnaround ever—but the deadline made her drawing, as Irving put it, "looser and more alive." While she was adapting the novels, Telgemeier was also working on her own comics, most notably *Smile*.

SMILE (2010) AND *DRAMA* (2012)

Smile, an autobiographical tale about Telgemeier losing her two front teeth, started out as web comic on a site called *Girlamatic*. "[It] was born out of a need to get the whole experience down on paper, since I spent so much time telling people about it," Telgemeier wrote on her personal website *Go Raina!* (2009). She began with a clear plan for at least twenty pages, and began posting one page a week. As readers responded to the pages, Telgemeier expanded her idea. "I realized I was creating something that actually resonated with some people," she told Irving. The book took Telgemeier nearly five years to write, though when she was finished, Graphix was eager to publish it. It told the true story of

Telgemeier's teeth—when she was in the sixth grade, she tripped and fell walking out of a Girl Scout meeting, smacking her face on the pavement. One of her front teeth fell out. The other was pushed up into her gums. So began Telgemeier's traumatizing, years-long dental saga, which began, of course, just as she was entering middle school. The book was an unexpected best seller, and Elizabeth Bird, who reviewed it for the *New York Times* (14 May 2010), praised Telgemeier's wit and attention to detail, comparing her to beloved young adult author, Judy Blume. "Drawing in a deceptively simple style, Telgemeier has a knack for synthesizing the preadolescent experience in a visual medium," Bird wrote.

The success of *Smile* made Telgemeier realize that she loved writing for young audiences. She began writing her second book, *Drama* (2012), soon after. *Drama*, unlike *Smile*, was not a story from Telgemeier's life, though she drew on several high school experiences to write it. In *Drama*, Callie is a set designer for her middle school's production of the (fictional) musical *Moon over Mississippi*. She befriends twin brothers and develops a crush on one of them, only to discover that he is gay. Ada Calhoun, who reviewed the book for the *New York Times* (23 Aug. 2012), wrote that it was more subtle and sophisticated than *Smile*. "Telgemeier's work is part of a boom in smart, wholesome comics for young people. . . . In her stories, relatable girls make the first move, add and shed friends according to a niceness-ocracy, and roll with setbacks."

SISTERS (2014)

Telgemeier's most recent comic book, *Sisters* (2014), is an autobiographical story about a family road trip. Fans had been dogging Telgemeier to write a sequel to *Smile*. "It took me awhile to realize what people were really asking for were more anecdotes from my childhood, drawn from my point of view," she told Michael Cavna for the *Washington Post* (16 May 2014). The story was inspired by Telgemeier's competitive relationship with her younger sister. Growing up, both girls were artists, and Telgemeier was often miffed by Amara's greater success. In her story, their barbed relationship comes to a head on a family road trip when Telgemeier is fourteen. The girls contend with sullen cousins—their destination is a family reunion—and an escaped pet snake, all while keeping one eye on their parents' unraveling marriage. Telgemeier worked with her sister to hone the first draft of the book. *Sisters* was darker than Telgemeier's previous works, but just as well received. Maya Van Wagenen praised Telgemeier's depiction of sibling rivalry and family conflict for the *New York Times* (22 Aug. 2014), writing that the lens through which she views familiar subjects is "uncomfortable yet transcendent." Like Telgemeier's other books, *Sisters* ends on a happy if bittersweet note, though Telgemeier struggled to come to terms with her parents' divorce. "I don't write stories to tell a message, but choose the stories I do if the story will make the reader feel better about themselves," she told Huval.

PERSONAL LIFE

Telgemeier is married to fellow comics artist Dave Roman. Roman also writes for children and young adults. Among his books is *Astronaut Academy: Zero Gravity* (2011), about a young intergalactic hero who gives up his day job to go to middle school. The couple met at the School of Visual Arts, and share the same birthday. Norman proposed to Telgemeier with a homemade comic that had "Will You Marry Me?" written on the second-to-last page. She wrote the last page herself: "Yes." They live in the Astoria neighborhood of Queens in New York City.

SUGGESTED READING

Baylen, Ashley. "Exclusive Interview with Graphic Novelist, Raina Telgemeier." *Shalom Life*. Shalom Life, 8 Nov. 2012. Web. 10 Dec. 2015.

Bird, Elizabeth. "Blood, Sweat and Teeth." Rev. of *Smile*, by Raina Telgemeier. *New York Times*. New York Times, 14 May 2010. Web. 10 Dec. 2015.

Calhoun, Ada. "Life Backstage." Rev. of *Drama*, by Raina Telgemeier. *New York Times*. New York Times, 23 Aug. 2012. Web. 10 Dec. 2015.

Cavna, Michael. "Raina Telgemeier: Bestselling 'Smile' Graphic Novelist Comes to Gaithersburg Book Festival with Fans' Wish: More True Tales of Childhood." *Washington Post*. Washington Post, 16 May 2014. Web. 10 Dec. 2015.

Huval, Rebecca. "New Graphic Novel 'Sisters' Captures the Joys and Troubles of Sisterhood." *Bitch Media*. Bitch Media, 8 Sept. 2014. Web. 10 Dec. 2015.

Irving, Christopher. "Raina Telgemeier and Her Well-Deserved Smile." *NYC Graphic Novelists*. Author, 16 Feb. 2010. Web. 10 Dec. 2015.

Maloney, Jennifer. "The New Wave of Graphic Novels." *Wall Street Journal*. Dow Jones, 31 Dec. 2014. Web. 10 Dec. 2015.

SELECTED WORKS

Smile (2010); *Drama* (2012); *Sisters* (2014)

—*Molly Hagan*

Klay Thompson

Born: February 8, 1990
Occupation: Basketball player

Like his superstar backcourt partner Stephen Curry, the Golden State Warriors' shooting guard Klay Thompson has followed in his father's footsteps of playing in the National Basketball Association (NBA). Along with Curry, Thompson makes up a duo known around the league as the "Splash Brothers," so named because of their effortless ability to consistently make all-net three-pointers. The duo has established new NBA records for most combined three-pointers among teammates every year since the 2012–13 season.

Aside from making up one half of the most prolific three-point tandem in NBA history, Thompson has emerged as a superstar in his own right since being drafted by the Warriors in 2011. Regarded as "one of the greatest shooters the league has ever seen," as Rob Mahoney wrote for *Sports Illustrated* (29 May 2016), Thompson made 1,060 three-pointers during his first five full seasons with the Warriors, the most in NBA history by a player in his first five seasons in the league. In 2015 he set an NBA record for most individual points scored in a quarter (thirty-seven) and powered the Warriors to an NBA championship, the team's first since 1975.

During the 2016 NBA playoffs, Thompson set another league record for most three-pointers made in a single postseason game (eleven), en route to leading the Warriors to their second consecutive berth in the NBA Finals. Known as much for his shooting prowess as for

Ezra Shaw/Getty Images

his defensive versatility, Thompson has grown into one of the league's best two-way guards. He earned All-Star and All-NBA Third Team selections in both 2015 and 2016.

EARLY LIFE AND EDUCATION

The middle of three sons, Klay Alexander Thompson was born on February 8, 1990, in Los Angeles, California. His father, Mychal, who hails from the Bahamas, was selected first overall in the NBA Draft, going number one to the Portland Trail Blazers in 1978. A six-foot-ten center-forward, Mychal Thompson spent twelve seasons in the NBA, winning consecutive titles as a member of the Los Angeles Lakers in 1987 and 1988. Thompson's mother, Julie, was a volleyball player at the University of San Francisco.

Thompson spent his childhood and elementary school years in Lake Oswego, Oregon, where his father moved the family after ending his playing career. Thompson naturally gravitated to basketball at an early age, though his father never pushed him into the sport. He grew up playing backyard battles with his father and two brothers, Mychel and Trayce, which helped accelerate his basketball development. "Usually one of us would quit before the game even ended, because it would get pretty heated," Thompson recalled to Abe Schwadron for *SLAM* (25 Feb. 2014).

During his youth, Thompson was as firmly dedicated to baseball as he was to basketball. He was a standout shortstop and pitcher and played on Little League All-Star teams with current Cleveland Cavaliers forward Kevin Love. In 2001 the duo helped lead the Lake Oswego Lakers to a state title, finishing just several games shy of making the Little League World Series. "Klay always had a quiet confidence about him," Love said to Connor Letourneau for the *San Francisco Chronicle* (5 June 2016). "There was something about Klay that separated him from the rest of the group."

After finishing elementary school, Thompson moved with his family to Orange County, California. There, his father began working as a color analyst for the Lakers' radio broadcasts and cohosting a morning radio talk show. Thompson attended Santa Margarita Catholic High School, a private college prep school. As a freshman, he played on the school's junior varsity basketball squad and also played football and baseball.

Thompson gave up the latter two sports after his freshman year to concentrate on basketball. He was Santa Margarita's starting varsity shooting guard his sophomore through senior seasons. As a senior, Thompson teamed up with his brother Trayce, then a junior, to lead Santa Margarita to the 2008 Division III state title. That same year he earned first-team all-state honors and was named Division III player of the year.

During his high-school career, Thompson grew from a one-dimensional, albeit exceptional, long-range shooting threat to an all-around talent. By the end of his senior season, he had established himself as one of the top prep players in Southern California. Thompson was not heavily recruited by Division I basketball schools, however, due to concerns over his defensive skills. Those concerns notwithstanding, Thompson "was an undeniable talent," his high-school coach, Jerry DeBusk, told Sean Ceglinksy for *ESPN.com* (10 Feb. 2011). "He had a good feel for the game and had that little something extra" that separated him from other players.

WASHINGTON STATE TO GOLDEN STATE WARRIORS

Thompson ultimately accepted a scholarship to Washington State University (WSU), a Division I school not known for its basketball prowess. Any doubts about Thompson's abilities were put to rest during his freshman season, when he started all thirty-three games for the Cougars and was the team's leader in free-throw percentage (.902) and three-point field goal percentage (.412).

As a sophomore, Thompson averaged a team-best 19.6 points and was selected for the All-Pacific-10 (Pac-10) Conference First Team. He again earned first-team all-conference honors as a junior in 2010–11, when he led the Cougars and the Pac-10 in scoring (21.6 points per game) and in three-point field goals made (98). That season Thompson also set the Cougars' single-season scoring record with 733 points. He was nonetheless suspended for his final regular-season game after being cited for misdemeanor marijuana possession. The transgression drew the ire of Thompson's father, who candidly berated him on his radio show.

Controversy aside, Thompson opted to forgo his senior season to enter the 2011 NBA Draft. Regarded as one of the best shooters in the draft, he was selected by the Golden State Warriors in the draft's first round, as the eleventh overall pick. Thompson finished his college career at WSU as the school's all-time leader in three-pointers made, with 242.

Thompson was expected to make immediate contributions off the bench for the Warriors during his rookie 2011–12 season, which was shortened from eighty-two to sixty-six games due to an NBA lockout. Despite a lackluster preseason, he eventually settled into a backup role for the Warriors' veteran starting guard Monta Ellis. Thompson was thrust into the Warriors' starting lineup in March 2012 after Ellis was traded to the Milwaukee Bucks.

Thompson appeared in all sixty-six games, averaging 12.5 points, 2.4 rebounds, and 2.0 assists. He led all rookies in three-point percentage

(.414) and three-pointers made (111), and was named to the NBA All-Rookie First Team. During the season, the Warriors' first-year coach, the former NBA point guard Mark Jackson, said of Thompson to Rusty Simmons for the *San Francisco Chronicle* (17 Feb. 2012): "The guy is not afraid. He takes tremendous pride, not just in his shooting, but in his entire game. . . . He's a silent assassin."

RECORD-SETTING TANDEM

Thompson built on his strong rookie campaign in a big way in 2012–13, when he teamed up with the Warriors' starting point guard Stephen Curry to form the most prolific shooting tandem in NBA history. The duo earned the nickname the "Splash Brothers," as they combined to hit 483 three-pointers, then the highest combined total among teammates since the NBA instituted the three-point line in 1979–80. While Curry hit an NBA-record 272 three-pointers, Thompson finished third in the league with 211 baskets from beyond the arc. He also ranked third on the Warriors in scoring, averaging 16.6 points in eighty-two games (all starts).

Thompson and Curry's record-breaking backcourt production helped propel the Warriors to a 47–35 record and to their first playoff berth in six years. The Warriors advanced to the Western Conference Semifinals, where they lost to the San Antonio Spurs in six games. In the second game of that series, Thompson recorded thirty-four points and fourteen rebounds, becoming only the fourth guard to reach those point and rebound totals in a playoff game in the previous twenty-five years; the others are Michael Jordan, Kobe Bryant, and Vince Carter.

Prior to the 2013–14 season, Jackson boldly declared that Thompson was among the top five shooting guards in the league. Thompson gave serious credence to that declaration as he complemented his already-outstanding shooting ability with first-rate defensive play. Throughout that season, he regularly lived up to the task of defending the opposing team's best perimeter player. "At 6-7," Abe Schwadron wrote, "[Thompson] gives smaller guards fits with his size on both ends of the floor, and bigger players struggle with his constant off-the-ball activity and quick feet."

On the offensive end, Thompson improved his scoring average to 18.4 points per game and ranked second in the NBA in three-pointers (223), finishing only behind Curry. Thompson and Curry eclipsed their own NBA record by hitting a combined 484 three-pointers, as they became the first pair of teammates in league history to finish as the top-two three-point leaders in a single season. The Warriors, meanwhile, improved to 51–31 and earned their second consecutive playoff berth.

NBA ALL-STAR AND WORLD CHAMPION

During the summer of 2014, Thompson captured a gold medal as a member of the US men's national basketball team at the FIBA Basketball World Cup. That summer he found himself the subject of several NBA trade rumors, among which included the Warriors sending him to the Minnesota Timberwolves in exchange for Kevin Love, his former Little League teammate. Love was ultimately dealt to the Cavaliers in a three-team trade, while Thompson remained with the Warriors in what was "one of the most important non-moves in franchise history," Letourneau wrote.

At the beginning of the 2014–15 season, the Warriors showed their commitment to Thompson by signing him to a four-year, $70 million contract extension. Thompson wasted little time rewarding the Warriors' faith in him: in the second game of the season, he scored a then career-high forty-one points against the Los Angeles Lakers. Thompson would surpass that performance in historic fashion on January 23, 2015, when he broke the NBA record for points in a quarter by scoring thirty-seven points in the third quarter against the Sacramento Kings. He also hit an NBA-record nine three-pointers in the quarter, en route to finishing with a career-high fifty-two points in a 126–101 Warriors victory.

Thompson averaged 21.7 points, 3.2 rebounds, and a career-high 2.9 assists in seventy-seven games, and again finished second in the league to Curry in three-point field goals, with 239. He earned his first career All-Star selection, as a reserve for the Western Conference, and was named to the All-NBA Third Team. Thompson and Curry, who would win the 2015 NBA Most Valuable Player Award, combined to hit 525 three-pointers, thus surpassing their league record for the third consecutive year.

Guided by first-year coach Steve Kerr, another former NBA guard who replaced Jackson after the 2013–14 season, Thompson and Curry anchored the Warriors to an NBA-best and franchise-record sixty-seven regular-season wins. The Warriors lost only three games in the first three playoff rounds before facing the Cleveland Cavaliers in the NBA Finals. The Warriors defeated the Cavaliers in six games to claim their first NBA championship in forty years. Thompson started in all of the team's twenty-one postseason games, averaging 18.6 points, 3.9 rebounds, and 2.6 assists. He also hit fifty-seven three-pointers, the third-highest total in a single NBA postseason.

2015–16 SEASON

Thompson solidified his status as one of the best two-way guards in the league during the 2015–16 season, in which he averaged career-highs in points (22.1) and rebounds (3.8). He also finished with a career-high 276 three-point field goals, the third-highest total in NBA history. For the third straight season, Thompson finished second in the league in three-pointers to Curry, who made an astounding 402 baskets from beyond the arc. Thompson and Curry again established another league record for combined three-pointers in a season, with 678. Thompson was selected to his second straight All-Star team and won his first three-point contest during 2016 NBA All-Star Weekend. He was also named to the All-NBA Third Team for the second consecutive year.

The Warriors, meanwhile, made a strong case for being the greatest team in NBA history. They opened the 2015–16 season by winning a record twenty-four straight games and finished with seventy-three wins overall, overtaking the 1995–96 Chicago Bulls for the most regular-season wins in league history. Despite breaking numerous NBA records during the regular season, the Warriors came within a game of being eliminated from the playoffs after falling into a three-games-to-one deficit against the Oklahoma City Thunder in the Western Conference Finals. Thompson played a vital role in helping the Warriors win the next three games in the series to return to the NBA Finals.

In the Warriors' 108–101 game 6 victory, Thompson scored a playoff career-high forty-one points and hit a playoff-record eleven three-pointers. Following that game, coach Steve Kerr commented on Thompson and Curry's aggressive and at times fearless shooting approach. As quoted by Mahoney, Kerr explained, "They kind of walk that fine line between lethal and crazy, and we have to live with some crazy shots, some crazy misses because they make more than their fair share."

2016 NBA FINALS

The Warriors went head to head against the Cleveland Cavaliers, led by LeBron James, in the 2016 NBA Finals. Although the Warriors had a 3–1 lead going into game 5, the Cavs won games 5 and 6, and were able to force a winner-take-all final game 7. During a press conference on June 16, 2016, Thompson noted the pressure the team was under to win their second straight championship: "We expected to win the NBA Championship coming into the season. It's either win the whole thing or bust for us. . . . A lot at stake, but that's when we're going to rise up and be at our best."

Unfortunately for the Warriors, the team fell short of their best in game 7, and lost both the game and the championship. With four minutes and thirty-nine seconds on the clock, Thompson's two-pointer brought the score to a tie at 89–89, but his shot turned out to be the Warriors' last of the game, and the Cavs prevailed with a final score of 93–89. Of the loss, Thompson said, as quoted by Jeff Faraudo for the *Mercury News* (19 June 2016), "It's the hardest thing I've ever had to go through in my sports career." But Thompson was hopeful for the future, too, saying, "We're going to be better from this. I promise you that. It won't be the last time we're on this stage."

PERSONAL LIFE

Thompson has been extensively involved in charitable activities with the Warriors since making his NBA debut. His older brother, Mychel, is also a professional basketball player, making his NBA debut with the Cleveland Cavaliers in 2011–12 and playing in the NBA Development League with the Warriors' affiliate, the Santa Cruz Warriors, from 2013 to 2015. Thompson's younger brother, Trayce, meanwhile, is a professional baseball player who currently plays for Major League Baseball's Los Angeles Dodgers.

SUGGESTED READING

Ceglinsky, Sean. "Look at Them Now: Klay Thompson." *ESPN.com*. ESPN Internet Ventures, 10 Feb. 2011. Web. 30 May 2016.

Faraudo, Jeff. "NBA Finals: Klay Thompson Deals with the Pain." *Mercury News*. Digital First Media, 19 June 2016. Web. 20 June 2016.

Letourneau, Connor. "Klay Thompson, Kevin Love Go from Little League to NBA Finals." *San Francisco Chronicle*. Hearst Communications, 5 June 2016. Web. 6 June 2016.

Mahoney, Rob. "How Klay Thompson's Historic Night Saved the Warriors' Season." *Sports Illustrated*. Time, 29 May 2016. Web. 30 May 2016.

Schwadron, Abe. "Under the Rainbow Jumper." *SLAM*. Enthusiast Network, 25 Feb. 2014. Web. 30 May 2016.

Simmons, Rusty. "Warriors' Klay Thompson Growing into a Top Shooter." *San Francisco Chronicle*. Hearst Communications, 17 Feb. 2012. Web. 30 May 2016.

—*Chris Cullen*

Tessa Thompson

Born: October 3, 1983
Occupation: Actor

Television audiences first became familiar with Tessa Thompson in 2005 during her guest appearance on an episode of the CBS crime drama *Cold Case* and a season-long stint on the United

Monica Schipper/FilmMagic/Getty Images

Paramount Network (UPN) teen detective series *Veronica Mars*, which had a dedicated cult following over three short seasons. Over the next five years, she remained a small-screen fixture, with notable roles in the hit dramas *Grey's Anatomy*, *Private Practice*, and *Heroes*. She strove to make her first real mark on the big screen in the 2010 film *For Colored Girls*.

However, it was Thompson's breakout performance as opinionated young activist Sam White in the indie comedy *Dear White People* (2014) that impressed critics, as well as the film's director. "To be a dramatic actress who can also headline a satire is very tricky and difficult to do," Justin Simien told Tre'vell Anderson for the *Los Angeles Times* (1 Dec. 2015). "That says a lot about what an actor can do. She can exist in a lot of different worlds and genres." Since then, Thompson has made a career of playing strong, outspoken characters in powerful and high-profile films, including *Selma* (2014) and *Creed* (2015).

EARLY LIFE AND EDUCATION

Tessa Thompson was born on October 3, 1983, in Los Angeles, California, to a mother of Mexican European descent and a Panamanian father. In addition to being multiracial, she hails from a creative family. Her maternal grandfather is Mexican American bandleader and singer Bobby Ramos, who produced and cohosted *Latin Cruise*, a Latin American television variety series on KTLA. Her father, a New York City–based singer and songwriter, founded the musical collective Chocolate Genius and composed scores for film and theater. Growing up in Los Angeles,

she spent summer and winter breaks visiting her father in Brooklyn, where she could often be found in his basement music studio.

Thompson first truly caught the acting bug in the fifth grade, while playing a dancing wolf in a school play. "Since childhood, acting was always something I was doing; it was the only thing I cared about being good at," she recalled to Krista Smith for *Vanity Fair* (Dec. 2015). During her sophomore year at Santa Monica High School, she graduated to more serious fare, landing the role of Hermia in a modern take of William Shakespeare's *A Midsummer Night's Dream*. Upon graduating from high school, she majored in cultural anthropology at Santa Monica College.

Thompson's interest in linguistics led her to attend a workshop hosted by the LA Women's Shakespeare Company (LAWSC), a nonprofit, all-female acting troupe that stages productions of the playwright's works. After she inquired about an internship with LAWSC, Lisa Wolpe, the company's artistic director, convinced Thompson to audition instead and then invited her to participate in a table reading. She was subsequently cast, alongside two other actors, as the sprite Ariel in the company's 2002 production of *The Tempest*.

PROFESSIONAL STAGE DEBUT AND GETTING NOTICED

At the urging of LAWSC company members, Thompson attended an open casting call for *Romeo and Juliet: Antebellum New Orleans, 1836*, the debut production for Pasadena's Boston Court Theater. She impressed one of the venue's artistic directors, Michael Michetti, who tapped her for the female lead after catching her in a performance of *The Tempest*. "While Tessa did not have an enormous amount of experience, she had the skills coming in," he recalled to Deborah Behrens for *@ This Stage* (11 July 2012). "She knew how to use her voice, work with text and take direction. She was not just raw material." Thompson made her stage debut in September 2003 and scored an NAACP (National Association for the Advancement of Colored People) Theatre Award nod for her performance as well as prospective agent and manager contacts.

Determined to pursue an acting career, Thompson took a break from college and continued to build up stage credits. In 2004 she headlined the cast of Charles Mee's romantic comedy *Summertime* and also appeared as Olivia in A Noise Within's production of Shakespeare's *Twelfth Night*. The following summer, she took on the lead role of a house cat in love with an alley cat in *Indoor/Outdoor*, which made its West Coast debut at the Colony Theatre in Burbank, California.

STARTING SMALL

Despite her developing stage career, Thompson struggled to support herself with odd jobs. Therefore, she heeded a friend's advice and enlisted the help of a talent agent, who arranged auditions for her. "Eventually, when I realized that [commercials] were not for me, I finally started going out for television roles, and stuff just started happening," she told Shannon M. Houston for *Paste* (28 May 2014). Within two weeks, she had landed her first television role—a guest spot on a May 2005 episode of CBS's *Cold Case*, in which she played a lesbian bootlegger during the Prohibition era. Later that year, her profile increased considerably when she joined the second season of the UPN teen detective series *Veronica Mars* as Jackie Cook, a foil for the title character.

Thompson got her first taste of film work with her supporting role in *When a Stranger Calls* (2006), a remake of the 1979 cult horror classic that grossed nearly $67 million worldwide. Although her role in *Veronica Mars* lasted only one season, she continued to appear in popular network shows, including a two-episode arc on ABC's long-running medical drama *Grey's Anatomy*. In 2007, she returned to episodic television on the CW (CBS/Warner Bros.) Television Network's short-lived summer drama *Hidden Palms*, playing rich, troubled teen Nikki Barnes.

In 2009, Thompson starred as a gifted but disadvantaged pianist yearning to attend college in *Mississippi Damned*, an independent drama from Tina Mabry, another first-time director. This performance was followed by guest appearances on the medical dramas *Mental* and *Three Rivers*, as well as multi-episode arcs on two hit series, ABC's *Private Practice* and NBC's *Heroes*.

STRUGGLING TO MAKE A MAINSTREAM IMPRESSION

Thompson soon made the transition to more adult roles, playing the naïve love interest of a charismatic, young spiritual leader in *Everyday Black Man*, which premiered at the 2010 San Diego Black Film Festival. Pushing the envelope further, she appeared in the dramatic web series *Blue Belle*, which revolves around a high-school teacher secretly working as a call girl. That summer, she returned to the theater stage in the role of Cordelia in the Antaeus Theatre Company's double-cast performance of *King Lear*, the ensemble troupe's first full production of a Shakespeare play.

In November 2010 Thompson starred alongside Whoopi Goldberg, Janet Jackson, and other notable actors in an ensemble project that could have served as a breakout opportunity—Tyler Perry's big-screen adaptation of a work she first read as a little girl, Ntozake Shange's classic 1976 feminist play *For Colored Girls Who Have Considered Suicide / When the Rainbow is Enuf*. Highly anticipated, *For Colored Girls* served as Perry's dramatic directorial debut, and he hoped to attract a broader audience and achieve more critical acclaim than with his previous comedic oeuvre. Still trying to establish her footing in the industry, Thompson was almost not cast in the film. "I think then Tyler was still in talks with people of note," she told Yolanda Sangweni for *Essence* (3 Nov. 2010). "Then it came back into my life in a series of serendipitous . . . events where I had the opportunity to send a tape to Tyler directly . . . and I did the two monologues I did in the film and much to my surprise and great happiness he said, 'Okay.'" However, although the film achieved a respectable opening weekend, it largely did not manage to draw in audiences outside of Perry's typical demographic, garnered mixed reviews, and did not receive the Oscar nods originally anticipated.

BREAKING OUT WITH *DEAR WHITE PEOPLE*

Thompson returned once more to her Shakespearean roots in July 2012, with her acclaimed portrayal of Rosalind in the Shakespeare Center of Los Angeles's limited engagement of *As You Like It*. She also joined ABC's supernatural drama *666 Park Avenue* as media consultant Laurel Harris, a recurring character. The series lasted only one season and aired its final episode the following summer.

In a surprising move that same year, Thompson took on the more serious role of Sara Freeman, a doctor's wife and runaway slave in BBC (British Broadcasting Corp.) America's first original scripted show, *Copper*, a crime series set in Civil War–era New York. However, after the second season's ratings failed to match the first season's viewership, the gritty period drama ended in September 2013.Thompson took a self-imposed sabbatical following *Copper*'s cancellation. "I just didn't want to work on anything until it was something I burned for," she told Eric Eidelstein for *Complex* (27 Nov. 2015).

Thompson immediately felt that passion when she first read the script for *Dear White People* (2014), in which she portrays Samantha White, a politically active college student and popular campus radio host who secretly grapples with her own racial identity. She lobbied hard for the part, auditioning via Skype while shooting *Copper* and also writing a heartfelt letter to director and writer Simien.

The satirical indie drama debuted at the 2014 Sundance Film Festival, earning Thompson widespread critical acclaim. "Thompson emerges as the heart and soul of *Dear White People*," Michael Phillips wrote for the *Chicago Tribune* (23 Oct. 2014). In his review for *Variety* (19 Jan. 2014), Justin Chang singled her out as "perhaps the standout as the film's sharpest and most enigmatic figure." Thompson's performance earned her the breakthrough actor prize at the 2014 Gotham Awards, and she described the character to Eidelstein as "the new barometer for me," explaining that she would not settle for any less powerful roles.

SELMA AND *CREED*

The caliber of her subsequent two projects illustrated Thompson's commitment to that philosophy. Race relations was also the subject of her next major film, Ava DuVernay's *Selma* (2014), which chronicles the epic 1965 African American voting rights marches from Selma to Montgomery, Alabama. In the historical drama, she plays civil rights activist Diane Nash, a founder of the Student Nonviolent Coordinating Committee (SNCC). Despite being mentioned as a major awards contender, *Selma* only won best original song at the 2015 Golden Globes and Oscars, raising questions regarding the lack of diversity in Hollywood. This issue was further compounded when Thompson was mistaken for costar Carmen Ejogo on the Academy Award's Instagram page touting *Selma*'s best picture nod.

Thompson then teamed up with Michael B. Jordan and Ryan Coogler, the star and director of 2013's *Fruitvale Station*, respectively, for *Creed* (2015), the latest installment in the Rocky Balboa franchise. She worked with Coogler to flesh out the character of Bianca, an aspiring singer struggling with hearing loss who also becomes romantically involved with the title character, Apollo Creed (Jordan), a boxer and the son of Rocky's best friend and former rival.

Writing and performing several of the film's songs, inspired by Aaliyah, FKA Twigs, and Pink, Thompson ensured that Bianca would not be a one-dimensional or merely supportive character. "I wanted to give people a palpable sense of a real living person that has a life before she meets him, and will have a life after," she shared with Lindsay Peoples for *New York* (12 Feb. 2016). "I love that the audience got to wonder about Bianca's world, and that was much stronger than having her ringside holding a water bottle."

Although *Creed* was a critical and commercial success, the film became shrouded in controversy after Jordan and Coogler were snubbed during the 2016 awards season in favor of Sylvester Stallone's Rocky, who earned Oscar and Golden Globe supporting nods. In early 2016, Thompson also appeared in the British police comedy *War on Everyone* (2016), as well as the Off-Broadway play *Smart People*. Upcoming projects include *Westworld*, HBO's adaptation of Michael Crichton's 1973 film of the same name, and *Thor: Ragnarok* (2017), the third of Marvel's Thor films.

PERSONAL LIFE

Thompson is a frontwoman of the electronic duo Caught a Ghost, which provided songs for the *Dear White People* soundtrack. Between filming, she also enjoys traveling to places such as Paris, France, and India.

SUGGESTED READING

Anderson, Tre'Vell. "Tessa Thompson Welcomed the Challenges of Playing a Hearing-Impaired Musician in *Creed*." *Los Angeles Times*. Tribune, 1 Dec. 2015. Web. 12 Apr. 2016.

Eidelstein, Eric. "*Creed* Isn't Just Michael B. Jordan's Movie—Say Hello to Tessa Thompson." *Complex*. Complex Media, 27 Nov. 2015. Web. 12 Apr. 2016.

Houston, Shannon M. "Tessa Thompson Breaks the Mold." *Paste*. Paste Media, 28 May 2014. Web. 12 Apr. 2016.

Peoples, Lindsay. "Tessa Thompson on Race, Hollywood, and Her Impending Stardom." *New York*. New York Media, 12 Feb. 2016. Web. 12 Apr. 2016.

Sangweni, Yolanda. "Tessa Thompson on *Colored Girls* and Tyler Perry." *Essence*. Essence Communications, 3 Nov. 2010. Web. 12 Apr. 2016.

Smith, Krista. "Tessa Thompson's *Creed* Character Won't Just Be 'a Ringside Cheerleader.'" *Vanity Fair*. Condé Nast, Dec. 2015. Web. 12 Apr. 2016.

SELECTED WORKS

Veronica Mars, 2005–6; *For Colored Girls*, 2010; *Copper*, 2012–13; *Dear White People*, 2014; *Selma*, 2014; *Creed*, 2015; *War on Everyone*, 2016

—Bertha Muteba

Kip Thorne

Born: June 1, 1940
Occupation: Astrophysicist

Kip Thorne has been heralded for dedicating a half-century of his life to the understanding and detection of gravitational waves, which had been predicted to exist by Albert Einstein in his general theory of relativity in 1915. A century later, in September 2015, Thorne's efforts received complete validation when the first direct detection of gravitational waves was made by a pair of detectors at the Laser Interferometer Gravitational-Wave Observatory (LIGO), which recorded the gravitational waves created by a pair of spinning black holes colliding more than 1.3 billion years ago. Thorne and fellow physicists Rainer Weiss and Ronald Drever had initially proposed LIGO

as a means of detecting gravitational waves in the 1980s.

Thorne has also sought to popularize the understanding of physics by working as a scientific adviser and executive producer for *Interstellar* (2014), the critically acclaimed sci-fi movie directed by Christopher Nolan. Although he retired from the California Institute of Technology (Caltech) in 2009 after more than forty years of teaching, Thorne continues to write and lecture about science. He is even drafting a science-fiction novel based on his decades of research. "I can't imagine not being in a phase where I'm trying to understand something or create something," Thorne said to Josh Rottenberg for the *Los Angeles Times* (21 Nov. 2014). "That's the essence of life."

EARLY LIFE AND EDUCATION
Kip Stephen Thorne was born on June 1, 1940, in Logan, Utah, into a Mormon family. His parents, D. Wynne Thorne and Alison C. Thorne, were both professors. Although he grew up in an academic home, he admitted to having no scholarly aspirations during his childhood. "I wanted to be a snowplow driver when I was a kid," he told Rottenberg. "Growing up in the Rocky Mountains, that's the most glorious job you can imagine. But then my mother took me to a lecture about the solar system when I was eight and I got hooked."

That lecture helped change the course of his life. He became passionately interested in understanding the fundamentals of the universe and began studying physics in earnest. He

earned his bachelor of science in physics from Caltech in 1962. He enrolled at Princeton University, where he earned a master's degree and PhD in physics in 1963 and 1965, respectively. After doing a postdoctoral fellowship in physics at Princeton from 1965 to 1966, he returned to Caltech, his alma mater, where he became a research fellow in physics from 1966 to 1967. After completing his fellowship, he became an associate professor of theoretical physics at Caltech.

PROFESSORIAL CAREER AND AREAS OF SCIENTIFIC STUDY
In 1970, Thorne became the one of the youngest full professors in the history of the university. His early success was due in large part to his work studying the behavior of curved space-time, which is a key component of the general theory of relativity that Albert Einstein had developed in the early part of the twentieth century. In the late 1960s and early 1970s Thorne made major contributions to the study of the pulsations of relativistic stars and their gravitational waves. He further cemented his reputation in the 1970s and 1980s by developing mathematical formulas to analyze the generation of gravitational waves and by laying the groundwork for developing the scientific tools and data analysis techniques to detect gravitational waves. "I got a lot of notoriety early on," Thorne told Rottenberg. "Much of my career I was just trying to prove I was as good as the world thought I was."

Thorne served the William R. Kenan Jr. Professor of Physics at Caltech from 1981 until 1991, the year he was elevated to the post of Feynman Professor of Theoretical Physics, which he held until his retirement. During his career as an educator, he also served as an adjunct professor of physics at the University of Utah from 1971 to 1988 and as the Andrew D. White Professor at Large at Cornell University from 1986 to 1992. During his research career in theoretical physics, gravitational physics, and astrophysics, Thorne served as a mentor for fifty-two doctoral physicists.

DETECTING GRAVITATIONAL WAVES WITH LIGO
Although many parts of Einstein's theory of relativity have been proved in the century since he proposed it, one key aspect—gravitational waves—had only been inferred to exist and never directly detected. According to Einstein's theory, gravity and acceleration are one in the same: gravity is an effect of the warping of space-time as objects move through it. So for example, the reason a planet orbits a star is because space-time is warped around the planet's parent star. Detecting gravitational waves has been a key aspect of Thorne's work for decades. In the 1960s one of Thorne's mentors, Joseph Weber, believed

he had detected gravitational waves by suspending a six-foot-long aluminum bar that he insulated from vibrations. Unfortunately, Weber was never able to reproduce his proof. "We had to wait another forty years," Thorne said, as quoted by Joel Achenbach of the *Washington Post* (11 Feb. 2016), for gravitational waves to be detected conclusively by the LIGO in September 2015. "It does validate Weber in a way that's significant. He was the only person in that era who thought that this could be possible."

In 1975 Thorne shared a room with Rainer Weiss of the Massachusetts Institute of Technology (MIT) during a conference in Washington, DC. The pair stayed up all night discussing various experiments they could run to search for gravitational waves in the hopes of finding proof for general relativity. Thorne then made contact with a fellow scientist at Caltech, Ronald Drever, to start an experimental gravitation group at Caltech. Each agreed that such waves would likely compress space in one direction and stretch it in another as they rippled outward in all directions from their source. They also believed that carefully positioned mirrors and lasers could detect the motion of gravitational waves as they passed through Earth. The MIT and Caltech groups worked somewhat imperfectly together on the process until 1984, when the National Science Foundation asked the two teams to merge. Thorne acted as chair of the steering committee that oversaw LIGO from 1984 to 1987, when a single director was appointed to oversee the program in 1987.

In 2000 the project finally began the first phase of experimentation: Initial LIGO was set up with two detectors, one in Hanford, Washington, and the other in Livingston, Louisiana. After running for ten years and proving that such an experiment was workable, Advanced LIGO began in earnest. Using two L-shaped antennas with perpendicular arms measuring two-and-a-half miles long, the facilities shoot a laser beam down each vacuum tunnel; each beam is then reflected off a mirror hung by glass threads at the end of an arm and returns to the same point. If a gravitational wave passes through Earth, the beam in one arm would arrive back slightly later because the gravitational wave would have stretched one part of the tube and therefore have changed the distance the laser beam traveled.

Advanced LIGO was built to detect changes in the length of the arms as small as one ten-thousandth the diameter of a proton, a subatomic particle. Many scientists were skeptical that so slight a detection would ever occur. Then, on September 14, 2015, the seemingly impossible happened: LIGO detected a gravitational wave passing through Earth. A loud signal came into the Livingston site and then hit the Hanford site

seven milliseconds later. The wave had emanated from the collision of two spinning black holes that had merged together more than 1.3 billion light-years ago. Through January 2016, the LIGO detectors recorded at least four more instances of gravitational waves.

The discovery not only proves the existence of gravitational waves as proposed by Einstein's theory of relativity; it gives researchers a new way to study the universe. "Until now, we scientists have only seen warped space-time when it's calm," Thorne said in an e-mail quoted by Dennis Overbye in an article for the *New York Times* (11 Feb. 2016). "It's as though we had only seen the ocean's surface on a calm day but had never seen it roiled in a storm, with crashing waves."

INTERSTELLAR

Thorne has long been an admirer of so-called "hard" science fiction novels, a subgenre that emphasizes scientific accuracy. Not many Hollywood productions, however, have sought to depict the science behind science fiction accurately, the few exceptions being such films such *2001: A Space Odyssey* (1968) and *Contact* (1997), a movie based on the 1985 novel of the same name by astrophysicist Carl Sagan. In 1980 Sagan had set Thorne up on a blind date with Lynda Obst, a film producer who was then a science editor for the *New York Times Magazine*. Though no romance blossomed, a friendship did, and years later Obst proposed that Thorne help her develop a treatment for a film that would employ hard scientific facts about traveling through a wormhole in order to get to a different part of the galaxy. The work on that film treatment, which began in 2005, ultimately culminated in the critically acclaimed film *Interstellar*, which Christopher Nolan directed and cowrote with his brother Jonah.

In agreeing to work with the Nolan brothers on the film, Thorne insisted that nothing in the movie violate established physical laws and that any wild speculation came from scientific theory. The brothers agreed, and the trio began a lengthy collaborative process that Thorne saw as successful overall, particularly because he hoped that the film would inspire young viewers to dive into science. Christopher Nolan also found the collaboration to be successful, telling Rottenberg, "I was worried that he would just be the science police, telling me what I could and couldn't do with my story. But what I rapidly realized in talking to him was that he was able to offer me tremendously exciting narrative possibilities."

In the plot of the film, astronauts must use a traversable wormhole to explore a distant point of the galaxy in the hopes of bringing most of humanity to a new planet, as crops on Earth are dying from blight. In no part of the film do the astronauts move faster than light; therefore, as they travel to a distant planet at speeds reaching the speed of light, time slows for them while it accelerates on Earth. So, for example, for each hour the astronauts spend on one planet located near a black hole, seven years pass on Earth. Thorne believes that while traversing wormholes is not necessarily in humankind's immediate future, he does believe that interstellar travel could be possible in the future and outlines several kinds in his book *The Science of Interstellar* (2014). Thorne noted to Lee Billings for *Scientific American* (28 Nov. 2014): "I have this chapter in the book on interstellar travel and give far-out examples of how one could undertake interstellar voyages. Nuclear-pulse propulsion, laser-powered light sails, binary black hole slingshots, things like that. And as crude and far-out as they may be, they convince me that the time will come when humans travel between the stars."

PROFESSIONAL ACCOLADES

Thorne holds elected memberships in a number of prestigious societies, including the American Physical Society (APS), the American Academy of Arts and Sciences, the National Academy of Sciences (NAS), the American Association for the Advancement of Science (AAAS), and the International Society on General Relativity and Gravitation (ISGRG). He is also the recipient of numerous scientific awards. These include the 1992 Richtmyer Memorial Award from the American Association of Physics Teachers, the 1996 Julius Edgar Lilienfeld Prize from the American Physical Society, the 2005 Common Wealth Award for science and invention, the 2009 Albert Einstein Medal from the Albert Einstein Society, the 2010 UNESCO Niels Bohr Gold Medal, and the 2013 Howard Vollum Award for Science and Technology from Reed College.

PERSONAL LIFE

Thorne is the father of two children, Kares Anne and Bret Carter. His first marriage, to Linda Jean Peterson, began in 1960 and ended in divorce in 1977. He married Carolee Joyce Winstein on July 7, 1984. Winstein is a professor of biokinesiology and physical therapy at the University of Southern California (USC).

SUGGESTED READING

Achenbach, Joel. "A Brief History of Gravity, Gravitational Waves and LIGO." *Washington Post*. Washington Post, 11 Feb. 2016. Web. 10 July 2016.

Billings, Lee. "Parsing the Science of Interstellar with Physicist Kip Thorne." *Scientific American*. Scientific American, 28 Nov. 2014. Web. 8 July 2016.

"Kip S. Thorne: The Feynman Professor of Theoretical Physics." *Caltech.edu*. California Inst. of Technology, 11 May 2016. Web. 8 July 2016.

Overbye, Dennis. "Gravitational Waves Detected, Confirming Einstein's Theory." *New York Times*. New York Times, 11 Feb. 2016. Web. 10 July 2016.

Rottenberg, Josh. "Meet the Astrophysicist Whose 1980 Blind Date Led to 'Interstellar.'" *Los Angeles Times*. Los Angeles Times, 21 Nov. 2014. Web. 8 July 2016.

—*Christopher Mari*

Henry Threadgill

Born: February 15, 1944
Occupation: Composer, musician

Prolific Pulitzer Prize–winning composer and musician Henry Threadgill is regarded as one of the most influential musicians of the twentieth century. Threadgill, a saxophonist, began his career as an early member of the Association for the Advancement of Creative Musicians (AACM), a nonprofit cooperative group of free-thinking musicians who pioneered experimental music in Chicago in the 1960s. In the 1970s, he performed with the successful jazz trio Air. Reviewing a performance of Threadgill's ensemble group Zooid, jazz critic Howard Reich wrote for the *Chicago Tribune* (20 Dec. 2004), "It would be difficult to overestimate Henry Threadgill's role in perpetually altering the meaning of jazz. As composer, bandleader, and organizer, the former Chicagoan has given the music more than just new sounds and purposes—he has changed our underlying assumptions of what jazz can and should be."

In interviews Threadgill speaks of creating musical languages as opposed to merely playing jazz. "Music is something that has an applicative base and people always forget that," Threadgill told Hank Shteamer for the British music magazine the *Wire* (July 2010). "You know, you don't play wedding music at a damn dance. The music that they play in a funeral home is not the music for a disco and not the music that you want to eat your dinner by. And people forget about these things." With these different applications in mind, Threadgill created a number of groups for a number of reasons. The Society Situation Dance Band in the 1980s, for instance, never recorded an album because their sole purpose was to play live music. As he told Shteamer, "It was

Taylor Hill/Getty Images for Big Hassle Media

not music for listening; it was music that you were supposed to be able to react to."

EARLY LIFE AND MUSIC

Henry Luther Threadgill was born in the Bronzeville neighborhood of Chicago, Illinois, on February 15, 1944. Growing up on the South Side, he listened to an eclectic stew of blues, gospel, boogie-woogie, classical, and Serbian and Polish music on the radio. Several of his extended family members were musicians, including his aunt, at the time an aspiring opera singer, and his uncle Nevin Wilson, a bassist who played with jazz pianist Ahmad Jamal. Threadgill began playing the piano around age four or five, taking lessons when his family could afford it but otherwise teaching himself.

By the time he was a student at Englewood High School, Threadgill knew he wanted to be a musician himself. Surrounded by a group of likeminded youngsters, he embraced all different kinds of music. At school, he took up the saxophone and the clarinet, studying with John Hauser, who had played with jazz legend Charlie Parker. Not satisfied with performing in the school band, Threadgill played wherever he could—with polka bands, classical orchestras, and marching bands, as well as at blues clubs such as the Blue Flame, where he was in the house band. "My experience is much like that of a lot of my contemporaries," he told Nate Chinen for the *New York Times* (6 Nov. 2009). "We got interested in the idea of music, not the idea of jazz. And that means all music, any place where you can get information."

Threadgill began attending Woodrow Wilson Junior College (now Kennedy-King College) in 1963, during a particularly fruitful period for the African American arts movement in Chicago. "We read poetry and philosophy," Threadgill recalled to Greg Sandow, who interviewed the musician as part of Columbia Records' press kit for *Carry the Day* (1995), Threadgill's first album released with the label. "When school was over, we'd go across the street to a church and open up rooms for poetry readings, for bands to rehearse in, for art exhibits."

While at Wilson Junior College, Threadgill met musicians Joseph Jarman and Roscoe Mitchell and began playing with them in Muhal Richard Abrams's Experimental Band, a rehearsal band with a large and revolving membership that would later give rise to the AACM. However, in 1963, two years before the AACM was created, Threadgill dropped out of school and left the Experimental Band for a stint playing gospel music. He spent nearly two years with Horace Shepherd's traveling evangelical Christian band before joining the army in 1966, hoping that serving as an army musician would prevent him from seeing active duty in Vietnam. He returned to Chicago in 1968.

AACM AND ACM

In 1965, while Threadgill was traveling with Shepherd's evangelical troupe, Abrams and three other musicians from the Experimental Band—trumpeter Phil Cohran, pianist Jodie Christian, and drummer Steve McCall—founded the Association for the Advancement of Creative Musicians, or AACM, and invited the other Experimental Band members to join. Other original AACM members included Mitchell and Jarman; when Threadgill returned from the service, he had a spot waiting for him.

In addition to playing with the AACM, mostly with the group's big band, Threadgill also took the opportunity to pursue further music education, first at nearby Governors State University and then at Chicago's American Conservatory of Music (ACM). "I knew what I didn't know, how much I couldn't take apart theoretically," he told the *Nation* music columnist Gene Santoro, for an article later reprinted in Santoro's book *Dancing in Your Head: Jazz, Blues, Rock, and Beyond* (1994). "I wasn't in those programs the way most students were, to get their degree; I was there just to take everything they had."

At the ACM, Threadgill studied flute, piano, and composition with Stella Roberts. He had begun writing his own music in high school, but Roberts was his first formal composition teacher. She was an enormously influential force in the young musician's life; her own mentor, Nadia Boulanger, was a French composer whose students had included Aaron Copland and Philip

Glass. Roberts encouraged Threadgill to continue to look outside of music—to art, architecture, or photography—for inspiration for his writing.

AIR

In 1971 Threadgill teamed up with two other AACM members, McCall and bassist Fred Hopkins, to form a jazz trio titled Reflection, in response to a request from Columbia College Chicago's theater department for a modern take on the music of Scott Joplin, the early twentieth-century king of ragtime. Although Reflection disbanded the following year, the three reunited in New York in 1975 under the name Air. Their first album, *Air Song*, was recorded and released that year. It consisted of four long songs, the shortest clocking in at just over eleven minutes, all composed by Threadgill.

Air Song was originally released by the short-lived Japanese jazz label Why Not Records; it was rereleased on CD in 2009 by Candid Records, which had bought the rights to Why Not's catalog the year before. In a review of the rerelease for the *Guardian* (23 July 2009), John Fordham wrote that the tracks "[evolve] in a free-conversational manner, though Threadgill's rough-hewn and sinewy sound cuts through." He also lamented that the group was not more widely known, concluding, "Air deserved a lot more exposure as a leading free-jazz ensemble of its day, and [*Air Song* is] the imposing evidence."

Air thrived in New York and on tour in Europe. Throughout the trio's tenure, Threadgill played a variety of reed instruments, as well as on occasion the hubkaphone, a percussion instrument he had invented himself and built out of hubcaps. Over the next ten years they released a handful of records, including *Air Raid* (1976), *Air Time* (1977), and *Open Air Suit* (1978). Their 1979 album *Air Lore*, featuring improvisational interpretations of compositions by Joplin and ragtime pianist Jelly Roll Morton, was voted album of the year by *Down Beat* magazine's critic's poll. The group's last album recorded with their original line-up was *80° Below '82* (1982). They then released two more albums under the name New Air, featuring drummer Pheeroan ak-Laff in the place of McCall, who had left.

OTHER GROUPS

In 1979, Threadgill released a solo album called *X-75 Volume 1*, featuring eight supporting musicians: four woodwinds (including Threadgill himself), four basses, and vocals by Amina Claudine Myers. Soon after, he formed the seven-member Henry Threadgill Sextet, consisting of a trumpet, trombone, bass, cello, two drums, and Threadgill on saxophone, flute, and clarinet; he called the group a sextet rather than a septet because he counted the two drums as one unit. They recorded three albums—*When*

Was That? (1981), *Just the Facts and Pass the Bucket* (1983), and *Subject to Change* (1984)—before going on hiatus so Threadgill could record with New Air. He then reformed the group as the Henry Threadgill Sextett (two *t*s) to record *You Know the Number* (1986), *Easily Slip into Another World* (1987), and *Rag, Bush and All* (1988).

In the 1990s Threadgill formed another septet, Very Very Circus, which featured two tubas, two guitars, either a trombone or a French horn, and drums, plus Threadgill on saxophone and flute. Kevin Whitehead, in an episode of the National Public Radio (NPR) show *Fresh Air* (4 Jan. 2011), described the band as "hint[ing] at New Orleans parade bands" with a dose of "African pop." They released their first album, *Spirit of Nuff . . . Nuff*, in 1990, followed by *Too Much Sugar for a Dime* in 1993. *Carry the Day* (1995) featured a number of guest musicians, including Wu Man on the pipa, a Chinese stringed instrument similar to a lute. Their last album was *Makin' a Move* (1995), which was half Very Very Circus songs and half compositions performed by guest musicians on guitars and cellos.

Threadgill and some of his fellow Very Very Circus musicians then formed a quintet called Make a Move; they released *Where's Your Cup?*, their debut album, in 1996. For their second and final studio album, *Everybodys Mouth's a Book* (2001), Threadgill began experimenting with a new system of composition he had devised, which he described to Chinen as "a serial intervallic language" based on mathematical principles and inspired by the work of the French-born American composer Edgard Varèse, who conceived of sound in spatial terms.

After debuting his new system with Make a Move, Threadgill took the concept further with Zooid, a sextet (later a quintet) that he formed in 2000. Zooid's first two albums, *Up Popped the Two Lips* (2001) and *Pop Start the Tape, Stop* (2004), featured an acoustic guitar, a tuba, a cello, drums, and an oud, a North African and Middle Eastern stringed instrument; on the next three albums—*This Brings Us to Volume I* (2009), *This Brings Us to Volume II* (2010), and *Tomorrow Sunny / The Revelry, Spp* (2012)—the oud was replaced with a bass guitar.

IN FOR A PENNY, IN FOR A POUND

In 2016, Threadgill won the Pulitzer Prize for music for Zooid's album *In for a Penny, In for a Pound* (2015). The Pulitzer jury, as quoted by Patrick Jarenwattananon for the NPR Music blog *A Blog Supreme* (18 Apr. 2016), described *In for a Penny* as "a sonic tapestry that seems the very expression of modern American life." The album, released as a double CD, consists of four movements, each of which highlights the style of a different member of the now-quintet: José Davila on trombone and tuba, Liberty Ellman on guitar, Christopher Hoffman on cello, and Elliot Humberto Kavee on drums. Zooid, Threadgill pointed out to Jarenwattananon, is his longest-running ensemble project to date, and in a sense the album is a tribute to their successful collaboration. "It's not about the number of years—it's about 100 percent to 150 percent that they give," Threadgill said. "So they were in for a penny, you see. And if you're in for a penny, you're in for a pound."

SUGGESTED READING

Chinen, Nate. "Master of the Mutable, in an Idiom All His Own." *New York Times*. New York Times, 6 Nov. 2009. Web. 13 Aug. 2016.

Fordham, John. Rev. of *Air Song*, by Air. *Guardian*. Guardian News and Media, 23 July 2009. Web. 13 Aug. 2016.

Sandow, Greg. "Fried Grapefruit: The Life of Henry Threadgill." 1995. *Greg Sandow's Archived Writings*. Author, n.d. Web. 13 Aug. 2016.

Santoro, Gene. "Child Is Father to the Music." *Dancing in Your Head: Jazz, Blues, Rock, and Beyond*. New York: Oxford UP, 1994. 248–53. Print.

Threadgill, Henry. "Henry Threadgill Unedited." Interview by Hank Shteamer. *Wire*. Wire Magazine, July 2010. Web. 13 Aug. 2016.

Threadgill, Henry. Interview by Studs Terkel. 1988. *And They All Sang: Adventures of an Eclectic Disc Jockey*. By Terkel. New York: New Press, 2005. 161–63. Print.

Whitehead, Kevin. "Henry Threadgill's No-Groove Groove." *Fresh Air*. NPR, 4 Jan. 2011. Web. 13 Aug. 2016.

SELECTED WORKS

Air Song, 1975; *Air Lore*, 1979; *X-75 Volume 1*, 1979; *Spirit of Nuff . . . Nuff*, 1990; *Everybodys Mouth's a Book*, 2001; *In for a Penny, In for a Pound*, 2015

—*Molly Hagan*

Thundercat

Born: October 19, 1984
Occupation: Musician

The Los Angeles–based musician Thundercat has earned a reputation as one of the music world's most versatile and sought-after bass players. Described by Jeff Weiss in an article for *Rolling Stone* (2 Apr. 2015) as a "consummate session man," Thundercat is known for

Rick Kern/GettyImages

his virtuosic, genre-hopping bass style, eccentric sartorial tastes, and open-minded approach to the music industry. He began his career as a sideman, touring with and performing session work for such artists as Suicidal Tendencies, Snoop Dogg, Sa-Ra, and Erykah Badu, before forming a creative partnership with experimental electronic producer Flying Lotus in 2009. He has since released three Flying Lotus–produced solo albums: *The Golden Age of Apocalypse* (2011), *Apocalypse* (2013), and *The Beyond/Where the Giants Roam* (2015). He has also served as a major contributor to three Lotus studio albums. In 2015 Thundercat was widely recognized for his contributions to hip-hop artist Kendrick Lamar's third studio album, *To Pimp a Butterfly*.

EARLY LIFE AND EDUCATION

Born Stephen Bruner on October 19, 1984, in Los Angeles, California, Thundercat was raised in various neighborhoods throughout the city. He comes from a family of distinguished musicians. His father, Ronald Bruner Sr., is an internationally recognized jazz drummer who has played with Diana Ross, Gladys Knight, and the Temptations. His brother, Ronald Bruner Jr., is a Grammy Award–winning drummer who has played with a wide range of artists, from jazz bassist Stanley Clarke to the thrash metal band Suicidal Tendencies. His mother was also musical, performing in churches as a flutist and percussionist.

Thundercat grew up surrounded by music and musicians. He began playing the bass at the age of four. Though his father and brother were drummers, Thundercat told Aaron Frank for the music blog *Passion of the Weiss* (14 Oct. 2011) that taking up the bass fell "right in line with what was going on at my house." He learned how to play the instrument by listening to Clarke and two other influential bass players, Marcus Miller and the late Jaco Pastorius. Thundercat's musical style was further shaped by an eclectic mix of influences, which included video game music. Still, as he explained to Brooke Jackson-Glidden for the *Boston Globe* (26 Sept. 2015), "My whole being sonically comes from my dad's understanding of music." Meanwhile, all of his "weird creative energy" comes from his mother, as he told Frank.

Thundercat attended 32nd Street Visual and Performing Arts Magnet, a public alternative school in Los Angeles, where he was a classmate of future Hollywood actor Shia LaBeouf. He then enrolled at Locke High School, located in Los Angeles's rough-and-tumble Watts neighborhood. At Locke, Thundercat was mentored by Reggie Andrews, a legendary music instructor who has taught such acclaimed musicians as Ndugu Chancler, Patrice Rushen, and Tyrese Gibson. In an interview with E. E. Bradman for *Bass Player* (21 Dec. 2011), Thundercat credited Andrews, who retired from teaching in 2010, with teaching him "everything I know about being a musician."

EARLY MUSIC CAREER

During his freshman year at Locke, Thundercat began performing professionally as a member of the short-lived boy band No Curfew, who, according to several sources, had a minor hit in Germany before disbanding. Then, at age sixteen, he was recruited to replace Josh Paul as the bassist in Suicidal Tendencies. Thundercat joined his brother in the group, which is noted for being one of the first bands to meld hardcore punk and metal. "I'd do a concert at night and then come to class and just lay my head on the desk," he recalled to Frank. Thundercat toured extensively with the group over the next decade and played bass on three of their albums: *Year of the Cycos* (2008), *No Mercy Fool!/The Suicidal Family* (2010), and *13* (2013).

Concurrently with Suicidal Tendencies, Thundercat formed a bebop quartet, called Young Jazz Giants, with his brother, saxophonist Kamasi Washington, and pianist Cameron Graves. The quartet, which was selected from among a group of young jazz talents at a workshop in southern California, released its only album, the self-titled *Young Jazz Giants*, in 2004.

By the mid-2000s, Thundercat's reputation as a bass prodigy landed him touring and session work with musical artists all over Los Angeles. Among them was rapper Snoop Dogg, who hired him to join his touring band. Thundercat

also came to the attention of Sa-Ra, an alternative hip-hop group composed of Shafiq Husayn, Om'Mas Keith, and Taz Arnold. He became fast friends with the group's members and started hanging out regularly at their studio in Silver Lake, which for a time served as "the Los Alamos of the L.A. underground music scene," as Weiss noted. Thundercat went on to contribute bass work to Sa-Ra's first two studio albums, *The Hollywood Recordings* (2007) and *Nuclear Evolution: The Age of Love* (2009).

It was through Sa-Ra that Thundercat first met singer-songwriter Erykah Badu, the so-called queen of neo-soul. Impressed with his contributions for the group, Badu commissioned Thundercat to play in her live touring band and had him perform session work for her acclaimed *New Amerykah* concept albums, released in 2008 and in 2010, respectively. Around this time, Thundercat started going by his stage name, which is a reference to his favorite 1980s animated television series.

FLYING LOTUS PARTNERSHIP AND SOLO DEBUT

Thundercat first met experimental electronic music producer Steven Ellison, better known as Flying Lotus, in 2009, while he was performing with the music duo J*Davey at the South by Southwest music festival in Austin, Texas. Bonding "over a love of jazz-fusion, anime, and South Korean cult films," as Weiss noted, the two immediately hit it off and launched a creative partnership. In an interview with Ryan Dombal for the music website *Pitchfork* (1 Sept. 2011), Thundercat said his chance encounter with Lotus was "like Jay and Silent Bob meeting for the first time," referring to writer-director Kevin Smith's cinematic comedy duo. He added, "Musically, he's the person I've bonded with most other than my brother."

The first fruits of Thundercat's partnership with Lotus materialized in May 2010, with the release of the latter's highly acclaimed third studio album, *Cosmogramma*. Thundercat played bass and provided lead vocals on the album's unofficial lead single, "MmmHmm," and was credited with having a strong sonic influence on many other tracks, one of which featured guest vocals by Radiohead's Thom Yorke. Lotus ultimately nudged Thundercat into making solo albums, and in 2011, he produced the bassist's solo debut, *The Golden Age of Apocalypse*.

Released on Lotus's Brainfeeder label, the album combined a wide variety of influences, from 1970s jazz fusion and classic R&B to modern gospel and progressive electronica. It featured the songs "Daylight," the George Duke cover "For Love I Come," and "Is It Love?" as well as contributions from many of Thundercat's previous collaborators. Among them were Sa-Ra,

Erykah Badu, J*Davey, multi-instrumentalist Georgia Ann Muldrow, violinist Miguel Atwood-Ferguson, and pianist Austin Peralta.

The Golden Age of Apocalypse received widespread praise from critics, most of whom singled out Thundercat's exceptional bass guitar work. Bradman called the album "a feast for bass fanatics: Bruner's upfront lines and fluid chording technique are the meat of every tune." Meanwhile, in a review for *LA Weekly* (1 Sept. 2011), Ian Cohen called Thundercat's bass playing "virtuosic" and "laid-back but never passive; in its own zone but hardly stoned."

APOCALYPSE

In 2012 Thundercat contributed to Lotus's widely acclaimed electronic jazz album *Until the Quiet Comes*, which drew predominantly on concepts related to the dream state. He also contributed extensively to Lotus's next album *You're Dead*, which was released in 2014. The album confronted the theme of death through Lotus's sorrowful experiences of losing both of his parents and other loved ones during the span of its making.

One of those loved ones was creative collaborator Austin Peralta, who in November 2012 died suddenly at the age of twenty-two of viral pneumonia. The son of skateboarding legend and documentary filmmaker Stacy Peralta, Austin Peralta had established a reputation as one of the Los Angeles music scene's brightest young piano talents and had formed close friendships not only with Lotus but also with Thundercat, whose sophomore album, *Apocalypse*, paid tribute to him.

Released in July 2013 on Brainfeeder and again produced by Lotus, *Apocalypse* offered a darker and more mature departure from Thundercat's debut. Many of the album's songs, including "Without You," "We'll Die," and "A Message for Austin/Praise the Lord/Enter the Void," dealt explicitly with grief and loss. Others, though, retained Thundercat's humorous and light-hearted side, most notably "Oh Sheit It's X," which chronicled an epic New Year's Eve party. Thundercat told Reggie Ugwu for *Billboard* (11 June 2013), "Music has no boundaries. The more people get to see that, the more they can connect to how free spirited music can be."

Apocalypse garnered widespread critical acclaim. Nate Chinen, writing for the *New York Times* (10 June 2013), called the album "an outlet for [Thundercat's] instrumental prowess, his taste in soulful retro-futurism, and his slyly ingenuous songwriting" and affirmed that it was "bolder and clearer, less blissed-out, and more grippingly immediate" than the bassist's debut. Rob Tannenbaum proclaimed for *Rolling Stone* (17 June 2013) that *Apocalypse* was the most original album of the year and wrote

that it was "both esoteric and outlandish, built around Bruner's rubbery, odd-metered bass-guitar excursions, sparse grooves, and trippy falsetto musings." Furthermore, Ugwu commented that Thundercat's songs "walk the line between virtuosity and vulnerability" and described the album as a "funk-drenched, intermittently electronic record."

TO PIMP A BUTTERFLY AND *THE BEYOND/WHERE THE GIANTS ROAM*

Following *Apocalypse*, Thundercat collaborated with hip-hop artist Kendrick Lamar on his wildly acclaimed third studio album, *To Pimp a Butterfly*, which was released in March 2015. The album featured a mix of jazz, funk, and spoken-word poems, and a wide range of contributors, including Flying Lotus, George Clinton, Snoop Dogg, Ronald Isley, and Pharrell Williams, among others. Thundercat served as a writer and coproducer of the song "Wesley's Theory," on which he provided vocals alongside Lamar and Clinton, and he also lent his voice to the song "These Walls." Weiss credited Thundercat with supplying "the celestial ecclesiastical architecture undergirding" the album, which debuted at number one on the US Billboard 200 album chart.

In June 2015 Thundercat released his third studio effort, *The Beyond/Where the Giants Roam*. Coproduced by Lotus, the sixteen-minute jazz-funk album featured six tracks and contributions from Kamasi Washington, Miguel Atwood-Ferguson, and the legendary jazz pianist Herbie Hancock. Also in 2015 Thundercat played electric bass on Washington's debut studio album, *The Epic*. Washington told Weiss that watching Thundercat work was "like seeing a great painter with a canvas that looks like a lot of nothing, and then one little stroke goes and you're like, 'Wow you saw that the whole time?'"

Thundercat, who lives in Los Angeles's Koreatown neighborhood, has earned much attention for his bizarre onstage outfits. He has been known to wear Native American headdresses, armored shoulder pads, billowing scarves, and an assortment of wide-brimmed hats.

SUGGESTED READING

Thundercat. "From Jazz to Punk and Beyond, Thundercat Plays to Win." Interview by Brooke Jackson-Glidden. *Boston Globe*. Boston Globe Media, 26 Sept. 2015. Web. 18 Nov. 2015.

Thundercat. "Rising: Thundercat." Interview by Ryan Dombal. *Pitchfork*. Condé Nast, 1 Sept. 2011. Web. 2 Nov. 2015.

Thundercat. "Question in the Form of an Answer: Thundercat." Interview by Aaron Frank. *Passion of the Weiss*. Passion of the Weiss, 14 Oct. 2011. Web. 2 Nov. 2015.

Thundercat. "Thundercat: Future Soul." Interview by E. E. Bradman. *Bass Player*. NewBay Media, 21 Dec. 2011. Web. 2 Nov. 2015.

Thundercat. "Thundercat Q&A: Coping with Loss, Surprising Snoop, and the Jazz Roots of Mac Miller." Interview by Reggie Ugwu. *Billboard*. Billboard, 11 June 2013. Web. 2 Nov. 2015.

Weiss, Jeff. "Meet Thundercat, the Jazz-Fusion Genius behind Kendrick Lamar's 'Butterfly.'" *Rolling Stone*. Rolling Stone, 2 Apr. 2015. Web. 2 Nov. 2015.

SELECTED WORKS

The Golden Age of Apocalypse, 2011; *Apocalypse*, 2013; *The Beyond/Where the Giants Roam*, 2015

—*Chris Cullen*

Wendy Redfern/Redferns/Getty Images

Torres

Born: January 23, 1991
Occupation: Singer, songwriter, and musician

Torres is the stage name of the up-and-coming singer, songwriter, and musician Mackenzie Scott. Born and raised in Macon, Georgia, Torres first began performing in Nashville before moving to Brooklyn, New York, in 2013. That year, on her debut album *Torres*, the singer impressed critics with her unusual and beguiling voice. Jayson Greene, for *Pitchfork* (30 Apr. 2015), described it as "the sound of poorly contained things exploding, full of expert glottal hitches and capable of constricting or yawning open in the space of a note." Torres's music is deeply personal and often explores aspects of her strict upbringing in the Baptist church. On her latest record, *Sprinter* (2015), she reveals her consuming fears about death and her struggles to come to terms with her religious faith. For Torres, honest, well-wrought lyrics are exhausting and difficult to create, but they are essential to her work. Her writing influences—science fiction novelist Ray Bradbury, essayist Joan Didion, and poet Sylvia Plath, among others—are as diverse as her musical influences, which range from Kurt Cobain, the late front man of the grunge band Nirvana, to country singer Johnny Cash, to the Irish musician Enya. Musician and artist St. Vincent, also known as Annie Clark, inspired Torres's stage name, which is the surname of her late maternal grandfather. As Torres transitioned from acoustic guitar to electric, she adopted a persona to match.

EARLY LIFE

Mackenzie Scott was born in Macon, Georgia, on January 23, 1991. Her birth mother was attending a bible study class when she was pregnant with Torres and asked the teacher of the class to adopt her unborn child. The teacher, who had been adopted herself, agreed and became Torres's mother. In addition to Torres, her parents also have a son and another daughter.

Torres met her birth mother only once, when she was eight, but she has a journal that her birth mother wrote when she was pregnant. The contents of that notebook were the inspiration for Torres's song "Moon & Back" from her debut album. Torres's parents are very active in the Baptist church, and Torres was raised with a strong religious influence. Torres attended youth group and sang and played guitar during church services, but she was never able to connect with the enthusiasm for religion that her peers felt. "The thing that I remember most about those years is the pressure to feel something, the pressure to . . . lift my hands in front of everyone and pray publicly," she told Kate Hutchinson for the *Guardian* (12 May 2015). Torres explained to Greene that although she has not abandoned her faith, her viewpoint is different than it once was. She considers herself a "Christ-following mystic."

Singing in the church choir gave way to an interest in musical theater. After visiting New York City with her family when she was fourteen, Torres became enamored with the musical *The Phantom of the Opera*, which then inspired her to begin performing in school plays all the while dreaming of appearing on Broadway. When she was sixteen, however, she learned to play the guitar, and her focus shifted. Her first performances were singing hymns at local nursing homes.

BECOMING A SONG WRITER

Just as quickly as she began playing guitar, Torres began writing her own songs, but she was hesitant to seriously pursue a career as a songwriter. As a freshman at the Belmont University School of Music in Nashville, Tennessee, in 2010, she was still unsure of her choice or her future. A turning point occurred that summer when Torres saw one of her idols, the alternative country singer Brandi Carlile, perform. After the show, Torres met the singer, and Carlile was enthusiastic and supportive when Torres told her that she was considering becoming a songwriter. The two spoke at length, with Carlile asking Torres what she liked to write and sing about. Torres recalled to Elise Lasko for the Nashville magazine *Native* (1 June 2013) that Carlile told her in parting, "I can't wait to hear you someday." The small kindness bolstered Torres's confidence and resolve to follow a songwriting path. "She'll never know that something so . . . insignificant completely gave me the kick in the pants and the self-confidence boost that I needed," Torres said.

Torres's musical awakening came in college. She started listening to classic country and rock acts and began following local bands. "I didn't go to concerts in my hometown, and all of a sudden I was in basements every night with a Coke and whiskey in my hand, you know, watching bands play house shows," Torres recalled to Amelia Mason for the *ARTery* (24 June 2015). "And it was honestly some of the best times that I think I'll ever have in my life. . . . I'll never get to do that again, be that excited about music for the first time."

TORRES (2013)

Torres began recording her first album, which was self-titled and self-released, at the Nashville home studio of musician Tony Joe White. She recorded ten songs in five days, retaining most of her first-take performances in order to maintain a more intimate feel for the album. At the time, Torres was still in school, but in anticipation of the album's January 2013 release and the touring that would accompanying it, she graduated a semester early in December 2012 with a degree in songwriting and a minor in English.

Torres was met with rave reviews from music critics and outlets like *Pitchfork*, for which Greene wrote on January 24, 2013, "Her record is an overwhelming rush of feeling, and it connects with throat-seizing immediacy." The album's second song and breakout track, "Honey," was featured on the *Pitchfork* website as a Best New Track, which is a major coup for a debut, self-released album. The song slowly builds momentum and power over its repeated and heartbreaking chorus, "Honey, while you were ashing in your coffee, I was thinking 'bout telling you

what you've done to me." Other songs on the album include "Moon & Back," which is written from the perspective of her birth mother and includes the lyrics, "I'm writing to you from 1991, the year I gave you to a mama with a girl and a son." In his review for the *Nashville Scene* (22 Jan. 2013), Steve Haruch praised Torres for eschewing the polished sound of other Nashville singers, and he wrote that her debut album was "promising and occasionally staggering." But in truth, Torres never felt as if she fit in the Nashville scene in the first place: She found it hard to succeed in the country music mecca because her sound was so difficult to quantify. Her frustration led her to move to the Bushwick neighborhood of Brooklyn, New York, in 2013.

SPRINTER (2015)

Torres released her second album, *Sprinter*, in 2015. On the title track, she writes about a pastor who betrayed her trust, which then leads her to examine her religious beliefs more closely. The word "sprinter" is a nod to Torres's time as a high school track-and-field sprinter, and it is also a reference to a line from Ray Bradbury's *Zen in the Art of Writing*. In Bradbury's book, which was a twenty-third birthday gift to Torres from singer-songwriter Sharon Van Etten, he describes his youthful self as a sprinter who had not yet learned to pace himself. The description resonated with Torres who sings the songs chorus at a much slower tempo than the rest of the song, thus accentuating the lyrics, "Cause I was a sprinter then."

While *Torres* featured only the singer with her guitar, Torres recorded *Sprinter* with a full band in a former children's nursery in Dorset, England, and in a recording studio in Bristol. She worked with producer and arranger Rob Ellis, who is widely known for his studio work with British singer-songwriter PJ Harvey. Adrian Utley of the English band Portishead provided guitar and synthesizers.

DEEPER AND MORE PERSONAL SONGWRITING

The songs on *Sprinter* are much darker and, with a few exceptions, more abstract than the songs on *Torres*. After the release of the first album, Torres was frustrated with being labeled as a confessional writer, but in speaking with Frank Valish for *Under the Radar* (19 June 2015) about *Sprinter*, she said, "I think I'm still spilling my guts a good deal, but I didn't want the whole record to be about that."

The most overtly personal song on the record is the closing track—the raw, eight-minute "The Exchange," which is about her adoption and also her mother's adoption. She reveals that her mother's birth records were lost in a flood, singing, "My mother lost her mother twice." Richard Bienstock of *Rolling Stone* (17 Dec. 2015) described the song as "the album's most arresting track." It features only Torres and an acoustic guitar, and in the song she expands on the images of water and, singing, "Mother, father, I'm underwater and I don't think you can pull me out of this." Torres was nervous to perform the song in front of others in the studio, so she recorded it alone on a portable Zoom recorder, outside under a tree. She is unsure whether she will ever perform the song live.

Other songs on the record include "New Skin," which Van Etten helped shape. In it Torres sings, "I am a tired woman. In January I will be just twenty-three." The line is indicative of the heavy subject matter on *Sprinter* and how a conservative childhood followed by a hard-charging young adulthood have left her feeling like a stranger to herself. On "Son, You Are No Island," she expands this sense of isolation by incorporating mystical references to voids, oceans, and sixteenth-century poet John Donne. As Jillian Mapes for *Pitchfork* (7 May 2015) wrote, the song is reminiscent of a Celtic hymn and suggests an age-old battle to understand something larger than oneself.

Like *Torres* before it, *Sprinter* was well-received by critics. Zach Schonfeld, for *Paste* magazine (5 May 2015), wrote, "After spending just a month and a half with *Sprinter*, it already feels like these songs have been around for a long time, which is a reasonable indication that they will be with us for a while."

SUGGESTED READING

Bienstock, Richard. "Meet Torres: The True Confessions of Mackenzie Scott." *Rolling Stone.* Rolling Stone, 17 Dec. 2015. Web. 14 Mar. 2016.

Greene, Jayson. "I'm Drowning But I'm OK: The Revelations of Torres' Mackenzie Scott." *Pitchfork.* Condé Nast, 30 Apr. 2015. Web. 14 Mar. 2016.

Hutchinson, Kate. "Torres: 'You're Not Really an American Anymore When You're in the Ocean.'" *Guardian.* Guardian News and Media, 12 May 2015. Web. 14 Mar. 2016.

Mapes, Jillian. Rev. of *Sprinter*, by Torres. *Pitchfork.* Condé Nast, 7 May 2015. Web. 14 Mar. 2016.

Mason, Amelia. "The Awakenings of Torres' Mackenzie Scott." *WBUR.* NPR, 24 June 2015. Web. 14 Mar. 2016.

Valish, Frank. "Torres—Mackenzie Scott on 'Sprinter.'" *Under the Radar.* Under the Radar Magazine, 19 June 2015. Web. 14 Mar. 2016.

—Molly Hagan

Justin Trudeau

Born: December 25, 1971
Occupation: Prime minister of Canada

When Justin Trudeau took office as prime minister of Canada in November 2015, many observers in Canada and around the world were struck by a sense of déjà vu: for the second time, a Trudeau would lead the nation. Trudeau's father, Pierre, became prime minister in the late 1960s and served for much of the following two decades, during which time he ushered in an era of liberal reforms that shaped the country into the twenty-first century—reforms that some liberal Canadians believe had been dismantled or undermined by Conservative prime minister Stephen Harper, the younger Trudeau's predecessor. But even as he sought to uphold his father's legacy, Trudeau was equally concerned with making it clear to voters that he is very much his own person. "My whole life has been about figuring out the balance between knowing who I am and being who I am and accepting that people will come to me with all sorts of preconceptions," he told John Powers for *Vogue* (9 Dec. 2015).

In his first months as prime minister, Trudeau sought to address key issues such as immigration, the rights of First Nations Canadians, and climate change in addition to surrounding himself with a cabinet that is more diverse in terms of gender and ethnicity than any before. Above all, he hopes to ensure that Canada's government and policies represent what he sees as the essential spirit of its people. "There is no

A.k.fung at English Wikipedia/Wikimedia Commons

core identity, no mainstream in Canada," he told Guy Lawson for the *New York Times Magazine* (8 Dec. 2015). "There are shared values—openness, respect, compassion, willingness to work hard, to be there for each other, to search for equality and justice."

EARLY LIFE

Justin Pierre James Trudeau was born on December 25, 1971, in Ottawa, Ontario. He was the first of three sons born to Pierre and Margaret Sinclair Trudeau. The couple separated when Trudeau was young and ultimately divorced in 1984; Trudeau and his brothers, Alexandre (Sacha) and Michel, remained with their father.

At the time of Trudeau's birth, his father was serving as Canada's fifteenth prime minister, having ascended to the position when the Liberal Party took power in the federal election of 1968. Pierre Trudeau remained in office until 1979, when he became leader of the official Opposition following the Liberal Party's electoral defeat, and resumed the role from 1980 to 1984. Because of their father's position, Trudeau and his brothers grew up at the prime minister's residence at 24 Sussex Drive in Ottawa, the Canadian capital. The young Trudeau began his schooling in Ottawa, attending Rockcliffe Park Public School and later the French-speaking Lycée Claudel.

As a young child, Trudeau was perplexed by his father's work. "I was eight or nine years old before I had a firm grasp of my father's career and what he did when he wasn't at home with us," he wrote in his 2014 memoir *Common Ground*, noting that as a child he had once referred to his father as "the boss of Canada." In 1979, the Liberals lost the federal election and Joe Clark became the Canadian prime minister. "Almost overnight 24 Sussex was no longer our home, and we packed up and moved a few blocks away to Stornoway, the official opposition leader's residence. That's when I understood that the real boss of Canada was the Canadian people," Trudeau wrote in his memoir. The Trudeau family returned to 24 Sussex Drive when the Liberal Party regained power but left the residence for good in 1984, settling in Montreal, in Pierre's home province of Quebec.

EDUCATION AND EARLY CAREER

After moving to Montreal, Trudeau enrolled in the Collège Jean-de-Brébeuf, the private secondary school from which his father had graduated. After completing secondary school, he attended McGill University, where he studied literature before earning his bachelor's degree in 1994. Initially unsure of his career path, he spent a year traveling the world with friends but ultimately returned and decided to pursue a bachelor's degree in education, hoping to become a teacher. He earned his degree in 1998 from the University of British Columbia; while he went on to take additional courses at McGill and l'École Polytechnique de Montréal, he did not complete a postgraduate degree.

As a young man, Trudeau worked a number of jobs, including stints as a snowboard instructor and a nightclub bouncer. Eventually, he found work as a teacher in Vancouver, British Columbia, teaching subjects such as math and French. He also became chair of Katimavik, a national youth service program, and advocated for various causes. Perhaps the most personal of those was avalanche awareness, a particularly important cause to him following the death of his younger brother Michel in an avalanche in 1998.

ENTERING POLITICS

After teaching in Vancouver for several years, Trudeau decided to return to Quebec, where he hoped to settle down and start a family. The move also provided him with the opportunity to become more active in politics. Like his father before him, Trudeau became deeply involved in Canada's Liberal Party, a center-left party that is generally considered to fall between the Conservative Party and the social democratic New Democratic Party on the political spectrum. He initially devoted himself to drawing voters to the party, chairing a task force on attracting young voters, but in 2007 he began his first run for office. Seeking a position in the House of Commons, Trudeau secured the Liberal Party's nomination for member of parliament (MP) for the riding, or electoral district, of Papineau, located within Montreal. The incumbent MP for the riding was a member of the Bloc Québécois, a political party focused heavily on issues of particular concern to the province, and Trudeau thus faced a significant challenge. However, he won the 2008 election by about 1,200 votes, becoming MP for Papineau and a member of the official Opposition party. He was reelected to the post in 2011.

As a member of the House of Commons, Trudeau devoted himself to causes such as immigration, multiculturalism, and youth issues, as well as to the needs of the residents of the Papineau riding. "It was hard work, but I loved every minute of it," he wrote for the Liberal Party's official website (2016). "Most of all, I loved the interaction with the people of Papineau. So much of politics is fleeting and ephemeral. But the connections you make with the people who invest their hope and trust in you, that's what gets you through all of the rest. That's what makes it worth doing." While many of his victories came at the ballot box and in the House of Commons, in early 2012 he fought for his party in an entirely different sphere, defeating Conservative senator Patrick Brazeau in the third round of a charity boxing match.

In late 2012, following Liberal Party leader Michael Ignatieff's resignation from the position, Trudeau announced that he planned to run for leadership of the party. This move, like nearly all of Trudeau's political actions before it, sparked perhaps inevitable comparisons between the young politician and his father, who had died in 2000. In fact, his moving eulogy to his father had garnered significant attention and prompted some speculation that he would one day also hold the nation's top position. Such comparisons both helped and hindered Trudeau—some Canadians remembered his father's administration fondly, while others objected to Pierre Trudeau's policies or to the concept of a political dynasty. In addition to campaigning for party leadership, then, Trudeau was also tasked with distinguishing himself from his father while still upholding his legacy. "My father's values and vision of this country obviously form everything I have as values and ideals," Trudeau told Jonathon Gatehouse for *Maclean's* (11 Oct. 2012). "But this is not the ghost of my father running for the leadership of the Liberal Party. This is me." Trudeau's efforts were ultimately successful, and he was elected leader of the party in the spring of 2013.

PRIME MINISTER

In the Canadian political system, voters elect MPs for their respective ridings, and the party that receives the most seats forms the government; the leader of the party, in most cases, becomes the country's prime minister. Trudeau's election to the Liberal Party leadership, then, raised the possibility that he could soon become the second Trudeau prime minister—if the Liberal Party could secure enough seats in the 2015 federal election. Although the party had lost many seats in the election of 2011, it began to gain additional traction following Trudeau's election to the leadership, perhaps in part because of his overall popularity. Perhaps more important to many liberal Canadians, however, was the possibility of unseating Conservative prime minister Harper, who was widely viewed as having dismantled many of the liberal reforms put in place by earlier prime ministers, including Pierre Trudeau. "People decided to line up behind whoever was going to beat Stephen Harper," Trudeau told Lawson. "I was of the mind that even if there was uncertainty about my own personal ability to run the economy, there was the feeling that the party had a team and history that meant we'd get the compromises and balances you have to make. So I could take much bigger risks to challenge the orthodoxy."

Liberal Party candidates won 184 of a possible 338 seats on October 19, 2015, placing the party in control of the Canadian government and Trudeau in the position of prime minister. He was sworn in just over two weeks later, on November 4. In the months since taking office, Trudeau has worked to improve the diversity of Canadian government, appointing an equal number of men and women to his cabinet as well as increasing that body's ethnic diversity. Asked about his reasons for doing so, Trudeau was widely quoted as saying simply, "Because it's 2015." As prime minister, he seeks to improve Canada's infrastructure, tackle global issues such as climate change, and address the needs of the country's First Nations population, among other goals. Although a committed Liberal, Trudeau has likewise stated that he wants to combat partisanship and encourage the sharing of ideas for the betterment of the country. "I don't believe in surrounding myself with people who are afraid of me or worried about offending me with the wrong idea," he told Christopher Curtis for the *Montreal Gazette* (21 Aug. 2015). "That approach of not telling me what you think is a quick way to lose my trust."

PERSONAL LIFE

Trudeau first met his wife, former television personality Sophie Grégoire, as a child, and the two later reconnected while cohosting the Starlight Children's Foundation gala in 2003. They married in the spring of 2005. They have three children and live in Ottawa. As the traditional prime minister's residence and Trudeau's childhood home, 24 Sussex Drive, is in need of significant repairs, Trudeau opted to move his family into Rideau Cottage, a smaller government-owned residence nearby.

SUGGESTED READING

Curtis, Christopher. "Electric in a Crowd, Guarded in Private, Justin Trudeau Sticks to His Script." *Montreal Gazette*. PostMedia Network, 21 Aug. 2015. Web. 14 Mar. 2016.

Gatehouse, Jonathon. "On His Own Terms: Justin Runs for the Liberal Leadership." *Maclean's*. Rogers Media, 11 Oct. 2012. Web. 14 Mar. 2016.

Lawson, Guy. "Trudeau's Canada, Again." *New York Times Magazine*. New York Times, 8 Dec. 2015. Web. 14 Mar. 2016.

Powers, John. "Justin Trudeau Is the New Young Face of Canadian Politics." *Vogue*. Condé Nast, 9 Dec. 2015. Web. 14 Mar. 2016.

Reid, Stuart. "Canada's Contender." *Atlantic*. Atlantic Monthly Group, May 2015. Web. 14 Mar. 2016.

Trudeau, Justin. *Common Ground*. Toronto: HarperCollins, 2014. Print.

Trudeau, Justin. "Meet Justin Trudeau." *Liberal*. Liberal Party of Canada, 2016. Web. 14 Mar. 2016.   —Joy Crelin

Sophie Turner

Born: February 21, 1996
Occupation: Actor

Sophie Turner is an English actor best known for her role as Sansa Stark on the award-winning HBO drama *Game of Thrones*. Turner, who started playing Sansa when she was just thirteen, has grown up alongside her character. "I probably know her better than I know myself," she told Jessica Salter for the *Telegraph* (13 Apr. 2015). Based on the popular novels by George R. R. Martin, *Game of Thrones* is an epic set in a sprawling fantasy world featuring dragons, political intrigue, and ample gore. Sansa is the oldest daughter of Lady Catelyn and Lord Eddard Stark. Over the course of the series, Sansa evolves from an innocent young girl into a battle-tested heroine. As Laura Miller of *Slate* (27 June 2016) put it, "She expected nothing more from life than to marry a strong, handsome knight and have a castle full of kids, and instead she got the trials of Job." After enduring three ill-fated marriages and a brutal beating and rape—the scene is among the show's most controversial—Sansa has emerged as a political force, as well as one of the most beloved characters on the show. *Game of Thrones*, which premiered in 2011, has become a touchstone of contemporary popular culture, embraced by audiences and critics alike. In 2016, the finale of its sixth season drew in 8.89 million viewers—a record for the show. In addition to her role on *Game of Thrones*, Turner has appeared in a handful of films, and in 2016, played Jean Grey, a teenager with telekinetic powers, in the summer blockbuster *X-Men: Apocalypse*.

Steve Granitz/WireImage/Getty Images

EARLY LIFE AND AUDITION

Sophie Turner was born in rural England on February 21, 1996, and grew up on a farm with her parents and brothers near Leamington Spa in central Warwickshire. Her mother Sally is a nursery school teacher, and Turner has two older brothers: James, a doctor, and Will, a graduate student. Turner knew she wanted to be an actor since she began taking classes at the age of three. She was also a talented dancer. As a child in Leamington Spa she performed in productions at the Playbox Theatre. At age eleven, she turned down a spot at the prestigious Royal Ballet School in London to study drama at The King's High School for Girls in Warwick and focus on her acting career. While studying drama, Turner had her first leading role in a production at the Playbox called *Scary Play* in 2009. When she was twelve, her school drama teacher told her about an audition for a twelve-year-old character named Sansa for a television show called *Game of Thrones*. "I had been for other auditions

before, and didn't get them," Turner told Salter, adding that the audition, "was the first audition that I didn't really try very hard for." It was the ease in her performance that attracted the attention of the producers. D. B. Weiss, one of the show's creators, told Jeremy Egner for the *New York Times* (1 Apr. 2015) Turner "didn't seem like she was acting." Turner auditioned four more times before being cast.

It was an exciting moment for the young actor but her parents were hesitant. The show, based on the popular books by George R. R. Martin, is extremely violent and sexually explicit—but content was not their only worry. Accepting the role meant breaking up the family. In the end, both parents pledged their support. Sally Turner quit her teaching job for three years to act as her daughter's chaperone on set in Croatia and other filming locations.

GAME OF THRONES

Game of Thrones is based on a series of fantasy novels by George R. R. Martin collectively called *A Song of Fire and Ice*. The first novel in the series, *A Game of Thrones*, was published in 1996 and had a significant following.

The official pilot debuted on HBO in April 2011. The show drew in the existing book fan base, but viewership grew as the first season progressed. Critical reviews were largely positive and praised many aspects of the show, including the performances of its young cast members. Turner was the victim of some fan ire in the first season (and a few seasons after) as Sansa became one of the most hated characters on the show for her naiveté, docility, and the ways those qualities affected her family. No matter how fans felt about her character, Turner connected with and was affected by Sansa's story from the beginning. As she told Salter, "When I read the script my heart just breaks. I don't need to imagine something sad, because to me what is happening to her is so real."

In interviews, Turner recalls the difficulty of navigating her schoolwork—with the help of an on-set tutor she had until she was sixteen—and her career. Turner returned to school at home when not filming, which posed additional challenges. Even while filming, Turner was learning; she has noted that working with her costars has taught her a lot about acting. She told Salter that she learned the most from watching Lena Headey (Cersei): "She's so fascinating to watch. She can convey so much with just her eyes."

Turner and her costars have also become something of a family, and she is particularly close with Maisie Williams, who plays Sansa's younger sister Arya Stark. Turner and Williams bonded through the often-isolating experience of filming for long hours each day and months at a time on location, an experience that their friends from home simply do not understand. "People say, 'Do you ever miss being a normal teenager? And we don't really know what that is, I guess," Williams told Egner. "Because this is normal."

As the seasons of the show progressed, Sansa became the show's resident victim; the narrative path for the character has been the source of controversy. "I swear, this show, after the first season when people were hating on Sansa. Showrunners [David Benioff and Dan Weiss] must have been like, 'Okay, let's do everything we can to make her the most abused, manipulated character!'" she quipped to James Hibberd in an interview for *Entertainment Weekly* (17 May 2015). Sansa's misery and the controversy around it came to a head after the season five episode "Unbowed, Unbent, Unbroken" in which Sansa is brutally beaten and raped on her wedding night. It was not the first time a character had been raped or humiliated on the show, but this particular scene disturbed many viewers, particularly those who decried the show for its frequent violence against women and the choice to make rape a plot point. (There is a similar rape scene in Martin's book, but it does not involve Sansa.) A few public *Game of Thrones* admirers, like Missouri Senator Claire McCaskill washed their hands of the show, and the website *Deadspin* published an article the next day called "Game of Thrones Is Gross, Exploitative, and Totally Out of Ideas" (18 May 2015). But the show's producers, and Turner, defended the scene. "When I read that scene, I kinda loved it," Turner told Hibberd. "It was all so messed up."

Sansa gets her comeuppance, in true *Game of Thrones* fashion, in the show's sixth season.

Sansa has become one of the show's most powerful political players. "She's a powerful young woman now," Turner told Egner. "Rather than being a pawn in everyone else's game, she's playing her own." What was more, the sixth season was entirely new even to readers of the novels; the last book was published in 2011 and the next book is still being written. The show had moved past the end of the fifth book and introduced entirely new material, which critics loved and finally brought audiences onto Sansa's side, making her a fan favorite."

X-MEN: APOCALYPSE

In 2013, Turner starred in a poorly received British thriller called *Another Me*, and in 2015, she appeared, alongside Hailee Steinfeld, Samuel L. Jackson, and Jessica Alba, in a comedy called *Barely Lethal*. In 2016, she made her high-profile big screen debut as teenage mutant Jean Grey in *X-Men: Apocalypse*. Turner first heard about the role on social media and after some persuasion from fans and friends, inquired about the part. Grey is an extraordinarily powerful Marvel superhero with telekinetic powers and a dark side, but *X-Men: Apocalypse*, which also stars Michael Fassbender, Jennifer Lawrence and Oscar Isaac, is a prequel, featuring a younger, more vulnerable Grey. "She has no idea how to control her powers," Turner told Meredith Woerner for the *Los Angeles Times* (27 May 2016). "She's too strong for her own good." The film was released in May 2016, but received lackluster reviews from critics, as well as a less-than-stellar box office debut, taking in about $65 million in sales, 29 percent less than the last film in the franchise. Citing Turner as a new addition to the cast, Geoff Berkshire of *Variety* (9 May 2016) wrote that *X-Men: Apocalypse* "isn't short on talent or charisma" but that its writer and director "give the players precious little to sink their teeth into."

PERSONAL LIFE

When not filming, Sophie Turner lives in London. She is close with her parents and two brothers and has maintained friendships with all of her school friends, whom she goes to visit at university when she gets the chance. HBO announced in 2016 that *Game of Thrones* will end after its eighth season. Turner says she does not know what her plans will be after *Thrones*, but she has expressed a desire in interviews to attend university.

SUGGESTED READING

Berkshire, Geoff. Rev. of *X-Men: Apocalypse*. *Variety*. Variety Media, 9 May 2016. Web. 16 Aug. 2016.

Egner, Jeremy. "Sophie Turner and Maisie Williams Have Grown Up on *Game of Thrones*."

New York Times. New York Times, 1 Apr. 2015. Web. 13 Aug. 2016.

Hibberd, James. "Game of Thrones: Sophie Turner Says She 'Loved' That Horrifying Scene." *Entertainment Weekly.* Entertainment Weekly, 17 May 2015. Web. 16 Aug. 2016.

Miller, Laura. "What Does Sansa Stark *Really* Want? The *Game of Thrones* Season Finale Offered a Few Clues." *Slate.* Slate, 27 June 2016. Web. 15 Aug. 2016.

Salter, Jessica. "Game of Thrones's Sophie Turner: 'I've Grown Up with Sansa Stark—I Really Feel What She Feels.'" *Telegraph.* Telegraph Media, 13 Apr. 2015. Web. 13 Aug. 2016.

Windolf, Jim. "The Gathering Storm." *Vanity Fair.* Condé Nast, 24 Mar. 2014. Web. 16 Aug. 2016.

Woerner, Meredith. "With 'X-Men: Apocalypse' and 'Game of Thrones,' Sophie Turner Is Coming into Her Own." *Los Angeles Times.* Los Angeles Times, 27 May 2016. Web. 16 Aug. 2016.

—*Molly Hagan*

Manuel Valls

Date of birth: August 13, 1962
Occupation: Prime minister of France

Manuel Valls is the prime minister of France. A member of the French Socialist Party, he aligns himself more with the ideology of social democracy in other European countries, which has resulted in many French residents considering him an outlier in his own party.

EARLY LIFE AND EDUCATION
Manuel Carlos Valls Galfetti was born on August 13, 1962, in Barcelona, Spain. As was the custom in Spain, Valls was given both parents' surnames. His father, Xavier Valls Subirà, was a Barcelona-born painter who had lived in France in the 1940s and 1950s; his mother, Luisangela Galfetti, was a Swiss artist. Valls grew up in Spain, but he spent many holidays and summers in Ticino, Switzerland, where his maternal grandparents lived. He moved to France when he was a teenager.

When he was seventeen, Valls joined the French Socialist Party. In his late teens, he decided to become a French citizen and dropped Galfetti from his surname. He became a citizen of France through naturalization in 1982. He attended the Panthéon-Sorbonne University at Tolbiac, where he studied history.

POLITICAL CAREER
Valls began his political career in 1983 by working as a parliamentary attaché for Robert Chapuis. Three years later, he was elected the regional councillor for Île-de-France, a position he held simultaneously with other elected positions until 2002. From 1989 to 1998, for example, he was the deputy mayor of Argenteuil in the northwestern suburbs of Paris.

Valls was the special advisor to the prime minister's office during Michel Rocard's term (1988–91). He then became the deputy interministerial delegate to the Winter Olympics in Albertville, a position he held until 1993. Following Lionel Jospin's appointment as prime minister in 1997, he worked as the head of communications and media relations in the prime minister's office until 2001.

Valls's participation in the French Socialist Party increased beginning in the 1990s. He served as first secretary of the Val d'Oise department of the Socialist Federation from 1990 to 2000, as the party's national secretary for communications from 1993 to 1994 and 1995 to 1997, and as the national secretary for organization from 2003 to 2004.

In 2001, Valls was elected mayor of Évry, a multicultural suburb of Paris, a position he held until 2012. He was elected to the National Assembly for the First Essonne constituency in 2002, and reelected in 2007 and 2012. He ran in the Socialist's 2011 presidential primary, but he failed to garner more than 5.6 percent of the vote.

In May 2012, Valls became the minister of the interior in French president François Hollande's administration. There he gained a reputation for taking a hard stance on economic policies, public spending, immigration, and crime. While some party members considered Valls's views inconsistent with those of the traditional Socialist Party and accused him of being a closet right-wing conservative, his popularity soared among others. Valls appeared undeterred by the criticism and called on the Socialist Party to abandon many of its traditional views, which he considered old-fashioned and restrictive. As the interior minister, Valls supported tighter controls on spending to reduce France's large deficit and create a more stable economy. He also called for tighter controls on immigration.

Following the February 2014 elections in which the ruling Socialist Party lost to the center-right Union for a Popular Movement and the far-right National Front, President Hollande appointed Valls prime minister. He took office on March 31, 2014, and faced the challenges of a country with a stagnant economy, high unemployment, and a huge deficit. Another challenge was to heal rifts in the sharply divided Socialist Party.

Valls tried to gain his party's—and the rest of the National Assembly's—support for pro-business reforms, but he often faced opposition from both hard-liner left Socialist Party members and others. Some Socialists sought reforms to improve workers' conditions while Valls sought reforms to promote economic growth and reduce the deficit. While agreeing to make worker rights reforms, Valls refused to change the work week or raise the minimum wage. He argued that support of business was necessary to create wealth, which would promote economic growth. Other reforms included liberalizing professions such as pharmacists and dentists and cutting public spending and welfare. Many of his proposals, such as a social-security budget, have narrowly passed.

In his first month of office, Valls survived a no-confidence vote. Four months later, facing criticism of his austerity policies and economic reforms, he resigned. At President Hollande's request, he then set up a new cabinet and survived another no-confidence vote a few weeks later. Opposition to his reforms continued, and in February 2015 Valls invoked special powers in order to approve pro-business legislation. Valls survived another no-confidence vote in June 2015.

IMPACT

Despite passing several economic reforms, France's economic woes have persisted. Valls's popularity fell as the approval ratings for Hollande plummeted. In the first round of the December 2015 elections, which were held weeks after the November terrorist attacks in Paris that killed 130 people, the far-right National Front party gained the largest share of votes, presenting a serious challenge to the two mainstream parties. The Socialist Party withdrew from two regions, and the mainstream parties rebounded with the second-round vote. The Republicans, led by former president Nicolas Sarkozy, won seven regions and the Socialist Party held on to five regions. These results position the Republicans to regain the government in the 2017 presidential race if Valls's economic reforms fail to bear fruit.

PERSONAL LIFE

Valls is married to concert violinist Anne Gravoin and has four children from a previous marriage. He speaks French, Italian, Catalan, and Castilian.

SUGGESTED READING

Ganley, Elaine. "French Prime Minister Wins Confidence Vote." *Huffington Post.* TheHuffingtonPost.com, 16 Sept. 2014. Web. 21 Dec. 2015.

"The Last Valls." *Economist.* Economist Newspaper, 4 Oct. 2014. Web. 21 Dec. 2015.

"Prime Minister: Manuel Valls." *Gouvernement. fr.* Government of France, n.d. Web. 21 Dec. 2015.

"Profile: France's Prime Minister Manuel Valls." *BBC.* BBC, 26 Aug. 2014. Web. 21 Dec. 2015.

Samuel, Henry. "Manuel Valls, France's New Prime Minister: Profile." *Telegraph.* Telegraph Media Group, 31 Mar. 2014. Web. 21 Dec. 2015.

—*Barb Lightner*

Alicia Vikander

Born: October 3, 1988
Occupation: Actor

By winning the 2016 Academy Award for best supporting actress for her role in *The Danish Girl* (2015), Alicia Vikander became the first Swede to win an Oscar since 1975, when legendary actor Ingrid Bergman won for *Murder on the Orient Express* (1974). In the press, Vikander is often compared to Bergman, for both their uncommon beauty and their substantial depth as actors. Vikander was able to put her talents on considerable display in 2015, as she appeared in a number of films released that year. Among her most notable performances—in addition to the one in *The Danish Girl*, in which she plays a woman coming to grips with her husband's desire to undergo sex reassignment surgery—were her turns as a pacifist in *Testament of Youth* and as a possibly manipulative robot in *Ex Machina*.

Many filmgoers and critics saw 2015 as Vikander's great breakout year, one that all but guaranteed that she would have her pick of choice roles going forward in her career. She told Rob Haskell for *Vogue* (14 Dec. 2015), "It's a mixed feeling when everything you've ever wanted in making films is coming true, and yet you feel scared because it's happening all at once. Suddenly you're in rooms with people you've looked up to for years, the Judi Denches. You wonder if you're good, if you have what it takes. You carry an anxiety around with you—I've met many actors now who will say this—and the lonely feeling that this could be your one chance."

EARLY LIFE AND EDUCATION

Alicia Vikander was born on October 3, 1988, in Gothenburg, Sweden. Her mother, Maria Fahl Vikander, a successful stage actor, and her father, Svante Vikander, a psychiatrist, divorced

Frankie Fouganthin/CC BY-SA 3.0/Wikimedia Commons

when she was just an infant. Her father eventually remarried, giving Alicia five additional half-siblings. Developing a love of performance early in life, Vikander convinced her mother to let her audition for the stage musical *Kristina from Duvemåla*. She got the part and spent the next three years performing in that production, which was written by the creators of the classic *Mamma Mia!*, in a number of roles.

She later took to the stage in a different way, when she moved to Stockholm on her own at age fifteen to enroll in the Royal Swedish Ballet School. The days were long—beginning at six o'clock in the morning and ending at ten o'clock at night—but she and all of her classmates were dedicated to their work. "In ballet school we all had very good grades," Vikander recalled to Haskell, "but not because you needed to be smart to dance. It was because ballet is about perfection, and if you weren't perfect, it was like the world was falling apart. I experienced a lot of stress around that. I went to therapy without telling my parents."

By the time she had completed the three-year ballet program and experienced several injuries, Vikander's interest had again shifted back to acting. She went to numerous auditions for films and television and ultimately found work on a Swedish soap opera. Despite that success, she felt she needed to hone her craft, applying to drama school; however, she was rejected twice. Feeling that she was floating without a plan for her life, she applied for law school and got in, before landing a role that would help launch her career.

EARLY ROLES

The film was *Pure* (2009), directed by Swedish director and screenwriter Lisa Langseth. For her lead performance as a young woman who is changed by listening to Mozart, Vikander earned the Guldbagge Award for best actress, a Swedish award that is comparable to an Academy Award. With the success of her film debut, she found that returning to the ballet world would be almost impossible. "I still love the ballet," she told Kathryn Shattuck for the *New York Times* (29 May 2015). "Any time the curtains go up, I think, 'What if?' and I get sucked into that world again. But . . . I don't think I could have gone on and done it my entire life."

Vikander's next major role was in the 2012 historical drama *A Royal Affair*, in which she portrays eighteenth-century Danish queen Caroline Matilda. She learned to speak Danish in order to portray the famed queen, who had an affair with Johann Friedrich Struensee, the royal physician, after her husband, King Christian VII of Denmark, became mentally ill. The queen and the royal doctor then began to implement reforms that reduced the power of the aristocracy and ended the royal practices of torture and censorship. The film, which was nominated for an Academy Award for best foreign language film, was the first to bring Vikander to the attention of American moviegoers and critics.

Vikander also received attention for her portrayal of Kitty in the 2012 adaptation of Leo Tolstoy's classic *Anna Karenina* and in the supporting role of Anke Domscheit-Berg in *The Fifth Estate* (2013), a film based on the life of Julian Assange and his news-leaking website WikiLeaks.

BREAKING OUT IN HOLLYWOOD

Vikander's breakout year in Hollywood came in 2015, when she appeared in no less than seven films, all of which had been shot over a period of three years. These films included the sci-fi thriller *Ex Machina*, in which she portrays a female robot; *Testament of Youth*, in which she plays the real-life writer and pacifist Vera Brittain; *The Man from U. N. C. L. E.*, a lighthearted spy thriller that takes place in the early 1960s; *Son of a Gun*, an action adventure; *Burnt*, in which she stars opposite Bradley Cooper; the fantasy bomb *Seventh Son*; and *The Danish Girl*, in which she portrays real-life painter Gerda Wegener, who helps her husband transition to life as a woman.

Vikander's memorable appearances in so many films in a single year caused a number of critics to describe her as an upcoming star. The actor, however, notes that her seeming omnipresence was not a calculated transition to stardom, but an accident of all of the movies getting assigned release dates at the same time. "People have seen the films that have come out, but they haven't seen all the auditions and the constant tryouts and the meetings that didn't work out," she explained to Shattuck.

Among the most celebrated of these performances was in *Ex Machina*, which was the directorial debut of the celebrated novelist and screenwriter Alex Garland. Vikander plays a humanoid robot named Ava, who may be more manipulative than she appears. During the film, the viewer is unsure whether Ava is displaying genuine human emotions, or if her apparent feelings are part of an elaborate ruse to escape the laboratory in which she was built. Vikander received considerable acclaim for her eerie performance in the film, including a nomination for a Golden Globe Award.

One of her other notable performances of the year was her role as the real-life author Vera Brittain in *Testament of Youth*, a film adaptation of Brittain's 1933 memoir of the same title. Brittain, who served as a nurse during World War I, bore witness to the war's incredible costs, which included the deaths of her brother, two close friends, and her fiancé. After the war, she became an outspoken pacifist. Critics were impressed by Vikander's performance as Brittain. Reviewing the film for National Public Radio (4 June 2015), Ella Taylor raved, "Vikander crisply holds the screen as a naive rebel transformed by unspeakable suffering into a mature, independent young woman who remains open to the possibility of a new love and a rebuilt England. . . . She caught the moment, then rode the wave, and Britain loved her for it. Vikander makes us see why."

In addition to her many performances on the big screen, Vikander also gained visibility when she was selected as the new model for Louis Vuitton, first appearing on magazine pages for the fashion giant's fall 2015 ad campaign.

OSCAR WINNER

The Danish Girl, the film in which Vikander portrays Gerda Wegener, would become the film that would cement her standing as an outstanding up-and-coming actor. In this biographical drama, she plays the real-life painter as a woman who is struggling to come to terms with her husband's desire to become a woman. Eddie Redmayne plays opposite Vikander as the first person to undergo successful sex reassignment surgery, ultimately becoming a woman named Lili Elbe. The movie chronicles the development of their relationship as their marriage comes to an end at the same time that Vikander's character becomes her former husband's greatest supporter. "It's about them going through a transition, not just him," Vikander remarked to Guy Lodge for the *Guardian* (13 Dec. 2015). "In any relationship, when you go through any big change, you struggle to find your new constellation, your new

ground. It takes a while to determine what the new relationship between you is. I could relate to that. That got to me immediately."

For her performance, Vikander received numerous accolades, the greatest of which was winning the Academy Award for best supporting actress in 2016. Although the award was considered somewhat controversial, as her part was large enough to have competed in the best actress award category, the win was still seen as a capstone for Vikander's remarkable year. "Thank you for giving me the belief that anything can happen," she said in her acceptance speech, as quoted by Amy Kaufman in the *Los Angeles Times* (28 Feb. 2016). "Even though I would never have believed this."

2016 FILMS

Vikander has roles in a number of films scheduled to be released in 2016, including the period drama *Tulip Fever*; the next installment in Matt Damon's Jason Bourne spy series, *Jason Bourne*; and *The Light between Oceans*, a drama about a childless couple who adopt a baby they find adrift in a rowboat on the ocean. "Alicia has this ripe internal world, and when the camera points to her, you can see the tornadoes inside. It's spellbinding. She's not afraid to be ugly, to be unlikable, to fail. And she gave me as much on the thirtieth take as on the first," director Derek Cianfrance said to Haskell about her performance in *The Light between Oceans*.

In April 2016, it was announced that Vikander would be taking on the role of video game character Lara Croft in a reboot of the Tomb Raider film series.

PERSONAL LIFE

According to interviews, Vikander is dedicated to keeping her personal life out of the limelight. "I think it can be quite good for everybody to have a bit of privacy. That is something in whatever work you do, I think it's everybody's clear right," she told Kara Warner for *People* (26 Feb. 2016). As of early 2016, she was living primarily in London and reportedly dating fellow actor Michael Fassbender, whom she met on the set of *The Light between Oceans*.

SUGGESTED READING

Haskell, Rob. "Alicia Vikander: *The Danish Girl* Star Jumps Out of a Plane and Talks Overnight Fame." *Vogue*. Condé Nast, 14 Dec. 2015. Web. 6 May 2016.

Kaufman, Amy. "Alicia Vikander's Supporting Actress Oscar Caps Off a Whirlwind Year." *Los Angeles Times*. Tribune, 28 Feb. 2016. Web. 6 May 2016.

Lodge, Guy. "Alicia Vikander: 'I Made Five Films in a Row Before I Had a Scene with Another

Woman.'" *Guardian*. Guardian News and Media, 13 Dec. 2015. Web. 6 May 2016.

Shattuck, Kathryn. "Alicia Vikander, Who Portrayed Denmark's Queen, Is Screen Royalty." *New York Times*. New York Times, 29 May 2015. Web. 6 May 2016.

Taylor, Ella. "A Strong Central Performance Elevates a Pacifist's Story." *NPR*. NPR, 4 June 2015. Web. 6 May 2016.

SELECTED WORKS

Pure, 2009; *A Royal Affair*, 2012; *Anna Karenina*, 2012; *The Fifth Estate*, 2013; *Testament of Youth*, 2015; *Ex Machina*, 2015; *The Man from U. N. C. L. E.*, 2015; *The Danish Girl*, 2015; *The Light between Oceans*, 2016

—Christopher Mari

Shannon Walker

Date of birth: June 4, 1965
Occupation: Astronaut

Shannon Walker is the first Houston-born astronaut. She traveled into space in 2010 and lived aboard the International Space Station (ISS) for an extended period.

EARLY LIFE AND EDUCATION

Shannon Walker was born on June 4, 1965, in Houston, Texas. One of four children born to Robert Walker, a physics professor, and Sherry Walker, she developed a strong interest in space at a young age. Growing up in Houston, the home of the Johnson Space Center, talk of space was a familiar and ever-present part of her childhood. So, too, was science, as her father was involved in the founding of the University of Houston's College of Natural Sciences and Mathematics. Determined to work in a space-related field, she took classes in elementary and high school to prepare for a career in rocket science.

After graduating from Westbury Senior High School in 1983, Walker attended Rice University in Houston. She earned a bachelor's degree in physics in 1987.

CAREER AS AN ASTRONAUT

Walker joined the Rockwell Space Operations at the Johnson Space Center as a robotics flight controller in 1987. After working as the flight controller for several Space Shuttle missions, she left the Johnson Space Center for about three years to attend graduate school. She earned a master's degree in astrophysics in 1992 and a PhD in astrophysics in 1993, also from Rice University. Walker joined the National Aeronautics and Space Administration (NASA)

in 1995 and worked at the Johnson Space Center. She worked on the design and construction of robotics hardware for the International Space Station (ISS). She then became a manager at the Mission Evaluation Room in 1998, where her responsibilities included coordinating solutions for problems aboard the ISS.

In 1999, Walker left her hometown to work with the Russian Space Agency in Moscow. She learned Russian and familiarized herself with Russian space equipment. Returning to Houston in 2000, she became the deputy manager of the On-Orbit Engineering Office and technical lead for the Mission Evaluation Room for ISS.

In 2004, Walker was selected to the astronaut candidate training program. After eighteen months of intensive training, she became an astronaut in February 2006 and was qualified to fly on the Space Shuttle and ISS. She later qualified for extravehicular activity and as a mobile servicing system robotics operator for the Canadian Space Agency.

Walker served as the crew support astronaut and spacecraft communicator for the ISS Expedition 14 crew, which spent seven months in space in 2006 and 2007. She served as the point person for all communications between the astronauts aboard the ISS and the ground crew. She was then promoted to the lead spacecraft communicator for a Space Shuttle mission.

In 2007, Walker began training for a long-duration flight aboard the ISS. She was chosen as a backup crewmember for several missions before being selected as the flight engineer, or copilot, of the Russian Soyuz TMA-19 spacecraft for the twenty-fourth expedition to the ISS. That expedition involved a two-day flight through space to the ISS and living aboard the Space Station for almost six months.

Having learned Russian proved to be advantageous as Walker needed to be able to communicate with her Russian crewmates. She traveled to Russia and trained with the Russian Federal Space Agency prior to the expedition. On June 16, 2010, Walker took her first space trip, lifting off from the Baikonur space center in Kazakhstan along with Russian cosmonaut Yury Yurchihin and NASA astronaut Douglas Walker. Two days later, they docked at the ISS and joined three other astronauts living there. For the next five-and-a-half months, Walker conducted research experiments and performed maintenance on the ISS. Walker also held live talks with students at several schools from space. During one live downlink, she chatted with students attending her former elementary, middle, and high schools in Houston.

She also carried objects that held a special significance to her into space. One such object was a watch that had been owned by Amelia

Earhart, a pioneer in aviation. She also carried a poster about her father and a plaque honoring her alma mater, Rice University. After 161 days aboard the ISS, Walker boarded a Soyuz spacecraft for the return trip to Earth. She served as the flight engineer during the November 25, 2010, landing.

In October 2011 Walker became an aquanaut when she participated in the NASA Extreme Environment Mission Operations (NEEMO) program on the NEEMO 15 mission. The program tests potential methods for asteroid exploration underwater. The mission took place at the Aquarius Reef Base, which is located off the east coast of Florida. During the thirteen-day mission, Walker and her colleagues tested a number of vehicles for their effectiveness with sample and data collection.

IMPACT

Following her space expedition and the NEEMO mission, Walker continued to work at NASA. She often gives presentations to the public to inform them about her space travels and to encourage students to take courses in science, technology, engineering, and math. In 2015, she helped to promote openings for astronaut candidates, participating in an online federal job board forum to answer individuals' queries about the application process and how to prepare for a career as an astronaut.

PERSONAL LIFE

Walker married fellow astronaut Andy Thomas in 2005. They live in Seabrook, a community near Houston, Texas. She is a member of the Ninety-Nines International Organization of Women Pilots and the Aircraft Owners and Pilots Association.

SUGGESTED READING

"Biographical Data: Shannon Walker." *Lyndon B. Johnson Space Center*. NASA, Mar. 2015. Web. 13 Jan. 2016.

"Houston, We (Finally) Have an Astronaut." *SPACE.com*. Purch, 14 June 2010. Web. 13 Jan. 2016.

"Next ISS Crew Confirmed for June 16 Launch." *Sputnik News*. Sputnik, 14 June 2010. Web. 13 Jan. 2016.

Pearlman, Robert Z. "Amelia Earhart's Watch Brought to International Space Station." *Christian Science Monitor*. Christian Science Monitor, 18 June 2010. Web. 13 Jan. 2016.

Williams, Mike. "Shannon Walker Preps for Six-Month Stint at International Space Station." *Wiess School of Natural Sciences*. Rice U, 2009. Web. 13 Jan. 2016.

—*Barb Lightner*

Luke Walton

Born: March 28, 1980
Occupation: Basketball coach

Golden State Warriors assistant coach Luke Walton has basketball in his blood. The son of veteran basketball player Bill Walton, who followed a successful career with the San Diego Clippers and Boston Celtics with more than two decades as a prominent sportscaster, Walton established himself as a talented player early in life, amassing impressive statistics during his years playing for the University of Arizona. His success playing for the Los Angeles Lakers and the Cleveland Cavaliers provided further proof that Walton is not only his father's son but also a talented player in his own right. "Luke is one of these people who was born with an innate understanding of the game of basketball," Bob Myers, the general manager of the Golden State Warriors, explained to Diamond Leung for the Bay Area News Group (4 Oct. 2015).

Walton's most impressive accomplishments, however, have perhaps come not on the basketball court but beside it: in the role of coach. Hired as an assistant coach for the Golden State Warriors in 2014, he stepped up to the position of interim head coach in late 2015 when head coach Steve Kerr took a leave of absence for medical reasons. Walton led the team in a record-breaking start to the 2015–16 season. Despite this impressive achievement, Walton has expressed that he tends to emphasize his strong working relationships with his players rather than his own personal efforts. "Players

Jason Miller/Stringer/Getty Images

expect honesty, and as long as we have a relationship and they feel that I'm not trying to get anything over on them, I can be laid-back, and then I can still pull them aside and tell them that they're messing up, that they need to do something better," he told Leung. "They respect it, and they respond to it."

EARLY LIFE AND EDUCATION

Luke Theodore Walton was born on March 28, 1980, in San Diego, California. The third of four sons born to Bill and Susie Walton, Walton spent his early years in southern California where his father played professional basketball. Bill Walton had begun his National Basketball Association (NBA) career with the Portland Trail Blazers and at the time of Walton's birth was playing for the San Diego Clippers; he went on to play for the Boston Celtics and, after retiring from the sport in 1987, began a second career as a sports commentator.

Growing up as the son of a championship winner and respected sportscaster was sometimes difficult, but it also had its perks: Walton has recalled in interviews that some of his strongest childhood memories involve attending his father's games and meeting famed players such as Larry Bird. "I don't think every kid would enjoy the childhood that I had, but I loved the childhood I had," he told Mary Schmitt Boyer for *Cleveland.com* (25 Mar. 2013). "We had freedom, but we had discipline. It was a little chaotic over there. But I enjoyed that. I wouldn't trade it." Basketball was a key part of life for Walton and his brothers, even after they moved in with their mother following their parents' divorce, and all four boys enjoyed playing the game. Nevertheless, their father sought to ensure that they never felt pressured to pursue the sport professionally. "Obviously, he knew more about the type of pressure we were going to be having being his kids," Walton explained to Boyer. "But he'd ask you if you wanted advice on the game. Sometimes you were mad and you didn't want to hear it from your dad. Other times you'd say yes and he'd break down what he saw and what he thought you should work on. But he'd always ask you first and he'd always make the point of telling us that it was our lives and not to feel obligated to play basketball."

Walton attended the University of San Diego High School, where he was considered for the varsity basketball team early on. Walton's father, with whom he lived during that period, encouraged the coach to place the teenage Walton on the junior varsity team instead. Walton filled the position of point guard on the junior varsity team and later went on to play varsity basketball, helping his team obtain a state title during his senior year. After graduating from high school in 1998, Walton enrolled in the University of Arizona (UA), from which he earned his bachelor's degree in 2003. He continued to play basketball at the university, joining the school's Arizona Wildcats. A prolific player, Walton ranked in first place in the Pacific-10 Conference for number of games played two seasons in a row. He ultimately scored more than 1100 points for the Wildcats over the course of his four-year career and in his senior year aided the Wildcats in becoming regular-season Pac-10 champions.

PROFESSIONAL BASKETBALL

Walton's professional basketball career began in June 2003 when he was drafted by the Los Angeles Lakers in the second round of that year's NBA draft. Entering the world of professional basketball had some unexpected consequences for Walton, who, as the son of a sports commentator who never shied away from criticizing players when necessary, faced some scrutiny for his father's comments. "Sometimes I had teammates' moms come up to me and tell me, 'Tell your dad to leave my son alone,'" he recalled to Boyer. "I was like, 'Listen I can't control that man. He's going to do what he does.'" Although he occasionally faced some uncomfortable conversations with teammates' families, Walton soon came to be seen as a player in his own right rather than Bill Walton's son, and his teammates opted to treat Walton differently because of his father's at-times critical words.

Walton made his debut with the Lakers on October 28, 2003, playing for seven minutes in the season's opening game in which the Lakers ultimately defeated the Dallas Mavericks by sixteen points. After playing as a power forward during the 2003–4 season, he later transitioned into the role of small forward, filling that position throughout much of his professional career. Walton remained with the Lakers for nearly a decade and played for the team into early 2012. During his tenure with the Lakers, the team won the NBA Finals two years in a row, in 2009 and 2010.

In March of 2012, the Lakers traded Walton to the Cleveland Cavaliers. Returning to the position of power forward, he played for the team from March 2012 to April 2013. Following the end of the 2012–13 season, Walton retired from play but not from professional basketball, transitioning into the role of coach.

A COACH IN THE MAKING

Walton first developed an interest in coaching in 2010 when a pinched nerve in his back sidelined him for much of the season. During that period, doctors cautioned Walton that he might not be able to continue playing basketball at a professional level if he did not recover fully, a concept that left Walton distressed. Aware of Walton's difficulties, Lakers coach Phil Jackson stepped in and encouraged Walton to become more involved in the coaching side of the sport. "Phil saw that I was pretty depressed and he invited me in to start hanging out with his coaching staff that season," he told Ben Golliver for *Sports Illustrated* (9 Nov. 2015). "He had me tracking plays on the bench with the staff. For the first time, I had to think about what I would do if I couldn't play basketball any more. I really enjoyed what Phil and his staff were doing. I thought it might be something I wanted to do once it was all said and done."

The 2011 NBA lockout, a six-month contract dispute prompted by the expiration of the league's previous collective bargaining agreement, provided Walton with his first opportunity to work as a coach, and he took a position with the University of Memphis (UM) during that period. When he retired from the Cavaliers in late 2013, he was hired as a player development coach for the Los Angeles D-Fenders, a minor-league basketball team affiliated with the Lakers. Walton was tasked with developing talented players with the goal of preparing them to join major-league basketball teams one day.

GOLDEN STATE WARRIORS

The following summer, Walton joined the Golden State Warriors, a professional team based in Oakland, California, as an assistant coach. He approached the position with an open mind. "I didn't really have expectations," he told Tim Kawakami for the *Mercury News* blog Talking Points (19 May 2015). "I came in, I told [head coach Steve Kerr] I wanted to be as involved as possible; I wasn't going to come in and overstep any boundaries. I was just going to kind of watch how things played out and do what was asked of me until I kind of felt the groove of what they wanted and what was going to be my role."

In October 2015, Walton's role with the team shifted dramatically when Kerr took a leave of absence following back surgery and named Walton interim head coach. In that position, Walton led the Warriors to significant success in the beginning of the 2015–16 season when the team achieved a twenty-four-game winning streak that did not end until December. Although Walton filled the role of head coach during the Warriors' incredible autumn, NBA regulations stipulated that Kerr would be credited for the success as the team's official head coach. Although fans objected to the policy and argued that Walton should be recognized for his leadership, the interim coach focused more on the collaborative efforts of the entire team than his own contributions. "I'm completely okay with the fact that the wins don't count on any record book for me," he told Golliver. "Our concern here is getting the wins and the team continuing to get better while Steve isn't able to coach. It's an atmosphere that

was built when he got here: none of us are out here doing it for credit, none of us are out here doing it for ourselves. It's what we're trying to accomplish as a group."

Walton remained interim coach for the Warriors until January 2016 when Kerr returned from his leave of absence. Having demonstrated his capabilities as a head coach, Walton became the focus of much attention during the months, with numerous commentators speculating about whether he would take a head coach position with another team following the end of the 2015–16 NBA season, and if so, which team.

PERSONAL LIFE

While attending the University of Arizona, Walton met Bre Ladd, a varsity volleyball player. The two began dating several years later and married in 2013. They live in California.

SUGGESTED READING

Boyer, Mary Schmitt. "Cleveland Cavaliers Forward Luke Walton: The Most Interesting Man in the NBA?" *Cleveland.com*. Advance Ohio, 25 Mar. 2013. Web. 8 Apr. 2016.

Golliver, Ben. "Luke Walton Q&A: Warriors' Dominant Start, Filling in for Steve Kerr and More." *Sports Illustrated*. Time, 9 Nov. 2015. Web. 8 Apr. 2016.

Kawakami, Tim. "Luke Walton on the Warriors' Coaching Staff: 'We Don't Want to Act Like We're Stressed or Freaking Out.'" *Talking Points*. Mercury News, Bay Area News Group, 19 May 2015. Web. 8 Apr. 2016.

Killion, Ann. "Warriors Youngest Coach Luke Walton with Big Responsibility." *SFGATE*. Hearst Communications, 25 Mar. 2015. Web. 8 Apr. 2016.

Leung, Diamond. "Luke Walton, Suddenly Warriors Interim Coach, Has Basketball Pedigree." *Mercury News*. Digital First Media, 4 Oct. 2015. Web. 8 Apr. 2016.

"NBA Hall of Famer Bill Walton Talks about Luke, John Wooden." *SFGATE*. Hearst Communications, 2 Apr. 2016. Web. 8 Apr. 2016.

—*Joy Crelin*

Kamasi Washington

Born: 1981
Occupation: Musician

Kamasi Washington is a tenor saxophonist and jazz composer with the fan base of a rock star. He played on and wrote the string arrangements for rapper Kendrick Lamar's *To Pimp a Butterfly* (2015), one of the most acclaimed albums of the year. (*To Pimp a Butterfly* was nominated

for eleven Grammy Awards and won five in 2016.) Washington released his own critically acclaimed, three-disc jazz epic called, appropriately, *The Epic*, in May 2015. Influenced by jazz legends of the 1960s and 1970s such as John Coltrane and Pharoah Sanders, the Los Angeles musician draws on grooves that are suggestive of that era of spiritualism, Afro-futurism, and black consciousness. A rare crossover talent, Washington has become a major figure in the black arts renaissance that has been energized by the Black Lives Matter movement. The writer Greg Tate described Washington to Adam Shatz for the *New York Times* (21 Jan. 2016) as the "jazz voice of Black Lives Matter," adding that his music serves as "a healing force, a place of regeneration when you're trying to deal with the trauma of being black in America."

EARLY LIFE

Washington, the second of three boys, was born in Los Angeles in 1981 and raised in a rough part of South Central on 74th and Figueroa. It was the dawn of the crack epidemic and the era of the Bloods and the Crips; pervasive police brutality in the area came to a head with the riots sparked by the beating of Rodney King in 1992. A young Washington learned quickly how to live with fear—his father once found a woman's body in the family's backyard. Washington's parents divorced when he was three and moved to separate houses in better parts of town. Washington's mother, Valerie, a chemistry teacher, stayed in the South Central area. His father Rickey, a saxophonist and flutist who supported the family through his work as a music teacher,

moved to Inglewood. Washington split his time between the two houses while growing up.

As a student, he excelled at math and science. He harbored a secret fascination with gang life, but the charm wore off after he read *The Autobiography of Malcolm X*. (Washington's *The Epic* includes a tribute to the late civil rights leader.) The book changed Washington's worldview. "I realized I didn't want to be a part of our self-destruction," he told Shatz. "I wanted to be a positive force in the world."

Washington had begun playing the drums when he was three years old and the clarinet at age nine. He listened almost exclusively to hip-hop music until he was eleven, but then a friend introduced him to the 1940s jazz bandleader Art Blakey. Washington liked what he heard, and suddenly realized that he was surrounded by his father's jazz record collection. ("Kamasi was hearing [Coltrane's] *A Love Supreme* before he even knew what he was listening to," his father told Shatz.) Using the collection for reference, Washington taught himself how to play songs on his soprano saxophone, and when he was thirteen he told his father he wanted to become a jazz musician. At first, his father was wary. He asked his son to sing—not play—a Charlie Parker solo. "I knew if you couldn't sing it, you couldn't play it," his father explained to Shatz. Washington delivered a flawless rendition of Parker's "Blues for Alice" and was rewarded with a new alto saxophone: a Conn 6M, just like Parker's. Washington played the instrument every week at church and then switched to a tenor saxophone a year later, taking his father's Selmer Mark VI tenor saxophone. It is the only tenor saxophone Washington has ever played.

MUSICAL EDUCATION

Washington attended the prestigious Alexander Hamilton High Music Academy near Culver City in Los Angeles County. There he was discovered by a man named Reggie Andrews, a music teacher at Locke High School in the predominantly black neighborhood of Watts. Andrews formed a band of young musicians, culled from schools around the city, called the Multi-School Jazz Band. The most talented student musicians were bused outside of South Central to magnet schools. "So you wouldn't know the talented musicians who lived around the corner from you," Washington explained to Ben Ratliff for the *New York Times* (24 Apr. 2015). "Reggie used to figure out who was talented around Central L.A., and he'd pick us up after school." The band practiced at Locke but performed all over the city. Washington recalls being shocked when white kids, drawn by the group's local fame and talent, began showing up at practice asking to join. "The amazing thing is that white kids were coming down to Locke to rehearse because the band was so good and they wanted to be in it," he recalled to Shatz. "It was kind of ironic, since we were being bused to their schools."

The Multi-School Jazz Band laid the foundations for the Los Angeles underground jazz scene in which Washington cut his teeth. Other performers included Washington's bandmate and pianist Cameron Graves, and the Bruner brothers, sons of Ronald Bruner Sr., a former drummer for the Temptations, among others. Ronald Bruner Jr., a virtuosic drummer and Grammy Award winner, plays with Washington, as does Stephen Bruner (better known as Thundercat), a bassist and singer who contributed heavily to Lamar's *To Pimp a Butterfly* and was nominated for a Grammy for his single "These Walls." In addition to the Multi-School Jazz Band, Washington found another haven in Leimert Park, a black neighborhood in South Central that was home to the Black Arts movement in the 1960s. Washington and his bandmates jammed there after rehearsal as teenagers in the mid-1990s and saw jazz legends perform at the town's World Stage, a nonprofit performing arts gallery.

Washington won a full scholarship to the University of California, Los Angeles, in 1999. He studied with Gerald Wilson, a composer who had worked with Duke Ellington and Ella Fitzgerald. He also landed a spot in rapper Snoop Dogg's touring band in 2000. Washington jumped at the chance to go on the road. Washington, used to the technicalities of learning harmonically complex jazz compositions, received a crash course in grooving on a hip-hop beat. "It wasn't like the compositional elements in Stravinsky. It wasn't about counterpoint or thick harmonies. It was more about the relationships and the timing. . . . I started to hear music in a different way, and it changed the way I played jazz," he told Shatz. "The question was *how* to play it, with the right articulation and timing and tone." He began to see the relationship between hip-hop and jazz, broadening his understanding of music in general and leading him to his current philosophy that music should exist outside of constrictive categories. Washington later toured with rapper and singer Lauryn Hill and R&B singer Raphael Saadiq.

THE EPIC

In 2009, Washington and a handful of musicians from the Multi-School Jazz Band formed a collective called the West Coast Get Down. They performed at the Piano Bar in Hollywood, drawing diverse crowds with eclectic musical tastes. In 2011, the collective pooled money to rent a studio space, and within the span of one month they recorded 192 songs for each other's individual projects. Washington led forty-five of those songs; he chose seventeen of them, fourteen of which he had composed, for *The Epic*. While

Washington was on tour with Chaka Khan, he began fleshing out the music on *The Epic*, writing parts for a choir and a string orchestra. The editing process took three years. The finished product was finally released through Brainfeeder, an independent record label founded by rapper, producer, and musical wunderkind Steven Ellison, who records under the name Flying Lotus, in May 2015.

The first song on the album, "Change of the Guard," is an ode to his father and the jazz musicians with whom he played. Though Los Angeles was home to a number of musicians in his father's era, few truly made it in the larger industry. (With Lamar, Thundercat, Flying Lotus, and Washington putting the city at the forefront of their new and distinctive sound, the opposite could be said to be true in 2016.) Washington's father, for one, gave up his musical dreams to help raise his children. "Change of the Guard," Washington told Shatz, was for those musicians like his father who "had something to say but never had a chance to say it." The album also includes a version of Claude Debussy's "Clair de Lune" and an ode to Malcolm X called "Malcolm's Theme," which features a sung version of actor Ossie Davis's famous eulogy for the slain leader. Washington's inspirations while making the record included Igor Stravinsky's neoclassical "Symphony of Psalms," the compilation album *Charlie Parker with Strings*, and soul singer Marvin Gaye's landmark 1971 album *What's Going On*. The concept for *The Epic*, Washington has said, was a nights-long dream he had about a group of warriors battling to take the place of a guard—note the song title "Change of the Guard"—at the top of a mountain. Washington has said he plans to write a graphic novel that tells the story of the dream. In 2016, Washington toured the world with his band, the Next Step.

Critics lavished praise on *The Epic*, and Shatz hailed Washington as "the most-talked-about jazz musician since Wynton Marsalis." Patrick Jarenwattananon for NPR's *First Listen* (26 Apr. 2015) wrote that the term epic, while hyperbolic, was appropriately deployed in the case of Washington's record. "It seems intentionally to overwhelm, in an immersive way; it's music to be swept up by and revisited after the wave subsides." *Pitchfork* named it one of the top ten albums of 2015. Seth Colter Walls wrote for *Pitchfork* (8 May 2015), "Instead of a self-conscious attempt to seize someone else's idea of the zeitgeist, it's a large and generous canvas, clearly created in the hopes of attracting new visitors to the post-Coltrane wing of the jazz museum. At this point, that project is its own form of radicalism." Washington won the inaugural American Music Prize, worth $25,000, for *The Epic* in 2016.

PERSONAL LIFE

Washington lives and records in his childhood home, which he rents from his father, in the Inglewood neighborhood of Los Angeles. He converted the home's garage into a studio. His girlfriend, Tiffany Wright, is the founder of a private elementary school called the Wright Academy.

SUGGESTED READING

Jarenwattananon, Patrick. Rev. of *The Epic*, by Kamasi Washington. *First Listen*. NPR, 26 Apr. 2015. Web. 14 July 2016.

Ratliff, Ben. "Los Angeles Jazz with Kamasi Washington and Others." *New York Times*. New York Times, 24 Apr. 2015. Web. 13 July 2016.

Shatz, Adam. "Kamasi Washington's Giant Step." *New York Times*. New York Times, 21 Jan. 2016. Web. 12 July 2016.

Walls, Seth Colter. Rev. of *The Epic*, by Kamasi Washington. *Pitchfork*. Condé Nast, 8 May 2015. Web. 13 July 2016.

Weiner, Natalia. "Kamasi Washington on Winning First-Ever American Music Prize and How Jazz Doesn't Have to Be 'Daunting.'" *Billboard*. Billboard, 7 Mar. 2016. Web. 12 July 2016.

—*Molly Hagan*

J. J. Watt

Born: March 22, 1989
Occupation: Football player

Houston Texans defensive end J. J. Watt is indisputably regarded as one of the best defensive players in the National Football League (NFL). Standing at six feet five inches and weighing 290 pounds, Watt has frequently drawn comparisons to the New York Giants legend and Pro Football Hall of Famer Lawrence Taylor, widely considered to be the best defensive player ever, for his rare combination of size and speed and for his relentless on-field play. Elizabeth Merrill, writing for ESPN.com (28 Oct. 2012), called Watt "an electrifying, disruptive force" who "does things that only agile and fleet-footed athletes are supposed to do."

Since being drafted by the Texans in 2011, Watt burst into the national consciousness during his sophomore season in 2012, when he led the NFL with 20.5 sacks and won the Associated Press (AP) NFL Defensive Player of the Year Award. In 2014 Watt won his second Defensive Player of the Year award after becoming the first player in league history with multiple seasons of twenty-plus sacks. "What he is," Wade Phillips, who served as the defensive coordinator for

Andy Lyons/GettyImages

the Texans from 2011 to 2013, declared to Tim Layden for *Sports Illustrated* (17 Nov. 2014), "is the perfect football player."

EARLY LIFE

Justin James "J. J." Watt was born on March 22, 1989, in Waukesha, Wisconsin. The oldest of three brothers, he grew up in a middle-class home in Pewaukee, Wisconsin, a small town located about an hour east of the state capital of Madison. Watt's father, John, served with the Waukesha Fire Department for several years, rising to the rank of lieutenant; his mother, Connie, worked for a building inspection company, rising from secretary to vice president. Watt has said that his parents instilled in him and his brothers the importance of a strong work ethic. "Every day, we were trying to be somebody," he told John McClain for the *Houston Chronicle* (18 June 2015). "We wanted to be somebody that could be remembered, somebody that could really make a change in the world."

From the time Watt was young, being "somebody" meant aspiring to greatness as an athlete. Watt's first love was hockey, and he started skating at the age of three. He grew up rooting for the University of Wisconsin–Madison (UW) hockey team, the Badgers, and regularly attended their games at the Kohl Center, which opened in 1998. One of Watt's favorite childhood pastimes was playing a pickup game of hockey, called shinny, with his brothers, Derek and T. J., in the family basement.

Watt also developed an early passion for football, which he started playing in fourth grade. It was then that he first expressed the desire to play in the NFL. Still, Watt remained heavily involved in hockey throughout his youth, playing on travel teams that competed in tournaments in Canada and Germany. He stopped playing the sport at age thirteen, primarily for financial reasons.

HIGH SCHOOL FOOTBALL

Watt attended Pewaukee High School, where he was a four-sport standout in football, basketball, baseball, and track. Tall but scrawny as a freshman, Watt served as a backup quarterback on Pewaukee's football team during his first two years of high school. He began to undergo a physical transformation as a sophomore, when he overhauled his diet and started weight training at NX Level Sports Performance, a gym in Waukesha owned and operated by Brad Arnett, a former college strength coach.

During his junior season, Watt was converted into a tight end and defensive end by Pewaukee's then first-year coach Clay Iverson, who recognized his burgeoning size, relentless work ethic, and unwavering drive to succeed. The transition proved seamless; as a senior, he earned first-team all-state and all-conference honors at both positions.

Watt also won the Division II state shot put title as a senior with a then record-breaking throw of nearly sixty feet. But his focus remained exclusively on football. Despite his outstanding senior season, Watt, who by then had reached his current height of six feet five inches and filled out to nearly 230 pounds, was not heavily recruited by major college football programs. This was largely due to the debilitating bout of mononucleosis he had during the summer before his senior season, which prevented him from attending college camps.

Offered only walk-on opportunities at major colleges, Watt instead accepted a scholarship to play tight end at Central Michigan University. "The thing that hurt me the most was that nobody got to see my work ethic up close and personal," Watt said to Jeffri Chadiha for ESPN. com (7 Apr. 2011). "But I kept working my tail off because I always wanted to be the best player on the field."

FROM PIZZA DELIVERY BOY TO WISCONSIN STANDOUT

At Central Michigan, Watt was used mostly as a run-blocking tight end in the Chippewas' spread offense. Consequently, he only recorded eight receptions for seventy-seven yards in his fourteen starts. Faced with the prospect of being moved to the offensive line during his sophomore season, Watt opted to return home and try his luck as a walk-on at UW.

In order to walk on at his dream school, Watt had to ask his parents for tuition money. He promised them that he would either quit or pay for his tuition himself if he did not earn a scholarship after a year. Over the following six months, he took classes at a community college in Waukesha and developed his body under Arnett at NX Level.

During this time, Watt took a delivery job at Pizza Hut to make extra money. On one occasion, in an oft-reported if somewhat apocryphal story, he delivered pizza to a perplexed young boy who remembered him being a star football player at Pewaukee High. Embarrassed, Watt returned to his car dejected, but contrary to some erroneous reports, "I never cried," he asserted to Tania Ganguli for the *Houston Chronicle* (13 Oct. 2012). "But it re-instilled the drive in me to become great again, to become that kid's role model again."

When Watt arrived at Wisconsin in the fall of 2008, he had upped his weight to 280 pounds, prompting his immediate move to defensive end. Though he was redshirted for the 2008 season, Watt became a standout on the Wisconsin Badgers' scout team, disrupting plays "so consistently that the first-team offense would have to run them two or three times," Chadiha noted. He was named the Badgers' defensive scout team player of the year and earned a scholarship.

Watt started thirteen games at defensive end for the Badgers during the 2009 season, finishing second on the team in tackles for loss (15.5) and third in sacks (4.5). He emerged as a defensive force for the Badgers in 2010, when he led the team in tackles for loss (21), sacks (7), forced fumbles (3), and blocked kicks (3). Watt helped lead the Badgers to a co-Big Ten championship title and a berth in the 2011 Rose Bowl.

HOUSTON TEXANS

Watt opted to forgo his senior season to enter the 2011 NFL Draft. Many scouts and analysts initially projected Watt to be a late first-round to early second-round pick, but his draft stock rose after he participated in that year's NFL Scouting Combine. His combination of size and speed impressed Phillips, who helped convince the Houston Texans to select him with the eleventh overall pick in the draft. The pick, however, did not go over well with Texans fans, who booed his selection on draft day and, like some members of the media, expressed doubts about his ability. "There were a lot of people saying I was just a big white guy," Watt explained to Ganguli, "that the team was taking a high character guy, not the best football player."

As a rookie during the 2011 season, Watt was immediately inserted into the Texans' starting lineup at right defensive end. He rewarded their faith in him by recording 5.5 sacks and recovering 2 fumbles in sixteen games. The Texans finished with a 10–6 record, won their first ever

American Football Conference (AFC) South title, and clinched their first play-off berth.

It was during the Texans' 31–10 victory over the Cincinnati Bengals in the AFC wild-card play-off round when Watt first earned serious attention around the league. With one minute left in the first half of that game, Watt intercepted a pass from Bengals quarterback Andy Dalton and returned it for a twenty-nine-yard touchdown.

RECORD-BREAKING SEASONS

During the 2012 season, Watt posted arguably one of the best statistical seasons by a defensive player in NFL history. Starting all sixteen games for the second consecutive season, he finished with a league-best 20.5 sacks, 39 tackles for loss, 42 quarterback hits, 4 forced fumbles, 2 fumble recoveries, and 16 passes defensed, the latter of which set a league record for defensive linemen. He became only the ninth player in history to record at least 20 sacks in a season and the first with at least 15 sacks and 15 passes defensed in the same season.

Watt's mesmerizing play propelled the Texans to a franchise-best 12–4 record and to their second straight AFC South title. Though the Texans would lose again in the AFC divisional play-off round, Watt was widely recognized for his accomplishments. He was voted the Texans' most valuable player (MVP), was a unanimous selection to the All-Prof (AP) First Team, and earned his first Pro Bowl selection, as a starter for the AFC squad. Unsurprisingly, Watt won the AP NFL Defensive Player of the Year Award. He became the first defensive lineman to receive the honor since the Miami Dolphins' Jason Taylor in 2006 and the first Texans player to win a league-wide player of the year award.

Watt fortified his status as the NFL's best defensive player in 2013, when he led the league in quarterback hits (46) and finished second in tackles for loss (22). He also recorded 10.5 sacks, 4 forced fumbles, and 2 fumble recoveries. Named to his second straight AP All-Pro First Team, he also earned his second straight Pro Bowl selection. The Texans, however, finished with a disastrous 2–14 record.

On September 2, 2014, Watt signed a six-year contract extension with the Texans worth $100 million. The contract included $51.8 million in fully guaranteed money, and at the time, made him the highest-paid defensive player in the league.

SECOND DEFENSIVE PLAYER OF THE YEAR AWARD

Watt justified his new contract in a big way during the 2014 season, which again saw him make history as he showcased his all-around versatility. Despite routinely facing double- and even triple-teams, he finished second in the NFL with 20.5 sacks, becoming the first player in league history with 20 or more sacks in two different seasons. He also recorded 4 forced fumbles and a career-high 5 fumble recoveries. In addition, Watt scored two defensive touchdowns, one on an interception return and another on a fumble recovery, and three offensive touchdowns as a tight end in goal-line situations. He became the first defensive lineman since 1944 to score five touchdowns in a single season. The Texans, meanwhile, finished second in the AFC South with a 9–7 record.

For his historic regular-season performance, Watt was named to his third straight All-Pro team and third consecutive Pro Bowl. He became the first player to be unanimously selected for the AP NFL Defensive Player of the Year Award. He also finished second to Green Bay Packers quarterback Aaron Rodgers in the voting for the NFL MVP award.

Through week thirteen of the 2015 season, Watt was leading the league with 13.5 sacks and was the frontrunner to win his third defensive player of the year award. He is just one of a handful of players in league history to receive the honor more than once.

PERSONAL LIFE

Prior to the 2015 season, Watt purchased a minimalistic, 4,500-square-foot log cabin situated on thirty-five acres of land in Summit, Wisconsin. He holds endorsement deals with and has appeared in commercials for such high-profile brands as Gatorade, Reebok, and Verizon. In his interview with McClain, Watt said, "Obviously, I'm trying to take advantage of all these great opportunities, but the thing I'll always be most proud of is . . . I'm still just that kid from Pewaukee."

SUGGESTED READING

Chadiha, Jeffri. "J.J. Watt Is Determined to Deliver." *ESPN*. ESPN Internet Ventures, 7 Apr. 2011. Web. 11 Dec. 2015.

Ganguli, Tania. "The Life and Times of J.J. Watt." *Houston Chronicle*. Hearst, 13 Oct. 2012. Web. 11 Dec. 2015.

Layden, Tim. "J.J. Watt, NFL's Best Defensive Player, Really Cares Most about the Next Play." *Sports Illustrated*. Time, 17 Nov. 2014. Web. 11 Dec. 2015.

Mays, Robert. "All Work and No Play for J.J. Watt." *Grantland*. ESPN Internet Ventures, 29 July 2014. Web. 11 Dec. 2015.

McClain, John. "Texans' Watt Credits Father for his Work Ethic." *Houston Chronicle*. Hearst, 18 June 2015. Web. 11 Dec. 2015.

—Chris Cullen

The Weeknd

Born: February 16, 1990
Occupation: Musician

In February 2011, a user of the video-sharing website YouTube uploaded several videos showcasing songs by an unknown artist going by the name the Weeknd. Little was known about the Weeknd's identity at the time, but within months, his music was the talk of the Internet, and by spring, the mystery of the artist's identity was solved. Born Abel Tesfaye, the Weeknd is a young Toronto native who is making atmospheric, experimental, indie R&B. Though initially posted to the Internet with little fanfare, his music quickly captured the attention of numerous critics and tastemakers, perhaps most notably the Canadian rapper Drake, who helped popularize the Weeknd's first extended play (EP), *House of Balloons*.

The Weeknd released two additional EPs as well as a studio album, *Kiss Land*, but it was the 2015 release of his sophomore album, *Beauty behind the Madness*, that garnered him his most critical and popular attention. The album hit number one on the Billboard 200 chart, and both the album itself and two of its songs were nominated for Grammy Awards. That would be an impressive accomplishment for any musician, but the Weeknd, who counts pop superstars such as Michael Jackson among his biggest influences, has even greater aspirations. "These kids, you know, they don't have a Michael Jackson," he told Jon Caramanica for the *New York Times Magazine* (27 July 2015). "They don't have a Prince. They don't have a Whitney [Houston]. Who else is there? Who else can really do it at this point?"

EARLY LIFE AND EDUCATION

The Weeknd was born Abel Makkonen Tesfaye on February 16, 1990. The son of parents who immigrated to Canada from Ethiopia in the 1980s, he grew up in Scarborough, a neighborhood of Toronto, Ontario. His father, Makkonen, left the family when the Weeknd was young, and he was raised primarily by his mother, Samra. Because his mother was often working, for a time as a nurse, he was frequently cared for by his maternal grandmother, who taught him to speak Amharic, the official language of Ethiopia.

A lover of music from an early age, the Weeknd grew up listening to a wide array of musical genres, from the R&B, pop, and rap of the late 1990s and early 2000s to classic rock and traditional Ethiopian music. "I was the kid wearing the Pink Floyd shirt and listening to Ginuwine in my ear," he told Josh Eells for *Rolling Stone* (21 Oct. 2015) of his diverse tastes. Perhaps the most influential figure in shaping the

Taylor Hill/GettyImages

young Weeknd's musical tastes, however, was Michael Jackson. In addition to being a pop phenomenon, Jackson took on a special significance in the Weeknd's family. "People forget—'We Are the World' is for Ethiopia," he explained to Eells, referring to the 1985 charity single cowritten by Jackson. "At home, if it wasn't Ethiopian music, it was Michael. He was our icon."

After completing his primary education, during which he took some French immersion classes, the Weeknd attended Birchmount Park Collegiate Institute, a high school in Scarborough, for a time. He dropped out of high school at the age of seventeen and left home, moving in with two friends in the Toronto neighborhood of Parkdale. As a teenager living away from home for the first time, he reveled in his newfound freedom; the rental home he shared with his friends gained a reputation as a party house, and his experiences with drugs and women during that period, which he described to Eells as his "hazy years," helped shape the content and aesthetic of his later work. When the need for money became urgent, the Weeknd took a job at the clothing retailer American Apparel.

EARLY CAREER

Long a lover of music, the Weeknd had experimented with performing but had not seriously considered pursuing a career in the field. "I've been singing my whole life," he explained to Anupa Mistry for *Pitchfork* (31 Aug. 2015). "I'd randomly sing in the hallways at high school, and all my friends would be like, 'You should sing on Canadian Idol!' It definitely gassed me! So then I got a microphone and a s—— computer and started recording these corny songs with my friends. . . . I would listen to it and I thought I sounded okay, but I was still shy, you know?"

As a young adult, the Weeknd began writing songs, initially as part of the hip-hop group Bulleez N Nerdz, for which he took on the moniker Kin Kane, and later with a group known as the Noise. Success came when he partnered with producer Jeremy Rose, who had created some instrumental tracks that he played for the Weeknd, who later recorded vocals for them. Originally taking on the name the "Weekend," the Weeknd dropped the final "e" from the name to avoid confusion with an existing band, and posted the first few songs to YouTube in early 2011. He soon followed those initial works with three independently released mixtapes—*House of Balloons*, *Thursday*, and *Echoes of Silence*—which he combined into a single release, *Trilogy*, the following year.

As the Weeknd's music, an experimental and eclectic take on R&B, found listeners through the Internet, the artist himself cultivated an air of mystery about his identity, refusing interviews and keeping a low profile. Although his reticence to interact with the press was in part related to his mysterious persona, it likewise had roots in the Weeknd's discomfort with being in the public eye. "I think I really avoided questions because I felt uncomfortable. I get naturally uncomfortable when I'm put under a magnifying glass," he told Will Welch for *GQ* (18 Aug. 2015). "I think I'm a little less awkward now."

GROWING FAME

Among the Weeknd's most influential early listeners was the Canadian rapper Drake, who introduced the artist's music to a wider audience when he posted about it on Twitter. The two soon became frequent collaborators, with the Weeknd contributing to a number of songs on Drake's 2011 album, *Take Care*. They went on to perform together on several songs, including "Crew Love," from *Take Care*, and "Live For," from the Weeknd's album *Kiss Land*.

The Weeknd's first studio album, *Kiss Land*, was released in September 2013. Although the album was relatively successful, hitting the number-two spot on the Billboard 200 sales chart, its sales and critical reception did not meet the Weeknd's expectations. "It humbled me a bit," he admitted to Eells. "I can be honest about it. Nobody wants to put out music where the reception's not great." Nevertheless, he gained additional public attention during the following years for the singles "Love Me Harder," a collaboration with pop singer Ariana Grande, and "Earned It," from the soundtrack to the 2015 film *Fifty Shades of Grey*.

BEAUTY BEHIND THE MADNESS

Somewhat disappointed by *Kiss Land*'s performance, the Weeknd opted to head in a different, more commercially accessible artistic direction for his next album, *Beauty behind the Madness*. He enlisted the help of various producers and songwriters, most notably including Max Martin, the Swedish songwriter and producer behind chart-topping hits by artists such as Britney Spears, the Backstreet Boys, Katy Perry, and Taylor Swift. As an artist with roots in experimental, independent R&B, the Weeknd initially resisted writing songs that conformed to traditional musical structures, preferring instead to create music that worked outside of such boundaries. For *Beauty behind the Madness*, however, he learned to work within such structures, creating radio-friendly music that remained faithful to his unique musical sensibilities. "I was always a punk: 'I hate major chords. I hate structure. I want this song to be eight minutes long,'" he told Caramanica of his shift in attitude. "My headspace now is, I love choruses."

Beauty behind the Madness was released in August 2015. The first single, "Often," was only a moderate success, peaking at number fifty-nine on the Billboard Hot 100 chart. Later singles, however, proved incredibly popular; both "The Hills" and "Can't Feel My Face," the latter cowritten and produced by Martin, hit number one. The album was ultimately nominated for two Grammy Awards, for album of the year and best urban contemporary album, while "Can't Feel My Face" and "Earned It" were nominated for five Grammy Awards, collectively.

The Weeknd acknowledges that *Beauty behind the Madness* is in some ways a departure from his earlier work, a fact that may upset some of his longtime fans. "The music I make on this album is definitely matured," he told Mistry. "It's a bit of a different state of mind even though it's the same person. You grow and you grow and you don't know what the next album is going to be about. You never know what I'm going to say." While some fans might consider his new, more commercial direction to be a negative, for the Weeknd it is all part of his evolution as an artist. "I owe it to myself to show the world how versatile I can be, because that's not all I can do," he explained to Mistry. "Why can't I try something that challenges me as an artist?"

PERSONAL LIFE

The Weeknd lives in Los Angeles, California, but returns from time to time to his native Toronto, where his mother lives in a house he purchased for her. He met his girlfriend, model and equestrian Bella Hadid, while searching for a model to appear on *Beauty behind the Madness*'s album artwork. She declined, but the two began dating shortly thereafter. Although those familiar with the Weeknd's music, which features mentions of liaisons with numerous women, might be surprised by his turn toward monogamy, he has noted in interviews that his relationship with Hadid reflects his own personal growth. "If I'd met someone two years ago, I probably would've f—— it up," he told Eells. "But I'm more—how do I say it?—clear-thinking now."

SUGGESTED READING

Caramanica, Jon. "Can the Weeknd Turn Himself into the Biggest Pop Star in the World?" *New York Times Magazine*. New York Times, 27 July 2015. Web. 11 Dec. 2015.

Eells, Josh. "Sex, Drugs and R&B: Inside the Weeknd's Dark Twisted Fantasy." *Rolling Stone*. Rolling Stone, 21 Oct. 2015. Web. 11 Dec. 2015.

Ehrlich, Brenna. "The Weeknd Reveals How He Got His Name . . . and Where the 'E' Went." *MTV News*. MTV, 13 Sept. 2013. Web. 11 Dec. 2015.

Helmore, Edward. "With Dark Tales of Sex and Drugs, Is the Weeknd the Next Face of R&B?" *Guardian*. Guardian News and Media, 1 Aug. 2015. Web. 11 Dec. 2015.

Jancelewicz, Chris. "He Has Seven Grammy Nominations, but Who Is the Weeknd?" *Global News*. Shaw Media, 8 Dec. 2015. Web. 11 Dec. 2015.

Mistry, Anupa. "The Dark Knight Returns: A Conversation with the Weeknd." *Pitchfork*. Pitchfork Media, 31 Aug. 2015. Web. 11 Dec. 2015.

Welch, Will. "The Weeknd Talks Kanye West, Music, Drugs, and Joe DiMaggio's Sperm." *GQ*. Condé Nast, 18 Aug. 2015. Web. 11 Dec. 2015.

SELECTED WORKS

House of Balloons, 2011; *Thursday*, 2011; *Echoes of Silence*, 2011; *Trilogy*, 2012; *Kiss Land*, 2013; *Beauty behind the Madness*, 2015

—Joy Crelin

Jessica Williams

Born: July 31, 1989
Occupation: Actor, comedian

Jessica Williams is an actor and comedian who is best known for her role as a correspondent on the satirical news program *The Daily Show*. Williams joined the show in 2012 when she was twenty-two, and since then she has become one of its most popular correspondents. When longtime host Jon Stewart retired in 2015, fans lobbied for Williams to replace him. At the age of

Stephen Lovekin / Stringer/ GettyImages

twenty-five, however, she felt she was not ready and did not want to be considered for the job.

Williams continues to appear on *The Daily Show* while pursuing various side projects such as acting in the independent film *People Places Things* (2015) in which she plays an aspiring artist who encourages her single mother to date her college professor, who is played by Jemaine Clement of the New Zealand comedy duo Flight of the Conchords.

Williams got her start in show business when she was fifteen years old in the role of Vida in the 2006 Nickelodeon comedy about a girls' soccer team called *Just for Kicks*. Although the show was created by veteran comedian Whoopi Goldberg, it only lasted one season. The opportunity and exposure, however, inspired Williams to pursue comedy—sketch comedy in particular—and cemented her future career path. She insists she has never had a back-up plan if comedy did not work out. "I still don't have it all figured out," she told Darla Murray for *Cosmopolitan* magazine (25 Feb. 2015), "but I don't want to be doing anything else."

EARLY LIFE AND EDUCATION

Williams was born in Los Angeles, California, on July 31, 1989. Her family is deeply religious, and both of her parents are conservative Christian ministers. When she was a young teenager, she participated in a "purity ceremony," in which participants pledge to delay having sex until they are married. The ceremony left Williams feeling as if her body was not her own, she has said, and prompted her to attend therapy sessions as an adult.

Growing up, Williams idolized her grandmother. The two often watched *Saturday Night Live* together, and early exposure to the comedy sketch show influenced Williams's ambitions. Williams recalled to Murray that she was in the first or second grade when she realized she was funny. She had a favorite day care instructor who started having children, and a jealous Williams made a witty comment after the woman lamented about being pregnant again. "I don't even remember thinking about it and I don't think I fully comprehended what I said, but I remember being like, *I'm funny*," she explained.

EARLY CAREER

After a young Williams approached her parents about becoming an actor and received their support, she got an agent and began going on auditions. When she was fifteen, she landed a lead role on a Nickelodeon show called *Just for Kicks*, which was produced by comedian Whoopi Goldberg. Unfortunately, the show was short-lived. Matthew Gilbert for the *Boston Globe* (7 Apr. 2006) called the show "solid but unoriginal." *Just for Kicks* was canceled after one season.

Williams was crushed when the show ended, but later, as she explained to Murray, she realized that it "allowed me to see what I was capable of doing." She tried out for her high school improv troupe and discovered her passion for comedy. In college at California State University, Long Beach, Williams joined the improv and sketch group Upright Citizens Brigade (UCB). She studied film in college, but her success with UCB encouraged her to start auditioning again. At an audition in 2011 for a Will Ferrell movie, she met casting director Allison Jones. Jones told Williams that although she would not be a good fit for the part in the movie, she might have more success auditioning for *The Daily Show*—the popular satirical news program, which first aired on *Comedy Central* in 1996 and was interested in hiring another correspondent to join its cast. Williams agreed to submit a tape, and a few days later she received a call from New York: Jon Stewart, the longtime host of the show, had seen her tape and wanted her to audition in person. Williams was shocked. At the time, she was studying political satire in class, and her professor showed clips from *The Daily Show* to demonstrate the concept.

THE DAILY SHOW

Before joining the cast of *The Daily Show* in January 2012, Williams worked a handful of minimum-wage jobs, first at a mall and then as a security guard. Based on previous job interviews, she was surprised when Stewart put her immediately at ease. "That was such an amazing thing because I'd been on so many . . . interviews for things like jobs at the mall where the guys interviewing me . . . knew they had something that I wanted," she told Murray. "With Jon, it was not that at all. I could just relax and be myself. As soon as we were done with that audition, I knew it was mine." Though she was confident in her abilities, the transitions from college to career, Los Angeles to New York, and from a relatively unknown child actor to a prominent role on popular daily television program were more difficult than she anticipated.

Williams was given a tour of *The Daily Show* offices on her first day of work, and the next day Stewart asked her to perform on the show that night. Although she felt confident and self-assured, she says that watching her early episodes makes her cringe.

At the time she was hired, Williams was the youngest correspondent in the show's history as well as its first black female correspondent. As she explained to Lauren Williams for *Mother Jones* (1 Jan. 2014), however, she does not think too deeply about what those achievements may mean. "I'm not walking around feeling black all the time," she said. "That would stress me out. . . . Some days I do feel that pressure. . . . Ultimately, when I deliver something, a lot of times it will be from a black woman's perspective, but other times it will be just from a satirical, goofy perspective."

ON-AIR SUCCESS

Williams joined the cast of *The Daily Show* in time for the lead-up to the 2012 US presidential election, and as the show's format is primarily political satire, the juggernaut of candidate gaffes, debates, and conventions afforded Williams a lot of on-air time, and she soon became a fan favorite. In 2015, *Rolling Stone* magazine ranked the twenty-five best correspondents in the show's history, and Williams was listed at number five. "The former Nickelodeon star has not only taken on touchy subjects like stop-and-frisk procedures and the depressing double standards behind Florida's Stand Your Ground law (complete with the show's greatest mic drop moment), she's done so with an attack that can go from faux-daffy to blistering in a heartbeat," Steve Ciabattoni and David Fear wrote for the magazine (4 Aug. 2015).

A segment that many feel is one of Williams's best was called "Frisky Business" and aired on August 13, 2013. In the segment, Williams takes on the New York City Police Department's highly contentious stop-and-frisk program. The program, which has been criticized for disproportionately targeting young black and Latino men, allows city police officers to stop and question anyone without cause and then pat them down for weapons or illegal contraband. In response to Mayor Michael Bloomberg's comment that more black and Latino men are stopped because they belong to racial groups more likely to commit crimes, Williams flipped the scenario on its head: She supported the program, she said, and she wanted it to extend to what she believed was one of New York City's most criminal neighborhoods—Wall Street. She suggested that police stop and frisk all men wearing tailored suits who have slicked-back hair and "always need sunscreen, if you know what I'm saying." When the host of that episode, John Oliver, said that such targeting would be a rights violation, Williams quipped, "I know this is uncomfortable, but if you don't want to be associated with white-collar crime, maybe you shouldn't dress that way." Williams later told Murray that the bit was a turning point for her on-screen persona. "I like to expose hypocrisies," she said. Williams credits the show with making her more political and familiarizing her with the plights of people across the country.

PERSONAL LIFE
Williams lives in Brooklyn, New York, and when she is not performing on *The Daily Show*, she can be found entertaining audiences at colleges and universities. In her act, which is part standup comedy and part personal confession, she talks about her religious upbringing, her career and hopes for the future, and incidents of racism she has experienced. One incident, which was reported by Abby Rinaldi for the *Oracle* (25 Oct. 2015), eventually brought Williams to tears after a New York City cab driver drove past her to instead pick up her white boyfriend. Williams got in the cab with her boyfriend, said "Surprise!" to the cab driver and attempted to get him to admit that he had intentionally driven past her. When Williams later asked to roll down her window and he refused and would not tell her why, she protested and the driver called the police. Williams was not in trouble with the police, but she did tell the driver that he had hurt her feelings. He responded by asking her to get out of his cab. Williams explained that she "felt so heavy for something [she] could not change."

OTHER PROJECTS
Williams has also appeared as a guest star on the HBO comedy *Girls* (2014). She and the show's creator, Lena Dunham, are reportedly working on a project together, though no details have been released. In 2015, Williams costarred in the film *People Places Things*, written and directed by James C. Strouse. The romantic comedy premiered at the Sundance Film Festival to less-than-stellar reviews. In a review for the *New York Times* (13 Aug. 2015) Stephen Holden called it a "winsome trifle of a comedy" that "can't make up its mind about where to go or how to get there."

SUGGESTED READING
Ciabattoni, Steve, and David Fear. "25 Best 'Daily Show' Correspondents." *Rolling Stone*. Rolling Stone, 4 Aug. 2015. Web. 17 Nov. 2015.

Gilbert, Matthew. "'Just for Kicks' Shows Girls How to Get Along." *Boston Globe*. Boston Globe Media Partners, 7 Apr. 2006. Web. 16 Nov. 2015.

Holden, Stephen. "Review: In 'People Places Things,' Jemaine Clement Navigates Life as a Newly Single Dad." *New York Times*. New York Times, 13 Aug. 2015. Web. 17 Nov. 2015.

Murray, Darla. "How Jessica Williams Became a Key Member of the 'Daily Show' Team." *Cosmopolitan*. Hearst Communications, 25 Feb. 2015. Web. 18 Nov. 2015.

Williams, Lauren. "The Daily Show's Jessica Williams on Race, Comedy, and Her Role in 'Girls.'" *Mother Jones*. Mother Jones and the Foundation for National Progress, 1 Jan. 2014. Web. 17 Nov. 2015.

SELECTED WORKS
Just for Kicks, 2006; *The Daily Show*, 2012– ; *Girls*, 2014; *People Places Things*, 2015

—Molly Hagan

Katherine Willis
Born: 1964
Occupation: Biologist

A professor at England's Oxford University and the founder of that institution's Biodiversity Institute, Katherine Willis has dedicated her career to researching how the world's flora has changed over time. Coinciding with much of that work has been a strong interest in making science, particularly biology, both accessible and understandable. In 2013 Willis joined the Royal Botanic Gardens, Kew, as its science director and soon embarked on a mission to reorganize the institution in the wake of painful budget cuts and to expand Kew's educational and public-outreach efforts. "I think one of the things that we have to be much more realistic about is what do we work on? What is it that Kew does that's unique?" she told Jim al-Khalili for the podcast *The Life Scientific* (10 Nov. 2015) of her challenging yet exciting opportunity. "Going forward, I think that Kew has huge potential, but also we need to be partnering more with industries, with universities, with other academic bodies to ensure that we do have funding."

EARLY LIFE AND EDUCATION

Katherine Jane Willis, widely known as Kathy, was born in England in 1964. She grew up in London and has a sister who also went into academia. Willis enjoyed studying topics such as biology and geography while in school, and when considering potential careers, she was told that she should become a farmer. She was not particularly interested in pursuing farm work. However, her growing fascination with plants led her to pursue studies in environmental science at the University of Southampton, a research university in southern England.

While at university, Willis was introduced to fieldwork, often traveling with her classmates and professors into the New Forest. A large area of forested and meadow land located near the University of Southampton, the New Forest is one of the few natural areas of its kind in the United Kingdom. With her classmates, Willis learned about a variety of different environmental research techniques. "We'd go out for a Wednesday afternoon, we'd go into the New Forest, and we'd be digging around, and we'd be measuring stream flow, and we'd be looking at microorganisms in the soil," she recalled to al-Khalili.

Of all the techniques she studied, she was most fascinated by the practice of studying sediment cores taken from the New Forest's peat bogs. Similar to the practice of taking core samples from glaciers or other large bodies of ice, the process of collecting sediment cores allows scientists to examine pollen and other materials that are trapped within the peat. Such studies can allow researchers to gain an understanding of the ways vegetation in a particular region has changed over time. Some of the samples Willis worked with during her time in Southampton included sediment that was as many as ten thousand years old; she would later have the opportunity to examine samples whose ages could be measured in millions of years. Intrigued by the possibilities presented by such research, Willis decided to pursue further education in plant sciences following her graduation from the University of Southampton in 1985. She went on to complete her doctoral research at the University of Cambridge, earning her PhD in 1989. Her thesis was titled *Late Quaternary Vegetational History of Epirus, Northwest Greece*.

EARLY CAREER

After completing her doctorate, Willis initially looked for work outside of academia, in part due to the urging of her parents. She took a position with Cambridge University Press, where she worked on acquiring scientific manuscripts. However, as a lover of field research, she was ill-suited for an office job and left after a year. She confessed to al-Khalili that she had been so desperate to find new work that she scoured an issue of *Nature* magazine for job listings and applied to nearly every one.

Beginning in 1990, Willis took on a series of research fellowships, beginning with the Trevelyan Research Fellowship at Selwyn College, Cambridge. She remained a fellow there for four years while also completing a postdoctoral fellowship sponsored by the Natural Environment Research Council (NERC). She later became a Royal Society University research fellow as well as a tuition fellow and director of studies for Selwyn College.

RESEARCH AND TEACHING

As a researcher, Willis has studied a wide range of plant-related topics, usually focusing on environmental change over time and the ways in which external factors affect plant life. Some of her most memorable research took place in the Galápagos Islands, where she investigated the effects that reintroducing giant tortoises to the islands would have on plant life. Once common on the islands, tortoises became scarce after years of being used as a food source by sailors. Although some tortoises remain in protected areas, their numbers are small, and some have championed their reintroduction to the Galápagos as part of an attempt to return the islands to their prediscovery conditions. Willis found, however, that reintroducing giant tortoises to the islands could have unforeseen effects on their ecosystems. On nearby islands, tortoises live in greater numbers and survive by grazing on the surrounding plants. Because of their lack of tortoises, the Galápagos Islands feature areas of plant life, such as bracken and peat bogs, that do not exist on the other islands. Reintroducing tortoises to the islands would thus result in the destruction of some of the islands' existing ecosystems. Like much of Willis's research, her studies into the Galápagos Islands underscore the ways in which different plants and animals are deeply interconnected.

After spending nearly a decade as a research fellow at several institutions, Willis joined the University of Oxford as a lecturer in 1999. She also served as a tutorial fellow for one of the colleges within the university and later took on the role of reader. She was named a full professor at Oxford in 2006. Over the following years, she took on a number of additional positions, including multiple professorial fellowships at Oxford, and in 2009 she was named a professor of biodiversity within the university's Martin School.

BIODIVERSITY INSTITUTE

In addition to teaching at Oxford, Willis also played a key role in the development of its biodiversity program, becoming the founding director of the school's Biodiversity Institute. The primary goal of the institute was to bring together researchers from a variety of specialties to examine the complex intersections between different areas of the natural world. "Within the university you'd got people in computing sciences, people in geography, people in zoology, people in plant sciences, and the role of the Biodiversity Institute was to pull that together so that you could start to address these really big questions," she explained to al-Khalili.

As a researcher and teacher, Willis has long been aware that environmental research and conservation efforts often come into conflict with elements of the natural world (as in the case of the Galápagos tortoises) and various human organizations (such as oil companies and nongovernmental organizations) working in environmentally vulnerable regions. She has noted in interviews that even well-meaning organizations do not always see eye-to-eye with researchers like herself. "One of the problems, I think, is . . . everyone's always working at a massive rush, and they're always driven by budgets," she told al-Khalili. "But quite often, very basic ecological concepts are used to manage landscapes, which might not be most appropriate for the landscape." It is Willis's hope that through further research and collaborative efforts, such as through the Biodiversity Institute, a better understanding of the interactions between plants and other factors as well as the changes that occur to plant life over time will become more widespread.

JOINING KEW

In 2013, Willis took a partial leave of absence from Oxford to accept the position of director of science at the Royal Botanic Gardens, Kew, a government-sponsored educational and research body located in London. The role of director of science was a new one, and Willis was thrilled to have the opportunity to fill the position. "Kew is just an absolutely extraordinary place," she told al-Khalili. "It's a global asset. The collections there are extraordinary. . . . To me that seemed like a really attractive place to go and work."

Willis was forced to tackle a serious challenge soon after taking the position when the institution faced serious budget cuts that threatened to severely curtail its work. To keep Kew running, Willis made a number of difficult decisions about which research to continue and how the organization should be structured, introducing a new science strategy that focused on a select few topics, including climate change, food security, and other areas of immediate concern to humankind. She also worked to expand Kew's educational offerings through initiatives such as a children's science festival and a plant-of-the-month program, in which visitors learn about a particular plant each month through guided tours of the institution's collections and gardens. Above all, Willis prioritized improving Kew's transparency and making more of its research and resources accessible to the public.

KEW PROJECTS

In reconfiguring Kew's science strategy, Willis has worked to emphasize research that draws from the institution's existing resources. "Kew, over 255 years, has built up this extraordinary collection, both living and dried, of plants," she told Rebecca Morelle for BBC News (23 Feb. 2015). "But we've never really looked at what can we do with these collections, what global questions, what critical challenges can be addressed using this incredible resource."

In addition, Willis has worked to call attention to Kew's research that would be of concern to the general public. One such project involves coffee and its survival in the Earth's increasingly warm climate. "Coffee, after oil, is the second most important global commodity," she explained to Sarah Knapton for the *Telegraph* (28 Feb. 2015). "There are 125 species in the world, but we just drink one. *Coffea arabica* is from Ethiopia, but it doesn't like it when it gets too hot, and it dies." There are numerous varieties of coffee that thrive in hotter climates and could potentially replace *Coffea arabica* in the event that global climate change results in the destruction of these plants. However, more research will need to occur before any other variety can become a true contender. "We need to know if they will grow, and importantly, what do they taste like?" Willis explained to Knapton.

PUBLICATIONS AND RECOGNITION

In addition to her teaching and research work and her leadership at Kew, Willis has published numerous papers on topics such as biodiversity and environmental change. She is the coauthor of the books *The Evolution of Plants* (2002) and *Plants: From Roots to Riches* (2014). Willis has also been a member of a number of committees and panels and in 2015 was awarded the prestigious Michael Faraday Prize by the Royal Society of London. The prize honors scientists for their achievements in communicating scientific ideas to a general audience.

SUGGESTED READING

Knapton, Sarah. "Kew Quest to Prevent Coffee Dying Out." *Telegraph*. Telegraph News and Media, 28 Feb. 2015. Web. 10 June 2016.

Martin, Jane. "Professor Katherine Willis (M1986) Natural Sciences Awarded the 2015 Michael Faraday Prize." *Corpus Christi College*. Corpus Christi College Cambridge, 1 Sept. 2015. Web. 10 June 2016.

Morelle, Rebecca. "Kew Gardens Unveils Science Strategy." *BBC News*. BBC, 23 Feb. 2015. Web. 10 June 2016.

"Professor Kathy Willis, Director of Science." *Kew*. Royal Botanic Gardens, Kew, n. d. Web. 10 June 2016.

Willis, Katherine. "Kathy Willis." *Department of Zoology*. U of Oxford, n. d. Web. 10 June 2016.

Willis, Katherine. "Kathy Willis." Interview with Jim al-Khalili. *The Life Scientific*. BBC, 10 Nov. 2015. Web. 10 June 2016.

—*Joy Crelin*

G. Willow Wilson

Born: August 31, 1982
Occupation: Writer

In terms of overall impact, writer G. Willow Wilson is perhaps one of the most significant figures working in comics. The author of the critically acclaimed graphic novel *Cairo* (2007), Wilson has spent nearly a decade creating comics and graphic novels, as well as a prose novel and a memoir, that consider issues of religion, politics, and the intersections of folklore and modern life. An American who spent several years living and working in Egypt, Wilson has devoted particular attention to creating layered, true-to-life portrayals of a diverse array of Muslim characters, from the titular hacktivist of her novel *Alif the Unseen* (2012) to the wildly popular Pakistani American superhero Kamala Khan, who assumed the mantle of Ms. Marvel with the launch of the comic of the same name in 2014.

Perhaps one of the most important side effects of the popularity of Wilson's works has been the conversations about diversity—be it religious, ethnic, or gender diversity—that they have sparked. "I feel very strongly about these things and about the need to create space in which it is okay to talk about them," she told interviewer Arun Rath for National Public Radio's (NPR) *All Things Considered* (23 Feb. 2015). "Because by the time my own children are old enough to begin to start grappling with these things, I would love for there to be a canon of literature there that they can turn to see that they are not alone. That there are people that came before, and not only survived, but thrived, and hopefully went on to make the world a better place."

EARLY LIFE AND EDUCATION

Gwendolyn Willow Wilson was born in Longbranch, New Jersey, on August 31, 1982, the first of two daughters. She and her family moved to Colorado when she was young, and she grew up primarily in the city of Boulder. An avid reader as a child, particularly of fantasy novels, Wilson also developed an early interest in comics. "I at some point was given this ten-page public service announcement (PSA) anti-smoking comic in health class," she explained to Abraham Riesman for *Vulture* (20 Mar. 2014). "Y'know, someone thinking, 'This is how to reach kids!' It was incredibly dumb. . . . It took me years to realize how ironic it is to have chain-smoking [*X-Men* character] Wolverine in an anti-smoking comic." Yet Wilson was still struck by the ability of such superheroes to do good. "What stuck with me was these amazing characters with these costumes who could swoop in and morally adjust the world," she told Riesman. In addition to superhero comics, she became a fan of the innovative comics being published by DC Comics imprint Vertigo at the time, such as Neil Gaiman's *Sandman* series (1989–96).

Wilson settled on her preferred career path early in life. "Writing was the only thing I wanted to do, once I figured out it was something that you *could* do," she told *Locus Online* (16 Oct. 2013). However, she found that many of those around her were skeptical of that path. "When you're a certain age people say, 'Oh, you want to be a creative writer, that's fantastic. Why don't you take a creative writing class?'" she told *Locus*. "And then you go to high school, and then college, and you still want to write, and they're like, 'We didn't actually *mean* it. We thought you were going to be a doctor or a lawyer.'" Wilson's parents encouraged her pursuits, though she added that they did "gently suggest that it might be good to have a broad range of possibilities."

After graduating from Boulder High School in 1999, at the age of sixteen, Wilson enrolled in Boston University (BU) to study history. Having developed an interest in the Middle East, she focused on Middle Eastern history and the Arabic language. She also launched her professional writing career shortly after starting college by becoming a freelance music critic for the *Weekly Dig*, a Boston-based alternative newspaper. Wilson earned her bachelor's degree from BU's College of Arts and Sciences in 2003.

CAIRO

After graduating from BU, Wilson traveled to Cairo, Egypt, where she obtained a job teaching English. Her trip served dual purposes: first, it enabled her to work while exploring a new place, a common desire among new college graduates; and second, living in Egypt allowed her to explore life as a Muslim, having privately converted to Islam while in college. After teaching English for a semester, Wilson built on her previous writing experience to begin a career as a freelance journalist, publishing articles in American newspapers such as the *New York Times* and Egyptian publications such as *Cairo Magazine*.

Soon after arriving in Cairo, Wilson began to develop the idea for her first full-length project, one that took inspiration from her experiences in the city as well as from Middle Eastern folklore. The project ultimately took the form of a graphic novel titled *Cairo*, published in 2007 by Vertigo. Illustrated by M. K. Perker, with whom Wilson would later collaborate on the series *Air* (2008–10), *Cairo* tells the stories of several very different characters whose lives become intertwined in a series of events involving both crime and magic. Wilson's debut graphic novel won critical acclaim and was named one of the best graphic novels of the year by several organizations, including the American Library Association.

In addition to inspiring *Cairo*, Wilson's experiences in Egypt likewise became the foundation for a memoir, *The Butterfly Mosque*, published in 2010. Wilson was initially resistant to the idea of writing a memoir, feeling that she had not yet achieved the age and level of experience she considered necessary for such a work. However, the long e-mails she sent to friends and relatives while in Egypt had captured their attention, and they urged her to turn them into a book. Though initially conceived as more of a travelogue, *The Butterfly Mosque* ultimately became primarily about Wilson's exploration of Islam, as well as the development of her relationship with her husband, Omar, whom she met while teaching in Egypt.

BUILDING A CAREER

Following the success of *Cairo*, Wilson built a productive career in comics, writing lengthy series as well as individual issues for both DC Comics and its Vertigo imprint. Her next major project was *Air*, illustrated by Perker and published by Vertigo as a monthly series between 2008 and 2010. Later collected in four trade paperbacks, *Air* follows a flight attendant whose life takes a series of increasingly strange turns after she becomes embroiled in a terrorist plot. Though relatively well received by critics, the series was canceled in 2010 because of low sales. Wilson also wrote the 2008 limited series *Vixen: Return of the Lion*, about the established DC Comics superhero Vixen. She began working for Marvel Comics in 2010, contributing to the first issue of the limited-run anthology series *Girl Comics*, and went on to write a four-issue follow-up to Marvel's title *Mystic* (2000–), published in 2011.

In addition to her comics work, Wilson published her debut prose novel, *Alif the Unseen*, in 2012. Set in a fictional Middle Eastern city, the novel merges elements of Middle Eastern folklore, including the legendary beings known as jinn, with adventures of a hacker who is devoted to bypassing government censorship. In many ways the novel, with its emphasis on hacker activism, was a particularly timely one; its publication in 2012 fell during a period in which widespread protests in the Middle East and North Africa, conducted in part through online activity, led to regime changes in several countries, including Egypt. Although Wilson had moved to the United States with her husband several years before, she remained acutely aware of the political and cultural upheaval in Egypt and the surrounding region, and this awareness shines through in her novel. *Alif the Unseen* received positive reviews from critics and readers alike and was nominated for a number of awards, including the World Fantasy Award for best novel, which it won in 2013.

MS. MARVEL

Wilson's next major comics project began when she was approached by two editors from Marvel Comics, Sana Amanat and Stephen Wacker, who wanted to create a young, female, Muslim superhero to headline the publisher's *Ms. Marvel* series. As Wilson had extensive experience in comics as well as a personal connection to the subject matter, she was a natural choice to write the series. Wilson worked closely with Amanat, who is also Muslim, to create the character of Kamala Khan, a sixteen-year-old Pakistani American girl from New Jersey who must balance her school and family life with her newly manifested superpowers. One of several characters to go by the name Ms. Marvel, Khan is a fan of the original Ms. Marvel, Carol Danvers, who took on the moniker of Captain Marvel in a new ongoing series launched in 2012. Following its debut in 2014, *Ms. Marvel* became one of Marvel's most popular series, and the collected editions of the comics became *New York Times* best sellers. The first volume of the series won the 2015 Hugo Award for best graphic story.

To Wilson, the popularity of *Ms. Marvel* and Kamala Khan was indicative of an overall shift toward greater diversity in comics, which had long been dominated by white male characters, creators, and fans. "More and more women and minorities are starting to read comics and become comic book fans," she told Maria Werdine Norris for *LSE Human Rights* (3 Feb. 2015), a blog run by students of the London School of Economics and Political Science. "Comic book conventions here in the United States are now a 50/50 split between men and women in attendance. It used to be overwhelmingly male, now it's a more even mixture. With that has come a demand for different stories and a dissatisfaction with the idea that female superheroes are just there to be arm candy for guys, or to provide motivation for the male characters and not to stand in their own right with their own stories." *Ms. Marvel* also received significant praise for its nuanced depictions of Muslim characters, each of whom has a different relationship with his or her religious and cultural background and represents one of a multitude of viewpoints. "When it comes down to it, this is why representation matters," Wilson told Norris. "You want people who are in a position to tell authentic stories."

OTHER WORK

In addition to her best-known work, Wilson has worked on numerous other comic book titles, including the Marvel series *X-Men* and *Women of Marvel*, as well as the "Grounded" story arc of the DC Comics series *Superman*, which ran from 2010 to 2011. In 2015 she teamed up with fellow writer Marguerite Bennett to create *A-Force*, a new series for Marvel Comics about an alternate-universe team of female superheroes, including She-Hulk, Captain Marvel, and the new character Singularity. Wilson remained with the project for the first several issues.

PERSONAL LIFE

Wilson's faith plays a significant role in much of her work, particularly in her desire to create nuanced portrayals of Muslim characters. Raised in an atheist household, she studied a number of religions as a young woman and was ultimately drawn to Islam, to which she converted while in her early twenties. For Wilson, one of the most compelling aspects of the religion was its largely personal nature. "What . . . appealed to me is that to become a Muslim is sort of a deal between you and God," she explained to Lisa Wangsness for the *Boston Globe* (20 June 2010). "You don't need to be witnessed [by] any particular priest; there's no ceremony you have to go through; there is no test."

Wilson met her husband, Omar, while living in Cairo. The couple later settled in Seattle, Washington, where they live with their two children.

SUGGESTED READING

Wilson, G. Willow. "About the Author: Meet G. Willow Wilson." Interview by Niall Alexander. *Speculative Scotsman*. Blogger, 4 Sept. 2012. Web. 11 Mar. 2016.

Wilson, G. Willow. "Beneath the Veil." Interview by Lisa Wangsness. *Boston.com*. Boston Globe Media Partners, 20 June 2010. Web. 11 Mar. 2016.

Wilson, G. Willow. "Comics and Human Rights: An Interview with G. Willow Wilson." Interview by Maria Werdine Norris. *LSE Human Rights*. London School of Economics and Political Science, 3 Feb. 2015. Web. 11 Mar. 2016.

Wilson, G. Willow. "G. Willow Wilson: Landscape of the Imagination." *Locus Online*. Locus, 16 Oct. 2013. Web. 11 Mar. 2016.

Wilson, G. Willow. "Islam Sci-Fi Interview of G. Willow Wilson (Part I)." Interview by Rebecca Hankins. *Islam and Science Fiction*. Islam and Science Fiction, 25 Mar. 2015. Web. 11 Mar. 2016.

Wilson, G. Willow. "Meet G. Willow Wilson, the Muslim Woman Revolutionizing Superhero Comics." Interview by Abraham Riesman. *Vulture*. New York Media, 20 Mar. 2014. Web. 11 Mar. 2016.

Wilson, G. Willow. "The Woman behind Marvel's Newest Team of Heroines." Interview by Arun Rath. *NPR Books*. NPR, 23 Feb. 2015. Web. 11 Mar. 2016.

SELECTED WORKS

Cairo, 2007; *Vixen: Return of the Lion*, 2008–9; *Air*, 2008–10; *The Butterfly Mosque*, 2010; *Mystic*, 2011; *Alif the Unseen*, 2012; *Ms. Marvel*, 2014–; *A-Force*, 2015–16

—*Joy Crelin*

Robin Wright

Born: April 8, 1966
Occupation: Actor

When the first season of the political thriller *House of Cards* premiered on Netflix in the winter of 2013, fans and critics alike were struck

Georges Biard/CC BY-SA 3.0/Wikimedia Commons

by actor Robin Wright's portrayal of icy, driven Claire Underwood, a powerful figure in the realm of Washington, DC, nonprofits and a key player in husband Francis Underwood's rise to political power. The show's popularity thrust Wright into the spotlight, and she was nominated for numerous awards for her work.

The role of Claire was a breakout role that any new actor would envy, but Wright was no newcomer—far from it. A professional actor for nearly thirty years at the time of the premiere of *House of Cards*, Wright first entered the public consciousness through popular films such as *The Princess Bride* (1987) and *Forrest Gump* (1994), but she put her career largely on hold during the 1990s and 2000s as she raised a family and struggled with being typecast as poorly developed wife and mother characters. With *House of Cards*, however, Wright made a triumphant return to the forefront. "You hear people say how they have 'arrived,' but it was just always there, waiting to come out. For me, it just took a long time," she told Sam Kashner for *Vanity Fair* (31 Mar. 2015). "I'm finally a person. I think I'm finally ready."

EARLY LIFE AND EDUCATION
Robin Wright was born in Dallas, Texas, on April 8, 1966, the second child born to Freddie and Gayle Wright. Her father worked in pharmaceutical sales, while her mother would eventually become one of the first door-to-door salespeople for the newly formed Mary Kay cosmetics company. Her parents divorced when she was two years old, and Wright and her older brother, Richard, lived with their mother, who remarried

after several years. The family lived in Los Angeles, California, and later moved to the La Jolla neighborhood of San Diego.

As a child and teen, Wright was drawn to performing. She and her brother gave humorous performances for their mother, and they were both passionate about dance; Richard studied ballet, whereas Wright studied modern jazz and hoped one day to dance in a Broadway production. Despite her love of performing, however, Wright was not initially interested in acting, avoiding community theater and other venues in which actors often get their start. "I think I always viewed acting as a kind of exhibitionism if you were going to show your heart in that way," she explained to veteran filmmaker Francis Ford Coppola for *Interview* magazine (28 Apr. 2009). "And it was unfathomable to me. How could you do that? How could you be that vulnerable with strangers? And yet, what I think it was is that acting seemed verbal, and I'm a very physical, tactile person. I always loved to dance and move."

Wright attended William Howard Taft High School in Los Angeles and, after her family's move, completed her education at La Jolla High School. She did not enjoy school, as she struggled with dyslexia. Although she considers herself to have been unpopular as a teenager, Wright was nevertheless crowned homecoming queen one year. "I actually thought it was going to be like the scene in *Carrie*, with the pig's blood," she recalled to Coppola, referring to the memorable prom scene in the 1976 horror film. "That's what it felt like—like I was being set up."

EARLY CAREER
As a teenager Wright found work as a model, traveling to Europe and Asia and also appearing in commercials for products such as Doritos. After graduating from high school, she opted to forgo college—a decision she has said she regrets—and instead pursue a career in film and television. She had a difficult time breaking into the field at first, going on countless auditions but obtaining little work.

Needing money, she found a job working on a tour boat. However, she never actually left land, having learned prior to her first trip that she had secured the role of Kelly Capwell in the new soap opera *Santa Barbara*, a role for which she would earn a Daytime Emmy nomination three years in a row. Following the dramatic lives of wealthy families in the titular California city, *Santa Barbara* aired on NBC from July 1984 until January 1993. Wright left the show in 1988, and the character of Kelly was recast several times after her departure.

BREAKOUT ROLE

Wright's role in *Santa Barbara* proved life-changing, bringing her the opportunities her early auditions had not. She made her first film appearance in the 1986 film *Hollywood Vice Squad*, but it was her next feature-film part that proved to be her breakout role. Wright starred as Buttercup in *The Princess Bride*, a 1987 film directed by Rob Reiner and based on the 1973 William Goldman novel of the same name. The film, which blends comedy and romance with fantasy adventure, tells the story of the epic romance between Buttercup, the titular princess bride, and the farm boy Westley (Cary Elwes) and the adventures that follow when Buttercup is betrothed to the scheming Prince Humperdinck (Chris Sarandon). Though not particularly successful at the box office, the film became a cult classic and introduced Wright to a wider audience. For Wright, working on *The Princess Bride* proved to be a formative experience, as she had the opportunity to work alongside established actors such as Mandy Patinkin, Wallace Shawn, and Christopher Guest, as well as the wrestler André the Giant. She "fully immersed [herself] in the role," as she told Mary Kaye Schilling for *Town & Country* (June 2014), and has admitted that she developed a crush on Elwes, her on-screen romantic partner, while filming. "I did not act," she explained to Schilling. "It was mostly telling myself, 'Don't be an idiot in front of Mandy Patinkin and Christopher Guest.'"

Over the following years, Wright played major roles in a number of films, including the 1990 crime drama *State of Grace*, which starred Wright's future husband Sean Penn. Perhaps her most significant role during the early 1990s, however, was that of Jenny Curran, the lifelong love of the 1994 film *Forrest Gump*'s titular protagonist. Wright was nominated for the Screen Actors Guild (SAG) and Golden Globe Awards for best supporting actress for her performance as Jenny.

BEING TYPECAST

Following the birth of her two children and her 1996 marriage to Penn, Wright continued to work but put her career largely on the back burner, taking mainly supporting roles. She told journalists that her decision to take a step back from acting was based on an agreement she made with Penn. "We agreed as parents that we'd not work at the same time, so that one of us was always with the kids," she explained to Kashner. "He was making more money than I was at the time, so it was a simple decision: 'You go work—I'll stay with the kids.'" The family settled in northern California, away from the crowds and stress of Los Angeles. Wanting to share a last name with her children, Wright changed her name to Robin Wright Penn both legally and

professionally, and she is credited as such in her films from that period, which include *She's So Lovely* (1997), *Unbreakable* (2000), *White Oleander* (2002), and *The Private Lives of Pippa Lee* (2009).

Although she worked steadily throughout the late 1990s and the first decade of the twenty-first century, usually appearing in one or two films or other projects per year, Wright was dissatisfied with the types of roles she was typically offered. "I always look for variety. I always want to run the gamut. Play a character who's completely far-out and fabulous, and then the very understanding wife who's got her husband f—— around on her," she told actor Rita Wilson in an interview for *Harper's Bazaar* (18 Mar. 2014). "But the problem is, I was typecast for most of my career and still am today. I always get offered the role of wounded, soulful, understanding mother and wife."

HOUSE OF CARDS

In 2011, in addition to an appearance in the sports drama *Moneyball* alongside Brad Pitt, Jonah Hill, Chris Pratt, and Philip Seymour Hoffman, Wright played a supporting role in the thriller *The Girl with the Dragon Tattoo*, based on the best-selling novel by Swedish writer Stieg Larsson and directed by award-winning filmmaker David Fincher. Fincher, who was in the process of developing the television series *House of Cards* for the streaming-video service Netflix, was impressed by Wright's work during the shooting of the film, which began in 2010, and in the summer of 2011 cast her in one of the show's lead roles. An American adaptation of the 1990 British television miniseries of the same name, in turn based on the novel by Michael Dobbs, *House of Cards* is a political thriller focusing on politician Francis Underwood (Kevin Spacey) and the lengths to which he will go to amass political power. Wright plays Claire Underwood, Francis's wife and frequent collaborator in his political machinations.

Wright was initially reluctant to join the cast of *House of Cards*, in part because she preferred the medium of film. "I started out doing daytime TV, and I didn't want to go back there," she told Lucy Broadbent for the *Telegraph* (9 Feb. 2014). "I also don't watch much TV." However, *House of Cards* and other so-called prestige shows are widely considered to have elevated the medium to the point that television work has become attractive to many actors who otherwise avoided it. "Television is not what it used to be," Wright admitted to Broadbent. "The material, most of the time, is better than a lot of film."

In addition to her concerns about the medium, Wright worried that taking the role of Claire, the wife of the show's protagonist, would further perpetuate the typecasting that had shaped much of her career. However, she was ultimately won over by the part's potential, and the show's writers reworked the character with Wright's input. Critical response to the character following the show's premiere on Netflix in February 2013 was largely positive, with reviewers praising Wright's performance as the icy, pragmatic Claire. Although some viewers saw the character as merely cruel, Wright's take on Claire is more nuanced. "I don't see Claire as cruel," she told Broadbent. "I see her as calculating. She's a businesswoman. If you're the head of a business, there's a protocol that people have to follow. If you get in her way, or you mess up, or you're late for work, you're out. Sorry."

Wright was nominated for numerous awards for her performance, including the Emmy Award for outstanding lead actress in a drama series. She also directed several episodes of the show, beginning with the tenth episode of the second season. Shortly before the second season began streaming on Netflix, in January 2014, she walked on stage to accept the Golden Globe Award for best performance by an actress in a television series—drama, marking Netflix's first Golden Globe win.

PERSONAL LIFE

Wright married *Santa Barbara* costar Dane Witherspoon in 1986; they divorced two years later. In 1996 she married actor Sean Penn, whom she had met on the set of 1990's *State of Grace* and with whom she had two children, Dylan and Hopper. The couple separated and reconciled on several occasions but ultimately divorced in 2010. Wright announced her engagement to actor Ben Foster in 2014 and again in 2015, but the pair later ended their engagement both times.

A longtime resident of northern California, Wright has spent much of her time on the East Coast of the United States since being cast in *House of Cards*. She is a committed philanthropist and is involved in a variety of charities, including the Enough Project, which seeks to combat crimes against humanity.

SUGGESTED READING

Broadbent, Lucy. "Robin Wright on *House of Cards*, Botox and Getting Married Again." *Telegraph*. Telegraph Media Group, 9 Feb. 2014. Web. 11 Jan. 2016.

Carr, David. "This Time, Ready to Take Charge." *New York Times*. New York Times, 5 Feb. 2014. Web. 11 Jan. 2016.

Kashner, Sam. "Robin Wright on Her Role as Claire Underwood and Her Marriage to Sean Penn." *Vanity Fair*. Condé Nast, 31 Mar. 2015. Web. 11 Jan. 2016.

Schilling, Mary Kaye. "Our June/July Cover Star: Robin Wright." *Town & Country*. Hearst Communications, June 2014. Web. 11 Jan. 2016.

Wright, Robin. "The Blonde Having More Fun." Interview by Rita Wilson. *Harper's Bazaar*. Hearst Communications, 18 Mar. 2014. Web. 11 Jan. 2016.

Wright, Robin. "Robin Wright Penn." Interview by Francis Ford Coppola. *Interview*. Interview, 28 Apr. 2009. Web. 11 Jan. 2016.

SELECTED WORKS

Santa Barbara, 1984–88; *The Princess Bride*, 1987; *Forrest Gump*, 1994; *She's So Lovely*, 1997; *Unbreakable*, 2000; *White Oleander*, 2002; *The Private Lives of Pippa Lee*, 2009; *Moneyball*, 2011; *The Girl with the Dragon Tattoo*, 2011; *House of Cards*, 2013–

—Joy Crelin

Hanya Yanagihara

Born: 1975
Occupation: Author, editor

Hanya Yanagihara's second novel *A Little Life* (2015) was one of the most widely read and celebrated books of 2015, and was nominated that year for two prestigious literary prizes, the Man Booker Prize and the National Book Award for fiction. The 700-plus-page tome follows the lives of four men who attend college together in Massachusetts and then move to New York City where they achieve varying levels of success. *A Little Life* explores themes of male friendship as well as the lasting effects of trauma. It was celebrated for its rich portrayal of the emotional lives of gay men, and for its harrowing treatment of childhood sexual abuse. *A Little Life*, John Powers wrote for National Public Radio (*NPR*) (20 Mar. 2015), "is long, page-turny, deeply moving, sometimes excessive, but always packed with the weight of a genuine *experience*. As I was reading, I literally dreamed about it every night." Yanagihara's debut novel, *The People in the Trees*, was based on the true story of medical researcher Dr. D. Carleton Gajdusek and published to critical praise in 2013. She has edited for *Condé Nast Traveler* and *T Magazine*, a fashion and lifestyle magazine owned by the *New York Times*.

EARLY LIFE AND EDITING CAREER

Yanagihara was born in Los Angeles in 1975, though her family is from Hawaii. She is a fourth-generation Hawaiian, and she is part of the first generation of her family to never have worked in the fields there. Yanagihara grew up in a number of cities including Honolulu, Hawaii; Baltimore, Maryland; Irvine, California; and Tyler, Texas.

David Levenson/Getty Images

The family moved because of her father's job—he worked as a researcher and as a hematologist and oncologist—and because of his restlessness. When Yanagihara was ten or eleven and the family was living in Texas, she expressed an interest in drawing and art. Her father enthusiastically introduced her to a pathologist who took her to the morgue so that she could draw the cadavers. (For many years afterward, her parents hoped she would become a cartoonist.) Yanagihara attended Punahou High School in Honolulu and graduated from Smith College in Northampton, Massachusetts, in 1995.

After graduation, Yanagihara moved to New York City where she got a job as a sales assistant at Ballantine Books. After that, she worked as a publicist for several publishing companies before taking a job with a now-defunct media magazine called *Brill's Content* in 1999. Later, she took a job as editor-at-large with *Condé Nast Traveler*. Yanagihara described the kind of writing she did for the luxury travel magazine as service writing, which emphasizes efficiency over style, though most of her career there was spent as an editor. Yanagihara does not have an MFA degree in writing. She attributes some of her success to her lack of formal training. "Not knowing what you're not supposed to do is very freeing," she told Alexander Nazaryan for *Newsweek* (19 Mar. 2015).

THE PEOPLE IN THE TREES (2013)

Yanagihara began writing her first novel, *The People in the Trees*, in 1996 when she was twenty-one-years-old and working as an assistant at Vintage Books. She did not tell anyone

she was writing a novel until a decade later, in 2007, and then told only her best friend, Jared Hohlt, an editor at *New York Magazine*. "I think at first I didn't tell anyone I was writing something because I found so tedious the people who did," she told her editor, Gerry Howard, in a conversation published by *Slate* (5 Mar. 2015). She recalled specifically a colleague who used to print pages of his manuscript at work, "always, it seemed, when we were in the midst of closing the issue and needed the printer the most," she said. But as time passed, her silence became a way to live more fully in the world of the novel, free from outside input. After she told Hohlt her secret however, she gave him each chapter as she finished writing it. She worked closely with him, writing and rewriting, for the next several years.

The People in the Trees, which was published by Doubleday in 2013, purports to be the memoir of Dr. Norton Perina, a Nobel Prize-winning scientist. (Perina is based on Dr. D. Carleton Gajdusek, a medical researcher, who won the Nobel Prize and was convicted as a sexual predator some twenty years later.) Perina, looking back on his life from prison, recalls his early days at Harvard Medical School, but focuses on his years researching the inhabitants the fictional island Ivu'ivu, located in Micronesia. The novel's title is a reference to Perina's own book, *The People in the Trees: The Lost Tribe of Ivu'ivu*. This lost tribe—whom Perina calls "the dreamers"—live in the forest. Certain members of the tribe live for hundreds of years. Their longevity comes from eating the meat of turtles native to the island, though only members of the tribe over sixty are allowed to partake. There's one catch, however. Although elderly dreamers remain physically vigorous, their brains deteriorate over time. Perina, a chilling and prickly character, becomes obsessed by the possibility of such long-lasting life. He steals some of the turtle meat and a few young members of the tribe, taking them back to the United States for study. Perina is rewarded for these studies, but later, like Gajdusek, is accused and subsequently convicted of sexually abusing one of his Ivu'ivu charges. The manuscript is edited by Perina's protégé, Dr. Ronald Kubodera, who adds an introduction, footnotes, and other supplementary information to Perina's narrative. *The People in the Trees*, which appeared on several best books of the year lists, "examines issues of moral relativism, Western hubris, colonization and ecological disruption in the name of science as it charts the disappearance of the wondrous flora and fauna and the grievous harm done to the indigenous people," Carmela Ciuraru wrote for the *New York Times* (27 Sept. 2013). Ciuraru described the novel as "provocative and bleak," adding: "It is exhaustingly inventive and almost defiant in its refusal to offer redemption or solace—but that is arguably one of its virtues."

A LITTLE LIFE (2015)

Yanagihara spent years writing *The People in the Trees*, but wrote her second novel, *A Little Life* (2015), in a mere eighteen months—though the seed of the book was planted years before that. When Yanagihara was twenty-six, she began collecting photographs. This collection served, Yanagihara wrote for *Vulture* (28 Apr. 2015), as "a sort of tonal sound check," visually guiding her narrative and illustrating the world of her characters. Pieces included everything from a Diane Arbus photograph ("The Backwards Man in His Hotel Room," 1961) to a piece of ombré cloth because she wanted her story to become deeper and darker as the book went on. While writing *A Little Life*, Yanagihara adopted a strict schedule of writing three hours on working days, and six hours on days off. "Physically it was a hard book to write," she told James Kidd for the *National* (16 July 2015), a newspaper in the United Arab Emirates. "I would work all day and write at night. It was about staying up and typing, typing, typing. It was just not sustainable. I don't think I could do it again." Again, Hohlt was her first reader, though he is more intimately attached to the subject-matter of *A Little Life* than that of Yanagihara's first novel. Much of the book grew out of Yanagihara's intense, weekly conversations with Hohlt, and its narrative core—the friendship, over three decades, among four male friends—was inspired by Hohlt's relationship to his college friends. Yanagihara argues that men have smaller emotional vocabularies than women do—meaning that, while men feel a full range of human emotions, societal strictures give them fewer ways to express those emotions. In that context, she wanted to write a novel exploring male friendship, treating adult friendship with a level of seriousness most writers reserve for marriage or romantic relationships.

The book follows the after-college lives and careers of Willem, a Midwestern waiter and aspiring actor; Malcolm, a wealthy, biracial architect; Jean-Baptiste (JB), a Haitian artist; and Jude, a lawyer with a traumatic past. The narrative takes place in present times but also, curiously, out of time—reviewer Jon Michaud of the *New Yorker* (28 Apr. 2015) noted the peculiar lack of historical context in the form of events or names. This absence, Yanagihara has said in several interviews, is intentional. "I wanted it to reach a level of truth by playing with the conventions of a fairy tale, and then veering those conventions off path," Yanagihara told Howard. "I wanted the experience of reading it to feel immersive by being slightly otherworldly, to not give the reader many contextual tethers to steady them." The men succeed in their various fields, but soon the book shifts focus, training its lens more directly on Jude. The reader discovers that Jude, an orphan, was raised in a monastery where he was sexually abused. "And with Jude at its center, *A Little Life* becomes a surprisingly subversive novel—one that uses the middle-class trappings of naturalistic fiction to deliver an unsettling meditation on sexual abuse, suffering, and the difficulties of recovery." Michaud wrote. "And having upset our expectations once, Yanagihara does it again, by refusing us the consolations we have come to expect from stories that take such a dark turn."

A Little Life was widely praised, but its few critics found fault in Yanagihara's decision to depict Jude's abuse as brutally as she does. Gerry Howard, Yanagihara's editor, raised similar concerns when he first read her manuscript, but the author eventually quelled them. Howard and Yanagihara also disagreed on the book's cover—another battle that Yanagihara eventually won. The cover features a photograph by the late Peter Hujar. Part of his Orgiastic Man series, it depicts a man at the height of orgasm. Yanagihara told Claiborne Smith for *Kirkus* (16 Nov. 2015), "It's a really striking image, and I think the tone of it is just right." The novel was short-listed for the Man Booker Prize, and was a finalist for the National Book Award for fiction in 2015.

PERSONAL LIFE

In June 2015, several months after the publication of *A Little Life*, Yanagihara became the deputy editor at *T Magazine* in 2015. She is single and plans to abstain from marriage. She lives in the Soho neighborhood of New York City.

SUGGESTED READING

Ciuraru, Carmela. "Bitter Fruit." Rev. of *The People in the Trees* by Hanya Yanagihara. *New York Times*. New York Times, 27 Sept. 2013. Web. 10 Dec. 2015.

Kidd, James. "The Long Read: Rising Literary Star Hanya Yanagihara's *A Little Life* Is Sure to Be a Prize-Winner." *National*. Abu Dhabi Media, 16 July 2015. Web. 10 Dec. 2015.

Michaud, Jon. "The Subversive Brilliance of *A Little Life*." Rev. of *A Little Life* by Hanya Yanagihara. *New Yorker*. Condé Nast, 28 Apr. 2015. Web. 10 Dec. 2015.

Nazaryan, Alexander. "Author Hanya Yanagihara's Not-So-Little-Life." *Newsweek*. Newsweek, 19 Mar. 2015. Web. 10 Dec. 2015.

Powers, John. "*A Little Life*: An Unforgettable Novel about the Grace of Friendship." Rev. of *A Little Life* by Hanya Yanagihara. *NPR*. NPR, 20 Mar. 2015. Web. 10 Dec. 2015.

Yanagihara, Hanya. "How I Wrote My Novel: Hanya Yanagihara's *A Little Life*." *Vulture*. New York Media, 28 Apr. 2015. Web. 10 Dec. 2015.

Yanagihara, Hanya, and Gerry Howard. "The *Slate Book Review* Author-Editor Conversation." *Slate*. Slate, 5 Mar. 2015. Web. 10 Dec. 2015.

—*Molly Hagan*

OBITUARIES

Bhumibol Adulyadej

(Rama IX, King of Thailand)
Born: Cambridge, Massachusetts; December 5, 1927
Died: Bangkok, Thailand; October 13, 2016
Occupation: King of Thailand

Somdet Phra Yu Hua Bhumibol Adulyadej was the ninth sovereign of the Chakri dynasty. He was the longest reigning monarch in the world at the time of his death, a source of stability in an otherwise unstable political environment, for seven decades.

Adulyadej's father, Mahidol, was a student at Harvard Medical School when his third child was born. Mahidol's father, Adulyadej's grandfather, had been the King of Siam depicted in Margaret Landon's Anna and the King of Siam. After completing medical school, he returned to Thailand, but died several months later. Adulyadej was just two years old when his father died. The current Thai monarch, Pradhipok, and uncle to Adulyadej and his brother, Ananda Mahidol, had the children sent to Switzerland for their education. Adulyadej attended the École Nouvelle de la Suisse Romande, a preparatory school. The boys could not visit their homeland until after World War II in late 1945. Adulyadej's brother, Ananda, was to ascend the throne, however he was found dead from a gunshot wound. Adulyadej was named his brother's successor by an act of Parliament. A two-man regency council ruled in his stead while Adulyadej returned to Switzerland to complete his education. He received his Bachelor of Letters from the Gymnase de Lausanne in 1945, having planned to become an architect. However, following his brother's death, he studied law at the University of Lausanne.

Adulyadej was formally crowned on May 5, 1950. Though his role was largely ceremonial, he did play an important role through several political crises during his reign. In 1973 when protests against the dictatorship turned bloody, and protesters died, Adulyadej managed to persuade the generals, Thanom Kittikachorn and Praphas Charusathien, to relinquish their power. Similarly, in 1992 when a military junta toppled the government, Adulyadej intervened, calling for a "caretaker" government to rule until elections could be held.

In Thailand the monarch is revered as close to divine. At the time of his death, most Thais never knew a different king. Adulyadej's presence helped make Thailand a development success. His stable presence held the country together through twenty attempted or successful coups.

Bhumibol Adulyadej, Rama IX, king of Thailand, leaves behind his wife, Sirikit, and three children. His only son and heir, Crown Prince Maha Vajiralongkorn, will ascend the throne.

See Current Biography 1950

Edward Albee

Born: Virginia; March 12, 1928
Died: Montauk, New York; September 16, 2016
Occupation: Playwright, educator

Edward Albee was a three-time winner of the Pulitzer Prize for Drama for his plays *A Delicate Balance, Seascape,* and *Three Tall Women.* Ironically, Albee's most recognized play, *Who's Afraid of Virginia Woolf?,* did not win a Pulitzer, and stirred considerable controversy when the Pulitzer board defiantly refused to award a prize for drama that year, leading to the resignation of two members, in protest. In 1962 the play earned two Tony Awards, a New York Drama Critics Circle Award, and an Outer Circle Award. In 1966 the movie version of the play was nominated for thirteen Academy Awards, including Best Picture, winning five awards. In 2005 Albee was awarded a special Tony Award for Lifetime Achievement.

Little is known about Edward Albee's birth parents. At two weeks old he was adopted by Reed and Francis Albee, members of a well-known, wealthy New York City–based theatrical family. As such, Edward Albee was exposed to theater at an early age. He apparently had decided to become a playwright by the age of six. He was sent to boarding schools when he was eleven (including a disastrous year at the Valley Forge Military Academy) and attended three semesters at Trinity College in Hartford, Connecticut. His subsequent move to Greenwich Village in New York City marked his estrangement from his family whose values and lifestyle he abhorred. (He did remain close with his maternal grandmother.) He became enamored with the work of the European dramatists Samuel Beckett, Eugene Ionesco, and Jean Genet. After holding a series of odd jobs to support himself, including that of messenger for Western Union, in 1959 he committed himself to writing. His first play, *Zoo Story,* premiered in Germany (in German) and eventually was staged at the Provincetown Playhouse in New York City. The play won Albee a reputation as a playwright to watch, and won him an Obie award.

In 1962 Albee's reputation was secured with his first full-length play, *Who's Afraid of Virginia Woolf?* In 1967 Albee won his first Pulitzer for *A Delicate Balance.* He won his second Pulitzer in 1975 for *Seascape.* Though he continued to write, it would be several decades before he earned acclaim with his Pulitzer Prize-winning *Three Tall Women*.

As a gay writer, Albee was criticized for his avoidance of gay characters. Most of his work plumbed the depths of the human psyche, portraying people who are unable to communicate or achieve intimacy with one another, perhaps a reflection of his relationships with his family. He shared his several residences with his long-time companion, the sculptor Jonathan Thomas who predeceased him in 2005. In 1964 Albee created the Edward Albee Foundation, a summer retreat that provides living and workspace for six artists. He also taught playwriting at the University of Houston.

Edward Albee leaves no known survivors.

See Current Biography 1996

Muhammad Ali

Born: Louisville, Kentucky; January 17, 1942
Died: Paradise Valley, Arizona; June 5, 2016
Occupation: Boxer, civil rights activist

Muhammad Ali is often considered the boxing world's greatest champion. He was the first prizefighter ever to win the world heavyweight championship by challenge three times. He became a cultural icon, as much for his civil rights battles as for his boxing prowess.

Muhammad Ali was born Cassius Marcellus Clay Jr., the eldest of two sons born to his father, Cassius Marcellus Clay Sr. and Odessa (Grady) Clay. By most genealogical accounts, Ali's maternal grandfather was a white Irish-American and his paternal great-great-grandfather was a freed slave who took the name of his former master, Cassius Marcellus Clay. Ali became interested in boxing after his bicycle was stolen when he was twelve. He reported the theft to a white policeman, Joe Elsby Martin, who was a supervisor of a local boxing gym. He began training daily under Joe Martin and Fred Stoner of the Grace Community Center. He developed a method of wearing down his opponents by enticing them to throw punches. He picked up the art of "ring chatter" while participating in the Olympic Games in Rome, Italy where he took the light heavyweight title. He turned professional in 1960, training under Archie Moore and Angelo Dundee, who remained his long-time trainer. Ali developed his showman's strategy, abrasively attracting public attention through loud-mouthed braggadocio.

In February of 1964 Ali earned the chance to go up against the heavyweight champion, Sonny Liston, a hulking, stone-faced "monster," goading him into clumsy rushes, then peppering him with hard punches. Ali's famous quote, "float like a butterfly, sting like a bee," dates from that fight.

That same year, Ali announced that he had joined the Black Nationalist Nation of Islam, viewed by mainstream white Americans as a subversive "race hate" sect. He also adopted the name Muhammad Ali. The year 1965 was the finest of his career as he defended his title against five challengers. In 1966 Ali became a conscientious objector to the Vietnam War, saying, "I ain't got no quarrel with those Vietcong. . . . They never called me n__ __ __." The comment was devastating to his image in the mainstream press. When he formally refused to enter the Selective Service, the World Boxing Association (WBA) stripped him of his title and license. Ali would lose three critical years of boxing. His stance made him a folk hero, a spokesman of resistance to injustice and oppression and for social change, and his popularity spread throughout the world. His appeal to his sentence went all the way to the US Supreme Court, which eventually resolved the case in his favor.

Other key battles included his rematch against Joe Frazier who had won the championship title in 1971, and his "rumble in the jungle" against George Foreman in 1974. The event was documented in a film, *When We Were Kings*, which won an Academy Award in 1996.

In 2001 Ali was awarded the Presidential Citizen's Medal, and he served as a United Nations Messenger of Peace. In 2005 Ali was awarded the Medal of Freedom. *Time* magazine named Ali one of the hundred most important people of the twentieth century, and *Sports Illustrated* named him sportsman of the century.

In the mid-1980s Ali was diagnosed with Parkinson's disease, a likely result of repeated head injuries. Muhammad Ali was married four times and had nine children. His children and fourth wife, Lonnie, survive.

See Current Biography 1978

Hassan al-Turabi

Born: Kassala; February 1, 1932
Died: March 5, 2016
Occupation: Sudanese religious and political leader

An early mentor of his nephew, terrorist leader Osama bin Laden (who was married to Turabi's niece), Hassan al-Turabi was a major figure in instigating the resurgence of Muslim fundamentalism in Sudan, imposing his interpretation of strict Islamic law (sharia) on the war-weary country. He was the founder of the radical political party called the National Islamic Front

(NIF), and he helped found the Sudanese branch of the Muslim Brotherhood. It was Turabi who declared, in 1997, "America incarnates the devil for all Muslims."

Hassan al-Turabi was born in the remote Kassala province to a Sufi sheik. He studied law in Khartoum and at the University of London. He earned a doctorate in constitutional law from the Sorbonne in Paris in the early 1960s. He is said to have memorized the entire Qur'an and was an authority on Islamic law. For several years he was the dean of the law faculty at the University of Khartoum, and was elected to the Sudanese Parliament as a representative of the Muslim Brotherhood in 1965. However, following a coup led by Gaafar Nimeiri, Turabi spent six years in prison and then three years in exile in Libya, though he later returned to serve as Nimeiri's attorney general. After unrest toppled Nimeiri's government, Turabi emerged as the power behind Omar al-Bashir's unelected, theocratic regime. He helped instigate a brutal civil war against southern secessionists that claimed the lives of two million, and displaced another four million citizens.

In 1991 Sudan was declared an Islamic state, and in 1992 Amnesty International and Africa Watch accused the Sudanese regime of using torture, and in early 1993, Egyptian President Hosni Mubarak accused Sudan of hosting at least seventeen terrorist training camps staffed by revolutionary guards from Iran. The US Department of State added Sudan to its list of nations sponsoring terrorism, and six Sudanese were charged with involvement in the 1993 bombing of the World Trade Center in New York. Strangely, in the late 1990s, Turabi reinventing himself as a proponent of democracy, called for al-Bashir's overthrow. He was arrested again in 2011 after the "Arab Spring" uprisings. At the time of his death, Turabi was seeking reconciliation with President Omar al-Bashir.

Hassan al-Turabi died on March 5, 2016. His wife and son survive him.

See Current Biography 1999

Gene Amdahl

Born: Flandreau, South Dakota; November 16, 1922
Died: Palo Alto, California; November 10, 2015
Occupation: Computer pioneer, electronics engineer

As a research engineer for International Business Machines (IBM), Gene Amdahl helped usher in the computer era, more out of his understanding of economics and IBM's customer base, than of computer engineering savvy, though he was an accomplished engineer, becoming an IBM fellow and heading IBM's advanced computer systems laboratory in the late 1960s. After leaving IBM, out of frustration with the company's administrators, he founded his own successful rival company, Amdahl Corporation, in 1970. His architecture for replacing IBM mainframe computers with high-performance emulators became known as "Amdahl's Law."

While studying theoretical physics as a graduate student at the University of Wisconsin, Amdahl found the conventional slide rule and calculator to be nearly useless in studying atomic particles, so he invented a computer. He joined IBM in 1952 as a project manager, but quit in 1955 and moved to California. However, in 1960, he returned to IBM where he headed the technical team for the IBM 360 series—IBM's most profitable product at that time. Once more, a decade later, Amdahl failed to persuade IBM's administrators of the benefits of parallel processing in building new computer products—a design that became known as "Amdahl's Law," which has been widely accepted across the industry. He left the IBM behemoth to form his own computer-manufacturing company, Amdahl Corporation, which served customers like NASA, Ford Motor Company, and AT&T. Ten years later, he formed Trilogy Systems Corporation, which focused on silicon wafers for large computer systems.

Gene Amdahl is survived by his wife, three children, and five grandchildren.

See Current Biography 1982

Don L. Anderson

Born: Frederick, Maryland; March 5, 1933
Died: Cambria, California; December 2, 2014
Occupation: Scientist

Don Anderson was considered a pioneer in "deep earth" research, developing sophisticated tools for exploring the Earth's interior composition. He won numerous awards from the American Geophysical Union (AGU), the National Aeronautics and Space Administration (NASA), the Royal Astronomical Society of Great Britain (RAS), and the Royal Swedish Academy of Sciences. In 1998 he was awarded the Crafoord Prize, the equivalent of a Nobel Prize in earth sciences, astronomy, and mathematics. In 1998 Anderson also received the US National Medal of Science.

Anderson received his bachelor's degree in geology and geophysics from Rensselaer Polytechnic Institute (RPI) in 1955. As a member of the Reserved Officers' Training Corps (ROTC), he joined the US Navy and moved to Greenland to study the properties of sea ice. In 1962 he earned his doctorate in mathematics and geophysics at the California Institute of Technology (Caltech), where he continued as a research fellow. By 1968 he was a full professor, and from 1967 to 1989, Anderson was the head of Caltech's seismology laboratory.

Anderson's most significant contribution to science was a new model for Earth's mantle. Rather than the model where Earth, like a baseball, comprises three layers of crust, mantle, and core, Anderson's conception is much more complex. Along with Harvard's Adam Dziewonski, Anderson established what is now the most widely accepted theory of the structure of Earth's interior, one that scientists use as a standard comparison when new data appear.

Don Anderson was well-loved by his colleagues, and he established the Caltech institution of morning and afternoon coffee breaks where scientists and their students gathered on a regular basis to discuss their research. Anderson died of cancer on December 2, 2014. His wife of fifty-eight years, Nancy Ruth Anderson, their two children, and four grandchildren survive.

See Current Biography 2002

Pinochet Ugarte. By 1976 human rights abuses grew so widespread and flagrant that the United States suspended all weapons sales to the military government. Confident that most Chileans would vote for stability under the current military rule, Pinochet agreed to hold free elections. Aylwin helped found an opposition bloc known as the Coalition of Parties for Democracy. Pinochet was soundly defeated, and Patricio Aylwin emerged as a promising presidential candidate. He won the election, and on March 11, 1990, was sworn in as president of Chile, though Pinochet retained power over the military, making Aylwin's task like that of walking through a mine field. Eventually, and over Pinochet's objections, Aylwin created the Truth and Reconciliation Commission to investigate charges of torture and other human rights abuses under Pinochet's regime. Aylwin remained Chile's president until 1994.

Patricio Aylwin married the former Leonor Oyazun in 1948, and the couple had five children. Aylwin's daughter, Mariana, was a congresswoman and a cabinet minister. Aylwin's wife and five children survive him.

See Current Biography 1990

Patricio Aylwin

Born: Valparaiso, Chile; November 26, 1918
Died: Santiago, Chile; April 19, 2016
Occupation: Former president of Chile, law professor

In large measure, Patricio Aylwin is credited with bringing democracy to Chile following nearly two decades of brutal rule under General Augusto Pinochet. Aylwin was instrumental in Chile's avoiding another bloody coup like the one that put Pinochet in power. Under Aylwin's presidency, Chile experienced a period of strong economic growth and political stability.

Patricio Aylwin was born to a family of Spanish Basque and Welsh heritage, with his Welsh great grandfather serving as a British consul in Chile. His father was the president of the Chilean Supreme Court. Aylwin attended law school at the University of Chile, and spent some years teaching administrative law. In 1965 Aylwin was elected to the Senate as a member of the Christian Democratic party. He would eventually serve six terms as the party president. In the early 1970s the self-avowed Marxist president, Salvadore Allende, plunged the country into economic chaos when he nationalized banks, large farms, and industrial plants. After widespread protest strikes, he imposed martial law. A bloody coup ensued leading to Allende's death and a new military regime under General Augusto

John Backe

Born: Akron, Ohio; July 5, 1932
Died: Gladwyne, New Jersey; October 22, 2015
Occupation: Broadcasting executive

In 1977, at the age of forty-four, John Backe replaced CBS broadcasting's founder, William S. Paley, as the chief executive officer, charged with the task of reclaiming CBS's status as the number one broadcasting network in the United States, after it lost that spot to ABC.

Backe's rise to chief executive officer at CBS was meteoric. In 1973, CBS president, Arthur R. Taylor, convinced Backe to sign on as president of the CBS publishing group, and corporate vice president, a move that boosted the publishing group's sales from $140 million per year to $400 million, in three short years, which caught the eye of network founder, William Paley. In 1976, Paley elevated Backe to CBS president and, only a few months later, to chief executive. Backe is said to have embraced new technology and pressed CBS to expand into cable, made-for-TV movies, and video production. Paley was uncomfortable about such moves, and in 1980, John Backe resigned from CBS. He went on to form the Backe Group, a broadcast management firm, specializing in technology for broadcasting and publishing.

Backe attended Miami University in Oxford, Ohio on an ROTC (Reserve Officers' Training

Corps) scholarship. After graduation he served as a B-47 pilot with the Strategic Air Command. Backe went to school at Xavier University in Cincinnati, earning a master's in business administration. In 1955 he married Katherine Elliott, who passed away in 2014. Backe's son, a daughter, six grandchildren, a great-grandson, and a sister survive him.

See Current Biography 1978

Journal-American stating, "Unchecked brutality in the National Hockey League is going to kill someone." For his public denunciation of violence in the game, Bathgate was fined $500.

Andy Bathgate suffered from Parkinson's disease and Alzheimer's disease. He passed away on February 26, 2016. His survivors include his wife, Merle, two children, and six grandchildren.

See Current Biography 1964

Andy Bathgate

Born: Winnipeg, Manitoba, Canada; August 28, 1932
Died: Brampton, Ontario, Canada; February 26, 2016
Occupation: Professional hockey player

Andy Bathgate was a hockey super star who set numerous scoring records. He played in eight all-star games and won the National Hockey League's (NHL's) Hart trophy as the league's Most Valuable Player (MVP) in 1959. He was inducted into the Hockey Hall of Fame in 1978.

Andy Bathgate was one of five children born to a Scottish immigrant, who died before his son reached his teens. The young Bathgate began playing organized hockey when he was nine years old, and by the age of twelve, he was playing on six different teams and coaching one. He was a great fan of the New York Rangers, explaining that when the Rangers arrived for preseason training in Winnipeg, he and his friends would "scrounge sticks." The Blueshirts chased the kids, but were kind, giving a kid a cracked stick on a near daily basis. Bathgate passed up two hockey scholarships, one with the University of Denver and the other with the University of Colorado, to play professionally. During his first full season with the New York Rangers, he scored an astonishing twenty goals. In the following season he scored nineteen goals and added forty-seven assists for a point total of sixty-six, breaking the twenty-six year-old team record of sixty-two. *New York Daily News* writer Pat Leonard summed up Bathgate's career, writing, "He captained the Blueshirts from 1961 until his trade on Feb. 22, 1964, was the first Ranger to score 40 goals in a season, and still holds the franchise record for goals scored in 10 straight games (11 goals) in 1962-63. He scored 349 goals and 973 points in 1,069 NHL games" (February 27, 2016).

Bathgate's career was not without controversy. His published views on fair play and sportsmanship in ice hockey once placed him in jeopardy with the National Hockey League. In 1959 he collaborated in writing an article with Dave Anderson, a hockey writer for the *New York*

Brian Bedford

Born: Morley, Yorkshire, England; February 16, 1935
Died: Santa Barbara, California; January 13, 2016
Occupation: English actor and director

Brian Bedford is considered theater royalty with seven Tony Award nominations, six Drama Desk Awards, and one Obie Award. He starred in over eighteen Broadway productions, and was a fixture at the world-renowned Stratford Festival in Ontario, Canada, where he performed and directed for twenty-nine seasons. One of his last roles was that of Lady Bracknell in Stratford's production of *The Importance of Being Earnest*, which then moved to Broadway, winning Bedford another Tony Award nomination. His early mentor was the legendary Sir John Gielgud, and his classmates included Albert Finney and Peter O'Toole.

Brian Bedford had a difficult start in life, born into poverty on February 16, 1935. His father was a Protestant postal worker who married an Irish Catholic girl. Two of his three brothers died of tuberculosis while he was still a boy. His parents fought often, and his father eventually committed suicide. Bedford attended the all-boys St. Bede's grammar school. He was a poor student and left high school at fifteen. However, he had a passion for acting, and at eighteen he auditioned at the Royal Academy of Dramatic Art. His ten lines from *Romeo and Juliet* won him a scholarship to the prestigious school, where he studied Method acting. He made his stage debut at twenty-one, playing Shakespeare's *Hamlet*.

He first came to the United States with a production of *The Five Finger Exercise*, costarring Jessica Tandy, and in 1963 he came to stay. In addition to his many stage appearances, he acted in a number of film and television productions.

His first film appearance was in *Miracle in Soho* in 1957, and his first television credits include the 1966 film, *Grand Prix* with James Garner. He also played cameo roles on a number of television series, including the 1994 miniseries *Scarlett*, and in a 1989 episode of *Hitchcock Presents*. He also played the part of Clyde Tolson in the 1995 Oliver Stone film, *Nixon*. Bedford was inducted into the American Theater Hall of Fame in 1997.

Brian Bedford battled cancer for the last few years of his life. He lost that battle on January 13, 2016. His partner of thirty years, and husband since July of 2013, actor Tim MacDonald, survives him.

See Current Biography 1998

John Belle

Born: Cardiff, Wales; June 30, 1932
Died: Remsenburg, New York; September 8, 2016
Occupation: Architect

John Belle was a founding member of the renowned architectural firm Beyer Blinder Belle. In an era of "urban removal," where historical landmarks were being destroyed and replaced with modern structures, Beyer Blinder Belle became known for the notion of restoration that was also functional. Belle's most important contributions to the cityscape of New York include the Grand Central Terminal, the Ellis Island Museum of Immigration, and the South Street Seaport Museum.

John Belle was born to a working class family. His father was a clerk in a teashop and his mother was a housewife. Belle received his diploma from the Portsmouth School of Architecture in England, and the Architectural Association in London. He moved to the United States in 1959 where he began his professional career working for Josep Lluis Sert, the dean of the Harvard University Design School. In 1968 Belle partnered with Harvard graduates, Richard Blinder and John Beyer to form Beyer Blinder Belle. The firm focused on community planning projects.

With the addition of James Marston Fitch as a partner in 1979, Beyer Blinder Belle came to the forefront of preservation-oriented architecture. The company's website reveals, "Under John's philosophy, the firm advanced a contemporary approach to preservation that promoted authenticity over replication and building insertions that were both contextual and of their time." In 1990 the firm earned wide praise for its restoration of the abandoned Ellis Island immigration station, which became the Ellis Island National Museum of Immigration. Several years later Belle restored the Haupt Conservatory at the botanical garden in the Bronx.

Though a 1978 ruling preserved Grand Central Terminal as an historic landmark, many New Yorkers were doubtful that a restoration was feasible. The underground city shared its halls with drug dealers and the homeless. Under Belle's directions, natural sunlight was restored,

with astonishing results. The entire complex was cleaned, revealing a startling teal ceiling with stars, constellations and zodiac signs in gold-leaf contrast. John Belle co-authored *Grand Central: Gateway to a Million Lives*, the account of the Grand Central restoration, which won a medal from The Chartered Institute of Building Literary Awards.

Belle was married twice. Both wives predeceased him. He is survived by two sons, three daughters, and eight grandchildren.

See Current Biography 2002

Helen Delich Bentley

Born: Ruth, Nevada; November 28, 1923
Died: Timonium, Maryland; August 6, 2016
Occupation: US congresswoman, chairwoman of the Federal Maritime Commission, journalist

When President Richard Nixon promoted Helen Delich Bentley to chair the Federal Maritime Commission, he made her the highest-ranking woman in the executive branch at that time. In 1984 Bentley was elected to Congress where she won seats on influential House committees such as the appropriations committee. She earned a reputation as a tough, no-nonsense trade protectionist and blue-collar worker's advocate.

Helen Delich Bentley was born and raised in the remote Nevada desert where her father worked in a copper mine. He died from silicosis, an occupational hazard, when she was eight years old. She began working to help support her family when she was twelve. Later she supported herself and financed her education at the University of Nevada and the University of Missouri through scholarships and by working while she attended school. During this time, Bentley worked for James Scrugham's senate campaign, and later moved to Washington DC to work as a secretary. In June of 1947 Bentley became a reporter for the *Baltimore Sun* where she focused on labor matters. She became the maritime editor in 1952. She wrote a syndicated column "Around the Waterfront," and also wrote and produced her own television show called *The Port that Built a City and State*. Through her work as a journalist, Bentley became a leading authority on the maritime industry.

In 1969 then President Richard Nixon selected her to be the chairman of the Federal Maritime Commission. She worked in that capacity until 1984 when she won a seat in the US Congress. Though she was a conservative, she was a trade union advocate. She supported the Equal Rights Amendment, but opposed abortion rights. In 1994 she vacated her seat in congress to run for Maryland's governor, a gamble that she lost.

It was Bentley's greatest honor when the city of Baltimore renamed its harbor in her honor. She co-authored *The Great Port of Baltimore: Its First 300 Years* in 2006. Bentley's husband of forty-four years, William Bentley, predeceased her in 2003. The couple had no children. Her survivors include one niece.

See Current Biography 1971

Sandy Berger

Born: Sharon, Connecticut; October 28, 1945
Died: Washington, District of Columbia; December 2, 2015
Occupation: US national security advisor

President Bill Clinton appointed Sandy Berger as the deputy advisor on national security affairs during his first term in office, from 1993 to 1997. Berger then became the national security advisor during Clinton's second term, attending meetings of the National Security Council, an inner-Cabinet group made up of the president, vice president, and secretaries of state and defense. Late in his career, as Clinton's liaison to the 9/11 Commission, Berger was caught smuggling classified files from the National Archives. His sentence was relatively light: a $50,000 fine, two years of probation, and one hundred hours of community service. He relinquished his law license, voluntarily, in 2007.

Sandy Berger was born in rural Connecticut on October 28, 1945, but grew up in the small, upstate town of Millerton, New York. His father passed away when Berger was just eight years old. He attended Cornell University, and graduated with a law degree from Harvard University, cum laude, in 1971. In 1972 he became a speechwriter for George McGovern, the Democratic presidential nominee, building a life-long friendship with Bill Clinton during that campaign. Berger worked in the Carter administration as the deputy director of policy planning at the state department. During the early 1980s, Berger gained significant experience in international trade as a partner in the law firm, Hogan & Hartson. He was instrumental in convincing Bill Clinton, Arkansas' little-known governor, to run for president in the 1992 election. After his win, Clinton asked Berger to head the transition from the Bush administration on matters of foreign policy and national security. He is credited with opening trade and the integration of Eastern and Western Europe without increasing tension with Russia.

Sandy Berger succumbed to cancer of the bile ducts on December 2, 2015, leaving behind his wife, Susan, three children, five grandchildren, and a sister.

See Current Biography 1998

Daniel Berrigan

Born: Virginia, Minnesota; May 9, 1921
Died: New York, New York; April 30, 2016
Occupation: American priest, poet, and peace activist

Daniel Berrigan and his brother, Philip Berrigan, were the first Roman Catholic priests to receive federal sentences for peace agitation during the 1960s and 1970s. Though a talented poet and devoted Jesuit priest, Daniel Berrigan will likely be remembered for his role in the 1968 raid on a US military recruitment station in Catonsville, Maryland where he and seven others (including his brother, Philip) burned draft files in protest of American involvement in Vietnam. His actions earned him three years in jail. He fled after refusing to passively accept the legal consequences of his law-breaking because "there [was] no machinery of recourse with [US] law about this war." He became the first priest to occupy the FBI's most-wanted list. The Cantonsville incident was portrayed in the off-Broadway play, *The Trial of the Cantonsville Nine*, and was made into a film, produced by Gregory Peck, earning the Berrigan brothers a place on the cover of *Time* magazine.

Perhaps Berrigan inherited his spirit of activism from his father, Thomas Berrigan, who moved to New York to found the Electrical Workers Union local in Syracuse, New York. Daniel and his brother, Philip, were the youngest of six sons born to Thomas and Frieda Berrigan. The young Daniel Berrigan had been drawn to the priesthood from a very young age. After his rigorous thirteen-year course of spiritual training, he studied philosophy at Woodstock College. In 1945 he served as a military chaplain in Germany. Following his ordination in 1952, Berrigan spent the last stage of his Jesuit training in a year of spiritual retreat. From 1957 to 1963, Berrigan taught at the Jesuits' Le Moyne College in Syracuse where he formed an elite cadre of young followers dedicated to pacifism, civil rights, and radical social work. One of his students, David Miller, became the first convicted draft card burner in the United States. With fellow priest and poet, Thomas Merton, Berrigan co-founded the Interfaith Coalition against the Vietnam War. He taught at numerous universities, including Loyola University, Columbia, Cornell, and Yale.

Berrigan received numerous awards for this writing, including the Lamont Prize for his first collection of poetry, *Time Without Number*. He published over fifty books of poetry, personal essays, and an autobiography.

See Current Biography 1970

Stephen Birmingham

Born: Hartford, Connecticut, May 28, 1929
Died: New York, New York; November 15, 2015
Occupation: American author

Stephen Birmingham is most remembered for his bestseller *Our Crowd*, and similar immigrant histories, that chronicle the lives of the ultra-wealthy in New York City.

Stephen Birmingham was not born to wealth, but he grew up in the rarefied air of America's immigrant dynasties. Born in Hartford, Connecticut, and raised in nearby Andover, Birmingham, he attended the elite Hotchkiss prep school with the likes of the Mellons and Vanderbilts. He graduated from Williams College in Williamstown, Massachusetts, in the early 1950s, with a bachelor's degree in English. After a stint in the Army during the Korean War, Birmingham moved to New York City, where he worked as a copywriter for Gimbals department store, and attended swank parties amidst the rich and famous. He began writing human-interest stories during his spare time, for magazines like *McCall's, Good Housekeeping,* and *Redbook*. In 1967, he came out with his third book, *Our Crowd,* which became a bestseller. Well-known author, John P. Marquant, became Birmingham's mentor, having recognized Birmingham's talent and recommended Birmingham to his agent.

Our Crowd is a social history of the entrepreneurial German Jews, who immigrated to the United States during the Civil War, and went on to earn enormous fortunes in banking, forming a new American aristocracy. Birmingham's second bestseller, *The Right People,* was a similar survey of the ultra-wealthy Anglo-Saxon social establishment in Newport, Boston, Philadelphia, and New York. *The Grandees*, published in 1971, followed a community of Sephardic Jews who immigrated in 1654 after their expulsion from Spain. With the publication of *Certain People,* a history of America's African American "elite" however, Birmingham's career took a hit as he was sharply criticized for his intrusion into a society he knew nothing about. Birmingham also wrote an unauthorized biography about Jacqueline Kennedy Onassis.

Overall, Stephen Birmingham published thirty books, the last of which was *The Wrong Kind of Money*, published in 1997. He died from lung cancer at his home in New York. His three children, a granddaughter, a sister, and long-time partner of forty-two years, Edward Lahniers, survive him.

See Current Biography 1974

Pierre Boulez

Born: Montbrison, Loire, France; March 26, 1925
Died: Baden Baden, Germany; January 5, 2016
Occupation: Composer, conductor

Sometimes referred to as a maverick for his radical modernist compositions aimed at moving beyond classical traditions, which he considered a burden, Pierre Boulez has been characterized as the most influential figure in avant-garde French music, and one of the greatest minds of the twentieth century.

The son of a steel manufacturer who had intended that his son become an engineer or mathematician, Boulez grew up in Montbrison, near Lyon, in Nazi-occupied France. He studied with Olivier Messiaen at the Paris Conservatory, graduating in 1945 at the top of his class. He earned the support of Jean-Louis Barrault and Madeleine Renaud to conduct a series of concerts he named "Domaine Musical," which were devoted to the avante garde. Shortly thereafter, he became the musical director of Barrault and Renaud's Paris theatre company. Though he was originally a composer, he turned to conducting to ensure a competent interpretation of his highly esoteric music. He was sharply critical of Arnold Schoenberg for stopping short of seeing his serial technique to its natural conclusions, in toto, particularly in regard to form and rhythm, and as a musical revolution. For Boulez an apt analogy was that of scientific evolution, where tonal music was akin to Newton's theory of gravity, and atonal, or serialization, was more like the leap in Einstein's theories.

Boulez became chief conductor of the BBC Symphony Orchestra in 1971, and also succeeded Leonard Bernstein as the music director of the New York Philharmonic where he remained for six years. He remained closely associated with the Cleveland Orchestra where he had made his US debut in 1964. Having alienated himself from the French musical scene in the late 1970s, Boulez returned to direct the nation's Institut de Recherche et Coordination Acoustique/Musique (IRCAM).

The maverick composer and conductor died on January 5, 2016. Boulez fiercely guarded his private life, and information about his survivors is unavailable.

See Current Biography 1969

Boutros Boutros-Ghali

Born: Cairo, Egypt; November 14, 1922
Died: Cairo, Egypt; February 16, 2016
Occupation: Secretary General of the United Nations

In 1992, Boutros Boutros-Ghali became the sixth secretary general of the United Nations (UN), and the first African diplomat to hold the post. He was the Egyptian foreign minister under President Anwar Sadat, and was the deputy prime minister for foreign affairs under President Hosni Mubarak.

Boutros Boutros-Ghali was born into one of Egypt's most distinguished Coptic-Christian families. His was a political family as well. His father once served as the finance minister for Egypt, and his grandfather, Boutros Pasha Ghali, had served as Egypt's prime minister from 1906 to 1910 when he was assassinated by a radical Muslim student. Boutros-Ghali earned a law degree from Cairo University in 1946, and a doctorate in international law from the University of Paris in 1949. He was a Fulbright scholar at Columbia University in New York City from 1954 to 1955. He was a professor of international law and international relations at Cairo University, and headed the university's political science department.

Boutros-Ghali jumped into the fray of Egyptian politics only days before President Anwar Sadat's historic journey to Jerusalem in 1977. Boutros-Ghali stood at Sadat's side when he signed the formal peace treaty that ended the thirty-one-year state of war between Egypt and Israel. Boutros-Ghali practically embodied progressive internationalism. He was a Coptic-Christian in a largely Muslim country, who married a woman from a prominent Jewish family. He was fluent in English, French, and Arabic. He authored more than one hundred books and articles on Arab and African regional issues.

While he began his tenure at the UN with an attempt at sweeping administrative reforms, his achievements as secretary general were mixed. He was heavily criticized for his failure to act on the genocide in Rwanda. He angered Western powers by suggesting that the conflict in the Balkans was a "rich man's war," and that there were other nations experiencing far greater carnage. Several events put Boutros-Ghali at odds with the United States, which was frustrated by the perceived lack of support that contributed to the deaths of eighteen US army rangers in Somalia, though operations there were under US command, not that of the UN (United Nations). Likewise, the United States blamed Boutros-Ghali for the deaths of about eight thousand Bosnian Muslims at Srebrenica. In return, Boutros-Ghali blamed the United States for abandoning Africa's poor once the Cold War had ended. The Americans used their Security Council veto to prevent Boutros-Ghali from serving for a second term. After stepping down as secretary general, Boutros-Ghali wrote a book, *Unvanquished: A US-UN Saga* about his term with the UN. He later became the chairman of the South Centre, a group of forty-six developing countries intent on protecting their common interests with the international community. He was also the secretary general of the International Organisation of la Francophonie, an association of French-speaking nations.

Boutros-Ghali died in Cairo on February 16, 2016. His wife, Leia survives.

See Current Biography 1992

David Bowie (David Jones)

Born: London, England; January 8, 1947
Died: New York, New York; January 10, 2016
Occupation: Rock musician, songwriter, actor

Calling rock-n-roll icon David Bowie a maverick would be an understatement. He was highly creative, and constantly reinvented himself, always a step ahead of creative stagnation. He was driven by experimentation, in his music and in his identity, as he pioneered glitter-rock, disco, and new-wave styles of music and fashion. He was nominated for at least sixty-three awards, from Grammys and MTV music awards to daytime Emmy Awards. He was recognized with a Lifetime Achievement Grammy Award in 2006.

David Bowie was born in Brixton, a rough neighborhood in South London, and his upbringing was decidedly middle-class. His father was a publicist for Dr. Barnardo's, a children's services organization, while his mother worked at various part-time jobs from waitressing to modeling. Bowie himself worked as a graphic artist for an advertising agency for a short while. His family had a history of mental illness, including schizophrenia, leading Bowie to fear for his own sanity from time-to-time. His older half-brother, Terry, had been institutionalized, and eventually committed suicide.

Elvis Presley and Little Richard were Bowie's first inspirations to pursue a career as a performer. His early career was marked by his membership in a series of bands. He changed his name from Jones to Bowie after the rock group "The Monkees," which included singer Davy Jones, gained notoriety. (Fascinated by the American Wild West, he chose the name "Bowie" after Jim Bowie, a Texas adventurer and the creator of the single-edged hunting knife.)

After releasing several albums that earned lukewarm acceptance, Bowie's song "Space

Oddity," became a hit single. As usual, his timing was impeccable. The song was released only nine days before Apollo 11 landed on the moon. Space travel and the possibility of space aliens helped Bowie soar into super-stardom with the creation of Bowie's alter ego, "Ziggy Stardust." Bowie hit upon the idea of actually embodying the fictional characters he wrote and sang about. Ziggy was an androgynous rock musician, a blameless being professing a message of hope, who, according to the song's lyrics, "took it too far, but, boy could he play guitar." Bowie would repeat his self-invention again, as the "thin white duke," "Major Tom," and "Aladdin Sane" (which also reads "a lad insane"). Each new persona had wildly different physical attributes like hair color and style. Years later, Bowie acknowledged that his various personae were ways of hiding from himself. In addition to his music career, he also played the lead role in the Broadway's *Elephant Man* in 1980. His final project was the musical *Lazarus*, which was staged for a limited run by the New York Theater Workshop.

The world was shocked upon learning of Bowie's death on January 10, 2016, just two days after his sixty-ninth birthday and the release of his final album, *Blackstar*, which is heavily laced with themes of death and mortality. His eighteen-month battle with cancer had been a fiercely guarded secret. His second wife, Iman Mohamed Abdulmajiid, and two children survive.

See Current Biography 1994

John Brademas

Born: Mishawaka, Indiana; March 2, 1927
Died: New York, New York; July 11, 2016
Occupation: American congressman, university president, educator

As a veteran politician, John Brademas was largely responsible for the passage of significant education bills, including the 1965 Elementary and Secondary Education Act, and he sponsored or promoted bills designed to increase the availability of technical education in two-year colleges. He also sponsored legislation to create the National Endowment for the Arts (NEA) and the National Endowment for the Humanities (NEH). Following his political career, Brademas became the president of New York University (NYU), where his efforts transformed the college from a local commuter school to a major, world-renowned research institution, one of the best in the country.

John Brademas was born and raised in Mishawaka, an industrial city just outside of South Bend, Indiana. After graduating from high

school in 1945, he enrolled in the officers' training program of the US Navy at the University of Mississippi. The following year he transferred to Harvard University, attending on a Veterans National Scholarship. In 1949 he attended Oxford University as a Rhodes Scholar, earning a doctorate in social studies in 1954. To gain political experience, Brademas worked as legislative assistant to US Senator Patrick McNamara, Representative Thomas Ashley, and Democratic Presidential nominee Adlai Stevenson. He also taught political science at St. Mary's College.

In 1958 Brademas was elected to Congress where he served on the House Committee on Education and Labor, as well as the House Administration and the Joint Committee on the Library of Congress. He led a special educational advisory group, which helped enact the Higher Education Acts of 1965, 1972, and 1976, doubling the federal government's annual allowance for education. After losing his House seat in 1980, Brademas was named the president of NYU, transforming the school into a world-class institution.

John Brademas married Mary Ellen Briggs in 1977. She survives him along with her three children and six grandchildren.

See Current Biography 1977

John Bradshaw

Born: Houston, Texas; June 29, 1933
Died: Houston, Texas; May 8, 2016
Occupation: Writer, educator, theologian, counselor, management consultant

A recovering alcoholic and former novice in the Catholic priesthood, John Bradshaw became a self-help guru and counselor who espoused the necessity of healing the damaged "inner child" before one could lead a fulfilling, productive life.

John Bradshaw was born to an abusive alcoholic who worked as a railroad clerk at the Southern Pacific railroad. When Bradshaw was ten years old, his father, John McCollough Bradshaw, abandoned the family leaving his wife, Norma Claire, to raise her three children alone. By the time he was thirteen, Bradshaw had become a heavy drinker himself. By the time he was a junior in high school, he was a regular patron of brothels as well as bars. Still, he excelled in school, winning three academic medals and a scholarship to the University of St. Thomas in Houston. He dropped out in his second year and hoped to become a Catholic priest. He was accepted into the novitiate at the Basilian seminary in Toronto, Canada. Nine years later, he left the seminary on the day he was to be ordained. He entered the University of Toronto and graduated magna cum laude with a bachelor's degree in theology and a master's degree in philosophy. In 1965 he checked himself into the Austin state hospital. He joined Alcoholics Anonymous (AA) and began a three-year regimen of daily twelve-step meetings. He credited the organization with saving his life.

In 1964 Bradshaw launched his ongoing career as a management-training consultant, holding workshops for Exxon, Philips Petroleum, Ogilvy and Mather, Inc., and Harrah's in Reno. In addition to speaking engagements, Bradshaw also taught at Sacred Heart Dominican College, Strake Jesuit College Preparatory School, and held a teaching fellowship at Rice University. He also hosted several Public Broadcasting shows, including *Spotlight*, a one-hour, weekly television talk show, and a series called *The Eight Stages of Man*. Bradshaw eventually had his own PBS series called *Bradshaw On: The Family*. He created a series of workshops using his numerous books with titles like *Bradshaw On: Healing the Shame That Binds You* and *Homecoming: Reclaiming and Championing Your Inner Child*. His titles occupied a spot on the *New York Times* bestseller list for decades.

Bradshaw leaves behind his wife, the former Karen Buntzel Mabray, two children, three grandchildren and two great-grandchildren.

See Current Biography 1993

Oscar Brand

Born: Winnipeg, Manitoba, Canada; February 7, 1920
Died: Great Neck, New York; September 30, 2016
Occupation: Folk singer, songwriter, author, producer

Oscar Brand was a folksinger and songwriter who produced over one hundred albums and wrote songs for popular entertainers like Doris Day, Harry Bellefonte, and Ella Fitzgerald. He hosted the longest-running radio program in history.

Oscar Brand was born on a wheat farm. His father was an interpreter for Native Americans for the Hudson's Bay Company and later, ran a theatrical supply store. Brand's love of music stemmed from his extended family. His parents and grandparents were singers. When he was seven, the family moved to the United States, eventually settling in Brooklyn, New York. After graduation from high school, Brand travelled around the country with his banjo, working as a farm hand. He graduated from Brooklyn College with a degree in abnormal psychology in 1942. Brand joined the US Army in 1942, serving as a section chief of the psychological section of the Army induction station in New York, and later became the editor of a newspaper for psychiatric patients.

Following the war Brand began his award winning, WNYC "Folk Song Festival," the longest-running radio program in history. His show featured such singers as Bob Dylan, Arlo Guthrie, Joan Baez, and Judy Collins. According to Brand's website, "his name is to be found among the credits of seventy-five documentary films." Brand directed music for a number of top-rated television programs, and was on the advisory panel for the children's show *Sesame Street*. Brand also wrote the musical that celebrated America's bicentennial, the Kennedy Center's *Sing America Sing*. He was a co-founders of the Newport Folk Festival. Over the course of his career, Brand earned a Peabody Award in 1982, a personal Peabody in 1997, and an Emmy Award.

Oscar Brand was married twice and had four children. His second wife, four children, and numerous grandchildren survive.

See Current Biography 1962

Anita Brookner

Born: London, England; July 16, 1928
Died: March 10, 2016
Occupation: Art historian, novelist

Anita Brookner was a highly regarded, widely published art historian when, at the age of fifty-three, she decided to try writing a novel, thus launching a second highly successful career that lasted until the end of her life.

Anita Brookner was born and raised in London, the only child of Polish immigrants, Newson and Maude (Shiska) Brookner. She described herself as a "sort of Jewish exile" who, though born in London, always felt like an outsider. Her father, a struggling businessman who once owned a library, directed her to the works of Charles Dickens and H. G. Wells. Brookner studied history at Kings College of the University of London. She continued her studies at the Courtauld Institute of Art where she earned a doctorate in art history under the tutelage of director Anthony Blunt, who was later revealed to be a KGB recruiter and spy.

Brookner received a scholarship to the École du Louvre where she studied throughout the 1950s. (Her "desertion" left her estranged from her extended family for years.) In 1959 Brookner returned to London as a visiting lecturer of art history at the University of Reading, before transferring to the Courtauld Institute of Art where she earned the status of "Reader." She was the first woman to receive the Slade Professorship at Cambridge University. Though she began her career as a novelist later in life (at the age of fifty-three) she published twenty-five novels, earning the coveted Booker Prize for her best-selling novel *Hotel du Lac* in 1984. She received the Commander of the Order of the British Empire (CBE) in 1990.

An intensely private person, Brookner never married and had no children.

See Current Biography 1989

Jerome Seymour Bruner

Born: New York, New York; October 1, 1915
Died: New York, New York; June 5, 2016
Occupation: Psychologist, educator

Jerome Bruner was a world-renowned psychologist whose studies about learning and cognition helped shape American educational reform and the developmental aspects of cognitive growth in children. He co-founded Harvard's Center for Cognitive Studies in 1960, and served on the educational panel of the President's Science Advisory Committee under the administrations of both John F. Kennedy and Lyndon B. Johnson. He advised the National Science Foundation (NSF), the National Institutes of Health (NIH), the Educational Testing Service, and the American Academy of Arts and Sciences (AAAS). He was a founding fellow of the National Academy of Education (NAEd).

Jerome Bruner was born, the youngest of four children, to Jewish-Polish immigrants Herman and Rose (Glucksmann) Bruner. His father was a watch manufacturer who, shortly before his death in 1927, sold his business to Bulova leaving the family relatively well off. The family moved often and Bruner attended a half-dozen public high schools. He attended Duke University in Durham, North Carolina, remaining there for one year of graduate study before transferring to Harvard University where he received his graduate degrees.

Upon graduation in 1941, Bruner accepted a position with the newly established Foreign Broadcast Monitoring Service of the Federal Communications Commission (FCC) where he analyzed the radio broadcasts of the Axis powers. Bruner had been born blind but cataract surgery when he was two left him with some limited eyesight. However, his vision precluded him from fighting in World War II, so he became an "assimilated" major in the Psychological Warfare Division of the Supreme Headquarters Allied Expeditionary Force. He later became an associate director of the Office of Public Opinion Research in Princeton, New Jersey. After the war, Bruner taught at Harvard becoming a full professor in 1952.

Burner and several colleagues formulated a revolutionary theory of perception that suggested factors such as values and needs strongly influenced a man's perception of his environment. With a grant from the Carnegie Corporation, Bruner and fellow psychologist, George A. Miller, opened the Center for Cognitive Studies on the Harvard campus. Bruner became involved in education reform after the Soviet Union launched Sputnik, leading Americans to question the quality of education in the United States. His work helped develop the Head Start early education program.

In addition to his work at Harvard, Dr. Bruner taught as a Watts Professor of Psychology and a Fellow of Wolfson College, a newly founded Graduate institution at Oxford University. He spent the last three decades of his life teaching at New York University's law school about the impact of story telling in understanding the world.

Dr. Bruner was married three times. His third wife, Carol Feldman, predeceased him. His survivors include two children from his first marriage and three grandchildren.

See Current Biography 1984

Dale Bumpers

Born: Charleston, Arkansas; August 12, 1925
Died: Little Rock, Arkansas; January 1, 2016
Occupation: Former governor of Arkansas, senator

Dale Bumpers earned the moniker "Giant Killer" after winning several elections against powerful, incumbent candidates. In the 1970 Arkansas gubernatorial race, Bumpers unseated the liberal Republican Governor, Winthrop Rockefeller. In the 1974 senatorial race, he won against the popular chairman of the Senate Foreign Relations Committee, J. William Fulbright. Bumpers won an astonishing 65.2 percent of the vote, over incumbent Fulbright's 34.8 percent, carrying seventy-one of seventy-five counties. As both the governor and senator from Arkansas, Bumpers won the respect of his colleagues, on both sides of the isle, with his country charm and disarming manner. In every political campaign, Bumpers refused to engage in personal attacks or negativity, preferring to garner votes based on his own merits.

Dale Bumper's wholesome image was not just his public personae. He was brought up in a small farming community in the foothills of the Ozark Mountains. His was a tight-knit, Christian family with a strong work ethic and commitment to a good education. His father served a term in the state legislature and instilled a love of history and politics in his three children. He later owned and ran the town hardware store. Dale Bumpers served as a Marine sergeant in World War II before earning his bachelor's degree from the University of Arkansas in 1948. He earned his law degree from Northwestern University in 1951. However, both of his parents were killed in a car crash in 1949. After graduation, Bumpers returned home and took over his father's hardware store. He eventually established a law practice in town.

Many in the Democratic Party considered Dale Bumpers to be a good candidate for a run at the presidency, but Bumpers felt his best chances were in 1976 when Jimmy Carter was in the White House. Late in his career, Bumpers came to national attention when senate leaders and President Bill Clinton asked him to make the closing statements, in the president's defense, at Clinton's impeachment trial. Bumper's son Brendt characterized his father as a staunch defender of the Constitution and he fought against numerous efforts at Constitutional amendments.

Dale Bumpers died on January 1, 2016, in Little Rock, Arkansas. His wife of sixty-six years, Betty, his two sons and a daughter survive him.

See Current Biography 1979

Dean Chance

Born: Wooster, Ohio; June 1, 1941
Died: Wooster, Ohio; October 11, 2015
Occupation: Professional baseball player

For twenty years Dean Chance was the youngest baseball player to win the Cy Young Award for best pitching in major league baseball. He played for the Los Angeles Angels that year, 1964, winning twenty games out of twenty-nine pitched. Eleven of these games were shutouts.

Chance was a Midwestern farm boy, raised in Wayne (near Wooster), Ohio. Born on June 1, 1941, Chance spent much of his childhood helping his father, Wilmer, Sr., on the farm, but his passion was baseball. He began pitching for a sandlot team. His high school coach recalls how Chance was a natural. They never messed with his unusual pitching style—Chance began his windup with his back turned, full on, to the batter. Once he began his windup, he never looked at home plate. In high school, he was virtually unbeatable, winning fifty-one games out of fifty-two; eight of these were no-hitters. Chance was also a basketball star and, as he graduated from high school, he was offered basketball scholarships from no fewer than thirty colleges. But he accepted a $30,000.00 bonus offer from baseball's Baltimore Orioles.

The 1960 season saw the creation of two new franchises and the existing teams were required to make some of their players available. The Los Angeles Angels drafted Chance for $75,000.00. In 1961, the Angels farmed him to Dallas-Fort Worth as a relief pitcher. The following year he started for the Angels, but complained about his team's fielding and batting support, winning him no friends on the team. In 1964, after a 5-5 record, but an incredibly low ERA—1.65, a still unbroken franchise record as of 2015, —he was named to the American League All-Star team. In addition to the Angels, Chance played for the Minnesota Twins, Cleveland Indians, New York Mets, and Detroit Tigers. In 1967, he threw a no-hitter while playing for Minnesota, and threw a perfect five-inning game that same year.

Dean Chance had a reputation as something of a bad boy, often breaking curfew with his on-the-road roommate, Bo Belisky. He was known to associate with Frank Sinatra, Dean Martin, and Marilyn Monroe. After retiring from baseball, in the 1970s and 1980s, Chance was a barker at carnivals and fairs, and raised cattle and hogs for market, on his eighty-three-acre farm. He married Judy Larson in 1960.

Dean Chance died of heart failure, just two months after being inducted into the Angels Hall of Fame. His marriage ended in divorce. He is survived by a son, a sister, and three grandchildren.

See Current Biography 1969

Joseph V. Charyk

Born: Canmore, Alberta, Canada; September 9, 1920
Died: Delray Beach, Florida; September 28, 2016
Occupation: Aeronautical scientist, business executive

A pioneer in the field of global telecommunications, Joseph Charyk is considered the founder of the geosynchronous communications satellite industry. He was the president, CEO and chairman of the Communications Satellite Corporation (Comsat) from 1963 to 1985.

Born and raised in Canmore, Alberta, Canada, Joseph Charyk migrated to the United States after graduating from the University of Alberta with a degree in engineering physics. He hoped to study with the renowned Hungarian scientist, Theodore von Karman, at the California Institute of Technology (Caltech). By 1946 Charyk graduated with his masters and doctorate degrees. During his last year of study, he taught aeronautics and was a section chief of the jet propulsion laboratories (JPL) at Caltech. From 1946 to 1955 he served on the faculty at Princeton University as a professor of aeronautics. While there he helped establish the Guggenheim Jet Propulsion Center and the Forrestal Research Center. He became the director of the aerophysics and chemistry laboratory of Lockheed Aircraft's missile systems division in 1955, where he helped start the Polaris Missile program. Shortly thereafter, he and a group of colleagues broke away to form a new company that would eventually become Aeronutronic Systems, Inc., a division of Ford Motor Company.

Charyk became involved with the US government when he accepted a one-year appointment as chief scientist of the US Air Force. A year later, he would become the secretary of research and development for the Air Force. In 1963 President Kennedy chose Charyk as the president of the Communications Satellite Corporation (Comsat), working in cooperation with the Department of Defense and the National Space and Aeronautics Administgration (NASA). Charyk played a critical role in telecommunications during the Cuban Missile Crisis.

In 1974 Charyk received the International Emmy Directorate Award, and in 1987, President Ronald Reagan awarded Charyk the National Medal of Technology and Innovation.

Joseph Charyk met the former Edwina Elizabeth Rhodes while they were both studying at Caltech. They married in 1945 and had three children. Edwina predeceased Joseph in 2013. Survivors include their children and their spouses, nine grandchildren, and seven great-grandchildren.

See Current Biography 1970

Michael Cimino

Born: New York, New York; February 3, 1939
Died: New York, New York; July 2, 2016
Occupation: Motion picture writer-director

Michael Cimino is most remembered as the co-author and director of *The Deer Hunter*, a 1978 blockbuster that garnered nine Academy Award nominations, winning five, including one for best director (Cimino) and best picture. The film also earned Cimino best director awards from the Golden Globes, the Director's Guild, and the Los Angeles Film Critics Association.

Michael Cimino was an intensely private eccentric whose directorial work helped define, then destroy, an era in Hollywood movie making. He attended Yale University, earning a degree in fine arts. Shortly thereafter, Cimino enlisted in the US Army Reserve where he was stationed at Fort Dix, New Jersey, for about six months. He studied acting and ballet while working for a small documentary producer in New York City.

In the late 1960s Cimino began directing television commercials. In 1971 he moved to Hollywood where he began his screenwriting career. He came to some notoriety for his collaboration with John Milius' *Magnum Force* starring Clint Eastwood as Harry Callahan, also known as "Dirty Harry." He directed Clint Eastwood in another hit, *Thunderbolt and Lightfoot*. But Cimino's magnum opus was *The Deer Hunter*, about a trio of close steelworker friends, representative of Middle American "ethnic" types who go off to fight in Vietnam as a matter of patriotic course. The movie was a three-hour epic starring Robert DeNiro, Christopher Walken, and John Savage. Unfortunately, Cimino's perfectionism, which barred no expense, led to the unmitigated failure of *Heaven's Gate*, which not only destroyed Cimino's career, it nearly bankrupt United Artists (UA), which eventually merged with Metro Goldwyn Mayer (MGM). Cimino would never regain the success of his earlier work.

The French awarded Cimino a Chevalier des Arts et des Lettres after the publication of his novel *Big Jane*. Michael Cimino never married. There is no information about his survivors.

See Current Biography 1981

Natalie Cole

Born: Los Angeles, California; February 6, 1950
Died: Los Angeles, California; December 31, 2015
Occupation: Singer

Natalie Cole, daughter of Nat King Cole, struggled for years to step outside her famous father's shadow, but when she finally succeeded, she became a singing sensation in her own right. She was awarded nine Grammys out of twenty-one nominations, three American Music Awards, two NAACP Image Awards, and a Hitmaker Award from the Songwriters Hall of Fame.

While being the daughter of a music celebrity may have helped open some doors for Natalie Cole, she struggled to make a name for herself beyond "Nat King Cole's daughter." Cole was born the second of five children to Nat King Cole and Maria (Hawkins) Cole who had been a vocalist with the Duke Ellington orchestra. She had a comfortable childhood, though the family experienced racism when they became the first African American family to live in the tawny Hancock Park neighborhood. Her father's death in 1965, when Natalie was just fifteen, was devastating. Her mother remarried and the family moved to Massachusetts where Cole attended the University of Massachusetts, graduating in 1972 with a degree in child psychology. She was an ardent rock-n-roll fan (which had bothered her father). While looking for a summer waitressing job, she found the band "Black Magic" (all except Cole were white), which needed her voice, and she discovered how much she loved performing. In 1974 Cole auditioned with producers Chuck Jackson and Marvin Yancy. They were enthusiastic about promoting Cole's talent, but numerous major record labels turned them down. Finally, Capitol offered her a contract, and in 1975 she recorded her first album, which was an instant hit with her songs "This Will Be," and the title track, "Inseparable." Her next six albums would top the charts. In 1976 Cole married her producer, Marvin Yancy, and Cole gave birth to their son, Adam, in 1978. In 1979 she was awarded a star on Hollywood's Walk of Fame.

Cole's life spun quickly out of her control, however, and in the early 1980s, she became heavily addicted to drugs and alcohol. Her talent also suffered, and her next two albums sold in relatively paltry numbers. In November of 1983, Cole checked into the Hazelden Hospital in Minnesota, and stayed there for six months.

The year 1987 saw Cole's comeback. Remarkably, in her best-selling 1991 album, *Unforgettable,* Cole sang duets with old recordings of her father's voice. In 2008, Cole announced she had hepatitis C, a result of her earlier drug use, and needed a kidney transplant. Her health continued to decline and she died from heart failure on December 31, 2015. Her son, Robert Yancy, survives.

See Current Biography 1991

Pat Conroy

Born: Atlanta, Georgia; October 26, 1945
Died: Beaufort, South Carolina; March 4, 2016
Occupation: Novelist

Best-selling novelist Pat Conroy penned twelve books, including one cookbook. Four of his novels were made into feature-length films. With irony, Conroy thanked his parents for his abusive childhood that provided fodder for the stories that captured a loyal following among American readers.

Though he is recognized as a "southern" writer, Pat Conroy spent much of his childhood moving from place-to-place. By the time he was fifteen, Conroy had lived in twenty-three different places, and had attended eleven schools. His father was a brutal, authoritarian fighter pilot with the US Marine Corp. Once Conroy famously quipped, "One of the greatest gifts you can get as a writer is to be born into an unhappy family." Conroy's mother was a class-conscious social climber who refused to acknowledge her husband's physical abuse. Pat Conroy was

offered several football scholarships from colleges, but at his father's insistence, Conroy accepted the offer by the Citadel, a military academy well known for its strict code of discipline. He graduated with a degree in English in 1967. He became a high-school English teacher, and accepted a job teaching disadvantaged African American children on the small, isolated island of Daufuskie, off the South Carolina coast. Upon finding most of the children were illiterate, Conroy took it upon himself to jettison the outdated books, teaching them about the world outside the small island. In 1970 he was fired for not adhering to standard curriculum.

Conroy wrote and self-published his first novel, *The Boo,* in 1969. It was a fictionalized account of what he considered the unjust firing of the Citadel's Lieutenant Colonel Thomas Nugent Courvoisie, affectionately known as "the boo." Only a few years later, *The Water is Wide* was published, winning Conroy the Anisfield-Wolf Award from the Cleveland Foundation for "its contribution towards improving relations between the races." His next novel, *The Great Santini,* was autobiographic, about his harsh father. In 1979 the novel became a commercial success at the box office in the film version of the story, starring Robert Duval who was nominated for an Academy Award for his performance. Conroy's 1980 novel, *The Lords of Discipline,* was nominated for the Robert Kennedy Book Award. It was later made into the film *The Lords of Discipline,* starring David Keith. Conroy's arguably most recognized work was *The Prince of Tides,* which became a runaway best seller. It too was made into a blockbuster movie directed by, and starring, Barbra Streisand.

Pat Conroy suffered several mental breakdowns throughout his adulthood. He was married three times. On February 15, 2016, Conroy announced he had pancreatic cancer. He died only weeks later, on March 4, 2016. His survivors include his third wife, Cassandra King, two daughters, stepchildren from his first two marriages, and several of his brothers.

See Current Biography 1996

Marlow Cook

Born: Akron, New York; July 27, 1926
Died: Sarasota, Florida; February 4, 2016
Occupation: United States senator from Kentucky

Marlow Cook was a one-term senator from Kentucky, but the brevity of his stay in the US Senate belies the significance of his impact.

Born in Akron, New York, Marlow Cook and his family moved to Louisville, Kentucky when he was sixteen. Upon graduation from high school, Cook joined the US Navy and served aboard the submarine, the US Sea Poacher. By 1950 he had graduated from the University of Louisville with an LL.B degree. He was an attorney with the law firm of Hottell & Stephenson. Over the following decade, Cook became more involved in Republican politics on both state and national levels. During this time, Kentucky was firmly in the hands of the Democrats. In 1957 he was elected to the state House of Representatives. At that time, moderate Republicans like Cook were more likely to support civil rights reform than Democrats. Under Republican leadership, Louisville became the first big city south of the Mason Dixon Line to pass a public accommodations law. In 1961 Cook ran for the office of Jefferson County Judge and became the equivalent of a county chief executive. To set the tone for his administration Cook purchased an old steamboat, rechristened the Belle of Louisville, which has since become one of the city's greatest icons. He was narrowly defeated in his bid for governor in 1967, and a year later, he became the first Republican senator from Kentucky to be elected statewide.

In the US Senate, Cook was a progressive who sat on the powerful Senate Judiciary Committee, which was responsible for screening federal court nominees, including those for the US Supreme Court. Then President Richard Nixon nominated G. Harrold Caswell, a judge from Georgia, for the Supreme Court. With a clear history of racism and misogyny, Cook voted against Nixon's nominee, earning him Nixon's scorn. (His action also earned him a spot on the cover of *The New York Times*.) He was a leader in supporting a Constitutional amendment supporting equal rights for women. Cook was quite outspoken in criticizing his former aid, Mitch McConnell, as McConnell shifted toward the extreme right. Cook lambasted McConnell for his opposition to the Affordable Care Act, claiming that McConnell was out of touch with the needs of his constituency. Later in life, though he remained a Republican, Cook supported more Democrats than he did Republicans. He went so far as to support Democrat John Kerry in the 2004 election, expressing deep disappointment in President Bush's first term.

Marlow Cook died in Sarasota, Florida on February 4, 2016. His wife of nearly sixty years, Nancy Remmers, his five children, and grandchildren survive.

See Current Biography 1972

Andre Courreges

Born: Pau, Aquitaine, France; March 9, 1923
Died: Neuilly-sur-Seine, France; January 7, 2016
Occupation: Fashion designer

One of the greatest fashion designers of the twentieth century, Andre Courreges has been credited with creating the mini-skirt and knee-high "go-go" boots craze of the 1960s. A contemporary of Pierre Cardin and Paco Rabanne, Courreges has dressed the wealthy and famous for decades, from Jacqueline Kennedy to Miley Cyrus. Courreges was forward thinking, embracing the "space age" in his unique designs, and touted as a designer for "tomorrow."

Andre Courreges was born in France where his father was the head butler in a wealthy British home. Though he was drawn to art and wanted to become an artist, his parents insisted that he pursue a more practical career. He studied civil engineering, but eventually switched to architecture and textiles. During World War II he served as a pilot in the French Air Force. In 1950 Courreges apprenticed with couture icon, Cristóbal Balenciaga, where he remained for eleven years. In 1961 he opened his own studio with another Balenciaga student, Coqueline Barrière. The two married two years later. It was Courreges who predicted women would eventually wear trousers as much as men, and he began designing pants suits. Mini skirts, hip-hugging, bell-bottomed trousers, and tops that exposed a woman's midriff were among his innovations. The boldness and simplicity of his designs made copycatting easy, and Courreges was incensed as he moved to maintain some sense of control over his designs.

When he wasn't active in the world of couture, Courreges was a sculptor. Andre Courreges died on January 7, 2016 at his home in Neuilly-sur-Seine, outside Paris. His wife and daughter survive.

See Current Biography 1970

Robert Craft

Born: Kingston, New York; October 20, 1923
Died: Gulf Stream, Florida; November 10, 2015
Occupation: Conductor, author, music critic

Though an accomplished conductor himself, Robert Craft is most remembered for his twenty-three year relationship with the renowned Igor Stravinsky, as his adviser and assistant, co-conductor, intellectual stimulus, almost constant companion, and surrogate son.

Robert Craft began studying and collecting the works of Igor Stravinsky, arguably the twentieth century's greatest composer, at a very young age. He studied music at Tanglewood, in Lenox, Massachusetts, at Columbia University, and the Julliard School of Music, where he graduated in 1946. Shortly thereafter, he founded the New York Chamber Art Society. He met Stravinsky after writing to the composer, requesting a copy of his "Symphonies of Wind Instruments," which was not available, locally, at the time. The letter made an impression on Stravinsky, and the two met on March 31, 1948 at the Raleigh Hotel in Washington. Stravinsky and his wife had an immediate affinity with Craft, inviting him to their California home to catalogue his manuscripts. They remained close for the rest of their lives, as Craft lived with the Stravinskys, becoming something of a surrogate son. He is credited with convincing Stravinsky to consider dodecaphony, after the elder lamented that his days of composition were over because he could not comprehend Schoenberg, the father of the twelve-tone school. With Craft's assistance, Stravinsky went on to re-instrument his Concertino for String Quartet, and several months later, Stravinsky had completed both that orchestration and the initial section of the "Cantata." Craft helped the native Russian composer write seven books.

Craft was heavily criticized for what some in the music world, and Stravinsky's personal manager, Lillian Libman, in particular, considered a false image of Stravinsky. He admitted that Stravinsky would speak, and he, Craft, would formulate the words, saying he never claimed to quote Stravinsky verbatim.

Following Stravinsky's death in 1971, Craft continued his close relationship with the widow, Vera Stravinsky. While closely guarding Stravinsky's private life from would-be biographers, Craft wrote six volumes of conversations, photograph albums and memoirs of Stravinsky's life. In 1976, Craft received an award from the American Academy of Arts and Letters for his work.

Robert Craft married Stravinsky's Danish nurse, Rita Christiansen in 1971, but the union ended in divorce. They had one son, Robert Alexander Craft, who lives in Copenhagen. Craft married his second wife, Alva Rodriquez Minoff, in 1993. Robert Craft died from prostate cancer on November 10, 2015. His son, wife, and two stepchildren survive him.

See Current Biography 1984

Johan Cruyff

Born: Amsterdam, Holland, Netherlands; April 25, 1947
Died: Barcelona, Spain; March 24, 2016
Occupation: Professional soccer player

Dutch soccer player Johan Cruyff was arguably the greatest soccer player in the game's long history. He was hailed as the "savior" of North American soccer when he joined the Los Angeles Aztecs in 1979. He had led European teams to six league championships, three European titles, and one world club team championship.

Johan Cruyff literally grew up on a soccer field. After his father's death, while Cruyff was still a small boy, his mother worked as a charwoman at Amsterdam's Ajax Stadium. When he was ten he outplayed two hundred other young players to win membership on the Ajax Juniors. He signed his first professional contract in 1965, as a forward and midfielder, leading his team to six league titles, four national cups, and three consecutive European championships. He was named the Dutch Player of the Year in 1967, 1968, and 1969, and was the European Player of the Year in 1971 and 1973. In his nine years with the Ajax he scored 256 goals in 350 games. In 1974 Cruyff captained the national team to the World Cup Final and was named Most Valuable Player (MVP). He was sold to Barcelona, by his own choice, in 1973, for tax purposes. Barcelona reportedly paid $2,250,000, the highest transfer sum in soccer history at that time. However, his enjoyment there was short-lived. The pressure from fans was extraordinary. He was vilified in the press if he underperformed, and his family received death threats. He retired in June of 1978. He did sign on with the New York Cosmos for some exhibition games, but in 1979 he signed on with the Los Angeles Aztecs in a two-year contract worth more than $1 million annually. He was, once more, voted the Most Valuable Player by the North American Soccer League. In 1980 he played for the Levante club in Valencia, Spain. After returning to the NASL Diplomats in 1981, Cruyff was plagued by injuries.

Cruyff retired from play and began coaching for the Ajax in the late 1980s. (He would eventually coach his own son, Jordi Cruyff.) He underwent heart bypass surgery in 1991 following a lifetime of heavy smoking, and became an anti-smoking advocate. In October of 2015, Cruyff announced he had lung cancer. He died on March 24, 2016. His wife of more than fifty years, Danny Coster, their three children, and numerous grandchildren survive.

See Current Biography 1981

Bill Cunningham

Born: Boston, Massachusetts; March 13, 1929
Died: New York, New York; June 25, 2016
Occupation: Fashion photographer, writer

Bill Cunningham was a legendary fashion icon best known for bringing the real-world fashion he observed on the streets of New York City to the world of haute couture. He wrote several style columns for the Sunday *New York Times*. His pictures also appeared in the *SoHo Weekly News* and the New York *Daily News*.

Bill Cunningham was born the second of four children to an Irish Catholic family in Boston, Massachusetts. As a teenager he worked as a stock boy at the Bonwit Teller department store. He attended Harvard University, but dropped out at the age of nineteen, then moved to New York City where his uncle, an advertising executive at Bonwit Teller, got him a job in the advertising department where his passion for fashion bloomed. Under pressure from family to choose a career path, Cunningham decided to become a milliner, creating his own brand, William J. He gained a reputation through his affiliation with the Chez Ninon dress shop, which catered to a socialite crowd that included members of the Vanderbilt, Astor, and Kennedy families.

Cunningham was drafted into the US Army during the Korean War. After two years in the military, he opened a small salon on West 54th Street. In the early 1960s, when fashion was dropping hats from its collections, Cunningham was asked to write for the trade journal *Women's Wear Daily*, which was widely considered the bible of the fashion industry. In the 1960s, he developed an interest in photography after the photographer, David Montgomery, gave him an Olympus camera. He was particularly interested in street fashion. His primary goal was to document clothes he found interesting, regardless of who was wearing them. In the late 1970s, Cunningham began writing a weekly column for the *New York Times* Style section. He became a New York icon, traveling through the streets by bicycle with his camera slung across his back.

In 2008 the French government honored Cunningham as an officer of the Order of Arts and Letters. In 2009 the New York Landmarks Conservancy declared Cunningham a "living" New York Landmark. In 2012 he was awarded the Carnegie Hall Medal of Excellence. Cunningham lived alone for his entire life, most of it in a small rent-controlled studio above Carnegie Hall. There are no immediate survivors.

See Current Biography 2011

Phyllis Curtin

Born: Clarksburg, West Virginia; December 3, 1921
Died: Great Barrington, Massachusetts; June 5, 2016
Occupation: Singer, educator

Although Phyllis Curtin was a naturally gifted opera singer, she will likely be most remembered for her role as teacher and dean of Boston University's College of Fine Arts, a role she played from 1983 to 1991. In 1987 she also founded the School of Music Opera Institute. She taught at the Boston University Tanglewood Institute for fifty-one years, and at Yale University from 1974 to 1983.

Phyllis Curtin began music studies as a child, learning to play the violin. Though she played in the high school orchestra, music was not necessarily her primary interest. She attended Monticello Junior College in Alton, Illinois for two years, and then enrolled at Wellesley College where she graduated with a degree in political science. It wasn't until her junior year at Wellesley that she began to consider studying voice. One of her early voice teachers was the Russian soprano, Olga Averino. In 1946 Curtin appeared with Leonard Bernstein at Tanglewood, Massachusetts and the New England Opera Theatre under Boris Goldovsky. Before long she was taking featured roles with the Boston Symphony, the Philadelphia Orchestra, and the New York Philharmonic. Though she certainly had the skill, critics speculate she never reached the notoriety of her contemporaries Beverly Sills, Joan Sutherland, and Maria Callas, because she was so drawn to performing and supporting contemporary, modern composers. She performed in the world's most notable venues, including La Scala. In Hamburg, Germany in 1964 Curtin received a twenty-minute standing ovation for her interpretation of "Arias and Lieder" by Richard Strauss.

Her famous protégés include Dawn Upshaw, Simon Estes, Gina Davis, and Stephanie Blythe. Curtin married Phillip Curtin in 1946, but the marriage ended in divorce. In 1956 Curtin married *Life* magazine editor and photographer, Eugene Cook who predeceased her in 1986. Phyllis Curtin leaves behind her daughter, Claudia d'Alessandro, and three grandchildren.

See Current Biography 1964

Gordon Davidson

Born: New York, New York; May 7, 1933
Died: Los Angeles, California; October 2, 2016
Occupation: Former artistic director of the Mark Taper Forum

Gordon Davidson was the artistic director of the Mark Taper Forum of the Los Angeles County Music Center, nurturing the new venture to become one of the finest regional theaters in the country. He was also the director and producer of the Ahmanson Theatre.

Gordon Davidson was born into the world of entertainment. His father taught theater at Brooklyn College for forty-six years, and his mother was a concert pianist. Davidson graduated as the valedictorian of the Brooklyn Technical High School, and earned several scholarships and admission to Cornell University, where he intended to study engineering, though he later changed his major to theater. After graduation, Davidson earned his MA degree in directing from Case Western Reserve University. He began his career as an apprentice stage manager at the American Shakespeare Festival in Stratford, Connecticut, and then took a job on Broadway as the stage manager of the Phoenix Theater. In 1964 director, producer, and playwright John Houseman hired Davidson to assist with the production of *King Lear* at the University of California in Los Angeles (UCLA). Davidson eventually succeeded Houseman as managing director. In 1967 Davidson was asked to become the first artistic director of the Marc Taper Forum in Los Angeles.

Davidson seemed to welcome controversy. The theater's first production, *The Devils*, was about a promiscuous priest and the sexual fantasies of a Catholic nun. The production was nearly shut down by the county board of supervisors. Davidson later won an Obie Award for best director, and received a Tony Award nomination for his work on *The Catonsville Nine*. (A rare venture into the movie industry had Davidson directing the movie version of the play produced by Gregory Peck.) In 1989 Davidson took on the post of artistic director and producer of the Ahmanson Theater. In 1994 three out of the four Tony Award nominees for best play had been developed and staged at the Taper.

Davidson received numerous awards for his work, including the Governor's Award for the Arts and an LA Stage Alliance Ovation Award. He was inducted into the Theater Hall of Fame on Broadway in 2002. Gordon Davidson married his college sweetheart, Judith Swiller. She and their two children survive him.

See Current Biography 2005

Peter Maxwell Davies

Born: Salford, England; September 8, 1934
Died: Orkney, Scotland; March 14, 2016
Occupation: Composer, conductor

Peter Maxwell Davies was a man of rare talent, writing compositions for ballet, string quartets, theater, and even for children. He was knighted in 1987, and was made "Master of the Queen's Music" in 2004 (the equivalent of a poet laureate). He was a conductor with the BBC Philharmonic, and the royal philharmonic orchestra.

Peter Maxwell Davies was slow to begin his music education. The headmaster at the Leigh Grammar School was a Quaker who considered music sinful. However, from 1952 to 1957 Davies worked toward an honors degree at the Royal Manchester College of Music, and Manchester University, which is where he met Alexander Goehr, Harrison Birtwistle, and John Ogdon. Together, with Davies, they made the so-called "Manchester School" helping to shape the future of British music. He then taught music to children, encouraging improvisation as a method for learning music. A few years later, on the recommendation of American composer, Aaron Copland, Davies attended Princeton University from 1962 to 1964, as a Harkness Fellow. He composed continuously during this time. His first recognized composition was the "Sonata for Trumpet and Piano" in 1955. He received a grant from the Italian government to study under Goffredo Petrassi in Rome. In 1959 his composition, "Prolation" earned Davies the Olivetti Prize.

Davies liked to experiment, injecting diverse elements, from Renaissance polyphony to jazz and electronic effects. He was known to "push the envelope," and the results were not always well received. Many complained that his early work was unplayable. In 1969 the audience chanted "rubbish" during the performance of his opera "Eight Songs for a Mad King." Another audience simply walked out. Davies' moved to the Orkney Islands, which had a calming effect on his compositions.

Davies was an outspoken champion of numerous environmental causes. He lived in a cottage in Orkney with no electricity or running water. There he founded the highly successful St. Magnus Festival. His most widely acclaimed composition was his opera, "The Martyrdom of St. Magnus" and his chamber symphony, "A Mirror of Whitening Light," which was inspired by his home on the isle of Hoy. He received the Koussevitzky Award, the Cobbett Medal for services to chamber music, and the Gulliver Award for Performing Arts in Scotland. He was appointed to the order of the British Empire (CBE) in 1981, and was knighted in 1987.

Davies announced he had leukemia in May of 2013, but he continued to work throughout his illness and treatment. He died on March 14, 2016. There are no known survivors.

See Current Biography 1980

Ales Debeljak

Born: Ljubljana, Slovenia; December 25, 1961
Died: Gorenjsko, Slovenia; January 29, 2016
Occupation: Slovenian poet, literary critic

Ales Debeljak was a world-renowned poet and literary critic who taught at the University of Ljubljana.

Ales Debeljak was born in a country that no longer exists—Yugoslavia—a circumstance that informed his writing as he explored the boundaries of cultural identity. He attended the University of Ljubljana where he studied philosophy and comparative literature, and where he was the editor in chief of the student-run bi-monthly, *Tribuna*. He was forced to resign his editorship after the local League of Communists banned two issues due to controversial content. He published his first collection of poetry in 1982 when he was just twenty-two years old. He graduated summa cum laude, and his thesis received the University Preseren Award, a student version of Slovenia's highest award for arts and culture. He received his master's degree in cultural studies, and pursued his doctorate in the United States at the Maxwell School of Citizenship and Public Affairs at Syracuse University in New York. He married American Erica Johnson.

Debeljak published fourteen collections of essays, and eight books of poetry, and his writing has been translated into twenty languages. He was also a prolific translator himself. Debeljak won numerous accolades and awards, including a senior Fulbright fellowship that funded his year at the University of California, Berkeley. Debeljak received the Miriam Lindberg Israel Poetry for Peace, and the Slovenian National Book Award. He has been a guest professor at a number of universities, including the University of Klagenfurt in Austria, and in the United States he was a visiting professor at Fairleigh Dickinson University and at Northwestern University. He also served as an expert for the Korber Stiftung, a foundation focused on promoting international dialogue.

Ales Debeljak was killed in an automobile accident on January 29, 2016. His wife and three children survive.

See Current Biography 2007

Mattiwilda Dobbs

Born: Atlanta, Georgia; July 11, 1925
Died: Atlanta, Georgia; December 8, 2015
Occupation: Opera singer

Named after her grandmother, Mattie Wilda, Mattiwilda Dobbs was an African American coloratura soprano who helped break the color barrier in the world of opera.

Mattiwilda Dobbs was born in Atlanta, Georgia, to an early civil rights activist and railroad mail clerk, John Wesley Dobbs, who, after making his own way through three years of college, saw that each of his six daughters had a college education. Mattiwilda began piano lessons when she was seven year old, and several years later, began discovering her voice in the choir of the First Congregational Church. She entered Spelman College and began voice lessons with Naomi Maise and Willis James. After graduating from Spelman as the class valedictorian, Dobbs moved on to Columbia University Teachers College in New York, where she earned her masters degree in Spanish (a career backup should she need it). While in New York, Dobbs also studied at the Mannes School of Music after receiving two scholarships, and in Massachusetts at the Berkshire Music Center. She received a $3,000 John Jay Whitney Opportunity Fellowship to study in Paris for two years with Pierre Bernac. In October of 1950, Dobbs competed against hundreds of singers from four continents, winning the prestigious International Music Competition held in Geneva, Switzerland.

Dobbs performed on the world's most distinguished stages, from La Scala where she was the first black singer to perform, to the Glyndebourne Opera Festival. The Royal Opera Company sent her to Covent Garden to appear in "Le Coq d'Or," before an audience that included British and Swedish royalty. Just four days prior to her performance, she learned that her husband, Luis Rodriguez, a journalist and scriptwriter, had died. The two had been married just over a year. She decided to perform and was awarded Sweden's Order of the North Star by King Gustaf VI. Her American debut was with the Little Orchestra Society in New York, followed a few years later with a performance as Gilda in "Rigoletto," at New York's Metropolitan Opera where, by 1964, she performed in twenty-nine roles. Following the lead of popular singer, Paul Robeson, Dobbs refused to perform before a segregated audience, a move that cost the American South the privilege of seeing her on stage until 1962 when the Atlanta Municipal Auditorium was de-segregated. The Atlanta mayor presented her with roses.

Dobbs was married a second time, to the Swedish newspaper journalist, Bengt Janzon, who died in 1997. Her nephew, Maynard Jackson, was the first African American mayor of Atlanta, and Dobbs sang at his inauguration.

Mattiwilda Dobbs died on December 8, 2015. The cause was cancer. Survivors include her sister, June Dobbs Butts, and niece, Michele Jordan.

See Current Biography 1955

Patty Duke

(Anna Marie Patricia Duke)
Born: New York, New York; December 14, 1946
Died: Coeur d'Alene, Idaho; March 29, 2016
Occupation: American actress, mental health advocate

Patty Duke came to fame as a child actress, starring in the 1959 Broadway hit, *The Miracle Worker*, where she played the blind and deaf Helen Keller opposite Anne Bancroft's Annie Sullivan. She won a Golden Globe Award for the "Most Promising Newcomer" for her role. The film adaptation of the play won Duke an Oscar as "Best Supporting Actress" when she was just sixteen years old—the youngest person to win an award at that time. She would soon land her own television show *The Patty Duke Show,* in which she portrayed two identical cousins. In the first year, the show earned Duke a top twenty hit in the Neilson Ratings, and an Emmy nomination in 1963.

While most of her fan base during her early acting career would consider Patty Duke to be living a charmed life, nothing could have been farther from the truth. She was born to a heavy-drinking cab driver and a chronically depressed mother who kicked her husband out by the time Patty Duke, the youngest of three children, was six years old. Her mother essentially handed her over to the greedy, controlling talent scouts John and Ethel Ross, who isolated her from her family. John Ross prepared Duke for the role of Helen Keller for over a year, having her wear a blindfold at home, and challenging her not to flinch at loud noises. The Ross home became more dysfunctional as John and Ethel began drinking heavily, sexually abusing their charge. When Duke's father died, she was not allowed to attend his funeral.

In addition to having her own television show, Duke also released several record albums. Her first single, "Don't Just Stand There," rose to the top of the Billboard charts. As she matured, Duke revealed that she suffered from bipolar disorder and depression, becoming an advocate

for mental health, and writing about her experience in her 1987 autobiography, *Call Me Anna: the Autobiography of Patty Duke*. She was the president of the Screen Actors Guild for five years, from 1983 to 1988.

Duke was married four times. While her first marriages were short-lived, her final marriage to drill sergeant Michael Pearce, whom she met on the set of A Time to Triumph, lasted thirty years. Patty Duke passed from sepsis from a ruptured intestine at age 69. Pearce, three children and several grandchildren survive her.

See Current Biography 1963

Umberto Eco

Born: Alessandria, Italy; January 5, 1932
Died: Milan, Italy; February 19, 2016
Occupation: Professor of semiotics, Italian novelist

A world-renowned scholar of semiotics—the study of signs as cultural phenomena and their meanings—Umberto Eco became a best-selling author late in life. He wrote his first novel, *The Name of the Rose,* in 1985 when he was forty-three. A few years later, the book was made into a movie starring Sean Connery.

Umberto Eco considered his childhood experiences of World War II in the medieval fortress city of his birth, Alessandria, to be an exciting time, and his experiences helped mold the thought processes that would eventually make him a scholar of semiotics. Reading American literature was an anti-Fascist statement, and American jazz came to signify resistance and defiance. Eco studied philosophy at the University of Turin where he earned his doctorate in 1954. He had a passion for the Middle Ages, and his early work explored the work of Saint Thomas Aquinas. (His first novel is set in the Middle Ages.) He became closely associated with a group of writers known as Gruppo 63, who formed an avant-garde literary movement that flourished in Italy in the 1950s and 1960s. Eco's study of aesthetics, and his first scholarly book, *Opera aperta* (*The Open Work*) became a "theoretical manifesto" for the Gruppo 63. A concern for social betterment was the foundation of Eco's approach to issues relating to mass culture and the mass media. Eco was a professor of visual communications at the University of Florence from 1966 to 1969. He taught for a short time at Milan Polytechnic then became a professor of semiotics at the University of Bologna where he established a chair in semiotics. Eco published seven novels, and at the time of his death, had just finished editing a collection of his essays. His first novel, *The Name of the Rose,* earned him two prestigious literary prizes: the Prix Medici and the Premio Strega. He received countless academic titles and honorary degrees.

Umberto Eco died from cancer at his home in Milan. His survivors include his wife of fifty-three years, Renate Ramge Eco, and two grown children.

See Current Biography 1985

Ronit Elkabetz

Born: Beersheba, Israel; November 27, 1964
Died: Tel Aviv, Israel; April 19, 2016
Occupation: Israeli actress and director

Ronit Elkabetz was an Israeli actress, screenwriter, and director widely recognized as the face of Israeli cinema. She acted in a variety of Israeli and French films, receiving three acting Ophir Awards from the Israeli Academy of Film and Television, and has been referred to as an Israeli Meryl Streep.

Ronit Elkabetz was born to Moroccan Jewish parents who had immigrated to Israel in 1963 from Essaouir on Morocco's Atlantic coast. She and her three younger brothers were raised in a deeply religious, working-class household, where Hebrew, Arabic, and French were spoken. Elkabetz originally planned a career in fashion design, but after two years of compulsory military service, she began modeling and appearing in commercials. Though she had never acted before, a commercial director suggested she audition for a role in Daniel Wachsmann's *Hameyu'ad (The Appointed)*. She was cast in the starring role. After reaching critical prominence in Israel, Elkabetz moved to Paris, France where she began working with the French stage director Ariane Mnouchkine's acclaimed Parisian acting troupe, Le Theatre du Soleil. In 2001 Elkabetz won her second Ophir Award for her role in *Late Marriage*, which also won the Ophir Award for best film and was submitted for an Academy Award for best foreign film. Shortly thereafter, Elkabetz traveled to New York to begin a creative partnership with her brother, Slomi. The two began a trilogy of films loosely based on their parents' troubled relationship. These became known as the Viviane Amsalem trilogy, the last of which Elkabetz completed with the 2014 film, *Gett: The Trial of Viviane Amsalem.* The film's premier at the 2014 Cannes Film Festival earned plaudits from critics for its powerful acting, bold directorial moves, and strong message about Israel's unequal divorce laws. *Gett* received twelve Ophir Award nominations and earned a Golden Globe

Award nomination for best foreign language film and was Israel's official submission to the Academy Awards. In 2015 Elkabetz was selected to preside over the jury for the International Critics' Week portion of the Cannes Film Festival.

In 2010 Elkabetz received a lifetime achievement award from the Israeli Film Academy, the same year she married architect Avner Yasharon with whom she had twins, a son and a daughter. Her husband and children survive.

See Current Biography 2016

Robert (Bob) Elliott

Born: Boston, Massachusetts; March 26, 1923
Died: Cundy's Harbor, Maine; February 2, 2016
Occupation: Radio personality, satirist

Bob Elliott was half of the popular radio duo, Bob and Ray, whose wit and skill in ad-libbed dialogue won them the affection of radio listeners of the 1950s and 1960s, as well as two Peabody Awards, America's highest honor in radio and television achievement. His son, Chris Elliott, and granddaughter, Abby Elliott, continue his legacy as accomplished comedians in their own right.

Bob Elliott was an only child, born in Boston, Massachusetts. In high school, he put on radio shows over the school's public address system. He attended the Feagin School of Drama and Radio in New York City, while also working as an usher at Radio City Music Hall, and as a page at NBC. In 1943 Elliott joined the US Army, serving with the 27th Infantry Division. His teaming up with Ray Goulding happened by accident when the two worked for WHDH in Boston. Elliott was a disc jockey and Ray delivered newscasts. After delivering his newscasts, Ray would stay on and the two began to banter back and forth. By popular demand, WHDH gave the pair a half-hour show called "Matinee with Bob and Ray." The two went to New York in 1951 to audition with Charles Barry, vice-president in charge of NBC radio programs. The two created a motely cast of characters who populated skits that mocked popular culture, their wit aimed at advertising in particular, and they named themselves "critics at large" when NBC inaugurated the program known as "Monitor." According to radio critic Melvin Maddocks, writing for the *Christian Science Monitor* (30 July 1957), "Monitor's most valuable feature is Bob and Ray. Radio had no funnier, and no more effective lampooners of serial dramas, inept or pretentious announcers and audience participation programs." They were given a George Foster Peabody Award in 1952 as the "foremost satirists in radio." They received three Peabody Awards over the course of their careers, and were inducted into the Radio Hall of Fame in 1995. In 1984 the pair performed in front of sold-out audiences at Carnegie Music Hall.

Elliott married his colleague Jane Underwood in 1943. The two had four children. Their son, Chris Elliott, became an accomplished comedian himself, best known for his work with David Letterman. Ray Goulding died from kidney cancer in 1990. Bob Elliott died from throat cancer on February 2, 2016. Survivors include three children from his first marriage, two adopted daughters, eleven grandchildren, and five great-grandchildren.

See Current Biography 1957

Thorbjörn Fälldin

Born: Vastby, Sweden; April 24, 1926
Died: Högsjö, Ångermanland, Sweden; July 23, 2016
Occupation: Former Swedish prime minister

Thorbjörn Fälldin, leader of Sweden's Center Party, served for two years as the first non-Social Democratic prime minister of Sweden in 1976. He was elected again in 1979 and served until 1982.

Thorbjörn Fälldin was born on the family farm in Vastby in north central Sweden where his parents were active members of the Agrarian (now Center) Party. Fälldin was largely self-educated in that he had to postpone secondary school to help with the farm work after his father's health declined. He finished his formal education with correspondence courses and biweekly classes at a nearby village. At that time, Fälldin was the only Swedish political party leader without a university education. He was still a teenager when he became the chairman of the Youth League district committee. After serving for two years in the compulsory military service as a reserve army officer, he became, at twenty-two, the Angermanland district committee general secretary, and served as it's president from 1950 to 1955. In 1958 Fälldin was elected to the Lower Chamber of the Riksdag (parliament). In 1969 he became the first vice-chairman of the Center party, and became its chairman in 1971.

At that time Swedes were widely dissatisfied with the centralized, bureaucratized, industrialized, and highly taxed society that had developed under four decades of Social Democratic rule. As leader of the largest opposition party, Fälldin ran for prime minister, appealing to voters by proposing tax cuts and measures to stimulate rural area industry, in addition to his strong stand against environmental pollution and Sweden's rising unemployment rate. His party also took a strong anti-nuclear stance. The 1976 election, one of the closest elections in Swedish history, put Fälldin in the prime minister's seat. However, before the year was over, Fälldin found it necessary to retreat from his nuclear power position, leaving voters feeling betrayed. Fälldin was forced to take other unpopular moves as inflation ran at about twelve percent. Despite his promises to expand the welfare system while cutting taxes, he was forced to cut spending, boost taxes, and nationalize the bankrupt shipbuilding industry. The Center Party was defeated in 1982, and Fälldin returned to his family farm in Högsjö, Ångermanland, just north of Sundsvall. Fälldin married Solveig Oberg in 1956. She and their three children survive.

See Current Biography 1978

Zelda Fichandler

Born: Boston, Massachusetts; September 18, 1924
Died: Washington, DC; July 29, 2016
Occupation: Theatre producer, director

Zelda Fichandler was the co-founder and artistic director of Washington, DC's Arena Stage, a venture that gave rise to a nationwide regional-theater movement.

Zelda Fichandler was born in Boston into a middle-class Jewish family where she was considered the outlier or maverick. She claimed she never fit in. By the age of nine, she had already decided she would become an actress. She attended Columbia University where she studied Russian language and literature. For a short while after World War II, Fichandler worked as a research analyst in the Russian division of military intelligence. At the same time she earned an MA degree in theatre arts at George Washington University. In 1950 she lamented that there were no professional theatres in Washington. (The National Theatre had closed down because of a dispute over racial segregation.) She and her husband, Thomas Fichandler, an economist who served in the Social Security Administration (SSA), teamed with her former drama professor, Edward Magnum, and founded the Arena Stage, Washington's first integrated professional theatre. Fichandler began the practice of giving a second chance to promising plays that had met with financial disaster on the New York stage. After several location changes, the Arena found its permanent home in 1961, after Fichandler decided to choose a not-for-profit status, meaning she could look for funding from foundations and other charitable organizations. As such, Fichandler created a national regional-theatre movement.

The Arena Stage became a complex with several stages: a 180-seat cabaret called the "Old Vat Room," and the 130-seat Scene Shop, which she used for exploratory work, in addition to the 800-seat Arena stage. Fichandler's main goal with the Arena Stage was to discover new plays and develop untried playwrights. A major break-through came in the form of Howard Sackler's interracial love drama *The Great White Hope*, starring James Earl Jones and Jane Alexander. The play later won several Tony Awards and a Pulitzer Prize after it moved onto Broadway.

The Fichandlers separated in 1975, but they continued to work together. Thomas Fichandler died in 1997. That same year, President Clinton awarded Zelda Fichandler the National Medal of Arts. Her survivors include her two sons, a sister, and two grandchildren.

See Current Biography 1987

Dario Fo

Born: Sangiano, Italy; March 24, 1926
Died: Milan, Italy; October 13, 2016
Occupation: Italian playwright, satirist, actor

Dario Fo was an Italian playwright and actor whose satirical, avant-garde, razor-tongued plays were the scourge of bureaucrats and politicians. He wrote more than seventy plays (a number of them co-written with his wife, Rame) and he wrote two illustrated novels. He won the 1997 Nobel Prize for literature.

Dario Fo was born and raised in northern Italy, in a "town of smugglers and fishermen." His interest in theater arose during his child-hood as he spent hours listening to the tales told by local fishermen or by itinerant storytellers and balladeers that roamed the countryside. During World War II he helped his father in the Resistance, guiding escaped Allied prisoners of war across the border into Switzerland. Following the war he entered the Academy of Fine Arts in Milan to study painting, but he felt irresistibly drawn to theater. He left the academy without a degree and joined a small theatrical troupe, run by the popular radio personality Franco Parenti, performing semi-improvised sketches for local audiences. He would continue in this vein for the rest of his career. From 1952 through 1958, Fo and two colleagues, formed their own revue company called I Dritti (The Stand-ups). His style has been likened to the sketches by Ameri-can comics Sid Caesar, Mel Brooks, and the Smothers Brothers. In 1958 Fo met and married

the actress Franca Rame, and the two collabo-rated on their creative endeavors until her death in 2013. Fo characterized their work as "unof-ficial leftism."

In 1968 the two founded the theatre coop-erative Nuova Scena (New Scene) touring the industrial north, performing for working-class audiences. In the climate of popular unrest, Fo's political satire found a ready audience. During this time Fo wrote and performed in one of his greatest plays, *Mistero buffo* ("comical mystery"), which the Vatican condemned as "the most blasphemous show in the history of television." Another of Fo's most widely performed plays was called "Accidental Death of an Anarchist," inspired by the actual death of a suspected ter-rorist, Giuseppe Pinelli, who mysteriously fell from a fourth story window at the Milan police station.

In addition to writing over seventy plays, Fo enjoyed directing opera, and wrote several man-uals about theater. When accepting the 1997 Nobel Prize, Fo credited his wife, Franca Rame as his muse. She predeceased her husband in 2013. Their son, Jacopo, survives.

See Current Biography 1986

Joe Garagiola

Born: St. Louis, Missouri; February 12, 1926
Died: Scottsdale, Arizona; March 23, 2016
Occupation: Professional baseball player, broadcaster

Though his success as a professional baseball catcher was somewhat unexceptional, Joe Gara-giola's greatest accomplishment was as a broad-caster following his baseball career. He was widely recognized in American households for his folksy, self-deprecating humor in the broad-cast booth, and eventually, as a television talk show host.

Joe Garagiola was born to Italian immigrants who settled in St. Louis, Missouri. His father was a bricklayer. He characterized his mother as a loving, simple woman who could not speak English. Garagiola lived in the Italian-American section of St. Louis, known as "The Hill," where he grew up with another baseball great, Law-rence Peter Berra, better known as "Yogi Berra." Regarding his less than impressive career as a professional player, Garagiola once quipped, "Not only was I not the best catcher in the ma-jor leagues, I wasn't even the best catcher on my street." In fact, Garagiola was considered the more promising player at the time he signed up with the Cardinals at the age of fifteen. (Berra went on to play with the New York Yankees, becoming a baseball legend.)

Garagiola was drafted into the army during World War II, but the war ended before he saw combat. He was then stationed as a military policeman in Manila. His closest friend in the army was Joe Ginsberg who also played professional baseball with the New York Mets. Garagiola was at the top of his game in the 1946 season when the Cardinals were up against the Boston Red Sox. Garagiola batted .316 and tied an all-time record, getting four hits in one game. The Cardinals went on to win the series in seven games. In 1950 Garagiola sustained a shoulder injury from which he never fully recovered. He was shunted to four different teams in as many years before he retired. The Anheuser-Busch beer company hired Garagiola as a color commentator at Cardinals' games. For the next two decades he went on to host "Game of the Week" for NBC. He also had a daily radio program. In 1973 Garagiola was awarded the prestigious Peabody Award for his pregame show. He branched out beyond the sports world when he became a host of NBC's "Today" show. He even appeared as a guest host, on a regular basis, for "The Tonight Show," interviewing such guests as John Lennon and Paul McCartney, Henry Kissinger, and Vice President Hubert Humphrey. He was also a game show emcee on "He Said, She Said," and "To Tell the Truth." For nearly ten years, Garagiola hosted the Westminster Kennel Club Dog Show. In 1991 he received the Baseball Hall of Fame's Fred D. Frick Award for his contribution to sports broadcasting. He also wrote three books about baseball.

Garagiola met his wife of more than sixty years, Audrie Ross, at the Cardinal's ballpark where she was the game organist. She, their three children, and eight grandchildren survive him.

See Current Biography 1976

Clifton Canter Garvin, Jr.

Born: Portsmouth, Virginia; December 22, 1921
Died: Easton, Maryland; April 17, 2016
Occupation: US corporate executive

Clifton Garvin became the president of Exxon Corporation in 1972, and was appointed chairman and chief executive officer in 1975. He retained his position until his retirement in 1986.

Clifton Garvin was born in Portsmouth, Virginia, where his father worked as a divisional controller for the Safeway Stores, Inc. food chain. He graduated from Virginia Polytechnic Institute in 1943 with a degree in chemical engineering. He then spent three years with the US Army Corp of Engineers in the South Pacific. After the war, he returned to Virginia Tech, earning his MS degree in 1947. Soon afterward he joined Esso Standard Oil Company as a process engineer. Recognized for his leadership skills, Garvin was recruited into the company's managerial development system, nicknamed "the Academy" in Baton Rouge, Louisiana. After twelve years in Baton Rouge, he was sent to New York to head the East Coast supply department. The following year he became the executive assistant to Michael Haider, the president of Standard Oil. He was elected to the board of directors as the executive vice-president in 1968.

Clifton Garvin became the voice of the industry during the tumultuous 1970s when oil prices spiraled out of control, and the industry was vilified in the court of public opinion. In 1981 President Ronald Reagan appointed Garvin to sit on the National Productivity Advisory Committee. In 1997 the Virginia Tech Board of Visitors awarded him the William H. Ruffner Medal, the university's highest honor.

Clifton Garvin married Thelma E. Volland of Washington, DC on March 3, 1943. Garvin's wife, Thelma, their four children, ten grandchildren, and thirteen grandchildren survive.

See Current Biography 1980

Hans-Dietrich Genscher

Born: Reideburg, Saxony-Anhalt, Germany; March 21, 1927
Died: Wachtberg-Pech, Germany; March 31, 2016
Occupation: Former vice-chancellor and foreign minister of the Federal Republic of Germany

Hans-Dietrich Genscher was an important figure in the reunification of Germany and a strong advocate of European unity. He served as the chairman of the liberal Free Democratic Party (FDP) from 1974 to 1985, and was West Germany's foreign minister and vice chancellor from 1974 to 1992.

Genscher was born to Kurt Genscher, a prosperous small farmer and lawyer who died when Genscher was still quite young. When he was ten years old, Genscher joined the Hitler Youth, and in 1943, he was drafted into the Luftwaffe (air force) auxiliary. By the end of the war Genscher was a prisoner of war with American forces. He went on to study law and economics at Martin Luther University in Halle, and at the University of Leipzig. Genscher became involved in politics while attending school, joining the Liberal Democratic party (LDP), not so much for any liberal leanings, as to stand up against socialism. His anti-socialist convictions pitted him against the East German Communist authorities, and he was forced to flee to the West in 1952. He joined the FDP and became the state deputy chairman of the Jungdemokraten (Young Democrats). Genscher was named the party's general secretary from 1959 to 1965, serving on a national level from 1962 to 1964. Genscher was elected to the Bundestag in 1965. In the late 1960s he played a key role in the fifteen-member Brandt-Scheel Cabinet, as Minister of the Interior, with responsibility for internal security, protection of the environment, and relations between the government and the Bundesrat. In June of 1972 he released a report on the increase in political extremism and called for improvement in the internal security apparatus. Only a few months later, Genscher personally participated in negotiations with Palestinian terrorists who kidnapped and eventually killed eleven Israeli athletes who were in Munich to compete in the Olympic games.

As a foreign minister, Genscher advocated a halt to the east-west arms race, a strong North Atlantic Treaty Organization (NATO) alliance and strengthening the European Union (EU). According to Hella Pick, writing for *The Guardian* (April 1, 2016), Genscher could claim "credit for being ahead of his country's partners in recognizing that Gorbachev's glasnost ("openness") and perestroika ("restructuring") would have a profound effect on Europe's political map and the end of the division of Europe."

Genscher's second wife, Barbara, and a daughter from his first marriage survive him.

See Current Biography 1975

André Glucksmann

Born: Boulogne-Billancourt, France; June 19, 1937
Died: Paris, France; November 10, 2015
Occupation: French philosopher, activist

Though a proponent of Marxism at the tender age of thirteen, André Glucksmann later became disillusioned with the militant tactics of Communist regimes, and became a seminal member of "the new thinkers," along with the likes of Pascal Bruckner, Bernard-Henri Lévy, and Jean-Marie Benoist. He became an advocate for the super oppressed, and denounced ideological labels like "left" and "right."

André Glucksmann was born to two leftist Zionists just as Nazism was gaining purchase in Germany. His father, Rubin, was born in Czernowitz, in present-day Ukraine, and his mother, Martha, was from Prague. The two had immigrated to Palestine, but the Communist Party sent them to Germany to join the anti-Nazi underground. A few years later, they moved to France where their son, André, was born. Glucksmann joined the Communist Party at a young age and, as a young man, became a militant advocate for a Marxist revolution. He studied at the elite École normale supérieure de Saint-Cloud in Lyon, earning certification to teach philosophy. He received his doctorate from the Centre National de la Recherche Scientifique (the National Center for Scientific Research). In the early 1970s, he joined the Maoist Proletarian Left, as he cheered student revolts at the Sorbonne, where he taught, protests that nearly resulted in the collapse of the French government.

In what many on the Left perceived as a massive betrayal, Glucksmann's leftist, Communist ideals took an about-face after two pivotal events: the kidnapping and murder of eleven Israeli Olympic athletes in Munich, Germany by a group closely associated with the Palestinian Liberation Organization (PLO), and the publication of Aleksandr Solzhenitsyn's *Gulag Archipelago* in 1973. By the middle of the decade, Glucksmann went so far as to draw a direct link between Marxist thought and the rise of Nazism and Soviet Communism. Regarding Glucksmann's most influential work, *The Master Thinkers*, William Grimes for the *New York Times* notes that Glucksmann claimed Marx, Hegel, Fichte, and Nietzsche "erected the mental apparatus which [sic] is indispensable for launching the grand final solutions of the 20th century" (November 11, 2015). Glucksmann and other young, French writers like him became known as "the new philosophers." Often considered a traitor to the Left, Glucksmann was reviled for supporting US President, Ronald Reagan's strategy of nuclear deterrence, as well as the US–led wars against Iraq's Saddam Hussein. To the Lefts horror, he originally supported French President Nicolas Sarkozy (a stance that he later acknowledged was a mistake). In the ensuing decades, Glucksmann would come to the conclusion that any black and white thinking, or "Left or Right" thinking, is an illusion and a "sin against the spirit." He became an advocate for the oppressed: the Vietnamese "boat people," the Bosnians in the former Yugoslavia who were facing genocide, the Chechen rebels who were fighting for independence from Russia, and marginalized gay men during the AIDS crisis. Rather than promoting an ideology aimed at building a better future, he espoused eradicating the evil in this world, today.

André Glucksmann died on November 10, 2015. He had been battling cancer for some time. He is survived by his wife, Francoise (Fanfan), and his son, Raphaël.

See Current Biography 2006

William M. Gray

Born: Detroit, Michigan; October 9, 1929
Died: Fort Collins, Colorado; April 16, 2016
Occupation: Meteorologist

William Gray was one of the world's foremost authorities on hurricanes and other tropical storms: how they form, their structure, the paths they take, their frequency, and global factors affecting their intensity. With remarkable accuracy Gray's annual predictions for hurricane activity were reported across the globe.

William Gray grew up in Washington DC, and attended George Washington University where he earned a BS degree in geography in 1952. In an effort to avoid being drafted into active combat in the Korean War, he preemptively signed on with the meteorological program in the air force, which would also pay for his graduate work at the University of Chicago. He became a protégé of Herbert Riehl, sometimes referred to as the father of modern meteorology. When Riehl moved to Colorado State University, Gray followed in 1961. The two scientists identified several factors that influenced the patterns and strengths of hurricanes—factors occurring far from the East Coast of the United States.

Gray is also well known for his association with United Nations World Meteorological Organization (WMO), though he often differed with fellow scientists about the causes of global climate change. Gray was adamant in his assertion that rising global temperatures are a part of a natural cycle of heating and cooling caused by thermohaline circulation, also known as the global ocean conveyor. He was contentious with his assertions, and publicly accused fellow scientists of knowingly carrying out flawed experiments, and even lying, for the sake of funding.

For his many accomplishments, Gray received the Jule G. Charney Award from the American Meteorological Society (AMS), and the Banner I. Miller Award from the Atlantic Oceanographic and Meteorological Laboratory (AOML). He had been an academic advisor to over seventy graduate students at Colorado State University.

Gray married Nancy Price in 1954 and they had four children. Nancy and a daughter, Ann, predeceased him. His survivors include two daughters, a son, and two grandsons.

See Current Biography 2010

Andrew S. Grove

Born: Budapest, Hungary; September 2, 1936
Died: Los Altos, California; March 21, 2016
Occupation: Former chairman, CEO, and COO of Intel

Andrew Grove co-founded Intel, the foremost microchip manufacturer, in the new, growing computer industry, eventually capturing ninety-percent of the market. With revenues exceeding $26.8 billion in 2002, Intel became the most profitable business in the world at that time.

Andrew Grove was born to a Jewish family in Budapest, Hungary, at a time when the Nazis were rising to power. After his father was arrested and sent to a concentration camp, the eight-year-old Grove (whose birth name was Andras Grof) and his mother obtained false identity papers and were sheltered by a neighbor. Miraculously, they were reunited with Grove's father, George Groff after the war. Grove realized his parents' dream that he earn a college education by first taking college courses in Hungary, but he had to flee when the Soviet Union invaded. He escaped across the border to Austria, then managed passage to the United States where he lived with relatives. He graduated with a degree in chemical engineering from the City University of New York (CUNY). He earned his doctorate in chemical engineering from the University of California at Berkeley. He worked for a startup computer company called Fairchild Semiconductor where he studied the uses of silicon in transistors. When several of his colleagues asked him to join them for their own startup, Grove jumped at the chance. In 1964 Grove, Bob Noyce, and Gordon Moore created Integrated Electronics, better known as Intel.

The company's success owed much to Andrew Grove. He was a harsh taskmaster. Employees arriving late had to sign in on a roster. In 1971 he sent what has become known as the "Scrooge memo" to his employees, making it clear that December 24 was to be a full workday. However, he lived by the same rules he imposed. Though he was the chairman and CEO, he ran the company from a nine-by-eight-foot cubicle. Over the course of his career, Grove published a number of books with titles like *High Output Management* (1983) and *One-on-One with Andy Grove: How to Manage Your Boss, Yourself, and Your Coworkers* (1988), and *Only the Paranoid Survive* (1996). Grove received a great number of honors and accolades including the "Technology leader of the Year" award from *Industry Week*, the *Chief Executive* magazine named him CEO of the year. *Time* magazine named him the 1997 "Man of the Year." Grove was also a philanthropist donating $26 million to the City University of New York, and supporting numerous medical research organizations.

In 1958 he married a fellow Hungarian refugee, Eva Kastan. She and their two daughters survive.

See Current Biography 1998

Zaha Hadid

Born: Baghdad, Iraq; October 31, 1950
Died: Miami, Florida; March 31, 2016
Occupation: Iraqi architect

Zaha Hadid designed some of the world's most innovative and unusual structures. She was dubbed "the queen of the curve" as she avoided straight edges and hard angles in her designs. Hadid's numerous awards included the Royal Institute of British Architect's Royal Gold Medal for her lifetime's work, the Pritzker Architecture Prize (architecture's highest honor), and the Royal Institute of British Architects' Royal Gold Medal, the first female to be so honored.

Zaha Hadid was raised in Iraq during a time when there were few limitations on women. She attended boarding school in Switzerland and then earned a BS degree in Mathematics from the American University of Beirut, in Lebanon. She continued graduate work at the London Architectural Association School of Architecture (AA). In 1979 she formed her own architectural firm, winning a variety of international architecture competitions, including designs for the Peak Club in Hong Kong, and the Kurfurstendamm office building in Berlin, Germany. While critics claimed her work was more artistic than practical, structures that could only exist on the canvas, engineers confirmed that Hadid's designs, though radical, were possible to build. Though her designs had firm foundations in the principles of modern architecture, they were also unconventional. Her first significant architectural design was the Vitra Fire Station in Weil am Rhein, Germany.

In addition to her many constructed works, Hadid's designs have appeared in art galleries for their artistic innovation. Such a display appeared at the Guggenheim Museum in New York, under the title "The Great Utopia" in 1992, and "Wish Machine: World Invention" at the Vienna Kunsthakke in 1996. The end of the millennium was a turning point for Hadid's career as more of her award-winning designs were actually being built. She taught architecture at such prestigious institutions as Yale University (which also hosted the Zaha Hadid Laboratory, an exhibit of her works), Columbia University, the University of Chicago, and Hochschule für bildende Künste (HFBK)

in Hamburg Germany. In addition, Hadid held the Kenzo Tange Chair at Harvard University's Graduate School of Design.

In 2002 Hadid was made a Commander of the British Empire (CBE), one of Britain's highest honors. She received the 2010 Riba Stirling Prize, the highest such honor in the United Kingdom.

Hadid never married or had children. Her brother, Haytham, survives her.

See Current Biography 2003

Merle Haggard

Born: Oildale, California; April 6, 1937
Died: Palo Cedro, California; April 6, 2016
Occupation: American country singer, songwriter, musician

Merle Haggard was a country music legend whose most widely recognized work is the "redneck" anthem "Okie from Muskogee," the pop hit that brought him to national attention in 1969, but his repertoire was more varied, and his musicianship was highly regarded. Writing for *USA Today*, (April 2, 1996), David Zimmerman declared, "Haggard may be the most graceful and sophisticated musical commentator in all of country music."

Merle Haggard was born to a lower, middle-class, working family. Though accounts of his upbringing vary, Haggard was born near Bakersfield, California, in a makeshift house that had been converted from a railroad boxcar. His father worked as a carpenter for the Santa Fe Railroad. Haggard's father died when he was just nine, leaving his mother, Flossie, to raise the family alone. Haggard would later draw on his relationship with his mother in his hit single, "Mamma Tried." Haggard considered himself a "general screw up" in his early teens when he was habitually truant from home as well as from school, riding the rails and hitching rides up and down the West Coast, doing migrant farm labor, oilfield work, odd jobs, and getting into ever-increasing trouble with the law. Twenty-seven months in San Quentin prison turned his life around.

Haggard unwittingly placed himself in the middle of a cultural, social fray with his song "Okie from Muskogee." Right-wingers claimed it as their anthem and some liberals accused Haggard of contributing to the polarization of the country occasioned by the war in Vietnam. He thought people were reading more into the song than he intended, and he refused to perform it publicly for many years. Writing for *Rolling Stone*, Jim Miller declared, "Haggard stands out [as] country western's foremost musical maverick." Haggard was also a fan of rock and roll. Major rock artists, ranging from Gram Parsons and John Fogerty to the Grateful Dead, covered his songs.

In 1965 Haggard was voted the most promising newcomer by the Academy of Country Music, and for the next three years, Haggard and his wife, Bonnie Owens, were voted the best vocal duet. In the early 1970s Haggard rejected overtures to campaign for Governor George Wallace of Alabama, but was proud to perform at the White House for the President and Mrs. Nixon. He walked off the set of an Ed Sullivan special when producers tried to choreograph his performance. A Haggard single hit the top ten list each year, for twenty-four years straight. He received an Award of Merit for lifetime achievement at the American Music Awards ceremonies, and three years later was inducted into the Country Music Hall of Fame.

Haggard was married five times. His fifth wife, Theresa Lane, his six children, and numerous grandchildren survive him.

See Current Biography 1996

Curtis Hanson

Born: Reno, Nevada; March 24, 1945
Died: Hollywood Hills, California; September 20, 2016
Occupation: Film director, producer, screenwriter

Curtis Hanson is most remembered as the director of the 1992 film, *The Hand That Rocks the Cradle* and the 1994 film, *The River Wild*. His screen adaptation of James Ellroy's novel, *L.A. Confidential*, won Hanson an Academy Award in 1998.

Though born in Reno, Nevada, Curtis Hanson grew up in the San Fernando Valley outside of Los Angeles. Hanson grew up with a passion for reading crime stories and at a young age, dreamed of becoming a screenwriter. His uncle Jack Hanson owned a clothing shop on Rodeo Drive in Beverly Hills, catering to some of the biggest names in Hollywood, thus exposing his nephew to elite actors and the film industry's biggest names. Hanson dropped out of high school to work as a gopher for *Cinema* magazine. When the magazine fell onto hard times, Hanson's uncle Jack not only bought the magazine, but he made his nephew the editor. Their venture succeeded and Hanson's experience there helped when he decided to go into directing and screenwriting.

Hanson's 1983 film *Losin' It* was notable not so much for his skill as a writer, but more

because it was the first film to feature Tom Cruise in a lead role. Hanson's first big success was the 1992 film, *The Hand That Rocks the Cradle*, starring Rebecca De Mornay and Annabella Sciorra. *The River Wild*, another big success, followed to wide acclaim. His decision to join fellow screenwriter, Brian Helgeland, in adapting James Ellroy's 500-page novel, *L.A. Confidential*—about drugs, prostitution, organized crime, and murder—etched Hanson's name into Hollywood history. The film featured established stars like Danny De Vito, Kim Basinger, and Kevin Spacey, but Hanson chose two relatively unknown actors, Russell Crowe and Guy Pearce, as the other principals. *L.A. Confidential* won the awards for best picture and best director from the National Society of Film Critics, the Boston Film Critics, the Los Angeles Film Critics, the National Board of Review, and the New York Film Critics Circle. The film also won the 1998 Academy Award for best-adapted screenplay. In 2002 Hanson worked with rap star Eminem on a somewhat biographical story about the rapper's life. It was Hanson's biggest commercial hit.

Curtis Hanson's survivors include his companion, Rebecca Yeldham, and their son.

See Current Biography 1998

Nikolaus Harnoncourt

Born: Berlin, Germany; December 6, 1929
Died: St. Georgen, Austria; March 5, 2016
Occupation: Music conductor, musician

Nikolaus Harnoncourt was a world-renowned symphony conductor who focused on any given composer's likely intentions for the sound he was trying to create in his music. Harnoncourt created the performance group, the Concentus Musicus of Vienna, who used period instruments to capture a composer's intended sound.

Nikolaus Harnoncourt was born into nobility. His mother came from Hapsburg stock, and his father, Eberhard Harnoncourt, held the title of count. He began his music career early, learning to play the cello first from Paul Grummer, and later, he studied under Emanuel Brabec at the Musikakademie of Vienna. In 1948 he began performing with the Vienna Symphony Orchestra. Early on, Harnoncourt recognized the limitations of musical notation, which fell short of communicating pitch, tempo, or the length of the notes. He began studying historic manuals on performance style to gain some knowledge about the historical context in which a piece was composed. Part of this quest for authenticity (though he would bristle at the use of the word) was to perform with period instruments. To that end, he and several colleagues created their own group, the Concentus Musicus of Vienna, with the aim of enlivening their music through the use of authentic, period instruments. They debuted in 1957 in a baroque palace in Vienna, carefully selected for its performance conditions. They continued to perform across Europe, the United States and Canada, to mixed reviews.

According to Bradley Klapper of the *Washington Post* (March 6, 2016), Harnoncourt completed "an eighteen-year project to record the complete cycle of Bach cantatas with the Concentus Musicus Wien. . . . and conducted orchestras in Berlin, London, [and] Vienna. . . . He also recorded all nine Beethoven symphonies with the Chamber Orchestra of Europe." In addition to his orchestral work, Harnoncourt taught at the Salzburg Mozarteum for over twenty years. Among his many honors and awards are the Erasmus Prize in 1980, and a Grammy for his rendition of Bach's "St. Matthew Passion."

Harnoncourt met his wife, Alice, when the two were both performing with the Concentus Musicus of Vienna. Alice played the violin. The two had four children, one of whom died in 1990. Their daughter is mezzo-soprano Elisabeth von Magnus. Nikolaus Harnoncourt is survived by his wife, their three adult children, seven grandchildren, and three great grandchildren.

See Current Biography 1991

was a librarian at Harvard University.) Harrison attended Michigan State University where he met Thomas McGuane and the two developed a lifelong friendship. With his master's degree in comparative literature, Harrison taught for one year at State University of New York at Stony Brook (SUNY), but decided to work as a writer full time. During his stay in New York, Harrison had a brush with the Beat writers, as an acquaintance of Jack Kerouac. While visiting Tom McGuane, on the movie set of *The Missouri Breaks,* Harrison met and befriended Jack Nicholson, who would later front him a loan of $15,000 so Harrison could write *Legends of the Fall.* In addition to his fiction and poetry, Harrison had a food column with *Esquire* and wrote about the outdoors for *Sports Illustrated.*

Harrison received numerous awards and accolades throughout his writing career. He received grants from the National Academy of the Arts for three years, from 1967 through 1969. He received a Guggenheim fellowship in 1969. In 2007 Harrison was elected to the Academy of Arts and Letters. He received the Saturn Award for Best Writing for his screenplay version of his novel, *Wolf.* In all, Harrison wrote a dozen novels, eighteen collections of poetry, and eight novella trilogies.

Harrison's wife of more than fifty years, Linda, died in 2015. Jim Harrison's two daughters survive.

See Current Biography 1992

Jim Harrison

Born: Grayling, Michigan; December 11, 1937
Died: Patagonia, Arizona; March 19, 2016
Occupation: Writer

Sometimes compared to Ernest Hemingway, critics considered the writer Jim Harrison a man's writer, often examining the confluence of the natural world, American history, and a man's character. He published over thirty books including eighteen collections of poetry, and twenty works of fiction. He is most recognized for his novella trilogy, *Legends of the Fall,* which was made into a feature film starring Brad Pitt and Anthony Hopkins. (The film won the 1995 Academy Award for cinematography.) His best-selling novel was *True North,* published in 2004.

Jim Harrison was born and raised in northern Michigan where he grew up learning to hunt and fish. His father was an agriculture inspector who specialized in soil quality. Both of his parents were avid readers and passed their love of literature on to their son who decided, at sixteen, he wanted to be a writer. (His brother

Donald Henderson

Born: Lakewood, Ohio; September 7, 1928
Died: Towson, Maryland; August 19, 2016
Occupation: Epidemiologist, director of the federal Office of Public Health Preparedness

A former dean of the Johns Hopkins School of Public Health, Donald Henderson was credited with having eradicated smallpox after the World Health Organization (WHO) appointed him to lead the group charged with eliminating the disease worldwide. The defeat of smallpox was officially announced to the world on May 8, 1980. Henderson later turned his attention to the potential use of viral agents as large-scale biological weapons after he was appointed as the director of the newly created Office of Public Health Preparedness, advising the president on issues related to bioterrorism. In 2002 Henderson received the Presidential Medal of Freedom, the nation's highest civilian award.

Donald Henderson attended Oberlin College, graduating with a degree in chemistry in 1950. He earned his MD in 1954 from the

University of Rochester School of Medicine, and served his internship at the Mary Imogene Bassett Hospital in Cooperstown, New York. While there, he was confronted with an outbreak of Polio, which served to drive Henderson toward a focus on public health. He went to Atlanta, Georgia as the assistant chief of the US government's Epidemic Intelligence Service at the Communicable Disease Center (CDC), now called the Centers for Disease Control and Prevention. He continued his education at Johns Hopkins University where he earned a master's degree in public health in 1960. Shortly thereafter, the WHO appointed Henderson to lead the group charged with eradicating smallpox worldwide—a feat most experts considered an impossibility. With his success, he became a hero of international stature. He then became the dean at the Johns Hopkins School of Hygiene and Public Health, and in 1998 he became the founding director of the Johns Hopkins Center for Civilian Biodefense Strategies, a biological-terrorism think tank. In 1990 he became a presidential adviser in the Office of Science and Technology Policy under President George Herbert Walker Bush, and in 1993, he became the deputy assistance secretary in the Department of Health and Human Services under President Bill Clinton. Though he was in semiretirement in November 2001, after the September 11 terrorist attacks and subsequent spate of viral anthrax attacks, he was appointed director of the Office of Public Health Preparedness.

In addition to the Presidential Medal of Freedom and more than a dozen honorary degrees, Henderson won such prestigious awards as the Public Welfare Medal from the National Academy of Sciences (NAS), the Albert Schweitzer International Prize for Medicine, and the 1986 National Medal of Science.

Donald Henderson's wife, Nana (nee Bragg), and their three children survive.

See Current Biography 2002

Geoffrey Howe

Born: Port Talbot, Wales; December 20, 1926
Died: Idlicote, United Kingdom; October 9, 2015
Occupation: British Chancellor of the Exchequer, foreign secretary, and deputy prime minister

Lord Howe's resignation from Prime Minister Margaret Thatcher's cabinet became a defining moment, not only in his long and illustrious career in Britain's seat of power, but also in the prime minister's career. Following his resignation in 1990, Thatcher stayed in power for nine days.

Geoffrey Howe took office as Chancellor of the Exchequer in 1979, and went on to become the longest-serving cabinet minister in Thatcher's conservative government, serving, at various times, as her foreign secretary, leader of the House, and deputy prime minister. For over a decade, the two made a formidable pair, who inherited a grim economy. He played a leading role in creating "Thatcherism" with its faith in free markets and small government, which helped pull Britain's economy out of a deep recession. He also played a key role in the negotiations for handing Hong Kong to China. But he and Thatcher eventually crossed swords over Britain's role in the European exchange rate mechanism. The acrimonious rupture in the relationship, and Thatcher's intransigence, spelled the end of the Thatcher era.

Geoffrey Howe was Welsh-born, a native of Port Talbot in Glamorgan County, South Wales. His father was a solicitor and a coroner, and his mother was a justice of the peace. His experiencing the massive unemployment in Wales, during his formative years, likely played some role in his choice of career. He attended the prestigious Winchester College, graduating in 1945. After taking courses in physics and mathematics at Exeter College, he was sent to East Africa as a lieutenant in the Royal Signals. In 1948 he studied classics at Trinity Hall, Cambridge University, where he earned his master of arts degree, and his Legum Baccalaureus. He was called to the bar in 1952.

His mild manner belied his ferocity. Colleague, Dennis Healy, famously quipped that a battle with Howe was like "being savaged by a dead sheep." But, Howe's role in Britain's economic turn-around is undeniable.

Geoffrey Howe married Elspeth Morton Shand in 1953. In 2001 Lady Howe was made life peer of the realm, in her own right, having served as chair of the Equal Opportunities Commission and chair of the Broadcasting Standards Commission. The couple had three children. Lord Geoffrey Howe died of an apparent heart attack. His wife and three children survive him.

See Current Biography 1980

Gordie Howe

Born: Floral, Saskatchewan, Canada; March 31, 1928
Died: Sylvania, Ohio; June 10, 2016
Occupation: Professional hockey player

Gordie Howe was a legendary ice hockey player who, for most of his career, played with the Detroit Red Wings. The team won four Stanley

Cups while Howe wore the jersey. Over his career he scored 801 goals and 1,850 points—a record that held until Wayne Gretzky broke it in 1989. Howe won six Hart Trophies, the National Hockey League's (NHL) Most Valuable Player (MVP), and six Art Ross Trophies as the league's top scorer. He held the league record for the most games played: 1,767. In 2008 Howe won the league's first lifetime achievement award. He was also known by the moniker, "Mr. Hockey."

Gordie Howe was born on the Canadian prairie in Saskatchewan, the fifth of nine children. The family had a hockey rink in their own back yard. When he was just fifteen, Howe was much sought after by scouts. In 1944 Fred Pinckney of the Detroit Red Wings saw Howe and, even though he was too young to play professionally, he had Howe practice with the team until he came of age in 1946. Howe's career was almost cut short by a nearly fatal collision on the ice that left him with a severe concussion. The concussion forced doctors to drill a hole in his skull to relieve pressure on the brain. He was a tough player, to the extent that any time a player scored a goal, got an assist, and got into a fight in a single game, it was known as a "Gordie Howe Hat Trick." Over the course of his career, Howe had over five hundred stiches to his face alone.

Howe married Colleen Joffaa in 1953 and the couple had four children. Colleen became Howe's agent. She predeceased Howe in 2009. Howe's son, Mark, was also inducted into the NHL Hall of Fame in 2011. Gordie Howe's survivors include his four children, two sisters, numerous grandchildren, and great-grandchildren.

See Current Biography 1962

Shirley Hufstedler

Born: Denver, Colorado; August 24, 1925
Died: Glendale, California; March 30, 2016
Occupation: First US Secretary of Education

In October of 1979, President Jimmy Carter named Shirley Hufstedler, a distinguished federal appellate jurist, as the first secretary of education. Until President Jimmy Carter's defeat in 1980, many considered Hufstedler a likely candidate for the first female United States Supreme Court justice.

Shirley Mount was born to a construction contractor who lost everything in the Great Depression. The family had to travel throughout the West through the 1930s, so Shirley and her brother changed schools often. Between the second and seventh grade, the two children attended twelve schools. The Mounts finally settled in Albuquerque, New Mexico where Hufstedler

earned a bachelor's degree in business administration in just two years. She then attended Stanford law where she worked on the Stanford Law Review. (She was a classmate of the former Deputy Secretary of State Warren Christopher.) She graduated tenth in her class and married Seth Hufstedler (who graduated at the top of the class). She then set up a general civil law practice in Los Angeles.

California's governor, Pat Brown, appointed Hufstedler to the Los Angeles County Superior Court in 1960, and then to the California State Court of Appeals for the Second District in 1966. Following Hufstedler's two-year stint there, President Johnson elevated her to the US Court of Appeals for the Ninth Circuit. Hufstedler quickly gained a reputation as a brilliant, admirable, and courageous jurist.

At the same time, the National Education Association was lobbying for the creation of a Department of Education. The Department of Education was officially opened on May 4, 1980, with Shirley Hufstedler at the helm as the first US Secretary of Education, overseeing a budget of $14.2 billion and 17,239 employees.

The Hufstedlers had one son. Shirley Hufstedler is survived by her husband, son, and three grandchildren.

See Current Biography 1980

Anne Jackson

Born: Millvale, Pennsylvania; September 3, 1925
Died: New York, New York; April 12, 2016
Occupation: American actress

Anne Jackson performed in over twenty-eight Broadway shows, often teaming with her equally talented husband, Eli Wallach. In 1956 Jackson was nominated for a Tony Award for her role in Paddy Chayefsky's *Middle of the Night*.

Anne Jackson was born in rural Pennsylvania, just outside of Pittsburgh, the youngest of three daughters born to a Croatian immigrant father. When she was seven, the family moved to Brooklyn, New York. After graduating from high school Jackson attended the New School for Social Research. She made her acting debut in the 1944 adaptation of the musical *The New Moon*. She met her future husband, Eli Wallach, when the two were performing in Tennessee Williams' *This Property Is Condemned*. The two married in 1948. Throughout the 1950s, Jackson studied under the tutelage of the famous Lee Strasberg, long considered the "father" of method acting in America. Eli Wallach and Anne Jackson often appeared together, winning an Obie Award in 1963 for their performances in *The Tiger*. Jackson also has many television credits including appearances on the popular shows *Gunsmoke, Law & Order, ER,* and the children's show, *Reading Rainbow.* Her most notable movie credits include *Sticks and Bones* and *The Shining.* Jackson also wrote a memoir called *Early Stages.*

Anne Jackson and Eli Wallach had three children. Their son, Peter, once quipped that when the children heard their parents arguing, they never knew whether they were having a genuine (though rare) fight or were just rehearsing. Eli Wallach predeceased Anne in 2013. Survivors include a son, Peter Wallach, a film animator, and two daughters, Roberta and Katherine, who both became actresses.

See Current Biography 1980

Joe Jamail

Born: Houston, Texas; October 19, 1925
Died: Houston, Texas; December 23, 2015
Occupation: US trial lawyer

With a net worth of more than $1.5 billion, the wealthiest trial lawyer in the country, Joe Jamail, was often referred to as the "King of Torts" due to his record of winning settlements in malpractice, negligence, and product-liability cases. He holds the record for winning the largest payout—nearly $11 billion—in history. Jamail won five awards over $100 million and more than two hundred for at least $1 million.

Joe Jamail was the second of five children, born to a Lebanese family that settled in Houston in the early twentieth century, and developed a thriving chain of produce markets. Jamail's future was not promising. Graduating high school at sixteen, he enrolled at Texas A&M University, transferred to the University of Texas (UT), and promptly flunked all of his premed courses. Forging his parents' signatures, he joined the Marines, serving in the Pacific during World War II. Upon his return, he entered the Southwest Louisiana Institute in another try at college. A family friend in Lafayette sparked his interest in law. Ironically, he failed his course in tort law. However he graduated from UT's law program, having never taken the entrance exam. Even before graduation he had tried and won his first case.

Jamail's name is included in the *Guinness Book of World Records* for the largest-ever personal-injury payout, in *Coates v. Remington Arms* with a $6.8 million settlement. In *Pennzoil v. Texaco,* Jamail won a nearly $11 billion verdict, making his win the largest lawsuit award in history. In addition to his huge success rate, a number of Jamail's cases ended with product recalls. In one case the gun manufacturer, Remington Arms, recalled its Mohawk 600 rifle after it was proven faulty design led to an accidental shooting. In another, the drug manufacturer, Sandoz Pharmaceutical, pulled its drug Parlodel after Jamail's case confirmed the drug could cause a stroke.

Though he amassed a fortune, he was also generous with his donations. In 1986 he founded the Lee and Joseph D. Jamail Foundation, which donated over $216 million to education, medical research, and the arts. One donation of $10 million to the University of Texas is the largest in the school's history.

Joe Jamail married his college sweetheart, Lillie Mae "Lee" Hage in 1949. She died in 2007. Joe Jamail died from complications of pneumonia on December 23, 2015. He was ninety years old. His survivors include his three sons, Joseph, Randall, and Robert.

See Current Biography 2008

Deborah Jin

Born: Stanford, California; November 15, 1968
Died: Boulder, Colorado; September 15, 2016
Occupation: Physicist

Deborah Jin was a world-renowned physicist with an unusually long list of accomplishment for such a young scientist. One of her greatest achievements was deemed by the journal *Science* as one of the top ten scientific breakthroughs for the year 1999. Jin succeeded in cooling atoms of an isotope of the element potassium to a temperature significantly closer to absolute zero than had ever been achieved. According to science writer Martin Well of the *Washington Post* (September 20, 2016), Jin's breakthrough resulted in "new states of matter to stand alongside the traditional solids, liquids, and gases." The website for the Joint Institute for Laboratory Astrophysics (JILA) describes her as "a pioneer in polar molecule quantum chemistry." In 2002 *Discover* magazine listed Jin among the fifty most important women in science.

Deborah Jin was born into physics. Both of her parents were physicists. Her mother worked as an engineer, while her father taught at a university in Florida. Jin attended Princeton University where, in her senior year, she won Princeton's Allen G. Shenstone Prize for her academic performance in physics, and she graduated magna cum laude in 1990. She held a National Science Foundation Graduate Fellowship in physics from 1990 to 1993, and earned her PhD from the University of Chicago in 1995. That same year she secured a position as a National Research Council (NRC) associate at JILA, and two years later she became a fellow at the National Institute of Standards and Technology (NIST). According to the JILA website, Jin also "developed innovative technical systems to study the behavior of ultra cold Fermi gases."

Dr. Jin's awards and accolades were many. In 2003, she received a MacArthur Fellowship, and in 2004 *Scientific American* named her the Research Leader of the Year." She earned the Benjamin Franklin Medal in Physics in 2008, and the Institute of Physics awarded her the Isaac Newton Medal in 2014. Deborah Jin was just forty-seven when she died from cancer. She was married and had one daughter. Her husband and daughter survive.

See Current Biography 2004

Anker Jørgensen

Born: Copenhagen, Denmark; July 13, 1922
Died: Copenhagen, Denmark; March 20, 2016
Occupation: Prime Minister of Denmark

Anker Jørgensen was the Danish prime minister from 1972 to 1973, and again from 1975 to 1982. His comfortable, "down home" manner won him popularity among his countrymen in spite of the sharp economic downturn and political turmoil during his leadership.

Orphaned at the age of four, Anker Jørgensen was raised by his paternal aunt who worked in a tobacco factory. He attended school at the strict Copenhagen School for Orphans before going to work at a lock factory when he was fourteen. During World War II, he served with the Royal Danish Hussars at Næstved until German troops disarmed the Danish military. He then joined the Resistance. Though he never attended high school, he qualified for a general certificate of education in 1945. He began his trade union career in 1947 as a salaried vice-president of the 5,000-member Warehouse Workers Union in Copenhagen. From 1956 to 1962, he was the union's president. After completing a course in trade union activities at the Roskilde Workers' Folk High School, he attended a three-month course in economics and labor market problems at Harvard University.

Throughout the 1960s, Jørgensen was a union manager in the Dansk Arbejtmans og Specialarbejderforbund (DASF), the country's largest union, and was active in the Social Democratic party. He was an early protester against the US military action in Vietnam, and was a consistent advocate of diplomatic recognition of East Germany. Though Jørgensen had very little

political experience, retiring Prime Minister Jens Otto Krag named him as his successor in 1972. Upon becoming prime minister, Jørgensen refused to move to Marienborg, the traditional home of the prime minister. He remained in his working class, three-room apartment where he entertained world dignitaries. His first term as prime minister was plagued by a crippling three-week strike by some 280,000 workers, and because he expressed sympathy for Israel, Denmark was adversely affected by the Arab oil boycott. Under his watch, inflation in Denmark doubled, and unemployment increased an astonishing seven-fold, leaving the economy in a deep recession. Jørgensen retired from politics in 1987.

Anker Jørgensen died on March 20, 2016. His wife, Ingrid died in 1997. Their four children survive.

See Current Biography 1978

Ellsworth Kelly

Born: Newburgh, New York; May 31, 1923
Died: Spencertown, New York; December 27, 2015
Occupation: American painter, sculptor

Sometimes referred to as a master of abstraction, Ellsworth Kelly was a prominent artist, an icon of twentieth-century American art, and a progenitor of abstract, hard-edge painting. His aim was to create a visceral, instinctive, physical response in those who viewed his art. He claimed to be more interested in the space between a work of art and its viewer, than in any particular form. He was among the first artists to use irregularly shaped canvases. Although his greatest work is not representational, Kelly claimed he learned the most, and was inspired the most, by real-life observations, rather than through studying the works of others. His paintings replicate the shapes and shadows, the visual encoding, of everyday objects.

After graduating from high school in Englewood, New Jersey, Kelly attended the Pratt Institute in Brooklyn, New York, but his education was interrupted by a stint in the US Army Engineer Corps from 1943 to 1945. Kelly was part of the "Ghost Army," a decoy, camouflage unit charged with the task of misdirecting enemy soldiers. This experience would have a significant impact on his later artwork. For a short time he attended the Boston Museum School where he studied with Karl Zerbe. Feeling that Boston was a "dead end," Kelly went to Europe on the GI Bill to study at the École des Beaux-Arts in Paris. His earliest paintings were figurative and small. While visiting the Musee d'Art Moderne in Paris, Kelly found himself drawn more to windows, doors, shadows and light, than he was to the artwork. It was a turning point to Kelly's art. He returned to New York where he joined a community of artists at Coenties Slip that included James Rosenquist, Agnes Martin, and Jack Youngerman.

Kelly had his first one-man show (the first of many) in 1956 at the Betty Parsons Gallery in New York. In 1958 he was one of seventeen artists whose work was selected for exhibition in the American Pavilion of the Brussels World's Fair. In 1963, the Metropolitan Museum of Art purchased one of Kelly's paintings, making him one of the youngest American artists to have work purchased for its permanent collections. He also created public art on commission. In 1969 he did a mural for UNESCO (United Nations Educational, Scientific and Cultural Organization) in Paris, and in 1978 he created a sculpture for the city of Barcelona. He did an installation for the Holocaust Memorial Museum in Washington, DC in 1993.

The artist received a number of awards and honorary degrees from Bard College, Annandale-on-Hudson, the Royal College of Art, Harvard University, Brandeis University, and Williams College. In 2013 US President, Barack Obama awarded him the National Medal of Arts. He received the equally prestigious Ordre des Arts et des Lettres from France.

Ellsworth Kelly died at home from natural causes. His long-time companion and husband, photographer, Jack Shear, survives.

See Current Biography 1970

Thanat Khoman

Born: Bangkok, Thailand; May 9, 1914
Died: Bangkok, Thailand; March 3, 2016
Occupation: Thai diplomat

Thanat Khoman was the foreign minister of Thailand from 1959 to 1971. He was the deputy prime minister of Thailand from 1980 to 1982, and cofounded the Association of Southeast Asian Nations (ASEAN).

Thanat Khoman studied law at the University of Paris, graduating with a doctor of laws degree in 1940, after which, he immediately joined the Foreign Ministry. During World War II, Thailand was under virtual Japanese occupation and Thanat joined the anti-Japanese underground. Following the war he served as a foreign diplomat in Washington, DC for two years, and as the Thai ambassador to the United States from 1957 through 1958. He was instrumental in creating the Rusk-Thanat Communique of 1962, establishing the two countries as allies, allowing the United States to establish military bases to support the Vietnam War effort, in exchange for development aid from the United States. However, in the late 1960s it was clear the United States would eventually withdraw from Vietnam, and Khoman advised an alliance with China. He would later become a vocal critic of US policies.

Thanat Khoman passed away due to old age—he was 101—on March 3, 2016. He had been the last surviving member of the ASEAN. Khoman's survivors include his daughter-in-law, Sirilaksana Khoman, an anti-corruption activist.

See Current Biography 1958

Abbas Kiarostami

Born: Tehran, Iran; June 22, 1940
Died: Paris, France; July 4, 2016
Occupation: Iranian filmmaker

Abbas Kiarostami was a world-renowned Iranian filmmaker who used the strict system of Iranian censorship to stimulate his imagination, inventing unique methods for depicting otherwise forbidden characters and activities. He won the prestigious Palme d'Or at the 1997 Cannes Film Festival for his film *Taste of Cherry*.

Abbas Kiarostami became interested in the arts after winning a painting competition at the age of eighteen. He studied at Tehran University's Faculty of Fine Arts, becoming a designer and illustrator who also made commercials, credit titles for films, and children's books. His filmmaking career started in 1969 when he helped establish the filmmaking department at the Institute for Intellectual Development of Children and Young Adults, a government organization that is better known in Iran as "Kanoon." The institute has become one of Iran's most famous film studios. For the first twelve years of his career, Kiarostami created a mix of short and long films, though he focused on feature-length films in his later career. His reputation was sealed with three films that have been dubbed the Earthquake Trilogy, shot in a village in northern Iran that was struck by a quake in 1990. The second film in the series, *And Life Goes On*, won the Rossellini Prize at Cannes in 1992. Kiarostami told Romain Maitra for the *UNESCO Courier* (February 1998), "my films never tell a story which begins at one point and ends at another. A new story always begins somewhere along the way. And the stories are blended together to such an extent that it's impossible to separate them. In fact, they are all part of a single story."

Abbas Kiarostami's death has sparked some debate in Iran over patient's rights. In Iran it is not uncommon for physicians to withhold information about a patient's diagnosis and prognosis. In Kiarostami's case, his physicians' secrecy prevented him from seeking medical advice outside of Iran until it was too late. His two sons, Ahmad and Bahman, survive him.

See Current Biography 1998

Kim Young-sam

Born: Koje-gun, South Kyongsang, Korea; December 20, 1927
Died: Seoul, South Korea; November 22, 2015
Occupation: Former president of South Korea

Kim Young-sam was the president of South Korea from 1993 to 1998, and is credited with helping to usher in his country's peaceful, post-military democracy. When US President, Bill Clinton considered military action against North Korea's Nyongbyon nuclear reactor, Kim advocated a peaceful resolution. Following his presidency, Kim traveled the world, promoting democracy.

Kim Young-sam was the only son of a prosperous fishing and shipping merchant. Though he was hardly a scholar, Kim attended the prestigious Kyongnam High School. He attended Seoul National University, but his education was interrupted by the Korean War in 1950. He served as a propagandist for the Seoul government, and attained a post in President Syngman Rhee's administration. He won a seat in the national assembly as a representative of Pusan, becoming the youngest member of Korea's National Assembly, at the age of twenty-seven. From the start, Kim fought against those who would ignore or re-write the country's constitution, earning a reputation as a rebel, and an advocate of free speech and government transparency. He assumed leadership of the New Democratic Party in 1974, and immediately called for President Park's resignation after Park drafted a new constitution, granting himself unlimited authority, and severely limiting freedom of speech. In 1979 General Park had Kim expelled from the National Assembly after Kim gave sanctuary to fired wig-factory workers. Riots followed and Park's own intelligence chief killed him.

Kim Young-sam and fellow New Democratic Party (NDP) rival, Kim Dae Jung, (the two were referred to as the "two Kims") joined forces in 1984, and founded the New Korean Democratic Party (NKDP), which called for direct presidential elections. In 1987, the two then ran opposing campaigns that split the party's vote, handing victory to the ruling party's candidate, General Roh Tae-woo. (The two Kims were sharply criticized for putting personal ambition above the party's well being.) For the 1992 election, Kim Young-sam shocked everyone when he joined with Roh Tae-woo, ensuring an election victory for himself and the general. However, soon thereafter, it was discovered that Roh had extorted slush funds from family conglomerates and was charged with having planned a coup, thus opening the way for Kim's presidency. His term was plagued by an economic financial crisis, which ended with an International Money Fund (IMF) bailout. The former president retired shortly thereafter, leaving the presidency open to Kim Dai Jung.

Kim Young-sam died from sepsis and heart failure on November 22, 2015. His wife, Myung-soon, their five children, and Kim's five sisters survive.

See Current Biography 1995

Florence King

Born: Washington, DC; January 5, 1936
Died: Fredericksburg, Virginia; January 6, 2016
Occupation: Writer, satirist

Florence King was a witty, acerbic, conservative writer who published dozens of books and, from 1991 to 2002, wrote a column known as "The Misanthrope's Corner" in the *National Review*.

King's father was a trombone player in a traveling jazz band, and her mother was a foul-mouthed tomboy who worked as a telephone operator. For the most part, King's maternal grandmother raised her, and tried to mold the irascible girl into a model of feminine southern charm. She failed. King's most celebrated book was a memoir titled *Confessions of a Failed Southern Lady*. She graduated from American University with a bachelor's degree in history, and briefly trained at the Women Officer Candidate School in Quantico, Virginia. She attended the University of Mississippi where she had a brief but intense love affair with a woman who was killed in a car accident, an experience that led her to more introspection, and an eventual writing career. She began her career writing "true confession" stories, leading her to eventually write over thirty-five soft porn novels. (Her pseudonym was Ruding Upton King.) From 1964 to 1967, King worked for the Raleigh, North Carolina *News and Observer*, and won the North Carolina Press Woman Award for her reporting. She moved to Seattle, Washington and, in 1975, penned her first novel using her real name, *Southern Ladies and Gentlemen*. She established her reputation as a satirist of the feminist movement with the novel *When Sisterhood Was in Flower*, in 1982.

She published several volumes of essays, establishing herself as an acerbic, sometimes harsh, social critic, bemoaning "helpism," political correctness, and what she viewed as effeminacy and oversensitivity. She declared that stress had become a status symbol, making Americans feel busy, important, and simultaneously deprived, ignored, and victimized. She came out of retirement briefly, in the August 7, 2006 edition of the *National Review* to criticize ultra-conservative media personality, Ann Coulter, whom King saw as "smart as a whip but dumb as a post, educated but not learned, sexy but not sensuous, all at the same time."

Florence King died in Fredericksburg, Virginia the day after her eightieth birthday. She had no survivors.

See Current Biography 2006

Tim LaHaye

Born: Detroit, Michigan; April 27, 1926
Died: San Diego, California; July 25, 2016
Occupation: Christian televangelist, minister, author

Tim LaHaye is most remembered for his role in writing the "Left Behind" evangelical Christian series of novels about his interpretation of the rapture, or "end times" as depicted in the Bible's New Testament book of Revelations. He served on the original board of the Moral Majority, a conservative, fundamentalist Christian political-action group founded in 1979. He worked with Pat Robertson in the 1980s, and started the American Coalition for Traditional Values in 1984.

Tim LaHaye's father died when LaHaye was just nine years old, leaving the boy's mother to support her three children by working in the Ford factory. While working at a summer camp, LaHaye discovered a love of preaching. He attended Bob Jones University in Greenville, South Carolina, earning a bachelor's degree in 1950. He received a doctorate in ministry from Western Theological Seminary, and served a Minneapolis congregation until 1956, when he moved to head the evangelical Scott Memorial Church in San Diego, California. He helped found the Christian Heritage College in Nearby El Cajon, and the Christian Unified Schools of San Diego. In 1987 LaHaye co-chaired the US Republican congressman, Jack Kemp's bid for the presidency. LaHaye wrote over fifty books, from self-help titles on marriage to religious primers with titles like *How to Win Over Depression, Anger Is a Choice*, and *The Unhappy Gays* (in which he judges homosexuality as

"vile.") *Time* magazine named LaHaye one of the twenty-five most influential evangelicals in America.

LaHaye won broad fame through his partnership with novelist Jerry Jenkins when the two created a popular series of novels that depicted the "rapture," according to LaHaye's interpretation of the Bible's prophecies about the end of days. Beginning with the 1995 title *Left Behind*, the sixteen-book series was the most commercially successful Christian fiction series in publishing history. In their partnership, LaHaye would write thirty- to fifty-page outlines for the novels based on biblical texts, and Jenkins would write fictional drafts based on LaHaye's outlines.

Tim LaHaye married the former Beverly Davenport in 1947. She co-founded the Concerned Women for America, a conservative public-policy group.

The two had four children. In addition to his wife, LaHaye's four children, nine grandchildren, and sixteen great-grandchildren survive him.

See Current Biography 2003

Harper Lee

Born: Monroeville, Alabama; April 28, 1926
Died: Monroeville, Alabama; February 19, 2016
Occupation: American author

Harper Lee penned one of America's most cherished and enduring novels, *To Kill A Mockingbird*, which won her a Pulitzer Prize for fiction in 1961, and sold over forty million copies. The novel has been translated into more than forty languages, and is considered one of the most influential books ever printed. In 1962 a film adaptation of the novel was released, starring Gregory Peck who won an Academy Award for his role. (The movie also earned an Academy Award for best art direction and for best writing adapted screenplay.) The American Film Institute later named Atticus Finch the greatest movie hero of the twentieth century.

Harper Lee was the youngest of three children born to Amasa Coleman and Frances Lee. She studied law at the University of Alabama, but left before earning a degree, moving to New York City where she worked as an airline reservation clerk, and wrote in her spare time. She had a lifelong friendship with fellow writer Truman Capote who encouraged Lee's work. (She traveled to Kansas to help with his research for his novel *In Cold Blood*.) Capote and Lee acknowledge that the character Dill Harris is based on Capote as a boy. Likewise, the story's narrator, Scout, is based on Lee as a young girl. Two main themes that run throughout the novel are the joys and sorrows associated with growing up in a small Southern town in the 1930s, and the wisdom inherent in a child's perspective. The book also addresses the challenges white southerners faced when seeking justice for African Americans in their community. Although the novel is ostensibly a children's book, some schools have banned it because the central crime in the story is rape, and there is some description of a white woman's attraction to the African American defendant, Tom Robinson.

Following the book's publication, overwhelmed by the attention and notoriety the novel garnered, Lee became somewhat reclusive, rarely granting interviews. In 2015, shortly before her death, a second book, *Go Set a Watchman*, was published amidst some controversy, especially for those who saw Atticus Finch as a hero. In the second novel, which takes place twenty years after *To Kill A Mockingbird* ended, Atticus is a bigot and a segregationist. In truth, *Go Set A Watchman* was Lee's first novel, but an early editor suggested she rewrite the book from the perspective of Scout as a child.

In addition to the 1961 Pulitzer, Lee has been awarded numerous honors and accolades. She was appointed to the National Council on the Arts in 1966. In 2007 President George W. Bush awarded Lee the Presidential Medal of Freedom, and in 2010 President Barack Obama awarded Lee a National Medal of the Arts for her contribution to American literature.

Lee suffered a stroke in 2011 that left her confined to a wheelchair. She died on February 19, 2016. There are no immediate survivors.

See Current Biography 1961

Lee Kuan Yew

Born: Singapore; September 16, 1923
Died: Outram, Singapore; March 23, 2015
Occupation: First prime minister of Singapore

Sometimes referred to as the "father of Singapore," Lee Kuan Yew was Singapore's prime minister for thirty-one years, from 1959 to 1990, developing a thriving nation out of an impoverished British colony. Lee was the world's longest-serving prime minister and was considered one of its most adept politicians.

Of Chinese descent, Lee Kuan Yew's father was a depot superintendent for the Shell Oil Company and his mother was a well-known cooking instructor. Lee studied economics, mathematics, and English literature at Raffles College (later known as the University of Singapore). After World War II Lee studied law at Fitzwilliam College at Cambridge University in England. He was admitted to the British bar in 1950. Lee began his career in Singapore as a legal representative for trade unions, but quickly found himself leading an anticolonialist movement. In 1954 Lee was named secretary general to the People's Action Party (PAP), which he helped found.

To reach his goal of self-rule for Singapore, Lee temporarily aligned himself with Singapore's Communists, but soon after rising to power, he purged the PAP of its Communists. In 1962 the State of Singapore joined the Federation of Malaysia for greater economic stability, and Lee instituted aggressive policies to entice foreign businesses in shipping, shipbuilding, oil-rig-construction, printing, and electronics, making Singapore an important center for international finance. In somewhat draconian fashion, Lee brought about urban reform, bulldozing slums to build blocks of uniform apartments. Political opposition was stifled as Lee's government revoked the right to habeas corpus, and forbade political activism by organizations that had not received express government approval. He had a strong belief in the tradition of the extended family, claiming the movement toward the nuclear family weakened the chain of survival. He set about improving Singapore's "genetic outlook," taking steps to discourage poorly educated, low-income mothers from having more than one or two children.

In the 1990s Lee put Singapore at loggerheads with the United States when an American student, Michael Fay, was sentenced to caning after he was caught in various acts of vandalism. During an interview for *Time* (May 9, 1994) Lee claimed, "If we do not cane [Michael Fay] because he is an American, I believe we'll lose our moral authority and our right to govern." In another case against an American, Singapore police interrogated Christopher Lingle, a university professor, for his criticism of "Asian states" as being "intolerant regimes." Lingle fled the country under threat of criminal charges.

Lee Kuan Yew married fellow Cambridge law student, Kwa Geok Choo, who headed the law firm of Lee and Lee. They had three children and numerous grandchildren.

See Current Biography 1995

Meadowlark Lemon

Born: Wilmington, North Carolina; April 25, 1932
Died: Scottsdale, Arizona; December 27, 2015
Occupation: Basketball performer with the Harlem Globetrotters

Dubbed the "Clown Prince of Basketball," Meadowlark Lemon became a household name, widely recognized for his athletic ability and sense of humor, as he led the Harlem Globetrotters exhibition team for over twenty-four years. When asked who the best basketball player of all time was, basketball legend, Wilt Chamberlain, (who also played for the Globetrotters for a year) declared it was Meadowlark Lemon.

Meadowlark's real name was Meadow George Lemon, and he credits much of his athletic ability to the necessity of running from kids who made fun of his name. Born on April 25, 1932, Lemon was raised by an aunt and uncle, and shared his hometown with Michael Jordon, who came to fame thirty years later. By the time he was eleven years old, Lemon knew what he wanted to be, and he worked diligently to achieve his goal, practicing eight to twelve hours each day. Unable to afford a basketball and hoop, he devised a makeshift hoop using an onion sack and wire coat hanger. His basketball was an empty evaporated milk can. He was named all-state high school player, and for a short time, played for Florida A & M.

He first contacted the Globetrotters in 1952, but was drafted into the military. After serving two years, he headed to Globetrotter training camp and signed a contract to play for the Kansas City Stars (a Globetrotter development team). In the 1950s and 1960s, the Globetrotters had a lasting impact on the world of basketball. The National Basketball Association (NBA) had only been integrated for a few years, and Globetrotter comedy drew people to the game and showcased African American talent. Comedy skits, known as "reems," often included taunting referees, faking injuries, and lining up in football or baseball formation.

Following his retirement from the Globetrotters, Lemon appeared as himself in several movies and television shows. He became an ordained minister and fronted Meadowlark Lemon Ministries, based in Scottsdale, Arizona. His marriage to Willie Maultsby ended in divorce. As he was inducted into the basketball Hall of Fame, Lemon apologized to his family for his grueling schedule that kept him away as he toured the globe. Lemon had ten children. In 1994 he married Dr. Cynthia Lemon.

Meadowlark Lemon passed away on December 27, 2015 in Scottsdale, Arizona. He was eighty-three years old.

See Current Biography 2002

Drew Lewis

Born: Philadelphia, Pennsylvania; November 3, 1931
Died: Prescott, Arizona; February 10, 2016
Occupation: Former US Secretary of Transportation

Drew Lewis was a close confidante of former US President Ronald Reagan who appointed Lewis to his cabinet as the US Secretary of Transportation. Lewis is most remembered for his handling of the 1981 walkout of the nation's air traffic controllers after negotiations collapsed.

Drew Lewis grew up on a farm north of Philadelphia, in the same area where future US Secretary of Health and Human Services, Richard Schweiker, grew up. The two were close friends and attended the same church. He received a bachelor's degree in economics from Haverford College in Pennsylvania, and a master's degree from Harvard's Graduate School of Business. He also took postgraduate courses at the Massachusetts Institute of Technology. His first venture into business was in utilities contracting. When he encountered his first electricians strike, his answer was to fly to Madrid and hire Spanish electricians to complete the striking workers' tasks.

Lewis became active in Pennsylvania state politics in the 1960s, serving as chairman of the Republican state finance committee. A decade later, he was considered one of the most influential power brokers in the country. He was a delegate to the Republican national conventions in 1968 and 1972. He ran for Governor of Pennsylvania, unsuccessfully, in 1974, and later managed Gerald Ford's Presidential primary. In 1979 he became the assistant campaign manager for Ronald Reagan, and deputy chairman of the Republican National Committee (RNC). He was instrumental in convincing Reagan to adopt George Bush as his running mate. In January of 1981, President Reagan made him the nation's seventh Secretary of Transportation who commanded a bureaucracy with a budget of $22 billion and 68,000 employees in eight transportation administrations. He personally oversaw the negotiations when the nation's air traffic controllers threatened to shut down air traffic by walking out. Though he and the union came to a tentative agreement, air traffic controllers still walked out, a defining moment in Reagan's presidency.

Lewis's wife of sixty-five years, Marilyn Stoughton Lewis, was also active in state politics, serving two terms in the Pennsylvania legislature. Drew Lewis died from complications of pneumonia. His wife, two children, fourteen grandchildren, and six great-grandchildren survive.

See Current Biography 1982

Robert Loggia

Born: New York, New York; January 3, 1930
Died: Los Angeles, California; December 4, 2015
Occupation: Actor

Robert Loggia was considered one of the most talented character actors in Hollywood. Though he was often cast in a supporting role, rather than the lead, he had a reputation for making his lead counterparts look good. His roles covered a broad range of personalities, from drug kingpin, Fran Lopez in *Scarface* (1983) to the open toy-store executive, MacMillan, in *Big* (1988) who dances across a giant keyboard with Tom Hanks in a playful rendition of the song "Heart and Soul." He was nominated for an Academy Award for his portrayal of Detective Sam Ransom in the 1985 thriller *Jagged Edge*.

Robert Loggia was born to two Sicilian immigrants, Benjamin and Elena Blandino, in New York on January 3, 1930. He spent his early childhood on the streets of "Little Italy," on Manhattan's Lower East Side. He received a football scholarship to Wagner College on Staten Island, and also played the lead role in the schools production of *The Taming of the Shrew.* He eventually transferred to the University of Missouri to study journalism. He was drafted into the Army and served two years, stationed in Panama during the Korean conflict. In 1955, he was accepted into the prestigious Actor's Studio at the New School for Social Research (now the New School University), under the tutelage of renowned acting coach, Stella Adler. He was not credited on his first movie role as Freddie Peppo, in the 1956 film *Somebody Up There Loves Me.* Through the 1960s, Loggia made more than forty television appearances, including the lead, Elfego Baca, in Disney's television series *The Nine Lives of Elfego Baca.* He had guest roles on some of the decade's most popular shows, including *Gunsmoke, Alfred Hitchcock Presents, The Untouchables,* and *Rawhide.*

In addition to his nomination for the Academy's Best Supporting Actor, he was also nominated for an Emmy Award for his acting in the lead role, Nick Mancuso, in the series Mancuso FBI (though the series was canceled after just one season).

Robert Loggia was married twice, first to Marjorie Sloan with whom he had three children. That marriage ended in divorce in 1981. In 1982 he married Audrey O'Brien who brought a daughter to the marriage. Loggia died from complications of Alzheimer's disease on December 4, 2015. His wife and children survive.

See Current Biography 2001

Jonah Lomu

Born: Auckland, New Zealand; May 12, 1975
Died: Auckland, New Zealand; November 18, 2015
Occupation: Professional rugby player

A former winger for New Zealand's All Blacks national rugby union team, Jonah Lomu was the youngest man ever to play in a sanctioned international contest, becoming one of New Zealand's most beloved sports icons. On New Zealand's 1995 national squad for the Rugby World Cup in South Africa, Lomu scored seven tries (the equivalent of a touchdown in American football) in five matches, in what is "still considered to be the single most extraordinary individual performance in the. . . . history of international rugby union," according to Chris Hewett, writer for *The Independent.* Lomu is credited with redefining the game of rugby.

Jonah Lomu had a difficult childhood, having been sent to a distant aunt and uncle (whom he thought were his parents) in the family's native Tonga, in the Auckland region of New Zealand. He was sent back to his abusive parents' home at the age of seven. His father was a violent alcoholic who frequently abused him and his mother. As an adolescent, he became involved in street gangs and petty crime, until an uncle and cousin were murdered by a rival Samoan gang. Lomu realized he had a similar fate in store if he did not change. His mother sent him to Methodist Wesley College, a strict boarding school that is one of the oldest in New Zealand. This is where he became involved in sports.

As an adult, Lomu stood at six feet five inches, and weighed 280 pounds, making him a formidable foe on any playing field. In 1993 he played for the Counties Manukau Steelers in the National Provincial Championship—New Zealand's top domestic rugby competition. In 1994 he won a spot on New Zealand's All Blacks national rugby union team, becoming the youngest All Blacks player in history. He was selected to New Zealand's national squad for the 1995

Rugby World Cup in South Africa, where he earned superstar status. Despite his team's loss, Lomu was named player of the tournament, becoming one of the most recognizable rugby players in the world. Lomu became the face of the sport, winning multi-million dollar contracts and endorsement deals.

Unfortunately, Lomu suffered from an energy-depleting kidney disease called nephrotic syndrome, forcing him to retire in 2003 when he had to undergo daily dialysis, which caused severe nerve damage to his legs and feet. Though he attempted a comeback, his condition and injuries prevented his playing as a top performer. Though he underwent two kidney transplants, one in 2004 and the second in 2011, he passed away from heart failure related to his kidney disease. His wife, Nadine Quirk, and their two sons, Brayley and Dhyreille survive.

See Current Biography 2012

Murray Louis

Born: New York, New York; November 4, 1926
Died: New York, New York; February 1, 2016
Occupation: Dancer, choreographer

Murray Louis was the avant-garde director of his own dance group, and the associate director of the Henry Street Playhouse Company, which became a major dance institution. His partnership with fellow choreographer, and Henry Street Playhouse partner, Alwin Nikolais, was legendary.

Murray Louis was one of five children born to his father, a baker in Brooklyn, New York. The family was so impoverished during the Depression that Louis was placed in an orphanage, which is where his initial interest in music originated. After graduating from Tilden High School in Brooklyn, Louis was drafted into the US Navy as a seaman first class. Following the war, he enrolled in a class with Ann Halprin who suggested he attend a summer workshop at Colorado College, which is where he met his lifelong mentor and companion, Alwin Nikolais. The two became co-directors of the Henry Street Playhouse while Louis took dance classes at New York University (NYU) where he earned a bachelor of science degree in speech and theatre. Louis established his own dance company in 1953, while also working as a principal dancer in the Alwin Nikolais Dance Company. (The two merged their dance companies in 1989.) As a young dancer, he was known for his perfect muscular control, capturing meaning of body movement, investing every gesture with maximum significance.

Murray Louis staged works for the Batsheva Dance Company, the Royal Danish Ballet, the Scottish Ballet, and the Hamburg Ballet. He received two Guggenheim fellowships, and grants from the Rockefeller and Ford foundations. He published two collections of essays about dancers: *Inside Dance* (St. Martins Press, 1980) and *On Dance* (A Cappella Books, 1992).

Murray Louis died on February 1, 2016 at the age of 89.

See Current Biography 1968

Patrick Manning

Born: San Fernando, Trinidad and Tobago; August 17, 1946
Died: San Fernando, Trinidad and Tobago; July 2, 2016
Occupation: Former prime minister of Trinidad and Tobago

Patrick Manning served several terms as the prime minister of the island nation of Trinidad and Tobago, twice from 1991 and 2010, and again in 2012, making him the longest-serving member of the country's parliament.

Manning was born into relatively modest circumstances, the only son out of five children. His mother, Elaine, was a teacher, and his father, Arnold, was a worker in the country's large petrochemical industry. He was also the chairman of the People's National Movement (PNM), a local political party, and Manning grew up surrounded by politicians who visited his home. Thanks to a scholarship from Texaco, Manning attended the University of the West Indies, graduating with a degree in geology. He began his career as a geologist at Texaco in 1969.

When Manning was just twenty-four, the prime minister (and fellow PNM member) Eric Williams encouraged him to seek office as a parliamentary representative for the San Fernando East district. With Williams' support, and aided by the opposition's electoral boycott, Manning won his first of nine consecutive elections. He would occupy his seat in parliament until his retirement from politics in 2015. In the early 1980s Manning served as the minister of information and later as the minister of energy and natural resources. When fellow PNM leader and Prime Minister George Chambers was booted from office, Manning became the party leader. In 1991, with the defeat of the opposition, United National Congress (UNC), Manning became the prime minister. He immediately proposed a budget and worked to improve economic relations with the country's neighbors and defeating crime. In 2001 President A.N.R. Robinson appointed Manning prime minister once again.

According to the Caribbean news source *LOOP,* Manning is credited with establishing the University of Trinidad and Tobago, the "development of the waterfront, the Government campus in downtown Port-of-Spain, the water taxi from Port-of-Spain to San Fernando. . . . and the Northern Academy of the Performing Arts (NAPA). . . . among others."

Manning leaves behind his wife, Hazel, and his two sons, Brian and David.

See Current Biography 2006

Marisol

Born: Paris, France; May 22, 1930
Died: New York, New York; April 30, 2016
Occupation: Artist

A Venezuelan-American sculptor and painter, Marisol's multimedia constructions often incorporated her own face and features in a delightful, whimsical, wryly satirical commentary on the clichés of contemporary American life.

Marisol was born Maria Sol Escobar. Her father, Gustavo Escobar, was a wealthy real estate agent, and the family enjoyed a comfortable, nomadic life in Europe, Venezuela, and the United States. Her mother, the former Josefina Hernandez, committed suicide when Marisol was eleven years old. The family lived in Caracas during World War II, and then moved to Los Angeles where Marisol attended the Westlake School for Girls. At sixteen, Marisol knew she wanted to be an artist, studying under the tutelage of Howard Warshaw at the Jepson School. She later studied at the Académie des Beaux-Arts in Paris in 1949. The following year she studied at the Art Students League in New York under Yasuo Kuniyoshi. Marisol acknowledged that her mentor, Hans Hofmann, the well-known abstract expressionist, had the greatest impact on her art. Though much of her early work was in painting, she began to study techniques of sculpture on her own, especially using molding, carving, and carpentry. Her work was inspired by pre-Columbian sculpture and South American folk art.

Her work was first exhibited at the Tenth Street galleries, including the Tanager. At this time, she discarded her last name, Escobar, reportedly because it was too masculine. Her show at the Stable and Sidney Janis galleries made her a star. In 1961 the Museum of Modern Art in New York City gave her a room of her own in its "Art of Assemblage" showcase "Americans 1963." Shortly thereafter, she was profiled in *Glamour* magazine. It was her confrontal-countenanced family groups, a portrait of a farm family of the dust bowl that helped assure Marisol's fame in her 1962 one-woman exhibition at the Stable Gallery. The Museum of Modern Art quickly picked up "The Family," an eighty-three-inch-tall construction of wood and mixed media. Marisol was a friend of Andy Warhol who starred Marisol in his underground movie *The Kiss.* She also appeared in his film, *13 Most Beautiful Girls.*

Marisol received a number of accolades over the course of her career; she was elected to the American Academy of Arts and Letters in 1978, and won the 1997 Premio Gabriela Mistral from the Organization of American States.

Marisol died of pneumonia on April 30, 2016. There are no immediate survivors.

See Current Biography 1968

Neville Marriner

Born: Lincoln, England; April 15, 1924
Died: London, England; October 2, 2016
Occupation: British conductor

Neville Marriner was one of the world's foremost music conductors who worked with many of the world's leading orchestras. He founded the Academy of St. Martin in the Fields. He created the soundtrack for the Academy Award Winning movie *Amadeus,* which topped the music charts in 1984, selling well over 6.5 million copies.

Neville Marriner's father introduced him to music at an early age, instructing him in violin and piano. He studied violin with the well-known teacher, Frederick Mountney. At thirteen, he was recommended for study at London's Royal College of Music, but was allowed to enter on scholarship only after graduating from the Lincoln School in 1939, when he was fifteen. His training in music was interrupted as he joined the army reconnaissance from 1941 to 1943, and he spent five months in the hospital recovering from injuries. He received his ARCM degree from the Royal College of Music in 1944, after capturing the coveted Tagore gold medal. He continued his studies at the Paris Conservatory, and became a professor at the Royal College of Music. His first orchestral experience was as a violinist with the London Philharmonic in the early 1950s, and four years later he joined the London Symphony Orchestra.

Marriner founded the Academy of St. Martin in the Fields, a chamber music group that won high acclaim in the late 1950s, and grew rapidly into one of the most innovative and highly paid ensembles in the world. Marriner's growing critical acclaim led to his founding and directorship of the Los Angeles Chamber Orchestra in 1969. For most of the 1980s, Marriner was the principal conductor for the Minneapolis Symphony Orchestra and the Südwest Deutsche Radio Orchestra.

Neville Marriner's academy has one of the largest discographies of any chamber orchestra in the world, with over five hundred albums. He was an honorary fellow of the Royal Academy of Music and has received some of Europe's top recording awards, including the Grand Prix du Disque, the Edison Award, and the Mozart Gemeinde prize. He was created a Knight Bachelor in 1985, and was appointed a Commander of the Order of the British Empire (CBE).

Neville Marriner was married twice, with his first marriage ending in divorce. He had two children. Information about survivors was unavailable.

See Current Biography 1978

Garry Marshall

Born: New York, New York; November 13, 1934
Died: Burbank, California; July 19, 2016
Occupation: Filmmaker, television producer, writer

Garry Marshall was an entertainment industry icon in both television and at the box office for over four decades, producing such all-time great shows as *The Odd Couple, Happy Days, Laverne and Shirley,* and *Mork and Mindy.* His movie credits include *The Flamingo Kid, Pretty Woman,* and *Frankie and Johnny.* He is credited with launching the careers of such Hollywood icons as Julia Roberts, Henry Winkler, and Robin Williams.

Garry Marshall was born into an Italian family in the Bronx, New York, where his immediately family (his parents and two siblings) shared an apartment with his grandparents. His father had anglicized their surname from Masciarelli to Marshall. Marshall's parents were loosely associated with show business. His mother ran a tap-dancing school, and his father directed industrial movies. While serving in the army during the Korean War, Marshall wrote for the service publication *Stars & Stripes,* and was the production chief of the Armed Forces Radio Network. Some time later he earned a degree in journalism from Northwestern University.

Back in New York, Marshall worked for the *Daily News* while also writing part-time for Jack Paar, the host of the *Tonight Show.* With writing partner Jerry Belson, Marshall began writing for sitcoms of the 1960s including *The Dick Van Dyke Show* and *The Lucy Show* (a follow-up

to *I Love Lucy,* starring Lucille Ball). In 1969 Marshall became a television producer and director, as well as a writer, when his show *The Odd Couple* (based on a Neil Simon play of the same name) debuted. In 1973 he scored a major hit with *Happy Days,* which offered pure escapist fare for eleven years. He created several successful spin-offs including *Laverne and Shirley* (starring his sister, Penny Marshall). For the week of January 28, 1979, four of the five most-watched television shows were Garry Marshall situation comedies.

Though he had written and produced several films, his filmmaking career really took off in 1982 when Marshall directed *Young Doctors in Love,* a light-hearted spoof of television soap operas. He soon followed up with several mega-hit movies that included *Pretty Woman, Runaway Bride,* and *The Princess Diaries.*

Garry Marshall's survivors include his wife of fifty-three years, Barbara, two sisters, three children, and six grandchildren.

See Current Biography 1992

Kurt Masur

Born: Brieg, Silesia, Germany; July 18, 1927
Died: Greenwich, Connecticut; December 19, 2015
Occupation: Music conductor

Kurt Masur was the music director of the Gewandhaus Orchestra of Leipzig for over twenty years, and the New York Philharmonic for ten. Though a skilled conductor, he will likely be remembered also for the humanist quality of his leadership. In 1989, when anti-government protesters were gathering on Karl-Marx Platz, outside the Gewandhaus concert hall, and police were setting up water cannons, Masur called an emergency meeting, which included Communist party officials. He broadcasted a public statement urging calm. The result was a bloodless revolution, and the eventual dismantling of the Iron Curtain. A dozen years later, in New York City, Masur conducted a moving arrangement of Brahms's *Ein Deutsches Requiem,* and arranged for orchestra musicians to perform around Ground Zero following the 2001 terrorist attacks. Even today, music-lovers can enjoy the free Annual Memorial Day Concert in New York.

Born near present-day Brzeg, Poland to an engineer father and music-minded mother, Masur began his music career at the age of seven by teaching himself to play the piano. Some time in his adolescence, he also learned to play the cello. He enrolled at the National Music School in Breslau in 1942, as an advanced pianist and cellist, and four years later, moved to the Leipzig Conservatory to study piano, composition, and conducting. Masur suggested that German artists didn't just lose morale following World War II; they also lost their sense of beauty, their "capacity to live life poetically."

In the 1960s, as the chief conductor for the Dresden Philharmonic, Masur, of necessity, cultivated the image of a government loyalist, feeling there was no other way to advance oneself in the highly regimented society of the German Democratic Republic. However, offers to conduct orchestras abroad became a source of friction between Masur and the Honecker government. His travel restrictions were eventually lifted, and Masur's reputation as an accomplished artist grew. In 1970 he was named artistic director of the Gewandhaus Orchestra of Leipzig, the most esteemed musical ensemble in East Germany and the oldest, busiest orchestra in Europe. In 1974 Masur and the Gewandhaus Orchestra made its first tour in America.

In March of 1990 Masur accepted an offer to succeed Zubin Mehta as music director of the New York Philharmonic, with its reputation for being unruly. Masur tamed that lion while, at the same time, maintaining his position with the Gewandhaus.

On December 19, 2015, Kurt Masur died at his home in Greenwich, Connecticut. His survivors include his third wife, Japanese soprano Tomoko, and his five children.

See Current Biography 1990

Melissa Mathison

Born: Los Angeles, California; June 3, 1950
Died: Los Angeles, California; November 4, 2015
Occupation: Screenwriter

Melissa Mathison is most remembered for writing the script for the 1982 blockbuster film, *E.T. The Extra-terrestrial*, that earned her an Oscar nomination for best screenplay. Other Mathison screenplays include a rewrite of *The Black Stallion*, and the 1995 hit, *The Indian in the Cupboard*. She was married to the movie star, Harrison Ford for twenty-one years.

Mathison's father, Richard Mathison, was a journalist who worked for *The Los Angeles Times*, and became the Los Angeles bureau chief for *Newsweek* magazine. One of her earliest jobs was that of babysitter for neighbor, Francis Ford Coppola who later recruited her as his assistant on the set of *The Godfather, Part II*. He enlisted her help again in 1996, this time as his executive assistant on *Apocalypse Now*, where she met her

future husband, Harrison Ford, who had a minor role in the movie. The two were married in 1983. Through Harrison Ford, Mathison met Steven Spielberg who approached her with the idea of writing a screenplay for a children's movie about a gentle alien stranded on Earth. They drew up a plot line in five minutes, and just eight weeks later, Mathison handed over the screenplay for *E.T., The Extra-terrestrial*. The movie received four Academy Awards and two Golden Globe Awards. She wrote the screenplay for the 1997 movie, *Kundun*, about Tenzin Gyatso, the 14th Dalai Lama, whom she met several times while working on the movie. Mathison's final project, a screen adaptation of Roald Dahl's *The B.F.G.*, is due to be released in 2016.

In 2000, Mathison and Ford announced that they were separating. Melissa Mathison died on November 4, 2015 from neuroendocrine cancer. Her two children, two brothers, and two sisters survive.

See Current Biography 2001

John McLaughlin

Born: Providence, Rhode Island; March 29, 1927
Died: Washington, District of Columbia; August 16, 2016
Occupation: Political commentator, broadcaster

Though born into a family of Catholic Democrats, John Joseph McLaughlin made a name for himself as a provocative political pundit of the Republican right with his hugely popular television show *The McLaughlin Group*, in which McLaughlin hosted a panel of four prominent print journalists in discussions on a range of issues, from the economy to East-West relations.

John McLaughlin attended Catholic schools as a child, and entered the Society of Jesus when he was eighteen. He began his thirteen years of training for the priesthood in the order at Weston College, the Jesuit seminary in Weston, Massachusetts. He earned both a BA degree, then an MA degree in philosophy and education at Boston College. After teaching briefly at prep schools in Connecticut, he moved to New York City to pursue a doctoral degree in communications at Columbia University, while making his way up the editorial ladder at *America*, the Manhattan-based Jesuit weekly journal of opinion. He attracted the attention of the Nixon White House with his article "Public Regulation and the News Media," in which he supported the notion that broadcasting was dominated by liberal ideologues. Patrick Buchanan, who worked on Nixon's speechwriting team, contacted McLaughlin and introduced him to the White House speechwriter Raymond Price.

In 1969 McLaughlin re-established Rhode Island residency and ran, unsuccessfully, for the US Senate as a "peace" candidate. In 1971 he joined Nixon's speechwriting team. During the Watergate scandal, Father McLaughlin vigorously defended the president, arguing that future historians would regard Nixon as a great moral leader. At that time, McLaughlin's future wife, Ann Dore, was the director of communications with the Committee to Reelect the President. The two married in 1974 after McLaughlin successfully petitioned Pope Paul VI for laicization. She eventually became the Secretary of Labor in President Ronald Reagan's cabinet.

In 1982 McLaughlin launched McLaughlin & Company, a public affairs and media relations consulting firm. McLaughlin began hosting a weekend radio talk show over WRC in Washington, on which he interviewed and argued with such guests as Barry Goldwater and Eugene McCarthy, and took phone calls from the audience. The politically conservative Edison Electric Institute financed a television pilot of *The McLaughlin Group*, which became a mainstay of weekend news programming for the next three decades.

John McLaughlin was married and divorced twice. There are no immediate survivors.

See Current Biography 1987

James Alan McPherson

Born: Savannah, Georgia; September 16, 1943
Died: Iowa City, Iowa; July 27, 2016
Occupation: Writer, educator

Though he earned a law degree from Harvard University, James McPherson is remembered as a writer of fiction. He won a Pulitzer Prize for his collection of short stories called *Elbow Room*, and worked on the faculty at the prestigious Iowa Writers Workshop at the University of Iowa from 1981 until his retirement in 2014, more than three decades.

James McPherson was born into a poor, working-class family in Savannah, Georgia. He attended Morris Brown College, a historically black school, graduating with a BA degree in English and history in 1965. During this time, McPherson worked during summers as an employee for the railroad, riding across the Pacific Northwest from Chicago to Seattle. He was able to attend the 1962 World's Fair in Seattle, and the experience had a major impact on his psyche. With almost every nation on earth represented in some way, McPherson found this convergence of cultures inspiring. In 1965 he entered and won first prize in a writing contest, co-sponsored by the United Negro College Fund and Reader's Digest, using the scholarship to attend law school at Harvard University. He earned his LL.B degree in 1968.

That same year McPherson's short story "Gold Coast" won an award and was published by the *Atlantic*. Soon thereafter McPherson entered the University of Iowa, and one year later, he saw his first collection of short stories, *Hue and Cry* published. The book was well received and won an award from the National Institute of Arts and Letters. The dust jacket of *Hue and Cry* contained an enthusiastic endorsement from the African-American literary icon Ralph Ellison, who had befriended and become a mentor to McPherson. He earned his MFA degree from the University of Iowa in 1972. During the mid 1970s McPherson taught at several universities including Harvard, Morgan State University, and the University of Virginia. He was also a guest lecturer at colleges and universities in Japan.

The mid-1970s saw the publication of McPherson's *Railroad: Trains and Train People in American Culture*, a collection of fiction, nonfiction, poetry and illustrations. And in 1977, McPherson's collection of short stories, *Elbow Room* was published, winning McPherson a Pulitzer Prize for fiction, the first African American to win a Pulitzer for fiction. Though he contributed essays and reviews to many publications, including the *New York Times*, the *Nation*, *Playboy*, *Ploughshares*, and *Reader's Digest*, he spent the rest of his career teaching at the Iowa Writer's Workshop. He retired in 2014.

James McPherson's survivors include his daughter, Rachel McPherson, and his son, Benjamin Miyamoto.

See Current Biography 1996

Fatima Mernissi

Born: Fez, Morocco; September 27, 1940
Died: Rabat, Morocco; November 30, 2015
Occupation: Moroccan sociologist, author

Fatima Mernissi was a world-renowned sociologist and feminist who introduced the world to the lives of Islamic women "behind the veil"— the title of her first groundbreaking study of women and gender relations in Islamic societies. She became an outspoken defender of women's rights in the Islamic world, and introduced the world to the otherwise closed society of the harem.

Mernissi was born into a domestic harem, which is a gender-separated home, as opposed to an imperial harem, which houses women for the sexual fancies of a prestigious man. Her father rejected polygamy, but still kept his wife and daughters isolated from the outside world. Females were only allowed access to the outside world for religious instruction and to attend the mosque. Yet, Mernissi's mother and grandmother imbued in her a desire to see a life beyond the traditional confines of her home. The women in her life were illiterate, and Mernissi's mother rebelled by dressing her daughter in Western clothes. In the mid-1950s, Moroccan nationalists won freedom from Spanish and French colonial rule, and women were allowed to seek a secular education. Mernissi was educated in a secular primary school and eventually earned a master's degree in political science at Mohammed V University. In 1973 she completed her doctorate in sociology from Brandeis University where her dissertation, *Beyond the Veil: Male-Female Dynamics in Modern Muslim Society* was published and widely read, though it was banned in Morocco. She argued that Muslim scholars justified the oppression of women in Islamic society based on the purportedly chaotic nature of women's sexuality.

Mernissi worked as a professor of sociology at the University of Rabat, then moved to Mohammed V University where she taught sociology and became a member of the research center. She also directed studies for a number of international organizations, including the United Nations Educational, Scientific and Cultural Organization, the International Labour Organization (ILO), and the United Nations Population Fund. While many of her publications focused on the lives of Muslim women, she has been praised for her contributions to all women. In particular, Mernissi introduced the idea of the harem as a metaphor, relating how a cruel shopping experience, an encounter with a salesperson, made her realize that "maybe 'size 6' is a more violent restriction imposed on women than is the Muslim veil. . . . Framing youth as beauty and condemning maturity, is the weapon used against women in the West." Mernissi has worked as a visiting lecturer at Harvard University and the University of California at Berkeley. Her books have been published in at least twenty-eight countries. She was awarded the Erasmus Prize in 2004 for contributions to culture, society, and social science.

Fatima Mernissi died on November 30, 2015 in Morocco's capital city, Rabat.

See Current Biography 2005

Abner Mikva

Born: Milwaukee, Wisconsin; January 21, 1926
Died: Chicago, Illinois; July 4, 2016
Occupation: Congressman, federal judge, White House counsel

Abner Mikva was one of very few individuals to have served the public from high office in all three branches of the federal government. He was an Illinois state legislator for five terms beginning in 1956; a five-term US congressman beginning in 1968; a judge for the US court of appeals in Washington, DC in 1979; and he served as White House counsel under President Bill Clinton beginning in 1994. Mikva was often considered a strong contender for the US Supreme Court.

Abner Mikva was born to poor Jewish immigrants from Eastern Europe and grew up speaking mostly Yiddish at home. He entered the US Army Air Force as a private in 1944 and served as a navigator with the Air Force training command. He attended the University of Wisconsin and Washington University in St. Louis, and even though he never graduated, the University of Chicago Law School accepted him in 1948, and he worked as an editor for the university's law review. Shortly after receiving his law degree, Mikva spent a year clerking for US Supreme Court Justice Sherman Minton. He then joined a labor law firm in Chicago. He won election to the Illinois House of Representatives in 1956, and ten years later he captured a seat in the US House of Representatives. In 1979 President Jimmy Carter nominated Mikva for the US Court of Appeals for the District of Columbia, arguably the most important court outside the Supreme Court. In 1994 President Clinton offered Mikva a post as White House Counsel. It was a tumultuous time with the Whitewater probe investigating Clinton's failed land deal in Arkansas. Mikva left the White House a year later and took a post as professor at the University of Chicago Law School and at Northwestern University. He was a founding board member of the Office of Congressional Ethics.

Mikva and his wife, Zoe, founded the Mikva Challenge, a charity aimed at involving young people in public service. Mikva was a mentor to powerful Democratic rising stars early in their careers, including Supreme Court Justice Elena Kagan, Chicago's Mayor Rahm Emanuel, and President Barack Obama who awarded Mikva the Presidential Medal of Freedom in 2014.

Abner Mikva married Zorita "Zoe" Wise in 1948. The couple had three daughters. Mikva's survivors include his wife, three daughters, and seven grandchildren.
See Current Biography 1980

Marvin Minsky

Born: New York, New York; August 9, 1927
Died: Boston, Massachusetts; January 4, 2016
Occupation: Computer scientist, educator

Marvin Minsky was a world-renowned research scientist in the field of artificial intelligence. For over thirty years he taught at the Massachusetts Institute of Technology (MIT) where he co-founded and directed the school's artificial intelligence laboratory. Along with his colleague, John McCarthy, Minsky coined the phrase "artificial intelligence."

Marvin Minsky was born in New York City to an eye surgeon who was also a musician and painter. At one time, Minsky's father, Dr. Henry Minsky, was the director of the ophthalmology department at New York's Mount Sinai Hospital. Minsky attended several special schools for gifted children, including the Bronx High School of Science and Phillips Academy in Andover, Massachusetts. After graduation in 1945, Minsky enlisted in the US Navy and was sent to the Great Lakes Naval Training Center north of Chicago. In 1946 he entered Harvard University where he began exploring genetics, neurology, physics, and the nature of intelligence. He graduated with a degree in mathematics. He then attended graduate school at Princeton University where he devised an electronic learning machine (a neural network simulator) known as SNARC, in collaboration with Dean Edmonds. Minsky returned to Harvard on a three-year junior fellowship. At that time, there was no name for the field Minsky was exploring. In 1958 he became an assistant professor of mathematics at MIT where he and his colleague, John McCarthy, founded the MIT Artificial Intelligence Project. He remained an MIT professor of media arts and sciences, electrical engineering and computer science for the rest of his life.

One of his greatest contributions to the field was his book *Perceptrons*, co-written with fellow scientist Seymour Papert, which explored artificial neural networks. The two collaborated on a theory called the "society of mind," that explored the nature of intelligence. (In 1986, they published a book called *The Society of Mind*.)

Marvin Minsky received many awards and accolades as a pioneer in this new field of study, including the ACM Turing Award, the MIT Killian Award, the Japan Prize, the Rank Prize, the Robert Wood Prize for Optoelectronics, and the Benjamin Franklin Medal. He was married to his wife, Gloria Anna Rudisch, a pediatrician, for more than sixty years. In addition to his wife, Minsky's survivors include their three children, and four grandchildren.

See Current Biography 1988

George E. Mueller

Born: St. Louis, Missouri; July 16, 1918
Died: Irvine, California; October 12, 2015
Occupation: NASA engineer, physicist

Sometimes referred to as the undisputed boss of manned space flight, George E. Mueller was unique in that he was a leading scientist who was also a skilled administrator. He is credited with ensuring that the National Aeronautics and Space Administration (NASA) would get an American to the moon before President Kennedy's deadline of 1970, with his insistence on testing rocket components all at once—a practice that became known as "all up." At the same time, he was charged with the task of restoring morale and eliminating differences within NASA, and was named the associate administrator for manned space flight. One official referred to him as the "moon czar."

Born in St. Louis, Missouri, he attended the School of Mines and Metallurgy at the University of Missouri. After receiving his bachelor of science degree in engineering, he obtained a research fellowship at Purdue University, earning him a master of science degree in electrical engineering. His first work was in video amplification, television, and microwave research at Bell laboratories. He taught electrical and system engineering at Ohio State University, while simultaneously earning his doctorate in 1951. He worked as a consultant to Thompson Ramo Wooldridge Inc. (TRW) developing missile-guided radar and the intercontinental ballistic missiles (ICBM).

Mueller was elected fellow of the Institute of Electronic and Electrical Engineers (IEEE), and an associate fellow of the American Institute of Aeronautics and Astronautics (AIAA). He was awarded six honorary doctorate degrees over his lifetime, received the National Medal of Science in 1971, and in 2011 the Smithsonian National Air and Space Museum honored him with a lifetime achievement award. George Mueller died from congestive heart failure on October 12, 2015. His second wife, Darla Hix Schwartzman and four children survive him.

See Current Biography 1964

Patrice Munsel

Born: Spokane, Washington; May 14, 1925
Died: Schroon Lake, New York; August 4, 2016
Occupation: American opera singer

Patrice Munsel was the youngest singer ever signed by the Metropolitan Opera. She startled the musical world in December 1943 with her debut at age eighteen.

Patrice Munsel was the only child of Dr. Audley and Eunice Munsil. (She changed her name to Munsel for ease of pronunciation.) Her father was a successful dentist, and her mother took great interest in her daughter's singing career from a very early age. Munsel attended Lewis and Clarke High School where she was the captain of the girl's football team and a star of the school's theatrical productions. She also took tap and ballet classes as a child. Her first claim to fame was as a "virtuoso of artistic whistling," something she claimed was invaluable in her singing career for the training it gave her in breath control and phrasing. When she was sixteen, Munsel and her mother moved to New York City where Munsel began a rigorous training schedule under the tutelage of William Herman and Renato Bellini. She also studied Italian and acting with Antoinette Stabile. Her opera coach, Giacomo Spadoni, brought his young pupil to the attention of Wilfred Pelletier, who was the program conductor of the Metropolitan Auditions of the Air. She won first prize, which included a contract with the Metropolitan. Thus, Munsel became the youngest singer ever to sign with the opera house. She gave her first professional concert in June of 1943.

Munsel remained with the Metropolitan Opera until 1958, leaving a record of 225 performances. She continued her career in acting and singing on television and road-show musicals like *Kiss Me Kate* and *Mame*. She was a frequent guest on the *Bell Telephone Hour*. Munsel married a public relations executive, Robert Schuler, in 1952. The couple had four children. Her husband and one son predeceased her. Survivors include her three remaining children.

See Current Biography 1945

Mark Murphy

Born: Fulton, New York; March 14, 1932
Died: Englewood, New Jersey; October 22, 2015
Occupation: American jazz singer

Jazz singer Mark Murphy was a well-known artist and favorite among the jazz-world's elite who saw him as an innovator who took classic songs and made them brand new. He released over four-dozen albums and was a Grammy nominee six times over.

Murphy was born in Fulton (near Syracuse), New York, to a musical family. Both of his parents sang. In addition, his father, Dwight Martin, was a trained vocalist and Methodist choirmaster. Murphy began piano lessons at the age of seven, and studied music and theater at Syracuse University.

Sammy Davis Jr. is credited with "discovering" Mark Murphy while Murphy sang at a local jam session in Syracuse, going so far as to have Murphy join him on stage during his own performance. Murphy took matters into his own hands by introducing himself to the *Tonight Show* host, Steve Allen, as someone whose music Davis admired. Allen became one of Murphy's greatest supporters, and the musician moved to New York in 1954, performing at the Apollo Theater, and landing deals with such big labels as Decca and Riverside. He released his first album *Meet Mark Murphy* in 1956.

Through his unique scat improvisation, Murphy gained a reputation as a performer's performer. Ella Fitzgerald is said to have considered him her equal. He was something of a beatnik, releasing his unique album *Bop for Kerouac*, which blended lines from Kerouac's novel *On the Road*. (He thought Kerouac's style had the cadence and rhythm of jazz.) In his *A Biographical Guide to the Great Jazz and Pop Singers*, Will Friedwald wrote that Murphy had a knack for taking an old song, "turning it inside out, spilling its guts and finding the feeling underneath."

Murphy's long-time partner, Eddie O'Sullivan, died in 1990. Mark Murphy died at the Lillian Booth Actors Home in Englewood, New Jersey, from complications of pneumonia. His sister survives.

See Current Biography 2004

Yitzhak Navon

Born: Jerusalem, Israel; April 9, 1921
Died: Jerusalem, Israel; November 7, 2015
Occupation: Former president of Israel

Yitzhak Navon was the fifth president of Israel, and the first to have been born in Israel. His family roots in the Holy Land reached back twelve generations with his father's family having been expelled from Spain in 1492, settling in Turkey until they immigrated to Palestine in the seventeenth century. His mother's family arrived from Morocco in 1742. As loved by Israel's Palestinian population as by fellow Jews, Yitzhak Navon was considered a unifying figure. He was fluent in Arabic (as well as Hebrew, English, Spanish, Ladino, and Yiddish), and often addressed Palestinians in their native language.

Upon graduating from Hebrew University, Navon taught at his former high school, Beit Hakerem. He later became the director of the Arabic department at Haganah, a paramilitary precursor to the Israel Defense Force. The government sent him to South America as secretary at the Israel legations in Uruguay and Argentina, becoming secretary of the foreign minister in 1951. In 1952 Prime Minister Ben-Gurion needed a Spanish tutor, and Navon was selected. Ben-Gurion was so impressed that Navon was soon named head of the bureau of the prime minister, where he remained for ten years, eventually taking the position of director at the Ministry of Education and Culture where he worked to eradicate illiteracy. He ran for Israel's parliament, Knesset, in 1965. In 1973 Navon was elected chairman of the World Zionist Council, and in 1978 he was elected as Israel's fifth president, a largely ceremonial position.

He was very popular among Jews and Arabs alike. After Israel's war with Lebanon in 1982, he called for an investigation into the massacre of thousands of Palestinians at Sabra and Chatilla refugee camps. The report revealed that much of the blame rested on defense minister Ariel Sharon, who soon resigned. While visiting Egypt's President Anwar Sadat, Navon captured the hearts of the Egyptian people by addressing them in their own language, underscoring his personal commitment to normalizing relations between Egypt and Israel. Upon his retirement in 1992, he became the national authority on Ladino, working to preserve Jewish-Ladino traditions. He also wrote numerous plays.

Yitzhak Navon had been in declining health for years and had been on dialysis for several months before his death on November 7, 2015. His first wife, Ofira Erez died in 1993.

Navon's second wife, Miri Shafir Navon, his two children, and several grandchildren survive.

See Current Biography 1982

Gloria Naylor

Born: New York, New York; January 25, 1950
Died: US Virgin Islands; September 28, 2016
Occupation: Author

Gloria Naylor's most recognized novel is *The Women of Brewster Place*, the first story in a "novel Quartet" that also included the novels *Mama Day, Linden Place*, and *Bailey's Café*.

Gloria Naylor has credited her mother with instilling in her a love of reading and writing. Naylor was born in New York City after her father, a transit worker, and her mother, a telephone operator, migrated north from rural Mississippi. Her mother, Alberta, had been denied borrowing privileges from her local library because of her race, and was determined to raise her children in the less segregated North. After the death of Reverend Martin Luther King, Jr., in an effort to make a difference with her life, Naylor decided to postpone college in order to work as a Jehovah's Witness missionary. Following seven years of traveling and evangelizing throughout the eastern United States, Naylor attended Brooklyn College where she learned about the rich history of celebrated African-American female authors like Zora Neale Hurston and Tony Morrison. She earned a degree in English literature and was awarded a scholarship to attend Yale University. At the same time, Naylor began writing short stories. Her first stories were published in a 1980 issue of *Essence* magazine. These stories evolved into the novel *The Women of Brewster Place*.

In addition to her novels, Naylor wrote a number of essays and screenplays. She founded One Way Productions, an independent film company, in order to bring her third book, *Mama Day* to the screen. Her first novel, *The Women of Brewster Place*, won the American Book Award for best first novel. Later Oprah Winfrey would produce a two-part television series based on the book. Naylor received fellowships from both the National Education Association (NEA) and the Guggenheim Foundation. She served as a visiting professor at numerous universities, including Princeton University, New York University (NYU), and Brandeis University.

Gloria Naylor was briefly married, but determined not to remarry or have children as her solitude was too important to her. Her sister, Bernice Harrison, survives.

See Current Biography 1993

James Morton Nederlander

Born: Detroit, Michigan, March 31, 1922
Died: Southampton, New York; July 25, 2016
Occupation: Theater executive

James Nederlander was the head of one of the country's largest theater companies with nine theaters on Broadway, three on the West End, seventeen more nationwide, and two theaters in London. His theaters have been home to some of the greatest shows of the last century including *Annie, Wicked, The Lion King*, and *Hamilton*.

James ("Jimmy") Nederlander was born into a close-knit family of five boys and one girl. His father, David Nederlander, was a jeweler, but in 1912 he decided to try his hand at theater management when he bought the lease on the old Detroit Opera House. Knowing nothing about the business, Nederlander partnered with Lee and Jacob Shubert. (The relationship between the two families would eventually turn acrimonious, as they became stiff competitors.) Though James Nederlander had attended the Detroit Institute of Technology hoping for a law degree, World War II intervened. Ironically, his tour of duty as an Air Force cadet included an assignment to the staff that was mounting the Broadway production of *Winged Victory*, Moss Hart's salute to the Air Force. When he returned home he began managing the Lyceum in Minneapolis for eight years. By the time David Nederlander died in 1965, the Nederlanders had acquired several theatres in Detroit and Chicago. That same year, they expanded their chain to Broadway by buying the legendary vaudeville house, The Palace. By 1971 the Nederlanders were operating seventeen theaters in five American cities. In 1977 they produced the Broadway hit *Annie*, which Nederlander reported had transformed his initial $150,000 into well over a million dollars. In the early 1990s, Nederlander established a lucrative partnership with the Disney Corporation, bringing *Beauty and the Beast* to Broadway. Many more Disney productions would follow.

James Nederlander won twelve Tony Awards as a producer or co-producer. In 2014 he was awarded a special Tony for Lifetime Achievement. Nederlander instituted a new program called the National High School Musical Theater Awards. Known as the "Jimmy Award," Nederlander's legacy enabled a winning high school troupe to be flown to New York and mentored by some of Broadway's leading performers.

In 1969 he married Charlene Saunders. They had three children. His wife, two sons, a stepdaughter, and four grandchildren survive.

See Current Biography 1991

Yukio Ninagawa was born in the Japanese city of Kawaguchi, northwest of Tokyo. After graduating from high school, he applied to Tokyo's University of the Arts as a painting student, but failed the entrance exam. He decided to pursue acting instead, and in 1955 he joined the Sehai, a Japanese repertory company in which he performed for twelve years. He also felt drawn to directing, and after seeing two Royal Shakespeare Company productions in the late 1960s, Ninagawa was inspired to direct Shakespeare. In the early 1970s Ninagawa began working with the theater and film producer, Tadeo Nakane, who invited Ninagawa to direct a production of *Romeo and Juliet*. In 1975 Ninagawa staged a seventy-five-person Japanese-language production of *King Lear*.

Ninagawa came to international prominence at the 1985 Edinburgh International Festival in Scotland, where he directed Shakespeare's *Macbeth* as the tale of a medieval samurai. The play was performed in Greece, Italy, France, Canada, New York, and Kuala Lumpur. Writing for *The Guardian* (19 September, 1987) Michael Billington wrote: "In my whole theatergoing lifetime, I have never seen a production as achingly beautiful as Yukio Ninagawa's *Macbeth*." Other Shakespeare plays included *Hamlet, Romeo and Juliet*, and *Richard III*. Often lavishly designed, his sets blended theatrical Eastern styles, especially the Japanese noh and kabuki, with Western elements. In 1986 he brought an all-male version of Euripides's *Medea* to the Edinburgh Festival. In 1987 Ninagawa was nominated for a best director prize at London's Laurence Olivier Awards. In 1990 he brought Yukio Mishima's modern noh play *Sotoba-Komachi*, to the Edinburgh Festival, winning the 1990 Edinburgh Festival Critics Award.

In addition to his theatrical awards and nominations, Ninagawa was named a Commander of the Order of the British Empire (CBE) in April of 2002. In 2010 he was awarded Japan's Order of Culture. Yukio Ninagawa's wife, Tomoko Mayama, and his two daughters survive.

See Current Biography 2003

Yukio Ninagawa

Born: Kawaguchi, Saitama, Japan; October 15, 1935
Died: Tokyo, Japan; May 12, 2016
Occupation: Japanese theater director

Yukio Ninagawa was a highly celebrated Japanese theater director who brought Western classics like Shakespeare and Euripides to the Japanese stage.

Agnes Nixon

Born: Chicago, Illinois; December 10, 1922
Died: Haverford, Pennsylvania; September 28, 2016
Occupation: Television writer

Agnes Nixon was a scriptwriter who helped usher in the new world of daytime soap operas. She created two of the most popular shows, *One Life* to *Live* and *All My Children*. She was inducted into the Television Hall of Fame in 1993.

Soon after Agnes Nixon's birth her parents divorced and Agnes moved to Nashville, Tennessee, to live with her mother and her extended family. Her grandmother Dalton was a prim, severe Irish Catholic, and her Aunt Emma loved to tell tall tales about the romantic lives of their Irish ancestors. Eventually, Nixon began devising her own stories. She attended St. Cecelia's Academy where she wrote and staged plays in the school auditorium. Though her father had been estranged from the family, he did finance Nixon's college education at Northwestern University, where she focused on dramatic writing. Following graduation Nixon's father had hoped to bring her into the family business of manufacturing burial garments. To discourage her about a career in writing, he arranged for her to meet with Ima Phillips who had created the first radio soap opera. Ironically, the encounter landed Nixon her first writing job. By 1950 television opened new doors for the soap-opera genre. Nixon moved to New York and continued her career, working for a number of the most popular shows on daytime television, including *Search for Tomorrow*, *The Guiding Light*, and *As the World Turns*. In 1967 the ABC network offered Nixon the opportunity to create her own show. *One Life to Live* was a runaway success, and Nixon was again invited to create a new show. The Wildly popular *All My Children* was the result.

Agnes Nixon won many honors and accolades for her work. She received five awards from the Writers' Guild of America, five Daytime Emmy Awards, and the National Academy of Television Arts and Sciences honored her with a lifetime achievement award, dubbing her "the grand dame of daytime serial drama."

Nixon's husband, Robert Nixon, predeceased her in 1996. Her survivors include her four children, ten grandchildren, and three great-grandchildren.

See Current Biography 2001

Marni Nixon

Born: Altadena, California; February 22, 1930
Died: New York, New York; July 24, 2016
Occupation: Singer, dubber, actress, educator

Marni Nixon has easily earned the sobriquet, with some irony, of "unsung hero." Though her name is unfamiliar to most movie fans, her voice is not. Nixon dubbed the voices for a number of Hollywood's greatest films, including that of Deborah Kerr in *The King and I*, Natalie Wood in *West Side Story*, Audrey Hepburn in *My Fair Lady*, and even for Marilyn Monroe in *Diamonds Are a Girls Best Friend*. Nixon recorded over two-dozen albums and won four local Emmy Awards for her hit children's television series, *Boomerang*. She was twice nominated for a Grammy Award.

Marni Nixon was born into a musical family. Everyone in the family of six played an instrument. Her father was a singer who toured with trios and quartets for several years. At the age of four, Marni began violin lessons. After only four lessons she was accepted into Karl Moldrem's Hollywood Baby Orchestra. Shortly thereafter, she began playing for the City Schools Youth Orchestra. Nixon made her screen debut in 1937, and over the next decade she appeared in minor roles or as an extra in over fifty films. In 1946 Nixon placed second in a singing competition under the famous choral director, Roger Wagner. At his invitation she joined his Los Angeles Concert Youth Chorus, performing regularly with the Los Angeles Philharmonic Orchestra. In the late 1940s, Nixon performed Stravinsky's cantata *Los Noces (The Wedding)*, and thereby forged a life-long friendship with Stravinsky and his wife. She landed her first major ghosting role in 1955, dubbing for *The King and I*. Her contract specified that she would receive no royalties or credits in the film, nor on the record jacket. She was ordered to keep her role a secret. In 1961 Nixon sang in *West Side Story*. The soundtrack won a Grammy Award. In 1964 the film version of *My Fair Lady* won eight Oscars. In the early 1980s Nixon moved to New York where she earned a Drama Desk Award for her role for the musical, *Taking My Turn*.

Marni Nixon married for the first time in 1950. She and her husband, Ernest Gold, had three children. Their marriage ended in divorce. Nixon married twice more. Her survivors include two daughters, six grandchildren, and three great-grandchildren.

See Current Biography 2009

Hugh O'Brian

Born: Rochester, New York; April 19, 1925
Died: Beverly Hills, California; September 5, 2016
Occupation: Actor

Hugh O'Brian is most remembered for his television role as Wyatt Earp, the marshal of Dodge City, Kansas, on *The Life and Legend of Wyatt Earp* in the mid- to late-1950s. He was also the founder of a youth leadership program known as the Hugh O'Brian Youth Leadership Organization, commonly referred to as HOBY.

Though born in Rochester, New York, Hugh O'Brian spent most of his childhood in Lancaster, Pennsylvania, Chicago, and Evanston, Illinois. The family moved often as O'Brian's father, a retired captain of the US Marine Corp, was a sales executive for the Armstrong Cork Company. O'Brian attended several schools in the Chicago area, and a military school in Boonville, Missouri. He entered the University of Cincinnati, but his education was interrupted by World War II. At the age of seventeen, O'Brian was one of the youngest drill instructors in the history of the Marine Corps. Upon leaving the military, O'Brian considered a law degree from Yale University, but his plans were interrupted when an actor friend in Los Angeles became ill and asked O'Brian to replace him. His reviews were so favorable, he decided to pursue an acting career. In 1950 he was selected to play a polio victim in the movie *Never Fear*. Between 1951 and 1954, O'Brian appeared in eighteen movies. He played opposite some of the biggest names in Hollywood, including Patricia Neal, Rock Hudson, and Spencer Tracy.

In 1958 O'Brian founded his youth organization, HOBY, after he and his friend, Norman Cousins, accompanied the Nobel Prize-winning physician and missionary Albert Schweitzer, to one of his clinics in Africa. O'Brian was so inspired by the experience that he wanted to create his own philanthropic organization. Among the program's famous alumni are basketball star, Shane Battier, actor James Van Der Beek, and Arkansas Governor Mike Huckabee.

Hugh O'Brian stayed single for most of his life, though he had numerous, high-profile relationships. After a paternity suit, he acknowledged he had fathered a son in 1953. He was eighty-one years old when he married longtime girlfriend, Virginia Barber. She and O'Brian's brother survive him.

See Current Biography 1958

Maureen O'Hara (FitzSimons)

Born: Milltown, Ireland; August 17, 1920
Died: Boise, Idaho; October 24, 2015
Occupation: Irish American actress

Though never nominated for an Academy Award, Maureen O'Hara received an honorary Academy Award in 2014, for a lifetime as one of Hollywood's leading actresses. The beautiful actress was noted for her flaming red hair, green eyes, and spicy demeanor. Longtime friend, John Wayne famously quipped, "she's a great guy."

Born outside of Dublin, in Milltown, Ireland, O'Hara's real name was Maureen FitzSimons.

She was the second of six children, all of whom have appeared onscreen, with the exception of one sibling who became a Sister of Charity. She graduated from the famed Abby Theater in 1937, with the dream of becoming an opera singer. However, Charles Laughton convinced her to audition for Alfred Hitchcock's British film, *Jamaica Inn* (1939). Shortly thereafter, under contract with Laughton, (contracting with an actor rather than a film studio was not unusual at the time) she appeared with him in *The Hunchback of Notre Dame*. A few years later she starred in *How Green Was My Valley*, directed by John Ford, which won six Academy Awards in 1941. Directors who championed her work include Jean Renoir, Henry King, Frank Borzage, and John Ford, who considered her the greatest leading lady of her time. She starred in five films under John Ford's direction, and the two shared a tumultuous friendship. (Ford is said to have punched her, but she refused to hit back, claiming she wanted to prove she could take a hit.) She shared a more peaceful, lifelong friendship with John Wayne.

O'Hara played opposite a number of Hollywood's leading men including John Wayne, James Stewart, Henry Fonda, Alec Guinness, Tyrone Power, and Rex Harrison. She was also an athlete, who reportedly had considered a career as a football player. She was one of only a handful of actresses to perform her own stunts, from swordplay to fisticuffs.

Maureen O'Hara was married three times, the first two marriages lasting only a few years. She gave birth to a daughter, Bronwyn, in her first marriage, when she was twenty-three. After marrying for the third time, to famous pilot Charles Blair, she retired to the Virgin Islands where she helped run their commuter seaplane service, Antilles Airboats. O'Hara remained head of the airline after Blair died in a plane accident. (She was the first female to run a scheduled airline service.)

Maureen O'Hara died at home in Boise, Idaho. She was ninety-eight years old. At the time of her death, Maureen O'Hara had over sixty film credits to her name. Her daughter, a grandson, and two great-grandchildren survive.

See Current Biography 1954

Arnold Palmer

Born: Latrobe, Pennsylvania; September 10, 1929
Died: Pittsburgh, Pennsylvania; September 25, 2016
Occupation: Professional golfer

Arnold Palmer was one of the greatest golfers in the history of the game, winning sixty-two PGA Tour titles. His charisma and easy-going manner helped usher in a new era of golf. He was among the few golfers to achieve the "Grand Slam," winning the US British Open twice, the Masters four times, and the US Open once. In 1974 he was inducted into the World Golf Hall of Fame. Palmer was the only golfer to be awarded both the Presidential Medal of Freedom, and the Congressional Gold Medal.

Arnold Palmer was born to a working-class family, one of four children. His father, Milfred Deacon ("Deac") Palmer, was a groundskeeper and teaching professional at the Latrobe Country Club near their home. Palmer was only three years old when his father first put a club (a sawed-off women's club) into his hands. Deac Palmer was his son's only coach. By the time he was nine, Palmer had shot nine holes at forty-five. He attended the Latrobe High School where he played on the school's golf team. In 1947 his friend, Bud Worsham, suggested he could attend Wake Forest College in North Carolina on a golf scholarship. Palmer jumped at the chance. Unfortunately, Palmer was devastated when Worsham was killed in an automobile accident. He left school and joined the Coast Guard. He briefly returned to Wake Forest in 1954, but did not graduate.

In 1954, the same year that he married Winnie Walzer, Palmer went professional, signing a contract with Wilson Sporting Goods. According to Adam Schupak of *Golf Week* (25 September 2016), Palmer's agent, Mark McCormack, deserves a lot of credit for selling "the Palmer personality and the values he represented," with Palmer's "matinee-idol looks, charisma, and blue-collar background." Palmer's business empire included a golf course design company, car dealerships, and a chain of dry cleaners. He designed more than three hundred courses, and owned the Bay Hill Club in Orlando, Florida. He also purchased the Latrobe Country Club where he learned to golf.

Palmer's fist wife, Winnie, predeceased him in 1999. His survivors include his second wife, Kathleen (Kit) Gawthrop, his two daughters, six grandchildren, and nine great-grandchildren.

See Current Biography 1960

Shimon Peres

Born: Wiszniew, Poland; August 16, 1923
Died: September 28, 2016
Occupation: Former Israeli prime minister, president, minister of defense

Shimon Peres was a dominant political figure for decades beginning in the 1950s when he served as the minister of defense under Israel's first prime minister, David Ben-Gurion. He was largely responsible for developing Israel's weapons and defense industries. He was Israel's prime minister in 1984. Peres negotiated a settlement of Israel's long-standing conflict with its Arab neighbors and Palestinian population, and played a key role in negotiations that led to the historic Oslo Peace Accord, for which, along with Yasir Arafat and Yitzhak Rabin, he was awarded the 1994 Nobel Peace Prize. Shimon Peres was Israel's president from 2007 to 2014.

Shimon Peres was born in a small village in Poland. His parents were non-religious, Zionist Jews, and the family moved to Israel in 1933. Peres attended the Balfour primary school in Tel Aviv, and received a scholarship to attend the Ben Shemen Agricultural School where he met his mentor, Berl Katznelson, an intellectual in the Labor movement. Peres joined Haganah, the underground Jewish defense organization. In 1946 he attended the twenty-second World Zionist Congress in Switzerland where he met the future first Prime Minister David Ben-Gurion, who would eventually send Peres to the United States as the head of a mission to acquire weapons for Israel. While in the US he attended the New School for Social Research, New York University (NYU), and Harvard University. Upon his return, Peres was appointed director-general of the ministry of defense, responsible for the development of Israel's government-owned weapons industry. He also forged a strong relationship with France—a crucial step in Israel's capture of the Sinai Peninsula from Egypt. Later, as Ben-Gurion's deputy minister of defense, Peres persuaded the United States to sell Israel its Hawk antiaircraft missile system, making the United States Israel's main source of arms.

In 1969 Peres was appointed to the new prime minister, Golda Meir's cabinet. After her ouster in 1974, the new prime minister, Yitzak Rabin (Peres's staunch political opponent) appointed him as minister of defense. He was heavily involved in the 1975 disengagement agreement with Egypt. A 1983 tie between the Likud and Labor parties brought about a novel power-sharing agreement where Peres served as prime minister for half of a term, from 1984 to 1986. He was particularly adept at handling a major economic crisis in the early 1980s, by cutting government spending, convincing the labor federation to cut wages, and convincing employers to freeze prices.

In the early 1990s the United States began to pressure Israel to make peace with its Arab neighbors and Palestinian population. Peres, as foreign minister under Prime Minister Yitzhak Rabin, held secret talks with Palestinian leader Yasir Arafat and the Palestinian Liberation Organization (PLO) to discuss possible self-government for Palestinians. The resulting "Declaration of Principles on Interim Self-Government" became known as the Oslo Peace Accords. In 1994 Peres, Yitzhak Rabin, and Yasir Arafat were jointly awarded the Nobel Prize for Peace. In 1995 Prime Minister Rabin was assassinated, and Peres became the prime minister until he lost the election, later that year, to Benjamin Netanyahu. A decade later, the Knesset would elect Shimon Peres to Israel's presidency, a largely honorific role, where he remained from 2007 to 2014.

Shimon Peres married the former Sonia Gelman in 1945. She predeceased him in 1999. Their four children, eight grandchildren, and three great-grandchildren survive.

See Current Biography 1995

Ivo Pitanguy

(Ivo Helcio Jardim de Campos Pitanguy)
Born: Belo Horizonte, Minas Gerais, Brazil; July 5, 1923
Died: Rio de Janeiro, Brazil; August 6, 2016
Occupation: Brazilian plastic surgeon

Ivo Pitanguy was arguably the most famous plastic surgeon in the world, known for his technical mastery in refurbishing the bodies of state and Hollywood royalty. He was the first plastic surgeon to be admitted to the Brazil's National Academy of Medicine, providing a sense of medical legitimacy to the field. He pioneered numerous plastic surgery techniques and trained a generation of plastic surgeons from all over the world.

Ivo Pitanguy was the son of a surgeon who encouraged his son to enter the medical field. Pitanguy lied about his age to gain admittance to the Universidad Federal de Minas Gerais. (He was sixteen at the time.) He finished medical school at the University of Brazil (now known as the Federal University of Rio de Janeiro). He practiced his medical training on soldiers returning from Europe during World War II. In the late 1940s Pitanguy traveled to the United States and Europe as a visiting surgeon at some of the world's most prestigious hospitals. In the early 1950s Pitanguy founded Brazil's first clinic that specialized in hand surgery at the Santa Casa de Misericordia General Hospital. He later founded the hospital's plastic surgery department. In 1960 Pitanguy opened a clinic for the poor. (He was known to devote one day each week to those who couldn't pay for his treatment.)

Pitanguy was very open about the techniques he developed and became something of a celebrity himself after working on such stars as Sophia Loren, Jacqueline Kennedy Onassis, and Jordan's King Hussein. Plastic surgery became something of a social movement in Brazil, a national obsession, in large measure to Dr. Pitanguy. Pitanguy authored several books, including a memoir and a groundbreaking textbook that continues to be influential in the field. The Ivo Pitanguy Study Center, part of the Ivo Pitanguy Clinic, trains plastic surgeons from around the world. Pitanguy claimed his greatest honor was when Pope John Paul II awarded him the Culture and Peace prize for his work with the Red Cross, helping deformed children.

Pitanguy was married to Marilu Nascimento and they had four children.

See Current Biography 2004

Imre Pozsgay

Born: Kóny, Győr-Moson-Sopron, Hungary; November 26, 1933
Died: Budapest, Hungary; March 25, 2016
Occupation: Hungarian politician

Though a high-ranking member of Hungary's Communist Party, Imre Pozsgay was an early proponent of democracy in Hungary. He served as the minister of culture in the late 1970s, the minister of education in the early 1980s, and the minister of state in the late 1980s. He was a member of Hungary's parliament from 1983 to 1994. He was well placed to become Hungary's first post-Communist president, except for his failed attempt to create a third, left-leaning party, an effort that angered those on either side of the political divide.

Imre Pozsgay was born into poverty. His mother was Catholic and worked to instill non-Communist principles in her children. Pozsgay studied at the Lenin Institution to prepare for a career in teaching. Like most young people at the time, he joined the Communist Party when he was seventeen, but the popular uprising of 1956, which was crushed by the Soviet Union, led him to question the legitimacy of Communist rule. He decided to work for change within the Communist structure. In the early 1970s, Pozsgay became the director of press affairs for the party, then the minister of culture. Later, education came under his purview, but he ran afoul of party hardliners. Under his administration the arts were freed of official censorship. In 1980 he was named to the Communist Party Central Committee. He was elevated to the Politburo and became the minister of state, becoming a radical voice in the ruling government, and earning the support of the Hungarian people. By the late 1980s, Pozsgay was the most popular politician in the country. In 1989 the Hungarian Socialist Workers Party was dissolved and a new congress of 1,256 delegates vowed to create a Western-style market economy. In 1989 Pozsgay visited US President George Bush at the White House, asking that trade restrictions with Hungary be lifted. He co-sponsored the "Pan-European Picnic," which allowed several hundred East Germans to defect across the Austrian/Hungarian border. He was a key figure in creating a "Europe without borders" and the fall of the Iron Curtain.

Information about survivors is not available.

See Current Biography 1990

Prince

(Prince Rogers Nelson)
Born: Minneapolis, Minnesota; June 7, 1958
Died: Chanhassen, Minnesota; April 21, 2016
Occupation: Singer, songwriter, instrumentalist

Prince was an unusually gifted musician, mastering more than a dozen musical instruments, including the saxophone. His guitar riffs were often compared to those of the legendary Jimi Hendrix. He earned seven Grammy Awards, an Academy Award, a Golden Globe, and was inducted into the Rock and Roll Hall of Fame in 2004.

Prince Rogers Nelson was named after his father's jazz group, the Prince Rogers Trio. His mother was a singer with the group. His father John Nelson worked at a local Honeywell electronics plant. After his parents divorced, Prince lived with his mother for a time, but she married a man who did not support Prince's musical ambitions, and the boy was informally "adopted" by a friend's mother, Bernadette Anderson, who encouraged him to continue playing as long as he maintained good grades in school. In 1976 Prince met Chris Moon who gave Prince free use of his small recording studio, and introduced him to Owen Husney who became the artist's first manager. For his first recording contract with Warner Brothers, Prince insisted on being able to produce his own album. *For You*, his first album came out in 1978. Astonished critics took notice when they learned that the youngest

himself had produced it, written all of the music, performed all of the vocals, and laid down all the instrumental tracks. In 1982 Prince's album *1999* went triple-platinum and included the song "Little Red Corvette," which became a classic rock song of the 1980s. In 1984 Prince released the movie and soundtrack, *Purple Rain*. Produced on a budget of about $7 million, the movie grossed $75 million, and the soulful song "When Doves Cry" occupied the number one spot simultaneously on the pop, dance, and soul charts. At the 1985 Academy Awards ceremonies *Purple Rain* won an Oscar for best original song score.

In 1992 Prince cut a $100 million deal with Warner Brothers, but the deal soured when Prince learned the contract deprived him of ownership of his new recordings. He changed his name to a "love symbol" and performed with the word "slave" written across his face. He became known as "the artist formerly known as Prince."

In 1996 Prince married one of his backup singers, Mayte Garcia, and the two had a son, Gregory. But the child died within a week of his birth due to a rare skull deformity. The couple divorced in 2000. In 2006 Prince was honored with a Webby Lifetime Achievement Award, as the first major artist to release an album solely on line. Prince was also married for five years to Manuela Testolini. Prince died on April 21, 2016 from an accidental overdose of the prescription opiate, Fentanyl. His sister, Tyka, survives.

See Current Biography 1986

Gregory Rabassa

Born: Yonkers, New York; March 9, 1922
Died: Branford, Connecticut; June 13, 2016
Occupation: Literary translator, educator

One of the most important translators of the twentieth century, Gregory Rabassa translated more than three-dozen books from Spanish and Portuguese into English, among them the works of the Nobel laureate Gabriel Garcia Marquez, who declared that Rabassa's translation actually improved on the original novel. His translation of Marquez's *One Hundred Years of Solitude* sparked a worldwide interest in Latin American literature.

Gregory Rabassa was the youngest of three sons born to his Cuban father, Miquel Rabassa and the American-born Clara (Macfarland) Rabassa. Though born in New York, Rabassa grew up in New Hampshire. He began "collecting languages" as a student at Dartmouth College in New Hampshire, where he learned German, Russian, and Portuguese. In 1942 Rabassa volunteered to serve in the US Army in North Africa and Italy, where he worked as a code-breaker and interrogator for the Office of Strategic Studies (OSS) (the precursor of the Central Intelligence Agency (CIA)). While there he translated Dante's *Divine Comedy*.

After the war Rabassa attended Columbia University in New York where he earned a master's degree in Spanish literature, and his PhD in Portuguese. After finishing school Rabassa became the editor for *Odyssey Review*, a literary magazine that featured new work from Europe and Latin America. An editor for Pantheon Publishing Company saw Rabassa's work and asked him to translate the experimental novel *Rayuela* (titled *Hopscotch* in English) by Argentine novelist, Julio Cortazar. The translation won the first National Book Award for Translation. Cortazar introduced Rabassa to Gabriel Garcia Marquez, the author of *One Hundred Years of Solitude*.

Though Rabassa was a highly successful translator, in order to earn a living he was a Distinguished Professor of Hispanic Languages and Literature at Queens College in New York City. He published his own book, *If This Be Treason: Translation and its Dyscontents*, in 2005. In addition to the National Book Award, he was awarded the translation prize from the writers' organization PEN (Public Education Network), the Bulbenkian Award, the Alexandar Gode Award from the American Translator's Association. In 2006 he was given the US National Medal of Arts.

Rabassa was married twice with both marriages ending in divorce. His two daughters and two grandaughters survive.

See Current Biography 2005

Simon Ramo

Born: Salt Lake City, Utah; May 7, 1913
Died: Santa Monica, California; June 27, 2016
Occupation: Engineer, scientist, author

An electrical engineer who was considered the "father" of the intercontinental ballistic missile (ICBM) at the height of the Cold War, Simon Ramo was the co-founder of the Ramo-Wooldridge Corporation, which eventually became the aerospace, electronics giant, TRW.

Born in Salt Lake City, Utah, Simon Ramo was an over-achiever from an early age, skipping several grades in school, and earning his PhD in electrical engineering and physics, from the University of Utah, by the time he was twenty-three. He had earned a full scholarship to the university based on his virtuosity with the violin. He also earned a three-year fellowship to study at the California Institute of Technology

(Caltech), a premiere electronics research institution, where he met his future business partner, Dean Wooldridge. His first job was working for General Electric (GE), helping to develop the electron microscope. By the time he left the company he had over twenty-five patents to his name. He avoided active duty in World War II because of his involvement in military research programs. Following the war, he moved to Hughes Aircraft in California. In 1953 Ramo left Hughes and teamed up with his former colleague, Dean Wooldridge when the Eisenhower administration asked the two scientists, who had formed the Ramo-Wooldridge Corporation, to develop the ICBM, a sophisticated weapons system designed to deliver nuclear warheads across the globe in a matter of minutes. In 1957 Ramo and Wooldridge were featured on the cover of *Time* magazine, which dubbed them the "face of a new age." By the time Northrop Grumman acquired TRW in 2002, TRW had over 100,000 employees.

Though he retired in 1978, Ramo continued to advise US presidents, cabinet members, and Congress on major weapons and aerospace systems. He penned dozens of books with titles that varied from *Tennis By Machiavelli* to *Meetings, Meetings, and More Meetings: Getting Things Done When People Are Involved*. In 2007 the Space Foundation awarded Ramo the General James E. Hill Lifetime Space Achievement Award. He was also honored with the Smithsonian Institution's National Trophy for Lifetime Achievement, and NASA's Distinguished Public Service Medal. In 1983 President Ronald Reagan awarded Ramo the Presidential Medal of Freedom.

Simon Ramo married Virginia May Smith in 1937 and they had two sons. Virginia predeceased Ramo in 2009. Their two sons, Jim and Alan, survive.

See Current Biography 1958

Nancy Reagan

Born: New York, New York; July 6, 1921
Died: Los Angeles, California; March 6, 2016
Occupation: Wife of President Ronald Reagan

As the wife of US President Ronald Reagan, Nancy Reagan was the First Lady from 1981 to 1989.

Nancy Reagan was born with the name Anne Frances Robbins, but was nicknamed Nancy in infancy. Her mother, Edith Robbins, was a mildly successful actress and her father was a car salesman who left while Nancy was still an infant. During her early childhood, Nancy's Aunt

Virginia raised her as her mother traveled with a theater group. On May 21, 1929, Edith married the prominent neurosurgeon Dr. Loyal Davis, who eventually adopted Nancy. Nancy Davis attended Girls' Latin School in Chicago, and then earned a bachelor's degree in theater from Smith College. She landed her first professional role as an actress in the mid-1940s with a touring company, and in 1956 she was cast in *Lute Song*, starring Mary Martin and Yul Brynner. A Metro Goldwyn Mayer (MGM) film scout saw her performance and offered her a screen test in Hollywood. She received roles alongside movie greats such as Barbara Stanwyck, Glenn Ford, and Janet Lei.

During the McCarthy era, her name appeared on a list of Communist sympathizers. She contacted the president of the Screen Actors Guild, Ronald Reagan, to help her resolve the mix-up. The two were married on March 4, 1952. They had two children. Many believe it was Nancy's far right political views (something she likely inherited from her father, Dr. Davis) that led Democrat Ronald Reagan to switch to the Republican Party. He rose quickly in the party and by 1966 he was elected Governor of California. Ten years later, after eight years as governor, Ronald Reagan ran for the presidency. He lost his first bid, but won the election in 1980.

The Washington press corps did not treat Mrs. Reagan well. She had established a reputation as something of a dilettante. As first lady of California she had refused to live in the old governor's mansion because she thought it felt like a funeral home and was a fire hazard. She was castigated when she wore a $25,000 gown to the inaugural ball, and raised $882,000 to redecorate the White House. What's more, when British Prime Minister Margaret Thatcher was about to visit, Nancy realized they didn't have a complete set of china large enough to accommodate their guests. She ordered four thousand pieces to the tune of $200,000. For Nancy, such sums were an investment in American heritage, while others regarded her actions as selfish, especially when social services were on the chopping block due to the economic recession.

She was fiercely protective of her husband, especially after he survived an attempted assassination. She oversaw his schedule and calendar to be sure he wasn't overtaxed. By all accounts, the president was a "big picture" thinker, while Nancy was concerned with the details. Some felt she had too much influence over the president's decisions. When the president fired his chief of staff, Don Regan, pundits claimed it was Nancy's call. Hardliners blamed Nancy when the president reached out to Mikhail Gorbachev to create an arms treaty.

In 1994 Ronald Reagan announced he was suffering from Alzheimer's disease, something his wife suspected much earlier. Against the ideology of many Republicans, Nancy became an advocate for stem cell research. She remained fiercely protective, keeping her husband's care and well-being her top priority. He died in 2004.

Nancy Reagan died from congestive heart failure on March 6, 2016. Survivors include her two children and a stepson.

See Current Biography 1982

Terry Redlin

Born: Watertown, South Dakota; July 11, 1937
Died: Watertown, South Dakota; April 24, 2016
Occupation: American artist

Terry Redlin's prints depicting wildlife and the outdoors made him one of the most popular artists in the United States. From 1990 to 1999, *US Art Magazine* named Redlin "the most popular artist" based on surveys from art galleries across the country.

Terry Redlin was born in 1937 in Watertown, South Dakota, where his childhood was filled with hunting, fishing, and drawing. When he was fifteen, Redlin lost his leg in a motorcycle accident, which also derailed his ambitions to be a forest ranger. After marrying his high school sweetheart, Helene Marie Langenfeld, the young couple moved to St. Paul, Minnesota, where Redlin attended the St. Paul School of Associated Arts. After his graduation, Redlin spent two decades working as a graphic artist, layout artist, art director, and illustrator.

In 1977 Redlin sold his first painting, "Winter Snows," to *The Farmer* magazine, which published it on the cover. Two years later, he quit his job as art director at the Webb Publishing Company to paint full-time. By the mid-1980s, limited-edition prints of his work, depicting wildlife, landscapes, and changing seasons had become popular with art collectors. In 1987 Redlin published a book discussing his work, *The Art of Terry Redlin: Opening Windows to the Wild.* In 1992 he produced his most acclaimed work, a series of prints for each stanza of "America the Beautiful."

Redlin was a three-time winner of the Minnesota Duck Stamp competition, and he won Minnesota Bass Stamp competition in 1982. He was a three-time winner of "lithograph of the year" by *U.S. Artist Magazine,* and was inducted into *U.S. Artist Magazine's* Hall of Fame in 1992. Over his lifetime, Redlin raised more than $28 million for wetland conservation. In 1997 he opened the Redlin Art Center in his hometown of Watertown, home to over one hundred and fifty original paintings, prints, and sketches.

In 2007 Redlin retired from painting due to the complications from Alzheimer's disease. His wife, three children, two grandchildren, and one great-grandchild survive him.

See Current Biography 2000

Alan Rickman

Born: London, England; February 21, 1946
Died: London, England; January 14, 2016
Occupation: Actor, director

Alan Rickman was an actor who will likely be most remembered for his portrayal of Severus Snape in the series of movies based on J. K. Rowling's series of Harry Potter novels. He was often cast as a villain, though he fought hard to avoid being typecast.

Alan Rickman was born and raised in London, England. His father died when he was just eight, leaving his mother to raise three sons and a daughter on her own. Rickman's original aspiration was to become an artist. In 1957 he received a scholarship to attend Latymer Upper School in West London, where he also began participating in acting with the school's Gild Drama Club. Unsure which of his passions he should pursue, he took a three-year course in art and design at the Chelsea College of Art, graduating in 1968. While working as a graphic designer he also participated in repertory theater. At age twenty-five, Rickman wrote to the Royal Academy of Dramatic Art (RADA), asking for an audition. He was accepted and eventually won numerous acting prizes, including the Forbes Robertson Prize, the Bancroft Gold Medal, and the Emile Litter Prize. His "big break" came in 1982 when he was cast in the role of Obadiah Slope, a nasty political character in the BBC production of *The Barchester Chronicles*. He continued to garner attention for his roles in theater and television, winning a Tony Award nomination for his role as Vicomte de Valmont in *Les Liaisons Dangereuses (Dangerous Liaisons)*. His foray into Hollywood began with his role as terrorist Hans Gruber in the 1988 action film *Die Hard*, starring Bruce Willis. Other roles he will be most remembered for include his Sheriff of Nottingham in *Robin Hood: Prince of Thieves*. Many critics believed he stole the show from lead actor Kevin Costner, winning Rickman a British Academy Award for best actor. He won the moniker "thinking woman's sex symbol" for his portrayal of deceased cellist who reappears to comfort his lover in the 1991 film *Truly, Madly, Deeply.*" His role as Rasputin in the HBO television movie about

the "holy man" at the court of Czar Nicholas II, earned him numerous best actor awards in 1997, including a Screen Actor's Guild Award, a Golden Satellite Award, and a Golden Globe Award.

Rickman met his lifetime partner, Rima Horton, while attending the Chelsea College of Art. The two had known each other for forty-seven years when they were married in a secret ceremony in 2012. They never had children. Alan Rickman died after a private battle with cancer. His survivors include his wife, Rima Horton, and three siblings.

See Current Biography 2001

Michel Rocard

Born: Courbevoie, France; August 23, 1930
Died: Paris, France; July 2, 2016
Occupation: Prime minister of France

Had it not been for political rival François Mitterrand, leader of the Socialist Party, the Socialist politician Michel Rocard may have risen to the office of president. As it stood, he served as the prime minister in Mitterrand's cabinet from 1988 to 1991. Rocard had been the minister of economic planning and development from 1981 to 1983, the minister of agriculture from 1983 to 1985, and was the mayor of Conflans-Sainte-Honorine from 1977 to 1994. He was a member of the European Parliament from 1994 to 2009 where he served on the Committee on Development and Cooperation from 1997 to 1999, and the Committee on Employment and Social Affairs from 1999 to 2002.

Michel Rocard was born the son of Yves Rocard, a physics professor who helped develop radar in Great Britain and the atomic bomb in France. At the age of nineteen, Michel Rocard joined the National Federation of Socialist Students while he was studying at the Institut d'Études Politiques de Paris. Jacques Chirac was one of his classmates. He continued his education at the École nationale d'administration (ENA). After graduation Rocard won a prestigious position as a senior economic official in the French Finance Ministry. In 1958, after the experience of Algeria's fight for independence, he quit the Socialist Party and helped found the Unified Socialist Party (PSU). He won his first term in the National Assembly in 1969. In 1974 he rejoined the Socialist party, bringing most of the PSU's supporters with him. Rocard was a popular politician, sometimes garnering more public support than did Mitterrand. In 1979 he outpolled Mitterrand forty percent to twenty-seven percent. However, Mitterrand was more powerful within the party and outmaneuvered

Rocard at every turn. By the early 1990s, Mitterrand's policies were more discredited. According to Julian Jackson of *The Guardian* (6 July 2016), "Rocard was a genuine political visionary and the French Socialist party would be in a better state today had he been listened to earlier."

Michel Rocard and his first wife, Genevieve Pujol, had two children. They divorced and in 1972, he married Michele Legendre, and they had two sons. That marriage also ended in divorce. Michel Rocard's third wife, Sylvie Pelissier, and his four children survive him.

See Current Biography 1988

Sonia Rykiel

Born: Neuilly-sur-Seine, France; May 25, 1930,
Died: Paris, France; August 25, 2016
Occupation: French fashion designer

Often considered one of the most sensuous and elegant women in the world, Sonia Rykiel redefined high fashion, from her innovative "inside-out" designs with seams exposed and hems unfinished, to the "fanny wrapper," a wide sash wound tightly around the hips, her creations brought fun to the catwalk.

Sonia Rykiel was of Russian and Romanian descent. Her father was a watchmaker. As Jews living in France during World War II, the family moved to various houses in the woods, keeping a low profile. Rykiel claimed to be an incredible tomboy as a child. She claimed the only clothes she liked were old clothes. Her first job was working in a Paris dry-goods store. While she was arranging colorful scarves for a window design, she realized an old man was watching. He turned out to be Henri Matisse who came in, bought most of the scarves, and paid personal compliments to Rykiel. With this incident, she realized her creativity could best be expressed by working with fabric.

Her first designs she made for herself when she was pregnant with her second child in 1962. At that time, she was working in her husband's boutique. She had married Sam Rykiel who owned the women's boutique called Laura. Her maternity designs unabashedly celebrated the pregnant figure. That same year she came out with small, tight "poor-boy" sweaters, which became a sensation. By 1968 she opened her own boutique in Glaeries Lafayette, a leading department store in Paris. She earned a reputation as the "Queen of knits," and developed her "unfinished look," featuring exposed seams and no hems, designed for freedom of movement and reversibility.

Rykiel was also a writer. Her first book, *Et Je La Voudrais Nue* (*I Would Like Her Naked*) was published in 1979. She also published several books about fashion, a series of children's stories, and was a regular contributor to fashion columns. In 1986 she received the fashion World's "Oscar" from Fashion Group International, and was made an Officer of l'Ordre des Arts et des Lettres in 1993. In 1996 she was made an Officer of l'Ordre National de la Legion d'Honneur.

In 1996 Rykiel learned that she had Parkinson's disease, which eventually claimed her life. Her two children, Nathalie and Jean-Philippe, survive her.

See Current Biography 1990

Morley Safer

Born: Toronto, Ontario, Canada; November 8, 1931
Died: New York, New York; May 19, 2016
Occupation: Broadcast journalist

Morley Safer was among the most recognized newscasters in American households. He was the longest-serving reporter on *60 Minutes*, CBS's perdurable news magazine. He came to prominence as a television reporter in Vietnam in the late 1960s where he almost singlehandedly ushered in the era of "the living-room war," to use Michael Arlen's phrase, with his graphic footage of the destruction of the hamlet of Cam Ne by US Marines in August of 1965.

Safer was born to Max and Anna (Cohn) Safer, Jewish-Austrian immigrants who owned a small upholstery shop. Safer graduated from the University of Western Ontario in 1953 and immediately began to write for the *Woodstock (Ontario) Sentinel Review* and the *London (Ontario) Free Press*. Having received a Commonwealth Press Union grant, Safer spent a year in London working for the *Oxford Mail & Times*. Returning to Canada, Safer became a Canadian Broadcasting Corporation (CBC) correspondent, covering guerrilla warfare in the Mideast, Cypress, and the Algerian revolution, occasionally appearing on the *CBC News* magazine, the oldest news program in Canada.

Safer's big break came when he worked as a correspondent in Vietnam. Rather than relying on press briefings, Safer and his cameraman/interpreter went "jungle bashing" with the US troops. He accompanied a group of Marines who had orders to "waste" the village of Cam Ne. Safer reported, "The Viet Cong were long gone. . . . The action wounded three women, killed one baby, wounded one marine, and netted four old men as prisoners." His shocking story first broke on the CBS's morning radio program, *World News Roundup*, and later that evening, was broadcast uncut on the *CBS Evening News*. According to David Halberstam, author of *The Powers That Be* (1979), Safer's film "not only helped legitimize pessimistic reporting. . . . it prepared the way for a different perception of the war among Americans at large. . . . Overnight one correspondent with one cameraman could become as important as ten or fifteen or twenty senators."

For his coverage of the war, Safer won three Overseas Press Club awards, a George Foster Peabody award, a George Polk Memorial award, and a Paul White Memorial award "for his courage in seeking and reporting the truth as he sees it." He also won twelve Emmys and four duPont-Columbia University Awards. Safer went on to write a book about his experiences, Flashbacks: On Returning to Vietnam (1990), which went on to become a best seller. Safer officially joined the 60 Minutes team in 1970. With his witty, stylish essays, he provided a perfect compliment to the hard-hitting exposé submitted by Mike Wallace.

Morley Safer married American anthropologist Jane Fearer and they had one daughter, Sarah. His wife, daughter, and three grandchildren survive him.

See Current Biography 1980

Antonin Scalia

Born: Trenton, New Jersey; March 11, 1936
Died: Shafter, Texas; February 13, 2016
Occupation: United States Supreme Court justice

The United States' Supreme Court Justice, Antonin Scalia, was an archconservative protector of executive powers and an advocate of judicial restraint. He espoused an "originalist" approach to interpreting the US Constitution, meaning it was his duty to interpret the intent of the original framers. He maintained a narrow interpretation of free speech protections, and opposed racially based affirmative action programs, and a constitutional right to an abortion. He wrote scathing rebukes against rulings with which he disagreed, launching acerbic, personal attacks on those who disagreed with him. He was the first Italian-American Supreme Court justice, and at the time of his death, he was the longest serving, having occupied his seat on the country's highest court for nearly thirty years.

Antonin Scalia was the only child of Sicilian immigrant, Eugene Scalia, and a second generation Italian American, Catherine Louise Panaro Scalia. His father was a professor of Romance languages at Brooklyn College and his mother taught elementary school. He was a brilliant student, graduating first in his class from the Catholic military academy, Xavier High School. He graduated, again first in his class, from Georgetown University with a degree in History, and attended Harvard Law School where he was the editor of the *Harvard Law Review*. He received his LL.B in 1960. After working several years as a lawyer, Scalia accepted a teaching position as the University of Virginia Law School where he developed expertise in administrative law. At the height of the Watergate controversy, President Richard Nixon promoted him to the post of assistant attorney general in charge of the Justice Department's Office of Legal Counsel, where he unsuccessfully argued that Richard Nixon, not the federal government, owned the Watergate tapes and documents. Following Democrat Jimmy Carter's election, Scalia taught at Georgetown Law Center, and was a scholar in residence at the conservative think tank, the American Enterprise Institute. In 1977 he became a law professor at the University of Chicago Law School.

In 1977 President Ronald Reagan nominated Scalia to the Supreme Court, along with William Rehnquist. Scalia's most controversial decisions and dissents have included his support for the death penalty and the scaling back of Miranda rights. In the 2000 presidential election, Scalia supported a stop on hand counting votes cast in Florida after the race proved too close to call. He claimed the count undermined the legitimacy of George Bush's presidency; those on the side of Al Gore felt the ruling was an obstruction to finding out which candidate actually had the most votes.

Antonin Scalia's death was unexpected. He was found dead at the Cibolo Creek Ranch, a Texas hunting lodge. The exact cause of death was not determined because the family declined an autopsy. He leaves behind his wife, nine children, and numerous grandchildren.

See Current Biography 1996

Sydney Schanberg

Born: Clinton, Massachusetts; January 17, 1934
Died: Poughkeepsie, New York; July 9, 2016
Occupation: Journalist

Sydney Schanberg is most remembered as the journalist whose experiences in the Cambodian capital of Phnom Penh, as it was being overrun by the Khmer Rouge, and those of his fellow journalist and interpreter, Dith Pran, inspired the 1984 award-winning movie, *The Killing Fields*. In 1976 Schanberg was awarded a Pulitzer Prize for international reporting.

Schanberg attended Harvard University on several scholarships, working his way through college at odd jobs. He graduated in 1955 with a BA degree. He was drafted in 1956 and spent his two years of service as a writer on the newspaper of the Third Armored Division in Frankfurt, Germany. After his discharge, he held a Nieman Fellowship at Harvard for one year before joining the *New York Times* as a copyboy in 1959. He was promoted quickly, and by 1967 he was the bureau chief for the state capital in Albany, New York. His first foreign assignment was from 1969 to 1972 as the bureau chief in New Delhi, India.

As the *New York Times* Southeast Asian correspondent based in Singapore from 1973 to 1975, Schanberg frequently reported on Cambodia's civil war. In 1972 he met fellow journalist and translator, Dith Pran, who acted as a guide. Cambodia was being ravaged by secret American bombing of North Vietnamese sanctuaries in Cambodian territory. In April of 1975 the two journalists, at great risk to their lives, refused to evacuate when the US embassy personnel left the country. Schanberg was eventually evacuated to Thailand, but Pran could not leave. The separation haunted Schanberg for years, until 1979 when he finally received word that Pran had survived. Pran would eventually join his family in the United States, and train as a photographer for the *New York Times*. Schanberg became an editor at the paper. Schanberg recounted the Cambodian ordeal in a lengthy article in the *New York Times Magazine* (20 January 1980). The article was released as the book *The Death and Life of Dith Pran* in 1980, which inspired the Award-winning film, *The Killing Fields*.

On May 3, 1976, Schanberg was awarded the Pulitzer Prize for international reporting "at great risk." He received the Elijah Parish Lovejoy Award in 1992, and was awarded an honorary doctorate from Colby College.

Schanberg was married to Janice Freiman. They had two daughters who survive him.

See Current Biography 1990

Walter Scheel

Born: Solingen, Germany; July 8, 1919
Died: Bad Krozingen, Germany; August 24, 2016
Occupation: German foreign minister, president

Under West Germany's Chancellor Willy Brandt, Walter Scheel served as Germany's foreign minister from 1969 to 1974, and as the country's president, a largely ceremonial role, from 1974 to 1979.

Walter Scheel was born in Solingen. His father was a wheelwright and a carriage builder.

In 1939 Scheel was drafted into the German Luftwaffe where he served as a pilot. He earned two Iron Crosses and was discharged in 1945 with the rank of first lieutenant. Motivated by concern for rebuilding the nation's economy, he entered politics in 1948 when he was elected to the city council of Solingen, and two years later, he won election to the Landtag (state legislature) of North Rhine-Westphalia, at Dusseldorf, where he devoted much of his effort to economic reconstruction and regional planning. He was elected to the Bundestag, the lower house of the federal legislature, in 1953. From 1961 to 1966, Scheel was the minister of economic cooperation, working to normalize relations with the Soviet Union and Poland. He also worked to strengthen ties with North Atlantic Treaty Organizations (NATO) countries of Europe and with the United States. At the time of his retirement in 1979, Scheel enjoyed a seventy-percent approval rating .

In 1970 Scheel became the first West German official to visit Auschwitz since the end of the war, and he was heard to utter, "Words escape me." And though he wielded little power as president, according the *Washington Post* (24 August 2016), Scheel "became the voice of moral authority, urging Germans to take responsibility" for the Nazi horrors.

Strangely, Scheel who was also a gifted singer, recorded an old folk song, "High Up on the Yellow Wagon," which shot to the top of the European pop charts in 1970. Scheel was married three times. His first wife, the former Eva Kronenberg, died in 1966, and they had one son. He married his second wife, Dr. Mildred Wirtz, a radiologist, in 1969. The widow brought one daughter to their marriage, and she later gave birth to the couple's daughter. She died in 1985 and Scheel married his third wife, Barbara Wiese who survives him.

See Current Biography 1971

Phyllis Schlafly

Born: St. Louis, Missouri; August 15, 1924
Died: St. Louis, Missouri; September 5, 2016
Occupation: Politician, conservative activist, author

Phyllis Schlafly was a leading foe of the Equal Rights Amendment (ERA), considering it "anti-family and "anti-American." She founded the "Stop ERA," organization, which became the conservative Eagle Forum. She was ardently antifeminist and anticommunist, helping Senator Joseph McCarthy in his mission to weed out communist sympathizers. She also founded the Cardinal Mindszenty Foundation.

Phyllis Schlafly was the eldest daughter of John Bruce and Odile (Dodge) Stewart. She attended the Academy of the Sacred Heart, a Roman Catholic school in St. Louis, where she graduated as the class valedictorian in 1941. She attended Maryville College of the Sacred Heart and, two years later, she transferred to Washington University in St. Louis. She helped fund her education by working the night shift at a federal small arms factory, firing rifles and machine guns to test ammunition. Schlafly graduated Phi Beta Kappa and was awarded a substantial grant for graduate work at Radcliffe where she earned her MA in political science. She would later earn a law degree from Washington University in 1978. In 1949 she married John Fred Schlafly, a lawyer from a wealthy family, who shared her conservative political ideology. Schlafly devoted much of her time to volunteer work, and was the director of the local chapter of the National Conference of Christians and Jews, and frequently appeared as a commentator on a weekly radio broadcast.

In 1952 Schlafly made her first unsuccessful bid for political office, and she was a delegate for the Republican National Convention (RNC) in 1956. She was an enthusiastic supporter of the conservative Arizona Senator Barry Goldwater's Presidential aspirations. In 1964 she published her first book, *A Choice Not an Echo*, which became a best seller. That same year she was the first vice-president of the National Federation of Republican Women (NFRW). It was in the February 1972 issue of the *Phyllis Schlafly Report* that Schlafly first attacked the ERA, which had nearly been ratified by then, as a threat to family life and American women.

Phyllis Schlafly wrote or edited twenty books, and published the monthly newsletter, *Phyllis Schlafly Report*. The *Ladies Home Journal* named her one of the most important women of the twentieth century.

Schlafly's husband died in 1993. Her survivors include six children, sixteen grandchildren, and three great-grandchildren.

See Current Biography 1978

Helmut Schmidt

Born: Hamburg, Germany; December 23, 1918
Died: Hamburg, Germany; November 10, 2015
Occupation: Former Chancellor of the Federal Republic of Germany

Helmut Schmidt was the fifth Chancellor of West Germany from 1974 to 1982. Though he spent eight years in the Wehrmacht, and was conscripted into the Nazi Labour Front, fighting in both the east and west battlefronts, his father was actually half Jewish, a closely guarded secret within his family. He was a prisoner of war, held by the British in Belgium for a brief period.

Upon his return to Hamburg after the war, he enrolled at the University of Hamburg, studying political science and economics, and joined the Social Democratic Party (SPD). He gained a reputation as a skilled debater and rhetorician, and in 1956, he was elected parliamentary executive for the party. He later served as Hamburg's minister of transport, and still later, minister of the interior. He proved his mettle during the 1962 floods that killed over three hundred people, organizing rescue and cleanup operations. In 1968, Schmidt became the deputy chairman of the SPD, and a year later, was appointed minister of defense by then chancellor, Willy Brandt. Schmidt incurred the ire of a number of military brass when he instituted sweeping reform of the Bundeswehr (defense force). By 1974, Schmidt was filling the positions of both minister of finance and minister of economics, when Chancellor Brandt was implicated in a spy scandal, leaving the reluctant Schmidt the obvious successor when Brandt resigned.

As a chancellor, Schmidt was a pioneer of the European Union (EU) when, in reaction to the frailty of the US dollar, he agreed with six of the nine European Economic Community (EEC) to link their currencies in a common float against the dollar. Schmidt had a close friendship with the French president, Valery Giscard d'Estaing, and the two helped create the European currency unit (Ecu), a precursor to the Euro. Schmidt was heavily criticized for his "twin-track" strategy of allowing the United States to install medium-range nuclear missiles in West Germany, while also negotiating arms reductions with Leonid Brezhnev of the Soviet Union. Two major terror events tested his leadership. In the fall of 1977, Palestinian terrorists hijacked a Lufthansa flight as it left Mallorca Spain, and demanded the release of Red Army Faction (RFA) German prisoners. As the flight landed in Mogadishu, Somalia, Schmidt ordered a German police unit to storm the plane. With the exception of the murdered pilot, passengers and crew were rescued unharmed. The RAF prisoners staged a mass suicide in their cells. In another related terror event, RAF terrorists kidnapped the businessman, Hanns Martin Schleyer. Under intense pressure from Schleyer's family, friends and colleagues, Schmidt refused to negotiate and Schleyer was eventually murdered.

After his political career ended, Schmidt became a writer and publisher, and as an accomplished pianist, he released recordings of Mozart and Bach. He was married to Hannelore ("Loki") nee Glaser for sixty-eight years. Loki died in

2010. They had one son who died in infancy, and one daughter, Susanne, who survives following her father's death on November 10, 2015.

See Current Biography 1974

Charles Schultze

Born: Alexandria, Virginia; December 12, 1924
Died: Washington, DC; September 27, 2016
Occupation: Economist

Charles Schultze was a leading expert and advisor to the federal government, including Presidents Kennedy, Johnson, and Carter. He was a senior fellow at the Brookings Institution, a Washington think tank, for over four decades.

Charles Schultze was born across the Potomac from Washington in Alexandria, Virginia. His college education was interrupted by World War II, where he served in the Army for three years, earning a Purple Heart and a Bronze Star. After the war, he graduated with a bachelor's degree, and later, a master's degree in economics from Georgetown University. He was awarded a PhD in economics from the University of Maryland in 1960. Schultze worked for the Democratic National Committee (DNC) and the government in a series of offices, including the Korean War-era Office of Price Stabilization, followed by a six-year stint as a staff economist with the Council of Economic Advisors. He was the assistant director of the Bureau of the Budget under President Kennedy, advancing to director under President Johnson, and was the chairman of the Council of Economic Advisors under President Carter. Between his stints on Capitol Hill, Schultze taught economics at the University of Maryland and at the Brookings Institution. During the Carter years, Schultze assembled a stimulus plan to fight rising inflation, but was blocked on political grounds. He was a frequent contributor to the American Economic Review, The Brookings Review, and Brookings Papers on Economic Activity.

Schultze married Rita Hertzog in 1947. The couple had six children. Rita Schultze predeceased her husband in 2014. Their six children, sixteen grandchildren, and five great-grandchildren survive.

See Current Biography 1970

Carolyn See

Born: Pasadena, California; January 13, 1934
Died: Santa Monica, California; July 13, 2016
Occupation: Novelist, literary critic, professor

Carolyn See authored seven novels, four works of non-fiction, and several additional novels under the pseudonym Monica Highland, a name she shared with her novelist daughter, Lisa See, and long-time companion, John Espey. She was a long-time book critic working primarily for the *Washington Post*, but she also contributed to the *Los Angeles Times*, and the *New York Times*. She taught at the University of California at Los Angeles (UCLA) and at Loyola University.

Born Carolyn Penelope Laws, Carolyn See did not have a happy childhood, and her memoirs are full of accounts of a chronically dysfunctional family, prone to alcoholism and drug addiction. Her father left when she was eleven, and her mother kicked her out when she was sixteen. But in See's words, "There's something to be said for free fall, the wild life. . . . It's given us our stories; and made us who we are." She attended Los Angeles City College and completed her undergraduate degree at California State University at Los Angeles (UCLA), where she won the Samuel Goldwyn Creative Writing Contest in 1958. See earned her graduate degree from UCLA in 1963.

See's work was often autobiographical. Her first novel, *The Rest Is Done with Mirrors*, was about graduate students at UCLA. Her novel *Mothers, Daughters*, involves the reasons for divorce. See was twice divorced. In addition to writing books, See worked at the *Washington Post* as a book critic for twenty-seven years, and sat on a number of review boards, including those of the National Book Critics Circle and PENWest International. She herself received a Guggenheim Fellowship and a Getty Center fellowship.

See was twice married and divorced, and had two daughters. Her eldest daughter, Lisa See, is also a successful novelist. She was a long-time companion of writer John Espey beginning in 1974 until his death in 2000. Carolyn See's survivors include her two daughters, a brother, three grandsons, and a great-grandson.

See Current Biography 1997

Richard Selzer

Born: Troy, New York; June 24, 1928
Died: North Branford, Connecticut; June 15, 2016
Occupation: Writer, surgeon

Richard Selzer managed to create two very successful careers in one lifetime. He was a surgeon and he was an accomplished writer, penning over a dozen books and two plays. A new collection, *Blood and Ink: A Richard Selzer Reader* is slated for release by the University of Delaware Press.

Richard Selzer was born, the younger of two sons, to Julius and Gertrude Selzer who instilled in their son a passion for literature, learning, and medicine. His father was a physician whose office was located in what would have been the front parlor. Richard, nicknamed "Dickie," accompanied his father on house calls, and on rounds at the local hospital. He had a voracious appetite for reading, finding special inspiration in Aesop's fables and Greek myths. Julius Selzer died unexpectedly from a heart attack when his son was twelve years old. Immediately after his father's death, Selzer committed himself to follow in his father's footsteps, writing "I gave myself to medicine the way a monk gives himself to God."

Selzer graduated from Union College, in New York in 1948, and received his MD from Albany Medical College. That same year, Selzer entered the Yale University School of Medicine to begin his internship and residency. However, his residency was interrupted when he was recruited for military service in Korea, commissioned to an army medical company. He contracted malaria and dysentery while there and was sent to Japan, where he remained for more than a year, to regain his strength. He returned to Yale and in 1961 and accepted a position as an instructor in surgery—a position he maintained for two decades. He established a practice with Dr. Bernie S. Siegel (author of *Love, Medicine, and Miracles*), which would eventually become a group practice.

However, Selzer couldn't overcome a sense of restlessness that could only be relieved by writing. His first short story was published in 1971. Thus began Selzer's second career. He continued writing short stories, which continued to be published by various popular magazines. He often focused on the human body, and drew from his experiences as a surgeon. His literary "breakthrough" came with the publication of his second book, *Mortal Lessons: Notes on the Art of Surgery*. Soon after, Selzer won a National Magazine Award for his collection of *Esquire* essays. He then produced three collections. In 1986 he decided to leave his medical career in order to write full time. Soon thereafter he published two collections of short stories, and a personal account of his near-death from Legionnaires' disease in 1991.

Richard Selzer won the Pushcart Prize for fiction, the American Medical Writer's Award, and a Guggenheim Fellowship. He leaves behind his wife of sixty-one years, Janet White Selzer, three children, and seven grandchildren.

See Current Biography 1993

Peter Shaffer

Born: Liverpool, England; May 15, 1926
Died: County Cork, England; June 6, 2016
Occupation: British playwright

Peter Shaffer was a highly acclaimed playwright whose biggest hits—*Equus* and *Amadeus*—were adapted for motion pictures.

Peter Shaffer and his twin brother, Anthony, were born into a family of orthodox Jews. (A younger brother was born later.) His father, Jack, made his living in real estate. After graduation from St. Paul's, a prestigious public school in London, Peter and Anthony were conscripted as coal miners for three years, working in the mines of Yorkshire and Kent until 1947. Peter Shaffer went on to attend Trinity College, Cambridge, where he had won a scholarship to read history. After a brief relocation to New York, and upon returning to London, Peter and Anthony wrote several mystery novels together under the pseudonym Peter Anthony.

Shaffer's first play, *Five Finger Exercise*, opened in 1958 at the Comedy Theatre in London, under the direction of John Gielgud, earning Shaffer a reputation as a playwright. It opened in New York at the Music Box Theatre in 1959. Shaffer's *The Royal Hunt of the Sun* premiered at the National Theatre at the 1964 Chichester Festival, and premiered in New York in 1965 to universal acclaim. Shaffer would establish a common theme for much of his work, which was humanity's search for fulfillment through God. *Equus*, considered one of Shaffer's best plays, opened at the Old Vic Theatre in London in 1973, and went on to Broadway at the Plymouth Theatre in 1974, winning a Tony Award for best play. He wrote the play *Lettice and Lovage* specifically as a vehicle for the star Maggie Smith, who also won a Tony Award in 1990. Shaffer's play *Amadeus* opened at the National Theatre in London in 1979, and then went on to Broadway where it ran for three years, winning another Tony Award for best play. In 1984 Shaffer wrote the screenplay for a movie version, directed by Milos Forman. The movie, *Amadeus*, won eight Oscar Awards, including one for

Shaffer for best adapted screenplay, and another for best picture. Shaffer's screen adaptation of *Equus* was also nominated for an Oscar in 1978.

Shaffer was made a Commander of the British Order (CBE) in 1978, and was knighted in 2001. His survivors include a brother, Brian, and several nieces and nephews.

See Current Biography 1988

Garry Shandling

Born: Chicago, Illinois; November 29, 1949
Died: Los Angeles, California; March 24, 2016
Occupation: Comedian, writer, actor

Garry Shandling created and starred in several popular television shows in the 1990s, at the dawn of the cable era, including *The Larry Sanders Show*, and *It's Garry Shandling's Show*. He received two Golden Globe nominations, eighteen Emmy nominations, and won the Primetime Emmy Award for Outstanding Writing for a Comedy Series. He was a popular television emcee, hosting the Grammy Awards in 1990, 1993, and 1994, and the Emmy Awards in 2000 and 2004. He was a regular substitute host for Johnny Carson on *The Tonight Show*.

Garry Shandling was raised in Tucson, Arizona, where the family moved for the benefit of Shandling's older brother who suffered from cystic fibrosis. His brother's death ten years later had a major impact on Shandling. He studied electrical engineering at the University of Arizona, but soon realized he couldn't tolerate sitting in a lab all day. He graduated with a degree in marketing and did postgraduate work in creative writing. He approached comedian George Carlin with some of his comedy writing, and was encouraged to continue. Shandling moved to Hollywood to pursue a career in comedy. He found work writing for situation comedies like *Sanford and Son*, *Welcome Back Kotter*, and *Three's Company*. After a near-fatal accident, Shandling pursued his real dream and became a standup comedian. A talent scout for the *Tonight Show* saw Shandling and he became a regular on the show. He would later collaborate with Alan Zweibel, former head writer for the original *Saturday Night Live* program, to create *It's Garry Shandling's Show*, which was picked up by the ShowTime network and lauded as one of the most original television series at that time. Later, Shandling's very successful show, *Larry Sanders*, a mock talk show, broke ground by eliminating the laugh track, using real-life guest stars who are interviewed by the fictional Larry Sanders. Shandling's methods paved the way for highly rated shows like *The Office*, *30 Rock*, and *Modern Family*.

In the early 1990s Shandling was offered several lucrative hosting positions on popular late-night programs, which he turned down. In addition to a number of serious movie roles, Shandling was a voice actor on a number of animated movies.

Shandling never married and had no children. Information about survivors is unavailable.

See Current Biography 1989

Aaron Shikler

Born: New York, New York; November 12, 1922
Died: New York, New York; November 12, 2015
Occupation: Artist

Before painting his iconic portraits of President John F. Kennedy and the former first lady, Jacqueline Kennedy Onassis, Aaron Shikler had painted portraits for a number of celebrities, including Lauren Bacall's children and Paul Newman's children. It is surmised that he first came to Jacqueline Onassis's attention after he completed portraits of her nieces and nephew, the children of Peter Lawford and Patricia (Kennedy) Lawford. He portrayed the former president Kennedy as a man lost in thought, looking down, arms crossed at his chest. Though he never met President Kennedy, Shikler used photographs to capture Kennedy's essence. He told Sarah Booth Controy of the *Washington Post* (5 February 1971) that he "wanted to show him as a president who was a thinker. . . . to show a courage that made him humble." In 1980 *Time* magazine commissioned Shikler to paint a portrait of president-elect Ronald Reagan for its cover of the "Man of the Year" issue.

Aaron Shikler was born in Brooklyn, New York, to a middle-class Jewish family. He had four older sisters. He graduated from the High school of Music and Art in Manhattan in June of 1940. He continued his education at Temple University and at the Barnes Foundation, though his education was interrupted in 1943 when Shikler was drafted into the Army Air Corps as a mapmaker. He married a fellow art student, Barbara Lurie with whom he had two children.

Early in his career, Shikler made a living painting clowns and ballerinas for a wholesale distributor, but he signed his work "Phil I. Steen" in protest. An Army friend, Leroy Davis, opened an art gallery in 1953, and began showing Shikler's work, which critics note for his control of "quite magical lighting." When other critics complained about a "gloomy" quality to his work, he responded, "It certainly stands out among all those God-forsaken postage-stamp portraits hanging in the White House" (William Grimes for the *New York Times*, November 16, 2015). Aaron Shikler has received numerous awards throughout his long career.

Aaron Shikler died from kidney failure on his ninety-third birthday, November 12, 2015. His two children and five grandchildren survive him.

See Current Biography 1971

Malick Sidibé

Born: Soloba, French Sudan; 1936
Died: Bamako, Mali; April 14, 2016
Occupation: Malian photographer

Malick Sidibé was an African photographer of international renown whose work has been showcased in the finest art galleries and museums from Berlin to New York, Chicago to Milan. His work has been lauded both as historical fact and high art, and praised for exposing the depth of his subjects, repudiating the stereotype of the "simple" African. He is said to have captured the joyous spirit of an era.

The date of Malick Sidibé's birth is uncertain, but he knew it was in 1935 or 1936. He was born into the Fulani ethnic group in a small village in Mali (then called French Sudan). When he was ten, Sidibé began attending school in Bougouni where his artistic talents were noticed, and he was encouraged to attend the Ecole des Artisans Soudanais (School for Sudanese Craftsmen, now called the National Institute for Art), in the Malian capital of Bamako. In 1955 he received a degree in jewelry making. While still attending college, he met a successful French photographer living in Bamako, Gerard Guillat, who visited the college's campus to find an artist to paint a mural in his studio, the "Photo Service Boutique." Guillat first hired Sidibé to only paint the mural, but then took him on as his apprentice. Sidibé bought his first camera, a "Brownie," in 1956, taking pictures of Guillat's patrons on a commission basis. In 1962 he took a position as an official government photographer. He also hired himself out to take pictures of private events, and began attending Bamako's burgeoning party scene where, with permission from partygoers, he documented all-night dances that, after dawn, would continue on the beaches of the Niger River. He also took pictures of city streets, soccer matches, and boxing bouts, and became popular enough that his studio became a popular hangout.

In 1991 Sidibé was "discovered" by Andre Magnin, an art curator and historian as he toured West Africa with fellow French photographer, Jean Pigozzi. Magnin began promoting Sidibé's work. In 1996 Sidibé was one of the 30 African-born photographers whose work was displayed at the Solomon R. Guggenheim Museum in New York, in an exhibit entitled "In/sight: African Photographers, 1940 to the Present." In 1997 and 1998 his work was shown in galleries in San Francisco, Stuttgart, Barcelona, and Munich. Also in 1998, a collection of Sidibé's work compiled by Andre Magnin, titled *Malick Sidibé*, was published. In recent years he has taken fashion photos for *Vogue*, *Elle*, *Cosmopolitan*, and the *New York Times Magazine*. In March 2003 Sidibé was awarded the prestigious Hasselblad Foundation International Award for Photography, which carries a purse of nearly $58,000 and a gold medal. Other awards include the Golden Lion Award for Lifetime Achievement by the Venice Biennale Foundation (the first artist to be so honored), the Infinity Award for Lifetime Achievement from the International Center of Photography, and the New York World Press Photo World Press award.

See Current Biography 2004

Elwyn Simons

Born: Lawrence, Kansas; July 14, 1930
Died: Peoria, Arizona; March 6, 2016
Occupation: Paleontologist, primatologist, biological anthropologist, educator, conservationist

Considered the father of contemporary primatology, Elwyn Simons is credited with providing key insight into the science of human origins. Dr. Simons led more than ninety scientific expeditions around the globe, from Egypt to India, and Madagascar to Wyoming. His experiences across the globe made him an avowed wildlife conservationist.

Elwyn Simons was born in Lawrence, Kansas, but he was raised in Houston, Texas, where his father taught economics at Rice University. Simons was born with a natural curiosity about history, biology, and anthropology. He was also a talented artist, a trait he inherited from his mother, Verna Irene (Cuddleback) Simons, who trained at the Art Institute of Chicago. At the age of nine, Simons won a scholarship to attend classes at the Houston Museum of Fine Arts. In high school, Simons held the position of junior curator at the Houston Natural History Museum. He received a BS degree from Rice University, and attended Princeton University where he earned doctorates in both biology and geology. He won a Fulbright fellowship to attend Utrecht University in the Netherlands, but instead attended Oxford University on a General George C. Marshall scholarship, studying primate history under Sir Wilfred Edward Le Gros Clark and

Joseph Weiner who exposed "Piltdown Man" as a hoax. As a Boise Fund fellow Simons earned a PhD from Oxford in anthropology, archeology, and anatomy in 1959.

Simons' early career had him teaching at Princeton University and the University of Pennsylvania. He joined the faculty at Yale University when he became the curator of the Division of Vertebrate Paleontology at Yale's Peabody Museum of Natural History, and was a professor of paleontology in Yale's department of Geology and Geophysics. He began leading expeditions, teaching collecting techniques, in the hunt for primate fossils. Margalit Fox, writing for the *New York Times* (16 March 2016) explains Simons' "most seminal find, made in the Fayum [region of Egypt] in the mid-1960s, was the skull of a cat-size, tree-dwelling primate he called Aegyptopithecus. The creature—about 33 million years old—was. . . . the earliest known common forebear of apes, monkeys, and man," a fossil find that predates the split between hominids (our human forebears) and cercopithecoids, or Old World monkeys. Another important find, was Simons' discovery of an ancient whale's hind feet and legs thus proving that 50 million years ago, whales still had vestigial lower limbs.

Simons later became the director of the Duke University Primate Center, and reintroduced lemurs (a variety of primate) to Madagascar. He helped establish a conservation center there and was knighted by the National Order of the Republic of Madagascar.

Elwyn Simons was married twice. He had an adopted daughter and a son from his first marriage, and two daughters from his second marriage to Fridrun Annursel Ankel, another primate scientist. Simon's eldest daughter died in 2009. He is survived by his wife, his remaining children, and five grandchildren.

See Current Biography 1994

Robert Stigwood

Born: Adelaide, South Australia; April 16, 1934
Died: London, England; January 4, 2016
Occupation: Entertainment mogul, record producer, talent manager

Robert Stigwood's innovation in merging rock music with other performing arts made superstars of artists like John Travolta, the Bee Gees, and Eric Clapton; he brought the rock musicals *Hair, Tommy,* and *Jesus Christ Superstar* to the stage; and he produced the 1970s blockbusters *Saturday Night Fever* and *Grease.* Robert Stigwood established a profitable crossover pattern in which a record album pre-sold a theater production or a motion picture and vice versa. He was also instrumental in bringing television's hit series *All in the Family* and *Stanford and Son* into America's living rooms.

Born and raised in South Australia, it wasn't until he settled himself "in a cupboard in Charing Cross Road," that Robert Stigwood realized the tremendous potential in commercial television that others seemed to overlook. In the course of a few short years, Stigwood was handling half the casting for English commercials. His big break occurred when he hit upon the idea of casting the musician John Leyton—a young rocker whose talent EMI, Decca, and Pye records had overlooked—as a pop singer on the popular television series *Harper West One.* In one episode, Leyton sang his single "Johnny Remember Me" on the show. Afterwards, EMI agreed to distribute the song, which shot up to the top of the charts, selling a million copies. In this way, Stigwood became Britain's first independent record producer.

In 1967 he bought the British rights to Hair, which filled London theaters for six years. He sought the television producer, Norman Lear, to create an Americanized version of Britain's popular Till Death Do Us Part and Steptoe and Son. Their partnership resulted in the popular shows All in the Family and Stanford and Son. In 1970 Stigwood joined Tim Rice and Andrew Lloyd Weber to create the first Broadway musical based on a music recording. That highly successful show was Jesus Christ Superstar, which was nominated for five Tony Awards. After it closed, Stigwood created a traveling theater group to perform the play worldwide, and he made a film version. Other successful combined musical/theater hits include Tommy (originally a recorded concert by The Who), Joseph and the Amazing Technicolor Dreamcoat, and Evita. Capitalizing on disco fever, Stigwood contracted with the Bee Gees to record the music for his movie Saturday Night Fever, followed up a year later with Grease. In 1979, at the suggestion of the Bee Gees, Stigwood masterminded a televised rock spectacular as a benefit for the United Nations International Children's Emergency Fund (UNICEF), which included the music of the Bee Gees, John Denver, and Rod Stewart.

Robert Stigwood died in London on January 4, 2016. Information on survivors is not available.

See Current Biography 1979

Maurice Strong

Born: Oak Lake, Manitoba, Canada; April 29, 1929
Died: Ottawa, Canada; November 28, 2015
Occupation: Environmentalist, UN official

Maurice Strong was the first to sound the clarion call for global unity in fighting global climate change, and the poverty that he sometimes considered its greatest contributor. He was the founding director of the United Nations' (UN) environment program, and organized its first environmental conference in Stockholm, Sweden in 1972.

Maurice Strong was born into poverty in the prairie town of Oak Lake, Manitoba, Canada. His early experience with "the destructiveness of poverty" had a profound effect on his choice of his life's work. He considered over-population, and its attendant poverty, to be the greatest contributing factor to environmental destruction. He felt there is an inherent interdependence for the Earth's population, which is at the heart of caring for the environment.

Early in his career, after achieving some success as a financial adviser and assistant to the president of Dome Explorations, Strong gave into his wanderlust, and spent his accumulated earnings on a two-year world tour, spending a full year in East Africa, where he was impressed with the work of the YMCA and Christian churches. He became a fund-raiser for the YMCA International and then served as president of the Canadian YMCA. At the same time, he helped found the Overseas Institute of Canada.

Ironically, Strong gained much of his business acumen, and his wealth, in natural resource development as the vice-president and treasurer of Dome Petroleum Ltd., and eventually, as the president of the Power Corporation of Canada. In 1966 he became the director general of the Canadian government's External Aid Office, which Strong renamed the Canadian International Development Agency (CIDA), shifting its focus to long-range projects aimed at making recipient nations more self-sufficient. In 1971 Strong joined the United Nations as undersecretary general, responsible for environmental affairs, under the guidance of Secretary General U Thant. Rather than embarking on a paternalistic dispensing of goods, Strong embarked on an educational mission teaching poorer nations how to handle problems associated with squandered mineral resources, soil erosion, man-made diseases, and water shortages. He helped establish Earthwatch as an international pollution-monitoring network, and urged affluent nations to lessen the gap between "haves" and "have-nots." He was considered a pioneer in the concept of sustainable development. In 2005 Strong

stepped down from his UN post amid allegations he was involved in corrupt practices in his role with the UN Oil-for-Food program.

Strong married Pauline Olivette Williams in 1950, and the couple had four children. Maurice Strong died on November 28, 2015, in Ottawa, just days before the World Climate Summit in Paris, France. His wife and five children survive.

See Current Biography 1973

Pat Summitt

Born: Clarksville, Tennessee; June 14, 1952
Died: Knoxville, Tennessee; June 28, 2016
Occupation: College basketball coach

Pat Summitt was the winningest college basketball coach in Division I history. She was named the NCAA coach of the year seven times, and led her team, the Lady Vols, to twenty-two final four championships.

Born in Henrietta, Tennessee, Pat Summitt was the fourth of five children. Her father was a strict authoritarian, a style Summitt copied as a coach. By all accounts she was considered an intense or harsh coach. Her father, aware of her basketball talent, moved the family so his daughter could attend Cheatham County High School, which had a women's basketball program. Summitt went on to attend the University of Tennessee at Martin, where she led the team to a 64-29 record during her four years at the school. She graduated with a degree in physical education. In 1972 Summitt received an invitation to try out for the US Olympic team. She made the cut, competing in the 1976 Olympic Games where the team captured a silver medal. In 1984 Summitt returned to the Olympics, this time as a coach, winning a gold medal.

In the 1997 season, the University of Tennessee Lady Vols became the first team in the National Collegiate Athletic Association (NCAA) history to win the title after suffering more than six losses during the regular season, and only the second ever to win back-to-back championships. The extraordinary season became the subject of a television documentary, A Cinderella Season: The 1997 Lady Vols Fight Back, which aired on HBO in 1998, the same year that Summitt published a book, Raise the Roof, about the extraordinary season.

In 2011 Summitt announced she was suffering from early onset Alzheimer's dementia. She retired the following year. In her honor, the University of Tennessee renamed the basketball court at Thompson-Boling Arena "The Summit," and a bronze statue of Summitt was erected at Pat Summitt Plaza. She was inducted into the Naismith Memorial Basketball Hall of Fame and, that same year, was named the Naismith Coach of the Century. In 2012 President Barack Obama awarded Summitt the Presidential Medal of Freedom.

Pat Summit's son, Tyler Summitt, her mother, three brothers, and a sister survive her.

See Current Biography 2005

Elizabeth Swados

Born: Buffalo, New York; February 5, 1951
Died: New York, New York; January 5, 2016
Occupation: Writer, composer, director, musician

Elizabeth Swados is most remembered for her innovation in theater. Her most successful endeavor was *Runaways,* a musical performed by actual teenage runaways. They sang their stories of abuse, child prostitution, and their struggles to make it on the streets, to the tune of haunting lullabies and nursery rhymes, which Swados composed. She became the first person ever to receive five Tony Award nominations for a single show. Columbia Records released a recording of *Runaways,* and Twentieth Century-Fox purchased the film rights. Her work pushed the boundaries of form, as in one of her earliest productions (with Andre Serban), an audacious adaptation of *Medea* presented, not in English but in a combination of the original Greek of Euripides and the Latin of Seneca, her words chosen, not for their meaning but for their sound and for their ability to elicit strong emotions in her audience. With cartoonist, Garry Trudeau, Swados orchestrated a stage adaptation of the comic strip, *Doonesbury.* And a very young Meryl Streep starred in Swados's *Alice at the Palace.*

Elizabeth Swados was born into a family of entertainers. Her father, Robert Swados, trained to be an actor before deciding to become a lawyer. (He was also the vice-president of the Buffalo Sabres hockey team.) Her mother was an actress and poet, and her maternal grandfather was a concertmaster and violinist in Russia. Her paternal grandmother was a concert violinist. Unfortunately, mental illness also ran in her family. Her violinist grandmother had to undergo a lobotomy, and her brother, Lincoln, was diagnosed with schizophrenia. (He died in 1989.) Her mother succumbed to depression and alcoholism, committing suicide in 1974, just as Swados was gaining notoriety for her talent.

At age sixteen, Swados entered Bennington College where she studied creative writing and music, but she left before graduation to work with Andrei Serban on his audacious adaptation of *Medea.* Swados's work won her a Village Voice

Obie for her musical score for the production. She was just twenty years old. While she was still in college, she worked with Appalachia Volunteers, Inc., living with a mining family for four months. She spent two summers singing with Pete Seeger aboard his sloop Clearwater on the Hudson River in New York.

Elizabeth Swados died prematurely from complications after surgery for cancer. Her spouse, Roz Lichter, survives.

See Current Biography 1979

Fred Thompson

Born: Sheffield, Alabama; August 19, 1942
Died: Nashville, Tennessee; November 1, 2015
Occupation: US senator, actor

Thompson first gained prominence when he served as minority counsel on the Senate Select Committee on Presidential Campaign Activities in 1973. It was Thompson's questioning of former White House aide, Alexander Butterfield, about the White House recording system that led to the eventual resignation of President Richard Nixon.

Thompson was a natural athlete, but his marriage to Sarah Lindsey at the age of seventeen got him kicked off the highschool basketball team. Thompson claimed to have not had much ambition in life until he read the autobiography of Clarence Darrow, which inspired him to seek a law degree. He graduated from Vanderbilt University in 1967.

He became involved with prominent Tennessee Republicans, working on US attorney general, John Mitchell's, campaign to oust Al Gore, Sr. from his senate seat. Another prominent Republican, Lamar Alexander, asked Thompson to run Senator Howard Baker's reelection campaign. His relationship with Baker led to Thompson's appointment as minority counsel with the senate committee in the Watergate investigation. Over the next twenty years, Thompson continued to serve as counsel on a number of legislative committees.

In 1977, Thompson found himself representing a whistleblower, Marie Ragghianti, who refused to grant parole to inmates who, it was later learned, paid then-Governor Ray Blanton. Blanton fired Ragghianti, who then sued with Fred Thompson as her legal counsel. The case was made into a movie and Thompson was offered the position of playing himself, thus launching a very successful career as an actor. Thompson played big roles in a number of hit movies, including *Days of Thunder, The Hunt for Red October,* and *Diehard 2.* He also enjoyed a five-year run on the hit television series *Law & Order*, playing Manhattan District Attorney, Arthur Branch. He was the first active US senator to simultaneously play a fictional role on television. He considered his acting career a welcome diversion from the Washington mileau. In 2008, Thompson made a short-lived bid for the role of Republican presidential candidate.

Fred Thompson died from a recurrence of lymphoma. He had first been diagnosed in 2004. Survivors include wife, Jeri Kehn Thompson, his four children, and five grandchildren.

See Current Biography 1999

Lester Thurow

Born: Livingston, Montana; May 7, 1938
Died: Westport, Massachusetts; March 25, 2016
Occupation: American economist, educator

Lester Thurow has been described as the most famous economist in the country, as well as the most influential economist of his generation.

Born in Livingston, Montana, to a Methodist minister and a high school mathematics teacher, Lester Thurow spent most of his childhood moving from one small Montana town to another as the Methodist administration moved the family every few years. His childhood was rich with the experiences of fishing and hiking in the Montana wilderness. He also spent four summers working in the Butte copper mines, which exposed him to the rigors of a life of manual labor. He attended Williams College in Williamstown, Massachusetts, graduating Phi Beta Kappa, and winning a Rhodes Scholarship to Balliol College at Oxford University where he received his master's degree.

After completing a PhD at Harvard in 1964, Thurow moved to Washington DC, where he joined the staff of the President's Council of Economic Advisers. He was quickly disillusioned as the country plunged into war in Vietnam without being willing to pay for it. He served as an assistant professor at Harvard from 1965 to 1968, then moved to the Massachusetts Institute of Technology where he became a full professor of economics and management before the age of thirty-three.

When Thurow was overlooked for a position on President Jimmy Carter's cabinet, he focused on informing the wider population about the dangers of growing income inequality and the ever-widening trade deficit. He came under some criticism from more conservative colleagues who considered his work less than thorough in his attempts to communicate complex ideas to a broader audience. As something of an advocate

for the middle and lower classes, he emphasized the necessity of creating an educated workforce. He was widely published, contributing regularly to popular publications like *Newsweek* and *US News and World Report*, and speaking on popular news programs. Thurow also was the author of a dozen books on economics, with titles like *The Zero-Sum Society: Distribution and the Possibilities of Change* (1980) and *Head to Head: the Coming Economic Battle Among Japan, Europe, and America* (1993).

Lester Thurow's first wife, Emily Jane Fooks, died in 1972. He married Anna Soldinger in 1998. He had two children with his second wife, Gretchen Pfuetze.

His wife and two children survive him.

See Current Biography 1990

Alvin Toffler

Born: New York, New York; October 4, 1928
Died: Los Angeles, California; June 27, 2016
Occupation: Author, futurist

Writer Alvin Toffler is best known for his remarkably prescient book *Future Shock*, and later, *The Third Wave*, which forecast the impact of technology in changing human culture. With more than fifteen million copies sold, *Future Shock*, maintained its spot on the bestseller list for seventy-eight weeks, and has been widely translated. Toffler coined the term "information overload."

Alvin Toffler was born in Brooklyn, New York, to working class Polish-Jewish immigrants. His father was a furrier. Toffler had always wanted to be a writer. In high school he worked on the school newspaper, and as a student at Washington Square College of New York University (NYU), he founded and edited an intercollegiate literary magazine, *Compass*. Following graduation, Toffler worked at numerous blue-collar jobs that included work as an auto assembly line welder, truck driver, and punch press operator. He began writing and editing for several industrial trade journals, eventually making his way as a labor columnist with *Fortune* magazine, where he wrote his seminal essays, "The Culture Consumers" and "The Future as a Way of Life." He coined the term "future shock" to "describe the shattering stress and disorientation" induced by subjecting individuals "to too much change in too short a time." His ideas eventually became his seminal work, *Future Shock*. Toffler was eerily accurate with his predictions about an era of instant and "throw-away" goods and the fractured family. He anticipated computer technology and the advent of the Internet. He likewise predicted key geo-political events like the fall of the Soviet Union and the dismantling of the Iron Curtain.

With his wife, Heidi, Toffler wrote over a dozen books about the cultural and technological revolutions he foresaw. Toffler was awarded a number of prestigious prizes, including the McKinsey Foundation Book Award, and the de L'Ordre des Arts et des Lettres. Both Toffler and his wife were awarded Brown University's "Independent Award." Alvin and Heidi Toffler had one daughter who predeceased them in 2000. Heidi Toffler survives her husband.

See Current Biography 1975

Michel Tournier

Born: Paris, France; December 19, 1924
Died: Choisel, France; January 18, 2016
Occupation: Novelist, philosopher

Michel Tournier was one of the most distinguished French writers of the late twentieth century. His work explored collective human experience through archetypes of the ogre, the saint, and the castaway by retelling old myths from new perspectives. He received the French Academy's prestigious Grand Prix for his first novel, *Vendredi* (*Friday,* in English) in 1967, and in 1970 he won the Prix Goncourt for his second novel, *Le Roi des Aulnes* (*The Erl King,* in English). He was elected to the Academie Goncourt (the Goncourt Literary Society) in 1972.

Tournier's parents had met as graduate students of German at the Sorbonne. During World War II, twenty-two German soldiers were garrisoned at their home. While the family occupied the ground floor, young Michel Tournier moved to the attic with the soldiers, claiming that he was set free by the chaos of the era. The family eventually abandoned the house and moved to the Paris suburb of Neuilly. Though Tournier was a poor student, he was accepted—to everyone's surprise, including Tournier's—at the Sorbonne where he studied philosophy and law. However, he failed the qualifying exam that would have allowed him to teach at university. He worked as a producer for radio and television, and translated German novels. He eventually became the literary director of Éditions Plon publishing house. In his spare time, he worked on his overambitious novel about the Hitler Youth Movement's annual conscription of one million ten-year-old girls and boys, something Tournier likened to an ogre who devoured children. The story eventually became his second novel. Michel Tournier was sometimes referred to as a "hyperrealist" in the vein of Gabriel Marquez

and Salmon Rushdie. In his retelling of Defoe's Robinson Crusoe, which would become his first published novel, the native named Friday, leaves the island for "civilization," while Crusoe is "freed" from Western society's constraints and remains on the island. In 1954 Tournier moved to Choisel, near Versailles, where he lived for the rest of his life.

Michel Tournier never married or had children. His godson, Laurent Feliculis, who was like a son to him, survives.

See Current Biography 1990

John Trudell

Born: Omaha, Nebraska; February 15, 1946
Died: Santa Clara County, California; December 8, 2015
Occupation: Native American activist, poet, actor

Native American activist John Trudell was once the leader of the American Indian Movement (AIM), an organization devoted to improving the lives of Native Americans and educating the American public about issues important to indigenous cultures. He was a spoken-word performer and poet who was befriended and promoted by a number of celebrities like Jackson Browne, Jane Fonda, and Bob Dylan.

John Trudell was born on a Sioux reservation in northwestern Nebraska. His mother died when he was just six years old, leaving him in the care of his grandparents who lived on the reservation. His father lived in Omaha, Nebraska. Trudell joined the Navy in 1963, the experience teaching him that what was happening to him as an Indian, "a prisoner of America," was happening to others all over the world." In 1969 he joined a coalition of organizations known as the Indians of All Tribes (IAT) that occupied the island and abandoned prison on Alcatraz, off the California coast, for eighteen months. Trudell became the spokesperson for the group, which aimed to establish their own government and provide an environment to realize their vision of an ideal society. After fire ravaged four historical buildings, a number of the occupiers left the island voluntarily. US Marshalls forcibly removed Trudell and fourteen others. However, their actions led to major policy changes, including the passage of the Indian Self-Determination and Education Act, the Indian Financing Act, the Indian Health Act, and the establishment of the office of the Assistant Interior Secretary for Indian Affairs.

After the end of his first marriage, Trudell moved to Oklahoma and married Palute activist

Tina Manning. Heavily involved in AIM activities, Trudell's file with the FBI had amassed 17,000 pages. (One statement reportedly called Trudell "extremely eloquent and therefore extremely dangerous.") In February of 1979 Trudell burned an American flag at a protest at FBI headquarters in Washington, DC. Within hours, Trudell's wife, her mother, and the couple's three children were killed in a suspicious fire. Trudell claimed they were killed in an act of war.

To cope with the loss, John Trudell turned to writing. He met Jackson Browne at a uranium mine protest in New Mexico, and the two became friends. In 1983 he recorded his first album, *Tribal Voice*, at Browne's studio. He met the famous guitarist, Jesse Ed Davis, a Kiowa Indian, who wrote music to accompany Trudell's poetry, and the two created the Graffiti Band. Trudell noted that Bob Dylan told *Rolling Stone* magazine he considered Trudell's work to be revolutionary, and proclaimed Trudell's *A.K.A. Graffiti Man* to be the 1986 album of the year. He played it during set breaks for his 1987 tour with The Grateful Dead. Trudell also appeared in a number of films including *Thunderheart* (1992), and Robert Redford produced the documentary *Incident at Oglala*, which included an interview with John Trudell who died on December 8, 2015 after a long illness.

See Current Biography 2001

In 1950 Verdy performed the title role in the motion picture *Ballerina* (Memnon Films). In 1954 Verdy accompanied the Ballets de Paris on its first tour of the United States, stopping in Hollywood the following year to appear in *The Glass Slipper* (MGM). After the Ballets de Paris disbanded, Verdy worked with George Balanchine, director of the New York City Ballet from 1958 to 1976, who created dozens of roles for her. By the end of her time with Balanchine, Verdy had appeared in nearly fifty of the works in City Ballet's extensive repertory.

Plagued by injuries, Verdy moved to the Boston Ballet as the associate artistic director. She was a dance professor at Indiana University's Jacobs School of Music for twenty years, beginning in 1996. Verdy won numerous accolades and awards, including the French government's Chevalier de l'Ordre des Arts et Lettres in 1971 and the Chevalier de l'Ordre National de la Légion d'honneur in 2009. She performed for the President and Mrs. Gerald Ford at the White House in 1976, and the School of American Ballet honored her with an Artistic Achievement Award.

Violette Verdy was married briefly to filmmaker, Colin Clark, the son of noted art historian, Kenneth Clark. She had no children, and no known survivors.

See Current Biography 1980

Violette Verdy

Born: Pont-l'Abbe, Brittany, France; December 1, 1933
Died: Bloomington, Indiana; February 8, 2016
Occupation: Ballerina, ballet company manager

Violette Verdy is remembered as one of the twentieth century's finest ballerinas. Born Nelly Guillerm, Verdy was the only child of a merchant of maritime supplies, who died before she was even a year old. Her mother was an iron-willed schoolteacher who devoted herself to raising her frail daughter. Noticing Verdy's interest in music, she provided piano and violin lessons, and when a physician suggested physical activity to help the insomniac child sleep, Verdy began taking daily ballet lessons. She was undeniably a natural, gifted dancer who studied with Madame Rousane Sarkissian, an exponent of the Russian Method. Verdy was just twelve years old when she first performed as a professional dancer, with Roland Petit's Ballets des Champs-Elysees (having rejected a rare invitation to study at the Paris Opera Ballet School). Throughout that first year, she continued to study with ballet master, Victor Gsovsky, who taught her leading classical roles.

Lillian Vernon

Born: Leipzig, Saxony, Germany; March 18, 1927
Died: New York, New York; December 14, 2015
Occupation: Business entrepreneur

Lillian Vernon became a household name in American homes, after she developed a catalogue retail business that started at her kitchen table and grew to annual sales of $260 million in 1987. Vernon sold the business for $60.5 million in 2003.

Born in Leipzig, Germany, to a Jewish industrialist and his wife, Lillian Vernon's family fled to the Netherlands, when she was just five years old. They made their way to New York City five years later, and Vernon's father started a zipper manufacturing business. He later sold leather goods. Vernon married Samuel Hochberg in 1949, and while she was pregnant with their first son, she started a business selling personally monogrammed belts and handbags, using her father as a reliable supplier of the leather goods. After her initial 1951 advertisement in *Seventeen* magazine, her business grew so quickly that by 1954, she had outgrown her home. She rented three buildings—a warehouse, a shipping department, and a monogramming workshop—in Mount Vernon, New York. She eventually set up a light manufacturing plant and, rather than placing more and more ads in magazines, she published a mail-order catalogue. By the end of the 1950s she was providing customized goods to cosmetic companies such as Revlon, Avon, Elizabeth Arden, and Max Factor. She renamed the business Lillian Vernon Corporation in 1965. By 1970 she posted sales of $1 million. In 1987 Vernon listed her company on the American Stock Exchange, the first woman to do so. She sold thirty-five percent of her company to the public. Annual sales had reached $112 million.

Lillian Vernon's first marriage ended in divorce, and in 1970 she married Robert Katz, and was known as Lillian Vernon Katz for twenty years. She changed her legal name to Lillian Vernon in 1990 following her second divorce. She was married a third time to Paolo Martino, a salon owner. Vernon established an endowment with the Lillian Vernon Writer's House, home to the prestigious writing program at New York University (NYU). She sat on the board of a number of philanthropic organizations such as Lincoln Center and Citymeals-on-Wheels, and established the charitable Lillian Vernon Foundation. Vernon died on December 14, 2015.

See Current Biography 1996

George Voinovich

Born: Cleveland, Ohio; July 15, 1936
Died: Cleveland, Ohio; June 12, 2016
Occupation: US Senator, governor of Ohio, mayor of Cleveland

A moderate Republican who often bucked his more conservative Republican colleagues, George Voinovich was widely respected for his bipartisan, no nonsense style of leadership. As the mayor of Cleveland, Voinovich rescued the ailing city from the verge of bankruptcy. Only two years later, the National Municipal League named Cleveland one of its ten "All American" cities. He was a two-term Republican governor in a state often considered a Democratic stronghold, and served two terms as a US senator.

George Voinovich was born the grandson of Serbian and Slovenian immigrants. He attended Cleveland's Collinwood High School, and went on to earn a BA in government from Ohio University, and a degree in law from Ohio State University College of Law. He passed the Ohio bar in 1961. In 1963 he joined the Ohio State Attorney General's office as an assistant attorney general. In 1966 he won a seat on the Ohio House of Representatives where he helped

create the Ohio Environmental Protection Agency in a region with a long history of heavy industry, and helped curtail oil drilling in Lake Erie. From 1978 to 1979, he served as lieutenant governor of Ohio. Campaigning on a platform of fiscal responsibility, he became the first candidate in nearly twenty years to win a majority of votes cast by both black and white voters, many of whom were registered Democrats. He was Cleveland's mayor for a decade, and in 1990, he began the first of two four-year terms as Ohio's governor. He served twelve years as the US Senator from Ohio. To the chagrin of his Republican colleagues, Voinovich supported a federal bailout of the US auto industry that employed thousands of Ohio citizens. During the Bush administration, he was among the first to propose raising taxes to help pay for the war in Iraq and hurricane Katrina relief.

Voinovich married his wife, Janet, in 1962, and the couple had four children. Sadly, their nine-year-old daughter was struck by a car and killed in 1979. Janet and their three remaining children, as well as nine grandchildren, survive.

See Current Biography 1997

Andrzej Wajda

Born: Suwalki, Poland; March 6, 1926
Died: Warsaw, Poland; October 9, 2016
Occupation: Polish filmmaker

A Polish filmmaker at the height of Communist power in Poland, Andrzej Wajda turned out a series of defiant and courageous, prize-winning films, winning numerous international film awards including three grand prizes at the Moscow International Film Festival and three Academy Award nominations. He received an honorary Oscar in 2000. His last film, *Afterimage*, is Poland's entry for the category of best foreign language film for the 2017 Oscars.

Andrzej Wajda was born in northeast Poland. His father, Jakub, was a cavalry officer killed at the "Katyn massacre," a national tragedy, and a subject Wajda would eventually cover in his later years with the movie *Katyn* (2007). He was a young teenager when Germany invaded Poland in 1939. Wajda joined the Home Army, a resistance arm of the Polish government-in-exile. In 1946 Wajda enrolled at the Academy of Fine Arts in Krakow to study painting, but soon realized it wasn't for him and he transferred to the School of Theatre and Cinematography in Lodz. He graduated in 1952 and was hired by the veteran film director, Aleksander Ford, to assist with the production of *Five Boys From Barska Street*. A year later, under Ford's tutelage, Wajda made *A Generation*, based on a novel about a left-wing resistance group during the Nazi occupation. (While making the film, he hired an unknown actor, Roman Polanski who would later become a celebrated film director himself.) The film became the first in a trilogy of controversial movies about the effects of war on Poland's youth. *Generation* won the State Prize for Wajda. The next film *Kanal* was about the Warsaw Uprising of 1944. The film won a Silver Palm at the 1957 Cannes Film Festival. The final film of the trilogy, *Ashes and Diamonds*, based on a popular novel about civil unrest and Communist rule following World War II, was arguably Wajda's best, winning the Fipresci Prize at the Venice Film Festival, and it was named the best foreign film of the year by the British film critics. His later film, *Man of Iron* was filmed during the actual events surrounding Poland's struggle for Solidarity.

Andrzej Wajda was married four times, with his first three marriages ending in divorce. His fourth wife, Krystyna Zachwatowicz, and his daughter from his third marriage, survive.

See Current Biography 1982

Olene S. Walker

Born: Ogden, Utah; November 15, 1930
Died: Holladay, Utah; November 28, 2015
Occupation: Former governor of Utah

Olene Walker was a lawmaker in the Utah House of Representatives for eight years, from 1980 to 1988. During her last term in the house, she was the Republican Party whip. She served as Utah's lieutenant governor for nearly eleven years, from 1993 to 2003. When Utah Governor Michael Leavitt accepted a post as head of the federal Environmental Protection Agency (EPA) in 2003, Walker became the first female governor of Utah.

Born in Ogden, Utah, Walker was raised on a family farm. She earned bachelor's and master's degrees from Brigham Young University (BYU) and Stanford University, respectively, and a doctorate in education administration from the University of Utah. She was fifty-five and the mother of seven children when she earned her PhD, graduating the same day her son graduated from medical school, and her youngest daughter graduated from college. She was a tireless worker, who apparently got by on little sleep, and was known to put in nineteen-hour days. She claimed she wrote her dissertation during the hours of 11:00 p.m. and 3:00 a.m.

Walker was a great proponent of education, going to battle with conservative Utahns,

by vetoing the Carson Smith Special Needs Scholarship program—a private school voucher initiative—because of the murky constitutionality of using public funds for private education. She fought for low-income housing. Her grandmotherly charm led some colleagues to call her "Aunt Bea" after the down-home and disarming demeanor of the television character on *The Andy Griffith Show.*

In 2005 Walker and her husband were named UN missionaries for the Church of Jesus Christ of Latter-Day Saints (the Mormon church), spending part of the summer of 2005 in New York, speaking with ambassadors from countries that had barred Mormons from entering their territory. In 2012 Walker created the Olene S. Walker Institute of Politics & Public Service at Weber State University, in support of students who are preparing for careers in public service.

Olene Walker's husband, Myron, her seven children, twenty-five grandchildren, and twenty-five great-grandchildren survive her.

See Current Biography 2005

Gerald Wasserburg

Born: New Brunswick, New Jersey; March 25, 1927
Died: Florence, Oregon; June 13, 2016
Occupation: Geophysicist, educator

Gerald Wasserburg was a world-renowned astro-geophysicist, a John D. MacArthur Professor of Geology and Geophysics, Emeritus at the California Institute of Technology (Caltech) in Pasadena. There he produced some of the most critical measurements in the history of geophysics, significantly influencing theories about the creation of the solar system. It was Wasserburg who definitively dated the oldest rocks—brought back from the Apollo 11 lunar landing—to be 4.6 billion years.

Gerald Wasserburg was born to a lower-middle class family in New Brunswick, New Jersey. As a child, his prospects were not promising. He essentially flunked "everything," including science as a student, and dropped out of high school. He forged a birth certificate and joined the US Army, serving as a rifleman on the European front in World War II. His service won him a Combat Infantryman's Badge and a Purple Heart. Upon returning home, Wasserburg earned a high school diploma and enrolled at Rutgers University under the GI Bill. He transferred to the University of Chicago where he worked with Enrico Fermi and the Nobel laureate, Harold Urey, who were bent on determining the age and origin of the solar system. The problem of discovering and reading the geological "time-keepers" of the solar system would occupy Wasserburg for the rest of his career. He earned his PhD in 1954 and remained at the University of Chicago as a research associate at its Institute for Nuclear Studies, working to improve the accuracy of the mass spectrometer. He moved to Caltech in 1955 where he joined a team of scientists intent on developing an advanced mass spectrometer in anticipation of Apollo 11's haul of lunar rocks following its moon landing. The indispensability of his mass spectrometer to the study and analysis of lunar material was proved when Wasserburg was one of only eleven geophysicists to be given a sample of Apollo 12 rocks, one of which he dubbed "Mr. Special." This sample dated the moon's formation at 4.6 billion years.

The National Association and Space Adminisgtration (NASA) twice awarded Dr. Wasserburg its Exceptional Scientific Achievement Award. Wasserburg received the National Academy of Science's Arthur L. Day Prize and Lectureship. Among his other honors are the J. F. Kemp Medal for Distinguished Public Service from Columbia University, the Meteoritical Society's Leonard Medal, and the Gold Medal of the Royal Astronomical Society (RAS), among many others.

Gerald Wasserburg leaves behind his wife of more than sixty years, Naomi, and two sons.

See Current Biography 1986

Papa Wemba

(Jules Shungu Wembadio Pene Kikumba)
Born: Lubefu, Kasai, Belgian Congo; June 14, 1949
Died: Abidjan, Ivory Coast; April 24, 2016
Occupation: Congolese singer

Sometimes referred to as the "king of rumba rock," Papa Wemba was one of the most popular musicians in Africa, creating a style that would greatly influence future young performers. He was also a cultural trail blazer, setting trends in fashion, creating the commune Société des Ambianceurs et des Personnes d'Élégance (the Society of Atmosphere-setters and Elegant People) also known as "La Sape."

Jules Shungu Wembadio Pene Kikumba was born into the Tetela ethnic tribe in the southern Kasai region of the Congo. His mother was a "pleureuse"—a professional funeral mourner, a traditional job that entailed both crying and singing at funerals and wakes. In a certain sense, she was a performer, and her son often accompanied her at her work. His experience instilled in him a love of music. Wemba's father, a soldier in the Belgian Army during World War II, discouraged his son's musical ambitions, but his death in 1966 left Wemba free to pursue his passion. He and several friends formed the group Zaiko Langa Langa in 1969. Their music fused traditional rhythms, popular Kinshasa radio tunes, and American soul and funk music harmonies. Deciding not to have one lead singer, the group combined many voices singing different harmonies and chants.

When President Mombutu's policies of 'L'Authenticity' attempted to keep out Western influences, including music, Wemba considered it an opportunity to use traditional music. He ran afoul of the government though when he tried to form a commune outside of Kinshasa, call the "Village of Molokai." The residents formed an organization, roughly translated as "the society of cool and elegant people," shortened to the acronym, SAPE. The Sapeur movement, a group of rebellious youth, was a direct affront to the president's "authenticity" philosophy.

In 2003 Wemba was accused of trying to smuggle native people from the Democratic Republic of Congo into Europe. He spent three and a half months in jail before bail was posted. His prison sentence was later suspended.

Papa Wemba also became a movie actor, playing the lead role in a Zairian film, La Vie est Belle (Life is Rosy). Though he acted in several other movies that was his only lead role. He also created soundtracks for a number of films.

In April of 2016 Wemba collapsed on stage while performing at the Festival des Musiques Urbaines d'Anoumabo (FEMUA) urban music festival. In 1970 he had married Marie-Rose Luzolo and the couple had six children. His survivors include his wife (commonly referred to as Mama Rosa), thirty-three children, and nearly two-dozen grandchildren.

See Current Biography 2003

Arnold Wesker

Born: London, England; May 24, 1932
Died: Brighton, England; April 12, 2016
Occupation: English playwright

Although Arnold Wesker is most remembered for his "Wesker Trilogy," comprised of three plays, *Chicken Soup with Barley, Roots*, and *I'm Talking About Jerusalem*, he published fifty plays, four volumes of short stories, numerous essays, poetry, and his autobiography, *As Much As I Dare*.

Arnold Wesker was born in London's East End, the son of Joseph Wesker, a Russian-Jewish tailor's machinist who was often unemployed. His mother, Leah (Perimutter) Wesker, an ardent Communist, often had to support the family by working in kitchens. During World War II, Wesker was evacuated and spent six years with foster parents at various sections of the English countryside. At a very young age, Wesker wanted to become an actor, so he left school when he was fourteen, working any number of odd jobs to support himself. He earned enough to enter the London School of Film Technique where Lindsay Anderson was his mentor. He began writing plays, and on July 7, 1958, his first play, *Chicken Soup with Barley*, appeared at the Belgrade Theatre in Coventry, winning Wesker a London Evening Standard award as the most promising British dramatist of that year. Wesker's next two plays were part of the "Wesker trilogy," which was produced in its entirety at the Royal Court Theatre in London in the summer of 1960. His plays were primarily about working class, Jewish families, and their responses to Communism during the mid-1930s. His work celebrated working-class life, the challenges of low-wage labor, and an attack on the British class system. In 1966 Wesker's play *The Kitchen* was an off-Broadway hit that starred Rip Torn.

However in the 1970s Wesker's career started to decline. Actors refused to perform his play *The Journalist,* claiming there were too many characters without any starring roles. Wesker sued claiming their refusal to work was political in nature. He was eventually awarded damages, but not before he had exiled himself to the margins of theater society.

Arnold Wesker's daughter, Tanya, predeceased him. His survivors include his wife, Dusty, and three children.

See Current Biography 1962

Haskell Wexler

Born: Chicago, Illinois; February 6, 1922
Died: Santa Monica, California; December 27, 2015
Occupation: Cinematographer, filmmaker

Considered one of the top ten cinematographers of all time, maverick Haskell Wexler received five nominations for Academy Awards, winning two: one for *Who's Afraid of Virginia Woolf in 1967*, and another for *Bound for Glory* in 1977. He was one of the few cinematographers with a star on Hollywood's Walk of Fame, and was the first cinematographer ever to receive a Lifetime Achievement Award from the American Society of Cinematographers (ASC). In 2007 he was honored with two more Lifetime Achievement

Awards, one from the Independent Documentary Association (IDA) and the other from the Society of Operating Cameramen.

Haskell Wexler was born to a well-to-do family in Chicago, Illinois. His father was one of the founders of Allied Radio, which later became Radio Shack. As early as eighth grade, the budding liberal agitator began photographing striking unionists for the Newspaper Guild. This experience generated a life-long pro-labor stance. He organized a strike at his father's electronics factory when he was seventeen, and while attending the University of California at Berkeley, was asked to leave after agitating for the right of assembly for the American Students Union. At the onset of World War II, he joined the Merchant Marines, briefly meeting fellow sailor, Woody Guthrie. (Some years hence, Wexler would win an Academy Award for his work on the film *Bound for Glory,* about the folk singer.) After Wexler's tanker was torpedoed off the coast of South Africa, he survived ten days in a lifeboat with nine crewmembers before being rescued.

Following the war, Wexler's father helped finance a film studio for him, but the venture failed. However, it served as an unofficial film school. While he did freelance work, McCarthy-era witch hunters blacklisted him due to his leftist political views. He did a number of short works—documentaries, television commercials, and docudramas. His big break came when he caught the eye of famous filmmaker Elia Kazan who asked Wexler to be the cinematographer for *America, America.*

By all accounts, Wexler was difficult to work with. He was demanding and intractable (he was fired from the set in several movie productions), but he was also highly innovative in producing striking effects. For his work on *Who's Afraid of Virginia Woolf,* Wexler used a handheld camera to capture the intense emotions and instability of the main couple's relationship (the same method he used early in his career to film a car chase). The film won Academy nominations in every category it was eligible for, winning five awards. In *The Thomas Crown Affair* he stretched silks over the tops of sets and aimed 10-Kelvin lights at their centers to enhance the juxtaposition of light and dark. For the climactic heist scene, he installed hidden cameras and captured the genuine reactions of bystanders who didn't know the scene was being filmed for a movie.

Haskell Wexler lived to be ninety-three. His wife, two sons, and a daughter survive.

See Current Biography 2007

Robert M. White

Born: Boston, Massachusetts; February 13, 1923
Died: Chevy Chase, Maryland; October 14, 2016
Occupation: American meteorologist

Robert White was the United States' top weatherman for decades, serving under the leadership of five presidents. He was a pioneer in the use of satellites to predict the weather, and was among the first scientists to raise alarm regarding greenhouse gases and global climate change.

White was born in Boston, Massachusetts, to a Russian immigrant lawyer. He was one of four children. (His older brother, Theodore, became a Pulitzer Prize–winning journalist.) Though both parents worked, they often had little money to buy shoes. His father died when he was eight. White attended Harvard University on a series of scholarships—the Burroughs Newsboy Scholarship, and the Edwards Scholarship—with a degree in geology. He became interested in meteorology after working at the Blue Hill Observatory in Milton, Massachusetts, as an aviation cadet for the US Army Air Corps. He obtained his master of science degree in meteorology from Massachusetts Institute of Technology (MIT), in 1949, and his doctorate in 1950.

White began his career as the president of the Travellers Research Center in Hartford, Connecticut—an arm of the Traveler's Insurance Group. In 1963 President John Kennedy appointed him director of the US Weather Bureau, and only two years later, President Lyndon Johnson made him chief of the new Environmental Science Services Administration (ESSA), which became of National Oceanic and Atmospheric Administration (NOAA), in 1970. White continued in that capacity until 1977. He was the president of the National Academy of Engineering (NAE) from 1983 to 1995.

Robert White came to prominence just as extraordinary leaps in technology were transforming his entire industry, and he welcomed innovation. Under his leadership, the first weather-monitoring satellites were launched, and, as technology became capable of processing massive amounts of data, White helped facilitate a global exchange of weather information, even with the Soviet Union at the height of the Cold War. He was one of the first scientists to ring the alarm about greenhouse gasses and global warming. As the leader of the National Academy of Sciences (NAS) research board, White chaired the first World Climate Conference in Geneva, in 1979.

Dr. White died at home in Chevy Chase, Maryland, on October 14, 2016, from complications of dementia. He is survived by his wife of sixty-seven years, Mavis Seagle White, and his two children.

See Current Biography 1964

Elie Wiesel

Born: Sighet Marmatiei, Romania; September 30, 1928
Died: New York, New York; July 2, 2016
Occupation: Author, educator, Nobel laureate

Elie Wiesel is best known as the author of *Night*, a true account of his imprisonment and survival at the Nazi concentration camp at Buchenwald, Germany. His father, mother, and sister perished, and Wiesel considered it his sacred duty to remember and tell his story. He was the first writer to use the term "holocaust" to describe the killing of some six million Jews and other "undesirables" at the hands of the German Nazis during World War II.

Elie Wiesel was born into a deeply religious Jewish family in northern Transylvania, near the Ukrainian border. His mother urged him to study the Torah, the Talmud, and the mystical teachings of Hasidism, and he was inspired by his Hasidic maternal grandfather. Wiesel's childhood ended in the spring of 1944 when Sighet's 15,000 Jews were transported to the concentration camp at Auschwitz, where his mother and younger sister died in the gas chambers. Wiesel and his father were later transferred to Buchenwald, where his father died from dysentery and starvation. After the liberation of Buchenwald on April 11, 1945, Wiesel moved to France where he studied literature, philosophy, and psychology at the Sorbonne. He became a journalist for L'Arche, a French newspaper, and also worked as a foreign correspondent for the Israeli paper, Yedioth Ahronoth. In 1954 Wiesel interviewed the Roman Catholic writer and Nobel laureate, François Mauriac, who urged Wiesel to relate his death-camp experiences. The result was the short memoir Night.

With the publication of *Night*, Wiesel turned his literary attention to survival after the holocaust, with a series of short semi-autobiographical novels in which the author explored such themes as suicide, madness, killing, political action, hate, indifference and faith, and the relationship between humanity and God. Wiesel wrote over fifty books, both fiction and non-fiction.

In 1978, President Jimmy Carter appointed Wiesel to head the President's Commission on the Holocaust. (The commission would eventually create the US Holocaust Memorial Museum.) In 1985, US President Ronald Reagan presented Wiesel with the Congressional Medal of Achievement for his contributions to literature and in recognition of his leadership as the chairman of the US Holocaust Memorial Council. Wiesel took the opportunity to urge the president to forego his plan to visit the military cemetery at Bitburg, West Germany, where members of the Nazi elite, the SS, were buried. He is credited as a pioneer of the movement in support of Soviet Jews amidst increasing anti-Semitism in the USSR. Wiesel was outspoken about human rights abuses across the globe, including the plight of the victims of ethnic cleansing in Kosovo, and he was a powerful critic of South African apartheid. Wiesel was awarded the Nobel Peace Prize in 1986 with the Nobel Committee naming him a "messenger to mankind."

Elie Wiesel leaves behind his wife of forty-seven years, Marion Erster Rose, who is also a holocaust survivor, and a son, Shlomo Elisha.

See Current Biography 1986

Gene Wilder

Born: Milwaukee, Wisconsin; June 11, 1933
Died: Stamford, Connecticut; August, 29, 2016
Occupation: Actor, director, writer

The movie roles that helped define Gene Wilder's career included that of Leo Bloom, a neurotic accountant in *The Producers*, the first film Mel Brook's wrote and directed; Willy Wonka in *Willy Wonka and the Chocolate Factory*; the alcoholic gunslinger, the Waco Kid, in Mel Brook's *Blazing Saddles*; and the young Dr. Frankenstein in another Mel Brook's hit, *Young Frankenstein*. Wilder won an Oscar Award nomination for his role in *The Producers*.

Gene Wilder was born Jerome Silberman. His father was a Russian immigrant and his mother was a native of Chicago. His mother suffered a debilitating heart attack when Wilder was just six years old, and from then on the child worked to entertain her with comedy. (A physician had explained to the child that if he caused her any anger it could kill her.) Wilder graduated from Washington High School in Milwaukee in 1951, and earned a BA degree from the University of Iowa in 1955. After graduation Wilder enrolled in the Old Vic Theatre School in Bristol, England, where he studied judo, fencing, gymnastics, and voice. After being inducted into the US Army, where he was assigned to Valley Forge Hospital in Pennsylvania, Wilder studied drama at the Herbert Berghof Studio in New York. His fencing skills enabled him to work as a fencing choreographer. In 1961, for his first professional

role, Wilder won the Clarence Derwent Award for his performance in Arnold Wesker's *Roots*. Wilder's career took off in 1961 after he was introduced to the writer and director, Mel Brooks, with whom he established a close partnership that resulted in some of the best comedies of the 1970s that shaped his career for the rest of his life.

Wilder's first two marriages, first to Mary Mercier and then to Joan Schutz, ended in divorce. In 1984 he married comedian Gilda Radner. She died of misdiagnosed ovarian cancer at the age of forty-two. Wilder became an advocate for cancer patients, speaking before a Congressional committee. In 1993 Wilder created "Gilda's Club," a cancer support center in New York City.

In his later years, Gene Wilder wrote three novels, a memoir, and a collection of essays. He appeared as a guest on the TV sitcom, *Will & Grace*, for which he earned an Emmy Award. He married his fourth wife, Karen Boyer, in 1991. She survives him.

See Current Biography 1978

Martha Wright (Wiederrecht)

Born: Seattle, Washington; March 23, 1923
Died: Newburyport, Massachusetts; March 1, 2016
Occupation: Actress

Martha Wright it most remembered for her Broadway performances in *South Pacific* and *The Sound of Music* during the 1950s.

Martha Wright was born to a family of performers. Her grandmother, Cora C. Wright, was a music teacher, and a graduate from the Boston Conservatory of Music. Wright's parents belonged to a local Gilbert and Sullivan repertory group. She entered the University of Washington in Seattle, when she was sixteen, but left after her sophomore year to work on a morning radio program. In her spare time she performed for the Seattle Repertory Playhouse. (She adopted her mother's maiden name, Wright, as her performance name.) Her entry into New York theater occurred in the summer of 1947 when the touring company of *Up In Central Park* visited Seattle, and one of the chorus members dropped out. Wright auditioned for Sammy Lambert, the general stage manager, and got the role. She continued through a circuit of New York agents, earning minor and understudy roles. In 1951 she was offered the job of replacing Mary Martin in the Ensign Nellie Forbush role for *South Pacific*. By the end of a three-year run, Wright had sung the role of Nellie Forbush 1,080 times—180 times more than Mary Martin. In 1954 she had her own fifteen-minute television program, *The Martha Wright Show*. In 1961 Wright succeeded Mary Martin again in the role of Maria von Trapp in *The Sound of Music*.

Martha Wright was married twice. Her second husband, football star George Manuche, Jr. predeceased her. Her survivors include her three daughters and a son.

See Current Biography 1955

Harry Wu

Born: Shanghai, China; February 8, 1937
Died: Honduras; April 26, 2016
Occupation: Chinese-American dissident, human rights activist, writer

Branded a "counterrevolutionary rightist" who spent nineteen years in a Chinese Gulag-like prison, Harry Wu exposed China's Laogai forced labor camps to the world. He founded the Laogai Research Foundation in 1992 to raise awareness about human rights abuse in China.

Harry Wu was the third of eight children born to a well-to-do banker. Wu's mother died in 1942 when he was a small child. Because Wu's father was from a bourgeois family, he was demoted after the Communists came to power, and the family had to adjust to a lower standard of living. Wu studied geology at Beijing College. In 1957 the Chinese ruler Mao Zedong initiated the "Hundred Flowers Campaign," which invited Chinese citizens to criticize the party in an effort to improve party operations. Taking the party at its word, Wu complained that the party treated the upper classes too harshly during the 1955 campaign against counterrevolutionaries. Taken aback by the intensity of the public's discontent, Mao Zedong initiated a "rectification movement." Through his complaint, Wu established himself as a "counterrevolutionary rightist," and he was arrested, without a trial, in 1960, and had to be "re-educated through labor." Wu also spent eleven days in solitary confinement in a three-by-six-foot cell. By August of 1961, Wu's health was so deteriorated that he weighed just eighty pounds when he was admitted to a unit for sick prisoners. As his friends died around him, Wu realized he had to use his life purposefully, in an effort to change the society. After being moved to the Wangzhuang coal mine, Wu was allowed to marry and live outside of the prison barracks. He and his wife, Shen Jiarui (another prisoner) moved to a cave on the hillside above the mine.

In 1979 Wu was told his sentence had been "corrected" and he was free to go. He immigrated to the United States and began looking for ways to make Westerners aware of the Chinese forced labor camps. His first book, *Laogai: The Chinese Gulag* was published in 1992. Wu had visited China in an effort to obtain incontrovertible proof that goods produced by prisoners were sold for profit on the world market. He was re-arrested in 1995, charged with spying as he attempted to enter the country from the former Soviet Republic of Kazakhstan. He was held incommunicado for several weeks. News of his detention became a major story in the American press and was one of several incidents that strained diplomatic relations between the United States and China.

Harry Wu had married several times. His son, Harrison Wu of Vienna, Virginia, survives him.

See Current Biography 1995

Alan Young

Born: North Shields, Northumberland, England; November 19, 1919
Died: Los Angeles, California; May 19, 2016
Occupation: Actor, comedian, radio personality

Alan Young is most remembered for his role in the 1960s television comedy *Mr. Ed*, a series about a bumbling architect who discovers that his newly acquired backyard barn is home to a talking horse named Mr. Ed.

Alan Young was born in England, but the family moved to Vancouver, Canada, when he was a small boy. Due to bronchial asthma, Young had to spend a lot of his childhood at home, where he loved to listen to radio programs like the *Jack Benny Program* and other comedy acts. By the time he had graduated from high school, Young had become a well-known local radio personality himself, with his own program called *Stag Party*, broadcast over the Canadian Broadcasting Corporation network. During World War II Young volunteered for the Canadian Navy, but resigned when he learned his job would be to write a radio program. Young's asthma kept him from joining the Army.

Young was "discovered" accidently by a New York talent agent, Frank Cooper, who brought him to New York to appear in his own program, *The Alan Young Show*. The trade paper, *Radio Daily*, named Young the "male star of tomorrow." He was also selected to co-star with Jimmy Durante on his radio program. Young's own television show debuted in April of 1950. In 1951 the Academy of Television Arts and Sciences cited him as the best television actor of that year, and he received the Academy's television equivalent of an Oscar. *TV Guide* later dubbed Young the

"Charlie Chaplin of television," and his show earned an Emmy Award for best variety show. In 1961 Young signed on to play Wilbur Post opposite the talking horse, Mr. Ed. The show became one of the most popular on television in the 1960s. Young quit show business in the late 1960s, and became the communications director for the Christian Science headquarters in Boston. He occasionally did voice work for animated shows like *The Smurfs* and *Alvin and the Chipmunks*.

Alan Young was married twice and had four children. Information about survivors was not immediately available.

See Current Biography 1953

Ahmed Zewail

Born: Damanhur, Egypt; February 26, 1946
Died: Pasadena; California; August 2, 2016
Occupation: Nobel laureate, chemist

Nobel laureate Ahmed Zewail was a pioneer in the field of femtochemistry, the study of chemical acts that occur in a femtosecond, or one quadrillionth of a second. Considered the "father of femtochemistry," he used laser technology to capture the creation and destruction of molecules. Prior to Zewail, scientists were unable to observe these miniscule molecular reactions because no camera was fast enough. His research group created a kind of motion picture of chemical reactions by taking a series of frames of a chemical reaction.

Ahmed Zewail was born in Egypt and studied at Alexandria University, earning both a BS and an MS degree. He was encouraged to study abroad for his PhD. He traveled to the United States where he studied at the University of Pennsylvania on a scholarship. Following graduation, he did his post-doctoral research at the University of California at Berkeley. In 1976 he joined the California Institute of Technology (Caltech) where he conducted his pioneering research. One of his earliest discoveries, as reported in *BBC News* (12 October 1999 on-line), "was the realisation that as chemical reactions proceed intermediate products are formed that are quite distinct from the reactants and final products." Until Zewail's breakthrough, no camera was fast enough to capture these actions. Later in his career, he worked on four-dimensional electron microscopy using some of the technology from his earlier work.

Zewail received numerous honors for his work. He was named Caltech's first Linus Pauling Professor. He won the 1999 Nobel Prize for Chemistry, as well as the Nobel Laureate Signature Award. He won the King Faisal International Prize in Science. Egyptian President Mubarak presented him with the Order of Merit, first class, and later, the Order of the Grand Collar of the Nile.

Late in his career, Zewail served on President Obama's advisory panel, and as the United States special envoy for science to the Middle East. In Egypt, a research institute—the Zewail City of Science and Technology—bears his name. He was also outspoken regarding the necessity for Egyptian leaders to protect education and science from political turmoil.

Ahmed Zewail married Dema Zewail, a physician in public health, in 1989. They had four children, all of whom survive him, along with his wife, Dema.

See Current Biography 1999

Vilmos Zsigmond

Born: Szeged, Csongrad, Hungary; June 6, 1930
Died: Big Sir, California; January 1, 2016
Occupation: Cinematographer, director

Vilmos Zsigmond was one of the most influential cinematographers in history. He earned five Academy Award nominations, winning one for his work on *Close Encounters of the Third Kind*, and he received several awards from the British Academy of Film and Television Arts (BAFTA).

Vilmos Zsigmond was born in Szeged, Hungary, to the legendary soccer player, also named Vilmos Zsigmond, who encouraged his son's early interest in cinematography, sending him to the Budapest Academy of Theater and Film Arts. When Soviet troops marched in the capital in 1956, Zsigmond secretly filmed the event and narrowly escaped with fellow cinematographer, László Kovács. The two sold their film to a Hungarian-German producer who used it in his documentary Hungary Aflame. Zsigmond made his way to Hollywood, California, where he built his career in cinematography. He made his first film in America, Wild Guitar, in 1962. His big break came in 1971, when he met director Robert Altman and the two collaborated on McCabe and Mrs. Miller starring Warren Beatty and Julie Christie. Zsigmond's soft lighting and monochromatic filming made him a star in industry circles.

Zsigmond worked with a number of legendary Hollywood directors, including Stephen Spielberg, Robert Altman, and Martin Scorsese. He was nominated for Academy Awards for his work on *The Deer Hunter, The River, The Black Dahlia*, and he won the Oscar for *Close Encounters of the Third Kind*. He won an Emmy Award for the 1992 miniseries, *Stalin*, and received another nomination for his work on *The Mists of Avalon* in 2001. In 1999 he received a lifetime achievement award from the American Society of Cinematographers (ASC). Zsigmond was also a distinguished member of the board of governors for the Academy of Motion Picture Arts and Sciences. In 2012 he co-founded the Global Cinematography Institute with Yuri Neyman.

Vilmos Zsigmond died on New Year's Day at his home in Big Sur, California. His second wife, director Susan Roether, and two daughters survive.

See Current Biography 1999

CLASSIFICATION BY PROFESSION

ACADEMICS
Lila Abu-Lughod
John Lewis Gaddis

ACTIVISM
Michelle Alexander
David Bossie
Mary Kay Henry
DeRay Mckesson

ARCHITECTURE
Shigeru Ban
Neil Denari

ART
Kate Beaton
Nicole Eisenman
LaToya Ruby Frazier
Randall Munroe
Noelle Stevenson
Raina Telgemeier

BUSINESS
Mary Barra
Katia Beauchamp
Heather Boushey
Mary Kay Henry
Amy Hood
Natalie Massenet
Christine McCarthy
Sheri McCoy
Satya Nadella
Ross Richie
Bhaskar Sunkara

COMEDY
Aidy Bryant
Wyatt Cenac
Rob Delaney
Ron Funches
Beppe Grillo
Abbi Jacobson
Trevor Noah
Jessica Williams

DANCE
Sarah Hay

EDUCATION
Andrew Bacevich
Carmen Fariña

ENGINEERING
Kartik Chandran

ENTERTAINMENT
Mallory Ortberg

FASHION
Cara Delevingne

FICTION
Eleanor Catton
Han Kang
Tom McCarthy
Noelle Stevenson

FILM
Lenny Abrahamson
Michael Cerveris
Nuri Bilge Ceylan
Chai Jing
Ryan Coogler
Cara Delevingne
Pete Docter
Adam Driver
Ronit Elkabetz
Aunjanue Ellis
Rick Famuyiwa
Domhnall Gleeson
Renée Elise Goldsberry
Alfonso Gomez-Rejon
Eva Green
Danai Gurira
Armando Iannucci
Oscar Isaac
Michael B. Jordan
Ellie Kemper
Regina King
Brie Larson
Rami Malek
Tatiana Maslany
Kate McKinnon
Steve McQueen
George Miller

Wagner Moura
László Nemes
Lupita Nyong'o
Leslie Odom Jr.
David Oyelowo
Teyonah Parris
Simon Pegg
Bel Powley
Eddie Redmayne
Daisy Ridley
Gina Rodriguez
Peter Sarsgaard
Jill Soloway
Paolo Sorrentino
Tessa Thompson
Sophie Turner
Alicia Vikander
Robin Wright

GOVERNMENT
Mhairi Black
Robert Califf
Deb Fischer
Michael Daniel Higgins
Sally Jewell
Michelle K. Lee
Frank Luntz
Moncef Marzouki
Denis McDonough
Ernest Moniz
Robby Mook
Ayman Odeh
Penny Pritzker
Catherine Samba-Panza
Gayle Smith
Justin Trudeau
Manuel Valls

HISTORY
Mary Beard
Elizabeth Fenn
John Lewis Gaddis

JOURNALISM
José Eduardo Agualusa
Radley Balko
Jamelle Bouie
Elizabeth Stoker Bruenig
Chai Jing
Steve Coll
Robert Costa
Stefan Fatsis

Greg Howard
Ezra Klein
Wesley Lowery
David Muir
Pete Souza
Bhaskar Sunkara

LITERATURE
José Eduardo Agualusa
Mary Beard
Stefan Fatsis
Lauren Groff
Chris Jackson
Marlon James
Lisa Kron
Robin Coste Lewis
Helen Macdonald
Sy Montgomery
Randall Munroe
Sara Nović
Chigozie Obioma
Chinelo Okparanta
Sunjeev Sahota
G. Willow Wilson
Hanya Yanagihara

MUSIC
Julien Baker
Courtney Barnett
Carter Burwell
Isaac Brock
Alessia Cara
Andra Day
Mac DeMarco
Jason Derulo
Diplo
FKA twigs
Rhiannon Giddens
Lalah Hathaway
Judith Hill
Vijay Iyer
Jamie xx
Tori Kelly
Elle King
Lorde
Flying Lotus
Laura Marling
K. Michelle
Paul Moravec
James Murphy
Joanna Newsom
Leslie Odom Jr.

Of Monsters and Men
Kevin Parker
Rachel Platten
Kevin Puts
Dawn Richard
Ryuichi Sakamoto
Romeo Santos
Caroline Shaw
Sia
Phillipa Soo
Chris Stapleton
Sufjan Stevens
Henry Threadgill
Thundercat
Torres
St. Vincent
Kamasi Washington
The Weeknd

PHILOSOPHY
Nick Bostrom

POLITICS
David Bossie
Jeremy Corbyn
Isaac Herzog
Megyn Kelly
Sadiq Khan
Federica Mogherini

RADIO
Hugh Hewitt

SCIENCE
Bruce A. Beutler
Kartik Chandran
Emmanuelle Charpentier
Matthew Desmond
Katherine Freese
Gabriela González
Serge Haroche
Joanne Liu
Phil Plait
Pardis Sabeti
Alan Stern
Lorenz Studer
Kip Thorne
Shannon Walker
Katherine Willis

SPORTS
Jozy Altidore

Eniola Aluko
Jake Arrieta
Mario Balotelli
Bruce Bochy
Christine Jensen Burke
Mirinda Carfrae
Carlos Correa
Kirk Cousins
Stephen Curry
Genzebe Dibaba
Josh Donaldson
Elena Delle Donne
Pauline Ferrand-Prévot
Joe Flacco
Paul Goldschmidt
Rob Gronkowski
Simona Halep
Yuzuru Hanyu
James Harden
Katinka Hosszú
Andre Iguodala
Dallas Keuchel
Katie Ledecky
Stacy Lewis
Damian Lillard
Kyle Lowry
Marcus Mariota
Kim Ng
Salvador Pérez
Kristaps Porziņģis
Agnieszka Radwańska
Megan Rapinoe
Claressa Shields
Giancarlo Stanton
Brad Stevens
Breanna Stewart
Klay Thompson
Luke Walton
J. J. Watt

TELEVISION
Uzo Aduba
Annaleigh Ashford
Peter Capaldi
Wyatt Cenac
Michael Cerveris
Adam Driver
Ronit Elkabetz
Aunjanue Ellis
Julian Fellowes
Domhnall Gleeson

Renée Elise Goldsberry
Eva Green
Danai Gurira
Sarah Hay
Armando Iannucci
Oscar Isaac
Michael B. Jordan
Megyn Kelly
Ellie Kemper
Regina King
Brie Larson
Rami Malek
Tatiana Maslany
Kate McKinnon
Wagner Moura
Trevor Noah
Emily Nussbaum
Lupita Nyong'o
Leslie Odom Jr.
David Oyelowo
Teyonah Parris
Simon Pegg
Daisy Ridley

Gina Rodriguez
Peter Sarsgaard
Jill Soloway
Tessa Thompson
Sophie Turner
Robin Wright

THEATER
Annaleigh Ashford
Michael Cerveris
Aunjanue Ellis
Cynthia Erivo
Domhnall Gleeson
Renée Elise Goldsberry
Danai Gurira
Oscar Isaac
Lisa Kron
Ruthie Ann Miles
Leslie Odom Jr.
Bel Powley
Phillipa Soo
Tessa Thompson

LIST OF PROFILES